PORK (OVEN TEMPERATURE 350°F)

CUT AND WEIGHT Start with meat at refrigerator temperature. **Remove** roast from oven when it reaches 5° to 10°F below desired doneness; temperature will continue to rise as roast stands.			MEAT THERMOMETER READING	APPROXIMATE COOKING TIME (MINUTES PER LB)
Fresh pork	Crown roast	6–10 lbs	160°F	20 mins
	Center loin roast (with bone)	3–5 lbs	160°F	20 mins
	Boneless top loin roast	2–4 lbs	160°F	20 mins
	Whole leg (fresh ham)	12 lbs	160°–170°F	25–30 mins
	Leg half, shank or butt portion	3–4 lbs	160°–170°F	40 mins
	Boston butt	3–6 lbs	160°–170°F	45 mins
	Tenderloin (roast at 425°–450°F)	½–1½ lb	160°F	25–35 mins total
Smoked, cook before eating	Whole ham	14–16 lbs	160°F	15–18 mins
Smoked fully cooked pork (heat at 325°F)	Whole ham	14–16 lbs	130°–140°F	1–1¾ hours total
	Half ham	6–8 lbs	130°–140°F	1 hour total

LAMB (OVEN TEMPERATURE 325°F)

CUT AND WEIGHT Start with meat at refrigerator temperature. **Remove** roast from oven when it reaches 5° to 10°F below desired doneness; temperature will rise as it stands.		APPROXIMATE COOKING TIME (MINUTES PER LB)		
		Medium-rare (145°F)	Medium (160°F)	Well done (170°F)
Whole leg	5–7 lbs	15 mins	20 mins	25 mins
	7–9 lbs	20 mins	25 mins	30 mins
Leg shank half	3–4 lbs	30 mins	40 mins	45 mins
Leg sirloin half	3–4 lbs	25 mins	35 mins	45 mins
Leg roast (boneless)	4–7 lbs	20 mins	25 mins	30 mins
Rib roast or rack (cook at 375°F)	1½–2½ lbs	30 mins	35 mins	40 mins
Crown roast, unstuffed (cook at 375°F)	2–3 lbs	25 mins	30 mins	35 mins
Shoulder roast	4–6 lbs	20 mins	25 mins	30 mins
Shoulder roast (boneless)	3½–6 lbs	35 mins	40 mins	45 mins

THE
Good Housekeeping
STEP-BY-STEP
COOKBOOK

THE
Good Housekeeping
STEP-BY-STEP
COOKBOOK

Edited by Susan Westmoreland

Food Director

Good Housekeeping

with the assistance of

Susan Deborah Goldsmith

Associate Food Director

and Elizabeth Brainerd Burge

HEARST BOOKS
A DIVISION OF
WILLIAM MORROW AND COMPANY, INC.
NEW YORK

GOOD HOUSEKEEPING

Editor-in-Chief Ellen Levine
Food Director Susan Westmoreland
Associate Food Director Susan Deborah Goldsmith

A CARROLL & BROWN BOOK

Designed and produced by
Carroll & Brown Limited
5 Lonsdale Road
London NW6 6RA
England

Publishing Director Denis Kennedy
Art Director Chrissie Lloyd

Project Editor Theresa Reynolds

Editors Janet Charatan, Paula Disbrowe, Kate Fryer, Valerie Cipollone, Madeline Weston
Assistant Editors Joanne Stanford, Simon Warmer

US Cooking Consultant Elizabeth Brainerd Burge

Senior Art Editor Sally Powell
Designers Paul Stradling, Simon Daley, Hallam Bannister

Photography David Murray, Jules Selmes

Production Christine Corton, Wendy Rogers, Clair Reynolds

Nutrition Consultant Michele C. Fisher, Ph.D., R.D.

This edition first published in the United States by
William Morrow and Company, Inc.
1350 Avenue of the Americas
New York, New York 10019

First edition September 1997
1 2 3 4 5 6 7 8 9 10

Library of Congress Cataloging-in-Publication Data
The Good Housekeeping Step-by-Step Cookbook / edited by
Susan Westmoreland, with the assistance of Susan Deborah
Goldsmith and Elizabeth Brainerd Burge.
p. cm.
Includes index
ISBN 0-688-14716-X
1. Cookery. I. Westmoreland, Susan.
II. Goldsmith, Susan Deborah. III. Burge, Elizabeth Brainerd.
IV. Good Housekeeping.
(New York, N.Y.)
TX714.G663   1997
641.5–dc21   97-11375
CIP

Reproduced in Singapore by Colourscan
Printed and bound in the United States of America by
Quebecor Printing Hawkins

FOREWORD

As the mother of a three-year-old, cooking has come full circle for me. At about my son's age, I began to cook with my grandmother, a tiny lady who could make almost anything – and make it seem like fun. I had a special chair that I moved from counter to stove to get the best vantage point for watching, stirring, and tasting. From sautéing garlic to kneading bread, she had special tricks to show me. While I can't offer you my grandmother, I'm very pleased to present Good Housekeeping's first cookbook that is organized by technique, *The Good Housekeeping Step-by-Step Cookbook*.

It's the next best thing to having a wise and patient grandmother who's a great cook and teacher. We start with a basic technique: Want to panfry chicken-breast cutlets? Our step-by-step photos will show you the way and – voilà – the finished dish. With the turn of a page you'll have eight more recipes – all using the same technique. You'll also find preparation and cooking times and a full nutritional profile with each recipe. As always, every recipe has been thoroughly tested in Good Housekeeping's Test Kitchens.

Whether you are a working mom like me who also has to have dinner on the table every night, a curious beginner who wants to learn the basics, or an experienced cook in search of culinary inspiration, you'll find dishes that you want to make. With photos to instruct and entice, the recipes range from how to make perfect pie crust, to great crab cakes, to a Thai beef with basil stir-fry that you can put together while you cook the rice to go with it.

Dig in – enjoy the recipes, the photos, the wealth of "Know-How" information and cooking tips. Our aim at Good Housekeeping is to give you the sort of information and recipes that make cooking a pleasure.

Susan Westmoreland

Susan Westmoreland
Food Director
Good Housekeeping

CONTENTS

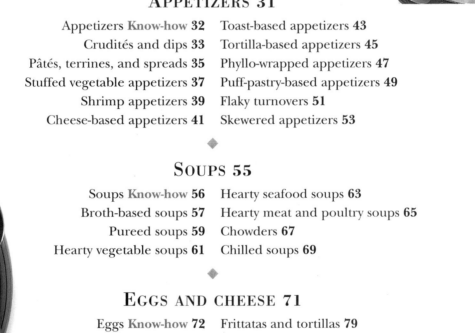

◆

POULTRY 131

◆

MEAT 179

◆

VEGETABLES 267

◆

SALADS 313

◆

PASTA 347

◆

GRAINS AND BEANS 369

◆

QUICK AND YEAST BREADS 391

EQUIPMENT KNOW-HOW

There's a piece of equipment out there for every cooking method imaginable. No one needs every new gadget on the market, but there are certain items that make kitchen life easier and more enjoyable. Here are all of our favorites, from time-honored basic cookware to specialized utensils for adventuresome home cooks.

SHOPPING TIPS

Quality cookware can be expensive. But if you get the best, you'll have a lifetime investment that's reliable, durable, and a pleasure to use. The first step in judging quality? Check the price: Finer metals and manufacturing typically mean you'll pay more. (But not always; cast-iron pans, for instance, are cheap, heavy, and durable.) Invest in a few quality pieces, especially knives and sturdy pots and pans. Don't skimp on nonstick pans for low-fat cooking. You can cut corners on items like pasta pots, which simply boil water. Get extra mileage from your cookware by choosing products that work equally well in the oven and on the stove-top.

STOVE-TOP STAPLES

Pots and pans come in many materials. Stainless steel is easy to care for but does not conduct heat well, so manufacturers often add an aluminum or copper core to improve its heat-conducting qualities. By contrast, copper is a superb heat conductor and a pleasure to cook in – but it's heavy, expensive, and a nuisance to polish. Aluminum and cast iron are much less costly and easier to care for; both are efficient heat conductors but can react with acidic foods, causing them to taste metallic or discolor.

In general, look for pots and pans with thick bottoms, which guard against scorching, and heatproof handles (or ones designed to stay cool). You're better off investing in pieces you know you'll use and avoiding prepackaged sets, which may contain some pans you won't need. For a well-equipped kitchen, you'll need the following:

Saucepan You'll need at least 3 or 4 (ranging from 1-quart to 4-quart), each between 3½ and 4 inches deep. They should have tight-fitting lids and ovenproof handles.

Dutch oven Great for the stove-top or oven; heavy ones are best, and enameled pans are pretty enough to serve in. A 5-quart size is most useful.

Skillets Have at least 3 sizes: small (8-inch), medium (10-inch), and large (12-inch). A good nonstick skillet is a must if you're trying to cook with less fat.

Saucepot This deep, wide, fairly light pot is used for soups, stews, and cooking pasta. A 5-quart saucepot with a tight-fitting lid will serve most needs.

Stockpot A tall, narrow pot used for cooking soups and stocks as well as bulky foods like corn on the cob and lobster. A 6- or 8-quart stockpot is recommended.

Stockpot

Double boiler A set of two saucepans that allows for gentle cooking of foods (in the upper pan) over simmering water (in the lower pan). If you don't own one, it's easy to improvise a double boiler: Just nest a metal mixing bowl in a saucepan of simmering water, or stack two saucepans of about the same diameter.

Double boiler

Grill pan This combination griddle/grill provides an excellent way to cook foods with little or no fat. The bottom surface is ridged, allowing fat to drip away from foods. Use over high heat for best results.

SEASONING A CAST-IRON PAN

Regular (not enamel-coated) cast-iron skillets require seasoning before the first use to create a nonstick finish. Wash in hot, soapy water; dry. Using a cloth soaked in vegetable oil, rub the entire surface – even exterior and lid. Heat upside down in a 350°F oven 1 hour. Turn off oven; cool completely in oven.

FOR THE OVEN

Roasting and baking results depend on how long the food bakes and at how high a temperature, and the dimensions of the vessel. Many materials will do the job: enameled cast-iron, which is easy to clean and transmits heat well; enameled steel, which is a reasonably priced, lightweight choice for roasting pans; stainless steel, which is durable and inexpensive; and heat-resistant glass and glass-ceramic, which can go directly from the freezer or refrigerator to the oven. Earthenware and stoneware are especially good for long, slow baking. For most cakes, shiny metal pans will yield the most delicate crusts. The following is a round-up of essentials.

Baking dish A large, fairly shallow, coverless oval or rectangular dish with sides about 2 inches high; usually made of glass or ceramic. Choose a variety in different sizes.

Baking pan Like a baking dish, but made of metal; the sides of this pan are 1½ to 2 inches high. Essential: an 8" by 8" square; a 9" by 9" square; a rectangular 13" by 9" pan.

Casserole Round, oval, square, or rectangular, this dish may be made of glass, ceramic, or enameled metal, and may have a lid. Have several sizes.

Roasting pan A large, deep pan typically made of stainless or enameled steel or aluminum. A low, open roasting pan with a rack is the most versatile.

Cake pan No baker should be without an assortment of round cake pans (8-inch and 9-inch), plus several square and rectangular baking pans (see page 10). Depending on your baking needs, also consider the following: springform pan (9" by 3" and 10" by 2½" are useful sizes); tube pan (9- to 10-inch); Bundt pan (10-inch); fluted tube pan (6-cup).

Loaf pan Essential for quick breads and tea cakes and useful for meat loaves. Standard sizes are 9" by 5" and 8½" by 4½".

Pie plate The standard size is 9 inches; deep-dish plates are 9½ inches. Glass, dark metal, or dull metal pans make the best piecrusts – crisp and nicely browned.

Tart pan This shallow pan with fluted sides and a removable bottom comes in all shapes and sizes; 11" by 1" and 9" by 1" round pans are especially useful. Tartlet pans (1¾-inch to 4-inch) are nice for individual desserts.

Other baking equipment The following also come in handy: jelly-roll pan (15½" by 10½", with low rim all around); baking sheets and cookie sheets (with low lip on one or more edges); muffin pan; custard cups (6-ounce capacity).

Cookie sheet   Roasting pan with rack   Metal baking pan

Casserole   Jelly-roll pan   Glass baking dish

CARE AND CLEANING

Aluminum Scrub with a mild abrasive cleanser. If pan has darkened, fill with water and vinegar or lemon juice; boil 15 minutes.

Cast iron Wash cast iron briefly so you don't wash away the seasoning (see box, page 10). Clean with boiling water and a paper towel or soft cloth, or use a nylon pad to scrub off food. Dry at once.

Copper Wash in hot, soapy water; dry immediately. Copper tarnishes quickly; use a polish to brighten. Most traditional copper pans are lined with tin and will need relining from time to time (reline if you can see copper through the tin).

Earthenware or stoneware Cool completely before washing to prevent cracking. Scrub with nylon pad, rinse, and air dry. Glazed stoneware is dishwasher-safe.

Enameled metals Soak in hot, soapy water; avoid abrasives.

Glass, glass-ceramic, porcelain Soak in hot, soapy water. All are dishwasher-safe.

Nonstick surfaces Clean with a sponge and warm, soapy water. Avoid abrasives.

Stainless steel Wash in hot, soapy water with a nylon pad. A stainless steel cleaner will help remove stubborn stains.

HOW TO MEASURE PANS

To measure the size of a baking dish or pan, measure across the top of the dish from inside edge to inside edge. Measure depth on the inside of the pan as well, from the bottom to the top of the pan.

PAN SUBSTITUTIONS

Cakes and breads are usually baked in metal baking pans. But in a pinch, you can substitute a glass or ceramic dish – just reduce the oven temperature by 25 degrees, since cakes bake faster in these materials than in metal. That way, the outside of the cake won't be over-baked before the center is cooked.

PAN VOLUMES	
PAN SIZE	APPROXIMATE VOLUME
2½" by 1¼" muffin pan cup	¼ cup
8½" by 4½" by 2½" loaf pan	5 to 6 cups
8" by 8" by 1½" baking pan	1½ quarts
9" by 9" by 1½" baking pan	2 quarts
9" by 1" pie plate	1 quart
11" by 7" by 1½" baking pan	2 quarts
13" by 9" by 2" baking pan	3½ quarts
15½" by 10½" by 1" jelly-roll pan	2½ quarts

MICROWAVE TIPS

• Remember that the size of the food affects cooking time. Small or thin pieces cook faster than large or thick ones.
• Avoid microwaving large cuts of on-the-bone meat. The bones attract microwaves and the meat will cook unevenly.
• Pierce eggs and foods with tight skin (eggplant, potatoes). If not, they may explode from a buildup of steam.
• Use a dish that's large enough for stirring and boiling. Think of how full you'd want a saucepan, not a casserole.
• Don't reheat baked goods in the microwave – they'll be tough. However, you can thaw them in a paper towel.
• Use medium power (the microwave will cycle on and off) for delicate tasks, such as melting chocolate.
• Clean the oven with soapy water or multi-purpose cleaner.

MICROWAVE SAFETY

• Use paper products only for cooking less than 10 minutes, or they could ignite. Don't use recycled paper, which can contain metal bits that will spark, or dyed paper products – the dye could leach into food.
• Don't use the twist ties that come with plastic storage bags – the metal could spark and possibly ignite. Also beware of glass or porcelain with a metal trim, or the metal content of some ceramic glazes.
• For safety, use plastic wrap designed for microwave use, and don't let the plastic touch the food.
• Always remove a tight cover carefully, opening it away from your face – steam can build up under the cover.
• Sugar attracts microwaves, so sweet foods can become extremely hot – be careful when you take a bite.

UTENSIL ESSENTIALS

Bristle brushes Have at least two: one for cleaning pots, and one for scrubbing vegetables. Nylon bristles last the longest.
Colander This sink staple is indispensable for draining pasta and vegetables. Large colanders are best; look for one with solid feet at the base.
Cooling racks Have 2 or 3 if you bake a lot of cakes or cookies. Avoid racks with large gaps between the wires.
Cutting boards To avoid cross-contamination, have one board for raw

Cooling rack

poultry, fish, and meat, and another for bread, vegetables, and cheese. Scrub with hot soapy water after use, and sterilize weekly in a solution of 1 tablepoon bleach mixed with 1 gallon water. Sanitize plastic boards in the

dishwasher. You may want to reserve a board just for fruit, to avoid tragedies like garlic-flavored apple pie.

Cutting boards

Grater This flat or box-shaped tool can grate (fine holes), shred (medium holes), or slice (large slots) many foods. Stainless steel won't rust.
Measuring cups Use a glass or plastic set for liquids and a nested metal or plastic set, with cups that can be leveled, for dry ingredients.
Measuring spoons Stainless steel are the most durable. For liquids, fill to the rim. For dry ingredients, fill and level off.
Mixing bowls A set of these all-purpose bowls is invaluable. Typically made of stainless steel, glass, or plastic, they range from tiny to 8 quarts. Avoid using plastic bowls to beat egg whites.
Rolling pins Heavy pins, hardwood or marble, work best for rolling dough out smoothly, with less effort. Don't wash wooden pins in the dishwasher.
Sieve/Strainer Sifts dry ingredients or strains liquids. Have a few in various sizes and with different gauges of mesh.

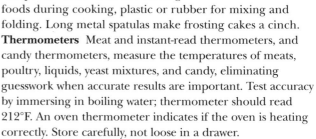
Grater   Sieve

Spatulas Use wooden or heatproof rubber ones for turning foods during cooking, plastic or rubber for mixing and folding. Long metal spatulas make frosting cakes a cinch.
Thermometers Meat and instant-read thermometers, and candy thermometers, measure the temperatures of meats, poultry, liquids, yeast mixtures, and candy, eliminating guesswork when accurate results are important. Test accuracy by immersing in boiling water; thermometer should read 212°F. An oven thermometer indicates if the oven is heating correctly. Store carefully, not loose in a drawer.
Tongs Use to pick up foods that are hot, slippery, or messy, or turn meats without piercing them.
Vegetable peeler Easier than a paring knife for peeling potatoes, apples, and other fruit and vegetables, and great for shaving cheese and making chocolate curls. A swivel blade removes less peel than a fixed blade since it conforms to the vegetable's shape.
Whisk A must for mixing smooth sauces, gravies, vinaigrettes, and cake batters. Have several sizes for different tasks.

Rubber   Metal   Tongs   Whisk
spatula spatula

ALL THE RIGHT KNIVES

Quality knives are made of high-carbon stainless steel. If the knife has a tang (the narrower metal part at the base of the blade) that goes right through the handle, it's solidly made. A good knife should feel comfortable in your hand.

Essential knives include a chef's knife (for chopping, slicing, dicing, and mincing; a 6- to 8-inch blade is the most popular), a small paring knife (for fruits and vegetables), and a large serrated knife (for breads, cakes, and even tomatoes). Useful extras include a carving knife for slicing meats – these often come in a set with a carving fork– and a boning knife. A slicing knife has a scalloped edge and rounded tip, and is good for ham and other cooked meats.

Sharp knives are easier to use and safer too because they'll be less likely to slip. Take a cue from chefs, who sharpen their knives every day. For directions on how to use a sharpening steel, see page 180.

Paring knife   Chef's knife   Serrated knife   Carving fork and knife   Slicing knife

BLENDING AND MIXING OPTIONS

Blenders and food processors can be used for similar tasks, but they each have their own advantages. The blender makes pureed soups, silky sauces, and smooth drinks with ease; its tall, narrow container holds more liquid than a food processor and makes smoother soups. Processor bowls will leak at the base if overloaded. On the other hand, a food processor is better at chopping, shredding, and grating; it can also make pastry dough in a flash. If you want a small, portable, hand-held blender option, consider an immersion blender. This fits right into the cooking pot and, as a benefit, gives you fewer bowls to clean.

For whipping cream, beating egg whites, and mixing cake batters, an electric mixer does the job best. A handheld mixer is convenient because it's light and can be moved around the kitchen. But holding it can be tiring, and it can stall with stiff doughs. A heavy-duty standing mixer easily handles large amounts of thick batter, cold butter, and bread dough, and will free you up to do other things; this type is best for serious bakers. Most standing mixers offer mixing paddles, dough hooks for kneading, and balloon whisks for beating eggs and cream. Other accessories range from a food grinder to a sausage stuffer.

THE LITTLE EXTRAS

Apple corer This cylindrical tool neatly cores apples as well as pears. Buy the larger size so you don't miss any core.

Decorating bag For decorating cakes and pies and forming spritz cookies and beautifully shaped pastries.

Egg beater This hand-powered mixer can also be used for whipping cream. Crank gears spin the metal beaters.

Ice cream maker They come as manual and electric; used for ice cream, sorbet, and frozen yogurt.

Juicer A device to extract fruit or vegetable juices – from a simple ridged cone onto which a halved citrus fruit is pressed to elaborate electric models used for carrot juice.

Kitchen scissors For cutting kitchen string, snipping fresh herbs, and trimming artichoke leaves. Shears, which are larger and spring-loaded, make sectioning poultry simple. Buy sturdy models made of stainless steel.

Melon baller Besides scooping perfect globes of melon, this tool cores apples and pears. A large one is most useful.

Mortar and pestle For grinding spices, herbs, and nuts. You crush with the pestle (a bat-like tool) in a mortar (the bowl).

Pastry blender The metal wires on this tool cut the cold fat into flour for pastry without warming it, as your hands would.

Pastry brush Used to brush doughs with butter or egg and apply glazes to baked goods; great for dusting off excess flour. Wash right after using (especially at the base of the bristles); dry thoroughly. When buying, look for well-anchored bristles.

Potato masher Perfect for mashing potatoes, other root vegetables, and cooked beans into a slightly chunky puree.

Ruler Handy for measuring the size of baking pans, and the thickness of meat and fish to gauge cooking times.

Salad spinner Uses centrifugal force to dry greens.

Skewers A must for making kabobs and trussing turkeys; small, decorative varieties are great for appetizers.

Steamer The collapsible metal style can fit into pots and pans of various sizes. A two-tier steamer pan looks like a double boiler (see page 10) but the top half has a perforated base to allow steam through. Bamboo steamers fit in a wok or over a pot of simmering liquid.

Toothpicks Great for testing cakes and quick breads for doneness. Also handy for serving appetizers and for securing stuffed foods, such as chicken breasts.

Zester Pulled across citrus fruit, it removes only the outer peel, avoiding the bitter pith underneath.

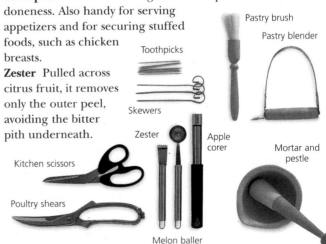

Toothpicks

Pastry brush

Pastry blender

Skewers

Zester

Apple corer

Mortar and pestle

Kitchen scissors

Poultry shears

Melon baller

COOKING BASICS KNOW-HOW

Confidence in the kitchen begins with the basics – such as mastering the proper techniques for simple procedures like measuring. The following tips and tricks form an essential foundation for success and promise to make any recipe more manageable. Turn to these pages when you need to clarify a cooking method, convert ingredient measurements, or seek out ingredient substitutions you can use in a pinch.

ALL THE RIGHT MEASURES

Careful measuring of ingredients means you'll get consistent results every time you prepare a recipe. For liquids, always measure in a glass or plastic cup designed for liquids, with a pouring lip. Read the measurement at eye level; for accurate results, place the cup on a flat surface. For dry ingredients, use a stainless steel or plastic cup that can be leveled off. These come in graduated sets of 1 cup, ½ cup, ⅓ cup, and ¼ cup; some sets also include ¾ cup and ⅔ cup measures. Measuring spoons, metal or plastic, come in sets of 1 tablespoon, 1 teaspoon, ½ teaspoon, ¼ teaspoon, and, sometimes, ⅛ teaspoon.

Measuring spoons

Liquid measuring cups   Dry measuring cups

MEASURING SHORTENING

1 If not using sticks, spoon the shortening into a dry measuring cup. With spoon, pack firmly into the cup.

2 Use the blade edge (not the flat side) of a knife or metal spatula to level off the shortening.

MEASURING FLOUR

1 Flour tends to pack down during storage. Stir the flour to loosen and aerate it before measuring.

2 Lightly spoon flour into a dry measuring cup (don't use the cup to scoop flour, and don't pack or shake the measuring cup).

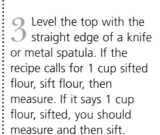

3 Level the top with the straight edge of a knife or metal spatula. If the recipe calls for 1 cup sifted flour, sift flour, then measure. If it says 1 cup flour, sifted, you should measure and then sift.

MEASURING BROWN SUGAR

For the most accurate results, always pack brown sugar firmly into a dry measuring cup before leveling off. It should hold its shape when turned out of the cup.

HINTS AND TIPS

• When measuring syrupy foods (e.g., molasses, honey, corn syrup), first coat the measuring spoon or liquid measuring cup with vegetable oil; the syrup will easily slip out.
• Check the volume of a casserole or soufflé dish by measuring water into the dish, to the top of the dish.
• When measuring ingredients, don't hold the cup or spoon over the bowl of other ingredients in case of spillage.
• For ingredients like nuts, coconut, and chopped dried fruits, fill a dry measuring cup and level with your fingers.
• Margarine and butter math: 1 stick = 8 tablespoons = ½ cup = ¼ pound (4 ounces).

CUT TO SIZE

Chop To cut food into small, irregular pieces about the size of peas. Roughly cut up food, then mound pieces in a pile. Hold the handle of a chef's knife with one hand and the tip with the other, and chop with a rocking motion.

Mince To cut food into tiny irregular pieces, less than ⅛ inch. Proceed as for chopping, but cut food smaller.

Dice These are small, uniform cubes of about ¼ inch in size. To dice, first cut food into matchsticks or shreds. Bundle pieces together; slice crosswise into uniform cubes.

Julienne These are thin matchsticks about 2 inches long. First cut food into slices about 2 inches long and ⅛ inch thick. Stack slices; cut lengthwise into ⅛-inch-wide sticks.

CHOPPING AN ONION

1 Halve onion through the root end; place on cutting board. Make horizontal cuts parallel to board, cutting to, but not through, the root.

2 Make lengthwise vertical cuts, almost but not quite through the root.

3 Now cut across the width of the onion to chop into small pieces.

EMERGENCY SUBSTITUTIONS

Asian fish sauce (nuoc nam) For each 1 tablespoon, use 2 teaspoons soy sauce and 1 teaspoon anchovy paste.

Baking powder For each 1 teaspoon called for, substitute ¼ teaspoon baking soda and ½ teaspoon cream of tartar (make fresh for each use).

Cake flour For each 1 cup called for, use 1 cup minus 2 tablespoons all-purpose flour.

Chives Substitute green onions, including the tops.

Herbs For each 1 tablespoon fresh, use ½ teaspoon dried.

Light brown sugar For each 1 cup, substitute 1 cup granulated sugar and 1 tablespoon molasses; or use dark brown sugar.

Mustard For each 1 tablespoon prepared mustard, use 1 teaspoon dry mustard mixed with 2 tablespoons wine vinegar, white wine, or water.

Pancetta Substitute Canadian bacon or ham.

Pine nuts Use walnuts or almonds.

Prosciutto Use ham, preferably Westphalian or country ham.

Shallots Use onion.

Vanilla extract Use brandy or an appropriate flavored liqueur.

SMALL VOLUME EQUIVALENTS

SPOONS	CUPS	FLUID OUNCES
1 tablespoon/3 teaspoons		½ fl oz
2 tablespoons	⅛ cup	1 fl oz
4 tablespoons	¼ cup	2 fl oz
5 tablespoons + 1 teaspoon	⅓ cup	2⅔ fl oz
6 tablespoons	⅜ cup	3 fl oz
8 tablespoons	½ cup	4 fl oz
10 tablespoons + 2 teaspoons	⅔ cup	5⅓ fl oz
12 tablespoons	¾ cup	6 fl oz
14 tablespoons	⅞ cup	7 fl oz
16 tablespoons	1 cup	8 fl oz

LARGER VOLUME EQUIVALENTS

CUPS	FLUID OUNCES	PINTS/QUARTS
1 cup	8 fl oz	½ pint
2 cups	16 fl oz	1 pint
3 cups	24 fl oz	1½ pints/¾ quart
4 cups	32 fl oz	2 pints/1 quart
6 cups	48 fl oz	3 pints/1½ quarts
8 cups	64 fl oz	2 quarts/½ gallon
16 cups	128 fl oz	4 quarts/1 gallon

The following guidelines are ones that no cook should be without. Keeping food in good condition isn't difficult and shouldn't be daunting. But a safe kitchen does call for a few precautions. Here, we outline safety essentials, including the right way to handle raw meats, and how long you can safely store a range of foods.

GOLDEN RULES OF FOOD SAFETY

• Keep a clean kitchen. Any area can harbor harmful bacteria, so always wash and dry your hands before handling food. Frequently wash kitchen towels, cloths, and sponges. Rinse fresh fruits and vegetables before eating. Wash cutting boards, knives, and other utensils with hot soapy water after every use – especially after handling raw meat and poultry. Wash cutting boards occasionally with a solution of 1 tablespoon bleach per 1 gallon water to sterilize them.
• Don't put cooked meat (or any ready-to-eat food) on a plate that has come in contact with raw meat, poultry, or fish.
• To kill harmful bacteria that may be present in raw eggs, fish, poultry, and meat, it's essential to cook these foods thoroughly. A thermometer is the safest method for checking doneness. For a visual check, follow these guidelines: Cook red meat at least to medium-rare (pink but not red in center); pork until juices run clear and meat retains just a trace of pink; poultry until juices run clear; fish just until opaque throughout; and egg yolks and whites until firm and set. Cook ground meat until no pink remains.
• It's unwise to cook foods in stages. Don't start to cook food, stop, and then return to it later. Even when food is stored in the refrigerator between cooking periods, safe temperatures might not be maintained and bacteria may develop.
• Refrigerate leftovers as soon as possible. Do not leave at room temperature longer than 2 hours. Divide large amounts among small, shallow containers for quicker cooling.
• In hot weather, don't leave protein foods such as chicken, egg salad, etc., out of the refrigerator for more than 1 hour.

PACKING A SAFER PICNIC

• Use 2 small coolers rather than one large one – one that will be opened frequently (for fruit and beverages), and one for perishable items like meat, poultry, salads, and cheese.
• Chill foods thoroughly before placing them in a cooler (the cooler cannot chill foods that aren't already cold). To preserve the chill, don't open the lid longer than necessary.
• If you're taking raw meat to a cookout, double-wrap it in zip-tight plastic bags to prevent juices from tainting other foods.
• Pack perishable items next to ice packs. Keep delicate fruits and lettuce away from ice to prevent freezing.

WRAP IT UP

Aluminum foil This provides optimal protection, molds easily, and can withstand extreme temperatures. The heavy-duty version is ideal for long-term storage.
Freezer paper This old-fashioned favorite protects food from freezer burn and is very easy to label.
Plastic bags Food storage bags are intended for room-temperature or refrigerated foods. Freezer bags are the thickest and sturdiest, and can even endure a quick zap in the microwave for defrosting and warming.
Plastic wrap The best offer a tight seal and protect food against moisture loss and odor transfer. Thinner wraps often cling better and are ideal for leftovers and brief microwave reheats (but should not be in direct contact with food when microwaved). For freezer storage, choose a heavy plastic wrap intended for that purpose.

PANTRY STORAGE

Unless otherwise noted, these pantry staples fare best in a cool, dry place. For more information on basic ingredients (e.g., flour, pasta, grains), see appropriate Know-How pages.
Baking powder Once opened, keep it well sealed and it should be effective for up to 6 months. To test it, add 1 teaspoon to 1 cup hot water; it should bubble vigorously.
Bread crumbs Store dried bread crumbs in the pantry up to 6 months, or – for better flavor – refrigerate up to 2 years.
Honey It will last indefinitely; if it has crystallized, place opened jar in bowl of hot water. Stir until crystals dissolve.
Hot-pepper sauce After opening, store at room temperature up to 3 months, or refrigerate for longer storage.
Olive oil Keep in a cool, dark place up to 6 months. Don't buy more than you can use; it may become rancid, especially if stored in a warm place.
Pancake syrup This will keep up to 9 months (after that, syrup thins and flavor weakens). It can also be refrigerated. Pure maple syrup should be refrigerated after opening, or can be frozen. Store in glass jars, not plastic or metal containers.
Peanut butter Unopened, it will last for a year in your cupboard. Refrigerate after opening to avoid rancidity.
Soy sauce Unopened, it will keep in the pantry for a year. Once opened, refrigerate to keep for an additional year.
Spices and dried herbs Keep in lightproof containers in a cool place up to 1 year. Store red spices (paprika, ground red pepper), poppy seeds, and sesame seeds in the freezer.
Vegetable oil Store in a cool, dark place (for 6 months).
Vinegar Unopened, it will keep indefinitely. Sediment that may appear is harmless and can be strained off. Once opened, store in the pantry for 6 months. Vinegar with added flavorings (e.g., fruits, herbs) should be strained into a clean bottle when vinegar level drops below top of ingredients.

THE RIGHT WAY TO REFRIGERATE

• Make sure your refrigerator temperature remains between 33° and 40°F.
• To prevent spoilage, keep foods on a rotating system. Place new items at the back of the shelves and move older purchases to the front.
• Date all leftovers so you know how long you've had them.
• If you're unsure whether a food is safe to eat, discard it.
• Put packages of fresh meat, poultry, and fish on a plate in the refrigerator if you plan to cook them within a day or two; otherwise freeze them immediately.
• Keep eggs in their carton so they don't absorb other food odors. For the same reason, store cheese, cream, milk, yogurt, margarine, and butter tightly closed or covered.

FREEZER FACTS

• Frozen foods retain their color, texture, and nutrients better than foods preserved by other methods.
• Check the temperature of the freezer with a freezer thermometer to be sure that it is at 0°F. (Higher temperatures will draw moisture from the food, resulting in a loss of texture and taste.)
• It's time to defrost whenever there is ½ inch of frost on the sides of the freezer. If the frost has not solidified into hard ice, a plastic scraper makes light work of this job.
• Don't overload your freezer or add more than 2 pounds of food for each cubic foot of space in a 24-hour period. Either will cause temperature changes that may damage food.
• To avoid ice crystals, color or texture changes, or freezer burn, seal foods in airtight containers, or wrap them tightly in a wrap intended for freezer storage.
• Small "piece" foods such as individual appetizers (e.g., tartlets, phyllo triangles), drop cookies, or strawberries keep best when "tray," or "dry," frozen. This method freezes foods so they remain separate and you can remove only as many as you need. Simply spread the unwrapped food on a baking sheet; freeze just until firm, then package in zip-tight plastic bags. Tray-freezing is also ideal for firming foods such as cakes and pies so packaging material will not adhere to them.
• Liquid and semiliquid foods must be stored in leakproof containers; leave headspace for expansion of liquid during the freezing process (for wide-mouth containers, leave ½ inch for pints and 1 inch for quart cartons; for narrow-mouth containers, leave ¾ inch for pints and 1½ inches for quarts).
• Don't freeze raw vegetables (they'll lose crispness unless you blanch them first) or fried foods (they'll turn soggy). Also avoid freezing soft cheeses, mayonnaise, sour cream, custard, and pumpkin pies – they'll become watery or may separate.
• Label and date food packages, and note the weight of meats and poultry and number of portions.
• Prepare frozen foods right after thawing; growth of bacteria can occur rapidly in thawed foods left at room temperature (especially casseroles, pot pies, and gravy).

STORING FRESH HERBS

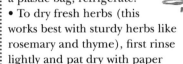
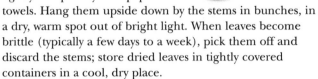

• Most fresh herbs are highly perishable, so buy them in small quantities as needed. To store them for a few days, immerse roots or freshly cut stems in about 2 inches of water. Cover the leaves with paper towels or a plastic bag; refrigerate.
• To dry fresh herbs (this works best with sturdy herbs like rosemary and thyme), first rinse lightly and pat dry with paper towels. Hang them upside down by the stems in bunches, in a dry, warm spot out of bright light. When leaves become brittle (typically a few days to a week), pick them off and discard the stems; store dried leaves in tightly covered containers in a cool, dry place.
• To freeze herbs, rinse lightly, pat dry, remove the stems, and place in plastic containers or bags. The frozen herbs will darken in color, but the flavor will be fine. There's no need to thaw frozen herbs; just add them directly to the food you are cooking. Or, place a few herbs (leaves only) in ice cube trays; add just enough water to cover leaves and freeze. Simply add the cube to simmering soups or sauces.

REFRIGERATOR AND FREEZER STORAGE GUIDE

FOOD	IN REFRIGERATOR	IN FREEZER
Raw poultry, fish, and meat (small pieces)	2–3 days	3–6 months
Raw ground meat or poultry	1–2 days	3 months
Cooked whole roasts or whole poultry	2–3 days	9 months
Cooked poultry pieces	1–2 days	1 month (6 months in broth or gravy)
Bread	—	3 months
Ice cream	—	1–2 months
Soups and stews	2–3 days	1–3 months
Casseroles	2–3 days	2–4 weeks
Cookies	—	6–8 months

Don't put good eating habits – for yourself or your family – on hold. Forming poor dietary habits when you're young can lead to health problems later. It's essential to go beyond the "basic four" food groups. The Food Pyramid illustrated below will help you choose what and how much to eat from a variety of food groups to get the nutrients you need without too many calories, or too much fat, saturated fat, cholesterol, sugar, or sodium.

DIETARY GUIDELINES FOR AMERICANS

• Eat a variety of foods to get the calories, protein, vitamins, minerals, and fiber needed.
• Balance the food you eat with physical activity to maintain or improve your weight.
• Choose a diet low in fat, saturated fat, and cholesterol.
• Choose a diet with plenty of vegetables, fruits, and grain products (these fill you up healthfully).
• Use sugar, salt, and alcohol only in moderation.

THE USDA FOOD PYRAMID

The Food Pyramid is an outline of what to eat each day. The research-based plan, developed by the United States Department of Agriculture, is meant to serve as a general guide – not a rigid prescription – that encourages you to pick and choose from a vast range of foods to create a healthful diet that's right for you.

• The Pyramid calls for eating a variety of foods to get the nutrients you need along with the right amount of calories to maintain a healthy weight. The Pyramid focuses on controlling fat intake, because most American diets are too high in fat, especially saturated fat.

• The Pyramid emphasizes foods from five major food groups shown in the three lower sections of the Pyramid. Each group provides some – but not all – of the nutrients you need for a balanced diet. Foods in one category can't replace those in another (and no one group is more important than another); for good health you need them all.

• When planning meals, choose fresh foods whenever possible. Processed foods tend to have fewer nutrients and higher amounts of sugar, fats, and sodium than home-prepared ones. When you eat packaged foods, check labels to see that the fat content fits your fat budget (see box, page 19).

Bread, cereal, rice, and pasta These foods – all from grains – form the base of the Pyramid. You need the most servings (6 to 11) of these foods each day.

Fruits and vegetables The next level up also comes from plants. Eat fruits (2 to 4 servings daily) and vegetables (3 to 5 servings daily) for vitamins, minerals, and fiber.

Meats and dairy foods Most of the foods on this level of the Pyramid come from animals. The "meat" group foods include meat, poultry, fish, dry beans, eggs, and nuts. Meats, poultry, and fish are rich in protein, B vitamins, iron, and zinc. Dry beans, eggs, and nuts provide protein along with other vitamins and minerals. Dairy foods – mainly milk, yogurt, and cheese – provide protein, bone-building calcium, and other nutrients. In general, animal foods are higher in fat than plant foods, but it's not necessary to cut out all meat and dairy products just to keep fat intake low. Low-fat versions of dairy foods and lean, well-trimmed meat and skinless poultry provide the same amounts of vitamins and minerals as their fattier counterparts. Most individuals should aim for 2 to 3 servings daily from each of these 2 groups. Vegetarians who do not eat animal foods can substitute extra servings of dry beans and nuts for their protein needs but will also need fortified foods, extra servings of other plant foods, or supplements to get adequate calcium, iron, and vitamin B_{12}.

Fats, oils, and sweets At the small tip of the Pyramid are foods such as oils, cream, butter, margarine, sugars, soft drinks, candies, and desserts. To maintain a healthy weight, eat them sparingly.

Fats, oils, sweets (use sparingly)

"Meat" group (2–3 servings)   Dairy group (2–3 servings)

Fruit group (2–4 servings)   Vegetable group (3–5 servings)

Bread, cereal, rice, and pasta group (6–11 servings)

WHAT IS A SERVING?

The Pyramid suggests a range of servings for each food group. The number that's right for you depends on your calorie needs, which in turn depends on your age, sex, size, and how active you are. What counts as a serving? There's no need to measure everything, but here are some guidelines:

Bread, cereal, rice, and pasta 1 slice bread; 1 ounce ready-to-eat cereal; ½ cup cooked rice, pasta, or cereal.

Vegetables 1 cup salad greens; ½ cup chopped cooked or raw vegetables; ¾ cup vegetable juice.

Fruits 1 medium apple, banana, orange, pear, or peach; ½ cup cooked, canned, or frozen fruit; ¼ cup dried fruit; ¾ cup fruit juice (100 percent juice).

Dairy foods 1 cup milk or yogurt; 1½ ounces natural cheese; 2 ounces process cheese.

Meat group 2 to 3 ounces cooked lean boneless meat, fish, or poultry (3 ounces is the size of a deck of playing cards). Or, count as 1 ounce of meat any of the following: ½ cup cooked dry beans; 1 egg; ⅓ cup nuts; 2 tablespoons peanut butter.

It's easy to overdo calorie-dense foods like meat and cheese. Try measuring out the suggested portions at least once; you may be surprised at their size.

GETTING ENOUGH CARBS

Breads, cereals, grains, and pasta provide complex carbohydrates (an important source of energy), vitamins, minerals, and fiber. The recommendation of 6 to 11 servings may seem high, but it adds up more quickly than you'd think: A generous bowl of cereal or pasta or a hefty bagel could equal 2, 3, or even 4 servings each! Starchy foods are often blamed for adding extra pounds, but high-fat toppings (butter on bread, cream sauce on pasta) are the more likely culprits. Stick with lean carbohydrates like peasant bread or pita instead of rich croissants and buttery crackers. Whole-grain breads and cereals offer the most fiber.

FRUITS AND VEGETABLES

Five servings of fruits and vegetables daily (at least) is the rule to remember. Follow these ideas to help get your daily quota:
• For the best range of nutrients – and for delicious variety – don't eat the same fruits and vegetables day after day.

• Include choices high in vitamin C (citrus fruits, kiwifruit, strawberries), and those rich in vitamin A (carrots, winter squash, spinach, kale, cantaloupe).
• Research links cruciferous vegetables such as broccoli, cabbage, cauliflower, and Brussels sprouts with reduced risk for certain cancers, so have them several times a week.
• Frozen produce is convenient, and it may be more nutritious than fresh that has been stored or shipped.

CHOOSING YOUR PROTEINS

Top of the class Chicken and turkey without skin, fish, and dry beans and peas are the slimmest selections.

Leanest red meats *Beef* eye round, top round, tenderloin, top sirloin, flank steak, top loin, ground beef (90 to 93 percent); *veal* cutlets (from leg), loin chop; *pork* tenderloin, boneless top loin roast, loin chop, boneless sirloin chop; *lamb* boneless leg shank half, loin roast, loin chop, leg and shoulder cubes for kabobs.

Super seafood Most fish and seafood is low in fat and rich in helpful Omega-3 oils.

Go easy on egg yolks They're high in cholesterol. Many health experts recommend a limit of 4 egg yolks per week.

Don't go nuts Nuts and seeds like sesame or sunflower are high in fat; eat in moderation.

IS THERE A "GOOD" FAT?

Yes. No healthy diet is without some fat; however, all fats in foods are a mixture of three types of fatty acids: saturated, monounsaturated, and polyunsaturated. *Saturated* fat, found in meat and dairy products and coconut, palm, and palm kernel oil, should be limited to 10 percent of calories (about one third of your total fat intake) or less; too much raises cholesterol and the risk of heart disease. *Monounsaturated* fats (found in olive, peanut, and canola oil), and *polyunsaturated* fats (found mainly in safflower, sunflower, corn, soybean, cottonseed oils, and some fish), are healthier.

WHAT'S YOUR FAT LIMIT?

Here's an easy way to calculate the maximum amount of fat you should consume each day. For a diet containing 30 percent fat calories, divide your ideal body weight by 2. So if your ideal weight is 120 pounds, limit your total fat intake to 60 grams (120 lbs ÷ 2 = 60). For a diet with 20 percent fat calories, divide your ideal body weight by 3. Fat is an essential nutrient, so don't cut it out completely. Remember that it's your average intake over a few days – not in a single food or meal – that's important. If you eat a high-fat food or meal, balance it with low-fat foods the rest of the day or the next day.

THE MEDITERRANEAN DIET

For centuries the traditional diet of the sunny countries around the Mediterranean has succeeded in prolonging life and preventing disease. Health experts have taken notice – and suggested that the culinary habits of these countries could help Americans in their quest to cut fat and eat more nutritiously. The result: The "Mediterranean Pyramid," a plan not too different from the USDA Pyramid. Both have a foundation of grains, fruits, and vegetables. But the Mediterranean model highlights beans and other legumes, limits red meat to a few times per month, and promotes the use of olive oil. The model also encourages daily exercise – and even a glass of wine with dinner.

Go with grains (and pasta!) Bread, pasta, bulgur, and rice are staples on the Mediterranean table. This is a jump-start to good health, because grains are naturally high in complex carbohydrates and low in fat. Whole grains boast another healthy bonus – fiber.

Pack in the produce The Mediterranean diet abounds in seasonal fresh fruits and vegetables – significantly more than the typical American diet.

Amazing olive oil For centuries, people in Mediterranean countries have enjoyed generous amounts of olive oil with no evidence of harm. They cook with it, drizzle it in soup and on salads, and even use it on bread in place of butter. What makes olive oil so great? The main difference between olive oil and other fats is that it's predominantly a heart-healthy monounsaturated fat. When substituted for fats that are more saturated, "mono" fats tend to lower artery-clogging LDL cholesterol while maintaining levels of the protective HDL cholesterol. But remember, all types of fat are high in calories and excess weight increases the risk of heart disease.

Focus on fish Red meat is saved for special occasions (and then usually used in small amounts in grain and vegetable dishes). Fish – low in saturated fat and rich in healthful Omega-3 fatty acids – is eaten several times a week instead.

Get lean with beans A key ingredient in Mediterranean salads, soups, and stews, these inexpensive foods are low in fat and high in protein, fiber, and complex carbohydrates.

Savor wines Wine with meals is traditional in Mediterranean cultures, but overindulgence is rare. Studies have shown that moderate drinking (usually defined as 1 drink per day for women, 2 for men) raises "good" cholesterol levels and may make blood less likely to form clots in arteries. But moderation is the key – "one drink" is a 4-ounce glass of wine (½ cup), a 12-ounce serving of beer, or 1 ounce of hard liquor.

Finish with fruit Sweets have a place in the Mediterranean diet, but meals typically end with fresh or dried fruit rather than sugar-laden, high-fat desserts.

Let yourself relax Quality of life can't be overlooked as a contributing factor to health and happiness. Meals are savored slowly with family and friends, and physical activity is part of daily life.

LEARNING FROM FOOD LABELS

Food labels help consumers make informed choices and understand how a particular food fits into their daily diet.

• The Percent Daily Values on labels tell you the percentage of the recommended daily amount of a nutrient in a serving (based on 2000 calories daily). You can "budget" your intake of nutrients simply by adding up these percentages. For example, the label below shows a food containing 20 percent of the daily value for fat. If the next food you eat has a 10 percent daily value for fat, you've had 30 percent of your total fat allowance for the day. For fat, saturated fat, sodium, and cholesterol, it's good to keep daily values below 100 percent. Fiber, vitamins A and C, calcium, and iron are listed because American diets often fall short. For these, do aim for the 100 percent mark. Other vitamins and minerals may also appear on some labels.

• The Daily Values footnote includes a chart that shows some Daily Values for diets containing 2000 and 2500 calories. Use these numbers as a guide. Your own daily values may be higher or lower depending on your calorie needs.

Nutrition Facts

Serving Size 1 cup (228g)
Servings per Container 2

Amount per serving

Calories 260   Calories from Fat 120

	% Daily Value*
Total Fat 13g	20%
Saturated Fat 5g	25%
Cholesterol 30mg	10%
Sodium 660mg	28%
Total Carbohydrate 31g	10%
Dietary Fiber 0g	0%
Sugars 5g	
Protein 5g	

Vitamin A 4% • Vitamin C 2%
Calcium 15% • Iron 4%

*Percent Daily Values are based on a 2000-calorie diet. Your daily values may be higher or lower depending on your calorie needs:

	Calories:	2000	2500
Total Fat	Less than	65g	80g
Sat Fat	Less than	20g	25g
Cholesterol	Less than	300mg	300mg
Sodium	Less than	2400mg	2400mg
Total Carbohydrate		300g	375g
Dietary Fiber		25g	30g

Calories per gram:
Fat 9 • Carbohydrate 4 • Protein 4

• Food labels must also carry an ingredient list. Ingredients are listed on food labels in descending order according to their weight. This allows you to, for example, choose muffins with flour, not sugar, at the top of the list.

USING THE NUTRITIONAL VALUES IN THIS BOOK

With each recipe, you'll find nutritional information that can help you plan a balanced diet. To help you use this information, see "Learning from Food Labels" (above) for recommended daily nutrient levels. Aim to balance higher-fat recipes with leaner choices: For example, serve lasagna with a green salad and a glass of skim milk.

• Our nutritional calculations do not include optional ingredients or garnishes.

• When alternative ingredients are listed (e.g., margarine or butter), our calculations are based on the first one mentioned.

• Unless otherwise noted, whole milk has been used.

TIPS FOR LOW-FAT COOKING

• Choose lean cuts of meat and trim visible fat before cooking. Remove skin from poultry before or after cooking.
• Broil meats on a rack so the fat can drip away.
• Chill soups and stews overnight so you can easily remove and discard the hardened fat from the top.
• Be skimpy with fat. Use nonstick pans or nonstick cooking spray, or "sauté" in a small amount of broth or water. Don't pour oil into a skillet – it's easy to add too much. Measure, or use a pastry brush to coat the pan with a thin layer of oil. When baking, coat pans with a spritz of nonstick cooking spray instead of oils or fats.
• Experiment with low-fat or skim milk, low-fat versions of sour cream and cheese, and nonfat yogurt; they provide the same calcium and protein as whole-milk varieties, with less fat.
• Use fresh herbs and zesty seasonings liberally to replace some of the flavor lost when you slash fat.

SMART SUBSTITUTIONS

• Use nonfat yogurt in dips instead of sour cream.
• Substitute Canadian bacon for regular bacon and save about 115 calories per ounce.
• Substitute ground chicken or turkey breast for ground beef. (Be sure the package is labeled *meat only* – if not, it may contain skin and can have as much fat as ground beef.)
• Substitute cooked fiber- and protein-packed dried legumes like beans and lentils for meat in casseroles.
• Replace the cream in cream soups or sauces with evaporated skim milk.
• For a leaner hamburger, substitute shredded carrots or cooked rice for a third of the meat.
• Choose angel food cake instead of pound cake.
• To reduce fat and cholesterol, use 2 egg whites for 1 whole egg.
• Replace sour cream with buttermilk or yogurt in baking.

SAMPLE MENUS

The following menus show 3 days of healthy, satisfying meals that meet the dietary requirements suggested by the USDA: 2000 calories a day with no more than 30 percent calories from fat. (These values are for a moderately active adult; your calorie requirement may vary from this depending on your metabolism and your level of activity.) The page numbers are listed for the recipes given in this book; all other items are generic. Remember that the key to good health is how you eat over time – not the fat and calorie content of a single dish or meal.

THREE DAYS OF BALANCED MENUS

	BREAKFAST	LUNCH	DINNER
Day 1	¾ cup orange juice or orange sections Toasted bagel with 1 tablespoon jam 1 cup skim or 1% milk	Mushroom-Barley Soup (page 61) Crusty bread or saltine crackers 2 ounces Cheddar cheese 1 apple	Five-Spice Salmon (page 114) Lime Couscous (page 380) Steamed spinach Peach Sorbet (page 484) Almond-Anise Biscotti (page 518) 1 cup skim or 1% milk
Day 2	Cantaloupe wedge 1 Apple-Buttermilk Muffin (page 397) 1 cup skim or 1% milk	Turkey sandwich: 2 ounces turkey, 2 slices rye bread, tomato and onion slices, mustard 1 cup low-fat yogurt	Tenderloin au Poivre (page 199) Steamed new potatoes with dill or parsley Steamed broccoli and carrots Sugar 'n' Spice Angel Food Cake (page 536) Fresh orange segments and strawberries 1 cup skim or 1% milk
Day 3	¾ cup bran-flakes cereal 1 cup skim or 1% milk 1 banana	Spinach salad: 3 cups spinach leaves, 1 hard-cooked egg, sliced, 1 slice bacon, cooked and crumbled, ¼ cup crumbled feta cheese, sliced raw mushrooms, balsamic vinegar 2 breadsticks ½ cup grapes 1 cup skim or 1% milk	Country French Chicken (page 155) Steamed green beans Lemon-Parsley Rice (page 376) Green salad, with Buttermilk-Chive Dressing (page 346) Baked Pears with Marsala (page 454)

GRILLING KNOW-HOW

Backyard patios, beaches, or a shady spot in a park: No matter where you're playing grill master, barbecues will bring together enthusiastic appetites and happy people. Here, every juicy detail for finger-licking results, quick ways to light the coals, the right cooking method for every cut, and essential equipment, plus inspired ways to boost flavor.

GETTING STARTED

It's easy to become a pro at getting the fire going. To light a standard charcoal grill, use a charcoal chimney (a metal cylinder with a rack that stacks briquettes over crumpled newspaper), or an electric starter, which nestles a hot coil among coals. Or, stack coals in a pyramid (for good air circulation) and douse with lighter fluid (instant-lighting briquettes have been pretreated with lighter fluid). Use enough charcoal to reach 1 inch beyond the area the food will cover – plus a few more briquettes if it's a cold and windy day. The coals will take about 20 minutes to reach desired temperature; when they are ready for cooking, they will appear ash gray (during the daytime) or have a slight red glow (at night). Before setting the grill rack in place, spread the coals in a single layer, or bank them on either side of grill for indirect heat. (Follow the manufacturer's instructions to light gas and electric grills.)

SAFETY TIPS

Location, location Place your grill on a flat, level surface so it won't tip over, and away from overhangs, fences, and shrubbery that could be ignited by a sudden flare-up.
Avoid contamination Use separate dishes for carrying raw and cooked foods. Wash all utensils, containers, cutting boards, and work surfaces with hot soapy water after they come in contact with uncooked foods.
Charcoal smarts To avoid a build-up of toxic fumes, position the grill in a well-ventilated location – and never barbecue indoors. It's dangerous to add lighter fluid to flames or hot coals. Gasoline or kerosene are off-limits – both can cause an explosion.
Cut the fat To avoid grease fires, trim excess fat from meats.
Stay out of the black A charred, blackened crust on foods is unhealthy.
Play it cool Once you've finished cooking, cover the grill, close the vents, and allow the coals to burn out completely. Let the ashes cool at least 48 hours and dispose of them in a noncombustible container. If you dispose of coals before they've cooled, remove them with long-handled tongs and bury them in sand or put in a bucket of water.

THE BEST WAY TO MARINATE

Nice and easy Zip-tight bags provide a great no-fuss method – simply add marinade ingredients and meat, poultry, or fish, then seal shut, pressing out excess air, and refrigerate. If using a bowl or pan, be sure it's made of a nonreactive material (glass, ceramic, stainless steel) that won't be affected by the acid in the marinade.
The raw deal Never let marinades that you've used for raw meat, poultry, or fish come in contact with cooked food. Marinate foods (except vegetables) in the refrigerator – never at room temperature, unless marinating time is 30 minutes or less. If using a marinade as a sauce, boil for at least 2 minutes before serving. Discard any unused marinade – do not use again.
Deepening flavor Most meat and poultry needs 1 to 3 hours to marinate; seafood, 15 to 30 minutes. But timing also depends on ingredients. The more acid (e.g., lemon juice, vinegar, yogurt) used in your marinade, the less time it will take. Marinating for too long can result in a mushy texture. Marinades penetrate about $\frac{1}{2}$ inch deep, so don't expect them to flavor the center of thick cuts.
Rub it in! Seasoning rubs are blends of dried herbs and spices that add flavor (without fat) to grilled meats and other foods. Common ingredients: rosemary, thyme, crushed red pepper, fennel seeds, garlic, dill, and cracked peppercorns. Just mix and rub onto meat, pressing it in place, either hours or minutes before grilling.

SKEWER STRATEGIES

• If you favor using metal skewers, you'll have best results with ones that are twisted or square – not round. The reason? Foods tend to twirl on round skewers when you try to turn them, making it difficult to ensure even cooking. (Wooden and skinny bamboo skewers aren't slippery, so their round shape doesn't pose a problem.)
• Be sure to soak wooden or bamboo skewers in water for at least 15 minutes before using, so that they won't burn when exposed to the grill's heat and flames. Then pat them dry.
• To ensure even cooking, don't jam pieces of food up against each other on the skewer – leave a small space between items when you thread them together. Additional safeguards: Cut even-size pieces, and combine foods with similar cooking times on the same skewer.

Unwieldy items like large, thick onion slices won't fall apart and slip through the grill rack if you thread them onto 2 parallel skewers.

DIRECT AND INDIRECT GRILLING

Different foods require specific heat sources. Follow these guidelines to pick the right method for what you're making. **Direct-heat grilling** For this method, food is cooked directly over the heat source, and must be turned in order to expose both sides to the fire. Direct grilling is best for foods that take less than 30 minutes to cook, such as boneless chicken, steaks, fish fillets, hamburgers, turkey cutlets, and hot dogs. **Indirect-heat grilling** Similar to oven-roasting, this method is for foods that take longer than 30 minutes to cook, including roasts, whole turkeys, bone-in chicken, ribs, and briskets; it must be done on a covered grill. Bank charcoal briquettes on one or both sides of a drip pan on the lower rack. When the coals are ready, place food on the grill centered over the pan. For extra moisture, you can add water, broth, or fruit juice to the drip pan. Close the grill lid and keep it closed until the end of cooking time or until you need to add coals (at least an hour); there's no need to turn the food. For a 22½-inch grill, use about 25 briquettes on each side of the drip pan (50 briquettes total) for up to an hour of cooking. For foods that require over an hour to cook, add 8 new briquettes to each side for each additional hour of cooking.

MAKING A FOIL PACKET

Foil packets create a handy pouch for grilling small, delicate foods like seafood or vegetables (good if you don't own a grill topper). You can add flavor by including ingredients such as olive oil, citrus zest, prosciutto, or fresh herbs. To make a foil packet, center food on a double thickness of heavy-duty foil. Close package with a double fold on top and ends (leave space for steam expansion). To avoid punctures, use tongs to turn packets.

ADDING A DISTINCTIVE FLAVOR

• Infuse chicken, ham, fish, pork, or beef with a hint of citrus by scattering orange, lemon, lime, or even grapefruit peels over coals in the last few minutes of grilling.
• For smoky flavor, add aromatic wood chips (soak them in water first to bring out their flavor and prolong burning time). Mesquite and hickory are popular choices. More exotic varieties to seek out: alder, fruit-tree woods, and grapevines. (Add large chips at the start of grilling, small chips near the end to keep the fire going.) Even easier: Buy briquettes that are embedded with wood chips.
• Great with grilled fruits like nectarines, plums, pineapple, and peaches: the seductively sweet and smoky flavor of

cinnamon sticks, whole cloves, star anise, or allspice berries. Simply soak a few in water and add them to the coals.
• Enhance the flavor of meats, seafood, or vegetables by sprinkling one of the following over coals at the end of cooking time: sturdy herb sprigs (rosemary, thyme); bay leaves; dampened, unpeeled garlic cloves; or wet corn cobs.

FEEL THE HEAT

• To estimate the temperature of the grill, place your hand, palm side down, about 6 inches over the heat source. Count the seconds ("one thousand one, one thousand two," etc.) until the heat forces you to pull your hand away. If you can keep it in place for 2 seconds, the grill is hot (375°F or more); 3 seconds, it's medium-hot (350°–375°F); 4 seconds, it's medium (300°–350°F); 5 seconds, it's low (200°–300°F).
• If the fire is too hot: Raise the cooking rack and spread out the charcoal. In a covered cooker, close vents halfway.
• Need more heat? Lower cooking rack; tap ashes from charcoal and push closer together. Add more coals to the edges of hot briquettes. In covered cooker, open vents fully.

HELPFUL EQUIPMENT

Long-handled tongs Indispensable for turning food and arranging coals. Don't turn meat or poultry with a fork; this can pierce the flesh, releasing juices and flavor.
Basting brush For applying sauce or oiling grill racks.
Fish flipper (or two flat metal spatulas) Ideal for supporting delicate-textured fish (fillets and whole), which otherwise may fall apart as they are being turned.
Grill brush Stiff wire bristles make the job easy; V–shaped models clean both sides of the grill in one sweep.
Insulated mitts Look for mitts that are elbow-length and flameproof.
Hinged grill basket A wire basket makes it easy to flip whole fish and other delicate foods.
Grill topper A small-hole or fine-mesh grid that's a must for grilled vegetables, seafood, and delicate fish fillets.

CLEANING YOUR GRILL

For easiest cleanup, clean grill right after cooking with metal-bristle brush. Let rack cool slightly, then soak it in hot soapy water to loosen grime. If the rack is too large for your sink, let it stand for an hour wrapped in wet paper towels; scrub clean. To clean a gas grill after use, turn heat to high and let grill run for 10 to 15 minutes with lid closed. Then use a metal-bristle brush to remove any baked-on food. A trick of the trade: To prevent foods from sticking to grill racks, rub rack with vegetable oil or spray with nonstick cooking spray before grilling.

Parties are terrific for bringing together favorite foods and friends. What's more, dazzling your guests can take surprisingly little effort. Whether you're an experienced party planner or a beginner, you'll find hints and tips galore on these pages. Read on for ways to get organized, strategies for choosing no-worry menus, how to create the prettiest tables – and more.

RULES FOR SUCCESS

Keep it simple A few well-planned dishes are more appealing than loads of fussy or rich foods. Remember, the bigger the crowd, the simpler the food should be.

Do it ahead The more you can do in advance, the more time you'll have to relax and enjoy your guests.

Be generous You're safer having too much food than running out. Don't forget, you can usually freeze the extras.

Go with the season Fruits and vegetables in season are fresher and cost less, so highlight them as much as possible.

Make lists This is a superb way to get organized. Write a guest list, a menu list, and two shopping lists (for nonperishables and perishables). Make a menu preparation timetable that can be checked off as you go.

Keep a record To avoid repeating the same dishes for the same people, write everything down in an entertaining notebook. It's also a useful reminder of which dishes or menus have worked well in the past.

EASY ENTERTAINING STRATEGIES

• The more dishes you can make ahead, the better. Many soups and stews will actually improve in flavor. It's also smart to include some dishes that freeze well, such as Spicy Cheese Sticks (see page 50), pound cakes, or cookies. For some items, components can be made ahead and stored separately for later assembly.

• Buffets are great for entertaining because once the food is out, all that's needed is to keep the serving bowls and platters full. Don't leave food at room temperature for more than 2 hours (1 hour in hot weather); replenish the table with fresh platters rather than adding more to half-empty ones.

• Create a menu of all room-temperature dishes. Try marinated vegetables; savory tarts and quiches; pâtés and terrines; crostini and bruschetta; cold sesame noodles; frittatas; dips and salads; thin-sliced roast beef, turkey, or ham; cold poached chicken or fish.

• Feature one centerpiece dish – elegant stuffed roast veal, a hearty pan of lasagna, or a big tureen of chili – and partner with simple side dishes like crisp tossed green salad and crusty bread or rolls.

• Keep prepared foods on hand for easy appetizers. Good bets include: jarred caponata; marinated artichokes; olivada or other spreads; a good pâté; cornichons; jumbo olives; nuts (macadamias, pistachios, cashews); pita breads; a selection of crackers; etc.

• Plan finishing touches to brighten any menu. A swirl of sour cream on creamy carrot soup; sprigs of fresh herbs on a roast chicken platter; zigzag-cut lemon halves alongside fish; candied violets strewn on a dark chocolate cake – these turn simple into sensational.

• Do as much advance prep as you can to avoid last-minute jitters. Make croutons and hold in an airtight tin at room temperature; rinse, trim, and cut vegetables for side dishes and salads (wrap in damp paper towels in plastic bags in the refrigerator); prepare salad dressings; and so on.

• Use the food processor and microwave to save time: Shred a mountain of cabbage, grate cheese, reheat sauces, etc.

• Avoid labor-intensive tasks. For example, for big parties you may find it easier to buy skinless, boneless chicken breasts than to bone them yourself.

• Use helpers to cook and serve. For example, delegate grill duty or recruit someone to pass the hors d'oeuvres tray.

DETAILS, DETAILS

• When inviting your guests, be specific about appropriate dress, the extent of the food and drink, and the expected duration of the party.

• Up to a week ahead, check your supply of chairs, glasses, serving dishes, and utensils. Rent, borrow, or buy extras if needed. For a large party, you may want to line up help like waiters or bartenders.

• Check recipes for any special cooking equipment you may need, such as parchment paper.

• Decide on the music in advance. Soft jazz or classical competes less with conversation than other kinds.

• Make sure your bar is stocked; include enough choices (soft drinks, lemonade, fruit juice, sparkling water, etc.) for nondrinkers. Choose wines to go with dinner.

• Buy enough ice – more than you think you need.

• Make fruited ice cubes to enliven drinks. Freeze tiny strawberries or raspberries in ice cubes. They're lovely in lemonade, iced tea, or a glass of white wine.

• If the refrigerator is full, use an ice chest for storing cold drinks, ice, and salads.

• Arrange flowers a day ahead so they'll be in full bloom for the day of the party.

• Set the table early in the day or the night before.

• If you're serving messy foods like corn on the cob or ribs, have little finger bowls at each place setting – float slices of lemon in warm water in small dishes or custard cups.

• If necessary, put out small bowls to be used for olive pits, toothpicks, etc.; put in a pit or pick so people will know.

STRESS-FREE MENU PLANNING

Stick with the tried and true To minimize potential hitches, serve mostly recipes that you've tried and loved before.
Consider your guests It's important to know of any food restrictions or preferences (e.g., vegetarian, low-cholesterol diet, no fish). Don't forget to ask about food allergies.
Harmony and order The best menus feature foods that complement each other in terms of flavors, colors, textures, and richness. Follow a spicy entrée with a refreshing salad; a creamy soup with a simple roast instead of a heavily sauced main dish; a light starter salad with a hearty stew. Try to avoid repeating ingredients and flavors. For example, don't have olives in both the salad and the stew.
Think ahead Include as many dishes as possible that can be prepared in advance. Soups, stews, casseroles, mousses, and sorbets are all good choices. Try not to have more than two dishes that need last-minute attention.
Room-temperature ready It can be tricky to get all the hot foods on the table before something else cools down, so plan at least some dishes to serve at room temperature.
Bite size is best Foods for the hors d'oeuvres tray should be small enough to be eaten in one bite (or easy to dip).

SEASONAL ENTERTAINING

Each season brings its own inspiration for party ideas. In spring and summer, think of colorful foods, fresh, light flavors, and firing up the barbecue grill. Winter parties call for richer flavors and heartier foods. Here are some ideas to help you take advantage of seasonal delights.

Summer/spring sensations
• Celebrate spring with a buffet of favorites – asparagus spears; grilled salmon; baby vegetables; Strawberry-Rhubarb Pie (see page 490).
• Rub glass rims with lemon wedges and dip in coarse salt (for margaritas or bloody Marys) or sugar (for mint juleps).
• Make an outdoor party especially festive by stringing tiny white lights around shrubs and small trees.
• Have an old-fashioned crab boil with corn on the cob – and lots of napkins.
• Decorate cakes lavishly with nontoxic flowers and berries.

Autumn/winter fancies
• Have a pre-game tailgate party with heroes and hearty soups.
• Scent the house by simmering cinnamon sticks on the stove.
• Warm up winter with meat-and-potatoes menus: meat loaf with creamy mashed potatoes, or beef tenderloin with roasted potatoes.
• Roast chestnuts (slash the flat side of each first) in a 400°F oven for 20 minutes – eat hot.
• Bring out hot chocolate with the after-dinner coffee.
• Decorate tables with votive candles and baskets of pine cones and holly sprigs.

ENTERTAINING MENUS

We've created a sampler of menus that both you and your guests will love. That's because each is filled with festive and delicious dishes that are simple to make, and many of the recipes can be prepared in advance. Adapt the menu choices as you like to suit individual preferences.

Healthy Entertaining for 6
Marinated Goat Cheese (page 41)
Stove-Top Eye Round with Spring Vegetables (page 188)
Crusty bread
Apricot Soufflé (page 461)
•

Spring Dinner for 8
Asparagus with Parmesan Vinaigrette (page 285)
Salmon and Vegetables in Parchment (page 125; double the recipe)
New potatoes with dill
Green salad, with Mustard-Shallot Vinaigrette (page 345)
Panna Cotta with Raspberry Sauce (page 475)
•

Summer Barbecue for 10 to 12
Roasted Eggplant Dip (page 34), **with pita wedges**
Grilled Pesto Lamb with Tomato-Cucumber Bruschetta (page 261)
Barley Salad with Nectarines (page 331)
Green Beans with Toasted Sesame Seeds (page 318)
Cherry Tomato-Lemon Salad (page 322)
Nectarine and Cherry Crisp with Oatmeal Topping (page 452), **with vanilla ice cream**
•

Autumn Dinner for 8
Pumpkin and Roasted Garlic Dip (page 34), **with focaccia strips**
Roast Duck with Cherry-Port Sauce (page 141; double the recipe)
Mashed Root Vegetables (page 294)
Green beans
Fennel, Pear, and Endive Salad (page 319)
Cappuccino Mousse (page 476)
Anise Wafers (page 505)
•

Winter Buffet for 12 to 16
Smoked Salmon Terrine (page 36)
Apricot-Glazed Smoked Ham (page 247)
Vegetables Vinaigrette (page 276)
Baked Rigatoni and Peas (page 364)
Spinach and Tangerine Salad (page 319)
Sweet Potato Biscuits (page 402)
Raspberry-Pear Trifle (page 473)
Coconut-Almond Macaroons (page 508)
Chocolate and Hazelnut Truffles (page 524)

SETTING A PROPER TABLE

A pretty table can set the mood for the meal to follow. Here, a brief guide to setting it right.
• Place a dinner plate in the center of each setting. Add flatware in the order it will be used, beginning on the outside. (The more formal the setting, the more flatware there is likely to be, but all settings should follow the order-of-use rule.) Place forks on the left and knives on the right, cutting edge turned in. Place spoons to the right of knives.
• If you have enough pieces, dessert utensils go above the plate (spoon next to plate, handle to the right, fork above spoon, handle to the left). If not, clear the table completely and serve dessert flatware with dessert.
• Set bread plates to the left of the plates, above the forks. Butter knives may be placed on the plates, handle to the right. Place salad plates, if using, to the left of the forks.
• Glasses go on the right, above the knives. Place the water glass closest to the plate, then the white-wine glass, and then the red-wine glass, if you're serving two wines.
• Place napkins either to the left of the forks, or in the center of the dinner plate.

WHICH TABLE COVERING?

Tablecloths Measure the table before you buy. For a formal tablecloth, add 16 to 24 inches to both the length and width of the table. For a round table, add 36 inches to the diameter. Except for the most formal occasions, choose a tablecloth as you like: bright or pastel, textured or patterned. Linen or lace in white and neutrals are most versatile, and always look elegant.
Place mats These come in all colors, sizes, shapes, and materials – from plastic and straw to linen and even metal. The mat should be large enough to hold the entire place setting, but not overlap with the next one.
Napkins As with tablecloths, fine cloth napkins in white or neutral colors are the most formal. Otherwise, choose napkins as desired to complement tablecloths or mats.

SUPER CENTERPIECES

Any table looks better with a stylish centerpiece. It's possible to make one from the simplest of raw materials; see the suggestions that follow. Keep the centerpiece low, so guests can see each other across the table. Don't forget to walk around the table so you can check it from all sides.
• Mix flowers, fruits, vegetables, and herbs together for a lovely effect. Try shiny plum tomatoes with scarlet poppies; small purple and white eggplants with flowering herbs; pale peaches with lemons and sage leaves.
• Line a basket with an antique cloth; fill with perfect pears.
• Fill a crystal bowl with nuts in their shells.
• Place pots of small flowering plants in a wooden box.
• For a winter party, place chestnuts, pinecones, and evergreen boughs in a wide silver bowl.
• Combine small gourds and squash in a wicker basket.
• Set orange and red bell peppers in a turquoise bowl.
• Arrange an assembly of cacti in a shallow basket.

BUFFET BASICS

A buffet is one of the easiest ways to serve a group of eight or more. You can set it up in advance, then enjoy with your guests – all you have to do is replenish the food as necessary. If you have room, organize drinks and food in separate places so there's less of a crowd at either place. For a basic buffet, arrange foods in a circle on the table in a logical order: main dish, vegetables, salad, bread. Stack large dinner plates at the start of the buffet and put napkins and flatware at the end so your guests are freer to fill up their plates. For easy serving, wrap individual place settings (knife and fork) in the napkins.

   A two-line buffet is a similar arrangement that's ideal for a bigger crowd. Since you organize the food in two identical lines, one on each side of the table, everyone gets served more quickly. Remember that you'll need double the amount of serving dishes and utensils. For a smaller group, try arranging the buffet on a sideboard or table against the wall.

WINE KNOW-HOW

Enjoyed the world over, wine can be one of the most pleasurable parts of a meal. Besides being savored at the table, with dinner or before, wine can also enhance cooking. Following is a guide to serving, storing, and using wine – plus what to expect from some of the more popular varieties.

SERVING SMARTS

• Stemmed glasses are traditional because the large base allows you to swirl the wine, which helps release its aroma and flavor. Holding the glass by its stem also means you're less apt to warm the wine with the heat of your hand. Fill glasses no more than two-thirds full (for swirling room).
• In general, serve red wines at room temperature. Some young and fruity reds, such as Beaujolais Nouveau, are best slightly chilled. Most wine does not need to "breathe." If you do wish to aerate wine before serving, decant it or pour it into glasses so that the wine actually comes in contact with air.
• White wines and sparkling wines should be served chilled.
• To quick-chill white wine, submerge the bottle in a bucket or pot filled with half ice and half water for 20 minutes.
• When pairing wine and food, try to match flavor intensities. For example, serve a light wine with a delicate entrée, a spicy, robust wine with a deeply flavored dish.
• Light wines are best with summer meals, or earlier in the day. Offer heavier wines with winter meals, or late in the day.
• If in doubt, go with the old rule: red wines with meats and cheese, white wines with fish, poultry, and vegetable dishes.

HOW TO STORE

• For long-term storage, keep wine in a cool, humid, dark place (e.g., cupboard, cellar). Store bottles on their side to prevent corks from drying and shrinking, which will let in air.
• It's fine to store leftover wine (without fancy equipment). It may even improve as it has a chance to aerate and release its bouquet. Refrigerate white wine and keep red at room temperature for up to 48 hours, with the original cork.

COOKING WITH WINE

• Use a decent wine for cooking or marinating – not your absolute best, but something you wouldn't hesitate to drink.
• When adding wine to a sauce or stove-top dish, let it cook to allow the flavor to mellow and to cook off the alcohol.
• Marinating in wine is a good way to add flavor to meats and poultry. Also, the acid in wine acts as a tenderizer.
• For subtle flavor, use wine in moderation when cooking.
• You can substitute vinegar, broth, or juice for wine in recipes.

KNOW YOUR WINES

WHITE WINES
Sauvignon Blanc This refreshing, clean-flavored wine has a grassy, herbaceous aroma. In California, it's sometimes called Fumé Blanc. Serve with fish and shellfish.
Chardonnay One of the most popular white wines, it's produced the world over. Most Chardonnays are fresh, fruity, and fairly dry; they are often flavored by aging in oak. Very good with light summer foods such as grilled salmon.
Chenin Blanc A dry, crisp wine with a spicy, slightly sweet flavor; it complements chicken as well as vegetable entrées.
Gewürztraminer A specialty of Alsace, France, though it's produced in other countries as well. A spicy, crisp wine, it can be dry or semisweet. Try dry versions with fish, poultry, and spicy foods, sweeter ones with desserts.
Riesling This favorite has a fruity, slightly sweet taste and a floral fragrance that's faintly like honey. It pairs nicely with veal and shellfish as well as most Asian foods.
Sauternes A rich, sweet wine made primarily from Semillon grapes. The grapes develop a beneficial mold that shrivels them and concentrates their sweetness. Serve as a dessert wine or with rich foods, such as pâté, duck, or Roquefort cheese.

RED WINES
Bordeaux This classic from western France can be light and fruity or rich and fragrant. Roast lamb is the ideal partner.
Cabernet Sauvignon Produced in many countries, this well-known wine is full-bodied, fruity, and complex. It complements hearty meats, chicken, and pasta.
Chianti The famous Italian red wine. Sturdy and dry, it goes nicely with pasta dishes, steak, burgers, and grilled foods.
Gamay (**Beaujolais**) Pleasantly light, this dry, fruity red wine is excellent with meats as well as poultry and pasta.
Merlot Rich, fragrant, and smooth-bodied. Serve with robust foods like lamb, sausages, and Cornish hens.
Pinot Noir This spicy, intensely flavored wine can be light and fresh or rich and smooth. It goes with almost any food, but is especially good with salmon, ham, and cheeses.
Zinfandel A uniquely California wine, it has a spicy, fruity, slight raspberry flavor. It can stand up to hearty foods like steaks, lamb, veal chops, hamburgers, and lobster.

OTHER WINES
Fortified Madeira, sherry, and port are all wines that are fortified with a spirit (usually brandy) to increase their alcohol content. They make a fine aperitif or dessert wine.
Rosé These wines get their pale pink color and light-bodied character from a very brief contact with grape skins. Serve rosés well chilled, before dinner or with light foods.
Sparkling These bubbly, mild-flavored wines range from slightly sweet to dry. Champagne is the most famous. Sparkling wines go nicely with many foods, from oysters and smoked salmon to desserts.

GLOSSARY

Al dente Italian for "to the tooth," describes perfectly cooked pasta and vegetables. If pasta is al dente, it is just tender but offers a slight resistance when it is bitten.

Baste To spoon or brush a liquid over food – typically roasted or grilled meats and poultry – during cooking to keep it moist. The liquid can be a sauce or glaze, broth, melted butter, or pan juices.

Beat To briskly whip or stir a mixture with a spoon, whisk, or electric mixer until it is smooth and light.

Blanch To cook foods briefly in boiling water. Blanching locks in textures for tender-crisp vegetables, loosens tomato and peach skins for peeling, and mellows salty foods. Begin timing as soon as the food hits the water – the water needn't return to a boil – then cool in cold water to stop the cooking.

Blend To combine two or more ingredients until smooth or uniformly mixed. Blending can be done with a spoon, or an appliance such as an electric mixer or a blender.

Blind bake To bake a piecrust before it's filled to create a crisper crust. To prevent puffing and slipping during baking, the pastry is lined with foil and filled with pie weights, dry beans, or uncooked rice; these are removed shortly before the end of baking time to allow the crust to brown.

Boil To heat a liquid until bubbles break vigorously on the surface. You can boil vegetables, cook pasta in boiling water, or reduce sauces by boiling them. Never boil meats (they'll be tough) or custard sauces (they'll curdle).

Braise To cook food in a small amount of liquid in a tightly covered pan, either in the oven or on the stove-top. Braising is an ideal way to prepare less-tender cuts of meat, firm-fleshed fish, and vegetables.

Broil To cook food with intense, direct dry heat under a broiler. For broiled meats, use a rack so the fat drips away. Always preheat the broiler, but don't preheat the pan and rack, or the food could stick.

Broth A thin, clear liquid produced by cooking poultry, meat, fish, or vegetables in water, and used as a base for soups, stews, sauces, and many other dishes. Canned broth is always convenient as a substitute for homemade.

Brown To cook food quickly on top of the stove (in fat), under a broiler, or in the oven to develop a richly browned, flavorful surface and help seal in natural juices.

Butterfly To split a food, such as shrimp or a boneless lamb leg or pork chop, horizontally in half, cutting almost but not all the way through, then opening (like a book) to form a butterfly shape. Butterflying exposes more surface area so the food cooks evenly and more quickly.

Caramelize To heat sugar in a skillet until it becomes syrupy and deep amber brown. Sugary toppings on desserts like crème brûlée can also be caramelized (by heating under the broiler until melted), as can onions (by sautéing slowly until deep golden and very tender).

Chop To cut food roughly into small, irregular pieces about the size of peas.

Core To remove the core or center of various fruits and vegetables. Coring eliminates small seeds or tough and woody centers (as in pineapple).

Cream To beat a fat, such as margarine or butter, alone or with sugar, until it's fluffy and light in color. This technique whips air into the fat, creating light-textured baked goods. An electric mixer makes short work of creaming.

Crimp To pinch or press dough edges – especially piecrust edges – to create a decorative finish and/or to seal two layers of dough so the filling doesn't seep out during baking. The edges of a parchment or foil packet may also be crimped to seal in food and its juices during cooking.

Curdle To coagulate, or separate, into solids and liquids. Egg- and milk-based mixtures are susceptible to curdling if they're heated too quickly or combined with an acidic ingredient, such as lemon juice or tomatoes.

Cut in To work a solid fat, such as shortening, butter, or margarine, into dry ingredients by using a pastry blender or two knives used scissor-fashion. The fat and flour should form pea-size nuggets or coarse crumbs for flaky pastry.

Deglaze To add a liquid (e.g., water, wine, broth) to a skillet or roasting pan in which meat or poultry has been cooked to release the caramelized meat juices. After removing the meat, pour the liquid into the pan and heat, scraping up the flavorful brown bits from the bottom, to make a quick sauce.

Devein To remove the dark intestinal vein of a shrimp. Use the tip of a sharp knife, then rinse the shrimp with cold water.

Dice To cut food into small cubes of about ¼ inch.

Dot To scatter bits of margarine or butter over a pie, casserole, or other dish before baking. This adds extra richness and flavor and helps promote browning.

Dredge To lightly coat food with a dry ingredient, typically flour or bread crumbs. Meats and fish are dredged to create a deliciously crisp, browned exterior. Be sure to shake off excess coating before browning.

Drizzle To slowly pour a liquid, such as melted butter or a glaze, in a fine stream, back and forth, over food.

Dust To sprinkle very lightly with a powdery ingredient, such as confectioners' sugar (on cakes and pastries) or flour (in a greased cake pan).

Eau-de-vie French for "water of life," describes any colorless brandy distilled from fermented fruit juice. Kirsch (cherry) and framboise (raspberry) are two popular varieties.

Emulsify To bind liquids that usually can't blend smoothly, such as oil and water. The trick is to add one liquid, usually the oil, to the other in a slow stream while mixing vigorously. You can also use natural emulsifiers – egg yolks or mustard – to bind mixtures like vinaigrettes and sauces.

Ferment To bring about a chemical change in foods and beverages; the change is caused by enzymes produced from bacteria or yeasts. Beer, wine, yogurt, buttermilk, vinegar, cheese, and yeast breads all get their distinctive flavors from fermentation.

Fold To incorporate a light, airy mixture (such as beaten egg whites) into a heavier mixture (a cake batter). To fold, use a rubber spatula to cut through the center of the mixture. Scrape across the bottom of the bowl and up the nearest side. Give the bowl a quarter turn, and repeat just until blended.

Fork-tender A degree of doneness for cooked vegetables and meats. You should feel just a slight resistance when the food is pierced with a fork.

Julienne To cut food, especially vegetables, into thin, uniform matchsticks about 2 inches long.

Knead To work dough until it's smooth, either by pressing and folding with the heels of the hands or in a food processor or an electric mixer with a dough hook. Kneading develops the gluten in the flour, an elastic protein that gives yeast breads their structure.

Leavening Any agent that causes a dough or batter to rise. Common leaveners include baking powder, baking soda, and yeast. Natural leaveners are air (when beaten into eggs) and steam (in popovers and cream puffs).

Liqueur A sweet, high-alcohol beverage made from fruits, nuts, seeds, spices, or herbs infused with a spirit, such as brandy or rum. Traditionally served after dinner as a mild digestive, liqueurs can also be used in cooking.

Marinate To flavor and/or tenderize a food by letting it soak in a liquid that may contain an acid ingredient (e.g., lemon juice, wine, or vinegar), oil, herbs, and spices.

Mince To chop or cut food into tiny, irregular pieces.

Panfry To cook food in a small amount of hot margarine, butter, or oil in a skillet until browned and cooked through.

Parboil To cook a food partially in boiling water. Slow-cooking foods, such as carrots, are often parboiled before they're added to a mixture made of quicker-cooking foods.

Pare To cut away the skin or rind of a fruit or vegetable. You can use a vegetable peeler or a paring knife – a small knife with a 3- to 4-inch blade.

Pasteurize To sterilize milk by heating, then rapidly cooling it. Most milk sold in the U.S. is pasteurized, which both destroys bacteria that can cause disease and improves shelf life. Ultrapasteurized (UHT) milk is subjected to very high temperatures – about 300°F – and vacuum-packed for extended storage. It will keep without refrigeration for up to 6 months, but must be refrigerated once it's opened. Ultrapasteurized cream, however, is not vacuum-packed and should be refrigerated even when unopened.

Pinch The amount of a powdery ingredient you can hold between your thumb and forefinger – about 1/16 teaspoon.

Pipe To force a food (typically frosting or whipped cream) through a pastry tip to use as a decoration or garnish, or to shape dough, such as that for éclairs. You can also use a zip-tight plastic bag with a corner snipped off.

Poach To cook food in gently simmering liquid; the surface should barely shimmer. If you plan to use the cooking liquid for a stock or sauce afterward, poach in a pan just large enough to hold the food. That way, you can add less liquid and avoid diluting flavors.

Pound To flatten meats and poultry to a uniform thickness using a meat mallet or rolling pin. This ensures even cooking and also tenderizes tough meats by breaking up hard-to-chew connective tissue. Veal and chicken cutlets are often pounded.

Prick To pierce a food in many or a few places. You can prick a food to prevent buckling – an empty piecrust before it's baked, for example – or bursting – a potato before baking, or sausages before cooking.

Proof To test yeast for potency: If you're not sure yeast is fresh and active, dissolve it in warm water (105° to 115°F) with a pinch of sugar. If the mixture foams after 5 to 10 minutes, the yeast is fine to use. Proofing also refers to the rising stage for yeast doughs.

Punch down To deflate yeast dough after it has risen, which distributes gluten (the elastic protein in flour that gives bread its strength) and prevents dough from overrising. Punch your fist into the center of dough, then pull the edges toward the center.

Puree To form a smooth mixture by whirling food, usually a fruit or vegetable, in a food processor or blender, or straining through a food mill.

Reduce To rapidly boil a liquid, especially a sauce, so a portion cooks off by evaporation. This creates a thicker sauce with a deeper, more concentrated flavor. If you use a wide pan, the liquid will evaporate faster.

Render To slowly melt animal fat (e.g., duck and chicken skin, pork rinds) until it separates from its connective tissue. The clear fat is strained before being used in cooking. The crisp, brown bits left in the skillet – delicious but high in fat – are called cracklings.

Roast To cook food in the oven, in an uncovered pan, by the free circulation of dry heat, usually until the exterior is well browned. Tender cuts of meat as well as poultry and fish are suitable for roasting; so are many vegetables, such as potatoes, parsnips, peppers, and even tomatoes.

Sauté To cook or brown food quickly in a small amount of hot fat in a skillet; the term derives from the French *sauter* ("to jump"), and refers to the practice of shaking food in the pan so it browns evenly.

Scald To heat milk until tiny bubbles just begin to appear around the edge of the pan – it should not boil. Before milk was pasteurized, scalding was a safeguard used to destroy bacteria and prolong freshness. Today's recipes specify scalding for other reasons, such as dissolving sugar or melting shortening.

Score To make shallow cuts (usually parallel or crisscross) in the surface of foods before cooking. This is done mainly to aid flavor absorption, as for marinated meats, chicken, and fish, but sometimes also for decorative purposes, as for hams and breads.

Sear To brown the surface of meat quickly in a hot pan or in the oven, to caramelize the meat and enrich flavor.

Shred To cut, tear, or grate food into narrow strips. For some recipes, cooked meat is shredded by pulling it apart with 2 forks.

Shave To cut wide, paper-thin slices of food, especially Parmesan cheese, vegetables, or chocolate. Shave off slices with a vegetable peeler and use as a garnish.

Shuck To remove the shells of oysters, mussels, or clams, or the husks of corn.

Sift To pass ingredients such as flour or confectioners' sugar through a fine-mesh sifter or sieve. This incorporates air, removes lumps, and helps the flour or sugar to mix more readily with liquids.

Simmer To cook liquid gently, alone or with other ingredients, over low heat so it's just below the boiling point. A few small bubbles should be visible on the surface.

Skim To remove fat or froth from the surface of a liquid, such as stock or boiling jelly. A skimmer, with a flat mesh or perforated bowl at the end of a long handle, is the ideal tool for the job.

Steam To cook food, covered, in the vapor given off by boiling water. The food is set on a rack or in a basket so it's over, not in, boiling water – since it's not immersed, it retains more nutrients, bright colors, and fresh flavor.

Stir-fry To cook small pieces of food quickly in a small amount of oil over high heat, stirring and tossing almost constantly. Vegetables cooked in this way retain more nutrients because of the short cooking time. Stir-frying is much used in Asian cooking; a wok is the traditional pan, though a skillet or Dutch oven will do just as well.

Temper To heat food gently before adding it to a hot mixture so it doesn't separate or curdle. Often eggs are tempered by mixing with a little hot liquid to raise their temperature before they're stirred into a hot sauce or soup.

Tender-crisp The ideal degree of doneness for many vegetables, especially green vegetables. Cook them until they're just tender but still retain some texture.

Toss To lift and drop pieces of food quickly and gently with two utensils, usually to coat them with a sauce (as for pasta) or dressing (as for salad).

Whip To beat an ingredient (especially cream) or mixture rapidly, adding air and increasing volume. Whip with a whisk, egg beater, or electric mixer.

Whisk To beat ingredients (e.g., cream, eggs, salad dressings, sauces) with a fork or the looped wire utensil called a whisk so as to mix or blend, or incorporate air.

Zest To remove the colored peel of a citrus fruit. Use a grater, zester, or vegetable peeler to remove the outermost part, avoiding the bitter white pith underneath. The peel itself is often referred to as zest.

Mail-Order Sources

Broadway Panhandler
477 Broome Street
New York, NY 10013
212–966–3434

Cooking and baking supplies and equipment (including adjustable-blade slicers)

Dean & DeLuca
Order Department
560 Broadway
New York, NY 10012
800–221–7714

Herbs, spices, dried chiles, canned chipotle chiles, vinegars, dry beans, dried porcini mushrooms

The King Arthur Flour Baker's
  Catalogue
P.O. Box 876
Norwich, VT 05055
800–827–6836

Flour (including semolina flour), baking equipment and ingredients, thermometers

Mo' Hotta Mo' Betta
P.O. Box 4136
San Luis Obispo, CA 93403
800–462–3220

Dried chiles, canned chipotle chiles, Asian fish sauce (nuoc nam), unsweetened coconut milk, curry paste

Shepherd's Garden Seeds
Order Department
30 Irene Street
Torrington, CT 06790
860–482–3638

Seeds for vegetables (including tomatillos), lettuces, herbs, chiles

Penzeys, Ltd.
P.O. Box 933G
Muskego, WI 53150
414–679–7207

Spices

Sweet Celebrations
P.O. Box 39426
Edina, MN 55439
800–328–6722

Baking and decorating equipment and supplies (including meringue powder, food color pastes)

White Lily Foods Co.
P.O. Box 871
Knoxville, TN 37901
800–264–5459

Southern soft-wheat flour

Wilton Industries
2240 West 75th Street
Woodridge, IL 60517
800–772–7111

Baking and decorating equipment and supplies (including meringue powder, food color pastes)

A 1 PPETIZERS

Whether you're throwing a big cocktail party or an intimate dinner for a few friends, appetizers should entice the eye and spark the taste buds. Beyond that, just a few simple rules apply: The flavors, textures, and colors of the foods should complement each other – and the courses that will follow. There should always be a light option, such as fresh salsa or raw vegetables. Need inspiration? Check out what's in season and plentiful at the market.

PLANNING FOR A PARTY

• To create a festive feel, serve a variety of colorful appetizers in assorted shapes.
• Make it easy on yourself: Prepare as many appetizers in advance as possible. When appropriate, make separate components ahead of time, such as a stuffed-vegetable filling, and then refrigerate for later assembly.
• Make only 1 or 2 hot appetizers, which demand last-minute attention, and serve some that require no work at all, like a cheese plate, nuts, grapes, or assorted salamis.
• If you're passing around an hors d'oeuvres platter, fill it with bite-size morsels that can be easily and neatly eaten.
• Arrange back-up platters; cover with plastic wrap and refrigerate to replenish your table when supplies dwindle.
• How much should you prepare? Figure on roughly 10 to 12 small hors d'oeuvres per guest if no meal follows. Otherwise, allow about 4 to 5 per guest.
• For maximum flavor, remove cold appetizers from the refrigerator about 30 minutes before serving.

STOCKING UP

• Prepare vegetables for crudités up to 1 day ahead. Cook any vegetables that need to be blanched (lightly cooked) as directed and rinse with cold running water, and cut up raw vegetables. Wrap in damp paper towels, seal in plastic bags, and refrigerate.
• Most pâtés and terrines are best made 1 or 2 days ahead; wrap tightly in plastic wrap or foil and refrigerate.
• Freeze pastry appetizers (such as the phyllo-wrapped ones on pages 47 and 48, or the puff-pastry Olive Sticks and Crabmeat Bites, unfilled, on pages 49 and 50), raw or baked, up to 1 month ahead. Bake uncooked pastries straight from the freezer as the recipe directs; warm cooked ones in a 350°F oven for about 10 minutes.

SERVING WITH STYLE

Choose interesting serving dishes and garnishes that complement the food. Here are a few eye-catching ideas:
• Serve crudités on a tray or in a large basket lined with plastic wrap and a bed of arugula, red cabbage, purple kale, spinach, or other leafy salad greens.
• Serve cheese on a platter decorated with bunches of fresh herbs, such as thyme or rosemary.
• Serve an assortment mezze of crackers (e.g., sesame, herb, wheat) and breads in wicker baskets lined with colorful napkins.
• Use nontoxic flowers and leaves (see pages 316 and 551) as a lovely garnish. Flowers are even available at some supermarkets; see your florist for lemon leaves and the like.
• For party food that will be served on a buffet, use broad, flat dishes to create the most dramatic presentation.

ALMOST-INSTANT APPETIZERS

When unexpected guests drop in, don't panic. These quick appetizers can be made in a flash from pantry staples:
White bean and tuna dip In a blender or food processor with the knife blade attached, whirl a can of tuna, drained, with a can of white kidney beans (cannellini), rinsed and drained, a little olive oil, lemon juice, and some coarsely chopped flat-leaf parsley and garlic until smooth.
Stuffed dates Break off chunks of good Parmesan cheese; use to stuff large pitted dates.
French-style radishes Set out radishes with stems still attached and provide small bowls of softened butter and coarse salt for dipping.
Quick quesadillas Sandwich shredded cheese and chopped green onions or salsa between flour tortillas. Heat in a skillet, turning once, until just beginning to brown on both sides. To serve, cut into wedges.
Super salsa Liven up bottled salsa with chopped fresh cilantro, or swirl in some sour cream.
Herbed nuts Toss walnuts or pecans with a little melted margarine or butter, crushed dried rosemary, and salt. Spread nuts on a cookie sheet and bake at 350°F for 10 minutes, or until toasted.
Quick dips In a blender, combine mayonnaise and sour cream with prepared pesto, drained jarred roasted red peppers, or dried tomatoes (rehydrated in boiling water if dry-packed, then drained) and process until smooth.
Mediterranean mezze platter Assemble bowls of store-bought hummus, eggplant dip, and olives; serve with wedges of pita bread, cucumber sticks, and carrots.
Pizza pronto Top a large Italian bread shell with one of the following, bake at 450°F for 10 minutes, and cut into small squares: olive oil and crushed dried rosemary; chopped marinated dried tomatoes and mozzarella or goat cheese; crumbled cooked bacon and Cheddar cheese.

CRUDITÉS AND DIPS

Crudités – bite-size whole or cut-up vegetables, raw or lightly cooked – are usually served with a dip or sauce. For the prettiest effect, choose a colorful variety of vegetables. Ideal for parties or buffets, most crudités can be prepared up to one day in advance. To store, wrap vegetables separately in damp paper towels, place in plastic bags, and refrigerate.

CRUDITÉS BASKET

◆◆◆◆◆◆◆◆◆◆◆◆◆

Prep: 45 minutes
Cook: 8 to 10 minutes
Makes 12 appetizer servings

Moroccan Spice Bean Dip (shown above top right) and Parmesan Dip (shown above far right), or other dips of your choice (see page 34)
1 bunch broccoli
8 ounces snow peas or sugar snap peas
2 pounds asparagus
3 bunches baby carrots with tops
1 bunch small radishes with tops
2 large red peppers
2 large yellow peppers
2 heads Belgian endive
1 large head radicchio
2 large heads red leaf or romaine lettuce

1 Prepare dips; cover and refrigerate until ready to use. Cut tough stems from broccoli. Cut broccoli into 2" by 1" pieces. Remove stem and strings along both edges of each pea pod. Bend base of asparagus stalks; ends will break off where stalks are tough. Discard ends; trim scales if stalks are gritty.

◆◆◆◆◆◆◆◆◆◆◆◆◆

USING BROCCOLI STEMS

Use broccoli stems as well as flowerets for crudités. Peel any stems that seem tough with a vegetable peeler; cut into sticks.

◆◆◆◆◆◆◆◆◆◆◆◆◆

2 Peel carrots; trim stems. Trim radish stems. Cut peppers into ½-inch strips. Separate leaves of endive, radicchio, and lettuce.

3 In 4-quart saucepan, in *1 inch boiling water*, cook broccoli 3 to 5 minutes. With slotted spoon, place in colander. Drain, rinse with cold running water, and drain again. Repeat with asparagus, cooking 3 minutes, then with snow peas, cooking 1 minute.

4 Line a large shallow basket with plastic wrap or foil. Arrange radicchio and lettuce leaves in basket. Arrange prepared vegetables on top; serve with dips.

EACH SERVING WITHOUT DIP: ABOUT 75 CALORIES, 4g PROTEIN, 16g CARBOHYDRATE, 1g TOTAL FAT (0g SATURATED), 0mg CHOLESTEROL, 45mg SODIUM

MOROCCAN SPICE BEAN DIP

Prep: 10 minutes   Makes about 1⅓ cups

1 teaspoon paprika
¼ teaspoon fennel seeds, crushed
¼ teaspoon ground ginger
¼ teaspoon ground cumin
⅛ teaspoon ground red pepper (cayenne)
Pinch ground cinnamon
1 can (15 to 19 ounces) garbanzo beans,
    rinsed and drained
2 tablespoons olive oil
1 tablespoon fresh lemon juice
½ teaspoon salt
¼ teaspoon ground black pepper

◆ In 1-quart saucepan, heat first 6 ingredients over medium-low heat, stirring, 1 to 2 minutes, until very fragrant. Remove from heat.

◆ In food processor with knife blade attached, combine garbanzo beans, olive oil, lemon juice, salt, black pepper, toasted spices, and ¼ *cup water*; blend until smooth. Transfer to small serving bowl.

Each tablespoon: About 25 calories, 1g protein, 3g carbohydrate, 1g total fat (0g saturated), 0mg cholesterol, 100mg sodium

PARMESAN DIP

*Prep: 10 minutes plus chilling
Makes about 1¼ cups*

⅔ cup sour cream
⅓ cup mayonnaise
¼ cup freshly grated Parmesan cheese
1 tablespoon fresh lemon juice
3 anchovy fillets, mashed
½ teaspoon coarsely ground black
    pepper

In small bowl, with fork or wire whisk, mix all ingredients. Cover and refrigerate about 2 hours for flavors to blend.

Each tablespoon: About 50 calories, 1g protein, 1g carbohydrate, 5g total fat (2g saturated), 7mg cholesterol, 70mg sodium

GUACAMOLE

Prep: 15 minutes   Makes about 1½ cups

2 ripe avocados
2 tablespoons minced onion
2 tablespoons chopped fresh cilantro
1 tablespoon fresh lime juice
2 serrano or jalapeño chiles, seeded and
    minced
½ teaspoon salt
¼ teaspoon ground black pepper
1 plum tomato, finely chopped

◆ Cut each avocado in half; remove seeds. With spoon, scoop flesh from peel into medium bowl.

◆ Add next 6 ingredients. With potato masher, coarsely mash avocados. Stir in tomato. Transfer to small serving bowl.

Each tablespoon: About 30 calories, 0g protein, 2g carbohydrate, 3g total fat (0g saturated), 0mg cholesterol, 45mg sodium

PUMPKIN AND ROASTED GARLIC DIP

*Prep: 10 minutes plus cooling
Bake: 45 minutes   Makes about 2 cups*

1 whole head garlic
1 can (16 ounces) solid-pack pumpkin
    (not pumpkin-pie mix)
2 tablespoons olive oil
1½ teaspoons salt
1 tablespoon chopped fresh parsley

◆ Preheat oven to 450°F. Discard papery outer layer from garlic; do not separate cloves. Wrap garlic in foil.

◆ Roast garlic 45 minutes, or until tender. Remove from oven; cool.

◆ When cool, squeeze garlic from skin. In food processor with knife blade attached, puree garlic, pumpkin, oil, and salt. Stir in parsley. Transfer to small serving bowl.

Each tablespoon: About 15 calories, 0g protein, 2g carbohydrate, 1g total fat (0g saturated), 0mg cholesterol, 100mg sodium

ROASTED EGGPLANT DIP

*Prep: 15 minutes plus draining   Roast: 1 hour
Makes about 2 cups*

2 small eggplants (1 pound each)
2 garlic cloves, cut into thin slivers
2 tablespoons olive oil
4 teaspoons fresh lemon juice
1 teaspoon salt
¼ teaspoon ground black pepper
2 tablespoons chopped fresh parsley
2 tablespoons chopped fresh mint

◆ Preheat oven to 400°F. Cut slits all over eggplants; insert garlic. Place eggplants on jelly-roll pan and roast 1 hour, or until collapsed. Remove from oven; cool.

◆ When cool, cut each eggplant in half. With spoon, scoop flesh from skin into colander set over bowl; discard skin. Let drain 10 minutes.

◆ Transfer eggplant to food processor with knife blade attached. Add oil, lemon juice, salt, and pepper and blend, pulsing processor on and off, until coarsely chopped.

◆ Add herbs; pulse to combine. Transfer to small serving bowl.

Each tablespoon: About 15 calories, 0g protein, 2g carbohydrate, 1g total fat (0g saturated), 0mg cholesterol, 70mg sodium

HONEY-MUSTARD DIP

Prep: 10 minutes   Makes about ⅔ cup

¼ cup Dijon mustard
¼ cup honey
1 tablespoon soy sauce
1 tablespoon minced green onion
2 teaspoons minced, peeled fresh ginger

In small bowl, with fork or wire whisk, mix all ingredients.

Each tablespoon: About 30 calories, 0g protein, 7g carbohydrate, 0g total fat, 0mg cholesterol, 235mg sodium

PÂTÉS, TERRINES, AND SPREADS

Welcome additions to any appetizer table, pâtés, terrines, and sumptuous spreads can be smooth and satiny or chunky and coarse. Some are cooked and some are not. A food processor can ensure a smoothly blended, spreadable mixture, but for a coarser texture, use a wooden spoon or potato masher. Smoked fish and sautéed chicken livers are classic ingredients for pâtés. Cream cheese is a natural base for quick spreads – try the savory pâté here, or the Chipotle Spread on page 36, flavored with fresh lime juice and zesty chiles.

SMOKED TROUT PÂTÉ

◆◆◆◆◆◆◆◆◆◆◆◆◆◆◆◆◆◆◆◆◆◆◆◆◆◆◆◆◆◆◆◆

Prep: 30 minutes   *Makes* about 3 cups

3 whole smoked trout (about 1¼ pounds)
1 container (8 ounces) whipped cream cheese
¼ cup light mayonnaise dressing
3 tablespoons fresh lemon juice

⅛ teaspoon ground black pepper
1 tablespoon minced fresh chives or green onion
Chives for garnish
Melba Triangles (see page 36) or crackers for serving
Cucumber slices (optional)

1 Place smoked trout on cutting board; cut head and tail from each smoked trout. Carefully remove skin and discard.

2 With tweezers, remove bones from trout. In food processor with knife blade attached, blend trout, cream cheese, mayonnaise dressing, lemon juice, and black pepper until mixture is smooth.

3 Spoon trout mixture into medium serving bowl; stir in minced chives until well combined. Smooth top. Cover and refrigerate up to 1 day if not serving right away.

4 If it has been refrigerated, allow pâté to stand at room temperature 15 minutes to soften slightly before serving. Garnish with chives. Serve spread on Melba Triangles with cucumber slices, if you like.

SMOKED FISH PÂTÉS AND SPREADS
◆◆◆◆◆◆◆◆◆◆◆◆◆◆◆◆◆◆◆◆◆◆◆◆◆◆◆◆◆◆

Smoked fish makes wonderfully flavorful pâtés and spreads. Those high in natural oils and fat, such as salmon, mackerel, and trout, are the ones to look for. Or, if you live near a good deli, seek out smoked whitefish. As well as being delicious, they're all tender enough to be worked to a smooth consistency. Saltiness and smokiness vary; taste, then adjust the seasoning accordingly. Smoked fish is also good in salads and soufflés. Depending on size, it is sold whole or by the fillet. It can be frozen for up to 2 months.

EACH TABLESPOON PÂTÉ: ABOUT 35 CALORIES, 3g PROTEIN, 0g CARBOHYDRATE, 2g TOTAL FAT (1g SATURATED), 14mg CHOLESTEROL, 115mg SODIUM

CHICKEN LIVER PÂTÉ

Prep: 15 minutes plus chilling   *Cook:* 6 minutes
Makes about 2 cups

1 pound chicken livers,
  trimmed (see page 134)
8 tablespoons butter
⅓ cup minced shallots
½ teaspoon salt
¼ teaspoon dried thyme

⅛ teaspoon ground nutmeg
⅛ teaspoon ground black
  pepper
¼ cup sweet vermouth
Toasts, crackers, or thin apple
  slices for serving

◆ Pat chicken livers dry with paper towels. In 10-inch skillet, melt 1 tablespoon butter over medium heat. Add shallots and cook, stirring frequently, 1 minute. Increase heat to high; stir in livers, salt, thyme, nutmeg, and pepper. Cook, stirring often, 4 minutes, or until livers are just slightly pink in center. Stir in vermouth; cook 30 seconds.

◆ Transfer mixture to food processor with knife blade attached and blend until smooth. With motor running, add remaining butter through feed tube, 1 tablespoon at a time.

◆ Spoon into serving bowl or crock and refrigerate 6 hours, or until cold. Serve with toast, crackers, or apple slices.

Each tablespoon pâté: About 50 calories, 4g protein, 1g carbohydrate, 4g total fat (2g saturated), 97mg cholesterol, 70mg sodium

---

TOASTS FOR PÂTÉS, TERRINES, AND SPREADS

Team spreads and pâtés with one of the specialty toasts suggested below. All should be baked at 375°F.

Melba triangles Named in honor of the turn-of-the-century Australian opera singer Nellie Melba. Serve with delicate pâtés and spreads. Remove crusts from very thin slices of white bread; cut each slice diagonally in half. Bake 15 minutes, or until crisp and edges curl slightly, turning once.

Garlic toast Delicious with robust pâtés and spreads. Cut French bread into thin slices. Bake 10 minutes, or until lightly toasted, turning once. Peel and halve a garlic clove; immediately rub one side of each slice of warm toast with cut side of garlic.

Pita toast Serve with Middle Eastern spreads, such as taramasalata (cod roe spread), tzatziki (cucumber yogurt dip), or our Moroccan Spice Bean Dip (see page 34). Cut pita bread into wedges. Bake 15 minutes, or until golden, turning once.

Italian toast Ideal with tomato or olive spreads. Slice ciabatta or focaccia (Italian flat breads) into strips. Bake 15 minutes, or until golden, turning once.

SMOKED SALMON TERRINE

Prep: 40 minutes plus chilling
Makes 32 appetizer servings

2 tablespoons capers, drained
  and chopped
1 tablespoon chopped fresh
  dill or ¾ teaspoon dillweed
½ teaspoon coarsely ground
  black pepper
4 packages (8 ounces each)
  cream cheese, softened
4 tablespoons milk

2 tablespoons fresh lemon
  juice
¾ pound sliced smoked
  salmon, finely chopped
Lemon slices and parsley or
  dill sprigs for garnish
Cocktail pumpernickel bread
  and assorted crackers for
  serving

◆ In medium bowl, with wooden spoon, blend capers, dill, pepper, half of cream cheese, half of milk, and half of lemon juice until smooth.

◆ In another medium bowl, with wooden spoon, blend smoked salmon, remaining cream cheese, remaining milk, and remaining lemon juice until smooth.

◆ Line 8½" by 4½" loaf pan with plastic wrap. Using metal spatula, evenly spread half of caper mixture into bottom of loaf pan. Evenly spread half of smoked-salmon mixture on top. Repeat layering with remaining mixtures. Cover terrine with plastic wrap and refrigerate at least 4 hours, or overnight, until firm.

◆ To serve, invert loaf pan onto platter; remove pan and plastic wrap. With metal spatula, smooth sides of terrine if necessary. Let terrine stand at room temperature 30 minutes to soften slightly. Garnish with lemon slices and parsley sprigs and serve with bread and crackers.

Each appetizer serving: About 115 calories, 4g protein, 1g carbohydrate, 11g total fat (6g saturated), 34mg cholesterol, 190mg sodium

---

CHIPOTLE SPREAD

Prep: 10 minutes   *Makes* about ¾ cup

1 package (8 ounces) cream
  cheese, softened
2 teaspoons minced canned
  chipotle chiles in adobo
  (see page 30)

2 teaspoons fresh lime juice
Crackers or cucumber slices
  for serving

In food processor with knife blade attached, blend cream cheese, chipotles, and lime juice until smooth. Serve with crackers or cucumber slices.

Each tablespoon spread: About 65 calories, 1g protein, 1g carbohydrate, 7g total fat (4g saturated), 21mg cholesterol, 65mg sodium

STUFFED VEGETABLE APPETIZERS

Bite-size vegetables, such as cherry tomatoes, mushrooms, or even tiny potato halves, make delicious, fresh vehicles for a variety of scrumptious fillings. Party plans? Most vegetable stuffings can be prepared up to a day in advance, covered tightly with plastic wrap, and kept refrigerated. You can stuff vegetables a few hours before serving.

EGGPLANT-STUFFED CHERRY TOMATOES

◆◆◆◆◆◆◆◆◆◆◆◆◆

Prep: 45 minutes plus cooling
Cook: 20 minutes
Makes about 48

½ small (1-pound) eggplant
1½-inch piece fresh ginger
2 tablespoons vegetable oil
2 tablespoons soy sauce
2 teaspoons sugar
1 teaspoon Asian sesame oil
1 pint cherry tomatoes

1 With large chef's knife, dice eggplant. Peel and finely mince ginger (you should have about 1 tablespoon).

2 In heavy 2-quart saucepan, heat vegetable oil over medium heat. Add eggplant and ginger; stir to coat. Add soy sauce, sugar, and ⅓ *cup water*; heat to boiling over high heat. Reduce heat to medium-low.

3 Cover; cook 15 minutes, or until eggplant is very tender, stirring occasionally and mashing with back of spoon. Stir in sesame oil. Cool to room temperature. Cover and refrigerate if not using right away.

OTHER FILLINGS
◆◆◆◆◆◆◆◆◆◆

• Chopped Kalamata olives and feta cheese

• Guacamole (see page 34)

• Chopped basil, pine nuts (pignoli), Parmesan, and toasted bread crumbs

4 Meanwhile, cut each tomato in half; scoop out and discard seeds, leaving a tomato "shell."

5 Drain tomato halves, cut side down, on paper towels. With small spoon, fill cherry-tomato halves with eggplant mixture.

EACH PIECE: ABOUT 10 CALORIES, 0g PROTEIN, 1g CARBOHYDRATE, 1g TOTAL FAT (0g SATURATED), 0mg CHOLESTEROL, 45mg SODIUM

SMOKED SALMON BOATS

Prep: 30 minutes   Makes about 36

1 package (8 ounces) cream
  cheese, softened
¼ pound sliced smoked salmon
1 tablespoon chopped fresh
  dill or 1 teaspoon dillweed
4 heads Belgian endive

1 jar (3 ounces) red lumpfish
  caviar
Small dill sprigs, mâche, and
  zigzag lemon (see page 130)
  for garnish

◆ In food processor with knife blade attached, process
cream cheese and smoked salmon just until well blended.
Add dill; pulse just until mixed. Separate endive leaves. Select
large leaves; reserve small leaves for another use. Rinse leaves
with cold running water; gently pat dry with paper towels.

◆ Spoon salmon mixture
into decorating bag with
medium star tip (or zip-tight
plastic bag; snip one corner
for hole). Pipe onto wide end
of each leaf. Cover and
refrigerate if not serving right
away. Just before serving, top
with caviar and garnish.

Each piece: About 30 calories, 2g protein, 1g carbohydrate,
3g total fat (1g saturated), 17mg cholesterol, 50mg sodium

PROSCIUTTO-PARMESAN BOATS

Press ½ cup ricotta cheese through a sieve into small bowl; mix in
⅓ cup freshly grated Parmesan cheese and 2 tablespoons milk. Cut
6 ounces sliced prosciutto crosswise into thin strips; place a few
strips on wide end of each of 36 Belgian endive leaves. Top each
with a teaspoon of cheese mixture; sprinkle with ground nutmeg.

Each piece: About 20 calories, 2g protein, 1g carbohydrate,
1g total fat (0g saturated), 5mg cholesterol, 80mg sodium

CAPONATA-STUFFED MUSHROOMS

Prep: 50 minutes   Bake: 10 minutes
Makes about 48

2 pounds medium
  mushrooms
About 4 tablespoons olive oil
½ small (1-pound) eggplant,
  coarsely chopped
1 small onion, coarsely
  chopped
1 small celery stalk, coarsely
  chopped

½ cup chili sauce
1 tablespoon capers, drained
¼ teaspoon dried basil
1 tablespoon chopped
  fresh parsley
Salt
2 tablespoons toasted slivered
  almonds, finely chopped

◆ Remove stems from mushrooms. Coarsely chop stems;
set caps aside. In 10-inch skillet, heat 3 tablespoons olive oil
over medium-high heat; add mushroom stems, eggplant,
onion, and celery and cook, stirring frequently, 15 minutes,
or until tender and browned. Stir in chili sauce, capers, and
basil. Reduce heat to low; cover and simmer 10 minutes.
Remove from heat; stir in parsley.

◆ Preheat oven to 350°F. Brush mushroom caps lightly with
olive oil and sprinkle with salt. Spoon 1 heaping teaspoon
filling into each mushroom cap (use any leftover filling to
serve on crackers another day). Place in jelly-roll pan; bake
10 minutes, or until mushrooms are tender and hot. To
serve, sprinkle with almonds.

Each piece: About 20 calories, 1g protein, 2g carbohydrate,
1g total fat (0g saturated), 0mg cholesterol, 40mg sodium

POTATO TOP HATS

Prep: 30 minutes   Cook: 20 minutes
Makes 36

⅓ cup heavy or whipping
  cream
4 ounces cream cheese,
  softened
1 tablespoon prepared white
  horseradish

1 tablespoon chopped chives
18 small red potatoes (about
  1½ pounds), boiled and
  chilled
½ (2-ounce) jar salmon caviar
Chopped chives for garnish

In small bowl, with mixer at medium speed, beat cream
until stiff peaks form. In another small bowl, with mixer at
low speed, beat cream cheese, horseradish, and chopped
chives until blended. With rubber spatula, fold whipped
cream into cream-cheese mixture. Cut each potato in half.
With small melon baller, scoop out cavity in each potato
half; spoon in cream-cheese mixture. Cover loosely and
refrigerate if not serving right away. Just before serving, top
each potato half with some caviar and garnish with chives.

Each piece: About 35 calories, 1g protein, 4g carbohydrate,
2g total fat (1g saturated), 7mg cholesterol, 15mg sodium

SHRIMP APPETIZERS

It's no wonder shrimp is one of our favorite appetizer foods. A guaranteed crowd-pleaser, it's festive, quick to prepare, and incredibly versatile. That's because the mild, sweet taste of shrimp is complemented by myriad other flavors. Our Mexican Shrimp, for instance, has a tart, zippy dressing of lime juice, cilantro, and mild green chiles. Cocktail Shrimp and Olives has a decidedly Mediterranean spirit, while Potted Shrimp, enhanced with sherry, is a creamy, distinctive creation that's delicious served with crackers or toasted rounds of bread.

MEXICAN SHRIMP

◆◆◆◆◆◆◆◆◆◆◆◆◆◆◆◆◆◆◆◆◆◆◆◆◆◆◆◆◆

Prep: 45 minutes   Cook: 3 minutes
Makes 20

40 large shrimp (about 1¾ pounds), shelled and deveined (see page 90)
1 can (4 to 4½ ounces) chopped mild green chiles
2 tablespoons fresh lime juice
1 tablespoon chopped fresh cilantro or 1 teaspoon dried cilantro
1 tablespoon olive or vegetable oil

¾ teaspoon salt
½ teaspoon sugar
½ teaspoon ground black pepper
2 medium avocados
20 (12-inch) bamboo skewers
Lime and lemon wedges for garnish

1 In 4-quart saucepan, heat *8 cups water* to boiling over high heat; add shrimp and heat to boiling. Cook 1 to 2 minutes, or until shrimp turn opaque throughout. Drain.

2 In large bowl, mix green chiles with their liquid, lime juice, cilantro, oil, salt, sugar, and black pepper. Stir in shrimp to coat thoroughly with dressing. If not serving kabobs right away, refrigerate shrimp mixture. Just before serving, cut each avocado lengthwise in half. With sharp knife, remove seed of each avocado (see below). Peel and cut avocados into 1¼-inch chunks.

3 Gently stir avocado chunks into shrimp mixture to coat thoroughly with chile dressing, being careful not to bruise avocado.

4 On each bamboo skewer, thread 2 shrimp and 2 chunks of avocado. Arrange skewers on large platter. Serve immediately, garnished with lime and lemon wedges.

◆◆◆◆◆◆◆◆◆◆◆◆◆◆◆◆◆◆◆◆◆◆◆◆◆◆◆◆◆

SEEDING AVOCADOS

1 Seeding an avocado doesn't need to be a slippery business. For neat results, with sharp knife, cut avocado lengthwise around seed; twist gently to separate halves.

2 Strike the seed with the blade of a chef's knife, so the blade lodges in seed; twist gently and lift out seed.

◆◆◆◆◆◆◆◆◆◆◆◆◆◆◆◆◆◆◆◆◆◆◆◆◆◆◆◆◆

EACH PIECE: ABOUT 70 CALORIES, 7g PROTEIN, 2g CARBOHYDRATE, 4g TOTAL FAT (1g SATURATED), 61mg CHOLESTEROL, 170mg SODIUM

COCKTAIL SHRIMP AND OLIVES

Prep: 20 minutes plus chilling   *Cook:* 3 minutes
Makes about 12 appetizer servings

1½ pounds medium or large shrimp, shelled and deveined, leaving tail part of shell on, if you like (see page 90)
1 jar (9½ ounces drained weight) large green olives, drained, or 1 can (7½ ounces drained weight) large ripe olives, drained
2 tablespoons olive or vegetable oil
1½ teaspoons curry powder
½ teaspoon ground ginger
½ teaspoon salt
¼ teaspoon coarsely ground black pepper
2 tablespoons fresh lemon juice
1 tablespoon finely chopped fresh parsley
Lemon slices and celery leaf for garnish

◆ In 4-quart saucepan, heat *8 cups water* to boiling over high heat; add shrimp and heat to boiling. Cook 1 to 2 minutes, or until shrimp turn opaque throughout. Drain well. Place shrimp and olives in 13" by 9" glass baking dish.

◆ In 1-quart saucepan, heat oil over medium heat; add curry powder, ginger, salt, and pepper and cook, stirring constantly, 1 minute. Remove saucepan from heat; stir in lemon juice and parsley. Pour warm marinade over shrimp and olives in baking dish.

◆ Cover and refrigerate at least 2 hours, until well chilled, tossing occasionally. Place shrimp and olives on platter; garnish with lemon slices and celery leaf. Serve with cocktail picks.

Each serving: About 90 calories, 10g protein, 1g carbohydrate, 6g total fat (1g saturated), 87mg cholesterol, 725mg sodium

SHRIMP WITH TARRAGON DIPPING SAUCE

Prep: 20 minutes   *Cook:* 3 minutes
Makes about 8 appetizer servings

1 pound medium shrimp, shelled and deveined (see page 90)
½ cup sour cream
¼ cup mayonnaise
¼ cup loosely packed fresh parsley leaves
1 tablespoon chopped fresh tarragon
1 teaspoon anchovy paste
¼ teaspoon ground black pepper

◆ In 3-quart saucepan, heat *6 cups water* to boiling over high heat; add shrimp and heat to boiling. Cook 1 to 2 minutes, or until shrimp turn opaque throughout. Drain.

◆ Prepare tarragon dipping sauce: In blender, combine sour cream, mayonnaise, parsley, tarragon, anchovy paste, and pepper; blend until smooth. Transfer dipping sauce to small serving bowl. Cover sauce and shrimp separately and refrigerate if not serving right away. Arrange shrimp with dipping sauce on platter.

Each serving: About 125 calories, 10g protein, 1g carbohydrate, 9g total fat (3g saturated), 98mg cholesterol, 155mg sodium

POTTED SHRIMP

Prep: 15 minutes plus chilling   *Cook:* 3 minutes
Makes about 2 cups

8 tablespoons unsalted butter, softened
1 pound medium shrimp, shelled and deveined (see page 90)
¾ teaspoon salt
¼ teaspoon ground red pepper (cayenne)
2 tablespoons dry sherry
Crackers or toasts (see page 36) for serving

◆ In 10-inch skillet, melt 1 tablespoon butter over medium-high heat. Add shrimp, salt, and ground red pepper; cook, stirring often, 2 minutes, or until shrimp turn opaque throughout. Add sherry and boil 30 seconds.

◆ Transfer mixture to food processor with knife blade attached and blend, pulsing processor on and off, until shrimp are finely chopped. Cut up remaining 7 tablespoons butter, add to processor, and blend until combined.

◆ Transfer shrimp mixture to small crock or bowl. Cover and refrigerate up to 24 hours if not serving right away. If chilled, let potted shrimp stand at room temperature about 1 hour before serving. Serve with crackers or toasts.

Each tablespoon: About 40 calories, 2g protein, 0g carbohydrate, 3g total fat (2g saturated), 30mg cholesterol, 75mg sodium

CHEESE-BASED APPETIZERS

Just a little dressing up turns cheese into party fare. For a sit-down appetizer, marinate creamy goat cheese with herbs to grace delicate greens; for Tex-Mex taste, take a tortilla chip and scoop up our spicy cheese melt – it's all irresistible.

MARINATED GOAT CHEESE

◆◆◆◆◆◆◆◆◆◆◆◆◆◆◆◆◆

Prep: 20 minutes plus marinating
Makes 12 appetizer servings

3 logs (3½ ounces each) goat cheese, such as Montrachet
¼ cup oil-packed dried tomatoes, drained
2 teaspoons fresh thyme leaves
2 teaspoons fresh rosemary leaves
¼ teaspoon cracked black pepper
1 cup extra-virgin olive oil
24 Homemade Croûtes (see below)
6 cups mixed baby salad greens

1 Hold knife under hot water; wipe dry. With warm knife, cut each cheese log into 8 rounds. Cut dried tomatoes into thin strips.

2 In 1-pint jar with tight-fitting lid (a short, wide-mouth jar is best), layer one-fourth of each of the following: goat-cheese rounds, dried-tomato strips, thyme leaves, rosemary leaves, and cracked black pepper. Repeat layering 3 more times.

◆◆◆◆◆◆◆◆◆◆◆◆◆◆◆◆◆◆◆◆◆◆◆◆◆

HOMEMADE CROÛTES

Croûtes are the ideal base for creamy cheeses. Use a 2½-inch cookie cutter to cut shapes or rounds from slices of whole-wheat, white, or other bread. Place on cookie sheet. Bake at 375°F, turning once, 10 to 15 minutes, until golden. For added flavor, rub the toasted croûtes with a cut clove of garlic, or top with a drizzle of olive oil and chopped fresh rosemary. Croûtes can also be served with soups, stews, and pâtés.

3 Pour olive oil over all. Cover and refrigerate overnight or up to 1 week, turning jar over occasionally for even marinating (oil will thicken). Allow cheese to stand at room temperature 30 minutes. Prepare croûtes.

4 Remove cheese from marinade. Toss baby greens with some oil from jar; divide greens among plates. For each serving, place 2 croûtes on top of greens; top each with a slice of goat cheese.

◆◆◆◆◆◆◆◆◆◆◆◆◆◆◆◆◆◆◆

EACH SERVING: ABOUT 310 CALORIES, 9g PROTEIN, 19g CARBOHYDRATE, 23g TOTAL FAT (7g SATURATED), 19mg CHOLESTEROL, 335mg SODIUM

FIESTA CHILES CON QUESO

Prep: 15 minutes Bake: 20 minutes
Makes 24 appetizer servings

1 tablespoon vegetable oil
1 large garlic clove, minced
1 teaspoon ground cumin
1 can (15 to 19 ounces) pinto
  beans, rinsed and drained
12 ounces Monterey Jack
  cheese, shredded (3 cups)

1 fully cooked chorizo
  sausage (3 ounces), finely
  chopped, or ¾ cup finely
  chopped pepperoni
1 can (4 to 4½ ounces)
  chopped mild green chiles
Tortilla chips for serving

◆ Preheat oven to 300°F. In 10-inch skillet, heat oil
over medium heat. Stir in garlic and cumin and cook
30 seconds. Add pinto beans and *¼ cup water*; cook,
mashing beans with back of spoon, 2 to 3 minutes, until
thick. Remove from heat.

◆ In large bowl, toss shredded cheese, chorizo, and green
chiles until combined. Press half of cheese mixture evenly
onto bottom of 9-inch pie plate. Spoon pinto-bean mixture
evenly on top. Top with remaining cheese mixture, pressing
gently. Bake 20 minutes, or just until cheese melts. Serve
with tortilla chips.

**Each serving without chips: About 75 calories, 5g protein,
3g carbohydrate, 6g total fat (3g saturated), 13mg cholesterol,
165mg sodium**

ROASTED PEPPER AND MOZZARELLA SANDWICHES WITH BASIL PUREE

Prep: 30 minutes Cook: 20 minutes
Makes 16 appetizer servings

3 medium red peppers,
  roasted and peeled (see
  page 310), or 1½ jars
  (7 ounces each) roasted red
  peppers, drained
⅓ cup olive oil
2 cups packed fresh basil or
  watercress leaves

½ teaspoon salt
1 loaf French bread
  (12 ounces)
1 pound fresh mozzarella
  cheese balls or 1 package
  (16 ounces) mozzarella
  cheese, cut into ¼-inch-thick
  slices

◆ Cut each roasted pepper half lengthwise into thirds; set
aside. In blender or food processor with knife blade
attached, blend oil, basil, and salt until almost smooth.

◆ Cut French bread horizontally in half. Remove and
discard some soft bread from each half. Evenly spread basil
mixture on cut side of both halves. Arrange mozzarella-
cheese slices on bottom half of loaf; top with roasted
peppers. Replace top half of loaf and cut into thin slices.

**Each serving: About 185 calories, 8g protein, 13g carbohydrate,
11g total fat (4g saturated), 22mg cholesterol, 300mg sodium**

FAST CHEESE APPETIZERS

SMOKY MOZZARELLA SKEWERS Cut smoked mozzarella into
1-inch cubes. On short bamboo skewers, thread oil-packed dried
tomatoes, squares of yellow pepper, fresh basil leaves, and
mozzarella. Brush cheese with some oil from the dried tomatoes.

GORGONZOLA-STUFFED DATES Mix equal amounts of
Gorgonzola and cream cheese, softened. Split one side of Medjool
or other large dates lengthwise in half and remove pits. With small
knife, spread a small amount of cheese mixture into each date (or
use a pastry bag to pipe the cheese); top cheese with a walnut half.

HERB-AND-SPICE-COATED GOAT CHEESE Roll logs of goat
cheese in chopped fresh herbs, such as parsley, rosemary, thyme,
or dill, and/or cracked black pepper. First spread desired coatings
on waxed paper, then roll well-chilled cheese logs over until
completely covered. Lift up corners of paper to press in coatings
gently if necessary. Wrap logs in plastic wrap until ready to serve.

PROSCIUTTO AND GOAT CHEESE ROLL-UPS Mix 8 ounces
mild goat cheese, softened, 2 tablespoons minced green onions, and
1 garlic clove, minced. Cut 12 thin slices prosciutto crosswise in half.
Spoon 2 tablespoons of cheese mixture across base of each strip; top
with a basil leaf. Roll prosciutto around cheese. Sprinkle with fresh
lemon juice and olive oil, and ground black pepper, if you like.

Smoky mozzarella
skewers

Gorgonzola-stuffed
dates

Herb-and-spice-coated
goat cheese

Prosciutto and goat
cheese roll-ups

Toast-Based Appetizers

Firm-textured country- or French-bread slices toast beautifully, and make crispy bases for tasty toppings. Ordinary white bread also lends itself to making delicious toasted miniature sandwiches. Depending on the topping and the size of the toast base, these can work nicely for cocktail parties or as a sit-down first course.

Broccoli Rabe Bruschetta

◆◆◆◆◆◆◆◆◆◆◆◆◆

Prep: 20 minutes
Cook: 6 minutes
Makes 8

1 round loaf crusty bread (16 ounces)
¼ cup plus 2 tablespoons freshly grated Parmesan cheese
2 bunches broccoli rabe (about 1 pound each), tough stems trimmed
¼ cup olive oil
3 garlic cloves, each cut in half
¾ teaspoon salt
¼ teaspoon crushed red pepper

1 In 5-quart Dutch oven, heat *4 quarts water* to boiling over high heat. Meanwhile, preheat broiler. Cut four ⅜-inch-thick slices from center portion of bread (save remainder for use another day); cut each slice crosswise in half. Place bread slices on rack in large broiler pan. Place pan in broiler at closest position to heat source. Broil bread 1 to 2 minutes until lightly toasted.

2 Turn bread; sprinkle with ¼ cup Parmesan. Broil 1 to 2 minutes longer, until cheese melts and edges of bread are lightly toasted. Set aside. Add broccoli rabe to boiling water; cook 2 minutes. Drain; coarsely chop. Wipe Dutch oven dry.

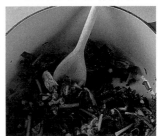

3 In same Dutch oven, heat oil over medium heat; add garlic and cook until lightly browned. Add broccoli rabe, salt, and red pepper; cook over medium-high heat, stirring, about 5 minutes, until tender.

CROSTINI AND BRUSCHETTA

Crostini are thin slices of toasted bread topped with a savory mixture. Bruschetta (bru-sket-ta) are thicker slices of grilled or toasted country bread. Either can be rubbed with a cut clove of garlic (see right) and drizzled with fruity olive oil.

4 Discard garlic cloves, if you like. Spoon broccoli rabe on top of toasted bread slices. Sprinkle bruschetta with remaining Parmesan. Serve bruschetta warm or at room temperature.

EACH PIECE: ABOUT 230 CALORIES, 8g PROTEIN, 29g CARBOHYDRATE, 10g TOTAL FAT (2g SATURATED), 4mg CHOLESTEROL, 585mg SODIUM

CHICKEN LIVER AND SAGE CROSTINI

Prep: 15 minutes   Cook: 15 minutes
Makes 30

1 loaf French bread
   (8 ounces), cut into 30 thin
   diagonal slices
1 tablespoon margarine or
   butter
1 tablespoon olive oil
1 medium onion, finely
   chopped
1 garlic clove, minced
¼ cup all-purpose flour

1 pound chicken livers,
   trimmed (see page 134) and
   each cut in half
½ teaspoon dried sage
½ teaspoon salt
¼ teaspoon ground black
   pepper
1 tablespoon red wine vinegar
2 tablespoons chopped
   fresh parsley

◆ Preheat oven to 400°F. Place bread slices on cookie sheet and bake 5 minutes, or until lightly toasted. Meanwhile, in 10-inch skillet, melt margarine with oil over medium heat. Add onion; cook 5 minutes, or until tender. Stir in garlic.

◆ Place flour on waxed paper. Toss chicken livers with flour to coat; shake off excess. Add chicken livers to skillet with sage, salt, and pepper. Cook, stirring frequently, 4 minutes, or until livers are browned but still slightly pink in center. Stir in vinegar; remove from heat. Stir in parsley; mash livers coarsely with back of spoon. Spread 1 tablespoon chicken-liver mixture on each toast slice.

Each piece: About 60 calories, 5g protein, 5g carbohydrate, 2g total fat (0g saturated), 95mg cholesterol, 95mg sodium

RICOTTA-SALATA BRUSCHETTA

Prep: 20 minutes   Makes 8

8 slices (½ inch thick) crusty
   country bread, toasted
1 garlic clove, cut in half
1 pound ripe plum tomatoes,
   seeded and diced
4 ounces ricotta salata or
   feta cheese, cut into ½-inch
   cubes
2 tablespoons extra-virgin
   olive oil

1 tablespoon finely chopped
   red onion
1 tablespoon chopped fresh
   basil
2 teaspoons balsamic vinegar
¼ teaspoon salt
¼ teaspoon coarsely ground
   black pepper

◆ Lightly rub one side of each warm toast slice with cut sides of garlic.

◆ In medium bowl, combine tomatoes with remaining ingredients; toss to blend. Spoon tomato-and-cheese mixture over garlic-rubbed sides of toast slices.

Each piece: About 140 calories, 4g protein, 15g carbohydrate, 7g total fat (3g saturated), 12mg cholesterol, 360mg sodium

BLUE-CHEESE TOASTS

Prep: 25 minutes   Bake: 12 minutes
Makes 64

16 slices firm white bread,
   crusts removed
4 ounces blue cheese,
   softened and rind removed,
   if any

2 tablespoons margarine or
   butter
2 tablespoons finely chopped
   fresh basil

◆ Preheat oven to 400°F. Grease large cookie sheet. With rolling pin, roll each bread slice paper-thin. Spread about 2 teaspoons softened blue cheese over 1 slice of bread; top with second slice, pressing gently to make a sandwich. Repeat with remaining bread and cheese.

◆ In small saucepan, melt margarine over low heat. Remove from heat; stir in basil. Brush some basil mixture over top of each sandwich. Cut each sandwich diagonally into quarters; cut each quarter in half. Arrange triangles on cookie sheet. Bake 12 minutes, or until golden. Serve hot.

Each piece: About 25 calories, 1g protein, 3g carbohydrate, 1g total fat (0g saturated), 1mg cholesterol, 65mg sodium

MEDITERRANEAN CHEESE TOASTS

Prep: 25 minutes   Broil: 2 minutes
Makes 60

½ cup Mediterranean olives,
   pitted and finely chopped
2 teaspoons capers, drained
   and finely chopped
4 anchovy fillets, finely
   chopped

1 tablespoon Dijon mustard
1 loaf French bread
   (16 ounces)
6 fresh mozzarella cheese
   balls (1½ ounces each), cut
   into very thin slices

Preheat broiler. In small bowl, mix first 4 ingredients. With serrated knife, cut bread into 60 very thin slices. Place half of bread slices in 15½" by 10½" jelly-roll pan; broil 1 minute, or just until golden. Cool on wire rack. Repeat with remaining bread slices. Place 2 slices cheese on toasted side of each bread slice; top with about ¼ teaspoon olive mixture.

Each piece: About 35 calories, 2g protein, 4g carbohydrate, 1g total fat (1g saturated), 4mg cholesterol, 85mg sodium

TORTILLA-BASED APPETIZERS

Tortillas make the perfect no-fuss base for easy appetizers. Soft, chewy flour tortillas can be rolled around savory fillings and sliced to create pinwheels, or layered with enticing ingredients and crisped for quesadillas. Use large corn tortilla chips to make individual nachos or dip in our Garden Salsa.

CORN AND POBLANO QUESADILLAS

◆◆◆◆◆◆◆◆◆◆◆◆◆

Prep: 25 minutes plus standing
Cook: 12 to 16 minutes
Makes 32

2 poblano chiles
2 medium ears corn, husks and silk removed
2 teaspoons vegetable oil
4 green onions, sliced
¼ teaspoon ground cumin
¼ teaspoon salt
¼ teaspoon ground black pepper
2 tablespoons chopped fresh cilantro
8 flour tortillas (6 to 7 inches)
4 ounces Monterey Jack cheese, shredded (1 cup)
Flat-leaf parsley and lime wedges for garnish
Mixed pickled chiles (optional)

1 Preheat broiler. Place poblanos on rack in broiling pan. Place pan in broiler as close as possible to heat source. Broil poblanos, turning occasionally, 10 to 15 minutes, until charred.

2 Transfer poblanos to brown paper bag; seal and let stand 15 minutes. When cool enough to handle, remove and discard skin and seeds. Chop poblanos. Cut corn kernels from cobs.

3 In 10-inch skillet, heat oil over medium heat. Add corn, green onions, cumin, salt, and pepper and cook, stirring, 4 to 5 minutes, until corn is tender-crisp. Remove from heat; stir in cilantro and chopped poblanos. Place 4 tortillas on work surface. Spread corn mixture evenly on top, sprinkle with cheese, then top with remaining tortillas.

4 Heat 10-inch skillet over medium-high heat. Add 1 quesadilla and cook, turning once, 3 to 4 minutes, until tortilla is lightly browned and cheese melts. Transfer quesadilla to cutting board. Repeat with remaining quesadillas. Cut each into 8 wedges. Arrange on platter; garnish and serve warm, with pickled chiles, if you like.

GARDEN SALSA

From 1 lime, grate ½ teaspoon peel and squeeze 1 tablespoon juice. In medium bowl, mix grated lime peel, lime juice, 1½ pounds tomatoes, diced, ½ small red onion, diced, 1 small jalapeño chile, seeded and finely diced, 2 tablespoons chopped fresh cilantro, ¾ teaspoon salt, and ¼ teaspoon coarsely ground black pepper. Serve with tortilla chips. Makes 3 cups.

Each tablespoon: About 5 calories, 0g protein, 1g carbohydrate, 0g total fat, 0mg cholesterol, 45mg sodium

---

EACH PIECE: ABOUT 50 CALORIES, 2g PROTEIN, 6g CARBOHYDRATE, 2g TOTAL FAT (1g SATURATED), 3mg CHOLESTEROL, 80mg SODIUM

NACHOS

Prep: 20 minutes Bake: 5 minutes each batch
Makes 36

36 large corn tortilla chips	1 fully cooked chorizo
3 large plum tomatoes,	sausage (3 ounces), finely
finely chopped	chopped, or ¾ cup finely
⅓ cup chopped fresh	chopped pepperoni
cilantro	1 can (15 to 19 ounces)
¼ teaspoon salt	black beans, rinsed and
1 tablespoon vegetable oil	drained
1 medium onion, finely	4 ounces Monterey Jack
chopped	cheese, shredded (1 cup)
1 garlic clove, minced	2 pickled jalapeño chiles,
½ teaspoon ground cumin	very thinly sliced

◆ Preheat oven to 400°F. Arrange tortilla chips in single layer on 2 or 3 large cookie sheets. In small bowl, combine tomatoes, cilantro, and salt; set aside. In 10-inch skillet, heat oil over medium heat. Add onion, garlic, cumin, and chorizo; cook, stirring frequently, 5 minutes, or until onion is tender. Stir in black beans until combined; heat through.

◆ Place 1 tablespoon black-bean mixture on each tortilla chip. Sprinkle cheese over beans and top each nacho with 1 slice jalapeño chile. Bake 5 minutes, or until cheese begins to melt. Spoon about 1 teaspoon tomato mixture onto each nacho. Transfer nachos to platter and serve warm.

Each piece: 45 calories, 3g protein, 5g carbohydrate, 3g total fat (1g saturated), 3mg cholesterol, 55mg sodium

TOMATO AND GOAT CHEESE QUESADILLAS

Prep: 5 minutes Cook: 12 to 16 minutes
Makes 32

8 flour tortillas (6 to	1 medium tomato, finely
7 inches)	chopped
3 ounces goat cheese,	½ teaspoon cracked black
crumbled (¾ cup)	pepper

◆ Place 4 tortillas on work surface. Sprinkle with goat cheese, then chopped tomato and cracked black pepper. Top with remaining tortillas.

◆ Heat heavy 10-inch skillet over medium-high heat. Add 1 quesadilla and cook, turning once, 3 to 4 minutes, until tortilla is lightly browned and cheese just begins to melt. Transfer to cutting board and cut into 8 wedges. Repeat with remaining quesadillas. Serve warm.

Each piece: 40 calories, 1g protein, 5g carbohydrate, 1g total fat (1g saturated), 2mg cholesterol, 55mg sodium

TORTILLA PINWHEELS

Prep: 15 minutes plus chilling
Makes about 54

4 large flour tortillas (8 to	8 ounces very thinly sliced
10 inches)	baked ham
6 ounces cream cheese,	¼ cup hot pepper jelly
softened	
4 green onions, finely	
chopped	

◆ Place tortillas on work surface. In small bowl, mix cream cheese with green onions; spread evenly on tortillas. Arrange layer of ham on top, then spread jelly over ham. Roll each tortilla up tightly, jelly-roll fashion. Wrap each in plastic wrap; refrigerate at least 4 hours, or overnight.

◆ Just before serving, unwrap tortillas and trim ends neatly. Cut each tortilla roll crosswise into ½-inch slices. To serve, arrange slices on platter.

Each piece: 30 calories, 1g protein, 3g carbohydrate, 2g total fat (1g saturated), 5mg cholesterol, 70mg sodium

CORN VERSUS FLOUR TORTILLAS

◆◆◆◆◆◆◆◆◆◆◆◆◆◆◆◆◆◆◆◆◆◆◆◆◆

Corn and flour tortillas vary in size, taste, and texture. Corn tortillas are made from finely ground, soaked and treated corn (called masa harina) and water. They're about 5 inches in diameter and the traditional choice for tacos, enchiladas (rolled-up tortillas filled with meat or cheese and baked), and tostadas (salad-topped fried tortillas). Flour tortillas are made from wheat flour and water, and enriched with lard or vegetable shortening. They are usually 6 to 10 inches in diameter and have a soft, chewy texture – making them ideal "wrappers" for burritos (folded tortilla "sandwiches") and chimichangas (deep-fried burritos).

PHYLLO-WRAPPED APPETIZERS

Phyllo can be layered and wrapped around fillings of all sorts – keep it covered while you work to prevent it from drying out. Freeze these phyllo appetizers, unbaked, up to 1 month, and bake from frozen, allowing a little more baking time.

MINI SPRING ROLLS

◆◆◆◆◆◆◆◆◆◆◆

Prep: 40 minutes
Bake: 15 minutes
Makes 36

Shrimp and Vegetable Filling (see right)
12 sheets (about 16" by 12" each) fresh or frozen (thawed) phyllo (about 8 ounces)
4 tablespoons margarine or butter, melted
Soy sauce for serving

1 Grease two 15½" by 10½" jelly-roll pans. Prepare filling; set aside. Arrange phyllo sheets in one stack. Cut crosswise into 3 strips. Place strips on waxed paper; cover with plastic wrap.

3 Roll strip with filling one-third of the way up, then fold left and right sides over and continue rolling to end.

2 Place 1 strip phyllo on work surface. Brush top lightly with some melted margarine. Drain any liquid from filling. Place 1 scant tablespoon filling in center at end of strip.

4 Place roll, seam-side down, in jelly-roll pan; brush lightly with melted margarine. Repeat with remaining phyllo strips, filling, and melted margarine, placing rolls about 1 inch apart in pans. If not serving right away, cover with foil and refrigerate. Preheat oven to 375°F. Bake spring rolls 15 minutes, or until golden. Serve hot with soy sauce.

1 tablespoon cornstarch
1 tablespoon dry sherry
1 tablespoon soy sauce
¼ teaspoon sugar
4 tablespoons vegetable oil
2 cups packed, finely sliced napa cabbage (Chinese cabbage)
¼ cup chopped green onions
½ cup chopped mushrooms
½ pound medium shrimp, shelled and deveined (see page 90), chopped
½ teaspoon grated, peeled fresh ginger
½ cup bean sprouts, chopped
½ cup chopped, drained, canned bamboo shoots
4 ounces cooked ham, chopped

1 In cup, mix first 4 ingredients; set aside. In 4-quart saucepan, heat 2 tablespoons oil over high heat. Add napa cabbage, green onions, and mushrooms and cook, stirring frequently, about 1 minute, just until tender-crisp. With slotted spoon, transfer to large bowl.

2 In same saucepan, heat 2 more tablespoons oil over high heat. Add shrimp and ginger; cook, stirring constantly, 30 seconds, or until shrimp turn opaque throughout. Pour in cornstarch mixture and stir until thickened. Add shrimp mixture to bowl with vegetables. With paper towels, pat bean sprouts and bamboo shoots dry; add to vegetables with ham and mix.

EACH PIECE: ABOUT 55 CALORIES, 2g PROTEIN, 4g CARBOHYDRATE, 3g TOTAL FAT (1g SATURATED), 11mg CHOLESTEROL, 120mg SODIUM

GREEK CHEESE BUNDLES

Prep: 40 minutes   Bake: 15 to 20 minutes
Makes 50

4 ounces feta cheese, crumbled (about 1 cup)	1 large egg
½ cup part-skim ricotta cheese	8 sheets (about 16" by 12" each) fresh or frozen
2 tablespoons chopped fresh parsley	(thawed) phyllo (about 5 ounces)
¼ teaspoon coarsely ground black pepper	4 tablespoons margarine or butter, melted

◆ Grease two 15½" by 10½" jelly-roll pans. In medium bowl, with fork, mix first 5 ingredients. Arrange phyllo sheets in one stack. Cut lengthwise into 5 strips; cut each strip crosswise into 5 rectangles. Place cut phyllo on waxed paper; cover with plastic wrap to prevent phyllo from drying out.

◆ Place 2 rectangles of phyllo on top of each other on work surface; brush top lightly with melted margarine. Place 2 more rectangles crosswise on top of first 2 rectangles; brush lightly with more margarine. Place 1 rounded teaspoon filling in center; crimp phyllo around filling to form a bundle. Repeat with remaining phyllo, margarine, and filling.

◆ Place bundles, crimped-side up, in jelly-roll pans. Brush with melted margarine. If not serving right away, cover and refrigerate. Preheat oven to 400°F. Bake cheese bundles 15 to 20 minutes, until golden. Serve hot.

Each piece: About 25 calories, 1g protein, 2g carbohydrate, 2g total fat (1g saturated), 7mg cholesterol, 50mg sodium

MUSHROOM TRIANGLES

Prep: 45 minutes   Bake: 10 to 12 minutes
Makes 35

2 tablespoons vegetable oil	¼ teaspoon dried thyme
2 pounds mushrooms, minced	7 sheets (about 16" by 12" each) fresh or frozen
1 large onion, minced	(thawed) phyllo (about 5 ounces)
1 teaspoon salt	
2 tablespoons freshly grated Parmesan cheese	3 tablespoons margarine or butter, melted

◆ In nonstick 12-inch skillet, heat oil over medium-high heat; add mushrooms, onion, and salt and cook about 15 minutes, until mushrooms and onion are golden and all liquid has evaporated. Remove skillet from heat; stir in Parmesan cheese and thyme.

◆ Arrange phyllo sheets in one stack. Cut stack lengthwise into 5 strips. Place cut phyllo on waxed paper; cover with plastic wrap to prevent phyllo from drying out.

◆ Place 1 phyllo strip on work surface; brush top lightly with melted margarine. Place about 2 teaspoons mushroom mixture at end of strip. Fold one corner of strip diagonally over filling so that short edge meets long edge of strip, forming a right angle. Continue folding over at right angles to form a triangular-shaped package.

◆ Repeat with remaining phyllo strips and mushroom mixture, brushing each strip with some melted margarine. Place triangles, seam-side down, in ungreased 15½" by 10½" jelly-roll pan; brush with remaining margarine. If not serving right away, cover and refrigerate. Preheat oven to 425°F. Bake triangles 10 to 12 minutes, until golden. Serve hot.

Each piece: About 35 calories, 1g protein, 4g carbohydrate, 2g total fat (0g saturated), 0mg cholesterol, 100mg sodium

◆◆◆◆◆◆◆◆◆◆◆◆◆◆◆◆◆◆◆◆◆◆◆◆◆

DECORATIVE TOUCHES FOR PHYLLO

If you like, for the Mushroom Triangles above, when you reach the last fold at the end of the phyllo strip, place a tiny sprig of fresh thyme, flat-leaf parsley, or other herb on the phyllo, and then fold the phyllo over to complete the triangular-shaped package. The herb will lend a pleasantly subtle fragrance and flavor.

◆◆◆◆◆◆◆◆◆◆◆◆◆◆◆◆◆◆◆◆◆◆◆◆◆

PUFF-PASTRY-BASED APPETIZERS

Puff pastry is made of hundreds of layers of pastry, which puff up during baking. It can be twisted and baked to make savory, flaky sticks, formed into layers or rounds, or baked until golden, then sandwiched with a flavorful filling.

OLIVE STICKS

◆◆◆◆◆◆◆◆◆◆◆◆◆

Prep: 30 minutes
Bake: 12 to 15 minutes per batch
Makes about 56

1 package (8 ounces) feta cheese, well drained and crumbled
⅓ cup minced fresh parsley
⅓ cup olive paste or ½ cup Kalamata olives, pitted and pureed with 1 tablespoon olive oil
2 large egg whites
1 package (17¼ ounces) frozen puff-pastry sheets, thawed

1 Preheat oven to 400°F. In small bowl, with fork, mix feta cheese, minced parsley, olive paste, and egg whites until thoroughly blended. On lightly floured surface, unfold 1 pastry sheet (keep other sheet refrigerated). With floured rolling pin, roll pastry sheet into 16" by 14" rectangle.

2 Cut pastry crosswise in half. Spread half of olive mixture evenly over 1 pastry half; top with remaining pastry half.

3 With rolling pin, gently roll over pastry layers to seal them together.

OLIVE PASTE
◆◆◆◆◆◆◆◆◆◆◆◆◆

This pungent puree is known as tapenade in the South of France and olivada in Italy; it is traditionally made from black or green olives, garlic, capers, anchovies, herbs, and olive oil. Olive paste is delicious slathered on toasted bread, added to sandwiches of grilled vegetables or creamy cheeses, or stirred into mayonnaise to make a dip for crudités.

4 Grease large cookie sheet. With large chef's knife, cut pastry rectangle crosswise into ½-inch-wide strips, taking care not to tear pastry.

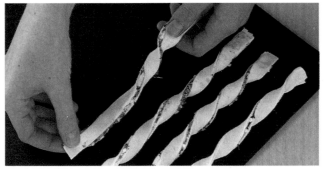

5 Place pastry strips, about 1 inch apart, on cookie sheet, twisting each strip 3 or 4 times. Bake strips 12 to 15 minutes, until pastry is puffed and lightly browned. With pancake turner, transfer sticks to wire rack to cool. Repeat with remaining pastry sheet and olive mixture. Serve at room temperature. Store in tightly covered container.

EACH PIECE: ABOUT 55 CALORIES, 1g PROTEIN, 5g CARBOHYDRATE, 4g TOTAL FAT (1g SATURATED), 4mg CHOLESTEROL, 80mg SODIUM

SPICY CHEESE STICKS

Prep: 30 minutes   Bake: 15 to 20 minutes per batch
Makes 40

1 package (17¼ ounces)
  frozen puff-pastry sheets,
  thawed
8 ounces Monterey Jack
  cheese with jalapeño
  chiles, shredded (2 cups)

1 teaspoon chili powder
1 teaspoon salt
1 large egg, beaten

◆ Preheat oven to 375°F. Grease large cookie sheet. On lightly floured surface, unfold 1 pastry sheet (keep other sheet refrigerated). With floured rolling pin, roll pastry sheet into 15-inch square; cut in half. Sprinkle half of shredded cheese onto half of pastry sheet; top with remaining pastry half. Roll pastry into 15" by 10" rectangle.

◆ Sprinkle rectangle with half of chili powder and half of salt; press in gently with rolling pin. Turn rectangle over and brush with some beaten egg. Cut rectangle crosswise into twenty 10" by ¾" strips. Place pastry strips, ½ inch apart, on cookie sheet, twisting each strip 3 or 4 times. Bake 15 to 20 minutes, until cheese sticks are crisp and lightly browned. Transfer to wire rack to cool.

◆ Repeat with remaining pastry sheet, cheese, chili powder, salt, and egg. Serve warm or at room temperature; store in tightly covered container.

Each piece: About 85 calories, 2g protein, 7g carbohydrate, 5g total fat (2g saturated), 11mg cholesterol, 135mg sodium

CRABMEAT BITES

Prep: 20 minutes   Bake: 15 minutes
Makes 42

½ (17¼-ounce) package
  frozen puff-pastry sheets
  (1 sheet), thawed
½ pound lump crabmeat,
  flaked and picked over
¼ cup mayonnaise

1 tablespoon fresh lemon
  juice
2 teaspoons chopped fresh
  tarragon
¼ teaspoon ground
  black pepper

Preheat oven to 400°F. On lightly floured surface, unfold pastry sheet. With 1½-inch scalloped biscuit-cutter, cut out 42 rounds; place on ungreased large cookie sheet. Bake 15 minutes, or until golden. Transfer to wire rack to cool. In bowl, mix crabmeat, mayonnaise, lemon juice, tarragon, and pepper. Cut each pastry puff horizontally in half; remove top halves. Place 1 level teaspoon crabmeat mixture on each bottom half; replace tops.

Each serving: About 45 calories, 1g protein, 3g carbohydrate, 3g total fat (1g saturated), 4mg cholesterol, 45mg sodium

STILTON AND APPLE NAPOLEONS

Prep: 30 minutes   Bake: 17 to 20 minutes
Makes about 36

½ (17¼-ounce) package
  frozen puff-pastry sheets
  (1 sheet), thawed
3 tablespoons unsalted
  butter, softened
2 large Golden Delicious
  apples, peeled, cored, and
  chopped
2½ ounces Stilton cheese,
  softened (⅓ cup)

¼ cup walnuts, toasted
  and finely chopped
1 tablespoon chopped
  fresh parsley
Thin apple slices, walnuts,
  and parsley sprigs for
  garnish

◆ Preheat oven to 400°F. On lightly floured surface, unfold pastry sheet. With floured rolling pin, roll sheet into 17" by 13" rectangle. Transfer to ungreased large cookie sheet. Using ruler as guide, cut pastry lengthwise into six 17" by 2" strips. Discard trimmings. Place second cookie sheet on top of pastry to keep it flat. Bake 17 to 20 minutes, until pastry is golden. Transfer to wire rack to cool.

◆ In 10-inch skillet, melt 1 tablespoon butter over medium heat. Stir in apples; cover and cook 10 to 15 minutes, until tender and beginning to brown. Remove from heat and mash with back of spoon.

◆ In small bowl, stir cheese with remaining 2 tablespoons butter until blended. Stir in chopped walnuts and parsley.

◆ Spread cheese mixture evenly on 2 pastry strips. Spread apple mixture evenly on another 2 pastry strips. Stack apple layers on cheese layers; top with remaining pastry strips. With serrated knife, trim ends and cut pastry crosswise into ¾-inch slices. Garnish and serve at room temperature.

Each piece: About 55 calories, 1g protein, 5g carbohydrate, 4g total fat (1g saturated), 4mg cholesterol, 50mg sodium

FLAKY TURNOVERS

Our easy-to-make basic recipe for turnover pastry can be used to enfold a tempting assortment of delicious fillings, from a feisty Mexican meat mixture to an Indian-spiced vegetable blend. Perfect for entertaining, these inviting little appetizers can all be prepared ahead, frozen for up to 1 month, and reheated, still frozen, at 425°F for about 10 minutes.

SPICY BEEF EMPANADITAS

◆◆◆◆◆◆◆◆◆◆◆◆◆◆◆◆◆◆◆◆◆◆◆◆◆◆◆◆◆◆

Prep: 1 hour 15 minutes   Bake: 12 minutes per batch
Makes about 60

2 teaspoons vegetable oil
1 small onion, finely chopped
1 large garlic clove, minced
¼ teaspoon ground cinnamon
¼ teaspoon ground red pepper (cayenne)
¼ pound ground beef
¼ teaspoon salt
3 tablespoons chopped golden raisins

3 tablespoons chopped pimiento-stuffed olives
1 cup canned tomatoes with their juice
Flaky Turnover Pastry (see page 52)
1 large egg

1 Prepare filling: In 12-inch skillet, heat oil over medium heat. Add chopped onion and cook, stirring often, 5 minutes, or until tender. Stir in minced garlic, cinnamon, and ground red pepper; cook 30 seconds. Add ground beef and salt; cook, stirring often, 5 minutes, or until beef begins to brown.

2 Stir in raisins, olives, and tomatoes; break up tomatoes with back of spoon. Increase heat to high and cook 10 minutes, or until almost all liquid evaporates. Remove from heat.

3 Preheat oven to 425°F. Prepare pastry; divide into fourths. On lightly floured surface, with floured rolling pin, roll one-fourth of pastry less than ¹⁄₁₆ inch thick (keep remainder covered with plastic wrap).

4 With 3-inch round biscuit cutter, cut out as many rounds as possible, reserving trimmings to re-roll.

5 With metal spatula, carefully transfer pastry rounds to ungreased large cookie sheet. Place 1 level teaspoon filling in center of each round; fold rounds in half to enclose filling. Crimp pastry edges together with fingers or tines of fork to seal.

6 In cup, beat egg with *2 tablespoons water.* Brush egg glaze lightly over turnovers. Bake turnovers 12 minutes, or until golden. Transfer to wire rack. Repeat with remaining pastry and filling. Serve warm.

EACH EMPANADITA: ABOUT 80 CALORIES, 1g PROTEIN, 7g CARBOHYDRATE, 5g TOTAL FAT (1g SATURATED), 5mg CHOLESTEROL, 105mg SODIUM

MUSHROOM TURNOVERS

Prep: 1 hour 15 minutes   *Bake:* 12 minutes per batch
Makes about 60

2 tablespoons margarine or
   butter
1 medium onion, finely
   chopped
8 ounces white mushrooms,
   thinly sliced
4 ounces shiitake mushrooms,
   stems discarded, thinly
   sliced
¾ teaspoon salt
¼ teaspoon ground black
   pepper

⅛ teaspoon dried thyme
1 garlic clove, minced
½ cup heavy or whipping
   cream
2 tablespoons chopped
   fresh parsley
Flaky Turnover Pastry
   (see below)
1 large egg, beaten with
   2 tablespoons water, for
   glaze

◆ Prepare filling: In 12-inch skillet, melt margarine over
medium-high heat. Add onion and cook, stirring often,
3 minutes, or until tender. Stir in white and shiitake
mushrooms, salt, pepper, and thyme; cook, stirring often,
10 minutes, or until liquid evaporates. Stir in garlic and
cook 30 seconds. Stir in cream and boil 5 minutes, or until
mixture is reduced and thickened. Remove from heat and
stir in chopped parsley.

◆ Prepare pastry. Cut out, fill, and bake as directed in
Steps 3 through 6 of Spicy Beef Empanaditas (see page 51).

**Each turnover: About 90 calories, 1g protein, 8g carbohydrate,
6g total fat (2g saturated), 6mg cholesterol, 105mg sodium**

SAMOSAS

Prep: 1 hour 15 minutes   *Bake:* 12 minutes per batch
Makes about 60

1 tablespoon vegetable oil
1 medium onion, finely
   chopped
2 medium all-purpose
   potatoes, peeled and diced
   (1½ cups)
1 tablespoon minced, peeled
   fresh ginger
1 large garlic clove, minced
1 teaspoon curry powder
½ teaspoon ground cumin

¼ teaspoon ground red
   pepper (cayenne)
1 teaspoon salt
½ cup frozen baby peas
¼ cup chopped fresh
   cilantro
Flaky Turnover Pastry
   (see below)
1 large egg, beaten with
   2 tablespoons water, for
   glaze

◆ Prepare filling: In 10-inch skillet, heat oil over medium
heat. Add onion and cook 5 minutes, or until tender. Add
potatoes; cook, stirring often, 10 minutes, or until beginning
to brown. Stir in ginger and next 4 ingredients; cook
30 seconds. Add salt and *1 cup water*; heat to boiling. Reduce
heat to medium-low; cover and simmer 10 to 15 minutes,
until potatoes are tender. Stir in peas and cook, uncovered,
until liquid evaporates. Remove from heat; stir in cilantro,
mashing potatoes coarsely with back of spoon.

◆ Prepare pastry. Cut out, fill, and bake as directed in
Steps 3 through 6 of Spicy Beef Empanaditas (see page 51).

**Each samosa: About 80 calories, 1g protein, 7g carbohydrate,
5g total fat (1g saturated), 4mg cholesterol, 110mg sodium**

FLAKY TURNOVER PASTRY

◆◆◆◆◆◆◆◆◆◆◆◆◆◆

This pastry is extra light and
flaky, thanks to the baking
powder. To use a food
processor with the knife
blade attached: Blend dry
ingredients in work bowl;
add shortening and blend
until mixture resembles
coarse crumbs. Add *7 tablespoons ice water* all at once
and pulse just until dough
forms a ball.

4 cups all-purpose flour
2 teaspoons baking powder
2 teaspoons salt
1⅓ cups shortening

1 In large bowl, combine
dry ingredients. With
pastry blender or two knives
used scissor-fashion, cut in
shortening until mixture
resembles coarse crumbs.

2 Add about *8 table-
spoons ice water*,
1 tablespoon at a time,
tossing with fork, until
dough begins to hold
together. Transfer to lightly
floured work surface and
knead lightly to form ball.

WHAT'S IN A NAME?

◆◆◆◆◆◆◆◆◆◆◆

Fillings vary, but pastry
turnovers are common
to many cuisines. In
Spain and Mexico, the
empanada (Spanish for
"baked in pastry") or
empanadita, a smaller
version, can be stuffed
with either sweet or
savory fillings; a blend of
ground beef and tomato
is typical. In India, the
samosa is a common
roadside food. It can be
stuffed with meat or
vegetable fillings; a
spiced potato mixture is
the classic. Traditionally,
empanadas and samosas
are deep-fried.

SKEWERED APPETIZERS

Scallops, meatballs or strips of chicken threaded on bamboo skewers, sometimes with other ingredients, make ideal party or buffet fare. Satay is the Indonesian version – ours highlights marinated pork with a peanut dipping sauce.

SESAME CHICKEN

◆◆◆◆◆◆◆◆◆◆◆◆◆

Prep: 30 minutes plus marinating
Broil: 7 minutes
Makes 24

2-inch piece fresh ginger
1 green onion
1 tablespoon chopped fresh cilantro
3 tablespoons soy sauce
1 tablespoon dry sherry
1 tablespoon vegetable oil
4 large skinless boneless chicken-breast halves (1½ pounds)
Cilantro Sauce (see below)
24 (6-inch) bamboo skewers
4 teaspoons sesame seeds
Cilantro sprigs for garnish

CILANTRO SAUCE

In blender, combine ¼ cup water, 1 cup lightly packed fresh cilantro sprigs, 1 green onion, chopped, 1 jalapeño chile, seeded if desired and chopped, 1 teaspoon fresh lemon juice, ½ teaspoon sugar, ½ teaspoon minced, peeled fresh ginger, and ¼ teaspoon salt. Blend until smooth. Transfer to small bowl and refrigerate until serving time. Makes about ½ cup.

1 Peel and mince ginger (you should have about 4 teaspoons). Mince green onion. In large bowl, mix ginger, green onion, and chopped cilantro. Add soy sauce, sherry, and oil and mix until well combined.

2 On cutting board, cut each chicken-breast half lengthwise into six ½-inch-wide strips.

3 Add chicken to mixture in bowl and stir to coat; cover and refrigerate at least 2 hours, or up to 6 hours.

4 Prepare Cilantro Sauce. Soak skewers (see page 54). In nonstick skillet over medium heat, toast sesame seeds, shaking pan and stirring often, until golden. Remove from heat. Preheat broiler.

5 Thread 1 chicken strip on each skewer. Arrange on rack in broiling pan; sprinkle with half of toasted sesame seeds. Place pan in broiler at closest position to heat source; broil 4 minutes.

6 Turn skewers; sprinkle with remaining sesame seeds. Broil 3 minutes longer, or until chicken loses its pink color throughout. Arrange skewers on platter; garnish with cilantro sprigs. Serve hot with Cilantro Sauce.

EACH SKEWER: ABOUT 45 CALORIES, 7g PROTEIN, 1g CARBOHYDRATE, 2g TOTAL FAT (0g SATURATED), 17mg CHOLESTEROL, 170mg SODIUM

SCALLOPS WITH SAGE AND BACON

Prep: 15 minutes plus marinating Grill/Broil: 5 minutes
Makes 20

2 tablespoons olive oil	5 slices bacon
1 teaspoon grated lemon peel	20 (6-inch) bamboo skewers,
½ teaspoon coarsely ground	soaked (see below)
black pepper	1 bunch fresh sage
40 medium sea scallops	Salt
(about 1¼ pounds)	

◆ In bowl, combine oil, lemon peel, and pepper. Pull tough crescent-shaped muscle from side of each scallop. Add scallops to bowl and stir gently to coat. Cover and refrigerate at least 30 minutes or up to 6 hours.

◆ Prepare outdoor grill or preheat broiler. In 10-inch skillet, cook bacon over medium heat 5 minutes, or just until beginning to brown. Transfer to paper towels to drain. Cut each slice bacon crosswise into 4 pieces. On each skewer, thread 1 scallop, 1 small sage leaf (or ½ large leaf), 1 piece bacon, and another scallop. Sprinkle with salt. Grill or broil at closest position to heat source, turning once, 5 minutes, or just until scallops turn opaque throughout. Serve hot.

Each skewer: About 50 calories, 5g protein, 1g carbohydrate, 2g total fat (0g saturated), 11mg cholesterol, 70mg sodium

HERBED MEATBALLS

Prep: 20 minutes Grill/Broil: 8 to 10 minutes
Makes 24

2 slices firm white bread, torn	2 teaspoons salt
2 bunches green onions	¾ teaspoon ground black
2 pounds ground beef	pepper
2 large eggs	24 (6-inch) bamboo skewers,
¼ cup chopped fresh parsley	soaked (see right)
1 teaspoon dried mint	

◆ Prepare outdoor grill or preheat broiler. In blender or food processor with knife blade attached, process bread to fine crumbs; transfer to large bowl. Chop enough green onions to equal ½ cup and add to bowl; cut remaining green onions into 1-inch lengths.

◆ Add ground beef and next 5 ingredients to bowl with bread crumbs; mix until well combined. Shape mixture into forty-eight 1½-inch balls. On each skewer, thread 2 meatballs alternately with green-onion pieces. Grill or broil at closest position to heat source, turning once, 8 to 10 minutes, just until cooked through. Serve hot.

Each skewer: About 115 calories, 7g protein, 1g carbohydrate, 8g total fat (3g saturated), 46mg cholesterol, 220mg sodium

PORK SATAY

Prep: 25 minutes plus marinating Grill/Broil: 3 to 4 minutes per batch
Makes 24

½ pound lean boneless pork	2 teaspoons vegetable oil
loin roast	1 small onion, finely chopped
3 tablespoons soy sauce	½ teaspoon crushed red
1 tablespoon fresh lime juice	pepper
1 teaspoon grated, peeled	¼ cup peanut butter
fresh ginger	1 tablespoon light molasses
1 teaspoon sugar	24 (6-inch) bamboo skewers,
1 garlic clove, minced	soaked (see below)

◆ Slice pork ¼ inch thick; cut each slice lengthwise in half to make strips. In small bowl, mix 2 tablespoons soy sauce with lime juice, ginger, sugar, and garlic. Add pork, stirring to coat. Cover and refrigerate 1 to 4 hours.

◆ Prepare dipping sauce: In 1-quart saucepan, heat oil over medium heat. Add onion and cook, stirring frequently, 5 minutes, or until tender. Stir in crushed red pepper and cook 30 seconds. Transfer to blender; add peanut butter, light molasses, remaining 1 tablespoon soy sauce, and ¼ *cup water* and blend until smooth. Set aside until ready to serve.

◆ Prepare outdoor grill or preheat broiler. Thread pork strips loosely on skewers, accordion-style. Grill or broil pork strips at closest position to heat source, turning once, 3 to 4 minutes, just until pork is cooked through. Serve hot with dipping sauce.

Each skewer: About 40 calories, 3g protein, 2g carbohydrate, 2g total fat (1g saturated), 6mg cholesterol, 150mg sodium

---

SOAKING BAMBOO SKEWERS

◆◆◆◆◆◆◆◆◆◆◆◆◆◆◆◆◆◆◆◆◆◆◆◆

Delicate bamboo skewers are ideal for individual appetizer servings. Before using for cooking, soak bamboo skewers in water to keep them from burning on the grill or under the broiler. Fill a shallow bowl with water. Add skewers and soak at least 15 minutes; remove and pat dry.

SOUPS

2

SOUPS KNOW-HOW

Perhaps no dish is more inviting than a steaming bowl of homemade soup. Utterly comforting to eat and delightfully easy to prepare, most require little more than some initial chopping. Depending on richness, soup can play various roles in your weekly menus. A simple broth or puree makes an elegant first course; a hearty bean soup creates a meal on its own with crusty bread and a crisp salad. Garnishes are great – they add an extra blast of fragrance and color, making any soup more enticing. Add fresh herbs just before serving.

KNOW YOUR SOUPS

Bisque A rich, creamy soup with a velvety texture, usually made with shellfish.
Broth A flavorful liquid made by simmering meat, fish, poultry and/or vegetables. Broth makes a light soup on its own and an excellent base for most other soups.
Chowder A hearty soup containing chunks of fish, shellfish, and/or vegetables. Clam chowder has been popular in New England since colonial times.
Consommé A clear soup, made by reducing stock and then filtering it meticulously. Good consommé has a heady aroma and strong flavor.
Gumbo A signature of Cajun cuisine, gumbo is a thick soup served over rice. It may contain a variety of vegetables, seafood, and meats, and may be thickened with okra or filé (made from sassafras leaves). The name gumbo comes from an African word for okra.
Stock A rich, clear liquid made by simmering poultry, meat, or fish bones in water with vegetables. The strained mixture is used as a base for soups, stews, and sauces.

GARNISHING

• Stir chopped fresh parsley, dill, basil, or mint into sour cream or yogurt and dollop on a creamed soup.
• Toasted nuts or crunchy crumbled bacon are delicious sprinkled over Broccoli Soup (see page 60), or Split-Pea Soup with Ham (see page 66).
• Garlicky homemade croutons, grated Parmesan or Gruyère, pesto, and slices of fresh lemon or lime are other tasty options.
• As a pretty garnish for chilled soups, freeze ice cubes with tiny sprigs of fresh herbs or berries. Add just before serving.

STORING

• Cool leftover soup; refrigerate in a sealed container up to 3 days. Chilling can thicken soup, so add extra broth, water, cream, or milk when reheating.
• Most soups freeze well in airtight containers for up to 3 months. Place in a large, shallow container for quicker freezing; leave some headspace to allow for expansion.
• Don't add cream, yogurt, or eggs to soup bases before freezing; they'll curdle when soup is reheated.
• It's best to thaw frozen soup in the refrigerator before reheating. Freezing may diminish some flavors, so be sure to taste and adjust seasonings before serving, if needed.

QUICK HOMEMADE SOUPS

Making soup from scratch can be a cinch. Choose your favorite from the chart, then just follow the steps below.

1 In 3-quart saucepan, heat 1 tablespoon vegetable oil, margarine, or butter over medium heat. Add 1 medium onion, finely chopped; cook 5 minutes, or until tender.

2 Add Flavoring for chosen soup; cook 30 seconds. Add 1 can (13¾ to 14½ ounces) chicken or vegetable broth, 1 cup water, and ¼ teaspoon salt; heat to boiling over high heat.

3 Now stir in Vegetables. Return the mixture to boiling. Reduce heat to medium and cook 10 to 20 minutes, until vegetables are very tender. In blender, blend in small batches until smooth. Season to taste. Makes 4 first-course servings.

SOUP SELECTION

SOUP	FLAVORING	VEGETABLES
Spinach	1 garlic clove, minced	1 package (10 ounces) frozen spinach
Pea	1 garlic clove, minced, and pinch dried mint	1 package (10 ounces) frozen peas
Carrot	⅛ teaspoon ground nutmeg	2 cups chopped carrots
Potato	⅛ teaspoon ground nutmeg and ¼ teaspoon dried thyme	2 cups chopped potatoes
Zucchini	1 teaspoon curry powder	2 cups chopped zucchini

56 ◆ SOUPS KNOW-HOW

BROTH-BASED SOUPS

Broth-based soups may be light and clear – or they can be hearty main dishes loaded with tender meat and chunky vegetables. For instance, our Latin Chicken Soup creates an aromatic broth as chicken and vegetables gently simmer; fresh lime juice, cilantro, and crisp tortilla chips lend additional great taste. In other soups, such as the Ravioli in Broth with Vegetables, canned broth is a convenient shortcut that saves on cooking time but doesn't sacrifice flavor.

LATIN CHICKEN SOUP

Prep: 25 minutes   Cook: 1 hour 15 minutes
Makes 8 main-dish servings

1 chicken (3½ pounds) cut into 8 pieces (see page 134)
3 large celery stalks, each cut into thirds
3 medium carrots, each cut into thirds
2 medium onions, unpeeled, each cut into quarters
10 fresh cilantro sprigs
2 bay leaves
1 teaspoon whole black peppercorns

2½ pounds all-purpose potatoes, peeled
1 can (15¼ to 16 ounces) whole-kernel corn, drained
2 teaspoons salt
¼ cup fresh lime juice
¼ cup chopped fresh cilantro
Tortilla chips and lime wedges (optional)

1 In 8-quart Dutch oven, combine chicken, next 6 ingredients, 1 pound whole potatoes, and *10 cups water*; heat to boiling over high heat.

2 Reduce heat to low; cover and simmer 35 to 45 minutes, until chicken is cooked through and potatoes are fork-tender. With slotted spoon, transfer chicken and potatoes to separate bowls. Pour broth through sieve into large bowl; skim and discard fat. Return all but 1 cup broth to Dutch oven. Discard vegetables.

3 Add the 1 cup broth to potatoes in bowl and mash; add to broth in Dutch oven. Stir well. Dice remaining potatoes. Add to broth; heat to boiling over high heat.

4 Reduce heat to low; cover and simmer 10 minutes, or until potatoes are tender. Meanwhile, discard skin and bones from chicken; cut chicken into bite-size pieces.

5 Stir chicken pieces, corn kernels, and salt into broth; heat through. Stir lime juice and chopped cilantro into soup. Serve immediately with tortilla chips and lime wedges, if you like.

EACH SERVING: ABOUT 380 CALORIES, 33g PROTEIN, 39g CARBOHYDRATE, 10g TOTAL FAT (3g SATURATED), 82mg CHOLESTEROL, 835mg SODIUM

RAVIOLI IN BROTH WITH VEGETABLES

Prep: 10 minutes   *Cook:* 20 minutes
Makes 3 main-dish servings

1 package (13 ounces) frozen jumbo cheese ravioli
1 can (13¾ to 14½ ounces) reduced-sodium chicken or beef broth
1 medium carrot, cut into matchstick-thin strips
1 small zucchini (about 6 ounces), diced
2 teaspoons grated, peeled fresh ginger
¼ bunch watercress, tough stems removed

◆ Prepare ravioli as label directs; drain. Cover to keep warm.

◆ Meanwhile, in 3-quart saucepan, heat broth and carrot strips to boiling over high heat. Reduce heat to low; cover and simmer 5 minutes.

◆ Stir in diced zucchini and grated ginger; heat to boiling over high heat. Reduce heat to low; cover and simmer 5 minutes longer, or just until vegetables are tender.

◆ To serve, place watercress sprigs in 3 shallow bowls. Place ravioli in bowls with watercress. Spoon broth with vegetables over ravioli.

Each serving: About 250 calories, 15g protein, 31g carbohydrate, 9g total fat (4g saturated), 65mg cholesterol, 375mg sodium

MUSHROOM AND WILD RICE SOUP

Prep: 45 minutes   *Cook:* 1 hour
Makes 8 first-course servings

½ cup wild rice
1 package (½ ounce) dried mushrooms
2 tablespoons olive oil
2 medium celery stalks, finely chopped
1 large onion, finely chopped
1 package (10 ounces) white mushrooms, thinly sliced
2 cans (13¾ to 14½ ounces each) chicken broth
1 tablespoon soy sauce
½ teaspoon dried thyme
¼ teaspoon coarsely ground black pepper
¼ cup cream sherry

◆ In 3-quart saucepan, heat wild rice and *2½ cups water* to boiling over high heat. Reduce heat to low; cover and simmer 45 minutes, or until rice is tender and most of water is absorbed. Meanwhile, in 4-cup measuring cup, combine dried mushrooms and *2 cups boiling water*. Set aside.

◆ In nonstick 12-inch skillet, heat 1 tablespoon oil over medium heat. Add celery, onion, and *2 tablespoons water*; cook about 10 minutes, until vegetables are tender and lightly browned. Transfer to 4-quart saucepan. In same skillet, heat remaining 1 tablespoon olive oil over medium-high heat. Add sliced fresh mushrooms; cook about 10 minutes, until tender and lightly browned. Transfer to saucepan with celery mixture.

◆ With slotted spoon, remove dried mushrooms from liquid and coarsely chop; strain liquid. Add mushrooms and liquid to celery mixture; stir in broth, soy sauce, thyme, pepper, and wild rice with any cooking liquid; heat to boiling over high heat. Reduce heat to low; cover and simmer 5 minutes. Stir in sherry.

Each serving: About 120 calories, 4g protein, 15g carbohydrate, 5g total fat (1g saturated), 8mg cholesterol, 575mg sodium

MISO SOUP

Prep: 20 minutes   *Cook:* 35 minutes
Makes 5 main-dish servings

1 tablespoon vegetable oil
2 large carrots, thinly sliced
1 small onion, diced
2 garlic cloves, minced
1 tablespoon grated, peeled fresh ginger
1 small head napa cabbage (Chinese cabbage, about 1 pound), cut crosswise into ½-inch-thick slices (about 4 cups)
1 tablespoon seasoned rice vinegar
¼ teaspoon coarsely ground black pepper
¼ cup red miso
1 package (16 ounces) firm tofu, drained and cut into ½-inch cubes
2 green onions, thinly sliced

◆ In 5-quart Dutch oven, heat oil over medium heat. Add carrots, onion, garlic, and ginger and cook, stirring occasionally, about 10 minutes, or until onion is lightly browned.

◆ Add cabbage, vinegar, pepper, and *6 cups water*; heat to boiling over high heat. Reduce heat to low; cover and simmer 20 minutes, or until vegetables are tender. In cup, mix miso and *¼ cup hot water*; add to soup. Stir in tofu and heat through, about 5 minutes. Sprinkle with green onions.

Each serving: About 225 calories, 18g protein, 16g carbohydrate, 12g total fat (2g saturated), 0mg cholesterol, 545mg sodium

---

MISO

A highly concentrated fermented soybean paste, made from a combination of soybeans and grains such as rice or barley, miso is widely used in Japanese cooking – from sauces and soups to main dishes – and is made in different strengths, varying by color. Red miso (far right) has the strongest flavor, golden (right) is fairly mild, and white is mellow and slightly sweet. Look for miso in health food stores and Asian markets.

PUREED SOUPS

Perfectly smooth, silky-textured soups make an elegant opener to almost any meal. Blenders produce the smoothest soups; to avoid burns, puree the cooked mixture in small batches. Removing the center part of the blender lid will prevent overflow and splatter. Hand-held immersion blenders also work well; cool the soup slightly before using one.

WINTER SQUASH AND APPLE SOUP

◆◆◆◆◆◆◆◆◆◆◆

Prep: 35 minutes
Cook: 40 minutes
Makes 8 first-course servings

2 medium Golden Delicious apples (about 12 ounces)
2 medium butternut squash (about 1¾ pounds each)
2 tablespoons vegetable oil
1 small onion, chopped
1 can (14½ ounces) vegetable broth
1 tablespoon chopped fresh thyme or ¼ teaspoon dried thyme
1 teaspoon salt
⅛ teaspoon coarsely ground black pepper
1 cup half-and-half or light cream
Chopped fresh thyme or parsley for garnish

1 Peel, quarter, and core each apple. Cut into ¾-inch chunks.

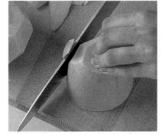

2 With large chef's knife, cut each squash into 2 pieces and slice off peel. Remove seeds.

3 Cut squash into ¾-inch chunks. In 4-quart saucepan, heat oil over medium heat; add onion and cook until tender.

4 Stir in apples, squash, broth, 1 tablespoon thyme, salt, pepper, and *1½ cups water*; heat to boiling over high heat. Reduce heat to low; cover and simmer, stirring frequently, 20 to 25 minutes, until squash is tender.

5 Spoon one-third of mixture into blender. Cover (with center part of blender lid removed) and blend at low speed until very smooth. Pour mixture into bowl. Repeat with remaining mixture.

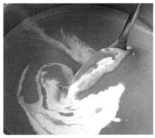

6 Return pureed mixture to saucepan, stir in half-and-half, and heat through over medium heat, stirring occasionally (do not boil). Serve garnished with chopped fresh thyme.

EACH SERVING: ABOUT 175 CALORIES, 3g PROTEIN, 29g CARBOHYDRATE, 7g TOTAL FAT (3g SATURATED), 11mg CHOLESTEROL, 305mg SODIUM

BROCCOLI SOUP

Prep: 10 minutes   Cook: 30 minutes
Makes 8 first-course servings

1 large bunch broccoli (1½ pounds)
1 tablespoon margarine or butter
1 medium onion, finely chopped
2 cans (13¾ to 14½ ounces each) chicken
   broth
½ teaspoon salt
¼ teaspoon ground black pepper
¼ teaspoon dried thyme
Pinch ground nutmeg
½ cup half-and-half or light cream

◆ Cut stems from broccoli; peel stems and thinly slice. Cut tops into flowerets. In 3-quart saucepan, melt margarine over medium heat. Add onion and cook, stirring often, 5 minutes, or until tender. Add broccoli stems and flowerets, broth, next 4 ingredients, and *2 cups water*. Heat to boiling over high heat; boil 15 minutes, or until broccoli stems are tender.

◆ Spoon small amount of broccoli mixture into blender; cover (with center part of blender lid removed) and blend at low speed until smooth. Pour mixture into bowl. Repeat with remaining broccoli mixture. Return mixture to saucepan. Stir in half-and-half and heat through over medium heat (do not boil).

Each serving: About 80 calories, 4g protein, 8g carbohydrate, 4g total fat (2g saturated), 13mg cholesterol, 615mg sodium

◆◆◆◆◆◆◆◆◆◆◆◆◆◆◆◆◆◆◆◆◆

CREAM GARNISH

Drizzle 1 tablespoon crème fraîche or slightly thinned sour cream in ring onto soup. Draw tip of knife through ring at intervals, alternately moving toward the center, then toward the outside, until it forms a flower shape.

◆◆◆◆◆◆◆◆◆◆◆◆◆◆◆◆

FRESH TOMATO AND BASIL SOUP

Prep: 15 minutes   Cook: 25 minutes
Makes 4 first-course servings

4 large ripe tomatoes (about 2 pounds)
1 medium bunch basil
2 tablespoons vegetable oil
1 large onion, chopped
1 small carrot, shredded
½ teaspoon sugar
1 can (13¾ to 14½ ounces) chicken broth
½ teaspoon salt
Sour cream (optional)

◆ Cut each tomato horizontally in half; squeeze out and discard seeds. Chop tomatoes. Reserve 4 small basil sprigs; chop enough remaining basil to equal ¼ cup.

◆ In 3-quart saucepan, heat oil over medium heat; add onion and carrot and cook, stirring occasionally, just until tender.

◆ Add chopped tomatoes and sugar; heat to boiling over high heat. Reduce heat to low; cover and simmer, stirring occasionally, 15 minutes, or until tomatoes are very soft.

◆ Spoon half of tomato mixture into blender; cover (with center part of blender lid removed) and blend at low speed until smooth. Pour mixture into bowl. Repeat with remaining tomato mixture. Return mixture to saucepan. Stir in chopped basil, broth, and salt and heat through over medium heat.

◆ Serve soup hot or cover and refrigerate to serve cold later. To serve, spoon soup into 4 soup bowls. Top each serving with a spoonful of sour cream, if you like. Garnish with basil sprigs.

Each serving: About 155 calories, 4g protein, 19g carbohydrate, 9g total fat (2g saturated), 8mg cholesterol, 725mg sodium

ROASTED GARLIC AND POTATO SOUP

Prep: 1 hour 5 minutes plus cooling
Cook: 30 minutes   Makes 6 first-course servings

1 whole head garlic
3 tablespoons olive or vegetable oil
2 medium onions, diced
4 medium all-purpose potatoes (about
   1¼ pounds), peeled and diced
1 can (13¾ to 14½ ounces) chicken broth
1 cup half-and-half or light cream
1¼ teaspoons salt

◆ Preheat oven to 350°F. Remove any loose papery skin from garlic, leaving head intact. Place garlic in small baking dish; pour oil over garlic. Cover with foil and bake garlic 1 hour, or until soft. Cool garlic until easy to handle. Separate garlic head into cloves. Press soft, cooked garlic from each clove into small bowl; discard skin. Reserve 1 tablespoon oil from baking dish.

◆ In 4-quart saucepan, heat reserved oil over medium-high heat; add onions and cook, stirring often, 10 minutes, or until golden brown and tender.

◆ Add potatoes to saucepan with garlic, broth, and *3 cups water*; heat to boiling over high heat. Reduce heat to low; cover and simmer, stirring occasionally, about 10 minutes, until potatoes are tender.

◆ Spoon half of potato mixture into blender; cover (with center part of blender lid removed) and blend at low speed until smooth. Pour mixture into bowl. Repeat with remaining potato mixture. Return soup to saucepan; stir in half-and-half and salt. Heat soup to boiling over medium-high heat, stirring constantly. Serve hot or cover and refrigerate to serve cold later.

Each serving: About 235 calories, 5g protein, 28g carbohydrate, 12g total fat (4g saturated), 20mg cholesterol, 755mg sodium

HEARTY VEGETABLE SOUPS

Chock-full of chunky vegetables and greens, as well as beans and grains, these long-simmered soups nourish body and soul. They're extremely simple, but substantial enough for supper – and so hearty, in fact, that you'll never miss the meat. There's a secret to thickening some of these soups: Puree a small amount of the soup, and then stir it back in.

MUSHROOM-BARLEY SOUP

◆◆◆◆◆◆◆◆◆◆◆◆◆

Prep: 20 minutes
Cook: 1 hour 15 minutes
Makes 6 main-dish servings

¾ **cup pearl barley**
1½ **pounds mushrooms**
5 **medium carrots**
2 **tablespoons olive oil**
3 **medium celery stalks, sliced**
1 **large onion, coarsely chopped**
2 **tablespoons tomato paste**
2 **cans (13¾ to 14½ ounces each) beef broth**
¼ **cup dry sherry**
Fresh oregano leaves for garnish
Crusty bread (optional)

1 In 3-quart saucepan, heat barley and *4 cups water* to boiling over high heat. Reduce heat to low. Cover; simmer 30 minutes. Drain.

2 Meanwhile, cut mushrooms into thick slices. Cut carrots lengthwise in half, then crosswise into ½-inch-thick slices.

3 In 5-quart Dutch oven, heat olive oil over medium-high heat. Add celery and onion and cook, stirring occasionally, 8 to 10 minutes, until golden brown. Increase heat to high; add sliced mushrooms and cook, stirring occasionally, 10 to 12 minutes, until all liquid evaporates and mushrooms are lightly browned.

4 Reduce heat to medium-high; stir in tomato paste and cook, stirring, 2 minutes. Add beef broth, carrots, sherry, barley, and *4 cups water*; heat to boiling over high heat. Reduce heat to low; cover and simmer 20 to 25 minutes, until carrots and barley are tender. Garnish and serve hot, with crusty bread, if you like.

◆◆◆◆◆◆◆◆◆◆◆◆◆◆◆◆◆◆◆◆◆◆◆

GARNISHING HEARTY SOUPS

Top steaming bowls of soup with one of the following for extra color, texture, or flavor: sour cream or yogurt; fresh herbs; crumbled bacon; thin strips of ham; chopped hard-cooked egg; shredded Gruyère; grated Parmesan; pesto tossed with chopped tomato; crumbled tortilla chips.

For crumbled bacon, cook bacon until crisp; break into tiny pieces to use as garnish.

Pesto tossed with chopped tomato

Chopped hard-cooked egg

Chopped fresh parsley

◆◆◆◆◆◆◆◆◆◆◆◆◆◆◆◆◆◆◆◆◆◆◆

EACH SERVING: ABOUT 220 CALORIES, 8g PROTEIN, 34g CARBOHYDRATE, 6g TOTAL FAT (1g SATURATED), 0mg CHOLESTEROL, 575mg SODIUM

LENTIL-VEGETABLE SOUP

Prep: 20 minutes   Cook: 40 minutes
Makes 4 main-dish servings

2 cans (13¾ to 14½ ounces
  each) reduced-sodium
  chicken or vegetable broth
½ cup lentils
2 tablespoons vegetable oil
2 medium carrots, cut into
  ½-inch thick slices
1 medium onion, coarsely
  chopped
1 medium zucchini, cut into
  ½-inch pieces

1 medium yellow straightneck
  squash, cut into ½-inch
  pieces
1 garlic clove, minced
½ medium head escarole,
  coarsely chopped
1 can (32 ounces) tomatoes
¼ cup seasoned dried bread
  crumbs

◆ In 4-quart saucepan, heat broth and lentils to boiling over high heat. Reduce heat to low; cover and simmer 20 minutes, or until lentils are almost tender.

◆ Meanwhile, in 12-inch skillet, heat oil over medium-high heat; add carrots and onion and cook about 5 minutes, until lightly browned. Add zucchini, yellow squash, and garlic; cook about 5 minutes, until lightly browned. Stir in escarole; cook about 2 minutes, until tender.

◆ To lentil mixture, add tomatoes with their juice, bread crumbs, vegetables in skillet, and *1 cup water*; heat to boiling over high heat, breaking up tomatoes with back of spoon. Reduce heat to low; cover and simmer 5 minutes.

Each serving: About 300 calories, 13g protein, 43g carbohydrate, 9g total fat (1g saturated), 0mg cholesterol, 675mg sodium

MINESTRONE WITH PESTO

Prep: 30 minutes plus soaking and cooking beans   Cook: 1 hour
Makes 6 main-dish servings

2 tablespoons olive oil
3 medium carrots, sliced
2 medium celery stalks, thinly
  sliced
1 large onion, diced
2 ounces sliced pancetta or
  bacon, diced
3 medium all-purpose
  potatoes (about 1 pound),
  peeled and cut into ½-inch
  cubes
2 medium zucchini, diced

½ (2-pound) head savoy
  cabbage, thinly sliced
1 large garlic clove, minced
2 cans (13¾ to 14½ ounces
  each) reduced-sodium
  chicken broth
1 can (14½ to 16 ounces)
  diced tomatoes
1⅓ cups dry Great Northern
  beans, soaked (see page
  370) and cooked
½ cup Pesto (see page 354)

◆ In 5-quart Dutch oven, heat oil over medium-high heat. Add carrots, celery, onion, and pancetta; cook, stirring occasionally, 10 minutes, or until onion begins to brown. Add potatoes, zucchini, cabbage, and garlic; cook, stirring, until

cabbage wilts. Add broth, tomatoes with their juice, and *1 cup water*; heat to boiling over high heat. Reduce heat to low; cover and simmer 30 minutes, or until vegetables are tender.

◆ In blender or food processor with knife blade attached, blend ½ cup cooked beans with 1 cup soup until pureed. Stir bean puree and remaining cooked beans into soup; heat to boiling over high heat. Reduce heat to low; cover and simmer 10 minutes. Serve hot with Pesto.

Each serving: About 450 calories, 19g protein, 54g carbohydrate, 19g total fat (4g saturated), 10mg cholesterol, 510mg sodium

BORSCHT

Prep: 25 minutes   Cook: 1 hour 15 minutes
Makes 4 main-dish servings

2 tablespoons margarine or
  butter
¼ (2-pound) head green
  cabbage, sliced
2 medium carrots, sliced
2 medium celery stalks, sliced
1 medium onion, diced
1 pound beets, peeled and cut
  into matchstick-thin sticks
1 can (14½ to 16 ounces)
  tomatoes in puree

2 cans (13¾ to 14½ ounces
  each) beef broth
1 tablespoon sugar
¼ teaspoon salt
⅛ teaspoon ground black
  pepper
Celery leaves for garnish
Pumpernickel bread
  (optional)

◆ In 5-quart Dutch oven, melt margarine over medium heat. Add cabbage, carrots, celery, and onion; cover and cook, stirring frequently, until tender and browned. Add beets, tomatoes with their puree, broth, sugar, salt, pepper, and *1½ cups water*; heat to boiling over high heat. Reduce heat to low; cover and simmer, stirring, 45 minutes, or until all vegetables are tender.

◆ Spoon 2 cups soup into blender; cover (with center part of blender lid removed) and blend at low speed until smooth. Return mixture to Dutch oven; heat through. Garnish and serve hot with pumpernickel bread, if you like. Or, cover and refrigerate to serve cold later.

Each serving: About 220 calories, 7g protein, 37g carbohydrate, 7g total fat (1g saturated), 0mg cholesterol, 1465mg sodium

HEARTY SEAFOOD SOUPS

Cook shellfish or tasty chunks of fish in a spicy, flavorful broth to produce sensational soups – from bouillabaisse, the classic Provençal one-pot feast, to gutsy Louisiana gumbo. Just add crusty bread and a fresh green salad to make a memorable meal.

BOUILLABAISSE

◆◆◆◆◆◆◆◆◆◆◆◆◆

Prep: 35 minutes
Cook: 30 minutes
Makes 12 main-dish servings

Rouille (see page 64)
1 pound sea scallops
1 dozen littleneck clams or
**   2 dozen Manila clams**
1 dozen medium mussels
1 pound large shrimp
2 tablespoons olive oil
3 medium leeks (about
**   1 pound), cut into ¾-inch**
**   pieces**
1 garlic clove, minced
1 teaspoon salt
¾ teaspoon dried thyme
½ teaspoon saffron threads
2 cans (14½ to 16 ounces
**   each) tomatoes**
2 pounds cod or scrod fillet,
**   cut into 1½-inch chunks**
2 tablespoons chopped
**   fresh parsley**

1 Prepare Rouille. Rinse scallops with cold running water to remove any sand, then pull tough crescent-shaped muscle from side of each scallop. Slice each scallop horizontally in half. With stiff brush, scrub clams and mussels under cold running water to remove any sand. Remove beards from mussels (see page 88). Shell and devein shrimp (see page 90); rinse.

2 In 8-quart Dutch oven or saucepot, heat *1 cup water* to boiling over high heat. Add clams and mussels; heat to boiling. Reduce heat to medium; cover and cook, stirring occasionally, about 5 minutes, just until shells open. Discard any clams or mussels that do not open.

3 With slotted spoon, transfer cooked shellfish to bowl.

4 Let broth stand until sand settles to bottom of Dutch oven. Ladle clear broth through sieve into measuring cup or bowl; discard remaining broth. Wipe Dutch oven dry.

5 In Dutch oven, heat oil over medium heat; add leeks and garlic and cook until tender. Add salt, thyme, saffron, tomatoes with their juice, clam broth, and *2 cups water*; heat to boiling over high heat, breaking up tomatoes with back of spoon.

6 Add cod, shrimp, and scallops; heat to boiling. Reduce heat to medium-low and cook, uncovered, 5 to 8 minutes, until seafood is opaque throughout. Add clams and mussels; heat through. Sprinkle with parsley. Top each serving with a dollop of Rouille.

EACH SERVING: ABOUT 230 CALORIES, 30g PROTEIN, 12g CARBOHYDRATE, 6g TOTAL FAT (1g SATURATED), 110mg CHOLESTEROL, 565mg SODIUM

PERUVIAN SEAFOOD SOUP

Prep: 30 minutes   Cook: 25 minutes
Makes 6 main-dish servings

1 tablespoon vegetable oil	⅛ teaspoon dried thyme
1 medium onion, chopped	½ medium lime
2 garlic cloves, minced	1 pound monkfish, dark
2 serrano chiles, seeded and	membrane removed, cut
minced	into 1-inch pieces
4 medium red potatoes	1 pound medium shrimp,
(about 1 pound), cut into	shelled and deveined (see
¾-inch chunks	page 90)
3 bottles (8 ounces each) clam	¼ cup chopped fresh cilantro
juice	Lime wedges for serving
¾ teaspoon salt	

◆ In 4-quart saucepan, heat oil over medium heat; add onion and cook 5 minutes, or until tender. Add garlic and chiles; cook 30 seconds. Add potatoes, next 3 ingredients, and *2 cups water*; heat to boiling over high heat. Boil 10 minutes.

◆ Add lime half and monkfish; cover and cook 5 minutes. Stir in shrimp; cover and cook 3 to 5 minutes longer, just until shrimp are opaque throughout. Remove lime half, pressing to squeeze juice into soup. Sprinkle soup with cilantro and serve with lime wedges.

Each serving: About 225 calories, 26g protein, 20g carbohydrate, 4g total fat (1g saturated), 135mg cholesterol, 665mg sodium

MUSSEL SOUP

Prep: 15 minutes   Cook: 20 minutes
Makes 4 main-dish servings

1 tablespoon olive oil	⅛ teaspoon crushed red
1 large onion, sliced	pepper
2 garlic cloves, minced	2 pounds small mussels,
1 can (28 ounces) tomatoes	scrubbed and beards
in puree	removed (see page 88)
1 bottle (8 ounces) clam juice	2 tablespoons chopped fresh
½ cup dry white wine	parsley

◆ In 5-quart Dutch oven, heat oil over medium heat; add onion and cook about 10 minutes, until golden. Add garlic; cook 2 minutes longer. Stir in tomatoes with their puree, next 3 ingredients, and *2 cups water*. Heat to boiling over high heat, breaking up tomatoes with spoon. Boil 3 minutes.

◆ Add mussels; return to boiling. Reduce heat to low; cover and simmer about 4 minutes, until mussels open. Discard any mussels that do not open. Stir in parsley.

Each serving: About 185 calories, 12g protein, 18g carbohydrate, 6g total fat (1g saturated), 21mg cholesterol, 1000mg sodium

RED-SNAPPER GUMBO

Prep: 20 minutes   Cook: 40 minutes
Makes 6 main-dish servings

1 cup regular long-grain rice	1 package (10 ounces) frozen
3 tablespoons vegetable oil	sliced okra
3 tablespoons all-purpose	1 package (10 ounces) frozen
flour	whole-kernel corn
1 medium green pepper,	1 tablespoon Worcestershire
chopped	sauce
1 medium celery stalk,	½ teaspoon salt
chopped	¼ teaspoon ground red
1 medium onion, chopped	pepper (cayenne)
1 can (14½ to 16 ounces)	⅛ teaspoon dried thyme
stewed tomatoes	1 bay leaf
1 can (13¾ to 14½ ounces)	10 ounces red snapper fillet,
chicken broth	cut into bite-size chunks

◆ Prepare rice as label directs; keep warm. Meanwhile, in 5-quart Dutch oven, heat oil over medium heat. Stir in flour and cook, stirring constantly, about 10 minutes, until flour is dark brown but not burned (mixture will be thick).

◆ To flour mixture, add green pepper, celery, and onion; cook, stirring occasionally, 8 to 10 minutes, until vegetables are tender. Gradually stir in tomatoes and broth. Stir in okra, next 6 ingredients, and *1 cup water*; heat to boiling over high heat. Reduce heat to low; cover and simmer 10 minutes.

◆ Stir in red snapper and cook until opaque throughout. To serve, discard bay leaf. Ladle soup into 6 soup bowls; top each with a scoop of rice.

Each serving: About 330 calories, 16g protein, 49g carbohydrate, 9g total fat (2g saturated), 22mg cholesterol, 705mg sodium

ROUILLE

Soak 1 slice firm white bread, crusts trimmed, in water to cover 5 minutes; squeeze out water. In blender or food processor, puree bread, 1 red pepper, roasted and peeled (see page 310), 2 tablespoons extra-virgin olive oil, and ⅛ teaspoon ground red pepper (cayenne).

Finely chop 1 garlic clove and mash to a paste with ¼ teaspoon salt; stir into bread mixture. Makes ½ cup.

Each tablespoon: About 40 calories, 0g protein, 2g carbohydrate, 4g total fat (0g saturated), 0mg cholesterol, 85mg sodium

HEARTY MEAT AND POULTRY SOUPS

A bowl of thick, steaming soup can be a wonderfully welcome meal in itself – or a cupful can team up with a sandwich or salad. Sweet sausage, smoked ham, and savory meatballs are so flavorful that a little goes a long way in these chunky soups. Each of these tasty specialties takes very little effort to prepare – just remember to allow plenty of simmering time so the flavors can mingle. If preparing in advance, add any leafy vegetables, such as spinach, just before serving.

ITALIAN SAUSAGE AND BEAN SOUP

◆◆◆◆◆◆◆◆◆◆◆◆◆◆◆◆◆◆◆◆◆◆◆◆◆◆◆

Prep: 15 minutes plus soaking and cooking beans   Cook: 1 hour
Makes 8 main-dish servings

1 pound sweet Italian-sausage links, casings removed
1 tablespoon olive oil
2 medium onions, chopped
2 garlic cloves, minced
1 can (28 ounces) plum tomatoes
2 cans (13¾ to 14½ ounces each) reduced-sodium chicken broth
1½ cups dry Great Northern beans, soaked (see page 370) and cooked

6 ounces ditalini or tubetti pasta (1 rounded cup)
½ (10-ounce) bag spinach, tough stems removed and leaves cut into 1-inch-wide strips
Crusty bread and Parmesan cheese shavings (optional)

1 Heat 5-quart Dutch oven over medium-high heat. Add sausage and cook, stirring frequently and breaking up with spoon, until browned. With slotted spoon, transfer sausage to bowl.

2 Reduce heat to medium. Add oil to drippings in Dutch oven; add onions and cook until golden. Add garlic; cook 1 minute. Stir in tomatoes with their juice, breaking up tomatoes with back of spoon.

3 Add broth, beans, and *2 cups water*; heat to boiling over high heat. Reduce heat to low; cover and simmer 30 minutes. Add cooked sausage.

4 Meanwhile, in 3-quart saucepan, prepare ditalini or tubetti as label directs but do not add salt to water. Drain pasta.

5 Add spinach and cooked pasta to soup. Stir well to mix; heat through. Serve hot with crusty bread and Parmesan cheese shavings, if you like.

ITALIAN SAUSAGE

Made from coarsely ground pork and often redolent of fennel seeds, Italian sausage packs plenty of flavor. The hot version is spiced up with ground red pepper. In their casings, Italian sausages can be panfried, grilled, or braised (be sure to fully cook). Or, remove the casings to crumble and sauté the meat as we've done for our hearty Italian Sausage and Bean Soup.

EACH SERVING: ABOUT 435 CALORIES, 24g PROTEIN, 45g CARBOHYDRATE, 18g TOTAL FAT (6g SATURATED), 44mg CHOLESTEROL, 900mg SODIUM

MEATBALL AND ESCAROLE SOUP

Prep: 20 minutes   Cook: 35 minutes
Makes 6 main-dish servings

1 pound lean ground beef
½ cup plain dried bread
   crumbs
¼ cup freshly grated
   Parmesan cheese
¼ teaspoon salt
¼ teaspoon ground black
   pepper
1 large egg
1 tablespoon olive or
   vegetable oil

2 green onions, thinly sliced
2 cans (13¾ to 14½ ounces
   each) beef broth
½ teaspoon dried marjoram
1 small head escarole (about
   8 ounces), cut into bite-size
   pieces
1 large tomato, cut into ½-inch
   pieces

◆ In large bowl, with hands, mix ground beef, bread crumbs, Parmesan cheese, salt, pepper, egg, and *¼ cup water*. Shape into 30 meatballs.

◆ In 5-quart Dutch oven, heat oil over medium-high heat; add meatballs, half at a time, and cook until browned, transferring them to clean bowl as they brown.

◆ In drippings remaining in Dutch oven, cook green onions 1 minute. Add broth, marjoram, meatballs, and *3 cups water*; heat to boiling over high heat. Reduce heat to low; cover and simmer 5 minutes. Stir in escarole and tomato and cook just until escarole is wilted.

Each serving: About 315 calories, 20g protein, 10g carbohydrate, 21g total fat (8g saturated), 95mg cholesterol, 820mg sodium

SPLIT-PEA SOUP WITH HAM

Prep: 10 minutes   Cook: 1 hour 15 minutes
Makes 6 main-dish servings

1 package (16 ounces) dry
   split peas
2 tablespoons vegetable oil
2 white turnips (about
   6 ounces each), peeled and
   cut into ½-inch cubes
2 medium carrots, diced
2 medium celery stalks, diced

1 medium onion, finely
   chopped
2 smoked ham hocks
¼ teaspoon ground allspice
1 bay leaf
1 teaspoon salt
Chopped fresh parsley for
   garnish

◆ Rinse split peas with cold running water and discard any stones or shriveled peas.

◆ In 5-quart Dutch oven, heat oil over medium-high heat. Add next 4 ingredients and cook, stirring frequently, 10 minutes, or until vegetables are tender-crisp. Add split peas, ham hocks, allspice, bay leaf, salt, and *8 cups water*; heat to boiling over high heat. Reduce heat to low; cover and simmer 45 minutes.

◆ Discard bay leaf. Remove ham hocks; discard skin and bones and finely chop meat. Return meat to Dutch oven. Heat through; garnish with parsley.

Each serving: About 415 calories, 30g protein, 54g carbohydrate, 10g total fat (2g saturated), 28mg cholesterol, 1115mg sodium

CHICKEN MINESTRONE

Prep: 15 minutes   Cook: 35 minutes
Makes 6 main-dish servings

2 skinless, boneless
   chicken-breast halves (about
   ¾ pound)
½ cup tubetti or ditalini pasta
1 tablespoon vegetable oil
1 medium onion, chopped
1 medium carrot, chopped
2 large tomatoes, chopped
8 ounces green beans,
   trimmed and each cut in half
2 cans (13¾ to 14½ ounces
   each) chicken broth

1 small yellow straightneck
   squash (about 8 ounces),
   cut into ½-inch-thick slices
1 can (15 to 19 ounces) white
   kidney beans (cannellini),
   rinsed and drained
1 package (10 ounces) frozen
   chopped spinach, thawed
Freshly grated Parmesan
   cheese (optional)

◆ Cut each chicken-breast half lengthwise in half, then cross-wise into ¼-inch-thick strips. Prepare tubetti as label directs; drain well. Meanwhile, in 5-quart Dutch oven, heat oil over medium-high heat; add chicken and cook, stirring frequently, just until it loses its pink color throughout. Transfer to bowl.

◆ In drippings in Dutch oven, cook onion and carrot over medium heat until tender but not browned. Add tomatoes, green beans, broth, and *2 cups water*; heat to boiling over high heat. Reduce heat to low. Cover; simmer 5 minutes. Add squash; simmer 5 minutes, or until vegetables are tender. Stir in chicken, tubetti, kidney beans, and spinach; heat through over medium-high heat. Serve with Parmesan, if you like.

Each serving: About 260 calories, 22g protein, 32g carbohydrate, 6g total fat (1g saturated), 45mg cholesterol, 920mg sodium

◆ ◆

COOKING WITH HAM HOCKS

Smoked ham hocks impart a depth of flavor to long-simmering stews and soups. After cooking, remove hocks from soup. With sharp knife, cut through skin; peel away skin and cut around bone to release meat. Chop the ham and return it to the soup.

◆ ◆

CHOWDERS

Named for the French cauldron used to cook the catch of the day, a chowder is a thick, creamy soup traditionally made with fish. Contemporary versions also feature corn or other vegetables. Versatile and warming, chowders can be served as the main dish or in mugs as a hearty prelude to a meal.

OYSTER-CORN CHOWDER

◆◆◆◆◆◆◆◆◆◆◆◆◆

Prep: 20 minutes
Cook: 10 minutes
Makes 8 first-course servings

3 medium ears corn, husks and silk removed, or 1 can (15¼ to 16 ounces) whole-kernel corn, drained

1 pint shucked oysters (about 24), with their liquor

4 medium all-purpose potatoes (about 1¼ pounds), peeled and diced

2 bottles (8 ounces each) clam juice

1 cup half-and-half or light cream

2 cups milk

1 teaspoon salt

¼ teaspoon coarsely ground black pepper

Chopped chives or parsley for garnish

1 If using fresh corn, holding each ear firmly on cutting board, with sharp knife, cut corn kernels away from cobs. With back of knife, scrape cobs to release milk.

2 Drain oysters, reserving ⅔ cup oyster liquor. In 4-quart Dutch oven, heat potatoes, clam juice, and reserved liquor to boiling over high heat. Reduce heat to low; cover and simmer about 10 minutes, until potatoes are fork-tender.

3 Remove Dutch oven from heat. With slotted spoon, transfer 1½ cups potatoes to blender. Cover (with center part of blender lid removed) and blend with half-and-half at low speed until smooth. Pour potato mixture back into Dutch oven. Stir in milk, corn kernels with their milk, salt, and pepper; heat just to boiling over medium-high heat.

4 Add oysters and cook, stirring often, 5 minutes, or until edges ruffle and centers are firm Garnish; serve immediately.

EACH SERVING: ABOUT 200 CALORIES, 8g PROTEIN, 29g CARBOHYDRATE, 7g TOTAL FAT (4g SATURATED), 36mg CHOLESTEROL, 500mg SODIUM

CORN CHOWDER

Prep: 20 minutes
Cook: 25 minutes
Makes 4 main-dish servings

1 tablespoon margarine or butter
1 medium onion, finely chopped
1 red pepper, finely chopped
3 medium all-purpose potatoes (about
   1 pound), peeled and cut into ½-inch
   chunks
1 can (13¾ to 14½ ounces) chicken broth
⅛ teaspoon dried thyme
¾ teaspoon salt
Ground black pepper
4 medium ears corn, husks and silk
   removed
1 cup half-and-half or light cream
3 slices bacon, cooked and crumbled

◆ In 4-quart saucepan, melt
margarine over medium heat. Add
onion and red pepper and cook,
stirring often, 5 minutes, or until
vegetables are tender.

◆ Add potatoes, chicken broth,
thyme, salt, ⅛ teaspoon pepper, and
1 cup water. Heat to boiling; boil
10 minutes, or until potatoes are
fork-tender.

◆ Meanwhile, cut corn kernels from
cobs (you should have about 2 cups).
With back of knife, scrape cobs to
release milk. Add corn kernels and
their milk to pan and cook 5 minutes.

◆ Stir in half-and-half; heat through
(do not boil). Spoon soup into bowls;
sprinkle with crumbled bacon and a
little black pepper.

**Each serving: About 380 calories,
11g protein, 59g carbohydrate, 14g total
fat (6g saturated), 34mg cholesterol,
975mg sodium**

GARDEN VEGETABLE CHOWDER

Prep: 20 minutes
Cook: 30 minutes
Makes 4 main-dish servings

1 tablespoon margarine or butter
2 medium leeks (about 6 ounces each),
   white and light green parts, each cut
   lengthwise in half and sliced ¼ inch thick
2 medium carrots, sliced ¼ inch thick
1 medium celery stalk, sliced ¼ inch thick
3 medium red potatoes (about 1 pound),
   cut into ½-inch chunks
1 can (13¾ to 14½ ounces) chicken or
   vegetable broth
⅛ teaspoon dried thyme
¾ teaspoon salt
⅛ teaspoon ground black pepper
2 ounces green or wax beans, cut into
   ½-inch pieces
1 medium zucchini (about 10 ounces),
   cut into ½-inch chunks
1 cup half-and-half or light cream
1 tablespoon chopped fresh dill

◆ In 3-quart saucepan, melt
margarine over medium heat. Stir in
leeks, carrots, and celery. Cover and
cook, stirring occasionally, 10 minutes,
or until vegetables are tender.

◆ Stir in potatoes, next 4 ingredients,
and *1 cup water*. Heat to boiling over
high heat; boil, uncovered, 5 minutes.
Stir in green beans; cook 5 minutes.
Stir in zucchini and cook 5 minutes
longer. Stir in half-and-half and heat
through (do not boil). Remove from
heat; stir in dill.

**Each serving: About 285 calories,
7g protein, 42g carbohydrate, 11g total fat
(5g saturated), 30mg cholesterol,
925mg sodium**

NEW ENGLAND-STYLE COD CHOWDER

Prep: 20 minutes
Cook: 30 minutes
Makes 5 main-dish servings

4 slices bacon
3 medium carrots, each cut lengthwise
   in half, then crosswise into slices
1 large fennel bulb (about 1 pound),
   diced, or 3 medium celery stalks, diced
1 medium onion, diced
3 medium all-purpose potatoes (about
   1 pound), peeled and cut into ½-inch
   chunks
3 bottles (8 ounces each) clam juice
1 can (13¾ to 14½ ounces) chicken broth
1 bay leaf
1 piece cod fillet (about 1 pound), cut
   into 1½-inch pieces
1 cup half-and-half or light cream
Chopped fresh parsley for garnish

◆ In 5-quart Dutch oven or saucepot,
cook bacon over medium heat until
browned. Transfer bacon to paper
towels to drain; crumble.

◆ Discard all but 2 tablespoons
bacon drippings from Dutch oven.
Add carrots, fennel, and onion and
cook, stirring occasionally, 6 to
8 minutes, until lightly browned. Add
potatoes, clam juice, chicken broth,
and bay leaf; heat to boiling over high
heat. Reduce heat to low; cover and
simmer 10 to 15 minutes, until
vegetables are tender.

◆ Add cod; cover and cook 3 to
5 minutes, until fish is opaque
throughout. Stir in half-and-half; heat
through (do not boil). Discard bay
leaf. Serve soup hot, topped with
crumbled bacon and chopped parsley.

**Each serving: About 320 calories,
24g protein, 35g carbohydrate, 10g total
fat (5g saturated), 68mg cholesterol,
850mg sodium**

CHILLED SOUPS

Chilled soups of all kinds make refreshing first courses or main dishes in the summer months; cold fruit soups make unusual desserts any time of year. Because they must be made in advance, they're ideal for easy entertaining. Chilling can diminish flavor, so always taste the soup before serving and add extra seasoning if it seems too bland.

SPICY CURRIED CARROT SOUP

◆◆◆◆◆◆◆◆◆◆◆◆◆

Prep: 30 minutes plus chilling
Cook: 1 hour
Makes 12 first-course servings

3 bags (16 ounces each) carrots
1 jumbo onion (about 1 pound)
1½-inch piece fresh ginger
2 tablespoons olive oil
4 teaspoons curry powder
2 cans (13¾ to 14½ ounces each) chicken broth
1½ teaspoons salt
1 cup half-and-half or light cream
Fresh cilantro for garnish

1 Peel carrots; cut into ¾-inch slices. Coarsely chop onion. With small paring knife, cut peel from ginger (see below). Grate 1 tablespoon ginger.

◆◆◆◆◆◆◆◆◆◆◆◆◆

PEELING GINGER

With paring knife, peel away the rough outer skin that covers the aromatic flesh. To prevent drying, peel only the amount to be grated.

◆◆◆◆◆◆◆◆◆◆◆◆◆

2 In 5-quart Dutch oven, heat oil over medium heat. Add onion and cook, stirring frequently, 15 to 20 minutes, until tender and golden.

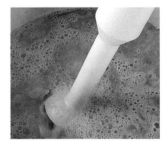

4 With hand-held immersion blender, blend soup in Dutch oven until pureed. (Or, in blender at low speed, with center part of blender lid removed, puree in small batches until smooth. Return to Dutch oven.)

3 Add curry powder and grated ginger to Dutch oven; cook, stirring constantly, 1 minute. Add sliced carrots, broth, salt, and *2 cups water*; heat to boiling. Reduce heat to low; cover and simmer 30 to 40 minutes, until carrots are very tender. Remove Dutch oven from heat; allow soup to cool slightly.

5 Stir in half-and-half and *4 cups water*. Cover and refrigerate at least 4 hours, or until very cold. Garnish with cilantro. (This soup is also good served hot. After adding half-and-half and water, heat through over medium heat; do not boil.)

EACH SERVING: ABOUT 120 CALORIES, 3g PROTEIN, 16g CARBOHYDRATE, 6g TOTAL FAT (2g SATURATED), 13mg CHOLESTEROL, 605mg SODIUM

CALIFORNIAN SPICY AVOCADO AND VEGETABLE SOUP

Prep: 20 minutes plus chilling
Makes 5 main-dish servings

2 large tomatoes	¼ cup red wine vinegar
1 medium yellow pepper	¼ teaspoon salt
1 medium cucumber	1½ teaspoons chopped
1 large celery stalk	fresh cilantro or parsley
½ bunch radishes	½ teaspoon chili powder
2 medium avocados	
1 bottle (32 ounces) spicy cocktail vegetable juice, chilled	

◆ Seed and coarsely chop tomatoes. Cut yellow pepper into ½-inch pieces. Cut cucumber lengthwise in half, scoop out seeds, and cut into ½-inch pieces. Thinly slice celery. Finely chop radishes. Halve, seed, and peel avocados; cut into ¾-inch pieces.

◆ Transfer vegetables to large bowl. Add spicy cocktail vegetable juice, red wine vinegar, salt, cilantro, and chili powder and stir well to combine.

◆ Cover and refrigerate soup at least 30 minutes, or until very cold.

Each serving: About 195 calories, 4g protein, 22g carbohydrate, 12g total fat (2g saturated), 0mg cholesterol, 825mg sodium

PEACHY MELON SOUP

Prep: 15 minutes
Makes 5 appetizer or dessert servings

1 small cantaloupe (about 2½ pounds), chilled	2 tablespoons fresh lime juice
1 cup peach nectar or apricot nectar, chilled	Lime slices for garnish

◆ Cut cantaloupe in half. With spoon, scoop out and discard seeds. Cut rind away from cantaloupe. Cut cantaloupe into bite-size chunks.

◆ In blender at medium speed (with center part of blender lid removed), blend cantaloupe, peach nectar, and lime juice until smooth. Increase speed to high; blend 1 minute.

◆ If not serving right away, pour soup into large bowl; cover and refrigerate up to 6 hours. Garnish with lime slices.

Each serving: About 100 calories, 2g protein, 25g carbohydrate, 0g total fat, 0mg cholesterol, 50mg sodium

PEAR AND RED WINE SOUP

Prep: 10 minutes plus chilling   Cook: 15 to 20 minutes
Makes 5 appetizer or dessert servings

1 cup red wine	4 fully ripe pears
½ cup sugar	(1½ pounds), peeled, cored,
1 lemon	and each cut into quarters

◆ In 2-quart saucepan, heat red wine, sugar, and *1 cup water* to boiling over high heat, stirring frequently to dissolve sugar.

◆ Meanwhile, with vegetable peeler or small sharp knife, remove two 3-inch strips peel from lemon; squeeze 1 tablespoon juice.

◆ Add pears and lemon peel to saucepan; heat to boiling. Reduce heat to low and simmer 10 to 15 minutes, until pears are very tender. Remove and discard peel.

◆ In blender at low speed (with center part of lid removed), blend pear mixture in batches until smooth. Transfer to bowl; stir in lemon juice. Cover and refrigerate soup at least 4 hours, or until very cold.

Each serving: About 195 calories, 1g protein, 44g carbohydrate, 1g total fat (0g saturated), 0mg cholesterol, 30mg sodium

◆◆◆◆◆◆◆◆◆◆◆◆◆◆◆◆◆◆◆◆◆◆◆◆◆◆◆◆◆

USING LEMON PEEL

The outer, yellow part of lemon rind contains a fragrant oil that imparts a zesty flavor to all kinds of savory and sweet dishes. Remove the peel with a vegetable peeler or small sharp knife, taking care to leave behind the white pith, which is unpleasantly bitter. (The same holds true for lime and orange peels.)

◆◆◆◆◆◆◆◆◆◆◆◆◆◆◆◆◆◆◆◆◆◆◆◆◆◆◆◆◆

3

EGGS & CHEESE

EGGS KNOW-HOW

Whether they're whipped into a cloud-like meringue or simply boiled, fried, poached, baked, or scrambled, eggs are one of our most versatile foods. As a cooking ingredient, their uses are virtually endless – from thickening and enriching custards to aerating cakes and puffy soufflés. Nutritionally speaking, eggs are a good (and inexpensive) source of protein, iron, and vitamins. And, while the yolks are relatively high in fat and cholesterol, egg whites are completely fat- and cholesterol-free.

Treat eggs with care – their delicate structure is sensitive to handling and heat. To ensure that your egg dishes have a fluffy, light texture, use low to medium heat and do not overcook, or the yolks may toughen and the whites become rubbery.

BUYING, STORING, AND USING

• When buying eggs, pass on any that are dirty, cracked, or leaking. Move each egg in the carton to make sure it isn't stuck to the bottom.
• The color of an egg – white or brown – is determined by the breed and diet of the hen and has no bearing on taste, nutritional value, or cooking performance.
• The "pack date" on the carton is the day the eggs were packed. It runs from 001 (for January 1) through 365 (for December 31). Eggs can be used up to 5 weeks beyond the pack date. In some states and localities, the carton also indicates an expiration date after which the eggs should not be sold.
• A blood spot does not signal a fertilized or bad egg. It can, in fact, be an indication of freshness. It means that while the egg was forming, a blood vessel ruptured on the egg's surface. The spot can be removed with the tip of a knife.
• Store eggs in the coldest part of the refrigerator – not in the refrigerator door. Keep them in their carton to prevent the porous shells from absorbing other refrigerator odors.
• Store eggs pointed end down to keep the yolk centered.
• For baked goods, bring eggs out of the refrigerator about 30 minutes before you'll use them, or place them in a bowl of warm (not hot) tap water for 5 minutes (room-temperature eggs will beat to a greater volume, yielding lighter cakes). However, cold eggs are easier to separate; so do this right when you take them out of the refrigerator. For all other recipes, use refrigerator-cold eggs.
• Cover leftover egg yolks (unbroken) with cold water and refrigerate to use within 2 days. Drain before using.

• Refrigerate leftover egg whites in a tightly covered container; use within 4 days.
• You can safely refrigerate hard-cooked eggs in their shells for up to 7 days (mark to identify them as cooked).
• All recipes in this book use large eggs.
  1 large egg white = about 2 tablespoons
  1 large egg yolk = about 1 tablespoon
  5 large eggs = about 1 cup
  8 large egg whites = about 1 cup

FREEZING FACTS

To freeze extra raw eggs, beat to blend the whites and yolks, transfer to a freezer container, and seal. Egg whites can be frozen on their own. So can egg yolks, but you must add salt or sugar or corn syrup (depending on whether they'll be used in a sweet or savory dish) to prevent the yolks from thickening on freezing. For every 4 yolks, stir in ⅛ teaspoon salt or 1½ teaspoons sugar or corn syrup, then freeze as usual. Thaw frozen eggs in the refrigerator.

TESTING FOR FRESHNESS

Crack the egg onto a saucer. A fresh egg has a round yolk and a thick, translucent white. An older egg's yolk is flat, the white thin and runny. For poaching or frying, use a fresh egg so it holds its shape. Use older eggs for scrambling or baking.

To test without breaking the egg, place in a glass of cold water: If fresh, it will stay on the bottom or stand upright (if less fresh). If older, it will float. For hard-cooking, a less-fresh egg is easier to peel.

EGGS TO ORDER

Scrambled For each serving, beat together 2 eggs, 2 tablespoons milk, and salt and pepper to taste just until blended. In 8-inch skillet, heat 2 teaspoons margarine or butter over medium heat until hot. Add eggs and, as they begin to set, draw an inverted pancake turner across the bottom of the pan, forming large soft curds; stir occasionally. Continue cooking until eggs are thickened and set.
Poached In skillet, heat 1 to 1½ inches of water to boiling. Reduce heat so water gently simmers. Break cold eggs, 1 at a time, into a cup; holding cup close to water, slip in eggs. Cook 3 to 5 minutes, until whites are set and yolks begin to thicken. With a slotted spoon, lift out each egg; drain in the spoon over paper towels.

Fried In 8-inch skillet, melt 1 tablespoon margarine or butter over medium-high heat. Break 2 eggs into pan; reduce heat to low. For "sunny-side up," cover and cook slowly until whites are set and yolks have thickened. For "over easy," carefully turn eggs to cook second side.
Cooked in shell Place eggs in saucepan with cold water to cover by at least 1 inch. Cover and quickly heat just to boiling. Remove from heat. Let eggs stand, covered, 4 to 5 minutes for soft-cooked eggs, or 15 minutes for hard-cooked eggs. To cool hard-cooked eggs, immediately run cold water over them to keep them from overcooking.

SMART SEPARATING

Many recipes call for separated eggs. An egg separator can be used, but the half-shell method (below) works just as well.
• It is easiest to separate refrigerator-cold eggs.
• Remove any trace of egg yolk in the whites using a half-shell as a scoop.
• When separating several eggs, transfer the whites to a different bowl as you go in case a yolk breaks.

Sharply tap the egg on the side of the bowl to crack the shell. With your thumbs, carefully pull open shell along the crack, letting some of the white run into the bowl. Transfer the yolk carefully back and forth from one half-shell to the other until all the white has run into the bowl.

EGG WHITE MAGIC

• For maximum volume, use room-temperature whites.
• Fat inhibits whites from foaming; for fullest volume, avoid all traces of yolk. Don't use plastic bowls; they absorb fat.
• If whites are underbeaten, the result will not be as light. If overbeaten, they won't blend easily with other ingredients.
• Soft peaks: When beaters are lifted, peaks form and curl over slightly.
• Stiff peaks: Whites do not slip when bowl is tilted.
• To salvage overbeaten whites, stir an additional unbeaten white in a small bowl, then stir in some of overbeaten whites. Add mixture to overbeaten whites; beat 30 seconds.
• When folding beaten whites into another mixture, first fold a small amount of whites into the heavier mixture to lighten it. To fold, with rubber spatula, cut through center of mixture to bottom of bowl, then lift mixture up side of bowl. Repeat, giving bowl a quarter-turn after each stroke.
• Cream of tartar helps stabilize beaten egg whites.
• Meringue powder and powdered egg whites have been pasteurized and are a safe substitute for raw eggs in recipes calling for uncooked whites.

EGGS AND SALMONELLA

The overall risk of salmonella (a bacterium that can cause food poisoning) is low and can be avoided by thorough cooking; most cases come from eating undercooked eggs or foods containing raw eggs. People most at risk are the elderly, pregnant women, infants, and anyone who is ill or whose immune system is compromised. To ensure safety, cook eggs to 140°F and hold at that temperature for 3½ minutes, or cook to 160°F.

CHEESE KNOW-HOW

The incredible range in the taste and texture of individual cheeses is the result of the type of milk used, the manufacturing process, and the length of aging (in general, the longer cheese has been aged, the stronger the flavor, the harder the cheese, and the longer it will keep). Ideal with bread and wine, cheese also has myriad culinary uses: it can be spread, piped, sliced, grated, melted, and mixed into batters and doughs. The ubiquitous pizza and gratin topper, cheese is also a central ingredient in soups, tarts, and casseroles, and more.

KNOW YOUR CHEESES

To make cheese, milk is usually combined with a starter, such as rennet, so that it separates into curds (solids) and whey (liquid). The whey is drained off; the curds are used as fresh cheese or cured by pressing, cooking, or adding bacterial cultures. Most cheese falls into the following categories:
• Hard-grating, such as Parmesan and Romano.
• Hard (or semi-firm), such as Cheddar and Swiss.
• Semi-soft, such as Gouda and Monterey Jack.
• Soft, such as Brie and Camembert; this category includes double- and triple-cream cheeses such as Saga Blue.
• Fresh, including such perishable mild-tasting cheeses as ricotta, cottage cheese, mascarpone, and cream cheese.
• Goat and sheep milk cheeses, which may be fresh and mild or aged and sharp.

• Blue-veined cheeses, such as Roquefort and Stilton, injected or sprayed with *penicillium* molds.
• Processed cheese, made by combining one or more cheeses with an emulsifier and pasteurizing the mixture; process cheese spreads have ingredients added to make them soft, moist, and spreadable.

BUYING

• When choosing hard or semi-firm cheeses, avoid those with small beads of moisture on the surface or dry, cracked rinds.
• Pass on any cheese that smells ammoniated. Be sure packaged cheeses are not wet or sticky.
• If possible, sample first.
• Semi-soft or soft cheeses should be slightly springy to the touch and soft in the middle (or very soft for immediate use). Any "bloomy" (white and powdery) rind should be even in color and slightly moist.

SERVING AND STORING

Before serving most cheeses, let stand at room temperature about 1 hour to bring out their full flavor and texture. Fresh cheeses, such as cottage and ricotta, should be eaten chilled.
• As a rule of thumb, the harder the cheese, the longer it will keep. Fresh soft cheeses, particularly goat cheese, should be eaten as soon as possible. Firmer, drier cheeses, such as Cheddar, will keep for a month or longer if well wrapped. Hard grating cheeses will last several months.
• Store all cheese in the refrigerator, tightly wrapped to prevent drying. Leave the original wrapping intact, or rewrap in waxed paper or foil and plastic wrap. Change the wrapping every few days to prolong the life of the cheese.
• Strong-smelling cheeses, such as Limburger, should be wrapped and placed in an airtight container.
• Even when stored correctly, the surface of hard cheese may turn moldy; simply cut off the moldy part or scrape the surface clean. The cheese will be fine to eat. However, soft cheeses with mold should be discarded, as the mold may have permeated the cheese.
• If cheese has dried out in the refrigerator, shred or grate it and use in cooking.
• Hard or semi-firm cheeses can be frozen up to 3 months if wrapped tightly in moisture-proof wrapping. Cheeses that are frozen may lose moisture and become crumbly – use them for cooking rather than eating.

TO GRATE OR NOT TO GRATE

How you prepare cheese – by grating, shredding, or shaving – affects the qualities it lends to a dish.
Finely grated The classic for pasta. Hard-grating cheeses such as Parmesan or Romano work best to coat noodles evenly.

Coarsely shredded Cheeses prepared this way hold their own in salads and add noticeable texture to pasta dishes. Coarse shreds melt evenly to create smooth sauces or gooey toppings.
Cheese shavings Thick, sturdy curls of hard-grating cheese such as Parmesan add strong, individual bites of flavor that create an interesting element in many salads and pasta dishes.

Cheese shavings are simple to make. Use a vegetable peeler to pare off pieces from a block of hard-grating cheese such as Parmesan.

COOKING SUCCESS

• Cheese reacts quickly when heated. Cook briefly over low heat for best results; high heat or long cooking can make cheese tough and leathery. Processed cheese melts smoothly without becoming grainy or stringy.
• Shred, grate, or slice cheese for quick, even melting. For easier shredding, use cold cheese; if shredding a soft cheese such as mozzarella, put it in the freezer for about 30 minutes.
• Stir cheese into sauces at the end of cooking time and heat just until cheese melts and blends in. Don't overheat, or sauce may become stringy. If reheating, use a double boiler.
• Sprinkle cheese toppings over skillet dishes when they're fully cooked. Remove the pan from the heat and cover; the heat from the food will melt the cheese.
• Broil cheese toppings several inches from the heat, just until melted.
• To blend cream cheese with other ingredients, let it stand, wrapped, at room temperature to soften. Alternatively, unwrap the cheese and microwave for 15 to 20 seconds.
• If substituting cheese in a recipe, use one with a similar fat and moisture content. For example, replace a full-fat Cheddar with Swiss or Fontina, not a low-fat goat cheese.
• Reduced-fat cheeses need extra care in cooking to prevent them from turning rubbery.

ASSEMBLING A CHEESE BOARD

A cheese board works nicely as an appetizer or elegant dessert. To create a nice variety, choose at least three different types of cheese. Make sure they vary in flavor from mild to sharp, and in texture from soft or creamy to firm. Include wedges of blue-veined cheese, soft cheese, and hard or semi-firm cheese, and perhaps a log of goat cheese.

Avoid crowding the board, and accompany with crackers, toasts, or thinly sliced French or Italian bread. Add fresh fruit, if desired, such as seedless grapes or apple or pear wedges.

BAKED EGGS

Adorned with fruit or enriched with cheese, baked egg dishes encompass a wide range of deliciously comforting treats, perfect for brunch or even supper. For true convenience, the bread pudding below can be assembled the night before and baked in the morning for a hearty breakfast.

BRUNCH BREAD PUDDING

◆◆◆◆◆◆◆◆◆◆◆◆◆

Prep: 20 minutes plus chilling
Bake: 45 minutes
Makes 8 main-dish servings

1 loaf unsliced rich egg
   bread such as challah
   (about 1 pound), cut into
   1-inch-thick slices
3 cups milk
½ teaspoon salt
10 large eggs
¼ cup plus 1 tablespoon sugar
1 teaspoon ground cinnamon
2 tablespoons margarine
   or butter
Maple-Banana Sauce (see
   below right)
Cooked bacon (optional)

1 Grease shallow 3½- to 4-quart baking dish. Arrange bread slices, overlapping slightly, in dish. In medium bowl, whisk milk, salt, eggs, and ¼ cup sugar until well mixed. Slowly pour over bread.

2 Prick bread with fork so it absorbs egg mixture. Spoon any unabsorbed egg mixture over bread. In a cup, mix cinnamon with remaining 1 tablespoon sugar; sprinkle over bread and dot with margarine. Cover and refrigerate at least 30 minutes, or overnight.

MAPLE-BANANA SAUCE

In nonstick 12-inch skillet, melt 2 tablespoons margarine or butter over medium-high heat. Add 6 medium firm bananas, thinly sliced; cook about 3 minutes, until lightly browned. Add 1 cup maple syrup; boil 2 to 3 minutes, until slightly thickened. Serve warm. Makes 3 cups.

3 Preheat oven to 325°F. Uncover bread pudding and bake 45 minutes, or until knife inserted in center comes out clean. Meanwhile, prepare Maple-Banana Sauce. Serve bread pudding warm with sauce, and bacon, if you like.

EACH SERVING: ABOUT 570 CALORIES, 17g PROTEIN, 85g CARBOHYDRATE, 19g TOTAL FAT (6g SATURATED), 307mg CHOLESTEROL, 605mg SODIUM

PUFFY APPLE PANCAKE

Prep: 25 minutes   Bake: 15 minutes
Makes 6 main-dish servings

6 medium Granny Smith or
   Newtown Pippin apples
   (2 pounds)
2 tablespoons margarine
   or butter
½ cup plus 2 tablespoons
   sugar

3 large eggs
¾ cup milk
¾ cup all-purpose flour
¼ teaspoon salt

◆ Peel and core apples; cut each into 8 wedges. Preheat oven to 425°F. In 12-inch skillet with oven-safe handle, heat margarine, ½ cup sugar, and ¼ *cup water* to boiling over medium-high heat. Add apple wedges to mixture in skillet; cook, stirring occasionally, about 15 minutes, until apples are golden and sugar mixture begins to caramelize.

◆ Meanwhile, in blender at medium speed or in food processor with knife blade attached, blend eggs, milk, flour, salt, and remaining 2 tablespoons sugar until smooth. When apples are golden and lightly caramelized, pour egg mixture over. Place skillet in oven; bake pancake 15 minutes, or until puffed and golden. Serve immediately.

Each serving: About 310 calories, 6g protein, 57g carbohydrate, 8g total fat (2g saturated), 111mg cholesterol, 180mg sodium

PUFFY PEAR PANCAKE

Prepare Puffy Apple Pancake as above, but substitute 6 ripe Bosc pears (about 2 pounds) for the apples, and add 1 tablespoon pear-flavored liqueur and a generous pinch of ground nutmeg to the egg mixture when blending.

Each serving: About 355 calories, 6g protein, 66g carbohydrate, 8g total fat (2g saturated), 111mg cholesterol, 180mg sodium

BAKED CHEDDAR GRITS

Prep: 20 minutes   Bake: 45 minutes
Makes 6 main-dish servings

2 tablespoons margarine
   or butter
1 teaspoon salt
3½ cups milk
1¼ cups quick-cooking grits
8 ounces Cheddar cheese,
   shredded (2 cups)

1 teaspoon hot-pepper
   sauce
¼ teaspoon ground black
   pepper
5 large eggs

◆ Preheat oven to 325°F. Grease shallow 2½-quart casserole.

◆ In 3-quart saucepan, heat margarine, salt, 1½ cups milk, and *2 cups water* to boiling over medium-high heat. Gradually stir in grits, whisking constantly to prevent lumping.

◆ Reduce heat to low; cover and cook, stirring occasionally, 5 minutes. (Grits will be very stiff.) Remove saucepan from heat; stir in cheese until blended.

◆ In large bowl, with wire whisk or fork, mix hot-pepper sauce, pepper, eggs, and remaining 2 cups milk until blended. Gradually stir grits mixture into egg mixture.

◆ Pour grits mixture into casserole. Bake 45 minutes, or until knife inserted in center comes out clean. Serve immediately.

Each serving: About 455 calories, 23g protein, 33g carbohydrate, 25g total fat (13g saturated), 237mg cholesterol, 760mg sodium

CHILES RELLENOS

Prep: 20 minutes   Bake: 35 minutes
Makes 4 main-dish servings

3 cans (4 to 4½ ounces each)
   whole green chiles, drained
8 ounces Monterey Jack
   cheese

5 large eggs
½ cup all-purpose flour
½ cup milk

◆ Preheat oven to 350°F. Grease shallow 2-quart casserole. Discard seeds from chiles (do not cut); pat chiles dry with paper towels. Slice cheese into same number of pieces as there are chiles. Insert 1 slice of cheese in each chile. Arrange stuffed chiles in casserole.

◆ In medium bowl, beat eggs, flour, and milk until blended. Pour egg mixture over chiles in casserole. Bake 35 minutes, or until top is golden brown and knife inserted in center comes out clean. Serve immediately.

Each serving: About 405 calories, 24g protein, 19g carbohydrate, 25g total fat (13g saturated), 321mg cholesterol, 1050mg sodium

OMELETS

A perfectly plump, golden omelet is one of the most enticing dishes, and one of the fastest to prepare. To ensure a light, fluffy texture, cook the eggs quickly and keep the mixture moving freely in the skillet. This is easiest to accomplish in a nonstick skillet.

1 In medium bowl, with wire whisk or fork, beat eggs, pepper, ½ teaspoon salt, and ⅓ cup water until blended. In nonstick 12-inch skillet, heat 1 tablespoon oil over medium-high heat. Add onion, green pepper, and ¼ teaspoon salt and cook until vegetables are tender. Add ham and heat through. Transfer mixture to bowl; keep warm.

2 In same skillet, heat 1 tablespoon oil; add mushrooms and cook until tender. Transfer to another bowl; keep warm.

3 In same skillet, heat remaining 1 tablespoon oil over medium heat. Add eggs; cook until edge sets. Gently lift edge as it sets, tilting skillet so uncooked egg runs underneath.

BIG WESTERN OMELET

◆◆◆◆◆◆◆◆◆◆◆◆

Prep: 15 minutes
Cook: 15 minutes
Makes 3 main-dish servings

6 large eggs
¼ teaspoon ground black pepper
Salt
3 tablespoons vegetable oil
1 small onion, diced
1 medium green pepper, diced
¼ pound sliced ham, diced
8 ounces mushrooms, each cut in half
Tomato wedges, shredded fresh basil, and flat-leaf parsley sprigs for garnish

NONSTICK SKILLETS

The specially formulated surface on nonstick skillets requires a bit of respect. For best results, use wooden, plastic, or other nonmetal utensils to prevent scratching, do not use over extremely high heat, and never plunge the hot pan into cold water.

4 Shake skillet occasionally to keep omelet moving freely in pan. When omelet is set but still moist, spoon ham and vegetable mixture over half of omelet.

5 Tilt skillet and, with spatula, fold omelet in half. To serve, cut omelet into 3 pieces; top with mushrooms. Garnish with tomato wedges, basil, and parsley.

EACH SERVING: ABOUT 365 CALORIES, 23g PROTEIN, 10g CARBOHYDRATE, 26g TOTAL FAT (6g SATURATED), 437mg CHOLESTEROL, 1095mg SODIUM

BASIC OMELET

◆ ◆ ◆ ◆ ◆ ◆ ◆ ◆ ◆ ◆ ◆ ◆ ◆

Prep: 2 minutes   Cook: 2 to 3 minutes
Makes 1 serving

2 large eggs
Pinch each salt and ground
**   black pepper**

2 teaspoons margarine
**   or butter**

1 In small bowl, whisk eggs, salt, pepper, and *2 tablespoons water*. Heat nonstick 10-inch skillet over medium-high heat. Add margarine, swirling to coat pan. Add egg mixture and stir quickly.

2 With handle of pan toward you, place filling on half of eggs; cook 30 seconds, or until almost set. With heatproof rubber spatula, loosen omelet and roll, starting from unfilled side, onto warm plate.

Each serving: About 220 calories, 13g protein, 1g carbohydrate, 18g total fat (5g saturated), 426mg cholesterol, 320mg sodium

RATATOUILLE OMELET

Prep: 15 minutes   Cook: 40 minutes
Makes 4 main-dish servings

1 tablespoon olive oil
1 small onion, minced
½ small (1-pound) eggplant,
**   cut into ½-inch pieces**
½ teaspoon salt
⅛ teaspoon ground black
**   pepper**
½ yellow or red pepper, diced
1 small zucchini (about
**   4 ounces), diced**

1 large garlic clove, minced
1 cup canned tomatoes with
**   juice**
Pinch dried thyme
2 tablespoons chopped fresh
**   basil or parsley**
4 Basic Omelets (see above)
4 tablespoons freshly grated
**   Parmesan cheese (optional)**

◆ In nonstick 12-inch skillet, heat oil over medium heat. Add onion; cook until tender. Add eggplant, salt, and black pepper. Cook, stirring often, 10 minutes, or until eggplant begins to brown. Stir in diced pepper, zucchini, and garlic; cook 1 minute. Stir in tomatoes with their juice and thyme, breaking up tomatoes with back of spoon. Heat to boiling. Reduce heat to low; cover and simmer 15 minutes, or until eggplant is tender. Remove from heat; stir in basil.

◆ Prepare Basic Omelets. Fill each omelet with about ½ cup of ratatouille mixture, and 1 tablespoon grated Parmesan cheese, if you like.

Each serving: About 240 calories, 11g protein, 12g carbohydrate, 17g total fat (4g saturated), 320mg cholesterol, 895mg sodium

SPINACH, CHEDDAR, AND BACON OMELET

Prep: 5 minutes   Cook: 5 minutes
Makes 4 main-dish servings

1 medium bunch spinach
**   (10 to 12 ounces)**
4 ounces Cheddar cheese,
**   shredded (1 cup)**

4 slices bacon, cooked crisp
**   and crumbled**
4 Basic Omelets (see left)

Wash spinach. In 2-quart saucepan, cook spinach with water clinging to its leaves over high heat, stirring frequently, just until wilted. Drain in colander, pressing out excess liquid. Coarsely chop spinach; set aside. Prepare Basic Omelets. Fill each omelet with one-fourth of spinach, cheese, and bacon.

Each serving: About 335 calories, 21g protein, 5g carbohydrate, 26g total fat (11g saturated), 355mg cholesterol, 765mg sodium

LIGHT TOMATO OMELET

Prep: 5 minutes   Cook: 5 minutes
Makes 4 main-dish servings

1 teaspoon olive oil
1 garlic clove, minced
4 large plum tomatoes, diced
¼ teaspoon salt
⅛ teaspoon ground black
**   pepper**

2 tablespoons chopped fresh
**   parsley**
4 Basic Omelets (see above
**   left)**
Tossed salad (optional)

In nonstick 10-inch skillet, heat oil over medium-high heat. Add garlic and next 3 ingredients; cook, stirring often, 5 minutes, or until almost dry. Remove from heat; stir in parsley. Prepare Basic Omelets, but, for each one, use 1 large egg and 1 large egg white instead of 2 large eggs and 1 teaspoon olive oil instead of margarine. Fill each with one-fourth of tomato mixture. Serve with salad, if you like.

Each serving: About 165 calories, 11g protein, 9g carbohydrate, 10g total fat (2g saturated), 213mg cholesterol, 530mg sodium

FRITTATAS AND TORTILLAS

A frittata is a flat Italian omelet; a tortilla is a flat Spanish omelet. They differ from French omelets in that the filling ingredients are set in the eggs as they cook, not rolled up in the omelet at the end. Frittatas and tortillas cook slowly, either on the stovetop or in the oven. You can brown the top of the frittata in the broiler before serving; just be sure the skillet and its handle are oven-safe. (Or, wrap a plastic handle in heavy-duty foil).

ASPARAGUS, TOMATO, AND CHEESE FRITTATA

◆◆◆◆◆◆◆◆◆◆◆◆

Prep: 30 minutes
Cook: 20 minutes
Makes 4 main-dish servings

12 ounces asparagus
1 medium onion
1 medium tomato
4 ounces Jarlsberg or
  Swiss cheese
2 tablespoons margarine
  or butter
8 large eggs
½ teaspoon dried
  marjoram
¼ teaspoon salt

1 Bend base of asparagus stalks; ends will break off where stalks are tough. Discard ends; trim scales if stalks are gritty. Cut stalks diagonally into 2-inch pieces.

2 Thinly slice onion. Cut tomato into 8 wedges; remove seeds. Shred Jarlsberg cheese (you should have about 1 cup).

3 In nonstick oven-safe 10-inch skillet, melt margarine over medium heat. Add asparagus and onion; cook 10 minutes, or until asparagus is tender-crisp.

4 Preheat broiler. In medium bowl, with fork, beat eggs, marjoram, salt, half of shredded cheese, and ¼ *cup water* until blended.

5 Pour egg mixture over vegetables in skillet; arrange tomato wedges on top. Cover and cook over medium heat 10 minutes, or until set. Sprinkle with remaining cheese.

6 Broil frittata at closest position to heat source 1 minute, or until cheese is bubbly. Loosen frittata and slide onto platter; cut into wedges. Serve hot or at room temperature.

EACH SERVING: ABOUT 340 CALORIES, 23g PROTEIN, 9g CARBOHYDRATE, 23g TOTAL FAT (4g SATURATED), 442mg CHOLESTEROL, 470mg SODIUM

POTATO AND HAM FRITTATA

Prep: 10 minutes   Cook: 50 to 55 minutes
Makes 6 main-dish servings

2 large all-purpose potatoes
(about 1 pound)
4 tablespoons vegetable oil
½ pound cooked ham, in one
piece, diced
1 medium sweet onion, cut
into ¼-inch-thick slices

Salt
8 large eggs
1 teaspoon dried thyme
¼ teaspoon coarsely ground
black pepper

◆ Peel potatoes; cut into ¼-inch-thick slices. In nonstick
10-inch skillet, heat 2 tablespoons oil over medium-high
heat; add ham and cook until browned. Transfer to plate.
Add onion to skillet; cook over medium heat until golden.
Transfer to another plate. In same skillet, heat remaining
2 tablespoons oil. Add potatoes and ½ teaspoon salt; cook
15 minutes, or until golden. Remove from heat. Spoon off
excess oil, if any. Stir ham into potatoes; sprinkle with onion.

◆ In medium bowl, beat eggs, thyme, pepper, ¼ teaspoon salt,
and ¼ *cup water*; pour into skillet. Cook, covered, over low heat
25 to 30 minutes, until set. Serve hot or at room temperature.

**Each serving: About 315 calories, 19g protein, 18g carbohydrate,
18g total fat (4g saturated), 305mg cholesterol, 855mg sodium**

LOW-FAT VEGETABLE FRITTATA

Prep: 30 minutes   Bake: 10 minutes
Makes 4 main-dish servings

Nonstick cooking spray
1 medium onion, diced
1 medium red pepper, diced
1 medium green pepper,
diced
1 medium zucchini (about
8 ounces), diced
1 teaspoon sugar
¾ teaspoon salt

¼ teaspoon coarsely ground
black pepper
4 tablespoons finely chopped
fresh basil
6 large egg whites
2 large eggs
2 ounces feta cheese,
crumbled (½ cup)

◆ Preheat oven to 375°F. Spray nonstick 12-inch skillet with
cooking spray. Add onion; cook over medium-high heat until
golden. Add peppers and next 4 ingredients; cook, stirring
frequently, until tender-crisp. Stir in ¼ *cup water*; heat to
boiling. Reduce heat to low; cover and simmer 10 minutes, or
until tender. Remove from heat; stir in 3 tablespoons basil.

◆ In medium bowl, with wire whisk or fork, beat egg
whites, eggs, ¼ cup feta, and remaining 1 tablespoon basil.
Spray 10-inch oven-safe skillet with cooking spray; add egg
mixture and cook over medium-high heat 1 to 2 minutes,
until it begins to set. Remove from heat. With slotted spoon,
spoon vegetable mixture over egg mixture; sprinkle with

remaining feta. Bake 10 minutes, or until set. If desired,
broil 1 to 2 minutes to brown top of frittata. Serve hot or at
room temperature.

**Each serving: About 140 calories, 12g protein, 10g carbohydrate,
6g total fat (3g saturated), 119mg cholesterol, 675mg sodium**

SPANISH POTATO TORTILLA

Prep: 20 minutes   Cook: 40 minutes
Makes 4 main-dish servings

4 medium all-purpose
potatoes (about 1¼ pounds)
4 tablespoons olive or
vegetable oil
1 medium red pepper, diced
1 medium green pepper, diced
1 onion, thinly sliced
Salt

5 large eggs
2 tablespoons freshly grated
Parmesan cheese
2 tablespoons chopped fresh
parsley
½ teaspoon coarsely ground
black pepper

◆ Peel potatoes; slice very thin. In nonstick 10-inch skillet,
heat 2 tablespoons oil over medium heat. Add potatoes,
peppers, onion, and ½ teaspoon salt; cook until vegetables
are slightly browned. Reduce heat to low; cover and cook,
turning occasionally, about 15 minutes, until vegetables are
fork-tender. Transfer to bowl to cool. Wipe skillet clean. In
large bowl, with wire whisk or fork, beat eggs, Parmesan,
parsley, pepper, and ½ teaspoon salt. Stir in vegetables.

◆ In skillet, heat 1 tablespoon oil over medium-low heat.
Add egg mixture; cook until set around edge. With spatula,
lift edge as it sets, tilting skillet to allow uncooked portion to
run under; shake skillet occasionally. When tortilla is set but
still moist on top, increase heat slightly to brown bottom.

◆ Loosen tortilla from skillet. Invert plate over skillet; flip
tortilla onto plate. Wipe skillet clean. Add remaining
1 tablespoon oil to skillet and heat over medium heat. Slide
tortilla into skillet, browned-side up. Cook about 5 minutes,
until bottom is golden; invert tortilla onto warm platter. Cut
into wedges. Serve hot or at room temperature.

**Each serving: About 345 calories, 12g protein,
35g carbohydrate,
18g total fat (4g saturated),
269mg
cholesterol,
680mg sodium**

CREPES

Our Basic Crepes (see page 82) can be stuffed with a variety of fillings. Here they're rolled into cylinders around a traditional rustic French mixture of sautéed peppers called pipérade, but they can also be folded over a hearty chicken and vegetable filling or an apple and Gruyère cheese combination. You can prepare the crepes ahead and refrigerate them overnight, or freeze them for up to 1 month.

CREPES WITH PIPÉRADE FILLING

◆◆◆◆◆◆◆◆◆◆◆◆◆

Prep: 40 minutes plus making crepes
Bake: 15 minutes
Makes 4 main-dish servings

8 Basic Crepes (see page 82)
1 tablespoon olive oil
1 medium onion, thinly sliced
1 medium red pepper, thinly sliced
1 medium yellow or green pepper, thinly sliced
¾ teaspoon salt
1 garlic clove, minced
⅛ teaspoon ground red pepper (cayenne)
1 can (14½ to 16 ounces) tomatoes
3 ounces Gruyère cheese, shredded (¾ cup)
2 tablespoons diced red and yellow pepper
1 tablespoon chopped fresh parsley

1 Prepare Basic Crepes. Prepare pipérade filling: In 10-inch skillet, heat olive oil over medium heat. Add sliced onion, sliced red and yellow peppers, and salt; cover and cook 15 minutes, or until vegetables are tender. Stir in minced garlic and ground red pepper; cook, uncovered, 30 seconds.

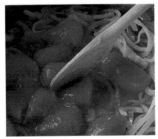

2 Stir in tomatoes with their juice, breaking up tomatoes with back of spoon. Cook, uncovered, 15 minutes, or until thick.

3 Preheat oven to 400°F. Place crepes on work surface; sprinkle evenly with cheese, leaving a 1-inch border.

QUICK CREPE FILLINGS

Filling a crepe can be as easy as assembling your favorite sandwich. Any combination of the following makes a tasty treat: thinly sliced ham or smoked chicken or turkey; diced tomatoes; chopped arugula; crumbled feta or goat cheese; chopped fresh herbs; sautéed sliced mushrooms; cottage cheese; or smoked fish.

4 Spread a generous ¼ cup pipérade filling down center of each crepe.

5 Roll up crepes and place, seam-side down, in 13" by 9" baking dish. Bake 15 minutes, or until heated through. To serve, sprinkle with diced pepper and chopped parsley.

EACH SERVING: ABOUT 345 CALORIES, 15g PROTEIN, 25g CARBOHYDRATE, 21g TOTAL FAT (10g SATURATED), 153mg CHOLESTEROL, 940mg SODIUM

CHICKEN AND VEGETABLE CREPES

Prep: 40 minutes plus making crepes   Bake: 15 to 20 minutes
Makes 4 main-dish servings

8 Basic Crepes (see right)
3 tablespoons margarine or
   butter
1 medium onion, minced
4 large skinless, boneless
   chicken breast halves (about
   1¼ pounds), cut into bite-
   size pieces
1 medium zucchini (about
   10 ounces), cut into ½-inch
   pieces

1 medium yellow squash
   (about 10 ounces), cut into
   ½-inch pieces
½ teaspoon salt
¼ teaspoon coarsely ground
   black pepper
½ cup milk
¼ cup all-purpose flour
4 ounces Jarlsberg or Swiss
   cheese, shredded (1 cup)

◆ Prepare Basic Crepes. Preheat oven to 400°F. In 3-quart saucepan, melt margarine over medium-high heat; add onion and cook until tender. Add chicken; cook, stirring frequently, about 3 minutes, until it loses its pink color. Stir in zucchini, squash, salt, and pepper. In small bowl, whisk milk with flour; stir into chicken mixture. Cook, stirring, until liquid thickens and boils. Stir in half of cheese.

◆ Place crepes on work surface. Spoon scant ½ cup chicken mixture onto each crepe; fold 2 sides over, slightly over-lapping. Place filled crepes, seam-side up, in 13" by 9" baking dish. Spoon any remaining mixture around crepes; sprinkle with remaining cheese. Bake 15 to 20 minutes, until chicken mixture is bubbly.

Each serving: About 600 calories, 49g protein, 30g carbohydrate, 31g total fat (9g saturated), 236mg cholesterol, 885mg sodium

APPLE AND GRUYÈRE CREPES

Prep: 15 minutes plus making crepes   Bake: 5 minutes
Makes 4 dessert servings

8 Basic Crepes (see right)
2 Golden Delicious apples
   (about 1 pound)
1 tablespoon margarine or
   butter

4 ounces Gruyère cheese,
   shredded (1 cup)

Prepare Basic Crepes. Preheat oven to 400°F. Grease large cookie sheet. Peel and core each apple; cut into thin slices. In nonstick 10-inch skillet, melt margarine over medium-high heat. Add apples and cook, stirring often, 5 minutes, or until tender and beginning to brown. Place crepes on work surface. Sprinkle cheese over half of each crepe. Arrange apple slices over cheese. Fold crepes in half to enclose filling; place on cookie sheet. Bake 5 minutes, or until hot.

Each serving: About 380 calories, 15g protein, 30g carbohydrate, 23g total fat (12g saturated), 161mg cholesterol, 425mg sodium

BASIC CREPES

◆ ◆ ◆ ◆ ◆ ◆ ◆ ◆ ◆ ◆ ◆ ◆

Crepes, made from a smooth egg batter, are used in both sweet and savory dishes. It's important to let the batter rest before cooking; the resting process relaxes the gluten in the flour for tender crepes. This recipe makes about 12 crepes; the leftovers can be frozen for later use or rolled up with jam and eaten as a quick snack.

Prep: 5 minutes plus chilling   Cook: 20 minutes

3 large eggs
1½ cups milk
⅔ cup all-purpose flour

½ teaspoon salt
About 4 tablespoons butter,
   melted

1 In blender at medium speed, mix eggs, milk, flour, salt, and 2 tablespoons melted butter until completely smooth and free from lumps.

2 Transfer to bowl and refrigerate at least 1 hour, or overnight. Whisk batter thoroughly just before using.

3 Heat nonstick 10-inch skillet over medium-high heat; brush lightly with melted butter. Pour scant ¼ cup batter into pan; tip pan to coat bottom. Cook crepe 1½ minutes, or until top is set and underside is lightly browned.

4 With plastic spatula, loosen crepe; turn and cook other side 30 seconds. Slip onto waxed paper. Repeat with remaining batter, brushing pan lightly with butter before cooking each crepe; stack cooked crepes.

Each crepe: About 80 calories, 3g protein, 6g carbohydrate, 4g total fat (2g saturated), 62mg cholesterol, 140mg sodium

SOUFFLÉS

Few dishes dazzle like a golden, high-rising soufflé. Eggs provide a rich flavor – and dramatic results. To begin, a cooked base of flour, butter (or margarine), and milk is enriched with egg yolks, cheese, and other flavorings. Then stiffly beaten egg whites are folded in to create a light, airy texture.

CRAB SOUFFLÉ

Prep: 20 minutes   *Bake:* 40 to 45 minutes
Makes 4 main-dish servings

½ pound lump crabmeat
4 tablespoons margarine or butter
¼ cup all-purpose flour
½ teaspoon dry mustard
1 cup milk
1 tablespoon dry sherry
2 ounces Swiss or Gruyère cheese, shredded (½ cup)

2 tablespoons coarsely chopped fresh parsley
1 tablespoon plain dried bread crumbs
4 large eggs, separated
1 large egg white (optional)
½ teaspoon cream of tartar

1 Pick over crabmeat to remove any pieces of shell or cartilage. Flake crabmeat. In 3-quart saucepan, melt margarine over medium heat.

2 With wooden spoon, stir in flour and mustard; cook, stirring, 1 minute. Gradually whisk in milk and sherry and cook, whisking constantly, until mixture thickens and boils. Remove from heat.

3 Gently stir in crabmeat, cheese, and parsley. Cool slightly. Meanwhile, preheat oven to 350°F. Grease 1½-quart soufflé dish; sprinkle with bread crumbs.

4 In medium bowl, with mixer at high speed, beat egg whites with cream of tartar until stiff peaks form.

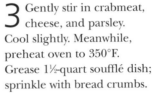

5 Stir egg yolks into cheese mixture; then, with rubber spatula, gently fold in egg whites, one-third at a time, just until blended. Pour into soufflé dish. Bake soufflé 40 to 45 minutes, until puffy and golden. Serve immediately.

MAKING A "TOP-HAT" SOUFFLÉ

If you want the center of your cooked soufflé to puff up dramatically, with the back of a spoon, make a 1-inch-deep indentation all the way around the top of the uncooked soufflé mixture, 1 inch in from the edge of the dish.

EACH SERVING: ABOUT 315 CALORIES, 22g PROTEIN, 9g CARBOHYDRATE, 21g TOTAL FAT (6g SATURATED), 250mg CHOLESTEROL, 720mg SODIUM

CORN-CHEESE SOUFFLÉ

Prep: 15 minutes   *Bake:* 40 to 45 minutes
Makes 4 main-dish servings

4 tablespoons margarine or butter
1 green onion, chopped
¼ cup all-purpose flour
½ teaspoon dry mustard
½ teaspoon salt
¾ cup milk
2 ounces Monterey Jack cheese with
   jalapeño chiles, shredded (½ cup)
1 can (8½ ounces) cream-style corn
4 large eggs, separated
1 large egg white (optional), see below
½ teaspoon cream of tartar

◆ In 3-quart saucepan, melt margarine
over medium heat. Add green onion;
cook until tender. Stir in flour,
mustard, and salt; cook, stirring,
1 minute. Gradually whisk in milk;
cook, whisking constantly, until
mixture thickens and boils.

◆ Stir in cheese and corn until cheese
melts. Remove from heat.

◆ Preheat oven to 350°F. Grease
1½-quart soufflé dish. Follow directions
in Steps 4 and 5 of Crab Soufflé (see
page 83).

**Each serving: About 330 calories,
13g protein, 20g carbohydrate,
22g total fat (7g saturated),
232mg cholesterol, 730mg sodium**

HAM AND SPINACH SOUFFLÉ

Prep: 15 minutes   *Bake:* 35 to 40 minutes
Makes 4 main-dish servings

4 tablespoons margarine or butter
¼ cup all-purpose flour
½ teaspoon dry mustard
1 cup milk
1 package (10 ounces) frozen chopped
   spinach, thawed and squeezed dry
4 ounces Cheddar cheese, shredded
   (1 cup)
2 ounces cooked ham, chopped (½ cup)
1 tablespoon plain dried bread crumbs
4 large eggs, separated
1 large egg white (optional), see below
½ teaspoon cream of tartar

◆ In 3-quart saucepan, melt margarine
over medium heat. Stir in flour and
mustard; cook, stirring, 1 minute.
Gradually whisk in milk; cook, whisking
constantly, until mixture thickens and
boils. Stir in spinach, cheese, and ham
until cheese melts. Remove from heat.

◆ Preheat oven to 350°F. Grease
1½-quart soufflé dish; sprinkle with
bread crumbs. Follow directions in
Steps 4 and 5 of Crab Soufflé (see
page 83), but bake only 35 to
40 minutes, until puffy and golden.

**Each serving: About 405 calories,
22g protein, 15g carbohydrate,
29g total fat (11g saturated),
259mg cholesterol, 665mg sodium**

TOMATO SOUFFLÉ

Prep: 45 minutes   *Bake:* 45 minutes
Makes 8 accompaniment servings

1 tablespoon vegetable oil
1 medium onion, chopped
2 pounds tomatoes, peeled and diced,
   juices reserved
½ teaspoon sugar
Salt
¼ teaspoon ground black pepper
4 tablespoons margarine or butter
¼ cup all-purpose flour
1¼ cups milk
1 tablespoon plain dried bread crumbs
6 large eggs, separated
2 tablespoons freshly grated Parmesan
   cheese

◆ In 12-inch skillet, heat oil over
medium heat. Add onion and cook
10 minutes, until tender. Add tomatoes
with their juice, sugar, ½ teaspoon salt,
and pepper. Increase heat to high and
cook, stirring often, 15 minutes, or
until juices evaporate. Meanwhile, in
2-quart saucepan, melt margarine over
medium heat. Stir in flour and
¾ teaspoon salt; cook, stirring,
1 minute. Gradually whisk in milk and
cook, whisking constantly, until
mixture thickens and boils. Remove
from heat; stir in tomato mixture.

◆ Preheat oven to 325°F. Grease
2-quart soufflé dish; sprinkle with
bread crumbs. In large bowl, beat egg
yolks slightly; beat in small amount of
tomato mixture. Gradually stir yolk
mixture into tomato mixture, stirring
rapidly to prevent lumping. Pour
mixture back into bowl.

◆ In medium bowl, with mixer at high
speed, beat egg whites to stiff peaks.
With rubber spatula, gently fold beaten
egg whites, one-third at a time, into
tomato mixture just until blended;
pour into soufflé dish. Sprinkle with
Parmesan. Bake 45 minutes, or until
puffy and golden. Serve immediately.

**Each serving: About 200 calories,
8g protein, 13g carbohydrate, 13g total fat
(4g saturated), 166mg cholesterol,
510mg sodium**

SOUFFLÉ TIPS

Extra volume Adding another egg
white gives the soufflé extra
lightness and will also lend volume
to the finished dish.

The right dish For a tall and
impressive-looking soufflé, use a
straight-sided casserole or soufflé
dish of medium depth. Fill the dish
three-quarters full to ensure the
soufflé puffs up well above the rim
during baking.

Make it ahead Prepare the soufflé
and let it stand in its dish at room
temperature for up to 30 minutes
before baking.

Keep it puffy During baking, avoid
opening the oven door to check the
soufflé or the cold draft could cause
the delicate mixture to collapse.
Always serve as soon as it has
finished baking, before it deflates.

SAVORY TARTS

Eggs, milk, and cheese bake together in a flaky pastry shell to make a classic tart. Here, mushrooms add contemporary flair to an old favorite. On the next page, you'll find tender cabbage spiked with mustard giving zip to one recipe, roasted tomatoes adding sweetness to another. Each tart is delicious served hot or at room temperature.

FARM-STAND MUSHROOM AND CHEESE TART

◆◆◆◆◆◆◆◆◆◆◆◆

Prep: 45 minutes plus chilling
Bake: 50 to 55 minutes
Makes 6 main-dish servings

Pastry for 11-inch Tart (see page 487)
5 large eggs
2 cups milk
1 tablespoon chopped fresh parsley
¾ teaspoon salt
¼ teaspoon coarsely ground black pepper
4 ounces Gruyère or Swiss cheese, shredded (1 cup)
1 tablespoon olive or vegetable oil
12 ounces shiitake mushrooms, stems removed and caps thinly sliced
4 ounces cremini or white mushrooms, thinly sliced
4 ounces oyster mushrooms, thinly sliced

1 Prepare Pastry for 11-inch Tart through chilling. Preheat oven to 400°F. On lightly floured surface, with floured rolling pin, roll pastry to 13-inch round. Ease into 11" by 1" round tart pan with removable bottom.

2 Trim pastry, leaving ½-inch overhang. Fold overhang in and press against side of tart pan to form a rim ⅛ inch above edge of pan.

3 Line tart shell with foil and fill with dried beans, pie weights, or uncooked rice. Bake 15 minutes; remove foil and beans. Return tart shell to oven; bake 10 minutes longer, or until golden.

4 Meanwhile, in medium bowl, with fork or wire whisk, beat eggs, milk, parsley, salt, and pepper until blended. Stir in half of shredded cheese.

5 In nonstick 12-inch skillet, heat oil over medium-high heat; add all mushrooms and cook, stirring frequently, about 15 minutes, or until tender and liquid evaporates.

6 Spoon mushrooms into tart shell; top with remaining cheese, then egg mixture. Bake 25 to 30 minutes, until custard is set and top is browned.

EACH SERVING: ABOUT 530 CALORIES, 18g PROTEIN, 36g CARBOHYDRATE, 35g TOTAL FAT (11g SATURATED), 209mg CHOLESTEROL, 690mg SODIUM

DIJON CABBAGE TART

Prep: 55 minutes plus chilling   *Bake:* 55 to 60 minutes
Makes 8 main-dish servings or 16 appetizer servings

Pastry for 11-inch Tart (see
  page 487), made with half-
  and-half or light cream
  instead of water
1 medium head green
  cabbage (2 pounds)
2 tablespoons vegetable oil
1 large onion, thinly sliced
3 large eggs
1 tablespoon chopped fresh
  parsley

3 tablespoons Dijon mustard
¾ teaspoon salt
¾ teaspoon coarsely ground
  black pepper
1 cup half-and-half or light
  cream
6 ounces Gruyère cheese,
  shredded (1½ cups)
Flat-leaf parsley and sliced
  tomatoes for garnish

◆ Prepare Pastry for 11-inch Tart through chilling. Thinly
slice cabbage; discard tough ribs (you should have 8 to
10 cups). In nonstick 12-inch skillet, heat oil over high heat;
stir in cabbage and onion until coated. Reduce heat to low;
cover and cook, stirring occasionally, 30 minutes, or until
cabbage is very tender. Preheat oven to 400°F. Follow
directions in Steps 1 through 3 of Farm-Stand Mushroom
and Cheese Tart (see page 85).

MUSTARD

When ground mustard seeds are combined with liquid, enzymes
react to form fiery mustard oil. Prepared mustard varies in
pungency, flavor, and color, depending on the type of mustard
seeds and additional ingredients used.
Varieties include grainy (made with
both ground and partly
crushed seeds), Dijon
(made with wine or sour
grape juice), and hot
English (made with flour
and turmeric).
Refrigerate prepared
mustard after opening.

Dijon

Grainy

English

◆ In medium bowl, with wire whisk or fork, whisk eggs with
next 5 ingredients. Stir in 1 cup Gruyère cheese. Sprinkle
remaining cheese over bottom of baked tart shell; top with
cabbage mixture, then egg mixture. Arrange a few parsley
leaves on top of tart.

◆ Bake tart 25 to 30 minutes, until custard is set and top is
browned. Serve hot, garnished with sliced tomatoes and
additional parsley. Or, cool completely on wire rack and
reheat to serve later.

**Each main-dish serving: About 445 calories, 14g protein,
27g carbohydrate, 32g total fat (11g saturated),
116mg cholesterol, 680mg sodium**

ROASTED TOMATO AND
CHEESE TART

Prep: 35 minutes plus chilling   *Bake:* 1 hour 15 minutes
Makes 9 main-dish servings

Pastry for 11-inch Tart (see
  page 487)
8 medium plum tomatoes
  (about 1½ pounds)
½ teaspoon coarsely ground
  black pepper
Salt

8 large eggs
3 cups milk
1 package (4 to 5 ounces) soft
  spreadable cheese with
  garlic and herbs, softened
½ cup chopped fresh basil

◆ Prepare Pastry for 11-inch Tart through chilling.
Meanwhile, preheat oven to 450°F. Grease 15½" by 10½"
jelly-roll pan. Cut each plum tomato crosswise into ½-inch-
thick slices. Arrange slices in 1 layer in jelly-roll pan;
sprinkle with pepper and ½ teaspoon salt. Bake 30 minutes,
or until tomatoes are lightly browned. Remove from oven;
turn oven control to 375°F.

◆ On lightly floured surface, with floured rolling pin, roll
dough into square 2 inches larger all around than inverted
8" by 8" square glass baking dish. Gently ease dough into
baking dish, allowing dough to hang over edges. Fold
overhang under to form stand-up edge; make fluted edge
(see page 488). Refrigerate while preparing filling.

◆ In large bowl, with wire whisk or fork, mix eggs, milk,
cheese, and ¼ teaspoon salt until blended. Reserve
1 tablespoon chopped basil for topping; stir remaining basil
into egg mixture. Pour egg mixture into tart shell. With
pancake turner, carefully remove tomatoes from jelly-roll
pan; arrange tomatoes over egg mixture. Sprinkle tart with
reserved basil. Bake tart 40 to 45 minutes, until knife
inserted in center comes out clean. Serve hot, or cool
completely on wire rack and reheat to serve later.

**Each serving: About 365 calories, 12g protein, 24g carbohydrate,
25g total fat (8g saturated), 212mg cholesterol, 530mg sodium**

S4HELLFISH

SHELLFISH KNOW-HOW

Shrimp, lobster, oysters, scallops...beautiful shellfish delights the eyes as well as the tastebuds. There are two main categories: mollusks (clams, mussels, oysters, scallops, squid), which have soft bodies and hard, rigid shells, and crustaceans (shrimp, crab, lobster), with long bodies and jointed shells. Like fish, shellfish is high in Omega-3 fatty acids, which can help lower cholesterol levels. Never overcook delicate shellfish, or its tender flesh will turn tough.

BUYING AND STORING

When buying, freshness is paramount, since shellfish is highly perishable. Buy only super-fresh specimens from a reliable source. Shellfish should be undamaged and, like fish, should have a fresh, clean odor. When buying frozen shellfish, look for firm, thoroughly frozen, undamaged packages. To thaw, place the shellfish in its wrapping on a plate to catch drips, and thaw overnight in the refrigerator. Cook shellfish quickly once thawed, and do not refreeze.

CLAMS

• When buying hard-shell clams such as littleneck, Manila, or cherrystone, be sure the shells are tightly closed and not broken. If slightly apart, they should snap shut when tapped; discard any that stay open. For soft-shell clams (such as steamers or long-necks), see that the neck-like siphon pulls in slightly when touched.
• Refrigerate live clams, covered with a damp kitchen towel, up to 3 days, and shucked, with their liquor, up to 1 day. Any dead clams should be discarded before cooking.
• Clean clams with rough shells by scrubbing with a stiff brush under cold running water to remove any sand. Small, smooth-shell clams may require only rinsing.
• Clams are shucked in the same way as oysters (see page 89).
• When cooking in the shell, discard any that do not open.
• To serve, figure on about 1 dozen per main-dish serving.

MUSSELS

• The blue mussel is the variety most commonly sold in the U.S.; it has a bluish-black shell. You may also come across New Zealand green mussels, which are larger with a bright green shell. They have a similar flavor to blue mussels.

• Mussels are at their best in the cold winter months, although imported and farmed varieties are available throughout the year.
• Buy mussels with undamaged, tightly closed shells or with shells that snap shut when tapped. Any that remain open should be discarded. Avoid those that feel heavy (they may be full of sand), and any that feel light and are loose when shaken (the mussel may be dead).
• Store live mussels, covered with a damp kitchen cloth, in a single layer in the refrigerator. Use within 2 days. Before cooking, discard any dead mussels.
• Always debeard just before you're ready to cook; once debearded, mussels soon die and spoil.
• After you've cooked the mussels, check that all shells have opened and discard any that have not.
• Plan on about 1½ dozen mussels per main-dish serving.

1 Scrub mussels with a stiff brush under cold running water to remove any sand. Scrape any barnacles off with a knife.

2 To debeard, grasp the hair-like beard with your thumb and forefinger and pull it away, or scrape it off with a knife.

OYSTERS

• Fresh oysters can be bought year-round but in most of the world are at their best during fall and winter.
• Buy oysters with undamaged, tightly closed shells.
• Fresh shucked oysters are also available. They should be plump and uniform in size, smell fresh, and be packed in clear, not cloudy, liquid.
• Cover live oysters with a damp kitchen towel and store flat, preferably on ice, in the refrigerator for up to 5 days. Refrigerate shucked oysters in a container with their liquor for up to 1 day. (The liquor should cover the oysters. If not, make your own to top it up by dissolving ½ teaspoon salt in 1 cup water.)
• Clean oysters by scrubbing with a stiff brush under cold running water to remove any sand.
• Shuck oysters just before serving or cooking; discard open or damaged oysters.
• For serving raw on the half-shell, allow 6 oysters per diner.

SHUCKING OYSTERS AND CLAMS

Oysters and clams are shucked using the same technique. An oyster knife (see page 96), which can be used for both, is shown here. You can also open clams (but not oysters) with a clam knife, which has a long blade and a rounded tip designed to accommodate the shape of the clam shell. To protect your hands, hold the oyster or clam in a heavy cloth or oven mitt. This will also make the shell easier to grip.

1 Hold oyster in oven mitt, flat side up. Insert point of oyster knife between top and bottom shells next to the hinge.

2 Push knife blade farther into the shell and then twist the knife to pry shells apart.

3 Taking care not to spill any liquor, carefully loosen flesh from top shell. Discard top shell.

4 Run knife blade under the oyster to loosen flesh from bottom shell. Remove any broken shell.

SCALLOPS

• Scallops are usually shucked at sea; the part we eat is actually the adductor muscle. Scallops in the shell are rarer; their crescent-shaped coral, or roe, is a delicacy.

To prepare scallops, first remove the tough little side muscle with your fingers. Rinse under cold running water to remove any sand from crevices, then pat dry with paper towels.

• Bay scallops are smaller, sweeter, and more expensive than sea scallops. Calico scallops are even smaller, but because they are shucked by commercial steaming, they are less tender and sweet.
• Choose sweet-smelling scallops that are almost "dry." Avoid those that have been soaked in phosphates (to plump and preserve them); these are bright white, wet, and shiny.
• Scallops shrink and toughen if overcooked. For best results, cook only until just opaque throughout.
• Figure on about ¼ pound scallops per person.

SQUID

• Buy whole squid (calamari) that are small with bright white flesh, clear eyes, and a mild ocean smell. Check that the skin and tentacles are intact.
• Fresh squid should be refrigerated in a tightly sealed container for no more than a day or two. Rinse thoroughly before and after cleaning.
• When estimating how much squid to buy, figure on about 1 pound of cleaned meat from 1½ pounds whole squid. Allow ¼ pound meat per serving.
• Although cleaned, ready-to-use squid is quite widely available at fish markets and some supermarkets, it's easy to clean your own – follow the simple steps below.

1 Hold squid body firmly in one hand, and grip head and tentacles with the other. Pull gently to remove the body contents.

2 Cut off tentacles in front of eyes. Remove and discard beak from center of tentacles. Discard head and ink sac.

3 Pull out the clear plastic-like quill from body pocket and discard.

4 Rub off thin dark outer skin from body; discard skin. Rinse body well inside and out with cold running water; rinse tentacles.

SHRIMP

• Around 95 percent of the shrimp sold in the U.S. has been previously frozen, so you can buy shrimp all year round.
• Depending on variety, shrimp shells can be light gray, brownish pink, or red, but when cooked all will turn reddish.
• Select raw shrimp with firm-looking meat and shiny shells that feel full. Avoid black spots, which are a sign of aging. Shrimp are usually sold without the heads; if not, gently pull the head away from the body before shelling. Cooked, shelled shrimp should be plump with white flesh and a mild odor.
• When buying shrimp in their shells, always buy more than you need to account for the shelled weight. For example, 1¼ pounds shrimp yields 1 pound shelled and deveined.
• Shrimp can be shelled before or after cooking. While shell-on shrimp can be more flavorful, it's often more convenient to shell before cooking.
• Deveining small and medium shrimp is optional. However, do remove the vein of large shrimp, which can contain grit.
• Although small shrimp are cheaper, they're harder to peel and, pound for pound, may not be as good value.
• Cook raw shrimp briefly, just until opaque throughout; heat cooked shrimp just until warmed through.
• Allow about ¼ pound shelled shrimp per serving.

When buying shrimp by the pound, remember the number of shrimp you'll get depends on their size. As a result, they are sold by "count." See the chart at right, which tells you the number you'll get per pound for different sizes.

SHRIMP SENSE

SIZE	SHRIMP PER LB
Small	36–45
Medium	31–35
Large	21–30
Extra large	16–20
Jumbo	11–15

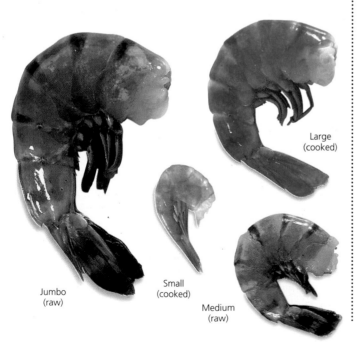

Jumbo
(raw)

Small
(cooked)

Medium
(raw)

Large
(cooked)

SHELLING AND DEVEINING

1 With kitchen shears or small knife, cut shrimp shell along outer curve, just deep enough into flesh to expose the dark vein.

2 Peel back shell from the cut and gently separate shell from shrimp. Discard shell (or use to make stock).

3 Holding shrimp under cold running water, remove vein with tip of a knife.

BUTTERFLYING

1 Shell shrimp as above, leaving tail segment in place. With kitchen shears or knife, cut shrimp along center back, about three-fourths of the way into the flesh.

2 Spread the flesh open, and remove the dark vein with tip of a knife. Rinse the butterflied shrimp under cold running water.

WHAT'S IN A NAME?

Jumbo shrimp (15 or fewer to the pound) are often sold as "prawns." Prawns are a separate species, however, and are part of the lobster family. Resembling miniature lobsters, they are also called saltwater crayfish, Dublin Bay prawns, or langoustines; their tails are used to make scampi. Freshwater shrimp look like a cross between shrimp and lobster, and are also, correctly, called prawns.

CRABS

- Fresh and saltwater crabs are popular for their succulent meat; saltwater varieties are more readily available.
- Crabs are sold whole, cooked or live, and as fresh or frozen cooked legs, lumpmeat (whole pieces from the body), or flaked meat (light and dark meat from the body and claws).
- When buying whole crabs, choose cooked ones with bright red shells or live crabs that are active. Cooked crabmeat should be white tinged with pink, and sweet-smelling; when preparing it, check for any small pieces of shell and cartilage. Frozen crabmeat is a convenient alternative to fresh.
- Hard-shell varieties of crab should be cooked before you remove the meat. Soft-shell crabs, which are available fresh only from May through mid-September, are eaten shell and all, and must be cleaned (see below right) before cooking.

1 To remove meat from a cooked hard-shell crab, first twist off legs and claws close to the body. Break each claw and leg with a nutcracker; remove meat using a lobster pick or skewer.

2 With your fingers, pull off the "apron" from underside of crab and discard it.

3 Holding crab in both hands, insert your thumb under shell by apron hinge. Pull body away from shell.

4 With a spoon, remove meat and roe from shell. Discard stomach bag located between eyes. Discard shell (or scrub to use as serving container).

5 Pull away the inedible feathery gills, or "dead man's fingers," from the body and discard.

6 With kitchen shears, cut body down center; trim any jagged edges of shell.

7 With fingers or lobster pick, remove meat from each body section.

CLEANING SOFT-SHELL CRABS

Soft-shell crabs are simply blue crabs that have shed their shells and are growing new ones. To clean, with kitchen shears, cut across each crab ¼ inch behind eyes; discard front portion. Cut off flat, pointed apron on underside. Bend back top shell on each side and pull off spongy gills. Rinse with cold running water; pat dry with paper towels.

LOBSTER

• There are two types of lobster: the American or Maine lobster, from the North Atlantic coast, which is the most popular, and the rock or spiny lobster. The rock lobster, commercially harvested off Florida, southern California, Australia, New Zealand, and South America, has no claws. It is mostly sold frozen as lobster tail.

• When buying a live lobster, pick it up near its head – the tail should curl under and the lobster should feel heavy for its size; if too light it is not fresh and the meat has had time to dry out. Check that both claws are intact.

• Purchase frozen lobster tails in untorn packages with no evidence of frost; the lobster meat should have no dry areas.

• Live lobsters must be purchased the day they'll be cooked because they can't be stored very long. Store for no more than a few hours, wrapped in a wet cloth or wet newspaper, on a bed of ice in the refrigerator.

• When buying whole lobsters, allow a 1¼- to 1½-pound lobster for each serving. If buying tails only, allow one 6- to 8-ounce tail or 2 or 3 smaller ones per serving.

BOILING LOBSTER

To boil live lobsters, in a large (12-quart) stockpot, heat enough water to cover lobsters to boiling over high heat. Add lobsters, head first. Reheat water to boiling, then reduce heat to medium; cover and simmer for about 10 minutes per pound (the lobster shells will turn red during cooking). With tongs, transfer cooked lobsters to a colander to drain.

1 To remove meat from a cooked lobster, break off claws and legs. With nutcracker or lobster cracker, crack large claws and remove meat.

2 Twist off head from tail. With kitchen shears, cut down center of thin shell on underside of tail to expose meat. Gently pull meat from shell in one piece.

3 Cut along outer curve of tail meat, about ¼ inch deep, to expose dark vein. Remove vein and discard.

4 Spoon any green tomalley (liver) or coral roe (found only in females) into a bowl, to serve with the lobster meat, if desired.

5 Lift out rigid portion from head shell, then spoon out any additional tomalley or roe and add to bowl. Remove and discard sac and spongy gills from head.

6 Break rigid portion into several pieces. Pick out meat with lobster pick or fork.

CLAMS AND MUSSELS

Cleaning mussels and clams is very simple and straightforward; once prepared, they take only minutes to cook. Hard-shell clams come in various sizes; medium-size cherrystones and smaller littlenecks are more tender than larger chowder clams and soft-shell steamers. Both cherrystones and littlenecks can be eaten raw on the half shell, and are also good in cooked dishes – from stuffed clams to richly flavored pasta sauces. The briny liquid they release adds wonderful flavor but varies in saltiness – taste after cooking and season accordingly.

1 With stiff brush, scrub clams under cold running water. Shuck clams and release meat from bottom shells (see page 89).

2 Preheat oven to 400°F. Place clams in bottom shells in small baking dish or jelly-roll pan. Refrigerate clams until ready to bake.

3 In food processor with knife blade attached or in blender, process bread to fine crumbs. Spread crumbs on cookie sheet and bake 5 minutes, or until golden. In nonstick 10-inch skillet, cook bacon over medium-low heat until browned. With slotted spoon, transfer bacon to paper towels to drain. Discard drippings from skillet.

4 Add oil to skillet; add onion and cook, stirring occasionally, 3 minutes, or until tender. Add garlic and pepper; cook 30 seconds. Remove from heat; stir in parsley, crumbs, and bacon.

5 Spoon crumb mixture evenly over clams in baking dish. Bake about 10 minutes, until topping is lightly golden and clams are just cooked through.

STUFFED CLAMS

◆◆◆◆◆◆◆◆◆◆◆◆◆

Prep: 20 minutes
Bake: 15 minutes
Makes 4 appetizer servings

1 dozen littleneck or cherrystone clams
2 slices white bread, torn
2 slices bacon, finely chopped
1 tablespoon olive oil
1 small onion, finely chopped
1 small garlic clove, minced
¼ teaspoon ground black pepper
2 tablespoons chopped fresh parsley

CLAM GLOSSARY

Littlenecks These small hard-shells (under 2 inches in diameter) are sweet and tender; try them in pasta, soup, or simply steamed.
Cherrystones Medium-sized hard-shells that are prepared like littlenecks; perfect for stuffing.
Manila A Pacific clam that tastes best when under 1 inch across.
Geoducks From the Pacific Northwest, this giant clam has an oval shell and long siphon; used in soups.

EACH SERVING: ABOUT 115 CALORIES, 6g PROTEIN, 10g CARBOHYDRATE, 6g TOTAL FAT (1g SATURATED), 12mg CHOLESTEROL, 135mg SODIUM

CLAMS AND MUSSELS IN BROTH

Prep: 25 minutes   Cook: 20 minutes
Makes 4 main-dish servings

2 dozen littleneck or small cherrystone clams	**3 medium carrots, diced**
2 dozen large mussels	**1 small onion, diced**
2 tablespoons margarine or butter	**1 bay leaf**
3 medium celery stalks, diced	**1 cup dry vermouth**
	Coarsely chopped celery leaves for garnish

◆ With stiff brush, scrub clams and mussels under cold running water to remove any sand. Remove beards from mussels (see page 88).

◆ In 8-quart Dutch oven or saucepot, melt margarine over medium heat; add celery, carrots, onion, and bay leaf and cook, stirring occasionally, 8 to 10 minutes, until vegetables are tender. Stir in vermouth, clams, and mussels; heat to boiling over high heat.

◆ Reduce heat to medium-low; cover and cook, stirring occasionally, about 10 minutes, until mussels and clams open; discard any mussels and clams that do not open. Remove and discard bay leaf. Serve clams and mussels in bowls with broth, garnished with chopped celery leaves.

Each serving: About 245 calories, 16g protein, 14g carbohydrate, 8g total fat (4g saturated), 65mg cholesterol, 300mg sodium

LINGUINE WITH CLAMS AND MUSSELS

Prep: 20 minutes   Cook: 20 minutes
Makes 6 main-dish servings

1 dozen cherrystone or littleneck clams	**1 garlic clove, minced**
1 dozen mussels	**4 tablespoons chopped fresh parsley**
1 package (16 ounces) linguine	**2 cans (14½ ounces each) diced tomatoes**
1 teaspoon salt	**1 can (6 ounces) tomato paste**
¼ cup dry white wine	**½ cup reduced-sodium chicken broth**
2 tablespoons olive or vegetable oil	**1 tablespoon sugar**

◆ With stiff brush, scrub clams and mussels under cold running water; remove beards from mussels (see page 88). Prepare linguine as label directs, using 1 teaspoon of salt in water; drain. Return linguine to saucepot; keep warm.

◆ Meanwhile, in 12-inch skillet, toss clams with wine, oil, garlic, and 2 tablespoons parsley. Cover skillet; cook over medium-high heat, stirring occasionally, 8 to 10 minutes, just until clams open. With slotted spoon, transfer clams to bowl as they open; discard any clams that do not open.

◆ Add mussels to liquid remaining in skillet; heat to boiling over high heat. Reduce heat to medium; cover and cook, stirring occasionally, 3 to 5 minutes, until shells open. With slotted spoon, transfer mussels to bowl with clams as they open; discard any mussels that do not open.

◆ In same skillet, heat remaining ingredients and remaining 2 tablespoons chopped parsley to boiling over medium-high heat. Stir in shellfish; heat through. Spoon sauce and shellfish over linguine and serve.

Each serving: About 445 calories, 17g protein, 73g carbohydrate, 9g total fat (1g saturated), 18mg cholesterol, 885mg sodium

ASIAN-STYLE ANGEL HAIR PASTA WITH CLAMS

Prep: 20 minutes   Cook: 25 minutes
Makes 4 main-dish servings

1 tablespoon olive oil	**2 dozen littleneck clams, scrubbed**
3 garlic cloves, cut in half	**½ (16-ounce) package angel hair pasta**
1½ teaspoons grated, peeled fresh ginger	**Salt**
¼ teaspoon crushed red pepper	**1¼ teaspoons cornstarch**
1 cup chicken broth	**2 tablespoons chopped fresh cilantro**
⅓ cup dry white wine	
3 strips (3" by ¾") lemon peel, finely sliced lengthwise	

◆ In nonstick 12-inch skillet, heat oil over medium heat. Add garlic, ginger, and crushed red pepper; cook, stirring, 3 minutes. Add chicken broth, wine, and lemon peel; heat to boiling over high heat.

◆ Add clams; heat to boiling. Reduce heat to medium-low; cover and cook 10 to 15 minutes, until clams open. With slotted spoon, transfer clams to bowl as they open; discard any clams that do not open.

◆ After clams have cooked about 5 minutes, prepare pasta as label directs, using 1 teaspoon salt in water. Drain pasta and divide among 4 large soup bowls.

◆ Meanwhile, in cup, mix cornstarch with *1 tablespoon water* until smooth. Whisk cornstarch mixture into broth mixture remaining in skillet; cook over medium heat until mixture boils. Boil, stirring, 1 minute. Discard garlic.

◆ Return clams to skillet; heat through. To serve, spoon clam sauce over pasta in bowls. Sprinkle with cilantro.

Each serving: About 310 calories, 15g protein, 47g carbohydrate, 5g total fat (1g saturated), 23mg cholesterol, 340mg sodium

OYSTERS

Shuck oysters just before using; be sure to save their flavorful liquor if making a sauce. The most popular way of eating oysters is raw on the half shell, but for a special occasion, try them warm topped with spicy spinach and bread crumbs, or baked in a creamy sauce. Ready-shucked oysters are convenient if you are going to cook them but don't need their shells.

OYSTERS ROCKEFELLER

◆◆◆◆◆◆◆◆◆◆◆◆◆

Prep: 30 minutes
Bake: 10 minutes
Makes 4 appetizer servings

1 dozen oysters, scrubbed
Rock or kosher salt (optional)
1 bunch (10 to 12 ounces)
  spinach
1 tablespoon plus 2 teaspoons
  margarine or butter
2 tablespoons minced onion
Pinch ground nutmeg
Pinch ground red pepper
  (cayenne)
Pinch salt
1 tablespoon Pernod or other
  anise-flavor apéritif
¼ cup heavy or whipping
  cream
2 tablespoons plain dried
  bread crumbs
Lemon wedges and dill sprigs
  for garnish

1 Preheat oven to 425°F. Shuck oysters and release meat from bottom shells (see page 89). Remove any pieces of broken shell.

ROCK SALT

Rock salt has a grayish color because it retains more minerals than other salts. It is not a food-grade salt, but it is used to make hand-cranked ice cream (slowly melting the ice surrounding the ice-cream mixture) and is traditionally used as a bed on which to serve baked oysters and clams.

2 Place oysters in bottom shells in jelly-roll pan on ½-inch layer of rock salt, if desired; this will keep the oysters flat. Refrigerate until ready to bake.

4 In same pan, melt 1 tablespoon margarine over medium heat; add onion and cook 3 minutes, until tender. Stir in spinach, nutmeg, red pepper, salt, and Pernod. Add cream to mixture and cook over high heat, stirring, until reduced and thick. Remove from heat. In small saucepan or microwave-safe cup, melt remaining 2 teaspoons margarine; stir in bread crumbs.

3 Wash spinach. In 2-quart saucepan, cook spinach with water clinging to its leaves over high heat, stirring, until wilted. Drain well; chop very fine.

5 Spoon spinach mixture evenly on top of oysters. Sprinkle with bread-crumb mixture. Bake 10 minutes. Serve garnished with lemon wedges and dill sprigs.

EACH SERVING: ABOUT 170 CALORIES, 6g PROTEIN, 9g CARBOHYDRATE, 12g TOTAL FAT (5g SATURATED), 43mg CHOLESTEROL, 270mg SODIUM

GLAZED OYSTERS WITH LEEK AND CARROT

Prep: 15 minutes   Broil: 2 to 3 minutes
Makes 4 appetizer servings

1 dozen oysters, scrubbed
Rock or kosher salt (optional)
Salt
1 medium leek, cut into
   matchstick-thin strips
1 medium carrot, cut into
   matchstick-thin strips

2 tablespoons minced shallots
2 tablespoons dry white wine
¼ cup heavy or whipping
   cream
Chopped fresh tarragon for
   garnish

◆ Preheat broiler. Shuck oysters and release meat from bottom shells (see page 89); save as much oyster liquor as possible. Arrange bottom shells in jelly-roll pan, on ½-inch layer of rock salt, if desired, to keep them flat. Refrigerate oysters, reserving their liquor.

◆ In 2-quart saucepan, heat *6 cups water* and 1 teaspoon salt to boiling over high heat. Add leek and carrot and cook 2 to 3 minutes, until tender. Drain.

◆ In 1-quart saucepan, boil shallots, wine, and reserved oyster liquor over high heat until liquid is reduced to about 1 tablespoon. Add cream and boil until mixture is reduced to ¼ cup. Remove from heat.

◆ Arrange leek and carrot strips evenly in oyster shells; place oysters on top. Spoon sauce on top. Place pan in broiler at closest position to heat source; broil 2 minutes. Serve garnished with chopped tarragon, if you like.

Each serving: About 115 calories, 4g protein, 9g carbohydrate, 7g total fat (4g saturated), 43mg cholesterol, 120mg sodium

---

OYSTER KNIFE

This knife is indispensable when it comes to opening oysters. It has a short blade and pointed end to pry the shells apart. Choose a knife with a guard that protects your fingers from the sharp edges of the shell. The short, stubby handle enables you to keep a firm grip, which is important when it comes to this difficult culinary task. It does become easier with practice. The knife can also be used for opening clams. Buy the sturdiest knife available; a flimsy one may break off in your hand.

OYSTERS WITH GINGER MIGNONETTE

Prep: 15 minutes   Makes 2 appetizer servings

1 dozen oysters, scrubbed
¼ cup rice vinegar
2 medium green onions,
   finely chopped

½ teaspoon grated, peeled
   fresh ginger
½ teaspoon coarsely ground
   black pepper

◆ Shuck oysters and release meat from bottom shells (see page 89); arrange in bottom shells on platter.

◆ In small bowl, combine rice vinegar, green onions, ginger, and pepper; stir until well combined. To serve, spoon mignonette sauce onto oysters.

Each serving: About 60 calories, 6g protein, 4g carbohydrate, 2g total fat (0g saturated), 46mg cholesterol, 95mg sodium

---

SCALLOPED OYSTERS

Prep: 15 minutes   Bake: 35 minutes
Makes 6 appetizer servings

½ (16-ounce) loaf unsliced
   white bread
4 tablespoons margarine or
   butter, melted
1 pint shucked oysters
½ cup heavy or whipping
   cream

¼ teaspoon salt
⅛ teaspoon ground black
   pepper
2 tablespoons chopped fresh
   parsley

◆ Preheat oven to 400°F. Tear bread into 1-inch pieces and place in jelly-roll pan. Drizzle with margarine and toss to coat. Bake 25 minutes, or until bread is golden and crisp. Set toasted bread aside.

◆ Drain oysters, reserving oyster liquor.

◆ In 1-quart saucepan, boil reserved oyster liquor over high heat until reduced to about 2 tablespoons. Add heavy cream, salt, and pepper and heat to boiling; remove cream mixture from heat.

◆ In 9" by 9" glass baking dish, combine toasted bread, oysters, and 1 tablespoon parsley. Pour cream mixture on top and toss to coat.

◆ Bake 10 minutes. Sprinkle with remaining 1 tablespoon chopped parsley and serve.

Each serving: About 285 calories, 8g protein, 24g carbohydrate, 18g total fat (7g saturated), 49mg cholesterol, 535mg sodium

SCALLOPS

Scallops, which come already shucked, are the easiest shellfish to prepare. Sea scallops, the largest variety, are the most widely available. Before using them, first remove and discard the hard muscle found on the side – the creamy white meat can then be lightly sautéed or quickly broiled. Accent the delicate flavor of scallops with a tangy vinaigrette or sauce, or complement their soft texture with a bread-crumb topping. Scallops become tough when overcooked, so cook them just until they turn opaque.

SCALLOPS AND SHRIMP VINAIGRETTE

◆◆◆◆◆◆◆◆◆◆◆◆◆◆◆◆◆◆◆◆◆◆◆◆◆◆◆◆◆◆

Prep: 25 minutes plus chilling   Cook: 5 minutes
Makes 6 main-dish servings

¼ cup plus 3 tablespoons olive or vegetable oil
¼ cup white wine vinegar
1½ teaspoons salt
1 teaspoon dried tarragon
1 teaspoon sugar
½ teaspoon hot pepper sauce
⅛ teaspoon ground black pepper

1 pound large shrimp
1 pound sea scallops
3 medium heads Belgian endive, sliced crosswise
¼ cup chopped fresh parsley
Arugula and sliced red onion (optional)

1 Prepare vinaigrette: In large bowl, whisk ¼ cup oil with white wine vinegar, salt, tarragon, sugar, hot pepper sauce, and black pepper until blended. Set vinaigrette aside.

2 Shell and devein shrimp (see page 90); rinse with cold running water. Rinse scallops under cold running water to remove any sand. Pull tough crescent-shaped muscle from side of each scallop. Pat shrimp and scallops dry with paper towels. Cut each scallop horizontally in half.

3 In 12-inch skillet, heat remaining 3 tablespoons oil over medium-high heat. Add shrimp and scallops; cook, stirring often, 5 minutes, or until opaque throughout. Add seafood to vinaigrette in bowl; toss to coat. Cover with plastic wrap; refrigerate at least 2 hours.

4 Just before serving, add endive and parsley to seafood mixture; toss well to combine. Serve with arugula and sliced red onion, if you like.

SCALLOPS

There are many species of scallops, but only three are common in the U.S. Bay scallops are about ½ inch in diameter and offer the sweetest flavor and most delicate texture. Harvested along the East Coast, they are the least plentiful and most expensive. Larger sea scallops are less delicate, but their meat is still sweet. Calico scallops, from the Gulf of Mexico, have speckled shells. Similar to bay scallops in size, they're tougher, with a less fine taste.

EACH SERVING: ABOUT 280 CALORIES, 26g PROTEIN, 5g CARBOHYDRATE, 17g TOTAL FAT (2g SATURATED), 142mg CHOLESTEROL, 800mg SODIUM

SCALLOPS WITH WATERCRESS AND LEMON-CAPER SAUCE

Prep: 10 minutes   Cook: 8 to 10 minutes
Makes 4 main-dish servings

1¼ pounds sea scallops	2 bunches watercress
6 tablespoons butter	1 tablespoon fresh lemon
⅛ teaspoon ground black	juice
pepper	1 tablespoon capers, drained
Salt	and chopped
1 tablespoon vegetable oil	

◆ Rinse scallops with cold running water to remove sand from crevices. Pull tough crescent-shaped muscle from side of each scallop. Pat dry with paper towels. In 10-inch skillet, heat 2 tablespoons butter over medium-high heat; add scallops, pepper, and ½ teaspoon salt and cook about 5 minutes, or until scallops are browned on both sides and opaque throughout.

◆ Meanwhile, in 5-quart Dutch oven or saucepot, heat oil over high heat; add watercress and ¼ teaspoon salt and cook, stirring, about 2 minutes, until watercress just wilts.

◆ Transfer scallops to 4 warm plates; keep warm. In same skillet, heat lemon juice, capers, and *2 tablespoons water* to boiling over medium-high heat.

◆ Reduce heat to medium; add remaining 4 tablespoons butter, 1 tablespoon at a time, beating with a wire whisk until butter just melts and mixture thickens. (Do not use margarine; sauce will not be thick.) Pour sauce over scallops; arrange watercress on plates.

Each serving: About 310 calories, 25g protein, 4g carbohydrate, 22g total fat (11g saturated), 93mg cholesterol, 895mg sodium

PEPPERY SCALLOPS

Prep: 10 minutes   Broil: 5 minutes
Makes 4 main-dish servings

1¼ pounds sea scallops	1 tablespoon chopped fresh
2 tablespoons margarine or	basil
butter, melted	½ teaspoon seasoned pepper
2 tablespoons plain dried	¼ teaspoon salt
bread crumbs	Lemon slices or wedges

Preheat broiler. Rinse scallops with cold running water to remove sand from crevices. Pull tough crescent-shaped muscle from side of each scallop. Pat dry with paper towels. In bowl, toss scallops with melted margarine to coat well. On waxed paper, mix bread crumbs, basil, pepper, and salt. Dip top of each scallop into bread-crumb mixture. Place scallops, breaded-side up, on rack in broiling pan. With pan at closest position to heat source, broil scallops, without turning, 5 minutes, or until topping is golden and scallops are opaque throughout. Serve with lemon slices.

Each serving: About 190 calories, 24g protein, 6g carbohydrate, 7g total fat (1g saturated), 47mg cholesterol, 455mg sodium

SAUTÉED SCALLOPS AND VEGETABLES

Prep: 25 minutes   Cook: 20 minutes
Makes 4 main-dish servings

2 bunches arugula	1 medium onion, thinly sliced
1 pound sea scallops	¾ pound medium
4 teaspoons olive or vegetable	mushrooms, quartered
oil	8 ounces sugar snap peas,
1 large red pepper, thinly	strings removed
sliced	2 tablespoons soy sauce

◆ Arrange arugula on platter; set aside. Rinse scallops with cold running water to remove sand from crevices. Pull tough crescent-shaped muscle from side of each scallop. Pat dry with paper towels. In nonstick 12-inch skillet, heat 2 teaspoons oil over medium-high heat. Add red pepper and onion; cook until onion is golden. Transfer red-pepper mixture to plate. In same skillet, heat 1 teaspoon oil; add mushrooms and cook until golden brown. Add sugar snap peas and cook, stirring, 2 minutes more, or until tender-crisp. Transfer to same plate.

◆ In same skillet, heat remaining 1 teaspoon oil over medium-high heat; add scallops and cook, stirring occasionally, about 3 to 4 minutes, until scallops are opaque throughout. Return vegetable mixture to skillet with scallops; stir in soy sauce. Heat through over medium-high heat. Spoon scallop mixture over arugula on platter.

Each serving: About 215 calories, 24g protein, 19g carbohydrate, 6g total fat (1g saturated), 37mg cholesterol, 780mg sodium

SQUID

Squid, also known by its Italian name, *calamari*, makes a special treat whether it is coated and panfried for crunch, simmered in a sauce, or quickly grilled. For speediest preparation, buy cleaned squid; if you clean it yourself (see page 89), allow 1½ pounds whole squid to yield 1 pound, cleaned. Cook squid either very briefly – less than a minute – or for more than 30 minutes to prevent it from turning rubbery.

CALAMARI WITH SPICY TOMATO SAUCE

◆◆◆◆◆◆◆◆◆◆◆◆

Prep: 30 minutes
Cook: 10 minutes
Makes 4 appetizer servings

1 tablespoon vegetable oil plus additional for frying
1 small onion, finely chopped
1 can (8 ounces) tomato sauce
3 tablespoons red wine vinegar
1½ teaspoons sugar
½ teaspoon salt
¼ teaspoon crushed red pepper
¼ teaspoon dried oregano
1 pound cleaned squid
1 large egg, lightly beaten
⅔ cup all-purpose flour
Lemon wedges and parsley sprigs for garnish

1 Prepare spicy tomato sauce: In 1-quart saucepan, heat 1 tablespoon oil over medium heat; add onion and cook until tender. Add tomato sauce and next 5 ingredients; heat to boiling.

2 Reduce heat to low; cover sauce and simmer 5 minutes. Keep warm. Slice squid bodies crosswise into ¾-inch-wide rings. Cut tentacles into several pieces if they are large.

3 In bowl, toss squid pieces with egg to coat. Measure flour onto waxed paper. In 10-inch skillet, heat ½ inch oil over medium heat. Dip squid in flour; add to skillet and cook in small batches until golden.

SQUID INK

If you clean and prepare squid yourself, you may see the ink sac; this contains a brownish-black liquid and is usually discarded. Squid and cuttlefish both have this sac; they squirt ink as a defensive mechanism to cloud the water around them.

In Italy, where squid is much more commonly eaten than it is here, cooks add squid or cuttlefish ink to pasta dough and risotto to give a deep black color and deep-sea flavor. If you live near a good Italian market, you may be able to find squid-ink pasta. For a dramatic presentation, try squid-ink pasta instead of linguine in our Linguine with Squid Sauce (see page 100).

4 With slotted spoon, transfer squid to paper towels to drain. Serve fried squid with warm tomato sauce, garnished with lemon wedges and parsley sprigs.

EACH SERVING: ABOUT 300 CALORIES, 22g PROTEIN, 24g CARBOHYDRATE, 13g TOTAL FAT (3g SATURATED), 317mg CHOLESTEROL, 680mg SODIUM

LINGUINE WITH SQUID SAUCE

Prep: 40 minutes   *Cook:* 1 hour 15 minutes
Makes 6 main-dish servings

2 pounds cleaned squid	1 can (28 ounces) plum
1 tablespoon olive oil	tomatoes
1 medium onion, chopped	Salt
2 large garlic cloves, minced	1 package (16 ounces)
1 teaspoon fennel seeds	linguine
¼ to ½ teaspoon crushed red	¼ cup chopped flat-leaf
pepper	parsley

◆ Slice squid bodies into ½-inch rings. Cut tentacles into several pieces if they are large.

◆ In 4-quart saucepan, heat oil over medium heat. Add onion and cook, stirring often, 5 to 8 minutes, until tender.

◆ Stir in garlic, fennel seeds, and crushed red pepper; cook 30 seconds. Stir in tomatoes with their juice and 1¼ teaspoons salt, breaking up tomatoes with back of spoon. Heat to boiling.

◆ Stir in squid pieces; heat to boiling. Reduce heat to low; cover saucepan and simmer 30 minutes. Uncover and simmer 30 minutes longer. Meanwhile, prepare linguine as label directs, using 2 teaspoons salt in water; drain. In large bowl, toss linguine with squid sauce and parsley.

Each serving: About 480 calories, 35g protein, 70g carbohydrate, 6g total fat (1g saturated), 352mg cholesterol, 735mg sodium

THAI SQUID SALAD

Prep: 30 minutes   *Cook:* 30 seconds
Makes 4 appetizer servings

Salt	1 medium carrot, shredded
3 tablespoons Asian fish sauce	1 pound cleaned squid
(nuoc nam, see page 30)	1 large head Boston lettuce,
3 tablespoons fresh lime juice	torn into bite-size pieces
1 tablespoon sugar	½ cup loosely packed fresh
¼ teaspoon crushed red	mint leaves
pepper	½ cup loosely packed fresh
½ small sweet onion such as	cilantro leaves
Vidalia or Walla Walla, very	
thinly sliced	

◆ In 4-quart saucepan, heat *3 quarts water* with 2 teaspoons salt to boiling over high heat.

◆ Meanwhile, prepare dressing: In large bowl, stir together fish sauce, lime juice, sugar, crushed pepper, and ¼ teaspoon salt until sugar dissolves. Stir in onion and carrot.

◆ Slice squid bodies into very thin rings. Cut tentacles into several pieces if they are large.

◆ Add squid pieces to boiling water and cook 30 seconds. Drain. Add to dressing in bowl. Add lettuce, mint, and cilantro and toss to coat.

Each serving: About 150 calories, 19g protein, 13g carbohydrate, 2g total fat (0g saturated), 264mg cholesterol, 565mg sodium

GRILLED SQUID

Prep: 15 minutes   *Grill:* 1 to 2 minutes
Makes 4 appetizer servings

1 pound cleaned squid	⅛ teaspoon ground black
1 tablespoon extra-virgin olive	pepper
oil	1 tablespoon chopped
1 tablespoon fresh lemon	flat-leaf parsley
juice	Lemon wedges for garnish
¼ teaspoon salt	

◆ Prepare outdoor grill. Slice squid bodies down one side to open flat. In medium bowl, toss bodies and tentacles with olive oil, lemon juice, salt, and pepper.

◆ Thread squid bodies on metal skewers so they lie flat; thread tentacles on separate skewers. Place on grill over high heat and cook 1 to 2 minutes, turning once, just until opaque throughout. Transfer from skewers to platter and sprinkle with parsley. Serve garnished with lemon wedges.

Each serving: About 135 calories, 18g protein, 4g carbohydrate, 5g total fat (1g saturated), 264mg cholesterol, 185mg sodium

SHRIMP

Sweet-tasting shrimp are the most popular of all shellfish. They can be cooked in or out of the shell, but are most often shelled and deveined before serving. Whether they are simply sautéed, lightly marinated and charcoal-grilled, or simmered in a flavorful tomato sauce, shrimp take only minutes to cook. As soon as they turn opaque throughout, they're done. Don't overcook – they'll toughen.

GARLIC SHRIMP AND BEANS

◆◆◆◆◆◆◆◆◆◆◆◆◆◆◆◆◆◆◆◆◆◆◆◆◆◆◆◆◆

Prep: 20 minutes   Cook: 20 minutes
Makes 4 main-dish servings

1¼ pounds large shrimp	1 cup chicken broth
2 tablespoons olive oil	1 tablespoon fresh lemon
1 small eggplant (12 ounces),	juice
cut into ¼-inch-thick slices	1 can (15 to 19 ounces) Great
2 garlic cloves, crushed with	Northern or cannellini
side of knife	beans, rinsed and drained
½ teaspoon salt	Capers, lemon wedges, and
1 tablespoon all-purpose flour	flat-leaf parsley sprigs for
¼ teaspoon crushed red	garnish
pepper (optional)	

1 Shell and devein shrimp (see page 90); rinse with cold running water. Preheat broiler; lightly oil rack in broiling pan. Brush eggplant with 1 tablespoon oil; place on rack.

2 Place pan in broiler at closest position to heat source; broil slices, turning once, 8 to 10 minutes, until tender. Transfer slices to plate; keep warm.

3 In nonstick 12-inch skillet, heat remaining 1 tablespoon oil over medium-high heat. Add garlic, shrimp, and salt; cook until shrimp begin to turn opaque.

4 Meanwhile, in small bowl, mix flour, crushed red pepper, if using, chicken broth, and lemon juice until smooth. Add lemon-juice mixture to shrimp in skillet.

5 Discard garlic from shrimp mixture; stir in beans. Heat to boiling over high heat, stirring. Boil, stirring, 1 minute, or until thickened. Serve shrimp mixture with eggplant; garnish with capers, lemon wedges, and parsley sprigs.

CRUSHING GARLIC

Garlic is crushed to make it easier to peel, and to release the cloves' aromatic oils. The crushed cloves can easily be removed from a finished dish. To crush, press clove with the flat side of a knife until skin breaks.

EACH SERVING: ABOUT 335 CALORIES, 32g PROTEIN, 30g CARBOHYDRATE, 10g TOTAL FAT (2g SATURATED), 218mg CHOLESTEROL, 690mg SODIUM

SHRIMP CURRY

Prep: 20 minutes   Cook: 8 to 10 minutes
Makes 4 main-dish servings

2 tablespoons margarine or
   butter
2 garlic cloves, minced
2 teaspoons minced, peeled
   fresh ginger
2 teaspoons curry powder
½ teaspoon ground coriander
½ teaspoon ground cumin
¾ cup heavy or whipping
   cream

Salt
1 medium zucchini (8 ounces)
1 pound medium shrimp,
   shelled and deveined (see
   page 90)
½ teaspoon ground black
   pepper
2 tablespoons chopped fresh
   cilantro
Hot cooked rice (optional)

◆ In 2-quart saucepan, melt 1 tablespoon margarine over
medium heat. Stir in garlic and next 4 ingredients; cook,
stirring, 1 minute. Stir in cream and ½ teaspoon salt;
increase heat to high and boil 5 minutes, or until thickened.

◆ Meanwhile, cut zucchini lengthwise in half; thinly slice.
In 10-inch skillet, melt remaining 1 tablespoon margarine
over medium-high heat. Add zucchini and cook, stirring,
2 to 3 minutes, until beginning to brown. Stir in shrimp,
½ teaspoon salt, and pepper; cook, stirring, 2 minutes, or
until shrimp are opaque throughout. Stir shrimp mixture
into sauce; sprinkle with cilantro. Serve over rice, if you like.

**Each serving: About 310 calories, 21g protein, 5g carbohydrate,
23g total fat (12g saturated), 236mg cholesterol, 815mg sodium**

GRILLED SHRIMP TOSTADAS

Prep: 30 minutes   Grill: 2 to 3 minutes
Makes 6 main-dish servings

1 large lime
3 to 4 avocados (2 pounds
   total)
2 small tomatoes, seeded and
   cut into ½-inch chunks
1 tablespoon drained pickled
   jalapeño-chile slices, chopped

Salt and coarsely ground
   black pepper
1½ pounds large shrimp
1 tablespoon olive oil
6 corn tortillas (6 inches)
Diced tomato and lime
   wedges for garnish

◆ Grate 1 teaspoon peel and squeeze 2 tablespoons juice
from lime. Peel and cube avocados; mash in bowl. Stir in
tomato chunks, 1 tablespoon lime juice, jalapeño chile

slices, ½ teaspoon salt, and ¼ teaspoon pepper. Press plastic
wrap directly onto surface of mixture to prevent browning
until ready to use.

◆ Shell and devein shrimp, leaving tail part of shell on, if
you like (see page 90). In bowl, toss shrimp, oil, ¾ teaspoon
salt, ½ teaspoon pepper, lime peel, and remaining
1 tablespoon lime juice.

◆ Place shrimp on grill topper on grill or thread on metal
skewers; grill over medium heat, turning occasionally, 2 to
3 minutes, until shrimp are opaque throughout. Place
tortillas directly on grill; cook 1 to 2 minutes per side, until
lightly browned.

◆ To serve, arrange tortillas on 6 dinner plates. Divide
avocado mixture and shrimp among tortillas. Garnish with
diced tomato and lime wedges.

**Each serving: About 420 calories, 23g protein, 26g carbohydrate,
27g total fat (4g saturated), 175mg cholesterol, 720mg sodium**

SHRIMP IN FETA-TOMATO SAUCE

Prep: 20 minutes   Cook: 50 minutes
Makes 4 main-dish servings

1 tablespoon olive oil
2 medium onions, chopped
1½ pounds all-purpose
   potatoes, peeled and cut
   into 1-inch pieces
1 large garlic clove, minced
Pinch ground red pepper
   (cayenne)
½ teaspoon salt

1 can (14½ to 16 ounces)
   tomatoes
1 pound medium shrimp,
   shelled and deveined (see
   page 90)
4 ounces feta cheese, diced
   (1 cup)
¼ cup chopped fresh dill

◆ In 10-inch skillet, heat oil over medium heat. Add onions
and cook, stirring often, 10 minutes, or until tender. Add
potatoes and cook, stirring occasionally, 10 minutes, or until
beginning to brown. Stir in garlic and ground red pepper
and cook 30 seconds.

◆ Stir in *¾ cup water* and salt; cover and simmer over low
heat 10 minutes, or until potatoes are almost tender.

◆ Add tomatoes with their juice, breaking up tomatoes
with back of spoon. Cook, uncovered, over medium heat
10 minutes, or until juices are slightly thickened.

◆ Stir in shrimp and feta. Cover and cook 3 to 5 minutes,
until shrimp are opaque throughout. Remove from heat
and stir in dill.

**Each serving: About 390 calories, 28g protein, 47g carbohydrate,
11g total fat (5g saturated), 200mg cholesterol, 955mg sodium**

SPICY STIR-FRIED SHRIMP

Prep: 15 minutes   Cook: 8 minutes
Makes 4 main-dish servings

¼ cup chili sauce
2 tablespoons soy sauce
2 tablespoons dry sherry
4 green onions
2 tablespoons vegetable oil
1¼ pounds large shrimp, shelled and deveined (see page 90)

¼ teaspoon crushed red pepper
1 tablespoon chopped fresh parsley

◆ In small bowl, mix chili sauce, soy sauce, and sherry until well combined. Cut green onions into 3-inch pieces.

◆ In 4-quart saucepan, heat oil over high heat; add green onions and cook, stirring frequently, about 3 minutes, until lightly browned.

◆ Stir in shrimp and crushed red pepper and cook, stirring constantly, 2 minutes. Stir in chili-sauce mixture; cook 2 minutes longer, or until shrimp turn opaque throughout.

◆ Remove from heat and stir in chopped parsley.

Each serving: About 205 calories, 24g protein, 5g carbohydrate, 8g total fat (2g saturated), 219mg cholesterol, 965mg sodium

SHRIMP WITH BLACK-BEAN SAUCE

Prep: 25 minutes   Cook: 25 minutes
Makes 6 main-dish servings

4 tablespoons vegetable oil
1 large onion, chopped
1 large celery stalk, diced
2 tablespoons chili powder
1 can (28 ounces) tomatoes
Salt
1¼ teaspoons dried oregano
⅜ teaspoon crushed red pepper

2 cans (15 to 19 ounces each) black beans, rinsed and drained
¼ cup chopped fresh parsley
2 tablespoons red wine vinegar
1¼ pounds large shrimp, shelled and deveined (see page 90)

◆ In 12-inch skillet, heat 2 tablespoons oil over high heat; add onion and celery and cook, stirring frequently, about 5 minutes, until tender and lightly browned. Add chili powder; cook 1 minute.

◆ Add tomatoes with their juice, 1 teaspoon salt, 1 teaspoon oregano, and ⅛ teaspoon crushed red pepper; heat to boiling, breaking up tomatoes with back of spoon.

◆ Reduce heat to low; simmer, stirring occasionally, 10 minutes. Stir in black beans, chopped parsley, and vinegar; heat through.

◆ Meanwhile, in 10-inch skillet, heat remaining 2 tablespoons oil over high heat; add shrimp, ½ teaspoon salt, remaining ¼ teaspoon oregano, and remaining ¼ teaspoon crushed red pepper, and cook, stirring constantly, just until shrimp are opaque throughout.

◆ To serve, spoon bean mixture onto 6 warm dinner plates; top with shrimp mixture.

Each serving: About 390 calories, 28g protein, 47g carbohydrate, 11g total fat (2g saturated), 117mg cholesterol, 920mg sodium

GINGERED SHRIMP AND ASPARAGUS

Prep: 20 minutes   Cook: 10 minutes
Makes 4 main-dish servings

1¼ pounds asparagus, tough ends removed
1 pound large shrimp
1 tablespoon balsamic vinegar
1 tablespoon soy sauce
2 tablespoons olive or vegetable oil

1 tablespoon minced, peeled fresh ginger
¼ teaspoon crushed red pepper
1 bunch arugula or watercress

◆ Cut asparagus into bite-size pieces. Shell and devein shrimp, leaving tail part of shell on, if you like (see page 90). In small bowl, mix balsamic vinegar, soy sauce, and *1 tablespoon water.*

◆ In nonstick 12-inch skillet, heat oil over medium-high heat; add asparagus and cook, stirring frequently, about 5 minutes, just until tender-crisp.

◆ Stir in shrimp, ginger, and crushed red pepper and cook, stirring constantly, about 4 minutes, until shrimp are opaque throughout and asparagus is tender. Stir in balsamic-vinegar mixture. To serve, arrange arugula on 4 warm dinner plates; top with shrimp mixture.

Each serving: About 195 calories, 23g protein, 5g carbohydrate, 9g total fat (1g saturated), 175mg cholesterol, 480mg sodium

BAKED LEMON-GARLIC SHRIMP

Prep: 25 minutes   *Bake:* 12 to 15 minutes
Makes 4 main-dish servings

1¼ pounds large shrimp
1 bunch (10 to 12 ounces) spinach,
  coarsely chopped
2 medium tomatoes, halved, seeded, and
  cut into ½-inch chunks
2 tablespoons olive or vegetable oil
Salt
1 garlic clove, minced
1 tablespoon chopped fresh parsley
1 tablespoon fresh lemon juice
½ teaspoon lemon-pepper seasoning salt
Parsley sprigs for garnish

◆ Preheat oven to 450°F. Shell and
devein shrimp (see page 90).

◆ In bowl, combine spinach, tomatoes,
1 tablespoon oil, and ½ teaspoon salt.
Toss to coat. Place spinach mixture in
four 1½-cup shallow casseroles.

◆ In same bowl, combine shrimp,
garlic, next 3 ingredients, remaining
1 tablespoon oil, and ½ teaspoon salt;
toss to coat shrimp. Arrange shrimp
mixture over spinach mixture. Bake
12 to 15 minutes, until shrimp are
opaque throughout. To serve, place
each casserole on plate and garnish
with parsley sprigs.

**Each serving: About 205 calories,
26g protein, 6g carbohydrate, 8g total fat
(1g saturated), 219mg cholesterol,
865mg sodium**

SHRIMP SHELLS FOR FISH STOCK

Instead of discarding shrimp shells,
use them to make stock: Place the
shells in a saucepan with water to
cover. Heat to boiling over high
heat; reduce heat to low and
simmer 30 minutes. Leave shells in
liquid to cool, then strain liquid
into bowl. Store up to 1 week in
an airtight container in the
refrigerator, or up to 3 months in
the freezer.

CREOLE SHRIMP AND PEPPERS

Prep: 35 minutes   *Bake:* 20 minutes
Makes 6 main-dish servings

1½ pounds large shrimp
1 large lemon
4 tablespoons margarine or butter
1 medium onion, chopped
2 medium celery stalks, thinly sliced
1 large red pepper, cut into 1-inch
  pieces
1 large green pepper, cut into 1-inch
  pieces
1 can (16 ounces) crushed tomatoes
1 teaspoon salt
1 teaspoon sugar
1 teaspoon dried basil
½ teaspoon hot pepper sauce
1 bay leaf
2 tablespoons chopped fresh parsley
Hot cooked rice (optional)

◆ Shell and devein shrimp (see page
90). Grate 1 teaspoon peel and
squeeze 2 teaspoons juice from lemon.

◆ Preheat oven to 375°F. In 12-inch
skillet, melt margarine over medium-
high heat; add onion and celery and
cook, stirring frequently, 5 minutes, or
until tender. Add peppers; cook,
stirring frequently, 10 minutes longer,
or until tender.

◆ Stir in lemon peel, lemon juice,
crushed tomatoes, salt, sugar, basil,
hot pepper sauce, and bay leaf; cook
1 minute. Stir in shrimp.

◆ Spoon shrimp mixture into shallow
2-quart casserole. Bake 20 minutes, or
until shrimp are opaque throughout.
Remove casserole from oven; remove
and discard bay leaf. Stir in parsley.
Serve with rice, if you like.

**Each serving: About 210 calories,
21g protein, 13g carbohydrate, 9g total fat
(2g saturated), 175mg cholesterol,
845mg sodium**

SEAFOOD AND SAFFRON-RICE CASSEROLE

Prep: 35 minutes   *Bake:* 40 minutes
Makes 6 main-dish servings

1 pound large shrimp
¾ pound medium sea scallops
2 teaspoons minced, peeled fresh ginger
  or ¼ teaspoon ground ginger
¼ teaspoon crushed red pepper
3 tablespoons coarsely chopped fresh
  parsley
Salt
2 tablespoons vegetable oil
1 medium onion, diced
1 medium red pepper, diced
1½ cups regular long-grain rice
1 can (13¾ to 14½ ounces) chicken broth
¼ teaspoon crushed saffron threads

◆ Shell and devein shrimp (see page
90). Rinse scallops with cold running
water to remove sand from crevices. Pull
tough muscle from side of each scallop.

◆ In bowl, toss shrimp and scallops
with ginger, crushed red pepper,
2 tablespoons chopped parsley, and
½ teaspoon salt. Cover and refrigerate.

◆ Preheat oven to 375°F. In 4-quart
saucepan, heat oil over medium-high
heat; add onion and red pepper and
cook until tender-crisp. Stir in rice,
broth, saffron, ½ teaspoon salt, and
1¼ cups water. Heat to boiling over high
heat; pour into deep 3-quart casserole.
Cover and bake 20 minutes.

◆ Remove casserole from oven.
Reserve 6 shrimp and 6 scallops; stir
remaining seafood into rice mixture.
Tuck reserved shrimp and scallops into
top of casserole. Bake, uncovered,
20 minutes longer, or until liquid is
absorbed and seafood is opaque
throughout. To serve, sprinkle with
remaining 1 tablespoon parsley.

**Each serving: About 345 calories,
26g protein, 42g carbohydrate, 7g total fat
(1g saturated), 141mg cholesterol,
870mg sodium**

CRAB

No one can resist the spicy, succulent experience of a crab boil, a dish that's guaranteed to spark any appetite. For this time-honored cooking method, whole crabs are plunged into a fragrant broth filled with aromatic vegetables and spices. The result? An adventure in eating – cracking open spice-coated shells to reveal sweet, tender nuggets of crabmeat. When serving fresh crab, provide nutcrackers, extra bowls for shells, and plenty of napkins. We've also created recipes using lump crabmeat, which provides the taste of real crab without the trouble of picking meat out of the whole crab.

1 Coarsely chop onions, carrot, and celery. Cut lemon into thin slices. Transfer onions, carrot, celery, and lemon slices to 12-quart stockpot or Dutch oven.

2 Add Old Bay seasoning, crushed red pepper, beer, salt, and *1 gallon (16 cups) water*. Heat to boiling over high heat; boil 15 minutes. In large colander, rinse crabs thoroughly with cold running water.

CRAB BOIL

◆◆◆◆◆◆◆◆◆◆◆◆◆◆◆◆◆◆◆◆◆◆◆◆◆◆◆◆◆◆◆◆◆◆

Prep: 5 minutes   Cook: 20 minutes
Makes 4 main-dish servings

2 medium onions
1 medium carrot
1 medium celery stalk
1 lemon
½ cup Old Bay seasoning or other crab boil seasoning
1 tablespoon crushed red pepper

1 can or bottle (12 ounces) beer
1 tablespoon salt
2 dozen live hard-shell blue crabs
Corn on the cob (optional)

3 Holding crabs from behind with tongs, add to stockpot. Cover pot tightly and heat to boiling over high heat.

4 Boil 5 minutes, or until crabs turn red. Transfer crabs to colander to drain. Serve crabs with corn on the cob, if you like.

OLD BAY SEASONING

The water for a crab boil is traditionally highly seasoned with anything from hot chiles, ginger, and bay leaves to whole allspice and peppercorns. The blend of herbs and spices can vary according to the place of origin, but Old Bay seasoning, from Maryland, is one of the more popular commercial blends available. It contains celery salt, cayenne pepper, and dry mustard, among other assorted herbs and spices. You should be able to find Old Bay seasoning in supermarkets and at many fish markets.

EACH SERVING: ABOUT 115 CALORIES, 23g PROTEIN, 2g CARBOHYDRATE, 1g TOTAL FAT (0g SATURATED), 96mg CHOLESTEROL, 395mg SODIUM

THIN PASTA WITH CRABMEAT SAUCE

Prep: 15 minutes   *Cook:* 30 minutes
Makes 6 main-dish servings

1 tablespoon olive or
vegetable oil
1 garlic clove, sliced
1 small onion, diced
2 medium plum tomatoes,
seeded and diced
2 bottles (8 ounces each)
clam juice
2 tablespoons dry sherry

¼ teaspoon white pepper
Salt
1 container (16 ounces) lump
crabmeat, picked over
¾ (16-ounce) package angel
hair pasta or thin spaghetti
1 tablespoon chopped fresh
parsley

◆ In 3-quart saucepan, heat oil over medium heat; add garlic and cook, stirring, until golden. With slotted spoon, remove and discard garlic. Add onion to oil; cook about 5 minutes, until tender and golden.

◆ Stir in tomatoes, clam juice, sherry, pepper, and ¾ teaspoon salt; heat to boiling over high heat. Reduce heat to low; cover and simmer 10 minutes. Stir in crabmeat; heat through, stirring occasionally, 1 to 2 minutes.

◆ Meanwhile, prepare angel hair pasta as label directs, using 2 teaspoons salt in water. Drain. To serve, place pasta in 6 pasta bowls; top with crabmeat mixture and sprinkle with parsley.

Each serving: About 320 calories, 21g protein, 47g carbohydrate, 4g total fat (1g saturated), 45mg cholesterol, 695mg sodium

SOFT-SHELL CRABS WITH LEMON-CAPER SAUCE

Prep: 15 minutes   *Cook:* 10 minutes
Makes 4 appetizer or 2 main-dish servings

1 small lemon
2 tablespoons chopped fresh
parsley
2 tablespoons capers, drained
4 live large soft-shell crabs
(about 6 ounces each)

2 tablespoons plus 2 teaspoons
margarine or butter
¼ cup all-purpose flour
¼ teaspoon ground black
pepper
¼ cup minced shallots

◆ With small knife, cut ends from lemon. Place upright on cutting board; cut off peel and white pith. Slice lemon ¼ inch thick, discarding seeds; finely chop. In cup, mix lemon, parsley, and capers. Set aside.

◆ To clean crabs, with kitchen shears, cut across each crab ¼ inch just behind eyes; discard front portion. Cut off flat, pointed apron on underside. Bend back top shell on each side and pull off spongy gills. Rinse crabs with cold running water; pat dry with paper towels.

◆ In nonstick 10-inch skillet, melt 2 tablespoons margarine over medium heat. Meanwhile, spread flour on waxed paper; coat crabs evenly with flour. Add crabs to skillet, sprinkle with pepper, and cook, turning once, 8 minutes, or until golden and cooked through. Transfer to serving platter; keep warm. Add remaining 2 teaspoons margarine and shallots to skillet; cook 1 minute. Stir in lemon mixture and heat through. Spoon over crabs.

Each appetizer serving: About 250 calories, 32g protein, 9g carbohydrate, 10g total fat (2g saturated), 130mg cholesterol, 750mg sodium

CRAB CAKES RÉMOULADE

Prep: 35 minutes   *Cook:* 10 minutes
Makes 4 main-dish servings

Rémoulade Sauce (see below)
3 tablespoons margarine or
butter
½ small onion, grated
1 large celery stalk, minced
½ small red pepper, minced
1 tablespoon all-purpose flour
1 teaspoon dry mustard

½ cup milk
1 container (16 ounces) lump
crabmeat, picked over
½ cup plain dried bread
crumbs
1 tablespoon fresh lemon
juice

◆ Prepare Rémoulade Sauce; cover and refrigerate. In 3-quart saucepan, melt 1 tablespoon margarine over medium heat; add onion, celery, and red pepper and cook, stirring occasionally, until tender. Stir in flour and mustard; cook, stirring, 1 minute. Gradually stir in milk; cook, stirring, until mixture thickens. Remove saucepan from heat; stir in crabmeat, bread crumbs, and lemon juice.

◆ In 12-inch skillet, melt remaining 2 tablespoons margarine over medium heat. Spoon 8 mounds of crab mixture into skillet; press into cakes. Cook 10 minutes, or until browned on both sides. Serve with Rémoulade Sauce.

Each serving: About 680 calories, 24g protein, 23g carbohydrate, 55g total fat (9g saturated), 103mg cholesterol, 1115mg sodium

RÉMOULADE SAUCE

In small bowl, mix 1 cup mayonnaise, ¼ cup catchup, ¼ cup minced fresh parsley, 1 tablespoon prepared white horseradish, 2 teaspoons distilled white vinegar, 1 teaspoon grated lemon peel, and 1 teaspoon hot pepper sauce. Makes about 1 cup.

LOBSTER

Be sure to buy lobsters the day you plan to serve them and to cook them live. Enjoy lobster meat straight from the shell, mix it with curry sauce for a light meal, or moisten with mayonnaise for a luxurious sandwich filling. Use the shells to flavor savory fish soups.

STUFFED LOBSTER

◆◆◆◆◆◆◆◆◆◆◆

Prep: 20 minutes
Bake: 12 to 15 minutes
Makes 2 main-dish servings

2 live lobsters (1¼ pounds each)
4 slices firm white bread, torn
3 tablespoons margarine or butter
¼ cup minced shallots
¼ cup chopped fresh basil
⅛ teaspoon salt
⅛ teaspoon ground black pepper
Lemon wedges

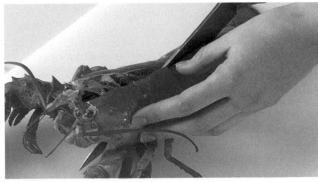

1 Preheat oven to 450°F. In 12-quart stockpot, heat *2 inches water* to boiling over high heat. Add lobsters, head down. Cover and heat to boiling over high heat; boil 2 minutes.

2 With tongs, transfer lobsters to colander to drain; allow to cool slightly. With large chef's knife or kitchen shears, cut each lobster in half lengthwise, cutting through shell as cleanly as possible.

3 Using tip of sharp knife, remove and discard head sac and intestinal vein; with spoon, remove green tomalley (see below). Place lobster halves, cut-side up, in jelly-roll pan.

4 In blender or food processor with knife blade attached, process bread to fine crumbs. In 10-inch skillet over medium heat, melt margarine. Add shallots to skillet and cook 2 minutes, or until tender. Remove from heat and stir in bread crumbs, basil, salt, and pepper. Spoon stuffing onto body cavities and tails of lobsters. Bake 12 to 15 minutes, until tail meat is opaque throughout. Serve with lemon wedges.

TOMALLEY AND CORAL

Tomalley is the green-colored liver of the lobster and is considered a great delicacy. The female lobster is prized for its roe, or eggs, otherwise known as coral. When raw, the coral is black in color but when cooked, it turns bright red. The tomalley and roe can be eaten alone, used in a sauce, or made into a flavored butter to spread on lobster before broiling.

EACH SERVING: ABOUT 560 CALORIES, 58g PROTEIN, 30g CARBOHYDRATE, 22g TOTAL FAT (4g SATURATED), 270mg CHOLESTEROL, 605mg SODIUM

LOBSTER IN COCONUT MILK CURRY

Prep: 20 minutes   Cook: 20 minutes
Makes 4 main-dish servings

2 live lobsters (1¼ to
  1½ pounds each)
2 limes
1 tablespoon margarine or
  butter
1 small onion, finely chopped
2 teaspoons minced, peeled
  fresh ginger
⅛ to ¼ teaspoon ground red
  pepper (cayenne)
1 can (14 ounces)
  unsweetened coconut milk
  (see page 30)

1 medium carrot, shredded
½ teaspoon salt
2 ounces snow peas, cut into
  matchstick-thin strips
¼ cup chopped fresh basil
Hot cooked jasmine or
  regular long-grain rice
  (optional)

◆ Cook lobsters and remove meat (see page 92); coarsely chop meat. With vegetable peeler, remove two 3-inch-long strips of peel from limes; squeeze 2 tablespoons juice.

◆ In 3-quart saucepan, melt margarine over medium heat. Add onion and cook, stirring frequently, 5 minutes, or until tender. Stir in ginger and ground red pepper; cook 30 seconds.

◆ Stir in coconut milk, carrot, salt, and lime peel; heat to boiling. Stir in lobster, lime juice, and snow peas; heat through. Remove from heat; stir in basil. Serve lobster over rice, if you like.

Each serving: About 420 calories, 30g protein, 16g carbohydrate, 28g total fat (22g saturated), 135mg cholesterol, 325mg sodium

THE ULTIMATE LOBSTER CLUB SANDWICH

Prep: 15 minutes   Cook: 12 minutes
Makes 2 main-dish servings

1 live lobster (1¼ to
  1½ pounds)
¼ cup mayonnaise
2 teaspoons chopped fresh
  tarragon
1 teaspoon fresh lemon juice
⅛ teaspoon ground black
  pepper

6 thin slices brioche or
  challah bread, toasted
½ avocado, thinly sliced
4 slices bacon, cooked crisp
4 slices tomato
2 lettuce leaves

◆ Cook lobsters and remove meat (see page 92); chop meat and place in small bowl. In cup, combine mayonnaise, tarragon, lemon juice, and pepper; stir 1 tablespoon mayonnaise mixture into chopped lobster meat. Spread remaining mayonnaise mixture on one side of each toasted brioche slice.

◆ Arrange avocado on 2 toast slices; top with bacon, then tomato. Place lettuce on another 2 brioche slices and top with lobster mixture; stack on top of avocado layer. Top with remaining brioche slices.

Each serving: About 710 calories, 40g protein, 47g carbohydrate, 41g total fat (8g saturated), 196mg cholesterol, 765mg sodium

LOBSTER BISQUE

Prep: 15 minutes   Cook: 1 hour 15 minutes
Makes about 5 cups or 4 appetizer servings

2 tablespoons margarine or
  butter
1 medium onion, chopped
1 medium carrot, chopped
1 medium celery stalk,
  chopped
1 garlic clove, minced
3 tablespoons tomato paste
Leftover shells and heads
  from 4 steamed lobsters
2 tablespoons cognac or
  brandy

2 bottles (8 ounces each) clam
  juice, or leftover water from
  steaming lobsters
3 parsley sprigs
⅛ teaspoon dried thyme
Pinch nutmeg
Pinch ground red pepper
  (cayenne)
¾ cup heavy or whipping
  cream
3 tablespoons all-purpose flour
French bread slices (optional)

◆ In 12-quart stockpot or Dutch oven, melt margarine over medium heat. Add onion, carrot, celery, and garlic and cook 5 minutes, or until tender. Stir in tomato paste.

◆ Increase heat to high and add lobster shells; cook, stirring occasionally, 5 minutes. Stir in cognac and cook until it has evaporated. Add clam juice, parsley, thyme, nutmeg, ground red pepper, and *6 cups water*; heat to boiling. Reduce heat to low; cover and simmer 30 minutes.

◆ Strain soup, discarding lobster shells and vegetables. Transfer soup to 4-quart saucepan and boil over high heat 10 to 15 minutes, until reduced to about 5 cups. Place cream in small bowl; whisk in flour until smooth. Whisk cream mixture into soup; return to boiling, whisking constantly. Reduce heat and simmer 2 minutes. Serve bisque with French bread slices, if you like.

Each serving: About 280 calories, 3g protein, 14g carbohydrate, 22g total fat (11g saturated), 61mg cholesterol, 440g sodium

F~ISH~ 5

FISH KNOW-HOW

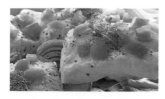

The tide has turned in America – and the popularity of fresh fish is on the rise. The reason? Supermarkets boast a greater variety of tempting fish, and the recognition of its nutritional value continues to grow. A rich source of protein, vitamins, and minerals, fish is also relatively low in fat and calories. Even fatty fish, such as tuna and salmon, contain only about 15 percent fat, far less than most meats, while white fish such as cod or flounder contain only 5 percent. Fish is highly perishable, so freshness (and a few simple guidelines for buying, storing, and handling) is key.

KNOW YOUR FISH

Fish are usually divided into two categories, "round" and "flat." They have very different bone structures and consequently are prepared and cut differently.

Round fish These have a plump, cylindrical shape, and eyes that lie on either side of the head. The backbone runs along the center of the fish, separating the two thick fillets on either side. Round fish are generally filleted or cut into steaks.

Red snapper fillet

Red snapper

Flat fish Almost two-dimensional, flat fish have both eyes on the same side of the head. The backbone runs through the center of the fish, with two lines of bones fanning out on either side, separating the top and bottom fillets. Flat fish are usually filleted but, if very large, like halibut, can be cut into steaks.

Flounder

Flounder fillet

FISH SENSE	
HOW FISH IS SOLD	HOW MUCH TO BUY
WHOLE Fish that has not been prepared in any way, sold fully intact with the head, scales, fins, and guts.	1 pound per serving
CLEANED AND SCALED A whole fish that has been gutted and scaled, with the gills removed.	1 pound per serving
CLEANED, SCALED, AND HEAD REMOVED A whole fish, gutted and scaled, with the gills, fins, head, and tail removed. (Smaller fish prepared this way may have the tail left on.)	½ to ¾ pound per serving
STEAKS Cross-section cuts from large fish, ¾ to 1¾ inches thick, usually containing a section of backbone and skin. If cut from very large fish, such as swordfish or tuna, the steaks are usually boneless and may be skinless as well.	¼ to ½ pound per serving
FILLETS The meaty sides of fish that are cut off the backbone. Fillets are boneless and may or may not be skinned. Although usually sold in single pieces, butterfly fillets (both sides of the fish taken off the bone held together by the skin) are also available.	¼ to ½ pound per serving

BUYING FRESH FISH

• Buy fresh fish from a reliable fish store with a quick turnover. The fish should be displayed on ice: whole fish on crushed ice, fillets and steaks on trays set on ice and stored in a refrigerated case. Packaged fish should have no visible liquid inside.

• Fresh fish should smell fresh and clean; avoid any with a strong or "fishy" odor.

• For whole fish, look for bright, clear, full eyes (if the eyes are cloudy or sunken, the fish is old), and shiny, brightly colored skin with scales tightly in place. The flesh should feel firm and spring back when pressed with a finger. Gills should be bright pink or red, not dull or brown, and should not show any white slime. The tail should not be curled up or look dried out.

• Fish fillets and steaks should be moist, firm, and dense rather than flaky (no gaps should be visible in the flesh), and appear freshly cut. They should look almost translucent rather than opaque. Some fish, such as tuna, take on a rainbow-like opalescence when handled improperly; it's best to avoid such fish. Pass on those showing signs of dryness, flaking, or discoloration. Any visible bones should be firmly embedded in the flesh.

STORING FRESH FISH

- Once you've chosen your fish, it's important to get it home in good condition, so if you're traveling any distance, or if the weather is extremely hot, have it packed in ice, or put it in a cooler.
- To store fresh fish, wrap it loosely and place in the coldest part of the refrigerator (no warmer than 35° to 40°F). Fresh fish is best used within 1 day.
- Always keep fish cold until you're ready to cook it – bacteria can multiply at room temperature. Don't leave it out while you're preparing the other ingredients.
- Do not store ungutted fish; bacteria in the guts will multiply and cause rapid spoilage.
- While you may be tempted to freeze a surplus of fresh fish, remember that home freezers are never as cold as commercial ones, and home freezing can spoil the flavor and texture of fish. This is due to the slow formation of ice crystals during the freezing process.
- If you must freeze fish, be sure it's impeccably fresh and of high quality. Rinse and dry, then carefully wrap it in moisture-proof and vapor-proof wrap, such as freezer paper, and freeze up to 3 months.
- Fish with the skin left on, whether whole (gutted) or steaks or fillets, freezes best, because the skin helps protect the flesh from the drying effects of the freezer. (To thaw or cook frozen fish, see below.)

BUYING, USING, AND STORING FROZEN FISH

- Packaged frozen raw fish should be tightly wrapped in moisture-proof and vapor-proof material; the flesh should be frozen solid. Avoid fish with white or discolored portions, which may indicate freezer burn or deterioration. There should be no detectable odor.
- Keep frozen fish for no more than 3 months.
- In many cases, frozen fish can be cooked while still frozen, but allow a few more minutes of cooking time.
- Thaw frozen fish overnight in the refrigerator (on a plate to catch drips) in its original wrapping. Once thawed, drain well and pat dry with paper towels before cooking. (If you're short of time, hasten thawing by placing the wrapped fish under cold running water.)
- Never thaw frozen fish at room temperature, or you'll run the risk of bacterial contamination. For the same reason, never thaw fish under warm water.
- Do not refreeze thawed fish.

SCALING A WHOLE FISH

Fresh whole fish are usually sold cleaned and scaled, but some may need additional scaling. Scaling can be messy, so it's best to work on newspapers in or near the sink or outdoors. Rinse frequently under cold running water as you go. You can also use a fish scaler, a small tool with a jagged-edged loop, to do the job.

Hold fish firmly by the tail (dip fingers in coarse salt or use a kitchen or paper towel to help grip more easily) and, holding back edge of a knife at a right angle to the body, scrape toward head to remove scales. Turn fish over and repeat on other side.

SKINNING A FISH FILLET

Round and flatfish fillets are skinned the same way; the procedure is not difficult to master. Use a knife with a long blade; a sharp blade is essential. Before you begin, dip your fingers in coarse salt for a better grip, or hold the tail end with a kitchen or paper towel.

1 Place fillet skin-side down on cutting board. Make a small cut through to skin at base of tail, then loosen flesh from skin just a little with the knife.

2 Pulling skin taut at tail end, use a gentle sawing motion to slide knife toward other end as you release flesh. With tweezers or needle-nose pliers, remove pin bones, if any.

COOKING SUCCESS

• Fish is best cooked briefly. Overcooking can toughen the flesh or cause it to fall apart; it can also ruin the flavor.
• Fish is done as soon as the flesh is no longer translucent and turns opaque all the way through. Remember that fish continues to cook after it has been removed from the heat.
• For steaks and fillets, test for doneness by inserting the point of a knife deep into the thickest part and gently parting the flesh, which should be just opaque throughout.
• For a whole fish, use a small knife and peek at the backbone to see if the flesh is opaque.
• To ensure that fish fillets cook evenly, tuck the thin end underneath if necessary to create a more uniform thickness.
• To estimate cooking time for whole, stuffed, or rolled fish as well as unsauced steaks and fillets, use the "10-minute rule." Allow 10 minutes of cooking time for every inch of thickness. Sauced or frozen fish require more time; see the chart below. (Do not use this rule for microwave or deep-frying, as these cooking methods are much quicker.) Use the rule only as a guideline, checking doneness just before the cooking time indicated.

To determine cooking time, measure the fish at the thickest part. Then time as directed at right.

COOKING TIMES	
Fresh fish	10 minutes per inch
Fresh fish in sauce	15 minutes per inch
Frozen fish	20 minutes per inch

FANTASTIC (NO-FUSS) FLAVORINGS

You don't have to coat fish in a rich, fancy sauce to give it flavor – here are some easy ways to add an exciting taste:
Add a little lemon Or any citrus fruit for that matter. Drape fish fillets with paper-thin lemon slices before baking; add citrus wedges to poaching liquid; or, simply top cooked fish with grated peel and a drizzle of juice for a hit of fresh flavor.
Get in a Mexican mood Serve broiled fish with red or green salsa and chopped fresh cilantro.
Low-fat and luscious Make a satisfying "creamy" sauce by swirling mustard, vinegar, herbs, capers, or green onions into plain low-fat yogurt or reduced-fat mayonnaise.
Veggie good Serve poached, baked, or broiled fish on a bed of sautéed spinach, sweet peppers, onions, or fennel. Or, serve the fish on a green salad; drizzle with citrus vinaigrette.
Think Asian Try poached or baked fish with Asian seasonings such as fresh ginger, green onions, and soy sauce.

SUBSTITUTING FISH

When you want to try a recipe but the tuna or salmon it calls for isn't available, don't worry. Substituting one fish for another is almost always an option, and doing so will add more variety to your recipes.

Fish, a naturally low-fat food, is generally categorized by its fat content, which ranges from lean to oily. As a rule, the oilier the fish, the darker and richer the flesh. Lean fish has delicate, whiter flesh. When choosing a substitute, go for a fish that falls in the same fat category as the one called for (see chart below). Before you make a decision, also consider the flavor and texture of the fish. Most thin, white-fleshed fish fillets, for example, are mild-tasting and flaky. And of course, if the recipe calls for fish steaks, it's best to stick with steaks, though in a pinch you could use firm fillets.
Lean fish The majority of readily available fish fall in this group. Fish with the lowest fat content, or lean fish, have the most delicate texture and mildest flavor. Their fat content may be as little as 2.5 percent, and most of the fat is concentrated in the liver (which is not generally eaten).
Moderately oily fish This category contains fish with a slightly higher fat content, about 6 percent. They have a moderately firm texture and fairly neutral flavor. Some fish, such as tuna, can be classed as moderately oily or oily, depending on the species.
Oily fish The average fat content of oily fish is 12 percent; their flesh is strong-tasting and meaty. Oily fish are rich in Omega-3 fatty acids. Unlike the saturated fats found in meat, Omega-3 fatty acids are a type of polyunsaturated fat that does not clog arteries.

THE FISH EXCHANGE		
LEAN	MODERATE	OILY
Cod, Scrod	Bluefin tuna	Butterfish
Flounder	Bluefish	Herring
Grouper	Catfish	Lake trout
Haddock	Rainbow trout	Mackerel
Hake	Striped bass	Pompano
Halibut	Swordfish	Salmon
Mahi mahi		Shad
Monkfish		Yellowfin tuna
Orange roughy		Whitefish
Pollock		
Red snapper		
Rockfish		
Sea bass		
Sole		
Tilefish		
Turbot		
Whiting		

BROILED FISH

Salmon, tuna, and swordfish are all high in natural oils, which means they remain moist and tender when quickly cooked under the broiler. Brushing the fish with a sauce beforehand will also keep it flavorful. The skin can be left on for easier handling; trim it off with a paring knife before serving, if you like.

SALMON WITH DILL AND CAPER SAUCE

◆◆◆◆◆◆◆◆◆◆◆◆

Prep: 10 minutes
Broil: 10 minutes
Makes 6 main-dish servings

Vegetable oil
1 small bunch fresh dill
2 tablespoons fresh lemon
   juice
¼ cup capers, drained and
   chopped
2 teaspoons sugar
2 teaspoons anchovy paste
1 salmon fillet (about
   2 pounds), with skin
¼ teaspoon salt
Lemon slices for garnish
Sautéed potatoes (optional)

1 Preheat broiler. Grease rack in broiling pan with oil. Prepare sauce: Chop 2 tablespoons dill. In small bowl, mix dill, lemon juice, and next 3 ingredients.

2 Place salmon fillet on work surface, skin-side down. With tweezers, remove any small bones from salmon. Sprinkle salmon fillet with salt on flesh side only.

ANCHOVY PASTE

◆◆◆◆◆◆◆◆◆◆◆◆◆◆◆◆◆◆◆◆◆

Available in tubes, anchovy paste has a slightly more delicate flavor than whole anchovy fillets. Made from pounded salt-cured anchovies mixed with vinegar and spices, it has many uses as a piquant seasoning ingredient. Use it to enhance the dill and caper sauce on this page; mix with margarine or butter to top broiled fish steaks; stir a little into dips and salad dressings; or add to fresh tomato pasta sauces. As a guide: ½ teaspoon paste is equivalent to 1 anchovy fillet.

3 Place salmon on rack in broiling pan; brush sauce on flesh side only. Place pan in broiler 4 to 6 inches from heat source. Broil 10 minutes, without turning, or until salmon is opaque throughout. Cut into 6 pieces. Garnish with dill sprigs and lemon slices and serve with sautéed potatoes, if you like.

EACH SERVING: ABOUT 195 CALORIES, 31g PROTEIN, 3g CARBOHYDRATE, 6g TOTAL FAT (1g SATURATED), 80mg CHOLESTEROL, 680mg SODIUM

SALMON WITH CORN-TOMATO SALSA

Prep: 10 minutes   *Broil:* 6 to 7 minutes
Makes 4 main-dish servings

2 ears corn, husked
1 tablespoon olive oil
1 small red onion, chopped
¼ teaspoon salt
1 medium tomato, diced
1 can (4 to 4½ ounces) chopped mild green chiles, drained
2 tablespoons chopped fresh parsley
2 tablespoons fresh lemon juice
1 teaspoon sugar
4 salmon fillets (about 6 ounces each), with skin
1 tablespoon teriyaki sauce
½ teaspoon coarsely ground black pepper

◆ Preheat broiler. Grease rack in broiling pan. Prepare salsa: Cut corn kernels from cobs. In 1-quart saucepan, heat oil over medium heat; add onion, corn, and salt and cook until onion is tender. Stir in tomato, chiles, parsley, lemon juice, and sugar; heat through. Keep warm.

◆ Place salmon fillets, skin-side down, on rack in broiling pan. Brush tops of fillets evenly with teriyaki sauce; sprinkle with black pepper.

◆ Place pan in broiler at closest position to heat source; broil salmon, without turning, 6 to 7 minutes, until golden brown and opaque throughout. Serve with corn-tomato salsa.

Each serving: About 295 calories, 36g protein, 16g carbohydrate, 9g total fat (1g saturated), 88mg cholesterol, 530mg sodium

HALIBUT WITH PARMESAN TOMATOES

Prep: 10 minutes   *Broil:* 14 minutes
Makes 4 main-dish servings

2 medium tomatoes
2 tablespoons plain dried bread crumbs
1 tablespoon freshly grated Parmesan cheese
1 tablespoon chopped fresh parsley
1 halibut steak, 1½ inches thick (1¼ pounds)
¼ cup mayonnaise
1 tablespoon chopped oil-packed dried tomato
Parsley sprigs and lemon wedges for garnish

◆ Preheat broiler. Cut each tomato in half. Place tomato halves, cut-side up, on rack in broiling pan. In small bowl, mix bread crumbs, Parmesan cheese, and parsley; sprinkle mixture on top of tomatoes.

◆ Place halibut steak on rack with tomatoes. Place pan in broiler about 5 to 7 inches from heat source; broil halibut and tomatoes 6 minutes. Meanwhile, in small bowl, mix mayonnaise with dried tomato.

◆ Turn halibut; cover tomatoes loosely with foil to prevent overbrowning. Broil 6 minutes longer or just until fish is opaque throughout.

◆ Remove pan from broiler; spread mayonnaise mixture on halibut. Continue broiling until topping is browned.

◆ To serve, arrange halibut and tomatoes on platter. Serve garnished with parsley and lemon wedges.

Each serving: About 290 calories, 31g protein, 6g carbohydrate, 15g total fat (2g saturated), 54mg cholesterol, 235mg sodium

FIVE-SPICE SALMON

Prep: 5 minutes   *Broil:* 6 to 7 minutes
Makes 4 main-dish servings

2 teaspoons Chinese five-spice powder
1 teaspoon all-purpose flour
½ teaspoon salt
¼ teaspoon cracked black pepper
4 pieces salmon fillet (about ¼ pound each), with skin

◆ Preheat broiler. Grease rack in broiling pan. In small bowl, mix Chinese five-spice powder, flour, salt, and cracked black pepper. Use to coat flesh side of salmon fillets.

◆ Place salmon fillets, skin-side down, on rack in broiling pan. Place pan in broiler at closest position to heat source; broil salmon, without turning, 6 to 7 minutes, until fish is opaque throughout.

Each serving: About 155 calories, 23g protein, 1g carbohydrate, 6g total fat (1g saturated), 59mg cholesterol, 370mg sodium

FIVE-SPICE POWDER

Used widely in Chinese cooking, five-spice powder may include cinnamon, cloves, fennel seeds, star anise, and Szechuan peppercorns, ground to a fine powder. It is available ready-made from Asian markets and many supermarkets. Every blend is different, and may not be exactly five spices.

  The blend lends pungency to Chinese red-cooked meats and poultry (pork, beef, chicken, or duck simmered in soy sauce with ginger), and is also used in marinades and dipping sauces. Sometimes the whole spices are tied like a bouquet garni in a muslin or cheesecloth bag and added to simmered dishes; the bag is discarded from the finished dish before serving.

GREEK-STYLE SWORDFISH

Prep: 10 minutes   Broil: 8 minutes
Makes 4 main-dish servings

4 swordfish steaks, each
¾ inch thick (about
6 ounces each)
1 tablespoon olive oil
1 can (14½ to 16 ounces)
Italian-style stewed
tomatoes

1 medium tomato, chopped
1 ounce feta cheese,
crumbled (¼ cup)
¼ cup pitted ripe olives,
sliced

◆ Preheat broiler. Brush both sides of swordfish steaks evenly with olive oil; place swordfish steaks on rack in broiling pan.

◆ Place pan in broiler at closest position to heat source; broil swordfish, turning once, 8 minutes, or until fish is opaque throughout.

◆ Meanwhile, in 2-quart saucepan, heat stewed tomatoes to boiling over medium-high heat; boil about 5 minutes, until mixture is slightly thickened.

◆ Spoon stewed tomatoes onto 4 warm dinner plates. Arrange swordfish on top of tomatoes; sprinkle with chopped tomato, feta cheese, and sliced olives.

Each serving: About 295 calories, 36g protein, 6g carbohydrate, 13g total fat (3g saturated), 72mg cholesterol, 480mg sodium

THYME-BROILED SWORDFISH STEAKS

Prep: 5 minutes   Broil: 8 minutes
Makes 4 main-dish servings

4 swordfish steaks, each
¾ inch thick (about
6 ounces each)
1 teaspoon fresh thyme
¾ teaspoon salt

½ teaspoon coarsely ground
black pepper
2 teaspoons olive oil
Thyme or parsley sprigs for
garnish

◆ Preheat broiler. Place swordfish steaks on waxed paper and sprinkle both sides with thyme, salt, and coarsely ground black pepper.

◆ Place swordfish steaks on rack in broiling pan. Drizzle each steak with ½ teaspoon olive oil.

◆ Place pan in broiler at closest position to heat source; broil, without turning, 8 minutes, or until fish is opaque throughout. Serve garnished with thyme sprigs.

Each serving: About 225 calories, 34g protein, 0g carbohydrate, 9g total fat (2g saturated), 66mg cholesterol, 550mg sodium

SWORDFISH STEAKS STUFFED WITH DRIED TOMATOES

Prep: 15 minutes   Broil: 11 to 13 minutes
Makes 4 main-dish servings

2 tablespoons finely chopped,
drained oil-packed dried
tomatoes
1 teaspoon grated lemon peel
4 swordfish steaks, each
1 inch thick (about
6 ounces each)

2 tablespoons margarine or
butter, softened
2 tablespoons chopped fresh
parsley
¼ teaspoon salt
Lemon slices for garnish
Cooked pasta (optional)

◆ Preheat broiler. Reserve 2 teaspoons chopped dried tomatoes and ½ teaspoon grated lemon peel for topping. In cup, stir together remaining chopped dried tomatoes and grated lemon peel.

◆ With knife, cut each swordfish steak horizontally through center along a long edge, almost but not all the way through, to form pocket. Spread some dried-tomato mixture from cup in each pocket.

◆ Place swordfish steaks on rack in broiling pan. Place pan in broiler at closest position to heat source; broil swordfish 5 minutes. Turn swordfish; broil 5 to 7 minutes longer, until opaque throughout.

◆ Meanwhile, in small bowl, mix margarine, chopped parsley, salt, and reserved chopped dried tomatoes and grated lemon peel. Spread parsley mixture over tops of broiled swordfish steaks; broil 1 minute longer. Garnish with lemon slices and serve with pasta, if you like.

Each serving: About 265 calories, 34g protein, 1g carbohydrate, 13g total fat (3g saturated), 66mg cholesterol, 360mg sodium

Fresh tuna and vegetable salad

Prep: 35 minutes   *Broil:* 8 minutes
Makes 4 main-dish servings

½ cup vegetable oil
3 large potatoes (about
  1½ pounds), peeled and cut
  into 1½-inch chunks
1 medium onion, chopped
Salt and ground black pepper
2 medium zucchini, cut into
  1½-inch chunks
1½ teaspoons fresh rosemary
  or ½ teaspoon dried
  rosemary, crushed
2 tuna steaks, each ¾ inch
  thick (about ½ pound each)

2 tablespoons chopped oil-
  packed dried tomatoes,
  2 tablespoons of oil
  reserved
3 tablespoons white wine
  vinegar
1½ teaspoons sugar
Boston lettuce leaves
2 medium tomatoes, cut into
  bite-size chunks

◆ In 12-inch skillet, heat 3 tablespoons vegetable oil over medium heat; add potatoes, onion, ½ teaspoon salt, and ¼ teaspoon pepper and cook, covered, about 20 minutes, until potatoes are golden and tender, turning potatoes occasionally. Transfer potato mixture to bowl.

◆ In same skillet, heat 1 tablespoon vegetable oil over medium-high heat. Add zucchini, rosemary, and ¼ teaspoon salt and cook, stirring frequently, until zucchini is lightly browned and tender-crisp. Transfer cooked zucchini to another bowl.

◆ Preheat broiler. Place tuna on rack in broiling pan. Spoon reserved oil from dried tomatoes into cup; brush tops of tuna steaks with some of the tomato oil; sprinkle lightly with salt and pepper.

◆ Place pan in broiler at closest position to heat source; broil tuna steaks 4 minutes. Turn tuna steaks; brush with remaining tomato oil. Sprinkle with salt and pepper and broil 4 minutes longer, or until pale pink in center when cut with knife for medium, or until desired doneness.

◆ Meanwhile, prepare vinaigrette: In small bowl, with wire whisk or fork, mix white wine vinegar, sugar, remaining ¼ cup vegetable oil, ¾ teaspoon salt, and ¼ teaspoon pepper.

◆ Assemble salad: With fork, break tuna steaks into large chunks. Arrange lettuce leaves on large platter; arrange tuna, tomato chunks, potato mixture, and zucchini on top.

◆ Sprinkle dried tomatoes over tuna. Drizzle vinaigrette over tuna and vegetables. Serve tuna salad at room temperature.

Each serving: About 795 calories, 32g protein, 48g carbohydrate, 54g total fat (10g saturated), 43mg cholesterol, 875mg sodium

Sicilian tuna

Prep: 30 minutes plus chilling   *Broil:* 8 minutes
Makes 8 main-dish servings

4 anchovy fillets, chopped
1 garlic clove, minced
¼ teaspoon dried thyme
⅛ teaspoon ground black
  pepper
6 tablespoons olive oil
5 tablespoons fresh lemon
  juice
8 tuna steaks, each ¾ inch
  thick (about 4 ounces each)

1 large celery stalk, sliced
3 medium plum tomatoes,
  diced
2 green onions, sliced
¼ cup pitted ripe olives, thinly
  sliced
2 tablespoons capers, drained
¼ cup chopped fresh basil

In baking dish, mix anchovies, garlic, thyme, pepper, 3 tablespoons oil, and 3 tablespoons lemon juice. Add tuna, turning to coat. Refrigerate, turning once, at least 45 minutes. Preheat broiler. In 2-quart saucepan, heat remaining 3 tablespoons oil over medium heat; add celery and cook 5 minutes. Add next 4 ingredients; cook 5 minutes. Stir in basil and remaining 2 tablespoons lemon juice; keep warm. Meanwhile, place tuna on rack in broiling pan. Broil at closest position to heat source, turning once, about 8 minutes, until pale pink in center when cut with knife for medium, or until desired doneness. Serve with sauce.

Each serving: About 275 calories, 28g protein, 3g carbohydrate, 17g total fat (3g saturated), 44mg cholesterol, 220mg sodium

Scrod with tomato relish

Prep: 10 minutes   *Broil:* 6 to 8 minutes
Makes 4 main-dish servings

3 teaspoons vegetable oil
1 small onion, diced
1 can (28 ounces) plum
  tomatoes, drained and cut
  into quarters
¼ cup red wine vinegar

2 tablespoons brown sugar
Salt
4 pieces scrod fillet (about
  6 ounces each)
¼ teaspoon coarsely ground
  black pepper

Prepare tomato relish: In 2-quart saucepan, heat 2 teaspoons oil over medium heat. Add onion and *2 tablespoons water*; cook 10 minutes, until onion is tender and golden. Stir in tomatoes, vinegar, brown sugar, and ¼ teaspoon salt; heat to boiling over high heat. Continue cooking, stirring frequently, 10 to 15 minutes, until relish thickens. Meanwhile, preheat broiler. Place scrod on rack in broiling pan. Sprinkle with pepper, ¼ teaspoon salt, and remaining 1 teaspoon oil. Broil at closest position to heat source, without turning, 6 to 8 minutes, until opaque throughout. To serve, spoon tomato relish over scrod.

Each serving: About 245 calories, 32g protein, 19g carbohydrate, 5g total fat (1g saturated), 73mg cholesterol, 685mg sodium

PANFRIED FISH

Dip fish in seasoned flour, cornmeal, or even shredded potatoes, then panfry to create a golden-crisp crust. These fish become fragile when cooked, so turn them only once.

COD WITH CRISPY POTATO CRUST

◆◆◆◆◆◆◆◆◆◆◆◆

Prep: 20 minutes
Cook: 20 to 30 minutes
Makes 4 main-dish servings

4 tablespoons olive or vegetable oil
1 medium onion, minced
2 large egg whites
⅛ teaspoon ground white pepper
3 tablespoons cornstarch
2 large baking potatoes (1 pound)
4 pieces cod or scrod fillet, each 1 inch thick (about 6 ounces each)
1 teaspoon salt
Balsamic Sauce (see below)
Green beans and oil-packed dried tomatoes (optional)

BALSAMIC SAUCE

In 1-quart saucepan, mix 1 tablespoon sugar, 2 tablespoons balsamic vinegar, ½ extra-large vegetable bouillon cube, 1 teaspoon cornstarch, and ¾ cup water. Heat to boiling, stirring constantly. Reduce heat and simmer 1 minute, stirring, or until sauce thickens slightly. Keep warm. Makes about ¾ cup.

1 In small saucepan, heat 1 tablespoon oil over medium-high heat; add onion and cook until lightly browned. Transfer to bowl; cool slightly. Stir egg whites, pepper, and 1 tablespoon cornstarch into onion.

2 Peel potatoes and shred onto kitchen towel. Wrap potatoes in towel and squeeze out as much liquid as possible. Stir potatoes into egg-white mixture in bowl.

3 Sprinkle cod fillets with salt. Place remaining 2 tablespoons cornstarch on sheet of waxed paper. Carefully dip cod into cornstarch, turning to coat both sides.

4 Spread scant ¼ cup potato mixture on top of each cod fillet, pressing firmly; turn fillets and spread each with another scant ¼ cup potato mixture.

5 In nonstick 12-inch skillet, heat 2 tablespoons oil over medium heat. Add 2 cod fillets; cook, turning once, 10 to 15 minutes, until opaque throughout. Transfer to plate; keep warm. Heat remaining 1 tablespoon oil; repeat with remaining cod. Meanwhile, prepare sauce. Serve cod with sauce, and green beans and dried tomatoes, if you like.

EACH SERVING: ABOUT 395 CALORIES, 34g PROTEIN, 38g CARBOHYDRATE, 11g TOTAL FAT (2g SATURATED), 74mg CHOLESTEROL, 830mg SODIUM

TROUT WITH A CORNMEAL CRUST

Prep: 25 minutes   *Cook:* 6 minutes
Makes 4 main-dish servings

Spicy Corn Relish (see below)
4 brook or rainbow trout fillets
  (¼ pound each)
¾ teaspoon salt
½ teaspoon ground black pepper
3 tablespoons yellow cornmeal
1 tablespoon all-purpose flour
1 teaspoon paprika
2 tablespoons vegetable oil

◆ Prepare Spicy Corn Relish; set aside.
Sprinkle fillets with salt and pepper.
On waxed paper, mix cornmeal, flour,
and paprika. Dip fillets into cornmeal
mixture, turning to coat both sides.

◆ In 12-inch skillet, heat oil over
medium-high heat; add fish fillets and
cook, carefully turning fillets once,
6 minutes, until fish is golden brown
and opaque throughout. Serve with
Spicy Corn Relish.

**Each serving: About 325 calories,
27g protein, 24g carbohydrate, 14g total
fat (2g saturated), 65mg cholesterol,
600mg sodium**

SPICY CORN RELISH

Cook 4 ears corn; cut kernels from cobs.
In medium bowl, mix corn, 1 large red
pepper, diced, 2 jalapeño chiles, minced,
2 tablespoons cider vinegar, 1 tablespoon
olive or vegetable oil, 1 tablespoon
chopped fresh cilantro, ½ teaspoon sugar,
and ¼ teaspoon salt. Makes about
2¼ cups.

ORANGE ROUGHY WITH CHICORY-ORANGE SALAD

Prep: 20 minutes   *Cook:* 5 minutes
Makes 2 main-dish servings

2 teaspoons red wine vinegar
2 tablespoons olive or vegetable oil
¼ teaspoon sugar
Salt
¼ small head chicory (about 4 ounces)
1 medium cucumber, seeded and cut into
  ½-inch chunks
1 navel orange, peeled and sliced
1 small red pepper, diced
1 small red onion, thinly sliced
2 teaspoons all-purpose flour
⅛ teaspoon ground black pepper
2 medium orange roughy fillets
  (6 ounces each)
2 tablespoons pesto

◆ Prepare chicory-orange salad: In
large bowl, mix red wine vinegar,
1 tablespoon oil, sugar, and ¼ teaspoon
salt until blended. Add chicory,
cucumber, orange, red pepper, and
onion; toss to coat. Set aside.

◆ On waxed paper, mix flour, black
pepper, and ¼ teaspoon salt. Dip
orange roughy fillets into flour
mixture, turning to coat both sides.

◆ In nonstick 10-inch skillet, heat
remaining 1 tablespoon oil over
medium-high heat; add orange roughy
fillets and cook, carefully turning fillets
once, about 5 minutes, until fish is
golden brown and opaque throughout.
Spread top of fillets with pesto.

◆ To serve, arrange orange roughy
fillets and chicory-orange salad on
2 plates.

**Each serving: About 420 calories,
30g protein, 26g carbohydrate, 23g total
fat (3g saturated), 36mg cholesterol,
800mg sodium**

RED SNAPPER WITH COLLARD GREENS

Prep: 15 minutes   *Cook:* 20 minutes
Makes 4 main-dish servings

2 tablespoons vegetable oil
1 medium onion, coarsely chopped
1 large bunch collard greens (about
  1¼ pounds), coarsely chopped
Salt
1 can (15 to 19 ounces) black-eyed peas,
  rinsed and drained
1 tablespoon all-purpose flour
1 teaspoon paprika
½ teaspoon dried thyme
⅛ teaspoon ground red pepper (cayenne)
4 red snapper fillets (¼ pound each),
  with skin
1 tablespoon fresh lemon juice
Lemon slices and parsley sprigs for
  garnish

◆ In 3-quart saucepan, heat
1 tablespoon oil over medium-high
heat. Add onion and cook, stirring
frequently, until tender; add collard
greens and ½ teaspoon salt and
continue cooking until vegetables
begin to brown. Add ¼ cup water.
Reduce heat to low; cover and simmer,
stirring occasionally, 5 minutes, or
until greens are tender. Stir in black-
eyed peas; heat through. Keep warm
over low heat.

◆ On waxed paper, combine flour,
paprika, thyme, red pepper, and
¾ teaspoon salt. Press flesh side of
fillets into flour mixture to coat.

◆ In nonstick 12-inch skillet, heat
remaining 1 tablespoon oil over
medium-high heat; add fillets and
cook, turning once, 5 to 7 minutes,
until fish is golden brown and opaque
throughout; transfer to warm platter.
Add lemon juice and *1 tablespoon water*
to skillet. Heat to boiling; pour over
snapper. To serve, arrange greens on
platter with snapper. Garnish with
lemon slices and parsley sprigs.

**Each serving: About 375 calories,
35g protein, 39g carbohydrate, 9g total fat
(2g saturated), 41mg cholesterol,
770mg sodium**

FISH CAKES

Delicate-flavored cod fillets make fantastic fish cakes, though other fish, such as fresh or even canned salmon, also provide delicious results. For fluffy cakes, chop fish fine by hand – ground fish becomes compact during mixing, making dense and heavy cakes.

CODFISH CAKES

◆◆◆◆◆◆◆◆◆◆◆◆◆◆

Prep: 20 minutes plus chilling
Cook: 10 to 12 minutes
Makes 4 main-dish servings

Tartar Sauce (optional, see below) `
3 tablespoons vegetable oil
2 large celery stalks, chopped
1 small onion, chopped
3 slices firm white bread
1 piece cod fillet (1 pound)
1 large egg
2 tablespoons light mayonnaise
1 tablespoon chopped fresh parsley
1 teaspoon cayenne-pepper sauce
1 teaspoon fresh lemon juice
½ teaspoon salt
Arugula for garnish
Lemon wedges (optional)

TARTAR SAUCE

In small bowl, combine ¼ cup light mayonnaise, 2 tablespoons chopped fresh parsley, 2 teaspoons Dijon mustard, 2 teaspoons sweet pickle relish, and 2 teaspoons fresh lemon juice until blended. Cover and refrigerate. Makes about ⅓ cup.

1 Prepare Tartar Sauce, if you like; set aside. In 12-inch skillet, heat 1 tablespoon oil over medium heat; add celery and onion and cook, covered, until tender and lightly browned, stirring occasionally. Remove from heat; set aside. In food processor with knife blade attached or in blender, process bread to fine crumbs. Place two-thirds of bread crumbs on sheet of waxed paper. Place remaining crumbs in bowl.

2 With tweezers, pull out bones from cod fillet, if any. With large chef's knife, finely chop fish; add to bowl with bread crumbs. Mix in celery and onion mixture, egg, mayonnaise, parsley, pepper sauce, lemon juice, and salt until well combined.

3 Shape fish mixture into four 3-inch round patties (mixture will be very soft and moist); refrigerate until firm (at least 30 minutes) for easier handling. Wipe skillet clean.

4 Carefully dip patties, one at a time, into crumbs on waxed paper, turning to coat both sides. In same skillet, heat remaining 2 tablespoons oil over medium-low heat.

5 Add patties to skillet and cook, turning once, 10 to 12 minutes, until cooked through. Garnish and serve with lemon and Tartar Sauce, if you like.

EACH SERVING: ABOUT 290 CALORIES, 24g PROTEIN, 14g CARBOHYDRATE, 15g TOTAL FAT (3g SATURATED), 105mg CHOLESTEROL, 475mg SODIUM

MEXICAN FISH CAKES

Prep: 25 minutes   *Cook:* 12 to 15 minutes
Makes 4 main-dish servings

2 tablespoons vegetable oil
1 medium onion, finely chopped
1 large garlic clove, minced
¼ teaspoon ground cinnamon
¼ teaspoon ground cumin
Pinch ground cloves
3 slices firm white bread
1 piece cod fillet (1 pound)
1 large egg
1 tablespoon fresh lime juice
1 jalapeño chile, seeded and minced
½ teaspoon salt
3 tablespoons chopped fresh cilantro
1 tablespoon margarine or butter
Lime wedges for serving

◆ In 12-inch skillet, heat 1 tablespoon oil over medium heat. Add onion and cook 5 minutes, or until tender. Stir in garlic, cinnamon, cumin, and cloves; cook 30 seconds. Place onion mixture in medium bowl; wipe skillet clean.

◆ In food processor with knife blade attached or in blender, process 1 slice bread to fine crumbs; place in bowl with onion mixture. Process remaining 2 slices bread to fine crumbs and place on waxed paper.

◆ With tweezers, pull out bones, if any, from fish. Finely chop fish; add to bowl with crumbs. Mix in egg, next 3 ingredients, and 2 tablespoons cilantro. Shape fish mixture into four 3-inch round patties. On waxed paper, toss remaining 1 tablespoon cilantro with crumbs; carefully dip patties, one at a time, into mixture, turning to coat both sides.

◆ In same skillet, melt margarine with remaining 1 tablespoon oil over medium-low heat. Add patties and cook, turning once, 12 to 15 minutes, until browned and cooked through. Serve with lime wedges.

Each serving: About 270 calories, 24g protein, 14g carbohydrate, 12g total fat (2g saturated), 103mg cholesterol, 500mg sodium

SALMON BURGERS

Prep: 15 minutes   *Cook:* 10 minutes
Makes 4 main-dish servings

Pickled Ginger (optional, see below)
1 piece salmon fillet (1 pound), skin removed, if any
2 green onions, thinly sliced
2 tablespoons soy sauce
1 teaspoon grated, peeled fresh ginger
¼ teaspoon ground black pepper
¼ cup plain dried bread crumbs
2 tablespoons sesame seeds
1 tablespoon vegetable oil

◆ Prepare Pickled Ginger, if you like. Set aside. With tweezers, pull out bones, if any, from fish. Finely chop fish. Place in bowl and mix in green onions, soy sauce, ginger, and pepper. Shape into four 3-inch round patties.

◆ On waxed paper, combine bread crumbs and sesame seeds; carefully dip patties, one at a time, into mixture, turning to coat both sides.

◆ In nonstick 10-inch skillet, heat oil over medium heat. Add patties and cook, turning once, 10 minutes, until browned and cooked through. Serve with Pickled Ginger, if you like.

Each serving: About 220 calories, 25g protein, 6g carbohydrate, 10g total fat (2g saturated), 59mg cholesterol, 650mg sodium

PICKLED GINGER

In 1-quart saucepan, combine 1 cup water, ½ cup white vinegar, and ¼ cup sugar. Heat to boiling over high heat. Add ¼ cup peeled, thinly sliced fresh ginger; reduce heat to low and simmer 30 minutes, or until tender. Drain.

SALMON PATTIES WITH CAPER SAUCE

Prep: 15 minutes   *Cook:* 5 to 10 minutes
Makes 6 main-dish servings

½ cup mayonnaise
1 tablespoon fresh lemon juice
1 tablespoon minced fresh parsley
1 tablespoon capers, drained and minced
2 slices firm white bread
3 cans (7½ to 7¾ ounces each) salmon, drained, skin and bones removed
1 large egg
3 green onions, chopped
¼ cup milk
2 tablespoons Dijon mustard
2 teaspoons Worcestershire sauce
¼ teaspoon hot-pepper sauce
½ cup plain dried bread crumbs
2 tablespoons vegetable oil
2 tablespoons margarine or butter

◆ Prepare caper sauce: In small bowl, stir together mayonnaise, lemon juice, parsley, and capers; refrigerate.

◆ In food processor with knife blade attached or in blender, process bread to fine crumbs; place in large bowl. Add salmon, egg, green onions, milk, mustard, Worcestershire, and hot-pepper sauce. Mix lightly until blended, leaving salmon in large chunks. Shape salmon mixture into six ½-inch-thick round patties.

◆ Place dried bread crumbs on waxed paper. Carefully dip patties, one at a time, into crumbs, turning to coat both sides.

◆ In 12-inch skillet, heat oil with margarine over medium heat; add patties and cook, turning once, 5 to 10 minutes, until browned and heated through. Serve patties with caper sauce.

Each serving: About 440 calories, 25g protein, 13g carbohydrate, 32g total fat (6g saturated), 106mg cholesterol, 1075mg sodium

POACHED AND STEAMED FISH

Delicate foods such as fish are often poached – cooked in gently simmering liquid. Poached fish can be served hot or cold. Steamed fish does not come in contact with the liquid but is cooked by a surrounding vapor bath. Both poached and steamed fish tend to be pale in color, so they are especially nice paired with colorful sauces.

COLD POACHED SALMON WITH SAUTÉED CUCUMBERS

◆◆◆◆◆◆◆◆◆◆◆◆◆◆◆

Prep: 10 minutes plus chilling
Cook: 12 to 15 minutes
Makes 4 main-dish servings

1 medium lemon
1 bunch watercress
½ cup light sour cream
2 teaspoons chopped fresh tarragon or ¼ teaspoon dried tarragon
1½ teaspoons sugar
Salt
4 salmon steaks (about 6 ounces each)
½ teaspoon coarsely ground black pepper
1 medium onion, sliced
1 tablespoon vegetable oil
3 medium cucumbers (about 1¾ pounds), seeded and cut into 1½-inch chunks
1 tablespoon soy sauce
¼ teaspoon crushed red pepper
Radishes and watercress sprigs for garnish

1 Squeeze 1 tablespoon juice from lemon; set juice and lemon shell aside. Prepare watercress sauce: Remove tough stems from watercress (you should have about 3 cups). In blender or in food processor with knife blade attached, blend watercress, sour cream, tarragon, 1 teaspoon sugar, 1 teaspoon salt, and reserved lemon juice until smooth. Cover and refrigerate. Rub salmon steaks with black pepper and ¾ teaspoon salt.

◆◆◆◆◆◆◆◆◆◆◆◆◆◆◆◆◆◆◆◆◆◆◆◆◆◆◆

SEEDING CUCUMBERS

Trim ends from cucumbers, then cut each lengthwise in half. With a small spoon, scoop out the seeds; discard. (Peeling is needed only if the skin seems very thick or tough, or tastes bitter. The peel adds color and helps the cucumbers hold their shape during cooking.)

◆◆◆◆◆◆◆◆◆◆◆◆◆◆◆◆◆◆◆◆◆◆◆

2 In 12-inch skillet, heat *½ inch water* to boiling over high heat. Add lemon shell, onion, and salmon; heat to boiling. Reduce heat to medium-low. Cover and simmer 5 to 8 minutes, until fish is opaque throughout.

3 Carefully transfer fish to platter; refrigerate about 30 minutes, until cool. Meanwhile, in 10-inch skillet, heat oil over medium-high heat. Add cucumbers, soy sauce, red pepper, and remaining ½ teaspoon sugar; cook, stirring constantly, until cucumbers are coated.

4 Reduce heat to medium; cook, stirring frequently, 5 minutes longer or until cucumbers are just tender-crisp. To serve, divide cucumbers and salmon steaks among 4 plates. Spoon watercress sauce over salmon; serve garnished with radishes and watercress sprigs.

EACH SERVING: ABOUT 315 CALORIES, 38g PROTEIN, 15g CARBOHYDRATE, 12g TOTAL FAT (2g SATURATED), 98mg CHOLESTEROL, 810mg SODIUM

MONKFISH ESCABÈCHE

Prep: 20 minutes plus chilling   Cook: 30 minutes
Makes 4 main-dish servings

1½ pounds monkfish or cod
   fillets
2 tablespoons fresh lemon
   juice
Salt
3 tablespoons olive or
   vegetable oil
1 small onion, finely chopped
1 medium red pepper, finely
   chopped

1 medium green pepper,
   finely chopped
1 small tomato, finely
   chopped
½ cup dry white wine
2 tablespoons red wine
   vinegar
1 teaspoon dried oregano
¼ teaspoon coarsely ground
   black pepper

◆ Pull tough, grayish membrane from monkfish fillets. Slice fillets crosswise into ¾-inch-thick pieces. In 12-inch skillet, heat monkfish, lemon juice, ½ teaspoon salt, and *1½ cups water* to boiling over high heat. Reduce heat to low; cover and simmer about 8 minutes, or until fish is pierced easily with knife. Transfer monkfish to paper-towel-lined plate to drain. Discard poaching liquid. Wipe skillet dry.

◆ In same skillet, heat oil over medium-high heat; add onion and red and green peppers and cook about 10 minutes, until tender. Add tomato, white wine, vinegar, oregano, pepper, and 1¼ teaspoons salt; heat to boiling. Cook, stirring frequently, about 5 minutes, or until liquid is reduced by half. Spoon half of sauce onto platter; arrange monkfish pieces on top. Spoon remaining sauce over monkfish. Cover and refrigerate until monkfish is well chilled.

Each serving: About 265 calories, 26g protein, 8g carbohydrate, 13g total fat (1g saturated), 42mg cholesterol, 730mg sodium

MEDITERRANEAN SWORDFISH

Prep: 15 minutes   Cook: 30 minutes
Makes 4 main-dish servings

1 swordfish steak, about
   1½ inches thick (1¾ pounds)
2 tablespoons olive or
   vegetable oil
1 pound small red potatoes,
   each cut into quarters
Salt
2 medium zucchini (about
   8 ounces each), thickly
   sliced
1 bunch radishes, each cut in
   half

1 tablespoon fresh lemon
   juice
1 tablespoon capers, drained
1 teaspoon chicken-flavor
   instant bouillon
½ teaspoon dried rosemary
¼ teaspoon ground black
   pepper
1 tablespoon minced fresh
   parsley
1 tablespoon grated lemon
   peel

◆ Remove skin and bone from swordfish, if any; cut fish into 1½-inch chunks. In 10-inch skillet, heat oil over medium-high heat. Add potatoes and cook about

10 minutes, until browned; with slotted spoon, transfer to bowl. In oil remaining in skillet, cook swordfish with ¼ teaspoon salt, stirring, about 1 minute, just until fish is lightly browned. Transfer fish to bowl with potatoes. In same skillet, cook zucchini and radishes with ¼ teaspoon salt, stirring, until tender-crisp; transfer to another bowl.

◆ Add lemon juice, next 4 ingredients, and *¼ cup water* to skillet. Return potatoes and swordfish to skillet; heat to boiling over high heat. Reduce heat to low; cover and simmer 10 to 12 minutes, until potatoes are tender and swordfish is opaque throughout. Stir in parsley and zucchini mixture; heat through. Sprinkle with lemon peel.

Each serving: About 420 calories, 43g protein, 27g carbohydrate, 15g total fat (3g saturated), 77mg cholesterol, 760mg sodium

STEAMED FLOUNDER

Prep: 15 minutes   Cook: 10 to 15 minutes
Makes 6 main-dish servings

2 large green onions
1 piece fresh ginger, about
   2 inches long, peeled
2 tablespoons dry sherry
2 teaspoons soy sauce

½ teaspoon chicken-flavor
   instant bouillon
6 flounder fillets (about
   1½ pounds)
1 tablespoon minced ham

◆ Slice green onions and ginger into 2-inch-long matchstick-thin strips. In large bowl, mix sherry, soy sauce, and bouillon. Add fish fillets, turning to coat; fold each fillet in half and arrange, slightly overlapping, in deep heatproof platter or shallow casserole that will fit in a large wok or roasting pan. Sprinkle green onions, ginger, and any remaining sherry mixture over fish.

◆ Pour *1 to 2 inches water* into wok. Place steamer or rack in wok. Set platter with fish on steamer. Heat water to boiling over high heat. Reduce heat to medium. Cover; steam fish 10 to 15 minutes, until opaque throughout. Sprinkle with ham.

Each serving: About 115 calories, 22g protein, 1g carbohydrate, 1g total fat (0g saturated), 56mg cholesterol, 300mg sodium

---

BAMBOO STEAMER

Instead of using a platter on a rack, use a traditional bamboo steamer. Line steamer with lettuce or cabbage leaves and arrange fish on top. Set steamer in wok over boiling water, cover, and steam as directed.

BAKED FISH

Baking is one of the easiest ways to cook fish. Mild fish, such as scrod, sole, and red snapper, gain added moisture and flavor when baked with vegetables. As is true for all fish recipes, the most important rule for baking is not to overcook the fish.

1 Preheat oven to 425°F. Cut each potato crosswise into thin slices.

2 Trim root end and stalks from fennel bulb and cut bulb crosswise into thin slices. In 2½-quart casserole, toss potatoes, fennel, garlic, olive oil, ¾ teaspoon salt, and ¼ teaspoon pepper.

BAKED SCROD WITH FENNEL AND POTATOES

◆◆◆◆◆◆◆◆◆◆◆◆◆

Prep: 15 minutes
Bake: 55 to 60 minutes
Makes 4 main-dish servings

4 large red potatoes (about 1½ pounds)
1 medium fennel bulb
1 garlic clove, minced
2 tablespoons olive oil
Salt and coarsely ground black pepper
1 piece scrod fillet (1¼ pounds), cut into 4 pieces
1 medium tomato, seeded and diced
Feathery fennel tops for garnish

3 Bake 45 minutes, or until vegetables are fork-tender and lightly browned, stirring once. Sprinkle scrod with ¼ teaspoon pepper and ⅛ teaspoon salt. Arrange scrod in a single layer on top of potato mixture.

4 Bake 10 to 15 minutes longer, until fish is opaque throughout. Sprinkle scrod with diced tomato and serve garnished with fennel tops.

WHAT'S IN A NAME?

◆◆◆◆◆◆◆◆◆◆◆◆◆

Although many people think of it as a different species, scrod is just small cod (under 2½ pounds). It is, however, more tender and sweet than full-sized cod. Small haddock and pollock are also sold as scrod. Broiled scrod is a specialty of New England.

EACH SERVING: ABOUT 365 CALORIES, 29g PROTEIN, 37g CARBOHYDRATE, 8g TOTAL FAT (1g SATURATED), 61mg CHOLESTEROL, 565mg SODIUM

SCROD WITH LEMON-GARLIC BREAD CRUMBS

Prep: 10 minutes   Bake: 10 to 15 minutes
Makes 4 main-dish servings

2 slices firm white bread
2 tablespoons margarine or butter
1 garlic clove, minced
4 pieces scrod or cod fillet (about 6 ounces each)
2 tablespoons fresh lemon juice
¾ teaspoon salt
Lemon wedges (optional)
Parsley sprigs for garnish

◆ Preheat oven to 450°F. In food processor with knife blade attached or in blender, process bread until fine crumbs form.

◆ In 10-inch skillet, melt margarine over medium heat. Add garlic; cook until golden. Add bread crumbs and cook, stirring often, until lightly toasted. Remove skillet from heat.

◆ In 13" by 9" glass baking dish, arrange scrod fillets; sprinkle with lemon juice and salt. Press bread-crumb mixture onto tops of fillets. Bake scrod 10 to 15 minutes, until fish is opaque throughout.

◆ To serve, arrange fish on platter; serve with lemon wedges, if you like, and garnish with parsley sprigs.

Each serving: About 225 calories, 31g protein, 7g carbohydrate, 7g total fat (1g saturated), 73mg cholesterol, 625mg sodium

RED SNAPPER WITH OLIVES

Prep: 20 minutes   Bake: 30 minutes
Makes 4 main-dish servings

1 medium lemon
1 small red pepper
⅓ cup Niçoise olives, pitted, or ½ cup pitted ripe olives, sliced
2 medium shallots or 1 small onion, thinly sliced and separated into rings
2 tablespoons capers, drained and chopped
2 tablespoons olive or vegetable oil
½ teaspoon salt
½ teaspoon ground black pepper
2 whole red snapper (about 1¾ pounds each), cleaned and scaled, with head and tail left on
1 cup reduced-sodium chicken broth
1 large tomato, seeded and diced
2 tablespoons chopped fresh parsley

◆ Preheat oven to 350°F. Grate peel and squeeze 2 tablespoons juice from lemon. Cut red pepper into matchstick-thin 1-inch-long strips. In small bowl, mix lemon peel, red-pepper strips, olives, shallots, capers, and 1 tablespoon oil. In cup, mix salt, black pepper, and remaining 1 tablespoon oil.

◆ Rinse fish with cold running water; pat dry with paper towels. Place fish in large roasting pan; brush with olive-oil mixture, then sprinkle with olive mixture. Pour broth and reserved lemon juice around fish; sprinkle diced tomato around fish.

◆ Bake 30 minutes, or until fish is opaque throughout. With pancake turners, carefully transfer fish to warm platter. Stir 1 tablespoon parsley into sauce in pan; spoon sauce around fish. Sprinkle fish with remaining 1 tablespoon parsley.

Each serving: About 400 calories, 60g protein, 10g carbohydrate, 13g total fat (2g saturated), 103mg cholesterol, 685mg sodium

EASY STUFFED SOLE

Prep: 20 minutes   Bake: 20 minutes
Makes 6 main-dish servings

½ pound sea scallops
1 bunch watercress, tough stems removed, leaves chopped
2 tablespoons plus 2 teaspoons margarine or butter
1 medium carrot, coarsely shredded
1 green onion, minced
1 large egg white
¼ teaspoon ground black pepper
1 tablespoon plus ½ cup dry white wine
Salt
4 sole fillets (about ½ pound each)
1 slice white bread, torn into tiny pieces

◆ Preheat oven to 350°F. Rinse scallops with cold running water; pull tough crescent-shaped muscle from side of each scallop. Pat dry. Reserve 1 tablespoon watercress. In 10-inch skillet, melt 1 tablespoon margarine over medium heat; add carrot, green onion, and remaining watercress and cook until tender. Remove skillet from heat.

◆ In food processor with knife blade attached, blend scallops to a paste. Blend in egg white, pepper, 1 tablespoon wine, and ½ teaspoon salt; slowly pour in ¼ *cup water* and blend just until mixed. Remove blade; stir in vegetable mixture.

◆ Grease 13" by 9" baking dish. Arrange 2 fillets in dish. Sprinkle with ⅛ teaspoon salt; spread evenly with scallop mixture. Top with remaining fillets; sprinkle with ⅛ teaspoon salt. Pour remaining ½ cup wine over; dot with 1 tablespoon margarine. Bake 15 minutes, basting occasionally.

◆ Meanwhile, melt remaining 2 teaspoons margarine over medium heat; add bread pieces and cook until golden. Remove from heat; stir in reserved watercress. Sprinkle bread mixture over fillets; bake 5 minutes longer, or until fish is opaque throughout. Serve with pan juices.

Each serving: About 255 calories, 36g protein, 5g carbohydrate, 7g total fat (1g saturated), 85mg cholesterol, 510mg sodium

Wrapped Baked Fish

Baking fish in a paper wrapping – *en papillote* – allows it to steam in its own juices, locking in moistness and delicious natural flavors. For even cooking, choose fillets of uniform thickness.

SALMON AND VEGETABLES IN PARCHMENT

◆◆◆◆◆◆◆◆◆◆◆

Prep: 15 minutes
Bake: 15 minutes
Makes 4 main-dish servings

2 medium carrots
½ bunch watercress
4 ounces mushrooms, sliced
¾ teaspoon lemon and herb seasoning
1 piece salmon fillet (1¼ pounds)
4 heart-shaped pieces or squares (12 inches) cooking parchment or foil (see below)
2 tablespoons margarine or butter, cut up

PAPER PACKAGES
◆◆◆◆◆◆◆◆◆◆◆

To make a heart, fold a 12-inch sheet of cooking parchment or foil in half, and draw half a heart shape with the center on the fold. Cut just inside the line; the open heart should be 3 inches larger than the fillet. Or simply use a 12-inch square of parchment or foil. Parchment makes the best presentation as it puffs nicely when baked.

1 Preheat oven to 400°F. With vegetable peeler, shave each carrot lengthwise into thin strips.

2 Remove tough stems from watercress. In bowl, toss watercress, carrots, mushrooms, and lemon and herb seasoning. Remove salmon skin, if any; cut salmon into 4 pieces.

3 Reserve one-fourth of watercress mixture. Arrange remaining watercress on half of each piece of parchment. Top with salmon, then reserved watercress mixture. Dot with margarine; fold other half of parchment paper over ingredients.

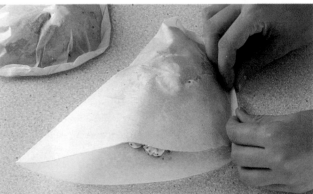

4 To seal packets, begin at one corner and fold edges of paper over about ½ inch all around, overlapping the folds. Place packets in jelly-roll pan. Bake 15 minutes. Cut packets open to serve.

EACH SERVING: ABOUT 240 CALORIES, 30g PROTEIN, 5g CARBOHYDRATE, 11g TOTAL FAT (2g SATURATED), 73mg CHOLESTEROL, 200mg SODIUM

RED SNAPPER IN PARCHMENT

Prep: 15 minutes *Bake:* 15 minutes
Makes 4 main-dish servings

1 tablespoon margarine or butter
1 large garlic clove, minced
1 pound plum tomatoes, seeded and
  finely chopped (2 cups)
Salt and ground black pepper
⅓ cup chopped fresh basil
4 red snapper fillets (6 ounces each),
  skin removed
4 squares (12 inches) cooking parchment
  or foil

◆ Preheat oven to 400°F. In 12-inch
skillet, melt margarine over medium-
high heat. Add garlic; cook, stirring,
30 seconds. Add tomatoes, ¼ teaspoon
salt, and ⅛ teaspoon pepper. Cook,
stirring often, 5 minutes or until pan is
almost dry. Remove from heat; stir in
chopped basil.

◆ Remove any bones from fish. Place
1 fillet on half of each parchment
square; sprinkle with salt and pepper.
Top with tomato mixture. Fold other
half of parchment over ingredients.

◆ To seal packets, begin at one corner
and fold edges of paper over ½ inch all
around, overlapping the folds. Place
packets in jelly-roll pan. Bake
15 minutes. Cut packets open to serve.

**Each serving: About 220 calories,
36g protein, 6g carbohydrate, 6g total fat
(1g saturated), 62mg cholesterol,
350mg sodium**

"EN PAPILLOTE" TIPS

◆◆◆◆◆◆◆◆◆◆◆◆◆◆◆◆

• Cut any firm vegetables (carrots
and peppers) into thin or small
pieces for even cooking. Precook
slow-cooking vegetables (potatoes
and cabbage).

• Fold the edges of the package
tightly so that no steam can escape.

• Take care when opening the
parcels to avoid escaping steam.

COD WITH SAVOY CABBAGE IN PARCHMENT

Prep: 20 minutes *Bake:* 20 minutes
Makes 4 main-dish servings

2 slices bacon, chopped
2 teaspoons vegetable oil
½ head savoy cabbage, thinly sliced
  (6 cups)
Pinch dried thyme
Salt and ground black pepper
4 squares (12 inches) cooking parchment
  or foil
4 pieces thick cod fillet (6 ounces each)
1 tablespoon margarine or butter, cut up

◆ Preheat oven to 400°F. In 12-inch
skillet, cook bacon over medium-low
heat until browned. With slotted
spoon, transfer bacon to paper towels
to drain. Discard drippings from skillet.

◆ In same skillet, heat oil over high
heat. Add savoy cabbage, thyme,
½ teaspoon salt, and ¼ teaspoon pepper
and cook, stirring often, until cabbage
is tender. Stir in cooked bacon.

◆ Arrange cabbage mixture on half of
each parchment square. Remove any
bones from cod; place cod on top of
cabbage. Sprinkle cod lightly with salt
and pepper and dot with margarine.
Fold other half of parchment over
ingredients.

◆ To seal packets, begin at one corner
and fold edges of paper over ½ inch all
around, overlapping the folds. Place
packets in jelly-roll pan. Bake
20 minutes. Cut packets open to serve.

**Each serving: About 230 calories,
33g protein, 6g carbohydrate, 8g total fat
(2g saturated), 77mg cholesterol,
565mg sodium**

SEAFOOD IN PARCHMENT PACKETS

Prep: 20 minutes *Bake:* 12 minutes
Makes 4 main-dish servings

12 small shrimp (about 6 ounces)
1 tablespoon vegetable oil
1 medium onion, chopped
1 pound mushrooms, sliced
Salt
2 tablespoons dry white wine
2 bunches arugula
4 squares (12 inches) cooking parchment
  or foil
4 small sole or flounder fillets (about
  ¼ pound each)
1 tablespoon capers, drained
1 tablespoon chopped fresh parsley

◆ Preheat oven to 450°F. Shell and
devein shrimp (see page 90). In
12-inch skillet, heat oil over medium-
high heat; add onion and cook until
lightly browned. Add mushrooms and
½ teaspoon salt; cook, stirring, about
10 minutes, or until mushrooms are
browned and liquid evaporates. Add
wine; cook 1 minute longer. Transfer
mushroom mixture to bowl.

◆ Add arugula and ¼ teaspoon salt to
skillet; cover and cook 1 minute, or
until arugula wilts. Remove from heat.

◆ Place arugula on half of each
square. Top with fish and mushroom
mixture. Place 3 shrimp on top of
each. Sprinkle with capers. Fold other
half of parchment over ingredients.

◆ To seal packets, begin at one corner
and fold edges of paper over ½ inch all
around, overlapping the folds. Place
packets in jelly-roll pan. Bake
12 minutes. Cut packets open to serve;
sprinkle seafood with parsley.

**Each serving: About 230 calories,
33g protein, 10g carbohydrate, 6g total fat
(1g saturated), 119mg cholesterol,
645mg sodium**

FISH CASSEROLES AND STEWS

When selecting fish for stews and casseroles, choose firm-textured fish that retain their shape during cooking – cod, red snapper, and monkfish are ideal, or use a variety, for contrasting tastes and textures. Accompany with some good crusty bread for mopping up all the delicious sauce.

SEAFOOD STEW

◆◆◆◆◆◆◆◆◆◆◆◆◆◆

Prep: 25 minutes
Cook: 45 to 55 minutes
Makes 10 main-dish servings

1¼ **pounds large shrimp**
1½ **pounds red snapper or cod fillets**
1 **pound sea scallops**
1 **medium lime, halved**
1 **teaspoon ground coriander**
3 **tablespoons olive or vegetable oil**
2 **large onions, diced**
2 **large celery stalks, diced**
2 **medium carrots, diced**
1 **medium red pepper, diced**
1 **can (35 ounces) Italian plum tomatoes**
1 **extra-large vegetable- or chicken-flavor bouillon cube**
½ **cup dry white wine**
1 **teaspoon sugar**
1 **teaspoon salt**
¼ **teaspoon crushed red pepper**
2 **tablespoons chopped fresh parsley**

1 Hold each shrimp curved-side up; insert tip of kitchen shears under shell; cut about ¼ inch deep along back through to tail to expose vein. Devein and rinse; do not remove shells.

2 Cut red snapper into 3" by 2" pieces. Rinse scallops to remove sand from crevices. Pull tough muscle from side of each scallop. Into large bowl, squeeze juice from lime; stir in coriander. Add shrimp, red snapper, and scallops; toss to coat. Set aside.

3 In 8-quart Dutch oven or saucepot, heat oil over medium heat; add diced vegetables and cook, stirring occasionally, about 25 minutes, until tender and browned.

4 Stir in tomatoes with their juice, next 5 ingredients, and ¾ *cup water*, breaking up tomatoes with back of spoon; heat to boiling over high heat.

5 Reduce heat to medium-low; cook 5 minutes to blend flavors. Stir seafood into tomato mixture; heat to boiling over high heat. Reduce heat to medium-low; cook, stirring occasionally, 5 to 10 minutes, until seafood is opaque throughout. Stir in parsley.

EACH SERVING: ABOUT 250 CALORIES, 33g PROTEIN, 12g CARBOHYDRATE, 6g TOTAL FAT (1g SATURATED), 127mg CHOLESTEROL, 790mg SODIUM

EASY COD STEW

Prep: 15 minutes   Cook: 25 minutes
Makes 4 main-dish servings

1 tablespoon olive or
   vegetable oil
1 large onion, halved and
   thinly sliced
¾ teaspoon salt
5 medium red potatoes
   (about 12 ounces), cut into
   ¾-inch chunks
1 can (14½ ounces) stewed
   tomatoes

1 can (13¾ to 14½ ounces)
   reduced-sodium chicken
   broth
1 piece cod fillet (about
   1¼ pounds), cut into
   1½-inch chunks
1 bunch (10 to 12 ounces)
   spinach, coarsely sliced

◆ In 4-quart saucepan, heat oil over medium heat; add onion and salt and cook until onion is tender but not browned.

◆ Add potatoes, tomatoes, broth, and *1 cup water*; heat to boiling over high heat. Reduce heat to low; cover and simmer 10 minutes, or until potatoes are almost tender.

◆ Stir in cod and spinach; cook 5 minutes longer, or until cod is opaque throughout and potatoes are fork-tender.

Each serving: About 290 calories, 31g protein, 31g carbohydrate, 5g total fat (1g saturated), 62mg cholesterol, 815mg sodium

LETTUCE-WRAPPED SEAFOOD

Prep: 25 minutes   Bake: 30 to 35 minutes
Makes 6 main-dish servings

½ pound sea scallops
½ pound large shrimp
⅓ cup all-purpose flour
½ teaspoon salt
2 pounds cod fillets, cut into
   6 pieces
3 tablespoons vegetable oil

2 cans (13¾ to 14¼ ounces
   each) reduced-sodium
   chicken broth
12 large iceberg or romaine
   lettuce leaves
3 green onions, sliced

◆ Preheat oven to 425°F. Rinse scallops with cold running water. Pull tough muscle from side of each scallop; cut each horizontally in half. Shell and devein shrimp (see page 90).

◆ On waxed paper, mix flour and salt. Dip cod fillets into flour mixture, turning to coat both sides.

◆ In 10-inch skillet, heat oil over medium-high heat; add cod fillets, 3 pieces at a time, and cook, turning once, until golden brown.

◆ Transfer cod to plate. Discard any oil remaining in skillet. Pour chicken broth into skillet; heat to boiling over high heat. Remove skillet from heat.

◆ Line shallow 2½-quart casserole with 8 lettuce leaves, allowing them to overhang side slightly; arrange cod, scallops, shrimp, and green onions on top.

◆ Pour broth over seafood; fold lettuce over top. Arrange remaining lettuce leaves on top. Cover and bake 30 to 35 minutes, until seafood is opaque throughout. To serve, fold back lettuce; spoon seafood and lettuce into bowls.

Each serving: About 295 calories, 42g protein, 8g carbohydrate, 9g total fat (2g saturated), 137mg cholesterol, 430mg sodium

LOUISIANA SEAFOOD CASSEROLE

Prep: 30 minutes   Bake: 45 to 50 minutes
Makes 8 main-dish servings

¾ pound hot Italian-sausage
   links
2 medium celery stalks, cut
   into ½-inch pieces
1 large red pepper, cut into
   ½-inch pieces
1 large green pepper, cut into
   ½-inch pieces
1 medium onion, diced
1 package (16 ounces)
   parboiled rice
2 cans (13¾ to 14½ ounces
   each) reduced-sodium
   chicken broth

1 can (14½ to 16 ounces)
   stewed tomatoes
1 bay leaf
½ teaspoon hot-pepper sauce
¼ teaspoon dried thyme
1 pound monkfish or scrod
   fillets
¾ pound large shrimp
¾ pound sea scallops
2 tablespoons chopped fresh
   parsley

◆ Preheat oven to 350°F. In 8-quart Dutch oven, cook sausage over medium-high heat until browned; with slotted spoon, transfer to paper towels to drain.

◆ In drippings in Dutch oven, cook celery, red and green peppers, and onion, stirring occasionally, until tender. Meanwhile, cut sausages into ½-inch-thick diagonal slices.

◆ Add rice to vegetables in Dutch oven; cook, stirring, until rice is opaque. Stir in broth, next 4 ingredients, and sausage; heat to boiling. Bake, covered, 25 minutes.

◆ Meanwhile, pull tough, grayish membrane from monkfish fillets; cut monkfish into 1½-inch pieces. Shell and devein shrimp (see page 90). Pull tough muscle from side of each scallop. Rinse shellfish with cold running water.

◆ Stir monkfish, shrimp, and scallops into rice mixture. Cover and bake, stirring occasionally, 20 to 25 minutes longer, until rice is tender and seafood is opaque throughout. Discard bay leaf. Stir in parsley and serve.

Each serving: About 500 calories, 37g protein, 56g carbohydrate, 13mg total fat (4g saturated), 127mg cholesterol, 720mg sodium

GRILLED FISH

The "meaty" flavor and firm texture of fish such as tuna, salmon, halibut, and red snapper make them wonderfully suited to grilling. Because fish contains little fat, it can dry out quickly on the grill. For best results, it should be either marinated or brushed with olive oil before cooking to keep it moist and flavorful. As a further safeguard, lightly grease the grill to prevent the flesh from sticking. As with all fish, freshness – and a brief cooking time – is paramount. While an outdoor barbecue is preferred for an authentic char-grilled taste, you can also grill fish on the stovetop in a ridged cast-iron grill pan.

CURRIED SEAFOOD KABOBS

Prep: 20 minutes   Grill: 7 to 8 minutes
Makes 6 main-dish servings

1 pound large sea scallops
⅓ cup mango chutney
¼ cup fresh lemon juice
1¼ teaspoons salt
1 teaspoon curry powder
1 piece salmon fillet
   (1 pound), skin removed if
   any, cut into 12 chunks

2 large red peppers, each cut
   into 9 pieces
6 (9-inch) bamboo skewers
Summer Salad with Chutney
   Dressing (see below right)
Lime wedges (optional)
Cooked parslied rice
   (optional)

1 Prepare outdoor grill. Rinse scallops with cold running water to remove sand from crevices. Pull tough crescent-shaped muscle from side of each scallop.

2 In food processor with knife blade attached or in blender, blend chutney, lemon juice, and salt until smooth. Reserve 3 tablespoons mixture for dressing for salad. Pour remaining mixture into large bowl; stir in curry powder until blended. Toss scallops, salmon, and red peppers with chutney mixture in bowl.

3 On skewers, alternately thread red peppers, salmon, and scallops. In cast-iron grill pan, cook kabobs over high heat, turning occasionally, 7 to 8 minutes, until seafood is opaque throughout. Meanwhile, prepare salad. Pour pan drippings over salad. Serve kabobs with salad, lime wedges, and rice, if you like.

CURRY POWDER

A premixed blend of up to 20 pulverized spices, herbs, and seeds, curry powder can vary widely in content. Dried red chiles give heat, and turmeric gives the characteristic rich yellow color; ginger, cumin, black pepper, and coriander seeds are also common. Curry powder is rarely used in India, where spices are freshly ground every day. It should be stored in an airtight container in the refrigerator for up to 6 months.

SUMMER SALAD WITH CHUTNEY DRESSING

In large bowl, place reserved chutney mixture; slowly beat in 2 tablespoons olive or vegetable oil until slightly thickened. Add 1 head red leaf lettuce, torn into bite-size pieces, 1 bunch watercress, tough stems removed, and ½ pound seedless green grapes; toss well to coat.

EACH SERVING: ABOUT 275 CALORIES, 29g PROTEIN, 22g CARBOHYDRATE, 8g TOTAL FAT (1g SATURATED), 64mg CHOLESTEROL, 635mg SODIUM

SALMON TERIYAKI WITH SQUASH

Prep: 15 minutes   Grill: 18 to 20 minutes
Makes 4 main-dish servings

¼ cup teriyaki sauce
1 cup grated, peeled fresh horseradish root
2 tablespoons olive or vegetable oil
2 medium zucchini (about 10 ounces each)
2 medium yellow squash (about 10 ounces each)
¼ teaspoon lemon-pepper seasoning salt
4 salmon steaks, each ¾ inch thick (about 6 ounces each)

◆ In cup, mix teriyaki sauce, ½ cup grated horseradish, and 1 tablespoon oil; set aside.

◆ Prepare outdoor grill.

◆ Cut each zucchini and yellow squash lengthwise in half. Brush halves with remaining 1 tablespoon oil; sprinkle with lemon-pepper seasoning salt. Place vegetables on grill over medium heat. Cook 12 to 15 minutes, or until tender, turning occasionally.

◆ Meanwhile, arrange salmon steaks on grill over medium heat. Cook, brushing occasionally with teriyaki-sauce mixture and turning once, 8 to 10 minutes, until salmon is opaque throughout. Transfer salmon and squash to platter. Serve with remaining ½ cup grated horseradish.

Each serving: About 325 calories, 38g protein, 14g carbohydrate, 13g total fat (2g saturated), 88mg cholesterol, 815mg sodium

◆◆◆◆◆◆◆◆◆◆◆◆◆◆◆◆◆◆◆◆◆◆◆◆◆◆◆◆◆

LEMON GARNISHES

Knots Score peel of lemon to divide it into quarters; remove peel. With tip of spoon, scrape away most of white pith. Stack pieces; cut into long, thin strips; tie into knots.

Scalloped slices Use a zester to cut lengthwise strips of peel from lemon to give striped effect; cut lemon crosswise into thin slices.

Twists Cut lemon into thin slices; cut slit from edge to center of each slice; twist into a curl.

Zigzags Draw zigzag pattern around center of lemon. With sharp knife, cut through pattern to halve lemon.

◆◆◆◆◆◆◆◆◆◆◆◆◆◆◆◆◆◆◆◆◆◆◆◆◆◆   ◆◆

GRILLED HALIBUT WITH FRESH DILL

Prep: 5 minutes plus marinating   Grill: 10 minutes
Makes 4 main-dish servings

¼ cup white-wine Worcestershire sauce
2 tablespoons fresh lemon juice
1 tablespoon olive or vegetable oil
1 tablespoon minced fresh dill or ¾ teaspoon dillweed
¼ teaspoon ground black pepper
2 halibut steaks, each 1 inch thick (about ¾ pound each)

◆ In 13" by 9" baking dish, mix Worcestershire, lemon juice, oil, dill, and pepper. Add halibut, turning to coat both sides. Cover and refrigerate at least 2 hours, turning once.

◆ Prepare outdoor grill. Place halibut on grill over low heat, reserving marinade. Cook, turning occasionally and basting frequently with reserved marinade, 10 minutes, or until opaque throughout.

Each serving: About 220 calories, 35g protein, 4g carbohydrate, 7g total fat (1g saturated), 54mg cholesterol, 240mg sodium

STUFFED RED SNAPPER

Prep: 20 minutes   Grill: 15 to 20 minutes
Makes 6 main-dish servings

1 large lemon
4 tablespoons olive or vegetable oil
2 medium carrots, shredded
1 medium onion, minced
⅛ teaspoon ground black pepper
Salt
¼ cup finely chopped fresh parsley
3 whole red snapper (1½ pounds each), filleted
Lemon wedges for garnish

◆ Prepare outdoor grill. Grate peel and squeeze juice from lemon. In 10-inch skillet, heat 2 tablespoons oil over medium-high heat. Add carrots, onion, pepper, and ½ teaspoon salt; cook until vegetables are tender and golden. Stir in parsley and lemon peel. Remove from heat. Arrange 3 fillets, skin-side down, on work surface; sprinkle with ½ teaspoon salt. Spread vegetable mixture on fillets; top with remaining fillets, skin-side up. Tie each snapper securely with string at about 2½-inch intervals.

◆ In cup, mix lemon juice and remaining 2 tablespoons oil; brush fish with some lemon-juice mixture. Place red snapper on greased grill topper or greased rack of grill. Cook snapper over medium heat, turning once and brushing frequently with remaining lemon-juice mixture, 15 to 20 minutes, until fish is opaque throughout. Remove string; garnish.

Each serving: About 410 calories, 63g protein, 7g carbohydrate, 13g total fat (2g saturated), 110mg cholesterol, 560mg sodium

P6OULTRY

POULTRY

All around the globe, poultry is prized for being simple to prepare and delicious combined with a vast range of flavors. Chickens, ducks, geese, turkeys, and Cornish hens – whether farmed or free-range – all fall under the heading of poultry. Low in fat, chicken and turkey are an ideal choice for those watching their waistline – white meat has less fat and fewer calories than dark meat, and skinless breast meat is the leanest of all. For maximum flavor and juiciness, cook poultry with the skin on – but remove it before eating, if you like, and you'll slash the fat content by about half.

BUYING

• Choose fresh whole birds that seem plump, with meaty breasts (meatier birds are a better buy because you're paying for less bone per pound). Chicken parts should also look plump.

• Poultry skin should be smooth and moist, and free of bruises or pinfeathers; bone ends should be pinkish-white. (The color of the skin can range from creamy white to yellow; it depends on the bird's feed and breed and has no effect on taste.)

• Avoid packages that are broken or leaking.

• The USDA inspection sticker or tag is a guarantee that the bird was reared and processed under strict conditions. Grade A birds, the most common variety sold in supermarkets, are the highest quality. More than 90 percent of all broiler-fryers (2½- to 4-pound chickens) are marketed under a brand name, a further assurance of quality.

• To check freshness, note the "sell-by" date on the package. You can safely buy poultry through that date, and then refrigerate it for up to 2 days afterward.

• Free-range chickens are those fed on a grain-only diet free of antibiotics and allowed to roam freely in the farmyard (unlike most chickens, which are caged). As a result, they develop more muscle, which creates fuller-flavored meat. Free-range chickens are usually much more expensive than regular chickens.

• When buying frozen poultry, be sure the meat is rock-hard and without signs of freezer burn. The quick commercial freezing process should guarantee that poultry hasn't absorbed excess water; check by making sure there are no ice crystals. The packaging should be tightly sealed and intact; frozen liquid in the bottom can mean the bird was thawed and refrozen.

POULTRY SENSE			
POULTRY/READY-TO-COOK WEIGHT		SERVINGS	STUFFING
Broiler-fryer	2½–3½ lbs	4	1–3 cups
Roasting chicken	5–7 lbs	6–7	3–6 cups
Capon	6–8 lbs	6–8	3–6 cups
Cornish hen	1–2 lbs	1–2	¾–1½ cups
Turkey	8–12 lbs	6–8	6–9 cups
	12–16 lbs	12–16	9–12 cups
	16–20 lbs	16–20	12–15 cups
	20–24 lbs	20–24	15–18 cups
Turkey breast	4–6 lbs	5–8	—
Turkey breast (boneless)	2½–3 lbs	6–9	—
Duckling	4–5 lbs	4	3–4 cups
Goose	10–12 lbs	6–8	6–9 cups

HANDLING AND STORING

• Raw poultry can harbor salmonella, a prime source of food poisoning, so always wash your hands, cutting board, and all utensils in hot, soapy water after handling it. Cutting boards should be bleached occasionally with a solution of 1 tablespoon bleach to 1 gallon water.

• Store raw poultry in its original wrapping in the coldest part of the refrigerator for no more than 2 or 3 days; keep it separate from cooked and ready-to-eat foods.

• If poultry is wrapped in butcher paper, or if the wrapping is leaking, unwrap it, place in a dish, and cover loosely with foil or waxed paper before refrigerating.

• Some wrappings can transfer their odor to poultry. After unwrapping, check that any smell disappears quickly. Do not use if any off odors linger.

• Rinse poultry inside and out with cold running water and pat dry with paper towels before using.

• Store any giblets separately in the refrigerator and use within a day. They are an excellent addition to gravy.

• Freeze whole uncooked poultry up to 6 months and pieces 3 to 6 months. Ground poultry will keep in the refrigerator 1 day, or in the freezer up to 3 months.

• Cool cooked poultry as quickly as possible, then cover and refrigerate 2 to 3 days, or wrap and freeze up to 3 months.

• Any leftover stuffing should be promptly removed from the bird (to avoid potential bacterial growth), covered and refrigerated separately, and used within 3 days. It can be frozen for up to 1 month.

THAWING

For safety, it's important to thaw poultry in one of two ways: either in the refrigerator or by immersing it in cold water (see below). Never thaw poultry on the kitchen counter, because bacteria can multiply rapidly at room temperature. Also, do not thaw a commercially stuffed frozen turkey before roasting – bacteria can flourish in the thawed stuffing. Follow the label instructions for cooking. Keep these important guidelines in mind:
• Frozen poultry should be thawed completely before cooking, so allow sufficient time, especially for large birds.
• Remove giblets as soon as possible during thawing, then wrap and refrigerate and use for stock or gravy, if desired.
• If all ice crystals have disappeared from the body cavity and the legs are soft and flexible, then the bird has thawed.
• Once thawed, cook the bird within 12 hours. Wipe out the body and neck cavities with paper towels; pat the skin dry.
• For reasons of texture, not safety, do not refreeze poultry once it has been thawed.

Thawing in the refrigerator For refrigerator thawing, leave the bird in its original wrapper and place it on a tray to catch drips. Thawing time will depend both on the size of the bird and the temperature of the refrigerator (ideally 35° to 40°F). As a general rule, allow about 6 hours per pound.

Thawing in cold water If there's no time to thaw the bird in the refrigerator, try the cold-water method, which takes less time but requires more attention. Place the bird (in its original wrapper or a watertight plastic bag) in a large pan or in the sink with cold water to cover. (Warm water thaws poultry too quickly and can cause bacteria to grow.) Change the water regularly – every 30 minutes – to maintain the temperature. Allow about 30 minutes of thawing time per pound, then add 1 hour to that total.

REFRIGERATOR		COLD WATER	
WEIGHT (POUNDS)	APPROXIMATE THAWING TIME	WEIGHT (POUNDS)	APPROXIMATE THAWING TIME
1–2	12 hours	1–2	1½–2 hours
2–4	12–24 hours	2–6	2–4 hours
4–6	24–36 hours	7–12	4½–7 hours
6–12	1½–2 days	12–20	7–11 hours
12–20	2–3 days	20–24	11–13 hours
20–24	3–3½ days	Parts	2–4 hours

STUFFING

Whole birds don't have to be stuffed. You can place a quartered onion or lemon inside the cavity or spread fragrant herbs or peppery spices under the skin. However, a traditional stuffing, deliciously flavored with sautéed vegetables, sausage, or other savory ingredients, will accent the flavor of the meat. Follow the rules below:
• Before stuffing, rinse the bird inside and out and pat dry.
• Cool any cooked stuffing (unless roasting immediately) before filling the bird.
• Stuff the bird just before roasting – never in advance. It's fine to prepare a stuffing recipe ahead, but remember to refrigerate it separately and then add it just before roasting.
• Lightly stuff the body and neck cavities; do not pack. Stuffing needs room because it expands during cooking.
• Stuffing temperature in body cavity should reach 165°F.
• Bake extra stuffing in a covered casserole with the bird for the last 30 minutes of roasting. Since this stuffing won't be as moist, you may want to drizzle the top with some broth or melted margarine or butter before heating.

Stand the bird, neck-end up, in a bowl just big enough to hold it upright. Lightly spoon stuffing into neck cavity. Secure neck flap over opening with skewers. Tuck wing tips under back of bird. Loosely stuff body cavity (left); fold skin over opening. Tie legs and tail together with string to enclose stuffing.

WHITE VERSUS DARK MEAT

The white breast meat is the most tender part of the bird – and the leanest. A 3½-ounce portion of breast meat without skin has about 4 grams of fat. (The same amount of skinless dark meat has about 10 grams of fat.) Remember that by removing the skin, before or after cooking, you'll trim the fat content by about 50 percent.

White meat is ideal for quick stir-frying and panfrying or moist cooking methods such as poaching. It also takes well to dry-heat methods like broiling or grilling, but take care not to overcook, because white meat can dry out quickly. The more richly flavored and moister dark meat remains succulent in casseroles and stews. Or, coat thighs and drumsticks with crumbs and bake or sauté. Dark meat pieces also cook nicely on the grill.

Boneless thighs and breasts cook more quickly and are often more convenient. However, poultry cooked on the bone has the best flavor and tends to be juicier; the bones also help the bird (or part of the bird) hold its shape.

CUTTING UP A CHICKEN

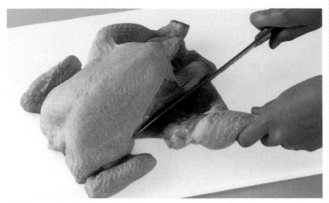

1 Place chicken breast-side up on cutting board. To remove leg-thigh portion, cut down between thigh and body. Bend leg portion back; twist to break hip joint. Cut through joint. Repeat for other leg.

2 To separate drumstick from thigh, place leg portion skin-side down and cut through joint. Repeat for other leg.

3 To remove wing, pull away from body, then cut between joint and breast. Repeat for other wing. Remove wing tips, if desired; freeze to use in stock.

4 Using poultry shears or kitchen scissors, cut through rib cage along one side of backbone from tail end to neck. Repeat on other side to remove backbone in one piece.

5 With skin-side down, cut breast in half by placing knife along one side of breastbone. Press knife down to cut through bone and meat. Cut each breast half crosswise, if you like.

SKINNING AND BONING A CHICKEN BREAST

1 To remove skin from chicken, grasp skin at thickest end of breast and pull it away. If you like, use a paper towel or dip your fingers in a little coarse salt for a better grip.

2 To bone a chicken breast, holding knife as close as possible to bone, work blade over rib bones, gently pulling meat away with the other hand.

3 The white tendon found on the underside of the breast is tough and should be removed. Holding end of tendon, scrape from meat with knife as you pull the tendon away.

TRIMMING CHICKEN LIVERS

Before cooking chicken livers, trim any fat and membranes with a small sharp knife. Any green-tinged portions should also be cut away.

QUARTERING A DUCKLING

1 Using poultry shears or kitchen scissors, cut away neck flap of duckling skin. Pull off any large pieces of fat (use fat to roast potatoes, if you like).

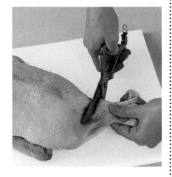

2 Keeping duckling breast-side up, and working from body cavity to neck, cut duckling along one side of breastbone.

3 Open duckling to expose rib cage and backbone. Cut along one side of backbone to split duckling into two halves.

4 Place duckling halves skin-side up. To divide into quarters, cut each half diagonally midway between wing and leg.

ROASTING AND CARVING POULTRY

Use the chart at right to estimate roasting times for poultry. To be sure a whole bird is fully cooked, always use a meat thermometer – even if the bird comes with its own pop-up thermometer. Before cooking, insert the meat thermometer inside the thigh, into thickest part of thigh (but not touching the bone) and pointing toward the body. When it reads 175° to 180°F, the bird is done (the temperature will continue to rise as you let the bird stand, so the final temperature will be 5 to 10 degrees higher than this). As a second test for doneness, insert a small knife into the thickest part of the thigh; the juices should run clear. Also check that the leg moves easily. The bones of very young chickens may remain pink even if thoroughly cooked.

Letting the bird rest after roasting results in firmer, juicier meat that's easier to carve. Poultry should stand at least 10 minutes before serving. To carve, select a knife with a slender blade that's long enough to slice off the breast of large birds like turkey or long-bodied birds such as duck and goose. The blade should extend about 2 inches beyond the meat on both sides to accommodate the sawing action of carving. For tenderest slices, carve across the grain rather than parallel to the fibers of the meat.

ROASTING TIMES (OVEN TEMPERATURE 350°F)

POULTRY TYPE AND WEIGHT		COOKING TIME (UNSTUFFED)	COOKING TIME (STUFFED)
Chicken	2½–3 lbs	1¼–1½ hrs	1¼–1½ hrs
	3–4 lbs	1½–1¾ hrs	1½–1¾ hrs
	4–6 lbs	1¾–2 hrs	1¾–2 hrs
Capon (at 325°F)	5–6 lbs	2–2½ hrs	2½–3 hrs
	6–8 lbs	2½–3½ hrs	3–4 hrs
Cornish hen	1–2 lbs	1–1¼ hrs	1–1¼ hrs
Turkey (at 325°F)	8–12 lbs	2¾–3 hrs	3–3½ hrs
	12–14 lbs	3–3¾ hrs	3½–4 hrs
	14–18 lbs	3¾–4¼ hrs	4–4¼ hrs
	18–20 lbs	4¼–4½ hrs	4¼–4¾ hrs
	20–24 lbs	4½–5 hrs	4¾–5½ hrs
Duckling	4–5 lbs	2½–2¾ hrs	2½–2¾ hrs
Goose	10–12 lbs	2¾–3¼ hrs	3–3½ hrs

ROASTING IT RIGHT

• Roast poultry on a rack in the roasting pan to allow heat to circulate freely under the bird.
• When roasting fattier birds such as duck or goose, prick the skin all over with a 2-tine fork so the fat can drain away. Spoon off the fat from the pan occasionally.
• For moist meat and crisp skin, baste poultry occasionally during cooking.
• If the skin is becoming too brown, cover the bird with a loose tent of foil.
• After roasting, transfer the bird to a warm platter and let the pan juices stand for a minute. Then spoon off most or all of the fat from the top. The degreased juices can be used to make a gravy or sauce.

CARVING A ROAST TURKEY
(TRADITIONAL METHOD)

1 To remove turkey leg, force it outward with a carving fork, then cut between thigh and body and through joint. If you like, cut drumstick from thigh through center joint.

2 To carve leg, holding it steady with carving fork, slice thigh meat parallel to the bone. Slice drumstick meat parallel to bone. Repeat with second thigh and drumstick.

3 To carve breast, make a horizontal cut above wing joint along the length of the bird, making sure it goes right to the bone.

4 With knife blade parallel to rib cage, beginning halfway up breast, cut thin slices. Continue slicing, starting a little higher each time. Cut off wing. Repeat on other side.

CARVING A ROAST TURKEY BREAST
(KITCHEN METHOD)

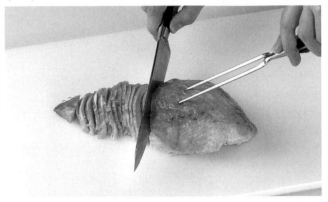

After removing turkey leg (see left), remove turkey breast half in one piece; transfer to cutting board. Hold meat steady with carving fork; beginning at tip of breast, carve thin slices.

CARVING A ROAST DUCK

1 To remove wing, cut through joint between wing and body. To remove leg, cut through skin around leg, then cut down between thigh and body to reveal joint; cut through joint to separate. Cut drumstick from thigh through center joint. Repeat with second wing and leg.

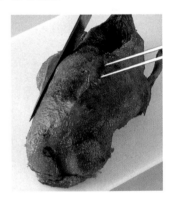

2 Holding knife blade at a 45° angle, cut long, thin slices from one side of breast. Repeat on other side.

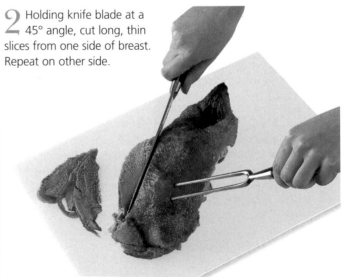

ROAST TURKEY AND GOOSE

A perfectly roasted bird has a rich, golden skin and tender, succulent meat. A meat thermometer will ensure your bird is fully cooked, and a foil tent will keep the breast meat moist. To avoid any bacterial growth, don't stuff birds until just before cooking.

GOLDEN ROAST TURKEY WITH GIBLET GRAVY

◆◆◆◆◆◆◆◆◆◆◆◆◆

Prep: 15 minutes plus standing and making stuffing and gravy
Roast: About 3 hours 45 minutes
Makes 14 main-dish servings

Cranberry-Pear Relish (optional, see page 138)
Country Sausage and Corn-Bread Stuffing (see page 138)
1 ready-to-stuff turkey (14 pounds), giblets and neck reserved for gravy
1½ teaspoons salt
½ teaspoon coarsely ground black pepper
Giblet Gravy (see page 138)
Roasted potato wedges and sugar snap peas (optional)

CHECKING TURKEY FOR DONENESS
◆◆◆◆◆◆◆◆◆◆◆

Turkey is done when thigh temperature reaches 180° to 185°F and leg moves up and down easily. (Breast temperature should be 170° to 175°F; stuffing temperature should be 165°F.)

1 Prepare relish, if you like, and stuffing. Preheat oven to 325°F. Rinse turkey; drain well. Spoon some stuffing lightly into neck cavity.

2 Fold neck skin over stuffing; fasten neck skin to back with 1 or 2 skewers. Spoon remaining stuffing lightly into body cavity. Fold skin over opening; skewer closed if necessary.

3 With string, tie legs and tail together. Place turkey, breast-side up, on rack in large roasting pan. Rub turkey all over with salt and pepper.

4 Insert meat thermometer into thickest part of thigh next to body, being careful that pointed end of thermometer does not touch bone. Cover turkey with loose tent of foil.

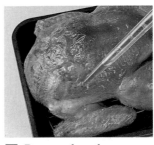

5 Roast turkey about 3¾ hours. Start checking for doneness during last hour of roasting (see left). To brown turkey, remove foil during last hour of roasting and baste with pan drippings occasionally.

6 Meanwhile, prepare broth for Giblet Gravy, Steps 1 and 2. Place turkey on warm large platter. Let stand 15 minutes for easier carving; keep warm. Reserve drippings. Prepare Giblet Gravy. Serve turkey with stuffing, gravy, relish, potato wedges, and sugar snap peas, if you like.

EACH SERVING WITHOUT GRAVY: ABOUT 390 CALORIES, 53g PROTEIN, 0g CARBOHYDRATE, 18g TOTAL FAT (5g SATURATED), 181mg CHOLESTEROL, 365mg SODIUM

COUNTRY SAUSAGE AND CORN-BREAD STUFFING

Prep: 45 minutes   Bake: 45 minutes
Makes about 12 cups

1 pound pork-sausage meat
4 tablespoons margarine or
   butter
3 medium celery stalks, diced
1 large onion, diced
1 medium red pepper, diced
1 can (13¾ to 14½ ounces)
   chicken broth

½ teaspoon coarsely ground
   black pepper
1 package (14 to 16 ounces)
   corn-bread stuffing mix
1 cup pecans, toasted and
   coarsely chopped
¼ cup chopped fresh parsley

◆ Heat 12-inch skillet over medium-high heat; add sausage meat and cook, stirring frequently to break up sausage, about 10 minutes, until browned. With slotted spoon, transfer sausage to large bowl.

◆ Discard all but 2 tablespoons drippings from skillet. Add margarine, celery, onion, and red pepper; cook, stirring occasionally, until vegetables are browned.

◆ Stir in broth, black pepper, and *¾ cup water*; heat to boiling, stirring to loosen brown bits from bottom of skillet.

◆ Add vegetable mixture, corn-bread stuffing mix, pecans, and parsley to sausage; mix well. Use to stuff 12- to 16-pound turkey. (Place any leftover stuffing in greased, covered casserole and add to oven 30 minutes before end of roasting time.)

Each ½ cup: About 150 calories, 4g protein, 15g carbohydrate, 9g total fat (2g saturated), 9mg cholesterol, 425mg sodium

CRANBERRY-PEAR RELISH

In 3-quart saucepan, heat 1 bag (12 ounces) cranberries, 1¼ cups packed brown sugar, ¼ cup balsamic vinegar, and ½ cup water to boiling over high heat, stirring. Reduce heat to low; simmer, uncovered, 8 minutes, or until most of cranberries pop. Add 1 pear, peeled, cored, and diced, to pan; cover and cook 2 to 3 minutes longer. Transfer to bowl, cover, and refrigerate relish about 4 hours, until chilled. If you like, transfer relish to airtight container and refrigerate up to 2 days. Makes about 3 cups.

Each tablespoon: About 30 calories,
0g protein, 7g carbohydrate,
0g total fat, 0mg cholesterol,
5mg sodium

GIBLET GRAVY

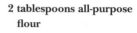

Turkey giblets and neck
Roast turkey pan drippings
½ teaspoon salt

2 tablespoons all-purpose
   flour

1 In 3-quart saucepan, heat turkey gizzard, heart, neck, and *water* to cover to boiling over high heat. Reduce heat to low; cover and simmer 45 minutes. Add liver; cook 15 minutes.

2 Strain broth into large bowl. Pull meat from neck; discard bones. Coarsely chop neck meat and giblets. Cover and refrigerate meat and broth separately.

3 Remove rack from roasting pan. Pour drippings through sieve into 4-cup measuring cup. Add 1 cup broth to roasting pan. Stir until brown bits are loosened; pour into drippings in cup. Let stand until fat separates from meat juice.

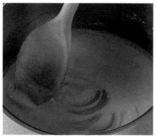

4 Spoon 2 tablespoons fat from pan drippings in cup into 2-quart saucepan. Skim and discard remaining fat. Into fat in saucepan, stir salt and flour. Cook over medium heat, stirring constantly, until golden.

5 Add remaining broth and enough *water* to pan drippings in cup to equal 3½ cups. Gradually stir into saucepan; cook, stirring, until gravy thickens and boils. Stir in reserved meat; heat through. Makes about 3¾ cups.

Each ¼ cup: About 50 calories, 4g protein, 1g carbohydrate,
3g total fat (1g saturated), 34mg cholesterol, 85mg sodium

TURKEY WITH PORT-WINE SAUCE AND RICE STUFFING

Prep: 35 minutes plus standing   Roast: About 3 hours
Makes 6 main-dish servings

1½ cups aromatic rice (such as Texmati or jasmine) or regular long-grain rice
Salt
3 medium celery stalks
1 medium onion
2 tablespoons vegetable oil
⅓ cup dried currants
1 ready-to-stuff turkey or capon (8 pounds), giblets and neck reserved for another use
½ teaspoon dried thyme
2 cups cranberry-raspberry juice
2 tablespoons brown sugar
¼ cup cranberries, sliced
2 tablespoons port wine
2 teaspoons cornstarch
½ teaspoon chicken-flavor instant bouillon

◆ Prepare stuffing: In 3-quart saucepan, prepare rice as label directs, using ¾ teaspoon salt. Meanwhile, thinly slice celery; finely chop onion. In 10-inch skillet, heat oil over medium heat; add celery and onion and cook until vegetables are lightly browned. Stir in *½ cup water*; heat to boiling over high heat. Reduce heat to low; simmer, uncovered, until water evaporates and vegetables are tender. Stir vegetable mixture into rice with currants. Set stuffing aside.

◆ Preheat oven to 350°F. Prepare turkey for roasting and stuff as in Steps 1 through 5 of Golden Roast Turkey with Giblet Gravy (see page 137), but rub turkey all over with dried thyme and 1 teaspoon salt and roast turkey 3 hours, or until meat thermometer inserted in thickest part of thigh registers 180° to 185°F. (Place any leftover stuffing in greased, covered casserole and add to oven 30 minutes before end of roasting time.)

◆ Prepare glaze: In 3-quart saucepan, heat cranberry-raspberry juice and brown sugar to boiling over high heat. Cook, uncovered, 15 minutes, or until mixture has reduced to ⅓ cup. Cover and set aside.

◆ Place turkey on warm platter. Let stand 15 minutes; keep warm. Reserve pan drippings.

◆ Prepare port-wine sauce: Remove rack from roasting pan; skim and discard fat from drippings. Add *½ cup water* to drippings; stir until brown bits are loosened. Strain mixture into 1-quart saucepan. Add cranberries and ¼ cup glaze. Heat to boiling over high heat; boil 1 minute, or until thickened. In cup, mix port, cornstarch, bouillon, and *⅓ cup water*. Stir into sauce; heat to boiling. Boil 1 minute; pour into gravy boat. Brush turkey with remaining glaze. Serve with sauce and stuffing.

Each serving: About 825 calories, 72g protein, 65g carbohydrate 28g total fat (8g saturated), 233mg cholesterol, 895mg sodium

APPLE-GLAZED TURKEY WITH MULTIGRAIN-BREAD STUFFING

Prep: 30 minutes plus standing and making gravy
Roast: About 3 hours 45 minutes
Makes 14 main-dish servings

3 tablespoons margarine or butter
7 medium celery stalks, chopped
3 medium onions, chopped
¾ teaspoon dried oregano
1½ loaves (24 ounces total) multigrain bread, cut into ½-inch cubes
1 can (13¾ to 14½ ounces) chicken broth
Coarsely ground black pepper
1 ready-to-stuff turkey (14 pounds), giblets and neck reserved for Giblet Gravy (see page 138)
1½ teaspoons salt
Apple Glaze (see below)

◆ Prepare stuffing: In 12-inch skillet, melt margarine over medium heat; add celery and onions and cook, stirring frequently, until golden. Stir in *¼ cup water*; reduce heat to low, cover, and cook until vegetables are tender. In very large bowl, toss vegetables with oregano, bread, broth, ¾ teaspoon pepper, and *¾ cup water*. Set aside.

◆ Preheat oven to 325°F. Prepare turkey for roasting and stuff as in Steps 1 through 5 of Golden Roast Turkey with Giblet Gravy (see page 137), but rub turkey all over with salt and ½ teaspoon pepper.

◆ Roast turkey 3¾ hours, or until meat thermometer inserted in thickest part of thigh registers 180° to 185°F. (Place any leftover stuffing in greased, covered casserole and add to oven 30 minutes before end of roasting time.)

◆ Meanwhile, prepare broth for Giblet Gravy. Prepare Apple Glaze. About 10 minutes before end of roasting time, brush turkey with glaze. Place turkey on warm platter. Let stand 15 minutes; keep warm. Reserve pan drippings.

◆ Prepare Giblet Gravy. Serve turkey with stuffing and gravy.

Each serving: About 630 calories, 61g protein, 36g carbohydrate, 25g total fat (7g saturated), 215mg cholesterol, 855mg sodium

APPLE GLAZE

In 1-quart saucepan, heat ½ cup apple jelly, 3 tablespoons balsamic vinegar, ½ teaspoon ground cinnamon, and ¼ teaspoon ground cloves to boiling over medium-high heat. Boil about 2 minutes, stirring constantly, until mixture thickens slightly.

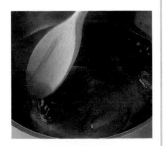

ROAST GOOSE WITH WILD RICE AND CHESTNUT STUFFING

Prep: 2 hours   *Roast:* 3 hours
Makes 8 main-dish servings

2 tablespoons margarine or
  butter
1 large Granny Smith apple,
  peeled, cored, and chopped
1 large celery stalk, diced
1 medium carrot, diced
1 small onion, diced
Salt and ground black pepper

¼ teaspoon dried thyme
2 cans (13¾ to 14½ ounces
  each) reduced-sodium
  chicken broth
⅔ cup wild rice, rinsed
1 cup parboiled white rice
1 pound fresh chestnuts
1 goose (12 pounds)

◆ Prepare stuffing: In 3-quart saucepan, melt 1 tablespoon margarine over medium heat; add apple and cook until softened. Transfer to bowl. In same saucepan, melt remaining 1 tablespoon margarine. Add celery, carrot, onion, ¼ teaspoon each salt and pepper, and thyme and cook, stirring frequently, until vegetables are golden.

◆ Stir in broth and wild rice; heat to boiling over high heat. Reduce heat to low; cover and simmer 35 minutes. Stir in parboiled rice; heat to boiling over high heat. Reduce heat to low; cover and simmer 25 minutes longer, or until liquid is absorbed and rice is tender.

◆ Meanwhile, prepare chestnuts: In 4-quart saucepan, heat chestnuts and *water* to cover to boiling over high heat. Reduce heat to medium; cook 10 minutes. Remove from heat. Transfer chestnuts, 3 or 4 at a time, to cutting board; cut each in half. Scrape out chestnut from shell (skin will stay in shell); chop any large pieces. When rice is done, stir in chestnuts and apple. Set stuffing aside.

◆ Preheat oven to 350°F. Remove giblets and neck from goose; discard fat from body cavity. Rinse goose with cold running water; drain well. Fasten neck skin to back with 1 or 2 skewers. With goose breast-side up, lift wings toward neck, then fold them under back of goose so they stay in place. Spoon stuffing lightly into body cavity. With string, tie legs and tail together.

◆ Place goose, breast-side up, on rack in large roasting pan; with 2-tine fork, prick skin in several places to drain fat during roasting. Rub goose with 1 teaspoon salt and ¼ teaspoon pepper. Insert meat thermometer into thickest part of thigh next to body, being careful that pointed end of thermometer does not touch bone. Roast goose 3 hours, spooning off fat from pan occasionally, or until thermometer reaches 180° to 185°F. During last hour of roasting, if necessary, cover goose with foil to prevent overbrowning. Place goose on warm large platter; let stand 15 minutes for easier carving.

Each serving: About 1180 calories, 83g protein, 47g carbohydrate, 71g total fat (22g saturated), 280mg cholesterol, 765mg sodium

CHRISTMAS GOOSE

Prep: 20 minutes   *Roast:* 3 hours to 3 hours 30 minutes
Makes 10 main-dish servings

1 goose (14 pounds)
1 teaspoon salt
½ teaspoon ground black
  pepper
½ teaspoon ground sage
3 tablespoons sugar
3 tablespoons soy sauce
3 tablespoons red wine
  vinegar

1 tablespoon minced, peeled
  fresh ginger or ¾ teaspoon
  ground ginger
3 tablespoons all-purpose
  flour
1 beef-flavor bouillon cube or
  envelope
Fresh sage leaves for garnish

◆ Preheat oven to 350°F. Remove giblets and neck from goose; discard fat from body cavity. Rinse goose with cold running water; drain well. With goose breast-side up, lift wings toward neck, then fold them under back of goose so they stay in place. With string, tie legs and tail together.

◆ Place goose, breast-side up, on rack in large roasting pan; with 2-tine fork, prick skin in several places to drain fat during roasting. Rub goose with salt, pepper, and ground sage. Insert meat thermometer into thickest part of thigh next to body, being careful that pointed end of thermometer does not touch bone. Roast 3 to 3½ hours, spooning off fat from pan occasionally, or until thermometer reaches 180° to 185°F. During last hour of roasting, if necessary, cover goose with foil to prevent overbrowning.

◆ Meanwhile, prepare glaze: In small bowl, stir sugar with soy sauce, vinegar, and ginger. After goose has roasted 2½ hours, with pastry brush, brush goose occasionally with glaze.

◆ Place goose on warm large platter. Let stand 15 minutes for easier carving; keep warm. Reserve pan drippings.

◆ Prepare gravy: Remove rack from roasting pan. Pour pan drippings through sieve into 8-cup measuring cup or large bowl. Set pan aside. Let drippings stand a few seconds, until fat separates from meat juice. Spoon 2 tablespoons fat from drippings into 2-quart saucepan; skim and discard remaining fat. Add ½ *cup water* to roasting pan; stir until brown bits are loosened. Add to meat juice in measuring cup with enough additional *water* to equal 2 cups.

◆ Into fat in saucepan, stir flour over medium heat. Gradually stir in meat-juice mixture and bouillon; cook, stirring constantly, until mixture thickens slightly and boils. Pour gravy into gravy boat. To serve, garnish platter with sage leaves. Serve with gravy.

Each serving: About 905 calories, 73g protein, 6g carbohydrate, 63g total fat (20g saturated), 263mg cholesterol, 810mg sodium

ROAST DUCK

The trick to producing crispy duck: Pierce the skin, and roast the duck on a rack, allowing the fat to drain. Serve as a festive company meal or for a treat on a winter evening.

ROAST DUCK WITH CHERRY-PORT SAUCE

◆◆◆◆◆◆◆◆◆◆◆◆◆

Prep: 10 minutes plus preparing broth
Roast: 2 hours 30 minutes
Makes 4 main-dish servings

1 duckling (4½ pounds), giblets and neck reserved for Giblet Broth (see below)
½ teaspoon dried thyme
¼ teaspoon salt
¼ teaspoon ground black pepper
2 Bosc pears, each cut into quarters and cored
2 teaspoons sugar
¼ cup minced shallots
⅓ cup port wine
¼ cup dried tart cherries
Roasted potatoes, Brussels sprouts, and carrots (optional)

GIBLET BROTH

In 2-quart saucepan, heat duckling giblets (except liver; discard) and neck, 1 can (13¾ to 14½ ounces) chicken broth, and 2 cups water to boiling over high heat. Reduce heat to low; simmer, uncovered, 1½ hours (if liquid evaporates too quickly, add ½ cup more water). Strain, discarding giblets. Makes ½ to ¾ cup.

1 Preheat oven to 350°F. Discard fat from body cavity of duckling. Rinse duckling and drain well. Lift wings toward neck; fold under back of duckling so they stay in place. With 2-tine fork, prick skin in several places to drain fat during roasting. Sprinkle ¼ teaspoon thyme inside body cavity.

2 With string, tie legs and tail together. Place duckling, breast-side up, on rack in medium roasting pan. Sprinkle with salt, pepper, and remaining ¼ teaspoon thyme.

3 Insert meat thermometer into thickest part of thigh next to body (pointed end should not touch bone). Roast 2½ hours, spooning off fat occasionally, or until thermometer reaches 180° to 185°F. Meanwhile, prepare Giblet Broth. After duckling has roasted 2 hours, place pears in small baking dish. Sprinkle with sugar; bake 30 minutes, or until tender. Transfer duckling and pears to platter. Let stand 15 minutes; keep warm.

4 Prepare Cherry-Port Sauce: Discard fat from roasting pan. Add shallots; cook over medium-high heat, stirring, 2 minutes. Stir in port, dried cherries, and Giblet Broth. Heat to boiling, stirring until brown bits are loosened; simmer 5 minutes. Pour into small bowl. Serve duckling with Cherry-Port Sauce, and vegetables, if you like.

EACH SERVING: ABOUT 790 CALORIES, 39g PROTEIN, 25g CARBOHYDRATE, 57g TOTAL FAT (19g SATURATED), 171mg CHOLESTEROL, 685mg SODIUM

ROASTED DUCK WITH CRANBERRY-DATE COMPOTE

Prep: 10 minutes   Roast: 2 hours 30 minutes
Makes 4 main-dish servings

1 duckling (4½ pounds), giblets and neck reserved for Giblet Broth (see page 141)	½ cup sugar
1 orange, cut into quarters	2 cups cranberries
¼ teaspoon salt	½ cup dry red wine
¼ teaspoon ground black pepper	½ cup chopped, pitted dates
	Flat-leaf parsley and orange slices for garnish
	Roasted potatoes (optional)

◆ Preheat oven to 350°F. Discard fat from body cavity of duckling. Rinse; drain well. Lift wings toward neck, then fold them under back of duckling so they stay in place. With 2-tine fork, prick skin in several places to drain fat during roasting. Place orange quarters in cavity. With string, tie legs and tail of duckling together.

◆ Place duckling, breast-side up, on rack in medium roasting pan. Sprinkle with salt and pepper. Insert meat thermometer into thickest part of thigh next to body, being careful that pointed end of thermometer does not touch bone. Roast 2½ hours, spooning off fat from pan occasionally, or until meat thermometer reaches 180° to 185°F. Transfer to platter. Let stand 15 minutes; keep warm.

◆ Meanwhile, prepare Giblet Broth. Prepare compote: In 10-inch skillet, cook sugar over medium-high heat, stirring, until melted and amber in color. Remove from heat; carefully stir in cranberries, wine, dates, and Giblet Broth (mixture will bubble). Cook over medium-low heat, stirring, until cranberries pop. Spoon into bowl.

◆ To serve, carve duckling (see page 136); garnish with parsley and orange slices and serve with compote, and potatoes, if you like.

Each serving: About 890 calories, 39g protein, 54g carbohydrate, 57g total fat (19g saturated), 171mg cholesterol, 705mg sodium

CHIPOTLE-GLAZED DUCK

Prep: 10 minutes   Roast: 2 hours 10 minutes
Makes 4 main-dish servings

1 duckling (4½ pounds), cut into quarters (see page 135)	2 tablespoons light molasses
2 tablespoons chopped canned chipotle chiles in adobo (see page 30)	

◆ Preheat oven to 350°F. Discard fat from duckling quarters. Rinse; drain well. With 2-tine fork, prick skin in several places to drain fat during roasting. Place duckling quarters, skin-side up, on rack in large foil-lined roasting pan. Roast 2 hours, spooning off fat from pan occasionally.

◆ Meanwhile, prepare glaze: Press chipotles through sieve into small bowl; discard skin and seeds. Stir molasses into chiles in bowl.

◆ Turn oven control to 450°F. Remove duckling from oven and brush on both sides with chipotle glaze. Return duckling to oven and roast 10 minutes longer.

Each serving: About 685 calories, 37g protein, 7g carbohydrate, 55g total fat (19g saturated), 163mg cholesterol, 165mg sodium

GINGER-GLAZED DUCK

Prep: 10 minutes   Roast: 2 hours 10 minutes
Makes 4 main-dish servings

1 duckling (4½ pounds), cut into quarters (see page 135)	3 teaspoons grated, peeled fresh ginger
½ teaspoon salt	2 tablespoons honey
¼ teaspoon ground black pepper	1 tablespoon soy sauce

◆ Preheat oven to 350°F. Discard fat from duckling quarters. Rinse; drain well. With 2-tine fork, prick skin in several places to drain fat during roasting.

◆ In cup, combine salt, pepper, and 1 teaspoon grated ginger; rub on inner side of duckling quarters. Place duckling quarters, skin-side up, on rack in large foil-lined roasting pan. Roast 2 hours, spooning off fat from pan occasionally.

◆ Meanwhile, in cup, combine remaining 2 teaspoons ginger with honey and soy sauce. Turn oven control to 450°F. Remove duckling from oven and brush on both sides with ginger glaze. Return duckling to oven and roast 10 minutes longer.

Each serving: About 695 calories, 37g protein, 9g carbohydrate, 55g total fat (19g saturated), 163g cholesterol, 640g sodium

ROAST CHICKEN

A crisp, golden roasted chicken is the ultimate comfort food: homey and succulently satisfying. Dress up the flavor with a simple stuffing or rich glaze, or by placing aromatic ingredients such as fresh herbs or thin slices of lemon under the skin. To keep the bird extra moist and juicy, baste it occasionally during roasting.

ROAST CHICKEN WITH LEMON AND HERBS

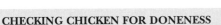

Prep: 15 minutes plus standing and making gravy   *Roast: About 2 hours*
Makes 8 main-dish servings

1 roasting chicken (about 7 pounds), giblets and neck reserved for another use	1 tablespoon chopped fresh thyme
4 thin slices lemon	½ teaspoon paprika
4 large fresh sage leaves	Pan Gravy (see page 144)
2 garlic cloves	Fresh sage leaves for garnish
1 lemon, cut in half	Roasted potatoes and broccoli (optional)
A few thyme and sage sprigs	

CHECKING CHICKEN FOR DONENESS

Chicken is done when thigh temperature reaches 175° to 180°F and juices run clear when thickest part of thigh is pierced with tip of knife.

1 Preheat oven to 375°F. Carefully push fingers between skin and meat of chicken breast to loosen skin. Place lemon slices and large sage leaves under loosened skin.

2 Place garlic, lemon halves, and thyme and sage sprigs inside cavity of chicken.

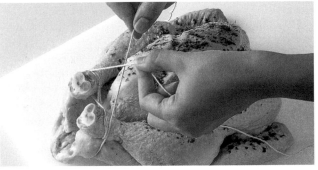

3 Sprinkle chicken with chopped thyme and paprika. With chicken breast-side up, lift wings up toward neck; fold under back of chicken so they stay in place. Tie legs together with string.

4 Place chicken, breast-side up, on rack in medium roasting pan. Insert meat thermometer into thickest part of thigh, next to body, being careful that end of thermometer does not touch bone.

5 Roast chicken, basting occasionally with pan drippings, about 2 hours. When chicken turns golden, cover loosely with tent of foil. Start checking for doneness during last 30 minutes of roasting (see above left).

6 When roast chicken is done, place on large warm platter. Let stand 15 minutes for easier carving; keep warm. Reserve pan drippings; prepare Pan Gravy. To serve, garnish platter with fresh sage leaves. Serve chicken with Pan Gravy, and roasted potatoes and steamed broccoli, if you like.

EACH SERVING: ABOUT 505 CALORIES, 53g PROTEIN, 5g CARBOHYDRATE, 29g TOTAL FAT (8g SATURATED), 211mg CHOLESTEROL, 375mg SODIUM

GRANNY'S ROAST CHICKEN WITH RICE AND SPINACH STUFFING

Prep: 35 minutes plus standing   *Roast: 2 hours 30 minutes*
Makes 8 main-dish servings

2 tablespoons vegetable oil
1 medium onion, diced
1 cup parboiled rice
1 package (10 ounces) frozen chopped spinach, thawed and squeezed dry
2 tablespoons fresh lemon juice
1 roasting chicken (7 pounds), giblets and neck reserved for another use

1 teaspoon grated lemon peel
1 teaspoon dried rosemary, crushed
1 teaspoon salt
½ teaspoon ground black pepper
Pan Gravy (see below)

◆ Prepare stuffing: In 3-quart saucepan, heat 1 tablespoon oil over medium heat. Add onion; cook until golden. In pan with onion, prepare rice as label directs, but do not use butter. Add spinach and lemon juice to cooked rice; mix well.

◆ Preheat oven to 350°F. Spoon some stuffing lightly into neck cavity of chicken. Fold neck skin over stuffing; fasten to back with 1 or 2 skewers. With chicken breast-side up, lift wings up toward neck, then fold them under back of chicken so they stay in place. Spoon more stuffing lightly into body cavity. Close by folding skin lightly over opening; skewer closed if necessary. With string, tie legs and tail together. (Bake any leftover stuffing in small covered casserole during last 30 minutes of roasting time.)

◆ Place chicken, breast-side up, on rack in medium roasting pan. In cup, mix lemon peel, rosemary, salt, pepper, and remaining 1 tablespoon oil. Rub chicken all over with herb mixture. Insert meat thermometer into thickest part of thigh, next to body, being careful that pointed end of thermometer does not touch bone.

PAN GRAVY

Remove rack from roasting pan. Add ¼ cup dry vermouth to roasting pan. Heat to boiling over high heat, stirring to loosen brown bits. Add 1¼ cups chicken broth and boil 3 minutes. Pour broth mixture into 2-cup measuring cup or gravy separator; let stand a few seconds until fat separates from liquid. Return 2 tablespoons fat to roasting pan; skim and discard remaining fat. Add 2 tablespoons all-purpose flour to roasting pan and cook over low heat, stirring, 1 minute. Gradually stir in broth mixture and ¼ teaspoon each salt and ground black pepper. Heat to boiling, stirring; boil 1 minute. Makes about 1¼ cups.

Each tablespoon: About 20 calories, 0g protein, 1g carbohydrate, 1g total fat (0g saturated), 2mg cholesterol, 90mg sodium

---

◆ Roast chicken, basting occasionally with pan drippings, about 2½ hours. When chicken turns golden, cover loosely with tent of foil. Start checking for doneness during last 30 minutes of roasting. Chicken is done when thermometer reaches 175° to 180°F and juices run clear when thickest part of thigh is pierced with tip of knife. Place chicken on warm platter; let stand 15 minutes. Keep warm. Reserve pan drippings. Prepare Pan Gravy. Serve chicken with stuffing and gravy.

Each serving: About 645 calories, 56g protein, 27g carbohydrate, 34g total fat (9g saturated), 215mg cholesterol, 925mg sodium

MAHOGANY ROAST CHICKEN

Prep: 10 minutes plus standing   *Roast: 1 hour 15 minutes*
Makes 4 main-dish servings

1 chicken (3½ pounds), giblets and neck reserved for another use
¾ teaspoon salt
½ teaspoon coarsely ground black pepper

2 tablespoons dry vermouth
2 tablespoons dark brown sugar
2 tablespoons balsamic vinegar

◆ Preheat oven to 375°F. Prepare chicken for roasting as in Steps 3 and 4 of Roast Chicken with Lemon and Herbs (see page 143), but sprinkle chicken with salt and pepper.

◆ Roast chicken 45 minutes. Meanwhile, prepare glaze: In small bowl, stir vermouth, brown sugar, and vinegar until sugar dissolves. After 45 minutes, brush chicken with some glaze. Turn oven control to 400°F and roast 30 minutes longer, brushing with glaze twice more during roasting, or until thermometer reaches 175° to 180°F and juices run clear when thickest part of thigh is pierced with tip of knife.

◆ Place chicken on warm platter; let stand 15 minutes. Keep warm. Reserve pan drippings. Meanwhile, add ¼ *cup water* to roasting pan; heat to boiling over medium heat, stirring until brown bits are loosened. Remove from heat; skim and discard fat. Serve chicken with pan juices.

Each serving: About 450 calories, 47g protein, 9g carbohydrate, 23g total fat (6g saturated), 186mg cholesterol, 540mg sodium

---

GRAVY SEPARATOR

This handy tool makes it easy to skim fat. Simply fill the cup with broth or pan juices and let it stand a moment. The fat will rise to the top, so the fat-free liquid can be poured out of the spout from the bottom.

ROAST CORNISH HENS

Cornish hens are a small, flavorful hybrid chicken. Weighing little more than 1 pound, each hen will feed one to two people. A favorite for entertaining, Cornish hens are easy to prepare and make an elegant entrée served alongside an innovative pilaf or colorful vegetables. Roasting offers the best results: crisp, golden skin and moist, tender meat.

CORNISH HEN WITH WILD-RICE PILAF

Prep: 60 to 65 minutes   Roast: 45 to 50 minutes
Makes 2 main-dish servings

1 tablespoon olive oil
1 large carrot, diced
1 medium yellow pepper, diced
1 medium onion, diced
½ cup wild rice, rinsed
Salt
1 garlic clove, minced

1 teaspoon chopped fresh oregano or ¼ teaspoon dried oregano
¼ teaspoon ground black pepper
1 Cornish hen (1¼ pounds), cut lengthwise in half (see page 146)

1 Prepare pilaf: In 2-quart saucepan, heat oil over medium-high heat. Add carrot, yellow pepper, and onion and cook, stirring frequently, until tender and lightly browned.

2 Stir in wild rice, ¼ teaspoon salt, and *1 cup water*. Heat to boiling over high heat. Reduce heat to low; cover and simmer 45 to 50 minutes, until wild rice is tender and liquid is absorbed. Keep warm.

3 Meanwhile, preheat oven to 425°F. In small bowl, mix garlic, oregano, ¼ teaspoon salt, and black pepper; rub over Cornish hen halves. Place hen halves, skin-side up, in small roasting pan.

4 Roast, brushing occasionally with pan drippings, 45 to 50 minutes, until hen halves are browned and juices run clear when hen is pierced with tip of knife. Transfer hen halves to 2 warm dinner plates; keep warm.

5 With large spoon, skim fat from drippings in roasting pan; discard fat. Stir *3 tablespoons hot water* into drippings in roasting pan. Stir until brown bits are loosened. Spoon pan juices over hen halves; serve with wild-rice pilaf.

WILD RICE

Prized for its nutty flavor and chewy texture, wild rice isn't really a rice at all. It's actually a marsh grass native to the northern states around the Great Lakes. Because it requires special harvesting methods, wild rice is expensive. You can stretch it, however, by combining it with other grains. Wild rice should always be rinsed before using. Depending on the variety of the rice used, it can take up to an hour to cook.

EACH SERVING: ABOUT 670 CALORIES, 43g PROTEIN, 45g CARBOHYDRATE, 36g TOTAL FAT (9g SATURATED), 203mg CHOLESTEROL, 655mg SODIUM

CORNISH HENS PROVENÇALE

Prep: 15 minutes   Roast: 45 to 50 minutes
Makes 6 main-dish servings

1 tablespoon olive or
  vegetable oil
1 small garlic clove, minced
½ teaspoon dried thyme
½ teaspoon salt
¼ teaspoon ground black
  pepper
3 Cornish hens (1¼ pounds
  each), each cut lengthwise
  in half (see below)

2 large onions, each cut into
  quarters
10 medium pitted ripe olives,
  coarsely chopped
3 large tomatoes, each cut
  into quarters

◆ Preheat oven to 425°F. In cup, mix oil, garlic, thyme, salt, and pepper. Rub Cornish hen halves with oil mixture; place skin-side up in large roasting pan.

◆ Arrange onions and olives around hens and roast 35 minutes, brushing hens occasionally with pan drippings. Add tomatoes and cook 10 to 15 minutes longer, or until juices run clear when hens are pierced with tip of knife. Transfer hens with olives and vegetables to platter. Skim and discard fat from pan juices; serve hens with pan juices.

Each serving: About 475 calories, 36g protein, 10g carbohydrate, 31g total fat (8g saturated), 203mg cholesterol, 335mg sodium

CITRUS-GLAZED CORNISH HENS

Prep: 10 minutes   Roast: 20 minutes
Makes 4 main-dish servings

2 refrigerated roasted Cornish
  hens (1¼ pounds each),
  each cut lengthwise in half
  (see below)

1 small lemon
¼ cup orange marmalade
2 teaspoons soy sauce

◆ Preheat oven to 450°F. Place hens, skin-side up, in large roasting pan. Roast hens 20 minutes. Meanwhile, grate 1 teaspoon peel and squeeze 1 tablespoon juice from lemon. In 1-quart saucepan, heat lemon peel, lemon juice, orange marmalade, and soy sauce over low heat until marmalade melts.

HALVING CORNISH HENS

◆◆◆◆◆◆◆◆◆◆◆◆◆◆◆◆◆◆◆◆◆◆◆◆◆◆

Cornish hens can be cut in half before or after cooking. It's easiest to use poultry shears, but a large knife will also work well. Place hen on a cutting board, back down. Slit closely along breastbone with a knife to loosen the meat. Cut along one side of the breastbone with shears. Turn bird over; cut along each side of backbone and discard it.

◆ Brush hen halves with marmalade mixture frequently during last 10 minutes of roasting time. Skim and discard fat from pan juices; serve hens with pan juices.

Each serving: About 460 calories, 35g protein, 15g carbohydrate, 28g total fat (8g saturated), 203mg cholesterol, 275mg sodium

CORNISH HENS WITH ACORN SQUASH

Prep: 20 minutes   Roast: 1 hour 15 minutes
Makes 6 main-dish servings

2 medium acorn squash
  (about 1¼ pounds each)
3 Cornish hens (1¼ pounds
  each)
¾ teaspoon salt
½ teaspoon coarsely ground
  black pepper

1 cup apple cider or apple
  juice
½ cup pitted prunes
  (3 ounces)
2 cinnamon sticks (3 inches
  each)

◆ Preheat oven to 375°F. Cut each acorn squash lengthwise in half; remove and discard seeds. Cut each squash half lengthwise into 3 wedges; cut each wedge diagonally in half.

◆ Lift wings of hens toward neck, then fold them under back of hens so they stay in place. With string, tie legs of each hen together.

◆ Place hens, breast-side up, in large roasting pan; rub with salt and pepper. Arrange squash in roasting pan around hens.

◆ Roast hens and squash 30 minutes. Add apple cider, prunes, and cinnamon sticks to pan. Roast, basting hens occasionally with pan juices, 45 minutes longer, or until squash is tender and juices run clear when hens are pierced with tip of knife.

◆ Cut each hen lengthwise in half (see below left). To serve, arrange hens, squash, prunes, and cinnamon sticks on large platter. Skim and discard fat from pan juices; serve hens with pan juices.

Each serving: About 490 calories, 32g protein, 36g carbohydrate, 25g total fat (7g saturated), 176mg cholesterol, 360mg sodium

POULTRY SHEARS

These curved shears are used to split both large and small birds. The serrated blades are spring-loaded, which forces them apart. After using, wash in hot, soapy water to avoid the risk of salmonella.

ROAST TURKEY BREASTS

Ideal for white-meat-only fans, a turkey breast is deliciously versatile. Pound it flat and roll around a flavorful filling, then slice and serve hot or cold for easy, elegant party fare. Or, for a smaller gathering, roast it whole and serve with all the traditional accompaniments.

STUFFED TURKEY BREAST WITH BASIL SAUCE

◆◆◆◆◆◆◆◆◆◆◆◆◆

Prep: 25 minutes plus standing
Roast: 1 hour 15 to 30 minutes
Makes 8 main-dish servings

1 skinless, boneless turkey-breast half (2 pounds)
1½ cups loosely packed fresh basil leaves
¼ pound thinly sliced cooked ham
4 ounces Jarlsberg cheese, thinly sliced
1 tablespoon olive oil
½ teaspoon dried basil
½ teaspoon coarsely ground black pepper
¼ teaspoon salt
Basil Sauce (see right)
Basil sprigs and cherry tomatoes for garnish

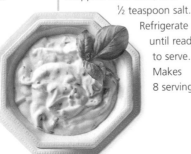

1 Preheat oven to 325°F. Holding knife parallel to work surface, and starting from a long side, cut turkey breast horizontally almost, but not all the way through.

2 Spread turkey breast open. With rolling pin or meat mallet, pound breast between 2 sheets of plastic wrap into 12" by 10" rectangle.

3 Cover turkey breast with basil leaves; top with ham, then cheese. Starting from a long side, roll turkey, jelly-roll fashion, to enclose stuffing completely.

BASIL SAUCE

In medium bowl, mix 1 cup mayonnaise, 2 teaspoons white wine vinegar, ½ teaspoon sugar, ¼ cup chopped fresh basil, and ½ teaspoon salt. Refrigerate until ready to serve. Makes 8 servings.

4 Tie turkey-breast roll securely with string at 1½-inch intervals; place on rack in small roasting pan. In cup, mix oil, dried basil, pepper, and salt; brush over turkey-breast roll.

5 Insert meat thermometer into center of roll. Roast turkey 1¼ to 1½ hours, brushing occasionally with pan drippings, until thermometer reaches 170°F. Meanwhile, prepare Basil Sauce. Transfer turkey to cutting board; discard string. Let stand 15 minutes for easier slicing. Cut roll crosswise into ½-inch-thick slices; arrange on warm large platter. Garnish with basil sprigs and cherry tomatoes. Serve with Basil Sauce.

EACH SERVING: ABOUT 415 CALORIES, 35g PROTEIN, 2g CARBOHYDRATE, 28g TOTAL FAT (4g SATURATED), 99mg CHOLESTEROL, 640mg SODIUM

TURKEY PINWHEELS

Prep: 45 minutes plus standing   *Roast:* 1 hour 15 to 30 minutes
Makes 12 main-dish servings

2 tablespoons plus
  2 teaspoons vegetable oil
1 bag (16 ounces) carrots,
  diced
2 medium onions, diced
1 large red pepper, diced
1 medium celery stalk, diced
Salt
2 tablespoons plain dried
  bread crumbs

2 tablespoons freshly grated
  Parmesan cheese
¼ cup chopped fresh parsley
1 skinless, boneless turkey-
  breast half (2½ pounds)
1 teaspoon coarsely ground
  black pepper

◆ In 12-inch skillet, heat 2 tablespoons oil over medium-high heat. Add carrots, onions, red pepper, celery, and 1 teaspoon salt and cook, stirring frequently, about 15 minutes, until vegetables are well browned.

◆ To vegetables in skillet, add *½ cup water*; heat to boiling over high heat. Reduce heat to low; cover and simmer 5 minutes, or until vegetables are tender. Remove cover; cook until any liquid in skillet has evaporated.

◆ Remove skillet from heat. Stir in bread crumbs, Parmesan cheese, and half of chopped parsley.

◆ Preheat oven to 325°F. On cutting board, holding knife parallel to work surface, and starting from a long side of turkey breast, cut breast horizontally almost, but not all the way through. Spread turkey breast open to make a butterflied breast.

◆ With rolling pin or meat mallet, pound butterflied breast between 2 sheets of plastic wrap into a 14" by 12" rectangle.

◆ Spread vegetable mixture evenly over entire turkey breast. Starting from a long side, roll turkey, jelly-roll fashion, to enclose stuffing completely. Tie turkey-breast roll securely with string at 1½-inch intervals; place on rack in small roasting pan.

◆ In cup, mix black pepper, ¾ teaspoon salt, and remaining 2 teaspoons oil and chopped parsley; pat over turkey-breast roll. Insert meat thermometer into center of roll. Roast turkey-breast roll 1¼ to 1½ hours, brushing occasionally with pan drippings, until thermometer reaches 170°F.

◆ Transfer turkey-breast roll to cutting board and discard string. Let roll stand 15 minutes for easier slicing. To serve, cut roll crosswise into ½-inch-thick slices. Arrange turkey slices on warm large platter.

Each serving: About 175 calories, 25g protein, 8g carbohydrate, 4g total fat (1g saturated), 60mg cholesterol, 405mg sodium

HERB-ROASTED TURKEY BREAST

Prep: 10 minutes plus refrigerating and standing
Roast: 2 hours to 2 hours 15 minutes
Makes 8 main-dish servings

¼ cup chopped fresh basil
1 tablespoon salt
1 teaspoon fennel seeds,
  crushed

¼ teaspoon coarsely ground
  black pepper
1 turkey breast (5 pounds)
Vegetable oil

◆ In small bowl, mix chopped basil, salt, fennel seeds, and pepper. Rub mixture all over turkey breast. Place turkey breast in large bowl; cover with plastic wrap and refrigerate overnight.

◆ Preheat oven to 325°F. Place turkey breast, skin-side up, on rack in medium roasting pan; rub skin with oil.

◆ Insert meat thermometer into thickest part of meat, being careful that pointed end of thermometer does not touch bone. Cover turkey breast with a loose tent of foil.

◆ Roast turkey breast 2 to 2¼ hours. Start checking for doneness during last 30 minutes of roasting. To brown turkey breast, remove foil during last 20 to 30 minutes of roasting; brush turkey breast generously with pan drippings for attractive sheen. Turkey breast is done when thermometer reaches 170°F.

◆ When turkey breast is done, place on warm large platter; let stand 15 minutes for easier slicing. Or, to serve cold, cover and refrigerate at least 3 hours. Cut turkey breast into thin slices.

Each serving: About 345 calories, 58g protein, 0g carbohydrate, 11g total fat (3g saturated), 108mg cholesterol, 870mg sodium

◆◆◆◆◆◆◆◆◆◆◆◆◆◆◆◆◆◆◆◆◆◆◆◆◆

BONING A TURKEY-BREAST HALF

1 Hold a sharp knife almost flat against the bone and rib cage; gently cut and scrape meat away, pulling it off in one piece as you cut.

2 Discard bones. Remove skin, then use knife to gently cut away the white tendon.

◆◆◆◆◆◆◆◆◆◆◆◆◆◆◆◆◆◆◆◆◆◆◆◆◆

ROASTED OR BAKED CHICKEN PIECES

Pan-roasting is terrific for chicken pieces coated with aromatic seasonings such as thyme, rosemary, and paprika, or enhanced with spicy marinades like our Indian-style yogurt mixture. Vegetables roasted along with the chicken and basted with the drippings are especially flavorful. Make sure your roasting pan is large enough so that the chicken pieces can roast evenly, and remove quicker-cooking breast pieces first. To keep cooked chicken warm, just cover the pieces loosely with a sheet of foil.

THYME-ROASTED CHICKEN AND VEGETABLES

Prep: 20 minutes   Roast: 50 minutes
Makes 4 main-dish servings

3 medium all-purpose
  potatoes (about 1 pound),
  unpeeled
1 large fennel bulb
  (1½ pounds)
1 large red onion
1 chicken (3 pounds), cut into
  8 pieces (see page 134) and
  skin removed
2 tablespoons olive oil

1 tablespoon chopped fresh
  thyme or 1 teaspoon dried
  thyme
1¼ teaspoons salt
¼ teaspoon ground black
  pepper
Thyme sprigs for garnish

1 Preheat oven to 450°F. Cut potatoes into 2-inch chunks. Trim fennel bulb, reserving some feathery tops, if any, for garnish; cut trimmed bulb into 8 wedges. Cut red onion into 8 wedges.

2 In large roasting pan, toss chicken and vegetables with olive oil; sprinkle with chopped thyme, salt, and pepper.

3 Roast chicken and vegetables 20 minutes; baste chicken and vegetables with pan drippings. Roast 20 minutes longer, basting once, until juices run clear when chicken breasts are pierced with tip of knife. Transfer chicken breasts to large serving bowl; keep warm.

4 Roast remaining chicken pieces and vegetables 10 minutes longer, or until juices run clear when chicken pieces are pierced with tip of knife and vegetables are tender. Transfer chicken and vegetables to serving bowl with chicken breasts.

5 To drippings in roasting pan, add *⅓ cup hot water*, stirring until brown bits are loosened. Spoon pan juices over chicken and vegetables. Garnish with thyme sprigs and reserved fennel tops.

EACH SERVING: ABOUT 430 CALORIES, 38g PROTEIN, 36g CARBOHYDRATE, 16g TOTAL FAT (3g SATURATED), 101mg CHOLESTEROL, 860mg SODIUM

BAKED LIME CHICKEN

Prep: 15 minutes   Roast: 50 minutes
Makes 4 main-dish servings

2 small limes
1 chicken (3½ pounds), cut
    into 8 pieces (see page 134)
3 tablespoons margarine or
    butter
¼ cup all-purpose flour
¾ teaspoon salt
½ teaspoon ground black
    pepper

2 tablespoons light brown
    sugar
1 can (13¾ to 14½ ounces)
    reduced-sodium chicken
    broth
Lime peel strips and lime
    wedges for garnish
Carrots and mashed potatoes
    (optional)

◆ Preheat oven to 400°F. Grate all peel and squeeze
2 tablespoons juice from limes. In large bowl, toss chicken
with lime juice. In large roasting pan, place margarine and
melt in oven. Remove pan from oven.

◆ On waxed paper, mix flour, salt, and pepper; use to coat
chicken pieces. Dip chicken pieces, one at a time, into
melted margarine in roasting pan, turning to coat. Arrange
chicken, skin-side up, in pan. (Do not use smaller pan and
crowd chicken pieces; they won't brown.)

◆ In cup, mix grated lime peel and brown sugar; sprinkle
over chicken pieces. Pour chicken broth into roasting pan
and bake 50 minutes, basting chicken with pan juices
occasionally, or until chicken is tender and juices run clear
when pierced with tip of knife.

◆ To serve, transfer chicken to 4 plates. Skim fat from pan
drippings. Spoon pan juices over chicken. Garnish with
lime peel strips and lime wedges. Serve with carrots and
mashed potatoes, if you like.

**Each serving: About 505 calories, 43g protein, 14g carbohydrate,
29g total fat (7g saturated), 166mg cholesterol, 650mg sodium**

HERB CHICKEN

Prep: 10 minutes   Roast: 40 minutes
Makes 8 main-dish servings

2 tablespoons chopped fresh
    thyme or 2 teaspoons dried
    thyme
2 tablespoons chopped fresh
    rosemary or 2 teaspoons
    dried rosemary, crushed
1 tablespoon olive oil
2 teaspoons paprika

1½ teaspoons salt
1 teaspoon coarsely ground
    black pepper
2 chickens (3½ pounds each),
    each cut into quarters
Fresh thyme and rosemary
    sprigs for garnish

◆ Preheat oven to 425°F. In cup, mix chopped thyme and
rosemary, olive oil, paprika, salt, and pepper; rub over
chicken quarters. Place chicken quarters, skin-side up, on
rack in large roasting pan. Roast chicken (do not turn)
40 minutes, or until golden and juices run clear when
pierced with tip of knife.

◆ Serve hot, or refrigerate to serve cold later. To serve,
arrange chicken on platter. Tuck thyme and rosemary sprigs
among chicken quarters.

**Each serving: About 380 calories, 42g protein, 1g carbohydrate,
22g total fat (6g saturated), 166mg cholesterol, 520mg sodium**

TANDOORI-STYLE CHICKEN

Prep: 10 minutes plus marinating   Roast: 30 minutes
Makes 6 main-dish servings

1 container (8 ounces) plain
    low-fat yogurt
½ small onion, chopped
2 tablespoons fresh lime juice
1 tablespoon minced, peeled
    fresh ginger
1 tablespoon paprika
1 teaspoon ground cumin
1 teaspoon ground coriander

¾ teaspoon salt
¼ teaspoon ground red
    pepper (cayenne)
Pinch ground cloves
6 chicken-breast halves (about
    3 pounds), skin removed
Lime wedges for garnish
Cooked basmati rice
    (optional)

◆ In blender at high speed or in food processor with knife
blade attached, blend all ingredients except chicken, lime
wedges, and rice until smooth. Place chicken in medium bowl
or in heavy-duty zip-tight plastic bag with yogurt marinade,
turning to coat. Marinate in refrigerator 30 minutes.

◆ Preheat oven to 450°F. Place chicken on rack in medium
roasting pan. Spoon half of marinade over chicken (discard
remaining marinade). Roast chicken 30 minutes, or until
juices run clear when pierced with tip of knife. Garnish with
lime wedges. Serve with basmati rice, if you like.

**Each serving: About 210 calories, 36g protein, 5g carbohydrate,
5g total fat (1g saturated), 94mg cholesterol, 375mg sodium**

OVEN-FRIED CHICKEN

You get all the crispness of fried chicken – without the extra fat and fuss of deep-frying – in the oven. Remove the skin before coating to cut fat further. Parmesan cheese and herbs make a savory, flavorful crust; or use a little cornmeal for some crunch.

CHICKEN MEXICANA

◆◆◆◆◆◆◆◆◆◆◆◆◆

Prep: 15 minutes
Bake: 40 to 45 minutes
Makes 8 main-dish servings

1 can (4 to 4½ ounces) chopped mild green chiles
½ cup Dijon mustard
1 tablespoon fresh lime juice
½ teaspoon ground black pepper
⅔ cup plain dried bread crumbs
⅔ cup yellow cornmeal
1 tablespoon paprika
2 tablespoons coarsely chopped fresh cilantro or parsley
½ teaspoon salt
1 teaspoon dried oregano
2 chickens (3 pounds each), each cut into 8 pieces (see page 134) and skin removed
2 tablespoons olive or vegetable oil
Tomato-Cucumber Salsa (optional, see right)
Lime slices, cilantro, and sliced pickled jalapeño chiles for garnish
Warm flour tortillas (optional)

1 In small bowl, mix green chiles, mustard, lime juice, and pepper until blended. On waxed paper, mix bread crumbs and next 5 ingredients.

2 Preheat oven to 425°F. Brush mustard mixture evenly onto chicken. Coat with bread-crumb mixture, firmly pressing crumb mixture onto chicken.

3 Grease 17" by 11½" roasting pan. Place chicken in roasting pan. With pastry brush, lightly dab oil onto chicken.

TOMATO-CUCUMBER SALSA

Cut 2 medium cucumbers, unpeeled, lengthwise in half, remove seeds, and dice. In large bowl, with wire whisk or fork, mix 3 tablespoons olive or vegetable oil, 3 tablespoons red wine vinegar, ¾ teaspoon sugar, ¾ teaspoon salt, and ½ teaspoon coarsely ground black pepper until blended. Stir in diced cucumbers, 4 medium tomatoes, seeded and diced, and 2 medium green peppers, diced, until well combined. Refrigerate until ready to serve. Makes 8 servings.

Each serving: About 75 calories, 1g protein, 7g carbohydrate, 5g total fat (1g saturated), 0mg cholesterol, 205mg sodium

4 Bake chicken (do not turn) 40 to 45 minutes, until crisp and juices run clear when pierced with tip of knife. Meanwhile, prepare Tomato-Cucumber Salsa, if desired. Garnish chicken; serve with salsa and tortillas, if you like.

EACH SERVING: ABOUT 365 CALORIES, 38g PROTEIN, 18g CARBOHYDRATE, 14g TOTAL FAT (3g SATURATED), 109mg CHOLESTEROL, 760mg SODIUM

"FRIED" CHICKEN

Prep: 25 minutes   Bake: 40 minutes
Makes 8 main-dish servings

4 chicken-breast halves (about 2½ pounds)
4 large chicken legs (about 2¼ pounds)
1 container (8 ounces) plain nonfat yogurt
1¼ teaspoons salt
1 cup plain dried bread crumbs
2 tablespoons chopped fresh cilantro or parsley
¾ teaspoon coarsely ground black pepper
Cilantro or parsley sprigs for garnish

◆ Preheat oven to 425°F. Remove skin and fat from chicken. Cut each leg at joint, separating drumstick from thigh.

◆ In pie plate, mix yogurt and salt. On waxed paper, mix bread crumbs, chopped cilantro, and pepper. Coat each piece of chicken lightly with yogurt mixture, then coat with bread-crumb mixture.

◆ Arrange chicken pieces in single layer in large roasting pan. Bake chicken (do not turn) 40 minutes, or until juices run clear when pierced with tip of knife.

◆ When chicken is done, if you like, turn oven control to broil. Broil chicken in roasting pan 4 to 5 minutes, until coating is golden brown. To serve, arrange chicken on warm large platter. Garnish with cilantro sprigs.

Each serving: About 365 calories, 43g protein, 12g carbohydrate, 15g total fat (4g saturated), 124g cholesterol, 580g sodium

"FRIED" CHICKEN WITH CORNMEAL CRUST

Prep: 15 minutes   Bake: 35 minutes
Makes 4 main-dish servings

Olive-oil nonstick cooking spray
½ cup plain dried bread crumbs
¼ cup freshly grated Parmesan cheese
2 tablespoons yellow cornmeal
½ teaspoon ground red pepper (cayenne)
1 large egg white
½ teaspoon salt
1 chicken (3½ pounds), cut into 8 pieces (see page 134) and skin removed

◆ Preheat oven to 425°F. Spray 15½" by 10½" jelly-roll pan with olive-oil nonstick cooking spray. On waxed paper, mix bread crumbs, Parmesan, cornmeal, and ground red pepper.

◆ In pie plate, beat egg white and salt. Coat each piece of chicken with egg-white mixture, then coat with bread-crumb mixture. Place chicken in jelly-roll pan; spray lightly with cooking spray.

◆ Bake chicken (do not turn the pieces) 35 minutes, or until coating is crisp and golden and juices run clear when chicken is pierced with tip of knife.

Each serving: About 370 calories, 47g protein, 14g carbohydrate, 13g total fat (4g saturated), 132mg cholesterol, 635mg sodium

CRISPY CHICKEN WITH PARMESAN TOMATOES

Prep: 15 minutes   Bake: 35 to 40 minutes
Makes 2 main-dish servings

¼ cup seasoned dried bread crumbs
1 tablespoon chopped fresh parsley
1 small garlic clove, minced
2 teaspoons olive or vegetable oil
Coarsely ground black pepper
2 tablespoons Dijon mustard
2 chicken-breast halves (about 1½ pounds)
3 medium plum tomatoes (about 12 ounces)
2 tablespoons freshly grated Parmesan cheese
1 teaspoon dried oregano

◆ Preheat oven to 400°F. In small bowl, mix first 4 ingredients and ¼ teaspoon pepper until blended. Brush mustard onto skin side of chicken-breast halves, then coat with crumb mixture, firmly pressing mixture onto chicken.

◆ Grease 11" by 7" glass or ceramic baking dish. Place chicken, skin-side up, in baking dish. Bake chicken (do not turn) 20 minutes.

◆ Meanwhile, cut each tomato lengthwise in half. On waxed paper, mix Parmesan cheese, oregano, and ¼ teaspoon pepper. Sprinkle Parmesan-cheese mixture evenly over tomato halves.

◆ Add tomatoes to baking dish with chicken; bake 15 to 20 minutes longer, until coating is crisp and browned and juices run clear when chicken is pierced with tip of knife.

Each serving: About 550 calories, 62g protein, 21g carbohydrate, 23g total fat (6g saturated), 161mg cholesterol, 1055mg sodium

COOKING SPRAYS

◆◆◆◆◆◆◆◆◆◆◆◆◆◆◆◆◆◆◆◆◆◆◆

Cooking sprays provide a quick, easy way to grease skillets, baking pans, and ceramic dishes and are especially helpful for ornate, fluted tube pans or barbecue grill racks (make sure to spray unheated rack). Although they add very little taste, olive-oil- or butter-flavored varieties are available. For an instant snack, lightly spray triangles of pita bread, top with crumbled oregano, and bake until golden.

STUFFED CHICKEN PIECES

Savory stuffings can dress up chicken pieces as well as whole birds. One technique is to form a "pocket" by separating the skin from the meat and then tucking the stuffing into the space formed. The skin will keep the filling next to the meat, infusing it with flavor. Alternatively, a flattened boneless chicken breast can be rolled around a filling and then secured with toothpicks. Aromatic basil and dried tomatoes, summer-ripe zucchini, and tangy feta cheese all feature in the stuffings given here.

CHICKEN BREASTS STUFFED WITH DRIED TOMATOES AND BASIL

◆◆◆◆◆◆◆◆◆◆◆◆◆◆◆◆◆◆◆◆◆◆◆◆◆◆◆◆

Prep: 20 minutes   *Bake:* 35 to 40 minutes
Makes 4 main-dish servings

1 bunch basil
¼ cup oil-packed dried
   tomatoes
2 tablespoons freshly grated
   Parmesan cheese
Coarsely ground black pepper
4 chicken-breast halves (about
   2½ pounds)

1 tablespoon oil from dried
   tomatoes
½ teaspoon salt
Zucchini Ribbons with Mint
   (optional, see page 304)

1 Preheat oven to 425°F. Chop enough basil to equal ¼ cup; reserve remaining for garnish. Coarsely chop dried tomatoes.

2 In small bowl, mix basil, tomatoes, Parmesan, and ½ teaspoon pepper. Push fingers between skin and meat of each chicken breast to form a pocket.

3 Place some basil mixture in each pocket. Place chicken breasts, skin-side up, in 13" by 9" glass baking dish.

4 Brush chicken with oil from dried tomatoes; sprinkle with salt and ½ teaspoon pepper. Bake chicken, basting occasionally with pan drippings, 35 to 40 minutes, until browned and juices run clear when chicken is pierced with tip of knife. Serve garnished with remaining basil, and zucchini ribbons, if you like.

FRESH BASIL

Fresh basil has a warm, sweet aroma quite unlike the dried herb (which has a more grassy, minty flavor). Purple opal basil is a pretty variety that has a spicier taste. To store, place basil in a jar, with stems in 2 inches water; cover with a plastic bag and secure with a rubber band.

EACH SERVING: ABOUT 365 CALORIES, 48g PROTEIN, 2g CARBOHYDRATE, 17g TOTAL FAT (5g SATURATED), 133mg CHOLESTEROL, 450mg SODIUM

CHEESE-STUFFED CHICKEN

Prep: 30 minutes   Bake: 45 minutes
Makes 6 main-dish servings

1 tablespoon olive oil
1 medium onion, minced
1 small carrot, shredded
1 bunch watercress, tough
   stems trimmed, chopped
1 container (8 ounces)
   ricotta cheese
¼ cup freshly grated
   Parmesan or Romano
   cheese

2 ounces Swiss cheese,
   shredded (½ cup)
⅛ teaspoon coarsely
   ground black pepper
3 chicken-breast halves (about
   1¾ pounds)
3 chicken-leg quarters (about
   1½ pounds)
½ teaspoon salt

◆ In 10-inch skillet, heat oil over medium heat; add onion and carrot. Cover and cook 5 minutes, stirring occasionally. Add watercress; cook, uncovered, until just wilted, stirring. Remove from heat; cool slightly. Preheat oven to 400°F.

◆ Stir all cheeses and pepper into vegetable mixture. Carefully push fingers between chicken skin and meat to form a pocket; fill with stuffing. Place chicken, stuffing-side up, in roasting pan; sprinkle with salt. Bake 45 minutes, basting frequently, or until juices run clear when chicken is pierced with tip of knife. Serve with pan juices.

Each serving: About 425 calories, 45g protein, 5g carbohydrate, 24g total fat (10g saturated), 143mg cholesterol, 420mg sodium

ZUCCHINI-STUFFED CHICKEN

Prep: 20 minutes   Bake: 50 minutes
Makes 4 main-dish servings

3 tablespoons margarine or
   butter
2 medium zucchini (about
   8 ounces each), shredded
3 slices white bread, torn
   into fine crumbs
2 ounces Swiss cheese,
   shredded (½ cup)

1 large egg
½ teaspoon salt
⅛ teaspoon ground black
   pepper
1 chicken (3 pounds), cut into
   quarters
2 tablespoons honey

◆ Preheat oven to 400°F. In 2-quart saucepan, melt margarine over medium heat; add zucchini and cook, stirring, about 2 minutes. Remove from heat. Stir in bread and cheese, then egg, salt, and pepper.

◆ Carefully push fingers between chicken skin and meat to form a pocket; fill with stuffing. Place chicken, skin-side up, in roasting pan; bake 50 minutes, or until juices run clear when chicken is pierced with tip of knife. Brush with honey.

Each serving: About 560 calories, 44g protein, 22g carbohydrate, 32g total fat (10g saturated), 208g cholesterol, 630g sodium

GREEK CHICKEN

Prep: 25 minutes   Cook: 25 minutes
Makes 6 main-dish servings

4 ounces feta cheese,
   crumbled (about 1 cup)
1 tablespoon fresh lemon
   juice
1 teaspoon dried oregano
6 skinless, boneless
   chicken-breast halves
   (about 2 pounds)
¾ teaspoon salt
¼ teaspoon ground black
   pepper

2 tablespoons all-purpose
   flour
2 tablespoons olive oil
1 teaspoon chicken-flavor
   instant bouillon
1 medium tomato, diced
½ (10- to 12-ounce) bunch
   spinach, coarsely sliced
   (2 cups loosely packed)
Toasted pita wedges
   (optional)

◆ In small bowl, with fork, mix feta cheese, lemon juice, and oregano until smooth. On work surface, with rolling pin or meat mallet, pound each chicken-breast half between 2 sheets plastic wrap to ½-inch thickness.

◆ With knife or small metal spatula, spread cheese mixture over each breast half to within ½ inch of edge. Fold each chicken breast crosswise in half to enclose filling; secure with toothpick. On sheet of waxed paper, mix salt, pepper, and 1 tablespoon flour; coat chicken with flour mixture.

◆ In 12-inch skillet, heat oil over medium-high heat; add chicken and cook until golden brown on both sides, turning once. Meanwhile, in cup, mix bouillon, remaining 1 tablespoon flour, and *1 cup water* until smooth. To chicken in skillet, add bouillon mixture, tomato, and spinach; heat to boiling over high heat. Reduce heat to low; cover and simmer 8 to 10 minutes, until juices run clear when chicken is pierced with tip of knife. To serve, remove and discard toothpicks. Serve chicken with pita wedges, if you like.

Each serving: About 285 calories, 37g protein, 5g carbohydrate, 12g total fat (5g saturated), 125mg cholesterol, 690mg sodium

PANFRIED POULTRY

Lean, quick-cooking cuts of poultry benefit from panfrying. Searing seals in the juices; a light coating of flour gives a golden crust. Use the flavorful pan drippings in a sauce, with a medley of mushrooms, or just a dash of wine and some broth.

COUNTRY FRENCH CHICKEN

◆◆◆◆◆◆◆◆◆◆◆◆

Prep: 20 minutes
Cook: 30 minutes
Makes 6 main-dish servings

1½ pounds chicken cutlets
3 tablespoons all-purpose flour
½ teaspoon salt
¼ teaspoon ground black
   pepper
2 tablespoons chopped fresh
   tarragon or 1 teaspoon
   dried tarragon
2 tablespoons olive oil
1 pound assorted mushrooms
   (white, cremini, shiitake),
   sliced
1 large shallot, minced
1 cup chicken broth
¼ cup dry white wine
Chopped fresh tarragon or
   parsley for garnish

SKILLETS

◆◆◆◆◆◆◆◆◆◆◆◆

A good skillet has a thick base so that heat spreads evenly, low sides so steam can escape, and a heat-safe handle. Stainless steel sandwiched with a copper core, anodized aluminum, and heavier cast iron are all excellent heat conductors.

1 If chicken cutlets are not evenly thin, pound to ⅛-inch thickness (see page 156). On waxed paper, mix flour, salt, pepper, and 1 tablespoon chopped tarragon; use to coat chicken cutlets.

2 In 12-inch skillet, heat 1 tablespoon oil over medium-high heat. Add mushrooms and shallot and cook, stirring often, 12 to 15 minutes, until any liquid evaporates. Transfer to bowl.

3 In same skillet, heat remaining 1 tablespoon oil. Add half of chicken; cook about 4 minutes per side, until golden. Transfer to platter; keep warm. Repeat with remaining chicken; transfer to platter.

4 To drippings in skillet, add chicken broth, white wine, mushroom mixture, and remaining 1 tablespoon chopped tarragon; boil 1 minute. Pour mushroom sauce over chicken cutlets; garnish with chopped tarragon.

EACH SERVING: ABOUT 230 CALORIES, 28g PROTEIN, 10g CARBOHYDRATE, 8g TOTAL FAT (2g SATURATED), 84mg CHOLESTEROL, 395mg SODIUM

CHICKEN WITH SHRIMP AND CAPERS

Prep: 25 minutes   Cook: 25 minutes
Makes 6 main-dish servings

1 pound large shrimp
1 pound chicken cutlets
3 tablespoons all-purpose flour
Salt
3 tablespoons olive or
   vegetable oil

1 package (10 ounces) large
   mushrooms, sliced
1 shallot or small onion,
   minced
¼ cup dry white wine
2 tablespoons capers, drained

◆ Shell and devein shrimp, leaving tail part of shell on, if you like (see page 90). If chicken cutlets are not evenly thin, pound to ⅛-inch thickness (see below). Cut chicken cutlets into 3" by 2" pieces. On waxed paper, combine 2 tablespoons flour and ¾ teaspoon salt; use to coat chicken.

◆ In nonstick 12-inch skillet, heat 1 tablespoon oil over medium-high heat; add mushrooms and cook, stirring often, 10 minutes, or until golden. With slotted spoon, transfer mushrooms to large bowl.

◆ In same skillet, heat 2 teaspoons oil over medium-high heat; add shrimp and shallot and cook, stirring often, until shrimp are opaque throughout. Transfer to bowl with mushrooms. In same skillet, heat 1 tablespoon oil over medium-high heat; add chicken, half at a time, and cook 2 to 3 minutes, until chicken loses its pink color throughout; transfer to same bowl.

◆ In drippings in skillet, heat remaining 1 teaspoon oil over medium-high heat. Stir in remaining 1 tablespoon flour; cook, stirring constantly, about 30 seconds, until flour begins to brown slightly. Gradually stir in wine, ½ teaspoon salt, and *1¼ cups water*. Cook over high heat until sauce thickens slightly and boils; boil 1 minute. Return chicken mixture to skillet; stir in capers and heat through.

Each serving: About 270 calories, 34g protein, 8g carbohydrate, 10g total fat (2g saturated), 171mg cholesterol, 690mg sodium

◆◆◆◆◆◆◆◆◆◆◆◆◆◆◆◆◆◆◆◆◆◆◆◆◆◆◆

POUNDING POULTRY CUTLETS

Gently pounding cutlets to a uniform thickness ensures even cooking and helps to tenderize the meat. Place each cutlet between two sheets of waxed paper or plastic wrap and pound with a rolling pin or meat mallet.

◆◆◆◆◆◆◆◆◆◆◆◆◆◆◆◆◆◆◆◆◆◆◆◆◆◆◆

SPRING TURKEY AND VEGETABLE PICCATA

Prep: 25 minutes   Cook: 20 minutes
Makes 6 main-dish servings

3 tablespoons olive or
   vegetable oil
1 large fennel bulb (about
   1¼ pounds), trimmed and
   cut into ¼-inch-thick slices
3 large carrots, cut into 3-inch-
   long matchstick-thin sticks
1 medium onion, diced
Salt

2 medium zucchini (about
   8 ounces each), cut into
   3-inch-long matchstick-thin
   sticks
1¼ pounds turkey cutlets
½ teaspoon coarsely ground
   black pepper
¼ teaspoon dried thyme
1 large lemon

◆ In nonstick 12-inch skillet, heat 2 tablespoons oil over medium-high heat; add fennel, carrots, onion, and ½ teaspoon salt and cook, stirring occasionally, until vegetables are lightly browned. Stir in zucchini; cook until vegetables are tender. Transfer vegetable mixture to bowl.

◆ If turkey cutlets are thick, pound to ⅛-inch thickness (see below left). Cut turkey cutlets into 3" by 2" pieces. Sprinkle with pepper, thyme, and ½ teaspoon salt.

◆ In same skillet, heat remaining 1 tablespoon oil over medium-high heat. Add turkey, a few pieces at a time, and cook 2 to 3 minutes, until turkey just loses its pink color throughout. Transfer to bowl with vegetables.

◆ Squeeze juice from half of lemon; slice remaining half for garnish. Pour lemon juice and ⅓ *cup water* into drippings in skillet, stirring until brown bits are loosened. Return turkey and vegetables to skillet; heat through. Serve garnished with lemon slices.

Each serving: About 245 calories, 27g protein, 18g carbohydrate, 8g total fat (1g saturated), 59mg cholesterol, 470mg sodium

COOKING WITH WINE

◆◆◆◆◆◆◆◆◆◆◆◆◆◆◆◆◆◆◆◆◆◆◆◆◆◆◆

Wine gives sauces, stews, and braised dishes an acid balance and a delicious depth of flavor. To avoid a sharp, raw taste, boil the wine to reduce it by at least half. This evaporates the alcohol and concentrates the wine, creating a mellow flavor. Wine can also be used to deglaze pan juices, or as a poaching liquid for fruit. It's essential to use a good-tasting wine, as the flavor in the bottle will be passed on to the final dish. White wines blend nicely with delicate poultry and fish; red wines create a deeper flavor and go well with red meats and game. Salty, smoked, or acidic foods can make wine taste flat. Avoid cooking wine in an aluminum pan, or the finished dish may have a metallic taste.

CHICKEN WITH LEMON-CAPER SAUCE

Prep: 15 minutes
Cook: 10 minutes
Makes 4 main-dish servings

2 tablespoons plus 1½ teaspoons all-purpose flour
½ teaspoon salt
1 large egg
4 skinless, boneless chicken-breast halves (about 1¼ pounds)
2 teaspoons olive or vegetable oil
2 tablespoons margarine or butter
½ cup chicken broth
¼ cup dry white wine
2 tablespoons fresh lemon juice
3 garlic cloves, crushed with side of knife
2 tablespoons capers, drained
Chopped fresh parsley for garnish

◆ On waxed paper, mix 2 tablespoons flour with salt. In pie plate, with fork, beat egg. Coat chicken with flour mixture, then dip in egg.

◆ In nonstick 12-inch skillet, heat oil and 1 tablespoon margarine over medium-high heat. Add chicken; cook 3 minutes. Reduce heat to medium; turn chicken and cook about 5 minutes longer, until juices run clear when chicken is pierced with tip of knife. Transfer to warm platter.

◆ In cup, mix chicken broth, wine, lemon juice, and remaining 1½ teaspoons flour until smooth. To drippings in skillet, add garlic; cook until golden. Stir in broth mixture and heat to boiling over high heat. Boil 1 minute. Stir in capers and remaining 1 tablespoon margarine until melted. Discard garlic. Pour sauce over chicken. Garnish with chopped parsley.

Each serving: About 290 calories, 34g protein, 5g carbohydrate, 13g total fat (3g saturated), 157mg cholesterol, 675mg sodium

CHICKEN BREASTS WITH TARRAGON SAUCE

Prep: 15 minutes
Cook: 25 minutes
Makes 4 main-dish servings

2 teaspoons plus 1 tablespoon olive or vegetable oil
2 large shallots, thinly sliced
1 teaspoon salt
1 tablespoon chopped fresh tarragon or ½ teaspoon dried tarragon
5 tablespoons all-purpose flour
4 chicken-breast halves (about 2½ pounds), skin removed
1 chicken-flavor bouillon cube or envelope

◆ In nonstick 12-inch skillet, heat 2 teaspoons oil over medium heat; add shallots and cook until tender and lightly browned. With slotted spoon, transfer shallots to small bowl.

◆ On waxed paper, mix salt, tarragon, and 3 tablespoons flour; use to coat chicken breasts. In same skillet, heat remaining 1 tablespoon oil over medium-high heat; add chicken and cook, turning once, until golden brown. Reduce heat to medium-low; cover and cook about 10 minutes longer, until juices run clear when chicken is pierced with tip of knife. Place chicken on 4 plates. Keep warm.

◆ In cup, mix remaining 2 tablespoons flour with *1½ cups water* until smooth. Add flour mixture, bouillon, and sautéed shallots to drippings in skillet; heat to boiling over high heat, stirring until brown bits are loosened. Boil 1 minute. Pour sauce over chicken.

Each serving: About 355 calories, 44g protein, 14g carbohydrate, 11g total fat (2g saturated), 114mg cholesterol, 860mg sodium

CHICKEN BREASTS WITH TOMATO-OLIVE SAUCE

Prep: 15 minutes
Cook: 20 minutes
Makes 4 main-dish servings

1 tablespoon olive or vegetable oil
4 skinless, boneless chicken-breast halves (about 1¼ pounds)
1 medium onion, finely chopped
1 tablespoon red wine vinegar
6 large plum tomatoes (about 1½ pounds) or 4 medium tomatoes, peeled, seeded, and chopped
½ cup Kalamata olives, pitted, or pitted ripe olives
Cooked pasta (optional)
Flat-leaf parsley sprigs for garnish

◆ In 12-inch skillet, heat oil over medium-high heat; add chicken-breast halves and cook about 8 minutes, until golden and juices run clear when chicken is pierced with tip of knife. Transfer chicken to plate.

◆ To drippings in skillet, add onion; cook over medium heat until tender-crisp. Add vinegar; cook until onion is very tender. Stir in tomatoes and olives; heat to boiling over high heat.

◆ Return chicken to skillet; heat through. Serve with pasta, if you like; garnish with parsley.

Each serving: About 300 calories, 34g protein, 13g carbohydrate, 13g total fat (2g saturated), 101mg cholesterol, 615mg sodium

SMOTHERED CHICKEN AND PEPPERS

Prep: 15 minutes   *Cook:* 30 minutes
Makes 4 main-dish servings

3 tablespoons all-purpose flour	1 pound medium red potatoes, each cut in half
Salt and ground black pepper	1 medium red pepper, diced
6 skinless, boneless chicken thighs (about 1¼ pounds), each cut in half	1 medium yellow pepper, diced
2 tablespoons olive oil	2 tablespoons brown sugar
	2 tablespoons cider vinegar

◆ On waxed paper, mix flour, 1 teaspoon salt, and ¼ teaspoon black pepper; use to coat chicken.

◆ In nonstick 12-inch skillet, heat oil over medium-high heat. Add chicken thighs and cook until golden brown; transfer to bowl. To drippings in skillet, add potatoes, diced peppers, ½ teaspoon salt, and ¼ teaspoon black pepper; cook until vegetables are golden.

◆ Return chicken to skillet. Reduce heat to medium; cover and cook, stirring often, 10 to 15 minutes, or until juices run clear when chicken is pierced with tip of knife and potatoes are fork-tender. Stir in brown sugar and vinegar; heat through.

Each serving: About 430 calories, 31g protein, 39g carbohydrate, 17g total fat (4g saturated), 132mg cholesterol, 930mg sodium

TURKEY CUTLETS WITH CHOPPED SALAD

Prep: 20 minutes   *Cook:* 8 to 10 minutes
Makes 4 main-dish servings

1 green onion, thinly sliced	4 large plum tomatoes (about 1 pound), cut into ¾-inch pieces
2 tablespoons freshly grated Parmesan cheese	
1 tablespoon red wine vinegar	2 bunches arugula, coarsely chopped
½ teaspoon Dijon mustard	
¼ teaspoon salt	4 large turkey cutlets (about 1 pound)
¼ teaspoon coarsely ground black pepper	
3 to 4 tablespoons olive or vegetable oil	⅓ cup seasoned dried bread crumbs

◆ In medium bowl, with wire whisk or fork, mix green onion with next 5 ingredients and 2 tablespoons oil. Add tomatoes and arugula; toss gently to mix well.

◆ Pound turkey cutlets to ¼-inch thickness (see page 156). Place bread crumbs on waxed paper; use to coat turkey cutlets. In nonstick 12-inch skillet, heat 1 tablespoon oil over medium-high heat. Add cutlets, 2 at a time; cook 2 to 3 minutes per side, until cutlets are golden and lose their

pink color throughout, adding remaining 1 tablespoon oil if necessary. To serve, place turkey cutlets on 4 plates; pile chopped salad on top.

Each serving: About 300 calories, 32g protein, 13g carbohydrate, 13g fat (2g saturated), 73mg cholesterol, 345mg sodium

POTATO-CRISP CHICKEN

Prep: 20 minutes   *Cook:* 15 minutes
Makes 2 main-dish servings

2 skinless, boneless chicken-breast halves (about ¾ pound)	Salt
	¼ teaspoon coarsely ground black pepper
1 large baking potato (about 10 ounces), peeled	2 tablespoons vegetable oil
	Parsley sprigs for garnish

◆ Pound chicken-breast halves to ¼-inch thickness (see page 156).

◆ With sharp knife, cut wide portion of potato crosswise into 24 paper-thin slices, immediately placing cut potato slices into bowl of cold water to prevent discoloration. Drain; pat dry with paper towels.

◆ On work surface, arrange 6 potato slices into an oval the same size as a chicken-breast half, overlapping slices to fit. Place chicken breast on top of potato slices; sprinkle with ⅛ teaspoon salt. Top chicken with another 6 potato slices. Repeat with remaining potato slices and chicken.

◆ In 12-inch skillet, heat oil over medium-high heat; add chicken and cook until potatoes are golden on bottom. Reduce heat to medium and cook 2 to 3 minutes longer, until potatoes are browned.

◆ With pancake turner, carefully turn chicken; sprinkle with pepper and ¼ teaspoon salt. Cook over medium-high heat until potatoes are golden on second side. Reduce heat to medium and cook 2 to 3 minutes longer, until potatoes are browned and fork-tender and juices run clear when chicken is pierced with tip of knife. To serve, arrange chicken breasts on 2 plates. Garnish with parsley sprigs.

Each serving: About 430 calories, 41g protein, 26g carbohydrate, 18g total fat (4g saturated), 122mg cholesterol, 460mg sodium

SKILLET-BRAISED CHICKEN

The secret to these full-bodied dishes is cooking the chicken in two steps. First sear it in hot oil to seal in juices and create a rich, browned flavor. Next simmer it, covered, in liquid until tender and cooked through. Pair these saucy dishes with vegetable purees, polenta, or risotto, to soak up all the delicious juices.

CHICKEN OSSO-BUCO STYLE

◆◆◆◆◆◆◆◆◆◆◆◆◆

Prep: 20 minutes
Cook: 45 minutes
Makes 4 main-dish servings

2 tablespoons vegetable oil
8 chicken thighs (about 2½ pounds), skin and fat removed
1 teaspoon salt
1 large onion
4 medium carrots
1 large celery stalk
1 can (14½ to 16 ounces) Italian-style stewed tomatoes
Chopped fresh parsley and grated lemon peel for garnish

1 In 12-inch skillet, heat oil over medium-high heat. Add chicken thighs; sprinkle with salt. Cook until golden on all sides. Transfer to bowl.

2 Meanwhile, on cutting board, coarsely chop onion. Dice carrots and celery. To drippings in skillet, add onion, carrots, and celery and cook, stirring frequently, 10 minutes, or until vegetables are lightly browned.

WHAT'S IN A NAME?
◆◆◆◆◆◆◆◆◆◆◆

Osso buco is the Italian name both for veal shanks and the classic Milanese method of cooking them: They are first braised with aromatic vegetables and tomatoes, then enlivened with a last-minute sprinkling of lemon peel, parsley, and garlic. You can achieve the same delicious flavor – in much less time – with chicken.

3 Return chicken thighs to skillet; stir in stewed tomatoes. Heat to boiling over high heat.

4 Reduce heat to low. Cover and simmer 25 minutes, or until juices run clear when chicken is pierced with tip of knife. Serve sprinkled with chopped parsley and grated lemon peel.

EACH SERVING: ABOUT 440 CALORIES, 42g PROTEIN, 18g CARBOHYDRATE, 21g TOTAL FAT (5g SATURATED), 190mg CHOLESTEROL, 935mg SODIUM

CHICKEN WITH OLIVES AND THYME

Prep: 15 minutes   Cook: 45 minutes
Makes 4 main-dish servings

1 tablespoon olive oil
8 skinless chicken thighs
  (about 2¼ pounds)
Salt
2 small onions (about
  4 ounces each), each cut
  into 6 wedges

¾ cup reduced-sodium
  chicken broth
½ cup Kalamata olives, pitted
1 teaspoon chopped fresh
  thyme or ¼ teaspoon dried
  thyme
2 teaspoons all-purpose flour

◆ In nonstick 12-inch skillet, heat oil over medium-high heat. Add chicken; sprinkle with ¼ teaspoon salt and cook until lightly browned on all sides. Transfer to plate.

◆ To drippings in skillet, add onions and cook, shaking skillet occasionally, until golden. Stir in chicken broth, olives, and thyme; return chicken to skillet. Reduce heat to low; cover and simmer 20 to 25 minutes, until juices run clear when chicken is pierced with tip of knife.

◆ Transfer chicken to warm platter. In cup, mix flour, ¼ teaspoon salt, and *1 tablespoon water* until smooth. Stir flour mixture into skillet. Heat to boiling over high heat, stirring; boil about 1 minute, until sauce thickens slightly. Pour sauce over chicken and serve.

Each serving: About 420 calories, 42g protein, 8g carbohydrate, 24g total fat (5g saturated), 190mg cholesterol, 1005mg sodium

ORANGE-ROSEMARY CHICKEN

Prep: 15 minutes   Cook: 30 minutes
Makes 4 main-dish servings

2 tablespoons olive or
  vegetable oil
6 skinless, boneless chicken
  thighs (about 1¼ pounds),
  each cut in half
1 large onion (8 ounces),
  thinly sliced
Salt

4 medium red potatoes
  (about 12 ounces)
1 medium orange
¼ cup chicken broth
1 tablespoon all-purpose flour
1 teaspoon chopped fresh
  rosemary or ¼ teaspoon
  dried rosemary

◆ In 12-inch skillet, heat oil over medium-high heat. Add chicken, onion, and 1 teaspoon salt and cook about 15 minutes, until onion is tender and chicken thighs are browned on all sides and lose their pink color throughout. With fork, transfer chicken to bowl, leaving onions in skillet.

◆ Meanwhile, cut potatoes into 1¼-inch chunks. With vegetable peeler, cut two 2½" by ¾" strips of peel from orange; reserve. Into 2-cup measuring cup, squeeze ¼ cup juice from orange; stir in broth, flour, and ¾ *cup water* until smooth.

◆ To skillet with onion, add potatoes, orange-juice mixture, and ¼ teaspoon salt; heat to boiling over high heat, stirring. Reduce heat to low; cover and simmer 10 minutes or until potatoes are almost tender.

◆ Return chicken thighs to skillet; stir in rosemary and cook until potatoes are tender and chicken is heated through. Meanwhile, cut reserved orange peel into thin strips. Serve garnished with orange peel.

Each serving: About 395 calories, 33g protein, 25g carbohydrate, 18g total fat (4g saturated), 144mg cholesterol, 865mg sodium

HARVEST SKILLET DINNER

Prep: 25 minutes   Cook: 40 minutes
Makes 6 main-dish servings

1 medium butternut squash
  (2 pounds)
1 jumbo onion (about
  1 pound)
1 small bunch kale (about
  1 pound)
1 teaspoon vegetable oil
6 chicken thighs (about
  2½ pounds), skin and fat
  removed

¾ teaspoon salt
1 can (13¾ to 14½ ounces)
  chicken broth
1 tablespoon all-purpose flour
¼ cup dried cranberries or
  raisins
Crusty bread (optional)

◆ Cut squash lengthwise in half and remove seeds; cut each half crosswise into 1-inch-thick slices. Cut peel from slices; cut into bite-size chunks. Cut onion into thick slices. Remove tough ribs from kale leaves; tear leaves into bite-size pieces. Meanwhile, in deep nonstick 12-inch skillet, heat oil over medium-high heat. Add chicken and cook until browned on all sides; transfer to plate.

◆ To drippings in skillet, add squash, onion, salt, and *2 tablespoons water*; cook until vegetables are browned. In small bowl, stir together broth and flour; add to skillet along with kale and cranberries. Return chicken to skillet; heat to boiling over high heat. Reduce heat to low; cover and simmer 20 minutes, or until vegetables are tender and juices run clear when chicken is pierced with tip of knife. Serve with bread, if you like.

Each serving: About 290 calories, 25g protein, 31g carbohydrate, 9g total fat (2g saturated), 100mg cholesterol, 655mg sodium

SWEET-AND-SPICY CHICKEN

Prep: 10 minutes
Cook: 40 minutes
Makes 6 main-dish servings

1 tablespoon vegetable oil
1 chicken (3½ pounds), cut into 8 pieces (see page 134)
1 medium onion, diced
1 medium green pepper, diced
½ cup blanched whole almonds
2 teaspoons chili powder
1 can (8 ounces) tomatoes
1 teaspoon salt
¼ teaspoon ground cinnamon
2 large sweet potatoes (about 2 pounds), peeled and cut into ½-inch-thick slices
1 large red cooking apple, cut into wedges
Cilantro sprigs for garnish

◆ In 12-inch skillet, heat oil over medium-high heat. Add chicken and cook about 10 minutes, until browned on all sides; transfer to plate.

◆ Discard all but 2 tablespoons drippings from skillet. To drippings, add onion, green pepper, and almonds; cook over medium heat about 10 minutes, until vegetables are tender and almonds are lightly browned.

◆ Stir in chili powder; cook, stirring constantly, 1 minute. Remove skillet from heat; stir in tomatoes with their juice, salt, cinnamon, and *1¼ cups water*, stirring until brown bits are loosened.

◆ In blender at low speed, blend tomato mixture until smooth. Return tomato mixture and chicken to skillet; add sweet potatoes. Heat to boiling over high heat. Reduce heat to low; cover and simmer, stirring occasionally, 20 minutes, or until juices run clear when chicken is pierced with tip of knife. Add apple wedges to skillet; heat through. Serve garnished with cilantro.

Each serving: About 520 calories, 34g protein, 49g carbohydrate, 22g total fat (5g saturated), 111mg cholesterol, 525mg sodium

CHICKEN AND MUSHROOMS

Prep: 5 minutes
Cook: 1 hour
Makes 4 main-dish servings

1 tablespoon vegetable oil
1 chicken (3½ pounds), cut into quarters
1 small onion, minced
1¼ teaspoons salt
¼ teaspoon dried thyme
1 pound small mushrooms
¼ cup all-purpose flour
½ cup half-and-half or light cream
1 small bunch dill
Hot cooked rice (optional)

◆ In 12-inch skillet, heat oil over medium heat; add chicken and cook until lightly browned on all sides. Transfer to plate. To drippings in skillet, add onion; cook until tender but not browned.

◆ Return chicken to skillet. Add salt, thyme, and *2 cups water*; heat to boiling over high heat. Reduce heat to low; cover and simmer 30 minutes.

◆ Add mushrooms to skillet; cover and simmer 15 minutes longer, or until chicken is tender.

◆ With slotted spoon, transfer chicken and mushrooms to warm large platter. Skim fat from liquid in skillet.

◆ In cup, stir flour and *⅓ cup water* until blended; slowly add to skillet and cook, stirring constantly, until sauce thickens slightly and boils. Stir in half-and-half; heat through.

◆ To serve, pour some sauce over chicken; pour remainder into sauceboat. Chop 1 tablespoon dill; sprinkle over chicken and mushrooms. Garnish with remaining dill. Serve with rice, if you like, and sauce.

Each serving: About 630 calories, 61g protein, 15g carbohydrate, 35g total fat (11g saturated), 237mg cholesterol, 850mg sodium

CHICKEN MOLE

Prep: 10 minutes
Cook: 45 minutes
Makes 6 main-dish servings

1 can (14½ ounces) diced tomatoes
1 can (4 to 4½ ounces) chopped mild green chiles
½ cup blanched whole almonds
½ small onion, cut into chunks
1 small garlic clove
1 tablespoon chili powder
1 teaspoon ground cumin
1 teaspoon ground coriander
1 teaspoon salt
¾ teaspoon ground cinnamon
½ teaspoon sugar
1 tablespoon olive oil
3 pounds bone-in chicken parts, skin removed
½ square (½ ounce) unsweetened chocolate, chopped
Chopped fresh cilantro for garnish
Sautéed peppers and onions (optional)

◆ Prepare mole sauce: In blender at high speed, blend first 11 ingredients until smooth.

◆ In nonstick 12-inch skillet, heat oil over medium-high heat. Add chicken in batches and cook until golden; transfer to plate. Add sauce, chocolate, and *¼ cup water* to skillet; cook, stirring, until chocolate melts. Add chicken; heat to boiling over high heat. Reduce heat to low; cover and simmer 30 to 35 minutes, until juices run clear when chicken is pierced with tip of knife. Garnish; serve with peppers and onions, if you like.

Each serving: About 305 calories, 38g protein, 10g carbohydrate, 13g total fat (2g saturated), 91mg cholesterol, 745mg sodium

CHICKEN WITH MUSSELS AND CLAMS

Prep: 10 minutes   *Cook:* 55 minutes
Makes 6 main-dish servings

1 chicken (3½ pounds), cut into 8 pieces (see page 134)
½ teaspoon ground black pepper
Salt
2 tablespoons vegetable oil
1 can (14½ to 16 ounces) stewed tomatoes
1 can (4 to 4½ ounces) chopped mild green chiles
1 tablespoon chili powder
1 teaspoon sugar
1 dozen littleneck clams
1 dozen small mussels
1 tablespoon chopped fresh parsley
1 tablespoon margarine or butter
¼ teaspoon ground turmeric (optional)
1 cup couscous (Moroccan pasta)
Parsley sprigs for garnish

◆ Remove skin from all chicken pieces except wings. Sprinkle chicken with pepper and ½ teaspoon salt. In 12-inch skillet, heat oil over medium-high heat. Add chicken and cook until browned on all sides; pour off fat from skillet. Stir in tomatoes, green chiles, chili powder, sugar, and *1 cup water*; heat to boiling over high heat. Reduce heat to low; cover and simmer 30 minutes.

◆ Meanwhile, with stiff brush, scrub clams and mussels with cold running water to remove any sand; remove beards from mussels (see page 88). To chicken in skillet, add clams and mussels; cover and cook 8 to 10 minutes, until shells open. Discard any that do not open. Sprinkle shellfish and chicken with chopped parsley.

◆ While shellfish is cooking, prepare couscous: In 2-quart saucepan, heat margarine, turmeric, ½ teaspoon salt, and *1½ cups water* to boiling over high heat. Stir in couscous. Cover saucepan and remove from heat; let stand 5 minutes. Fluff couscous with fork. Serve chicken with couscous. Garnish with parsley.

Each serving: About 490 calories, 40g protein, 32g carbohydrate, 22g total fat (5g saturated), 136mg cholesterol, 815mg sodium

SPICY PEANUT CHICKEN

Prep: 15 minutes   *Cook:* 1 hour
Makes 4 main-dish servings

1 teaspoon ground cumin
¼ teaspoon ground cinnamon
4 chicken-leg quarters (about 2¼ pounds), skin removed
1 tablespoon vegetable oil
1 medium onion, sliced
1 can (28 ounces) plum tomatoes, drained and chopped, juice reserved
¼ cup creamy peanut butter
¼ cup packed fresh cilantro leaves
2 garlic cloves
½ teaspoon salt
¼ teaspoon crushed red pepper

In cup, mix cumin and cinnamon; use to rub over chicken. In nonstick 12-inch skillet, heat oil over medium-high heat; add chicken and cook until browned. Add onion; cook 5 minutes. In blender at high speed, puree reserved tomato juice and remaining ingredients; pour over chicken. Stir in tomatoes; heat to boiling over high heat. Reduce heat to low; cover and simmer 40 minutes, or until juices run clear when chicken is pierced with tip of knife.

Each serving: About 385 calories, 35g protein, 16g carbohydrate, 21g total fat (5g saturated), 98mg cholesterol, 765mg sodium

CHICKEN RAGOUT

Prep: 15 minutes   *Cook:* 55 minutes
Makes 4 main-dish servings

3 tablespoons vegetable oil
1 chicken (2½ pounds), cut into quarters and skin removed
1 teaspoon salt
½ teaspoon dried thyme
¼ teaspoon coarsely ground black pepper
2 medium zucchini, cut into ¾-inch chunks
3 medium carrots, chopped
1 large onion, chopped
2 teaspoons all-purpose flour
1 can (28 ounces) plum tomatoes

◆ In nonstick 12-inch skillet, heat 1 tablespoon oil over medium-high heat. Add chicken; sprinkle with salt, thyme, and pepper and cook until browned. Transfer chicken to plate. To drippings in skillet, add zucchini. Cook until tender; transfer to bowl. In same skillet, heat remaining 2 tablespoons oil; add carrots and onion and cook until browned.

◆ In cup, mix flour and *2 tablespoons water* until smooth; add to skillet. Add tomatoes with their juice, breaking up tomatoes with back of spoon. Return chicken to skillet; heat to boiling over high heat. Reduce heat to low; cover and simmer 25 minutes, or until juices run clear when chicken is pierced with tip of knife. Stir in zucchini; heat through.

Each serving: About 390 calories, 34g protein, 24g carbohydrate, 19g total fat (4g saturated), 90mg cholesterol, 965mg sodium

POULTRY CASSEROLES AND STEWS

After browning chicken or duck – both to seal in the juices and to add a slightly caramelized flavor – you can leave it to simmer in a flavorful liquid with vegetables on top of the stove or in the oven. The family-pleasing result: A one-dish meal that is the very definition of comfort food. Fluffy rosemary dumplings sop up the broth here, while our delicate anise-perfumed bouillabaisse simply calls out for crusty French bread.

CHICKEN AND VEGETABLES WITH ROSEMARY DUMPLINGS

◆◆◆◆◆◆◆◆◆◆◆◆◆◆◆◆◆◆◆◆◆◆◆◆◆◆

Prep: 20 minutes   Cook: 1 hour
Makes 6 main-dish servings

2 tablespoons vegetable oil	1 can (13¾ to 14½ ounces) reduced-sodium chicken broth
6 chicken-breast halves (about 3¼ pounds), skin removed	¼ teaspoon ground black pepper
½ teaspoon salt	2 tablespoons all-purpose flour
4 large carrots, cut into ¼-inch-thick slices	1 cup milk
2 large celery stalks, cut into ¼-inch-thick slices	1 package (10 ounces) frozen peas, thawed
1 medium onion, diced	Rosemary sprigs and chopped fresh chives for garnish
Rosemary Dumplings (see below right)	

1 In 8-quart Dutch oven, heat 1 tablespoon oil over medium-high heat. Add chicken, half at a time, sprinkling each batch with ¼ teaspoon salt; cook 8 to 10 minutes, until lightly browned. Transfer to bowl.

2 In drippings in skillet, heat remaining 1 tablespoon oil; add carrots, celery, and onion and cook, stirring frequently, about 10 minutes, until browned and tender.

3 Meanwhile, prepare dumplings. Return chicken to Dutch oven; add broth, pepper, and *2 cups water*. Heat to boiling over high heat.

4 Drop dumpling mixture by rounded tablespoons into Dutch oven to make 12 dumplings. Cover Dutch oven; reduce heat to low and simmer 15 minutes.

5 With slotted spoon, transfer dumplings, chicken, and vegetables to large shallow bowl; reserve broth in Dutch oven. In small bowl, beat flour with milk; whisk into broth.

6 Heat to boiling over high heat; boil, stirring, 1 minute, or until sauce thickens slightly. Add peas and heat through. Pour sauce over chicken and vegetables; garnish and serve.

ROSEMARY DUMPLINGS

In small bowl, mix 2 teaspoons baking powder, 1½ teaspoons chopped fresh rosemary or ½ teaspoon dried rosemary, crushed, 1 cup all-purpose flour, and ½ teaspoon salt. In cup, with fork, beat ½ cup milk with 1 large egg. Stir milk mixture into flour mixture just until blended. Shape and cook as directed in Step 4, above. Makes 12 dumplings.

EACH SERVING: ABOUT 460 CALORIES, 46g PROTEIN, 37g CARBOHYDRATE, 13g TOTAL FAT (4g SATURATED), 143mg CHOLESTEROL, 585mg SODIUM

COUNTRY CAPTAIN CASSEROLE

Prep: 1 hour   Bake: 1 hour
Makes 8 main-dish servings

2 tablespoons plus 1 teaspoon
   vegetable oil
2 chickens (3½ pounds each),
   each cut into 8 pieces (see
   page 134) and skin removed
2 medium onions, chopped
1 large Granny Smith apple,
   peeled, cored, and diced
1 large green pepper, diced
3 large garlic cloves, minced
1 tablespoon grated, peeled
   fresh ginger

3 tablespoons curry powder
¼ teaspoon ground cumin
1 teaspoon salt
½ teaspoon coarsely ground
   black pepper
1 can (28 ounces) tomatoes in
   puree
1 can (13¾ to 14½ ounces)
   chicken broth
½ cup dark seedless raisins

◆ Preheat oven to 350°F. In 8-quart Dutch oven, heat 2 tablespoons oil over medium-high heat. Add chicken in batches and cook until browned; transfer to bowl. In drippings in Dutch oven, heat remaining 1 teaspoon oil; add onions and next 4 ingredients and cook, stirring frequently, 2 minutes. Reduce heat to low; cover and cook 5 minutes.

◆ Stir in curry powder and cumin; cook 1 minute. Stir in remaining ingredients. Return chicken to Dutch oven; heat to boiling over high heat. Boil 1 minute. Cover; bake 1 hour, or until juices run clear when chicken is pierced with tip of knife.

Each serving: About 400 calories, 44g protein, 22g carbohydrate, 16g total fat (4g saturated), 131mg cholesterol, 935mg sodium

CHINESE SPICED DUCK CASSEROLE

Prep: 30 minutes   Bake: 2 hours
Makes 4 main-dish servings

1 duckling (4½ pounds), cut
   into quarters (see page 135)
4 medium red onions, halved
¼ cup soy sauce
2 tablespoons dry sherry
1 tablespoon grated, peeled
   fresh ginger

1 teaspoon sugar
2 star anise or ¼ teaspoon
   anise seeds
2 containers (10 ounces each)
   Brussels sprouts, trimmed,
   each cut in half if large

◆ To 8-quart Dutch oven, add duckling and cook over high heat until browned; transfer to large bowl. Discard all but 1 tablespoon drippings from Dutch oven. To drippings in Dutch oven, add onions; cook 10 minutes, or until golden. Transfer to bowl with duckling.

◆ Preheat oven to 350°F. Into Dutch oven, stir soy sauce, sherry, ginger, sugar, star anise, and ¾ cup water. Heat to boiling over high heat, stirring until brown bits are loosened. Return duckling and onions to Dutch oven. Cover and bake, basting occasionally with cooking liquid, 1¼ hours.

◆ Stir in Brussels sprouts. Cover and bake 45 minutes longer, or until duckling is tender. Skim fat from liquid in Dutch oven before serving.

Each serving: About 740 calories, 57g protein, 30g carbohydrate, 43g total fat (13g saturated), 178mg cholesterol, 1205mg sodium

CHICKEN BOUILLABAISSE

Prep: 30 minutes   Bake: 1 hour
Makes 4 main-dish servings

1 tablespoon olive oil
8 chicken thighs (about
   2½ pounds), skin removed
2 large carrots, diced
1 medium onion, diced
1 medium fennel bulb,
   trimmed and sliced
3 garlic cloves, minced
1 can (14½ ounces) diced
   tomatoes
½ cup dry white wine

1 can (13¾ to 14½ ounces)
   reduced-sodium chicken
   broth
2 tablespoons Pernod or
   other anise-flavor apéritif
   (optional)
¼ teaspoon dried thyme
⅛ teaspoon ground red
   pepper (cayenne)
1 bay leaf
Pinch saffron threads

◆ In 5-quart Dutch oven, heat oil over medium-high heat. Add chicken thighs, half at a time; cook about 12 minutes, until browned. Transfer to bowl. To drippings in Dutch oven, add carrots and onion; cook, stirring occasionally, about 10 minutes, until tender and golden. Transfer to same bowl.

◆ Preheat oven to 350°F. Add fennel and ½ cup water to Dutch oven, stirring until brown bits are loosened. Cook, stirring occasionally, about 7 minutes, until fennel is tender and browned. Add garlic and cook 3 minutes longer.

◆ Return chicken and carrot mixture to Dutch oven; add tomatoes with their juice and remaining ingredients. Heat to boiling over high heat. Cover and bake 30 minutes, or until juices run clear when chicken is pierced with tip of knife. Remove bay leaf before serving.

Each serving: About 415 calories, 36g protein, 23g carbohydrate, 18g total fat (4g saturated), 116mg cholesterol, 555mg sodium

---

BAY LEAVES

Aromatic bay leaves, also called sweet bay or laurel, impart a deep, heady flavor to long-simmered dishes. Fresh leaves are vibrant green and deliver a sharp, pungent flavor. Bay leaves from California taste strongest (you may choose to use half a leaf), while Turkish bay leaves offer a sweeter, subtler taste. To avoid any danger of swallowing, always discard bay leaves before serving the food.

POACHED POULTRY

Poaching is the perfect low-fat cooking method, resulting in tender, flavorful meat. The aromatic vegetables and herbs that are simmered with the poultry infuse both the meat and the broth with delicious flavor. Reserve the broth to create a sauce for the dish, or use it as a base for soups or rice pilafs.

TURKEY AND SHRIMP BLANQUETTE

◆◆◆◆◆◆◆◆◆◆◆◆◆◆◆◆◆◆◆◆◆◆◆◆◆◆◆◆◆

Prep: 40 minutes plus cooling   Cook: 1 hour 30 minutes
Makes 10 main-dish servings

3 medium onions
1 bag (16 ounces) carrots
1 large celery stalk, thickly sliced
1 turkey-breast half (2½ pounds), skin removed
½ cup dry white wine
10 black peppercorns
1 whole clove
4 tablespoons margarine or butter
1 package (12 ounces) mushrooms, sliced

Salt
⅓ cup all-purpose flour
2 cups milk
1½ pounds large shrimp, shelled and deveined (see page 90)
1 package (10 ounces) frozen peas
2 tablespoons chopped fresh dill
Dill sprigs for garnish
Mashed potatoes and French bread (optional)

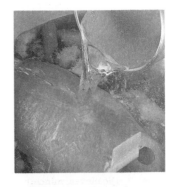

1 Thickly slice 1 onion and 1 carrot; set remainder aside. In 5-quart Dutch oven heat sliced vegetables, turkey, wine, peppercorns, clove, and *4 cups water* to boiling over high heat. Reduce heat to low; cover and simmer, turning turkey occasionally, 30 minutes, or until it loses its pink color throughout.

2 Meanwhile, dice remaining onions. Cut remaining carrots diagonally into ⅛-inch-thick slices. Transfer turkey to bowl; set aside. Strain turkey broth through sieve into 4-quart saucepan; discard cooked vegetable mixture.

3 Heat broth to boiling over high heat. Reduce heat to medium; cook about 30 minutes, until reduced to 2 cups.

4 When cool enough to handle, discard bones from turkey. Cut turkey into bite-size chunks. Return turkey chunks to bowl.

5 In same Dutch oven, melt 2 tablespoons margarine over high heat. Add sliced carrots, mushrooms, and ½ teaspoon salt; cook until carrots are tender. Transfer to bowl with turkey.

6 In same Dutch oven, melt remaining 2 tablespoons margarine over medium heat. Add diced onions and 1 teaspoon salt; cook until onions are tender but not browned. Stir in flour; cook, stirring constantly, 1 minute. Gradually stir in milk and turkey broth; heat, stirring, to boiling.

7 Reduce heat to low; simmer, stirring constantly, about 1 minute, until sauce thickens slightly. Stir in shrimp, turkey, carrots, mushrooms, and peas. Simmer just until shrimp are opaque throughout and blanquette is heated through. Stir in chopped dill. Garnish with dill sprigs and serve with mashed potatoes and French bread, if you like.

EACH SERVING: ABOUT 280 CALORIES, 31g PROTEIN, 20g CARBOHYDRATE, 8g TOTAL FAT (2g SATURATED), 152mg CHOLESTEROL, 590mg SODIUM

POULE AU POT WITH TARRAGON

Prep: 15 minutes   Cook: 1 hour
Makes 4 main-dish servings

1 chicken (3½ pounds),
    cut into 8 pieces (see
    page 134)
1 pound small red potatoes
1 bag (16 ounces) carrots,
    each quartered lengthwise
    then cut into 3-inch pieces
3 medium leeks, cleaned and
    cut into 3-inch pieces
1 can (13¾ to 14½ ounces)
    reduced-sodium chicken
    broth
½ teaspoon salt
¼ teaspoon ground black
    pepper
¼ teaspoon dried thyme
1 small bunch tarragon

◆ In 6- to 8-quart Dutch oven, combine chicken, potatoes, carrots, leeks, broth, salt, pepper, thyme, 1 large sprig tarragon, and *4 cups water*. Heat to boiling over high heat. Reduce heat to low; cover and simmer 45 minutes, or until chicken loses its pink color throughout.

◆ With slotted spoon, transfer chicken to plate; remove and discard skin. With slotted spoon, transfer vegetables to serving bowl; add chicken and 1 cup broth from Dutch oven (reserve remaining broth for use another day). Chop 1 tablespoon tarragon; sprinkle on top.

Each serving: About 570 calories, 48g protein, 45g carbohydrate, 22g total fat (6g saturated), 166mg cholesterol, 485mg sodium

TURKISH CHICKEN IN WALNUT SAUCE

Prep: 20 minutes plus cooling   Cook: 30 to 35 minutes
Makes 4 main-dish servings

4 chicken-breast halves
    (2½ pounds)
1 can (13¾ to 14½ ounces)
    chicken broth
1 small bunch parsley
1½ cups walnuts, toasted
3 slices firm white bread, torn
1 small garlic clove, minced
¾ teaspoon salt
½ teaspoon paprika
⅛ teaspoon ground red
    pepper (cayenne)

◆ In 4-quart saucepan, heat chicken, broth, 3 parsley sprigs, and *1 cup water* to boiling over high heat.

◆ Reduce heat to low; cover and simmer 20 to 25 minutes, until chicken loses its pink color throughout. Remove from heat; cool chicken in broth 30 minutes.

◆ Drain chicken breasts, reserving broth. Remove and discard skin and bones; cut meat into ½-inch-thick strips. Transfer to medium bowl.

◆ Prepare walnut sauce: In food processor with knife blade attached, blend walnuts and bread until walnuts are finely ground and mixture is smooth. Add 1 cup broth from saucepan (reserve remaining broth for use another day), garlic, salt, paprika, and ground red pepper; blend until well combined.

◆ Add half of walnut sauce to chicken in bowl; stir to combine. Spoon onto platter. Pour remaining walnut sauce on top. Garnish with parsley.

Each serving: About 575 calories, 51g protein, 19g carbohydrate, 34g total fat (4g saturated), 119mg cholesterol, 855mg sodium

CHICKEN BREASTS WITH TUNA SAUCE

Prep: 15 minutes plus chilling   Cook: 15 to 20 minutes
Makes 6 main-dish servings

6 skinless, boneless
    chicken-breast halves
    (1¾ pounds)
1 medium onion, thinly
    sliced
1 can (6 ounces) white tuna in
    oil
⅓ cup olive oil
3 tablespoons milk
2 tablespoons fresh lemon
    juice
2 tablespoons capers, drained
¼ teaspoon salt
1 bunch arugula or
    watercress
Lemon slices and capers
    for garnish

◆ In 10-inch skillet, heat chicken-breast halves, onion, and *2 cups water* to boiling over high heat.

◆ Reduce heat to low; cover and simmer 5 to 10 minutes, turning chicken once, until chicken loses its pink color throughout.

◆ Transfer chicken breasts to plate; cover and refrigerate until well chilled.

◆ Meanwhile, prepare tuna sauce: In food processor with knife blade attached or in blender at high speed, blend tuna with its oil, olive oil, milk, lemon juice, 2 tablespoons capers, and salt until smooth.

◆ To serve, line platter with arugula. Dip each piece of cold chicken into tuna sauce to coat and arrange over arugula. Pour any remaining sauce over chicken breasts. Garnish with lemon slices and capers.

Each serving: About 330 calories, 38g protein, 3g carbohydrate, 17g total fat (3g saturated), 104mg cholesterol, 355mg sodium

GROUND POULTRY

Ground poultry is as versatile as ground beef with a fraction of the fat – but be sure to read the label. Depending on the mix of white and dark meat, or even skin, in the product, its fat content can soar as high as 15%, which rivals red meat. All ground poultry should be thoroughly cooked.

1 Finely chop bread. Grate 1 tablespoon onion and set aside; chop remaining onion. Cut eggplant and zucchini into 1-inch chunks.

2 In medium bowl, with hands, combine bread, grated onion, turkey, Parmesan cheese, basil, egg, and salt. With wet hands, shape mixture into 25 meatballs.

3 In 12-inch skillet, heat 2 tablespoons oil over medium heat. Add meatballs, half at a time, and cook until browned; transfer meatballs to plate as they brown.

TURKEY MEATBALLS

◆◆◆◆◆◆◆◆◆◆◆◆

Prep: 30 minutes
Cook: 50 minutes
Makes 5 main-dish servings

2 slices firm white bread
1 medium onion
1 small eggplant (about 1 pound)
2 small zucchini (about 6 ounces each)
1¼ pounds ground turkey
2 tablespoons freshly grated Parmesan cheese
2 tablespoons chopped fresh basil or ¾ teaspoon dried basil
1 large egg
½ teaspoon salt
4 tablespoons olive or vegetable oil
1 can (28 ounces) plum tomatoes
½ teaspoon sugar
Olives and chopped flat-leaf parsley for garnish
Crusty bread (optional)

4 In drippings in skillet, heat remaining 2 tablespoons olive oil over medium-high heat. Add eggplant, zucchini, and chopped onion and cook, stirring frequently, 5 minutes, or until onion is golden. Stir in ¼ *cup water.* Reduce heat to low; cover and simmer, stirring occasionally, 10 minutes.

5 Add tomatoes with their juice and sugar, breaking up tomatoes with back of spoon. Return meatballs to pan; heat to boiling over high heat. Reduce heat to low; simmer meatballs, uncovered, 15 minutes, or until cooked through. Garnish; serve with crusty bread, if you like.

EACH SERVING: ABOUT 400 CALORIES, 27g PROTEIN, 23g CARBOHYDRATE, 23g TOTAL FAT (5g SATURATED), 134mg CHOLESTEROL, 695mg SODIUM

TURKEY MEATBALL PITAS

Prep: 15 minutes   Bake: 12 to 15 minutes
Makes 5 main-dish servings

1 pound ground turkey	½ large cucumber, peeled and
2 slices firm white bread,	cut into ¾-inch pieces
finely chopped	1 container (8 ounces) nonfat
2 tablespoons grated onion	plain yogurt
1 large egg white	2 tablespoons chopped fresh
1½ teaspoons ground cumin	cilantro
Salt	4 cups thinly sliced romaine
5 whole-wheat pitas (6 inches)	lettuce

◆ Preheat oven to 425°F. Grease 15½" by 10½" jelly-roll pan. In medium bowl, with hands, mix ground turkey, bread, onion, egg white, cumin, ¼ teaspoon salt, and *3 tablespoons water*. With wet hands, shape mixture into 25 meatballs. Place in jelly-roll pan and bake 12 to 15 minutes, until cooked through (meatballs will not brown).

◆ Meanwhile, cut off 1 inch across top of each pita. Wrap pitas in foil. After meatballs have baked 5 minutes, place pitas in oven to warm. In small bowl, combine cucumber, yogurt, cilantro, and ¼ teaspoon salt. Fill pitas with lettuce and meatballs; top with cucumber mixture.

Each serving: About 375 calories, 27g protein, 46g carbohydrate, 10g total fat (2g saturated), 73mg cholesterol, 745mg sodium

TEXAS CHICKEN BURGERS

Prep: 15 minutes   Cook: 12 to 15 minutes
Makes 4 main-dish servings

1 pound ground chicken	1 can (16 ounces) vegetarian
2 green onions, chopped	baked beans
1 small zucchini (about	1 tablespoon prepared
5 ounces), grated	mustard
1 medium carrot, grated	1 tablespoon light molasses
1 tablespoon chili powder	Nonstick cooking spray
¼ teaspoon ground cumin	4 whole-grain sandwich rolls,
⅛ teaspoon ground red	split
pepper (cayenne)	Lettuce leaves

◆ In medium bowl, with hands, mix ground chicken, green onions, zucchini, carrot, chili powder, cumin, and ground red pepper until well mixed. On waxed paper, with wet hands, shape mixture into four 3½-inch round patties; set aside.

◆ In 1-quart saucepan, heat baked beans, mustard, and molasses to boiling over medium heat, stirring occasionally.

◆ Meanwhile, spray heavy 12-inch skillet with nonstick cooking spray. Heat skillet over medium-high heat until very hot. With pancake turner, transfer chicken patties to hot skillet. Cook 5 minutes; turn patties and cook 5 minutes

longer, or until they lose their pink color throughout. Arrange patties on sandwich rolls with lettuce. Serve with baked beans.

Each serving: About 410 calories, 28g protein, 48g carbohydrate, 16g total fat (4g saturated), 154mg cholesterol, 745mg sodium

CHICKEN MEATBALL CHILI

Prep: 30 minutes   Cook: 45 minutes
Makes 10 main-dish servings

3 tablespoons vegetable oil	2 tablespoons chili powder
2 medium celery stalks, finely	1 can (28 ounces) plum
chopped	tomatoes
1 medium onion, finely	3 cans (15 to 19 ounces each)
chopped	white kidney beans
3 slices firm white bread,	(cannellini), rinsed and
finely chopped	drained
2 pounds ground chicken	Chopped fresh cilantro for
1 large egg	garnish
Salt	Corn bread (optional)
3 large carrots, thinly sliced	

◆ In 5-quart Dutch oven, heat 1 tablespoon oil over medium heat. Add celery and onion; cook, stirring occasionally, until tender. In large bowl, combine celery mixture with bread; with hands, mix in ground chicken, egg, ½ teaspoon salt, and ¼ cup water. With wet hands, shape mixture into 1½-inch meatballs.

◆ In same Dutch oven, heat remaining 2 tablespoons oil over medium heat. Add meatballs, half at a time, and cook until browned, transferring meatballs to bowl as they brown. To drippings in Dutch oven, add carrots and cook over medium-high heat 5 minutes, or until tender-crisp. Stir in chili powder, tomatoes with their juice, ¼ teaspoon salt, and *2 cups water*; heat to boiling over high heat.

◆ Return meatballs to Dutch oven. Reduce heat to low; cover and simmer 10 minutes. Stir in kidney beans; heat through over medium heat. Garnish with cilantro and serve with corn bread, if you like.

Each serving: About 345 calories, 23g protein, 31g carbohydrate, 15g total fat (4g saturated), 139mg cholesterol, 910mg sodium

STIR-FRIED POULTRY

Stir-frying is the world's fastest cooking technique. You don't need a wok; a large skillet or a Dutch oven works well. The secrets: Cut the food into small, even pieces for quick, uniform cooking; stir constantly; and don't be afraid of high heat. Since cooking is so quick, have all ingredients and utensils at hand before you begin.

INDONESIAN CHICKEN

Prep: 25 minutes plus marinating *Cook:* 10 minutes

Makes 4 main-dish servings

1 teaspoon plus 1 tablespoon vegetable oil
1 green onion, thinly sliced
1 garlic clove, minced
1 medium lime
1 medium orange
2 tablespoons soy sauce
1 tablespoon honey
½ teaspoon crushed red pepper

½ teaspoon ground cumin
½ teaspoon ground coriander
4 skinless, boneless chicken-breast halves (about 1 pound)
1 teaspoon cornstarch
Fresh cilantro leaves for garnish

1 In nonstick wok or large skillet, heat 1 teaspoon oil over medium heat. Add green onion and garlic and cook 2 to 3 minutes, until beginning to brown. Transfer to large bowl.

2 Grate peel and squeeze juice from lime and orange. Set aside orange juice. Add all peel and lime juice to bowl with green onion; stir in soy sauce, honey, crushed red pepper, cumin, and coriander.

3 Cut chicken-breast halves lengthwise into ½-inch-wide strips; add to soy-sauce mixture in bowl and stir to coat. Cover and let marinate 15 minutes. With slotted spoon, remove chicken from marinade; reserve marinade.

4 In same wok, heat remaining 1 tablespoon oil over medium-high heat. Add chicken strips and cook, stirring constantly, 5 minutes, or until chicken just loses its pink color throughout. Transfer chicken to clean bowl.

JUICING CITRUS FRUITS

For best yield, use room-temperature fruit. Before juicing, roll the fruit under the palm of your hand, which loosens inner membranes, helping to release as much juice as possible.

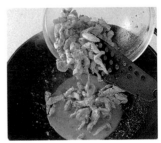

5 In small bowl, with fork, mix cornstarch with orange juice. Add to wok with reserved chicken marinade. Cook over medium heat, stirring constantly, until mixture boils and thickens slightly; boil 1 minute. Return chicken to wok; heat through. Serve garnished with cilantro.

EACH SERVING: ABOUT 220 CALORIES, 26g PROTEIN, 12g CARBOHYDRATE, 7g TOTAL FAT (2g SATURATED), 81mg CHOLESTEROL, 555 mg SODIUM

CHICKEN AND EGGPLANT

Prep: 20 minutes   Cook: 30 minutes
Makes 6 main-dish servings

2 tablespoons vegetable oil
6 skinless, boneless chicken-breast halves
    (about 1¾ pounds), cut lengthwise into
    ½-inch-wide strips
6 baby eggplants (about 2 pounds), each
    cut lengthwise in half
1 tablespoon grated, peeled fresh ginger
1 garlic clove, minced
¼ cup soy sauce
¼ cup red wine vinegar
3 tablespoons sugar
2 tablespoons Asian sesame oil
2 teaspoons cornstarch
¼ teaspoon crushed red pepper
Hot cooked rice (optional)

◆ In 12-inch skillet or wok, heat oil over high heat; add chicken and cook, stirring constantly, until it loses its pink color throughout. Transfer to bowl. In drippings in skillet, heat eggplants, ginger, garlic, and *½ cup water* to boiling over high heat. Reduce heat to medium-low; cover and cook, stirring occasionally, about 20 minutes, until liquid evaporates. In cup, mix soy sauce with next 5 ingredients.

◆ Return chicken to skillet; add soy-sauce mixture. Heat to boiling over high heat. Reduce heat to medium; cook, stirring, until sauce thickens slightly and boils. Serve with rice, if you like.

Each serving: About 310 calories, 32g protein, 18g carbohydrate, 12g total fat (3g saturated), 95mg cholesterol, 730mg sodium

EASY CHINESE CHICKEN AND VEGETABLES

Prep: 25 minutes   Cook: 12 minutes
Makes 4 main-dish servings

4 skinless, boneless chicken-breast halves
    (about 1¼ pounds)
¼ cup soy sauce
2 tablespoons balsamic vinegar
2 teaspoons brown sugar
2 tablespoons vegetable oil plus more if
    needed
5 medium carrots, thinly sliced
    diagonally
2 large red peppers, cut into 1½-inch
    pieces
1 bunch green onions, cut into 1-inch
    pieces
Green-leaf lettuce leaves (optional)
⅓ cup cashews

◆ With knife held in slanting position, almost parallel to cutting surface, slice each chicken-breast half into ⅛-inch-thick slices. In cup, mix soy sauce with vinegar and brown sugar.

◆ In 12-inch skillet or wok, heat 1 tablespoon oil over high heat; add chicken and cook, stirring constantly, just until chicken loses its pink color throughout. Transfer chicken to bowl.

◆ In same skillet, heat remaining 1 tablespoon oil over medium-high heat; add carrots and red peppers and cook, stirring frequently, 4 minutes. Add green onions; cook, stirring, until vegetables are tender-crisp, adding additional oil if necessary.

◆ Return chicken to skillet. Stir in soy-sauce mixture; cook 1 minute, or until chicken is heated through. To serve, arrange lettuce leaves on platter, if you like; spoon chicken mixture over lettuce leaves. Sprinkle with cashews.

Each serving: About 370 calories, 36g protein, 22g carbohydrate, 16g total fat (4g saturated), 101mg cholesterol, 1110mg sodium

CHICKEN WITH SESAME NOODLES

Prep: 20 minutes   Cook: 10 minutes
Makes 4 main-dish servings

8 ounces linguine
1 medium red pepper
1 medium cucumber
2 tablespoons cornstarch
¼ teaspoon salt
4 skinless, boneless chicken-breast halves
    (about 1 pound), cut crosswise into
    1-inch-thick strips
2 tablespoons vegetable oil
¼ cup creamy peanut butter
3 tablespoons soy sauce
1 tablespoon Asian sesame oil
1 tablespoon distilled white vinegar
2 teaspoons sugar
1 green onion, thinly sliced
¼ teaspoon crushed red pepper
    (optional)

◆ Prepare linguine as label directs; drain. Meanwhile, cut red pepper and cucumber into matchstick-thin strips.

◆ In medium bowl, combine cornstarch and salt. Add chicken strips to cornstarch mixture; toss to coat. In 12-inch skillet or wok, heat vegetable oil over high heat. Add chicken and cook, stirring constantly, until chicken loses its pink color throughout. Transfer to plate; keep warm.

◆ In same skillet, combine peanut butter, soy sauce, sesame oil, vinegar, sugar, and *¾ cup water*; cook over medium heat, stirring constantly, until mixture is smooth. Stir in linguine and heat through. Spoon linguine mixture onto warm platter. Top with red-pepper and cucumber strips, chicken strips, and green onion. Sprinkle with crushed red pepper, if you like. Toss to serve.

Each serving: About 570 calories, 38g protein, 56g carbohydrate, 22g total fat (4g saturated), 81mg cholesterol, 1025mg sodium

POULTRY PIES

Whether poultry is left over or cooked to order, it's guaranteed a welcome as the star of a savory pie. Combined with vegetables in a milk or cheese sauce and topped with a cornmeal, flour, or phyllo crust, it's a favorite winter dish.

CHICKEN POTPIE WITH CORNMEAL CRUST

❖❖❖❖❖❖❖❖❖❖❖❖

Prep: 1 hour
Bake: 35 to 40 minutes
Makes 10 main-dish servings

2 large all-purpose potatoes (about 1¾ pounds)
1 medium rutabaga (about 1¼ pounds)
3 medium carrots
1 large onion
2 large celery stalks
1 tablespoon olive or vegetable oil
½ teaspoon salt
1 package (10 ounces) frozen peas
3 cups bite-size pieces cooked chicken (1 pound)
1 cup milk
¼ cup all-purpose flour
3 cups chicken broth
¼ teaspoon ground black pepper
Cornmeal Crust (see page 172)
½ cup minced celery leaves
1 large egg white, lightly beaten
Celery leaves for garnish

1 Peel and dice potatoes and rutabaga; dice carrots, onion, and celery. In nonstick 12-inch skillet, heat oil over medium-high heat. Add rutabaga, carrots, and onion and cook 10 minutes. Stir in potatoes, celery, and salt and cook, stirring often, 10 minutes longer, or until vegetables are tender. Stir in peas and chicken; spoon mixture into 13" by 9" baking dish. In small bowl, with wire whisk or fork, beat milk and flour.

2 In 3-quart saucepan, heat chicken broth to boiling; stir in milk mixture and pepper. Cook, stirring, until sauce boils. Stir into chicken mixture. Preheat oven to 425°F.

3 Prepare Cornmeal Crust. On lightly floured surface, with floured rolling pin, roll dough into a rectangle 2 inches larger all around than top of baking dish; sprinkle with minced celery leaves. With rolling pin, press leaves into dough.

4 Place dough rectangle over filling; trim edge, leaving 1-inch overhang. Reserve trimmings. Fold overhang under; crimp edge. Brush crust with some egg white. Reroll trimmings; cut into leaves to decorate edge of pie. Brush pastry leaves with egg white.

5 Cut several slits in crust to allow steam to escape during baking. Tear off 15-inch piece of foil; crimp edges slightly. Place foil on oven rack directly below pie to catch any drips while baking. Bake pie 35 to 40 minutes, until crust is golden brown and filling is hot and bubbling; during end of baking time, cover edge of crust with foil to prevent overbrowning. Garnish with celery leaves.

EACH SERVING: ABOUT 455 CALORIES, 23g PROTEIN, 49g CARBOHYDRATE, 19g FAT (6g SATURATED), 47mg CHOLESTEROL, 755mg SODIUM

FIESTA TURKEY PIE

Prep: 55 minutes   Bake: 40 to 45 minutes
Makes 8 main-dish servings

2 cups all-purpose flour	1 medium onion, diced
8 ounces sharp Cheddar cheese, finely shredded (2 cups)	3 cups bite-size pieces cooked turkey (1 pound)
⅔ cup shortening or butter-flavor shortening	1 can (15 to 19 ounces) black beans, rinsed and drained
1 medium potato (about 8 ounces), peeled and cut into ½-inch pieces	1 can (14½ ounces) Mexican-style stewed tomatoes
1 tablespoon vegetable oil	1 can (11 ounces) whole-kernel corn, drained
	1 teaspoon chili powder

◆ In large bowl, mix flour and ½ cup cheese. With pastry blender or two knives used scissor-fashion, cut in shortening until mixture resembles coarse crumbs. Add *5 to 6 tablespoons cold water*, 1 tablespoon at a time, mixing with a fork after each addition, until dough is just moist enough to hold together. Shape into a ball. Cover with plastic wrap.

◆ In 2-quart saucepan, heat potato and *water* to cover to boiling over high heat. Reduce heat to low; cover and simmer 5 minutes, or until potato is tender. Drain. In 12-inch skillet, heat oil over medium-high heat; add onion and cook, stirring occasionally, until tender. Stir in turkey, black beans, tomatoes, corn, chili powder, and potato; heat to boiling over high heat. Remove from heat; stir in remaining cheese.

CORNMEAL CRUST

◆◆◆◆◆◆◆◆◆◆◆◆◆

¼ cup yellow cornmeal	1 teaspoon salt
1½ cups all-purpose flour	⅔ cup shortening

1 In large bowl, mix cornmeal, flour, and salt. With pastry blender or two knives used scissor-fashion, cut in shortening until mixture resembles coarse crumbs.

2 Sprinkle *6 to 7 tablespoons cold water*, 1 tablespoon at a time, into flour mixture, mixing with a fork after each addition until dough is just moist enough to hold together.

◆ Preheat oven to 400°F. On lightly floured surface, with floured rolling pin, roll out two-thirds of dough into a round 2½ inches larger all around than inverted 9½-inch deep-dish pie plate. Gently ease dough into pie plate; trim edge, leaving 1-inch overhang. Spoon filling into pie plate.

◆ Roll remaining dough into 11-inch round; lift onto pie. Trim edge, leaving 1-inch overhang. Fold overhang under; make fluted edge (see page 488). Cut several slits in crust to allow steam to escape during baking. Bake pie 40 to 45 minutes, until crust is golden and filling is bubbling.

Each serving: About 580 calories, 32g protein, 48g carbohydrate, 30g total fat (11g saturated), 77mg cholesterol, 620mg sodium

PHYLLO-CRUST CHICKEN POTPIE

Prep: 55 minutes   Bake: 20 to 25 minutes
Makes 4 main-dish servings

1 tablespoon vegetable oil	1¼ cups milk
1 medium onion, diced	2 tablespoons all-purpose flour
2 medium potatoes (about 8 ounces), peeled and cut into ½-inch pieces	3 cups bite-size pieces cooked chicken (1 pound)
2 medium carrots, sliced	3 sheets (about 16" by 12" each) fresh or frozen (thawed) phyllo (about 2 ounces)
1 teaspoon salt	
½ teaspoon ground black pepper	1 tablespoon margarine or butter, melted
¼ teaspoon dried tarragon	
1 cup frozen peas	

◆ In 10-inch skillet, heat oil over medium-high heat; add onion and cook until tender. Add potatoes, carrots, salt, pepper, tarragon, and *1 cup water*; heat to boiling. Reduce heat to low; cover and simmer 20 minutes, or until vegetables are tender. Stir in frozen peas.

◆ In small bowl, mix milk and flour until smooth; stir into liquid in skillet. Cook over medium heat, stirring constantly, until mixture boils and thickens. Stir in chicken; pour into four 10-ounce oven-safe custard cups or ramekins.

◆ Preheat oven to 425°F. On work surface, place 1 sheet of phyllo; lightly brush with some melted margarine. Top with second sheet, lightly brushing with more margarine. Top with remaining sheet, brushing with remaining margarine. Cut stack in half crosswise, then lengthwise to make 4 stacks.

◆ Gently arrange 1 stack on top of each custard cup, scrunching center so edge is within rim. Place custard cups in jelly-roll pan for easier handling. Bake 20 to 25 minutes, until crust is golden and filling is hot.

Each serving: About 455 calories, 43g protein, 35g carbohydrate, 15g total fat (4g saturated), 106mg cholesterol, 800mg sodium

USING COOKED POULTRY

Take cooked poultry and create satisfying meals with an international flair in no time. We've paired chicken and turkey with bold ethnic flavors to create a speedy, spicy Thai stir-fry, a cheesy layered tortilla dinner, zesty burritos, and even a French-style cassoulet. Always keep cooked poultry refrigerated until you are ready to use it.

THAI TURKEY

Prep: 20 minutes   *Cook:* 25 minutes
Makes 4 main-dish servings

1 cup regular long-grain rice
¾ teaspoon salt
¼ teaspoon coarsely ground black pepper
2 tablespoons chopped fresh parsley
¾ pound cooked turkey-breast meat
3 green onions
1 medium red pepper
1 garlic clove, minced
2 tablespoons soy sauce

1 tablespoon chopped fresh cilantro
1 tablespoon honey
1½ teaspoons curry powder
1 teaspoon Asian sesame oil
½ teaspoon cornstarch
¼ teaspoon crushed red pepper
1 tablespoon vegetable oil
Chopped fresh cilantro and sliced green onions for garnish

1 Prepare rice: In 2-quart saucepan, in *2 cups boiling water,* heat rice, salt, and black pepper to boiling over high heat. Reduce heat to low; cover and simmer 20 minutes, or until rice is tender and liquid is absorbed. Stir in parsley. Set aside and keep warm.

2 Meanwhile, coarsely shred turkey-breast meat (you should have 3 cups). Thinly slice green onions; cut red pepper into 2-inch-long matchstick-thin strips.

3 In small bowl, mix garlic, soy sauce, 1 tablespoon chopped cilantro, next 5 ingredients, and ⅓ cup water.

4 In wok or large skillet, heat vegetable oil over high heat. Add green onions and red pepper and cook, stirring frequently, until tender and golden. Stir in soy-sauce mixture and turkey and cook, stirring to coat turkey well, until heated through. Serve over rice; garnish with cilantro and green onions.

SOME LIKE IT HOT

Dried chiles are prized around the globe for their flavor – and fire. Ground red pepper (cayenne) blends easily with other ingredients; a pinch will heat up an entire dish. Crushed chiles can be sautéed or used as a condiment. Whole dried chiles are best suited to simmered dishes.

EACH SERVING: ABOUT 355 CALORIES, 30g PROTEIN, 45g CARBOHYDRATE, 6g TOTAL FAT (1g SATURATED), 71mg CHOLESTEROL, 965mg SODIUM

TRIPLE-DECKER TORTILLA MELT

Prep: 25 minutes   *Bake:* 12 to 15 minutes
Makes 4 main-dish servings

1 medium avocado	3 flour tortillas (8 inches)
3 tablespoons mayonnaise	1 can (4 to 4½ ounces)
1 tablespoon milk	chopped mild green chiles,
2 teaspoons fresh lemon juice	drained
¼ teaspoon salt	4 ounces Monterey Jack
⅛ teaspoon ground black	cheese, shredded (1 cup)
pepper	3 medium plum tomatoes,
1 package refrigerated	thinly sliced
roasted chicken breast	
(about 1 pound)	

◆ Cut avocado lengthwise in half; remove seed and peel. In small bowl, with fork, mash avocado with next 5 ingredients.

◆ Discard skin and bones from chicken; cut chicken into bite-size pieces. Preheat oven to 375°F. In 10-inch skillet, heat 1 tortilla over high heat, turning once, 40 seconds, or until slightly crisp. Repeat with remaining 2 tortillas.

◆ Place 1 tortilla on ungreased cookie sheet; top with half of chicken. Spread half of avocado mixture over chicken; sprinkle with half of chiles and one-third of cheese. Arrange one-third of tomato slices over cheese.

◆ Top with second tortilla; top with remaining chicken, avocado mixture, and chiles, then half of remaining cheese and half of remaining tomato slices. Top with third tortilla; arrange remaining tomato on top; sprinkle with remaining cheese. Bake 12 to 15 minutes, until heated through and cheese on top is browned. To serve, cut into 4 wedges.

Each serving: About 505 calories, 37g protein, 24g carbohydrate, 30g total fat (9g saturated), 101mg cholesterol, 650mg sodium

CHICKEN BURRITOS

Prep: 25 minutes   *Bake:* 35 minutes
Makes 4 main-dish servings

1 refrigerated roasted whole	8 flour tortillas (8 inches)
chicken (about 3 pounds)	6 ounces Monterey Jack
1 can (7½ ounces) tomatoes	cheese, shredded (1½ cups)
and jalapeño chiles	1 cup loosely packed sliced
¼ cup sour cream	iceberg lettuce
1 tablespoon chili powder	Avocado and lime slices for
1 can (16 ounces) nonfat	garnish
refried beans	

◆ Discard skin and bones from chicken and pull meat into thin shreds. In large bowl, mix shredded chicken, tomatoes and jalapeño chiles with their liquid, sour cream, and chili powder.

◆ Preheat oven to 425°F. Spread one-eighth of beans over each tortilla. Spoon one-eighth of chicken mixture across center of each bean-topped tortilla. Sprinkle half of cheese evenly over chicken; roll up tortillas and place, seam-side down, in baking dish. Cover with foil and bake 30 minutes, or until heated through. Remove foil; sprinkle burritos with remaining cheese. Bake 5 minutes longer, or until cheese melts. Serve with lettuce; garnish with avocado and lime slices.

Each serving: About 780 calories, 61g protein, 62g carbohydrate, 31g total fat (13g saturated), 163mg cholesterol, 1225mg sodium

QUICK TURKEY CASSOULET

Prep: 25 minutes   *Cook:* 40 minutes
Makes 8 main-dish servings

1 kielbasa (smoked Polish	2 cups bite-size pieces cooked
sausage), cut into ½-inch	turkey (about 10 ounces)
slices (1 pound)	1 can (14½ to 16 ounces)
2 tablespoons vegetable oil	tomatoes
1 bag (16 ounces) carrots, cut	1 beef-flavor bouillon cube or
into 1-inch pieces	envelope
2 large onions, sliced	1 bay leaf
2 medium celery stalks, sliced	½ cup fresh bread crumbs
3 cans (15 to 19 ounces each)	(1 slice firm white bread)
white kidney beans	1 tablespoon plus ¼ cup
(cannellini), rinsed and	chopped fresh parsley
drained	

◆ In 5-quart Dutch oven, cook kielbasa over medium heat until browned. Transfer to plate. In drippings in Dutch oven, heat 1 tablespoon oil over medium heat. Add carrots, onions, and celery and cook 10 minutes, or until tender. Return kielbasa to Dutch oven. Add beans, turkey, tomatoes with their juice, bouillon, bay leaf, and *1¾ cups water.* Heat to boiling over high heat. Reduce heat to low; simmer 15 minutes.

◆ Meanwhile, in 1-quart saucepan, heat remaining 1 tablespoon oil over medium-high heat. Add bread crumbs and 1 tablespoon parsley; cook until crumbs are golden. To serve, discard bay leaf. Stir remaining ¼ cup parsley into cassoulet; sprinkle with toasted bread crumbs.

Each serving: About 445 calories, 29g protein, 38g carbohydrate, 20g total fat (6g saturated), 67mg cholesterol, 1480mg sodium

BROILED POULTRY

Broiling is an ideal cooking method: It's simple, fast, and requires a minimum of fat. Make sure to preheat your broiler for 10 minutes before using. Broilers vary in the degree of heat they generate, so watch food carefully for doneness. To avoid flare-ups when broiling, never line the rack of the broiling pan with foil – the fat should be allowed to drip through into the pan below (if you like, for easy clean-up, line the broiling pan only).

ISLAND CHICKEN WITH FRUIT

Prep: 25 minutes plus marinating *Broil: 12 to 15 minutes*
Makes 4 main-dish servings

1 small onion, grated
1 container (8 ounces) plain low-fat yogurt
1 tablespoon vegetable oil
2 teaspoons grated, peeled fresh ginger
1 teaspoon salt
½ teaspoon ground cumin
¼ teaspoon chili powder
¼ teaspoon ground turmeric
¼ teaspoon ground cinnamon
4 skinless, boneless chicken-breast halves (about 1½ pounds)

½ small honeydew melon
2 large mangoes
2 tablespoons peach jam
1 tablespoon fresh lime juice
¼ teaspoon coarsely ground black pepper
Lime peel slivers for garnish
Couscous (Moroccan pasta, optional)

1 In 11" by 7" glass baking dish, mix first 9 ingredients. Add chicken-breast halves and turn to coat. Cover with plastic wrap and refrigerate 3 hours.

2 Preheat broiler. Lightly grease rack in broiling pan. Arrange chicken on rack. Spread any mixture remaining in baking dish over chicken.

3 Broil chicken 5 inches from heat source, without turning, 12 to 15 minutes, until chicken loses its pink color throughout.

4 Meanwhile, remove rind from melon; peel mangoes. Cut melon and mangoes into 1½-inch chunks. In large bowl, gently toss fruit with peach jam, lime juice, and pepper.

5 Slice each chicken-breast half on slight diagonal into 6 pieces. Place chicken-breast halves on 4 plates, keeping original shape intact. Spoon fruit mixture on the side, garnish with lime peel slivers, and serve with couscous, if you like.

EACH SERVING: ABOUT 420 CALORIES, 42g PROTEIN, 44g CARBOHYDRATE, 9g TOTAL FAT (3g SATURATED), 125mg CHOLESTEROL, 640mg SODIUM

BROILED CORNISH HENS WITH LEMON

Prep: 5 minutes *Broil:* 30 minutes

Makes 4 main-dish servings

2 Cornish hens (1¼ pounds each), each cut lengthwise in half (see page 146)	**½ teaspoon dried thyme**
Salt	**¼ teaspoon ground black pepper**
¼ teaspoon dried rosemary, crushed	**2 tablespoons fresh lemon juice**

◆ Preheat broiler. In small roasting pan, arrange Cornish hens, skin-side down; sprinkle with ¼ teaspoon salt. Place roasting pan in broiler 5 to 7 inches from heat source; broil hens 15 minutes.

◆ In cup, mix rosemary, thyme, pepper, and ½ teaspoon salt. Turn hens; sprinkle with herb mixture. Broil hens, basting once or twice with pan drippings, 15 minutes longer, or until golden and juices run clear when thickest part of hens is pierced with tip of knife. Transfer hens to warm platter; skim fat from pan drippings. Add lemon juice to roasting pan, stirring until brown bits are loosened; spoon over hens.

Each serving: About 405 calories, 35g protein, 1g carbohydrate 28g total fat (8g saturated), 203mg cholesterol, 500mg sodium

JAMAICAN JERK CHICKEN KABOBS

Prep: 20 minutes plus marinating *Broil:* 10 minutes

Makes 4 main-dish servings

2 green onions, chopped	**1 teaspoon dried thyme**
1 jalapeño chile, seeded and chopped	**3 teaspoons vegetable oil**
1 tablespoon chopped, peeled fresh ginger	**Salt**
	4 skinless, boneless chicken-breast halves (1 pound), cut into 12 pieces
2 tablespoons white wine vinegar	**2 medium red peppers, cut into 1-inch pieces**
2 tablespoons Worcestershire sauce	**4 long all-metal skewers**
1 teaspoon ground allspice	

◆ In blender at high speed, blend green onions, jalapeño chile, ginger, vinegar, Worcestershire, allspice, thyme, 2 teaspoons oil, and ½ teaspoon salt until combined.

◆ In small bowl, place chicken pieces; add green-onion mixture, stirring to coat. Cover with plastic wrap and refrigerate 30 minutes.

◆ Meanwhile, in small bowl, toss pepper pieces with remaining 1 teaspoon oil and ⅛ teaspoon salt; set aside.

◆ Preheat broiler. On 4 all-metal skewers, alternately thread chicken and pepper pieces. Place kabobs on rack in broiling pan; brush with any remaining marinade in bowl. Place pan in broiler at closest position to heat source; broil kabobs, turning once, 10 minutes, or until chicken just loses its pink color throughout.

Each serving: About 185 calories, 26g protein, 5g carbohydrate, 6g total fat (2g saturated), 81mg cholesterol, 485mg sodium

CHILI-SPICED CHICKEN LEGS

Prep: 15 minutes *Broil:* 45 to 50 minutes

Makes 8 main-dish servings

1 bottle (12 ounces) chili sauce	**2 teaspoons chili powder**
	1 teaspoon salt
1 small onion, grated	**½ teaspoon hot pepper sauce**
1 garlic clove, minced	**3 tablespoons chopped fresh parsley**
3 tablespoons brown sugar	
1 tablespoon white wine vinegar	**8 chicken-leg quarters (about 4½ pounds)**
1 tablespoon olive oil	

◆ Preheat broiler. In medium bowl, mix first 9 ingredients with 2 tablespoons chopped parsley and *1 tablespoon water* until blended. Arrange chicken legs, skin-side down, on rack in broiling pan; brush chicken with some chili mixture. Place pan in broiler 5 to 7 inches from heat source; broil chicken legs 25 minutes.

◆ Turn chicken legs; broil 20 to 25 minutes longer, brushing occasionally with chili mixture, until juices run clear when chicken is pierced with tip of knife. To serve, sprinkle with remaining 1 tablespoon chopped parsley.

Each serving: About 380 calories, 34g protein, 18g carbohydrate, 19g total fat (5g saturated), 116mg cholesterol, 955mg sodium

GRILLED POULTRY

Except for quick-cooking cutlets and boneless breasts, poultry should be grilled over medium-hot coals, so that it cooks through without charring or drying out. For safety, use long-handled tongs and basting brushes designed for barbecuing.

CORNISH HENS WITH FRUIT SALSA

◆◆◆◆◆◆◆◆◆◆◆◆

Prep: 30 minutes
Grill: 35 minutes
Makes 4 main-dish servings

1 large red or green jalapeño chile
2 medium peaches
2 medium kiwifruit
1 can (8 ounces) crushed pineapple in its own juice, drained
1 tablespoon minced fresh cilantro
½ teaspoon sugar
Salt
Grated peel of 1 medium lime
3 tablespoons fresh lime juice
2 garlic cloves, minced
4 teaspoons chili powder
1 tablespoon olive oil
2 Cornish hens (1¼ pounds each), each cut lengthwise in half (see page 146)

1 Prepare outdoor grill. Prepare fruit salsa: Cut jalapeño chile lengthwise in half; discard seeds and mince chile.

2 Peel, halve, and pit peaches; peel kiwifruit. Dice peaches and 1 kiwifruit. Slice remaining kiwifruit and place in medium bowl; with fork, coarsely crush.

3 Stir in diced peaches and kiwifruit, jalapeño chile, pineapple, minced cilantro, sugar, ½ teaspoon salt, lime peel, and 2 tablespoons lime juice. Cover and refrigerate.

JALAPEÑO CHILES

Jalapeño chiles spice up countless dishes from salsas to bean or grain salads and dips. Most of the heat lies in the ribs and seeds; for extra kick, leave them in. Green jalapeños have a green-pepper flavor. Red jalapeños are the ripe form of the green; they offer a sweeter flavor.

4 In small bowl, mix garlic, chili powder, olive oil, remaining 1 tablespoon lime juice, and 1 teaspoon salt. Use to rub over hens; place on grill over medium heat. Grill hens, turning often, 35 minutes, or until juices run clear when hens are pierced with tip of knife. Serve with fruit salsa.

EACH SERVING: ABOUT 525 CALORIES, 36g PROTEIN, 23g CARBOHYDRATE, 32g TOTAL FAT (8g SATURATED), 203mg CHOLESTEROL, 950mg SODIUM

HERBED TURKEY CUTLETS

Prep: 10 minutes   *Grill:* 5 to 7 minutes
Makes 4 main-dish servings

2 medium lemons
1 tablespoon chopped fresh
 sage or ¾ teaspoon dried
 sage
1 tablespoon vegetable oil
½ teaspoon salt
¼ teaspoon coarsely ground
 black pepper

1 garlic clove, crushed
1 pound turkey cutlets
Sage leaves and grilled lemon
 slices for garnish
Sautéed peppers and mâche
 (optional)

◆ Prepare outdoor grill. Grate 2 teaspoons peel from lemons. Cut each lemon in half; squeeze juice from 3 halves into small bowl. Into lemon juice, stir lemon peel, chopped sage, oil, salt, pepper, and garlic until combined.

◆ Place turkey cutlets on grill over high heat. Grill cutlets, brushing with lemon mixture often and turning once, 5 to 7 minutes, until turkey just loses its pink color throughout. Place turkey cutlets on 4 plates. Squeeze juice from remaining lemon half over turkey cutlets. Garnish with sage leaves and grilled lemon slices, and serve with sautéed peppers and mâche, if you like.

Each serving: About 175 calories, 29g protein; 3g carbohydrate, 4g total fat (1g saturated), 71mg cholesterol, 325mg sodium

◆◆◆◆◆◆◆◆◆◆◆◆◆◆◆◆◆◆◆◆◆◆

GRILLED CITRUS GARNISHES

Grilled slices of oranges, lemons, or limes make an attractive – and flavorful – garnish for grilled foods. Slice thinly; carefully remove seeds. Grill slices 2 to 5 minutes on each side, until grill marks appear.

◆◆◆◆◆◆◆◆◆◆◆◆◆◆◆◆◆◆◆◆◆◆

APRICOT-GINGER CHICKEN LEGS

Prep: 10 minutes   *Grill:* 35 minutes
Makes 6 main-dish servings

2 green onions, chopped
½ cup apricot jam
⅓ cup catchup
2 tablespoons cider vinegar
1 tablespoon plus 1 teaspoon
 grated, peeled fresh ginger

1 tablespoon plus 1 teaspoon
 soy sauce
6 chicken-leg quarters (about
 3¾ pounds)

◆ Prepare outdoor grill. In small bowl, mix chopped green onions, apricot jam, catchup, vinegar, ginger, and soy sauce.

◆ Place chicken legs on grill over medium heat; cook about 10 minutes, until golden on both sides. Then, to avoid charring, stand chicken legs upright, leaning one against the other. Cook about 25 minutes longer, rearranging pieces from time to time, until juices run clear when chicken is pierced with tip of knife.

◆ During last 10 minutes of cooking, brush chicken legs frequently with apricot mixture.

Each serving: About 425 calories, 37g protein. 26g carbohydrate, 19g total fat (5g saturated), 129mg cholesterol, 625mg sodium

SWEET-AND-SOUR CHICKEN WINGS

Prep: 5 minutes   *Grill:* 25 to 30 minutes
Makes 4 main-dish servings

¼ cup red wine vinegar
¼ cup soy sauce
¼ cup sugar
1 tablespoon cornstarch
2 tablespoons Asian sesame oil
2 pounds chicken wings
 (about 12)

¼ teaspoon ground black
 pepper
Chopped green onion for
 garnish

◆ Prepare outdoor grill. Prepare sweet-and-sour sauce: In 1-quart saucepan, combine vinegar, soy sauce, sugar, cornstarch, sesame oil, and *¼ cup water.* Cook over medium-high heat, stirring, until sauce boils and thickens; boil 1 minute. Remove saucepan from heat.

◆ Sprinkle chicken wings with pepper and place on grill over medium heat. Grill chicken wings 25 to 30 minutes, until tender and golden and juices run clear when chicken is pierced with tip of knife, turning wings frequently and brushing with sweet-and-sour sauce during last 10 minutes of cooking. To serve, sprinkle chicken wings with chopped green onion.

Each serving: About 440 calories, 31g protein, 17g carbohydrate, 29g total fat (8g saturated), 188mg cholesterol, 1140mg sodium

7 MEAT

MEAT KNOW-HOW

Whether you're preparing beef, pork, lamb, or veal, the same basic cooking techniques apply to all meats – the method you choose depends largely on the cut. Here is the essential information, from making the smartest choices at the supermarket to the easiest carving techniques.

BUYING AND STORING

• All meat sold in the U.S. is checked for wholesomeness by government inspectors. The USDA monitors quality by grading meat according to the age of the animal and the amount of marbling (streaks or flecks of fat) in the flesh.
• Select meat with a good color and even marbling; any fat should be creamy white. Check that bones are cut cleanly, with no obvious splintering. Be sure to note the sell-by date on the label; cuts in vacuum packaging have a longer shelf life.
• For boneless cuts and ground meat, figure about ¼ to ⅓ pound per serving. For cuts with some bone, such as chops, allow ⅓ to ½ pound; for bony cuts, such as ribs, ¾ to 1 pound.
• Store raw meat in the coldest part of the refrigerator (generally the bottom shelf), away from cooked and ready-to-eat foods. Refrigerate uncooked meats 2 to 3 days or freeze up to 6 months. Ground meat won't last as long; refrigerate only 1 to 2 days or freeze up to 3 months.
• For short-term storage (up to 2 days in the refrigerator or 2 weeks in the freezer), leave the meat in its original wrapping if intact. For longer freezing, or if wrapping is torn, carefully rewrap meat in freezer wrap, heavy-duty plastic wrap, or foil, pressing out air. Layer steaks, chops, and patties with freezer wrap before wrapping. Label packages with the name of the cut, the number of servings, and the date.
• Thaw frozen meat (on a plate to catch drips) overnight in the refrigerator – never on the counter. Use thawed meat as soon as possible; never refreeze, or the texture will suffer.

COOKING SUCCESS

Roasting
• When roasting boneless cuts, place the meat on a rack in the roasting pan. That way, the heat can circulate under the meat and prevent it from steaming in its juices. For some cuts, such as rib roasts, the bones act as a built-in rack.
• Use a meat thermometer to determine doneness. Insert it into the thickest part of the meat without touching bone.
• Remove the roast from the oven when it reaches 5°F to 10°F less than the desired temperature; the temperature will continue to rise as the meat stands.

Panfrying and sautéing
• Pat meat dry with paper towels; it will brown more easily.
• Use a heavy-bottomed pan, which will conduct heat evenly.
• Use just enough oil to prevent meat from sticking and make sure the pan is hot before adding the meat.
• Avoid crowding the skillet, or meat will steam, not brown.
• After cooking meat, pour off any fat and then deglaze the pan by adding a little liquid to release the caramelized meat juices and create a quick sauce.

Braising and stewing
• Cut meat into cubes of about the same size for uniform cooking, then pat dry with paper towels before browning.
• Simmer over low heat; do not boil, or meat will toughen.
• Use a pan with a tight-fitting lid to keep in steam.
• To test braised or simmered meat for doneness, pierce with a fork; the fork should slip in easily.
• Many stews taste even better if cooked a day ahead, then chilled overnight to allow flavors to build and mellow. Remove any surface fat before reheating.

Broiling and grilling
• Broil or grill thinner cuts close to the heat. Thicker cuts need more distance so the inside has time to cook through before the outside burns.
• To prevent flare-ups when broiling, do not line the rack with foil. The fat must be able to drip through. If you like, for easy clean-up, line the pan below the rack with foil.
• To avoid piercing meat and releasing its flavorful juices, use tongs rather than a fork to turn.

CARVING IT RIGHT

• Let steaks and roasts stand, covered with foil, for 10 to 15 minutes before slicing. The juices will settle, enriching the flavor and firming the meat so it's easier to carve.
• Place a cloth under the cutting board to prevent slipping.
• Always use a sharp knife.
• Carve across the grain, not parallel to the fibers of the meat – this produces shorter fibers for more tender meat.

SHARPENING A CARVING KNIFE

Rest one end of sharpening steel on work surface. Position heel of knife (widest part of blade) at a 20° angle on the underside of the steel near finger guard. Draw knife downward, pulling the handle toward you gradually, until you have sharpened the full length of the blade; repeat on other side of knife. Continue, alternating strokes, until sharp.

BEEF

Virtually any cut of beef can create a delicious meal if it's cooked right. What determines the best method? The quality of the cut; the part of the animal from which the cut comes; and the animal's age (older meat will be tougher). Read on for helpful hints and tips to ensure you get juicy, tender results from every cut you cook.

THE "LEAN" STORY

Thanks to improved ranching methods, trim butchering, and consumer demand for healthier foods, beef is leaner than in the past.

• Beef is graded by the USDA according to how much marbling (streaks of fat) the cut contains. Prime beef has the most marbling and is usually sold to restaurants. Choice beef has moderate marbling and is the grade most available in supermarkets. Select beef, the least expensive grade, has the least marbling and is often sold as a house brand.

• Cuts of beef including the words "round" or "loin" are lean – top round and tenderloin, for example.

• Ground beef is labeled with the percentage of lean meat to fat. This ranges from 75 percent lean to 90 percent extra-lean; 80 to 85 percent lean, juicy and flavorful, is the most popular.

• To eliminate the danger of E. coli and other bacteria, ground beef (lean or otherwise) should always be cooked to medium doneness – until barely pink in the center.

• To be tender, lean cuts should either be panfried or roasted briefly, just until medium-rare so they do not dry out, or else braised for a long time.

BUYING BEEF

• For all beef, color is a good indicator of quality. Beef should be bright to deep red. Any fat should be dry and creamy white. Cut edges should look freshly cut and moist, but never wet.

• Ground beef should look bright and cherry-red. Don't worry if the center of the package looks darker than the exterior. The darker color comes from a lack of oxygen; when exposed to air, the dark meat should return to red. Vacuum-packed beef is darker and more purple in color.

• All beef is aged to improve its texture and flavor; for supermarket beef the process is quite short. Traditional aging can take up to six weeks; such cuts are more expensive and are generally found only at fancy butchers and restaurants.

CHOOSING THE RIGHT CUT

With appropriate cooking methods, any cut of beef can be tender. Cook lean cuts by dry-heat methods (roasting, broiling, grilling, panfrying); for less-tender cuts use a moist-heat method (stewing, braising) until meat is butter-soft.

For broiling, grilling, or panfrying Lean, tender cuts work best for these quick methods. When broiling or grilling steaks 1 inch thick or more, position them farther from the heat source so the outside isn't charred before the inside is done.
Best bets Porterhouse steak (below), T-bone steak, top round, top loin, rib-eye, sirloin steaks, tenderloin, flank steak, ground beef.

Trim away excess fat before cooking

Steaks for broiling or grilling should be at least ¾ inch thick

Look for lightly marbled meat with fat in broken lines

For braising or stewing Less-tender cuts of beef become deliciously tender when simmered in a flavorful liquid for a long time. Such cuts are often less expensive too.
Best bets Chuck roast, bottom round (below), brisket, short ribs, shank cross-cuts, oxtails. Cubes for stew are usually cut from boneless beef round or chuck. Bones add flavor and body to stews.

Trim away excess fat before cooking in liquid

Whole cuts keep their shape during long, slow cooking

Coarse-grained, less-tender cuts require moist-heat cooking

For roasting Large, tender cuts with some internal fat will give best results. Roast boneless cuts on a rack in a shallow roasting pan so the meat doesn't stew in its juices; bone-in roasts don't need a rack.
Best bets Standing rib roast (below), tenderloin, rib-eye, or eye round.

A thin covering of fat ensures meat stays moist during cooking

Bones should be cleanly cut

Meat should have some marbling for tenderness

ROASTING BEEF

Roasting beef to perfection is as simple as can be – just watch its temperature. The roasting chart on the right gives guidelines for cooking a variety of cuts to medium-rare and medium. Start with the meat at refrigerator temperature, and **remove the roast from the oven when it reaches 5° to 10°F below the desired doneness; the temperature will rise as the roast stands.** For juiciest meat, allow the roast to stand for 15 minutes before carving.

ROASTING TIMES

CUT	OVEN TEMPERATURE	WEIGHT	APPROXIMATE COOKING TIME Medium-rare (145°F)	Medium (160°F)
Rib roast (chine bone removed)	350°F	4–6 lbs 6–8 lbs	1¾–2¼ hrs 2¼–2½ hrs	2¼–2¾ hrs 2¾–3 hrs
Rib eye roast	350°F	4–6 lbs	1¾–2 hrs	2–2½ hrs
Whole tenderloin	425°F	4–5 lbs	50–60 mins	60–70 mins
Half tenderloin	425°F	2–3 lbs	35–40 mins	45–50 mins
Round tip roast	325°F	3–4 lbs 6–8 lbs	1¾–2 hrs 2½–3 hrs	2¼–2½ hrs 3–3½ hrs
Eye round roast	325°F	2–3 lbs	1½–1¾ hrs	—

SLICING A FLANK STEAK

Use a 2-pronged carving fork to steady the meat. Cut steak across the grain for tender slices.

Starting at thin end of steak, position carving knife at a 45° angle to meat, with blade facing away from you. Use a sawing motion to cut slices along length of steak.

CARVING A RIB ROAST

The chine bone should be removed by your butcher so that you can carve the roast between the rib bones. Carving will be easier, and the meat will be juicier, if you allow the roast to stand for at least 15 minutes after you have removed it from the oven.

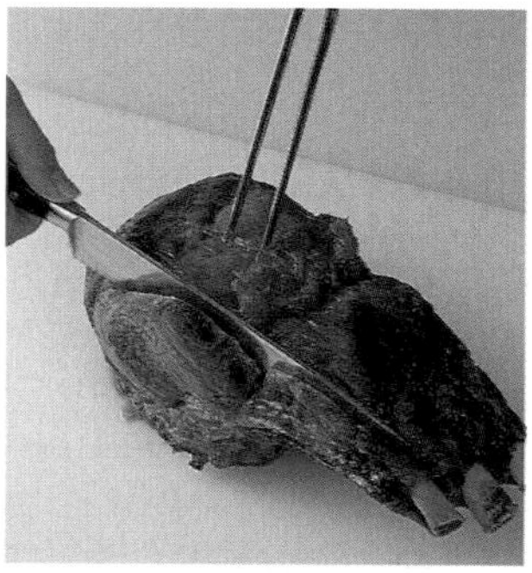

1 Place roast, rib-side down, on cutting board. With a carving knife, cut down toward ribs to make a slice about ¼ inch thick.

2 Release the meat slice by cutting along edge of rib bone. Transfer slice to warm platter.

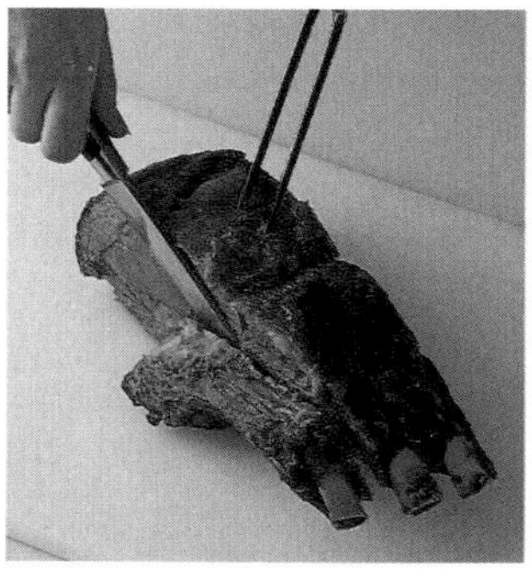

3 Repeat to cut more slices. As each rib bone is exposed, cut it away from roast and add to platter. This will make it easier to carve the rest of the roast.

STEAK SUCCESS

Cut into steaks to check for doneness, following our visual guide at right (always use a meat thermometer to check roasts).

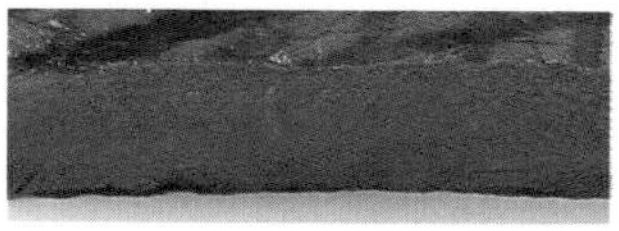

Rare steak

Medium-rare steak

Well-done steak

ROAST BEEF

Regal roast beef is superb when rubbed with an herb coating, which flavors the meat and the pan juices during cooking. The roasting pan should be kept uncovered; placing the meat fat-side up keeps it moist. Since no two roasts are exactly alike, a meat thermometer is the best guide to doneness.

BEEF RIB ROAST WITH MADEIRA GRAVY

Prep: 15 minutes plus standing and making Yorkshire Pudding
Roast: 2 hours 20 minutes
Makes 12 main-dish servings

1 tablespoon fennel seeds
1 teaspoon coarsely ground black pepper
1 teaspoon salt
2 tablespoons chopped fresh parsley
1 (3-rib) beef rib roast, about 7 pounds, chine bone removed
Yorkshire Pudding (optional, see page 184)

¼ cup Madeira wine or dry sherry
2 tablespoons all-purpose flour
1¼ teaspoons beef-flavor instant bouillon
Chopped fresh parsley for garnish
Zucchini and carrots (optional)

1 Preheat oven to 325°F. In mortar with pestle, crush fennel seeds. Stir in pepper, salt, and parsley. Pat roast dry with paper towels. Rub fennel mixture over roast. Place roast, fat-side up, on rack in large roasting pan.

2 Insert meat thermometer into center of roast. Roast beef 2 hours 20 minutes (20 minutes per pound), or until thermometer reaches 140°F. Internal temperature of meat will rise to 145°F (medium-rare) upon standing. Or, roast until desired doneness.

3 Transfer beef to warm large platter; let stand 15 minutes for easier carving. Keep warm. Remove rack from roasting pan. Pour pan drippings into 2-cup measuring cup; let stand a few seconds, until fat separates from meat juice. Skim 2 tablespoons fat from drippings into 2-quart saucepan. Skim remaining fat; discard or reserve for Yorkshire Pudding. Prepare Yorkshire Pudding, if you like.

4 Prepare gravy: Add Madeira and ½ *cup water* to roasting pan; stir over medium heat until brown bits are loosened. Add Madeira mixture to meat juice in measuring cup with enough *water* to equal 2 cups; set aside. Into fat in saucepan, stir flour until blended; cook over medium heat, stirring constantly, until flour turns golden.

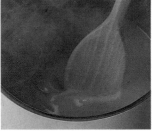

5 Gradually stir in meat-juice mixture and bouillon; cook, stirring, until gravy boils and thickens slightly. To serve, slice beef. Arrange slices on 12 plates; sprinkle with chopped parsley. Serve with gravy, and Yorkshire Pudding, zucchini, and carrots, if you like.

EACH SERVING: ABOUT 530 CALORIES, 70g PROTEIN, 1g CARBOHYDRATE, 24g TOTAL FAT (9g SATURATED), 167mg CHOLESTEROL, 320mg SODIUM

MUSTARD-CRUSTED
RIB-EYE ROAST

Prep: 25 minutes plus standing   *Roast: 1 hour 20 minutes*
Makes 12 main-dish servings

1 beef rib-eye roast
   (4 pounds)
½ teaspoon dried thyme
Salt and ground black pepper
6 medium red onions, each
   cut lengthwise in half
⅓ cup Dijon mustard with
   seeds

1 tablespoon prepared white
   horseradish
1½ pounds green beans, ends
   trimmed
2 tablespoons olive or
   vegetable oil
1 pound snow peas or sugar
   snap peas, strings removed

◆ Preheat oven to 350°F. Pat roast dry with paper towels. In cup, mix thyme, 1 teaspoon salt, and ½ teaspoon pepper; use to rub over roast. Place roast, fat-side up, in large roasting pan with onions. Insert meat thermometer into center of roast; roast 1 hour, turning onions in pan drippings occasionally.

◆ In small bowl, mix mustard and horseradish. When meat has roasted 1 hour, spread top with mustard mixture. Roast 20 minutes longer, or until thermometer reaches 140°F. Internal temperature of meat will rise to 145°F (medium-rare) upon standing. Or, roast until desired doneness. Transfer roast to warm large platter; let stand 15 minutes.

◆ Meanwhile, in 12-inch skillet, heat *1 inch water* to boiling over high heat. Add green beans; return to boiling. Reduce heat to low; cover and simmer 8 to 10 minutes, until tender-crisp. Drain. Wipe skillet dry. In same skillet, heat oil over high heat; add green beans and snow peas and cook, stirring constantly, until coated. Sprinkle with 1 teaspoon salt and ¼ teaspoon pepper; cook, stirring, 5 minutes longer, or until snow peas are tender-crisp. Slice roast; arrange onions and green-bean mixture on platter with roast.

Each serving: About 505 calories, 30g protein, 14g carbohydrate, 36g total fat (14g saturated), 103mg cholesterol, 545mg sodium

ROAST BEEF WITH TWO SAUCES

Prep: 25 minutes plus standing   *Roast: 1 hour 30 minutes*
Makes 8 main-dish servings

1 beef eye round roast
   (4 pounds)
2 teaspoons dried thyme
1 teaspoon ground sage
4 garlic cloves, minced
¼ teaspoon salt
Coarsely ground black pepper
¾ cup olive or vegetable oil
½ cup capers, drained and
   chopped

⅓ cup Dijon mustard
1 tablespoon chopped chives
1 jar (6 ounces) prepared
   white horseradish, drained
½ cup mayonnaise
1 teaspoon sugar
½ cup heavy or whipping
   cream

◆ Preheat oven to 325°F. Trim any fat from eye round roast; pat dry with paper towels. In cup, mix thyme, sage, minced garlic, salt, and 1¼ teaspoon pepper. Use to rub over roast. Place roast on rack in small roasting pan. Insert meat thermometer into center of roast.

◆ Roast beef 1½ hours, or until thermometer reaches 140°F. Internal temperature of meat will rise to 145°F (medium-rare) upon standing. Or, roast until desired doneness. Transfer roast to warm large platter; let stand 15 minutes.

◆ Meanwhile, prepare sauces. For caper sauce: In small bowl, mix oil, capers, Dijon mustard, chopped chives, ¾ teaspoon pepper and ¼ *cup water* until blended.

◆ For horseradish sauce: In small bowl, mix horseradish, mayonnaise, and sugar until blended. In small bowl, with mixer at medium speed, whip cream to stiff peaks; fold into horseradish mixture.

◆ Slice roast; serve with caper sauce and horseradish sauce.

Each serving: About 730 calories, 44g protein, 5g carbohydrate, 59g total fat (16g saturated), 153mg cholesterol, 1055mg sodium

YORKSHIRE PUDDING

◆◆◆◆◆◆◆◆◆◆◆◆◆

For individual puddings, use eighteen 2½" by 1½" muffin-pan cups; bake puddings only 12 to 15 minutes.

3 large eggs
1½ cups milk
1½ cups all-purpose flour
¾ teaspoon salt
3 tablespoons roast-beef pan
   drippings

1 Preheat oven to 450°F. In medium bowl, with wire whisk, beat eggs, milk, flour, and salt until smooth. Place roast-beef pan drippings in 13" by 9" metal baking pan; place in oven for 2 minutes. Remove pan from oven.

2 Pour milk mixture over hot drippings. Bake 25 minutes, or until puffed and lightly browned. Cut into squares; serve hot. Makes 8 accompaniment servings.

Each serving: About 160 calories, 6g protein, 19g carbohydrate, 6g total fat (3g saturated), 89mg cholesterol, 250mg sodium

ROAST BEEF TENDERLOIN

This premium cut of beef, a boneless strip from the loin, is the most tender and makes a wonderful roast. Unlike larger cuts of beef, the tenderloin roasts quickly at a high temperature. If cooking a whole, unstuffed tenderloin, tuck the thin end under so the roast is of an even thickness.

STUFFED BEEF TENDERLOIN

◆◆◆◆◆◆◆◆◆◆◆◆◆◆

Prep: 30 minutes plus standing
Roast: 45 to 50 minutes
Makes 10 main-dish servings

2 tablespoons vegetable oil
1 medium onion, minced
1 bunch (10 to 12 ounces) spinach, chopped
½ teaspoon salt
¼ teaspoon ground black pepper
¼ cup freshly grated Parmesan cheese
¼ cup oil-packed dried tomatoes, drained and finely chopped
1 center-cut beef tenderloin roast (3 pounds)
1 beef-flavor bouillon cube or envelope
¼ cup dry sherry
Chopped oil-packed dried tomatoes for garnish
Assorted sautéed vegetables (optional)

1 Preheat oven to 425°F. In 12-inch skillet, heat oil over medium heat. Add onion; cook until tender and golden. Add spinach, salt, and pepper; cook, stirring, until spinach just wilts.

2 Remove mixture from heat; stir in Parmesan cheese and ¼ cup dried tomatoes. Set aside. Make a lengthwise cut along center of tenderloin, cutting almost but not all the way through.

3 Ease tenderloin open. Spoon spinach-cheese mixture evenly into slit in tenderloin, pressing firmly. Close tenderloin, packing spinach mixture into slit.

4 With string, tie tenderloin securely in several places to hold cut edges of meat together. Place tenderloin, cut-side up, on rack in small roasting pan.

5 Roast tenderloin 45 to 50 minutes for medium-rare, or until desired doneness. After meat has roasted 30 minutes, if necessary, cover stuffing with foil to prevent drying out.

6 Transfer roast to cutting board. Let stand 10 minutes; keep warm. Meanwhile, remove rack from roasting pan. Skim and discard fat from drippings; add bouillon, sherry, and *1½ cups water* to roasting pan. Heat mixture to boiling over medium-high heat; stir until brown bits are loosened. To serve, remove strings from beef; slice beef. Arrange slices on 10 plates; garnish and pass gravy. Serve with sautéed vegetables, if you like.

EACH SERVING: ABOUT 270 CALORIES 31g PROTEIN, 4g CARBOHYDRATE, 13g TOTAL FAT (4g SATURATED), 73mg CHOLESTEROL, 335mg SODIUM

BEEF TENDERLOIN WITH WILD MUSHROOMS

Prep: 25 minutes plus standing   Roast: 45 to 55 minutes
Makes 8 main-dish servings

1 center-cut beef tenderloin
  roast (2½ pounds), tied
2 teaspoons vegetable oil
Salt and ground black pepper
Dried thyme
2 tablespoons margarine or
  butter
⅓ cup minced shallots
12 ounces white mushrooms,
  sliced
4 ounces shiitake mushrooms,
  stems discarded, sliced

4 ounces oyster mushrooms,
  each cut in half if large
⅓ cup Madeira wine
⅓ cup heavy or whipping
  cream
1 tablespoon chopped fresh
  parsley
Steamed snow peas and
  tomatoes (optional)

◆ Preheat oven to 425°F. Pat beef dry with paper towels. In cup, combine oil, 1 teaspoon salt, ¼ teaspoon pepper, and ¼ teaspoon thyme; use to rub over tenderloin.

◆ Place beef on rack in small roasting pan. Insert meat thermometer into center of thickest part of meat. Roast 45 to 55 minutes, until meat thermometer reaches 140°F. Internal temperature of meat will rise to 145°F (medium-rare) upon standing. Or, roast until desired doneness.

◆ Meanwhile, in 12-inch skillet, melt margarine over medium-high heat. Add shallots and cook, stirring often, 1 minute. Stir in all mushrooms, ¾ teaspoon salt, ⅛ teaspoon pepper, and ⅛ teaspoon thyme. Cook, stirring often, 10 minutes, or until mushrooms are lightly browned and liquid evaporates. Stir in Madeira and cook until pan is almost dry. Stir in cream; boil 1 minute. Remove from heat.

◆ Transfer tenderloin to warm large platter. Let stand 10 minutes; keep warm. Remove rack from roasting pan. Add ¼ cup water to pan and heat to boiling over medium-high heat. Stir until brown bits are loosened; stir into mushroom mixture with parsley.

◆ Thinly slice tenderloin; serve with mushrooms, and snow peas and tomatoes, if you like.

Each serving: About 360 calories, 34g protein, 15g carbohydrate, 17g total fat (7g saturated), 87mg cholesterol, 375mg sodium

ASIAN BEEF TENDERLOIN

Prep: 10 minutes plus marinating and standing   Roast: 50 to 60 minutes
Makes 16 main-dish servings

½ cup soy sauce
3 tablespoons grated, peeled
  fresh ginger
1½ teaspoons fennel seeds,
  crushed
½ teaspoon crushed red
  pepper

½ teaspoon cracked black
  pepper
¼ teaspoon ground cloves
1 beef tenderloin roast (about
  5 pounds), tied
1 tablespoon vegetable oil
Parsley sprigs for garnish

◆ In large zip-tight plastic bag, mix soy sauce, ginger, fennel seeds, crushed red pepper, black pepper, and cloves. Add tenderloin, turning to coat with marinade. Close bag securely and place in large baking dish or roasting pan; refrigerate 6 hours, or overnight, turning bag occasionally.

◆ Preheat oven to 425°F. Place tenderloin on rack in large roasting pan; discard marinade. Brush tenderloin with oil. Insert meat thermometer into center of thickest part of meat.

◆ Roast tenderloin 50 to 60 minutes, until meat thermometer reaches 140°F. Internal temperature of meat will rise to 145°F (medium-rare) upon standing. Or, roast until desired doneness.

◆ Transfer tenderloin to cutting board. Let stand 10 minutes; keep warm. Thinly slice tenderloin; arrange on warm large platter. Garnish with parsley sprigs.

Each serving: About 225 calories, 31g protein, 0g carbohydrate, 10g total fat (4g saturated), 74mg cholesterol, 195mg sodium

FENNEL SEEDS

Native to the Mediterranean, fennel has been prized for its delicate, licorice-like flavor for thousands of years. The bulb, feathery leaves, stems, flowers, and seeds were popular with the Romans and ancient Greeks, as well as in the cuisines of ancient China, India, and Egypt. Fennel seeds are small, greenish-brown ovals that are available whole and ground. They enhance sweet and savory dishes, such as fish soups, breads, sausages, roasted meats, curries, cabbage, and even apple pie. To better release the flavor, lightly crush the seeds in a mortar with a pestle before adding them to a dish. Indian restaurants often serve plain or sugar-coated fennel seeds after dinner as a digestive and breath freshener.

Braised beef

Braising, or pot-roasting, makes large, tough cuts of meat tender. The meat is first browned to seal in flavor, then gently simmered with vegetables and herbs in liquid. Serve the vegetables whole with the meat, or puree them to make a delicious savory sauce.

1 In cup, mix first 6 ingredients. Pat roast dry with paper towels. Rub 2½ teaspoons spice mix over roast; reserve remaining mix.

2 In 5-quart Dutch oven, heat oil over medium-high heat. Add roast and cook until well browned on all sides; transfer to plate.

3 To drippings in Dutch oven, add onions, celery, and green pepper; cover and cook, stirring often, over medium heat until tender.

CAJUN POT ROAST

◆◆◆◆◆◆◆◆◆◆◆◆◆

Prep: 15 minutes
Cook: 2 hours 30 minutes
to 3 hours
Makes 12 main-dish servings

1½ teaspoons salt
1 teaspoon paprika
1 teaspoon dry mustard
½ teaspoon dried thyme
½ teaspoon ground red pepper (cayenne)
½ teaspoon ground black pepper
1 beef bottom round roast (3 pounds)
1 tablespoon vegetable oil
2 medium onions, each cut into wedges
2 large celery stalks, sliced diagonally into 1½-inch pieces
1 medium green pepper, cut into 1½-inch pieces
1 can (14½ to 16 ounces) tomatoes
1 bay leaf
1 garlic clove, minced
2 packages (10 ounces each) frozen whole baby okra
Celery leaves for garnish

4 Stir in tomatoes with their juice, bay leaf, garlic, and remaining spice mix. Return roast to Dutch oven; heat to boiling over high heat. Reduce heat to low. Cover and simmer 2 to 2½ hours, until roast is fork-tender, turning roast occasionally. About 10 minutes before roast is done, add frozen okra to Dutch oven; heat through.

5 To serve, transfer roast and vegetables to warm deep platter. Discard bay leaf. Skim and discard fat from broth in Dutch oven. Slice roast; garnish and serve with broth and vegetables.

EACH SERVING: ABOUT 195 CALORIES, 23g PROTEIN, 8g CARBOHYDRATE, 7g TOTAL FAT (2g SATURATED), 66mg CHOLESTEROL, 190mg SODIUM

COUNTRY POT ROAST

Prep: 15 minutes   Cook: 3 hours to 3 hours 30 minutes
Makes 12 main-dish servings

1 boneless beef chuck cross-rib pot roast or boneless chuck eye roast (4 pounds)	2 large celery stalks, sliced
¼ cup all-purpose flour	2 garlic cloves, crushed
2 tablespoons vegetable oil	1 teaspoon dried oregano
1½ cups tomato juice	½ teaspoon salt
2 medium onions, chopped	¼ teaspoon ground black pepper
2 medium carrots, sliced	Mashed potatoes (optional)
	Flat-leaf parsley for garnish

◆ Pat roast dry with paper towels. Spread flour on waxed paper; coat roast with flour.

◆ In 5-quart Dutch oven, heat oil over medium-high heat. Add roast and cook until browned on all sides; discard fat in Dutch oven.

◆ Add tomato juice, onions, carrots, celery, garlic, oregano, salt, and pepper to roast in Dutch oven; stir to combine. Heat to boiling over high heat.

◆ Reduce heat to low; cover and simmer 2½ to 3 hours, until roast is fork-tender, turning roast occasionally.

◆ Transfer roast to warm large platter; keep warm. Skim and discard fat from broth in Dutch oven. Fill blender about half-full with broth and vegetables from Dutch oven. Cover (with center part of blender lid removed) and blend at low speed until mixture is smooth; pour into large bowl. Repeat until all of mixture is blended.

◆ Return gravy mixture to Dutch oven; heat to boiling over high heat. Thinly slice roast; serve with gravy, and mashed potatoes, if you like. Garnish with parsley.

Each serving: About 420 calories, 31g protein, 7g carbohydrate, 29g total fat (11g saturated), 117mg cholesterol, 285mg sodium

STOVE-TOP EYE ROUND WITH SPRING VEGETABLES

Prep: 25 minutes   Cook: 1 hour 10 minutes
Makes 8 main-dish servings

1 beef eye round roast (2 pounds), tied	1 bay leaf
½ teaspoon coarsely ground black pepper	½ teaspoon dried tarragon
2 teaspoons vegetable oil	1½ pounds baby carrots, trimmed
2 beef-flavor bouillon cubes or envelopes	1¾ pounds small white and/or red potatoes
1 garlic clove, cut in half	1½ pounds thin asparagus, tough ends removed

◆ Pat roast dry with paper towels; rub with pepper. In 5-quart Dutch oven, heat oil over medium-high heat; add roast and cook until browned on all sides.

◆ Add bouillon, garlic, bay leaf, tarragon, and *2½ cups water*; heat to boiling. Reduce heat to low; cover and simmer 20 minutes. Add carrots and potatoes; heat to boiling over high heat.

◆ Reduce heat to low; cover and simmer 30 minutes longer, or until vegetables are tender and temperature of roast reaches 140°F on instant-read meat thermometer inserted in thickest part of meat. Internal temperature of meat will rise to 145°F (medium-rare) upon standing. Transfer roast to warm large platter; keep warm.

◆ Meanwhile, in 12-inch skillet, heat *½ inch water* to boiling over high heat; add asparagus and cook 3 to 5 minutes, until tender-crisp; drain.

◆ Transfer carrots and potatoes to platter with roast, reserving broth in Dutch oven. Discard garlic and bay leaf. Skim and discard fat from broth. Thinly slice roast; serve with broth, carrots, potatoes, and asparagus.

Each serving: About 285 calories, 26g protein, 28g carbohydrate, 6g total fat (2g saturated), 55mg cholesterol, 310mg sodium

BEEF POTPIES

When a chill in the air demands heartier fare, these savory meat pies make the perfect dinner. Crusts flecked with herbs, enriched with cheese, or made with flaky puff pastry crown our flavor-loaded potpies.

BEEF CURRY PIE

◆◆◆◆◆◆◆◆◆◆◆◆◆◆

Prep: 1 hour 15 minutes
Bake: 35 minutes
Makes 6 main-dish servings

1 pound lean boneless beef chuck, cut into ½-inch cubes
3 teaspoons olive or vegetable oil
1 garlic clove, minced
2 tablespoons curry powder
2 medium carrots, sliced
1 medium onion, diced
1 beef-flavor bouillon cube or envelope
¾ teaspoon salt
1 tablespoon cornstarch
1 package (10 ounces) frozen peas
Parsley Crust (see below)

PARSLEY CRUST

In large bowl, mix 2 cups all-purpose flour, ½ cup chopped fresh parsley, and 1 teaspoon salt. With pastry blender or two knives used scissor-fashion, cut in ¾ cup shortening until mixture resembles coarse crumbs. Stir in 5 to 6 tablespoons cold water, 1 tablespoon at a time, mixing lightly with fork after each addition, until dough just holds together. Divide dough in half; shape each into a ball.

1 Pat beef dry with paper towels. In 10-inch nonstick skillet, heat 2 teaspoons oil over medium-high heat; add beef and cook until browned on all sides. Stir in garlic and curry powder; cook 1 minute longer. With slotted spoon, transfer beef mixture to bowl. In same skillet, heat remaining 1 teaspoon oil; add carrots and onion and cook 10 minutes, or until browned.

2 Add beef, bouillon, salt, and *1¼ cups water*; heat to boiling over high heat. Reduce heat to low; cover and simmer 30 minutes. In cup, mix cornstarch and *¼ cup water*; gradually add to skillet. Cook over high heat, stirring, until mixture thickens; boil 1 minute. Stir in peas; remove from heat.

3 Prepare Parsley Crust. Preheat oven to 425°F. On lightly floured surface, with floured rolling pin, roll half of dough into round 1½ inches larger all around than inverted 9-inch pie plate. Ease round into pie plate. Spoon filling into crust. Trim pastry edge, leaving 1-inch overhang.

4 Roll remaining dough into 10-inch round; cut into ½-inch-wide strips. Place half of strips about ¾ inch apart across pie; do not seal ends. Fold every other strip back halfway from center.

5 Place center cross strip on pie; replace folded part of strips. Fold back alternate strips; add second cross strip. Repeat to weave strips into lattice. Seal ends. Fold overhang under; make fluted edge (see page 488). Bake on cookie sheet 35 minutes, or until crust is golden and filling is bubbly.

EACH SERVING: ABOUT 645 CALORIES, 23g PROTEIN, 44g CARBOHYDRATE, 42g TOTAL FAT (13g SATURATED), 56mg CHOLESTEROL, 855mg SODIUM

DEEP-DISH BEEF PIE

Prep: 2 hours *Bake:* 25 to 30 minutes
Makes 8 main-dish servings

2 tablespoons vegetable oil
1 pound small onions, peeled
2 pounds beef for stew, cut
   into 2-inch chunks
1 can (13¾ to 14½ ounces)
   beef broth
1¼ cups ginger ale
1½ teaspoons salt
¼ teaspoon coarsely ground
   black pepper
1 pound small white or red
   potatoes, each cut into
   quarters

1 bag (16 ounces) carrots, cut
   into 2-inch pieces
3 medium parsnips (about
   8 ounces), cut into bite-size
   chunks
8 ounces green beans,
   trimmed, each cut in half
½ (17¼-ounce) package frozen
   puff pastry (1 sheet),
   thawed
1 large egg, slightly beaten
⅓ cup all-purpose flour

◆ In 8-quart Dutch oven, heat oil over medium-high heat. Add onions; cook until browned. With slotted spoon, transfer to plate. Pat beef dry with paper towels. Heat oil remaining in Dutch oven over medium-high heat. Add beef, one-third at a time; cook until well browned. Transfer to plate as it browns.

◆ Return all beef to Dutch oven; stir in broth, ginger ale, salt, and pepper. Heat to boiling over high heat. Reduce heat to low; cover and simmer 30 minutes. Add onions; heat to boiling. Cover and simmer 30 minutes. Add potatoes, carrots, parsnips, and green beans; heat to boiling. Cover and simmer, stirring occasionally, 30 minutes longer, or until meat and vegetables are tender.

◆ Meanwhile, on lightly floured surface, with floured rolling pin, roll pastry to 13-inch square. Trim pastry into round ½ inch larger all around than 3-quart round casserole. Brush round with beaten egg. Keep pastry cold.

◆ Preheat oven to 375°F. In small bowl, mix flour and *1 cup water*; stir into stew. Cook over medium-high heat, stirring gently, until mixture thickens and boils. Spoon stew into casserole. Place pastry round on casserole, leaving overhang; pinch edge to seal. Bake 25 to 30 minutes, until pastry is golden.

Each serving: About 525 calories, 32g protein, 53g carbohydrate, 21g total fat (6g saturated), 82mg cholesterol, 790mg sodium

CHEDDAR-CRUST CHILI CASSEROLE

Prep: 35 minutes *Bake:* 40 to 45 minutes
Makes 8 main-dish servings

1 tablespoon vegetable oil
1½ pounds lean ground beef
1 medium onion, coarsely
   chopped
2 tablespoons chili powder
1 can (15 to 19 ounces) red
   kidney beans, rinsed and
   drained
1 can (15 to 19 ounces) Great
   Northern beans, rinsed and
   drained
1 package (10 ounces) frozen
   cut green beans

1 can (14½ to 16 ounces)
   stewed tomatoes
1 package (10 ounces) frozen
   whole-kernel corn
1 tablespoon chopped fresh
   cilantro or parsley
2¾ cups all-purpose flour
2 ounces Cheddar cheese,
   shredded (½ cup)
½ teaspoon salt
1 cup shortening
1 large egg, lightly beaten

◆ In 12-inch skillet, heat oil over medium-high heat; add beef and onion and cook, stirring frequently, until pan juices evaporate and beef is well browned.

◆ Stir in chili powder; cook, stirring constantly, 1 minute. Stir in kidney beans, Great Northern beans, green beans, stewed tomatoes, corn, and cilantro.

◆ In small bowl, mix ¼ cup flour with *1¼ cups water*; stir into ground-beef mixture and heat to boiling over high heat. Spoon meat mixture into 13" by 9" glass or ceramic baking dish. Cool slightly. Preheat oven to 375°F.

◆ Meanwhile, prepare crust: In large bowl, with fork, mix cheese, salt, and remaining 2½ cups flour. With pastry blender or two knives used scissor-fashion, cut in shortening until mixture resembles coarse crumbs.

◆ Sprinkle *6 to 7 tablespoons cold water*, 1 tablespoon at a time, into flour mixture, mixing lightly with fork after each addition, until dough is just moist enough to hold together.

◆ On lightly floured surface, with floured rolling pin, roll dough into a rectangle about 2 inches larger all around than top of baking dish.

◆ Place dough on filling. Trim edge, leaving 1-inch overhang. Fold overhang under; make fluted edge (see page 488). Cut several slits in crust to allow steam to escape during baking. Brush crust with beaten egg. Bake on cookie sheet 40 to 45 minutes, until crust is golden.

Each serving: About 825 calories, 31g protein, 66g carbohydrate, 49g total fat (17g saturated), 97mg cholesterol, 585mg sodium

BEEF CASSEROLES AND STEWS

Rich, flavorful beef stew makes the perfect warming winter supper. It's also a great do-ahead meal, as the flavors improve the next day, and it's easier to skim off fat if the stew is refrigerated overnight. To avoid scorching, add a little water when reheating.

BEEF AND MIXED MUSHROOM STEW

Prep: 30 minutes   *Bake:* 1 hour 30 minutes
Makes 6 main-dish servings

1 package (½ ounce) dried mushrooms
2 pounds beef for stew, cut into 1½-inch chunks
2 tablespoons vegetable oil
1 pound mushrooms, each cut in half
1 large onion, diced
2 garlic cloves, minced
2 tablespoons tomato paste
1 cup chicken broth

¾ cup dry red wine
2 medium carrots, each cut lengthwise in half, then crosswise into thirds
¾ teaspoon salt
¼ teaspoon dried thyme
1 bay leaf
Chopped fresh parsley for garnish
Wide egg noodles (optional)

1 Place dried mushrooms in small bowl; add *1 cup boiling water.* Set mixture aside for about 30 minutes so mushrooms can soften. Meanwhile, pat beef dry with paper towels.

2 In 5-quart Dutch oven, heat 1 tablespoon oil over medium-high heat. Add fresh mushrooms and cook about 10 minutes, or until lightly browned and most of liquid evaporates; transfer to small bowl.

3 In same Dutch oven, heat remaining 1 tablespoon oil over medium-high heat. Add beef chunks, half at a time, and cook until well browned; transfer beef to plate as it browns.

4 With slotted spoon, remove dried mushrooms from soaking liquid and coarsely chop; strain liquid through sieve lined with cheesecloth or paper towel. Preheat oven to 350°F.

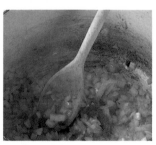

5 To drippings in Dutch oven, add onion and *2 tablespoons water* and cook over medium heat about 10 minutes, until onion is lightly browned. Add garlic and cook 30 seconds longer. Stir in tomato paste; cook, stirring constantly, 1 minute.

6 Return browned beef to Dutch oven; add dried mushrooms with their liquid, chicken broth, wine, carrots, salt, thyme, and bay leaf. Heat to boiling over high heat. Cover and bake 1¼ hours. Add sautéed mushrooms; bake 15 minutes longer, or until beef is tender. Skim and discard fat; discard bay leaf. Sprinkle with chopped parsley. Serve stew with egg noodles, if you like.

EACH SERVING: ABOUT 360 CALORIES, 37g PROTEIN, 13g CARBOHYDRATE, 16g TOTAL FAT (5g SATURATED), 77mg CHOLESTEROL, 610mg SODIUM

SAUERBRATEN STEW

Prep: 45 minutes   *Bake:* 1 hour 45 minutes
Makes 8 main-dish servings

2 pounds beef for stew, cut
   into 1½-inch chunks
2 tablespoons vegetable oil
1 large onion, sliced
1 small butternut squash
   (about 1½ pounds), peeled,
   seeded, and cut into 1½-inch
   chunks
6 small red potatoes (about 1½
   pounds), cut into quarters

1 cup cider vinegar
⅓ cup packed light brown
   sugar
2 teaspoons salt
1 bay leaf
½ cup fine gingersnap
   crumbs (about 8 cookies)
½ cup dark seedless raisins
1 pound green beans,
   trimmed

◆ Preheat oven to 350°F. Pat beef dry with paper towels. In 5-quart Dutch oven, heat oil over medium-high heat. Add beef, one-third at a time, and cook until well browned; with slotted spoon, transfer meat to plate as it browns. In drippings in Dutch oven, cook onion about 5 minutes, until tender. Stir in squash, potatoes, vinegar, brown sugar, salt, bay leaf, and *3 cups water*. Return meat to Dutch oven; heat to boiling over high heat. Cover and bake 1¼ hours, or until meat is tender.

◆ Stir in gingersnap crumbs and raisins until well blended; stir in green beans. Cover and bake 30 minutes longer, or until meat and vegetables are tender. Skim and discard fat; discard bay leaf before serving.

Each serving: About 420 calories, 29g protein, 52g carbohydrate, 12g total fat (4g saturated), 55mg cholesterol, 665mg sodium

BRAISED SHORT-RIB CASSEROLE

Prep: 30 minutes   *Bake:* 2 hours 30 minutes
Makes 6 main-dish servings

4 pounds beef chuck short
   ribs
1 tablespoon vegetable oil
1 bag (16 ounces) carrots, cut
   into 1-inch pieces
2 large onions, sliced
2 tablespoons all-purpose
   flour
1 can (14½ to 16 ounces)
   stewed tomatoes
1½ teaspoons salt

2 cans (15 to 19 ounces each)
   Great Northern or small
   white beans, rinsed and
   drained
Chopped fresh parsley and
   grated lemon peel for
   garnish
Hot cooked rice (optional)

◆ Preheat oven to 350°F. Pat short ribs dry with paper towels. In 5-quart Dutch oven, heat oil over medium-high heat. Add short ribs, half at a time, and cook until browned on all sides; transfer to bowl as they brown. In drippings in Dutch oven, cook carrots and onions, stirring occasionally, until lightly browned.

◆ In small bowl, mix flour and *1 cup water*. Return short ribs to Dutch oven; stir in flour mixture, tomatoes, and salt. Heat to boiling over high heat.

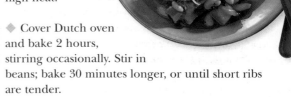

◆ Cover Dutch oven and bake 2 hours, stirring occasionally. Stir in beans; bake 30 minutes longer, or until short ribs are tender.

◆ Skim and discard fat. Sprinkle with chopped parsley and grated lemon peel and serve with rice, if you like.

Each serving: About 895 calories, 82g protein, 49g carbohydrate, 40g total fat (16g saturated), 174mg cholesterol, 875mg sodium

PAPRIKASH CASSEROLE

Prep: 30 minutes   *Bake:* 1 hour 15 minutes
Makes 6 main-dish servings

1½ pounds beef for stew, cut
   into 1¼-inch chunks
2 tablespoons vegetable oil
2 large onions, thinly sliced
1 package (12 ounces)
   medium mushrooms
2 tablespoons paprika

1 tablespoon all-purpose flour
1¼ teaspoons salt
½ cup light sour cream
2 tablespoons chopped fresh
   parsley
Wide egg noodles (optional)

◆ Preheat oven to 350°F. Pat beef dry with paper towels. In 5-quart Dutch oven, heat 1 tablespoon oil over medium-high heat. Add beef, half at a time, and cook until well browned; transfer meat to bowl as it browns.

◆ In drippings in Dutch oven and remaining 1 tablespoon oil, cook onions and mushrooms until lightly browned. Stir in paprika; cook 1 minute, stirring.

◆ In small bowl, mix flour and *1½ cups water*; stir into onion mixture with salt. Return meat to Dutch oven; heat to boiling over high heat. Cover Dutch oven and bake 1¼ hours, or until meat is tender, stirring once halfway through baking time.

◆ Skim and discard fat. Stir in sour cream. Sprinkle with parsley and serve with egg noodles, if you like.

Each serving: About 405 calories, 31g protein, 36g carbohydrate, 15g total fat (4g saturated), 61mg cholesterol, 555mg sodium

ORANGE BEEF AND BARLEY STEW

Prep: 35 minutes   *Bake:* 1 hour 30 to 45 minutes
Makes 6 main-dish servings

1½ pounds beef for stew, cut into 1½-inch chunks
2 tablespoons vegetable oil
4 medium carrots, cut into 2-inch pieces
2 medium onions, each cut into 6 wedges
2 garlic cloves, minced
1 can (28 ounces) plum tomatoes
1 can (13¾ to 14½ ounces) beef broth
1 cup dry red wine
3 strips orange peel (each 3" by 1")
1 bay leaf
½ teaspoon salt
¾ cup pearl barley

◆ Preheat oven to 350°F. Pat beef dry with paper towels. In 5-quart Dutch oven, heat 1 tablespoon oil over medium-high heat; add beef in batches and cook until browned; transfer to bowl. In drippings in Dutch oven, heat remaining 1 tablespoon oil; add carrots and onions and cook until browned. Add garlic; cook 1 minute, stirring. Return beef to Dutch oven; add tomatoes with their liquid, broth, wine, orange peel, bay leaf, and salt. Heat to boiling over high heat, breaking up tomatoes with back of spoon.

◆ Cover Dutch oven and bake 45 minutes. Stir in barley; cover and bake 45 to 60 minutes longer, until beef and barley are tender. Skim and discard fat; discard bay leaf.

Each serving: About 410 calories, 31g protein, 36g carbohydrate, 14g total fat (4g saturated), 55mg cholesterol, 750mg sodium

OXTAIL STEW

Prep: 15 minutes   *Cook:* 3 hours 30 minutes
Makes 6 main-dish servings

1 bag (16 ounces) carrots
6 medium celery stalks
4 pounds oxtails
1 tablespoon vegetable oil
1 large onion, finely chopped
2 garlic cloves, minced
2 tablespoons all-purpose flour
1 cup dry red wine
1 can (28 ounces) tomatoes in puree
1 teaspoon salt
¼ teaspoon ground black pepper
¼ teaspoon dried thyme
¼ teaspoon dried rosemary, crushed

◆ Finely chop 1 carrot and 1 celery stalk. Cut remaining carrots and celery lengthwise in half, then crosswise into 3-inch pieces; set aside.

◆ Pat oxtails dry with paper towels. In 5-quart Dutch oven, heat 1 teaspoon oil over medium-high heat. Add half of oxtails and cook until well browned; transfer to bowl. Repeat with 1 teaspoon oil and remaining oxtails. In drippings in Dutch oven, heat remaining 1 teaspoon oil; add finely chopped carrot, celery, and onion and cook 5 minutes, or until tender. Stir in garlic; cook 30 seconds. Add flour and cook, stirring, 1 minute. Stir in wine; heat to boiling, stirring, over high heat. Add tomatoes in puree, breaking them up with back of spoon. Return oxtails to Dutch oven. Add salt, pepper, thyme, and rosemary; heat to boiling over high heat.

◆ Reduce heat to low; cover and simmer 2½ hours, or until meat is very tender. Stir in reserved carrot and celery pieces; heat to boiling over high heat. Reduce heat to low; cover and simmer 30 minutes longer, or until vegetables are tender. Skim and discard fat before serving.

Each serving: About 535 calories, 61g protein, 22g carbohydrate, 19g total fat (6g saturated), 177mg cholesterol, 975mg sodium.

ROPA VIEJA

Prep: 30 minutes plus standing   *Cook:* 3 hours to 3 hours 30 minutes
Makes 6 main-dish servings

1 beef flank steak (1¾ pounds)
1 medium onion, chopped
1 medium carrot, chopped
½ bay leaf
Salt
4 teaspoons olive oil
1 large onion, sliced
1 red pepper, cut into strips
1 yellow pepper, cut into strips
1 green pepper, cut into strips
3 garlic cloves, minced
3 serrano or jalapeño chiles, seeded and minced
¼ teaspoon ground cinnamon
1 can (14½ to 16 ounces) tomatoes
Capers for garnish

◆ Cut steak crosswise in half. In 5-quart Dutch oven, heat steak, chopped onion, carrot, bay leaf, ½ teaspoon salt, and *5 cups water* to boiling over high heat. Reduce heat to low; cover and simmer 2½ to 3 hours, until meat is very tender. Remove from heat; let stand, uncovered, 30 minutes. Transfer beef to cutting board. Strain broth. With fork or fingers, shred beef into fine strips.

◆ In 12-inch skillet, heat oil over medium-high heat. Add sliced onion, peppers, and ½ teaspoon salt. Cook, stirring frequently, 10 minutes or until vegetables are tender. Stir in garlic, serranos, and cinnamon; cook 30 seconds. Stir in tomatoes with their liquid, breaking up tomatoes with back of spoon; cook 5 minutes. Stir in 2 cups broth (reserve remaining broth for use another day) and beef; simmer, stirring occasionally, 10 minutes. To serve, sprinkle with capers.

Each serving: About 305 calories, 28g protein, 13g carbohydrate, 16g total fat (6g saturated), 67mg cholesterol, 760mg sodium

BOEUF BOURGUIGNON

Prep: 30 minutes   *Cook:* 2 hours 15 to 45 minutes
Makes 6 main-dish servings

2 slices bacon, chopped
2 pounds boneless beef chuck, cut into 1½-inch pieces
1 to 2 teaspoons vegetable oil
1 large onion, finely chopped
2 medium carrots, finely chopped
2 garlic cloves, minced
2 tablespoons all-purpose flour
2 teaspoons tomato paste
2 cups dry red wine
½ bay leaf
¼ teaspoon dried thyme
Salt and ground black pepper
1 pound small white onions, peeled
1 teaspoon sugar
2 tablespoons margarine or butter
1 pound mushrooms, each cut into quarters if large
Chopped fresh parsley for garnish

◆ In 5-quart Dutch oven, cook bacon over medium heat until beginning to brown; transfer to bowl. Pat beef dry with paper towels. Add 1 teaspoon oil to drippings in Dutch oven; increase heat to medium-high. Add beef in batches and cook, adding 1 teaspoon more oil if necessary, until well browned; transfer to bowl with bacon.

◆ Reduce heat to medium. Add chopped onion, carrots, and garlic and cook, stirring often, until tender. Stir in flour and cook 1 minute. Stir in tomato paste and cook 1 minute. Add wine, bay leaf, thyme, 1 teaspoon salt, and ¼ teaspoon pepper; stir until brown bits are loosened.

◆ Return beef and bacon to Dutch oven and heat to boiling over high heat. Reduce heat to low; cover and simmer 1½ to 2 hours, until beef is very tender. Skim fat; discard bay leaf.

◆ Meanwhile, in 10-inch skillet, heat small white onions, sugar, 1 tablespoon margarine, and *1 cup water* to boiling over high heat. Reduce heat to low; cover and simmer 10 minutes, or until onions are tender. Uncover; cook over medium-high heat, shaking pan occasionally, until water evaporates and onions are golden.

◆ In 12-inch skillet, melt remaining 1 tablespoon margarine over medium-high heat. Add mushrooms and a pinch each salt and pepper; cook, stirring often, until mushrooms are tender and liquid evaporates. Stir onions and mushrooms into stew. Garnish and serve.

Each serving: About 560 calories, 35g protein, 20g carbohydrate, 32g total fat (12g saturated), 119mg cholesterol, 620mg sodium

SCANDINAVIAN BEEF STEW

Prep: 25 minutes   *Cook:* 2 hours 30 minutes to 3 hours
Makes 8 main-dish servings

2 pounds boneless beef chuck, cut into 2-inch pieces
2 teaspoons vegetable oil
1 large onion, finely chopped
1 tablespoon ground coriander
2 teaspoons ground ginger
¼ teaspoon ground nutmeg
1 teaspoon salt
¼ teaspoon dried thyme
¼ teaspoon ground black pepper
1 bag (16 ounces) carrots
2 large parsnips (8 ounces)
½ small rutabaga
1 pound small red potatoes

Pat beef dry. In 5-quart Dutch oven, heat 1 teaspoon oil over medium-high heat. Add half of beef; cook until browned. Transfer to plate. Repeat with remaining oil and beef. Reduce heat to medium. To drippings in Dutch oven, add onion; cook until tender. Stir in coriander, ginger, and nutmeg; cook 30 seconds. Add beef, salt, thyme, pepper, and *3 cups water*; heat to boiling over high heat. Reduce heat to low; simmer, covered, 1½ to 2 hours, until beef is tender. Meanwhile, cut vegetables into 1½-inch pieces. Add vegetables to pot and heat to boiling over high heat. Reduce heat to low; cover and simmer 30 to 40 minutes longer, until tender. Skim fat.

Each serving: About 400 calories, 26g protein, 26g carbohydrate, 21g total fat (8g saturated), 88mg cholesterol, 355mg sodium

CHINESE-SPICED BEEF STEW

Prep: 15 minutes   *Cook:* 2 hours to 2 hours 30 minutes
Makes 8 main-dish servings

2 pounds boneless beef chuck, cut into 2-inch pieces
2 teaspoons vegetable oil
⅓ cup dry sherry
3 tablespoons soy sauce
2 tablespoons sugar
¼ cup sliced peeled fresh ginger
2 garlic cloves, peeled
2 star anise
4 strips (3" by 1") orange peel
1 bunch broccoli (about 1½ pounds), cut into spears
4 ounces snow peas, trimmed
1 bunch green onions, each cut into 2-inch pieces

Pat beef dry. In 5-quart Dutch oven, heat 1 teaspoon oil over medium-high heat. Add half of beef; cook until browned. Transfer to plate. Repeat with remaining 1 teaspoon oil and remaining beef. Return beef to Dutch oven. Add sherry, next 6 ingredients, and *3 cups water*; heat to boiling over high heat. Reduce heat to low; simmer, covered, 1½ to 2 hours, until beef is very tender. Transfer beef to bowl; keep warm. Boil liquid in Dutch oven 10 minutes. Meanwhile, in 4-quart saucepan, heat *1 inch water* to boiling. Add broccoli. Cover; cook 5 minutes. Add snow peas and green onions; cook, covered, 1 minute longer. Drain; stir into Dutch oven. Spoon mixture over beef.

Each serving: About 355 calories, 27g protein, 11g carbohydrate, 22g total fat (8g saturated), 88mg cholesterol, 465mg sodium

CHILI

This hearty Southwest specialty originated in Texas, and has become one of America's favorite dishes. It is excellent whether made with cubes of beef or with ground meat; some chilies include beans and vegetables as well. Try leftover chili spooned over a baked potato or fluffy white rice.

TEXAS-STYLE CHILI

◆◆◆◆◆◆◆◆◆◆◆◆◆

Prep: 25 minutes
Cook: 2 hours 20 minutes
Makes 12 main-dish servings

3½ pounds beef for stew, cut into ½-inch cubes
¼ cup vegetable oil
3 medium green peppers, diced
2 medium onions, chopped
4 garlic cloves, minced
2 cans (28 ounces each) tomatoes
1 can (12 ounces) tomato paste
⅓ cup chili powder
¼ cup sugar
2 teaspoons salt
2 teaspoons dried oregano
¾ teaspoon cracked black pepper
Shredded Monterey Jack cheese and sliced green onions for garnish
Tortilla chips (optional)

1 Pat beef dry with paper towels. In 8-quart Dutch oven, heat oil over medium-high heat. Add beef, one-third at a time; cook until browned. Transfer beef to bowl as it browns.

2 Add green peppers, onions, and garlic to drippings in Dutch oven; cook over medium-high heat, stirring occasionally, 10 minutes.

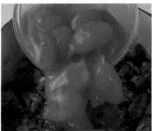

3 Return beef to Dutch oven; stir in tomatoes with their juice, tomato paste, chili powder, sugar, salt, oregano, and black pepper, breaking up tomatoes with back of spoon.

TOUCH OF SPICE

Deep red in color, with a hot and spicy flavor, chili powder may be purely one variety of chile, dried and ground, or more often, a seasoning blend of ground dried chiles, oregano, cumin, garlic, and salt. Depending on the brand, the flavor can range from mild to fiery hot, and the saltiness varies too. The best chili powders contain nothing but pure ground chiles, and are deep red in color, rather than brown. There are hundreds of different chiles, with different flavors and heat levels. Mexican and Southwestern cooks prefer to grind their own chiles. For freshness, store chili powder in the freezer.

4 Stir in *2 cups water*; heat to boiling over high heat. Reduce heat to low; cover and simmer, stirring occasionally, 1½ hours, or until beef is tender. To serve, spoon into bowls and garnish; serve with tortilla chips, if you like.

EACH SERVING: ABOUT 345 CALORIES, 33g PROTEIN, 21g CARBOHYDRATE, 15g TOTAL FAT (4g SATURATED), 64mg CHOLESTEROL, 910mg SODIUM

CHILI-BEEF CASSEROLE

Prep: 40 minutes   Bake: 1 hour
Makes 8 main-dish servings

3 tablespoons olive or vegetable oil	1 teaspoon salt
1 large onion, chopped	1 can (16 ounces) tomatoes in puree
1 small red pepper, diced	1 medium tomato, diced
1 small green pepper, diced	1 jar (3 ounces) small pimiento-stuffed olives
2 pounds beef for stew, cut into ½-inch pieces	½ cup dark seedless raisins
2 tablespoons all-purpose flour	¼ cup sliced almonds, toasted
2 tablespoons chili powder	

◆ In 5-quart Dutch oven, heat 1 tablespoon oil over medium-high heat; add onion and peppers and cook until tender and golden. With slotted spoon, transfer to bowl.

◆ Preheat oven to 400°F. Pat beef dry with paper towels. In large bowl, toss beef with flour, chili powder, and salt.

◆ In same Dutch oven, heat 1 more tablespoon oil over medium-high heat. Add half of beef and cook until browned; with slotted spoon, transfer to bowl with vegetables. Repeat with remaining beef and remaining 1 tablespoon oil.

◆ Return beef and vegetables to Dutch oven. Add tomatoes in puree and ¾ *cup water*; stir until brown bits are loosened. Heat to boiling over high heat. Cover Dutch oven; bake 45 minutes, or until beef is almost tender.

◆ Stir in tomato, olives, and raisins. Cover and bake 15 minutes longer, or until beef is tender. To serve, skim and discard fat and sprinkle with toasted almonds.

Each serving: About 415 calories, 26g protein, 17g carbohydrate, 28g total fat (9g saturated), 88mg cholesterol, 745mg sodium

CHILI CON CARNE

Prep: 10 minutes   Cook: 55 minutes
Makes 8 main-dish servings

2 pounds ground beef	1 can (28 ounces) tomatoes
1 large onion, diced	2 cans (15 to 19 ounces each) red kidney beans, rinsed and drained
1 garlic clove, minced	
¼ cup chili powder	
½ teaspoon ground black pepper	1 can (15 ounces) tomato sauce

◆ In 5-quart Dutch oven, cook ground beef, onion, and garlic, stirring often, over high heat until all pan juices evaporate and beef is well browned. Stir in chili powder and pepper; cook 1 minute.

◆ Stir in tomatoes with their liquid, beans, and tomato sauce; heat to boiling over high heat. Reduce heat to low; cover and simmer, stirring often, 30 minutes. Skim fat before serving.

Each serving: About 455 calories, 29g protein, 30g carbohydrate, 25g total fat (10g saturated), 84mg cholesterol, 955mg sodium

GREEN CHILE AND TOMATILLO STEW

Prep: 30 minutes plus standing   Bake: 2 hours 30 minutes to 3 hours
Makes 8 main-dish servings

4 poblano chiles or 2 green peppers	1 teaspoon ground cumin
1 bunch cilantro	¼ teaspoon ground red pepper (cayenne)
3 garlic cloves, minced	2 pounds tomatillos, husked, rinsed, and each cut into quarters
1½ teaspoons salt	
2 pounds boneless beef chuck, cut into ¾-inch pieces	1 can (15¼ to 16 ounces) whole-kernel corn, drained
2 medium onions, finely chopped	Sour cream (optional)
3 serrano or jalapeño chiles, seeded and minced	

◆ Preheat broiler. Line broiling pan with foil. Place poblanos in pan without rack. Place pan in broiler; broil at closest position to heat source, turning occasionally, about 15 minutes, until charred all over. Wrap foil around poblanos; let stand until cool enough to handle. Remove and discard skin and seeds; cut poblanos into 1-inch pieces.

◆ Turn oven control to 325°F. Chop ¼ cup cilantro leaves and stems; chop and reserve another ¼ cup leaves for garnish. On cutting board, mash garlic to a paste with salt; transfer to 5-quart Dutch oven. Add cilantro leaves and stems, beef, and next 4 ingredients; mix well. Cover and bake 1 hour. Stir in poblanos and tomatillos. Cover and bake 1½ to 2 hours longer, until beef is very tender. Stir in corn; cover and bake 5 minutes. Skim and discard fat. Sprinkle with reserved cilantro; serve with sour cream, if you like.

Each serving: About 385 calories, 26g protein, 23g carbohydrate, 22g total fat (8g saturated), 88mg cholesterol, 790mg sodium

---

TOMATILLOS

These small, pale green, tart-tasting fruits are encased in a slightly sticky papery husk, which is removed before use. They are most typically simmered until tender, and sometimes pureed to create a base for Mexican green sauces. While canned varieties are available, fresh tomatillos yield the best flavor.

PANFRIED BEEF

Panfrying is perfectly suited to tender filet mignon and sirloin, but it also works well for less-tender cuts – just take care not to overcook them, and slice the cooked meat thinly across the grain. The flavorful pan drippings can be used to create a quick sauce. Stir in a little liquid such as wine or broth, then boil until the sauce is reduced and the flavors are concentrated.

FILET MIGNON IN SHERRY SAUCE

Prep: 10 minutes   Cook: 15 minutes
Makes 4 main-dish servings

3 oil-packed dried tomatoes
1 bunch arugula
1 small head Boston lettuce
4 tablespoons margarine or
    butter
2 shallots, minced
½ teaspoon salt

¼ teaspoon coarsely ground
    black pepper
4 beef tenderloin steaks (filet
    mignon), each 1¼ inches
    thick (about 4 ounces each)
¼ cup dry sherry
Sourdough bread (optional)

1 Cut dried tomatoes into thin slices; set aside. Arrange arugula and Boston lettuce on 4 plates; set aside.

2 In 12-inch skillet, melt margarine over medium-high heat. Add shallots, salt, and pepper; cook, stirring, until lightly browned.

3 Pat steaks dry with paper towels. Add steaks to skillet; cook about 5 minutes, until underside of meat is browned. Turn and cook about 5 minutes longer for medium-rare, or until desired doneness.

4 Place steaks on salad greens on plates; sprinkle with dried tomatoes; keep warm. To skillet, add sherry; heat to boiling over high heat. Boil 1 minute; pour over steaks and salad greens. Serve with sourdough bread, if you like.

DRIED TOMATOES

These tomatoes, available packed in oil or dried, have an intense tomato flavor and pleasantly chewy texture. Those in oil can be used straight from the jar, while the dried must be rehydrated: Soak them in boiling water to cover about 5 minutes; drain. You can rehydrate a batch of dried tomatoes and store them in oil for future use: Squeeze out excess water, pack the tomatoes loosely in a jar, cover with olive oil, and add dried herbs, if you like. Store your "oil-packed" tomatoes in the refrigerator for up to 2 weeks.

Dried

Oil-packed

PER SERVING: ABOUT 435 CALORIES, 21g PROTEIN, 6g CARBOHYDRATE, 34g TOTAL FAT (11g SATURATED), 73mg CHOLESTEROL, 475mg SODIUM

FILET MIGNON WITH TOMATOES AND ROQUEFORT

Prep: 10 minutes   Cook: 30 minutes
Makes 4 main-dish servings

12 ounces French green beans (haricots verts) or green beans, ends trimmed
3 teaspoons margarine or butter
4 ounces oyster mushrooms or white mushrooms, sliced
2 teaspoons soy sauce
¾ teaspoon cornstarch
½ teaspoon beef-flavor instant bouillon
4 beef tenderloin steaks (filet mignon), each 1 inch thick (about 4 ounces each)
½ teaspoon salt
4 thick tomato slices
2 tablespoons dry white wine (optional)
1 ounce Roquefort or blue cheese, crumbled (¼ cup)
French bread (optional)

◆ In 4-quart saucepan, in *1 inch boiling water*, heat green beans to boiling over high heat. Reduce heat to low; cover and simmer 5 to 8 minutes, until tender-crisp. Drain; place in bowl. Wipe saucepan dry. In same saucepan, melt 2 teaspoons margarine over medium-high heat; add mushrooms and cook, stirring frequently, until golden. Stir in green beans and soy sauce; keep warm. In cup, mix cornstarch, beef bouillon, and *½ cup water* until blended. Set aside.

◆ Pat steaks dry with paper towels. In nonstick 10-inch skillet, melt remaining 1 teaspoon margarine over medium-high heat; add steaks with salt and cook 10 minutes, turning once, for medium-rare, or until desired doneness. Transfer to plate; keep warm. In drippings in skillet, cook tomato, turning once, just until hot. Transfer to 4 warm plates; keep warm.

◆ If using wine, add to skillet; cook 30 seconds, stirring. Stir in cornstarch mixture; boil 1 minute, stirring constantly, until sauce thickens slightly. Top each tomato slice with a steak. Spoon sauce over steaks; sprinkle with cheese. Serve with bean mixture, and bread, if you like.

Each serving: About 380 calories, 24g protein, 10g carbohydrate, 27g total fat (11g saturated), 78mg cholesterol, 700mg sodium

FILET MIGNON WITH SHIITAKE CREAM SAUCE

Prep: 10 minutes   Cook: 30 minutes
Makes 2 main-dish servings

2 beef tenderloin steaks (filet mignon), each 1 inch thick (about 4 ounces each)
1 tablespoon olive oil
4 ounces snow peas, strings removed
½ (6-ounce) bag radishes, each cut in half if large
Salt
4 teaspoons margarine or butter
1 small onion, diced
½ teaspoon chopped fresh thyme
4 ounces shiitake mushrooms, stems discarded
⅓ cup half-and-half or light cream

◆ Pat steaks dry with paper towels. In 3-quart saucepan, heat oil over high heat. Add snow peas, radishes, and ¼ teaspoon salt; cook, stirring often, until radishes are lightly browned and snow peas are tender-crisp. Keep warm.

◆ In 10-inch nonstick skillet, melt 2 teaspoons margarine over medium heat; add onion and cook until tender. Transfer to plate. Add steaks to skillet with thyme and ¼ teaspoon salt; cook over medium-high heat 10 minutes, turning once, for medium-rare. Transfer to 2 warm plates; keep warm.

◆ In same skillet, melt remaining 2 teaspoons margarine. Stir in shiitake mushrooms; cook until lightly browned. Stir in half-and-half and cooked onion; heat to boiling over high heat. Spoon mushroom sauce over steaks; serve with vegetable mixture.

Each serving: About 685 calories, 29g protein, 56g carbohydrate, 42g total fat (14g saturated), 87mg cholesterol, 700mg sodium

TUSCAN-STYLE STEAK

Prep: 5 minutes plus standing   Cook: 20 minutes
Makes 4 main-dish servings

1 beef sirloin steak, 1½ inches thick (about 1¾ pounds)
2 teaspoons olive oil
½ teaspoon dried rosemary
¼ teaspoon dried thyme
¼ teaspoon coarsely ground black pepper
Salt
1 lemon, cut into wedges

Pat steak dry with paper towels. In cup, mix oil, rosemary, thyme, and pepper. Use to rub over steak. Heat 10-inch skillet over medium-high heat until hot. Add steak; reduce heat to medium and cook 20 minutes, turning once, for medium-rare, or until desired doneness. Sprinkle steak generously with salt; transfer to warm large platter. Let stand 10 minutes; keep warm. Cut steak into thin slices and serve with lemon wedges.

Each serving: About 340 calories, 44g protein, 3g carbohydrate, 16g total fat (6g saturated), 93mg cholesterol, 220mg sodium

BLACK-PEPPER STEAK

Prep: 10 minutes   Cook: 12 minutes
Makes 8 main-dish servings

1 beef top round steak,
  1½ inches thick (about
  2½ pounds)
1 tablespoon cracked black
  pepper
1 teaspoon salt
2 tablespoons olive oil

¼ cup heavy or whipping
  cream
1 tablespoon all-purpose flour
1½ teaspoons beef-flavor
  instant bouillon
¼ cup brandy

◆ Cut steak crosswise into 4 pieces; then cut each piece horizontally in half to make 8 steaks, each ¾ inch thick. Pat steaks dry with paper towels. Sprinkle steaks on both sides with pepper and salt.

◆ In 12-inch skillet, heat oil over high heat. Add steaks and cook 8 to 10 minutes, turning once, for medium-rare, or until desired doneness. Transfer to platter; keep warm.

◆ Prepare sauce: In small bowl, whisk heavy cream, flour, bouillon, and ¾ *cup water*. Pour off fat from skillet. Add brandy to skillet; cook 1 minute, stirring until brown bits are loosened.

◆ Add cream mixture to skillet; heat to boiling over high heat. Reduce heat to medium and cook, stirring constantly, until sauce thickens slightly and boils. Pour sauce over steaks.

Each serving: About 315 calories, 27g protein, 2g carbohydrate, 20g total fat (7g saturated), 88mg cholesterol, 440mg sodium

TENDERLOIN AU POIVRE

Prep: 10 minutes   Cook: 10 minutes
Makes 4 main-dish servings

4 beef tenderloin steaks (filet
  mignon), each 1 inch thick
  (about 4 ounces each)
2 teaspoons cracked black
  pepper

½ teapoon salt
⅓ cup brandy
1 tablespoon Dijon mustard
  with seeds

◆ Pat steaks dry with paper towels. On waxed paper, mix pepper and salt; use to coat steaks. Heat nonstick 12-inch skillet over medium-high heat until hot. Add steaks and cook 8 to 10 minutes, turning once, for medium-rare, or until desired doneness.

◆ Transfer steaks to plate; keep warm. Add brandy and mustard to skillet and heat to boiling, stirring frequently; boil 30 seconds. Pour sauce onto 4 plates; place steaks on top.

Each serving: About 335 calories, 20g protein, 1g carbohydrate, 22g total fat (9g saturated), 73mg cholesterol, 415mg sodium

◆◆◆◆◆◆◆◆◆◆◆◆◆◆◆◆◆◆◆◆◆◆◆◆◆◆◆◆

CRACKING PEPPERCORNS

Cracked peppercorns give steak a crunchy and flavorful crust. Seal a handful of black peppercorns in a zip-tight plastic bag. With rolling pin, tap the peppercorns until they crack open but are not crushed.

◆◆◆◆◆◆◆◆◆◆◆◆◆◆◆◆◆◆◆◆◆◆◆◆◆◆◆◆

FLANK STEAK WITH RED-ONION MARMALADE

Prep: 10 minutes plus standing   Cook: 35 minutes
Makes 6 main-dish servings

3 tablespoons margarine or
  butter
2 medium red onions (about
  1 pound), thinly sliced
3 tablespoons sugar
3 tablespoons distilled white
  vinegar

Salt
1 beef flank steak (about
  1¾ pounds)
¼ teaspoon coarsely ground
  black pepper
Boiled parslied potatoes
  (optional)

◆ Prepare onion marmalade: In nonstick 12-inch skillet, melt 2 tablespoons margarine over medium heat. Add onions; cook, stirring occasionally, 15 minutes, or until tender. Stir in sugar, vinegar, and ½ teaspoon salt. Reduce heat to low; simmer 5 minutes. Spoon into small bowl; keep warm.

◆ Wash skillet and wipe dry. Pat steak dry with paper towels; sprinkle with black pepper and ½ teaspoon salt. In skillet, melt remaining 1 tablespoon margarine over medium-high heat. Add steak and cook 12 to 15 minutes, turning once, for medium-rare, or until desired doneness. Transfer steak to cutting board. Let stand 10 minutes; keep warm. Return onion marmalade to skillet; heat through. With knife almost parallel to cutting surface, thinly slice steak crosswise against the grain; serve with marmalade, and potatoes, if you like.

Each serving:
About 325 calories,
27g protein,
13g carbohydrate,
18g total fat (6g saturated),
67mg cholesterol,
505mg sodium

STEAK WITH RED-WINE SAUCE

Prep: 5 minutes
Cook: 15 minutes
Makes 4 main-dish servings

2 teaspoons vegetable oil	Pinch dried thyme
2 boneless beef top loin steaks, each 1 inch thick (about 10 ounces each)	2 tablespoons butter, cut up
	2 teaspoons chopped fresh tarragon or parsley
Salt and ground black pepper	Sautéed julienned vegetables (optional)
¼ cup minced shallots	
1 cup dry red wine	

◆ In 10-inch skillet, heat oil over medium-high heat until very hot. Pat steaks dry with paper towels. Sprinkle steaks with salt and pepper, add to skillet, and cook 7 to 8 minutes, turning once, for medium-rare, or until desired doneness. Transfer steaks to warm platter; keep warm.

◆ Pour off drippings from skillet. Add shallots to skillet; cook 1 minute, or until tender. Stir in red wine and thyme; boil over high heat about 5 minutes, until reduced to ⅓ cup. Remove from heat; stir in butter until incorporated.

◆ Cut steaks into thin slices and pour sauce on top. Sprinkle with tarragon. Serve with sautéed vegetables, if you like.

Each serving: About 345 calories, 32g protein, 3g carbohydrate, 18g total fat (8g saturated), 82mg cholesterol, 295mg sodium

❖❖❖❖❖❖❖❖❖❖❖❖❖❖❖❖❖❖❖❖❖❖❖❖❖❖

MINCING SHALLOTS

To mince a shallot, separate and peel the individual sections. Place each section, flat-side down, on the cutting board. Slice parallel to cutting board, keeping root end intact. Then slice shallot lengthwise, still keeping root end intact. Slice across the shallot at right angles to the previous cut, making a fine dice. Discard the root end. Chop onions the same way.

❖❖❖❖❖❖❖❖❖❖❖❖❖❖❖❖❖❖❖❖❖❖❖❖❖❖

RIB-EYE STEAKS WITH MADEIRA

Prep: 5 minutes   *Cook:* 15 minutes
Makes 4 main-dish servings

1 tablespoon olive or vegetable oil	¼ teaspoon salt
1 small onion, chopped	⅛ teaspoon cracked black pepper
2 beef rib-eye steaks, each ½ inch thick (8 ounces each)	2 tablespoons Madeira wine or beef broth

◆ In 10-inch skillet, heat oil over medium-high heat; add onion and cook, stirring often, until tender. Transfer to small bowl. Pat steaks dry with paper towels. In oil remaining in skillet, cook steaks, turning once, 6 to 8 minutes for medium-rare, or until desired doneness. Sprinkle steaks with salt and pepper. Transfer steaks to warm platter; keep warm.

◆ Pour off drippings from skillet. Add Madeira, onion, and *2 tablespoons water* to skillet; stir over medium heat until brown bits are loosened. Cut steaks into thin slices; pour Madeira sauce on top.

Each serving: About 250 calories, 25g protein, 3g carbohydrate, 14g total fat (5g saturated), 58mg cholesterol, 185mg sodium

BEEF TENDERLOIN WITH BROILED-TOMATO SAUCE

Prep: 30 minutes plus cooling   *Cook:* 15 minutes
Makes 4 main-dish servings

2½ pounds plum tomatoes, each cut lengthwise in half	1 teaspoon coarsely ground black pepper
1 medium onion, coarsely chopped	Salt
	1 tablespoon vegetable oil
4 beef tenderloin steaks (filet mignon), each 1½ inches thick (about 5 ounces each)	½ teaspoon sugar
	½ teaspoon dried basil

◆ Preheat broiler. Place tomatoes, cut-side up, and onion in broiling pan. Broil at closest position to heat source 15 to 20 minutes, or until tomatoes and onion are lightly charred. Remove pan from oven; set aside to cool. When tomatoes are cool enough to handle, peel and coarsely chop.

◆ Pat steaks dry with paper towels; sprinkle with pepper and 1 teaspoon salt. In 12-inch skillet, heat oil over medium-high heat; add steaks and cook 10 to 12 minutes, turning once, for medium-rare, or until desired doneness. Transfer to warm platter; keep warm. To drippings in skillet, add tomatoes, onion, sugar, basil, and ½ teaspoon salt; heat to boiling over high heat, stirring frequently. Spoon sauce onto warm platter; arrange steaks on sauce.

Each serving: About 460 calories, 28g protein, 18g carbohydrate, 32g total fat (11g saturated), 91mg cholesterol, 885mg sodium

STIR-FRIED BEEF

For speed and ease of preparation, nothing is better than a colorful stir-fry. Remember to cut the meat and vegetables into uniform pieces to ensure even cooking. Of course a wok is made for the job, but a large skillet with high sides or Dutch oven will work just as well.

ORANGE BEEF AND PEPPERS

◆◆◆◆◆◆◆◆◆◆◆◆◆◆◆◆◆◆◆◆◆◆◆◆◆◆◆◆◆

Prep: 25 minutes   *Cook:* 15 minutes
Makes 4 main-dish servings

1 beef top round steak, ¾ inch thick (about 1 pound)
2 tablespoons soy sauce
2 tablespoons vegetable oil
1 large red pepper, cut into ¼-inch-thick slices
1 large yellow pepper, cut into ¼-inch-thick slices
1 bunch green onions, cut into 2-inch pieces

1 teaspoon grated orange peel
½ cup fresh orange juice
1½ teaspoons grated, peeled fresh ginger
¾ teaspoon cornstarch
2 large oranges, peeled and white pith removed, cut lengthwise in half, and thinly sliced
2 bunches arugula

1 Cut steak lengthwise in half. With knife held in slanting position, almost parallel to cutting surface, slice each half of steak crosswise into ⅛-inch-thick slices. In medium bowl, toss steak with soy sauce.

2 In nonstick 12-inch skillet or wok, heat 2 teaspoons oil over medium-high heat. Add red and yellow peppers; cook, stirring frequently, until tender-crisp. Transfer peppers to bowl.

3 In same skillet, heat 1 teaspoon oil over medium-high heat. Add green onions; cook, stirring often, until tender-crisp. Transfer to bowl with peppers. In small bowl, mix orange peel and next 3 ingredients until smooth.

4 In same skillet, heat remaining 1 tablespoon oil over medium-high heat. Add half of beef mixture and cook, stirring constantly, just until beef loses its pink color; transfer to bowl with vegetables.

5 Repeat with remaining beef mixture. Return vegetables and all beef to skillet. Stir in orange-juice mixture and oranges; cook, stirring constantly, until liquid thickens and boils. Serve over arugula.

SOY SAUCE

The unique flavor of this ancient seasoning comes from fermented soybeans that are mixed with roasted wheat and aged up to two years. Dark soy sauce traditionally flavors and darkens hearty meat dishes; light-colored soy sauce is saltier with a less pungent flavor, and is preferred with seafood, vegetables, and soups.

EACH SERVING: ABOUT 330 CALORIES, 25g PROTEIN, 19g CARBOHYDRATE, 18g TOTAL FAT (5g SATURATED), 62mg CHOLESTEROL, 575mg SODIUM

GINGER BEEF

Prep: 25 minutes   Cook: 20 minutes
Makes 4 main-dish servings

1 beef flank steak (about
  1 pound)
2 tablespoons soy sauce
2 tablespoons dry sherry
2 teaspoons grated, peeled
  fresh ginger
1 garlic clove, minced
3 tablespoons vegetable oil
8 ounces mushrooms, sliced

1 large red pepper, thinly
  sliced
8 ounces sugar snap peas or
  snow peas, strings removed
2 large celery stalks, cut into
  1-inch pieces
1 medium onion, thinly sliced
8 ounces fresh bean sprouts
2 teaspoons cornstarch

◆ Cut steak lengthwise in half. With knife held in slanting position, almost parallel to cutting surface, slice steak crosswise into ⅛-inch-thick slices. In bowl, mix steak, soy sauce, sherry, ginger, and garlic; set aside.

◆ In nonstick 12-inch skillet or wok, heat 1 tablespoon oil over medium-high heat. Add mushrooms and red pepper; cook, stirring often, until liquid evaporates. Transfer to large bowl.

◆ In same skillet, heat 1 tablespoon oil over medium-high heat; add sugar snap peas, celery, and onion and cook, stirring, until tender-crisp. Stir in bean sprouts; cook 2 minutes, stirring. Spoon vegetables into bowl with mushroom mixture. In small bowl, mix cornstarch and ½ cup water until smooth.

◆ In same skillet, heat remaining 1 tablespoon oil over medium-high heat until very hot. Add half of steak mixture and cook, stirring constantly, until beef loses its pink color. Transfer to bowl with mushrooms. Repeat with remaining steak mixture. Return vegetables and all beef to skillet. Stir in cornstarch mixture and cook, stirring constantly, until liquid thickens slightly and boils.

Each serving: About 380 calories, 28g protein, 18g carbohydrate, 21g total fat (6g saturated), 58mg cholesterol, 620mg sodium

GRATING FRESH GINGER

Fresh ginger has a pungent, sweet-hot flavor. When buying, look for firm, heavy knobs. Grating ginger is easy, as the fibers remain in the grater. Simply rub the peeled ginger across a fine grating surface or a ginger grater (available from Asian markets).

THAI BEEF WITH BASIL

Prep: 15 minutes plus standing   Cook: 6 minutes
Makes 4 main-dish servings

3 tablespoons Asian fish sauce
  (nuoc nam)
1 tablespoon soy sauce
1 tablespoon brown sugar
1 beef top round steak (about
  1 pound)
1 jumbo sweet onion (1 pound)
1 tablespoon plus 1 teaspoon
  vegetable oil

3 long red or serrano chiles,
  seeded and cut into slivers
3 garlic cloves, minced
2 teaspoons minced, peeled
  fresh ginger
1 cup loosely packed fresh
  basil leaves

◆ In large bowl, mix first 3 ingredients. Cut steak lengthwise in half, then slice across grain into ⅛-inch-thick slices; stir into sauce mixture. Let stand 30 minutes.

◆ Thinly slice onion. In 12-inch skillet or wok, heat 1 tablespoon oil over high heat until very hot. Add beef mixture and cook, stirring constantly, 1 minute, or just until beef loses its pink color; transfer to plate. Add remaining 1 teaspoon oil to skillet. Add onion and cook, stirring, 3 minutes. Add chiles, garlic, and ginger; cook 30 seconds. Return beef to skillet with basil; heat through.

Each serving: About 280 calories, 29g protein, 20g carbohydrate, 10g total fat (3g saturated), 56mg cholesterol, 755mg sodium

SPICY BEEF BUNDLES

Prep: 15 minutes   Cook: 20 minutes
Makes 6 main-dish servings

3 tablespoons vegetable oil
8 ounces mushrooms, minced
4 green onions, minced
1 can (8 ounces) bamboo
  shoots, drained and minced
1½ pounds ground beef
1 tablespoon minced, peeled
  fresh ginger

¼ cup dry sherry
2 tablespoons cornstarch
3 tablespoons soy sauce
1 teaspoon sugar
½ teaspoon hot pepper sauce
Iceberg lettuce leaves
2 tablespoons toasted pine
  nuts (pignoli)

In 12-inch skillet or wok, heat 1 tablespoon oil over medium-high heat. Add mushrooms, green onions, and bamboo shoots; cook, stirring often, 10 minutes. Transfer to bowl. In same skillet, heat remaining 2 tablespoons oil over high heat. Add beef and ginger; cook until liquid evaporates and beef is browned. Return mushroom mixture to skillet. In cup, mix sherry and next 4 ingredients; stir into skillet. Cook over medium heat, stirring constantly, until thickened. Let each person spoon some beef mixture and pine nuts onto a lettuce leaf, fold over, and eat out of hand.

Each serving: About 435 calories, 23g protein, 9g carbohydrate, 33g total fat (11g saturated), 84mg cholesterol, 605mg sodium

MEAT LOAF

We've given an old-fashioned favorite enticing new flavor twists. There's meat loaf with a savory spinach-mushroom filling, and a spirited version with all the robust flavors found in a bowl of chili. To avoid a heavy, tough-textured loaf, don't over-blend the meat mixture.

MUSHROOM-AND-SPINACH-STUFFED MEAT LOAF

◆◆◆◆◆◆◆◆◆◆◆◆◆

Prep: 30 minutes
Bake: 1 hour
Makes 8 main-dish servings

2 tablespoons vegetable oil
2 medium celery stalks, chopped
1 medium onion, chopped
1 package (8 ounces) mushrooms, sliced
1 package (10 ounces) frozen chopped spinach, thawed
¾ cup pimiento-stuffed olives, chopped
1½ pounds ground beef or ground meat for meat loaf (beef, pork, and/or veal)
¾ cup quick-cooking or old-fashioned oats, uncooked
1 tablespoon Worcestershire sauce
1½ teaspoons salt
1 large egg
¾ cup chili sauce
Mashed potatoes and steamed sliced carrots (optional)

1 Preheat oven to 375°F. In 10-inch skillet, heat 1 tablespoon oil over medium heat; add celery and onion and cook, stirring occasionally, until very tender. Transfer to medium bowl.

2 In same skillet, heat remaining 1 tablespoon oil over medium-high heat; add mushrooms and cook, stirring occasionally, until golden brown. Remove mushrooms from heat. Squeeze spinach dry.

3 Stir spinach and chopped olives into mushrooms; set aside. In large bowl, mix ground beef, oats, Worcestershire, salt, egg, celery mixture, ¼ cup chili sauce, and ¼ *cup water.*

4 Fill and shape meat mixture into a roll: On sheet of waxed paper, pat meat mixture into 12" by 10" rectangle. Spread spinach mixture on meat rectangle.

5 From a long side, carefully roll meat mixture, jelly-roll fashion, lifting waxed paper and using long metal spatula to loosen meat from paper.

6 Place loaf, seam-side down, in roasting pan. Bake 50 minutes. Spread remaining ½ cup chili sauce over loaf; bake 10 minutes longer. Serve meat loaf with mashed potatoes and carrots, if you like.

EACH SERVING: ABOUT 350 CALORIES, 20g PROTEIN, 16g CARBOHYDRATE, 23g TOTAL FAT (8g SATURATED), 90mg CHOLESTEROL, 910mg SODIUM

CHILI MEAT LOAF

Prep: 20 minutes   Bake: 1 hour 15 minutes
Makes 8 main-dish servings

1 tablespoon vegetable oil
1 large celery stalk with
  leaves, chopped
1 medium onion, chopped
2 teaspoons chili powder
2 slices firm white bread
1½ pounds ground beef or
  ground meat for meat loaf
  (beef, pork, and/or veal)
1 can (15 to 19 ounces) red
  kidney beans, rinsed and
  drained

1 large egg
1 can (4 to 4½ ounces)
  chopped mild green chiles
1½ teaspoons salt
¼ teaspoon ground black
  pepper
¾ cup mild chunky salsa
1 container (8 ounces) sour
  cream

◆ Preheat oven to 350°F. In 10-inch skillet, heat oil over medium heat; add celery with leaves and onion and cook, stirring, until tender. Stir in chili powder; cook, stirring, 1 minute. Remove skillet from heat.

◆ Into large bowl, tear bread into crumbs; add celery mixture, ground meat, kidney beans, egg, green chiles with their liquid, salt, and pepper; mix well.

◆ In 13" by 9" roasting pan, shape meat mixture into a 10" by 4" loaf, pressing mixture firmly together. Spread ¼ cup salsa over loaf. Bake meat loaf 1¼ hours.

◆ With 2 pancake turners, carefully place meat loaf on platter. Serve warm or cover and refrigerate at least 3 hours to serve chilled.

◆ To serve, in small bowl, gently stir together sour cream and remaining ½ cup salsa until blended; serve sour-cream salsa with meat loaf.

Each serving: About 330 calories, 21g protein, 17g carbohydrate, 20g total fat (9g saturated), 92mg cholesterol, 955mg sodium

THE DEEP FREEZE

Meat loaf freezes beautifully, so consider doubling the recipe and making an extra loaf for stashing in the freezer. Cool completely, wrap tightly in plastic, then overwrap in heavy-duty foil or freezer paper, label, and date. Plan to use within 1 month. Thaw in the refrigerator or microwave oven before reheating. Or, serve at room temperature. For almost-instant sandwiches, freeze meat-loaf slices individually in heavy-duty foil or freezer paper. Make up the sandwiches in the morning with the still-frozen slices. By noon, the sandwiches will be thawed and ready to eat.

CONFETTI MEAT LOAF

Prep: 25 minutes   Bake: 1 hour 15 minutes
Makes 8 main-dish servings

2 tablespoons vegetable oil
2 large carrots, diced
1 large onion, diced
1¾ teaspoons salt
1 teaspoon fennel seeds
½ teaspoon coarsely ground
  black pepper
1 large egg

1½ pounds ground beef or
  ground meat for meat loaf
  (beef, pork, and/or veal)
1 can (7¼ to 8 ounces)
  whole-kernel corn, drained
1 cup frozen peas, thawed
¾ cup plain dried bread
  crumbs

◆ Preheat oven to 350°F. In 10-inch skillet, heat oil over medium-high heat. Add carrots, onion, salt, fennel seeds, and pepper; cook, stirring often, about 15 minutes, until tender.

◆ Transfer to large bowl. Add remaining ingredients and *½ cup water*; mix well. In 13" by 9" roasting pan, shape meat mixture into 9" by 6" loaf, pressing firmly. Bake meat loaf 1¼ hours. To serve, with 2 pancake turners, place meat loaf on warm platter.

Each serving: About 300 calories, 19g protein, 20g carbohydrate, 16g total fat (5g saturated), 79mg cholesterol, 715mg sodium.

MEAT LOAF WITH DRIED TOMATOES

Prep: 25 minutes   Bake: 1 hour 15 minutes
Makes 8 main-dish servings

1 tablespoon olive oil
2 medium carrots, shredded
1 medium celery stalk,
  chopped
1 medium onion, chopped
1 teaspoon salt
¼ teaspoon ground black
  pepper
1 bunch (10 to 12 ounces)
  spinach, coarsely chopped
  (2 cups packed)

1½ pounds ground beef or
  ground meat for meat loaf
  (beef, pork and/or veal)
½ cup drained oil-packed
  dried tomatoes, chopped
3 slices firm white bread,
  torn into small crumbs
2 tablespoons freshly grated
  Parmesan cheese
2 large egg whites

◆ Preheat oven to 350°F. In nonstick 12-inch skillet, heat oil over medium-high heat; add carrots, celery, onion, salt, and pepper and cook, stirring occasionally, until tender. Stir in spinach and cook, stirring constantly, until spinach wilts.

◆ Transfer vegetable mixture to large bowl. Add remaining ingredients; mix well. In 13" by 9" roasting pan, shape meat mixture into 8" by 5" loaf, pressing firmly. Bake 1¼ hours. To serve, with 2 pancake turners, place loaf on warm platter.

Each serving: About 250 calories, 19g protein, 11g carbohydrate, 15g total fat (5g saturated), 54mg cholesterol, 460mg sodium

BURGERS

Grilled or panfried, burgers should be handled as little as possible and cooked to medium (with just a trace of pink in the center).

TEX-MEX STUFFED BURGERS

◆◆◆◆◆◆◆◆◆◆◆◆◆

Prep: 20 minutes
Grill: 10 minutes
Makes 4 main-dish servings

1 pound ground beef
16 saltine crackers with unsalted tops, crushed (about ½ cup)
1 small green pepper, minced
1 small red pepper, minced
1 teaspoon grated onion
¾ teaspoon salt
¼ teaspoon coarsely ground black pepper
4 ounces Monterey Jack cheese or Monterey Jack cheese with jalapeño chiles, shredded (1 cup)
4 hamburger buns with sesame seeds, split
4 lettuce leaves
1 small tomato, diced
Potato chips, pickles, and tomato wedges (optional)
Flat-leaf parsley for garnish

TO BROIL IN OVEN
◆◆◆◆◆◆◆◆◆◆◆◆

Preheat broiler and place burgers on rack in broiling pan. Place pan in broiler at closest position to heat source and broil, turning once, about 10 minutes for medium, or until desired doneness; top with cheese as directed.

1 Prepare outdoor grill. In medium bowl, mix first 7 ingredients.

ROQUEFORT BURGERS

Mix 1 pound ground beef, 1 tablespoon Worcestershire sauce, and ½ teaspoon coarsely ground black pepper. Shape burgers as above; stuff with 2 ounces crumbled Roquefort or blue cheese. Grill; top with thinly sliced red onion, if you like. Makes 4 main-dish servings.

Each serving: About 475 calories, 28g protein, 22g carbohydrate, 30g total fat (13g saturated), 97mg cholesterol, 575mg sodium

2 Shape mixture into 4 balls, handling as little as possible. Make indentation in center of each ball; place 1 heaping tablespoon shredded cheese in each indentation. Shape beef mixture around cheese to enclose completely; flatten each ball into a ¾-inch-thick round patty. Place burgers on grill over medium heat.

3 Cook burgers, turning once, 10 minutes for medium, or until desired doneness. During last few minutes of cooking, top burgers with remaining shredded cheese and place buns, cut-side down, on grill; cook until cheese melts and buns are lightly toasted.

4 To serve, arrange lettuce leaves on bottom halves of toasted buns; top with burgers. Spoon diced tomato on top. Replace tops of buns. Serve with potato chips, pickles, and tomato wedges, if you like. Garnish with parsley.

EACH SERVING: ABOUT 590 CALORIES, 33g PROTEIN, 32g CARBOHYDRATE, 37g TOTAL FAT (15g SATURATED), 114mg CHOLESTEROL, 950mg SODIUM

CAJUN BURGERS WITH RÉMOULADE SAUCE

Prep: 20 minutes   Cook: 8 minutes
Makes 4 main-dish servings

1 tablespoon vegetable oil
1 small red pepper, minced
1 small onion, minced
2 garlic cloves, minced
¼ teaspoon dried thyme
Salt
Hot pepper sauce
1 pound ground beef
½ cup mayonnaise

1 tablespoon fresh lemon juice
1 tablespoon catchup
2 teaspoons prepared white horseradish
4 English muffins, split and lightly toasted
4 lettuce leaves
4 tomato slices

◆ In 10-inch skillet, heat oil over medium heat. Add red pepper, onion, garlic, thyme, ½ teaspoon salt, and ¼ teaspoon hot pepper sauce; cook, stirring occasionally, until vegetables are tender. Transfer to medium bowl. Add ground beef and mix just until blended. Shape beef mixture into four ¾-inch-thick round patties, handling meat as little as possible. In same skillet, cook patties over high heat, shaking skillet occasionally and turning patties once, 8 minutes for medium, or until desired doneness.

◆ Meanwhile, prepare rémoulade sauce: In small bowl, mix mayonnaise, lemon juice, catchup, horseradish, ¼ teaspoon salt, and ¼ teaspoon hot pepper sauce until well blended. To serve, spread rémoulade sauce on toasted muffins; sandwich with lettuce leaves, burgers, and tomato slices.

Each serving: About 690 calories, 26g protein, 34g carbohydrate, 50g total fat (13g saturated), 100mg cholesterol, 980mg sodium

---

SWEET-AND-TANGY ONIONS

Peel 6 medium red onions (about 1½ pounds); cut each into 8 wedges, leaving a little of the root end to help hold shape during cooking. In 10-inch skillet, heat onions, ½ cup water, ½ cup distilled white vinegar, ½ cup sugar, and 1 teaspoon salt to boiling over high heat. Reduce heat to low; cover and simmer 3 to 5 minutes, until onions are tender-crisp. Transfer to bowl; cover and refrigerate until well chilled. Drain to serve with your favorite burgers. Makes about 4 cups.

Each ½ cup: About 80 calories, 1g protein, 21g carbohydrate, 0g total fat, 0mg cholesterol, 270mg sodium

---

STEAKHOUSE BURGERS WITH HORSERADISH SOUR CREAM

Prep: 10 minutes   Cook: 6 minutes
Makes 4 main-dish servings

1¼ pounds ground beef
Salt and coarsely ground black pepper
2½ teaspoons prepared white horseradish

⅓ cup sour cream
4 English muffins, split and lightly toasted
4 Boston lettuce leaves

◆ Shape ground beef into four ½-inch-thick round patties, handling meat as little as possible. Sprinkle patties with ½ teaspoon salt, then with 1 teaspoon pepper, pressing pepper lightly into patties. Heat nonstick 12-inch skillet over medium-high heat until hot. Add patties and cook, shaking skillet occasionally and turning patties once, about 6 minutes for medium, or until desired doneness.

◆ Meanwhile, in small bowl, stir horseradish, ⅛ teaspoon salt, and ⅛ teaspoon pepper into sour cream. Serve patties on toasted muffins with lettuce and horseradish sauce.

Each serving: About 555 calories, 30g protein, 28g carbohydrate, 34g total fat (14g saturated), 113mg cholesterol, 745mg sodium

---

HAMBURGERS WITH MUSHROOM AND ONION TOPPING

Prep: 15 minutes   Cook: 20 minutes
Makes 4 main-dish servings

1 pound ground beef
Salt and coarsely ground black pepper
2 tablespoons olive oil
1 large onion, sliced

8 ounces mushrooms, sliced
¼ cup chopped fresh parsley
8 slices Italian bread, each ¼ inch thick, toasted
1 tomato, sliced

◆ Shape ground beef into four ¾-inch-thick round patties, handling meat as little as possible. In 10-inch skillet over high heat, cook patties, turning patties once and sprinkling with ¼ teaspoon each salt and pepper, 8 minutes for medium, or until desired doneness.

◆ Meanwhile, in another 10-inch skillet, heat oil over medium-high heat; add onion and cook until tender-crisp and golden. Stir in mushrooms, ½ teaspoon salt, and ¼ teaspoon pepper; cook over high heat, stirring often, until mushrooms are golden and tender. Stir in parsley.

◆ To serve, on each plate, arrange 2 toasted bread slices; top with 1 or 2 slices tomato, 1 hamburger, and some mushroom mixture to make open-faced sandwich.

Each serving: About 565 calories, 27g protein, 39g carbohydrate, 33g total fat (11g saturated), 84mg cholesterol, 840mg sodium

MEATBALLS

Panfried meatballs make an easy main dish. For best results, blend the meat mixture until the ingredients are just evenly combined – overmixing creates tough meatballs. Form the meat into uniform balls, and avoid crowding the skillet. Mashed potatoes, rice, or pasta are ideal side dishes for savory meatballs.

MEATBALLS IN LIGHT TOMATO SAUCE

◆◆◆◆◆◆◆◆◆◆◆◆◆◆◆◆◆◆◆◆◆◆◆◆◆

Prep: 25 minutes   *Cook:* 45 minutes
Makes 6 main-dish servings

1½ pounds ground beef
1½ cups fresh bread crumbs (3 slices firm white bread)
1 large egg
¼ teaspoon ground black pepper
Salt
2 tablespoons vegetable oil
1 medium onion, cut into thin wedges
1 medium carrot, sliced

1 medium celery stalk, sliced
1 can (14½ to 16 ounces) tomatoes
¼ cup dry white wine or chicken broth
½ teaspoon dried basil
1 tablespoon chopped fresh parsley
2 teaspoons grated lemon peel
Cooked pasta (optional)

1 In large bowl, mix ground beef, bread crumbs, egg, pepper, 1 teaspoon salt, and ¼ *cup water*. Shape meat mixture into 18 meatballs.

2 In 12-inch skillet, heat oil over medium-high heat; add meatballs, half at a time, and cook until browned on all sides. Transfer to plate.

3 To drippings in skillet, add onion, carrot, and celery and cook, stirring often, 10 minutes, or until vegetables are tender and lightly browned.

4 Add tomatoes with their juice, wine, basil, and ½ teaspoon salt, breaking up tomatoes with spoon. Return meatballs to skillet; heat to boiling over high heat.

FRESH TOMATO SAUCE

This recipe uses canned tomatoes, which are already peeled. However, peeled fresh tomatoes can easily be substituted, especially in summer when they are ripest. Peel 1 pound of tomatoes (see page 314), then proceed as directed in Steps 4 and 5 of the recipe. If the tomato sauce seems too thick at the end of simmering, stir in a little chicken broth or water to thin.

5 Reduce heat to low; cover and simmer, turning meatballs occasionally, 20 minutes, or until meatballs are cooked through. To serve, sprinkle meatballs with parsley and lemon peel. Serve with pasta, if you like.

EACH SERVING: ABOUT 425 CALORIES, 23g PROTEIN, 13g CARBOHYDRATE, 29g TOTAL FAT (11g SATURATED), 119mg CHOLESTEROL, 815mg SODIUM

SWEDISH MEATBALLS

Prep: 20 minutes   Cook: 20 minutes
Makes 6 main-dish servings

1 tablespoon plus 2 teaspoons margarine or butter
1 medium onion, finely chopped
2 slices firm white bread, torn
1½ pounds ground beef
1 large egg
1 teaspoon salt
¼ teaspoon ground black pepper
¼ teaspoon ground nutmeg
Pinch ground allspice
2 teaspoons vegetable oil
2 tablespoons all-purpose flour
1 can (13¾ to 14½ ounces) chicken broth
¼ cup heavy or whipping cream
¼ cup chopped fresh dill

◆ In 10-inch skillet, melt 1 tablespoon margarine over medium heat. Add onion and cook, stirring often, 8 minutes, or until tender. Transfer to large bowl and wipe skillet clean. Meanwhile, in blender or food processor with knife blade attached, process bread to fine crumbs. To onion in bowl, add bread crumbs, ground beef, and next 5 ingredients and mix until blended. Shape into 1½-inch meatballs.

◆ In same skillet, melt 1 teaspoon margarine with 1 teaspoon oil over medium heat. Add half of meatballs and cook, turning occasionally, 10 minutes, or until browned on all sides and just cooked through; transfer to plate and keep warm. Repeat with remaining 1 teaspoon each margarine and oil and remaining meatballs; transfer to plate.

◆ To drippings in skillet, add flour and cook, stirring constantly, 1 minute. Gradually whisk in chicken broth and cream; heat to boiling, stirring, over high heat. Reduce heat to low and simmer 5 minutes. Return meatballs to skillet, stirring gently to coat with sauce. Sprinkle with dill and serve.

Each serving: About 440 calories, 23g protein, 9g carbohydrate, 34g total fat (13g saturated), 138mg cholesterol, 820mg sodium

SHAPING MEATBALLS

To make uniform meatballs, try this: For 1-inch meatballs, pat the meat mixture out on waxed paper into a 1-inch-thick square. Cut the square into 1-inch cubes and, with wet hands, roll each cube into a ball. For 2-inch meatballs, cut a 2-inch-thick square into 2-inch cubes.

MEXICAN MEATBALLS

Prep: 20 minutes   Cook: 45 minutes
Makes 6 main-dish servings

1½ pounds ground beef
1 large egg
¾ cup plain dried bread crumbs
1 teaspoon salt
½ teaspoon ground black pepper
3 garlic cloves, minced
1 can (28 ounces) tomatoes
1 canned chipotle chile in adobo (see page 30)
2 teaspoons vegetable oil
1 small onion, minced
1 teaspoon ground cumin
1 cup chicken broth
¼ cup chopped fresh cilantro

◆ In large bowl, mix ground beef, egg, bread crumbs, salt, pepper, *¼ cup water*, and one-third of garlic until blended. Shape into 1-inch meatballs. In blender, blend tomatoes with their juice and chipotle until smooth.

◆ In 5-quart Dutch oven, heat oil over medium heat. Add onion and cook, stirring often, 5 minutes, or until tender. Stir in cumin and remaining minced garlic; cook 30 seconds. Stir in tomato mixture and chicken broth; heat to boiling over high heat.

◆ Add meatballs; heat to boiling. Reduce heat to low and simmer, uncovered, 30 minutes, or until meatballs are cooked through. Sprinkle with cilantro.

Each serving: About 425 calories, 25g protein, 19g carbohydrate, 27g total fat (10g saturated), 123mg cholesterol, 960mg sodium

CLASSIC ITALIAN MEATBALLS

Prep: 15 minutes   Cook: 15 minutes
Makes 6 main-dish servings

2 slices firm white bread, torn
1½ pounds ground beef
1 large egg
¼ cup chopped fresh flat-leaf parsley
¼ cup freshly grated Pecorino Romano or Parmesan cheese
1 garlic clove, minced
1 teaspoon salt
¼ teaspoon ground black pepper
2 teaspoons olive oil

◆ In blender or food processor with knife blade attached, process bread to fine crumbs. Transfer to large bowl. Add ground beef, egg, parsley, cheese, garlic, salt, and pepper. Mix until combined. Shape into twelve 2-inch meatballs.

◆ In 10-inch skillet, heat oil over medium heat. Add meatballs and cook, gently turning occasionally, 15 minutes, or until browned all over and just cooked through.

Each serving: About 370 calories, 24g protein, 5g carbohydrate, 27g total fat (11g saturated), 123mg cholesterol, 570mg sodium

Broiled Beef

Broil steaks close to the heat source – but don't overcook – and they will stay tender and juicy. The method is simple: Season the meat or spread it with an herb butter and broil it, turning the meat only once during cooking.

LEMON-PEPPER STEAK

◆◆◆◆◆◆◆◆◆◆◆◆

Prep: 10 minutes plus standing
Broil: 16 minutes
Makes 8 main-dish servings

2 tablespoons butter, softened
2 tablespoons grated lemon peel
2 teaspoons cracked black pepper
1½ teaspoons salt
1 garlic clove, minced
1 beef top round steak, 1¼ inches thick (about 2 pounds)
Steamed broccoli and sautéed mushrooms (optional)

1 Preheat broiler. Prepare lemon butter: In small bowl, mix butter, grated lemon peel, pepper, salt, and garlic until mixture is smooth and well blended.

2 Place steak on rack in broiling pan; spread with half of lemon butter. Place in broiler at closest position to heat source; broil 8 minutes.

3 With tongs, turn steak; spread with remaining lemon butter. Broil about 8 minutes longer for medium-rare, or until desired doneness.

A SAMPLER OF SAVORY BUTTERS

Parsley-caper butter In small bowl, mix 2 tablespoons butter, softened, 2 tablespoons chopped fresh parsley, 2 tablespoons chopped capers, 1 tablespoon minced shallot, ½ teaspoon salt, and ¼ teaspoon ground black pepper.

Chili-lime butter In small bowl, mix 2 tablespoons butter, softened, with 1 tablespoon grated lime peel, 2 teaspoons chili powder, ¾ teaspoon salt, and ⅛ teaspoon ground red pepper (cayenne).

Ginger-tarragon butter In small bowl, mix 2 tablespoons butter, softened, with 2 teaspoons grated, peeled fresh ginger, 2 teaspoons chopped fresh tarragon, ¾ teaspoon salt, and ¼ teaspoon ground black pepper.

4 To serve, transfer steak to cutting board. Let stand 10 minutes; keep warm. Cut steak across the grain into thin slices. Serve with broccoli and mushrooms, if you like.

EACH SERVING: ABOUT 180 CALORIES, 26g PROTEIN, 1g CARBOHYDRATE, 8g TOTAL FAT (4g SATURATED), 64mg CHOLESTEROL, 470mg SODIUM

STEAK WITH YELLOW-PEPPER CHUTNEY

Prep: 25 minutes plus standing **Broil:** *13 to 15 minutes*
Makes 6 main-dish servings

1 beef flank steak
  (1½ pounds)
Salt and coarsely ground
  black pepper
1 tablespoon vegetable oil
4 large yellow peppers, cut
  into ½-inch-thick slices
1 large onion, thinly sliced
½ pint cherry tomatoes, each
  cut in half

1 jar (8½ ounces) mango
  chutney
2 tablespoons chopped fresh
  parsley
2 pitas (each 6 inches)
2 teaspoons margarine or
  butter, softened
1 tablespoon freshly grated
  Parmesan cheese

◆ Preheat broiler. Place steak on rack in broiling pan; sprinkle with ¾ teaspoon salt and ½ teaspoon black pepper. Place pan in broiler at closest position to heat source; broil steak 5 minutes. Turn steak; sprinkle with ½ teaspoon salt and ¼ teaspoon black pepper and broil 8 to 10 minutes longer for medium-rare, or until desired doneness. Transfer to cutting board. Let stand 10 minutes; keep warm. Keep broiler on.

◆ Meanwhile, prepare yellow-pepper chutney: In nonstick 12-inch skillet, heat oil over medium-high heat; add peppers and onion and cook until tender-crisp. Stir in tomatoes, chutney, and ½ *cup water*; heat through. Remove from heat. Stir in parsley.

◆ Split each pita horizontally in half. Spread margarine over pita halves; sprinkle with cheese. Cut each half into 6 pieces. Place on cookie sheet. Place cookie sheet in broiler at closest position to heat source; broil until pita pieces are lightly toasted. To serve, thinly slice flank steak across the grain. Serve with chutney and pita.

Each serving: About 425 calories, 27g protein, 51g carbohydrate, 13g total fat (5g saturated), 59mg cholesterol, 670mg sodium

FILET MIGNON ON A BED OF GREENS

Prep: 20 minutes **Broil:** *14 to 15 minutes*
Makes 4 main-dish servings

1 medium head radicchio,
  coarsely chopped
1 large head Belgian endive,
  coarsely chopped
1 bunch watercress, coarsely
  chopped
2 tablespoons plain dried
  bread crumbs
1 tablespoon margarine or
  butter, softened
1 tablespoon grated lemon
  peel
1 tablespoon minced fresh
  parsley

¼ teaspoon coarsely ground
  black pepper
Salt
4 beef tenderloin steaks (filet
  mignon), each 1½ inches
  thick (about 4 ounces each)
⅓ cup olive or vegetable oil
2 tablespoons fresh lemon
  juice
1 tablespoon white wine
  vinegar
1½ teaspoons sugar

◆ Preheat broiler. In large bowl, mix radicchio, endive, and watercress; refrigerate. In small bowl, mix bread crumbs, margarine, lemon peel, parsley, pepper, and ½ teaspoon salt.

◆ Place steaks on rack in broiling pan; place pan in broiler at closest position to heat source. Broil steaks 8 minutes. Turn steaks; broil 3 to 4 minutes longer for medium-rare, or until desired doneness. Remove broiler pan from oven; spread tops of steaks with bread-crumb mixture. Broil steaks 3 minutes longer, or until topping is golden.

◆ Meanwhile, in 1-quart saucepan, heat oil, lemon juice, vinegar, sugar, and ½ teaspoon salt to boiling over medium heat. Pour over chopped salad; toss to mix well. Arrange salad on platter. To serve, arrange steaks on salad.

Each serving: About 505 calories, 22g protein, 9g carbohydrate, 43g total fat (12g saturated), 73mg cholesterol, 670mg sodium

◆◆◆◆◆◆◆◆◆◆◆◆◆◆◆◆◆◆◆◆◆◆◆◆◆◆◆

COATING STEAKS WITH CRUMBS

For a flavorful finishing touch and crunchy contrast, top broiled steaks with a savory bread-crumb mixture. Broil the steaks as directed above, turning once. A few minutes before they're done, use a heatproof rubber spatula to spread the tops of the steaks with the bread-crumb mixture. Then broil just until topping is golden.

◆◆◆◆◆◆◆◆◆◆◆◆◆◆◆◆◆◆◆◆◆◆◆◆◆◆◆

Sirloin Steak Oreganato

Prep: 10 minutes plus standing   *Broil: 12 to 15 minutes*
Makes 6 main-dish servings

1 medium lemon
2 garlic cloves, minced
1 tablespoon olive oil
1 teaspoon salt
1 teaspoon dried oregano
¾ teaspoon coarsely ground
    black pepper
1 boneless beef top sirloin
    steak, 1¼ inches thick
    (about 1½ pounds)

◆ Preheat broiler. Grate peel and squeeze juice from lemon. In 12" by 8" baking dish or deep ceramic platter, mix lemon peel, lemon juice, garlic, oil, salt, oregano, and pepper. Add steak, turning to coat both sides.

◆ Place steak on rack in broiling pan. Place pan in broiler at closest position to heat source. Broil steak, turning once and brushing with any remaining marinade after turning, 12 to 15 minutes for medium-rare, or until desired doneness.

◆ Transfer to platter. Let stand 10 minutes; keep warm. To serve, thinly slice steak. Spoon any juices from broiling pan over slices.

Each serving: About 190 calories, 23g protein, 3g carbohydrate, 10g total fat (3g saturated), 68mg cholesterol, 405mg sodium

Barbecue-style steak and onion rings

Prep: 25 minutes plus marinating and standing   *Broil: 16 to 20 minutes*
Makes 6 main-dish servings

¼ cup bottled steak sauce
2 tablespoons catchup
1 garlic clove, minced
1 beef top round steak,
    1½ inches thick (about
    2½ pounds)
Vegetable oil for deep-frying
2 large onions (about
    1½ pounds), cut crosswise
    into 1-inch-thick slices
½ cup milk
1½ cups all-purpose flour
1 teaspoon salt

◆ In 12" by 8" baking dish, mix first 3 ingredients. Add steak, turning to coat both sides. Cover and refrigerate at least 1 hour.

◆ In 3- to 4-quart saucepan, heat 2 inches oil over medium heat to 375°F on deep-fat thermometer (or heat oil in deep-fat fryer set at 375°F). Meanwhile, separate onion slices into rings. In small bowl, place milk. In medium bowl, mix flour and salt.

◆ Dip onion rings into milk, then into flour mixture. Repeat to coat twice. Add onion rings to hot oil in batches and cook, turning once, 3 to 5 minutes, until golden brown. Transfer onion rings as they brown to paper towels to drain thoroughly. Keep warm.

◆ Meanwhile, preheat broiler. Place steak on rack in broiling pan; broil 5 inches from heat source, brushing once with marinade, 10 minutes. Turn steak; broil, brushing with marinade, 6 to 10 minutes longer for medium-rare or until desired doneness. Transfer to cutting board. Let stand 10 minutes; keep warm. Thinly slice; serve with onion rings.

Each serving: About 530 calories, 47g protein, 31g carbohydrate, 23g total fat (6g saturated), 96mg cholesterol, 645mg sodium

Filet Mignon with Balsamic-Fruit Sauce

Prep: 20 minutes   *Broil: 14 to 15 minutes*
Makes 4 main-dish servings

1 teaspoon beef-flavor instant
    bouillon
1 teaspoon vegetable oil
2 medium shallots, minced
8 pitted prunes, coarsely
    chopped
¼ teaspoon cracked black
    pepper
1 tablespoon balsamic vinegar
1 teaspoon grated lemon peel
½ teaspoon sugar
4 small beef tenderloin steaks
    (filet mignon), each ¾ inch
    thick (about 3 ounces each)

◆ Preheat broiler. In cup, dissolve beef-flavor bouillon in *½ cup very hot water*. In 1-quart saucepan, heat oil over medium heat. Add shallots; cook until softened, adding bouillon mixture as needed to prevent shallots from sticking. Stir in prunes, pepper, and any remaining bouillon mixture; reduce heat to low and simmer 5 minutes. Stir in balsamic vinegar, lemon peel, and sugar; keep warm.

◆ Place steaks on rack in broiling pan; place pan in broiler at closest position to heat source. Broil steaks 4 minutes. Turn steaks and broil 4 to 6 minutes longer for medium-rare, or until desired doneness. To serve, arrange steaks on 4 warm plates; spoon balsamic-fruit sauce over.

Each serving: About 295 calories, 16g protein, 18g carbohydrate, 18g total fat (7g saturated), 55mg cholesterol, 255mg sodium

◆◆◆◆◆◆◆◆◆◆◆◆◆◆◆◆◆◆◆◆◆◆◆◆◆

LOW-FAT "SAUTÉING"

When sautéing shallots or onions, prevent them from sticking by adding a little liquid to a minimal amount of oil or butter – you'll save fat and calories. Here, we've used beef-flavor instant bouillon dissolved in very hot water.

◆◆◆◆◆◆◆◆◆◆◆◆◆◆◆◆◆◆◆◆◆◆◆◆◆

BEEF TENDERLOIN STEAKS WITH ONION AND RED-PEPPER CONFIT

Prep: 30 minutes   Broil: 12 minutes
Makes 4 main-dish servings

1 tablespoon olive or
   vegetable oil
2 medium onions, diced
1 large red pepper, diced
1 teaspoon sugar
½ teaspoon dried basil
Salt and coarsely ground
   black pepper

1 tablespoon red wine vinegar
1 tablespoon chopped fresh
   parsley
4 beef tenderloin steaks (filet
   mignon), each 1½ inches
   thick (about 4 ounces each)
Sautéed spinach (optional)

◆ Prepare red-pepper confit: In 2-quart saucepan, heat oil over medium heat; add onions and cook, stirring occasionally, until tender and golden.

◆ Stir in red pepper, sugar, basil, ¾ teaspoon salt, and ¼ teaspoon black pepper; cook, stirring frequently, until red pepper is tender-crisp. Stir in vinegar and *2 tablespoons water*; heat to boiling over high heat. Reduce heat to low; cover and simmer 5 minutes, or until red pepper is tender. Stir in parsley; keep warm.

◆ Preheat broiler. Place steaks on rack in broiling pan; place pan in broiler at closest position to heat source. Broil steaks 6 minutes. Turn steaks and sprinkle with ¾ teaspoon black pepper and ¼ teaspoon salt. Broil 6 minutes longer for medium-rare, or until desired doneness.

◆ To serve, transfer steaks to cutting board; slice each steak horizontally in half. Spoon red-pepper confit onto 4 plates, reserving ¼ cup. Arrange steaks over confit, slightly overlapping top and bottom halves; spoon reserved confit over steaks. Serve with sautéed spinach, if you like.

Each serving: About 355 calories, 21g protein, 10g carbohydrate, 25g total fat (9g saturated), 73mg cholesterol, 585mg sodium

STEAK AND PEPPER FAJITAS

Prep: 25 minutes plus standing   Broil: 12 to 14 minutes
Makes 4 main-dish servings

1 beef top round steak, 1 inch
   thick (about ¾ pound)
1 bottle (8 ounces) medium-
   hot chunky salsa
1 tablespoon vegetable oil
1 medium red onion, sliced
1 medium green pepper,
   sliced
1 medium red pepper, sliced

2 tablespoons chopped fresh
   cilantro
8 flour tortillas (6 to 7 inches),
   warmed according to
   package directions
1 container (8 ounces) light
   sour cream
4 ounces sharp Cheddar
   cheese, shredded (1 cup)

◆ Preheat broiler. Place steak on rack in broiling pan; spread steak with ¼ cup salsa. Place pan in broiler at closest position to heat source; broil steak 6 minutes. Turn steak and spread with ¼ cup salsa; broil 6 to 8 minutes longer for medium-rare, or until desired doneness. Transfer steak to cutting board. Let stand 10 minutes; keep warm.

◆ Meanwhile, in nonstick 12-inch skillet, heat oil over medium-high heat. Add red onion and both sliced peppers; cook, stirring often, until tender-crisp. Stir in cilantro. Spoon into serving bowl. To serve, with knife held almost parallel to cutting surface, thinly slice steak across the grain. Serve steak with pepper mixture, flour tortillas, sour cream, shredded cheese, and remaining salsa.

Each serving: About 590 calories, 35g protein, 51g carbohydrate, 25g total fat (9g saturated), 91mg cholesterol, 845mg sodium

HERBED SIRLOIN STEAK

Prep: 10 minutes plus standing   Broil: 13 to 17 minutes
Makes 6 main-dish servings

⅓ cup loosely packed fresh
   parsley, coarsely chopped
1 tablespoon chopped fresh
   thyme or ½ teaspoon dried
   thyme
2 tablespoons plain dried
   bread crumbs

1 tablespoon light mayonnaise
½ teaspoon coarsely ground
   black pepper
1 boneless beef top sirloin
   steak, 1¼ inches thick
   (1½ pounds)
½ teaspoon salt

◆ Preheat broiler. In cup, mix first 5 ingredients; set aside. Sprinkle steak with salt. Place steak on rack in broiling pan; place pan in broiler at closest position to heat source. Broil steak, turning once, 12 to 15 minutes for medium-rare, or until desired doneness. Remove broiling pan from oven; spread herb mixture on top of steak. Broil 1 to 2 minutes longer, until topping is golden. Transfer steak to cutting board. Let stand 10 minutes; keep warm. Thinly slice steak.

Each serving: About 180 calories, 23g protein, 2g carbohydrate, 8g total fat (3g saturated), 69mg cholesterol, 250mg sodium

GRILLED BEEF

Steaks, ribs, and kabobs all lend themselves to outdoor grilling, and they are even better when enhanced with a marinade, spice rub, or tangy sauce. The marinade serves the dual purpose of imparting flavor and making the meat more tender. If you're using a charcoal grill, prepare the fire 20 to 30 minutes before cooking to be sure the coals are good and hot. They are ready when a light-gray ash covers the coals (in daylight) or they glow red (at night).

PORTERHOUSE STEAK WITH GRILLED SALAD

◆◆◆◆◆◆◆◆◆◆◆◆◆

Prep: 10 minutes plus standing
Grill: 25 to 40 minutes
Makes 6 main-dish servings

1 large head radicchio
3 medium heads Belgian endive
3 tablespoons olive oil
1 tablespoon chopped fresh rosemary or 1 teaspoon dried rosemary, crushed
Salt
¼ cup chili sauce
¼ cup balsamic vinegar
1 garlic clove, crushed with side of knife
1 beef porterhouse steak, 2 inches thick (about 2¼ pounds)

1 Prepare outdoor grill. Prepare grilled salad: Cut radicchio into 6 wedges. Cut each head of endive lengthwise in half. In cup, mix oil, chopped rosemary, and ½ teaspoon salt. Set aside. In pie plate or deep dish, mix chili sauce, vinegar, ¾ teaspoon salt, and garlic until well combined.

2 Add steak to chili-sauce mixture; turn to coat. Place steak on grill over medium heat; brush with half of chili-sauce mixture.

3 Grill steak, turning occasionally, 20 to 30 minutes for medium-rare, or until desired doneness; brush with remaining chili-sauce mixture halfway through grilling. Transfer to cutting board. Let stand 10 minutes; keep warm.

4 Meanwhile, place vegetables on grill; brush with oil mixture. Grill, turning occasionally, 5 to 10 minutes, until tender-crisp. Thinly slice steak; arrange on serving platter with grilled salad.

BARBECUE EQUIPMENT

The long handles on these tools make it easier – and safer – to maneuver foods over hot fires. Shown here (left to right): a brush for basting; a fork for moving vegetables and meat (don't pierce meat, or you will lose juices); and tongs for turning and picking up. A spatula (or pancake turner) is indispensable for burgers. Another useful tool is a grill topper. This flat, perforated grate fits over a grill and is ideal for unskewered small foods such as scallops, shrimp, and vegetables, which can fall through the regular grid.

EACH SERVING: ABOUT 490 CALORIES, 33g PROTEIN, 9g CARBOHYDRATE, 35g TOTAL FAT (12g SATURATED), 104mg CHOLESTEROL, 675mg SODIUM

LIME BEEF WITH TORTILLAS

Prep: 25 minutes plus marinating and standing
Grill: 10 to 12 minutes
Makes 6 main-dish servings

4 medium limes
1 small onion, chopped
1 teaspoon chili powder
½ teaspoon salt
¼ teaspoon crushed red pepper
1 beef skirt steak or flank steak (1½ pounds)
¼ cup olive or vegetable oil

2 medium avocados, peeled, seeded, and cut into thin wedges
4 small tomatoes, cut into thin wedges
12 flour tortillas (6 to 7 inches), warmed according to package directions

◆ Grate peel and squeeze juice from limes. In 13" by 9" baking dish, mix grated lime peel and juice, onion, chili powder, salt, and crushed red pepper. Add steak to marinade and turn to coat. Cover and refrigerate steak at least 4 hours, turning occasionally.

◆ Prepare outdoor grill. Prepare lime dressing: Remove meat from marinade; pour marinade into 1-quart saucepan. Heat to boiling over high heat; boil 5 minutes. Pour marinade into small bowl. Gradually whisk oil into marinade in a thin stream; set dressing aside.

◆ Place steak on grill over medium-high heat; grill steak, turning once, 6 to 8 minutes for skirt steak, 10 to 12 minutes for flank steak, for medium-rare, or until desired doneness. Place steak on large cutting board. Let stand 10 minutes; keep warm.

◆ To serve, with knife held almost parallel to cutting surface, thinly slice steak across the grain. Arrange avocado and tomato wedges on cutting board. Place lime dressing and warm tortillas next to steak. Let each person arrange some sliced meat, avocado, and tomato on a tortilla, then spoon on some dressing, roll up tortilla, and eat out of hand.

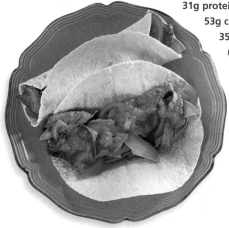

Each serving: About 640 calories, 31g protein, 53g carbohydrate, 35g total fat (8g saturated), 58mg cholesterol, 600mg sodium

SPICE-RUBBED BEEF TENDERLOIN

Prep: 5 minutes   *Grill:* 30 to 40 minutes
Makes 10 main-dish servings

1 tablespoon fennel seeds, crushed
2 teaspoons salt
½ teaspoon ground ginger

½ teaspoon crushed red pepper
1 beef tenderloin roast (about 2½ pounds)

◆ On waxed paper, mix first 4 ingredients. Use mixture to rub on beef. If you like, cover and refrigerate spice-rubbed beef overnight before grilling.

◆ Prepare outdoor grill. Grill beef, covered, over medium heat, turning occasionally, 30 to 40 minutes for medium-rare, or until desired doneness. Temperature on instant-read thermometer should reach 140°F (internal temperature of meat will rise to 145°F upon standing). Transfer beef to cutting board. Let stand 10 minutes; keep warm. Thinly slice.

Each serving: About 175 calories, 24g protein, 0g carbohydrate, 8g total fat (3g saturated), 59mg cholesterol, 480mg sodium

FILET MIGNON WITH RED-PEPPER AND ONION STUFFING

Prep: 35 minutes   *Grill:* 10 to 15 minutes
Makes 4 main-dish servings

1 tablespoon plus 2 teaspoons olive or vegetable oil
1 large onion, chopped
1 tablespoon red wine vinegar
1 teaspoon sugar
¾ teaspoon dried basil
Salt

½ (7-ounce) jar roasted red peppers, drained and chopped
4 beef tenderloin steaks (filet mignon), each 1½ inches thick (about 4 ounces each)
½ teaspoon coarsely ground black pepper

◆ In 2-quart saucepan, heat 1 tablespoon oil over medium-high heat; add onion and cook, stirring frequently, until golden. Stir in vinegar, sugar, basil, ¼ teaspoon salt, and *1 tablespoon water*; heat to boiling over high heat. Reduce heat to low; cover and simmer 15 minutes. Uncover; stir in roasted peppers and cook, stirring, until liquid evaporates. Remove from heat; cool to room temperature.

◆ Prepare outdoor grill. With knife, cut a horizontal slit in each steak, almost but not all the way through, to form a deep pocket. Spoon onion mixture into pockets. Brush steaks with remaining 2 teaspoons oil; sprinkle with black pepper and ½ teaspoon salt. Place on grill over medium heat; grill, turning once, 10 to 15 minutes for medium-rare, or until desired doneness.

Each serving: About 360 calories, 21g protein, 7g carbohydrate, 28g total fat (9g saturated), 73mg cholesterol, 455mg sodium

BEEF SATAY WITH PEANUT SAUCE

Prep: 20 minutes
Grill: 3 to 4 minutes
Makes 6 main-dish servings

30 (10- or 12-inch) bamboo skewers
1 medium lemon
1 small garlic clove, minced
1 tablespoon Dijon mustard
¼ teaspoon crushed red pepper
¼ cup plus 2 tablespoons soy sauce
1 tablespoon plus 1 teaspoon sugar
1 beef flank steak (about 1½ pounds)
¼ cup creamy peanut butter
1 tablespoon white wine vinegar

◆ Prepare outdoor grill. Soak bamboo skewers in *water* to cover for 15 minutes; drain and pat dry. Meanwhile, grate peel and squeeze 1 tablespoon juice from lemon.

◆ In 13" by 9" glass baking dish, mix lemon peel, lemon juice, garlic, mustard, crushed red pepper, ¼ cup soy sauce, and 1 tablespoon sugar. Holding knife almost parallel to work surface, cut flank steak crosswise into 30 slices, each about ¼ inch thick. Add steak to soy-sauce mixture in baking dish; toss to coat. Set aside.

◆ Prepare peanut sauce: In small saucepan, heat peanut butter, vinegar, ¼ *cup water,* and remaining 2 tablespoons soy sauce and 1 teaspoon sugar to boiling, stirring constantly, over medium-high heat. Reduce heat to low; simmer, stirring, until mixture is smooth. Remove saucepan from heat. Keep warm.

◆ On each skewer, loosely thread 1 slice flank steak, accordion-style. Place skewers on grill over medium heat. Grill skewers, turning once, 3 to 4 minutes for medium-rare, or until desired doneness. Arrange skewers on warm large platter. Serve with peanut sauce.

Each serving: About 280 calories, 26g protein, 9g carbohydrate, 16g total fat (6g saturated), 58mg cholesterol, 1215mg sodium

SIRLOIN STEAK KABOBS WITH CAESAR SALAD

Prep: 25 minutes
Grill: 10 to 12 minutes
Makes 6 main-dish servings

Caesar Salad (see below)
¼ cup catchup
3 tablespoons light molasses
2 tablespoons Worcestershire sauce
1 tablespoon spicy brown mustard
1 tablespoon grated onion
½ teaspoon salt
1 boneless beef top sirloin steak, 1¼ inches thick (about 2 pounds), cut into 2-inch chunks
6 (14-inch) all-metal skewers

◆ Prepare outdoor grill. Prepare Caesar Salad but do not toss with dressing; refrigerate. In large bowl, mix catchup and next 5 ingredients; add steak and toss to coat.

◆ On skewers, thread steak. Place skewers on grill over medium heat. Grill skewers, turning occasionally and brushing with remaining catchup mixture, 10 to 12 minutes for medium-rare, or until desired doneness. Toss salad with dressing; serve with kabobs.

Each serving: About 230 calories, 30g protein, 10g carbohydrate, 10g total fat (4g saturated), 91mg cholesterol, 445mg sodium

CAESAR SALAD

Tear or cut 2 heads romaine lettuce into 2-inch pieces; place in bowl with ½ (6-ounce) package plain croutons. In blender, blend ⅓ cup freshly grated Parmesan cheese, ¼ cup olive oil; 2 tablespoons fresh lemon juice, 2 teaspoons Dijon mustard, ½ teaspoon each salt and coarsely ground black pepper, 4 anchovy fillets, and 1 garlic clove until smooth. Add to salad; toss.

SPICY BEEF KABOBS

Prep: 15 minutes
Grill: 10 to 12 minutes
Makes 4 main-dish servings

1 tablespoon chili powder
1 tablespoon soy sauce
1 teaspoon jalapeño chile sauce
2 tablespoons vegetable oil
1 boneless beef top sirloin steak, 1¼ inches thick (1½ pounds), cut into 12 chunks
½ teaspoon salt
3 green onions, cut into 3-inch-long pieces
8 large mushrooms
1 medium zucchini (about 12 ounces), cut into bite-size chunks
4 (14-inch) all-metal skewers
8 cherry tomatoes
Couscous (Moroccan pasta, optional)

◆ Prepare outdoor grill. In medium bowl, with fork, mix chili powder, soy sauce, jalapeño chile sauce, and 1 tablespoon oil. Add beef chunks to chili mixture; stir to coat.

◆ In large bowl, mix salt and remaining 1 tablespoon oil. Add green onions, mushrooms, and zucchini; toss to coat.

◆ On skewers, alternately thread beef, green-onion pieces, mushrooms, zucchini, and tomatoes. Place skewers on grill over medium heat. Grill skewers, turning once, 10 to 12 minutes, until beef is medium-rare and vegetables are tender. Serve kabobs with couscous, if you like.

Each serving: About 450 calories, 37g protein, 24g carbohydrate, 22g total fat (7g saturated), 98mg cholesterol, 980mg sodium

SPICY BEEF RIBS WITH GRILLED PINEAPPLE

Prep: 20 minutes
Grill: 25 to 30 minutes
Makes 4 main-dish servings

1 garlic clove, minced
1 tablespoon olive or vegetable oil
1½ teaspoons coarsely ground black pepper
1½ teaspoons dry mustard
1½ teaspoons fennel seeds, crushed

1 teaspoon salt
½ teaspoon ground cloves
4 pounds beef back ribs, cut into 1-rib portions
1 medium pineapple
2 tablespoons brown sugar
Flat-leaf parsley sprigs for garnish

◆ Prepare outdoor grill. In small bowl, mix garlic, oil, pepper, dry mustard, fennel seeds, salt, and ground cloves. Use to rub over beef back ribs.

◆ Cut off rind from pineapple. Slice pineapple lengthwise in half, then cut each half crosswise into ¾-inch-thick slices; remove center core from each slice.

◆ Place ribs on grill over medium heat; cook, turning frequently, 15 to 20 minutes for medium-rare, or until desired doneness. Transfer ribs to board or large platter.

◆ In large bowl, toss pineapple slices with brown sugar. Place pineapple slices on grill; cook, turning frequently, 10 minutes, or until browned on both sides. Serve ribs with pineapple slices. Garnish with parsley sprigs.

Each serving: About 1070 calories, 105g protein, 25g carbohydrate, 59g total fat (24g saturated), 261mg cholesterol, 735mg sodium

GRILLED FRUIT

Grilled fruit makes a striking garnish or delicious dessert. Use firm-textured fruits that aren't overly ripe, such as nectarines, peaches, plums, or pineapple. Halve fruit or cut into fairly thick slices or wedges so it won't slip through the grill.

DOUBLE-CHILI BEEF KABOBS

Prep: 15 minutes   *Grill:* 9 to 11 minutes
Makes 4 main-dish servings

1 tablespoon vegetable oil
1 tablespoon chili powder
½ cup chili sauce
1 tablespoon honey
½ teaspoon salt
4 (10-inch) all-metal skewers

1 beef tri-tip roast (1¼ pounds), cut into 1-inch cubes
2 bunches green onions, cut into 2-inch pieces

◆ Prepare outdoor grill. Prepare double-chili sauce: In 1-quart saucepan, heat oil over medium heat. Add chili powder; cook, stirring constantly, 1 minute. Stir in chili sauce, honey, and salt; cook 1 minute longer. Remove from heat.

◆ On skewers, alternately thread beef cubes and green-onion pieces.

◆ Place skewers on grill over medium heat; grill skewers, turning once, 5 minutes. Brush with double-chili sauce; turn and grill, turning occasionally and brushing with remaining sauce, 4 to 6 minutes longer, until beef is medium-rare, or until desired doneness. To serve, transfer kabobs to large platter.

Each serving: About 325 calories, 29g protein, 14g carbohydrate, 17g total fat (6g saturated), 72mg cholesterol, 775mg sodium

KOREAN-STYLE SESAME-GINGER SHORT RIBS

Prep: 15 minutes plus marinating   *Grill:* 20 to 25 minutes
Makes 5 main-dish servings

4 pounds beef chuck short ribs, cut into 2-inch pieces
3 large garlic cloves, minced
½ cup soy sauce

4 teaspoons minced, peeled fresh ginger
2 teaspoons Asian sesame oil

◆ With sharp knife, slash meaty side of ribs at ½-inch intervals, ¼ inch deep.

◆ In large zip-tight plastic bag, combine garlic, soy sauce, ginger, and sesame oil. Add ribs, turning to coat well with mixture. Seal bag; place in 13" by 9" pan and refrigerate overnight, turning once.

◆ Prepare outdoor grill. Place ribs on grill over medium heat; brush with remaining marinade. Grill ribs, turning occasionally, 20 to 25 minutes for medium, or until desired doneness. To serve, transfer ribs to large platter.

Each serving: About 785 calories, 85g protein, 3g carbohydrate, 46g total fat (19g saturated), 209mg cholesterol, 1805mg sodium

Veal KNOW-HOW

No matter how you cook veal, do it with care. Lean and delicate, veal should actually be cooked more like poultry than beef. As with other meats, the proper cooking method depends on the cut. Whether you broil a thick, juicy chop or create a fragrant stew, remember not to overcook veal, or you'll toughen its delicate texture.

KNOW YOUR VEAL

Veal calves are raised to an age of 12 to 16 weeks. The finest and most expensive of all veal is milk-fed. It comes from animals that are fed on their mothers' milk or a special milk formula. The meat is light pink – almost white – and mildly flavored, with a firm but velvety texture.

Grain-fed veal comes from calves that are reared to a similar age but fed a diet of grain or grass. It has a rosier color and a slightly stronger flavor than milk-fed veal.

BUYING AND STORING

• Look for fine-textured veal that's pale to creamy pink with little marbling. Any fat should be firm and very white. The bones of milk-fed veal will have reddish marrow.
• Some veal carries a USDA grade of Prime, which is usually milk-fed veal, or Choice, typically from grain-fed calves and of slightly lower quality.
• Because veal is a moist meat, it is fairly perishable. It will last for only two days in the refrigerator, tightly wrapped.

STUFFING A VEAL BREAST

1 Make stuffing; cool. To make a pocket, work boning or paring knife between the two main layers of muscle. Extend the space until pocket is deep and wide.

2 Spoon stuffing into pocket (fill loosely because stuffing will expand during cooking). Thread a metal skewer through meat at pocket opening to secure.

CHOOSING THE RIGHT CUT

Veal is especially good cooked by moist-heat methods such as braising so the meat stays juicy and flavorful. Roasting at moderate temperatures also works well, and panfrying (in butter or oil) is ideal for thin cutlets.

For broiling, grilling, or panfrying These dry-heat methods are suitable for a variety of thin cuts. For broiling and grilling, choose fairly thick chops and steaks; cuts that are too thin will dry out. Use veal cutlets for panfrying only. Since they'll cook very quickly, keep a close watch.
Best bets Arm or blade steaks, loin chops, rib chops (below right), ground veal, and cutlets (below left).

Cutlets of even thickness cook uniformly – pound lightly if necessary

Trim fat to ¼ inch before cooking

Chops for broiling should be at least ¾ inch thick

For braising or stewing Bone-in pieces are especially suited to long cooking, as they yield the best flavor. Veal shanks have meaty-tasting marrow in the center, which helps enrich stews. When done, braised or stewed veal should be fork-tender.
Best bets Shanks, shank crosscuts (below right), arm or blade steak, breast, shoulder. Veal cubes for stew (below left) are cut from the leg or shoulder.

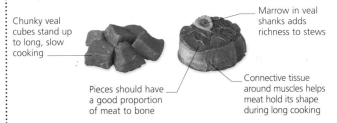

Chunky veal cubes stand up to long, slow cooking

Marrow in veal shanks adds richness to stews

Pieces should have a good proportion of meat to bone

Connective tissue around muscles helps meat hold its shape during long cooking

For roasting Many large cuts of veal will roast nicely. Since veal roasts are generally very lean, ensure juicy results by cooking only to medium doneness (160°F), basting occasionally with the flavorful pan juices.
Best bets Shoulder (below), rib roast, loin roast, round, and breast.

Veal has little internal fat, so should be basted during roasting

A well-trimmed roast should be free of cartilage, sinews, and membranes

Boneless roasts will keep their shape and cook evenly if they're tied or netted

ROASTING TIMES (OVEN TEMPERATURE OF 325°F)			
CUT AND WEIGHT Start with meat at refrigerator temperature. **Remove roast from oven when it reaches 5° to 10°F below desired doneness; temperature will rise as it stands.**		MEAT THERMOMETER READING	APPROXIMATE COOKING TIME (MINUTES PER LB)
Boneless shoulder roast	3–5 lbs	160°F	35–40 mins
Leg rump or round roast (boneless)	3–5 lbs	160°F	35–40 mins
Boneless loin roast	3–5 lbs	160°F	25–30 mins
Rib roast	3–5 lbs	160°F	30–35 mins

FLAVORS FOR VEAL

Many flavors marry well with delicate, elegant veal. Fresh herbs – tarragon, sage, or rosemary – are lovely. For zesty flavor, try lemon and capers (a must for veal piccata), tangy vinegars, tomatoes, olives, orange, and heady fortified wines such as Madeira or Marsala.

CARVING A VEAL BREAST ROAST

A veal breast is extra-easy to carve if the rib bones have been cracked by the butcher before cooking (but even if ribs aren't cracked, the breast should still be easy to carve after its long cooking). Place roast on a cutting board, cover with loose tent of foil, and let stand 15 minutes. Remove the metal skewer.

1 Steady veal roast with a 2-pronged carving fork. Carve slices from veal breast by cutting down through meat following the line of the rib bone.

2 Cut away exposed rib and continue carving even slices of meat, working along breast. Transfer slices to warm platter.

MAKING VEAL STOCK

Veal bones produce a rich and full-bodied stock that makes a wonderful substitute for canned chicken broth in soups, stews, and sauces. It becomes thick when reduced and has a depth of flavor that's a world away from canned broth. Ask your butcher for veal bones (have them cut into 2- to 3-inch pieces), or buy shoulder or blade chops and use the bones for stock and the meat for stew. This recipe makes about 2½ quarts.

4 pounds veal knuckle bones or other veal bones
4 carrots
2 celery stalks
2 onions, each cut in half
1 bay leaf
8 whole black peppercorns
½ teaspoon dried thyme

1 Rinse veal bones; place in 6-quart stockpot with 4 quarts cold water. Heat mixture to boiling over high heat. Reduce heat to low; skim and discard froth from top of mixture.

2 Add remaining ingredients; simmer 4 to 6 hours. (Do not boil vigorously, and do not stir, or stock will not be clear.) Continue to skim any froth that rises to top. Strain stock through colander; discard veal bones and vegetables. Strain stock through fine sieve. Transfer to small containers and refrigerate to use within 4 days, or freeze up to 4 months. Before using, skim and discard any surface fat.

ROAST VEAL

A naturally tender meat with a delicate flavor, veal is best roasted at a moderate temperature. Be sure to baste it from time to time while cooking – the result will be a most delicious roast. If you add potatoes or other vegetables to the roasting pan, they will also be flavored with the pan juices.

STUFFED VEAL WITH ROASTED POTATOES

◆◆◆◆◆◆◆◆◆◆◆◆◆

Prep: 50 minutes plus standing
Roast: 2 hours 15 minutes
Makes 8 main-dish servings

3 tablespoons olive or vegetable oil
12 ounces mushrooms, finely chopped
1 medium onion, finely chopped
Salt and coarsely ground black pepper
1 rolled boneless veal shoulder roast (3 pounds)
1 bunch spinach (10 to 12 ounces), stemmed, rinsed, and dried
1 teaspoon dried thyme
8 large all-purpose potatoes (about 3½ pounds), peeled and cut into 2-inch chunks
Thyme sprigs for garnish

1 In 12-inch skillet, heat 2 tablespoons oil over medium-high heat. Add mushrooms, onion, ½ teaspoon salt, and ¼ teaspoon pepper and cook, stirring often, until liquid evaporates.

2 Reduce heat to medium; cook until vegetables are golden. Set aside. Untie veal roast. To make veal evenly thick, pound veal, fat-side down, between 2 sheets plastic wrap or waxed paper into 12" by 10" rectangle.

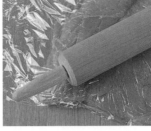

3 Preheat oven to 325°F. Arrange spinach over veal; top with mushroom mixture. Starting from a narrow end, roll veal, jelly-roll fashion. With string, tie roast at 2-inch intervals.

4 In small bowl, mix dried thyme, ¾ teaspoon salt, and ½ teaspoon pepper. Use to rub over veal; place roast on small rack in large roasting pan. Insert meat thermometer into center of roast.

5 Roast veal 1¼ hours, brushing occasionally with pan drippings. In large bowl, toss potatoes with remaining 1 tablespoon oil, ½ teaspoon salt, and ¼ teaspoon pepper.

6 Add potatoes to roasting pan, turning to coat with drippings. Roast veal and potatoes 1 hour longer, turning potatoes occasionally, or until potatoes are fork-tender and temperature on meat thermometer reaches 160°F for medium. Transfer veal with potatoes to warm large platter; let stand 10 minutes for easier carving. Keep warm. To serve, slice veal roast. Arrange veal and potatoes on 8 plates and garnish with thyme sprigs.

EACH SERVING: ABOUT 395 CALORIES, 33g PROTEIN, 41g CARBOHYDRATE, 12g TOTAL FAT (3g SATURATED), 112mg CHOLESTEROL, 600mg SODIUM

VEAL ROAST WITH ROSEMARY AND GARLIC

Prep: 20 minutes plus standing   Roast: 2 hours
Makes 8 main-dish servings

3 garlic cloves, minced
1 teaspoon dried rosemary
½ teaspoon dried thyme
1 teaspoon salt
½ teaspoon ground black pepper
1 rolled boneless veal shoulder roast (3 pounds), tied
1 tablespoon olive oil
1 small onion, finely chopped
1 medium carrot, finely chopped
½ cup dry white wine

◆ Preheat oven to 350°F. On cutting board, mash garlic, rosemary, thyme, salt, and pepper to a paste. Pat veal dry with paper towels. Rub paste all over veal and in crevices.

◆ In oven-safe 10-inch skillet, heat oil over medium-high heat. Add veal and cook 10 minutes, or until browned all over. Add chopped onion and carrot and place veal on top. Pour in wine. Insert meat thermometer into center of roast.

◆ Transfer skillet to oven and roast veal 2 hours, basting with pan juices every 30 minutes and adding *½ cup water* if skillet is dry, or until temperature on meat thermometer reaches 160°F for medium.

◆ Transfer veal to warm large platter; let stand 10 minutes for easier carving. Keep warm. Meanwhile, add *¾ cup water* to same skillet and heat to boiling; stir until brown bits are loosened. Simmer 2 minutes. Skim and discard fat from pan juices. Strain pan juices and vegetables through coarse sieve, pressing hard on vegetables. Discard chopped vegetables. Slice veal thin and serve with pan juices.

Each serving: About 205 calories, 27g protein, 3g carbohydrate, 8g total fat (3g saturated), 112mg cholesterol, 365mg sodium

STUFFED BREAST OF VEAL

Prep: 30 minutes plus cooling   Roast: 2 hours
Makes 6 main-dish servings

2 cans (13¾ to 14½ ounces each) reduced-sodium chicken broth
½ cup parboiled rice
2 tablespoons olive oil
1 medium onion, diced
1 large celery stalk, diced
1 small head escarole (about 12 ounces), chopped
¼ cup dark seedless raisins, chopped
1¼ teaspoons rubbed sage
Salt and ground black pepper
1 veal breast (6 pounds) with pocket (see page 217) for stuffing (ask your butcher to crack bones for easier carving)
Warm Plum-Tomato Salad (optional, below left)

◆ Prepare stuffing: In 1-quart saucepan, heat 1⅓ cups broth to boiling over high heat; stir in rice. Reduce heat to low. Cover; simmer 20 minutes, or until rice is tender and all liquid is absorbed.

◆ Meanwhile, in 12-inch skillet, heat 1 tablespoon oil over medium-high heat. Add onion and celery; cook, stirring occasionally, until lightly browned. Add escarole; cook, stirring, until escarole just wilts. Remove from heat; stir in rice, raisins, and ¼ teaspoon each sage, salt, and pepper. Cool to room temperature.

◆ Preheat oven to 350°F. Spoon stuffing into pocket of veal; skewer closed if necessary (see page 217). Place veal, meat-side up, in roasting pan. In cup, mix remaining 1 tablespoon oil with remaining 1 teaspoon sage, ¼ teaspoon salt, and ¼ teaspoon pepper. Use to rub over veal. Roast veal 1 hour. Pour remaining broth into roasting pan. Roast 1 hour longer, basting often, until tender when pierced with tip of knife.

◆ Just before veal is done, prepare tomato salad, if you like; keep warm. Place veal on warm large platter. Let stand 15 minutes for easier carving; keep warm. Pour broth in roasting pan into 2-quart saucepan; let stand a few seconds, until fat separates from broth. Skim and discard fat. Add *1½ cups water* to roasting pan; stir until brown bits are loosened; stir into broth in saucepan and heat through. Serve veal with sauce, and tomato salad, if you like.

Each serving: About 455 calories, 48g protein, 23g carbohydrate, 18g total fat (4g saturated), 193mg cholesterol, 435mg sodium

---

WARM PLUM-TOMATO SALAD

In 12-inch skillet, heat 3 tablespoons olive oil over medium heat. Add 1 small onion, minced; cook until tender. Add 12 small plum tomatoes, each cut in half, ½ teaspoon salt, and ¼ teaspoon cracked black pepper. Cook, stirring occasionally, until heated through. Just before serving, sprinkle with 2 tablespoons freshly grated Parmesan cheese and 1 tablespoon fresh lemon juice. Makes 6 accompaniment servings.

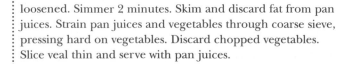

Each serving: About 105 calories, 2g protein, 8g carbohydrate, 8g total fat (1g saturated), 2mg cholesterol, 230mg sodium

PANFRIED VEAL

Delicate veal stays tender when it's panfried very quickly over fairly high heat. For moist and tender results, do not cook the meat beyond medium doneness. The mild flavor of veal is enhanced by fresh, lively flavors, such as the arugula and tomato salad accompanying it here.

VEAL WITH TOMATO AND ARUGULA SALAD

◆◆◆◆◆◆◆◆◆◆◆◆◆◆

Prep: 20 minutes
Cook: 5 minutes
Makes 4 main-dish servings

2 teaspoons fresh lemon juice
6 tablespoons olive oil
Salt and ground black pepper
1 large tomato, coarsely chopped
1 cup loosely packed fresh basil leaves
¼ cup coarsely chopped red onion
1 pound veal cutlets
2 large eggs
½ cup all-purpose flour
1 cup plain dried bread crumbs
1 bunch arugula
Toasted Italian bread (optional)

1 Prepare salad. In medium bowl, combine lemon juice, 2 tablespoons oil, ½ teaspoon salt, and ¼ teaspoon pepper. Stir in tomato, basil, and red onion until combined; set aside.

2 With rolling pin or meat mallet, pound veal between 2 sheets of waxed paper or plastic wrap to ⅛-inch thickness. Pat veal dry with paper towels. In pie plate, whisk eggs with ½ teaspoon each salt and pepper.

3 Spread flour on sheet of waxed paper; spread bread crumbs on another sheet of waxed paper. Dip veal, one piece at a time, first in flour, turning to coat and shaking off excess, then in egg, then in bread crumbs, shaking off excess.

4 In nonstick 12-inch skillet, heat 2 tablespoons oil over medium-high heat until very hot. Add half of veal; cook 1 minute per side, or until browned. Transfer to platter in single layer. Keep warm.

5 Repeat with remaining 2 tablespoons oil and remaining veal cutlets. Add arugula to tomato mixture in bowl; toss well to combine. To serve, spoon tomato and arugula salad on top of hot veal cutlets. Serve with toasted Italian bread, if you like.

EACH SERVING: ABOUT 565 CALORIES, 40g PROTEIN, 35g CARBOHYDRATE, 29g TOTAL FAT (5g SATURATED), 221mg CHOLESTEROL, 865mg SODIUM

VEAL CHOPS AU POIVRE WITH POTATO-CARROT PANCAKES

Prep: 20 minutes   Cook: 20 minutes
Makes 2 main-dish servings

1 large baking potato (about 12 ounces)	3 tablespoons olive or vegetable oil
1 large egg	2 veal rib chops, each
1 large carrot, shredded	1¼ inches thick (about
3 tablespoons all-purpose flour	12 ounces each)
1 tablespoon chopped fresh parsley	2 teaspoons cracked black pepper
Salt	3 tablespoons dry white wine

◆ Peel potato. Into medium bowl half-filled with cold *water*, coarsely shred potato. Drain potato, discarding water. Wrap potato in clean towel; squeeze to remove as much water as possible. In same bowl, beat egg. Stir in potato, carrot, flour, parsley, and ½ teaspoon salt until well mixed.

◆ In 12-inch skillet, heat 2 tablespoons oil over medium heat. Drop potato mixture into skillet by ¼ cups to make 6 mounds. With pancake turner, flatten each to make a 4-inch pancake. Cook pancakes about 4 minutes or until golden brown on bottom; turn and brown other side. Transfer to cookie sheet lined with paper towels to drain; keep warm in low oven.

◆ Pat veal chops dry with paper towels. Press cracked pepper and ¼ teaspoon salt into meat. In same skillet, heat remaining 1 tablespoon oil over medium-high heat; add veal chops and cook, turning once, until browned.

◆ Reduce heat to medium; cook 6 minutes longer for medium-rare, or until desired doneness. Place veal chops on 2 warm plates; keep warm. Skim and discard fat from drippings in skillet; stir in wine and simmer 1 minute. Spoon sauce over veal; serve with potato pancakes.

Each serving: About 725 calories, 53g protein, 45g carbohydrate, 35g total fat (8g saturated), 286mg cholesterol, 1025mg sodium

STUFFED VEAL CUTLETS

Prep: 25 minutes   Cook: 7 minutes
Makes 4 main-dish servings

3 tablespoons olive or vegetable oil	4 large veal cutlets, each ¼ inch thick (about 4 ounces each)
1 medium onion, thinly sliced	2 tablespoons plus ½ teaspoon all-purpose flour
¼ cup oil-packed dried tomatoes, drained and thinly sliced	½ teaspoon salt
1 tablespoon red wine vinegar	½ teaspoon chicken-flavor instant bouillon
Ground black pepper	¼ teaspoon dried basil
⅛ cup packed fresh basil leaves, thinly sliced, or 1 teaspoon dried basil	

◆ In 2-quart saucepan, heat 1 tablespoon oil over medium heat; add onion and cook, stirring occasionally, until very tender. Stir in dried tomatoes, vinegar, and ¼ teaspoon pepper. Cook, stirring, until vinegar evaporates; remove from heat. Stir in fresh basil.

◆ If veal cutlets are thick, with rolling pin or meat mallet, pound between 2 sheets of waxed paper or plastic wrap to ¼-inch thickness. Pat dry with paper towels. On waxed paper, combine 2 tablespoons flour, salt, and ¼ teaspoon pepper.

◆ Onto half of each veal cutlet, spoon one-fourth of onion mixture; fold other half of cutlet over filling. Carefully dip veal into flour mixture, turning to coat; shake off excess. In 12-inch skillet, heat remaining 2 tablespoons oil over medium-high heat; add veal and cook 5 minutes, or until browned all over. Transfer veal to warm platter.

◆ Into drippings in skillet, stir bouillon and dried basil. In cup, mix remaining ½ teaspoon flour and ½ cup *water* until blended; stir into skillet. Heat to boiling; boil 30 seconds, or until pan juices thicken slightly. Pour pan juices over veal.

Each serving: About 305 calories, 32g protein, 9g carbohydrate, 16g total fat (3g saturated), 114mg cholesterol, 455mg sodium

VEAL CUTLET SUBSTITUTE

Thin, tender veal cutlets are great for special occasions or everyday splurges. But if they're not available in the supermarket, or if you're watching your budget, try a favorite veal cutlet recipe using chicken or turkey cutlets. The results will be equally delicious. Cooking time for poultry will be a minute or two longer; while it's fine to serve veal on the medium side of doneness, poultry should always be fully cooked. For best results, buy chicken or turkey cutlets about ¼ inch thick. If they are thicker, simply pound them to a uniform thickness.

VEAL CASSEROLES AND STEWS

To transform veal into a sumptuous casserole or stew, the pieces are first browned in hot oil for best flavor and color, and then slowly simmered until very tender. The bone-in veal shanks make an especially delicious, full-bodied stew.

VEAL AND SPAETZLE CASSEROLE

Prep: 45 minutes   *Bake:* 1 hour 45 minutes to 2 hours
Makes 4 main-dish servings

3 tablespoons olive or vegetable oil
2 large celery stalks, cut into ½-inch-thick slices
2 medium carrots, cut into ½-inch-thick slices
1 large onion, cut into ½-inch pieces
4 veal shank cross cuts, each 2 inches thick (about 1 pound each)

1 can (14½ to 16 ounces) tomatoes
½ cup dry white wine
¼ teaspoon ground black pepper
¼ teaspoon dried oregano
1½ cups all-purpose flour
½ cup finely chopped fresh basil
2 large eggs
½ teaspoon salt

1 In 8-quart Dutch oven, heat oil over medium-high heat. Add celery, carrots, and onion and cook, stirring occasionally, until golden and tender-crisp; with slotted spoon, transfer to bowl.

2 Preheat oven to 375°F. Pat veal shanks dry with paper towels. In oil remaining in Dutch oven, cook veal shanks over high heat until browned on all sides. Return sautéed vegetables to Dutch oven.

3 Add tomatoes with their juice, white wine, pepper, and oregano, breaking up tomatoes with back of spoon; heat to boiling. Cover and bake 1¾ to 2 hours, or until veal is very tender.

4 When veal is almost done, prepare basil spaetzle: In 5-quart saucepot, heat *4 quarts water* to boiling over high heat. In medium bowl, with wooden spoon, beat flour, basil, eggs, salt, and *⅓ cup water* until smooth.

5 Reduce heat under saucepot to medium. Into simmering water, drop dough by measuring teaspoons, stirring water gently so spaetzle pieces do not stick together.

6 Cook spaetzle 2 to 3 minutes, until tender but firm; drain well. To serve, skim and discard any fat from liquid in Dutch oven. Gently stir in spaetzle and transfer casserole to large serving dish.

EACH SERVING: ABOUT 620 CALORIES, 56g PROTEIN, 47g CARBOHYDRATE, 20g TOTAL FAT (5g SATURATED), 278mg CHOLESTEROL, 590mg SODIUM

VEAL STEW WITH ORANGE GREMOLATA

Prep: 30 minutes   Bake: 1 hour 15 minutes
Makes 6 main-dish servings

2 pounds veal for stew, cut into 1½-inch
    chunks
2 tablespoons vegetable oil
4 medium carrots, cut into 2-inch pieces
1 medium onion, chopped
1 cup chicken broth
1 can (16 ounces) tomatoes in puree
¾ teaspoon salt
¼ teaspoon coarsely ground black pepper
¼ teaspoon dried thyme
2 garlic cloves, minced
2 tablespoons chopped fresh parsley
1 tablespoon grated orange peel

◆ Pat veal dry with paper towels. In
5-quart Dutch oven, heat 1 tablespoon
oil over medium-high heat. Add veal,
half at a time; cook until browned on all
sides. Transfer veal to bowl as it browns.

◆ Preheat oven to 350°F. In same
Dutch oven, heat remaining 1 tablespoon oil over medium heat. Add
carrots and onion; cook 10 minutes, or
until browned. Add broth, stirring until
brown bits are loosened. Return veal to
Dutch oven. Stir in tomatoes with their
puree, salt, pepper, and thyme; heat to
boiling over high heat. Cover; bake
1¼ hours, or until veal and vegetables
are tender. In cup, combine garlic,
parsley, and orange peel; stir into stew.

**Each serving: About 320 calories,
38g protein, 12g carbohydrate, 13g total
fat (3g saturated), 136mg cholesterol,
815mg sodium**

VEAL AND MUSHROOM STEW

Prep: 30 minutes
Bake: 1 hour to 1 hour 15 minutes
Makes 6 main-dish servings

1½ pounds veal for stew, cut into 1½-inch
    chunks
¾ teaspoon salt
¼ teaspoon ground black pepper
3 tablespoons vegetable oil
1 pound medium mushrooms, each cut
    in half
4 ounces shiitake mushrooms, stems
    removed
⅓ cup sweet Marsala wine
1 package (10 ounces) frozen peas

◆ Pat veal dry with paper towels;
sprinkle with salt and pepper. In
5-quart Dutch oven, heat 2 tablespoons
oil over medium-high heat. Add veal
chunks, half at a time, and cook until
browned on all sides. Transfer veal to
bowl as it browns.

◆ Preheat oven to 350°F. In same
Dutch oven, heat remaining 1 tablespoon oil over medium-high heat;
cook all mushrooms, stirring
occasionally, until lightly browned.
Return veal to Dutch oven; stir in
Marsala and *½ cup water*, stirring until
brown bits are loosened. Heat to
boiling over high heat. Cover and bake
1 to 1¼ hours, stirring occasionally, until
veal is tender. Stir in peas; heat through.

**Each serving: About 310 calories,
31g protein, 15g carbohydrate, 13g total
fat (3g saturated), 99mg cholesterol,
390mg sodium**

VEAL AND VEGETABLE RAGOUT

Prep: 25 minutes   Cook: 2 hours
Makes 10 main-dish servings

3 tablespoons olive oil
1 large onion, minced
3 pounds veal for stew, cut into 2-inch
    chunks
1 teaspoon salt
¼ teaspoon ground black pepper
5 tablespoons all-purpose flour
¼ cup dry red wine
1 envelope beef-flavor bouillon
1½ pounds turnips, peeled and cut into
    1½-inch wedges
1 bag (16 ounces) carrots, cut lengthwise
    in half, then crosswise into 2-inch pieces
6 medium celery stalks, cut into 2-inch
    pieces
1 pound medium mushrooms

◆ In 8-quart Dutch oven, heat oil over
medium-high heat. Add onion and
cook 10 minutes, or until tender;
transfer to bowl.

◆ Pat veal dry with paper towels. In
large bowl, mix salt, pepper, and
3 tablespoons flour; add veal and toss
to coat.

◆ Heat oil remaining in Dutch oven
over medium-high heat. Add veal, half
at a time, and cook until well browned
on all sides, adding more oil if
necessary; transfer veal to bowl with
onion as it browns.

◆ Return onion and veal to Dutch
oven. In cup, stir red wine, bouillon,
and 2 tablespoons flour until smooth;
add to Dutch oven with *2¼ cups water*;
heat to boiling, stirring. Reduce heat
to low; cover and simmer 45 minutes.

◆ Add turnips, carrots, celery, and
mushrooms to Dutch oven; heat to
boiling over high heat. Reduce heat to
low; cover and simmer 40 minutes, or
until veal and vegetables are tender.

**Each serving: About 305 calories,
35g protein, 15g carbohydrate, 11g total
fat (2g saturated), 119mg cholesterol,
465mg sodium**

◆◆◆◆◆◆◆◆◆◆◆◆◆◆◆◆◆◆◆◆◆◆◆◆◆◆◆◆◆◆◆

PATTING MEAT DRY

When searing meat, for the best
"browned" flavor and color, it must be
as dry as possible. This is easily done
by patting raw meat with paper towels.
This helps meat absorb seasonings,
and prevents any excess moisture from
creating steam, which inhibits the
browning process.

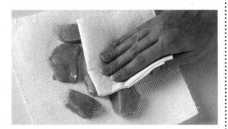

◆◆◆◆◆◆◆◆◆◆◆◆◆◆◆◆◆◆◆◆◆◆◆◆◆◆◆◆◆◆◆

BROILED VEAL

When a premium cut of veal is oven-broiled, it requires very few embellishments to enhance its flavor. Our selection uses a simple Fontina cheese and prosciutto stuffing, a caper and Dijon mustard topping, a quick sherry marinade with yellow peppers, and, easiest of all, a rub made of fresh sage and olive oil. Each sets off the elegant simplicity of veal.

VEAL STUFFED WITH FONTINA, PROSCIUTTO, AND BASIL

Prep: *15 minutes*   **Broil:** *10 to 12 minutes*
Makes *4 main-dish servings*

2 ounces Fontina cheese, shredded (½ cup)
1 ounce prosciutto, chopped (¼ cup)
¼ cup chopped fresh basil
Ground black pepper

4 veal rib or loin chops, each 1 inch thick (8 ounces each)
1 teaspoon olive oil
¼ teaspoon salt
Sautéed peppers and broiled tomatoes (optional)

1 Preheat broiler. In small bowl, mix Fontina, prosciutto, basil, and ⅛ teaspoon pepper until evenly combined.

2 Pat veal chops dry with paper towels. Holding knife parallel to work surface, cut a horizontal pocket in each chop.

PROSCIUTTO

The delicious salty tang of prosciutto lends flavor to the veal in this classic dish. Prosciutto is raw ham that has been cured, aged for up to 14 months, and air-dried. The best-known – and the finest – prosciutto comes from Parma, in northern Italy, though some prefer the saltier cure from San Daniele, near Venice.

Prosciutto is available in Italian food markets or at the deli counter in supermarkets. An ideal partner for chicken as well as veal, it can also be used in stuffings for pasta, or as an appetizer, served in paper-thin slices with fresh melon or figs.

3 Stuff one-quarter of cheese mixture into pocket in each chop. Rub chops with oil; sprinkle with salt and ¼ teaspoon pepper. Place chops on rack in broiling pan.

4 Place pan in broiler at closest position to heat source. Broil, turning once, 10 to 12 minutes for medium-rare. Serve with peppers and broiled tomatoes, if you like.

EACH SERVING: ABOUT 355 CALORIES, 37g PROTEIN, 1g CARBOHYDRATE, 22g TOTAL FAT (10g SATURATED), 151mg CHOLESTEROL, 470mg SODIUM

ZESTY VEAL CHOPS

Prep: 5 minutes   *Broil:* 10 to 13 minutes
Makes 4 main-dish servings

2 tablespoons capers, drained
  and chopped
1 tablespoon chopped fresh
  parsley
1 tablespoon Dijon mustard
1 tablespoon olive oil

4 veal loin or rib chops, each
  ¾ inch thick (about
  8 ounces each)
Parsley sprigs for garnish
Salad greens (optional)

◆ Preheat broiler. In small bowl, mix capers, chopped parsley, mustard, and oil.

◆ Place veal chops on rack in broiling pan. Place pan in broiler at closest position to heat source; broil veal chops 5 minutes. Turn veal chops; spoon caper mixture evenly over chops. Broil 5 to 8 minutes longer for medium, or until desired doneness. Place veal chops on 4 plates; garnish, and serve with salad greens, if you like.

Each serving: About 310 calories, 32g protein, 0g carbohydrate, 19g total fat (7g saturated), 130mg cholesterol, 375mg sodium

---

CAPERS

The flower buds of a shrub native to eastern Asia, capers are used only in their preserved form. Their firm texture and pungent taste make them ideal partners for smooth-textured or delicately flavored foods, such as veal. They are usually sold pickled in vinegar in jars, but can also be found layered in salt in Italian markets. In either case, you can rinse capers before using to remove excess salt. Capers keep well for months and are good in pasta sauces and pizza toppings, or with sautéed fish, lamb, beef, and poultry; they are also a classic ingredient in salad Niçoise and black butter sauce.

GINGERED VEAL CHOPS WITH SAUTÉED PEPPERS

Prep: 25 minutes   *Broil:* 10 to 12 minutes
Makes 4 main-dish servings

⅓ cup dry sherry
3 tablespoons soy sauce
2 tablespoons grated, peeled
  fresh ginger
4 veal rib chops, each
  ¾ inch thick (about
  8 ounces each)

1 tablespoon olive oil
4 medium yellow peppers, cut
  into 1-inch strips
½ teaspoon sugar
1 bunch arugula

◆ Preheat broiler. In 13" by 9" metal baking pan, mix sherry, soy sauce, and ginger. Add veal chops, turning to coat thoroughly with mixture.

◆ In 12-inch skillet, heat oil over high heat; add peppers and sugar and cook, stirring occasionally, 10 minutes, or until peppers are tender and lightly browned.

◆ Meanwhile, place baking pan with veal chops and sherry mixture in broiler at closest position to heat source; broil chops, turning once, 10 to 12 minutes for medium, or until desired doneness.

◆ To serve, line large platter with arugula leaves; spoon peppers evenly on top. Tuck veal chops into peppers; pour pan juices over chops and serve.

Each serving: About 345 calories, 36g protein, 16g carbohydrate, 13g total fat (3g saturated), 145mg cholesterol, 905mg sodium

BROILED SHOULDER CHOPS WITH SAGE

Prep: 5 minutes   *Broil:* 8 minutes
Makes 2 main-dish servings

2 veal shoulder blade chops,
  each ½ inch thick (12 to
  14 ounces each)
1 tablespoon chopped fresh
  sage

2 teaspoons olive oil
½ teaspoon salt
¼ teaspoon ground black
  pepper
Lemon wedges (optional)

◆ Preheat broiler. Pat veal chops dry with paper towels. In cup, mix chopped fresh sage, olive oil, salt, and pepper. Use to rub over chops.

◆ Place chops on rack in broiling pan. Place pan in broiler at closest position to heat source. Broil veal chops, turning once, 8 minutes for medium, or until desired doneness. Serve with lemon wedges, if you like.

Each serving: About 295 calories, 40g protein, 0g carbohydrate, 13g total fat (4g saturated), 168mg cholesterol, 675mg sodium

PORK

Versatile pork benefits from a vast range of seasonings and cooking methods. Today's pork is bred leaner than it used to be; to guarantee tenderness, cook it only to 160°F. It will have just a hint of pink in the center (with a deeper pink color near the bone) but the juices will be clear.

BUYING PORK

• Look for fresh pork that's pinkish-white to grayish-pink (leg and shoulder cuts tend to be darker than loin cuts). The flesh should be firm to the touch and moist but not wet. Fat marbling should be minimal; any fat should be white, firm, and well trimmed.
• Cured and smoked pork products are darker in color due to the curing process. They should be rosy pink.
• The quality of pork is so consistent that, unlike other meats, cuts are not graded according to their quality. Simply check the label for the cut you need, remembering that meat from the loin, especially the tenderloin, or leg is the leanest.

KNOW YOUR PORK PRODUCTS

Fresh Fresh pork has not been salted, brined, smoked, or cured in any way. Fresh ham is uncured leg of pork.
Cured Pork is cured by salting with a dry rub or brine; once cured, it can be smoked for added flavor. Curing and smoking were originally developed as methods of preserving pork, enabling it to be stored at room temperature; today they're mainly intended for flavor.
Smoked Smoking takes place after curing and is generally done as a separate process to impart flavor to the pork. Wrap and seal smoked products before storing.
Ham Cut from the hind leg of pork, ham is usually cured and then smoked. Some hams are aged several months for even more flavor. Country hams are heavily salted and require soaking before they are cooked. Italian prosciutto is cured, dried ham that is not smoked.
Bacon Pork belly is used to make bacon, which is cured and sometimes smoked. Smoked bacon has deeper pink meat and yellower fat than unsmoked bacon. Italian pancetta is a type of unsmoked bacon that is often sold rolled in a jelly-roll shape, then sliced.
Salt pork Like bacon, salt pork is cut from pork belly. It is salt-cured but not smoked, and is fattier than regular bacon.
Canadian bacon Closer in flavor and texture to ham than to bacon, Canadian bacon is cut from the loin rather than the belly, and is therefore much leaner than regular bacon.

CHOOSING THE RIGHT CUT

Pork doesn't vary as much in tenderness as beef, so many cuts are equally suitable for dry-heat and moist-heat cooking methods. If broiling, grilling, or roasting pork, take care not to overcook it, or it will be tough and dry.

For broiling, grilling, or panfrying A wide range of lean pork cuts lend themselves to these quick cooking methods.
Best bets Tenderloin (below left), rib chops (below right), loin chops, sirloin chops, sirloin cutlets, and blade chops are ideal. Spareribs, back ribs, and country-style ribs are good for broiling and grilling (after precooking).

Lean cuts like tenderloin are best for quick cooking methods

Chops for broiling or grilling should be at least ¾ inch thick

For braising or stewing Many cuts of pork stand up well to long, slow cooking in liquid. Well-marbled cuts are especially succulent when braised or stewed. Avoid using very lean cuts, such as tenderloin; they'll toughen from long cooking.
Best bets Rib chops, loin chops, sirloin, loin blade chops (below right), sirloin cutlets, pork or ham hocks, spareribs, back ribs, country-style ribs. Pork cubes for stew (below left) are cut from the shoulder or leg.

Moist-heat cooking makes less-lean cuts especially tender

Trim excess fat before cooking

For roasting Use tender cuts for roasting. Cuts from the loin (the back of the pig from shoulder to hip) are especially suitable. Good cuts also come from the leg and shoulder.
Best bets Rib crown roast, shoulder arm roast, arm picnic roast, leg (bone-in, i.e., fresh ham, and boneless), whole tenderloin, bone-in loin (below), boneless loin, spareribs, country-style ribs.

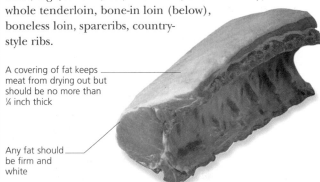

A covering of fat keeps meat from drying out but should be no more than ¼ inch thick

Any fat should be firm and white

TESTING PORK FOR DONENESS

Good news for pork lovers The rule used to be to cook pork until it was well done – and often overdone – to eliminate the risk of trichinosis, a disease caused by parasitic worms that are killed at 138°F. But modern production methods have virtually eradicated trichinosis. According to the USDA, today's fresh pork will be juicy and succulent – and perfectly safe to eat – if it's cooked to an internal temperature of 160°F (170°F for very large cuts, such as fresh ham).

Medium or well-done? Pork cooked to medium (160°F) has a pink-tinged center and is slightly deeper pink near any bone. Well-done pork (170°F) is less pink. Avoid cooking pork to a higher internal temperature, or the meat will be dry and tough. Ground pork should be cooked until no pink remains.

The right test To check pork chops and other small cuts for doneness, make a tiny slit near the center with a sharp knife. The meat is done if the juices run clear. To test roasts, use a meat thermometer inserted in the thickest part but without touching any bone (which would throw off the reading). Remove roast from the oven when the temperature reaches 5 degrees below the desired doneness, then let it stand 10 to 15 minutes. The meat will continue to cook as it stands.

ROASTING TIMES (OVEN TEMPERATURE 350°F)

CUT AND WEIGHT Start with meat at refrigerator temperature. **Remove roast from oven when it reaches 5° to 10°F below desired doneness; temperature will continue to rise as roast stands.**			MEAT THERMOMETER READING	APPROXIMATE COOKING TIME (MINUTES PER LB)
Fresh pork	Crown roast	6–10 lbs	160°F	20
	Center loin roast (with bone)	3–5 lbs	160°F	20
	Boneless top loin roast	2–4 lbs	160°F	20
	Whole leg (fresh ham)	12 lbs	160°–170°F	25–30
	Leg half, shank or butt portion	3–4 lbs	160°–170°F	40
	Boston butt	3–6 lbs	160°–170°F	45
	Tenderloin (roast at 425°–450°F)	½–1½ lb	160°F	25–35 total
Smoked, cook before eating	Whole ham	14–16 lbs	160°F	15–18
Smoked fully cooked pork (heat at 325°F)	Whole ham	14–16 lbs	130°–140°F	1–1¾ hours total
	Half ham	6–8 lbs	130°–140°F	1 hour total

REHEATING HAMS

Smoked hams labeled "fully cooked" can be bone-in or boneless, partially boned, boiled, canned, or picnic varieties. While such hams can be eaten as is, additional heating will improve their flavor and texture. For the best eating, and for thoroughly heated meat, bake ham until a meat thermometer inserted in the center registers 130° to 140°F. (Smoked hams that are not marked "fully cooked" must be cooked to an internal temperature of 160°F.)

CARVING A WHOLE HAM

1 Place cooked ham on cutting board. Using a carving fork to steady ham, cut a few slices from thin side of ham. Turn ham over onto cut surface; this will form a level base, making carving easier.

2 Cut out a small wedge of meat at shank end. Cut even slices along ham right to bone.

3 Use a sawing action to work blade under slices to release them from bone. Transfer to warm platter.

ROAST PORK

When it's party time, roast pork stars – as fresh ham for a buffet, or a magnificent loin (from crown roast to cabbage-clad) for sit-down fare. In a hurry? Roast a tenderloin with island spices. Be sure to use the flavorful pan drippings in the sauce. Today's pork tends to be quite lean, so to keep it moist and juicy; do not overcook it.

GOLDEN CROWN ROAST OF PORK

◆◆◆◆◆◆◆◆◆◆◆◆◆◆◆◆◆◆◆◆◆◆◆◆◆◆◆

Prep: 25 minutes plus standing   Roast: 3 hours
Makes 14 main-dish servings

1 pork rib crown roast (7 pounds), about 16 ribs
1 teaspoon dried thyme
½ teaspoon ground black pepper
Salt
Cranberry Corn-Bread Stuffing (see page 230)

3 tablespoons all-purpose flour
Sautéed cherry tomatoes and zucchini (optional)
Thyme sprigs and cranberries for garnish

1 Preheat oven to 325°F. Pat roast dry with paper towels. In cup, mix dried thyme, pepper, and 1 teaspoon salt. Use to rub inside and outside of roast. Place roast, rib-ends down, in large roasting pan. Roast 2 hours.

2 Meanwhile, prepare Cranberry Corn-Bread Stuffing. When pork has roasted 2 hours, remove from oven and turn rib-ends up. With large spoon, fill cavity of pork roast with stuffing.

3 Insert meat thermometer into thickest part of meat, being careful that pointed end does not touch bone. Roast pork 1 hour longer, or until thermometer reaches 155°F (internal temperature of meat will rise to 160°F upon standing). If stuffing browns too quickly, cover with foil.

4 Transfer roast to warm large platter. Let stand 15 minutes; keep warm. Meanwhile, prepare gravy: Pour pan drippings into 2-cup measuring cup; let stand a few seconds, until fat separates from meat juices.

5 Spoon 3 tablespoons fat from drippings into 2-quart saucepan; skim and discard remaining fat. Add *1 cup water* to roasting pan; stir over medium heat until brown bits are loosened.

6 Add liquid in roasting pan to meat juices in cup with enough *water* to equal 2 cups. Into fat in saucepan, stir flour and ½ teaspoon salt over medium heat; cook 1 minute. Gradually stir in meat-juice mixture and cook, stirring constantly, until gravy boils and thickens. Pour into gravy boat. Garnish roast; serve with stuffing and gravy, and cherry tomatoes and zucchini, if you like.

EACH SERVING: ABOUT 625 CALORIES, 38g PROTEIN, 38g CARBOHYDRATE, 35g TOTAL FAT (12g SATURATED), 84mg CHOLESTEROL, 730mg SODIUM

PORK ROAST WITH CARAWAY SEEDS

Prep: 15 minutes plus standing   Roast: 2 hours 30 minutes
Makes 10 main-dish servings

1 pork loin roast (6 pounds)
2 tablespoons caraway seeds, crushed
1 tablespoon vegetable oil
1 teaspoon salt
1 teaspoon dry mustard
½ teaspoon dried thyme
½ teaspoon dried oregano
3 tablespoons all-purpose flour
1 beef-flavor bouillon cube or envelope

◆ Preheat oven to 325°F. Pat pork dry with paper towels. In cup, mix caraway seeds with next 5 ingredients; use to rub over fat side of pork.

◆ Place roast, fat-side up, in 17" by 11½" roasting pan. Insert meat thermometer into center of roast, being careful that pointed end does not touch bone. Roast pork about 2½ hours, or until thermometer reaches 155°F (internal temperature of meat will rise to 160°F upon standing).

◆ Transfer roast to warm large platter. Let stand 15 minutes for easier carving; keep warm.

◆ Meanwhile, prepare gravy: Pour pan drippings through sieve into 4-cup measuring cup; let stand a few seconds, until fat separates from meat juices. Spoon 2 tablespoons fat from drippings into roasting pan; skim and discard any remaining fat. Add *water* to meat juices in cup to equal 2½ cups.

◆ Into fat in roasting pan, stir flour until blended over low heat. Gradually stir in meat-juice mixture and bouillon; stir until brown bits are loosened. Cook, stirring constantly, until gravy thickens and boils. Serve roast with gravy.

Each serving: About 375 calories, 45g protein, 2g carbohydrate, 20g total fat (6g saturated), 96mg cholesterol, 405mg sodium

CRANBERRY CORN-BREAD STUFFING

Chop 2 large celery stalks and 1 large onion. In 12-inch skillet, melt ½ cup margarine or butter over medium heat; add celery and onion; cook until tender. Meanwhile, in food processor with knife blade attached, coarsely chop 1 package (12 ounces) cranberries (3 cups) with ½ cup sugar. Remove skillet from heat; add 1 package (16 ounces) corn-bread stuffing, cranberry mixture, and 2½ cups water; mix lightly. Use to stuff Golden Crown Roast of Pork (see page 229); bake any leftover stuffing in small covered casserole with pork during last 40 minutes of roasting. Makes 14 accompaniment servings.

Each serving: About 230 calories, 4g protein, 37g carbohydrate, 8g total fat (2g saturated), 0mg cholesterol, 500mg sodium

CABBAGE-WRAPPED PORK ROAST

Prep: 30 minutes plus standing   Roast: 1 hour
Makes 10 main-dish servings

6 large outer leaves green cabbage
1 bunch green onions
1 boneless pork loin roast (3 pounds)
1 tablespoon minced fresh thyme or ½ teaspoon dried thyme
1 teaspoon salt
½ teaspoon ground black pepper
1 envelope chicken-flavor bouillon
2 teaspoons cornstarch

◆ In 5-quart Dutch oven or saucepot, heat *3 quarts water* to boiling over high heat. Meanwhile, trim tough ribs from cabbage leaves. Cut off root ends of green onions; separate into leaves. Add cabbage to boiling water and cook 3 to 5 minutes until wilted. With slotted spoon, transfer to colander to drain. Add green onions to boiling water; blanch 10 seconds, or until wilted. Drain green onions; pat dry with paper towels.

◆ Preheat oven to 350°F. Pat pork dry with paper towels. In cup, mix thyme, salt, and pepper. Use to rub over pork.

◆ Lay cabbage leaves flat, overlapping them. Place seasoned pork roast on cabbage; be sure leaves extend beyond roast on both ends. Lift leaves up over roast to enclose meat completely.

◆ To secure cabbage leaves, tie 2 blanched green onions together (they should be long enough to wrap around width of roast); slip onions underneath wrapped roast, pull ends up, and tie in a knot. Repeat with remaining onions, tying at 1-inch intervals.

◆ Place pork roast in 14" by 10" roasting pan. Insert meat thermometer into center of roast. In 2-cup measuring cup, mix bouillon with *2 cups hot water*; pour bouillon mixture into roasting pan. Roast 1 hour, or until meat thermometer reaches 155°F, basting occasionally with pan juices (internal temperature will rise to 160°F upon standing).

◆ Transfer pork to warm large platter. Let stand 15 minutes; keep warm. In cup, mix cornstarch with *2 tablespoons water*. Stir cornstarch mixture into drippings in roasting pan and heat to boiling over high heat; boil, stirring constantly, 1 minute. Spoon over pork.

Each serving: About 215 calories, 22g protein, 3g carbohydrate, 12g total fat (4g saturated), 66mg cholesterol, 355mg sodium

PORK ROAST WITH FRESH SAGE

Prep: 15 minutes plus standing   *Roast:* 2 hours to 2 hours 15 minutes
Makes 8 main-dish servings

2 garlic cloves, minced
¼ cup chopped fresh parsley
2 tablespoons chopped fresh sage
½ teaspoon dried thyme
1 teaspoon salt
½ teaspoon ground black pepper
1 pork loin roast (4 pounds)
⅓ cup dry white wine
⅔ cup chicken broth

◆ Preheat oven to 350°F. With flat side of chef's knife, on cutting board, mash garlic with parsley, sage, thyme, salt, and pepper to make a thick paste.

◆ Pat pork dry with paper towels. Place pork in small roasting pan; rub herb paste over pork. Insert meat thermometer into thickest part of roast, being careful that pointed end does not touch bone. Roast 2 to 2¼ hours, until thermometer reaches 155°F (internal temperature of meat will rise to 160°F upon standing).

◆ Transfer roast to warm large platter. Let stand 15 minutes for easier carving; keep warm. Add wine to roasting pan and heat to boiling over high heat; stir until brown bits are loosened. Add broth and heat to boiling. Skim and discard fat from pan juices. Serve roast with pan juices.

Each serving: About 305 calories, 37g protein, 1g carbohydrate, 15g total fat (5g saturated), 81mg cholesterol, 445mg sodium

FRESH HAM WITH TWO SAUCES

Prep: 30 minutes plus standing   *Roast:* 5 hours 30 minutes
Makes 30 main-dish servings

1 whole pork leg (15 pounds) (fresh ham)
2 teaspoons dried sage
2 teaspoons salt
1 teaspoon ground black pepper
1 tablespoon vegetable oil
3 green onions, thinly sliced
½ cup sour cream
⅓ cup Dijon mustard with seeds
⅓ cup milk
Mushroom Pan Gravy (see right)

◆ Preheat oven to 325°F. Remove skin and trim excess fat from pork leg, leaving thin covering of fat. Place pork, fat-side up, on rack in large roasting pan. Score fat on top of pork leg in shallow parallel lines. In cup, mix sage, salt, and pepper; use to rub over pork.

◆ Insert meat thermometer into center of thickest part of pork, being careful that pointed end does not touch bone. Roast pork about 5½ hours, or until meat thermometer reaches 160° to 170°F. If pork begins to brown too quickly, cover loosely with tent of foil. Pork near bone will be slightly pink.

◆ Meanwhile, prepare mustard sauce: In 2-quart saucepan, heat oil over medium-high heat; add green onions and cook 5 minutes, or until tender and lightly browned. Remove from heat. Stir in sour cream, mustard, and milk until blended. Refrigerate until ready to serve.

◆ When ham is done, transfer to warm large platter. Let stand 30 minutes; keep warm. Prepare Mushroom Pan Gravy. Thinly slice ham; serve with gravy and mustard sauce.

Each serving: About 385 calories, 55g protein, 1g carbohydrate, 16g total fat (6g saturated), 131mg cholesterol, 360mg sodium

MUSHROOM PAN GRAVY

◆◆◆◆◆◆◆◆◆◆◆◆◆

Pan drippings from Fresh Ham with Two Sauces (see left)
1 pound mushrooms, sliced
3 tablespoons all-purpose flour
Chicken broth (optional)

1 Remove rack from ham roasting pan; pour drippings into 4-cup measuring cup (set pan aside). Let drippings stand a few seconds until fat separates from meat juices; spoon 2 tablespoons fat into 12-inch skillet. Skim and discard remaining fat.

2 In fat in skillet, cook mushrooms over high heat until browned. Reduce heat to medium. Stir in flour; cook until lightly browned. Add *water* or chicken broth to juices in cup to equal 1¾ cups. Add about ½ cup juice mixture to roasting pan; stir over high heat until brown bits are loosened.

3 Stir liquid from roasting pan and remaining meat-juice mixture into mushrooms. Cook, stirring, over high heat, until gravy boils and thickens. Makes about 3 cups.

Each 2 tablespoons: About 20 calories, 1g protein, 2g carbohydrate, 1g total fat (0g saturated), 2mg cholesterol, 80mg sodium

SPICE-ROASTED PORK

Prep: 10 minutes plus standing
Roast: 1 hour to 1 hour 15 minutes
Makes 6 main-dish servings

1 boneless pork loin roast (2 pounds)
1 teaspoon salt
¾ teaspoon dried thyme
½ teaspoon ground cinnamon
½ teaspoon ground black pepper
⅛ teaspoon ground nutmeg
⅛ teaspoon ground cloves
⅓ cup dry white wine
⅔ cup chicken broth
Thyme sprigs for garnish
Peas and applesauce (optional)

◆ Preheat oven to 350°F. Pat pork dry with paper towels. In cup, mix salt and next 5 ingredients; use to rub over pork.

◆ Place pork in small roasting pan; insert meat thermometer into thickest part of pork. Roast 1 to 1¼ hours, or until thermometer reaches 155°F (internal temperature will rise to 160°F upon standing). Transfer to platter. Let stand 10 minutes; keep warm.

◆ Meanwhile, add wine to roasting pan. Heat to boiling over high heat; stir until brown bits are loosened. Add broth; heat to boiling. Boil 2 minutes. Skim fat from pan juices. Slice pork thin; garnish and serve with peas and applesauce, if you like, and pan juices.

**Each serving: About 235 calories,
24g protein, 1g carbohydrate, 13g total
fat (5g saturated) 75mg cholesterol,
525mg sodium**

JAMAICAN ROAST PORK TENDERLOINS

Prep: 10 minutes plus standing
Roast: 30 to 35 minutes
Makes 6 main-dish servings

2 pork tenderloins (12 ounces each)
1 garlic clove, minced
1 tablespoon brown sugar
1 teaspoon grated lime peel
½ teaspoon ground ginger
½ teaspoon salt
¼ teaspoon ground black pepper
⅛ teaspoon ground nutmeg
⅛ teaspoon ground allspice
⅛ teaspoon ground red pepper (cayenne)
2 teaspoons plus 2 tablespoons dark rum
1¼ cups chicken broth

◆ Preheat oven to 450°F. Pat pork dry with paper towels. Place pork in small roasting pan, tucking thin ends under for even thickness.

◆ In cup, mix garlic, brown sugar, lime peel, ginger, salt, black pepper, nutmeg, allspice, ground red pepper, and 2 teaspoons rum. Use to rub over pork. Insert meat thermometer into thickest part of pork. Pour ¼ cup chicken broth in pan around pork.

◆ Roast pork 30 to 35 minutes, or until thermometer reaches 155°F (internal temperature of meat will rise to 160°F upon standing), adding ¼ cup more broth to roasting pan after 10 and then after 20 minutes to prevent juices in pan from burning.

◆ Transfer pork to platter. Let stand 10 minutes; keep warm. Add remaining 2 tablespoons rum to roasting pan and heat to boiling over high heat; stir until brown bits are loosened. Boil 1 minute. Add remaining ½ cup broth to pan; heat to boiling. Slice pork thin and serve with pan juices.

**Each serving: About 170 calories,
24g protein, 3g carbohydrate, 5g total fat
(2g saturated), 70mg cholesterol,
445mg sodium**

ORANGE ROAST PORK WITH CUMIN

Prep: 15 minutes plus standing
Roast: 1 hour to 1 hour 15 minutes
Makes 6 main-dish servings

1 boneless pork loin roast (2 pounds)
1 garlic clove, minced
2 teaspoons grated orange peel
1 teaspoon salt
¾ teaspoon ground cumin
½ teaspoon dried oregano
½ teaspoon dried thyme
¼ teaspoon ground red pepper (cayenne)
1 medium onion, finely chopped
2 tablespoons cider vinegar
¾ cup chicken broth

◆ Preheat oven to 350°F. Pat pork dry with paper towels. With small knife, cut several ½-inch-deep slits in pork.

◆ In cup, mix garlic, orange peel, salt, cumin, oregano, thyme, and ground red pepper. Use to rub over pork, pressing into crevices and slits.

◆ Spread chopped onion in 11" by 7" roasting pan; place pork roast on top. Insert meat thermometer into thickest part of pork.

◆ Roast pork 1 to 1¼ hours, or until thermometer reaches 155°F (internal temperature of meat will rise to 160°F upon standing).

◆ Transfer pork to platter. Let stand 10 minutes; keep warm. Skim and discard fat from roasting pan. Add vinegar to pan and heat to boiling over high heat; stir until brown bits are loosened. Boil 1 minute.

◆ Add chicken broth to pan and heat to boiling; boil 3 minutes. Slice pork thin and serve with pan juices.

**Each serving: About 240 calories,
25mg protein, 4g carbohydrate, 13g total
fat (5g saturated), 76mg cholesterol,
535mg sodium**

PORK CASSEROLES AND STEWS

These hearty favorites have bold, exciting flavors that capture the tastes of the Southwest, Caribbean, or Eastern Europe. For best results, cut the pork into equal-sized cubes for even cooking, then brown them in batches to seal in the juices before finishing them in the oven or on top of the stove. Laden with fragrant spices such as chili powder, cumin, paprika, and allspice, pork shoulder makes an especially tender, succulent stew. The chili versions are even better the next day. Warm corn bread, noodles, or rice all make great accompaniments to soak up the delicious liquid.

PORK AND BLACK BEAN CHILI

◆◆◆◆◆◆◆◆◆◆◆◆◆◆◆◆◆◆◆◆◆◆◆◆◆

Prep: 50 minutes plus standing   Cook: 1 hour 45 minutes
Makes 10 main-dish servings

1 package (16 ounces) dry black beans
1½ pounds boneless pork shoulder blade roast (fresh pork butt)
3 tablespoons vegetable oil
1 large red pepper, cut into ½-inch pieces
1 large green pepper, cut into ½-inch pieces

1 medium onion, diced
⅓ cup chili powder
1 can (28 ounces) tomatoes in puree
1¾ teaspoons salt
Hot-pepper sauce
Corn bread (optional)

1 Rinse beans with cold running water; discard any shriveled beans. In 4-quart saucepan, heat beans and *6 cups water* to boiling over high heat; boil 3 minutes. Remove saucepan from heat; cover and let stand 1 hour. Drain and rinse beans. Cut pork into ½-inch cubes. Pat dry with paper towels.

2 Preheat oven to 375°F. In 5-quart Dutch oven, heat oil over medium heat; add pork, half at a time, and cook, stirring often, until browned. Transfer to bowl.

3 To drippings in Dutch oven, add peppers and onion; cook, stirring occasionally, until tender-crisp. Stir in chili powder; cook, stirring, 2 minutes.

4 Add tomatoes with their puree, stirring and breaking up tomatoes with back of spoon. Stir in salt, black beans, browned pork, and *4 cups water*. Heat to boiling over high heat. Cover and bake, stirring occasionally, about 1¾ hours, until pork is cooked through and beans are tender. Stir in hot-pepper sauce to taste. Serve chili in bowls, with corn bread, if you like.

HOT-PEPPER SAUCE

Hot-pepper sauce is made by steeping chiles in vinegar. This fiery condiment adds a kick to our pork and black bean chili, as well as other soups, stews, omelets, and marinades. The sauce is surprisingly strong, so add only a few drops and taste the dish to check the degree of heat. Refrigerate after opening.

EACH SERVING: ABOUT 315 CALORIES, 26g PROTEIN, 36g CARBOHYDRATE, 16g TOTAL FAT (5g SATURATED), 38mg CHOLESTEROL, 735mg SODIUM

ADOBO-STYLE CHILI

Prep: 15 minutes   *Cook:* 2 hours 30 minutes
Makes 6 main-dish servings

2 pounds boneless pork shoulder, cut into 2-inch chunks	¼ teaspoon ground cinnamon
2 teaspoons vegetable oil	¼ teaspoon ground red pepper (cayenne)
2 medium onions, finely chopped	⅛ teaspoon ground cloves
4 garlic cloves, minced	1 can (28 ounces) tomatoes
3 tablespoons chili powder	¼ cup cider vinegar
1 tablespoon ground cumin	¾ teaspoon salt
	½ teaspoon dried oregano
	1 bay leaf

◆ Pat pork dry with paper towels. In 5-quart Dutch oven, heat 1 teaspoon oil over medium-high heat. Add half of pork and cook until browned all over. Transfer to plate and repeat with remaining 1 teaspoon oil and remaining pork.

◆ Add onions to drippings in Dutch oven; cook 5 minutes over medium heat. Stir in garlic and next 5 ingredients; cook 1 minute. Add tomatoes with their juice, breaking up with spoon, vinegar, salt, oregano, bay leaf, and pork. Heat to boiling over high heat. Reduce heat to low; cover and simmer 2 hours. Discard bay leaf. Skim fat before serving.

Each serving: About 445 calories, 40g protein, 14g carbohydrate, 26g total fat (9g saturated), 96mg cholesterol, 630mg sodium

HUNGARIAN PORK GOULASH

Prep: 20 minutes   *Bake:* 1 hour 30 minutes
Makes 6 main-dish servings

2 tablespoons vegetable oil	1 can (14½ ounces) diced tomatoes
2 large onions, chopped	1 can (13¾ to 14½ ounces) beef broth
1 garlic clove, minced	¼ teaspoon ground black pepper
¼ cup paprika	1 container (8 ounces) light sour cream
2 pounds boneless pork shoulder blade roast (fresh pork butt), cut into 1½-inch chunks	Cooked egg noodles (optional)
1 package (16 ounces) sauerkraut, rinsed, drained	

Preheat oven to 325°F. In 5-quart Dutch oven, heat oil over medium heat. Add onions; cook 10 minutes, or until tender. Add garlic; cook, stirring, 1 minute. Add paprika; cook 1 minute. Add pork, sauerkraut, tomatoes with their juice, broth, and pepper; heat to boiling over high heat. Cover and bake 1½ hours, or until pork is tender. Remove from oven; stir in sour cream. Heat through over medium heat (do not boil). Serve over noodles, if you like.

Each serving: About 520 calories, 42g protein, 17g carbohydrate, 31g total fat (9g saturated), 109mg cholesterol, 960mg sodium

CARIBBEAN PORK CASSEROLE

Prep: 40 minutes plus marinating   *Bake:* 45 minutes
Makes 6 main-dish servings

4 green onions	½ teaspoon ground allspice
2 pork tenderloins (about 12 ounces each), cut into 1-inch-thick slices	½ teaspoon ground red pepper (cayenne)
2 tablespoons minced, peeled fresh ginger	3 medium sweet potatoes (1½ pounds), peeled and cut into ½-inch-thick slices
2 tablespoons soy sauce	1 large red pepper, cut into bite-size pieces
2 tablespoons Worcestershire sauce	2 tablespoons vegetable oil
1 tablespoon chopped fresh thyme or ½ teaspoon dried thyme	1 can (15¼ to 16 ounces) pineapple chunks in their own juice

◆ Preheat oven to 425°F. Mince 2 green onions. Cut remaining green onions into 2-inch pieces. In large bowl, toss minced green onions with pork, ginger, soy sauce, Worcestershire, thyme, allspice, and ground red pepper. Cover pork and marinate 30 minutes.

◆ In shallow 6-quart casserole, toss sweet potatoes, red pepper and green-onion pieces, and 1 tablespoon oil. Bake, uncovered, 15 minutes.

◆ While vegetables are baking, in 10-inch skillet, heat remaining 1 tablespoon oil over medium-high heat; add half of pork, reserving any marinade, and cook until browned. Transfer pork to bowl; repeat with remaining pork.

◆ Pour pineapple chunks with their juice into drippings in skillet; stir until brown bits are loosened. Add pineapple mixture, pork, and reserved marinade to vegetables in casserole. Bake, uncovered, stirring occasionally, 30 minutes longer, or until pork and vegetables are tender.

Each serving: About 330 calories, 26g protein, 36g carbohydrate, 9g total fat (2g saturated), 65mg cholesterol, 450mg sodium

SKILLET-BRAISED PORK

Pork chops of all kinds will stay moist and juicy when braised in liquid in a tightly covered pan. Maintain a gentle simmer for tender chops.

SICILIAN STUFFED PORK CHOPS

◆◆◆◆◆◆◆◆◆◆◆◆

Prep: 30 minutes
Cook: 1 hour 10 minutes
Makes 4 main-dish servings

12 ounces Swiss chard
1 teaspoon plus 1 tablespoon olive oil
1 garlic clove, minced
¼ cup golden raisins
2 tablespoons pine nuts (pignoli), toasted and chopped
Salt
4 pork loin chops, each 1½ inches thick (about 10 ounces each)
¼ teaspoon ground black pepper
1 cup reduced-sodium chicken broth
⅓ cup dry white wine
Confetti Pasta (see below)

CONFETTI PASTA

Cook 1 cup orzo (rice-shaped pasta) as label directs; drain. In nonstick 10-inch skillet, heat 2 teaspoons olive oil over medium heat. Add 2 medium carrots, shredded, 1 zucchini (8 ounces), shredded, 1 garlic clove, minced, ¾ teaspoon salt, and ¼ teaspoon ground black pepper. Cook 5 minutes. Stir in orzo; heat through. Makes 4 accompaniment servings.

1 Finely slice Swiss chard. In 2-quart saucepan, heat Swiss chard and *1 inch water* to boiling over high heat; cover and cook 5 minutes. Drain, pressing hard to squeeze out excess liquid.

2 In same saucepan, heat 1 teaspoon oil over medium heat. Add garlic and cook 30 seconds. Remove from heat; stir in chard, raisins, pine nuts, and ¼ teaspoon salt.

3 Cut a pocket from rib side of each chop, inserting knife near bone. Slice parallel to surface, widening pocket as you go. Do not cut through to edge.

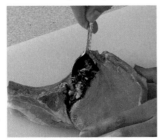

4 Fill pockets with chard stuffing; gently press closed. Pat chops dry with paper towels. Sprinkle with pepper and ¼ teaspoon salt. In 12-inch skillet, heat remaining 1 tablespoon oil over medium-high heat.

5 Add chops to skillet; cook until browned on both sides. Add broth and wine; heat to boiling. Reduce heat to low; cover and simmer 1 hour, or until chops are tender. Prepare Confetti Pasta; keep warm.

6 Transfer chops to platter; keep warm. Increase heat to high; boil pan juices until reduced to ¾ cup. Skim fat from juices. Serve chops with juices poured over, accompanied by Confetti Pasta.

EACH SERVING: ABOUT 725 CALORIES, 60g PROTEIN, 47g CARBOHYDRATE, 31g TOTAL FAT (9g SATURATED), 113mg CHOLESTEROL, 955mg SODIUM

ORANGE PORK CHOPS

Prep: 5 minutes
Cook: 50 minutes to 1 hour 5 minutes
Makes 4 main-dish servings

4 pork loin chops, each ¾ inch thick
   (about 6 ounces each)
1 tablespoon vegetable oil
2 large onions, cut into ¼-inch-thick slices
¼ cup dry sherry
¼ cup soy sauce
¼ cup orange marmalade
Orange slices for garnish
Steamed green beans (optional)

◆ Pat pork chops dry with paper towels. In 12-inch skillet, heat oil over medium-high heat. Add pork chops and cook until lightly browned on both sides; transfer chops to plate as they brown.

◆ To drippings in skillet, add onions; cook, stirring frequently, until lightly browned. Return chops to skillet. Stir in sherry, soy sauce, and marmalade; heat to boiling over high heat.

◆ Reduce heat to low; cover skillet and simmer 30 to 45 minutes, or until chops are tender. Remove cover; increase heat to medium-high and cook 3 minutes longer, or until liquid in skillet is almost evaporated.

◆ To serve, place chops on 4 plates. Garnish with orange slices. Serve with green beans, if you like.

Each serving: About 390 calories, 31g protein, 25g carbohydrate, 16g total fat (5g saturated), 64mg cholesterol, 1100mg sodium

PORK CHOPS WITH APPLES AND CREAM

Prep: 10 minutes
Cook: 1 hour to 1 hour 15 minutes
Makes 4 main-dish servings

4 pork loin chops, each ¾ inch thick
   (about 6 ounces each)
½ teaspoon salt
¼ teaspoon ground black pepper
2 teaspoons vegetable oil
1 small onion, finely chopped
¼ cup Calvados or applejack brandy
1 cup chicken broth
⅛ teaspoon dried thyme
3 medium Golden Delicious apples,
   peeled, cored, and each cut into
   quarters
½ cup heavy or whipping cream
Chopped fresh parsley for garnish

◆ Pat pork chops dry with paper towels. Sprinkle with salt and pepper.

◆ In 12-inch skillet, heat oil over medium-high heat. Add pork chops and cook until lightly browned on both sides. Transfer chops to plate as they brown.

◆ To drippings in skillet, add onion and cook over medium heat 3 minutes, or until tender. Add Calvados and cook until liquid is almost evaporated.

◆ Return chops to skillet. Add broth, thyme, and apples; heat to boiling over high heat. Reduce heat to low; cover skillet and simmer 30 to 45 minutes, until chops are tender.

◆ Transfer chops and apples to warm platter; keep warm. Increase heat under skillet to high; boil, uncovered, 5 minutes, or until liquid is reduced to ½ cup. Add cream; heat to boiling. Boil 3 minutes.

◆ To serve, spoon cream sauce over pork chops. Sprinkle with parsley.

Each serving: About 485 calories, 31g protein, 23g carbohydrate, 27g total fat (12g saturated), 110mg cholesterol, 610mg sodium

PORK CHOPS WITH BROCCOLI RABE

Prep: 5 minutes
Cook: 30 minutes
Makes 4 main-dish servings

2 tablespoons olive oil
1 garlic clove, cut in half
4 pork loin blade, rib, loin, or sirloin
   chops, each ½ inch thick (about
   5 ounces each)
⅓ cup dry vermouth or chicken broth
1 teaspoon sugar
¼ teaspoon ground black pepper
Salt
2 bunches broccoli rabe (about
   2 pounds), tough stems removed

◆ In 8-quart Dutch oven, heat *6 quarts water* to boiling over high heat. Meanwhile, in 12-inch skillet, heat 1 tablespoon oil over medium heat; add garlic and cook until lightly browned. With slotted spoon, remove garlic from skillet and discard.

◆ Pat pork chops dry with paper towels. To oil in skillet, add pork chops and cook over medium-high heat until well browned on both sides.

◆ Add vermouth, sugar, pepper, and ½ teaspoon salt to chops in skillet. Reduce heat to low; cover and simmer 20 minutes, or until pork chops are tender, turning chops once.

◆ Meanwhile, add broccoli rabe and 1 tablespoon salt to boiling water in Dutch oven. Return to boiling; boil 2 minutes. Drain thoroughly.

◆ In same Dutch oven, heat remaining 1 tablespoon oil over high heat. Add broccoli rabe and ¼ teaspoon salt and cook, stirring, until well coated. Set aside.

◆ When pork chops are done, add broccoli rabe to skillet; cover and cook until heated through.

Each serving: About 335 calories, 31g protein, 10g carbohydrate, 18g total fat (5g saturated), 54mg cholesterol, 765mg sodium

Panfried pork

Panfried pork chops offer their best flavor when simply prepared with herbs, spices, or a crispy coating. The following recipes run the gamut, from an Italian-style dish with ham and melted Swiss cheese to a spirited Southwestern variation using black beans and tomatoes, and served with a refreshing corn salad. To avoid tough meat, it's essential not to overcook the chops. To test for doneness without using a meat thermometer, make a small cut in the thickest part of the meat or near the bone: The inside should have just lost its pink color.

BONELESS PORK CHOPS WITH SAUTÉED APPLES

◆◆◆◆◆◆◆◆◆◆◆◆◆◆◆◆◆◆◆◆◆◆◆◆◆◆◆◆

Prep: 10 minutes   Cook: 25 minutes
Makes 4 main-dish servings

4 teaspoons vegetable oil
1 medium red onion, thinly sliced
4 boneless pork loin chops, each 1¼ inches thick (about 8 ounces each)
Salt
½ teaspoon dried thyme
¼ teaspoon coarsely ground black pepper

2 medium Golden Delicious apples, unpeeled, cored and cut into ¼-inch-thick wedges
1 tablespoon sugar
½ cup apple juice or apple cider
1 teaspoon cornstarch
Cooked pasta or mashed potatoes (optional)

1 In nonstick 12-inch skillet, heat 2 teaspoons oil over medium heat. Add onion; cook until tender. Transfer to small bowl.

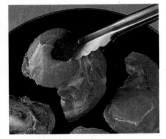

2 Pat chops dry with paper towels. In same skillet, cook chops 5 minutes over medium-high heat, or until underside is browned.

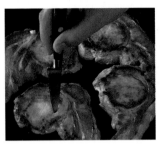

3 Sprinkle chops with ½ teaspoon salt. Turn chops; sprinkle with thyme, pepper, and ½ teaspoon salt. Cook 3 to 5 minutes longer, until pork just loses its pink color throughout.

4 Transfer chops to 4 warm plates; keep warm. In same skillet, heat remaining 2 teaspoons oil. Add apples. Sprinkle with sugar; cook until browned. Transfer to plates with chops.

5 In small bowl, mix apple juice and cornstarch. Stir apple-juice mixture and onion into skillet; heat to boiling over high heat, stirring. Boil 1 minute. Pour apple-juice mixture over pork chops and apple wedges. Serve with pasta or mashed potatoes, if you like.

EACH SERVING: ABOUT 510 CALORIES, 49g PROTEIN, 21g CARBOHYDRATE, 25g TOTAL FAT (8g SATURATED), 106mg CHOLESTEROL, 650mg SODIUM

PORK CHOPS ROMANO

Prep: 5 minutes   *Cook:* 15 minutes
Makes 6 main-dish servings

1 tablespoon all-purpose flour
1 tablespoon balsamic vinegar
6 boneless pork loin chops,
   each ¾ inch thick (about
   4 ounces each)
2 tablespoons vegetable oil

6 thin slices cooked ham
   (about 4 ounces)
6 thin slices Swiss cheese
   (about 4 ounces)
Steamed broccoli (optional)

◆ In measuring cup, with fork, mix flour, vinegar, and
¾ cup water until smooth; set aside.

◆ Place pork chops between 2 sheets of plastic wrap or
waxed paper. With rolling pin or meat mallet, pound each
chop into ¼-inch-thick cutlet; pat dry with paper towels.

◆ In 12-inch skillet, heat 1 tablespoon oil over medium-
high heat; add half of cutlets and cook about 4 minutes,
turning once, until browned on both sides and pork just
loses its pink color throughout. Transfer cutlets to plate.
Repeat with remaining 1 tablespoon oil and cutlets.

◆ Into drippings in skillet, stir vinegar mixture; cook over
medium heat, stirring constantly, until sauce thickens
slightly and boils.

◆ Top each cutlet with a slice of ham and cheese. Return
cutlets to skillet; cover and simmer until cheese just melts.
Serve with broccoli, if you like.

**Each serving: About 395 calories, 32g protein, 2g carbohydrate,
28g total fat (11g saturated), 77mg cholesterol, 320mg sodium**

BREADED PORK CHOPS

Prep: 10 minutes   *Cook:* 16 to 20 minutes
Makes 6 main-dish servings

½ cup plain dried bread
   crumbs
1 teaspoon salt
¼ teaspoon ground black
   pepper
2 tablespoons milk

1 large egg
6 pork loin, blade, rib, or
   sirloin chops, each ¾ inch
   thick (about 6 ounces each)
2 tablespoons vegetable oil

◆ On waxed paper, mix bread crumbs, salt, and pepper. In
pie plate, with fork, beat milk and egg. Dip pork chops in
milk mixture, then in bread-crumb mixture to coat.

◆ In 10-inch skillet, heat 1 tablespoon oil over medium-
high heat. Add half of chops; cook 8 to 10 minutes, turning
once, until golden brown on both sides and pork just loses
its pink color throughout.

◆ Transfer chops to platter; keep warm. Repeat with
remaining chops, adding remaining 1 tablespoon oil to skillet.

**Each serving: About 325 calories, 31g protein, 7g carbohydrate,
19g total fat (6g saturated), 99mg cholesterol, 510mg sodium**

CHILI PORK CHOPS WITH
CORN SALAD

Prep: 15 minutes   *Cook:* 8 minutes
Makes 4 main-dish servings

1 medium tomato, seeded
   and cut into 1-inch chunks
1 can (15¼ to 16 ounces)
   whole-kernel corn, drained
1 can (15 to 19 ounces) black
   beans, rinsed and drained
1 tablespoon chopped fresh
   cilantro or parsley
1 tablespoon fresh lime juice

½ teaspoon sugar
1 tablespoon all-purpose flour
1 tablespoon chili powder
¼ teaspoon salt
4 small pork loin chops,
   each ½ inch thick (about
   5 ounces each)
1 tablespoon vegetable oil

◆ Prepare corn salad: In medium bowl, combine first
6 ingredients; set aside.

◆ On waxed paper, mix flour, chili powder, and salt. Pat
pork chops dry with paper towels. Coat chops with chili-
powder mixture.

◆ In nonstick 12-inch skillet, heat oil over medium-high
heat; add pork chops and cook about 8 minutes, until
golden brown on both sides and pork just loses its pink
color throughout. Serve pork with corn salad.

**Each serving: About 420 calories, 34g protein, 41g carbohydrate,
16g total fat (4g saturated), 54mg cholesterol, 960mg sodium**

GROUND PORK

Deliciously imbued with herbs and spices from fresh ginger to delicate dill, ground pork is juicy and flavorful. It is the basis for favorites from around the world, such as Chinese dumplings, stuffed cabbage, or classic French pâté.

1 Prepare filling: In 2-quart saucepan, heat cabbage and *1 inch boiling water* to boiling over high heat. Cook 1 minute; drain. Immediately rinse with cold running water until cool.

2 Squeeze as much water out of cabbage as possible. Finely chop cabbage. Squeeze any liquid from chopped cabbage; place in bowl. Stir in pork and next 5 ingredients.

3 Arrange half of wonton wrappers on sheet of waxed paper. With pastry brush, brush each wrapper lightly with egg white. Spoon 1 rounded teaspoon filling onto center of each wrapper.

CHINESE DUMPLINGS

◆◆◆◆◆◆◆◆◆◆◆◆◆

Prep: 45 minutes
Cook: 5 minutes
Makes 4 main-dish servings

2 cups packed, sliced napa
   cabbage (Chinese cabbage)
½ pound ground pork
2 tablespoons soy sauce
1 tablespoon dry sherry
2 teaspoons cornstarch
1½ teaspoons minced, peeled
   fresh ginger
1 green onion, minced
36 wonton wrappers, 3½" by
   3¼" (three-quarters
   12-ounce package)
1 large egg white, beaten
Soy Dipping Sauce (below)
Sautéed asparagus and
   sesame seeds (optional)
Green onions for garnish

SOY DIPPING SAUCE

In small bowl, mix ¼ cup soy sauce, ¼ cup seasoned rice vinegar or white wine vinegar, and 2 tablespoons angel-hair-thin strips peeled fresh ginger. Makes about ½ cup.

4 Bring opposite corners of wrapper up over filling; pinch and pleat edges together to seal. Repeat with remaining wrappers, egg white, and filling.

5 In deep 12-inch skillet, heat ½ inch water to boiling over high heat. Place all dumplings, pleated edges up, in one layer in pan. Stir gently to prevent sticking.

6 Heat dumplings to boiling over high heat. Reduce heat to low, cover skillet, and simmer 5 minutes, or until dumplings are cooked through. Meanwhile, prepare Soy Dipping Sauce. With slotted spoon, transfer dumplings to 4 plates; serve with asparagus and sesame seeds, if you like. Garnish, and pass dipping sauce separately.

EACH SERVING: ABOUT 320 CALORIES, 22g PROTEIN, 46g CARBOHYDRATE, 4g TOTAL FAT (1g SATURATED), 42mg CHOLESTEROL, 2020mg SODIUM

STUFFED CABBAGE WITH DILL

Prep: 40 minutes   Bake: 1 hour
Makes 4 main-dish servings

1 medium head green
   cabbage (about 3 pounds)
½ cup regular long-grain rice
2 tablespoons margarine or
   butter
2 medium onions, finely
   chopped

1 pound ground pork
¼ cup chopped fresh dill
¼ teaspoon ground nutmeg
¼ teaspoon salt
Ground black pepper
1 can (28 ounces) tomatoes
1 teaspoon sugar

◆ In 8-quart saucepot, heat *6 quarts water* to boiling. Cut and discard core from cabbage. Add cabbage to boiling water, cut-side up. Using 2 large spoons, gently separate outer leaves as they soften slightly; remove 12 large leaves and drain on paper towels. (Drain and reserve remaining cabbage for another day.) Spread cabbage leaves on work surface; trim thick ribs almost to thinness of leaves, for easy rolling.

◆ Meanwhile, prepare rice as label directs. In 10-inch skillet, melt 1 tablespoon margarine over medium heat. Add half of onions and cook, stirring often, 5 minutes, or until tender. Transfer to medium bowl with rice, pork, dill, nutmeg, salt, and ¼ teaspoon pepper. Mix well. Preheat oven to 375°F. Place about ¼ cup filling in center of each cabbage leaf. Fold 2 sides of cabbage leaf over filling, overlapping edges, then roll up jelly-roll style. Arrange cabbage rolls in shallow 2-quart casserole.

◆ In 10-inch skillet, melt remaining 1 tablespoon margarine over medium heat. Add remaining onions and cook, stirring often, 5 minutes, or until tender. Add tomatoes with their juice, sugar, and ⅛ teaspoon pepper and heat to boiling, breaking up tomatoes with spoon. Pour evenly over cabbage rolls. Cover with foil and bake 1 hour.

Each serving: About 445 calories, 32g protein, 54g carbohydrate, 13g total fat (3g saturated), 65mg cholesterol, 675mg sodium

PREPARING CABBAGE ROLLS

Place blanched cabbage leaves, rib-side up, on work surface. Holding knife almost parallel to work surface, trim thick rib so leaves lie almost flat. Place about ¼ cup filling in center of each leaf. Fold sides over filling, overlapping edges, then roll leaf up to form a compact package.

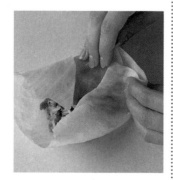

PORCUPINE MEATBALLS

Prep: 20 minutes   Cook: 45 minutes
Makes 4 main-dish servings

1 can (13¾ to 14½ ounces)
   reduced-sodium chicken
   broth
1 tablespoon dry sherry
¼ teaspoon Asian sesame oil
½ cup regular long-grain rice
4 green onions, chopped

1 pound ground pork
1 large egg
2 tablespoons soy sauce
2 teaspoons grated, peeled
   fresh ginger
¼ teaspoon ground black
   pepper

◆ In 10-inch skillet, heat broth, sherry, sesame oil, and *1½ cups water* to boiling over high heat. Meanwhile, in large bowl, combine uncooked rice with remaining ingredients; mix well. On waxed paper, form mixture into 1½-inch meatballs (mixture will be soft).

◆ Carefully place meatballs in broth mixture; heat to boiling. Reduce heat to low; cover and simmer 45 minutes. Serve meatballs with broth.

Each serving: About 285 calories, 28g protein, 21g carbohydrate, 9g total fat (3g saturated), 127mg cholesterol, 650mg sodium

COUNTRY PÂTÉ

Prep: 20 minutes plus chilling   Bake: 1 hour 45 minutes
Makes 30 appetizer servings

1 tablespoon margarine or
   butter
1 medium onion, finely
   chopped
1 pound chicken livers,
   trimmed (see page 134)
2½ pounds ground pork
2 large eggs

⅓ cup brandy
½ teaspoon dried thyme
¼ teaspoon ground nutmeg
⅛ teaspoon ground cloves
2½ teaspoons salt
½ teaspoon ground black
   pepper
2 bay leaves

◆ Preheat oven to 350°F. In 2-quart saucepan, melt margarine over medium heat. Add onion and cook, stirring, 4 minutes, or until tender. Transfer to blender. Add livers and blend until smooth. In large bowl, combine pork, eggs, brandy, thyme, nutmeg, cloves, salt, and pepper until evenly blended. Stir in liver mixture until smooth. Spoon into 9" by 5" loaf pan. Smooth top. Place bay leaves down center.

◆ Cover pan tightly with foil. Bake pâté on jelly-roll pan 1¾ hours, or until instant-read thermometer inserted in center reaches 160°F. Place on wire rack. Place a second loaf pan on top of pâté; weight down with heavy cans. Cool to room temperature. Refrigerate pâté, with weights, overnight. Unmold pâté, discarding bay leaves. Slice thin.

Each serving: About 85 calories, 11g protein, 1g carbohydrate, 3g total fat (1g saturated), 96mg cholesterol, 220mg sodium

STIR-FRIED PORK

Stir-frying is typically done over high heat, but when using a nonstick skillet, turn the burner to medium-high heat. An abundance of vegetables lends color and crunch.

SESAME PORK STIR-FRY

◆◆◆◆◆◆◆◆◆◆◆◆◆◆

Prep: 20 minutes
Cook: 20 minutes
Makes 4 main-dish servings

Watercress Rice (optional, see below)
1 pork tenderloin (about 12 ounces), cut into ½" by ¼" strips
2 tablespoons soy sauce
1 tablespoon minced, peeled fresh ginger
1 teaspoon Asian sesame oil
1 garlic clove, minced
¾ cup chicken broth
1¼ teaspoons cornstarch
2 teaspoons olive oil
3 medium carrots, cut into 2" by ¼" sticks
1 medium red pepper, cut into ¼-inch-wide strips
1 small zucchini (about 8 ounces), cut into 2" by ¼" sticks

1 Prepare Watercress Rice, if you like; keep warm. Meanwhile, in medium bowl, toss pork and next 4 ingredients. In small bowl, mix chicken broth and cornstarch; set aside.

2 In nonstick 12-inch skillet or wok, heat 1 teaspoon olive oil over medium-high heat. Add carrots and red pepper; cook, stirring, 5 minutes, or until lightly browned.

3 Add *1 tablespoon water;* cook 3 to 5 minutes longer, until tender-crisp. Transfer to bowl. In same skillet, heat remaining 1 teaspoon oil. Add zucchini; cook, stirring, 3 minutes.

WATERCRESS RICE

In 1-quart saucepan, heat 1½ cups water and ¾ cup regular long-grain rice to boiling over high heat. Reduce heat to low; cover and simmer 15 to 20 minutes, until rice is tender and water is absorbed. Stir in 1 cup loosely packed watercress leaves (½ bunch), coarsely chopped. Makes 4 accompaniment servings.

Each serving: About 130 calories, 3g protein, 28g carbohydrate, 0g total fat, 0mg cholesterol, 10mg sodium

4 Transfer zucchini to bowl with carrot and red-pepper mixture. In same skillet, cook pork mixture, stirring constantly, until pork just loses its pink color. Stir broth mixture; add to pork. Stir in vegetables; heat to boiling. Boil 1 minute, stirring, or until mixture thickens. Serve with Watercress Rice, if you like.

EACH SERVING: ABOUT 185 CALORIES, 20g PROTEIN, 11g CARBOHYDRATE, 7g TOTAL FAT (2g SATURATED), 53mg CHOLESTEROL, 770mg SODIUM

PORK LO MEIN

Prep: 30 minutes   *Cook:* 15 minutes
Makes 4 main-dish servings

1 pork tenderloin (about
  12 ounces), cut into very
  thin slices
2 tablespoons oyster sauce
2 tablespoons dry sherry
2 tablespoons soy sauce
1 teaspoon grated, peeled
  fresh ginger
8 ounces linguine
4 tablespoons vegetable oil
½ teaspoon salt

1 head bok choy (about
  1½ pounds), sliced crosswise
  into 1-inch-wide strips
1 bag (6 ounces) radishes,
  each cut in half if large
1 bunch green onions, cut
  into 2-inch pieces
1 can (15 ounces) Chinese
  straw mushrooms or 2 jars
  (7 ounces each) whole
  mushrooms, drained

◆ In medium bowl, mix pork, oyster sauce, sherry, soy
sauce, and ginger; set aside. In large saucepot, prepare
linguine as label directs.

◆ Meanwhile, in 12-inch skillet or wok, heat 2 tablespoons
oil over high heat. Add salt and bok choy and cook, stirring
frequently, until bok choy is tender-crisp; transfer to bowl.
To oil remaining in skillet, add 1 tablespoon oil; add
radishes and cook, stirring frequently, until tender-crisp.
Transfer to bowl with bok choy.

◆ To oil remaining in skillet, add remaining 1 tablespoon
oil; heat over high heat. Add green onions and cook,
stirring frequently, until tender-crisp. Add pork mixture;
cook, stirring constantly, about 3 minutes, until pork just
loses its pink color throughout. Return bok choy and
radishes to skillet. Add mushrooms and heat through.

◆ Drain linguine. Return linguine to saucepot and add
pork mixture; toss to mix well.

**Each serving: About 500 calories, 31g protein, 52g carbohydrate,
20g total fat (4g saturated), 115mg cholesterol, 1330mg sodium**

STIR-FRIED PORK WITH ASPARAGUS AND SHIITAKE MUSHROOMS

Prep: 25 minutes   *Cook:* 15 minutes
Makes 4 main-dish servings

1 pork tenderloin (12 ounces),
  cut into very thin slices
2 tablespoons soy sauce
1 tablespoon plus 2 teaspoons
  vegetable oil
8 ounces shiitake mushrooms,
  stems discarded, cut into
  wedges
8 ounces white mushrooms,
  each cut into quarters

2 pounds asparagus, trimmed
  and cut diagonally into
  1-inch pieces
4 teaspoons minced, peeled
  fresh ginger
1 garlic clove, minced
1 cup chicken broth
1 tablespoon hoisin sauce

◆ In medium bowl, toss pork with soy sauce. In 10-inch
skillet or wok, heat 1 tablespoon oil over high heat. Add
pork mixture and cook, stirring constantly, 2 minutes, until
pork just loses its pink color throughout. Transfer to plate.

◆ To drippings in skillet, add 1 more teaspoon oil; heat
over high heat. Add mushrooms and cook, stirring
frequently, 5 minutes, or until mushrooms are browned and
liquid has evaporated. Transfer to plate with pork.

◆ To skillet, add remaining 1 teaspoon oil; heat over high
heat. Add asparagus, ginger, and garlic; cook, stirring
frequently, 2 minutes. Stir in broth and hoisin sauce; heat to
boiling. Boil 2 to 4 minutes, until asparagus is tender-crisp.
Return pork and mushrooms to skillet; heat through.

**Each serving: About 270 calories, 26g protein, 24g carbohydrate,
10g total fat (2g saturated), 54mg cholesterol, 980mg sodium**

STIR-FRYING HINTS

• Have all ingredients cut and measured, and sauces or
thickening agents mixed, before you start cooking.

• Foods that are at room temperature will cook more
evenly than those that are cold. About 30 minutes
before cooking, bring out any refrigerated items.

• Cut ingredients into pieces of roughly the same size to
ensure even cooking.

• The oil should be very hot. To test, add a piece of
vegetable to the oil; if it sizzles, the oil is hot enough.

• Don't crowd the pan; the food will stew rather than fry.

• Stir the food almost continuously in the pan so
everything cooks evenly.

BROILED PORK

The tenderloin is both the leanest and most tender cut of pork. For a fast and low-fat meal, broil it with an Asian-style marinade, or rubbed with fragrant spices. Another enticing idea? Skewer cubes of pork with sweet red plums, then baste with apple jelly. Whatever your choice, in about fifteen minutes you'll have a sizzling, mouthwatering meal.

MARINATED PORK TENDERLOIN

Prep: 20 minutes plus marinating and standing   *Broil: 15 to 20 minutes*
Makes 4 main-dish servings

2 tablespoons soy sauce
2 tablespoons dry sherry
2 teaspoons grated, peeled fresh ginger
2 garlic cloves, minced
1 pork tenderloin (1 pound)
1 tablespoon vegetable oil
3 small zucchini (8 ounces each), each quartered lengthwise, then cut in 2-inch pieces
2 medium green onions, each cut lengthwise in half, then cut into 2-inch pieces
1 large red pepper, cut into thin 2-inch strips
½ teaspoon salt
1¾ teaspoons sugar
½ teaspoon cornstarch

1 In 11" by 7" glass baking dish, mix soy sauce, sherry, ginger, and garlic until well combined. Add pork tenderloin, turning to coat. Cover and refrigerate, turning tenderloin occasionally, 40 minutes. About 20 minutes before serving, preheat broiler. Place pork tenderloin on rack in broiling pan; reserve marinade in baking dish. Place pan in broiler 5 to 7 inches from heat source.

2 Broil pork 15 to 20 minutes, turning once, until browned and internal temperature of meat reaches 155°F on instant-read thermometer (temperature will rise to 160°F upon standing).

3 Place tenderloin on cutting board; let stand 10 minutes. Meanwhile, in nonstick 10-inch skillet, heat oil over medium-high heat. Add zucchini, green onions, red pepper, and salt; cook, stirring often, until golden and tender-crisp.

4 In small saucepan, heat reserved marinade and sugar to boiling over medium heat. In small bowl, mix cornstarch and *½ cup cold water*; stir into saucepan. Heat to boiling; boil, stirring, 1 minute.

5 Cut pork tenderloin on slight diagonal into ½-inch-thick slices. To serve, arrange vegetable mixture and pork on warm large platter; spoon sauce evenly over pork.

EACH SERVING: ABOUT 225 CALORIES, 26g PROTEIN, 11g CARBOHYDRATE, 8g TOTAL FAT (2g SATURATED), 65mg CHOLESTEROL, 835mg SODIUM

CHILI KABOBS WITH PLUMS

Prep: 15 minutes   Broil: 8 minutes
Makes 4 main-dish servings

2 teaspoons chili powder
1 teaspoon ground cumin
1 teaspoon brown sugar
⅛ teaspoon ground red
  pepper (cayenne)
½ teaspoon salt
1 pork tenderloin (12 ounces),
  cut into 1½-inch cubes

4 plums, each pitted and cut
  into quarters
4 (10-inch) all-metal skewers
3 tablespoons apple jelly,
  melted

◆ Preheat broiler. In medium bowl, mix first 5 ingredients. Pat pork dry with paper towels; add to spice mixture and toss to coat evenly.

◆ Thread pork alternately with plum quarters on skewers. Place skewers on rack in broiling pan.

◆ Place pan in broiler at closest position to heat source. Broil 7 minutes, turning once. Brush kabobs with half of apple jelly; broil 20 seconds.

◆ Turn kabobs and brush with remaining apple jelly. Broil kabobs 20 seconds longer, or until pork is browned and just cooked through.

Each serving: About 185 calories, 18g protein, 20g carbohydrate, 4g total fat (1g saturated), 49mg cholesterol, 320mg sodium

CURRIED PORK TENDERLOIN

Prep: 5 minutes plus standing   Broil: 15 to 20 minutes
Makes 4 main-dish servings

1 pork tenderloin (1 pound)
1 tablespoon curry powder
1 teaspoon ground cumin

¾ teaspoon salt
¼ teaspoon ground cinnamon
2 teaspoons vegetable oil

◆ Preheat broiler. Pat pork dry with paper towels. In small bowl, mix next 5 ingredients; use to rub over pork. Place pork on rack in broiling pan. Place pan in broiler 5 to 7 inches

from heat source; broil 15 to 20 minutes, turning once, until pork is browned and internal temperature reaches 155°F on instant-read thermometer (temperature will rise to 160°F upon standing).

◆ Transfer pork to platter. Let stand 10 minutes; keep warm. To serve, thinly slice pork.

Each serving: About 165 calories, 24g protein, 1g carbohydrate, 7g total fat (2g saturated), 65mg cholesterol, 450mg sodium

PORK WITH SAUTÉED VEGETABLES

Prep: 40 minutes plus standing   Broil: 15 to 20 minutes
Makes 6 main-dish servings

2 tablespoons brown sugar
1 tablespoon dry mustard
2 tablespoons balsamic
  vinegar
2 tablespoons soy sauce
2 pork tenderloins (12 ounces
  each)
3 teaspoons vegetable oil
5 large carrots, thinly sliced
1 medium onion, thinly sliced

4 large celery stalks, thinly
  sliced
1-inch piece fresh ginger,
  peeled and thinly sliced
Salt
2 large red peppers, cut into
  ¼-inch-wide strips
1 large green pepper, cut into
  ¼-inch-wide strips

◆ In 13" by 9" baking dish, mix first 4 ingredients. Add pork, turning to coat; set aside while cooking vegetables.

◆ In nonstick 12-inch skillet, heat 2 teaspoons oil over medium-high heat. Add carrots, onion, celery, ginger, and ½ teaspoon salt and cook 10 to 12 minutes, until vegetables are browned; transfer to bowl.

◆ Preheat broiler. In same skillet, heat remaining 1 teaspoon oil. Add peppers and ½ teaspoon salt; cook until browned. Return carrot mixture to skillet; keep warm.

◆ Brush rack in broiling pan with oil. Place pork on rack; reserve marinade. Place pan in broiler 5 to 7 inches from heat source; broil 15 to 20 minutes, turning once, until pork is browned and internal temperature of meat reaches 155°F on instant-read thermometer (temperature will rise to 160°F upon standing).

◆ Transfer pork to platter. Let stand 10 minutes; keep warm.

◆ Place marinade in 1-quart saucepan with ½ cup water; heat to boiling over high heat. Reduce heat to medium-low; boil sauce 3 minutes.

◆ Thinly slice pork; serve with vegetables and sauce.

Each serving: About 250 calories, 26g protein, 21g carbohydrate, 7g total fat (2g saturated), 65mg cholesterol, 805mg sodium

PORK RIBS

Finger-licking good, barbecued ribs are one of the joys of summer. Simmering them before grilling guarantees tenderness and removes excess fat. They're excellent whether rubbed with spices or brushed with a tangy glaze. Turn them often to avoid burning, especially with a sweet barbecue sauce. If the weather doesn't permit outdoor grilling, oven-broiling is just as fast.

TERIYAKI-GLAZED RIBS

◆◆◆◆◆◆◆◆◆◆◆◆◆◆◆◆◆◆◆◆◆◆◆◆◆◆◆

Prep: 1 hour 30 minutes   Grill: 15 minutes
Makes 5 main-dish servings

4 racks pork baby back ribs (1 pound each)	1 jar (12 ounces) quince or apple jelly
1 tablespoon olive or vegetable oil	5 medium nectarines, each cut in half and pitted
4 green onions, thinly sliced	2 tablespoons sugar
⅓ cup teriyaki sauce	Grilled French bread (optional)
2 tablespoons cornstarch	
3 tablespoons finely chopped, peeled fresh ginger	

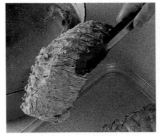

1 In 8-quart saucepot or Dutch oven, heat ribs and *water* to cover to boiling over high heat. Reduce heat to low; cover and simmer 45 to 60 minutes, until tender. Transfer to platter. If not serving right away, cover and refrigerate. Prepare outdoor grill.

2 Prepare glaze: In 1-quart saucepan, heat oil over medium heat. Add green onions and cook, stirring frequently, until golden. Stir in teriyaki sauce, next 3 ingredients, and ¼ cup *water*; cook, stirring, until mixture thickens and boils. Boil 1 minute. Sprinkle nectarines with sugar.

3 Place cooked ribs on grill over medium heat. Grill 15 minutes, turning frequently, and brushing with glaze during last 5 minutes of cooking, until heated through.

TERIYAKI SAUCE

A blend of Japanese wines, soy sauce, and sugar, this salty-sweet condiment gives a glossy sheen to grilled or broiled fish, chicken, and meats – baste near the end of cooking to avoid burning. Or, use as a marinade to give meat a delicious flavor and tenderize it too.

4 After ribs have cooked 5 minutes, add nectarines to grill. Cook 10 minutes, turning often, or until browned. Serve ribs and nectarines with French bread, if you like.

EACH SERVING: ABOUT 885 CALORIES, 47g PROTEIN, 77g CARBOHYDRATE, 44g TOTAL FAT (15g SATURATED), 164mg CHOLESTEROL, 850mg SODIUM

RIBS WITH CHILI-HERB COATING

Prep: 1 hour 30 minutes
Grill: 15 to 20 minutes
Makes 4 main-dish servings

4 pounds pork spareribs, cut into 2-rib
    portions
3 tablespoons chili powder
2 teaspoons dried oregano
1 teaspoon dry mustard
1 teaspoon salt
Chopped fresh parsley for garnish
Potato salad (optional)

◆ In 8-quart saucepot or Dutch oven,
heat spareribs and *water* to cover to
boiling over high heat. Reduce heat
to low; cover and simmer 45 to
60 minutes, or until ribs are tender.
Transfer to platter. If not serving right
away, cover and refrigerate. Prepare
outdoor grill.

◆ Pat ribs dry with paper towels. In
small bowl, mix chili powder, oregano,
mustard, and salt. Use to rub over ribs.

◆ Place spareribs on grill over
medium heat; grill 15 to 20 minutes,
turning spareribs often, until heated
through. Garnish, and serve with
potato salad, if you like.

**Each serving: About 720 calories,
57g protein, 4g carbohydrate, 52g total fat
(19g saturated), 205mg cholesterol,
730mg sodium**

SWEET-AND-SPICY RIBS

Prep: 1 hour 30 minutes
Grill: 15 to 20 minutes
Makes 4 main-dish servings

4 pounds pork spareribs, cut into 2-rib
    portions
½ cup chili sauce
½ cup hoisin sauce
¼ cup packed brown sugar
¾ teaspoon ground allspice
½ teaspoon hot-pepper sauce
4 medium-size ripe peaches, each cut in
    half and pitted
2 tablespoons peach jam

◆ In 8-quart saucepot or Dutch oven,
heat spareribs and *water* to cover to
boiling over high heat. Reduce heat to
low; cover and simmer 45 to 60 minutes,
or until ribs are tender. Transfer to
platter. If not serving right away, cover
and refrigerate. Prepare outdoor grill.

◆ In small bowl, mix chili sauce and
next 4 ingredients. Place spareribs on
grill over medium heat. Grill 15 to
20 minutes, turning ribs often and
brushing with sauce frequently during
last 10 minutes, until heated through.

◆ After spareribs have cooked
10 minutes, add peaches to grill. Grill
about 5 minutes, turning once and
brushing once with jam. Serve ribs
with peaches.

**Each serving: About 905 calories,
57g protein, 56g carbohydrate, 51g total
fat (19g saturated), 205mg cholesterol,
1630mg sodium**

ORANGE-ROSEMARY GLAZE

If you're having a big barbecue, you may
want to make a variety of glazes. This
recipe makes enough for 4 pounds of
spareribs. In small bowl, mix 1 cup
orange marmalade, ¼ cup fresh lemon
juice, 2 tablespoons chopped fresh
rosemary or 2 teaspoons dried rosemary,
crushed, and 1½ teaspoons salt until
combined. Makes about 1¼ cups.

COUNTRY-STYLE RIBS WITH JALAPEÑO BARBECUE SAUCE

Prep: 1 hour 30 minutes
Grill: 15 to 20 minutes
Makes 6 main-dish servings

4 pounds pork country-style ribs
½ cup cider vinegar
¼ cup chili sauce
2 tablespoons brown sugar
2 tablespoons drained, chopped canned
    green chiles
1 tablespoon drained, chopped pickled
    jalapeño chiles, stems and seeds
    removed
1 tablespoon vegetable oil
1 teaspoon salt
⅛ teaspoon dried oregano

◆ In 8-quart saucepot or Dutch oven,
heat ribs and *water* to cover to boiling
over high heat. Reduce heat to low;
cover and simmer 45 to 60 minutes, or
until ribs are tender. Transfer to
platter. If not serving right away, cover
and refrigerate. Prepare outdoor grill.

◆ Prepare barbecue sauce: In blender
at medium speed or in food processor
with knife blade attached, blend
remaining ingredients until smooth.
Place ribs on grill over medium heat.
Grill, turning often and brushing with
sauce during last 10 minutes, 15 to
20 minutes, until heated through.

**Each serving: About 610 calories,
65g protein, 9g carbohydrate, 34g total fat
(11g saturated), 134mg cholesterol,
645mg sodium**

THE INDOOR ALTERNATIVE

To broil rather than grill ribs, first
simmer as directed in recipes.
Arrange ribs meat-side down on
rack in broiling pan. Place pan in
broiler about 7 to 9 inches from
heat source; broil, turning and
brushing with glaze or sauce as
directed in recipe, 20 minutes, or
until heated through.

SMOKED PORK

Smoked pork is usually brine-cured, then flavored with hardwood smoke such as hickory or apple, or in some regions corncobs or mesquite; it is usually but not always fully cooked. Its robust flavor goes well with the sweet-sour combinations of preserves and mustard, apple juice and vinegar, or brown sugar and sauerkraut. Note that a fully cooked smoked ham can be served as is, but heating improves the flavor and texture.

APRICOT-GLAZED SMOKED HAM

◆◆◆◆◆◆◆◆◆◆◆◆◆◆◆◆◆◆◆◆◆◆◆◆◆◆◆◆◆◆

Prep: 10 minutes plus standing   *Bake:* 2 hours
Makes 12 main-dish servings

Half fully cooked smoked bone-in ham (7 pounds)
½ cup apricot jam
3 tablespoons Dijon mustard
½ teaspoon ground ginger
3 tablespoons all-purpose flour

1 can (13¾ to 14½ ounces) reduced-sodium chicken broth
Rosemary sprigs for garnish
Brussels sprouts and sweet potato wedges (optional)

1 Preheat oven to 325°F. Remove skin and trim all but ¼ inch fat from ham. Score fat, just through to the meat, into ¾-inch diamonds. Place ham on rack in medium roasting pan.

2 Insert meat thermometer into center of ham, being careful that pointed end does not touch bone. Bake 1½ hours. Meanwhile, prepare glaze: In cup, mix jam, mustard, and ginger until blended. Brush glaze over ham. Bake ham 30 minutes longer, or until thermometer reaches 140°F. Place on warm large platter. Let stand 15 minutes; keep warm.

3 Prepare gravy: Remove rack from roasting pan. Pour drippings through sieve into 4-cup measuring cup; let stand a few seconds, until fat separates from meat juice. Spoon 3 tablespoons fat from drippings into 2-quart saucepan; skim and discard remaining fat.

4 Add *1 cup water* to roasting pan; stir until brown bits are loosened. Pour through sieve into meat juice in measuring cup. Into fat in saucepan, stir flour over medium heat; cook 1 minute. Gradually stir in meat-juice mixture and broth; cook, stirring, until gravy thickens. Thinly slice ham; garnish and serve with gravy, and sprouts and sweet potatoes, if you like.

EACH SERVING: ABOUT 260 CALORIES, 34g PROTEIN, 12g CARBOHYDRATE, 8g TOTAL FAT (2g SATURATED), 76mg CHOLESTEROL, 1845mg SODIUM

SMOKED PORK-CHOP CASSEROLE

Prep: 30 minutes   Bake: 1 hour to 1 hour 15 minutes
Makes 6 main-dish servings

1 small head green cabbage
  (about 1½ pounds)
8 small red potatoes
  (1 pound)
2 tablespoons vegetable oil
3 large onions, each cut into
  quarters
6 smoked pork loin chops,
  each ½ inch thick (about
  5 ounces each)

½ cup apple juice
¼ cup cider vinegar
½ teaspoon coarsely ground
  black pepper
1 package (11 ounces) mixed
  dried fruit

◆ Preheat oven to 375°F. Cut cabbage into 6 wedges; remove core. Arrange cabbage and potatoes in shallow 15½" by 10½" casserole (5 quarts) or medium roasting pan.

◆ In 12-inch skillet, heat oil over medium-high heat; add onions and cook, stirring often, until golden brown. Transfer onions to casserole with cabbage and potatoes.

◆ Pat pork chops dry with paper towels. In oil remaining in skillet, cook chops, half at a time, until lightly browned on both sides. Tuck chops into vegetables in casserole.

◆ In drippings in skillet, heat remaining ingredients to boiling over high heat; stir until brown bits are loosened.

◆ Pour apple-juice mixture over pork chops and vegetables. Cover and bake 1 to 1¼ hours, basting meat and vegetables with liquid in casserole several times, until tender.

Each serving: About 515 calories, 30g protein, 68g carbohydrate, 16g total fat (5g saturated), 54mg cholesterol, 790mg sodium

FRUITED SMOKED PORK WITH CABBAGE

Prep: 40 minutes   Bake: 45 to 60 minutes
Makes 6 main-dish servings

1 medium head green
  cabbage (about 3 pounds)
3 tablespoons vegetable oil
2 large onions, each cut into
  8 wedges
1 smoked pork shoulder roll
  (2 pounds)
1 can (17 ounces) unpeeled
  apricots in heavy syrup

1 can (16 ounces) pear halves
  in heavy syrup
2 tablespoons brown sugar
3 tablespoons white wine
  vinegar
3 tablespoons prepared spicy
  mustard
½ teaspoon ground allspice

◆ Preheat oven to 325°F. Cut cabbage into quarters; remove core. Cut cabbage crosswise into 1-inch-wide slices; discard tough ribs.

◆ In 8-quart Dutch oven, heat oil over medium heat. Add onions; cook until tender. Stir in cabbage; cover and cook, stirring occasionally, 20 minutes, or until cabbage is tender. Meanwhile, remove stockinette casing (if any) from pork; cut pork into ¼-inch-thick slices. Drain canned fruit. Stir brown sugar, vinegar, mustard, and allspice into cabbage. Spoon cabbage mixture into 13" by 9" glass baking dish. Tuck pork and fruit into cabbage. Cover with foil; bake 45 minutes to 1 hour, until pork is tender.

Each serving: About 625 calories, 34g protein, 55g carbohydrate, 32g total fat (10g saturated), 84mg cholesterol, 1145mg sodium

SMOKED PORK-CHOP DINNER

Prep: 10 minutes   Cook: 50 minutes
Makes 4 main-dish servings

4 smoked pork loin or rib
  chops, each ¾ inch thick
  (about 7 ounces each)
1 tablespoon vegetable oil
1 medium Granny Smith or
  Rome Beauty apple,
  unpeeled
1 bag (16 ounces) carrots, cut
  into 1-inch pieces

¾ (32-ounce) bag sauerkraut,
  rinsed and drained
1 bottle or can (11 to
  12 ounces) beer or
  nonalcoholic beer
¼ cup packed brown sugar
2 teaspoons caraway or fennel
  seeds, crushed

◆ Pat chops dry with paper towels. In 12-inch skillet, heat oil over high heat; add chops and cook until browned on both sides. Meanwhile, grate half of apple; reserve remaining half. To skillet, add carrots, grated apple, sauerkraut, beer, brown sugar, caraway seeds, and *½ cup water.* Heat to boiling. Reduce heat to low; cover and simmer 35 minutes.

◆ Cut remaining apple into wedges; add to skillet. Cover and cook 10 minutes longer, occasionally spooning liquid over chops, or until carrots and pork are tender.

Each serving: About 500 calories, 37g protein, 41g carbohydrate, 19g total fat (6g saturated), 74mg cholesterol, 2195mg sodium

◆◆◆◆◆◆◆◆◆◆◆◆◆◆◆◆◆◆◆◆◆◆◆◆

SAUERKRAUT SECRET

Sauerkraut is shredded cabbage that has been pickled for several weeks in cabbage juice and salt, which gives it a unique sour taste. To mellow the pungent salty flavor, rinse sauerkraut with cold running water, then drain it well before using.

◆◆◆◆◆◆◆◆◆◆◆◆◆◆◆◆◆◆◆◆◆◆◆◆

PORK SAUSAGES

Pork sausage links run the gamut from sweet or spicy Italian sausage and smoked Polish kielbasa to coriander-flavored German bratwurst (made from pork and veal). Always cook fresh sausages thoroughly.

TORTA RUSTICA

◆◆◆◆◆◆◆◆◆◆◆◆◆◆

Prep: 40 minutes plus cooling
Bake: 25 minutes
Makes 6 main-dish servings

1 pound sweet Italian-sausage links, casings removed
1 large egg
1 container (8 ounces) ricotta cheese
2 packages (10 ounces each) refrigerated pizza crust
8 ounces mozzarella cheese, shredded (2 cups)
1 jar (7 ounces) roasted red peppers, drained, cut into ½-inch-wide slices, and patted dry with paper towels
½ cup packed fresh basil leaves

1 In 10-inch skillet, cook sausage over medium heat, stirring frequently to break up meat, until browned, about 20 minutes. With slotted spoon, transfer to paper towels to drain.

2 Separate egg, placing white in cup. Reserve egg white in refrigerator, covered. With fork, stir ricotta cheese into egg yolk until mixture is smooth and blended. Preheat oven to 425°F.

3 On lightly floured surface, with floured rolling pin, roll 1 package pizza crust to 13-inch square. Use to line 9½-inch deep-dish pie plate. Trim edge, leaving 1-inch overhang; reserve trimmings. Sprinkle half of mozzarella over crust; top with half of sausage. Add all of roasted red peppers, ricotta mixture, and basil.

4 Top layers with remaining sausage, spreading evenly, then remaining mozzarella.

5 On lightly floured surface, unroll second package pizza crust. With tip of knife, cut small slits in dough. Place on filling; fold overhang over top crust; pinch edges to seal.

6 From reserved trimmings, cut several leaves to decorate torta. Beat reserved egg white lightly with fork; brush top of torta with some egg white. Arrange leaves on top; brush with more egg white. Bake torta 15 minutes. Cover loosely with foil; bake 10 minutes longer. Transfer to wire rack to cool slightly. Serve warm or at room temperature. Or, cover and refrigerate torta to serve later.

EACH SERVING: ABOUT 610 CALORIES, 28g PROTEIN, 53g CARBOHYDRATE, 29g TOTAL FAT (13g SATURATED), 114mg CHOLESTEROL, 1350mg SODIUM

POLENTA AND SAUSAGE CASSEROLE

Prep: 1 hour 10 minutes   Bake: 35 minutes
Makes 8 main-dish servings

½ pound sweet Italian-sausage links, casings removed
½ pound hot Italian-sausage links, casings removed
1 tablespoon olive oil
1 large onion, chopped
1 large celery stalk, chopped
1 medium carrot, chopped
1 can (28 ounces) plum tomatoes in puree
2 cups yellow cornmeal

1 can (13¾ to 14½ ounces) reduced-sodium chicken broth
¼ teaspoon salt
½ cup freshly grated Parmesan cheese
8 ounces Fontina or mozzarella cheese, shredded (2 cups)
Celery leaves for garnish

◆ Prepare tomato-sausage sauce: In 5-quart Dutch oven, cook all sausages over medium-high heat until browned, stirring to break up. Transfer to bowl. In drippings in Dutch oven, heat oil over medium-high heat; add onion, celery, and carrot and cook, stirring often, until browned. Stir in sausage meat and tomatoes with their puree; heat to boiling over high heat. Reduce heat to low; cover and simmer 10 minutes. Remove cover and simmer 10 minutes longer, breaking up tomatoes with back of spoon.

◆ Preheat oven to 350°F. Prepare polenta: In 4-quart saucepan, with wire whisk, mix cornmeal, broth, and salt. Over medium-high heat, gradually add *4¼ cups boiling water*, whisking constantly, about 5 minutes, or until mixture thickens. Whisk in Parmesan cheese. Remove from heat.

◆ Grease 13" by 9" glass baking dish. Spread half of polenta in baking dish; top with half of tomato-sausage sauce, then half of Fontina cheese. Repeat with remaining polenta and sauce. Bake casserole, uncovered, 15 minutes. Sprinkle with remaining Fontina; bake about 20 minutes longer, or until casserole is hot and bubbling. Let stand 15 minutes for easier serving. Garnish with celery leaves.

Each serving: About 420 calories, 20g protein, 36g carbohydrate, 22g total fat (10g saturated), 64mg cholesterol, 1100mg sodium

KIELBASA WITH CABBAGE AND FRUIT

Prep: 10 minutes   Cook: 25 minutes
Makes 6 main-dish servings

1 small head Savoy or green cabbage (2 pounds)
1 tablespoon margarine or butter
1 medium onion, finely chopped
½ cup dry white wine
1 package (8 ounces) mixed dried fruit

½ cup reduced-sodium chicken broth
¼ teaspoon dried thyme
¼ teaspoon salt
¼ teaspoon ground black pepper
1 fully cooked kielbasa (Polish sausage), cut into 1-inch pieces (1 pound)

Cut cabbage into quarters; remove core. Thinly slice cabbage, discarding any tough ribs. In 8-quart Dutch oven, melt margarine over medium heat. Add onion and cook 5 minutes, or until tender. Add wine and dried fruit and heat to boiling over high heat. Stir in broth, thyme, salt, pepper, and cabbage. Cover and cook over high heat 5 minutes. Stir in kielbasa and cook 15 minutes longer, or until cabbage is tender and kielbasa is heated through.

Each serving: About 440 calories, 14mg protein, 40g carbohydrate, 25g total fat (10g saturated), 47mg cholesterol, 905mg sodium

BEER-BRAISED BRATWURST DINNER

Prep: 30 minutes   Bake: 1 hour 30 minutes
Makes 6 main-dish servings

1½ pounds bratwurst or country-style sausage links
1 small head green cabbage (about 2 pounds), cut into 6 wedges, core removed
1 tablespoon vegetable oil
3 medium red potatoes (1 pound), cut into 1½-inch chunks

2 medium onions, sliced
1 bottle or can (11 to 12 ounces) beer or nonalcoholic beer
1 tablespoon caraway seeds
1 teaspoon chicken-flavor instant bouillon
¼ teaspoon ground black pepper

◆ In 12-inch skillet, cook sausages over medium-high heat, turning frequently, until browned; drain on paper towels. Place sausages and cabbage in shallow 3½-quart casserole.

◆ Preheat oven to 375°F. In drippings in skillet, heat oil over medium-high heat. Add potatoes and onions; cook until lightly browned, stirring often; add to casserole. To skillet, add remaining ingredients. Heat to boiling over high heat; stir until brown bits are loosened. Pour over mixture in casserole. Cover and bake 1½ hours, or until vegetables are tender.

Each serving: About 385 calories, 13g protein, 30g carbohydrate, 24g total fat (9g saturated), 45mg cholesterol, 680mg sodium

LAMB

Whether you're roasting a whole leg for a festive holiday centerpiece or using lamb shanks for a homey weeknight stew, flavorful lamb is both elegant and earthy. Once a symbol of spring, lamb is now bred so it can be enjoyed all year round.

KNOW YOUR LAMB

Americans generally prefer the mild taste of young lamb – that's why most supermarket lamb is from sheep less than a year old. Baby lamb, or milk-fed lamb, has an even milder flavor and paler color; it comes from sheep that are between 3 to 5 months of age. Meat from sheep butchered between 12 and 24 months is sold as yearling lamb, and sheep over 2 years as mutton. These meats have a more gamey flavor than younger lambs, and are seldom sold in the U.S. except in ethnic markets. Most imported lamb comes from New Zealand, and the cuts are noticeably smaller since they come from a smaller – though not younger – animal.

BUYING AND SERVING

• Select lamb that's pinkish-red. Darker meat is from an older animal and will have a stronger flavor. Any fat should be white, firm, and waxy. Bones should be porous and unsplintered, with a reddish tinge at the cut end.
• A leg of lamb may be covered with "fell," a moist and pliable paper-thin membrane that surrounds the fat and may be strongly flavored. You can trim it off or not, as you prefer.
• Each 1 pound of raw lamb serves the following: Boneless roasts, 3 to 4 servings; bone-in roasts and chops, 2 to 3 servings; bony cuts like riblets and shanks, 1 to 2 servings.

MARINADES FOR LAMB

• Olive oil, red wine, thyme, and Dijon mustard
• Yogurt, garlic, cumin, and crushed cardamom seeds
• Balsamic vinegar, olive oil, garlic, fresh mint leaves, and rosemary
• Lemon juice, lemon peel, olive oil, fresh mint leaves, and oregano
• Paste of crushed fennel seeds, cumin seeds, coriander seeds, garlic, and olive oil
• Dry rub of chili powder, ground cumin, and thyme
• Soy sauce, garlic, and Chinese five-spice powder

CHOOSING THE RIGHT CUT

When preparing any cut of lamb, remember that it can dry out quickly if overcooked. So unless you prefer well-done meat, cook lamb just to medium-rare for the best results.

For broiling, grilling, or panfrying Tender cuts work best; avoid overcooking.
Best bets Rib chops, loin chops (below right), sirloin (below left), arm, and blade chops, leg steaks, butterflied leg.

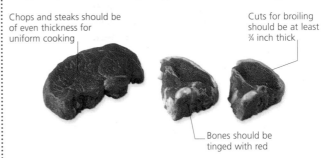

Chops and steaks should be of even thickness for uniform cooking

Cuts for broiling should be at least ¾ inch thick

Bones should be tinged with red

For braising or stewing These moist-heat cooking methods are best reserved for slightly less-tender – and more economical – cuts. Remember to cook at a gentle simmer.
Best bets Neck slices, arm chops, blade chops, bone-in shoulder pieces (below left), shanks (below right), breast, breast riblets. Lamb cubes for stew are cut from the shoulder.

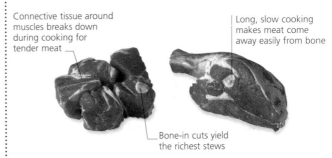

Connective tissue around muscles breaks down during cooking for tender meat

Long, slow cooking makes meat come away easily from bone

Bone-in cuts yield the richest stews

For roasting Many tender cuts of lamb are good for roasting, but the leg and rib sections are the most popular. Place lamb roasts fat-side up on a rack in a roasting pan, which will help keep the meat moist and flavorful.
Best bets Whole leg of lamb, leg shank half, rack (rib roast).

Layer of fell surrounding fat may be removed, if you like

Any bones should be cleanly cut, not splintered

Thin covering of fat keeps juices in

BONING AND BUTTERFLYING A LEG SHANK HALF

1 Place lamb, fat-side down, on cutting board. With sharp boning or paring knife, cut through meat to expose main leg bone.

2 Keeping knife blade against bone, scrape all meat around bone until you reach the knee joint.

3 Turn leg slightly and cut around knee joint. Continue to cut meat from knee down to second leg bone. Remove leg bone.

4 Since the boned leg of lamb is uneven in thickness, cut the thicker muscles horizontally almost in half, then open like a book to make meat flatter and a more even thickness. Trim excess fat from meat.

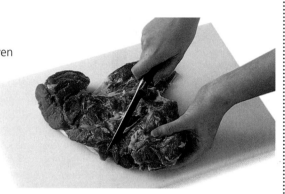

CARVING A LEG OF LAMB

1 So leg can lie flat for easier carving, cut a slice from thin side of leg; turn leg cut-side down. Holding meat steady with a carving fork, make a vertical cut to bone about 1 inch from shank. From shank end, make a horizontal cut parallel to bone to release the wedge of meat.

2 Cut even slices of meat, slicing perpendicular to bone and working along leg away from the shank.

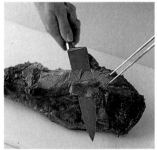

3 Turn leg over. With knife blade almost flat and working away from you, cut long slices following line of the bone.

ROASTING TIMES (OVEN TEMPERATURE 325°F)

CUT AND WEIGHT Start with meat at refrigerator temperature. **Remove roast from oven when it reaches 5° to 10°F below desired doneness; temperature will rise as it stands.**		APPROXIMATE COOKING TIME (MINUTES PER LB)		
		Medium-rare (145°F)	Medium (160°F)	Well done (170°F)
Whole leg	5–7 lbs	15 mins	20 mins	25 mins
	7–9 lbs	20 mins	25 mins	30 mins
Leg shank half	3–4 lbs	30 mins	40 mins	45 mins
Leg sirloin half	3–4 lbs	25 mins	35 mins	45 mins
Leg roast (boneless)	4–7 lbs	20 mins	25 mins	30 mins
Rib roast or rack (cook at 375°F)	1½–2½ lbs	30 mins	35 mins	40 mins
Crown roast, unstuffed (cook at 375°F)	2–3 lbs	25 mins	30 mins	35 mins
Shoulder roast	4–6 lbs	20 mins	25 mins	30 mins
Shoulder roast (boneless)	3½–6 lbs	35 mins	40 mins	45 mins

ROAST LAMB

From an elegant rack to a glorious leg, crowned with a crust of buttery crumbs or bistro-style on a bed of potatoes, lamb roasts beautifully. Rosemary, thyme, and garlic are classic complements to its delicate but distinctive flavor. For the juiciest, most flavorful lamb, roast just until the interior is still slightly pink.

ROASTED LEG OF LAMB WITH PISTACHIO-MINT CRUST

◆◆◆◆◆◆◆◆◆◆◆◆◆◆◆◆◆◆◆◆◆◆◆◆◆◆◆

Prep: 30 minutes plus standing Roast: 2 hours 15 to 30 minutes
Makes 14 main-dish servings

1 whole lamb leg (7 pounds)	2 tablespoons coarsely
2 large garlic cloves, sliced	chopped fresh mint
Salt	¼ teaspoon coarsely ground
2 tablespoons margarine or	black pepper
butter	½ cup port wine
1 small onion, chopped	3 tablespoons all-purpose flour
1½ slices firm white bread,	1 can (13¾ to 14½ ounces)
torn into ¼-inch crumbs	chicken broth
½ cup pistachios, finely	Asparagus and boiled
chopped	potatoes (optional)

1 Preheat oven to 325°F. Trim fat from lamb leg. With knife, cut about a dozen ½-inch-wide slits all over lamb; place a slice of garlic in each slit. Rub lamb with 1 teaspoon salt.

2 Place lamb, fat-side up, on rack in large roasting pan. Insert meat thermometer into thickest part of lamb, being careful that pointed end does not touch bone. Roast 1 hour.

3 Meanwhile, in small saucepan, melt margarine over medium heat. Add onion; cook about 10 minutes, until lightly browned and tender; remove from heat. Stir in bread crumbs, pistachios, mint, pepper, and ½ teaspoon salt.

4 After lamb has cooked 1 hour, carefully pat bread mixture on top. Roast 1¼ to 1½ hours longer, until thermometer reaches 140°F for medium-rare (internal temperature of meat will rise to 145°F upon standing).

5 Transfer to warm platter; let stand 15 minutes. Prepare gravy: Remove rack from roasting pan; pour pan drippings into 2-cup measuring cup. Add port to roasting pan. Heat to boiling over high heat; stir until brown bits are loosened.

6 Add port-wine mixture to meat juice in cup; let stand a few seconds, until fat separates from meat juice. Skim 2 tablespoons fat into roasting pan; discard any remaining fat. Stir flour into fat in roasting pan and cook over medium-high heat until blended. Gradually whisk in meat-juice mixture and broth and cook, stirring, until gravy boils and thickens slightly; boil 1 minute. Thinly slice lamb; serve with gravy, and asparagus and potatoes, if you like.

EACH SERVING: ABOUT 285 CALORIES, 33g PROTEIN, 6g CARBOHYDRATE, 13g TOTAL FAT (4g SATURATED), 99mg CHOLESTEROL, 460mg SODIUM

LAMB ROASTED OVER POTATOES

Prep: 15 minutes plus standing   *Roast:* 1 hour 30 to 45 minutes
Makes 8 main-dish servings

1 tablespoon margarine or butter	Salt
2 medium onions, sliced	Ground black pepper
1½ cups chicken broth	1 teaspoon olive oil
3 pounds all-purpose potatoes, peeled and thinly sliced	1 garlic clove, minced
	½ teaspoon dried thyme
	1 lamb leg shank half (3½ pounds)

◆ Preheat oven to 425°F. In 10-inch skillet, melt margarine over medium heat. Add onions; cook, stirring often, until tender. Stir in broth; heat to boiling over high heat. Remove from heat. In medium roasting pan, toss potatoes with onion mixture, ½ teaspoon salt, and ¼ teaspoon pepper; spread evenly in pan. Roast 15 minutes.

◆ Meanwhile, in cup, combine olive oil, garlic, thyme, ½ teaspoon salt, and ¼ teaspoon pepper; rub over lamb. Insert meat thermometer in thickest part of lamb, being careful that pointed end does not touch bone. Stir potatoes; place lamb on top. Roast 1¼ hours longer, stirring potatoes every 20 minutes, or until thermometer reaches 140°F for medium-rare (internal temperature of meat will rise to 145°F upon standing). Transfer lamb to warm large platter. Let stand 15 minutes; keep warm. (If potatoes are not yet tender, roast 15 minutes longer.) Thinly slice lamb; serve with potatoes.

Each serving: About 435 calories, 46g protein, 35g carbohydrate, 12g total fat (4g saturated), 133mg cholesterol, 590mg sodium

HERB-CRUSTED RACKS OF LAMB

Prep: 15 minutes plus standing   *Roast:* 1 hour 5 to 10 minutes
Makes 8 main-dish servings

2 lamb rib roasts, 8 ribs each (2½ pounds each; ask butcher to loosen backbone from ribs)	2 teaspoons dried rosemary, crushed
½ teaspoon salt	¼ teaspoon ground black pepper
4 slices firm white bread, torn	2 tablespoons minced fresh parsley
4 tablespoons margarine or butter	2 tablespoons Dijon mustard

◆ Preheat oven to 375°F. In large roasting pan, place lamb rib roasts, meat-side up. Sprinkle with salt. Insert meat thermometer into center of 1 roast, being careful that pointed end does not touch bone. Roast lamb 50 minutes.

◆ Meanwhile, in food processor with knife blade attached or in blender (in batches) at medium speed, process bread until fine crumbs form.

◆ In 10-inch skillet, melt margarine over medium heat. Add bread crumbs, rosemary, and pepper; cook until crumbs are golden brown. Stir in parsley.

◆ Remove roasting pan from oven. Spread tops of roasts with mustard. Carefully pat crumb mixture on top. Roast lamb 15 to 20 minutes longer, until thermometer reaches 140°F for medium-rare (internal temperature of meat will rise to 145°F upon standing). Transfer roasts to cutting board. Let stand 15 minutes; keep warm. Cut off backbone from ribs; place roasts on warm large platter. To serve, carve between ribs.

Each serving: About 485 calories, 46g protein, 7g carbohydrate, 29g total fat (9g saturated), 147mg cholesterol, 505mg sodium

ONION-STUFFED BUTTERFLIED LEG OF LAMB

Prep: 20 minutes plus standing   *Roast:* 1 hour 45 minutes
Makes 10 main-dish servings

4 tablespoons margarine or butter	1½ teaspoons dried thyme
1 large onion, minced	Ground black pepper
1 garlic clove, minced	3 pounds boneless butterflied lamb leg
Salt	1 tablespoon olive or vegetable oil
1½ teaspoons dried rosemary, crushed	½ cup dry white wine

◆ Preheat oven to 325°F. In 10-inch skillet, melt margarine over medium heat; add onion, garlic, 1 teaspoon salt, ¾ teaspoon rosemary, ¾ teaspoon thyme, and ¼ teaspoon pepper and cook until onion is tender. Remove from heat.

◆ Place lamb flat on work surface, cut-side up; spread onion mixture evenly over lamb. Roll lamb tightly. Cut three 24-inch strings and one 34-inch string. Place long string horizontally on work surface, and short strings vertically across it. Set lamb, seam-side up, lengthwise along long string. Tie strings securely around meat.

◆ Place lamb on rack in large roasting pan. Rub with oil and remaining ¾ teaspoon each rosemary and thyme; sprinkle with salt and pepper. Insert meat thermometer into center of lamb. Roast 1¾ hours, or until thermometer reaches 140°F for medium-rare (internal temperature of meat will rise to 145°F upon standing).

◆ Transfer lamb to warm large platter. Let stand 15 minutes; keep warm. Add wine and *½ cup water* to roasting pan. Heat to boiling over high heat; stir until brown bits are loosened. Skim and discard fat. Remove string from lamb; thinly slice and serve with gravy.

Each serving: About 250 calories, 29g protein, 2g carbohydrate, 13g total fat (3g saturated), 88mg cholesterol, 360mg sodium

LAMB SHANKS

Lamb shanks have excellent flavor but are not as tender as other cuts. The solution: Cook them by moist-heat methods such as braising, to yield falling-off-the-bone-tender meat in a rich sauce. Lemon, tomatoes, and dried fruit are some of the piquant ingredients that complement the robust taste of the shanks. Each shank gives enough meat for one serving.

BRAISED LAMB SHANKS WITH COUSCOUS

◆ ◆ ◆ ◆ ◆ ◆ ◆ ◆ ◆ ◆ ◆ ◆ ◆ ◆

Prep: 15 minutes
Cook: 2 hours 30 minutes
Makes 4 main-dish servings

2 teaspoons vegetable oil
4 small lamb shanks (about 1 pound each), patted dry with paper towels
2 medium carrots, cut into ¼-inch-thick slices
1 large celery stalk, cut into ¼-inch-thick slices
1 medium onion, coarsely chopped
1 can (28 ounces) tomatoes in puree
2 tablespoons chopped fresh rosemary or 2 teaspoons dried rosemary, crushed
2 teaspoons sugar
1 teaspoon beef-flavor instant bouillon
1 bay leaf
1 cinnamon stick (3 inches)
1 can (8 ounces) garbanzo beans, rinsed and drained
¾ cup couscous (Moroccan pasta)

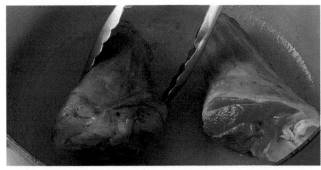

1 In 8-quart Dutch oven, heat oil over medium-high heat. Add lamb shanks, 2 at a time; cook until browned on all sides. Transfer shanks to bowl as they brown.

2 Reduce heat to medium. To drippings in Dutch oven, add carrots, celery, and onion; cook, stirring occasionally, until golden brown.

3 Add tomatoes with their puree, next 5 ingredients, and *1 cup water*; heat to boiling over high heat, breaking up tomatoes with back of spoon.

4 Return shanks to pan. Heat to boiling; reduce heat to low. Cover; simmer 2 hours, or until tender, turning meat once. Discard bay leaf and cinnamon stick; skim and discard fat. Add garbanzo beans to Dutch oven; heat through over high heat. Meanwhile, prepare couscous as label directs, but do not add margarine or butter. Serve lamb shanks and sauce with couscous.

EACH SERVING: ABOUT 490 CALORIES, 32g PROTEIN, 56g CARBOHYDRATE, 15g TOTAL FAT (5g SATURATED), 77mg CHOLESTEROL, 1180mg SODIUM

MOROCCAN LAMB SHANKS

Prep: 30 minutes   Bake: 2 hours
Makes 4 main-dish servings

4 small lamb shanks (about 1 pound each)
1 tablespoon plus 1 teaspoon vegetable oil
2 medium onions, finely chopped
3 garlic cloves, minced
1 teaspoon ground ginger
¼ teaspoon ground cinnamon
¼ teaspoon ground red pepper (cayenne)
1 can (13¾ to 14½ ounces) chicken broth
½ cup pitted prunes
⅛ cup dried apricots
1 teaspoon salt
¼ teaspoon ground black pepper
¼ cup chopped fresh cilantro

◆ Preheat oven to 350°F. Pat lamb shanks dry with paper towels. In 8-quart Dutch oven, heat 1 tablespoon oil over medium-high heat. Add shanks, 2 at a time; cook until browned on all sides. Transfer shanks to bowl as they brown.

◆ Reduce heat to medium. Add remaining 1 teaspoon oil and onions to Dutch oven; cook 5 minutes, or until onion is tender. Stir in garlic and next 3 ingredients; cook 30 seconds.

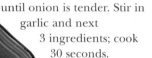

◆ Return shanks to Dutch oven; stir in broth, prunes, apricots, salt, pepper, and *1 cup water*. Heat to boiling over high heat. Cover and bake 2 hours, or until lamb is very tender, turning meat once.

◆ Skim and discard fat from sauce in Dutch oven. To serve, sprinkle with chopped cilantro.

Each serving: About 355 calories, 26g protein, 29g carbohydrate, 16g total fat (5g saturated), 85mg cholesterol, 1025mg sodium

LAMB AND BEAN CASSEROLE

Prep: 30 minutes
Bake: 2 hours
Makes 4 main-dish servings

4 small lamb shanks (about 1 pound each)
2 tablespoons all-purpose flour
2 tablespoons vegetable oil
1 large celery stalk, diced
1 medium onion, diced
1 can (14½ to 16 ounces) stewed tomatoes
1 can (13¾ to 14½ ounces) beef broth
1 garlic clove, minced
1 bay leaf
½ teaspoon dried thyme
½ teaspoon salt
¼ teaspoon coarsely ground black pepper
1 can (16 to 19 ounces) white kidney beans (cannellini), rinsed and drained
1 teaspoon chopped fresh parsley
1 teaspoon grated lemon peel

◆ Preheat oven to 350°F. Pat lamb shanks dry with paper towels. Coat shanks with flour. In 8-quart Dutch oven, heat oil over medium-high heat; add lamb shanks, 2 at a time; cook until browned on all sides. Transfer shanks to bowl as they brown.

◆ Reduce heat to medium. To drippings in Dutch oven, add celery and onion; cook until well browned. Return shanks to Dutch oven; stir in stewed tomatoes, broth, garlic, bay leaf, thyme, salt, and pepper; heat to boiling over high heat.

◆ Cover Dutch oven and bake 2 hours, or until lamb shanks are tender, turning meat once.

◆ Skim and discard fat from sauce in Dutch oven. Stir in kidney beans; heat through over medium heat. Discard bay leaf. To serve, sprinkle with parsley and lemon peel.

Each serving: About 395 calories, 30g protein, 29g carbohydrate, 18g total fat (6g saturated), 77mg cholesterol, 1000mg sodium

GREEK-STYLE LAMB SHANKS

Prep: 30 minutes
Bake: 2 hours 30 minutes
Makes 4 main-dish servings

4 small lamb shanks (about 1 pound each)
1 tablespoon vegetable oil
2 medium onions, diced
1 large carrot, diced
2 garlic cloves, minced
1 can (14½ ounces) diced tomatoes
1 cup chicken broth
¾ teaspoon salt
4 medium all-purpose potatoes (about 1¾ pounds), unpeeled, each cut into quarters
12 ounces green beans, ends trimmed and cut into 2-inch pieces
2 medium lemons
2 tablespoons chopped fresh dill
2 tablespoons chopped fresh parsley

◆ Preheat oven to 350°F. Pat lamb shanks dry with paper towels. In 8-quart Dutch oven, heat oil over medium-high heat. Add shanks, 2 at a time; cook until browned on all sides. Transfer shanks to bowl as they brown.

◆ To drippings in Dutch oven, add onions and carrot; cook over medium heat 12 minutes, or until tender and lightly browned. Add garlic; cook 1 minute longer.

◆ Return shanks to Dutch oven. Stir in tomatoes with their juice, broth, and salt; heat to boiling over high heat. Cover Dutch oven and bake 1¼ hours. Turn shanks over; add potatoes and green beans. Cover and bake 1¼ hours longer, or until lamb and potatoes are tender.

◆ Skim and discard fat from sauce in Dutch oven. Grate 1 tablespoon peel and squeeze 2 tablespoons juice from lemons. Stir lemon peel and juice, dill, and parsley into sauce.

Each serving: About 490 calories, 32g protein, 63g carbohydrate, 16g total fat (5g saturated), 81mg cholesterol, 1090mg sodium

LAMB CASSEROLES AND STEWS

Chopped fresh vegetables, a flavorful liquid, and some zesty herbs and spices transform simple chunks of lamb into a warming, hearty oven or stove-top meal. The long, slow cooking time both tenderizes the meat and allows the seasonings to permeate the lamb and vegetables.

LAMB CURRY

◆◆◆◆◆◆◆◆◆◆◆◆◆◆◆◆◆◆◆◆◆◆◆◆◆◆

Prep: 25 minutes   Cook: 2 hours 15 to 30 minutes
Makes 6 main-dish servings

2 tablespoons vegetable oil
4 pounds bone-in lamb shoulder, cut up for stew, patted dry with paper towels
6 medium onions, finely chopped
2 tablespoons minced, peeled fresh ginger
4 garlic cloves, minced
12 cardamom pods
1 cinnamon stick (3 inches)

2 teaspoons ground cumin
¼ teaspoon ground red pepper (cayenne)
2 tablespoons tomato paste
1½ teaspoons salt
2 pounds baking potatoes, peeled and cut into 1½-inch pieces
¼ cup chopped fresh cilantro
Naan bread (Indian flatbread) and steamed spinach (optional)

1 In 5-quart Dutch oven, heat 1 teaspoon oil over medium-high heat. Add one-third of lamb and brown all over; transfer to bowl. Repeat in 2 more batches with 2 teaspoons oil and remaining lamb.

2 To drippings in Dutch oven, add remaining 1 tablespoon oil; heat until hot. Stir in onions; cook, stirring often, 15 minutes, or until tender. Stir in ginger and next 5 ingredients; cook, stirring, 1 minute.

CARDAMOM

A member of the ginger family, cardamom is a spice prized for its aromatic seeds and is commonly used in Indian and Scandinavian cooking. Each whole pod, which may be pale green or bleached white, holds a cluster of tiny, hard black seeds, which have a flowery, lemony taste. Cardamom is sold in the pod or as ground seeds. The pods retain more fragrance than the ground version, which loses flavor quickly. Try adding whole pods, slightly crushed to release the fragrant oils, to a stew, curry, or rice – or let steep in a mug of tea.

3 Add tomato paste and cook, stirring, 1 minute. Return lamb to Dutch oven; stir in salt and *2 cups water*; heat to boiling over high heat. Reduce heat to low; cover and simmer 1½ hours.

4 Stir in potatoes; heat to boiling over high heat. Reduce heat to low, cover, and simmer 30 to 45 minutes, until potatoes are tender. Skim and discard fat. Sprinkle with cilantro. Serve with spinach and naan bread, if you like.

EACH SERVING: ABOUT 610 CALORIES, 62g PROTEIN, 43g CARBOHYDRATE, 20g TOTAL FAT (6g SATURATED), 183mg CHOLESTEROL, 710mg SODIUM

LAMB STEW PROVENÇAL

Prep: 45 minutes   Bake: 1 hour 15 to 30 minutes
Makes 6 main-dish servings

2 pounds boneless lamb, cut into 1½-inch pieces
2 teaspoons plus 1 tablespoon vegetable oil
4 medium onions, thinly sliced
2 red peppers, thinly sliced
1 teaspoon salt
3 garlic cloves, minced

1 can (14½ to 16 ounces) tomatoes
¼ teaspoon dried thyme
¼ teaspoon fennel seeds
¼ teaspoon ground black pepper
3 strips (3" by ½") orange peel
¼ cup chopped fresh basil

Preheat oven to 350°F. Pat lamb dry. In 5-quart Dutch oven, heat 1 teaspoon oil over medium-high heat. Add half of lamb; brown all over. With slotted spoon, transfer to plate. Repeat with 1 teaspoon oil and remaining lamb. To drippings, add 1 tablespoon oil and next 3 ingredients. Cook, stirring often, 25 minutes, or until very tender. Add garlic; cook 1 minute. Add tomatoes with their juice, stirring to break up, next 4 ingredients, and lamb. Heat to boiling. Cover; bake 1¼ to 1½ hours, until lamb is tender. Skim and discard fat. To serve, sprinkle with basil.

Each serving: About 325 calories, 40g protein, 15g carbohydrate, 14g total fat (4g saturated), 122mg cholesterol, 550mg sodium

ROMAN LAMB STEW WITH MARSALA

Prep: 15 minutes   Cook: 2 hours
Makes 6 main-dish servings

2 pounds boneless lamb, cut into 1½-inch pieces
3 teaspoons vegetable oil
1 bag (16 ounces) carrots
1 medium onion, finely chopped
1 celery stalk, finely chopped
1 garlic clove, minced
1 cup Marsala wine

1 can (14½ to 16 ounces) tomatoes
1¼ teaspoons salt
¼ teaspoon ground black pepper
¼ teaspoon dried rosemary
¼ teaspoon dried thyme
1 package (10 ounces) frozen peas

◆ Pat lamb dry with paper towels. In 5-quart Dutch oven, heat 1 teaspoon oil over medium-high heat. Add half of lamb and brown all over; with slotted spoon, transfer to plate. Repeat with 1 more teaspoon oil and remaining lamb. Meanwhile, finely chop 1 carrot. Cut remaining carrots lengthwise in half, then crosswise into 3-inch pieces.

◆ Reduce heat to medium. To drippings in Dutch oven, add remaining 1 teaspoon oil, chopped carrot, onion, and celery; cook 5 minutes, or until tender. Stir in garlic and cook 30 seconds. Add Marsala and heat to boiling over high heat. Stir in tomatoes with their juice, salt, pepper, rosemary, thyme, and lamb. Heat to boiling, breaking up tomatoes with back of spoon. Reduce heat to low; cover and simmer 1 hour. Stir in remaining carrots; cover and cook 30 to 45 minutes longer, until lamb and carrots are tender. Skim and discard fat. Stir in peas; cover and cook 5 minutes longer.

Each serving: About 405 calories, 42g protein, 21g carbohydrate, 13g total fat (4g saturated), 122mg cholesterol, 710mg sodium

LAMB AND VEGETABLE RAGOUT

Prep: 25 minutes   Cook: 1 hour 20 minutes
Makes 4 main-dish servings

1 pound boneless lamb, cut into 1-inch pieces
1 tablespoon vegetable oil
½ teaspoon salt
2 large celery stalks, chopped
1 large onion, chopped
1 can (14½ to 16 ounces) stewed tomatoes
1 can (13¾ to 14½ ounces) beef broth
3 large potatoes (1½ pounds)
3 medium turnips (12 ounces)

3 medium carrots, cut into ¾-inch chunks
1 tablespoon soy sauce
1 teaspoon sugar
¾ teaspoon browning and seasoning sauce (optional)
2 tablespoons all-purpose flour
1 package (10 ounces) frozen peas
2 tablespoons grated lemon peel

◆ Pat lamb dry with paper towels. In 5-quart Dutch oven, heat oil over medium-high heat. Add lamb and salt; brown lamb all over. With slotted spoon, transfer lamb to bowl. To drippings in Dutch oven, add celery and onion; cook until lightly browned. Stir in lamb, stewed tomatoes, beef broth, and *1 cup water*. Heat to boiling over high heat. Reduce heat to low; cover and simmer 25 minutes.

◆ Peel potatoes and turnips; cut into 1½-inch chunks. Stir into Dutch oven with next 4 ingredients. Heat to boiling over high heat. Reduce heat to low; cover and simmer 20 minutes longer, or until lamb and vegetables are tender.

◆ In cup, mix flour and *2 tablespoons water*; stir into ragout. Cook, stirring, over medium-high heat until mixture thickens and boils. Skim and discard fat. Stir in peas; cook 5 minutes longer. To serve, sprinkle with lemon peel.

Each serving: About 525 calories, 40g protein, 67g carbohydrate, 12g total fat (4g saturated), 92mg cholesterol, 1360mg sodium

LAMB CHOPS

Delicate rib chops and larger loin chops are luxury cuts, immensely satisfying to eat and easy to cook. Broiled with a fragrant rosemary and apple-jelly glaze or coated in a zippy mustard crust, panfried and served with a sweet walnut-fig sauce or a piquant pepper relish, they're a treat in any guise. More economical meaty shoulder chops are flavorful, but less tender; they're more suitable for braising. Once upon a time, lamb was only a springtime feast. Thankfully, it's now available for year-round enjoyment.

1 Preheat broiler. Rub both sides of each lamb chop with cut sides of garlic; discard garlic. Sprinkle lamb chops with rosemary, salt, and black pepper. In small bowl, mix apple jelly and balsamic vinegar until well combined.

GLAZED ROSEMARY LAMB CHOPS

Prep: 10 minutes   *Broil: 10 minutes*
Makes 4 main-dish servings

8 lamb loin chops, each
  1 inch thick (4 ounces each)
1 large garlic clove, cut in half
2 teaspoons chopped fresh
  rosemary or ½ teaspoon
  dried rosemary, crushed
¼ teaspoon salt

¼ teaspoon coarsely ground
  black pepper
¼ cup apple jelly
1 tablespoon balsamic vinegar
Rosemary sprigs for garnish
Italian green beans (optional)

2 Place chops on rack in broiling pan. Place pan in broiler at closest position to heat source; broil chops 4 minutes. Brush chops with half of jelly mixture; broil 1 minute. Turn chops and broil 4 minutes longer.

3 Brush on remaining jelly mixture and broil 1 minute longer for medium-rare. Transfer lamb to 4 plates; skim fat from drippings in pan. Garnish and serve with pan juices, and green beans, if you like.

BALSAMIC VINEGAR

This distinctive vinegar, from the area around Modena, Italy, is made from white Trebbiano grape juice. Aged in wooden barrels for at least 10 years, balsamic vinegar has an intense, tangy-sweet flavor that is especially good in marinades and salad dressings. Strawberries, peaches, and other fruits are also enhanced by a splash of balsamic vinegar.

EACH SERVING: ABOUT 350 CALORIES, 39g PROTEIN, 14g CARBOHYDRATE, 14g TOTAL FAT (5g SATURATED), 127mg CHOLESTEROL, 235mg SODIUM

LAMB CHOPS WITH WALNUT-FIG SAUCE

Prep: 5 minutes   *Cook:* 25 minutes
Makes 4 main-dish servings

4 lamb loin chops, each
   1½ inches thick (8 ounces
   each)
1 tablespoon vegetable oil
Salt

¼ cup coarsely chopped
   walnuts
¾ cup apple juice
8 dried Calimyrna figs, each
   cut in half

◆ Pat lamb chops dry with paper towels. In 10-inch skillet, heat oil over medium-high heat; add lamb chops and cook about 5 minutes, until browned on both sides. Reduce heat to low; cover and cook 12 to 15 minutes for medium-rare, or until desired doneness, turning chops occasionally.

◆ Transfer lamb chops to warm platter. Sprinkle with ¼ teaspoon salt; keep warm. Pour off all drippings in skillet. Add walnuts to skillet and cook over low heat, stirring frequently, until lightly toasted.

◆ Add apple juice, figs, and ¼ teaspoon salt to walnuts in skillet. Heat to boiling over high heat. Cook 2 to 3 minutes, until liquid is slightly thickened. Pour walnut-fig sauce over lamb chops.

Each serving: About 500 calories, 41g protein, 39g carbohydrate, 21g total fat (6g saturated), 127mg cholesterol, 370mg sodium

MINT JELLY

The fresh, zingy taste of mint makes it a perfect partner for lamb. In England, mint jelly or mint sauce is traditionally served with roast leg of lamb, but it works just as well with smaller cuts.

In cup, combine 1 tablespoon cider vinegar and 1 teaspoon dried mint; let stand 5 minutes. Meanwhile, in 1-quart saucepan, melt ½ cup apple jelly over medium heat. Stir in mint mixture and heat to boiling. Strain mixture through sieve. Makes ½ cup.

Each tablespoon: About 50 calories, 0g protein, 13g carbohydrate, 0g total fat, 0mg cholesterol, 5mg sodium

LAMB CHOPS WITH RED-PEPPER RELISH

Prep: 30 minutes   *Broil:* 10 minutes
Makes 4 main-dish servings

⅓ cup cider vinegar
¼ cup sugar
Pinch dried thyme
Pinch fennel seeds, crushed
Salt
1 medium Golden Delicious
   apple, peeled, cored, and
   diced

2 small red peppers, diced
2 jalapeño chiles, seeded and
   finely chopped
8 lamb loin chops, each
   1 inch thick (4 ounces each)

◆ In 2-quart saucepan, combine vinegar, sugar, thyme, fennel, and 1 teaspoon salt; heat to boiling over high heat. Add apple, peppers, and jalapeño chiles; heat to boiling.

◆ Reduce heat to medium-low; simmer, stirring occasionally, 15 to 20 minutes, until mixture is thickened and most of liquid has evaporated.

◆ Meanwhile, preheat broiler. Sprinkle lamb chops with ¼ teaspoon salt. Place chops on rack in broiling pan. Place pan in broiler at closest position to heat source; broil chops 5 minutes.

◆ Turn chops; broil 5 minutes longer for medium-rare, or until desired doneness. Serve with warm red-pepper relish.

Each serving: About 370 calories, 39g protein, 21g carbohydrate, 14g total fat (5g saturated), 127mg cholesterol, 970mg sodium

BROILED LAMB CHOPS WITH MUSTARD-PARSLEY CRUST

Prep: 10 minutes   *Broil:* 8 to 9 minutes
Makes 4 main-dish servings

8 lamb rib chops, each 1 inch
   thick (3 ounces each)
2 tablespoons plain dried
   bread crumbs
2 tablespoons Dijon mustard

2 tablespoons chopped fresh
   parsley
2 teaspoons olive or
   vegetable oil
½ teaspoon salt

◆ Preheat broiler. Place chops on rack in broiling pan. Place pan in broiler 4 to 5 inches from heat source; broil chops 5 minutes.

◆ Meanwhile, in small bowl, mix bread crumbs, mustard, parsley, oil, and salt. Turn chops; spread bread-crumb mixture over meaty portion. Broil chops 3 to 4 minutes longer for medium-rare, or until desired doneness.

Each serving: About 265 calories, 30g protein, 3g carbohydrate, 14g total fat (4g saturated), 97mg cholesterol, 570mg sodium

GRILLED BUTTERFLIED LAMB

Classic butterflied leg of lamb makes a spectacular company meal that is easy to prepare. Ask the butcher to butterfly and bone a 4- to 5½-pound half-leg, to yield 3 to 3½ pounds meat. The thickness of the piece will vary throughout; slice off the thinner pieces as soon as they are done.

GRILLED PESTO LAMB

◆◆◆◆◆◆◆◆◆◆◆◆◆

Prep: 25 minutes
Grill: 15 to 25 minutes
Makes 10 main-dish servings

3 cups loosely packed basil leaves (about 2 bunches)
⅓ cup pine nuts (pignoli)
⅓ cup freshly grated Parmesan cheese
3 tablespoons olive oil
2 tablespoons fresh lemon juice
¾ teaspoon salt
2 garlic cloves
3 pounds boneless butterflied lamb leg
Tomato-Cucumber Bruschetta (optional, see below)
Basil sprigs for garnish

1 Prepare outdoor grill. Prepare pesto: In food processor with knife blade attached or in blender, process basil leaves and next 6 ingredients until blended. Place lamb in 13" by 9" glass baking dish; spread pesto over both sides of lamb.

2 Place lamb on grill over medium heat; reserve any pesto in dish. Grill, brushing with reserved pesto several times and turning occasionally, 15 to 25 minutes for medium-rare, or until desired doneness. Cut off sections as they are done.

3 Transfer lamb to cutting board; let stand 10 minutes for easier carving. Meanwhile, prepare Tomato-Cucumber Bruschetta, if desired. Cut lamb into thin slices; garnish, and serve with bruschetta, if you like.

TOMATO-CUCUMBER BRUSCHETTA

In medium bowl, mix 1 medium tomato, seeded and chopped, 1 medium cucumber, peeled and chopped, 1 tablespoon olive oil, 2 teaspoons fresh lemon juice, and ¼ teaspoon ground black pepper. Cut 1 loaf (8 ounces) Italian bread diagonally into ½-inch-thick slices (reserve ends for another use). Toast slices on grill over medium heat, turning once. Spread slices with ¼ cup olive paste; top with tomato mixture. Makes 10 servings.

Each serving: About 100 calories, 2g protein, 13g carbohydrate, 4g total fat (1g saturated), 0mg cholesterol, 180mg sodium

---

PINE NUTS

The seed of a stone pine, pine nuts ("pignoli" in Italian) are a much-loved Mediterranean ingredient, used in stuffings for meat and grape leaves, pesto, vegetable sautés, and cakes and cookies. Because pine nuts are high in fat, they turn rancid quickly. To prolong flavor, buy the freshest nuts and store them in the freezer.

EACH SERVING: ABOUT 255 CALORIES, 31g PROTEIN, 2g CARBOHYDRATE, 14g TOTAL FAT (4g SATURATED), 91mg CHOLESTEROL, 290mg SODIUM

YOGURT-MARINATED BUTTERFLIED LEG OF LAMB

Prep: 10 minutes plus marinating
Grill: 15 to 25 minutes
Makes 10 main-dish servings

1 container (8 ounces) plain low-fat
   yogurt
¼ cup chopped fresh parsley
¼ cup fresh lemon juice
2½ teaspoons salt
2 teaspoons coarsely ground black
   pepper
2 garlic cloves, minced
3 pounds butterflied boneless lamb leg
Grilled peppers (optional)

◆ In 13" by 9" glass baking dish, mix first 6 ingredients. Add lamb, turning to coat with marinade. Cover dish with plastic wrap and refrigerate, turning lamb occasionally, at least 3 hours.

◆ Prepare outdoor grill. Place lamb on grill over medium heat, reserving marinade in dish. Grill, brushing with reserved marinade and turning occasionally, 15 to 25 minutes for medium-rare, or until desired doneness.

◆ Transfer lamb to cutting board; let stand 10 minutes for easier carving. Cut into bite-size chunks, and serve with grilled peppers, if you like.

Each serving: About 200 calories, 30g protein, 3g carbohydrate, 7g total fat (3g saturated), 90mg cholesterol, 615mg sodium

GRILLED LAMB WITH MINT AND OREGANO

Prep: 25 minutes plus marinating
Grill: 15 to 25 minutes
Makes 10 main-dish servings

1 large bunch fresh mint
1 large bunch fresh oregano
3 tablespoons plus ¼ cup olive oil
3 tablespoons plus ¼ cup fresh lemon
   juice
1 garlic clove, minced
Salt and ground black pepper
3 pounds butterflied boneless lamb leg

◆ Chop ¼ cup mint and ¼ cup oregano; reserve remaining mint and oregano to make sauce.

◆ In 13" by 9" glass baking dish, mix chopped mint and oregano, 3 tablespoons each olive oil and lemon juice, minced garlic, 1 teaspoon salt, and ½ teaspoon pepper; stir until well blended.

◆ Add lamb to dish, turning to coat with marinade and spooning marinade over. Cover dish with plastic wrap and refrigerate, turning lamb occasionally, at least 8 hours, or overnight.

◆ Prepare outdoor grill. Prepare sauce: Chop 2 tablespoons mint and 2 tablespoons oregano; stir into small bowl with remaining ¼ cup each olive oil and lemon juice, ½ teaspoon salt, and ¼ teaspoon pepper.

◆ Place lamb on grill over medium heat, discarding marinade in dish. Grill, turning lamb occasionally, 15 to 25 minutes for medium-rare, or until desired doneness.

◆ Transfer lamb to cutting board; let stand 10 minutes for easier carving. Cut lamb into thin slices and arrange on large platter. Spoon herb sauce on top of lamb; garnish with any remaining herbs.

Each serving: About 275 calories, 29g protein, 2g carbohydrate, 16g total fat (4g saturated), 88mg cholesterol, 390mg sodium

LEG OF LAMB WITH COCONUT COUSCOUS

Prep: 10 minutes   *Grill:* 15 to 25 minutes
Makes 10 main-dish servings

2 cups couscous (Moroccan pasta)
1 cup dried currants or seedless raisins
½ cup shredded coconut, toasted
1 tablespoon dried rosemary, crushed
1 tablespoon olive or vegetable oil
2 teaspoons salt
1 teaspoon coarsely ground black pepper
1 garlic clove, minced
3 pounds butterflied boneless lamb leg
Parsley sprigs for garnish
½ cup Kalamata olives, pitted, or pitted
   ripe olives

◆ Prepare outdoor grill. Prepare couscous as label directs; stir in currants and toasted coconut. Keep warm.

◆ In cup, mix rosemary, oil, salt, pepper, and minced garlic; rub over lamb. Place lamb on grill over medium heat. Grill, turning lamb occasionally, 15 to 25 minutes for medium-rare, or until desired doneness.

◆ Transfer lamb to cutting board; let stand 10 minutes for easier carving. Cut lamb into thin slices; arrange on large platter with couscous. Tuck parsley sprigs in between lamb slices. Scatter olives over top.

Each serving: About 420 calories, 34g protein, 43g carbohydrate, 12g total fat (4g saturated), 88mg cholesterol, 630mg sodium

TOASTING COCONUT

Toasted coconut has a sweet, nutty taste and an appealing crunchy texture. To toast shredded coconut, preheat the oven to 350°F. Spread coconut in a single layer in a shallow pan. Bake approximately 10 minutes or until coconut is lightly toasted, stirring occasionally so it browns evenly. Cool slightly before using.

GRILLED LAMB CUTS

When barbecuing calls for something on the elegant side, lamb kabobs, chops, and steaks fit the occasion. The meat can be marinated to absorb the flavors of herbs and spices, then grilled alongside colorful vegetables such as zucchini, tomatoes, and onions. A simple salad makes the perfect accompaniment.

1 In 3-quart saucepan, heat shallots with *water* to cover to boiling over high heat. Reduce heat to low; cover and simmer 5 minutes (15 minutes if using elephant garlic). Drain; peel.

2 In medium bowl, mix lemon juice, rosemary, oil, salt, and pepper. Add lamb, zucchini, and shallots; toss to coat. Cover; refrigerate, tossing occasionally, 2 hours.

3 Prepare outdoor grill. Prepare Greek salad, but do not toss with dressing. On skewers, thread lamb, zucchini, and shallots. Grill kabobs over medium heat, turning occasionally, 8 to 10 minutes for medium-rare.

LAMB KABOBS WITH GREEK SALAD

◆◆◆◆◆◆◆◆◆◆◆◆◆

Prep: 30 minutes plus marinating
Grill: 8 to 10 minutes
Makes 4 main-dish servings

12 to 16 large shallots or 2 heads elephant garlic, separated into cloves, unpeeled
3 tablespoons fresh lemon juice
1 tablespoon chopped fresh rosemary or 1 teaspoon dried rosemary, crushed
2 tablespoons olive oil
1 teaspoon salt
1 teaspoon coarsely ground black pepper
1½ pounds lamb cubes (1½ inches) for kabobs
2 small zucchini (6 ounces each), cut into 1-inch-thick slices
Greek Salad (see above right)
4 (10-inch) metal skewers
Rosemary sprigs for garnish

GREEK SALAD

In bowl, toss 1 small head romaine lettuce, cut into 2-inch pieces, 2 small tomatoes, cut into 1-inch chunks, 1 small cucumber, cut into ¼-inch-thick slices, ½ cup pitted Kalamata olives, and ½ small red onion, diced. Prepare dressing: In small bowl, mix 2 tablespoons red wine vinegar, 1 tablespoon olive oil, ½ teaspoon dried oregano, and ½ teaspoon each salt and ground black pepper. Chill salad and dressing separately. Just before serving, toss salad with dressing. Makes 4 servings.

Each serving: About 110 calories, 2g protein, 9g carbohydrate, 8g total fat (1g saturated), 0mg cholesterol, 580mg sodium

4 On large platter, arrange lamb kabobs. Garnish with rosemary sprigs. Toss Greek salad gently with dressing and serve with kabobs.

EACH SERVING (KABOBS ONLY): ABOUT 390 CALORIES, 45g PROTEIN, 11g CARBOHYDRATE, 18g TOTAL FAT (5g SATURATED), 137mg CHOLESTEROL, 630mg SODIUM

MARINATED LAMB CHOPS WITH GRILLED TOMATOES

Prep: 15 minutes plus marinating   Grill: 8 to 10 minutes
Makes 4 main-dish servings

2 garlic cloves, minced
¼ cup red wine vinegar
2 teaspoons dried rosemary, crushed
1¼ teaspoons salt
Coarsely ground black pepper
8 lamb rib chops, each 1 inch thick (3 ounces each)
2 large tomatoes, each cut horizontally in half
1 tablespoon olive or vegetable oil
2 tablespoons freshly grated Parmesan cheese
1 tablespoon chopped fresh parsley

◆ Prepare outdoor grill. In 13" by 9" glass baking dish, mix first 4 ingredients and ½ teaspoon pepper. Arrange lamb chops in 1 layer in baking dish, turning to coat with marinade. Let lamb chops stand, turning occasionally, 15 minutes.

◆ Place lamb chops on grill over medium heat, reserving marinade in dish. Brush tomatoes with oil; place tomatoes, cut-side down, on grill with chops. Grill 8 to 10 minutes for medium-rare, or until desired doneness, turning chops and tomatoes once, and brushing chops with reserved marinade halfway through cooking time. To serve, sprinkle tomato halves with Parmesan cheese, chopped parsley, and ¼ teaspoon pepper. Serve with chops.

Each serving: About 300 calories, 29g protein, 6g carbohydrate, 18g total fat (6g saturated), 91mg cholesterol, 815mg sodium

OREGANO LAMB STEAK

Prep: 15 minutes plus marinating and standing   Grill: 8 to 10 minutes
Makes 4 main-dish servings

2 tablespoons chopped fresh oregano or 1 teaspoon dried oregano
1 tablespoon red wine vinegar
1 garlic clove, minced
1 teaspoon grated orange peel
¼ teaspoon ground black pepper
1 tablespoon plus 1 teaspoon olive oil
Salt
1 lamb steak, 1 inch thick (1 pound)
2 small red onions, cut crosswise into ½-inch-thick slices
4 plum tomatoes, each cut lengthwise in half
4 pita breads (6 inches)

◆ In glass pie plate, combine oregano, vinegar, garlic, orange peel, pepper, 1 tablespoon olive oil, and ½ teaspoon salt. Add lamb, turning to coat with marinade. Cover and refrigerate at least 4 hours, or overnight.

◆ Prepare outdoor grill. Secure red onion slices with toothpicks to hold rings in place. In medium bowl, drizzle onions with remaining 1 teaspoon olive oil and toss gently to coat. Place lamb and onions on grill over medium heat. Grill 10 to 12 minutes for medium, or until desired doneness, turning lamb and onions once. Meanwhile, sprinkle tomatoes lightly with salt, place cut-side down on grill, and grill, turning once, 5 minutes. Grill pita breads 30 to 60 seconds on each side, until lightly toasted. Transfer lamb, vegetables, and pita breads to platter. Let lamb stand 10 minutes; keep warm. To serve, thinly slice lamb; cut each pita crosswise in half.

Each serving: About 505 calories, 26g protein, 42g carbohydrate 26g total fat (9g saturated), 80mg cholesterol, 985mg sodium

GRILLED LAMB STEAK WITH SPICE CRUST

Prep: 5 minutes plus standing   Grill: 8 to 10 minutes
Makes 4 main-dish servings

1 teaspoon coriander seeds
1 teaspoon cumin seeds
1 teaspon fennel seeds
½ teaspoon salt
½ teaspoon black peppercorns
1 lamb steak, 1 inch thick (1 pound)

◆ Prepare outdoor grill. In 1-quart saucepan, heat coriander, cumin, and fennel seeds over medium-low heat, shaking pan occasionally, 1 to 2 minutes, until very fragrant. Transfer to mortar with salt and peppercorns; coarsely crush spices. Or, place in heavy zip-tight plastic bag; crush with rolling pin.

◆ Pat lamb dry with paper towels. Press crushed spice mixture all over lamb. Place lamb on grill over medium heat. Grill 8 to 10 minutes, turning once, for medium, or until desired doneness. Transfer lamb to platter. Let stand 10 minutes; keep warm. To serve, thinly slice lamb.

Each serving: About 265 calories, 19g protein, 1g carbohydrate, 20g total fat (9g saturated), 80mg cholesterol, 320mg sodium

◆ ◆

MARINATING HINTS

When marinades contain acidic ingredients, such as vinegar, wine, or citrus juice, marinate food in nonreactive containers; glass, ceramic, and stainless steel are all suitable. Heavy-duty zip-tight plastic bags also work well. Do not use aluminum, which can react with the acid and create an unpleasant metallic taste. Foods can be marinated up to 30 minutes at room temperature. If longer marinating is called for, keep the food refrigerated.

◆ ◆

GROUND LAMB

Ground lamb makes comfort classics, from Mediterranean spicy meatballs and a delectable casserole with eggplant to British shepherd's pie. If you prefer, substitute beef.

EGGPLANT AND LAMB CASSEROLE

◆◆◆◆◆◆◆◆◆◆◆◆

Prep: 55 minutes
Bake: 35 to 40 minutes
Makes 10 main-dish servings

2 small eggplants (1¼ pounds each), cut lengthwise into ½-inch-thick slices
5 tablespoons olive oil
2 pounds ground lamb
1 large onion, chopped
2 garlic cloves, minced
1 teaspoon ground cumin
½ teaspoon ground cinnamon
Salt and coarsely ground black pepper
1 can (28 ounces) tomatoes in puree
⅓ cup all-purpose flour
3 cups milk
4 large eggs, lightly beaten
¼ teaspoon ground nutmeg
Crusty bread (optional)

1 Preheat oven to 450°F. Grease 2 small cookie sheets. Place eggplant slices on cookie sheets. Use 3 tablespoons oil to brush both sides. Bake 20 minutes, or until soft, switching position of sheets between racks after 10 minutes. Remove from oven; turn oven control to 375°F.

2 In deep 12-inch skillet, heat 1 tablespoon oil over medium-high heat; add lamb, onion, and garlic and cook 15 minutes, or until all are browned.

3 Stir in cumin, cinnamon, 1 teaspoon salt, and ¼ teaspoon pepper; cook 1 minute. Remove skillet from heat; add tomatoes with their puree, breaking them up with back of spoon.

4 In 3-quart saucepan, heat 1 tablespoon oil over medium heat; add flour and cook 1 minute. Gradually whisk in milk; cook about 15 minutes, until thick. Remove from heat.

5 Gradually whisk small amount of hot milk mixture into eggs. Return egg mixture to saucepan, whisking. Whisk in nutmeg, ½ teaspoon salt, and ¼ teaspoon pepper.

6 In shallow 3½- to 4-quart casserole or 13" by 9" glass or ceramic baking dish, arrange half of eggplant slices, overlapping slices to fit if necessary; top with half of lamb mixture. Repeat with remaining eggplant slices and lamb mixture; pour milk mixture evenly over top. Bake 35 to 40 minutes, until top is puffed and golden and casserole is heated through. Serve with crusty bread, if you like.

EACH SERVING: ABOUT 400 CALORIES, 24g PROTEIN, 20g CARBOHYDRATE, 25g TOTAL FAT (9g SATURATED), 160mg CHOLESTEROL, 700mg SODIUM

SHEPHERD'S PIE

Prep: 40 minutes   Bake: 20 minutes
Makes 4 main-dish servings

2 pounds all-purpose
   potatoes, peeled and cut
   into 1½-inch chunks
Salt
½ cup milk
3 tablespoons margarine or
   butter
¼ cup plus 1 tablespoon freshly
   grated Parmesan cheese
Ground black pepper
1 medium onion, chopped

2 carrots, finely chopped
1 pound ground lamb
2 tablespoons tomato paste
2 tablespoons all-purpose
   flour
¼ cup dry red wine
1 cup reduced-sodium
   chicken broth
¼ teaspoon dried thyme
1 cup frozen peas

◆ Preheat oven to 425°F. In 4-quart saucepan, heat
potatoes with ¼ teaspoon salt and *water* to cover to boiling
over high heat. Reduce heat to low; cover and simmer
20 minutes, or until potatoes are tender. Drain and return
to saucepan. With potato masher, mash potatoes with milk
and 2 tablespoons margarine. Stir in ¼ cup Parmesan
cheese and ¼ teaspoon pepper.

◆ Meanwhile, in 10-inch skillet, melt remaining 1 tablespoon
margarine over medium heat. Add onion and carrots; cook
until tender. Add lamb and cook over medium-high heat,
breaking it up with spoon, until no longer pink. Add
tomato paste; cook, stirring, 1 minute. Add flour and cook,
stirring, 1 minute. Stir in wine; cook until evaporated. Add
broth, thyme, ¼ teaspoon salt, and ⅛ teaspoon pepper; stir
until brown bits are loosened. Heat to boiling. Stir in peas.

◆ Spoon lamb mixture into 9-inch deep-dish pie plate; spoon
potatoes evenly on top. Sprinkle with remaining 1 tablespoon
Parmesan. Bake on cookie sheet 20 minutes, or until browned.

**Each serving: About 650 calories, 34g protein, 61g carbohydrate,
30g total fat (11g saturated), 97mg cholesterol, 745mg sodium**

TURKISH MEATBALLS

Prep: 15 minutes   Cook: 8 to 10 minutes
Makes 4 main-dish servings

1 slice firm white bread
1 pound ground lamb
1 large egg
¼ cup chopped fresh parsley
1 small garlic clove, minced
⅛ teaspoon ground red
   pepper (cayenne)

½ teaspoon ground cumin
½ teaspoon salt
2 tablespoons all-purpose
   flour
1 tablespoon vegetable oil

◆ In blender or food processor with knife blade attached,
process bread to fine crumbs. In large bowl, mix bread
crumbs with lamb and next 6 ingredients until combined.

◆ Shape mixture into 1½-inch meatballs. On waxed paper,
roll meatballs in flour to coat evenly. In 12-inch skillet, heat
oil over medium-high heat. Add meatballs and cook,
turning occasionally, 8 to 10 minutes, until just cooked
through. Transfer to paper towels to drain.

**Each serving: About 320 calories, 24g protein, 7g carbohydrate,
22g total fat (8g saturated), 135mg cholesterol, 390mg sodium**

LAMB IN PITAS WITH
YOGURT SAUCE

Prep: 20 minutes   Cook: 30 minutes
Makes 6 main-dish servings

2 tablespoons vegetable oil
2 medium onions, chopped
1¼ pounds ground lamb
1 small eggplant (about
   1¼ pounds), diced
1½ cups tomato juice
½ teaspoon coarsely ground
   black pepper
Salt

1 small cucumber, seeded and
   diced
1 container (8 ounces) plain
   low-fat yogurt
1 tablespoon chopped fresh
   dill or ¼ teaspoon dillweed
1 bunch watercress
3 whole-wheat pitas
   (6 inches), each cut in half

◆ In 12-inch skillet, heat 1 tablespoon oil over medium-high
heat. Add onions; cook 5 minutes. Add lamb, breaking it up
with spoon; cook until browned and juices have evaporated.

◆ Add eggplant and remaining 1 tablespoon oil; cook until
eggplant is tender. Stir in tomato juice, pepper, and
1 teaspoon salt; heat through.

◆ Meanwhile, prepare yogurt sauce: In small bowl, mix
cucumber, yogurt, dill, and ¼ teaspoon salt.

◆ Divide half of watercress among 6 plates. Tuck remaining
watercress into pita halves. Spoon lamb mixture into pitas.
Arrange filled pitas on plates with watercress. To serve,
spoon yogurt sauce over filling in pitas.

**Each serving: About 410 calories, 25g protein, 34g carbohydrate,
20g total fat (7g saturated), 70mg cholesterol, 930mg sodium**

V8EGETABLES

Vegetables KNOW-HOW

With hundreds of varieties to choose from, and countless ways to prepare them, there is a vegetable for practically every taste and occasion. Supermarkets offer myriad new and exotic vegetables alongside the basic broccoli, while farmers' markets bring top-notch local produce at its peak, in season, into the cities. Many of these markets offer heirloom produce – revivals of old-fashioned native varieties, particularly tomatoes, potatoes, and beans, that are generally more flavorful than their mass-market cousins.

BUYING AND STORING

As a rule, buy vegetables in season – you'll get them at their peak of flavor and freshness and prices will be lower too. In general, choose firm, brightly colored vegetables without blemishes or wilted leaves. Smaller vegetables tend to be sweeter and more tender. Avoid buying packaged vegetables if you can, because the quality is harder to check.

Most vegetables stay freshest if they're stored in the coldest part of the refrigerator – usually the bottom shelf or the crisper drawer – in loosely sealed paper or plastic bags. Don't wrap them airtight, because condensation can form on the surface and speed deterioration. Store potatoes, onions, garlic, and winter squash in a cool, dark, well-ventilated place. For most vegetables, the sooner you use them, the more flavorful and nutritious they'll be.

PREPARATION

• Shake or brush off loose dirt before washing, then use a soft vegetable brush for scrubbing. Lukewarm water is good for removing sand and grit from leafy vegetables and zucchini.
• Wash vegetables just before you use them.
• Peel off only a thin layer of skin, or don't peel at all, to cut the loss of vitamins, minerals, and fiber.
• Vegetables such as artichokes and celery root discolor quickly when cut. To reduce discoloration, use a stainless steel knife and rub the cut portions with a lemon half. Or, immediately place prepared vegetables in a bowl of acidulated water (combine 1 quart water with 3 tablespoons lemon juice).
• To revive limp cut vegetables or slightly wilted greens, soak them in ice water for about 15 minutes. Avoid soaking vegetables in water for longer than necessary, as it leaches out nutrients and creates waterlogged vegetables.

COOKING SUCCESS

• Most vegetables should be cooked as briefly as possible for the brightest color, best texture, and freshest flavor. Unless the recipe directs otherwise, cook in the minimum amount of lightly salted water so you don't drain away nutrients.
• Most vegetables can be cooked in the microwave. The short cooking time means that they retain their color and texture, as well as more of their nutrients.
• If you're cooking vegetables to serve cold or reheat later, after steaming or boiling, drain and then immediately rinse under cold running water to halt the cooking.
• Don't discard vegetable cooking water; it's full of nutrients. Save to use in sauces, soups, stocks, and stews.

THE RIGHT CUT

A sharp knife is essential for cutting vegetables. For speedy slicing, you can use an adjustable-blade slicer (see page 297) or a food processor.

Cut vegetables into same-sized pieces for even cooking and a more attractive finished dish.

Dice – small, even cubes

Julienne – fine strips the size of a matchstick

Chop – small, irregular-shaped pieces

ORGANIC VEGETABLES

Concern about chemicals in food has led to the wider availability of organic produce, with California leading the field. Produced without the use of chemical fertilizers and pesticides, these vegetables are not only healthful, but can be more flavorful as well. Production is labor-intensive and yields relatively low, however, so organic vegetables are more expensive than their supermarket counterparts. At present there are no consistent regulations guiding the standards of growers. If in doubt, ask what standards are being met – a reputable supplier will be happy to answer your questions.

CABBAGE FAMILY

Broccoli and broccoli rabe (rapini, broccoli di rape) Choose broccoli with firm, tightly closed buds (either dark green or purplish green) and no sign of yellowing or flowering. The stems should be firm; if they seem tough, peel away the outer layer with a vegetable peeler. Broccoli rabe has leafy stalks with clusters of tiny broccoli-like buds; the flavor is pleasantly bitter. Look for sturdy stalks and fresh, dark-green leaves.
Brussels sprouts Buy bright green, firm, tight heads. Small are best; large sprouts can be bitter. If boiling or steaming, cut an "x" in the base of each sprout first for even cooking.
Cauliflower and broccoflower When buying either cauliflower or broccoflower (a pale-green cross between broccoli and cauliflower with a mild flavor), choose firm heads that feel heavy for their size. Check that flowerets are tightly packed and unblemished; leaves should look fresh and green. The size of the head has no bearing on quality.
Chinese cabbage Resembling lettuce more than cabbage, napa (or simply "Chinese cabbage") has an elongated shape and pale green leaves that curl at the tips – look for crisp, firm leaves and a freshly cut stalk end. Bok choy has wide white or pale green stalks gathered in a loose head flowing to large green leaves. Choose bok choy with crisp, firm, stalks and moist, deep green leaves.
Head cabbage (green, red, savoy) Of these cabbages, savoy has the most mellow flavor. Buy heads that feel heavy for their size with fresh, unwilted leaves free of browning.

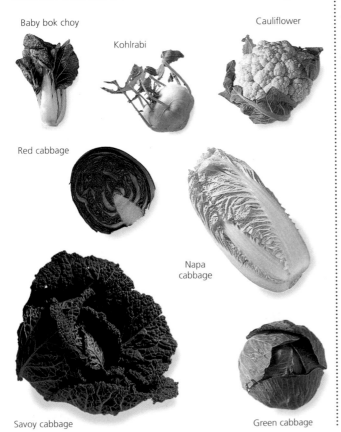

Baby bok choy

Kohlrabi

Cauliflower

Red cabbage

Napa cabbage

Savoy cabbage

Green cabbage

Kohlrabi This pale green or purple bulb has leafy shoots at the top; the bulb tastes like turnip, while the leaves have a spinach flavor. Choose small, heavy bulbs with dark green leaves; larger bulbs can be woody. Always peel before using.

LEAFY GREENS

Vitamin-rich leafy greens can be young and tender and eaten raw, or mature and strong-flavored and better cooked. Greens cook down substantially; a pound yields only ½ cup cooked. Look for crisp, unblemished, brightly colored greens; small leaves with thin stems are the most tender. To store, wash greens in several changes of water and pat dry with paper towels. Line a zip-tight plastic bag with a damp paper towel, loosely fill with greens, and use within 3 days.
• Mild-flavored greens include spinach, lettuce, and Swiss chard, with stalks that taste like celery and leaves that taste like spinach. Spinach is great in salads; chard is best cooked.
• For a moderately strong flavor, choose beet greens, collards, Belgian endive, and escarole.
• Pungent greens include chicory (curly endive), kale, dandelion greens, mustard greens, and turnip greens. Except when very young and tender, these greens are bitter raw, but are delicious sautéed with garlic and olive oil, or added (at the end of cooking time) to soups and stews.

ARTICHOKES, ASPARAGUS, CELERY, AND FENNEL

Artichokes Choose globe artichokes that feel heavy for their size, with compact heads and tightly closed green leaves. Heavily browned artichokes are old, but a little brown at the ends of the leaves (from frost) is fine. For baby artichokes, look for compact heads with soft leaves and soft stalks.
Asparagus Look for brightly colored, firm spears with tight buds; choose even-sized spears for uniform cooking. White asparagus is more expensive. Peeling is optional; if you do peel, remove only the tough peel at the stem end. You can also remove the scales with a paring knife, if you like. To store, trim ends and stand spears upright, loosely covered, in a tall glass with 1 inch of water in the bottom.
Celery A head of celery should look moist and crisp. Look for tight, compact heads with unblemished stalks and fresh leaves. In general, a darker color indicates a stronger taste. If you like, use a vegetable peeler to remove the outer strings.
Fennel (sometimes labeled anise) All parts of fennel are edible, from the bulb to the celery-like stalks and feathery leaves (add to salads or use as a garnish). Fennel can be eaten raw (slice it thin and add to salads or crudités platters) or cooked. Slow-cooking fennel by roasting or braising brings out its sweetness and tames the licorice flavor. Look for compact, uncracked, whitish-green bulbs free of discoloration; the leaves should look fresh and green. Bulbs that are spreading at the top indicate an older, tougher vegetable.

Carrots   Rutabaga   Celery root

BEANS, CORN, OKRA, AND PEAS

Beans The beans with edible pods include green beans, yellow wax beans, Italian green beans, and haricots verts, a slender French variety (see page 292). Beans should have a good color and firm, unblemished pods that snap crisply when bent (though haricots verts tend to be less crisp).

Corn Always cook corn soon after purchase, before the natural sugars turn to starch and reduce sweetness. Look for green, healthy husks that fit the cob tightly. The silk should be moist and fresh-looking – dry silk indicates old corn. Kernels should be plump and milky and grow in tight rows right to the tip. Pass on corn that's sold husked, since it deteriorates faster – shuck just before cooking.

Okra Buy small, bright green pods that are firm, not limp. Avoid large pods, which can be fibrous or tough. Okra becomes slippery when cooked and acts as a thickener for sauced dishes. Don't cook okra in a cast-iron or aluminum pot – these metals can cause okra to discolor.

Edible-pod peas These crisp treats are eaten pod and all. Snow peas have flat, almost translucent pods, while sugar snap peas have plumper, rounder pods. For either variety, look for firm, crisp pods with a good green color. Sugar snaps should be plump but not bursting at the seam.

Peas Choose fresh peas with plump, firm, bright green pods. The sugars in peas turn to starch soon after picking, so buy and cook as fresh as possible. Shell just before using. A pound of peas in the pod yields about 1 cup shelled peas.

ROOT VEGETABLES

Beets Loved for their sweetness, beets have the highest sugar content of any vegetable (however, they're very low in calories). Choose firm, unblemished, small to medium-sized beets. If possible, buy bunches with the green tops on, which can be cooked like spinach. The leaves should look fresh and healthy.

Carrots and parsnips Buy firm, smooth, slender roots without cracks or blemishes. Small parsnips have the sweetest flavor; large parsnips may have a woody center. Baby carrots look great on a plate, but mature, dark orange carrots actually have the sweetest taste and most vitamins.

Celery root (celeriac) This aromatic knobby root tastes like a cross between celery and parsley. Small, firm roots have the best texture;

Turnips

Beets

Parsnips

for easy peeling, look for a minimum of rootlets and knobs. Celery root can be shredded and dressed for salad; it's also delicious cooked in soups or purees.

Radish Look for smooth radishes that feel firm, not spongy. They vary in color (white, red, purple, black), shape (round, oval, elongated), and flavor (from peppery-hot to mild).

Rutabaga Choose firm, heavy rutabagas with smooth skin. When cooked, their yellow flesh takes on a creamy texture.

Sunchokes (Jerusalem artichokes) Look for small, firm sunchokes free of soft or green-tinged spots (see page 296).

Turnips Buy small turnips that feel heavy for their size, with smooth, unbruised skins. Large turnips can be woody.

POTATOES

Potatoes vary in their starch content, which makes a difference to the texture of the finished dish. Russet, or baking, potatoes have a fluffy, mealy texture that makes them good for frying and baking. Waxy potatoes – all-purpose round reds, round whites, and long whites – have less starch and hold their shape when cooked. They're ideal for boiling and salads. Tiny fingerlings are perfect steamed whole, while yellow-fleshed potatoes have a creamy texture.

Sweet potatoes can be yellow or orange. The yellow-fleshed variety is drier and less sweet than the orange-fleshed sweet potato, which is often incorrectly called a yam. (True yams are ivory-fleshed tropical tubers available in Latin markets.)

Whatever the variety, choose dry, smooth potatoes without sprouts. Pass on potatoes with a greenish cast (the result of prolonged exposure to light) because they'll taste bitter. Store potatoes in a cool, dark, well-ventilated place – not the refrigerator. Older potatoes will keep for about 2 weeks; new and sweet potatoes will keep for about a week.

Peeling or not is a matter of choice, but do cut off any green areas or sprouts.

Sweet potato

Baking potato

Red potato

Round white

ONION FAMILY

These vegetables range from "dry" ones with papery outer skins, such as onions and garlic, to "green" varieties that have a bulb at one end, such as green and spring onions. Dry onions are categorized either as storage onions, which are firm, compact, available year-round, and strong-flavored (freeze for 20 minutes before chopping for fewer tears), or sweet onions, like Vidalia and Walla Walla. Sweet onions, ripe in spring and summer, have a higher water and sugar content and are more fragile. Of all the onion family, leeks alone need thorough cleaning: Slit lengthwise from top to bottom and rinse well, fanning the leaves to remove all grit.

Choose dry onions that feel heavy for their size with dry, papery skins. Avoid any with sprouts or soft spots. Green onions should have clean white bulbs and fresh-looking tops. Store dry onions, preferably in a single layer, in a cool, dry, dark, airy place. Refrigerate green onions up to 2 weeks. (For more information on garlic, see page 351.)

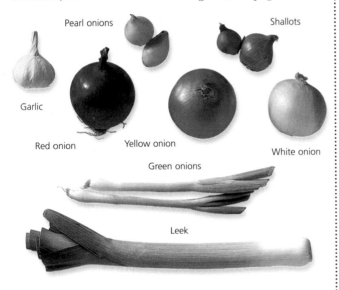

Pearl onions

Shallots

Garlic

Red onion

Yellow onion

White onion

Green onions

Leek

SQUASH

Squash are divided into two groups, summer and winter, but most are available year-round. Summer squash have tender flesh and seeds and soft edible skins. Winter squash have hard, thick skins and seeds and firm flesh. When buying summer squash, choose small ones that feel firm, not flabby. Winter squash should have hard, blemish-free skin. For either type, look for dry, well-shaped squash with good color; a squash should feel heavy for its size. Store summer squash in the refrigerator and winter squash in a cool, dry spot.

SUMMER SQUASH
Pattypan This small, pretty, bowl-shaped squash has a scalloped edge; it can be white, yellow, or pale green. The whimsical shape of this quick-cooking squash makes it perfect for grilling or, if large, for stuffing.

Yellow squash and zucchini Yellow squash comes as crookneck (with a curved neck) and straightneck. Besides regular zucchini, there are yellow and gray zucchini. Both vegetables can be eaten raw or cooked. Younger varieties tend to have the sweetest flavor (look for baby yellow squash and zucchini, which have a particularly sweet taste and crisp texture and look pretty on crudités platters or in stir-fries). Avoid fat, overgrown squash – they tend to have a bland flavor, large seeds, and a spongy texture.

WINTER SQUASH
Acorn This round, deeply ridged squash has a dark green skin, sometimes with an orange blotch, and a sweet orange flesh. There is also an orange-skinned variety. It is often stuffed with savory fillings or simply sliced and baked.
Butternut With one end shaped like a bulb, this large tan squash has deep orange flesh that's moist and sweet. It's used in soups and pies as well as served on its own.
Chayote Also called mirliton, this pear-shaped, pale green squash has a large center seed and a slight apple taste. Although it's a winter squash, prepare as you would zucchini.
Hubbard A very large greenish-gray squash, Hubbard is often sold in cut pieces. The flesh is dry but sweet, delicious roasted with herbs and root vegetables.
Pumpkin Jack-o'-lantern pumpkins have stringy flesh, which should be strained after cooking; pie pumpkins, with more flesh and fewer fibers, make better eating. Cut in half or into wedges, remove seeds, and bake as you would other squash. Buy blemish-free, heavy pumpkins.
Spaghetti This watermelon-shaped squash has yellow-gold flesh that separates into spaghetti-like strands when cooked. Look for pale yellow skin; if greenish, the squash is underripe.

Yellow zucchini

Acorn squash

Pattypan squash

Baby pumpkin

Spaghetti squash

MUSHROOMS

Fresh or dried, mushrooms come in great variety (see page 305). Buy plump, firm, unblemished fresh mushrooms with an even color. To store, refrigerate in a loosely closed paper bag (so they can breathe), loosely covered with a damp paper towel. Avoid storing in plastic bags – they'll become too moist, acquire a slimy texture, and deteriorate faster. Clean mushrooms just before using with a soft brush or a swipe of a damp cloth. Never subject mushrooms to a long rinsing or soak them in water – they'll absorb water and become soggy.

Dried mushrooms are available in many varieties. They have a more concentrated flavor and will add a woody depth to soups, stews, and sauces. Soak dried mushrooms in warm water for 20 minutes before using. Be sure to use the flavorful soaking liquid in your recipe (strain it first).

White (button) This common cultivated mushroom can also be cream or brown-colored. White mushrooms have a mild flavor, with caps that range from ½ to 3 inches in diameter.

Portobello A dark brown mushroom measuring as much as 6 inches in diameter. Portobellos have open caps with exposed gills and are prized for their rich flavor and meaty texture. The woody stems can be used in stocks.

Cremini A brown, full-flavored variation of the button mushroom. Portobellos are the mature form of cremini.

Shiitake A brown Asian mushroom with a flat cap and a rich, meaty flavor. The stems are usually too tough to eat.

Oyster A delicate-tasting Asian variety with a soft cream or gray color, large, ruffled top, and a short, fat stem.

Morel A golden-brown mushroom with a honeycombed, elongated cap and unusual spongy texture. Morels are available in specialty food stores; they have a hearty, woodsy flavor and tender texture when cooked.

Porcini Also called cèpes, these delicious mushrooms are pale brown and range in size from an ounce to a pound. They have a meaty texture and strong, woodsy flavor. They are expensive and rarely available fresh in the U.S. Dried porcini are widely available, however, and even a small quantity will add a lot of flavor to a dish.

Chanterelle A trumpet-shaped mushroom that ranges in color from bright yellow to orange. Chanterelles have a delicate, nutty flavor and chewy texture. When buying, avoid any that are broken or shrivelled. Cook gently and briefly.

EGGPLANT

This vegetable comes in many guises – including the ubiquitous pear-shaped Western eggplant, small baby Italian or long, slender Japanese eggplant, and elegant creamy-white varieties (see page 308). Choose eggplants that feel heavy for their size with smooth, glossy, taut skins free of soft or brown spots. Avoid hard eggplants, which are underripe. Unlike many vegetables, eggplant will not suffer if it's overcooked – it will simply have a softer texture. Peeling is optional; the skin is edible and adds a beautiful color to dishes.

PEPPERS AND CHILES

Although peppers are classed as fruits, sweet bell peppers are used as a vegetable, while chiles, the hot peppers, are used more as a seasoning. As sweet peppers ripen, they become even sweeter. Red peppers are simply green peppers that have been left on the vine to ripen. The sweetest pepper is the pimiento, which is sold canned or jarred.

Chiles vary widely in flavor and hotness, from mild to burning. As a broad rule, the smaller the chile, the hotter it is. Tiny Thai chiles, habaneros, and Scotch bonnets are searingly hot; jalapeños and serranos are less so. Large poblanos are quite mild. Capsaicin is the compound that gives chiles their heat, and most of the capsaicin is in the seeds and veins. To tame the fire, remove the seeds and veins, but take care – the oils released can irritate the skin. If you have sensitive skin, wear rubber gloves when preparing chiles, and wash your hands well when you are finished.

Choose sweet peppers and chiles with a bright color for their variety and firm, smooth skins. Pass on blemished or bruised peppers. Some chiles are also sold dried; soak them in hot water for about 30 minutes before using.

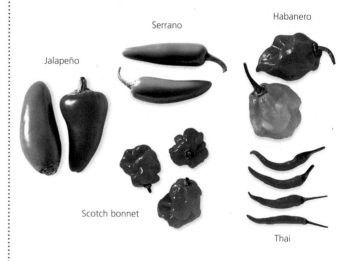

Serrano

Habanero

Jalapeño

Scotch bonnet

Thai

TOMATOES

Tomatoes come in many forms (see page 312) and vary in sweetness and acidity. Cherry tomatoes, red or yellow, are reliably sweet all year round. Yellow tomatoes are lower in acid than red varieties. Plum tomatoes have thick, meaty walls – they're ideal for cooked sauces.

Select firm (but not hard), heavy tomatoes with deeply colored, unblemished skins. Don't store tomatoes in the refrigerator, because cold kills their flavor; the only time to refrigerate a tomato is when it's overripe. Otherwise, store them at room temperature, but out of direct sunlight, where they can turn mushy. Unripe tomatoes can be placed in a paper bag with an apple to speed ripening.

Canned tomatoes are preferable to fresh in cooking when good-quality fresh tomatoes are unavailable.

CABBAGE FAMILY

The cabbage family includes green, red, savoy, and napa varieties, plus broccoli, Brussels sprouts, and cauliflower. A lesser-known member is kohlrabi, which resembles a knobby pale green beet and is a cross between cabbage and turnip. Best known for being nutritious and economical, these underrated vegetables are tasty both raw and cooked. The freshest vegetables have the mildest, most delicate flavor; with long storage or overcooking, they develop stronger "cabbage-y" flavor and odor. Red cabbage, with its sturdier structure, demands slightly longer cooking than green.

VEGETARIAN STUFFED CABBAGE

Prep: 50 minutes   Cook: 1 hour

Makes 6 main-dish servings

1 medium head savoy cabbage (3 pounds), tough outer leaves discarded

2 tablespoons vegetable oil

1 red pepper, finely chopped

1 yellow pepper, finely chopped

2 medium onions, finely chopped

1 tablespoon seasoned rice vinegar

1 garlic clove, minced

2 tablespoons soy sauce

2 tablespoons minced, peeled fresh ginger

½ cup regular long-grain rice, cooked as label directs

1 can (15 to 19 ounces) white kidney beans (cannellini), rinsed and drained

1 can (8 ounces) sliced water chestnuts, drained and finely chopped

1 can (28 ounces) tomatoes

French bread (optional)

1 Remove 2 large cabbage leaves; set aside. Cut out core and center of cabbage, leaving a 1-inch shell. Discard core and dice 2 cups cabbage from center leaves.

2 In nonstick 12-inch skillet, heat 1 tablespoon oil over medium-high heat. Add peppers and half of onions; cook, stirring often, 8 to 10 minutes, until tender.

3 Add diced cabbage, rice vinegar, garlic, 1 tablespoon soy sauce, and 1 tablespoon ginger; cook 5 minutes. Remove from heat; stir in rice, beans, and water chestnuts.

4 Fill cabbage shell with vegetable mixture, packing mixture firmly but gently. Cover opening with reserved cabbage leaves, overlapping slightly; tie with string. In 8-quart Dutch oven, heat remaining 1 tablespoon oil over medium heat. Add remaining onions and cook 5 minutes, or until tender. Add remaining 1 tablespoon ginger; cook 30 seconds.

5 Add tomatoes with their juice, remaining 1 tablespoon soy sauce, and *1 cup water*, breaking up tomatoes with back of spoon. Place stuffed cabbage, core-end down, in tomato sauce and heat to boiling over high heat. Reduce heat to low; cover and simmer 1 hour, basting cabbage occasionally. To serve, place cabbage in deep platter; discard string. Spoon sauce around cabbage. Cut into wedges. Serve with French bread, if you like.

EACH SERVING: ABOUT 295 CALORIES, 12g PROTEIN, 54g CARBOHYDRATE, 5g TOTAL FAT (1g SATURATED), 0mg CHOLESTEROL, 885mg SODIUM

KOHLRABI AND CARROTS WITH DILL

Prep: 25 minutes   Cook: 25 minutes
Makes 6 accompaniment servings

6 medium kohlrabi (about 2 pounds), peeled
1 bag (16 ounces) carrots
2 tablespoons vegetable oil
4 tablespoons margarine or butter

2 teaspoons all-purpose flour
1 chicken-flavor bouillon cube or envelope
1 tablespoon chopped fresh dill or ½ teaspoon dillweed

Cut each kohlrabi into ½-inch-thick slices; cut each slice into ½-inch-wide sticks. Cut each carrot crosswise into 3 pieces; cut each piece lengthwise into quarters. In 12-inch skillet, heat oil over medium-high heat; add vegetables and cook, stirring often, about 15 minutes, until browned. Add *⅓ cup water*; reduce heat to low. Cover and cook 10 minutes, or until vegetables are tender-crisp and liquid evaporates. Meanwhile, in 1-quart saucepan, melt margarine over low heat; stir in flour and cook 1 minute. Add bouillon; gradually stir in *½ cup water*; cook, stirring constantly, until mixture thickens slightly and boils. Pour sauce over vegetables and sprinkle with dill; gently toss to coat well.

Each serving: About 185 calories, 4g protein, 18g carbohydrate, 12g total fat (2g saturated), 0mg cholesterol, 295mg sodium

RED CABBAGE WITH APPLES

Prep: 15 minutes   Cook: 25 minutes
Makes 8 accompaniment servings

2 tablespoons olive oil
1 medium head red cabbage (about 2½ pounds), quartered, cored, and coarsely sliced
2 Golden Delicious apples, peeled, cored, and chopped

1 tablespoon sugar
2 tablespoons red wine vinegar
2 teaspoons salt
Chopped fresh parsley for garnish

In 12-inch skillet, heat olive oil over high heat. Add cabbage and apples; toss to coat. Stir in sugar, vinegar, and salt. Reduce heat to medium; cook, stirring occasionally, about 20 minutes, until cabbage is tender. To serve, sprinkle with parsley.

Each serving: About 90 calories, 2g protein, 15g carbohydrate, 4g total fat (1g saturated), 0mg cholesterol, 550mg sodium

SAUTÉED CABBAGE AND FRESH PEAS

Prep: 25 minutes   Cook: 15 to 20 minutes
Makes 6 accompaniment servings

3 tablespoons vegetable oil
1 medium onion, chopped
1 medium head green cabbage (about 2½ pounds), quartered, cored, and cut into ¾-inch-wide slices
2 pounds fresh peas, shelled (2 cups), or 1 package (10 ounces) frozen peas

1¼ teaspoons salt
¼ teaspoon crushed red pepper
1 tablespoon chopped fresh thyme or parsley

◆ In 5-quart Dutch oven, heat oil over medium heat; add onion and cook, stirring occasionally, 5 minutes, or until tender and golden.

◆ Stir in cabbage, peas, salt, crushed red pepper, and *2 tablespoons water*. Increase heat to high and cook, stirring frequently, 10 to 12 minutes, until cabbage is tender-crisp. To serve, sprinkle with thyme.

Each serving: About 135 calories, 4g protein, 16g carbohydrate, 7g total fat (1g saturated), 0mg cholesterol, 480mg sodium

CABBAGE AND ONION WITH CARAWAY

Prep: 10 minutes   Cook: 15 to 20 minutes
Makes 6 accompaniment servings

1 medium head green cabbage (about 2½ pounds)
2 tablespoons vegetable oil
1 large onion, diced
1 teaspoon salt

¾ teaspoon caraway seeds, crushed
¼ teaspoon ground black pepper

◆ Carefully remove several large cabbage leaves and use to line serving platter, if you like. Set platter aside.

◆ Cut cabbage into quarters; cut out core. Coarsely slice cabbage and discard tough ribs.

◆ In 5-quart Dutch oven, heat 2 tablespoons oil over medium heat; add onion and cook, stirring occasionally, 5 minutes, or until tender and golden.

◆ Stir in cabbage, salt, caraway seeds, and pepper. Increase heat to high and cook, stirring frequently, 10 to 12 minutes, until cabbage is tender-crisp. To serve, spoon cabbage mixture onto platter lined with cabbage leaves.

Each serving: About 100 calories, 3g protein, 13g carbohydrate, 5g total fat (1g saturated), 0mg cholesterol, 390mg sodium

SAUTÉED BRUSSELS SPROUTS

Prep: 15 minutes   Cook: 5 minutes
Makes 6 accompaniment servings

2 containers (10 ounces each)   ½ teaspoon salt
  Brussels sprouts, trimmed
3 tablespoons margarine or
  butter

Thinly slice Brussels sprouts. In 12-inch skillet, melt margarine over high heat. Add sliced Brussels sprouts; sprinkle with salt and cook, stirring, 5 minutes, or until sprouts are tender-crisp and beginning to brown.

Each serving: About 90 calories, 3g protein, 9g carbohydrate, 6g total fat (1g saturated), 0mg cholesterol, 265mg sodium

CURRIED CAULIFLOWER WITH POTATOES AND PEAS

Prep: 15 minutes   Cook: 30 minutes
Makes 8 accompaniment servings

1 tablespoon vegetable oil   ¼ teaspoon ground cumin
1 large onion, finely chopped   1 teaspoon salt
2 all-purpose potatoes, peeled   1 small head cauliflower
  and cut into ½-inch pieces   (2 pounds), cut into small
1 tablespoon minced, peeled   flowerets
  fresh ginger   1 cup frozen peas
2 garlic cloves, minced   ¼ cup chopped fresh cilantro
1 teaspoon curry powder

In 10-inch skillet, heat oil over medium heat. Add onion and cook 5 minutes, or until tender. Add potatoes and next 4 ingredients; cook, stirring, 2 minutes. Stir in salt and *1½ cups water*; heat to boiling over high heat. Reduce heat to medium; cover and cook 10 minutes. Stir in cauliflower; cover and cook 10 minutes longer, or until tender. Stir in peas and cook, uncovered, until most of liquid evaporates. To serve, stir in cilantro.

Each serving: About
120 calories, 5g protein,
21g carbohydrate,
2g total fat
(0g saturated),
0mg cholesterol,
295mg sodium

BRUSSELS SPROUTS WITH BACON

Prep: 15 minutes   Cook: 15 minutes
Makes 10 accompaniment servings

3 containers (10 ounces each)   ½ teaspoon salt
  Brussels sprouts, trimmed   ¼ teaspoon coarsely ground
6 slices bacon   black pepper
1 tablespoon olive oil   ¼ cup pine nuts (pignoli),
2 garlic cloves, minced   toasted

◆ In 4-quart saucepan, heat *1 inch water* to boiling over high heat. Add Brussels sprouts; heat to boiling. Reduce heat to low; cover and simmer 5 minutes, or until sprouts are tender-crisp. Drain.

◆ In nonstick 12-inch skillet, cook bacon over medium-low heat until browned. Transfer bacon to paper towels to drain; crumble.

◆ Spoon off all but 1 tablespoon bacon fat from skillet. Heat bacon fat and olive oil over medium-high heat. Add Brussels sprouts, garlic, salt, and pepper. Cook, stirring frequently, about 5 minutes, until sprouts are browned. To serve, sprinkle with pine nuts and crumbled bacon.

Each serving: About 85 calories, 4g protein, 9g carbohydrate, 5g total fat (1g saturated), 3mg cholesterol, 185mg sodium

PREPARING BRUSSELS SPROUTS

First, remove any yellow or wilted leaves, then trim the stem. If boiling the sprouts, use a small knife to make an X-shaped cut in the stem end for faster and more uniform cooking.

VEGETABLES VINAIGRETTE

Prep: 20 minutes   *Cook:* 25 to 30 minutes
Makes 8 accompaniment servings

⅓ cup olive or vegetable oil
¼ cup Dijon mustard with seeds
¼ cup white wine vinegar
¾ teaspoon salt
1 large head cauliflower (3 pounds), cut into 2½" by ¾" pieces

1 large bunch broccoli, cut into 2½" by ¾" pieces
1 bag (16 ounces) carrots, cut into ¼-inch-thick diagonal slices

◆ In large bowl, with fork or wire whisk, mix oil, mustard, vinegar, and salt until blended; set aside.

◆ In 8-quart saucepot, heat *1 inch water* to boiling over high heat. Add cauliflower; heat to boiling. Reduce heat to low; cover and simmer 5 to 7 minutes, until tender-crisp. With slotted spoon, transfer cauliflower to colander; rinse with cold running water.

◆ In water remaining in saucepot, heat broccoli to boiling over high heat. Reduce heat to low; cover and simmer 5 to 7 minutes, until tender-crisp. With slotted spoon, transfer to colander with cauliflower; rinse with cold running water.

◆ In water remaining in saucepot (adding more *water* if necessary to equal 1 inch), heat carrots to boiling over high heat. Reduce heat to low; cover and simmer 5 minutes, or until tender-crisp. Transfer to colander with cauliflower and broccoli; rinse with cold running water.

◆ Add drained vegetables to bowl with vinaigrette; toss until coated with vinaigrette. Serve vegetables warm; or, cover and refrigerate to serve cold later.

Each serving: About 180 calories, 7g protein, 19g carbohydrate, 10g total fat (1g saturated), 0mg cholesterol, 455mg sodium

WARM BROCCOLI AND POTATO SALAD

Prep: 15 minutes   *Cook:* 25 minutes
Makes 8 accompaniment servings

6 slices bacon, cut into ½-inch pieces
3 medium red potatoes, cut into ¼-inch-thick slices
1 medium onion, chopped
3 tablespoons red wine vinegar

2 teaspoons sugar
1½ teaspoons salt
¼ teaspoon crushed red pepper
1 large bunch broccoli, cut into 3" by 1" pieces

◆ In 12-inch skillet, cook bacon over medium-low heat until browned; drain on paper towels. Spoon off all but 3 tablespoons fat from skillet. Increase heat to medium. Add potatoes and onion; cook, turning potatoes occasionally, about 10 minutes, until browned. Add *½ cup water*; reduce heat to medium-low. Cover and cook 5 minutes longer, until potatoes are tender. Stir in vinegar and next 3 ingredients; cook, stirring, until liquid boils and thickens slightly.

◆ Meanwhile, in 5-quart saucepot, in *1 inch boiling water*, heat broccoli to boiling over high heat. Reduce heat to low; cover and simmer, stirring occasionally, 8 to 10 minutes, until tender-crisp. Drain broccoli. Stir broccoli and bacon into potato mixture until broccoli is coated with dressing.

Each serving: About 110 calories, 5g protein, 18g carbohydrate, 3g total fat (1g saturated), 4mg cholesterol, 505mg sodium

BROCCOLI AND RED-PEPPER AMANDINE

Prep: 10 minutes   *Cook:* 15 minutes
Makes 5 accompaniment servings

2 tablespoons olive or vegetable oil
1 red pepper, cut into ½-inch-wide strips
1 large bunch broccoli, cut into 2½" by 2" pieces

½ teaspoon salt
1 tablespoon fresh lemon juice
2 tablespoons sliced almonds, toasted

◆ In 12-inch skillet, heat 1 tablespoon oil over medium-high heat; add red pepper and cook until tender-crisp and browned. With slotted spoon, transfer to plate.

◆ In same skillet, heat remaining 1 tablespoon oil; add broccoli and cook, stirring constantly, until coated with oil. Add salt and *3 tablespoons water*. Reduce heat to medium; cover and cook 2 minutes. Uncover; stir-fry 5 minutes longer, or until broccoli is tender-crisp. Stir in red pepper. Spoon mixture onto platter. Sprinkle with lemon juice and almonds.

Each serving: About 110 calories, 5g protein, 9g carbohydrate, 7g total fat (1g saturated), 0mg cholesterol, 250mg sodium

LEAFY GREENS

Packed with flavor and nutrients, leafy greens range in texture and taste from tender and mild to assertive, resilient, and slightly peppery or bitter – depending on type, age, and growing conditions. Spinach is especially delicate and versatile, but you can mix and match most leafy greens for variety (tougher or stronger-flavored greens will need longer cooking). For speed, use prewashed fresh spinach or frozen spinach. Always squeeze excess moisture from cooked or thawed spinach to avoid a watery dish.

SPINACH AND RICOTTA DUMPLINGS

◆◆◆◆◆◆◆◆◆◆◆◆◆◆

Prep: 50 minutes
Bake: 15 to 20 minutes
Makes 4 main-dish servings

2 bunches (10 to 12 ounces each) spinach or 2 packages (10 ounces each) frozen chopped spinach, thawed and squeezed dry

1 container (8 ounces) ricotta cheese

2 large eggs

¼ teaspoon ground black pepper

1 cup freshly grated Parmesan cheese

½ cup plus 2 tablespoons all-purpose flour

2 tablespoons margarine or butter

2 cups milk

1 If using fresh spinach, remove tough stems; wash spinach well. In 5-quart Dutch oven, cook spinach with water clinging to leaves over high heat, stirring, until wilted. Drain. Squeeze dry; coarsely chop. Prepare dumplings: In large bowl, mix spinach, ricotta, eggs, pepper, ½ cup Parmesan, and ½ cup flour. With floured hands, shape spinach mixture into 2" by 1" ovals.

2 Meanwhile, fill 5-quart saucepot half-full with *water*. Heat to boiling over high heat. Reduce heat to medium. Add dumplings, half at a time.

3 Cook dumplings in simmering water, gently stirring occasionally, 3 to 5 minutes, until they float to the top. With slotted spoon, transfer dumplings to paper towels to drain. Preheat oven to 350°F.

4 Prepare white sauce: In 2-quart saucepan, melt margarine over medium heat. Stir in remaining 2 tablespoons flour; cook 1 minute. Gradually whisk in milk and cook, whisking constantly, until sauce thickens slightly and boils. Remove saucepan from heat; stir in ¼ cup Parmesan. Place dumplings in single layer in shallow 2-quart casserole; spoon sauce over. Sprinkle remaining ¼ cup Parmesan over top. Bake 15 to 20 minutes, until sauce is hot and bubbly.

EACH SERVING: ABOUT 475 CALORIES, 30g PROTEIN, 27g CARBOHYDRATE, 28g TOTAL FAT (14g SATURATED), 171mg CHOLESTEROL, 785mg SODIUM

ITALIAN SPINACH WITH GARBANZO BEANS AND RAISINS

Prep: 15 minutes   Cook: 6 minutes
Makes 4 accompaniment servings

1 tablespoon olive oil
1 garlic clove, crushed with side of knife
¼ teaspoon crushed red pepper
1 can (15 to 19 ounces) garbanzo beans, rinsed and drained

2 bunches (10 to 12 ounces each) spinach, washed and dried very well
¼ cup golden raisins
½ teaspoon salt

In 5-quart Dutch oven, heat oil with garlic over medium heat until garlic is golden; discard garlic. Add crushed red pepper to oil and cook 15 seconds. Stir in garbanzo beans and cook, stirring, 2 minutes, or until hot. Increase heat to high. Add spinach, raisins, and salt. Cook, stirring, 2 to 3 minutes, just until spinach wilts.

Each serving: About 200 calories, 9g protein, 31g carbohydrate, 6g total fat (1g saturated), 0mg cholesterol, 805mg sodium

INDIAN CREAMED SPINACH

Prep: 20 minutes   Cook: 12 minutes
Makes 4 accompaniment servings

1 tablespoon margarine or butter
1 medium onion, finely chopped
2 teaspoons minced, peeled fresh ginger
2 garlic cloves, minced
½ teaspoon ground coriander
½ teaspoon ground cumin

⅛ teaspoon ground red pepper (cayenne)
2 bunches (10 to 12 ounces each) spinach, washed and dried very well
½ teaspoon salt
¼ cup heavy or whipping cream

◆ In 5-quart Dutch oven, melt margarine over medium heat. Add onion and cook, stirring often, 5 minutes, or until tender. Add ginger, garlic, coriander, cumin, and ground red pepper and cook, stirring, 1 minute.

◆ Increase heat to high. Add spinach and salt; cook, stirring, 2 to 3 minutes, just until spinach wilts. Stir in cream and boil 2 minutes, until thickened.

Each serving: About 130 calories, 5g protein, 10g carbohydrate, 9g total fat (4g saturated), 20mg cholesterol, 420mg sodium

BAKED SPINACH AND RICE BALLS

Prep: 45 minutes   Bake: 25 to 30 minutes
Makes 4 main-dish servings

½ cup regular long-grain rice
2 bunches (10 to 12 ounces each) spinach or 2 packages (10 ounces each) frozen chopped spinach, thawed and squeezed dry
3 tablespoons olive or vegetable oil
2 large onions, diced
¼ teaspoon salt
Ground black pepper
½ cup freshly grated Parmesan cheese

¼ cup plain dried bread crumbs
1 large egg
1 large carrot, diced
½ teaspoon dried basil
1 can (14½ to 16 ounces) tomatoes
1 can (13¾ to 14½ ounces) vegetable or beef broth
2 teaspoons sugar

◆ In 1-quart saucepan, prepare rice as label directs. Meanwhile, if using fresh spinach, remove tough stems; wash spinach. Dry well; chop.

◆ In 12-inch skillet, heat 2 tablespoons oil over medium-high heat; add half of onions with salt and ½ teaspoon pepper and cook, stirring often, until tender and golden.

◆ Stir in spinach and cook, stirring, just until spinach wilts; remove skillet from heat. Stir in Parmesan cheese, bread crumbs, egg, and cooked rice until blended. Shape mixture into 12 balls; set aside.

◆ Preheat oven to 375°F. In 3-quart saucepan, heat remaining 1 tablespoon oil over medium-high heat; add carrot, basil, ¼ teaspoon pepper, and remaining onion and cook, stirring often, until onion and carrot are tender.

◆ Add tomatoes with their juice, broth, and sugar, breaking up tomatoes with back of spoon. Heat mixture to boiling over high heat and pour into shallow 2-quart baking dish.

◆ Arrange spinach balls in sauce in baking dish. Bake 25 to 30 minutes, until sauce is hot and bubbly and spinach balls are heated through.

Each serving: About 400 calories, 16g protein, 50g carbohydrate, 17g total fat (4g saturated), 63mg cholesterol, 765mg sodium

SPINACH WITH MUSHROOMS AND BACON

Prep: 20 minutes   Cook: 15 minutes
Makes 4 accompaniment servings

3 slices bacon
1 tablespoon olive oil
2 garlic cloves, crushed with
  side of knife
8 ounces mushrooms, cut into
  ¼-inch-thick slices
⅛ teaspoon ground black
  pepper

Salt
2 bunches (10 to 12 ounces
  each) spinach, washed and
  dried very well
1 tablespoon red wine vinegar
  (optional)

◆ In 5-quart Dutch oven, cook bacon over medium-low heat until browned; transfer to paper towels to drain. Discard drippings from Dutch oven.

◆ In same Dutch oven, heat oil with garlic over medium heat until garlic is golden; discard garlic. Add mushrooms, pepper, and ¼ teaspoon salt to oil; cook about 5 minutes, until mushrooms are tender and liquid has evaporated.

◆ Increase heat to high. Add spinach to Dutch oven, sprinkle with ¼ teaspoon salt, and cook, stirring, 2 to 3 minutes, just until spinach wilts. Stir in vinegar, if using. To serve, crumble bacon on top.

Each serving: About 105 calories, 7g protein, 8g carbohydrate, 6g total fat (1g saturated), 4mg cholesterol, 455mg sodium

ESCAROLE PIE

Prep: 50 minutes plus chilling and standing   Bake: 40 to 45 minutes
Makes 6 main-dish servings

Pastry for 2-Crust Pie (see
  page 487) or 1 package
  (10 to 11 ounces) piecrust
  mix, prepared as label
  directs
3 tablespoons olive oil
1 large onion, finely chopped
2 garlic cloves, minced
2 large heads escarole (about
  2½ pounds), cut into bite-
  size pieces

½ cup plus 2 tablespoons
  freshly grated Parmesan
  cheese
½ teaspoon crushed red
  pepper
½ teaspoon salt
2 tablespoons seasoned dried
  bread crumbs

◆ Prepare Pastry for 2-Crust Pie. Shape dough into 2 balls, one slightly larger. Wrap and chill 30 minutes, or overnight.

◆ Meanwhile, in 8-quart Dutch oven, heat 2 tablespoons oil over medium heat; add onion and garlic and cook 10 to 15 minutes, until onion is very tender. Increase heat to high. Stir in escarole; cook about 10 minutes, stirring often, just until escarole is tender. Drain well, pressing out excess liquid.

◆ Return escarole to Dutch oven; stir in ½ cup Parmesan, red pepper, salt, and remaining 1 tablespoon oil. Set aside.

◆ Preheat oven to 375°F. On lightly floured surface, with floured rolling pin, roll larger ball of dough 1½ inches larger all around than inverted 9-inch pie plate; use to line pie plate. Sprinkle crumbs over crust; top with escarole filling.

◆ Roll smaller ball of dough into 10-inch round. Cut several slits in dough; place over filling. Trim edge, leaving ½-inch overhang; fold overhang under and press gently all around rim to make stand-up edge. Sprinkle crust with remaining 2 tablespoons Parmesan. Bake 40 to 45 minutes, until crust is golden. Let pie stand 10 minutes; cut into wedges.

Each serving: About 540 calories, 15g protein, 45g carbohydrate, 35g total fat (8g saturated), 8mg cholesterol, 945mg sodium

BRAISED ENDIVE

Prep: 5 minutes   Cook: 15 to 25 minutes
Makes 6 accompaniment servings

6 large heads Belgian endive
2 tablespoons vegetable oil
2 tablespoons margarine or
  butter

1 teaspoon sugar
½ teaspoon salt
Fresh basil or parsley leaves
  for garnish

◆ Cut each endive lengthwise in half. In 12-inch skillet, heat oil and margarine over medium-high heat; arrange endive, cut-side down, in 1 layer in skillet. Cook, uncovered, 5 to 10 minutes, until cut sides are lightly browned.

◆ Turn endive cut-side up. Reduce heat to low; add *¼ cup water*. Sprinkle endive with sugar and salt; cover and cook 10 to 15 minutes longer, until tender. Transfer endive to warm large platter; garnish with basil.

Each serving: About 85 calories, 1g protein, 3g carbohydrate, 8g total fat (2g saturated), 0mg cholesterol, 235mg sodium

STIR-FRYING GREENS

One of the best ways to prepare leafy green vegetables is to stir-fry them – just enough to wilt them while retaining their bright color. Some of the tougher or more bitter greens, such as collard and mustard greens, should be blanched (cooked briefly in boiling water first) to mellow and tenderize them. See below for instructions on how to prepare, blanch, and stir-fry some of the most common varieties of greens. If you like, use a combination. The cooking times are short; be sure to keep an eye on the greens so they don't overcook.

Preparation and blanching Prepare 1 pound greens (see chart, right); discard discolored leaves, if any. To blanch, if recommended, add greens to 6 quarts boiling water; cook as directed and drain.

Stir-frying In 12-inch skillet or wok, heat 1 tablespoon olive oil over high heat. Add 2 garlic cloves, crushed with side of knife; cook, stirring frequently, until golden. Add ⅛ teaspoon crushed red pepper; cook 30 seconds. Add prepared greens (pan may splatter if greens are wet); sprinkle with ¼ teaspoon salt and cook, stirring. Discard garlic, if desired.

PREPARING AND STIR-FRYING GREENS

TYPE OF GREENS	PREPARE	BLANCH	STIR-FRY
Beet greens	Wash; chop stems	No	5 minutes
Bok choy (pak choi; pak choy; Chinese mustard cabbage)	Wash; thinly slice stems; cut leaves into 1-inch slices	No	5 minutes
Broccoli rabe (rape; rapini)	Wash; trim thick stems	Yes, for 5 minutes	5 minutes
Chicory (curly endive)	Wash; tear leaves	No	5 minutes
Collard greens	Wash; discard stems; cut leaves into 1-inch slices	Yes, for 3 minutes	5 minutes
Dandelion greens	Wash	Yes, for 3 minutes	5 minutes
Escarole	Wash; tear leaves	No	5 minutes
Kale	Wash; discard stems; tear leaves	Yes, for 5 minutes	5 minutes
Mustard greens	Wash	Yes, for 5 minutes	5 minutes
Napa cabbage (Chinese cabbage; celery cabbage)	Wash; thinly slice	No	3 minutes
Spinach	Wash very well	No	3 minutes
Swiss chard (chard)	Wash; thinly slice stems; cut leaves into 1-inch slices	No	3 minutes
Watercress	Wash	No	3 minutes

ARTICHOKES

With just a little more work than is required for most vegetables, fresh artichokes offer high rewards both in great taste and presentation.

STUFFED ARTICHOKES, CAESAR-STYLE

◆◆◆◆◆◆◆◆◆◆◆

Prep: 1 hour
Bake: 15 to 20 minutes
Makes 4 main-dish servings

4 large artichokes
4 slices firm white bread, torn into ¼-inch crumbs
2 tablespoons olive oil
1 large garlic clove, minced
4 anchovy fillets, chopped
½ cup pine nuts (pignoli), lightly toasted, or walnuts, toasted and chopped
⅓ cup freshly grated Parmesan cheese
2 tablespoons chopped fresh parsley
1 tablespoon fresh lemon juice
¼ teaspoon salt
¾ cup chicken broth
Flat-leaf parsley for garnish

1 Prepare and cook artichokes (see below). Preheat oven to 400°F. Bake bread crumbs in jelly-roll pan 5 minutes, or until golden. In 1-quart saucepan, heat oil over medium heat. Add garlic; cook 1 minute. Add anchovies; cook until almost dissolved and garlic is golden. Dice artichoke stems. In bowl, mix stems, crumbs, garlic mixture, pine nuts, next 4 ingredients, and ¼ cup chicken broth.

2 Pour remaining ½ cup chicken broth into shallow baking dish large enough to hold all artichokes (about 13" by 9"). Place artichokes in dish.

3 Spoon crumb mixture between artichoke leaves and into center cavities. Bake 15 to 20 minutes, until artichokes are hot. Served garnished with parsley.

◆◆◆

PREPARING AND COOKING ARTICHOKES

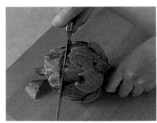

1 With sharp knife, cut 1 inch straight across top of each artichoke. Cut off stem; with vegetable peeler, peel stem. Reserve.

2 Pull loose dark green outer leaves from artichoke bottom. With kitchen shears, trim thorny tips of leaves.

3 Spread artichoke open; carefully cut around choke with small knife. Scrape out fuzzy center portion with spoon; discard.

4 Rinse artichoke well. In 5-quart saucepot, heat 1 tablespoon fresh lemon juice and 1 inch water to boiling over high heat. Add artichoke, stem-end down, with stem; heat to boiling. Reduce heat to low; cover and simmer 30 to 40 minutes, until knife inserted in center of artichoke goes through bottom easily. Drain.

◆◆◆

EACH SERVING: ABOUT 335 CALORIES, 16g PROTEIN, 33g CARBOHYDRATE, 19g TOTAL FAT (4g SATURATED), 14mg CHOLESTEROL, 915mg SODIUM

BRAISED BABY ARTICHOKES WITH OLIVES

Prep: 20 minutes   Cook: 15 minutes
Makes 8 first-course servings

16 baby artichokes (about
  2 pounds)
¼ cup olive oil
3 medium garlic cloves, sliced
½ teaspoon coarsely ground
  black pepper

½ teaspoon salt
⅓ cup oil-cured or Kalamata
  olives, pitted and coarsely
  chopped
Lemon wedges for garnish

◆ Trim baby artichokes: Bend back outer green leaves and snap off at base until leaves are half-green (at the top) and half-yellow (at the bottom). Cut off stems and across top of each artichoke at point where yellow meets green. Cut each artichoke lengthwise in half.

◆ In 12-inch skillet, heat *1 inch water* to boiling over high heat. Add artichokes and cook 5 minutes; drain.

◆ Dry skillet. In same skillet, heat olive oil over medium-high heat. Add garlic and cook, stirring, until lightly browned. Add artichokes; cook 2 minutes, until lightly browned. Stir in pepper, salt, and *1 cup water*; cover and cook about 5 minutes longer, until knife inserted in bottom of artichoke goes through easily. Stir in olives; heat through. Spoon into bowl; garnish with lemon wedges.

Each serving: About 100 calories, 2g protein, 6g carbohydrate, 8g total fat (1g saturated), 0mg cholesterol, 280mg sodium

ARTICHOKES WITH ROASTED RED PEPPER AND BASIL SAUCE

Prep: 25 minutes   Cook: 35 to 45 minutes
Makes 8 first-course or accompaniment servings

4 medium artichokes
¾ cup light mayonnaise
1 jar (7 ounces) roasted red
  peppers, drained
1 teaspoon sugar
¾ teaspoon salt
½ teaspoon hot-pepper sauce

1 tablespoon fresh lemon
  juice
½ cup chopped fresh basil or
  parsley
Shredded fresh basil for
  garnish

◆ Prepare and cook artichokes (see page 281), but omit Step 3. Meanwhile, in food processor with knife blade attached or in blender at medium speed, blend mayonnaise, roasted red peppers, sugar, salt, hot-pepper sauce, and lemon juice until smooth. Spoon red-pepper sauce into bowl; stir in chopped basil. Cover and refrigerate.

◆ Cut each artichoke into 4 wedges. Cut out and discard fuzzy centers. Serve artichokes warm or cover and refrigerate to serve cold later. To serve, arrange artichoke

wedges around bowl of red-pepper sauce on platter; garnish sauce with shredded basil. Let each person dip artichoke leaves and hearts in sauce.

Each serving: About 110 calories, 2g protein, 10g carbohydrate, 6g total fat (1g saturated), 8mg cholesterol, 300mg sodium

COUSCOUS-STUFFED ARTICHOKES

Prep: 1 hour   Bake: 15 to 20 minutes
Makes 4 main-dish servings

4 large artichokes
3 tablespoons olive oil
2 medium carrots, diced
2 garlic cloves, minced
¼ cup chopped fresh mint
3 tablespoons chopped fresh
  parsley

1 cup couscous (Moroccan
  pasta)
1½ cups chicken broth
½ teaspoon salt
¼ teaspoon coarsely ground
  black pepper
1 lemon, cut into wedges

◆ Prepare and cook artichokes (see page 281). Meanwhile, preheat oven to 400°F. In nonstick 10-inch skillet, heat 1 tablespoon olive oil over medium heat. Add carrots and cook about 10 minutes, until tender. Stir in garlic; cook 1 minute longer. Transfer carrots and garlic to medium bowl. Dice artichoke stems; add to carrot mixture with mint and parsley.

◆ Prepare couscous as label directs but use 1 cup chicken broth in place of water. When couscous is done, stir in salt, pepper, carrot mixture, and remaining 2 tablespoons oil.

◆ Pour remaining ½ cup chicken broth into shallow baking dish large enough to hold all artichokes (about 13" by 9"); place artichokes in dish. Spoon couscous mixture between artichoke leaves and into center cavities. Bake 15 to 20 minutes, until artichokes are heated through. Serve with lemon wedges.

Each serving: About 375 calories, 13g protein, 61g carbohydrate, 12g total fat (2g saturated), 7mg cholesterol, 830mg sodium

FENNEL AND CELERY

Cool, crunchy raw celery is a popular staple on crudité platters, but many people are not aware that cooking transforms it into an elegant side dish. Paired with parsnips, toasted walnuts, and a hint of brown butter, for example, it makes a delicate winter sauté. A relative of celery, fennel shares its crisp texture but offers a distinctive, sweet anise flavor. While fennel is delicious raw, simply sliced thin and drizzled with vinaigrette, cooked fennel has a more subtle flavor and melting texture. Roast it in olive oil to accompany roasted chicken or fish, or slice and layer it into a cheese-rich gratin. When purchasing either vegetable, choose firm, crisp varieties with fresh-looking leaves.

BRAISED FENNEL WITH TWO CHEESES

Prep: 15 minutes   *Cook:* 45 minutes plus broiling
Makes 6 accompaniment servings

3 small fennel bulbs
  (8 ounces each)
1 can (13¾ to 14½ ounces)
  chicken broth
6 ounces mozzarella cheese,
  shredded (1½ cups)

2 tablespoons freshly grated
  Parmesan cheese
1 tablespoon chopped fresh
  parsley

1. Rinse fennel bulbs with cold running water; cut off root end and stalks from bulbs. Slice each bulb lengthwise in half. In deep 12-inch skillet, heat chicken broth and *1½ cups water* to boiling over high heat. Add fennel; heat to boiling.

2. Reduce heat to low; cover and simmer 35 minutes, turning bulbs once, or until fennel is fork-tender; drain. Preheat broiler. Place fennel, cut-side up, in shallow broiler-safe 1½-quart casserole. In small bowl, mix mozzarella and Parmesan cheeses and parsley.

3. Sprinkle cheese mixture evenly over fennel in casserole. Place casserole in broiler at closest position to heat source. Broil 1 to 2 minutes, until cheese topping is golden and bubbly and fennel is heated through.

BRAISED CELERY WITH GRUYÈRE

Substitute 2 bunches celery for fennel; trim stalks from bases of celery. Cut each stalk in half to give 5- to 6-inch lengths. Proceed as directed, but simmer only 20 minutes in Step 2 and use 4 ounces Gruyère or Swiss cheese, shredded (about 1 cup), instead of mozzarella.

Each serving: About 125 calories, 8g protein, 7g carbohydrate, 8g total fat (4g saturated), 28mg cholesterol, 530mg sodium

EACH SERVING: ABOUT 135 CALORIES, 8g PROTEIN, 10g CARBOHYDRATE, 8g TOTAL FAT (4g SATURATED), 29mg CHOLESTEROL, 490mg SODIUM

ROASTED FENNEL

Prep: 5 minutes   Roast: 1 hour
Makes 6 accompaniment servings

3 large fennel bulbs (1¼ pounds each)	½ teaspoon salt
1 tablespoon olive oil	¼ teaspoon ground black pepper

◆ Preheat oven to 425°F. Trim fennel bulbs and cut each into 6 wedges. Place fennel in jelly-roll pan and toss with olive oil, salt, and pepper to coat evenly.

◆ Roast fennel about 1 hour, or until browned at edges and tender when pierced with tip of knife.

Each serving: About 110 calories, 4g protein, 21g carbohydrate, 3g total fat (0g saturated), 0mg cholesterol, 325mg sodium

CELERY AND PARSNIPS IN BROWN BUTTER

Prep: 20 minutes   Cook: 25 to 30 minutes
Makes 5 accompaniment servings

2 tablespoons coarsely chopped walnuts	6 stalks celery, cut into 3-inch-long matchstick-thin strips
1 tablespoon vegetable oil	¼ teaspoon salt
8 ounces parsnips, peeled and cut into 3-inch-long matchstick-thin strips	2 tablespoons butter

◆ In 10-inch skillet, toast walnuts over medium heat until lightly browned; transfer to small bowl. Wipe skillet clean with paper towels.

◆ In same skillet, heat oil over medium heat; add parsnips, celery, and salt and cook about 20 minutes, stirring frequently, until vegetables are tender.

◆ Transfer vegetables to warm platter; keep warm. In same skillet, melt butter; cook until butter turns golden, stirring (if butter gets dark, it will be bitter). Add walnuts; toss to coat. Spoon mixture over vegetables.

Each serving: About 120 calories, 2g protein, 11g carbohydrate, 9g total fat (3g saturated), 12mg cholesterol, 200mg sodium

FENNEL AND POTATO GRATIN

Prep: 20 minutes   Bake: 1 hour 20 minutes
Makes 8 accompaniment servings

1 large fennel bulb (1¼ pounds), trimmed, cored, and very thinly sliced (about 3½ cups)	¼ teaspoon ground black pepper
1½ pounds all-purpose potatoes, peeled and very thinly sliced (about 3½ cups)	1 cup heavy or whipping cream
	1 garlic clove, crushed with side of knife
	Pinch ground nutmeg
1 teaspoon salt	¼ cup freshly grated Parmesan cheese

Preheat oven to 400°F. In large bowl, toss fennel with potatoes, salt, and pepper. Spread evenly in shallow 2-quart baking dish. Cover tightly with foil and bake 1 hour. In 1-quart saucepan, combine cream, garlic, and nutmeg; heat to boiling over high heat. Discard garlic. Pour cream mixture over fennel mixture. Sprinkle with Parmesan. Bake, uncovered, 20 minutes longer, or until golden.

Each serving: About 215 calories, 4g protein, 23g carbohydrate, 12g total fat (7g saturated), 43mg cholesterol, 375mg sodium

◆ ◆

PREPARING FENNEL

Also known as anise, sweet anise, and finocchio, fennel is a vegetable valued for all its parts: bulb, leaves, stalks, and seeds. The bulb is the part most often eaten, but young fennel stalks can be served as crudités. The feathery leaves can be added to salads or used as a stuffing for fish; they also make an attractive garnish.

1 To prepare fennel, rinse the bulb in cold water. With a large chef's knife, trim root end.

2 Cut off stalks and feathery leaves, reserving them for other uses, if you like. Remove any bruised or discolored outer stalks, then halve or quarter, cut out core, if you like, and slice bulb as recipe directs.

◆ ◆

ASPARAGUS

Asparagus are at their best cooked simply and briefly, just until the spears are slightly limp. When buying, look for stalks with tips that are dry, tight, and purplish in color. The thickness of the spear makes no difference in the taste, but do select spears of uniform size so they cook evenly.

ASPARAGUS WITH PARMESAN VINAIGRETTE

◆◆◆◆◆◆◆◆◆◆◆◆◆◆

Prep: 20 minutes
Cook: 10 to 15 minutes
Makes 8 accompaniment servings

3 pounds asparagus
½ cup olive or vegetable oil
¼ cup red wine vinegar
1 tablespoon Dijon mustard
1 teaspoon salt
3 tablespoons freshly grated
**   Parmesan cheese**
2 ounces prosciutto or
**   cooked ham, chopped**
**   (about ¼ cup)**

1 Hold base of each asparagus stalk firmly and bend stalk; end will break off at spot where it becomes too tough to eat. Discard ends; trim scales if stalks are gritty.

2 In deep 12-inch skillet, in *1 inch boiling water*, heat asparagus to boiling over high heat. Reduce heat to medium-low; simmer 5 to 10 minutes, just until tender; drain well.

3 In 13" by 9" glass baking dish, prepare vinaigrette: With wire whisk or fork, mix oil, vinegar, mustard, salt, and 2 tablespoons Parmesan cheese.

PREPARING ASPARAGUS

◆◆◆◆◆◆◆◆◆◆◆◆◆◆◆◆◆◆

Asparagus may need only minimal trimming, but if the end of the stalk looks tough and woody, simply bend the stalk to snap the end off. Rinse the asparagus thoroughly under cold running water. You can trim the scales with a paring knife or vegetable peeler, if you like, though this is not really necessary – do so only if the stalks seem gritty.

Asparagus may be peeled for an elegant presentation or if the skin is thick and tough, but we prefer to leave them unpeeled; the outside of the stalk is rich in vitamin C, folic acid, and thiamine, which are lost in peeling. Store asparagus upright in 1 inch water, loosely covered, in the refrigerator.

4 Add asparagus to vinaigrette; turn to coat. Serve at room temperature or cover and refrigerate, turning occasionally, 2 hours. To serve, spoon asparagus and vinaigrette onto serving platter. Sprinkle with prosciutto and remaining 1 tablespoon Parmesan cheese.

EACH SERVING: ABOUT 180 CALORIES, 7g PROTEIN, 7g CARBOHYDRATE, 15g TOTAL FAT (2g SATURATED), 4mg CHOLESTEROL, 460mg SODIUM

ASPARAGUS GRATIN

Prep: 25 minutes   *Cook:* 10 to 15 minutes plus broiling
Makes 6 accompaniment servings

2 tablespoons plus
  2 teaspoons olive oil
1 large shallot, finely chopped
2 slices firm white bread
2 pounds asparagus, tough
  ends removed
Salt

¼ cup freshly grated
  Parmesan cheese
1 tablespoon chopped fresh
  parsley
1 tablespoon fresh lemon
  juice

◆ Preheat oven to 400°F. In 1-quart saucepan, heat
2 tablespoons olive oil over medium-low heat. Add shallot;
cook about 6 minutes, until golden. Remove from heat.

◆ In blender, process bread to fine crumbs; or tear bread
into small crumbs. Spread crumbs in jelly-roll pan; bake
3 to 6 minutes, until golden. Set aside.

◆ In 12-inch skillet, in *1 inch boiling water*, heat asparagus
and ½ teaspoon salt to boiling over high heat. Reduce heat
to medium-low and simmer, uncovered, 5 to 10 minutes, just
until asparagus are tender; drain. Place asparagus in shallow,
broiler-safe dish; drizzle with remaining 2 teaspoons oil.

GRATIN DISHES

Designed for broiling, or baking
at high temperatures, a gratin
dish is shallow so food heats
through quickly and achieves the
maximum browned top.

◆ Preheat broiler. In medium bowl, toss bread crumbs
with Parmesan cheese, parsley, lemon juice, shallot,
and ¼ teaspoon salt. Sprinkle bread-crumb mixture over
asparagus. Place dish in broiler 5 inches from heat source;
broil about 3 minutes, until crumbs are lightly browned.

**Each serving: About 130 calories, 6g protein, 11g carbohydrate,
8g total fat (2g saturated), 3mg cholesterol, 265mg sodium**

CHILLED ASPARAGUS WITH
WATERCRESS MAYONNAISE

Prep: 20 minutes plus chilling   *Cook:* 10 to 15 minutes
Makes 6 accompaniment servings

2 pounds asparagus, tough
  ends removed
1 bunch watercress
½ cup mayonnaise
2 tablespoons milk

2 tablespoons capers, drained
  and minced
1 tablespoon fresh lemon
  juice
Lemon slices for garnish

◆ In 12-inch skillet, in *1 inch boiling water*, heat asparagus to
boiling over high heat. Reduce heat to medium-low and
simmer, uncovered, 5 to 10 minutes, just until asparagus are
tender; drain. Place on serving platter; cover and refrigerate
2 hours, or until chilled.

◆ Prepare watercress mayonnaise: Chop ¾ cup watercress;
reserve remaining watercress for garnish. In medium bowl,
combine chopped watercress, mayonnaise, milk, capers, and
lemon juice; spoon over chilled asparagus. Garnish with
lemon slices and reserved watercress.

**Each serving: About 170 calories, 4g protein, 7g carbohydrate,
15g total fat (2g saturated), 11mg cholesterol, 235mg sodium**

SESAME STIR-FRIED ASPARAGUS

Prep: 5 minutes   *Cook:* 10 minutes
Makes 4 accompaniment servings

1 tablespoon sesame seeds
1 tablespoon vegetable oil
½ teaspoon Asian sesame
  oil

1 pound thin asparagus, tough
  ends removed and cut
  diagonally into 1-inch pieces
¼ teaspoon salt

In 10-inch skillet, toast sesame seeds over medium heat,
shaking pan frequently, 5 minutes, or until fragrant and
pale golden. Remove from skillet. In same skillet, heat
vegetable oil and sesame oil over high heat until very hot.
Add asparagus; sprinkle with salt and cook, stirring
constantly, 5 minutes, or until tender-crisp. To serve,
sprinkle with sesame seeds.

**Each serving: About 70 calories, 3g protein, 5g carbohydrate,
5g total fat (1g saturated) 0mg cholesterol, 145mg sodium**

CORN

Sweet corn on the cob is a perennial summer delight. For added flavor, tuck a fragrant herb sprig such as rosemary or sage right into the husk and grill the cob for a sweet, roasted flavor. Another appealing idea? Cut the fresh kernels from the cob and transform them into a quick sauté with chives, a savory corn pudding with a comforting texture, or an innovative succotash flavored with smoked Gouda. For the sweetest corn, cook it as soon as possible after buying, before its sugar content turns to starch. New hybrids of supersweet corn retain their sugars longer and can be stored for several days in the refrigerator.

1 Pull husks back from each ear of corn; cut off corn cobs and remove silk, leaving husks intact. In large bowl, soak husks and string in *water* to cover 20 minutes.

2 Meanwhile, cut 3 cups corn kernels from cobs; place in another large bowl (reserve remaining corn for another day). Stir in remaining ingredients.

ROASTED SUCCOTASH IN CORN HUSKS

◆◆◆◆◆◆◆◆◆◆◆◆◆◆◆◆◆◆◆◆◆◆◆◆◆◆

Prep: 30 minutes   Roast: 35 minutes
Makes 6 accompaniment servings

6 large ears corn with husks
6 pieces (10 inches each) string
1 package (10 ounces) frozen baby lima beans, thawed
1 large tomato, diced
4 ounces smoked Gouda cheese, shredded (1 cup)

3 tablespoons margarine or butter, melted
1 teaspoon sugar
½ teaspoon lemon-pepper seasoning salt
½ teaspoon salt

3 Preheat oven to 425°F. Remove husks and string from water. Shake excess water from husks. Carefully place about 1 cup succotash mixture in each husk.

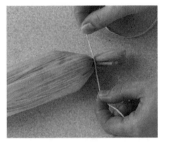

4 Bring husks together, being sure to enclose succotash filling completely; tie open end of each husk tightly with string; cut off loose ends of string.

5 Place filled corn husks in jelly-roll pan; roast 35 minutes, or until corn is tender and succotash is heated through. To serve, place filled corn husks on platter; remove string.

EACH SERVING: ABOUT 325 CALORIES, 13g PROTEIN, 47g CARBOHYDRATE, 12g TOTAL FAT (5g SATURATED), 22mg CHOLESTEROL, 535mg SODIUM

CREAMY CORN PUDDING

Prep: 30 minutes   Bake: 1 hour 15 minutes
Makes 8 accompaniment servings

2 medium ears corn, husks
  and silk removed, or
  1 package (10 ounces)
  frozen whole-kernel corn,
  thawed
2 tablespoons margarine or
  butter
1 small onion, minced

¼ cup all-purpose flour
1 teaspoon salt
¼ teaspoon coarsely ground
  black pepper
2 cups half-and-half or light
  cream
1 cup milk
4 large eggs

◆ Preheat oven to 325°F. Cut corn kernels from cobs. In 2-quart saucepan, melt margarine over medium heat. Add onion and cook, stirring occasionally, about 10 minutes, until tender and golden brown.

◆ Stir in flour, salt, and pepper until blended. Gradually stir in half-and-half and milk and cook, stirring constantly, until mixture thickens slightly and boils. Remove saucepan from heat; stir in corn.

◆ In deep 2-quart casserole or soufflé dish, beat eggs slightly. Gradually beat in corn mixture. Set casserole in larger baking pan; place pan on oven rack. Pour *boiling water* into pan to come halfway up side of casserole. Bake pudding 1¼ hours, or until knife inserted in center comes out clean.

Each serving: About 210 calories, 8g protein, 16g carbohydrate, 13g total fat (6g saturated), 133mg cholesterol, 375mg sodium

GRILLED SWEET CORN

Prep: 25 minutes plus soaking   Grill: 30 to 40 minutes
Makes 8 accompaniment servings

8 medium ears corn
  with husks
  8 teaspoons
    olive oil

Several sprigs each basil,
  rosemary, sage, and/or
  thyme

◆ Prepare outdoor grill. In 8-quart saucepot or bowl, place corn with husks and *cold water* to cover; let soak 15 minutes. (Soaking keeps husks from burning on grill.)

◆ Drain corn well. Gently pull back husks to about three-fourths way down; remove silk.

◆ With pastry brush, brush each ear of corn with 1 teaspoon olive oil. Tuck several sprigs of herbs into each ear.

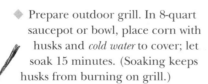

◆ Rewrap corn with husks, removing 1 strip of husk from each ear of corn and tying tops of husks together with strip of extra husk.

◆ Place corn on grill over medium heat; grill, turning corn occasionally, 30 to 40 minutes, until tender when pierced with tip of sharp knife.

Each serving: About 155 calories, 4g protein, 28g carbohydrate, 5g total fat (1g saturated), 0mg cholesterol, 5mg sodium

SAUTÉED FRESH CORN

Prep: 10 minutes   Cook: 5 minutes
Makes 4 accompaniment servings

6 medium ears corn, husks
  and silk removed
2 tablespoons margarine or
  butter
½ teaspoon salt

¼ teaspoon coarsely ground
  black pepper
¼ cup chopped fresh chives or
  thinly sliced green onions

Cut corn kernels from cobs. In 10-inch skillet, melt margarine over medium-high heat. Add corn, salt, and pepper and cook, stirring frequently, 4 minutes, or until corn is tender. Remove from heat; stir in chives.

Each serving: About 225 calories, 6g protein, 42g carbohydrate, 7g total fat (1g saturated) 0mg cholesterol, 340mg sodium

MAKE YOUR OWN HERB BRUSH

If you have an abundance of garden herbs, try making a fragrant herb brush, which can be used for brushing oil or melted margarine or butter over grilled or broiled fish, meat or poultry, garlic bread, or focaccia, as well as corn on the cob. Or, use to dab vinaigrette over salads and steamed vegetables. Choose herbs such as rosemary, sage, and thyme for your herb brush.

1 Tie a small bouquet of herb sprigs together at the stem end with a piece of string or another sprig.

2 Dip in olive oil or melted margarine or butter and brush over grilled corn on the cob or other food.

PEAS, SNAP PEAS, AND SNOW PEAS

Tender peas and snow peas are very easy to overcook; it's almost impossible to undercook them. Fresh green peas from a garden or farmstand are a spring and summer treat and well worth the extra time and effort of shelling; eat them as soon as possible after picking or buying, because, like corn, their sugars quickly convert to starch. Frozen peas are often sweeter than "fresh" peas that have been off the vine for some time. Both flat snow peas and plump sugar snap peas are meant to be eaten whole, pod and all – simply pull off the tough string first.

SWEET SUMMER PEAS

◆◆◆◆◆◆◆◆◆◆◆◆◆◆◆◆◆◆◆◆◆◆◆◆◆◆◆◆

Prep: 25 minutes   Cook: 8 to 10 minutes
Makes 6 accompaniment servings

2½ pounds fresh peas or
  2 packages (10 ounces each)
  frozen peas, thawed
¼ cup mayonnaise
1 tablespoon chopped fresh
  parsley
1 tablespoon tarragon vinegar

¾ teaspoon salt
⅛ teaspoon ground black
  pepper
1 bunch or 1 bag (6 ounces)
  radishes, finely chopped
Lettuce leaves

1 If using fresh peas, shell them (you should have about 2½ cups shelled peas). In 3-quart saucepan, heat *¾ cup water* to boiling over high heat; add fresh peas and heat to boiling.

2 Reduce heat to low; cover saucepan and simmer 3 to 5 minutes, just until peas are tender. Drain peas in a colander; rinse with cold running water until cool. Set aside.

3 Prepare dressing: In large bowl, with wire whisk or fork, mix mayonnaise, parsley, tarragon vinegar, salt, and pepper until mixture is smooth and well combined.

4 Add fresh or frozen thawed peas and radishes to dressing; toss to coat. Cover and refrigerate if not serving right away. To serve, line bowl with lettuce; spoon salad over lettuce.

HOMEMADE TARRAGON VINEGAR

Wash 4-cup-capacity bottle with cork in hot soapy water. Put bottle in large pot, and cork in small pan, and fill with water. Heat to boiling over high heat. Boil gently 5 minutes; drain. Place 3 or 4 sprigs tarragon in bottle; push in with skewer if necessary. In nonreactive saucepan, heat 4 cups white wine vinegar to boiling over high heat. Pour through funnel into bottle. Cork; let stand in cool, dark place 2 weeks.

  Strain through fine sieve into glass measuring cup. Discard tarragon sprigs. Return vinegar to bottle; add fresh tarragon. Vinegar can be stored up to 3 months at cool room temperature; if stored in a warm place, it may ferment and develop an off flavor. If the cork pops, discard the vinegar.

EACH SERVING: ABOUT 110 CALORIES, 3g PROTEIN, 9g CARBOHYDRATE, 8g TOTAL FAT (1g SATURATED), 5mg CHOLESTEROL, 370mg SODIUM

SNAP PEAS AND YELLOW PEPPERS

Prep: 20 minutes   *Cook:* 15 minutes
Makes 6 accompaniment servings

1 tablespoon plus 2 teaspoons olive or vegetable oil
1 large yellow pepper, cut into 2" by ¾" pieces
2 large celery stalks, cut diagonally into ¼-inch-thick slices
Salt
Coarsely ground black pepper
1 pound sugar snap peas or snow peas, strings removed

◆ In nonstick 12-inch skillet, heat 1 tablespoon oil over medium-high heat; add yellow pepper, celery, ¾ teaspoon salt, and ¼ teaspoon black pepper and cook, stirring frequently, about 10 minutes, until vegetables are tender and lightly browned.

◆ Transfer pepper mixture to bowl. In same skillet, heat remaining 2 teaspoons oil; add sugar snap peas, ½ teaspoon salt, and ¼ teaspoon black pepper and cook, stirring frequently, about 4 minutes, until peas are tender-crisp. Stir in pepper mixture until well combined.

◆ Spoon vegetable mixture onto platter. If not serving right away, cover and refrigerate to serve cold later.

Each serving: About 75 calories, 3g protein, 8g carbohydrate, 4g total fat (1g saturated), 0mg cholesterol, 460mg sodium

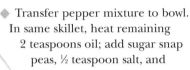

PREPARING SNOW AND SNAP PEAS

Rinse snow peas well. To remove the string, pull off the tip of the pod, keeping the string intact. Pull the string along the length of the pod. With sugar snap peas, the string runs along both sides of the pod.

MIXED PEA POD STIR-FRY

Prep: 15 minutes   *Cook:* 8 minutes
Makes 4 accompaniment servings

8 ounces green beans, ends trimmed
1 teaspoon salt
2 teaspoons vegetable oil
4 ounces snow peas, strings removed
4 ounces sugar snap peas, strings removed
1 garlic clove, minced
1 tablespoon soy sauce

◆ In 12-inch skillet, in *1 inch boiling water*, heat green beans and salt to boiling over high heat. Reduce heat to low. Simmer, uncovered, 3 minutes; drain in colander. Wipe skillet dry.

◆ In same skillet, heat oil over high heat until hot. Add green beans and cook, stirring often, 1 minute, or until beginning to brown.

◆ Add snow peas, sugar snap peas, and garlic; cook, stirring, 2 to 3 minutes, until peas are tender-crisp. Remove from heat and stir in soy sauce.

Each serving; About 60 calories, 3g protein, 8g carbohydrate, 2g total fat (0g saturated), 0mg cholesterol, 295mg sodium

SAUTÉED PEAS WITH GREEN ONIONS

Prep: 30 minutes   *Cook:* 15 minutes
Makes 6 accompaniment servings

4 pounds fresh peas, shelled (about 4 cups), or 1 bag (20 ounces) frozen peas, thawed
2 tablespoons margarine or butter
1 bunch green onions, cut into ¼-inch pieces (½ cup)
½ teaspoon salt
¼ teaspoon ground black pepper
¼ cup chopped fresh mint

◆ If using fresh peas, in 4-quart saucepan, heat *1 cup water* to boiling over high heat; add peas and heat to boiling. Reduce heat to low; cover and simmer 3 minutes, or just until peas are tender. Drain; set aside.

◆ In 10-inch skillet, melt margarine over medium heat. Add green onions and cook 2 minutes, or until tender. Add fresh or frozen thawed peas, salt, and pepper and cook, stirring often, 3 minutes longer, or until peas are hot. Remove from heat; stir in mint. Spoon into warm serving bowl.

Each serving; About 110 calories, 5g protein, 14g carbohydrate, 4g total fat (1g saturated), 0mg cholesterol, 305mg sodium

GREEN BEANS

Green beans take well to simple preparations – roasted in a very hot oven, blanched and then stir-fried with Asian seasonings, or sautéed in a little olive oil. Whatever variety you choose, buy firm, straight, slender beans without blemishes. To test for freshness, try breaking one in half: If it bends, the bean is past its prime; if it snaps easily, the bean should be tender and sweet.

ROASTED GREEN BEANS WITH DILL VINAIGRETTE

◆◆◆◆◆◆◆◆◆◆◆◆◆◆

Prep: 20 minutes
Roast: 20 to 30 minutes
Makes 8 accompaniment servings

2 pounds green beans, ends trimmed
3 tablespoons olive oil
Salt
2 tablespoons white wine vinegar
1½ teaspoons Dijon mustard
½ teaspoon sugar
½ teaspoon coarsely ground black pepper
2 tablespoons chopped fresh dill

1 Preheat oven to 450°F. In 17" by 11½" roasting pan, combine green beans, 1 tablespoon olive oil, and ½ teaspoon salt; toss until beans are coated with oil.

2 Roast green beans, uncovered, 20 to 30 minutes, until tender and slightly browned, stirring twice during roasting for even cooking. Meanwhile, prepare vinaigrette: In small bowl, with wire whisk or fork, mix vinegar, mustard, sugar, pepper, and ¼ teaspoon salt.

DILL

A member of the parsley family, dill is both an herb and a spice. Fresh dill has feathery green leaves and a slightly lemony anise flavor. It's a favorite for yogurt-based dips, cream sauces, soups, and salads, especially fish and cucumber salads. It loses its flavor quickly on heating, so when used in hot dishes it should be added towards the end of cooking time. (Dried dill, usually known as dillweed, does not have quite the same flavor.) Dill seeds are more pungent and are good in pickles, breads, and vegetable dishes.

3 Slowly whisk in remaining 2 tablespoons olive oil; whisk in dill. When beans are done, in large bowl, toss beans with vinaigrette. Serve warm or at room temperature.

EACH SERVING: ABOUT 75 CALORIES, 1g PROTEIN, 7g CARBOHYDRATE, 5g TOTAL FAT (1g SATURATED), 0mg CHOLESTEROL, 240mg SODIUM

ROMAN-STYLE GREEN BEANS

Prep: 15 minutes   *Cook:* 20 to 25 minutes
Makes 8 accompaniment servings

2 pounds green beans, ends trimmed
**4 ounces sliced pancetta or bacon, cut
    into ½-inch strips**
1 tablespoon olive oil
½ teaspoon salt
¼ cup pine nuts (pignoli), toasted

◆ In 5-quart saucepot in *1 inch boiling
water*, heat beans to boiling over high
heat. Reduce heat to low. Simmer,
uncovered, 5 to 10 minutes, until
beans are tender-crisp; drain. Wipe
saucepot dry.

◆ In same saucepot, cook pancetta,
stirring frequently, over medium heat
until golden. With slotted spoon,
transfer pancetta to paper towels to
drain. Set aside.

◆ To drippings in saucepot, add olive
oil; heat over medium-high heat until
hot. Add green beans with salt and
cook, stirring frequently, until beans
are lightly browned and tender.

◆ Spoon green beans onto warm
large platter; sprinkle with pancetta
and toasted pine nuts.

**Each serving: About 90 calories, 6g protein,
7g carbohydrate, 5g total fat
(1g saturated), 8mg cholesterol,
365mg sodium**

GREEN BEANS WITH HAZELNUTS

Prep: 20 minutes   *Cook:* 10 to 15 minutes
Makes 6 accompaniment servings

1½ pounds green beans, ends trimmed
Salt
2 tablespoons margarine or butter
**½ cup hazelnuts, toasted and skinned
    (see page 522)**
1 teaspoon grated lemon peel
¼ teaspoon ground black pepper

◆ In 5-quart saucepot, in *1 inch boiling
water*, heat beans and 2 teaspoons salt
to boiling over high heat.

◆ Reduce heat to low and simmer,
uncovered, 5 to 10 minutes, until
tender-crisp; drain. Wipe saucepot dry.

◆ In same saucepot, melt margarine
over medium heat. Add hazelnuts and
cook, stirring, 3 minutes, or just until
margarine begins to brown.

◆ Stir in lemon peel, pepper, beans
and ¼ teaspoon salt and cook, stirring,
5 minutes.

**Each serving; About 120 calories,
3g protein, 8g carbohydrate, 10g total fat
(1g saturated), 0mg cholesterol,
140mg sodium**

SESAME GREEN BEANS

Prep: 15 minutes   *Cook:* 10 to 15 minutes
Makes 8 accompaniment servings

2 pounds green beans, ends trimmed
1 tablespoon sesame seeds
2 tablespoons soy sauce
2 teaspoons Asian sesame oil
**1 tablespoon minced, peeled fresh ginger
    or ¾ teaspoon ground ginger**

◆ In 5-quart saucepot, in *1 inch boiling
water*, heat beans to boiling over high
heat. Reduce heat to low; simmer,
uncovered, 5 to 10 minutes, until
beans are tender-crisp.

◆ Meanwhile, in small saucepan, toast
sesame seeds over medium heat,
stirring and shaking pan frequently,
until golden brown.

◆ Drain beans. Wipe saucepot dry.
Return beans to saucepot. Stir in soy
sauce, sesame oil, and ginger; heat
through.

◆ Sprinkle beans with toasted sesame
seeds. Serve beans warm or cover and
refrigerate to serve cold later.

**Each serving: About 45 calories, 2g protein,
7g carbohydrate, 2g total fat
(0g saturated), 0mg cholesterol,
270mg sodium**

BEANS

Regular green beans are widely available;
Italian green beans may be easier to come
by at farmers' markets. Haricots verts, a
slender, tender but expensive
French bean, are increasingly
available at large supermarkets
and specialty markets. Feel free
to substitute a
different bean
in a favorite
recipe. Just
remember
that thicker
beans will take
longer to cook than
thinner beans.

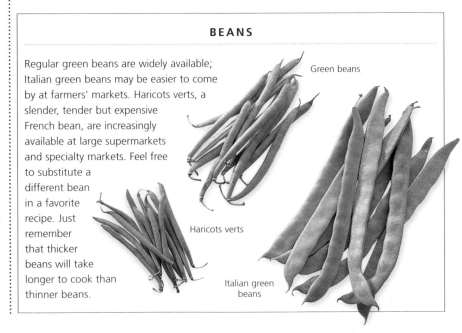

Green beans

Haricots verts

Italian green
beans

Root vegetables

Many of nature's edible gifts come from beneath the ground. Besides potatoes, which fall into their own category, carrots are perhaps the favorite root. But beets, turnips, parsnips, celery root (celeriac), rutabagas, and sunchokes (Jerusalem artichokes) are equally delicious – sweet and earthy – whether mashed, baked, roasted, or candied.

HARVEST CASSEROLE

◆◆◆◆◆◆◆◆◆◆◆◆◆

Prep: 40 minutes
Bake: 1 hour
Makes 8 accompaniment servings

5 tablespoons margarine or butter
1 jumbo onion (about 1 pound), cut into ¼-inch-thick slices
2 garlic cloves, minced
6 medium carrots (about 1 pound), peeled and thinly sliced
6 medium parsnips (about 1 pound), peeled and thinly sliced
1 small rutabaga (about 1 pound), peeled, cut into quarters, and thinly sliced
3 tablespoons all-purpose flour
1½ teaspoons salt
¼ teaspoon coarsely ground black pepper
¼ teaspoon ground nutmeg
2½ cups milk
¼ cup freshly grated Parmesan cheese
Chopped fresh parsley for garnish

1 Preheat oven to 375°F. In nonstick 10-inch skillet, melt 3 tablespoons margarine over medium heat. Add onion and garlic; cook 15 to 20 minutes, stirring often, until golden.

RUTABAGA

A cross between a cabbage and a turnip, rutabagas have yellow-orange flesh and a thick skin, which is often waxed to prevent drying out. They will keep for up to 2 weeks in the refrigerator, and can be prepared as for turnips.

2 In shallow 2½-quart casserole, toss carrots, parsnips, rutabaga, and onion mixture until well combined. Cover casserole and bake 45 minutes, or until vegetables are fork-tender.

3 Meanwhile, in 2-quart saucepan, melt remaining 2 tablespoons margarine over medium heat. Stir in flour and next 3 ingredients; cook, stirring, 1 minute.

4 Gradually stir milk into flour mixture in saucepan; cook, stirring constantly, until sauce thickens slightly and boils.

5 Stir sauce into vegetables. Sprinkle grated Parmesan cheese evenly on top. Bake casserole, uncovered, 15 minutes longer, or until sauce is bubbly and top is golden brown. To serve, sprinkle with parsley.

EACH SERVING: ABOUT 245 CALORIES, 7g PROTEIN, 32g CARBOHYDRATE, 11g TOTAL FAT (4g SATURATED), 13mg CHOLESTEROL, 615mg SODIUM

CELERY ROOT RÉMOULADE

Prep: 20 minutes plus chilling
Makes 6 accompaniment servings

2 tablespoons fresh lemon
juice
1½ pounds celery root
(celeriac)
½ cup mayonnaise

2 tablespoons Dijon mustard
1 tablespoon minced fresh
parsley
¼ teaspoon ground black
pepper

◆ Place lemon juice in large bowl. Peel celery root. With adjustable-blade slicer or mandoline, or very sharp knife, cut celery root into ⅛-inch-thick matchstick strips. As you cut it, add celery root to lemon juice in bowl and toss to coat to prevent browning.

◆ In small bowl, mix mayonnaise, mustard, parsley, and pepper until well combined. Add to celery root and toss to coat. Cover and refrigerate at least 1 hour, or overnight.

Each serving; About 160 calories, 2g protein, 6g carbohydrate, 15g total fat (2g saturated), 11mg cholesterol, 340mg sodium

MASHED ROOT VEGETABLES

Prep: 15 minutes   *Cook:* 25 minutes
Makes 8 accompaniment servings

2 pounds carrots, celery root
(celeriac), parsnips, white
turnips, and/or rutabaga
1 pound all-purpose potatoes
Salt

3 tablespoons margarine or
butter
Pinch ground nutmeg
¼ teaspoon ground black
pepper

◆ Peel root vegetables and potatoes and cut into 1-inch pieces. In 4-quart saucepan, combine root vegetables, potatoes, 2 teaspoons salt, and *water* to cover; heat to boiling over high heat. Reduce heat to low; cover and simmer 15 minutes, or until vegetables are tender. Drain; return to saucepan.

◆ Add margarine, nutmeg, pepper, and ½ teaspoon salt and mash with potato masher until smooth.

Each serving; About 135 calories, 2g protein, 23g carbohydrate, 5g total fat (1g saturated), 0mg cholesterol, 250mg sodium

VEGETABLE COBBLER

Prep: 30 minutes   *Bake:* 1 hour 15 minutes
Makes 6 main-dish servings

1 medium butternut squash
(about 2 pounds), peeled,
seeded, and cut into 1½-inch
chunks
3 large red potatoes (about
1 pound), cut into 1½-inch
chunks
3 medium parsnips (about
½ pound), peeled and cut
into 1-inch pieces
1 medium red onion, cut into
6 wedges
2 tablespoons olive oil
¼ teaspoon salt

½ teaspoon dried tarragon
1 can (13¾ to 14½ ounces)
chicken or vegetable broth
½ teaspoon grated lemon peel
1 small bunch (about
¾ pound) broccoli, cut into
2" by 1" pieces
½ cup plus ⅔ cup milk
1 tablespoon cornstarch
1¾ cups all-purpose baking
mix
½ cup yellow cornmeal
¾ teaspoon coarsely ground
black pepper

◆ Preheat oven to 450°F. In shallow 3- to 4-quart casserole or 13" by 9" glass baking dish, toss first 7 ingredients together until vegetables are well coated with oil. Bake, uncovered, 1 hour, or until vegetables are fork-tender and lightly browned, stirring once.

◆ Meanwhile, after vegetables have cooked about 45 minutes, in 3-quart saucepan, heat broth and lemon peel to boiling over high heat. Add broccoli; heat to boiling. Reduce heat to low; cover and simmer broccoli 1 minute.

◆ In cup, mix ½ cup milk with cornstarch; stir into broccoli mixture. Cook, stirring constantly, until mixture thickens slightly and boils; boil 1 minute.

◆ Pour broccoli mixture over vegetables; stir until brown bits are loosened from bottom of casserole.

◆ In medium bowl, mix baking mix, cornmeal, pepper, and remaining ⅔ cup milk until just combined. Drop 12 heaping spoonfuls of biscuit dough on top of vegetable mixture. Bake cobbler, uncovered, 15 minutes longer, or until biscuits are browned.

Each serving: About 450 calories, 11g protein, 79g carbohydrate, 12g total fat (2g saturated), 12mg cholesterol, 840mg sodium

CARROTS AND PARSNIPS AU GRATIN

Prep: 45 minutes   Bake: 20 minutes
Makes 8 accompaniment servings

1 bag (16 ounces) carrots, peeled and cut diagonally into ¼-inch-thick slices
1 pound parsnips, peeled and cut diagonally into ¼-inch-thick slices
2 tablespoons margarine or butter
1 small onion, minced
½ cup mayonnaise
2 tablespoons prepared white horseradish
¼ teaspoon salt
⅛ teaspoon ground black pepper
1 slice firm white bread, torn into ¼-inch crumbs

◆ In 12-inch skillet, in *1½ inches boiling water*, heat carrots and parsnips to boiling over high heat. Reduce heat to low; cover and simmer 20 minutes, or until vegetables are tender. Drain, reserving ¼ cup cooking liquid. Transfer vegetables to 1½-quart casserole.

◆ Preheat oven to 350°F. In 1-quart saucepan, melt 1 tablespoon margarine over medium heat; add onion and cook, stirring occasionally, until tender. Remove from heat.

◆ Stir in mayonnaise, horseradish, salt, pepper, and reserved cooking liquid. Gently fold sauce into vegetables.

◆ In small skillet, melt remaining 1 tablespoon margarine over low heat. Stir in bread crumbs; mix until coated with margarine and scatter over casserole. Bake 20 minutes, or until crumbs are browned and vegetables are hot.

Each serving: About 210 calories, 2g protein, 21g carbohydrate, 14g total fat (2g saturated), 8mg cholesterol, 260mg sodium

ROASTED CARROTS AND PARSNIPS

Prep: 15 minutes   Roast: 1 hour
Makes 8 accompaniment servings

1 bag (16 ounces) carrots, peeled and cut into 2-inch pieces
1 pound parsnips, peeled and cut into 2-inch pieces
8 ounces large shallots, peeled
1 tablespoon olive oil
⅛ teaspoon dried thyme
½ teaspoon salt
¼ teaspoon ground black pepper

Preheat oven to 425°F. In 14" by 10" roasting pan, toss carrots, parsnips, and shallots with olive oil, thyme, salt, and pepper until evenly coated. Roast 1 hour, or until vegetables are tender when pierced with knife.

Each serving; About 105 calories, 2g protein, 22g carbohydrate, 2g total fat (0g saturated), 0mg cholesterol, 160mg sodium

MAPLE-GLAZED CARROTS WITH PISTACHIOS

Prep: 30 minutes   Cook: 30 to 40 minutes
Makes 10 accompaniment servings

8 bunches (4 pounds) baby carrots, peeled or scrubbed, or 3 bags (16 ounces each) carrots, peeled and cut into 3" by ½" sticks
4 tablespoons margarine or butter, cut up
1 teaspoon salt
½ cup maple syrup
½ cup pistachios, chopped and toasted

◆ In 12-inch skillet, heat *1 inch water* to boiling over high heat. Add carrots; heat to boiling. Reduce heat to low; cover and simmer 8 to 10 minutes, until tender-crisp. Drain.

◆ Wipe skillet dry. Return carrots to skillet; add margarine and salt and cook, uncovered, over medium-high heat, gently stirring occasionally, 10 to 15 minutes, until carrots are glazed and golden.

◆ Add maple syrup; heat to boiling. Boil 2 minutes, stirring frequently, until carrots are lightly coated with glaze. Transfer to bowl; sprinkle with pistachios.

Each serving: About 175 calories, 3g protein, 25g carbohydrate, 8g total fat (1g saturated), 0mg cholesterol, 315mg sodium

PARSNIPS

Available all year round, parsnips are at their peak in winter. Their creamy texture lends itself beautifully to cold-weather favorites such as smooth mashes, purees, and soups, while their sweet nutty flavor makes them excellent in stews or roasted as an accompaniment. When buying, look for firm, smooth, medium-size parsnips without cracks. Large, older parsnips have a stronger flavor than younger ones; they may also have a woody core, which should be removed before cooking.

BEETS WITH BASIL VINAIGRETTE

Prep: 30 minutes plus cooling   Cook: 45 minutes
Makes 8 accompaniment servings

6 pounds beets with tops (about 12 medium beets)	2 teaspoons sugar
3 tablespoons cider vinegar	1 teaspoon salt
2 tablespoons olive or vegetable oil	¼ cup chopped fresh basil
	½ small onion, cut into paper-thin slices

◆ Trim stems and leaves from beets; reserve several leaves for garnish. With vegetable brush, scrub beets. In 5-quart saucepot, heat beets with *water* to cover to boiling over high heat. Reduce heat to low; cover and simmer 30 minutes, or until beets are tender when pierced with knife.

◆ Drain beets; cool until easy to handle. Peel beets and cut into bite-size chunks.

◆ In large bowl, with fork or wire whisk, mix vinegar, oil, sugar, and salt. Add basil, onion, and beets; toss to combine. Serve at room temperature or cover and refrigerate to serve cold later.

◆ To serve, line platter with reserved beet leaves; spoon beets on top.

Each serving: About 125 calories, 3g protein, 21g carbohydrate, 4g total fat (0g saturated), 0mg cholesterol, 410mg sodium

ROASTED BEETS WITH CARDAMOM SPICE BUTTER

Prep: 20 minutes plus cooling   Roast: 1 hour to 1 hour 30 minutes
Makes 4 accompaniment servings

3 pounds beets with tops (about 6 medium beets)	Pinch ground cloves
½ teaspoon ground cardamom	1 tablespoon margarine or butter
¼ teaspoon ground cumin	¼ teaspoon salt

◆ Preheat oven to 425°F. Trim stems and leaves from beets. With vegetable brush, scrub beets.

◆ Place beets in 14" by 10" roasting pan; cover tightly with foil. Roast 1 to 1½ hours, until tender when pierced with knife. Cool until easy to handle. Peel beets; cut into wedges.

◆ In 3-quart saucepan, heat cardamom, cumin, and cloves over low heat, shaking pan occasionally, 2 minutes, or until very fragrant. Add margarine and heat until bubbling. Add beets and salt; increase heat to medium and cook, stirring often, 5 minutes, or until hot.

Each serving: About 115 calories, 3g protein, 20g carbohydrate, 3g total fat (1g saturated), 0mg cholesterol, 310mg sodium.

CANDIED TURNIPS

Prep: 10 minutes   Cook: 20 minutes
Makes 6 accompaniment servings

1½ pounds turnips, peeled and cut into 1-inch wedges	2 tablespoons margarine or butter
1 teaspoon salt	⅓ cup sugar

◆ In 12-inch skillet, combine turnips with salt and *water* to cover; heat to boiling over high heat.

◆ Reduce heat to low; cover and simmer 7 to 10 minutes, just until turnips are tender when pierced with knife. Drain.

◆ Wipe skillet dry. In same skillet, melt margarine over high heat. Add sugar and cook, stirring occasionally, about 2 minutes, until amber in color. Add turnips and cook, stirring often, 5 minutes, or until well coated.

Each serving: About 95 calories, 1g protein, 16g carbohydrate, 4g total fat (1g saturated), 0mg cholesterol, 455mg sodium

ROASTED SUNCHOKES

Prep: 15 minutes   Roast: 1 hour
Makes 8 accompaniment servings

2 pounds sunchokes (Jerusalem artichokes)	¼ teaspoon ground black pepper
1 tablespoon olive oil	Chopped fresh parsley for garnish
1 teaspoon salt	

◆ Preheat oven to 425°F. With vegetable brush, scrub sunchokes. In 14" by 10" roasting pan, toss sunchokes with oil, salt, and pepper.

◆ Roast 1 hour, until sunchokes are tender when pierced with knife. To serve, sprinkle with parsley.

Each serving: About 100 calories, 2g protein, 20g carbohydrate, 2g total fat (0g saturated), 0mg cholesterol, 270mg sodium

SUNCHOKES (JERUSALEM ARTICHOKES)

Neither an artichoke nor from Jerusalem, this brown-skinned tuber is a member of the sunflower family. Crisp, nutty, and slightly sweet in taste, sunchokes are equally good served raw in a salad or cooked. Peel them or simply scrub the skin well before using. When shopping, choose firm, unblemished tubers free of soft spots and green-tinged portions.

POTATOES

Mashed, roasted, fried, or baked, potatoes are a supremely satisfying side dish in any guise. They can also be a tempting main course: Stuff a baked potato with a hearty filling, or create a rich potato pancake accented with artichokes.

TWO-POTATOES ANNA

◆◆◆◆◆◆◆◆◆◆◆◆◆◆

Prep: 45 minutes
Bake: 25 minutes
Makes 10 accompaniment servings

6 medium all-purpose
    potatoes (about 2 pounds)
4 medium sweet potatoes
    (about 2 pounds)
¼ cup vegetable oil
1 large onion, chopped
4 tablespoons margarine or
    butter
Salt
Ground black pepper
Parsley sprigs for garnish

ADJUSTABLE-BLADE SLICER

To slice, julienne, and waffle-cut vegetables easily, use an adjustable-blade slicer. These range from the classic all-metal mandoline to lightweight plastic models. Some have a selection of blades for different functions; the best are adjustable to paper-thinness. To protect your fingers, a safety shield holds the food in place as you slide it over the blade.

1 Peel all-purpose and sweet potatoes. Using an adjustable-blade slicer or sharp knife, thinly slice potatoes, keeping sliced white and sweet potatoes in separate piles.

2 In 10-inch cast-iron skillet with oven-safe handle (or wrap handle with double thickness of foil), heat oil over medium heat. Add onion; cook until tender. Transfer to bowl.

3 In same skillet, arrange white potatoes, overlapping them slightly. Sprinkle with onion; dot with 2 tablespoons margarine. Sprinkle with ¾ teaspoon salt and ¼ teaspoon pepper.

4 Arrange sweet-potato slices over white potatoes. Dot with remaining 2 tablespoons margarine; sprinkle with ¾ teaspoon salt and ¼ teaspoon pepper.

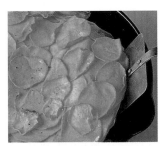

5 Cook layered potato mixture over medium heat 15 minutes, or until bottom layer of potatoes is lightly browned. Meanwhile, preheat oven to 450°F.

6 Place skillet on bottom rack in oven and bake 25 minutes, or until potatoes are tender when pierced with knife, pressing potatoes down with pancake turner occasionally. To serve, loosen edge of potatoes with pancake turner; carefully invert potatoes onto warm platter. Garnish with parsley sprigs; cut into wedges.

EACH SERVING: ABOUT 250 CALORIES, 3g PROTEIN, 37g CARBOHYDRATE, 10g TOTAL FAT (2g SATURATED), 0mg CHOLESTEROL, 385mg SODIUM

ROASTED POTATOES WITH GARLIC

Prep: 20 minutes   *Roast:* 1 hour
Makes 10 accompaniment servings

4½ pounds medium red
  and/or all-purpose
  potatoes, unpeeled and
  each cut into quarters
2 medium red onions, each
  cut into 6 wedges
¼ cup olive oil

1 tablespoon chopped fresh
  thyme or 1 teaspoon dried
  thyme
1¼ teaspoons salt
½ teaspoon coarsely ground
  black pepper
2 garlic cloves, minced

Preheat oven to 425°F. In 17" by 11½" roasting pan, toss potatoes with remaining ingredients. Roast, turning occasionally with metal spatula, 1 hour, or until golden and fork-tender. Serve warm or at room temperature.

Each serving: About 240 calories, 4g protein, 44g carbohydrate, 6g total fat (1g saturated), 0mg cholesterol, 275mg sodium

POTATO AND ARTICHOKE RÖSTI

Prep: 35 minutes   *Bake:* 20 to 25 minutes
Makes 4 main-dish servings

2½ pounds baking potatoes
  (about 4 large)
¾ teaspoon salt
¼ teaspoon coarsely ground
  black pepper
2 tablespoons olive oil

4 ounces Fontina or
  mozzarella cheese,
  shredded (1 cup)
1 jar (8¼ ounces) marinated
  artichoke hearts, rinsed,
  well drained, and sliced

◆ Preheat oven to 400°F. Peel and coarsely shred potatoes; pat dry. In large bowl, toss potatoes with salt and pepper.

◆ In nonstick 10-inch skillet with oven-safe handle (or wrap handle with double thickness of foil), heat 1 tablespoon oil over medium heat. Working quickly, add half the potatoes, patting with rubber spatula to cover skillet. Leaving ½-inch border, top potatoes with half the cheese, all the artichokes,

then remaining cheese. Cover with remaining potatoes, patting to edge of skillet. Cook 10 minutes, or until bottom is brown, shaking skillet occasionally to keep pancake moving freely. Carefully invert pancake onto large plate.

◆ Add remaining 1 tablespoon oil to skillet; slide pancake back into skillet. Cook 10 minutes, gently shaking skillet. Place in oven and bake 20 to 25 minutes, until potatoes are tender.

Each serving: About 475 calories, 15g protein, 71g carbohydrate, 16g total fat (6g saturated), 33mg cholesterol, 700mg sodium

CLASSIC MASHED POTATOES

Prep: 20 minutes   *Cook:* 30 minutes
Makes 8 accompaniment servings

3 pounds all-purpose potatoes
4 tablespoons margarine or
  butter

1½ teaspoons salt
1 cup hot milk

Peel potatoes and cut into 1-inch chunks. In 3-quart saucepan, heat potatoes and enough *water* to cover to boiling over high heat. Reduce heat to low. Cover and simmer 15 minutes, or until fork-tender; drain. Return potatoes to pan. With potato masher, mash potatoes with margarine and salt. Gradually add milk; mash until smooth.

Each serving: About 215 calories, 4g protein, 36g carbohydrate, 7g total fat (2g saturated), 4mg cholesterol, 490mg sodium

MASHED POTATOES PLUS

Garlic and lemon Prepare Classic Mashed Potatoes as above through draining. Meanwhile, in 1-quart saucepan, heat the margarine and salt with 2 cloves garlic, minced, over low heat 3 minutes. Add to potatoes; mash. Add milk as directed; stir in 2 tablespoons minced parsley and 1 teaspoon grated lemon peel.

Each serving: About 215 calories, 4g protein, 36g carbohydrate, 7g total fat (2g saturated), 4mg cholesterol, 490mg sodium

Horseradish Prepare Classic Mashed Potatoes as above, but add 2 tablespoons undrained prepared white horseradish with the milk.

Each serving: About 215 calories, 4g protein, 36g carbohydrate, 7g total fat (2g saturated), 4mg cholesterol, 530mg sodium

Parsnip Prepare Classic Mashed Potatoes as above, but substitute 1 pound parsnips, peeled and cut into 1-inch pieces, for 1 pound potatoes and use only ¾ cup milk.

Each serving: About 210 calories, 4g protein, 35g carbohydrate, 7g total fat (2g saturated), 3mg cholesterol, 490mg sodium

DELUXE STUFFED BAKED POTATOES

Prep: 15 to 25 minutes   Bake: 45 minutes
Makes 4 main-dish servings

4 large baking potatoes
(12 ounces each)

Choice of Baked Potato
Topping (see below)

Preheat oven to 450°F. Pierce potatoes with a fork. Bake potatoes directly on oven rack 45 minutes, or until fork-tender. Meanwhile, prepare Baked Potato Topping. When potatoes are done, slash tops, press to open slightly, and spoon on topping.

For nutritional values, see below.

CHUNKY HOME FRIES

Prep: 5 minutes   Cook: 25 minutes
Makes 4 accompaniment servings

1½ pounds medium red
potatoes

2 tablespoons olive oil
½ teaspoon salt

◆ Cut potatoes into 1½-inch chunks. In nonstick 12-inch skillet, heat oil over medium-high heat; add potatoes and salt and cook, turning occasionally, until golden brown.

◆ Reduce heat to medium; cover skillet and continue cooking potato chunks, turning once or twice, until potatoes are fork-tender.

Each serving: About 205 calories, 3g protein, 34g carbohydrate, 7g total fat (1g saturated), 0mg cholesterol, 275mg sodium

OVEN FRIES

Prep: 10 minutes   Bake: 45 minutes
Makes 4 accompaniment servings

3 medium baking potatoes or
sweet potatoes (about
1½ pounds), unpeeled
1 tablespoon vegetable oil

½ teaspoon salt
⅛ teaspoon ground black
pepper

◆ Preheat oven to 425°F. Cut each potato lengthwise into quarters, then cut each quarter lengthwise into 3 wedges.

◆ In 15½" by 10½" jelly-roll pan, toss potato wedges with oil, salt, and black pepper until evenly coated. Bake 45 minutes, or until potatoes are golden.

Each serving: About 195 calories, 3g protein, 38g carbohydrate, 4g total fat (1g saturated), 0mg cholesterol, 280mg sodium

BAKED POTATO TOPPINGS (EACH TOPS 4 POTATOES)

CHILI Heat nonstick 12-inch skillet over medium-high heat. Add ¾ pound ground beef and 1 small onion, chopped; cook, stirring, until meat is browned and onion is tender. Stir in 3 tablespoons chili powder; cook 1 minute. Add 1 can (14½ ounces) chili-style chunky tomatoes, ¾ cup water, and 1 teaspoon sugar; cook 1 minute longer.

Each serving: About 435 calories, 11g protein, 96g carbohydrate, 3g total fat (1g saturated), 4mg cholesterol, 500mg sodium

HAM AND EGG In nonstick 12-inch skillet, melt 2 tablespoons margarine or butter over medium heat. Add 1 medium green pepper, diced, and 1 medium onion, diced; cook until tender and browned. Stir in 4 ounces ham, diced, and 6 large eggs, beaten with ¼ cup water and ¼ teaspoon each salt and coarsely ground black pepper; stir until eggs are cooked.

Each serving: About 595 calories, 24g protein, 92g carbohydrate, 15g total fat (4g saturated), 328mg cholesterol, 645mg sodium

CHUNKY VEGETABLE Cut 1 small eggplant, 1 medium zucchini, and 1 large red pepper into ½-inch pieces. In nonstick 12-inch skillet, heat 2 tablespoons olive oil over medium-high heat. Add vegetables; cook 15 minutes. Stir in 1 can (14½ ounces) Italian-style stewed tomatoes, ¼ cup water, 1 tablespoon balsamic vinegar, and 1 teaspoon salt; heat through.

Each serving: About 490 calories, 10g protein, 99g carbohydrate, 7g total fat (1g saturated), 0mg cholesterol, 760mg sodium

SPINACH AND FETA In 2-quart saucepan, melt 2 tablespoons margarine or butter over medium heat; stir in 2 tablespoons all-purpose flour. Add 1⅓ cups milk; heat to boiling, stirring. Add 10 ounces frozen chopped spinach, thawed, ¼ teaspoon each dillweed and ground black pepper, and 2 ounces crumbled feta; heat through. Top with 2 ounces feta.

Each serving: About 590 calories, 18g protein, 99g carbohydrate, 16g total fat (8g saturated), 39mg cholesterol, 520mg sodium

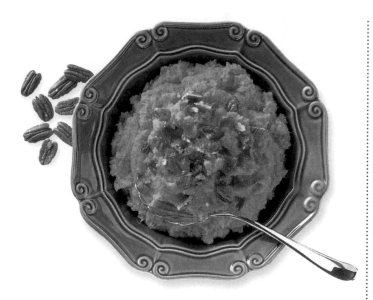

PRALINE SWEET POTATOES

Prep: 15 minutes plus cooling   *Cook:* 35 to 40 minutes
Makes 10 accompaniment servings

8 medium sweet potatoes
   (about 5 pounds), peeled
   and each cut crosswise into
   thirds
¼ cup sugar

1 cup pecans (about 4 ounces)
5 tablespoons margarine or
   butter
½ cup milk
1¼ teaspoons salt

◆ In 8-quart saucepot, heat sweet potatoes and enough *water* to cover to boiling over high heat. Reduce heat to low; cover and simmer 20 to 25 minutes, until sweet potatoes are fork-tender. Drain; return to saucepot.

◆ Meanwhile, grease cookie sheet. In 1-quart saucepan, heat sugar and ¼ *cup water*, stirring gently, over low heat until sugar dissolves. Increase heat to medium and boil rapidly, without stirring, about 7 minutes, until syrup turns a light golden brown.

◆ Working quickly, stir in pecans and 2 tablespoons margarine until combined. Spread pecan mixture in a thin layer on cookie sheet; cool.

◆ To saucepot with sweet potatoes, add milk, salt, and remaining 3 tablespoons margarine. With potato masher, mash sweet potatoes until almost smooth. Heat mixture through over low heat.

◆ To serve, spoon mashed sweet potatoes into large bowl. Break pecan mixture into small pieces; sprinkle on top of sweet potatoes.

Each serving: About 335 calories, 4g protein, 51g carbohydrate, 14g total fat (2g saturated), 2mg cholesterol, 360mg sodium

SWEET-POTATO CASSEROLE

Prep: 20 minutes   *Bake:* 60 to 70 minutes
Makes 8 accompaniment servings

5 large sweet potatoes
   (4 pounds), peeled and cut
   into ¾-inch-thick slices
⅓ cup packed dark brown
   sugar
Salt

¼ teaspoon coarsely ground
   black pepper
4 tablespoons margarine or
   butter, cut into small pieces
½ cup coarsely chopped
   walnuts

◆ Preheat oven to 400°F. In 13" by 9" ceramic or glass baking dish, arrange half of potato slices. Sprinkle with half of sugar, ¼ teaspoon salt, and all of pepper. Dot with half of margarine. Top with remaining potatoes. Sprinkle with remaining sugar and ¼ teaspoon salt; dot with remaining margarine.

◆ Cover with foil; bake 30 minutes. Uncover; sprinkle with walnuts and bake 30 to 40 minutes longer, until potatoes are tender, basting with syrup in dish 3 times during cooking.

Each serving: About 300 calories, 4g protein, 52g carbohydrate, 9g total fat (1g saturated), 0mg cholesterol, 225mg sodium

TWO-POTATO CASSEROLE

Prep: 1 hour plus cooling   *Bake:* 45 minutes
Makes 8 accompaniment servings

4 large baking potatoes
   (about 2 pounds), unpeeled
4 medium sweet potatoes
   (about 2 pounds), unpeeled
3 tablespoons margarine or
   butter
1 small onion, minced
3 tablespoons all-purpose flour

2 teaspoons salt
¼ teaspoon coarsely ground
   black pepper
2½ cups milk
2 packages (10 ounces each)
   frozen chopped spinach,
   thawed and squeezed dry

◆ In 8-quart saucepot, heat baking and sweet potatoes and enough *water* to cover to boiling over high heat. Reduce heat to low; cover and simmer 20 to 30 minutes, just until potatoes are fork-tender but not soft. Drain and cool.

◆ Preheat oven to 375°F. In 2-quart saucepan, melt margarine over medium heat; add onion and cook until tender. Stir in flour, salt, and pepper. Gradually whisk in milk and cook, whisking, until sauce boils. Set aside.

◆ Peel all potatoes; cut into ¼-inch-thick slices. In greased deep 2-quart casserole, arrange half of potato slices. Top with all of spinach; pour half of sauce on top. Repeat with remaining potatoes and sauce. Cover and bake 30 minutes. Uncover; bake 15 minutes longer, or until top is browned.

Each serving: About 335 calories, 9g protein, 61g carbohydrate, 7g total fat (3g saturated), 10mg cholesterol, 700mg sodium

ONION FAMILY

Leeks, garlic, and onions are the foundation of some irresistibly fragrant and appetizing side dishes. Leeks can be marinated in oil and herbs and then broiled to bring out their fresh, delicate onion flavor. Onions and garlic become sweet, succulent, and considerably milder in flavor when roasted or cooked with a bit of jelly or sugar in a skillet until they're nicely glazed. Try any of these recipes with roasted meats or poultry.

BROILED LEEKS

◆◆◆◆◆◆◆◆◆◆◆◆◆◆◆◆◆◆◆◆◆◆◆◆◆◆◆◆◆◆

Prep: 25 minutes plus marinating   Broil: 10 minutes
Makes 6 accompaniment servings

6 large leeks
Salt
¼ cup olive or vegetable oil
2 tablespoons tarragon
   vinegar
1½ teaspoons minced fresh
   oregano

½ teaspoon sugar
½ teaspoon coarsely ground
   black pepper
Oregano or parsley sprigs for
   garnish

1 Cut off roots from base and trim tops of leeks. Cut each leek lengthwise in half to within 2 inches of root ends.

2 Separate leaves slightly; rinse leeks thoroughly with cold running water to wash away all sand and grit.

3 In 8-quart saucepot over high heat, in *2 inches boiling water*, heat leeks and 2 teaspoons salt to boiling over high heat. Reduce heat to low; cover and simmer 5 to 10 minutes, just until leeks are tender. Drain in a colander; shake to remove excess water.

4 Prepare marinade: In shallow glass or ceramic baking dish, with wire whisk or fork, combine oil, vinegar, minced oregano, sugar, black pepper, and ½ teaspoon salt. Add leeks to dish and turn to coat. Cover and refrigerate at least 2 hours, turning leeks occasionally.

5 Preheat broiler. Place leeks on rack in broiling pan, reserving marinade. Broil leeks 7 to 10 inches from heat source 10 minutes, or until hot and lightly browned, turning once and brushing with marinade.

6 Transfer leeks to large platter. Pour pan juices in broiling pan over leeks. Serve warm or cover with plastic wrap and refrigerate to serve cold later. Garnish with oregano sprigs.

EACH SERVING: ABOUT 130 CALORIES, 1g PROTEIN, 13g CARBOHYDRATE, 9g TOTAL FAT (1g SATURATED), 0mg CHOLESTEROL, 230mg SODIUM

CARAMELIZED ONIONS

Prep: 45 minutes plus cooling
Cook: 30 minutes
Makes 4 accompaniment servings

1½ pounds small white onions
½ cup golden raisins
2 tablespoons sugar
2 tablespoons vegetable oil
½ teaspoon salt

◆ In deep 12-inch skillet, heat onions and *1 inch water* to boiling over high heat. Reduce heat to low; cover and simmer 15 minutes, or until onions are tender. Drain. Cool onions under cold running water; drain again.

◆ Peel onions, leaving a little of the root end on to help hold shape.

◆ Wipe skillet dry. In same skillet, cook onions, raisins, sugar, oil, and salt over medium-high heat, stirring and shaking skillet often, about 5 minutes, until onions are glazed and browned.

Each serving: About 210 calories, 3g protein, 37g carbohydrate, 7g total fat (1g saturated), 0mg cholesterol, 275mg sodium

GLAZED PEARL ONIONS

Prep: 45 minutes plus cooling   *Cook:* 25 minutes
Makes 6 accompaniment servings

2 pounds pearl onions
3 tablespoons margarine or butter
2 tablespoons red currant jelly
2 teaspoons sugar
¼ teaspoon salt

◆ In deep 12-inch skillet, heat onions and *1 inch water* to boiling over high heat. Reduce heat to low; cover and simmer 5 to 10 minutes, until onions are tender. Drain. Cool onions under cold running water; drain again.

◆ Peel onions, leaving a little of the root end of each to help hold shape. Wipe skillet dry.

◆ In same skillet, cook onions and remaining ingredients over medium-high heat, stirring and shaking skillet often, about 5 minutes, until onions are glazed and browned.

Each serving: About 130 calories, 2g protein, 19g carbohydrate, 6g total fat (1g saturated), 0mg cholesterol, 160mg sodium

OVEN-ROASTED ONIONS

Prep: 10 minutes   *Roast:* 1 hour 20 minutes
Makes 12 accompaniment servings

4 tablespoons olive or vegetable oil
4 jumbo red or white onions (about 1¼ pounds each), cut crosswise into ¾-inch-thick slices
Salt
2 tablespoons brown sugar
1 tablespoon cider vinegar

◆ Preheat oven to 400°F. Grease each of two 15½" by 10½" jelly-roll pans with 1 tablespoon oil. Place onion slices in single layer in jelly-roll pans.

◆ In cup, mix remaining 2 tablespoons oil with 1 teaspoon salt. Brush onion slices with half of oil mixture. Place jelly-roll pans on 2 oven racks and roast onions 45 minutes.

◆ With pancake turner, turn onion slices; brush with remaining oil mixture. Switch jelly-roll pans between upper and lower racks and roast onions 30 minutes longer.

◆ In cup, mix brown sugar, vinegar, and ½ teaspoon salt. Brush onion slices with brown-sugar mixture and roast 5 minutes longer, or until onions are tender and golden.

Each serving: About 110 calories, 2g protein, 19g carbohydrate, 4g total fat (1g saturated), 0mg cholesterol, 275mg sodium

PAN-ROASTED GARLIC

Prep: 15 minutes plus cooling   *Cook:* 30 minutes
Makes about 1 cup

4 heads garlic (about ¾ pound), separated into cloves, unpeeled
1 tablespoon sugar
1 tablespoon vegetable oil
½ teaspoon salt

◆ In 3-quart saucepan, heat garlic cloves and *6 cups water* to boiling over high heat. Reduce heat to low; cover and simmer 15 minutes, or until garlic cloves are fork-tender. Drain. Cool garlic under cold running water; drain again.

◆ Peel garlic cloves. In 10-inch skillet, cook garlic, sugar, oil, and salt over medium-high heat, stirring and shaking skillet often, about 5 minutes, until garlic cloves are glazed and browned. Use pan-roasted garlic as a condiment to sprinkle over salads or cooked vegetables, serve alongside roasted meats and poultry, or spread like butter on bread.

Each tablespoon: About 40 calories, 1g protein, 8g carbohydrate, 1g total fat (0g saturated), 0mg cholesterol, 70mg sodium

SQUASH

Squash are grouped into summer and winter varieties, although most are available year-round. Winter varieties (including butternut, acorn, and spaghetti squash) have hard skin and seeds, typically contain a firm, orange-colored flesh, and are equally good large or small. By contrast, soft-skinned summer squash, such as zucchini and yellow straightneck, have a creamy-white flesh and are most tender and flavorful when small. Cooking options for both are plentiful: Squash can be sliced and sautéed in garlic-flavored olive oil, shredded and fried for crisp, golden fritters, or halved and baked with a buttery pecan topping.

1 With coarse shredder, shred carrot, zucchini, and squash. Pat vegetables very dry with paper towels.

2 In medium bowl, mix shredded vegetables with flour, Parmesan cheese, salt, pepper, and egg.

VEGETABLE FRITTERS

❖❖❖❖❖❖❖❖❖❖❖❖❖❖❖❖❖❖❖❖❖❖❖❖

Prep: 20 minutes   Cook: 5 minutes per batch
Makes 4 accompaniment servings

1 large carrot
1 medium zucchini
　(10 ounces)
1 medium yellow straightneck
　squash (10 ounces)
⅓ cup all-purpose flour
⅓ cup freshly grated
　Parmesan cheese

½ teaspoon salt
⅛ teaspoon ground black
　pepper
1 large egg
½ cup vegetable oil

3 In 10-inch skillet, heat oil over medium heat. Gently drop one-eighth of vegetable mixture at a time (¼ cup) into oil in skillet, flattening slightly to about 3-inch round.

4 Cook 3 fritters at a time, turning once, 5 minutes, until golden brown. With pancake turner, transfer to paper towels to drain. Keep warm in low oven while cooking remainder.

MINI FRITTERS

Try tiny fritters with a basil dipping sauce. For sauce, in blender, process ⅔ cup sour cream, ⅔ cup loosely packed fresh basil, 1 teaspoon fresh lemon juice, and ¼ teaspoon each salt and black pepper until smooth. In Step 3, drop mixture into skillet 1 tablespoon at a time. Cook until golden, turning once. Makes about 32 mini-fritters.

Each fritter with 1 teaspoon sauce: About 40 calories, 1g protein, 2g carbohydrate, 3g total fat (2g saturated), 9mg cholesterol, 75mg sodium

EACH SERVING: ABOUT 245 CALORIES, 8g PROTEIN, 15g CARBOHYDRATE, 18g TOTAL FAT (4g SATURATED), 60mg CHOLESTEROL, 450mg SODIUM

ACORN SQUASH WITH BROWN SUGAR-PECAN TOPPING

Prep: 15 minutes   Bake: 45 minutes
Makes 4 accompaniment servings

2 small acorn squash (1 pound each)
½ teaspoon salt
½ cup pecans or walnuts (about 2 ounces), chopped
¼ cup packed light brown sugar
2 tablespoons margarine or butter, melted

◆ Preheat oven to 375°F. Cut each acorn squash lengthwise in half; discard seeds. Cut squash crosswise into 1-inch slices. Place slices, in a single layer, in 15½" by 10½" jelly-roll pan; sprinkle with salt. Drizzle *2 tablespoons water* around squash. Cover pan tightly with foil. Bake 30 minutes.

◆ Meanwhile, in small bowl, stir nuts with brown sugar and margarine until combined. Spoon nut mixture evenly over squash. Bake, uncovered, 15 minutes longer.

Each serving; About 320 calories, 4g protein, 49g carbohydrate, 15g total fat (2g saturated), 0mg cholesterol, 350g sodium

ZUCCHINI RIBBONS WITH MINT

Prep: 10 minutes   Cook: 3 minutes
Makes 4 accompaniment servings

4 very small zucchini (4 ounces each) or 2 medium zucchini (8 ounces each)
1 tablespoon olive oil
2 garlic cloves, crushed with side of knife
½ teaspoon salt
2 tablespoons chopped fresh mint
Mint sprig for garnish

◆ Trim ends from zucchini. With vegetable peeler or adjustable-blade slicer, shave zucchini lengthwise into long strips (if zucchini are wider than peeler, first cut each lengthwise in half). In 12-inch skillet, heat olive oil with garlic over medium heat until garlic is golden; discard garlic.

◆ Increase heat to high. Add zucchini and salt and cook, stirring, 2 minutes, or just until zucchini wilts. Remove from heat; stir in chopped mint. To serve, garnish with mint sprig.

Each serving; About 50 calories, 1g protein, 4g carbohydrate, 4g total fat (0g saturated), 0mg cholesterol, 270mg sodium

ROSEMARY-ROASTED BUTTERNUT SQUASH

Prep: 20 minutes   Roast: 35 minutes
Makes 10 accompaniment servings

4 tablespoons margarine or butter
3 medium butternut squash (about 1¾ pounds each)
1 medium onion, diced
1¾ teaspoons salt
1¼ teaspoons dried rosemary, crushed
½ teaspoon coarsely ground black pepper

◆ Preheat oven to 400°F. Place margarine in 17" by 11½" roasting pan; place roasting pan in oven until margarine melts. Meanwhile, cut each squash lengthwise in half; discard seeds. Cut squash into 2-inch chunks. Cut peel from chunks.

◆ Remove roasting pan from oven. Add squash, onion, salt, rosemary, and pepper; toss to coat with margarine. Arrange squash in single layer; roast 35 minutes, or until tender.

Each serving: About 145 calories, 2g protein, 27g carbohydrate, 5g total fat (1g saturated), 0mg cholesterol, 435mg sodium

THREE-SQUASH SAUTÉ

Prep: 20 minutes   Cook: 45 minutes
Makes 6 accompaniment servings

1 medium spaghetti squash
3 tablespoons olive oil
1 garlic clove, crushed with side of knife
1 small zucchini (6 ounces), cut into ½-inch pieces
1 small yellow straightneck squash (6 ounces), cut into ½-inch pieces
½ pint cherry tomatoes, each cut in half
2 tablespoons minced fresh basil
¾ teaspoon salt
¼ teaspoon ground black pepper
2 tablespoons pine nuts (pignoli), toasted

◆ Cut spaghetti squash lengthwise in half; discard seeds. In 8-quart Dutch oven, in ¾ inch boiling water, heat squash, cut-side up, to boiling over high heat. Reduce heat to low; cover and simmer 30 minutes, or until tender.

◆ Remove spaghetti squash from Dutch oven; drain. With 2 forks, gently scrape squash lengthwise, lifting out pulp as it becomes free. Drain pulp thoroughly on paper towels. Discard squash skin.

◆ Wipe Dutch oven dry. In Dutch oven, heat oil over medium-high heat; add garlic and cook until lightly browned. Discard garlic. Stir in zucchini and yellow squash; cook until tender. Add spaghetti squash, cherry tomatoes, basil, salt, and pepper; heat through. Sprinkle with pine nuts.

Each serving: About 110 calories, 2g protein, 9g carbohydrate, 9g total fat (1g saturated), 0mg cholesterol, 275mg sodium

MUSHROOMS

There's a world of mushrooms beyond the common cultivated white variety: Exotics such as shiitake and portobello, with their big, meaty flavor, and the delicate oyster mushroom are increasingly available.

WARM MUSHROOM SALAD

◆◆◆◆◆◆◆◆◆◆◆◆◆◆

Prep: 20 minutes
Cook: 35 minutes
Makes 6 first-course or accompaniment servings

1 bunch arugula
8 ounces shiitake mushrooms
3 tablespoons vegetable oil
1 large red onion, cut into
   ½-inch-wide wedges
2½ pounds cremini and/or
   white mushrooms, each cut
   in half if large
2 tablespoons soy sauce
2 tablespoons red wine
   vinegar
¼ cup pine nuts (pignoli),
   toasted (optional)
Parsley sprigs for garnish

1 Arrange arugula on platter; set aside. Cut and discard stems from shiitake mushrooms; cut shiitake caps into ½-inch-wide strips.

2 In nonstick 12-inch skillet, heat 1 tablespoon oil over medium heat. Add onion and cook just until tender; with slotted spoon, transfer to medium bowl.

3 In same skillet, heat 1 tablespoon oil over medium-high heat. Add half of all mushrooms; cook until liquid evaporates. Stir in 1 tablespoon soy sauce.

4 Transfer mushrooms to bowl with onion. Repeat with remaining 1 tablespoon oil, remaining mushrooms, and remaining 1 tablespoon soy sauce. Add vinegar to mushroom mixture in bowl; toss to coat. Spoon mushroom mixture on top of arugula on platter. Sprinkle with pine nuts, if using; garnish with parsley.

EXOTIC MUSHROOMS

These mushrooms generally have a more intense flavor than regular white button; use a selection to add interest to almost any mushroom recipe. Morels, porcini (cèpe in French), and shiitake are available fresh or dried. Don't throw away the soaking water from dried mushrooms – it is full of flavor and can be used in stocks, soups, and sauces.

Dried porcini (cèpe)
Cremini
Fresh shiitake
Dried morel
Chanterelle
Portobello
Dried shiitake
Oyster

EACH SERVING: ABOUT 150 CALORIES, 6g PROTEIN, 19g CARBOHYDRATE, 8g TOTAL FAT (1g SATURATED), 0mg CHOLESTEROL, 360mg SODIUM

MUSHROOM, ASPARAGUS, AND GRUYÈRE STRUDEL

Prep: 40 minutes plus cooling　*Bake:* 25 minutes
Makes 6 main-dish servings

12 ounces asparagus
Salt
7 tablespoons margarine or
　butter
1 pound mushrooms, thinly
　sliced
2 teaspoons fresh lemon juice
⅓ cup walnuts (about
　1½ ounces), toasted and
　finely chopped

2 tablespoons plain dried
　bread crumbs
12 sheets (about 16" by 12"
　each) fresh or frozen
　(thawed) phyllo (about
　8 ounces)
4 ounces Gruyère or Swiss
　cheese, shredded (1 cup)

◆ Cut asparagus into 6-inch-long spears. In nonstick 12-inch skillet, heat ½ *inch water* to boiling over medium-high heat. Add asparagus and ½ teaspoon salt; heat to boiling. Reduce heat to medium-low; cook 4 to 8 minutes, until asparagus are tender. Drain. Wipe skillet dry. In same skillet, melt 1 tablespoon margarine over medium-high heat. Add mushrooms and ½ teaspoon salt; cook until mushrooms are browned and liquid evaporates. Add lemon juice; cook 30 seconds. Transfer to plate; cool.

◆ Preheat oven to 375°F. Lightly grease cookie sheet. Melt remaining 6 tablespoons margarine. In small bowl, mix walnuts and bread crumbs. On work surface, place 1 phyllo sheet with a short side facing you; brush lightly with some melted margarine. Sprinkle all over with one-sixth of walnut mixture. Top with another phyllo sheet; brush with some margarine, being careful not to tear phyllo.

◆ Spoon one-sixth of cheese in a strip on phyllo 2 inches from edge facing you and leaving a 1½-inch border on both sides. Arrange one-sixth of asparagus on cheese; top with one-sixth of mushrooms. Fold bottom of phyllo over to enclose filling, then fold left and right sides in toward center. Roll up phyllo, jelly-roll fashion, forming a packet.

◆ Place packet, seam-side down, on cookie sheet. Brush lightly with some margarine. Repeat to make 5 more packets. Bake packets 25 minutes, or until slightly puffed and golden brown.

Each serving; About 375 calories, 13g protein, 28g carbohydrate, 25g total fat (7g saturated), 21mg cholesterol, 645mg sodium

GRILLED PORTOBELLO MUSHROOM SALAD

Prep: 15 minutes　*Grill/broil:* 8 to 9 minutes
Makes 4 first-course servings

1 wedge Parmesan cheese
2 bunches arugula
2 tablespoons balsamic
　vinegar
2 tablespoons olive oil
2 tablespoons minced shallots
2 tablespoons chopped fresh
　parsley

¼ teaspoon salt
⅛ teaspoon ground black
　pepper
1 pound portobello
　mushrooms, stems
　discarded

◆ Prepare outdoor grill or preheat broiler. With vegetable peeler, shave ½ cup (about 1 ounce) curls from Parmesan cheese; set aside. Reserve remaining Parmesan for use another day. Arrange arugula on platter.

◆ Prepare dressing: In small bowl, mix vinegar, oil, shallots, parsley, salt, and pepper. Place mushrooms, top-side up, on grill or rack in broiling pan at position closest to heat source. Brush mushroom tops with 1 tablespoon dressing. Grill or broil 4 minutes. Turn mushrooms; brush with 1 more tablespoon dressing. Grill or broil 4 to 5 minutes longer, until tender.

◆ Slice mushrooms and arrange on arugula. Spoon remaining dressing over salad. Top with Parmesan curls.

Each serving; About 150 calories, 6g protein, 14g carbohydrate, 10g total fat (2g saturated), 6mg cholesterol, 280mg sodium

SAUTÉED MIXED MUSHROOMS

Prep: 15 minutes　*Cook:* 10 minutes
Makes 4 accompaniment servings

2 tablespoons margarine or
　butter
¼ cup minced shallots
8 ounces medium white
　mushrooms, each cut into
　quarters
4 ounces shiitake mushrooms,
　stems discarded, cut into
　1-inch wedges

4 ounces oyster mushrooms,
　each cut in half if large
⅛ teaspoon dried thyme
¼ teaspoon salt
⅛ teaspoon ground black
　pepper
1 small garlic clove, minced
1 tablespoon chopped fresh
　parsley

In 12-inch skillet, melt margarine over medium-high heat. Add shallots; cook, stirring, 1 minute. Stir in all mushrooms. Sprinkle with thyme, salt, and pepper and cook, stirring often, until mushrooms are tender and liquid evaporates. Stir in garlic and parsley; cook 1 minute longer.

Each serving; About 100 calories, 3g protein, 10g carbohydrate, 6g total fat (1g saturated), 0mg cholesterol, 205mg sodium

EGGPLANT

Deep purple or creamy white, eggplant has a hearty, meaty texture and a neutral taste that readily absorbs the flavors of whatever ingredients are cooking along with it. Eggplant marries particularly well with strong flavors, such as garlic, olive oil, and balsamic vinegar. Be sure to purchase plump, shiny, unblemished eggplants that feel heavy for their size; light ones may be spongy.

ITALIAN EGGPLANT WITH GARLIC

Prep: 25 minutes   *Broil:* 40 minutes
Makes 10 accompaniment servings

½ cup olive oil
3 garlic cloves, sliced
¼ cup minced fresh basil
1½ teaspoons salt
½ teaspoon cracked black pepper

4 small eggplants (12 ounces each) or 10 baby eggplants (3 ounces each)
1 tablespoon grated lemon peel

1 In 1-quart saucepan, heat olive oil over medium heat; add garlic slices and cook, stirring occasionally, until lightly browned. Remove saucepan from heat; stir in minced basil, salt, and pepper.

2 Preheat broiler. Cut each eggplant lengthwise into ¾-inch-thick slices. Lightly score both sides of each slice in crisscross pattern. (If using baby eggplants, cut each lengthwise in half. Score cut sides only.)

3 Place half of eggplant slices in single layer on rack in broiling pan. Brush lightly with some olive-oil mixture from saucepan. (If using baby eggplant, place cut-side up. Brush cut sides with some olive-oil mixture, then turn cut-side down.) Broil eggplant 7 to 9 inches from heat source 10 minutes. Turn eggplant slices (or halves); lightly brush with some remaining olive-oil mixture, gently pressing garlic slices and minced basil into slits in eggplant.

4 Broil eggplant 10 minutes longer, or until fork-tender; transfer to platter. Repeat with remaining eggplant slices and olive-oil mixture. Sprinkle eggplant with lemon peel. Serve at room temperature or cover with plastic wrap and refrigerate to serve later.

EACH SERVING: ABOUT 135 CALORIES, 1g PROTEIN, 9g CARBOHYDRATE, 11g TOTAL FAT (1g SATURATED), 0mg CHOLESTEROL, 325mg SODIUM

EGGPLANT LASAGNA

Prep: 50 minutes plus standing   *Bake:* 40 minutes
Makes 10 main-dish servings

2 medium eggplants (about
   1½ pounds each), cut into
   ¼-inch-thick slices
5 tablespoons olive or
   vegetable oil
1 small onion, chopped
2 teaspoons sugar
1½ teaspoons salt
1 teaspoon dried basil

2 cans (28 ounces each)
   tomatoes
12 lasagna noodles (about
   two-thirds 16-ounce
   package)
¼ cup freshly grated
   Parmesan cheese
8 ounces mozzarella cheese,
   shredded (2 cups)

◆ Preheat broiler. Place half of eggplant slices on rack in
broiling pan; using 2 tablespoons oil, brush on both sides.
Place pan in broiler at closest position to heat source; broil
10 minutes, or until browned, turning once halfway through
cooking. Transfer to plate. Repeat with remaining eggplant
and 2 more tablespoons oil. Turn oven control to 375°F.

◆ While eggplants are broiling, prepare tomato sauce: In
4-quart saucepan, heat remaining 1 tablespoon oil over
medium heat; add onion and cook until tender. Stir in
sugar, salt, dried basil, and tomatoes with their juice; heat to
boiling over high heat, breaking up tomatoes with back of
spoon. Reduce heat to low; simmer, uncovered, 15 minutes,
stirring occasionally.

◆ Meanwhile, prepare lasagna noodles as label directs;
drain. In 13" by 9" glass or ceramic baking dish, spread
1 cup tomato sauce. Arrange half of noodles over sauce,
overlapping to fit. Arrange half of eggplant slices over
noodles; top with half of remaining sauce, then half of
Parmesan, and half of mozzarella. Repeat with remaining
noodles, eggplant, tomato sauce, Parmesan, and mozzarella.

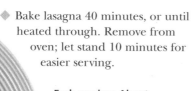

◆ Bake lasagna 40 minutes, or until
heated through. Remove from
oven; let stand 10 minutes for
easier serving.

**Each serving: About
325 calories, 12g protein,
41g carbohydrate, 14g total
fat (5g saturated),
20mg cholesterol,
715mg sodium**

SKILLET EGGPLANT STEW

Prep: 25 minutes   *Cook:* 30 to 35 minutes
Makes 8 accompaniment servings

3 tablespoons olive oil
1 large onion, cut into ¾-inch
   pieces
2 medium eggplants (about
   1½ pounds each), cut into
   2-inch pieces
½ cup pimiento-stuffed olives
2 tablespoons dark brown
   sugar
1 tablespoon balsamic vinegar

¾ teaspoon salt
1 package (9 ounces) fresh
   mozzarella cheese balls,
   drained and each cut in half
   (optional)
1 large tomato (about
   8 ounces), cut into ¾-inch
   pieces
¼ cup loosely packed basil
   leaves, coarsely chopped

◆ In nonstick 12-inch skillet (2 inches deep) or nonstick
5-quart saucepot, heat 1 tablespoon oil over medium heat.
Add onion; cook, stirring often, 10 minutes, or until golden.

◆ Increase heat to medium-high. Add remaining
2 tablespoons oil and eggplant to onion in skillet; cook,
stirring often, about 10 minutes, until eggplant is browned.
Stir in olives, next 3 ingredients, and *½ cup water*; heat to
boiling over high heat. Reduce heat to low; cover and simmer
10 to 15 minutes longer, until eggplant is tender. Remove
from heat; stir in mozzarella, if using, tomato, and basil.

**Each serving: About 125 calories, 2g protein, 18g carbohydrate,
6g total fat (1g saturated), 0mg cholesterol, 290mg sodium**

EGGPLANTS

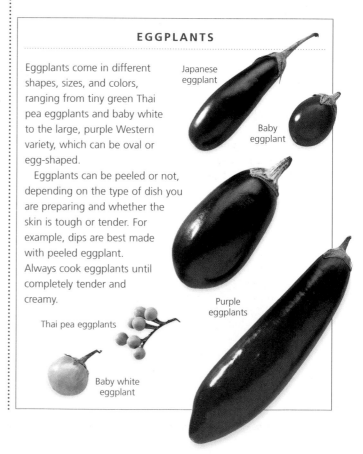

Eggplants come in different
shapes, sizes, and colors,
ranging from tiny green Thai
pea eggplants and baby white
to the large, purple Western
variety, which can be oval or
egg-shaped.

  Eggplants can be peeled or not,
depending on the type of dish you
are preparing and whether the
skin is tough or tender. For
example, dips are best made
with peeled eggplant.
Always cook eggplants until
completely tender and
creamy.

Japanese
eggplant

Baby
eggplant

Purple
eggplants

Thai pea eggplants

Baby white
eggplant

PEPPERS

Bright bell peppers can be green, red, yellow, orange, or even purple. Unlike hot peppers, or chiles, bell peppers lack a fiery bite since they contain no capsaicin, the chemical substance responsible for the heat. Roasting and broiling intensifies the subtle sweetness of bell peppers and makes them easy to peel. They are also natural candidates for stuffing and baking whole.

PEPPER AND EGGPLANT SALAD

◆◆◆◆◆◆◆◆◆◆◆◆

Prep: 30 minutes
Broil: 35 minutes
Makes 8 accompaniment servings

1 medium eggplant (about 1½ pounds)
1 medium onion
Salt
2 medium yellow peppers
2 medium red peppers
1 cup loosely packed basil leaves, cut into thin strips
2 tablespoons olive or vegetable oil
1 tablespoon fresh lemon juice
1 teaspoon sugar
½ teaspoon coarsely ground black pepper
Basil sprigs for garnish

1 Preheat broiler. Cut eggplant crosswise into ½-inch-thick slices; cut slices into ½-inch-wide strips. Cut onion in half through root end; cut each half into thin wedges, discarding tough root end.

2 In large bowl, toss eggplant and onion with ½ teaspoon salt. Spread on rack in large broiling pan. Broil at closest position to heat source, stirring occasionally, 20 minutes, or until eggplant is browned on all sides.

3 Meanwhile, cut yellow and red peppers into ½-inch-wide strips. In medium bowl, toss pepper strips with ½ teaspoon salt. When eggplant mixture is done, return mixture to large bowl.

4 Spoon pepper strips onto rack in broiling pan. Broil at closest position to heat source, stirring occasionally, 15 minutes, or until browned on all sides. Add to bowl with eggplant.

5 To vegetable mixture in bowl, add basil strips, next 4 ingredients, and *1 tablespoon water*; toss to mix. Spoon onto platter. Serve warm or cover and refrigerate to serve cold later. Garnish with basil.

EACH SERVING: ABOUT 80 CALORIES, 2g PROTEIN, 12g CARBOHYDRATE, 4g TOTAL FAT (0g SATURATED), 0mg CHOLESTEROL, 270mg SODIUM

BARLEY-STUFFED PEPPERS

Prep: 1 hour 15 minutes   *Bake: 1 hour*
Makes 6 main-dish servings

1 cup pearl barley
2⅔ cups vegetable or chicken
   broth
2 tablespoons olive or
   vegetable oil
1 large onion, chopped
3 medium carrots, shredded
½ teaspoon salt
1 cup frozen peas
2 tablespoons chopped fresh
   parsley

6 ounces sharp Cheddar
   cheese, shredded (1½ cups)
2 cans (14½ to 16 ounces
   each) Italian-style stewed
   tomatoes
2 medium red peppers
2 medium green peppers
2 medium yellow peppers

◆ In 3-quart saucepan, heat barley and broth to boiling over high heat. Reduce heat to low; cover and simmer 1 hour, or until barley is tender and liquid is absorbed.

◆ Meanwhile, in 10-inch skillet, heat oil over medium-high heat; add onion and cook, stirring often, until almost tender. Stir in carrots and salt; cook 5 minutes, or until vegetables are tender and lightly browned.

◆ When barley is done, stir in carrot mixture, peas, parsley, and 1 cup cheese. In food processor with knife blade attached or in blender at medium speed, blend tomatoes until almost smooth; pour into shallow 2½-quart casserole.

◆ Preheat oven to 350°F. Cut off top from each pepper; reserve tops for garnish. Remove seeds. Cut thin slice from bottom of each pepper, if necessary, so it will stand level. Fill peppers with barley mixture. Stand peppers in tomato sauce in casserole; sprinkle with remaining ½ cup cheese.

◆ Bake peppers 1 hour, or until tender when pierced with a knife. Loosely cover peppers with foil during last 30 minutes of baking to prevent overbrowning. To serve, arrange reserved pepper tops on stuffed peppers.

Each serving: About 405 calories, 15g protein, 55g carbohydrate, 15g total fat (7g saturated), 30mg cholesterol, 695mg sodium

RED AND YELLOW PEPPER SAUTÉ

Prep: 15 minutes   *Cook: 15 minutes*
Makes 6 accompaniment servings

2 tablespoons olive or
   vegetable oil
2 large red peppers, cut into
   1-inch-wide slices

2 large yellow peppers, cut
   into 1-inch-wide slices
½ teaspoon dried oregano
¼ teaspoon salt

In 12-inch skillet, heat oil over medium-high heat; add pepper slices, oregano, and salt, and cook, stirring frequently, until peppers are golden and tender-crisp.

Each serving: About 70 calories, 1g protein, 7g carbohydrate, 5g total fat (1g saturated), 0mg cholesterol, 90mg sodium

ROASTED PEPPER AND WALNUT DIP

Prep: 20 minutes plus standing   *Broil: 10 minutes*
Makes 1⅔ cups

½ cup walnuts (about 2 ounces)
½ teaspoon ground cumin
4 medium red peppers,
   roasted and peeled (see
   below)
2 slices firm white bread, torn

1 tablespoon olive oil
2 tablespoons raspberry
   vinegar
⅛ teaspoon ground red
   pepper (cayenne)
½ teaspoon salt

◆ Preheat oven to 350°F. Spread walnuts in pie plate; bake 8 to 10 minutes, until toasted. In 1-quart saucepan, toast cumin over low heat 1 to 2 minutes, until very fragrant.

◆ In food processor with knife blade attached, blend walnuts until ground. Add peppers, cumin, and remaining ingredients; blend until smooth. Transfer to bowl. Cover and refrigerate if not serving right away (remove from refrigerator 1 hour before serving).

Each tablespoon: About 25 calories, 1g protein, 2g carbohydrate, 2g total fat (0g saturated), 0mg cholesterol, 50mg sodium

◆◆◆◆◆◆◆◆◆◆◆◆◆◆◆◆◆◆◆◆◆◆◆◆◆◆◆◆◆

ROASTING PEPPERS

Preheat broiler; line broiling pan with foil. Cut peppers lengthwise in half; discard stems and seeds. Place peppers, skin-side up, on pan. Broil at closest position to heat source 10 minutes, or until charred all over. Wrap in foil; let stand 15 minutes. Remove foil; peel off skin.

◆◆◆◆◆◆◆◆◆◆◆◆◆◆◆◆◆◆◆◆◆◆◆◆◆◆◆◆◆

TOMATOES

It's worth waiting all year for garden-ripe juicy tomatoes. Here we celebrate them in a tomato and goat-cheese tart and broiled tomatoes topped with Parmesan. We even turn green tomatoes into a tempting treat, fried for a BLT. For maximum flavor, store tomatoes at room temperature rather than in the refrigerator, unless they are overripe.

SAVORY TOMATO TART

◆◆◆◆◆◆◆◆◆◆◆◆◆

Prep: 30 minutes
Bake: 35 minutes
Makes 6 main-dish servings

Pastry for 11-inch Tart (see page 487)
1 tablespoon olive or vegetable oil
3 medium onions (about 1 pound), thinly sliced
Salt
1 package (3½ ounces) goat cheese, crumbled
3 large tomatoes (about 1½ pounds), cut into ¼-inch-thick slices
½ teaspoon coarsely ground black pepper
¼ cup Kalamata olives, pitted and chopped
Sliced fresh basil leaves for garnish

1 Prepare Pastry for 11-inch Tart and use to line tart pan as directed. Preheat oven to 425°F. Line tart shell with foil; fill with pie weights, dry beans, or uncooked rice. Bake 20 minutes; remove foil with weights. Bake tart shell 10 minutes longer, or until golden. (If crust puffs up during baking, gently press it down with back of spoon.)

2 Meanwhile, in nonstick 12-inch skillet, heat oil over medium heat; add onions and ¼ teaspoon salt and cook, stirring frequently, about 15 minutes, until onions are tender and browned.

3 Turn oven control to broil. Spoon cooked onions in even layer over bottom of tart shell; sprinkle with half of goat cheese.

4 Arrange tomato slices in concentric circles over onion layer. Sprinkle black pepper and ¼ teaspoon salt over tomatoes. Sprinkle remaining goat cheese over top of tart. Place pan in broiler about 5 to 7 inches from heat source. Broil tart about 5 minutes, until cheese just melts. Sprinkle with chopped Kalamata olives and sliced basil leaves. To serve, cut tart into wedges.

EACH SERVING: ABOUT 415 CALORIES, 8g PROTEIN, 33g CARBOHYDRATE, 28g TOTAL FAT (7g SATURATED), 15mg CHOLESTEROL, 650mg SODIUM

CHERRY TOMATO GRATIN

Prep: 10 minutes
Bake: 20 minutes
Makes: 6 accompaniment servings

¼ cup plain dried bread
   crumbs
¼ cup freshly grated
   Parmesan cheese
1 garlic clove, minced
¼ teaspoon coarsely ground
   black pepper

1 tablespoon olive oil
2 pints cherry tomatoes
2 tablespoons chopped fresh
   parsley

◆ Preheat oven to 425°F. In small bowl, combine bread crumbs, Parmesan cheese, garlic, pepper, and olive oil.

◆ In 9-inch deep-dish pie plate, place cherry tomatoes. Sprinkle bread-crumb mixture on top of tomatoes. Sprinkle with parsley. Bake 20 minutes, or until crumbs are golden.

Each serving: About 85 calories, 3g protein, 9g carbohydrate, 4g total fat (1g saturated), 3mg cholesterol, 130mg sodium

BROILED PARMESAN TOMATOES

Prep: 10 minutes   Broil: 3 to 4 minutes
Makes: 4 accompaniment servings

1 tablespoon margarine or
   butter
1 small garlic clove, minced
¼ cup freshly grated
   Parmesan cheese

4 plum tomatoes (12 ounces),
   each cut lengthwise in half

◆ Preheat broiler. In 1-quart saucepan, melt margarine over low heat. Add garlic and cook just until golden; remove from heat.

◆ Spread Parmesan cheese on waxed paper. Dip cut side of each tomato half in melted margarine mixture, then in Parmesan; place on rack in broiling pan. Spoon any remaining cheese on top of tomatoes and drizzle with any remaining margarine mixture.

◆ Place pan in broiler at position closest to heat source; broil tomatoes 3 to 4 minutes, until cheese is golden brown.

Each serving: About 70 calories, 3g protein, 4g carbohydrate, 5g total fat (2g saturated), 5mg cholesterol, 155mg sodium

FRIED GREEN TOMATO SANDWICHES

Prep: 10 minutes   Cook: 20 minutes
Makes: 4 sandwiches

1 large egg white
¼ teaspoon salt
½ cup yellow cornmeal
Coarsely ground black pepper
3 medium green tomatoes,
   cut into ½-inch-thick slices
½ pound bacon

¼ cup low-fat mayonnaise
   dressing
¼ cup low-fat plain yogurt
2 tablespoons chopped fresh
   chives
8 slices white bread, toasted
4 green-leaf lettuce leaves

◆ In pie plate, beat egg white and salt. In another pie plate or on waxed paper, combine cornmeal with ¼ teaspoon pepper. Dip tomato slices in egg mixture to coat both sides, then dip into cornmeal mixture to coat both sides thoroughly. Place coated slices on waxed paper.

◆ In 12-inch skillet, cook bacon over medium-low heat until browned. Transfer bacon to paper towels to drain.

◆ Increase heat to medium-high. In drippings in skillet, cook tomato slices, a few at a time, until golden brown on both sides. Drain on paper towels.

◆ In small bowl, combine mayonnaise, yogurt, chives, and ¼ teaspoon pepper. Spread mayonnaise mixture on toast slices. Arrange lettuce, tomato slices, then bacon on 4 toast slices; top with remaining toast slices to make 4 sandwiches.

Each sandwich: About 350 calories, 12g protein, 45g carbohydrate, 13g total fat (3g saturated), 17mg cholesterol, 645mg sodium

---

TOMATOES

Tomatoes come in many shapes and sizes, especially at farmers' markets. Large red beefsteak tomatoes are juiciest, while cherry tomatoes are sweet all year round. Yellow tomatoes are less acidic than red ones, and can be mixed with the red for a pretty effect. For sauces, nothing can beat plum tomatoes, which have the meatiest flesh.

Yellow pear

Beefsteak

Cherry

Vine-ripened

Plum

9

S ALADS

Gone are the days when a salad meant skimpy diet fare. Today's creations are inspired mixtures of bold flavors, colors, and varied textures. Crisp green salads are the classic starter, but there are also more elaborate "chopped," composed, and warm salads that make substantial meals.

PREPARING SALAD INGREDIENTS

The most basic steps of salad preparation, such as washing and storing lettuce, are crucial. That's because fresh, uncooked ingredients hide few flaws – and nothing spoils a salad faster than biting down on a bit of grit. Tear lettuce into smaller pieces by hand; a knife may bruise the leaves. Most vegetables can be presliced a day in advance; sturdy ones (e.g., cabbage, carrots, or cooked beets) will keep longer. To retain moisture, store prepared vegetables wrapped in damp paper towels in food-storage bags in the crisper drawer. Don't chop fresh herbs in advance – they'll blacken.

PEELING TOMATOES

1 Cut a shallow X in the bottom end of each tomato; drop into pan of boiling water for 15 seconds.

2 With slotted spoon, transfer tomatoes to bowl of ice water. Use a knife to peel off the skin.

STORING AND PREPARING LETTUCE

Wash and dry lettuce leaves right after you bring them home from the store; you'll be able to assemble a beautiful salad in a flash. Remove and discard any bruised or spotted leaves, which will deteriorate quickly. A salad spinner makes short work of drying lettuce; the kind with a pull cord is especially fast. Be careful not to overload the spinner, or the lettuce will get crushed and bruised. To keep lettuce crisp, place clean, dry leaves in a zip-tight food storage bag, along with a few damp paper towels. Delicate varieties such as

butterhead will keep 2 to 3 days; iceberg and other sturdy heads will keep up to a week. Fresh herbs such as parsley, basil, chervil, or dill make delightful additions to salads, but don't chop the leaves in advance, or they'll blacken.

To avoid a soggy salad or diluted dressing, dry rinsed lettuce well before using. Place leaves on a clean kitchen towel; pat dry with another towel. (Or, simply pat leaves dry with paper towels or spin dry.)

CORING FIRM HEAD LETTUCE

With small, sharp knife, cut all the way around core in a cone shape. Holding lettuce head firmly with one hand, twist out the loosened core.

PREPARING LOOSE HEAD LETTUCE

1 Gently break off leaves at stem end. Discard any bruised or wilted leaves.

2 Swish leaves briefly in cold water. Lift out of bowl; grit will sink to bottom.

CHOOSING THE RIGHT LETTUCE

Lettuces fall into four basic types: Crisphead (iceberg) varieties are crisp but bland; butterhead (Bibb, Boston) are soft and delicate; loose-leaf (such as red oak leaf) are tender and sweet; and long-leaf lettuces (romaine) have a crisp, mild flavor. Mesclun encompasses many flavors – it's any mix of young, tiny salad greens.

ASSEMBLING SALADS

Whether you're tossing leafy greens or making a main-dish salad, aim for a balance of texture, color, and flavor. Cut or tear ingredients into manageable pieces, but don't make them too small. It's also important to pick the right serving dish. A jumble of curly leaves is most manageable in a bowl, while neatly arranged sliced ingredients can be shown off on a plate. Chilled plates help keep ingredients cool. To avoid a watered-down dressing, leafy greens – and all other vegetables – must be thoroughly dried. When making a salad of rice, beans, or potatoes, toss the cooked ingredients with the dressing while they're still warm so they'll soak it up.

SALAD MATH	
LETTUCE	APPROXIMATE YIELD
1 medium crisphead lettuce	10 cups prepared leaves
1 medium butterhead lettuce	4 cups prepared leaves
1 medium loose-leaf lettuce	8 cups prepared leaves
1 medium romaine lettuce	8 cups prepared leaves

SALAD LEAVES

Arugula An Italian favorite, this highly perishable green has a hot peppery taste that is stronger in older leaves. The leaves tend to be gritty and need thorough rinsing.

Spinach Sweet and earthy-tasting, spinach is delicious raw or cooked. Whether flat or crinkly, leaves should be crisp and dark with a fresh smell; spinach harbors grit, so rinse well.

Iceberg Juicy but bland-tasting leaves give this crisphead lettuce more crunch than flavor; great with creamy dressings.

Bibb lettuce A small butterhead with a sweet, succulent flavor, ranging in color from yellow-green to dark green.

Romaine The classic pick for Caesar salads, romaine has a crunchy texture and slightly nutty flavor. Its elongated leaves lighten at the pale, crunchy center.

Red endive A variety of Belgian endive with crimson-tipped leaves and a slightly bitter taste.

Mâche Also called lamb's lettuce or corn salad, this tender green has a nutty taste.

Belgian endive The shoots of a chicory root, with tightly packed leaves and a strong, slightly bitter taste.

Watercress This lively green has a peppery bite and can stand on its own or pair with other lettuces; also delicious used in sandwiches, soups, and omelets.

Radicchio Burgundy-colored leaves and a slightly bitter flavor make this Italian chicory a memorable addition to the salad bowl. In the Italian tradition, pair it with arugula and endive for a colorful and flavorful mix.

Frisée A member of the chicory family, frisée has slender, curly leaves that range in color from yellow-white to pale green; it has a delicately bitter flavor.

Red oak leaf This variety of loose-leaf lettuce has crisp, ruffled leaves with a fuller flavor than butterhead varieties.

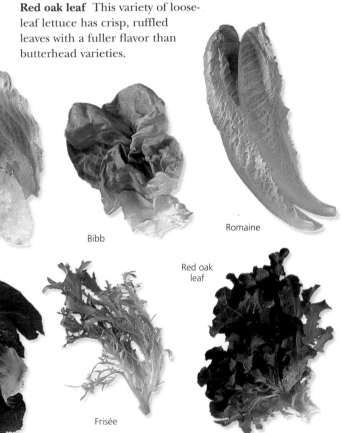

Arugula

Spinach

Iceberg

Bibb

Romaine

Red endive

Mâche

Red oak leaf

Belgian endive

Watercress

Radicchio

Frisée

THE BEST-DRESSED SALAD

Dressings should enhance but not overpower the taste and texture of salad greens. Sturdy lettuces such as romaine and iceberg stand up to thick creamy dressings such as blue cheese or Thousand Island. By contrast, delicate greens, such as leaf or butterhead varieties, pair best with simple vinaigrettes. For the crispest results, toss salads just before serving. To create a new taste, you can vary the oils and vinegars used in dressings. Extra-virgin olive oil is classic, or substitute walnut or hazelnut oil for half the olive oil, or add just a drop of Asian sesame oil. Vinegars range from dark, mellow balsamic to the more subtle varieties made from wine, champagne, cider, or sherry. Other delicious options include vinegars infused with fruit (e.g., raspberry or blueberry) or a fresh herb like tarragon.

The best way to emulsify a vinaigrette dressing is to first whisk together the mustard, vinegar or lemon juice, and seasonings. Than add the oil, while whisking constantly, in a slow, steady stream.

QUICK SALAD FIXINGS

Choose a basic ingredient, then pile on the flavor with pantry staples or quick-to-prepare add-ins:
Tossed greens Enliven with herb leaves or sprigs, warm garlic croutons, and Parmesan shavings; add substance with grilled meat or chicken strips or cubes of smoked ham.
Steamed new potatoes Dress with vinaigrette and add gutsy flavor with crumbled bacon, anchovies, capers, olives, or crumbled tangy cheese such as feta, blue, or goat cheese.
Rice or couscous Add sunshine with grapes, sliced apple or pear, orange chunks, or dried apricots or raisins. Toasted nuts or sunflower seeds give crunch.

SLIM SALADS

You can make low-fat salad dressings by substituting buttermilk or plain yogurt for mayonnaise or sour cream. A zesty salsa or Asian-style vinaigrette of seasoned rice vinegar, soy sauce, and citrus juice will boost flavor without any fat at all. When it comes to toppings, pile on crunchy veggies, but steer clear of fat sources like avocados, nuts, bacon, and cheese. For a main-dish salad, use skinless chicken, water-packed tuna, shrimp, or beans.

GLORIOUS GARNISHES

Edible flowers lend a unique flavor and dazzling color to salads. The fragile blossoms are typically left whole (tiny herb flowers should be plucked from the stem) and sprinkled on just before serving so they aren't discolored by the dressing. Always use the flowers sparingly, as some have a strong flavor. Small herb flowers, such as mint, thyme, oregano, or lavender blossoms, can be particularly pungent, so taste before using. You will need flowers that have not been treated with pesticides or other chemical sprays; flowers from the florist have usually been sprayed. Some supermarkets carry edible flowers, or check your own garden for unsprayed blossoms. However, not all flowers are edible, and some can be dangerous to eat. If you are not certain that a flower is edible, contact a local poison control center. Nontoxic flowers include carnations, pansies, borage, geraniums, nasturtiums, pinks, roses,

marigolds, cornflowers, baby's breath, and most herb flowers. Salad bowls aren't the only thing that benefit from these colorful blooms. Add them to iced punch, herbal teas, or desserts, or use to garnish soup, roasted fish, or meats. Flowers such as roses, pansies, or violets are often crystallized and used to garnish cakes.

Oregano flowers

Nasturtiums

Chive flowers

Pinks

Marjoram flowers

Mint flowers

Thyme flowers

VEGETABLE SALADS

Whether your supply of fresh produce is reaped from your own garden, a roadside farmstand, or the local supermarket, a warm or cold salad of tasty, vibrantly colored vegetables is sure to make an irresistible side dish. For the best texture, cook vegetables just until they are tender.

SUMMER BEET AND ASIAN PEAR SALAD

◆◆◆◆◆◆◆◆◆◆◆◆◆◆◆◆◆◆◆◆◆◆◆◆◆◆◆◆◆

Prep: 20 minutes   Cook: 40 minutes
Makes 6 accompaniment servings

8 medium beets (about 4 pounds with tops)
1 tablespoon light brown sugar
1 tablespoon red wine vinegar
1 tablespoon olive or vegetable oil
2 teaspoons Dijon mustard

½ teaspoon salt
1 large Asian pear or Red Delicious apple, peeled, cored, and cut into thin wedges
1 tablespoon chopped fresh parsley
Lettuce leaves

1 Trim stems and leaves from beets. With vegetable brush, scrub beets. In 4-quart saucepan, heat beets and enough *water* to cover to boiling over high heat. Reduce heat to low. Cover; simmer 30 minutes, or just until tender.

2 Drain cooked beets and cool thoroughly with cold running water. When beets are cool, with paring knife, peel beets; cut each beet in half or into quarters, if large.

3 Prepare vinaigrette: In large bowl, with wire whisk or fork, mix brown sugar, red wine vinegar, oil, Dijon mustard, and salt. Add beets, Asian pear, and chopped parsley to bowl with vinaigrette.

4 Toss beet mixture to coat with vinaigrette. Serve at room temperature or cover and refrigerate to serve cold later. To serve, line platter with lettuce leaves; spoon beet mixture on top.

ASIAN PEAR

This delicious fruit was first planted in the United States by Chinese prospectors during the Gold Rush, as they traveled through the Sierra Nevada. Asian pears can be smooth-skinned or speckled with a matte russeting. Unlike regular pears, they are low in acid and aroma, and quite hard even when ripe. This firm texture means that thin slices will hold up to tossing – making them perfect in salads. Asian pears can be stored in the refrigerator for at least 2 weeks. Crunchy and juicy at the same time, delicate in flavor, they make a light, refreshing dessert and remain crisp even when cooked.

EACH SERVING: ABOUT 130 CALORIES, 3g PROTEIN, 24g CARBOHYDRATE, 3g TOTAL FAT (0g SATURATED), 0mg CHOLESTEROL, 350mg SODIUM

CHUNKY VEGETABLE SALAD

Prep: 20 minutes   Makes 4 accompaniment servings

**2 tablespoons olive or
  vegetable oil**
**2 tablespoons red wine
  vinegar**
¾ teaspoon salt
½ teaspoon sugar
**¼ teaspoon coarsely ground
  black pepper**
**2 large tomatoes, cut into thin
  wedges**

**1 large yellow pepper, cut
  into bite-size chunks**
**1 medium cucumber,
  unpeeled, cut into bite-
  size chunks**
**½ small red onion, finely
  chopped**
**1 tablespoon chopped fresh
  chervil, cilantro, or parsley**

Prepare dressing: In medium bowl, with wire whisk or fork, mix first 5 ingredients until blended. Add remaining ingredients; toss to coat.

**Each serving: About 110 calories, 2g protein, 12g carbohydrate,
7g total fat (1g saturated), 0mg cholesterol, 410mg sodium**

WARM PEAS AND CARROTS SALAD

Prep: 15 minutes   Cook: 10 minutes
Makes 4 accompaniment servings

1 cup frozen peas
1 tablespoon vegetable oil
**3 medium carrots, thinly
  sliced**
1 small onion, thinly sliced

½ teaspoon salt
**1 tablespoon fresh lemon
  juice**
**1 small head romaine lettuce,
  washed and well dried**

◆ In small bowl, place frozen peas; cover with *boiling water* and let stand 5 minutes.

◆ Meanwhile, in nonstick 10-inch skillet, heat oil over medium-high heat; add carrots, onion, and salt and cook, stirring often, until vegetables are tender and lightly browned.

◆ Drain peas; stir into carrot-onion mixture in skillet. Stir in lemon juice; remove skillet from heat.

◆ Cut lettuce leaves crosswise into ¼-inch-wide strips (you should have about 4 cups loosely packed). In large bowl, toss lettuce with carrot mixture to mix well.

**Each serving: About 115 calories, 5g protein, 17g carbohydrate,
4g total fat (1g saturated), 0mg cholesterol, 330mg sodium**

GREEN BEANS WITH TOASTED SESAME SEEDS

Prep: 25 minutes   Cook: 20 minutes
Makes 8 accompaniment servings

3 tablespoons olive oil
**2 tablespoons fresh lemon
  juice**
2 teaspoons Dijon mustard
½ teaspoon salt

**2 pounds green beans, ends
  trimmed**
**1 tablespoon sesame seeds,
  toasted**

◆ Prepare dressing: In large bowl, with wire whisk or fork, mix olive oil, lemon juice, mustard, and salt until blended. Set aside.

◆ In 8-quart Dutch oven, in *1 inch boiling water*, heat green beans to boiling over high heat.

◆ Reduce heat to low and simmer, uncovered, 5 to 10 minutes, until beans are tender. Transfer beans to colander to drain well.

◆ Add warm beans to dressing in bowl; toss to mix well. Cover and refrigerate if not serving right away. Just before serving, toss beans with sesame seeds.

**Each serving: About 80 calories, 2g protein, 7g carbohydrate,
6g total fat (1g saturated), 0mg cholesterol, 180mg sodium**

◆◆◆◆◆◆◆◆◆◆◆◆◆◆◆◆◆◆◆◆◆◆◆◆

TOASTING SESAME SEEDS

Sesame seeds are the tiny, oval seeds of a tropical herb. They have a mild, nutty flavor that is best brought out by toasting: In a small skillet, toast sesame seeds over medium-low heat 1 to 2 minutes, stirring and shaking the pan often to prevent burning, until the seeds are lightly browned.

◆◆◆◆◆◆◆◆◆◆◆◆◆◆◆◆◆◆◆◆◆◆◆◆

BEET, ORANGE, AND WATERCRESS SALAD

Prep: 45 minutes   Cook: 40 minutes
Makes 10 accompaniment servings

10 medium beets (about 5 pounds
  with tops), trimmed
4 large navel oranges
¼ cup olive oil
¼ cup red wine vinegar
1 tablespoon Dijon mustard
1 teaspoon sugar
¾ teaspoon salt
¼ teaspoon coarsely ground black
  pepper
3 bunches watercress (about 12 ounces),
  tough stems removed
1 medium red onion, thinly sliced

◆ In 4-quart saucepan, heat beets and
enough *water* to cover to boiling over
high heat. Reduce heat to low; cover
and simmer 30 minutes, or until beets
are tender.

◆ Meanwhile, grate 1 teaspoon peel
from 1 orange; set aside. With knife,
cut peel and white pith from all
oranges; discard. Holding oranges
over large bowl to catch juice, cut
sections from oranges between
membranes. Place orange sections
on plate; reserve juice.

◆ Prepare dressing: Into orange juice
in bowl, with wire whisk or fork, mix
olive oil, vinegar, mustard, sugar, salt,
pepper, and grated orange peel.

◆ Drain beets and cool with cold
running water. Peel and cut each beet
lengthwise in half, then cut each half
crosswise into ¼-inch-thick slices.

◆ To dressing in bowl, add beets,
orange sections, watercress, and red-
onion slices; toss beet mixture to coat
with dressing.

**Each serving: About 150 calories,
4g protein, 23g carbohydrate, 6g total fat
(1g saturated), 0mg cholesterol,
310mg sodium**

FENNEL, PEAR, AND ENDIVE SALAD

Prep: 35 minutes
Makes 8 accompaniment servings

¼ cup extra-virgin olive oil
¼ cup tarragon vinegar
1 tablespoon Dijon mustard
¾ teaspoon salt
¼ teaspoon coarsely ground black
  pepper
5 medium Bartlett pears (about
  2 pounds), unpeeled, each cored and
  sliced into 12 wedges
2 large fennel bulbs (about
  1 pound each)
4 medium heads Belgian endive
  (2 red, if available)
¾ cup walnuts, toasted and coarsely
  chopped

◆ Prepare dressing: In small bowl,
with wire whisk or fork, mix olive oil,
tarragon vinegar, Dijon mustard, salt,
and pepper until blended; set aside.

◆ In large bowl, place pear wedges.
Trim top and bottom from each fennel
bulb. Slice each bulb lengthwise in
half; remove and discard core. Slice
fennel-bulb halves crosswise into
paper-thin slices; place in bowl with
pear wedges.

◆ Cut 2 heads of endive (1 yellow
and 1 red, if using both colors)
crosswise into ⅛-inch-thick slices; toss
with fennel mixture. Separate leaves
from remaining heads of endive.

◆ Add dressing to fennel mixture; toss
well to coat with dressing.

◆ Arrange endive leaves around edge
of large shallow bowl or platter; top
with fennel salad. Sprinkle with toasted
walnuts.

**Each serving: About 245 calories,
4g protein, 30g carbohydrate, 15g total fat
(2g saturated), 0mg cholesterol,
320mg sodium**

SPINACH AND TANGERINE SALAD

Prep: 30 minutes
Makes 8 accompaniment servings

4 medium tangerines or navel oranges
1 bunch (10 to 12 ounces) spinach,
  trimmed, washed, and well dried
2 small heads Bibb lettuce (about
  4 ounces each)
3 tablespoons extra-virgin olive oil
3 tablespoons cider vinegar
1 teaspoon sugar
1 teaspoon Dijon mustard
⅛ teaspoon salt
⅛ teaspoon coarsely ground black
  pepper

◆ Coarsely grate peel from
1 tangerine. Cut remaining peel and
white pith from all tangerines; discard.
Cut each tangerine in half (from top
to bottom), then cut each half crosswise into ¼-inch-thick slices. Tear
spinach and lettuce into bite-size pieces.

◆ Prepare vinaigrette: In large bowl,
with wire whisk or fork, mix olive oil,
vinegar, sugar, mustard, salt, pepper,
and grated tangerine peel.

◆ Add spinach, lettuce, and tangerine
slices to vinaigrette in bowl; toss well.

**Each serving: About 75 calories, 2g protein,
8g carbohydrate, 5g total fat
(1g saturated),
0mg cholesterol,
80mg sodium**

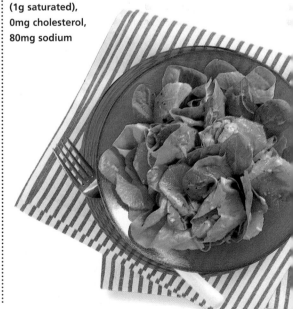

BABY-GREENS SALAD WITH GRAPEFRUIT VINAIGRETTE

Prep: 25 minutes   Makes 8 accompaniment servings

2 medium grapefruits
2 medium heads Belgian
  endive
1 tablespoon balsamic vinegar
1 tablespoon Dijon mustard
2 teaspoons capers, drained
½ teaspoon sugar

½ teaspoon salt
¼ cup olive or vegetable oil
1 pound mixed baby salad
  greens or mixed salad
  greens (about 12 cups
  loosely packed)

◆ With knife, cut peel and white pith from grapefruits; discard. Holding grapefruits over small bowl to catch juice, cut sections from grapefruits between membranes. Place grapefruit sections on plate; reserve juice in bowl. Cut each endive lengthwise into matchstick-thin strips.

◆ Prepare vinaigrette: In large bowl, combine balsamic vinegar, mustard, capers, sugar, salt, and 2 tablespoons grapefruit juice (reserve remaining juice for use another day). With wire whisk or fork, slowly beat in oil.

◆ Add greens, grapefruit sections, and endive to vinaigrette in bowl; toss to coat.

Each serving: About 105 calories, 2g protein, 10g carbohydrate, 7g total fat (1g saturated), 0mg cholesterol, 230mg sodium

GRILLED VEGETABLES VINAIGRETTE

Prep: 15 minutes   Grill: 15 to 20 minutes
Makes 4 accompaniment servings

6 tablespoons olive or
  vegetable oil
6 tablespoons white wine
  vinegar
2 tablespoons chopped fresh
  tarragon
1 teaspoon salt
1 teaspoon coarsely ground
  black pepper
1 teaspoon sugar
1 medium portobello
  mushroom (4 ounces) or
  4 jumbo white mushrooms,
  stems trimmed

1 medium red pepper, cut
  lengthwise into quarters
1 medium yellow pepper, cut
  lengthwise into quarters
2 small zucchini (6 ounces
  each), each cut lengthwise
  in half
2 baby eggplants (4 ounces
  each), each cut lengthwise
  in half
Tarragon sprigs for garnish

◆ Prepare outdoor grill. Prepare vinaigrette: In large bowl, with wire whisk or fork, mix oil and next 5 ingredients.

◆ Wipe mushroom clean with damp paper towel. Add mushroom, both peppers, zucchini, and eggplants to vinaigrette in bowl; toss to coat.

◆ Place vegetables on grill over medium heat. Grill, turning occasionally and brushing with some of vinaigrette remaining in bowl, until vegetables are browned and tender when pierced with a fork.

◆ To serve, slice mushroom; toss with vegetables and remaining vinaigrette. Garnish with tarragon sprigs.

Each serving: About 235 calories, 3g protein, 14g carbohydrate, 21g total fat (3g saturated), 0mg cholesterol, 540mg sodium

BABY GREENS WITH RASPBERRY VINAIGRETTE

Prep: 20 minutes   Makes 4 accompaniment servings

1 tablespoon sugar
3 tablespoons white wine
  vinegar
1 tablespoon Dijon mustard
½ pint raspberries (1 cup)
¼ cup extra-virgin olive oil
8 ounces mixed baby salad
  greens or mixed salad greens
  (6 cups loosely packed)

4 ounces ricotta salata or
  feta cheese, crumbled
  (about 1 cup)
8 quail eggs or 4 small eggs,
  hard-cooked and each cut
  lengthwise in half

◆ Prepare vinaigrette: In large bowl, combine sugar, vinegar, and mustard. Add ½ cup raspberries to vinegar mixture; with wire whisk or fork, crush berries slightly. Slowly beat in olive oil.

◆ Add salad greens to vinaigrette in bowl; toss to coat. To serve, place greens on 4 plates. Sprinkle with cheese and remaining raspberries; tuck eggs into greens.

Each serving: About 295 calories, 10g protein, 12g carbohydrate, 24g total fat (7g saturated), 185mg cholesterol, 470mg sodium

TOMATO SALADS

No flavor captures the essence of summer like vine-ripened tomatoes. Whether simply drizzled with vinaigrette or paired with hearty cubes of toasted bread and pancetta, they create an immensely satisyfying dish. We've even included an easy method for making home-dried tomatoes to perk up countless dishes all year round. Once cut, fresh tomatoes release juices that dilute dressings, so serve immediately.

DRIED TOMATO, GOAT CHEESE, AND ARUGULA

◆◆◆◆◆◆◆◆◆◆◆◆◆

Prep: 15 minutes plus preparing Home-Dried Tomatoes (optional)
Makes 6 accompaniment servings

Home-Dried Tomatoes (see right) or 24 oil-packed dried tomato halves
Coarsely ground black pepper
3 logs (3½ ounces each) goat cheese
2 tablespoons red wine vinegar
1 tablespoon extra-virgin olive oil
½ teaspoon dried basil
¼ teaspoon sugar
2 bunches arugula or watercress (about 3 cups loosely packed)

1 Prepare Home-Dried Tomatoes, if using. Sprinkle 2 tablespoons coarsely ground black pepper on waxed paper. Roll cheese logs in pepper; slice each log into 6 pieces.

2 Prepare vinaigrette: In small bowl, with wire whisk or fork, mix vinegar, olive oil, basil, sugar, and ¼ teaspoon coarsely ground black pepper until well combined.

3 Arrange arugula on 6 plates with goat cheese pieces. If using dried tomato halves in oil, drain well. Arrange tomatoes over arugula and goat cheese; drizzle with vinaigrette.

HOME-DRIED TOMATOES

◆◆◆◆◆◆◆◆◆◆◆◆◆

Store in a zip-tight plastic bag in the refrigerator up to 2 months or in the freezer up to 6 months. Makes 24 tomato halves.

12 plum tomatoes (3 pounds)
2 tablespoons extra-virgin olive oil
½ teaspoon dried basil
½ teaspoon dried thyme
½ teaspoon salt
¼ teaspoon coarsely ground black pepper

1 Preheat oven to 250°F. Peel tomatoes (see page 314). Cut each lengthwise in half; remove seeds. In large bowl, toss tomatoes with remaining ingredients.

2 Arrange tomatoes, cut-side down, on wire rack on cookie sheet. Bake 5½ hours, or until tomatoes are shriveled and partially dried. Cool completely.

EACH SERVING: ABOUT 220 CALORIES, 8g PROTEIN, 14g CARBOHYDRATE, 16g TOTAL FAT (1g SATURATED), 44mg CHOLESTEROL, 365mg SODIUM

PANZANELLA SALAD WITH TOMATO VINAIGRETTE

Prep: 30 minutes   Cook: 15 minutes
Makes 6 main-dish servings

¼ pound pancetta or bacon, cut into ¼-inch pieces
3 tablespoons olive oil
6 ounces sourdough bread, cut into ½-inch cubes (6 cups)
2 tablespoons freshly grated Parmesan cheese
Ground black pepper
1 small tomato (about 6 ounces), peeled (see page 314) and coarsely chopped
1 small shallot, chopped
1 tablespoon red wine vinegar

1 tablespoon balsamic vinegar
1 teaspoon sugar
1 teaspoon chopped fresh oregano
2 teaspoons Dijon mustard with seeds
¼ teaspoon salt
1 pound arugula (4 bunches)
1 pound red cherry and/or yellow pear-shaped tomatoes, each cut in half, or 1 pound medium tomatoes, cut into ½-inch chunks

◆ In nonstick 12-inch skillet, cook pancetta over medium heat until lightly browned. With slotted spoon, transfer pancetta to large bowl.

◆ Pour off all but 2 tablespoons drippings from skillet and add 1 tablespoon olive oil; add bread cubes and cook about 10 minutes, until lightly browned. Add toasted bread cubes to bowl with pancetta; toss with grated Parmesan and ¼ teaspoon pepper. Set aside.

◆ Prepare tomato vinaigrette: In blender at medium speed, blend peeled tomato, shallot, red wine vinegar, balsamic vinegar, sugar, oregano, mustard, salt, ¼ teaspoon pepper, and remaining 2 tablespoons olive oil until blended and smooth.

◆ Toss bread-cube mixture with tomato vinaigrette, arugula, and cherry tomatoes.

Each serving: About 225 calories, 10g protein, 25g carbohydrate, 11g total fat (2g saturated), 11mg cholesterol, 615mg sodium

TWO-TOMATO SALAD

Prep: 30 minutes   Cook: 10 seconds
Makes 8 accompaniment servings

¼ cup chopped fresh basil
2 tablespoons olive or vegetable oil
2 tablespoons white wine vinegar
1 teaspoon Dijon mustard

¾ teaspoon salt
½ teaspoon sugar
2 pints cherry tomatoes
2 medium tomatoes, sliced
Basil sprigs for garnish

◆ Prepare vinaigrette: In large bowl, with wire whisk or fork, mix chopped basil, oil, vinegar, Dijon mustard, salt, and sugar until blended. Set vinaigrette aside.

◆ In 5-quart saucepan, heat *3 quarts water* to boiling over high heat. Fill a large bowl with *ice water*. Meanwhile, cut small "x" in stem end of each cherry tomato.

◆ Add half of cherry tomatoes to boiling water; blanch 5 seconds. With slotted spoon, transfer tomatoes to ice water to cool. Repeat with remaining cherry tomatoes, heating water in saucepan to boiling before adding.

◆ Drain cherry tomatoes. With fingers, slip tomatoes from their skins, one at a time, and add to vinaigrette; toss to coat.

◆ To serve, arrange tomato slices on platter. Spoon cherry tomatoes and vinaigrette over tomato slices; garnish with basil sprigs.

Each serving: About 55 calories, 1g protein, 6g carbohydrate, 4g total fat (1g saturated), 0mg cholesterol, 225mg sodium

CHERRY TOMATO-LEMON SALAD

Prep: 20 minutes   Makes 8 accompaniment servings

2 medium lemons
2 pints red cherry tomatoes, each cut in half
1 pint yellow cherry tomatoes, each cut in half
1 tablespoon sugar
2 tablespoons chopped fresh chives

2 tablespoons extra-virgin olive oil
¾ teaspoon salt
½ teaspoon coarsely ground black pepper

◆ With knife, cut peel and white pith from lemons; discard. Cut each lemon crosswise into slightly less than ¼-inch-thick slices.

◆ In medium bowl, toss lemon slices, tomatoes, and remaining ingredients.

Each serving: About 65 calories, 1g protein, 9g carbohydrate, 4g total fat (1g saturated), 0mg cholesterol, 210mg sodium

POTATO SALADS

Dress up your basic burger or steak with a novel approach to potato salad: Toss potato chunks with roasted green beans and blue cheese; with fresh herbs and cool, crunchy celery; or with ripe olives, balsamic vinegar, and feta cheese. Red potatoes add color and, since you don't need to peel them, save time. As is true of most potato salads, these recipes are just as delicious when they are prepared several hours in advance. For the best flavor, remove the salad from the refrigerator about 30 minutes before serving to bring it to room temperature.

1 Preheat oven to 425°F. Peel shallots (if using onions, peel and cut each lengthwise in half). Cut potatoes into 1½-inch chunks.

2 In large roasting pan (about 17" by 11½"), combine shallots, potatoes, salt, and 1 tablespoon oil. Roast 30 minutes.

ROASTED POTATO SALAD

◆◆◆◆◆◆◆◆◆◆◆◆◆◆◆◆◆◆◆◆◆◆◆◆◆◆◆◆◆

Prep: 25 minutes   *Roast:* 45 minutes
Makes 6 accompaniment servings

16 shallots or 8 small white onions
2 pounds medium red potatoes (about 8)
1 teaspoon salt
3 tablespoons olive or vegetable oil
8 ounces French green beans (haricots verts) or green beans, ends trimmed

1 tablespoon fresh lemon juice
1 teaspoon Dijon mustard
1 ounce blue cheese, crumbled (about ¼ cup)

3 After vegetables have roasted 30 minutes, stir in green beans and 1 more tablespoon oil. Roast 15 minutes longer, or until vegetables are tender.

4 Meanwhile, prepare vinaigrette: In large bowl, with wire whisk or fork, mix lemon juice, Dijon mustard, and remaining 1 tablespoon oil. Add roasted vegetables to bowl, tossing to coat with vinaigrette. Serve salad warm or cover and refrigerate to serve later. To serve, place potato salad in serving dish or on platter; sprinkle with crumbled blue cheese.

GREEK ROASTED POTATO SALAD

Prepare salad as directed, but add ½ cup pitted Kalamata olives when tossing vegetables with vinaigrette, and 2 to 4 tablespoons chopped fresh oregano, mint, or parsley, if desired. Omit blue cheese; sprinkle salad with 2 ounces feta cheese, crumbled (about ½ cup).

Each serving: About 280 calories, 5g protein, 39g carbohydrate, 12g total fat (3g saturated), 8mg cholesterol, 700mg sodium

EACH SERVING: ABOUT 235 CALORIES, 5g PROTEIN, 37g CARBOHYDRATE, 8g TOTAL FAT (2g SATURATED), 3mg CHOLESTEROL, 455mg SODIUM

CLASSIC POTATO SALAD

Prep: 25 minutes plus cooling
Cook: 45 to 50 minutes
Makes 8 accompaniment servings

3 pounds medium all-purpose potatoes
  (about 9), unpeeled
Salt
2 large celery stalks, thinly sliced
1 cup mayonnaise
½ cup milk
2 tablespoons white vinegar
1 tablespoon grated onion
1 teaspoon sugar
¼ teaspoon coarsely ground black
  pepper

◆ In 4-quart saucepan, heat potatoes, 1 teaspoon salt, and enough *water* to cover to boiling over high heat. Reduce heat to low; cover and simmer 25 to 30 minutes, until potatoes are fork-tender. Drain potatoes; cool slightly. Peel and cut potatoes into ¾-inch cubes.

◆ In large bowl, gently toss potatoes with celery, mayonnaise, milk, vinegar, onion, sugar, pepper, and 2 teaspoons salt to coat well. If not serving right away, cover and refrigerate.

Each serving: About 360 calories, 4g protein, 37g carbohydrate, 23g total fat (4g saturated), 18mg cholesterol, 740mg sodium

MEDITERRANEAN POTATO SALAD

Prep: 15 minutes plus cooling
Cook: 40 to 45 minutes
Makes 6 accompaniment servings

2 pounds medium red potatoes
  (about 8)
Salt
½ cup pitted ripe olives, minced
3 tablespoons olive oil
2 tablespoons balsamic vinegar
½ (8-ounce) package feta cheese with
  dried tomatoes and basil, crumbled,
  or your favorite feta (1 cup)
Basil sprigs for garnish

◆ In 4-quart saucepan, heat potatoes, 1 teaspoon salt, and enough *water* to cover to boiling over high heat. Reduce heat to low; cover and simmer 20 to 25 minutes, until potatoes are fork-tender. Drain; cool slightly. Cut potatoes into ½-inch pieces.

◆ In large bowl, with fork, mix olives, olive oil, balsamic vinegar, ½ teaspoon salt, and half of feta cheese. Add potatoes; gently toss to coat. Sprinkle remaining feta cheese on top. If not serving right away, cover and refrigerate. Garnish with basil sprigs.

Each serving: About 320 calories, 9g protein, 34g carbohydrate, 17g total fat (7g saturated), 38mg cholesterol, 790mg sodium

LEMON-CHIVE POTATO SALAD

Prep: 25 minutes plus cooling
Cook: 30 to 35 minutes
Makes 12 accompaniment servings

5 pounds red potatoes, cut into
  1½-inch chunks
Salt
2 medium lemons
3 tablespoons olive oil
1 teaspoon sugar
¾ cup mayonnaise
½ cup milk
⅓ cup sour cream
5 large celery stalks, thinly sliced
½ cup chopped fresh chives or
  green-onion tops

◆ In 8-quart Dutch oven or saucepot, heat potatoes, 2 teaspoons salt, and enough *water* to cover to boiling. Reduce heat to low; cover and simmer 10 to 12 minutes, until potatoes are fork-tender.

◆ Meanwhile, prepare lemon dressing: Grate 1½ teaspoons peel and squeeze ¼ cup juice from lemons. In large bowl, with wire whisk or fork, mix lemon peel and juice, oil, sugar, and 1½ teaspoons salt until blended.

◆ Drain potatoes. Add hot potatoes to lemon dressing in large bowl. With rubber spatula, stir gently to coat thoroughly with dressing. Let potatoes cool at room temperature 30 minutes, stirring occasionally.

◆ In small bowl, stir mayonnaise, milk, sour cream, and ½ teaspoon salt until mixture is smooth. Add mayonnaise mixture, celery, and chopped chives to potatoes; stir gently to coat well. If not serving right away, cover and refrigerate.

Each serving: About 320 calories, 5g protein, 41g carbohydrate, 16g total fat (3g saturated), 12mg cholesterol, 505mg sodium

---

PERFECT POTATO SALADS

• All-purpose and red potatoes are ideal for salads because they retain their firm texture when cut. Avoid using baking potatoes, which can fall apart in salads.

• Choose potatoes of about the same size so they cook evenly.

• It's important that potatoes are neither under- nor overcooked. They are ready if just tender when tested with the tip of a knife. If overcooked, they will absorb too much dressing and fall apart.

• When adding the dressing, don't overdo it. Potatoes taste best when they are lightly coated rather than swimming in dressing.

• Always make potato salad with warm, freshly cooked potatoes. Cold leftover potatoes will not absorb the dressing as well.

• If your finished salad still needs a flavor fillip, try adding some crumbled cooked bacon, capers, anchovy fillets, dried tomatoes, or diced pickles.

VEGETABLE SLAWS

As good as basic coleslaw can be, slaw-style salads are not limited to cabbage and mayonnaise alone. Celery root and broccoli add their crunch and flavor, while cilantro and sesame oil lend Asian nuances to special slaws. There's even a cabbage-less slaw here: a crunchy carrot, apple, and date blend that's especially good with grilled meats.

THREE-C SLAW

◆◆◆◆◆◆◆◆◆◆◆◆◆

Prep: 1 hour plus chilling
Makes 10 accompaniment servings

½ cup light mayonnaise
¼ cup Dijon mustard with
    seeds
¼ cup fresh lemon juice
1 tablespoon sugar
1 tablespoon rice vinegar
¼ teaspoon salt
¼ teaspoon coarsely ground
    black pepper
2 small bulbs celery root
    (celeriac), about 8 ounces
    each (if you can't find
    celery root, use another
    3 medium carrots and
    ¼ teaspoon celery seeds)
3 medium carrots
1 small head green cabbage
    (about 1¼ pounds)

1 Prepare dressing: In small bowl, with wire whisk or fork, mix mayonnaise, mustard, lemon juice, sugar, vinegar, salt, and pepper.

2 Peel and finely shred celery root and carrots. With chef's knife, cut cabbage into quarters; cut out core. Thinly slice cabbage; discard tough ribs.

3 Place vegetables in large bowl. Add dressing and toss to coat well. Cover bowl with plastic wrap; refrigerate at least 1½ hours to allow flavors to blend.

◆◆◆◆◆◆◆◆◆◆◆◆◆◆◆◆◆◆◆◆◆◆◆◆◆◆◆◆◆◆◆◆◆◆◆◆◆◆◆

SMART SHREDDING

• Use a stainless steel knife for slicing cabbage; carbon steel may react with the juices in the cabbage, causing the cut edges to discolor (this will turn green cabbage black, and red cabbage blue).

• Slicing or shredding vegetables in advance causes a loss of vitamin C. If you must do this, seal the shredded vegetables tightly in a plastic bag and refrigerate.

• For shredding, use the coarse side of a grater, the shredding disk in a food processor, or an adjustable-blade slicer (right), which makes short work of shredding and gives attractive long, fine, uniform shreds.

◆◆◆◆◆◆◆◆◆◆◆◆◆◆◆◆◆◆◆◆◆◆◆◆◆◆◆◆◆◆◆◆◆◆◆◆◆◆◆

EACH SERVING: ABOUT 80 CALORIES, 2g PROTEIN, 10g CARBOHYDRATE, 4g TOTAL FAT (0g SATURATED), 4mg CHOLESTEROL, 250mg SODIUM

ASIAN COLESLAW

Prep: 40 minutes   Makes 12 accompaniment servings

⅓ cup seasoned rice vinegar
2 tablespoons vegetable oil
2 teaspoons Asian sesame oil
¾ teaspoon salt
1 bag (16 ounces) carrots, shredded

1 large head savoy cabbage (about 2½ pounds), thinly sliced and tough ribs removed
4 green onions, thinly sliced
½ cup chopped fresh cilantro

◆ Prepare vinaigrette: In large bowl, with wire whisk or fork, mix seasoned rice vinegar, vegetable oil, sesame oil, and salt until blended.

◆ Add carrots, cabbage, green onions, and cilantro to vinaigrette in bowl; toss to mix well.

Each serving: About 80 calories, 2g protein, 12g carbohydrate, 3g total fat (1g saturated), 0mg cholesterol, 280mg sodium

CABBAGE AND BEET-GREEN SLAW

Prep: 35 minutes plus chilling   Makes 12 accompaniment servings

1 medium head green cabbage (2 pounds)
1 medium head red cabbage (2 pounds)
1 medium red onion
¾ cup mayonnaise
¼ cup cider vinegar

2 tablespoons sugar
2 tablespoons Dijon mustard
1 teaspoon salt
½ teaspoon coarsely ground black pepper
3 cups loosely packed beet greens or spinach leaves

◆ Quarter, core, and thinly slice both cabbages; discard tough ribs. Place cabbage in large bowl. Cut red onion lengthwise in half, then cut each half crosswise into paper-thin slices. Add onion to cabbage in bowl.

◆ Prepare dressing: In small bowl, with wire whisk or fork, mix mayonnaise, cider vinegar, sugar, Dijon mustard, salt, and coarsely ground black pepper. Add dressing to cabbage mixture and toss to coat well. Cover bowl with plastic wrap and refrigerate at least 3 hours before serving to allow flavors to blend.

◆ Meanwhile, rinse beet greens with cold running water and pat dry with paper towels. Cut beet greens into julienne strips; wrap with plastic wrap and refrigerate until ready to serve slaw.

◆ To serve, add julienned beet greens to cabbage mixture; toss to mix well.

Each serving: About 160 calories, 3g protein, 14g carbohydrate, 12g total fat (2g saturated), 8mg cholesterol, 400mg sodium

CARROT AND APPLE SLAW WITH DATES

Prep: 20 minutes   Makes 6 accompaniment servings

1 tablespoon fresh lemon juice
1 teaspoon honey
¼ teaspoon dried mint
¼ teaspoon salt
1 bag (16 ounces) carrots, shredded

2 Granny Smith apples, peeled, cored, and shredded
⅓ cup chopped pitted dates
2 tablespoons chopped fresh parsley

◆ Prepare dressing: In large bowl, stir lemon juice, honey, mint, and salt until combined.

◆ Add carrots, apples, dates, and parsley to dressing in bowl; toss to mix well.

Each serving: About 90 calories, 1g protein, 23g carbohydrate, 0g total fat (0g saturated), 0mg cholesterol, 25mg sodium

SWEET BROCCOLI SLAW

Prep: 10 minutes   Makes 4 accompaniment servings

⅓ cup mayonnaise
¼ cup cider vinegar
4 teaspoons sugar
2 teaspoons celery seeds
1 bunch watercress

1 package (15 to 16 ounces) broccoli coleslaw or shredded cabbage mix for coleslaw

◆ Prepare dressing: In large bowl, with wire whisk or fork, mix mayonnaise, cider vinegar, sugar, and celery seeds.

◆ Remove tough stems from watercress. Add watercress and broccoli slaw to dressing in bowl; toss to mix well.

Each serving: About 185 calories, 2g protein, 14g carbohydrate, 15g total fat (2g saturated), 11mg cholesterol, 140mg sodium

HISTORIC FAVORITE

◆◆◆◆◆◆◆◆◆◆◆◆◆◆◆◆◆◆◆◆◆◆◆

Coleslaw was brought to the American colonies around 1627 by Dutch immigrants. Cabbage was an important staple of the pioneer cooks, who made good use of the sturdy vegetable that kept well through long winters in the root cellar. They called their creation of shredded cabbage, seasonings, and a boiled dressing *koolsla*, from the Dutch *kool*, for cabbage, and *sla*, for salad. By 1792, coleslaw had become a standard in kitchens all over America, and there are now many variations that include other vegetables besides cabbage. The cool, crisp, refreshing flavor of coleslaw makes it ideal with fried and barbecued foods.

PASTA SALADS

Pasta salads are terrific room-temperature dishes: They pack up nicely in a picnic basket, and are the ideal addition to any barbecue. They are best eaten the same day they're made because pasta continues to absorb dressing as it stands. For pasta salads, rinse the hot pasta under cold running water – this stops the cooking and ensures a firm texture.

SZECHUAN PEANUT-NOODLE SALAD

❖❖❖❖❖❖❖❖❖❖❖❖

Prep: 25 minutes
Cook: 12 minutes
Makes 5 main-dish or
8 accompaniment servings

1 package (16 ounces) linguine or spaghetti
4 ounces snow peas, strings removed
¾ cup creamy peanut butter
3 tablespoons soy sauce
2 tablespoons vegetable oil
1 tablespoon hot Asian sesame oil
1 tablespoon cider vinegar
2 teaspoons grated, peeled fresh ginger
1 medium red pepper, thinly sliced
Dry-roasted peanuts and chopped green onion (optional)

1 Prepare linguine as label directs. Drain, reserving 1 cup pasta cooking water. Rinse linguine with cold running water; drain well.

2 In 3-quart saucepan, in *1 inch boiling water*, heat snow peas to boiling over high heat. Reduce heat to low; simmer 1 minute, or until tender-crisp.

3 Rinse snow peas with cold running water to stop cooking; drain. Cut snow peas into matchstick-thin strips.

SESAME OIL

❖❖❖❖❖❖❖❖❖

Pressed from toasted sesame seeds, dark-amber Asian sesame oil has an intense, nutty aroma; use in preference to pale sesame oil, which is neutral in flavor. "Hot" Asian sesame oil is flavored with chiles. Refrigerate after opening to prolong freshness.

4 Prepare peanut-butter dressing: In large bowl, with wire whisk or spoon, mix peanut butter, soy sauce, vegetable oil, hot Asian sesame oil, cider vinegar, grated ginger, and reserved pasta cooking water until mixture is thoroughly blended and smooth.

5 Add linguine, snow-pea strips, and sliced red pepper to peanut-butter dressing in bowl; toss to coat well. Sprinkle with dry-roasted peanuts and chopped green onion, if you like. Serve noodle salad immediately or cover and refrigerate to serve later. If noodles become too sticky upon standing, toss with a little hot water until dressing is of desired consistency.

EACH MAIN-DISH SERVING: ABOUT 595 CALORIES, 21g PROTEIN, 62g CARBOHYDRATE, 32g TOTAL FAT (6g SATURATED), 101mg CHOLESTEROL, 835mg SODIUM

TORTELLINI SALAD

Prep: 25 minutes   *Cook: 10 to 15 minutes*
Makes 6 main-dish servings

2 packages (9 ounces each) refrigerated or 1 package (16 ounces) frozen cheese tortellini
¼ cup white wine vinegar
3 tablespoons extra-virgin olive oil
1 teaspoon sugar
½ teaspoon salt
¼ teaspoon coarsely ground black pepper
1 medium red pepper, cut into thin strips

1 medium yellow pepper, cut into thin strips
1 medium tomato, seeded and diced
1 jar (6 ounces) marinated artichoke hearts, drained and each cut in half
2 bunches arugula or watercress (about 3 cups lightly packed)

◆ Prepare tortellini as label directs. Drain and rinse with cold running water; drain well.

◆ Prepare dressing: In large bowl, with wire whisk or fork, mix white wine vinegar, olive oil, sugar, salt, and coarsely ground black pepper. Add red and yellow peppers, tomato, artichokes, and tortellini; toss to coat. Cover and refrigerate if not serving right away.

◆ To serve, set aside a few whole arugula leaves for garnish. Tear remaining arugula into bite-size pieces; toss with tortellini mixture. Garnish with arugula leaves.

Each serving: About 350 calories, 14g protein, 46g carbohydrate, 13g total fat (3g saturated), 40mg cholesterol, 540mg sodium

ORZO SALAD WITH FETA CHEESE

Prep: 20 minutes   *Cook: 10 minutes*
Makes 6 accompaniment servings

1½ cups orzo (rice-shaped pasta)
2 tablespoons fresh lemon juice
2 tablespoons olive oil
¾ teaspoon salt
½ teaspoon ground black pepper

¼ cup pitted, chopped Kalamata olives
¼ cup chopped fresh parsley
1 large ripe tomato, diced (1½ cups)
3 ounces feta cheese, crumbled (¾ cup)

◆ Cook orzo as label directs. Drain and rinse with cold running water; drain well.

◆ Prepare vinaigrette: In large bowl, with wire whisk or fork, mix lemon juice, olive oil, salt, and pepper.

◆ Add orzo to vinaigrette in bowl and toss to coat. Stir in chopped olives and parsley. Add diced tomato and feta cheese and toss gently, just until combined.

Each serving: About 260 calories, 9g protein, 33g carbohydrate, 10g total fat (3g saturated), 12mg cholesterol, 530mg sodium

MACARONI SALAD

Prep: 15 minutes   *Cook: 20 minutes*
Makes 6 accompaniment servings

1½ cups tubetti or ditalini pasta
3 medium carrots, diced (1 cup)
⅓ cup mayonnaise
¼ cup chopped fresh dill
1 tablespoon fresh lemon juice

½ teaspoon salt
½ teaspoon ground black pepper
3 medium celery stalks, diced (1 cup)
1 cup frozen peas, thawed

◆ In 5-quart Dutch oven, prepare tubetti as label directs, but cook only 8 minutes.

◆ Add carrots to tubetti and cook 3 minutes longer. Drain and rinse with cold running water. Drain well.

◆ Prepare dressing: In large bowl, mix mayonnaise, dill, lemon juice, salt, and pepper until blended.

◆ Add tubetti and carrots to dressing in bowl; toss to coat. Add celery and peas and toss to combine.

Each serving: About 225 calories, 5g protein, 28g carbohydrate, 10g total fat (2g saturated), 7mg cholesterol, 300mg sodium

RICE SALADS

Whether you're celebrating summer with a picnic or rounding out a holiday buffet, a rice salad is a side dish to consider. Vegetables or chunks of fresh or dried fruit make welcome additions. Tossing the hot rice with the dressing allows it to absorb maximum flavor as it cools. Rice salads are best eaten within two hours of preparation (rice hardens when it's refrigerated).

MINTED RICE SALAD WITH CORN

◆ ◆ ◆ ◆ ◆ ◆ ◆ ◆ ◆ ◆ ◆ ◆ ◆

Prep: 20 minutes plus cooling
Cook: 20 minutes
Makes 8 accompaniment servings

1 cup regular long-grain rice
Salt
2 tablespoons fresh lemon juice
2 tablespoons olive oil
¼ teaspoon ground black pepper
3 medium ears corn, husks and silk removed
¾ cup finely diced radishes
¾ cup frozen peas, thawed
¼ cup chopped fresh mint leaves

1 Prepare rice as label directs, using ½ teaspoon salt. Meanwhile, prepare vinaigrette: In large bowl, with wire whisk or fork, mix lemon juice, oil, pepper, and ¾ teaspoon salt.

2 Add cooked rice to vinaigrette in bowl and toss gently but thoroughly to coat. Let cool 30 minutes, tossing mixture occasionally with fork.

3 Meanwhile, in 5-quart Dutch oven, heat *3 quarts water* to boiling. Add corn; cook 5 minutes. Drain and cool.

ALMOST-INSTANT RICE SALADS

◆ ◆ ◆ ◆ ◆ ◆ ◆ ◆ ◆ ◆ ◆ ◆ ◆ ◆ ◆ ◆ ◆ ◆

Make a rice salad with any vinaigrette plus a few choice leftover meats or vegetables, or try the following:

• Canned tuna, diced tomatoes, capers, chopped flat-leaf parsley, and a lemon juice and olive oil vinaigrette.

• Diced cooked chicken, celery, apple, chopped walnuts, and a mayonnaise and lemon juice dressing.

• Rinsed and drained canned black beans, crumbled feta cheese, some diced avocado, and a dressing of fresh lime juice, olive oil, garlic, and cumin.

4 Cut corn kernels from cobs and add to rice mixture with diced radishes, peas, and chopped fresh mint; toss to combine.

EACH SERVING: ABOUT 160 CALORIES, 3g PROTEIN, 28g CARBOHYDRATE, 4g TOTAL FAT (1g SATURATED), 0mg CHOLESTEROL, 325mg SODIUM

WHITE AND WILD RICE SALAD

Prep: 20 minutes plus cooling   Cook: 50 to 60 minutes
Makes 8 accompaniment servings

½ cup wild rice
Salt
¾ cup regular long-grain rice
⅓ cup dried cranberries or
  currants
2 tablespoons red wine
  vinegar
2 tablespoons olive oil
½ teaspoon grated orange
  peel
¼ teaspoon ground black
  pepper

2 cups seedless red grapes,
  each cut in half
2 medium celery stalks, thinly
  sliced (1 cup)
2 tablespoons chopped fresh
  parsley
Lettuce leaves (optional)
½ cup pecans, toasted and
  coarsely chopped

◆ Prepare wild rice as label directs, using ½ teaspoon salt.
Meanwhile, cook long-grain rice as label directs, using
¼ teaspoon salt.

◆ In small bowl, combine dried cranberries with *boiling
water* just to cover; let stand 5 minutes. Drain.

◆ Prepare dressing: In large bowl, with wire whisk or fork,
mix vinegar, olive oil, orange peel, pepper,
and ¾ teaspoon salt.

◆ Add wild and long-grain
rices and cranberries to
dressing in bowl; toss to
coat. Let cool 30 minutes,
tossing occasionally
with fork.

◆ Add grapes, celery,
and parsley to rice mixture
in bowl; toss until evenly
combined. To serve, line
salad bowl or platter with
lettuce leaves, if you like.
Spoon in rice salad; sprinkle
with pecans.

**Each serving: About 205 calories, 4g protein, 32g carbohydrate,
8g total fat (1g saturated), 0mg cholesterol, 410mg sodium**

JAPANESE RICE SALAD

Prep: 20 minutes plus cooling   Cook: 20 minutes
Makes 8 accompaniment servings

1½ cups regular long-grain
  rice
Salt
3 tablespoons seasoned rice
  vinegar
2 tablespoons vegetable oil
1 teaspoon grated, peeled
  fresh ginger

¼ teaspoon ground black
  pepper
4 ounces green beans, ends
  trimmed, cut into ¼-inch
  pieces (1 cup)
2 medium carrots, shredded
3 green onions, thinly sliced
Watercress (optional)

◆ Prepare rice as label directs, using ½ teaspoon salt.

◆ Prepare dressing: In large bowl, with wire whisk or fork,
mix seasoned rice vinegar, oil, ginger, pepper, and
½ teaspoon salt.

◆ Add rice and toss to coat. Let cool 30 minutes, tossing
occasionally with fork.

◆ Meanwhile, in 2-quart saucepan, heat *2 cups water* to
boiling with 1 teaspoon salt; add green beans and cook
5 minutes. Drain and rinse with cold running water.

◆ Add green beans to rice with carrots and green onions;
toss to combine. To serve, arrange watercress, if using,
around edge of platter; spoon rice salad into center.

**Each serving: About 175 calories, 3g protein, 32g carbohydrate,
4g total fat (1g saturated), 0mg cholesterol, 395mg sodium**

BROWN RICE AND MANGO SALAD

Prep: 25 minutes   Cook: 1 hour
Makes 8 accompaniment servings

1 cup long-grain brown rice
Salt
1 large lime
2 tablespoons olive oil
¼ teaspoon ground black
  pepper

1 ripe mango, peeled and cut
  into ½-inch cubes
¼ cup chopped fresh cilantro
2 green onions, thinly sliced

◆ Prepare brown rice as label directs, using ½ teaspoon salt.
Rinse with cold running water; drain well. Meanwhile, grate
½ teaspoon peel and squeeze 2 tablespoons juice from lime.

◆ Prepare dressing: In large bowl, with wire whisk or fork,
mix lime peel, lime juice, olive oil, pepper, and ½ teaspoon
salt. Add rice and toss to coat. Add mango, cilantro, and
green onions; toss until evenly combined.

**Each serving: About 135 calories, 2g protein, 24g carbohydrate,
4g total fat (1g saturated), 0mg cholesterol, 205mg sodium**

GRAIN SALADS

Barley and wheat, both whole (wheat berries) and cracked (bulgur), make appearances in some wonderfully satisfying salads. Cooked (or soaked, for bulgur) until just tender but still slightly firm, they lend excellent texture and a delicately nutty flavor to these nutritious and irresistible combinations. If the grains in these recipes aren't available at the supermarket, look for them in health-food stores.

BARLEY SALAD WITH NECTARINES

◆◆◆◆◆◆◆◆◆◆◆◆◆◆◆◆◆◆◆◆◆◆◆◆◆◆

Prep: 30 minutes   Cook: 40 to 50 minutes
Makes 12 accompaniment servings

1 package (16 ounces) pearl barley	1½ pounds nectarines (about 4 medium), pitted and cut into ½-inch pieces
Salt	
3 to 4 medium limes	1 pound tomatoes (about 2 large), seeded and cut into ½-inch pieces
⅛ cup olive oil	
1 tablespoon sugar	
¾ teaspoon coarsely ground black pepper	4 green onions, thinly sliced
	½ cup chopped fresh mint

1 In 4-quart saucepan, heat *6 cups water* to boiling over high heat. Add barley and 1½ teaspoons salt; heat to boiling. Reduce heat to low; cover and simmer 35 to 45 minutes, until barley is tender and most of liquid is absorbed. Drain and rinse with cold running water. Drain well.

2 Meanwhile, prepare lime dressing: Grate 1 tablespoon peel and squeeze ½ cup juice from limes. Place grated lime peel and lime juice in large bowl. Add olive oil, sugar, pepper, and 1¼ teaspoons salt. With wire whisk or fork, mix until blended.

3 Add barley, nectarines, tomatoes, green onions, and mint to lime dressing; with rubber spatula, stir gently to coat. If not serving right away, cover and refrigerate.

BARLEY

This hearty, ancient grain is often identified with beer, breads, cereals, and soups, but it also makes delicious, healthy salads. When cooked until tender, the whole grain has a nutty taste and chewy texture, making it the perfect partner for bold vinaigrettes, herbs, crunchy vegetables, and even fruit. Instead of rice, try barley (or quick-cooking barley) as an easy side dish. Pearl barley is scoured six times to remove the bran and husk for quicker cooking.

EACH SERVING: ABOUT 230 CALORIES, 5g PROTEIN, 40g CARBOHYDRATE, 7g TOTAL FAT (1g SATURATED), 0mg CHOLESTEROL, 405mg SODIUM

WHEAT-BERRY SALAD WITH SPINACH

Prep: 15 minutes plus soaking   *Cook: 1 hour 15 minutes*
Makes 4 main-dish servings

1½ cups wheat berries
   (whole-grain wheat)
1 bunch (10 to 12 ounces)
   spinach, tough stems
   removed
1 medium tomato
10 dried tomato halves
   (about 1 ounce)
3 tablespoons olive oil

2 tablespoons red wine
   vinegar
1 teaspoon salt
½ teaspoon sugar
½ teaspoon Dijon mustard
¼ teaspoon coarsely ground
   black pepper
1 cup golden raisins

◆ In large bowl, soak wheat berries overnight in enough *water* to cover by 2 inches.

◆ Drain wheat berries. In 4-quart saucepan, heat *7 cups water* to boiling over high heat. Add soaked wheat berries; heat to boiling. Reduce heat to low; cover and simmer 1 hour, or until wheat berries are tender. Drain.

◆ Meanwhile, coarsely chop spinach. Dice tomato. Place dried tomato halves in small bowl; pour over *1 cup boiling water*. Let stand 5 minutes to soften; drain well. Coarsely chop dried tomatoes.

◆ Prepare dressing: In medium bowl, with wire whisk or fork, mix olive oil, red wine vinegar, salt, sugar, mustard, and coarsely ground black pepper. Add raisins, diced tomato, chopped dried tomatoes, spinach, and wheat berries; toss until blended.

Each serving: About 455 calories, 12g protein, 82g carbohydrate, 12g total fat (1g saturated), 0mg cholesterol, 625mg sodium

BARLEY SUCCOTASH SALAD

Prep: 15 minutes plus cooling   *Cook: 40 to 50 minutes*
Makes 6 accompaniment servings

¾ cup pearl barley
Salt
1 cup frozen baby lima beans
3 ears corn, husks and silk
   removed

2 tablespoons cider vinegar
1 tablespoon olive oil
¼ teaspoon ground black
   pepper
¼ cup chopped fresh parsley

◆ In 2-quart saucepan, heat *2½ cups water* to boiling over high heat. Add barley and ½ teaspoon salt; heat to boiling. Reduce heat to low; cover and simmer 35 to 45 minutes, until tender. Drain and rinse with cold running water. Drain well.

◆ Meanwhile, cook baby lima beans as label directs. Drain and rinse with cold running water; drain well. In 5-quart Dutch oven, heat *4 quarts water* to boiling over high heat. Add corn; cook 5 minutes. Drain corn and cool. Cut kernels from cobs.

◆ Prepare dressing: In large bowl, with wire whisk or fork, mix vinegar, olive oil, pepper, and ¾ teaspoon salt. Add barley, lima beans, corn kernels, and chopped parsley; toss until blended.

Each serving: About 180 calories, 6g protein, 35g carbohydrate, 3g total fat (0g saturated), 0mg cholesterol, 320mg sodium

TOMATO AND MINT TABBOULEH

Prep: 20 minutes plus standing and chilling
Makes 8 accompaniment servings

1½ cups bulgur (cracked
   wheat)
¼ cup fresh lemon juice
3 medium-size ripe tomatoes
   (about 1 pound), cut into
   ½-inch pieces
1 medium cucumber (about
   8 ounces), peeled and cut
   into ½-inch pieces

3 green onions, chopped
¾ cup loosely packed fresh
   parsley leaves, chopped
½ cup loosely packed fresh
   mint leaves, chopped
1 tablespoon olive oil
¾ teaspoon salt
¼ teaspoon coarsely ground
   black pepper

◆ In medium bowl, combine bulgur, lemon juice, and *1½ cups boiling water*, stirring to mix. Let mixture stand about 30 minutes, until liquid is absorbed.

◆ When bulgur mixture is cool, stir in tomatoes and remaining ingredients. Cover and refrigerate bulgur mixture at least 1 hour to blend flavors.

Each serving: About 125 calories, 4g protein, 24g carbohydrate, 2g total fat (0g saturated), 0mg cholesterol, 215mg sodium

BEAN SALADS

With their soft, creamy texture and mild taste, beans absorb the flavors of any dressing and make a wonderful foundation for a salad. If you cannot find one variety, simply substitute another. For the freshest taste and consistency – and to cut some of their sodium – always rinse canned beans before using. Keep your pantry stocked with a good assortment of canned beans and you'll always be able to prepare delicious salads at a moment's notice.

1 Trim ends from green beans; cut into 1½-inch pieces. In 3-quart saucepan, in *1 inch boiling water*, heat green beans to boiling over high heat. Reduce heat to low; cover and simmer 5 to 10 minutes, until tender-crisp. Drain. Prepare lima beans as label directs; drain. Meanwhile, chop onion.

FIESTA BEAN SALAD

◆◆◆◆◆◆◆◆◆◆◆◆◆◆◆◆◆◆◆◆◆◆◆◆◆◆◆

Prep: 20 minutes plus chilling   Cook: 20 minutes
Makes 12 accompaniment servings

1 pound green beans
1 package (10 ounces) frozen lima beans
1 small onion
¼ cup olive or vegetable oil
1 tablespoon chili powder
⅓ cup distilled white vinegar
1½ teaspoons sugar
1½ teaspoons salt
1 can (15 to 19 ounces) red kidney beans, rinsed and drained

1 can (15 to 19 ounces) white kidney beans (cannellini), rinsed and drained
1 can (15 to 19 ounces) black beans, rinsed and drained
1 can (16 to 17 ounces) whole-kernel corn, drained
¼ cup chopped fresh cilantro or parsley

2 In 2-quart saucepan, heat oil over medium-high heat; add chopped onion and cook, stirring, 10 minutes, or until tender.

3 Stir chili powder into onion; cook, stirring, 1 minute. Remove from heat; stir in vinegar, sugar, and salt.

4 Place red and white kidney beans and black beans in large bowl. Add corn, chopped cilantro, green beans, lima beans, and onion mixture; toss to coat. Cover with plastic wrap and refrigerate at least 1 hour to blend flavors.

◆◆◆◆◆◆◆◆◆◆◆◆◆◆◆◆

LEFTOVER CILANTRO

Left with half a bunch? Add cilantro to omelets, tuna salad, or mixed greens, or use it instead of basil in your favorite pesto recipe. To avoid discoloration, don't chop cilantro in advance.

◆◆◆◆◆◆◆◆◆◆◆◆◆◆◆◆

EACH SERVING: ABOUT 190 CALORIES, 9g PROTEIN, 32g CARBOHYDRATE, 5g TOTAL FAT (1g SATURATED), 0mg CHOLESTEROL, 790mg SODIUM

AVOCADO AND BLACK BEAN SALAD

Prep: 20 minutes

Makes 4 accompaniment servings

2 small avocados (8 ounces each)
2 medium plum tomatoes
2 medium navel oranges
1 can (15 to 19 ounces) black beans, rinsed and drained
1 tablespoon chopped fresh cilantro or parsley
1 teaspoon salt

Cut each avocado in half; discard seeds. Peel avocados. Cut avocados and tomatoes into bite-size chunks. Cut peel and white pith from oranges; discard. Cut each orange crosswise into ¼-inch-thick slices. In large bowl, with rubber spatula, toss avocados, tomatoes, orange slices, and remaining ingredients to mix well.

Each serving: About 325 calories, 10g protein, 35g carbohydrate, 20g total fat (3g saturated), 0mg cholesterol, 955mg sodium

GARBANZO SALAD

Prep: 20 minutes

Makes 4 accompaniment servings

2 tablespoons red wine vinegar
2 tablespoons olive oil
1 teaspoon Dijon mustard
¼ teaspoon salt
3 small tomatoes (about 12 ounces), each cut into 8 wedges
½ cup Kalamata olives, pitted and coarsely chopped
1 green onion, thinly sliced
1 can (15 to 19 ounces) garbanzo beans, rinsed and drained
2 tablespoons chopped fresh oregano, basil, or parsley

Prepare vinaigrette: In medium bowl, with wire whisk or fork, mix red wine vinegar, olive oil, mustard, and salt. To vinaigrette in bowl, add tomato wedges, olives, green onion, garbanzo beans, and oregano; toss to mix well.

Each serving: About 235 calories, 6g protein, 24g carbohydrate, 14g total fat (2g saturated), 0mg cholesterol, 900mg sodium

BLACK-EYED PEA SALAD

Prep: 10 minutes plus chilling   Cook: 20 minutes

Makes 8 accompaniment servings

2 packages (10 ounces each) frozen black-eyed peas
1 large red pepper, diced
½ cup chopped red onion
1 package (10 ounces) frozen peas, thawed
3 tablespoons cider vinegar
2 tablespoons olive oil
1 teaspoon sugar
1 teaspoon chopped fresh thyme or ¼ teaspoon dried thyme
¾ teaspoon salt
¼ teaspoon coarsely ground black pepper
1 large tomato

◆ Cook black-eyed peas as label directs; drain. Rinse with cold running water. In large bowl, toss black-eyed peas with remaining ingredients except tomato. Cover and refrigerate at least 3 hours to blend flavors.

◆ To serve, cut tomato into ¼-inch-thick slices. Arrange tomato slices and black-eyed pea salad on large platter.

Each serving: About 165 calories, 8g protein, 25g carbohydrate, 4g total fat (1g saturated), 0mg cholesterol, 235mg sodium

TWO-BEAN AND TOMATO SALAD

Prep: 20 minutes   Cook: 10 minutes

Makes 6 accompaniment servings

12 ounces French green beans (haricots verts) or green beans, ends trimmed
2 tablespoons extra-virgin olive oil
1 tablespoon fresh lemon juice
½ large shallot, finely chopped
½ teaspoon Dijon mustard
¼ teaspoon salt
¼ teaspoon coarsely ground black pepper
2 medium tomatoes, each cut into 12 wedges
1 can (15 to 19 ounces) Great Northern beans, rinsed and drained

◆ In 10-inch skillet, heat ¾ inch water to boiling over high heat. Add green beans; heat to boiling. Reduce heat to medium; cook, uncovered, 3 to 5 minutes, until beans are tender-crisp. Drain. Rinse beans with cold running water, then drain and pat dry with paper towels.

◆ Prepare dressing: In large bowl, with wire whisk or fork, mix olive oil, lemon juice, chopped shallot, mustard, salt, and pepper until blended.

◆ To dressing in bowl, add green beans, tomato wedges, and Great Northern beans; with rubber spatula, gently toss to mix well.

Each serving: About 145 calories, 6g protein, 21g carbohydrate, 5g total fat (1g saturated), 0mg cholesterol, 115mg sodium

Molded salads

A colorful, shimmering gelatin salad, studded with fruit, is a holiday classic, and the perfect do-ahead solution to easy entertaining. Infused with spices or flecked with herbs, these salads are cool and refreshing (in summer, try the simple tomato aspic). Always make sure the gelatin is completely dissolved: All granules must disappear.

SPICED WINE AND FRUIT MOLD

◆◆◆◆◆◆◆◆◆◆◆◆◆

Prep: 40 minutes plus standing and chilling
Cook: 30 minutes
Makes 16 accompaniment servings

1¼ cups sugar

3 cinnamon sticks (3 inches each)

2 teaspoons whole allspice

½ teaspoon salt

5 envelopes unflavored gelatin

1 bottle (750 ml) sauterne or other sweet white wine

2 tablespoons grenadine syrup

2 tablespoons fresh lemon juice

6 maraschino cherries

1 can (17 ounces) whole figs in syrup, drained

2 cans (16 ounces each) pear halves in syrup, drained

1 container (3½ to 4 ounces) green candied cherries, each cut in half, for garnish

Flat-leaf parsley sprigs for garnish

1 In 2-quart saucepan, heat first 4 ingredients and *1 cup water* to boiling over high heat. Reduce heat to low; simmer 15 minutes. Discard spices. In 2-cup measuring cup, sprinkle gelatin over *1½ cups cold water*; let stand 2 minutes to soften gelatin. Stir into syrup; cook over medium heat, stirring, until gelatin completely dissolves (do not boil). Remove from heat.

2 In large bowl, combine sauterne, grenadine, lemon juice, and *1½ cups water*. Stir in gelatin mixture. In bottom of 12-cup mold, arrange maraschino cherries and half of figs in pretty design.

3 Carefully pour ½ inch gelatin mixture over fruit in mold; place in large bowl of *ice water* until gelatin is set but not firm (it should be sticky to the touch). Add enough gelatin mixture to cover fruit in bottom of mold by ½ inch.

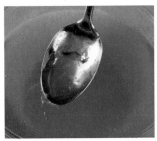

4 Let mold stand in ice-water bath until next layer is set but not firm. Meanwhile, place gelatin mixture in bowl in another large bowl of *ice water* just until it mounds slightly when dropped from spoon, stirring often. Reserve enough pears to fit around edge of mold.

5 Dice remaining pears and figs; gently fold into gelatin mixture in bowl. Ladle fruit mixture into mold in ice-water bath; edge should immediately gel (remove mold from ice-water bath if mixture sets too quickly).

6 Working quickly, arrange reserved pear halves around edge of mold, rounded-side out and pointed-end down. Refrigerate at least 6 hours, or until set. To serve, unmold gelatin salad onto chilled platter; garnish.

EACH SERVING: ABOUT 175 CALORIES, 2g PROTEIN, 35g CARBOHYDRATE, 0g TOTAL FAT, 0mg CHOLESTEROL, 75mg SODIUM

ROYAL CRANBERRY MOLD

Prep: 30 minutes plus standing and chilling
Makes 16 accompaniment servings

1 envelope unflavored gelatin
2 packages (4 servings each)
  strawberry-flavor gelatin
1 bag (12 ounces) cranberries
  (3 cups), coarsely chopped
1½ cups sugar

2 medium navel oranges, peel
  and white pith removed,
  coarsely chopped
1 can (29 ounces) sliced
  peaches, drained and diced

◆ In 2-quart saucepan, evenly sprinkle unflavored gelatin over *3 cups cold water*; let stand 2 minutes to soften gelatin slightly. Cook over medium heat, stirring frequently, until gelatin completely dissolves (do not boil). Remove from heat; stir in strawberry gelatin until completely dissolved.

◆ Pour gelatin mixture into large bowl; stir in *4 cups cold water*. Refrigerate gelatin mixture about 2 hours, just until it mounds slightly when dropped from spoon.

◆ Meanwhile, place cranberries in large bowl; stir in sugar until sugar completely dissolves, then stir in oranges and peaches. When gelatin mixture is ready, fold fruit mixture into thickened gelatin. Pour gelatin mixture into 10-inch Bundt pan or 12-cup mold. Cover and refrigerate at least 6 hours, until set.

◆ To serve, unmold gelatin salad onto chilled platter.

Each serving: About 170 calories, 2g protein, 43g carbohydrate, 0g total fat, 0mg cholesterol, 35mg sodium

BEET-SALAD MOLD

Prep: 20 minutes plus standing and chilling
Makes 16 accompaniment servings

1 can (16 ounces) sliced beets
2 envelopes unflavored gelatin
2 packages (4 servings each)
  lemon-flavor gelatin
½ cup cider vinegar

¼ teaspoon salt
1 medium carrot
3 tablespoons chopped fresh
  dill or 2 teaspoons dillweed

◆ Into 2-quart saucepan, drain liquid from beets. Add *2 cups cold water* to beet liquid. Evenly sprinkle unflavored gelatin over liquid and let stand 2 minutes.

◆ Cook over medium heat, stirring frequently, until gelatin completely dissolves (do not boil). Remove from heat; stir in lemon-flavor gelatin until completely dissolved.

◆ Pour gelatin mixture into large bowl; stir in cider vinegar, salt, and *3½ cups cold water*. Refrigerate gelatin mixture about 2 hours, just until it mounds slightly when dropped from spoon.

◆ Coarsely chop beets; shred carrot. When gelatin mixture is ready, fold beets, carrot, and dill into thickened gelatin. Pour into 12-cup mold. Cover and refrigerate at least 6 hours, until set. To serve, unmold onto chilled platter.

Each serving: About 55 calories, 2g protein, 12g carbohydrate, 0g total fat, 0mg cholesterol, 140mg sodium

TOMATO ASPIC

Prep: 10 minutes plus standing and chilling   Cook: 20 minutes
Makes 8 accompaniment servings

1 can or bottle (32 ounces)
  tomato juice
¼ cup celery leaves
6 whole allspice
2 whole cloves
2 envelopes unflavored gelatin
2 tablespoons fresh lemon
  juice

1 tablespoon sugar
½ teaspoon hot-pepper sauce
1 container (8 ounces) sour
  cream
2 tablespoons mayonnaise
2 tablespoons chopped
  fresh dill

◆ Pour ½ cup tomato juice into large bowl; set aside. In 3-quart saucepan, heat remaining 3½ cups tomato juice with celery leaves, allspice, and cloves to boiling over high heat. Reduce heat to low; simmer 15 minutes. Sprinkle gelatin over juice in bowl; let stand 2 minutes to soften gelatin slightly.

◆ Strain hot juice mixture over softened gelatin; stir until gelatin completely dissolves. Stir in lemon juice, sugar, and hot-pepper sauce. Pour into 8½" by 4½" loaf pan or 5-cup mold. Cover and refrigerate at least 6 hours, until set. To serve, unmold aspic onto chilled platter. In bowl, stir sour cream, mayonnaise, and dill; serve with aspic.

Each serving: About 120 calories, 3g protein, 8g carbohydrate, 9g total fat (4g saturated), 15mg cholesterol, 480mg sodium

EASY UNMOLDING

◆◆◆◆◆◆◆◆◆◆◆◆◆◆◆◆◆◆◆◆◆◆◆◆

To unmold a gelatin salad, dip the base of the mold or pan into a large bowl of warm water for 10 seconds – no longer, or the gelatin will begin to melt. Place a chilled serving platter that's been moistened with a little cold water over the mold, then, holding the two together tightly, invert them quickly, and give the mold a firm shake or tap to release the salad. (If the mold comes out off center, you can easily slide it into place on the moistened platter.) If the salad fails to come out, hold the mold on its side until the salad begins to loosen from the top side. Or, turn the mold right-side up and carefully run a knife between the gelatin mixture and mold. Then try again.

MAIN-DISH MEAT SALADS

Steak, smoked ham, prosciutto, and even ground beef team up with crisp greens, crunchy vegetables, and spicy dressings to make salads into main dishes. Fresh mint and cilantro round out Thai flavors in the most refreshing way, while juicy pears and shaved Parmesan provide the Italian answer to bitter greens…there's something to please every palate.

BEEF CAESAR SALAD

◆◆◆◆◆◆◆◆◆◆◆◆◆◆◆◆◆◆◆◆◆◆◆◆◆◆◆◆◆

Prep: 25 minutes plus standing   *Broil:* 12 to 15 minutes
Makes 4 main-dish servings

1 beef flank steak (1 pound)	2 tablespoons freshly grated Parmesan cheese
½ teaspoon salt	1 medium head romaine lettuce
½ teaspoon coarsely ground black pepper	1 medium head red leaf lettuce
3 tablespoons olive oil	1 medium cucumber
2 tablespoons mayonnaise	Parmesan shavings for garnish
1 tablespoon Dijon mustard	Crusty bread (optional)
1 tablespoon fresh lemon juice	
½ teaspoon anchovy paste	
1 garlic clove, minced	

1 Preheat broiler. Place flank steak on rack in broiling pan; sprinkle with salt and black pepper. Place pan in broiler at closest position to heat source; broil steak 12 to 15 minutes for medium-rare, or until desired doneness, turning steak once. Transfer to cutting board; let stand 10 minutes.

2 Meanwhile, prepare dressing: In large bowl, with wire whisk or fork, mix olive oil, mayonnaise, Dijon mustard, lemon juice, anchovy paste, minced garlic, and grated Parmesan cheese until blended.

3 Wash and thoroughly dry romaine and red leaf lettuce. Tear both lettuces into bite-size pieces; add to dressing in bowl and toss gently to coat.

4 Peel several strips of skin from cucumber, leaving some green. Thinly slice cucumber; toss with lettuce mixture. Place salad on 4 plates. Holding knife almost parallel to cutting board, slice steak thinly across the grain and arrange on salads. Sprinkle with Parmesan shavings; serve with crusty bread, if you like.

CAESAR SALAD PLUS

◆◆◆◆◆◆◆◆◆◆◆◆◆◆◆◆◆◆◆◆◆◆◆◆◆◆◆

Though originally concocted simply with romaine lettuce (in Tijuana, Mexico, in 1924), Caesar salad can be turned into a main dish by the addition of meat, such as the flank steak here. Other good choices are skinless, boneless chicken breasts, broiled or grilled and sliced, or skewered shrimp, broiled and piled on top.

EACH SERVING: ABOUT 395 CALORIES, 27g PROTEIN, 8g CARBOHYDRATE, 28g TOTAL FAT (7g SATURATED), 65mg CHOLESTEROL, 655mg SODIUM

THAI BEEF SALAD

Prep: 45 minutes   Cook: 10 minutes
Makes 4 main-dish servings

2 large bunches cilantro
2 large bunches fresh mint
¼ cup seasoned rice vinegar
3 tablespoons vegetable oil
4 teaspoons Asian fish sauce
   (nuoc nam, see page 30)
4 teaspoons grated, peeled
   fresh ginger
1 jalapeño chile, seeded and
   minced
Salt
1 large carrot, cut into 2-inch-
   long matchstick-thin strips

1 medium red pepper, cut
   into 2-inch-long matchstick-
   thin strips
2 large green onions, cut into
   2-inch-long matchstick-thin
   strips
1 pound ground beef chuck
1 garlic clove, minced
1 head Boston lettuce, torn
   into bite-size pieces

◆ From cilantro, remove ½ cup loosely packed leaves; set aside. Chop ¼ cup cilantro leaves. Repeat with mint. Prepare dressing: In medium bowl, with wire whisk or fork, mix chopped cilantro and mint, seasoned rice vinegar, next 4 ingredients, and ⅛ teaspoon salt. Spoon half of dressing into large bowl; set aside. To dressing remaining in medium bowl, add carrot, red pepper, and green onions.

◆ In nonstick 10-inch skillet, cook ground beef over medium-high heat until browned, breaking it up into nickel-size pieces. Spoon off and discard fat. Add garlic and ¼ teaspoon salt; cook 1 minute, stirring. Add to carrot mixture; toss well. To large bowl with dressing, add lettuce and reserved cilantro and mint; toss. Spoon onto 4 plates; top with beef mixture.

Each serving: About 380 calories, 20g protein, 12g carbohydrate, 27g total fat (8g saturated), 69mg cholesterol, 840mg sodium

QUESADILLA SALAD

Prep: 30 minutes   Cook: 10 minutes
Makes 4 main-dish servings

2 to 3 medium limes
¾ teaspoon chili powder
½ teaspoon ground coriander
½ teaspoon sugar
4 teaspoons olive oil
1 head romaine lettuce, cut
   crosswise into ¾-inch-wide
   strips
1 pint (12 ounces) cherry
   tomatoes, each cut
   in half

1 small avocado (about
   8 ounces), peeled and cut
   into ½-inch wedges
4 ounces sliced smoked ham,
   cut into ½-inch-wide strips
2 green onions, thinly sliced
8 flour tortillas (6 inches
   each)
6 ounces Monterey Jack
   cheese with jalapeño chiles,
   shredded (1½ cups)

◆ Prepare vinaigrette: Grate ¼ teaspoon peel and squeeze 3 tablespoons juice from limes. In large bowl, with wire whisk or fork, mix lime peel, lime juice, chili powder,

coriander, and sugar. Whisk in oil in thin stream until blended. Add lettuce and next 4 ingredients to vinaigrette; toss well. Arrange salads on 4 plates.

◆ Heat 10-inch skillet over medium heat. Place 1 tortilla in skillet. Sprinkle with one-quarter of cheese; top with second tortilla, pressing lightly. Cook quesadilla, turning once, about 2 minutes, until lightly toasted and cheese melts.

◆ Transfer to cutting board. Cut into 8 wedges; keep warm. Repeat with remaining tortillas and cheese. To serve, tuck quesadillas into salads.

Each serving: About 610 calories, 27g protein, 54g carbohydrate, 35g total fat (11g saturated), 62mg cholesterol, 950mg sodium

PROSCIUTTO AND PEAR SALAD WITH PARMESAN AND PECANS

Prep: 25 minutes   Makes 3 main-dish servings

1 chunk Parmesan cheese
1 tablespoon red wine vinegar
1 teaspoon Dijon mustard
¼ teaspoon ground black
   pepper
2 tablespoons olive oil
1 small head radicchio
   (4 ounces), torn into
   pieces

1 head Belgian endive,
   separated into leaves
1 bunch arugula
2 ripe pears, peeled, cored,
   and each cut into eighths
4 ounces thinly sliced
   prosciutto
¼ cup toasted pecans, broken
   into pieces

◆ With vegetable peeler, shave 1 cup loosely packed curls (about 2 ounces) from Parmesan; set aside. Prepare vinaigrette: In large bowl, with wire whisk or fork, mix vinegar, mustard, and pepper; slowly whisk in oil.

◆ Add radicchio, endive, arugula, and pears to vinaigrette; toss well. Arrange salad on 3 plates. Arrange prosciutto on top. Sprinkle with Parmesan curls and pecans.

Each serving: About 365 calories, 18g protein, 23g carbohydrate, 23g total fat (6g saturated), 26mg cholesterol, 845mg sodium

MAIN-DISH POULTRY SALADS

Use quick-cooking boneless chicken breasts, or simply purchase a roasted chicken from the supermarket for these no-fuss salads. We've added flavorful ingredients, such as lime, mango, fresh ginger, and tangy feta cheese, to complement the delicate taste of chicken. Each makes a colorful and scrumptious one-dish meal.

CURRIED CHICKEN SALAD WITH MANGO

◆ ◆ ◆ ◆ ◆ ◆ ◆ ◆ ◆ ◆

Prep: 25 minutes plus cooling
Cook: 15 minutes
Makes 4 main-dish servings

1 pound skinless, boneless chicken-breast halves
Salt
1 teaspoon curry powder
⅓ cup plain low-fat yogurt
¼ cup mayonnaise
2 tablespoons mango chutney, chopped
2 tablespoons fresh lime juice
¼ teaspoon ground black pepper
1 large ripe mango, diced (see right)
3 celery stalks, thinly sliced
¼ cup chopped fresh cilantro
Lettuce leaves
2 tablespoons sliced almonds, toasted (optional)

1 In 3-quart saucepan, heat chicken with 1 teaspoon salt and *water* to cover by 1 inch to boiling over high heat. Reduce heat to low; simmer 10 minutes, or until cooked through. Cool in liquid 30 minutes.

2 Meanwhile, in 1-quart saucepan, toast curry powder over low heat, stirring constantly with wooden spoon to prevent burning, 1 minute, or until very fragrant.

3 Prepare dressing: In large bowl, with wire whisk or rubber spatula, mix curry powder with yogurt, mayonnaise, chutney, lime juice, pepper, and ½ teaspoon salt.

◆ ◆

PREPARING A MANGO

Slice mango down both sides of long, flat seed. Run small paring knife between skin and flesh of each half, 1 inch deep, then turn back the 1-inch border of skin. Cut away rest of peel in a few strokes, then dice or slice as desired.

4 Drain chicken; cut into bite-size pieces. Toss chicken, mango, celery, and cilantro with dressing. Line platter with lettuce; top with salad, and almonds, if using.

◆ ◆ ◆ ◆ ◆ ◆ ◆ ◆ ◆ ◆ ◆ ◆ ◆ ◆ ◆ ◆ ◆ ◆ ◆ ◆

EACH SERVING: ABOUT 310 CALORIES, 28g PROTEIN, 18g CARBOHYDRATE, 14g TOTAL FAT (3g SATURATED), 90mg CHOLESTEROL, 560mg SODIUM

SESAME NOODLE SALAD WITH CHICKEN

Prep: 25 minutes   *Cook:* 12 to 15 minutes
Makes 4 main-dish servings

12 ounces linguine or spaghetti

6 ounces snow peas, strings removed, each cut crosswise into thirds

¼ cup creamy peanut butter

3 tablespoons seasoned rice vinegar

3 tablespoons soy sauce

1 tablespoon brown sugar

1 tablespoon minced, peeled fresh ginger

1 tablespoon Asian sesame oil

¼ teaspoon ground red pepper (cayenne)

1 small garlic clove, crushed

2 medium carrots, shredded

½ small head red cabbage, thinly sliced (3 cups)

¾ pound boneless roasted chicken, pulled into thin strips (about 1½ cups)

◆ Prepare linguine as label directs. During last minute of cooking, add snow peas. Drain linguine and snow peas; rinse with cold running water to cool. Drain again; set aside.

◆ Prepare peanut-butter sauce: In small bowl, with wire whisk or fork, mix peanut butter, next 7 ingredients, and *¾ cup very hot tap water* until blended. In large bowl, toss linguine, snow peas, carrots, red cabbage, and chicken with peanut-butter sauce. If not serving right away, cover and refrigerate. If noodles become too sticky upon standing, toss with a little *hot water* until dressing is of desired consistency.

Each serving: About 615 calories, 34g protein, 86g carbohydrate, 15g total fat (3g saturated), 44mg cholesterol, 1095mg sodium

SMOKED TURKEY, SPINACH, AND GARBANZO-BEAN SALAD

Prep: 25 minutes   *Makes* 4 main-dish servings

¼ cup fresh lemon juice

3 tablespoons olive oil

½ teaspoon sugar

½ teaspoon ground cumin

¼ teaspoon coarsely ground black pepper

1 small garlic clove, minced

3 medium nectarines, pitted and cut into ¼-inch wedges

1 can (15 to 19 ounces) garbanzo beans, rinsed and drained

½ pound sliced smoked turkey, cut into 2" by ½" strips

1 bunch (10 to 12 ounces) spinach, tough stems removed and leaves torn into 2-inch pieces

Prepare vinaigrette: In large salad bowl, with wire whisk or fork, mix lemon juice, olive oil, sugar, cumin, pepper, and garlic until blended. Add nectarines, garbanzo beans, turkey, and spinach to vinaigrette in bowl; toss to mix well.

Each serving: About 330 calories, 20g protein, 35g carbohydrate, 14g total fat (2g saturated), 26mg cholesterol, 920mg sodium

WARM CHICKEN, SPINACH, AND FETA SALAD

Prep: 20 minutes   *Cook:* 20 minutes
Makes 4 main-dish servings

5 tablespoons olive or vegetable oil

1 medium red pepper, cut into ¼-inch-wide strips

1 medium yellow pepper, cut into ¼-inch-wide strips

1½ pounds skinless, boneless chicken-breast halves, cut crosswise into 1-inch-wide strips

Salt

3 tablespoons white wine vinegar

1 teaspoon sugar

½ teaspoon coarsely ground black pepper

1 bunch (10 to 12 ounces) spinach, tough stems removed

4 ounces feta cheese (1 cup)

◆ In 12-inch skillet, heat 3 tablespoons oil over medium-high heat; add pepper strips and cook, stirring frequently, about 10 minutes, until tender and lightly browned. With slotted spoon, transfer pepper strips to large serving bowl.

◆ To oil remaining in skillet, add chicken strips and ½ teaspoon salt and cook, stirring frequently, about 10 minutes, until chicken is lightly browned and loses its pink color throughout. With slotted spoon, transfer chicken to bowl with peppers.

◆ Prepare dressing: Remove skillet from heat. To drippings remaining in skillet, add white wine vinegar, sugar, remaining 2 tablespoons oil, black pepper, and ¼ teaspoon salt; stir until brown bits are loosened.

◆ Add vinegar mixture and spinach to bowl with chicken; toss gently to mix. Finely crumble feta onto salad.

Each serving: About 460 calories, 45g protein, 10g carbohydrate, 27g total fat (8g saturated), 147mg cholesterol, 825mg sodium

MAIN-DISH FISH SALADS

Salmon and tuna make elegant salads, whether warm or chilled. Tuna grilled with fragrant thyme is redolent of the Mediterranean, and canned tuna with chunky vegetables comes straight from Tuscany. Salmon with asparagus simply celebrates spring, in a fresh, appealing way.

SALMON AND ASPARAGUS SALAD

◆◆◆◆◆◆◆◆◆◆◆◆◆

Prep: 30 minutes
Cook: 30 minutes
Makes 4 main-dish servings

⅓ cup fresh lemon juice

1 teaspoon grated lemon peel

2 tablespoons capers, drained and chopped

2 tablespoons Dijon mustard with seeds

2 tablespoons chopped fresh dill

1 teaspoon sugar

½ teaspoon salt

¼ teaspoon coarsely ground black pepper

⅓ cup olive oil

1 piece salmon fillet (1 pound), skin and small bones removed, if any

1 large lemon, sliced

1 teaspoon whole black peppercorns

1 pound small potatoes, unpeeled

1 pound asparagus, tough ends removed, cut into 2-inch pieces

1 medium head green leaf lettuce, torn into bite-size pieces

2 large hard-cooked eggs, each cut into quarters

1 Prepare lemon-caper dressing: In small bowl, combine first 8 ingredients. With wire whisk, slowly beat in olive oil until mixture thickens slightly. Set aside.

2 In 10-inch skillet, heat *1 inch water* to boiling over high heat. Add salmon and next 2 ingredients; heat to boiling. Reduce heat to low. Cover; simmer 8 minutes, or until opaque.

3 Drain cooked salmon; chill. Meanwhile, in 3-quart saucepan, heat potatoes and enough *water* to cover to boiling over high heat. Reduce heat to low; cover and simmer 15 to 20 minutes, until potatoes are fork-tender. Drain potatoes thoroughly; cut each in half, or into quarters if large. While potatoes are still warm, in medium bowl, toss with ¼ cup dressing.

4 In 2-quart saucepan, heat asparagus and *1 inch water* to boiling over high heat. Reduce heat to low; simmer, uncovered, 5 minutes, or until tender-crisp. Drain and chill briefly.

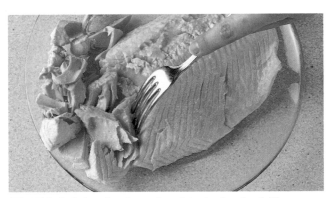

5 With fork, break salmon into 1-inch chunks. Add asparagus to potatoes in bowl; toss with ¼ cup dressing. Divide lettuce among 4 plates; arrange potato mixture, eggs, and salmon on lettuce. Drizzle with remaining dressing.

EACH SERVING: ABOUT 470 CALORIES, 31g PROTEIN, 32g CARBOHYDRATE, 25g TOTAL FAT (4g SATURATED), 164mg CHOLESTEROL, 750mg SODIUM

FRESH TUNA NIÇOISE

Prep: 25 minutes   Broil: 8 to 10 minutes
Makes 4 main-dish servings

4 medium plum tomatoes, peeled (see page 314), seeded, and diced	½ teaspoon coarsely ground black pepper
6 Kalamata olives, pitted and coarsely chopped	2 tablespoons olive oil
3 anchovy fillets, chopped	4 tuna steaks, 1 inch thick (about 6 ounces each)
2 tablespoons capers, drained	2 tablespoons cider vinegar
2 tablespoons chopped fresh parsley	¼ teaspoon salt
1 teaspoon dried thyme	1 small head frisée or 1 head chicory (inner leaves)
	1 bunch watercress

◆ Preheat broiler. In medium bowl, mix first 5 ingredients; set aside. In cup, mix thyme, pepper, and 1 tablespoon oil. Use to rub over tuna. Grease rack in broiling pan; place tuna on rack. Broil tuna at closest position to heat source, turning once, 8 to 10 minutes, until pale pink in center when cut with knife for medium.

◆ Meanwhile, in large bowl, with wire whisk or fork, mix vinegar, remaining 1 tablespoon oil, and salt. Add frisée and watercress; toss well. Arrange salad on 4 plates; place tuna on top. Spoon tomato mixture over tuna.

Each serving: About 400 calories, 45g protein, 16g carbohydrate, 18g total fat (4g saturated), 67mg cholesterol, 700mg sodium

WARM SALMON SALAD

Prep: 30 minutes   Cook: 8 minutes
Makes 4 main-dish servings

1 piece salmon fillet (1 pound), skin and small bones removed, if any	2 tablespoons balsamic vinegar
1 bunch green onions (about 4 ounces)	2 teaspoons brown sugar
4 large navel oranges	1 tablespoon olive oil
2 tablespoons light soy sauce	2 small heads Boston lettuce, torn
	2 small plum tomatoes, diced

◆ With knife held in slanting position, almost parallel to cutting surface, slice salmon crosswise into ¼-inch-thick slices. Cut green onions into 1-inch pieces.

◆ Cut peel and white pith from 3 oranges; discard. Holding 1 orange at a time over strainer set over 2-cup measuring cup, cut sections from oranges between membranes; drop sections into strainer and set aside. Squeeze juice from membranes into measuring cup. Squeeze juice from remaining orange to equal ¾ cup juice in all. Stir in soy sauce, vinegar, and sugar.

◆ In nonstick 12-inch skillet, heat olive oil over medium-high heat. Add salmon slices in batches; cook 1 to 2 minutes, until golden, carefully turning once. Transfer to plate. In drippings in skillet, cook green onions, stirring often, until golden; stir in juice mixture. Heat to boiling; boil 1 minute. To serve, arrange lettuce, orange sections, and salmon on 4 plates. Spoon green-onion mixture over salmon; sprinkle with diced tomatoes.

Each serving: About 275 calories, 25g protein, 28g carbohydrate, 8g total fat (1g saturated), 58mg cholesterol, 395mg sodium

TUSCAN TUNA AND BEAN SALAD

Prep: 25 minutes plus cooling   Cook: 10 minutes
Makes 4 main-dish servings

2 tablespoons plus ¼ cup olive oil	1 can (12 ounces) solid white tuna in water, drained and broken into large pieces
½ (8-ounce) long loaf Italian bread, cut into 1-inch cubes	1 can (15 to 19 ounces) white kidney beans (cannellini), rinsed and drained
2 large garlic cloves, crushed with side of knife	2 medium tomatoes, each cut into 8 wedges
8 ounces green beans, ends trimmed	1 head green leaf lettuce, torn
¼ cup red wine vinegar	½ small head chicory, torn
2 tablespoons capers, drained and chopped	1 small red onion, cut in half and thinly sliced
1 teaspoon sugar	
1 teaspoon Dijon mustard	
¼ teaspoon coarsely ground black pepper	

◆ Prepare croutons: In nonstick 12-inch skillet, heat 2 tablespoons olive oil over medium heat. Add bread cubes and garlic and cook, stirring occasionally, until bread is lightly browned. Remove skillet from heat; discard garlic.

◆ In 2-quart saucepan, in *1 inch boiling water*, heat green beans to boiling over high heat. Reduce heat to low; simmer, uncovered, 5 to 10 minutes, until beans are tender-crisp. Drain and rinse with cold running water to cool slightly. Prepare vinaigrette: In large bowl, with fork or wire whisk, mix vinegar, capers, sugar, mustard, pepper and remaining ¼ cup olive oil. Add remaining ingredients, green beans, and croutons; toss to serve.

Each serving: About 525 calories, 34g protein, 45g carbohydrate, 24g total fat (4g saturated), 35mg cholesterol, 1125mg sodium

Main-dish seafood salads

Salads made from crab, shrimp, and lobster create an instantly festive mood. Feel free to substitute other shellfish; for example, you can replace the crabmeat with cooked shrimp or surimi (imitation crabmeat).

Layered crab salad

Prep: 30 minutes   Cook: 5 minutes
Makes 4 main-dish servings

1 cup reduced-sodium chicken broth
⅔ cup couscous (Moroccan pasta)
1 medium tomato
1 small cucumber
2 tablespoons vegetable oil
1 small onion, minced
2 tablespoons dry white wine
1 container (16 ounces) lump crabmeat, picked over
1 tablespoon chopped fresh parsley

2 tablespoons mayonnaise
⅛ teaspoon ground black pepper
1 medium avocado, halved lengthwise, seeded, peeled, and thinly sliced
8 ounces mixed baby salad greens or mixed salad greens (about 6 cups loosely packed)
2 teaspoons white wine vinegar
¼ teaspoon salt

1 In 1-quart saucepan, heat broth to boiling over high heat. Stir in couscous; cover and remove from heat. Let stand 5 minutes. Uncover; fluff couscous with fork. Cool slightly.

3 In another bowl, mix crabmeat, onion mixture, parsley, mayonnaise, and pepper. Place can on plate; spoon in one-fourth of couscous mixture. Gently press with back of spoon.

VARIATION: LAYERED CRAB SALAD PLATTER

Prepare Layered Crab Salad as above, but to assemble salad, line a 6-cup soufflé dish or bowl with plastic wrap. Fill evenly with crab mixture and press down firmly with spoon. Arrange avocado slices on top. Spoon in couscous and spread over avocado layer; press down firmly. Carefully invert salad onto platter. Dress greens as in step 5 and arrange around crab salad.

2 Remove both ends from an empty food can (about 3 inches in diameter and 3 inches tall) to make a hollow cylinder. Wash and dry can thoroughly. Seed and dice tomato and cucumber. In bowl, combine couscous, tomato, and cucumber; set aside. In small skillet, heat 1 tablespoon oil over medium-high heat; add onion and cook, stirring occasionally, until very lightly browned. Stir in wine.

4 Top couscous with one-fourth of avocado slices, then one-fourth of crab mixture, pressing with spoon after each layer. While pressing with back of spoon, slowly lift off can. Repeat to make 3 more salads.

5 In bowl, toss greens with vinegar, remaining 1 tablespoon oil, and salt. Arrange greens around crab salads on plates.

EACH SERVING: ABOUT 450 CALORIES, 27g PROTEIN, 36g CARBOHYDRATE, 22g TOTAL FAT (4g SATURATED), 76mg CHOLESTEROL, 545mg SODIUM

SHRIMP AND WATERCRESS SALAD

Prep: 45 minutes   Cook: 1 to 2 minutes
Makes 4 main-dish servings

1 pound large shrimp, shelled
  and deveined (see page 90)
Salt
1 medium jicama (about
  1¼ pounds), peeled and cut
  into 1½" by ¼" sticks
2 bunches (about 4 ounces
  each) watercress, tough
  stems removed

2 medium navel oranges
1 large lime
1 cup loosely packed fresh
  cilantro leaves
¼ cup mayonnaise
1 teaspoon sugar
¼ teaspoon ground red
  pepper (cayenne)
½ cup plain low-fat yogurt

◆ Cut each shrimp horizontally in half; rinse with cold running water. In 3-quart saucepan, heat *3 inches water* to boiling over high heat. Add shrimp and 1 teaspoon salt; heat to boiling. Cook 1 minute, or until shrimp turn opaque throughout. Drain; rinse. Drain again and refrigerate.

◆ In large salad bowl, combine jicama and watercress. Cut peel and white pith from oranges; discard. Cut out sections between membranes and add (without juice) to salad bowl.

◆ Prepare yogurt dressing: Grate 1 teaspoon peel and squeeze 2 tablespoons juice from lime. In food processor with knife blade attached or in blender at medium speed, process lime peel, lime juice, cilantro, mayonnaise, sugar, ground red pepper, and ½ teaspoon salt 30 seconds, until blended. Add yogurt, pulsing just until blended. Just before serving, add shrimp to bowl with jicama mixture; add dressing and toss to combine.

Each serving: About 320 calories, 24g protein, 29g carbohydrate, 13g total fat (2g saturated), 185mg cholesterol, 720mg sodium

ITALIAN SEAFOOD SALAD

Prep: 50 minutes plus chilling   Cook: 20 minutes
Makes 8 main-dish servings

1 pound sea scallops
2 pounds cleaned squid
2 pounds large shrimp,
  shelled and deveined (see
  page 90)
1 small garlic clove, minced
⅔ cup fresh lemon juice
⅓ cup olive oil

2 tablespoons Dijon mustard
½ teaspoon coarsely ground
  black pepper
1 cup Kalamata olives, pitted
  and coarsely chopped
4 large celery stalks, sliced
¼ cup loosely packed fresh
  parsley leaves

◆ Rinse scallops with cold running water to remove sand from crevices. Pull tough crescent-shaped muscle from side of each scallop. Rinse squid; slice bodies crosswise into ¾-inch-thick rings. Cut tentacles into several pieces if large. In 5-quart saucepot, heat *2½ inches water* to boiling over high heat. Add shrimp; return to boiling. Reduce heat to

medium; cook 1 to 2 minutes, just until shrimp turn opaque throughout. With slotted spoon, transfer shrimp to colander to drain; place in large bowl.

◆ To boiling water in saucepot, add scallops; heat to boiling. Reduce heat to medium; cook 2 to 3 minutes, until scallops turn opaque throughout. With slotted spoon, transfer to colander to drain; add to bowl with shrimp. To boiling water in saucepot, add squid; heat to boiling. Squid should be tender and turn opaque throughout when water returns to boiling. If not, cook 30 seconds to 1 minute longer. Drain well in colander; add to bowl with shrimp and scallops.

◆ Prepare dressing: In small bowl, with wire whisk or fork, mix garlic and next 4 ingredients. To bowl with seafood, add dressing, olives, celery, and parsley; toss to combine. Cover and refrigerate at least 3 hours to blend flavors.

Each serving: About 390 calories, 47g protein, 10g carbohydrate, 17g total fat (2g saturated), 463mg cholesterol, 795mg sodium

LOBSTER AND MANGO SALAD

Prep: 30 minutes   Cook: 12 minutes
Makes 4 main-dish servings

2 live lobsters (1¼ to
  1½ pounds each) or
½ pound cooked lobster
  meat
1 medium cucumber, peeled,
  seeded, and diced
Salt
1 medium navel orange
2 tablespoons fresh lemon
  juice

⅛ teaspoon ground black
  pepper
2 tablespoons olive oil
1 mango, peeled and diced
  (see page 339)
1 tablespoon chopped fresh
  mint
4 ounces mixed baby salad
  greens (about 3 cups loosely
  packed)

◆ Cook live lobsters, if using, and remove meat from shells (see page 92). Chop lobster meat coarsely; set aside. In small bowl, toss cucumber with ¼ teaspoon salt. Transfer to sieve and set over bowl to drain.

◆ Prepare dressing: With vegetable peeler, remove several strips of peel from orange; cut 1 tablespoon very fine strips. Squeeze 2 tablespoons juice from orange. In small bowl, with wire whisk or fork, mix orange and lemon juice, pepper, and ½ teaspoon salt; slowly whisk in olive oil. Stir in peel.

◆ In small bowl, combine 2 tablespoons dressing with lobster. Pat cucumber dry; in another bowl, combine with mango, mint, and 2 tablespoons dressing. Arrange greens on 4 plates; spoon mango mixture in center. Arrange lobster on top. Drizzle remaining dressing over greens.

Each serving: About 185 calories, 13g protein, 18g carbohydrate, 7g total fat (1g saturated), 41mg cholesterol, 620mg sodium

SALAD DRESSINGS

Fast, fresh, and delicious, these salad dressings provide some intriguing possibilities. From a creamy buttermilk and chive dressing to a classic vinaigrette flavored with Dijon mustard and shallots, there's something here to suit every salad. Each of these dressings can be prepared a day or two in advance and refrigerated in a jar with a tight-fitting lid. If made ahead, bring the dressing to room temperature for fullest flavor, and shake the jar well before tossing the dressing with salad greens.

MUSTARD-SHALLOT VINAIGRETTE

Prep: 10 minutes   **Makes** *about ¾ cup*

6 tablespoons olive oil
⅓ cup red wine vinegar
4 teaspoons Dijon mustard
1 tablespoon minced shallot
½ teaspoon salt
½ teaspoon coarsely ground black pepper
½ teaspoon sugar

In small bowl, with wire whisk or fork, mix all ingredients.

Each tablespoon: About 65 calories, 0g protein, 1g carbohydrate, 7g total fat (1g saturated), 0mg cholesterol, 125mg sodium

JAPANESE MISO VINAIGRETTE

Prep: 10 minutes   **Makes** *about 1 cup*

2 tablespoons miso (fermented soybean paste, see page 58)
½ cup rice vinegar
¼ cup olive oil
1 tablespoon minced, peeled fresh ginger
1 tablespoon sugar

In small bowl, stir miso into vinegar until smooth. Add to blender with remaining ingredients; blend until smooth.

Each tablespoon: About 35 calories, 0g protein, 1g carbohydrate, 4g total fat (0g saturated), 0mg cholesterol, 80mg sodium

---

VINAIGRETTE VARIATIONS

Blue-cheese vinaigrette Prepare Mustard-Shallot Vinaigrette, adding 2 ounces blue cheese, crumbled (½ cup), to ingredients. Makes about 1 cup.

Each tablespoon: About 60 calories, 1g protein, 1g carbohydrate, 6g total fat (1g saturated), 3mg cholesterol, 140mg sodium

Balsamic vinaigrette Prepare Mustard-Shallot Vinaigrette, using balsamic vinegar instead of red-wine vinegar. Makes about ¾ cup.

Each tablespoon: About 70 calories, 0g protein, 2g carbohydrate, 7g total fat (1g saturated), 0mg cholesterol, 125mg sodium

---

HERB VINEGARS

Wash several 3- to 4-cup capacity bottles with corks (or jars with clamp-top lids) in hot soapy water. To sterilize, put bottles in large pot (and corks in small pan) with water to cover; heat to boiling over high heat. Boil 15 minutes; drain.

Place 3 or 4 sprigs of desired herbs (washed and dried) and other ingredients (see below) in each bottle; you may need a skewer to push them in. For each bottle, in nonreactive saucepan, heat vinegar (3 to 4 cups, depending on bottle size) to boiling. Pour through funnel into bottle. Cork; let stand in cool, dark place about 2 weeks (it is not necessary to refrigerate). Strain through fine sieve into measuring cup or pitcher. Discard herbs and fruits, return vinegar to bottle, and add sprigs of fresh herbs, if you like. Store at room temperature up to 3 months. If the cork pops, discard the vinegar.

Chive-garlic Rice vinegar, 2 to 3 peeled garlic cloves, chives

Dill-peppercorn Cider vinegar, 1 tablespoon whole black peppercorns, dill sprigs

Sage-rosemary Red wine vinegar, sage and rosemary sprigs

Basil-orange White wine vinegar, strips of peel of 1 orange, basil sprigs

Raspberry-mint (below left) White wine vinegar, 1½ cups fresh raspberries, mint sprigs

Chile-cilantro (below center) Distilled white vinegar, 1 to 4 fresh chiles, cilantro sprigs

Lemon-thyme (far right) White wine vinegar, strips of peel of 1 lemon, thyme sprigs

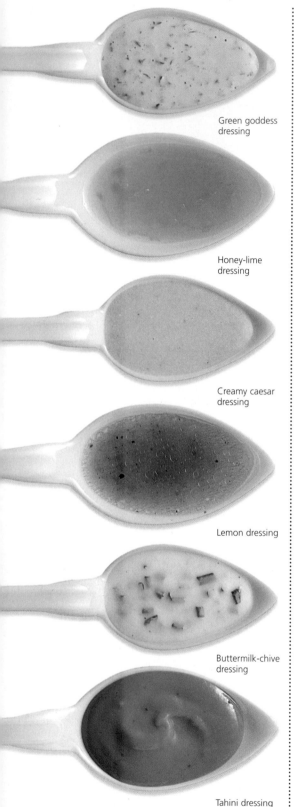

Green goddess
dressing

Honey-lime
dressing

Creamy caesar
dressing

Lemon dressing

Buttermilk-chive
dressing

Tahini dressing

GREEN GODDESS DRESSING

Prep: 10 minutes   Makes about ¾ cup

½ cup mayonnaise
½ cup loosely packed fresh parsley leaves
¼ cup sour cream
1 tablespoon red wine vinegar
1 teaspoon anchovy paste
¼ teaspoon ground black pepper

In blender, blend all ingredients until smooth, scraping sides as necessary.

Each tablespoon: About 80 calories, 1g protein, 1g carbohydrate, 9g total fat (2g saturated), 8mg cholesterol, 125mg sodium

HONEY-LIME DRESSING

Prep: 5 minutes   Makes about ½ cup

⅓ cup fresh lime juice
4 teaspoons honey
1 tablespoon rice vinegar
⅛ teaspoon salt

In small bowl, with wire whisk or fork, mix all ingredients.

Each tablespoon: About 15 calories, 0g protein, 4g carbohydrate, 0g total fat, 0mg cholesterol, 35mg sodium

BUTTERMILK-CHIVE DRESSING

Prep: 5 minutes   Makes about ¾ cup

½ cup buttermilk
2 tablespoons distilled white vinegar
2 tablespoons chopped fresh chives
1 tablespoon low-fat mayonnaise dressing
¼ teaspoon salt
¼ teaspoon coarsely ground black pepper

In small bowl, with wire whisk or fork, mix all ingredients.

Each tablespoon: About 10 calories, 0g protein, 1g carbohydrate, 0g total fat, 1mg cholesterol, 55mg sodium

LEMON DRESSING

Prep: 5 minutes   Makes about ¾ cup

¼ cup fresh lemon juice
½ teaspoon salt
¼ teaspoon ground black pepper
½ cup olive oil

In bowl, with wire whisk or fork, mix lemon juice, salt, and pepper. In thin, steady stream, gradually whisk in oil.

Each tablespoon: About 80 calories, 0g protein, 1g carbohydrate, 9g total fat (1g saturated), 0mg cholesterol, 90mg sodium

CREAMY CAESAR DRESSING

Prep: 10 minutes   Makes about 1¼ cups

⅓ cup olive oil
⅓ cup freshly grated Parmesan cheese
¼ cup fresh lemon juice
¼ cup mayonnaise
1 teaspoon anchovy paste
½ teaspoon coarsely ground pepper
1 small garlic clove, minced

In small bowl, with wire whisk or fork, mix all ingredients until smooth.

Each tablespoon: About 60 calories, 1g protein, 0g carbohydrate, 6g total fat (1g saturated), 3mg cholesterol, 90mg sodium

TAHINI DRESSING

Prep: 10 minutes   Makes about ¾ cup

⅓ cup tahini (sesame seed paste)
2 tablespoons fresh lemon juice
4 teaspoons soy sauce
1 tablespoon honey (optional)
½ teaspoon ground black pepper
½ small garlic clove, minced

In small bowl, with wire whisk or fork, mix all ingredients until smooth.

Each tablespoon: About 40 calories, 1g protein, 2g carbohydrate, 3g total fat (0g saturated), 0mg cholesterol, 115mg sodium

PASTA KNOW-HOW

Delicious, healthy, and easy to prepare, pasta is the perfect food for the way we eat today – and there have never been more enticing noodles to choose from. So whether you're cooking fresh fettuccine, dried penne, or an Asian pasta, here's how to get great results every time.

BUYING AND STORING

For the best taste and texture, buy dried pasta made from durum wheat or semolina flour (semolina is more coarsely ground durum wheat). Good-quality pasta will have a clear yellow color and feel hard and smooth. Stored in a cool, dry, dark place, dried pasta will keep up to 1 year (whole-wheat pasta up to 6 months). Store commercially made fresh pasta in the refrigerator according to package directions – or up to 1 week – or freeze up to 1 month.

HOMEMADE PASTA

It's easy to make your own fresh pasta. Although the dough can be rolled out with a rolling pin, a pasta machine makes it easy. A machine thins the dough gradually – through a series of thickness settings controlled by a knob – which results in an even, chewy texture. Support longer strips of dough as they come through the machine so they won't fold and stick together. Cut unwieldy lengths into more manageable pieces. You can refrigerate homemade pasta, tightly covered, up to 3 days, or freeze up to 1 month. Do not thaw before cooking.

1 With machine on widest setting, pass through portion of dough. Fold dough into thirds and roll again. Repeat folding and rolling 8 to 10 times, until dough is smooth and elastic.

2 Continue rolling dough (unfolded), reducing thickness setting by 1 notch each time, until it reaches the desired thickness; pass dough through cutting blades. Cut pasta into lengths.

THE SECRETS OF PERFECT PASTA

Start with plenty of water Use at least 4 quarts of water for every pound of pasta. Add the pasta – and salt – after the water comes to a rapid boil. (If the water stops boiling when you add the pasta, cover pot just until boil returns.)

Stir frequently This ensures even cooking and prevents strands from clumping or sticking to the bottom of the pot.

Check early (and often) for doneness Cooking times on packages are guides, not rules; start checking doneness early.

Test the texture Perfectly cooked pasta should feel firm to the bite. This texture is described in Italian as *al dente*, or "to the tooth." At this stage, the pasta will have no raw flour taste, but will reveal a tiny chalky-white center. (Residual heat will continue to cook pasta as it's drained and tossed, so gauge cooking time accordingly.)

Avoid a soggy sauce Drain cooked pasta thoroughly by shaking excess moisture through the colander. Unless it's indicated in a recipe, never rinse pasta. (Except for lasagna, pasta is rinsed only when it is to be used in a cold salad.)

Serve it hot Remember that pasta will wait for no one! The noodles tend to absorb liquid (creamy sauces can practically disappear), and the pasta will cool down quickly. So for best results, call everyone to the table while you're tossing, and serve the pasta in prewarmed bowls.

TO SALT OR NOT TO SALT

Almost all pasta recipes suggest adding salt to the pasta's cooking water – and purists wouldn't have it any other way. However, some people shy away from this step because they're worried about sodium. But in truth, the salt (we recommend 2 teaspoons per pound of pasta) added to the water isn't all absorbed by the noodles – it merely seasons them. When you drain the noodles, you're draining much of the sodium as well (only about 10 percent is absorbed by the pasta). The sodium analyses for all our pasta recipes are based on pasta cooked in salted water. Most important, salting the water results in noodles with a much fuller flavor.

FRESH VS. DRIED

There's no doubt that fresh, tender pasta is a delight to eat. But fresh pasta isn't superior to dried – it's simply different. Fresh noodles (typical of the cooking of northern Italy), are finer-textured and richer because they're made with eggs, and pair best with delicate sauces. By contrast, dried pasta (favored by southern Italian cooks), which is made from flour and water, is more economical, lower in fat, and the best choice for robust, highly flavored sauces.

A MORE NUTRITIOUS NOODLE

Storing pasta in a clear glass or plastic container on an open shelf or counter exposes it to light, which destroys riboflavin, a B vitamin and key nutrient in pasta. Instead, store pasta in an opaque container or in the cupboard. Buy pasta sold in cardboard cartons, which keep out the light.

COOKING LONG PASTA

1 Add pasta all at once to boiling water, pushing ends down as they soften until all strands are immersed. Cover pot until water returns to a boil.

2 To prevent noodles from sticking to the bottom of the pot, stir often. A spaghetti fork grips and separates strands, allowing for easier draining and neater serving.

COMMON PASTA DILEMMAS – SOLVED

How much do I make? Most packages list a 2-ounce serving size, but a more generous main-dish measure is 4 ounces dry pasta (3 ounces fresh) per person. For rich dishes you're apt to use less. The cooked yield depends on the shape: 4 ounces of dried *penne, ziti, corkscrews* = 2½ cups cooked; of *spaghetti, fettuccine, linguine* = 2 cups cooked; of *egg noodles* = 3 cups cooked.

How should I store leftover noodles? Toss them with a small amount of oil and store in a zip-tight plastic bag.

What's the best way to reheat noodles? Microwave them in a microwave-safe container or glass bowl on high for about 2 minutes, or simply place in a colander under hot running water just until warm; toss with hot sauce.

What can I do with leftover noodles? Layer them with sautéed vegetables and tomato sauce in a gratin dish, top with grated Parmesan cheese, and bake; use as an omelet or frittata filling; toss with salad dressing and a variety of crisp, colorful vegetables for a quick lunch.

How can I keep cooked lasagna noodles from sticking together? Rinse cooked noodles under cold running water, then return to saucepot with enough cold water to cover. Drain on a clean kitchen towel before using.

KNOW YOUR PASTA

These days pasta can be purchased in a dizzying array of shapes and sizes; each one has a special texture and its own cooking time. Many shapes have whimsical Italian names that reflect their shape: Ditalini means "thimbles"; penne, "quills"; orecchiette, "little ears"; manicotti, "sleeves"; and linguine, "little tongues." One shape may go by different names in different regions, and one name may refer to several different shapes.

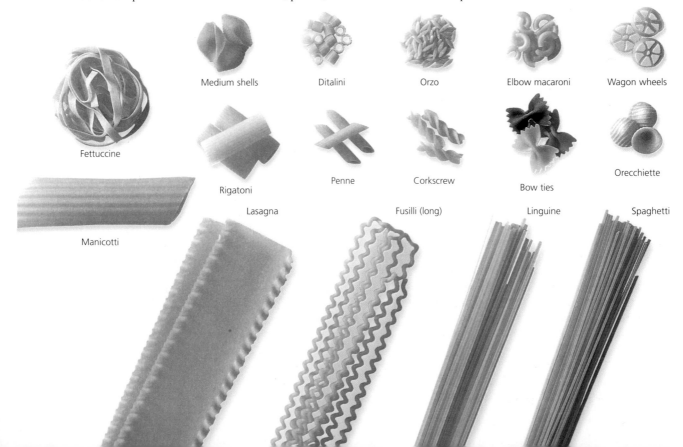

Fettuccine

Medium shells

Ditalini

Orzo

Elbow macaroni

Wagon wheels

Rigatoni

Penne

Corkscrew

Bow ties

Orecchiette

Manicotti

Lasagna

Fusilli (long)

Linguine

Spaghetti

PASTA PARTNERS

Tiny shapes and skinny strands Alphabets, acini di pepe, stars, ditalini, orzo, and vermicelli are excellent in soups, particularly well-seasoned homemade broths.

Long, thin strands Spaghetti or linguine goes well with smooth tomato or seafood sauces. You should use just enough sauce to keep the strands wet and slippery.

Sturdy, hollow, medium-sized shapes Rigatoni, ziti, and similar shapes are good for baked dishes, since their thick walls will hold up to prolonged cooking. Their sturdiness also makes them the perfect match for robust meat sauces and grilled vegetables.

Wide, flat noodles Pastas such as pappardelle, mafalde, and fettuccine are best with simple, rich sauces made with cream, butter, or a selection of cheeses.

Ridged, curved shapes Penne, farfalle, gemelli, fusilli, orecchiette, or small shells are designed to catch chunky sauces that contain chopped vegetables, olives, or chunks of cheese. These also make terrific pasta salads, because they cradle other ingredients and can stand up to lively vinaigrettes or creamy dressings.

Large shapes Manicotti and jumbo shells are strictly for stuffing with vegetables, meat, and/or cheese mixtures.

ALMOST-INSTANT PASTA DISHES

• Mix diced ham, frozen peas (add to the pasta cooking water just before draining pasta to thaw), some chopped fresh rosemary, Parmesan cheese, and olive oil with penne.

• Toss slivered jarred roasted red peppers, quartered oil-packed artichoke hearts, chunks of smoked mozzarella, and a generous amount of chopped flat-leaf parsley with rigatoni; moisten with chicken broth.

• Sauté shrimp or scallops in hot olive oil with some fresh bread crumbs and crushed red pepper; toss with spaghetti.

• Mix corkscrew pasta with chunks of deli-roasted turkey, a handful each of toasted pine nuts and golden raisins, some crushed red pepper, and a little olive oil.

• Toss bow ties with ricotta cheese, chopped toasted pecans, a spoonful of milk, and some grated Parmesan.

• Cook cheese-filled tortellini in chicken broth to cover until almost tender; stir in sliced spinach leaves until wilted. Serve in soup bowls with freshly grated Parmesan cheese.

• Heat garbanzo beans and diced salami in chicken broth; toss with wagon-wheel pasta. Then toss again with olive oil, freshly grated Parmesan cheese, and cracked black pepper.

KNOW YOUR ASIAN PASTA

Unlike most Western pastas, which are made from wheat flour, Asian noodles are made from a variety of flours, including rice and bean or vegetable starches such as yam, soybean, or potato. The versatility of these delicious noodles is limited only by your imagination. They can be served alongside meat and fish dishes, made into salads with tasty Asian-style vinaigrettes and other favorite ingredients (crisp vegetables, fresh herbs, seafood), or added to steaming broth to make a nourishing soup. Thinner noodles can be softened in hot water; others are boiled like spaghetti.

Soba These thin, brownish-gray noodles are made from buckwheat flour and served cold with a dipping sauce or steaming-hot in broth.

Flat rice noodles Made from rice flour, these noodles are typically boiled or stir-fried for salads or soups.

Rice stick noodles These thread-thin sticks can be softened in hot water for soups and salads, or deep-fried, which causes them to puff dramatically into crunchy strands used in salads.

Cellophane noodles When softened, these thin, translucent strands (made from mung bean flour) have a slippery texture and glassy look; they're used in stir-fries, soups, and salads.

Chinese-style egg noodles Made from wheat flour, these tender strands are similiar in texture and flavor to Western egg noodles. Available fresh or dried in a variety of widths, they're excellent added to soups, topped with meat, or eaten cold with sesame dressing.

Udon noodles These long, thick, chewy Japanese noodles made from wheat flour can be flat or round; they're usually eaten in soup.

Soba

Udon noodles

Chinese-style egg noodles

Rice stick noodles

Flat rice noodles

Cellophane noodles

TOMATO PASTA SAUCES

With a few choice ingredients or a clever cooking technique, a simple tomato sauce becomes the base for a sensational meal. We've roasted plum tomatoes and garlic, for example, to create a sauce of incredible depth and sweetness. There's also a fresh tomato sauce with chunks of mozzarella; a rich tomato-cream sauce; and a marinara with a host of tasty variations.

ROASTED TOMATO SAUCE

Prep: 20 minutes plus cooling   Roast: 50 to 60 minutes
Makes 4 main-dish servings

3 pounds medium-size ripe
  plum tomatoes
6 medium garlic cloves,
  unpeeled
2 tablespoons olive oil
¾ teaspoon salt

¼ teaspoon coarsely ground
  black pepper
1 package (16 ounces) penne
  or corkscrew pasta, cooked
Grated Romano cheese
  (optional)

1 Preheat oven to 450°F. Cut each plum tomato lengthwise in half. In 15½" by 10½" jelly-roll pan, toss plum tomatoes and garlic cloves with 1 tablespoon olive oil. Roast tomatoes and garlic 50 to 60 minutes, until tomatoes are well browned and garlic cloves are soft.

2 Let tomatoes and garlic cool 20 minutes in pan. When tomatoes and garlic are cool, over medium bowl, carefully peel tomatoes. Squeeze garlic cloves from skins into bowl.

3 With spoon, break up peeled tomatoes and garlic. Stir in salt, pepper, and remaining 1 tablespoon olive oil until blended. To serve, toss cooked pasta with sauce. Sprinkle with grated Romano cheese, if you like.

GARLIC

• Choose plump, rock-hard heads of garlic with dry, papery skins (avoid soft or moist heads, as well as those that are refrigerated at the grocery store).

• Store garlic in an open container in a cool, dry place up to 2 months. If any clove begins to sprout, cut it in half and simply cut out the bitter-tasting green core.

• For easy peeling, crush the clove with the flat side of a chef's knife to loosen the skin.

• When sautéing garlic, stir it often to prevent it from overbrowning and taking on a bitter taste.

• Raw, garlic is pungent (and its flavor in a dish builds if it sits); roasting or blanching sweetens and mellows it.

EACH SERVING: ABOUT 560 CALORIES, 18g PROTEIN, 102g CARBOHYDRATE, 10g TOTAL FAT (1g SATURATED), 0mg CHOLESTEROL, 545mg SODIUM

SUMMER TOMATO SAUCE WITH MOZZARELLA

Prep: 15 minutes plus standing   Makes 4 main-dish servings

2¼ pounds ripe tomatoes, cut into ½-inch pieces
8 ounces fresh mozzarella cheese, cut into ½-inch pieces
1 cup packed fresh basil leaves
1 tablespoon olive oil
1 tablespoon red wine vinegar
1 teaspoon salt
¼ teaspoon coarsely ground black pepper
1 package (16 ounces) penne or ziti, cooked

In medium bowl, combine tomatoes with their juice and remaining ingredients except pasta, stirring gently to mix well. Allow sauce to stand 15 minutes to develop flavor. To serve, toss cooked pasta with sauce.

Each serving: 665 calories, 28g protein, 99g carbohydrate, 18g total fat (8g saturated), 44mg cholesterol, 885mg sodium

MARINARA SAUCE

Prep: 10 minutes   Cook: 35 minutes
Makes 4 cups sauce or 4 main-dish servings

2 tablespoons olive oil
1 small onion, chopped
1 garlic clove, minced
1 can (29 to 35 ounces) plum tomatoes in juice
1 can (6 ounces) tomato paste
2 tablespoons chopped fresh basil or parsley (optional)
1 package (16 ounces) spaghetti or rigatoni, cooked

In 3-quart saucepan, heat oil over medium heat; add onion and garlic and cook until tender. Stir in tomatoes with their juice, tomato paste, and basil, if using; heat to boiling over high heat, breaking up tomatoes with back of spoon. Reduce heat to low. Partially cover pan; simmer, stirring occasionally, 20 minutes. To serve, toss cooked pasta with sauce, or use in your favorite recipe.

Each serving: About 570 calories, 18g protein, 104g carbohydrate, 9g total fat (1g saturated), 0mg cholesterol, 1130mg sodium

---

MARINARA PLUS

◆◆◆◆◆◆◆◆◆◆◆◆◆◆◆◆◆◆◆◆◆◆◆◆◆◆◆◆

Our Marinara Sauce is so versatile, it's worth doubling the recipe (use a 5-quart Dutch oven, and simmer 30 instead of 20 minutes) to freeze half. Try the following add-ins:

• 8 ounces mushrooms, sliced and sautéed

• 8 ounces Italian-sausage links (casings removed), crumbled, and cooked

• 2 green or red peppers, sliced and sautéed

CREAMY TOMATO SAUCE WITH PEAS

Prep: 10 minutes   Cook: 10 minutes
Makes 4 main-dish servings

1 tablespoon olive oil
1 medium onion, chopped
2 cans (14½ ounces each) diced tomatoes
1 package (10 ounces) frozen peas, thawed
¼ cup packed fresh basil leaves, chopped
½ cup heavy or whipping cream
½ teaspoon salt
¼ teaspoon crushed red pepper
1 package (16 ounces) medium shell or corkscrew pasta, cooked

◆ In 12-inch nonstick skillet, heat oil over medium heat; add onion and cook until tender.

◆ Add tomatoes with their juice and remaining ingredients except pasta; heat through, stirring constantly. To serve, toss cooked pasta with sauce.

Each serving: 665 calories, 21g protein, 108g carbohydrate, 17g total fat (8g saturated), 41mg cholesterol, 790mg sodium

TOMATO-SAGE SAUCE

Prep: 15 minutes   Cook: 1 hour
Makes 6 main-dish servings

2 tablespoons olive oil
1 small onion, finely chopped
3 pounds medium-size ripe plum tomatoes, peeled (see page 314) and chopped
½ cup chicken broth
⅓ cup dry white wine
2 tablespoons butter
1 tablespoon chopped fresh sage
1 teaspoon salt
1½ pounds spaghetti or cavatelli, cooked

◆ In 10-inch skillet, heat olive oil over medium-low heat. Add onion and cook 15 to 20 minutes, until very tender and slightly golden.

◆ Stir in tomatoes with their juice, chicken broth, and white wine; heat to boiling over high heat.

◆ Reduce heat to low; cover and simmer 30 minutes, stirring occasionally, and pressing on tomatoes with back of slotted spoon to crush.

◆ Uncover skillet and simmer, stirring occasionally, 25 minutes longer, or until sauce has reduced and thickened slightly. Add butter, chopped fresh sage, and salt and stir until butter melts. To serve, toss cooked pasta with tomato sauce.

Each serving: 420 calories, 12g protein, 69g carbohydrate, 11g total fat (3g saturated), 12mg cholesterol, 580mg sodium

OLIVE OIL PASTA SAUCES

A bottle of good olive oil comes in handy for creating a variety of easy pasta sauces. By adding a few flavorful ingredients such as broccoli rabe, anchovies, dried tomatoes, or Kalamata olives, you can whip up a splendid sauce in next to no time. Or, try our classic Italian pesto, a no-cook sauce that's packed with fresh basil taste. Because these sauces are simple, it's best to use good-quality ingredients so the pure flavors shine through.

LINGUINE WITH BROCCOLI RABE AND ANCHOVIES

◆◆◆◆◆◆◆◆◆◆◆◆◆

Prep: 5 minutes
Cook: 15 minutes
Makes 4 main-dish servings

1 package (16 ounces) linguine or spaghetti

2 bunches broccoli rabe (about 1 pound each)

2 teaspoons salt

3 tablespoons olive oil

3 garlic cloves, crushed with side of knife

1 can (2 ounces) anchovy fillets, undrained

¼ teaspoon crushed red pepper

½ cup golden raisins

1 Prepare linguine as label directs. Drain, reserving ¼ cup pasta cooking water. Return linguine to saucepot; keep warm. Meanwhile, trim ends of stems from broccoli rabe. In 5-quart Dutch oven, heat *4 quarts water* to boiling over high heat. Add broccoli rabe and salt; heat to boiling. Boil 2 minutes; drain. Wipe Dutch oven dry.

2 In same Dutch oven, heat oil over medium heat. Add garlic; cook until golden. Add anchovies with their oil and red pepper; cook, stirring, just until anchovies begin to dissolve.

3 Add broccoli rabe and raisins to anchovy mixture in Dutch oven; cook, stirring, until broccoli rabe is heated through and well coated with oil.

OLIVE OIL

The fragrant oil pressed from tree-ripened olives is prized around the world for cooking and salads. Olive oil is classified in categories that indicate color and taste. Extra-virgin, with a greenish hue, fruity aroma and taste, and the lowest acidity, is the finest. It is cold-pressed, a process that relies only on pressure and yields the most flavor. Virgin olive oil is slightly more acidic, and regular olive oil contains blends of refined and virgin oils. Light olive oil isn't low-fat, but instead has been filtered for a neutral aroma and taste. Stored in a cool, dark place, olive oil will last up to 6 months.

4 Add linguine and reserved pasta cooking water to broccoli rabe mixture in Dutch oven; toss well to combine.

EACH SERVING: ABOUT 660 CALORIES, 27g PROTEIN, 111g CARBOHYDRATE, 14g TOTAL FAT (2g SATURATED), 12mg CHOLESTEROL, 1075mg SODIUM

PESTO

Prep: 10 minutes   Makes 4 main-dish servings

2 cups loosely packed fresh
  basil leaves
¼ cup olive oil
¼ cup freshly grated
  Parmesan cheese
2 tablespoons pine nuts
  (pignoli) or chopped walnuts

½ teaspoon salt
1 package (16 ounces) long
  fusilli or linguine, cooked
Fresh basil leaves for garnish

In food processor with knife blade attached or in blender at medium speed, process basil, olive oil, Parmesan cheese, pine nuts, and salt with *¼ cup water* until smooth. To serve, toss cooked pasta with pesto; garnish.

Each serving: About 590 calories, 18g protein, 86g carbohydrate, 19g total fat (4g saturated), 5mg cholesterol, 500mg sodium

OIL AND GARLIC SAUCE

Prep: 10 minutes   Cook: 10 minutes
Makes 4 main-dish servings

¼ cup olive oil
1 large garlic clove, minced
2 tablespoons minced fresh
  parsley
2 tablespoons freshly grated
  Parmesan cheese
¼ teaspoon salt

¼ teaspoon ground black
  pepper
1 package (16 ounces)
  spaghetti or linguine,
  cooked
2 tablespoons pine nuts
  (pignoli), toasted (optional)

In 1-quart saucepan, heat olive oil over medium heat; add garlic and cook just until golden. Remove saucepan from heat; stir in parsley, Parmesan cheese, salt, and pepper. To serve, toss cooked pasta with sauce. Sprinkle pine nuts over pasta, if you like.

Each serving: About 555 calories, 16g protein, 85g carbohydrate, 16g total fat (3g saturated), 2mg cholesterol, 310mg sodium

SPINACH, GARBANZO, AND RAISIN SAUCE

Prep: 15 minutes   Cook: 10 minutes
Makes 4 main-dish servings

3 tablespoons olive oil
4 garlic cloves, minced
1 bunch (10 to 12 ounces)
  spinach, tough stems
  removed
1 can (15 to 19 ounces)
  garbanzo beans, rinsed and
  drained

½ cup golden raisins
¼ teaspoon salt
¼ teaspoon crushed red
  pepper
½ cup reduced-sodium
  chicken broth
1 package (16 ounces) penne
  or corkscrew pasta, cooked

In nonstick 12-inch skillet, heat oil over medium heat; add garlic and cook until golden. Increase heat to medium-high; stir in spinach, garbanzo beans, raisins, salt, and red pepper and cook until spinach wilts. Stir in chicken broth and heat through. To serve, toss cooked pasta with sauce.

Each serving: 700 calories, 23g protein, 122g carbohydrate, 14g total fat (2g saturated), 0mg cholesterol, 740mg sodium

DRIED TOMATO AND OLIVE SAUCE

Prep: 15 minutes   Cook: 15 minutes
Makes 4 main-dish servings

2 tablespoons olive oil
3 garlic cloves, minced
⅓ cup chopped dried
  tomatoes (1 ounce)
1 can (13¾ to 14½ ounces)
  chicken broth
½ cup Kalamata olives, pitted
  and chopped

¼ cup packed fresh parsley
  leaves, chopped
1 package (16 ounces)
  spaghetti or corkscrew
  pasta, cooked
2 ounces goat cheese,
  crumbled (½ cup)

In nonstick 12-inch skillet, heat oil over medium heat; add garlic and cook 30 seconds. Add dried tomatoes and chicken broth; heat to boiling over medium-high heat. Reduce heat to low and simmer 10 minutes. Stir in olives and parsley. To serve, toss cooked pasta with sauce; sprinkle with crumbled goat cheese.

**Each serving:
580 calories,
19g protein,
92g carbohydrate,
15g total fat
(4g saturated),
14mg cholesterol,
745mg sodium**

CREAMY PASTA SAUCES

Besides being rich and satisfying, cream-based pasta sauces generally take little time to prepare: In the time it takes to boil water and cook the pasta, the sauce can be ready and waiting. To keep fat and calories within reasonable limits, we've used light cream or half-and-half in most of the recipes here. Throw caution to the wind and enjoy the traditional Alfredo sauce made with real cream, or try a different but luscious light version accented with broccoli.

SMOKED SALMON AND CREAM SAUCE

◆◆◆◆◆◆◆◆◆◆◆◆◆◆◆◆◆◆◆◆◆◆◆◆◆◆◆◆

Prep: 10 minutes   Cook: 10 minutes
Makes 4 main-dish servings

1 large carrot	¼ teaspoon ground black
½ pound sliced smoked	pepper
salmon	1 tablespoon chopped fresh
⅓ cup dry vermouth or dry	dill
white wine	1 package (16 ounces) bowtie
1 cup half-and half or light	or medium shell pasta,
cream	cooked
½ teaspoon salt	Dill sprigs for garnish

SMOKED SALMON

Silken and seductive, smoked salmon requires a long, slow process. The fish is first cured, either with a dry rub of salt (and sometimes sugar and spices) for several hours or even days, or in a brine. It is then smoked, at a temperature of 90°F or less. Its flavor and texture vary with the species of salmon, the cure, the duration and temperature of the smoking process, and the wood used for smoking (usually alder in the Pacific Northwest, oak in Scotland, and juniper in Norway).

1 Shred carrot (you should have about 1 cup). In nonstick 10-inch skillet, heat carrot and *½ cup water* to boiling over medium-high heat. Cook 5 minutes, or until carrot is tender.

2 Meanwhile, cut salmon slices into 2-inch pieces. Add vermouth to carrot mixture. Heat to boiling; cook 1 minute. Add cream, salt, and pepper; heat to boiling, stirring constantly. Cook 1 minute longer.

3 Remove skillet from heat; stir in salmon pieces and chopped fresh dill. To serve, toss cooked pasta with salmon mixture until pasta is well coated; garnish with dill sprigs.

EACH SERVING: ABOUT 595 CALORIES, 27g PROTEIN, 90g CARBOHYDRATE, 11g TOTAL FAT (5g SATURATED), 35mg CHOLESTEROL, 860mg SODIUM

LIGHT ALFREDO SAUCE

Prep: 15 minutes   *Cook:* 15 minutes
Makes 4 main-dish servings

1 package (16 ounces) fettuccine	1 cup chicken broth
1 bunch broccoli, cut into small flowerets (optional)	3 tablespoons all-purpose flour
2 teaspoons vegetable oil	½ teaspoon salt
1 small onion, diced	¼ teaspoon coarsely ground black pepper
1 garlic clove, minced	½ cup freshly grated Parmesan cheese
2 cups skim milk	

◆ Prepare fettuccine as label directs. If using broccoli, when pasta has cooked 9 minutes, add broccoli flowerets to cooking water; cook 3 minutes longer. Drain.

◆ Meanwhile, in nonstick 12-inch skillet, heat oil over medium heat; add onion and garlic and cook until golden. In medium bowl, whisk milk, chicken broth, flour, salt, and pepper until blended; stir into skillet and cook until mixture thickens and boils. Stir in Parmesan cheese. To serve, toss cooked fettuccine and broccoli with sauce.

Each serving: About 495 calories, 23g protein, 78g carbohydrate, 11g total fat (3g saturated), 17mg cholesterol, 850mg sodium

CLASSIC ALFREDO SAUCE

Prep: 5 minutes   *Cook:* 10 minutes
Makes 6 main-dish servings

2 cups heavy or whipping cream	½ teaspoon salt
1 cup freshly grated Parmesan cheese	¼ teaspoon coarsely cracked black pepper
2 tablespoons margarine or butter	1 package (16 ounces) fettuccine, cooked

◆ In 2-quart saucepan, heat cream to boiling over medium-high heat, stirring frequently. Reduce heat to medium; gradually stir in ½ cup Parmesan cheese.

◆ Add margarine, 1 tablespoon at a time, stirring. Add salt and pepper. To serve, toss cooked pasta with sauce; sprinkle with remaining Parmesan cheese.

Each serving: About 605 calories, 17g protein, 45g carbohydrate, 41g total fat (22g saturated), 122mg cholesterol, 650mg sodium

MUSHROOM SAUCE

Prep: 10 minutes   *Cook:* 20 minutes
Makes 4 main-dish servings

2 tablespoons olive or vegetable oil	2 tablespoons soy sauce
1½ pounds mushrooms, thinly sliced	1 package (16 ounces) linguine or fettuccine, cooked
1 cup half-and-half or light cream	

◆ In 12-inch skillet, heat oil over high heat; add mushrooms and cook, stirring frequently, 15 minutes, or until browned and all liquid has evaporated.

◆ Stir in half-and-half and soy sauce; cook, stirring constantly, about 3 minutes, until sauce reduces slightly. To serve, toss cooked pasta with sauce.

Each serving: About 515 calories, 18g protein, 75g carbohydrate, 19g total fat (5g saturated), 22mg cholesterol, 675mg sodium

BLUE-CHEESE AND WALNUT SAUCE

Prep: 5 minutes   *Cook:* 10 to 15 minutes
Makes 6 main-dish servings

1 cup half-and-half or light cream	¼ teaspoon coarsely ground black pepper
¾ cup chicken broth	1 package (16 ounces) bow-tie or corkscrew pasta, cooked
4 ounces Gorgonzola or blue cheese, crumbled (1 cup)	½ cup chopped walnuts (2 ounces), toasted

◆ In 2-quart saucepan, heat half-and-half and broth to boiling over medium-high heat. Reduce heat to medium; cook 5 minutes. Add Gorgonzola and pepper and cook, whisking constantly, until melted and smooth.

◆ To serve, toss cooked pasta with sauce. Sprinkle with toasted walnuts.

Each serving: About 470 calories, 17g protein, 61g carbohydrate, 18g total fat (7g saturated), 31mg cholesterol, 505mg sodium

SEAFOOD PASTA SAUCES

From tender clams to meaty cubes of swordfish, the sweet, delicate flavors of seafood pair beautifully with pasta. These easy-to-make recipes rely on a few choice ingredients (olives, capers, fresh orange peel) that offer bold, exciting tastes. As with all seafood, it's essential not to overcook the fish or shellfish. In order not to interfere with the flavors of fish, Italians traditionally do not serve cheese with seafood pastas.

WHITE CLAM SAUCE

Prep: 15 minutes   Cook: 15 minutes
Makes 4 main-dish servings

2 dozen Manila or littleneck clams
½ cup dry white wine
¼ cup olive oil
1 large garlic clove, minced
¼ teaspoon crushed red pepper

¼ cup chopped fresh flat-leaf parsley
1 package (16 ounces) linguine or spaghetti, cooked

1 With stiff brush, scrub clams thoroughly with cold running water to remove any sand. Discard any clams that do not close tightly when shells are lightly tapped. In 5-quart Dutch oven, combine clams and wine. Cover and cook over high heat 5 minutes. With slotted spoon, transfer any opened clams to bowl.

2 Cover and cook all remaining unopened clams 3 to 5 minutes longer, removing clams as they open. Discard any clams that do not open.

3 Remove clams from shells and chop coarsely; set aside. Strain clam broth from Dutch oven through sieve lined with paper towel into small bowl; set aside.

4 Wipe Dutch oven clean. Add olive oil, garlic, and crushed red pepper to Dutch oven and cook over medium heat, stirring occasionally, just until garlic begins to turn golden.

5 Stir in chopped flat-leaf parsley, reserved clams, and reserved clam broth until well combined; heat just to simmering. To serve, toss clam sauce with cooked pasta.

MUSSEL SAUCE

Substitute 2 pounds fresh mussels for the clams. Scrub and debeard mussels (see page 88). Prepare as directed for clam sauce, but in Step 3, do not chop mussels; if you like, leave mussels in their shells. For a flavor twist, add one of the following, or a combination: the grated peel of 1 lemon or orange; ½ cup chopped fresh basil leaves; 4 plum tomatoes, chopped. Or, sprinkle the finished dish with fresh, coarse bread crumbs, lightly toasted.

Each serving: About 640 calories, 27g protein, 88g carbohydrate, 17g total fat (2g saturated), 48mg cholesterol, 365mg sodium

EACH SERVING: ABOUT 600 CALORIES, 22g PROTEIN, 87g CARBOHYDRATE, 16g TOTAL FAT (2g SATURATED), 18mg CHOLESTEROL, 150mg SODIUM

SICILIAN GRILLED SWORDFISH SAUCE WITH MINT AND ORANGE

Prep: 15 minutes plus standing   Grill/broil: 8 to 10 minutes
Makes 6 main-dish servings

2 large tomatoes, cut into
  ½-inch cubes (about
  2½ cups)
¼ cup chopped fresh mint
1 tablespoon red wine vinegar
1 small garlic clove, minced
3 tablespoons olive oil

Salt and coarsely ground
  black pepper
1 teaspoon grated orange peel
1 swordfish steak (1 pound),
  1 inch thick
1 package (16 ounces) penne
  or bowtie pasta, cooked

◆ In medium bowl, combine tomatoes with their juice, mint, red wine vinegar, garlic, 2 tablespoons olive oil, ¾ teaspoon salt, and ¼ teaspoon pepper. Let stand 30 minutes.

◆ Prepare outdoor grill or preheat broiler. In cup, mix orange peel, remaining 1 tablespoon olive oil, ¼ teaspoon salt, and ¼ teaspoon pepper until blended; use to brush over both sides of swordfish.

◆ Grill swordfish over medium-high heat, or broil on rack in broiling pan at position closest to heat source, turning once, 8 to 10 minutes, just until opaque throughout.

◆ Transfer swordfish to cutting board; cut into ¾-inch cubes. Add to tomato mixture in bowl. To serve, toss cooked pasta with sauce.

Each serving: About 445 calories, 25g protein, 59g carbohydrate, 11g total fat (2g saturated), 29mg cholesterol, 505mg sodium

SEAFOOD FRA DIAVOLO

Prep: 20 minutes   Cook: 1 hour
Makes 6 main-dish servings

1 tablespoon olive oil
1 large garlic clove, minced
¼ teaspoon crushed red
  pepper
1 can (28 ounces) tomatoes
½ teaspoon salt
8 ounces cleaned squid, cut
  into ¼-inch-thick rings
1 dozen mussels, scrubbed
  and debearded (see
  page 88)

8 ounces medium shrimp,
  shelled and deveined (see
  page 90), tail part of shell
  left on, if you like
¼ cup chopped fresh parsley
1 package (16 ounces)
  linguine or spaghetti,
  cooked

◆ In 4-quart saucepan, heat oil over medium heat. Add garlic and crushed red pepper; cook 30 seconds, just until very fragrant. Stir in tomatoes with their juice and salt, breaking up tomatoes with back of spoon. Heat to boiling over high heat. Add squid; heat to boiling. Reduce heat to low; cover and simmer 30 minutes. Uncover saucepan; simmer 15 minutes.

◆ Increase heat to high. Add mussels; cover and cook 3 minutes. Stir in shrimp; cover and cook 2 minutes longer, or until mussels open and shrimp turn opaque throughout. Discard any mussels that do not open. Stir in parsley. To serve, toss cooked pasta with sauce.

Each serving: About 420 calories, 27g protein, 65g carbohydrate, 5g total fat (1g saturated), 162mg cholesterol, 635mg sodium

TUNA, OLIVE, AND CAPER SAUCE

Prep: 20 minutes   Cook: 10 minutes
Makes 6 main-dish servings

2 tablespoons olive oil
1 large garlic clove, minced
1 pound tomatoes, cut into
  ½-inch cubes (3 cups)
¼ teaspoon salt
¼ teaspoon ground black
  pepper
1 can (12 ounces) solid white
  tuna in water, drained

⅓ cup Kalamata olives, pitted
  and chopped
⅓ cup chopped fresh flat-leaf
  parsley
2 tablespoons capers, drained
  and chopped
1 package (16 ounces) penne
  or corkscrew pasta, cooked

In 10-inch skillet, heat oil over medium heat. Add garlic; cook 30 seconds, just until very fragrant. Stir in tomatoes with their juice, salt, and pepper. Cook, stirring occasionally, 5 minutes. Stir in tuna, breaking up chunks with spoon, and cook until heated through. Stir in olives, parsley, and capers. To serve, toss cooked pasta with sauce.

Each serving: About 430 calories, 25g protein, 61g carbohydrate, 9g total fat (1g saturated), 23mg cholesterol, 575mg sodium

MEAT PASTA SAUCES

The heartiest pastas are the ones tossed with thick meat sauce. Classic Bolognese, enriched with red wine, cream, and tomatoes, is a sauce you'll want to use again and again. For something quite out of the ordinary, try the Sicilian sauce with pork and raisins. Both these recipes require plenty of simmering time so they can develop their wonderful depth of flavors. Quicker, but just as delicious, are the tasty sausage sauce with butternut squash and the amatriciana sauce, another Italian classic with a garlic-and-red-pepper kick.

CLASSIC BOLOGNESE SAUCE

Prep: 10 minutes   Cook: 1 hour 25 minutes
Makes 6 main-dish servings plus extra sauce

2 tablespoons olive oil
1 medium onion, finely chopped
1 carrot, finely chopped
1 celery stalk, finely chopped
1½ pounds ground meat for meat loaf or ½ pound each ground beef, veal, and pork
½ cup dry red wine
1 can (35 ounces) tomatoes, chopped, juice reserved

2 teaspoons salt
¼ teaspoon ground black pepper
⅛ teaspoon ground nutmeg
¼ cup heavy or whipping cream
1 package (16 ounces) spaghetti or fettuccine, cooked
Freshly grated Parmesan cheese (optional)

1 In 5-quart Dutch oven, heat olive oil over medium heat. Add onion, carrot, and celery and cook, stirring occasionally, about 10 minutes, or until tender.

2 Add ground meat to vegetables in Dutch oven and cook, stirring frequently to break up meat, until meat is no longer pink.

3 Stir red wine into meat mixture and heat to boiling over high heat. Stir in tomatoes with their juice, salt, pepper, and nutmeg.

4 Heat mixture to boiling; reduce heat to low and simmer, uncovered, stirring occasionally, 1 hour. Stir in cream and heat through, stirring constantly. To serve, use half of sauce to toss with cooked pasta (cool remaining sauce, then freeze for use another day). Serve with freshly grated Parmesan cheese, if you like.

BEYOND BOLOGNESE

Known to Italians as *il ragù*, Bolognese sauce is one of the very few recipes in Italy to have an official standard version. All cooks have their own variations, though: Try sautéing some chopped prosciutto or chicken livers with the meat. Stir in a little grated lemon peel or earthy dried porcini mushrooms with the tomatoes, or add chopped fresh herbs such as parsley or marjoram at the end of cooking.

EACH SERVING: ABOUT 475 CALORIES, 21g PROTEIN, 62g CARBOHYDRATE, 15g TOTAL FAT (5g SATURATED), 47mg CHOLESTEROL, 585mg SODIUM

SAUSAGE AND BUTTERNUT SQUASH SAUCE

Prep: 15 minutes   Cook: 20 minutes
Makes 6 main-dish servings

1 package (16 ounces)
   corkscrew or other short
   pasta
1 medium butternut squash
   (about 1¾ pounds)
¾ pound sweet Italian-sausage
   links, casings removed
¼ teaspoon salt

¼ teaspoon coarsely ground
   black pepper
⅓ cup packed fresh basil
   leaves, chopped
¼ cup freshly grated
   Parmesan cheese
Basil leaves for garnish

◆ Prepare pasta as label directs. Drain, reserving ¾ cup cooking water. Return pasta to saucepot; keep warm.

◆ Meanwhile, cut butternut squash into large chunks; cut peel from chunks and cut into ½-inch pieces. Set aside.

◆ In nonstick 12-inch skillet, cook sausage over medium-high heat, stirring frequently to break up, about 7 minutes, until browned. With slotted spoon, transfer sausage to bowl; discard all but 2 tablespoons drippings from skillet.

◆ To drippings in skillet, add butternut squash, salt, and pepper. Reduce heat to medium; cover and cook, stirring occasionally, about 10 minutes, until squash is tender.

◆ To serve, add chopped basil, Parmesan, sausage, and reserved pasta cooking water to skillet; toss pasta with sauce. Garnish with basil leaves.

Each serving: About 545 calories, 19g protein, 72g carbohydrate, 19g total fat (6g saturated), 47mg cholesterol, 770mg sodium

AMATRICIANA SAUCE

Prep: 10 minutes   Cook: 45 minutes
Makes 4 main-dish servings

1 tablespoon olive oil
4 ounces pancetta, chopped
1 small onion, finely chopped
1 garlic clove, minced
¼ teaspoon crushed red
   pepper

1 can (28 ounces) tomatoes
1 package (16 ounces)
   spaghetti or rigatoni,
   cooked
¼ cup chopped fresh parsley

◆ In 5-quart Dutch oven, heat oil over medium heat. Add pancetta and cook, stirring often, 5 minutes, or until lightly browned. Stir in onion; cook about 3 minutes, until tender. Stir in garlic and crushed red pepper; cook 15 seconds. Add tomatoes with their juice. Heat to boiling over high heat, breaking up tomatoes with back of spoon.

◆ Reduce heat to low and simmer, uncovered, stirring occasionally, 30 minutes. To serve, toss cooked pasta with sauce and parsley.

Each serving: About 545 calories, 23g protein, 97g carbohydrate, 8g total fat (1g saturated), 14mg cholesterol, 805mg sodium

HEARTY SICILIAN MEAT SAUCE

Prep: 15 minutes   Cook: 1 hour 45 minutes
Makes 6 main-dish servings

2 tablespoons vegetable oil
1½ pounds fresh pork butt,
   cut into 1½-inch cubes
2 large onions (8 ounces
   each), cut into ½-inch-thick
   slices
4 medium carrots, diced
1 can (28 ounces) tomatoes

1 tablespoon sugar
1 teaspoon salt
⅓ cup dark seedless raisins
2 tablespoons chopped fresh
   parsley
1 package (16 ounces)
   rigatoni or ziti, cooked

◆ In 5-quart Dutch oven, heat 1 tablespoon oil over medium-high heat; add pork cubes in batches and cook until browned; transfer pork to bowl as it browns.

◆ To drippings in Dutch oven, add remaining 1 tablespoon oil. Add onions and carrots; cook until lightly browned. Return pork to Dutch oven; stir in tomatoes with their juice, sugar, and salt. Heat to boiling over high heat, breaking up tomatoes with back of spoon. Reduce heat to low; cover and simmer 1¼ hours, or until pork is very tender.

◆ Using 2 forks, pull pork into shreds. Stir raisins and parsley into Dutch oven. Reduce heat to low; cover and simmer 5 minutes. To serve, toss cooked pasta with sauce.

Each serving: About 565 calories, 38g protein, 81g carbohydrate, 10g total fat (2g saturated), 57mg cholesterol, 750mg sodium

HOMEMADE PASTA

It is not at all difficult to make your own pasta, and the results are delicious as well as impressive. Use a pasta machine if you have one; or, follow our easy step-by-step directions for hand-rolling tortelli, pappardelle spiced up with lemon and pepper, or pretty herb squares.

HAM AND CHEESE TORTELLI

Prep: 1 hour 30 minutes plus standing **Cook:** *15 minutes*
Makes 6 main-dish servings

Spinach Pasta (see below)
1 container (15 ounces) ricotta cheese
8 ounces cooked ham, diced
⅛ teaspoon ground nutmeg
⅛ teaspoon ground black pepper

2 large eggs
All-purpose flour for dusting
1 teaspoon salt
6 tablespoons margarine or butter, melted
½ cup freshly grated Parmesan cheese

1 Prepare Spinach Pasta. Prepare filling: In small bowl, mix ricotta, ham, nutmeg, pepper, and 1 egg until blended; cover and refrigerate.When pasta dough has rested 30 minutes, cut dough in half; cover one half with plastic wrap. On well-floured surface, with floured rolling pin, roll remaining half of dough into 20" by 15" rectangle.

2 With knife or pastry wheel, trim edges and cut dough lengthwise into six 2½-inch-wide strips. Cut strips crosswise into 5 pieces, making thirty 2½" by 4" rectangles. Cover pasta with plastic wrap while you assemble tortelli.

3 Line 2 large jelly-roll pans with plastic wrap; dust with flour. Place 1 slightly rounded teaspoon filling in 2-inch-long strip lengthwise down center of each rectangle. In cup, beat remaining egg.

4 Fold 1 long side of pasta rectangle over filling. Lightly brush edge of other long side with egg; fold over filling. Pinch gently to seal; twist ends to close. Place tortelli in single layer in jelly-roll pan.

5 Repeat shaping with remaining pasta dough and filling. Cover jelly-roll pan loosely with plastic wrap; let tortelli dry 30 minutes, turning once.

6 To cook, in 8-quart saucepot, heat *6 quarts water* and salt to boiling over high heat. Add tortelli, stirring gently to separate; heat to boiling. Reduce heat to medium; cook 10 minutes, until tender but firm. Drain. Gently toss with melted margarine and half of Parmesan cheese. To serve, sprinkle with remaining Parmesan cheese.

SPINACH PASTA

In 2-quart saucepan, in ¼ inch boiling water, heat 4 ounces spinach (2½ cups), tough stems removed, to boiling. Reduce heat; simmer 1 minute. Drain; rinse with cold running water. Squeeze dry; finely chop. Place spinach in large bowl; stir in 4 large eggs and 1 teaspoon salt. Gradually stir in 3 cups all-purpose flour to make a stiff dough. On well-floured surface, knead about 20 times, until smooth and not sticky. Cover with plastic wrap. Let rest 30 minutes.

Each serving: About 265 calories, 11g protein, 45g carbohydrate, 4g total fat (1g saturated), 142mg cholesterol, 415mg sodium

EACH SERVING: ABOUT 605 CALORIES, 32g PROTEIN, 48g CARBOHYDRATE, 30g TOTAL FAT (12g SATURATED), 267mg CHOLESTEROL, 1030mg SODIUM

BASIC PASTA DOUGH

◆ ◆ ◆ ◆ ◆ ◆ ◆ ◆ ◆ ◆ ◆ ◆ ◆ ◆

Prep: 25 minutes plus standing
*Makes about 1 pound pasta, enough for 8 accompaniment
or 4 main-dish servings*

Follow the steps, or, in a food processor with knife blade
attached, blend ingredients 10 to 15 seconds to form a
smooth ball (do not knead). Cover; let rest 30 minutes.

About 2¼ cups all-purpose   **1 teaspoon salt**
flour   **2 large eggs**
1 tablespoon olive oil

1 In large bowl, stir
2¼ cups flour with olive
oil, salt, eggs, and ¼ *cup*
water to make a stiff dough.

2 On well-floured surface,
knead dough about
20 times, or until smooth
and not sticky. Cover with
plastic wrap; let rest
30 minutes for easier rolling.

**Each accompaniment serving: About 150 calories, 5g protein,
25g carbohydrate, 3g total fat (1g saturated), 53mg cholesterol,
335mg sodium**

HERB SQUARES

Prep: 30 minutes plus standing   Cook: 5 to 8 minutes
Makes 8 accompaniment or 4 main-dish servings

◆ Prepare Basic Pasta Dough.

◆ When dough has rested 30 minutes, cut in half. Follow
pasta machine instructions; roll to thinnest setting to make
2 equal strips. Or, place half of dough on well-floured surface
(keep remaining dough in plastic wrap). With floured rolling
pin, roll dough into 12" by 12" square. Cover with plastic
wrap. Repeat with other half of dough, but do not cover.

◆ Cover surface of 1 strip of dough, or uncovered square
of dough, with small pieces of herbs, such as parsley, dill,
chervil, or tarragon, stems removed. Remove plastic wrap
from first piece of dough and carefully place on top of
herb-covered dough.

◆ Roll dough strip through pasta machine or, with floured
rolling pin, roll dough square into 16" by 16" square. With
knife or pastry wheel, cut dough crosswise into eight 2-inch-
wide strips, then lengthwise into 8 pieces, making sixty-four
2-inch squares. Sprinkle pasta squares with all-purpose flour
to prevent sticking.

◆ Line jelly-roll pan with plastic wrap; dust with flour.
Place squares in jelly-roll pan, layering with plastic wrap. If
not cooking pasta immediately, cover pan with plastic wrap
and refrigerate.

◆ To cook, in 8-quart saucepot, heat *6 quarts water* and
2 teaspoons salt to boiling over high heat. Add pasta,
stirring gently to separate; heat to boiling. Reduce heat to
medium; cook 3 to 5 minutes, until tender but firm.

◆ Drain pasta well and serve with olive oil, butter, or
chicken broth.

LEMON-PEPPER PAPARDELLE

Prep: 25 minutes plus standing   Cook: 5 to 8 minutes
Makes 8 accompaniment or 4 main-dish servings

◆ Prepare Basic Pasta Dough, but add 1 tablespoon finely
grated lemon peel and ½ teaspoon coarsely ground black
pepper to dough.

◆ When dough has rested 30 minutes, cut in half. Follow
pasta machine instructions; roll to thinnest setting. Or,
place half of dough on well-floured surface (keep
remaining dough in plastic wrap). With floured rolling pin,
roll dough into 12" by 12" square.

◆ With knife or pastry wheel, cut dough into twelve 1-inch-
wide strips. Sprinkle strips with all-purpose flour to prevent
them from sticking.

◆ Line jelly-roll pan with plastic wrap; dust with flour. Place
strips in jelly-roll pan, layering with floured plastic wrap.
Repeat with remaining dough. If not cooking pasta
immediately, cover pan with plastic wrap and refrigerate.

◆ To cook, in 8-quart saucepot, heat *6 quarts water* and
2 teaspoons salt to boiling over high heat. Add pasta,
stirring gently to separate; heat to boiling. Reduce heat to
medium; cook 3 to 5 minutes, until tender but firm.

◆ Drain pasta well and serve with olive oil or butter.

BAKED AND STUFFED PASTA

Ever popular as a comforting family meal and for fuss-free entertaining, baked pastas are loved by all for their fragrant, zesty sauces and gooey strings of melted cheese. When cooking the pasta for these recipes, it's essential to undercook it slightly, so it doesn't become soft and mushy during baking.

ZUCCHINI AND CHEESE MANICOTTI

Prep: 40 minutes   Bake: 40 minutes
Makes 7 main-dish servings

1 package (8 ounces) manicotti shells (14 shells)
2 small zucchini (about 6 ounces each)
1 small onion
2 tablespoons olive oil
1 container (15 ounces) ricotta cheese
4 ounces mozzarella cheese, shredded (1 cup)
4 ounces Provolone cheese, shredded (1 cup)

2 large eggs
4 cups Marinara Sauce (see page 352) or 1 jar (30 ounces) chunky garden-style spaghetti sauce mixed with 1 cup water
1 tablespoon chopped fresh basil or parsley
Basil sprigs for garnish
Italian bread (optional)

1 Prepare manicotti shells as label directs but do not add salt to water. Drain. Meanwhile, shred zucchini and mince onion.

2 In 10-inch skillet, heat oil over high heat; add zucchini and onion and cook, stirring often, until lightly browned and all liquid evaporates. Remove from heat.

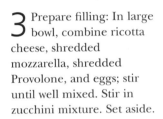

3 Prepare filling: In large bowl, combine ricotta cheese, shredded mozzarella, shredded Provolone, and eggs; stir until well mixed. Stir in zucchini mixture. Set aside.

4 Preheat oven to 375°F. Measure and reserve ½ cup marinara sauce. Spoon remaining sauce into bottom of 13" by 9" glass baking dish or shallow 3½- to 4-quart casserole; spread in even layer.

5 Spoon filling into cooked shells. Or, spoon filling into zip-tight plastic bag, snip off one corner of bag, and squeeze filling into shells. Arrange shells in sauce in casserole in single layer, making sure that shells do not touch sides of casserole.

6 Spoon reserved marinara sauce over top of filled manicotti shells. Cover casserole with foil and bake 40 minutes, or until pasta is heated through and sauce is bubbly. To serve, sprinkle with chopped basil. Garnish with basil sprigs. Serve manicotti with Italian bread, if you like.

EACH SERVING: ABOUT 485 CALORIES, 23g PROTEIN, 41g CARBOHYDRATE, 26g TOTAL FAT (12g SATURATED), 115mg CHOLESTEROL, 1010mg SODIUM

BAKED RIGATONI AND PEAS

Prep: 35 minutes   *Bake:* 30 to 35 minutes
Makes 8 main-dish servings

1 package (16 ounces)
  rigatoni or ziti
Salt
7 tablespoons margarine or
  butter
¼ cup all-purpose flour
3½ cups milk
1 cup freshly grated Parmesan
  cheese

1 package (10 ounces) frozen
  peas, thawed
1 can (14½ ounces) diced
  tomatoes
½ cup loosely packed fresh
  basil leaves, cut into strips
¼ cup plain dried bread
  crumbs

◆ Prepare rigatoni as label directs, using 2 teaspoons salt in water; drain. Return rigatoni to saucepot; keep warm. Preheat oven to 350°F. Meanwhile, in 2-quart saucepan, melt 5 tablespoons margarine over low heat. Stir in flour; cook, stirring constantly, 2 minutes. With wire whisk, gradually blend in milk. Increase heat to medium; cook, stirring frequently, about 15 minutes, until mixture thickens slightly and boils. Stir in 1 teaspoon salt and ¾ cup Parmesan.

◆ Pour sauce over rigatoni in saucepot, stirring to combine. Stir in peas, tomatoes with their juice, and basil. Spoon mixture into shallow 3½- to 4-quart casserole or 13" by 9" glass baking dish. In small saucepan, melt remaining 2 tablespoons margarine over low heat. Remove from heat; stir in bread crumbs and remaining ¼ cup Parmesan. Sprinkle topping on rigatoni. Bake 30 to 35 minutes, until top is golden brown.

Each serving: About 485 calories, 19g protein, 60g carbohydrate, 19g total fat (7g saturated), 24mg cholesterol, 870mg sodium

REDUCED-FAT MACARONI AND CHEESE

Prep: 30 minutes   *Bake:* 20 minutes
Makes 6 main-dish servings

12 ounces (about 3 cups)
  elbow macaroni twists
Nonstick cooking spray
1 container (16 ounces) low-
  fat cottage cheese (1%)
2 tablespoons all-purpose flour
2 cups skim milk
4 ounces sharp Cheddar
  cheese, shredded (1 cup)

1 teaspoon salt
¼ teaspoon ground black
  pepper
¼ teaspoon ground nutmeg
¼ cup freshly grated
  Parmesan cheese

◆ Prepare macaroni as label directs but do not add salt to water; drain. Preheat oven to 375°F. Spray shallow, broiler-safe 2½-quart casserole with nonstick cooking spray. In food processor with knife blade attached, blend cottage cheese until smooth. (Or, in blender at high speed, blend cottage cheese with ¼ cup of the milk called for in recipe.)

◆ In 2-quart saucepan, whisk flour with ¼ cup milk until smooth. Gradually stir in remaining milk until blended. Cook over medium heat, stirring frequently, until mixture thickens slightly and just boils. Remove saucepan from heat; stir in cottage cheese, Cheddar, salt, pepper, and nutmeg.

◆ Place macaroni in casserole; pour cheese sauce over. Bake, uncovered, 20 minutes. Remove casserole from oven; turn oven control to broil. Sprinkle Parmesan on top of macaroni. Place casserole in broiler at closest position to heat source; broil 2 to 3 minutes, until top is golden brown.

Each serving: About 400 calories, 26g protein, 51g carbohydrate, 9g total fat (6g saturated), 28mg cholesterol, 900mg sodium

SOUTHWESTERN-STYLE PASTA

Prep: 35 minutes   *Bake:* 15 minutes
Makes 4 main-dish servings

½ (16-ounce) package wagon
  wheel or corkscrew pasta
½ pound fully cooked chorizo
  sausage, thinly sliced
1 large green pepper, diced
1 large onion, diced
2 cans (14½ to 16 ounces
  each) stewed tomatoes
1 small zucchini (about
  6 ounces), diced

1 can (16 to 17¼ ounces)
  whole-kernel corn, drained
1 can (4 to 4½ ounces) diced
  mild green chiles
2 ounces Monterey Jack
  cheese, coarsely shredded
  (½ cup)

◆ Prepare pasta as label directs but do not add salt to water; drain. Meanwhile, preheat oven to 400°F. In 12-inch skillet, cook sausage, green pepper, and onion over medium-high heat, stirring frequently, until vegetables are tender. Spoon off and discard any fat in skillet.

◆ Stir in tomatoes, zucchini, corn, and chiles with their liquid; heat to boiling. Reduce heat to low; cook 5 minutes. Stir in pasta. Spoon mixture into shallow 2-quart casserole or 11" by 7" glass baking dish. Sprinkle with shredded cheese and bake 15 minutes, or until top is golden brown.

Each serving: About 445 calories, 31g protein, 86g carbohydrate, 29g total fat (11g saturated), 13mg cholesterol, 1305mg sodium

LASAGNA

A pan of hot, bubbly lasagna has timeless appeal. Here are recipes for every appetite, from a robust beef and sausage version to tempting cheese-filled lasagna rolls. Because lasagna freezes beautifully, it's a perfect make-ahead meal.

THREE-CHEESE LASAGNA ROLLS

◆◆◆◆◆◆◆◆◆◆◆◆◆

Prep: 35 minutes
Bake: 35 to 40 minutes
Makes 6 main-dish servings

½ (16-ounce) package curly lasagna noodles (9 noodles)

2 cans (14½ ounces each) stewed tomatoes

1 can (8 ounces) tomato sauce

1 container (15 ounces) part-skim ricotta cheese

6 ounces part-skim mozzarella cheese, shredded (1½ cups)

3 tablespoons freshly grated Parmesan cheese

½ teaspoon coarsely ground black pepper

4 tablespoons chopped fresh basil

2 teaspoons olive oil

1 small onion, chopped

1 small zucchini (4 ounces), diced

1 small tomato, diced

1 tablespoon capers, drained and chopped

1 Prepare lasagna noodles as label directs. Drain and rinse with cold running water. Return noodles to saucepot with *cold water* to cover. Meanwhile, in 3-quart ceramic or glass baking dish, combine stewed tomatoes and tomato sauce; break up tomatoes with back of spoon. Prepare filling: In large bowl, mix all cheeses, pepper, and 3 tablespoons chopped basil.

2 Preheat oven to 375°F. Drain lasagna noodles on clean kitchen towels. Spread rounded ¼ cup filling on each lasagna noodle and roll up jelly-roll fashion. Slice each rolled noodle crosswise in half.

3 Arrange lasagna rolls, cut-side down, in sauce in baking dish; cover loosely with foil. Bake 35 to 40 minutes, until hot.

4 Meanwhile, prepare topping: In nonstick 10-inch skillet, heat oil over medium heat. Add onion; cook until tender and browned. Stir in zucchini; cook until tender.

5 Stir in diced tomato, capers, and remaining 1 tablespoon basil; heat through. To serve, place sauce and lasagna rolls on 6 plates; spoon topping over lasagna rolls.

EACH SERVING: ABOUT 385 CALORIES, 24g PROTEIN, 43g CARBOHYDRATE, 14g TOTAL FAT (7g SATURATED), 40mg CHOLESTEROL, 910mg SODIUM

BEEF AND SAUSAGE LASAGNA

Prep: 1 hour plus standing   *Bake:* 45 minutes
Makes 10 main-dish servings

⅔ (16-ounce) package lasagna noodles (about 12 noodles)
½ pound hot Italian-sausage links, casings removed
½ pound ground beef
1 medium onion, diced
1 can (28 ounces) Italian plum tomatoes
2 tablespoons tomato paste
1 teaspoon salt

1 teaspoon sugar
¾ teaspoon dried Italian seasoning
1 container (15 ounces) part-skim ricotta cheese
1 large egg
¼ cup chopped fresh parsley
8 ounces part-skim mozzarella cheese, shredded (2 cups)

◆ Prepare lasagna noodles as label directs but do not add salt to water; drain and rinse with cold running water. Return to saucepot with *cold water* to cover. Set aside.

◆ Meanwhile, prepare meat sauce: In 4-quart saucepan, cook sausage, ground beef, and onion over high heat, stirring often to break up sausage, until meat is well browned. Spoon off and discard fat. Add tomatoes with their juice and next 4 ingredients. Heat to boiling, breaking up tomatoes with back of spoon. Reduce heat to low; cover and simmer, stirring occasionally, 30 minutes. Set aside.

◆ Preheat oven to 375°F. In medium bowl, mix ricotta, egg, and parsley. Drain noodles on clean kitchen towels.

◆ In 13" by 9" glass baking dish, arrange half of lasagna noodles, overlapping slightly; top with ricotta mixture. Sprinkle with half of mozzarella; top with half of meat sauce. Layer with remaining noodles and meat sauce; top with remaining mozzarella. Cover with foil; bake 30 minutes.

◆ Uncover and bake 15 minutes longer, or until sauce is bubbly and top is lightly browned. Let stand 15 minutes for easier serving.

Each serving: About 385 calories, 23g protein, 28g carbohydrate, 20g total fat (8g saturated), 82mg cholesterol, 800mg sodium

MUSHROOM LASAGNA

Prep: 1 hour plus standing   *Bake:* 50 minutes
Makes 12 main-dish servings

½ ounce dried porcini mushrooms
¾ (16-ounce) package lasagna noodles (about 16 noodles)
5 cups milk
5 tablespoons margarine or butter
⅓ cup all-purpose flour
Pinch ground nutmeg
Salt and ground black pepper
½ cup finely chopped shallots

1½ pounds white mushrooms, sliced
2 tablespoons chopped fresh parsley
1 container (15 ounces) ricotta cheese
1 package (10 ounces) frozen chopped spinach, thawed and squeezed dry
1 cup freshly grated Parmesan cheese

◆ In bowl, combine porcini and *¾ cup hot water*; let stand 30 minutes. With slotted spoon, remove porcini; rinse to remove any grit. Chop and set aside. Strain soaking liquid through sieve lined with paper towel; set aside. Meanwhile, prepare lasagna noodles as label directs, but do not add salt to water; drain and rinse with cold running water. Return noodles to saucepot with *cold water* to cover. Set aside.

◆ Prepare béchamel sauce: In 3-quart saucepan, heat milk to boiling over medium-high heat. Meanwhile, in 4-quart saucepan, melt 3 tablespoons margarine over medium heat. Stir in flour; cook, stirring, 1 minute. Gradually whisk in milk, nutmeg, ½ teaspoon salt, and ⅛ teaspoon pepper. Heat to boiling. Reduce heat to low; simmer 5 minutes, stirring. Remove from heat.

◆ In 12-inch skillet, melt remaining 2 tablespoons margarine over medium-high heat. Add shallots; cook 1 minute. Stir in white mushrooms, ½ teaspoon salt, and ⅛ teaspoon pepper and cook 10 minutes, or until liquid has evaporated. Stir in porcini and soaking liquid; cook until liquid has evaporated. Remove from heat; stir in parsley.

◆ Preheat oven to 375°F. In large bowl, mix ricotta, spinach, ¼ cup Parmesan, ½ teaspoon salt, ¼ teaspoon pepper, and ½ cup béchamel. Drain noodles on clean kitchen towels.

◆ In 13" by 9" glass baking dish, spread ½ cup béchamel. Arrange 4 lasagna noodles over sauce, overlapping slightly. Top with half of mushroom mixture, 1 cup béchamel, ¼ cup Parmesan, and 4 more noodles. Add all of ricotta mixture, 4 more noodles, remaining mushrooms, 1 more cup béchamel, and ¼ cup Parmesan. Top with remaining noodles, béchamel, and Parmesan. Cover with foil; bake 30 minutes.

◆ Uncover and bake 20 minutes longer, or until sauce is bubbly and top is lightly browned. Let stand 15 minutes.

Each serving: About 355 calories, 18g protein, 36g carbohydrate, 16g total fat (8g saturated), 38mg cholesterol, 580mg sodium

ASIAN PASTA

With a few specialty ingredients, it's surprisingly easy to create the exotic flavors of your favorite Asian noodle dishes in your own kitchen. Asian groceries and some supermarkets should carry any of the products called for in these recipes. But if you can't find rice noodles, you can substitute spaghetti or linguine.

CANTONESE NOODLE PANCAKE

❧❧❧❧❧❧❧❧❧❧❧❧❧

Prep: 25 minutes
Cook: 35 to 45 minutes
Makes 6 main-dish servings

1 package (16 ounces) Chinese-style egg noodles or spaghetti
1 pork tenderloin (about 12 ounces), thinly sliced
2 tablespoons dry sherry
4 tablespoons soy sauce
2 tablespoons plus 4 teaspoons vegetable oil
4 large green onions, cut into 1½-inch pieces
1 large red pepper, cut into 1-inch pieces
1 small head bok choy (about 12 ounces), cut crosswise into 2-inch pieces
4 ounces snow peas, strings removed
2 teaspoons cornstarch
2 tablespoons minced, peeled fresh ginger
1 can (15 ounces) Chinese straw mushrooms, drained

1 Prepare noodles as label directs but do not add salt to water. Drain. Meanwhile, in 11" by 7" glass baking dish, mix pork slices, sherry, and 2 tablespoons soy sauce; set aside. In nonstick 12-inch skillet, heat 1 tablespoon oil over medium heat. Place noodles in skillet to form 12-inch round pancake. Cook 5 to 8 minutes, until golden on bottom.

TOFU TOPPING

If you prefer, make a light and easy vegetarian version of this pancake by substituting 1 pound firm tofu for the pork tenderloin. Cut tofu into 1-inch cubes. Proceed as directed for pork, but cook tofu for about 5 minutes in Step 5.

2 Carefully invert pancake onto 12-inch plate. Slide pancake back into skillet; cook 5 to 8 minutes longer, until golden on other side. Transfer pancake to large warm platter; keep warm.

4 Transfer onion mixture to bowl. In same Dutch oven, heat 2 teaspoons oil; add bok choy and snow peas; cook until tender-crisp. Transfer to bowl with onion mixture.

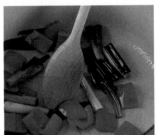

3 While pancake is cooking, in 5-quart Dutch oven, heat 2 teaspoons oil over medium-high heat; add green onions and red pepper and cook until tender-crisp.

5 In cup, mix cornstarch, *1 cup water*, and remaining 2 tablespoons soy sauce. In same Dutch oven, heat remaining 1 tablespoon oil. Add pork mixture and ginger; cook until pork loses its pink color. Return vegetables to Dutch oven; stir in cornstarch mixture and mushrooms. Cook over medium-high heat, stirring, until mixture thickens slightly and boils. Spoon pork mixture onto pancake; cut into wedges.

EACH SERVING: ABOUT 465 CALORIES, 25g PROTEIN, 64g CARBOHYDRATE, 11g TOTAL FAT (2g SATURATED), 33mg CHOLESTEROL, 945mg SODIUM

JAPANESE NOODLE SOUP

Prep: 25 minutes   Cook: 20 minutes
Makes 4 main-dish servings

1 tablespoon vegetable oil
6 ounces firm tofu, cut into
  1-inch pieces
3 medium green onions,
  thinly sliced on the
  diagonal
1 tablespoon grated, peeled
  fresh ginger
1 package (1.1 ounces) instant
  shiro miso soup mix (white
  soybean-paste soup) or
  2 extra-large vegetable
  bouillon cubes

8 ounces dried udon noodles
  (thick rice flour noodles) or
  linguine
1 large carrot, cut crosswise
  into thirds, then lengthwise
  into matchstick-thin strips
1 medium red pepper, cut
  into thin strips
3 strips (each 3" by ½") lemon
  peel
¼ teaspoon crushed red pepper
1 small bunch watercress,
  tough stems removed

◆ In nonstick 10-inch skillet, heat vegetable oil over
medium-high heat; add tofu, green onions, and ginger
and cook 5 minutes, or until golden. Set aside.

◆ In 4-quart saucepan, heat *8 cups water* to boiling over
high heat. Add soup mix, next 5 ingredients, and tofu
mixture; heat to boiling. Reduce heat to low; simmer 8 to
10 minutes, until noodles are cooked (linguine will take
slightly longer). Stir in watercress until it wilts. Serve
immediately (udon noodles absorb liquid quickly).

**Each serving: About 355 calories, 17g protein, 54g carbohydrate,
9g total fat (2g saturated), 0mg cholesterol, 540mg sodium**

THAI CHICKEN AND NOODLES

Prep: 25 minutes   Cook: 35 minutes
Makes 4 main-dish servings

½ (16-ounce) package flat
  dried rice noodles or
  linguine
1 stalk fresh lemongrass
4 large green onions
2 large skinless, boneless
  chicken-breast halves (about
  1 pound)
1 tablespoon vegetable oil
1 package (10 ounces)
  mushrooms, sliced

1 tablespoon minced, peeled
  fresh ginger
2 teaspoons red curry paste
  (see page 30)
2 tablespoons soy sauce
1 can (10 to 14 ounces) light
  or regular unsweetened
  coconut milk
1 medium red pepper
2 tablespoons chopped fresh
  cilantro

◆ Prepare noodles as label directs; drain. Return to
saucepot; keep warm. (If package has no directions, cook as
for regular pasta, 5 minutes, or just until tender.) Meanwhile,
remove outer layer from lemongrass. From bulb end, trim
and cut a 6-inch-long piece; discard top. Cut stalk lengthwise
in half. Slice 2 green onions into 1-inch pieces; reserve
remaining 2 for garnish. Cut chicken into 1-inch-wide strips.

◆ In nonstick 12-inch skillet, heat oil over medium-high
heat; add mushrooms and sliced green onions and cook
until golden. With slotted spoon, transfer to small bowl.

◆ To same skillet, add ginger and red curry paste; cook,
stirring, 1 minute. Add lemongrass, chicken strips, soy
sauce, coconut milk, and *1 cup water*; heat to boiling.
Reduce heat to low; cover and simmer 10 minutes, or until
chicken just loses its pink color throughout.

◆ While chicken is cooking, cut red pepper and reserved
green onions into 3-inch-long paper-thin strips. Remove
lemongrass from chicken mixture and discard. Stir in
mushroom mixture and cilantro; heat through. To serve,
arrange noodles in large bowl; top with chicken mixture.
Garnish with red-pepper and green-onion strips.

**Each serving: About 450 calories, 35g protein, 52g carbohydrate,
11g total fat (4g saturated), 81mg cholesterol, 660mg sodium**

PAD THAI

Prep: 25 minutes plus soaking   Cook: 5 minutes
Makes 4 main-dish servings

1 package (7 to 8 ounces) rice
  stick noodles, or 8 ounces
  angel hair pasta
¼ cup fresh lime juice
¼ cup Asian fish sauce (nuoc
  nam, see page 30)
2 tablespoons sugar
1 tablespoon vegetable oil
½ pound medium shrimp,
  shelled and deveined (see
  page 90), each cut
  lengthwise in half

2 garlic cloves, minced
¼ teaspoon crushed red
  pepper
3 large eggs, lightly beaten
6 ounces bean sprouts (about
  2 cups), rinsed
⅓ cup unsalted roasted
  peanuts, coarsely chopped
3 green onions, thinly sliced
½ cup fresh cilantro leaves
Lime wedges

◆ In large bowl, soak rice stick noodles, if using, in *hot water*
to cover 20 minutes. Drain; cut into 4-inch lengths. Or, break
angel hair pasta in half, cook as label directs; drain and rinse
with cold running water. In small bowl, mix lime juice, fish
sauce, and sugar. Assemble remaining ingredients before
beginning to cook.

◆ In 12-inch skillet, heat oil over high heat. Add shrimp and
next 2 ingredients and cook, stirring, 1 minute. Add eggs and
cook, stirring, 20 seconds, or just until set. Add noodles and
cook, stirring, 2 minutes. Add lime-juice mixture, half of
bean sprouts, half of peanuts, and half of green onions; cook,
stirring, 1 minute. Transfer noodle mixture to platter. Top
with remaining bean sprouts, peanuts, and green onions.
Sprinkle with cilantro; serve with lime wedges.

**Each serving: About 440 calories, 28g protein, 47g carbohydrate,
16g total fat (3g saturated), 297mg cholesterol, 1170mg sodium**

GRAINS & BEANS

11

GRAINS AND BEANS KNOW-HOW

Long a staple and source of protein in the cuisines of cultures around the globe, grains and beans have finally taken a prominent place on the American table – and it's easy to see why. Grains and beans are inexpensive, low in fat, rich in nutrients, and, if served together, form a complete protein. When it comes to meal planning, few foods are as versatile, creating satisfying side dishes and salads or hearty entrées in bold, robust flavors.

REASONS TO RINSE

There's no need to rinse most domestic packaged rice before cooking. That's because the rice has already been cleaned during milling – and you'll rinse away the starchy coating on enriched rice that contains nutrients such as thiamin, niacin, and iron. You should, however, rinse wild rice and imported varieties such as basmati or jasmine, which may be dirty or dusty.

By contrast, dry beans and lentils should be picked over to remove any shriveled beans, stones, or twigs, then rinsed with cold running water to remove dust before cooking. Canned beans of all kinds should also be rinsed, for best appearance and texture in the finished dish.

BUYING AND STORING

Dry beans and grains will keep for a year or longer, but they become less flavorful and drier with time. For best results, buy them in small quantities and use within 6 months. Avoid packages with any hint of dust or mold. Store grains and beans in airtight containers in a cool, dry place. The bran left in brown rice and other whole grains makes them more perishable, so refrigerate or freeze them for a longer shelf life.

Cooked beans can be refrigerated, tightly covered, for 4 or 5 days or frozen for 6 months (thaw them at room temperature for about 1 hour). Cooked grains can be refrigerated for up to 5 days. Since they keep so well, it's a good idea to cook extra beans and grains to use for fast salads, soups, pilafs, and stir-fries. Cooked rice becomes hard if refrigerated, but reheats beautifully in the microwave.

COOKING SUCCESS

• For the lightest texture, be sure to allow cooked rice a 5-minute "standing time" before fluffing and serving.
• For enhanced flavor, cook rice in broth.
• Don't lift the lid when cooking rice. This allows steam and heat to escape from the pan and results in a mushy texture.
• Never add anything acidic (e.g., tomatoes, vinegar, wine, or citrus juices) or salt to beans at the start of cooking. These can toughen the skins and result in a longer cooking time, so add toward the end of cooking.
• Test rice and beans for doneness by tasting: Freshness and variety can influence their cooking times. Rice should be soft and fluffy; beans should be creamy, not mushy, in texture.
• Cool cooked beans in their cooking liquid to prevent them from drying out.

SOAKING BEANS

There are two reasons to soak dry beans in water before they're cooked. The first is that this process softens and returns moisture to the beans, which will reduce cooking time. The second is that soaking allows some of the gas-causing oligosaccharides (complex sugars that the human body cannot digest) to dissolve in the water, which makes digestion easier. Always discard the soaking liquid and cook the beans in fresh water.

To soak, combine beans with enough cold water to cover by 2 inches. (Remember that beans will rehydrate to triple their dry size, so start with a large enough bowl or pot.) The standard soaking time is overnight, or about 8 hours. It's not true that longer is better, though; if left to soak too long, beans may start to ferment, so follow the recipe or package directions. When time is of the essence, you can use the quick-soak method instead. To do this, simply boil the water and beans for 3 minutes; remove from heat. Cover and set aside for 1 hour; discard the soaking liquid.

RICE COOKING METHODS

There are two basic methods of cooking rice, immersion and absorption. For the immersion method, rice is boiled like pasta, in a large amount of salted water until tender, then drained; the disadvantage is that nutrients are poured away with the cooking water. Good Housekeeping prefers the absorption method, where rice is cooked in a measured quantity of liquid, all of which is absorbed, thus conserving nutrients. (Rice cookers use the absorption method and have a built-in timer; some also double up as steamers for other foods.) The cooking time and amount of liquid will vary depending on the variety of rice (see chart on page 371). For long-grain white rice, combine 1 cup rice with 2 cups cooking liquid, 1 teaspoon salt (optional), and 1 tablespoon margarine or butter (optional) in a 2- to 3-quart saucepan. Heat to boiling. Reduce heat; cover and simmer 18 to 20 minutes. Remove from heat; let stand, covered, 5 minutes.

KNOW YOUR RICE

Regular long-grain Slender, polished white elongated grains; it cooks into dry grains that separate easily.

Parboiled (also called converted) Rice that has been steamed and pressure-treated; the grains remain firm and separate after cooking.

Instant Rice that has been partially or fully cooked, then dehydrated. It cooks in minutes but remains dry and chewy.

Arborio The traditional rice for Italian risotto; this fat, almost round grain has a high starch content and yields a moist, creamy texture. Vialone Nano and Carnaroli rice varieties have a similar starch content.

Brown The least processed form of rice; it has the outer hull removed but retains the nutritious, high-fiber bran layers that give it a light tan color, nutty flavor, and chewy texture.

Basmati A long-grain rice native to India; valued for its fragrant perfume, delicate taste, and fluffy texture. When cooked, the slender grains swell only lengthwise, resulting in thin, dry grains perfect for pilafs.

Wild rice Not truly a rice but the seed of an aquatic grass. The long, dark-brown grains have a chewy texture and nutty, earthy flavor; rinse well before cooking.

Regular long-grain   Instant   Arborio

Brown   Basmati   Wild

WHAT IS STICKY RICE?

Sticky, or glutinous, rice is a short-grain Asian rice with a slightly sweet taste and soft, sticky texture resulting from a high starch content. Typically used in dim sum, sushi, and desserts, it can be purchased in Asian or Caribbean markets.

RICE SENSE

RICE VARIETY (1 CUP)	AMOUNT OF LIQUID	COOKING TIME	COOKED YIELD
Regular long-grain	1¾–2 cups	18–20 mins	3 cups
Medium- or short-grain	1½–1¾ cups	18–20 mins	3 cups
Brown	2–2½ cups	45–50 mins	3–4 cups
Wild	2–2½ cups	45–60 mins	2⅔ cups

KNOW YOUR GRAINS

Couscous (Moroccan pasta) Grains of precooked semolina; in North African cooking, it is steamed and served with spiced meats and vegetables to make a dish of the same name.

Bulgur Wheat kernels that have been steamed, dried, and crushed. A staple in Middle Eastern cuisine and the grain for tabbouleh, bulgur has a tender, chewy texture.

Barley An ancient grain used to make cereal, bread, salads, and soups. Pearl barley has been polished to remove the outer hull; quick-cooking pearl barley has been pre-steamed.

Wheat berries Unprocessed whole wheat kernels with a chewy texture; used for salads, pilafs, breakfast porridge, or baking.

Quinoa A staple grain of the ancient Incas, quinoa is rich in protein and vital nutrients. The tiny seeds cook quickly; they have a slightly earthy taste and springy texture.

Cornmeal Dried corn kernels (yellow, white, or blue) ground to a fine, medium, or coarse texture. Much used in baking, it is also cooked to make polenta, a staple dish in Northern Italy. Stone-ground cornmeal has not been degerminated and has the best flavor; store in the freezer or refrigerator.

Couscous   Bulgur   Barley

Wheat berries   Quinoa   Cornmeal

Buckwheat A grain with an earthy flavor. The kernels, whole (groats) or ground (grits), may be cooked like rice. Kasha is roasted buckwheat kernels. Buckwheat flour is used in blinis.

KNOW YOUR BEANS

Black beans Also called turtle beans, these are a staple bean in Latin America and the Caribbean. With a slightly sweet taste, they're prized as the base for black bean soup, as a partner with rice, or as a robust filling for burritos.

Navy A small white bean, also called the pea or Yankee bean, these have long been a staple of the U.S. Navy. They're used for canned pork and beans, soups, and Boston baked beans.

Yellow or green split peas Dried peas that have been peeled and split in half, these have a slightly sweet flavor that pairs well with ham, and they can be cooked to a soft puree that makes excellent soup.

Cranberry These plump, beautiful beans are cream-colored with red streaks, but become uniform in color during cooking. Also called shell beans, they have a nutty flavor.

Pink A smooth, reddish-brown dry bean popular in the Southwest, where it's used to make refried beans and chili; interchangeable with pinto beans.

Great Northern These large white beans have a delicate flavor. Popular in soup and baked-bean dishes; they can be substituted for other white beans in most recipes.

Black-eyed peas Oval, beige-colored beans with a black circular "eye," also called cowpeas. Used to make Hoppin' John, a Southern specialty, as well as soups and salads; they have a mealy texture and earthy taste.

Garbanzo beans Also called chick-peas, they're perhaps best known as the base for hummus, a creamy Middle Eastern dip; they're also a favorite in Italian and Indian cooking. Their cooking time can vary greatly, so always taste for doneness.

Red kidney The choice for chili, this medium-size bean has a firm, burgundy-colored skin, pale flesh, and a sweet, meaty flavor.

White kidney Also called cannellini beans, they have a creamy texture and milder taste than the red variety. White kidney beans are common in Italian cooking, where they're used for soup or pasta dishes, or with tuna to make a salad.

Pinto Named for the Spanish word for "speckled," these pale pink beans are splotched with reddish-brown streaks. Grown in the Southwest and prized in most Spanish-speaking countries, they are used to make refried beans or in soup or stew. Pinto beans are interchangeable with pink beans.

Fava Also called broad beans, these flat, light brown beans resemble large limas. They have a tough skin that should be removed by blanching before cooking. Fava beans are popular in Mediterranean countries, where they are commonly used to make salads and soups.

Lima Also called butter beans, these large oval, cream-colored beans hold their shape well when cooked; often served alone as a hot vegetable or in salads.

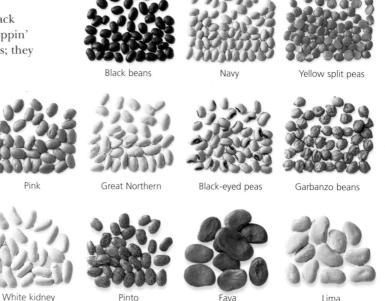

Black beans   Navy   Yellow split peas

Cranberry   Pink   Great Northern   Black-eyed peas   Garbanzo beans

Red kidney   White kidney   Pinto   Fava   Lima

KNOW YOUR LENTILS

Protein-packed lentils, one of our oldest cultivated crops, cook into countless savory, satisfying dishes including Indian dals and hearty stews and salads. They don't need to be presoaked and they cook faster than other dry beans.

Small green French lentils (Puy) These tiny, plump lentils are grown in central France. Considered to have the best flavor, they cook quickly, hold their shape, and have a nutty taste.

Red A smaller, round variety, these lighten to yellow and become very soft when cooked. They are often used in Indian dals.

Green lentils Popular in European cooking; they have a firm texture and a nutty, earthy taste.

Brown lentils The most common variety; they have a firm texture and a mild nutty flavor.

Puy   Red   Green   Brown

RICE

Perhaps the word's most versatile staple, rice is the basis of flavorful dishes from paella to jambalaya. In a hurry? A dash of herbs or spice transforms plain white rice into an exciting side dish.

VEGETABLE PAELLA

Prep: 40 minutes plus standing   Bake: 50 minutes
Makes 8 main-dish servings

1 small eggplant (1 pound), cut lengthwise in half, then crosswise into ½-inch-thick slices

2 tablespoons plus ¼ cup olive or vegetable oil

1 medium onion, diced

8 ounces mushrooms, each cut in half or quarters

2 small zucchini (about 6 ounces each), cut into 1-inch pieces

2 medium tomatoes, cut into ¾-inch pieces

3 cans (13¾ to 14½ ounces each) reduced-sodium vegetable broth

1 package (16 ounces) parboiled rice

1 package (10 ounces) frozen artichoke hearts, thawed

¼ teaspoon salt

½ teaspoon crushed saffron threads

¼ teaspoon ground black pepper

1 can (15 to 19 ounces) garbanzo beans, rinsed and drained

1 package (10 ounces) frozen peas

¼ cup pimiento-stuffed olives, rinsed and drained

½ teaspoon chopped fresh thyme

1 Preheat oven to 450°F. Brush eggplant slices on both sides with 2 tablespoons oil. Spread eggplant in jelly-roll pan. Bake 15 minutes, turning slices once. Set aside. Turn oven control to 350°F.

2 Meanwhile, in 12-inch skillet, heat remaining ¼ cup oil over medium-high heat; add onion and cook, stirring occasionally, until tender.

3 Add mushrooms to onion in skillet; cook, stirring occasionally, until tender and brown. Stir in zucchini and cook 1 minute.

4 Stir in tomatoes, vegetable broth, rice, artichoke hearts, salt, saffron, pepper, and eggplant; heat to boiling over high heat. Transfer rice mixture to shallow 4-quart casserole. Bake, uncovered, about 50 minutes, until rice is tender and liquid is absorbed.

5 Remove casserole from oven; stir in garbanzo beans, peas, olives, and thyme. Let paella stand 10 minutes to allow ingredients to heat through.

SAFFRON

The most expensive spice you can buy, saffron is the yellow-orange stigmas of the crocus flower, which are hand-picked and dried. Available as threads or powder, saffron should be used sparingly – too much produces a medicinal flavor. Use the threads in preference to powder, which loses its pungency in storage. The golden color and distinct flavor of saffron are traditional in paella, bouillabaisse, and risotto Milanese.

EACH SERVING: ABOUT 475 CALORIES, 12g PROTEIN, 78g CARBOHYDRATE, 13g TOTAL FAT (2g SATURATED), 0mg CHOLESTEROL, 660mg SODIUM

ARROZ CON POLLO

Prep: 15 minutes plus standing   Cook: 40 minutes
Makes 4 main-dish servings

1 tablespoon vegetable oil
1½ pounds chicken thighs,
  skin removed
1 medium onion, chopped
1 medium red pepper, cut
  into ½-inch pieces
1 garlic clove, minced
⅛ teaspoon ground red
  pepper (cayenne)
1 cup regular long-grain rice
1 strip (3" by ½") lemon peel

¼ teaspoon dried oregano
¼ teaspoon salt
1 can (13¾ to 14½ ounces)
  reduced-sodium chicken
  broth
1 cup frozen peas
¼ cup salad olives (chopped
  pimiento-stuffed olives)
¼ cup chopped fresh cilantro
Lemon wedges for garnish

◆ In 5-quart Dutch oven, heat oil over medium-high heat. Add chicken thighs and cook 8 to 10 minutes, turning once, until well browned. Transfer to bowl. Reduce heat to medium. To drippings in Dutch oven, add onion and pepper pieces; cook 5 minutes, or until tender. Stir in garlic and ground red pepper and cook 30 seconds. Add rice and cook, stirring, 1 minute. Stir in lemon peel, oregano, salt, and broth plus enough *water* to equal 2 cups.

◆ Return chicken to Dutch oven; heat to boiling over high heat. Reduce heat to low; cover and simmer 20 minutes, or until juices run clear when chicken is pierced with tip of knife.

◆ Stir in peas; cover and heat through. Remove from heat; let stand 5 minutes. Spoon into serving bowl and sprinkle with olives and cilantro. Serve garnished with lemon wedges.

Each serving: About 440 calories, 27g protein, 52g carbohydrate, 14g total fat (3g saturated), 77mg cholesterol, 450mg sodium

CHINESE FRIED RICE

Prep: 5 minutes   Cook: 30 minutes
Makes 4 main-dish servings

1 cup regular long-grain rice
  (or 3 cups cold cooked rice)
6 large eggs
½ teaspoon salt
3 tablespoons vegetable oil

4 ounces cooked ham, diced
  (1 cup)
½ cup frozen peas, thawed
1 tablespoon chopped green
  onion

◆ Prepare long-grain rice as label directs. Meanwhile, in medium bowl, with fork, lightly beat eggs and salt until just blended; set aside.

◆ In nonstick 12-inch skillet, heat 2 tablespoons oil over medium heat; add rice and stir gently until rice is well coated with oil. Push rice to one side of skillet.

◆ Add remaining 1 tablespoon oil to skillet and heat over medium-high heat until very hot. Pour in eggs and cook, stirring constantly, until eggs are the size of peas and leave side of pan.

◆ Stir rice into eggs. Stir in ham and peas; heat through. Sprinkle with green onion.

Each serving: About 430 calories, 21g protein, 41g carbohydrate, 20g total fat (5g saturated), 335mg cholesterol, 755mg sodium

JAMBALAYA

Prep: 20 minutes   Cook: 45 minutes
Makes 6 main-dish servings

8 ounces hot Italian-sausage
  links, pricked all over with
  fork
1 medium onion, finely
  chopped
1 medium green pepper, diced
1 medium celery stalk, diced
1 garlic clove, minced
⅛ teaspoon ground red
  pepper (cayenne)
1½ cups regular long-grain
  rice
⅛ teaspoon dried thyme

¼ teaspoon salt
1 can (13¾ to 14½ ounces)
  reduced-sodium chicken
  broth
1 can (14½ to 16 ounces)
  tomatoes, drained and
  chopped
1 pound medium shrimp,
  shelled and deveined (see
  page 90)
2 green onions, thinly sliced
Hot-pepper sauce (optional)

◆ In 5-quart Dutch oven, cook sausages over medium heat about 10 minutes, until browned all over. Transfer to paper towels to drain; cool. Slice sausages into ½-inch pieces.

◆ To drippings in Dutch oven, add onion, green pepper, and celery; cook 10 minutes, or until tender. Stir in garlic and ground red pepper; cook, stirring, 30 seconds.

◆ Add rice; cook, stirring, 1 minute. Stir in thyme, salt, and broth plus enough *water* to equal 3 cups. Return sausages to Dutch oven; heat to boiling over high heat. Reduce heat to low; cover and simmer 15 minutes.

◆ Stir in tomatoes; cover and cook 5 minutes. Stir in shrimp; cover and cook 5 minutes longer, or until shrimp turn opaque throughout.

◆ Spoon mixture into serving bowl and sprinkle with green onions. Serve with hot-pepper sauce, if you like.

Each serving: About 385 calories, 22g protein, 45g carbohydrate, 13g total fat (4g saturated), 152mg cholesterol, 710mg sodium

CUMIN RICE WITH BLACK BEANS

Prep: 10 minutes plus standing   Cook: 30 minutes
Makes 6 accompaniment servings

1 tablespoon vegetable oil
1 medium onion, finely chopped
1 garlic clove, minced
2 teaspoons cumin seeds
1½ cups regular long-grain rice
1 can (13¾ to 14½ ounces) chicken or vegetable broth
¼ teaspoon salt
1 can (15 to 19 ounces) black beans, rinsed and drained
2 tablespoons chopped fresh cilantro
Lime wedges

◆ In 3-quart saucepan, heat oil over medium heat. Add onion and cook 5 minutes, or until tender. Stir in garlic and cumin seeds; cook until fragrant. Add rice and cook, stirring, 1 minute.

◆ Stir in chicken broth plus enough *water* to equal 3 cups and salt; heat to boiling over high heat. Reduce heat to low; cover and simmer 15 minutes.

◆ Stir black beans into rice. Cover and simmer 5 minutes longer. Remove from heat and let stand 5 minutes. Spoon rice mixture into serving bowl and sprinkle with chopped cilantro. Serve with lime wedges.

Each serving: About 270 calories, 9g protein, 53g carbohydrate, 4g total fat (1g saturated), 5mg cholesterol, 650mg sodium

INDIAN-SPICED RICE

Prep: 2 minutes plus standing   Cook: 25 minutes
Makes 4 accompaniment servings

1 tablespoon vegetable oil
1 cinnamon stick (3 inches)
10 black peppercorns
6 cardamom pods
4 whole cloves
1 cup regular long-grain rice
½ teaspoon salt

◆ In 2-quart saucepan, heat oil over medium heat. Add cinnamon stick, peppercorns, cardamom, and cloves and cook, stirring often, just until spices begin to darken. Add rice and cook, stirring, 1 minute.

◆ Stir in salt and *2 cups water*; heat to boiling over high heat. Reduce heat to low; cover and simmer 20 minutes.

◆ Remove rice from heat and let stand 5 minutes. Fluff with fork.

Each serving: About 205 calories, 3g protein, 38g carbohydrate, 4g total fat (1g saturated), 0mg cholesterol, 270mg sodium

PERSIAN RICE PILAF

Prep: 10 minutes plus standing   Cook: 30 minutes
Makes 4 accompaniment servings

1 tablespoon margarine or butter
1 small onion, finely chopped
1 cup regular long-grain rice
1 can (13¾ to 14½ ounces) chicken or vegetable broth
¼ cup dried currants
Pinch ground cinnamon
⅛ teaspoon ground black pepper
½ teaspoon grated orange peel
¼ cup pine nuts (pignoli), toasted
¼ cup chopped fresh parsley

◆ In 2-quart saucepan, melt margarine over medium heat. Add onion and cook, stirring often, 4 minutes, or until tender. Add rice and cook, stirring, 1 minute.

◆ Stir in chicken broth plus enough *water* to equal 2 cups, currants, cinnamon, and ground black pepper; heat to boiling over high heat. Reduce heat to low; cover and simmer 20 minutes.

◆ Remove rice from heat and let stand 5 minutes. Add orange peel; fluff with fork until combined. Gently stir in pine nuts and parsley.

Each serving: About 285 calories, 7g protein, 49g carbohydrate, 8g total fat (2g saturated), 8mg cholesterol, 475mg sodium

WORLD OF RICE

◆◆◆◆◆◆◆◆◆◆◆◆◆◆◆◆◆◆◆◆◆◆

There are over 40,000 varieties of rice, and more than half the world's people eat rice as their main sustenance. Specialties come from all over: In the Near East and India, rice pilaf is prepared by browning rice in hot oil or butter before cooking it in broth, which helps keep the grains separate. Japanese cooks prefer a starchier variety of rice, while in northern Thailand, sticky rice holds together enough to be eaten with the hands. In China, rice is served as a breakfast porridge called congee.

Rijsttafel, Dutch for "rice table," is an adaptation of an Indonesian meal that's popular in Holland: A platter of hot spiced rice is accompanied by various small side dishes including fried seafood and meats, curries, and relishes. In Spain and Mexico, arroz con pollo, or "rice with chicken," may get added flavor from tomatoes, pimientos, onions, peppers, and peas. Paella is a Spanish rice dish that usually contains a combination of chicken, seafood, sausages, pork, and vegetables, with saffron for a bright yellow color. Jambalaya, the New Orleans version of paella, may include ham and shrimp, and replaces the saffron with cayenne pepper. "Dirty" rice was also created in New Orleans; it gets its "dirty" appearance from chicken livers.

ORANGE-CILANTRO RICE In 2-quart saucepan, heat 1 cup regular long-grain rice, 1 cup chicken or vegetable broth, ¾ cup water, and ¼ teaspoon salt to boiling over high heat. Reduce heat to low; cover and simmer 18 to 20 minutes, until rice is tender and liquid is absorbed. Stir in 2 tablespoons chopped fresh cilantro and ½ teaspoon grated orange peel. Makes 4 accompaniment servings.

Each serving: About 180 calories, 4g protein, 38g carbohydrate, 1g total fat (0g saturated), 5mg cholesterol, 400mg sodium

GREEN RICE In 2-quart saucepan, heat 1 cup regular long-grain rice, 1 cup chicken or vegetable broth, ¾ cup water, and ¼ teaspoon salt to boiling over high heat. Reduce heat to low; cover and simmer 15 minutes. Stir in 1 package (10 ounces) frozen chopped spinach, thawed and squeezed dry; cover and cook 5 minutes. Stir in 2 ounces feta cheese, finely crumbled (½ cup). Makes 4 accompaniment servings.

Each serving: About 235 calories, 8g protein, 42g carbohydrate, 4g total fat (2g saturated), 17mg cholesterol, 620mg sodium

Parsley-walnut rice

Soy-sesame rice

LEMON-PARSLEY RICE In 2-quart saucepan, heat 1 cup regular long-grain rice, 1 cup chicken or vegetable broth, ¾ cup water, and ¼ teaspoon salt to boiling over high heat. Reduce heat to low; cover and simmer 18 to 20 minutes, until rice is tender and liquid is absorbed. Stir in 2 tablespoons chopped fresh parsley and 1 teaspoon grated lemon peel until blended. Makes 4 accompaniment servings.

Each serving: About 180 calories, 4g protein, 38g carbohydrate, 1g total fat (0g saturated), 5mg cholesterol, 405mg sodium

PARSLEY-WALNUT RICE In 2-quart saucepan, heat 1 cup regular long-grain rice, 1 cup chicken or vegetable broth, ¾ cup water, and ¼ teaspoon salt to boiling over high heat. Reduce heat to low; cover and simmer 18 to 20 minutes, until rice is tender and liquid is absorbed. Stir in ¼ cup toasted walnuts (about 1 ounce), chopped, 2 tablespoons chopped fresh parsley, and 1 tablespoon margarine or butter until blended. Makes 4 accompaniment servings.

Each serving: About 250 calories, 5g protein, 39g carbohydrate, 8g total fat (1g saturated), 5mg cholesterol, 435mg sodium

SOY-SESAME RICE In 2-quart saucepan, heat 1 cup regular long-grain rice, 1 cup chicken or vegetable broth, and ¾ cup water to boiling over high heat. Reduce heat to low; cover and simmer 18 to 20 minutes, until rice is tender and liquid is absorbed. Stir in 2 green onions, chopped, 2 teaspoons soy sauce, and ¼ teaspoon Asian sesame oil. Makes 4 accompaniment servings.

Each serving: About 180 calories, 4g protein, 38g carbohydrate, 1g total fat (0g saturated), 5mg cholesterol, 575mg sodium

PEPPERED JACK RICE In 2-quart saucepan, heat 1 cup regular long-grain rice, 1 cup chicken or vegetable broth, ¾ cup water, and ¼ teaspoon salt to boiling over high heat. Reduce heat to low; cover and simmer 18 to 20 minutes, until rice is tender and liquid is absorbed. Stir in 2 ounces Monterey Jack cheese with jalapeño chiles, shredded (½ cup), and 3 green onions, thinly sliced. Makes 4 accompaniment servings.

Each serving: About 235 calories, 8g protein, 38g carbohydrate, 5g total fat (3g saturated), 20mg cholesterol, 500mg sodium

COCONUT RICE In 2-quart saucepan, heat 1 cup regular long-grain rice, 1 cup chicken or vegetable broth, ¾ cup water, and ¼ teaspoon salt to boiling over high heat. Reduce heat to low; cover and simmer 18 to 20 minutes, until rice is tender and liquid is absorbed. Stir in ½ cup unsweetened coconut milk, ½ teaspoon grated lime peel, and pinch ground red pepper (cayenne). Makes 4 accompaniment servings.

Each serving: About 245 calories, 5g protein, 39g carbohydrate, 8g total fat (7g saturated), 5mg cholesterol, 405mg sodium

LEMON-PARMESAN RICE In 2-quart saucepan, heat 1 cup regular long-grain rice, 1 cup chicken or vegetable broth, ¾ cup water, and ¼ teaspoon salt to boiling over high heat. Reduce heat to low; cover and simmer 18 to 20 minutes, until rice is tender and liquid is absorbed. Stir in ¼ cup freshly grated Parmesan cheese, 1 teaspoon grated lemon peel, and ¼ teaspoon ground black pepper. Makes 4 accompaniment servings.

Each serving: About 205 calories, 7g protein, 38g carbohydrate, 3g total fat (1g saturated), 10mg cholesterol, 520mg sodium

RISOTTO

Rich, creamy risotto, a specialty from Northern Italy, relies on starchy, short-grain Arborio rice – and a little patience. The grains of rice are first sautéed, then hot broth is added gradually, as it is absorbed. Almost constant stirring ensures even cooking. Perfect risotto is just tender, yet still slightly "al dente."

SPRING RISOTTO

◆◆◆◆◆◆◆◆◆◆◆

Prep: 30 minutes
Cook: 55 minutes
Makes 4 main-dish servings

1 can (13¾ to 14½ ounces) vegetable or chicken broth
2 tablespoons olive oil
3 medium carrots, diced
¾ pound asparagus, tough ends removed, cut into 2-inch pieces
6 ounces sugar snap peas, strings removed and each cut crosswise in half
¼ teaspoon coarsely ground black pepper
Salt
1 small onion, chopped
2 cups Arborio rice (Italian short-grain rice) or medium-grain rice
½ cup dry white wine
½ cup freshly grated Parmesan cheese
¼ cup chopped fresh basil or parsley

1 In 2-quart saucepan, heat broth and *3½ cups water* to boiling over high heat. Reduce heat to low to maintain simmer; cover. In 4-quart saucepan, heat 1 tablespoon olive oil over medium heat. Add carrots and cook 10 minutes. Add asparagus, sugar snap peas, pepper, and ¼ teaspoon salt; cover and cook about 5 minutes, until vegetables are tender-crisp. Transfer vegetables to bowl; set aside.

2 In same saucepan, heat remaining 1 tablespoon oil over medium heat. Add onion; cook 5 minutes, or until tender. Add rice and ¼ teaspoon salt; cook, stirring, until rice is opaque.

3 Add white wine; cook, stirring constantly, until wine is absorbed. Add about ½ cup simmering broth to rice mixture, stirring until liquid is absorbed.

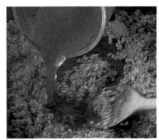

4 Continue cooking, adding simmering broth, ½ cup at a time, and stirring after each addition, about 25 minutes, until all liquid is absorbed and rice is tender but still firm.

5 When risotto is done (it should have a creamy consistency), stir in vegetables; heat through. Stir in Parmesan and basil. Spoon risotto into 4 shallow bowls; serve hot.

RISOTTO TIPS
◆◆◆◆◆◆◆◆◆◆◆

• Serve risotto at once; it continues to absorb liquid as it stands.

• Use a heavy pan with a thick base that heats evenly; maintain the rice at a steady, gentle simmer.

• Keep the broth at a constant simmer, or the risotto will cook too slowly and become gluey.

EACH SERVING: ABOUT 645 CALORIES, 18g PROTEIN, 107g CARBOHYDRATE, 12g TOTAL FAT (4g SATURATED), 18mg CHOLESTEROL, 965mg SODIUM

SHRIMP RISOTTO WITH BABY PEAS

Prep: 35 minutes   *Cook:* 35 minutes
Makes 4 main-dish servings

1 pound medium shrimp
1 can (13¾ to 14½ ounces) reduced-
  sodium chicken or vegetable broth
1 tablespoon margarine or butter
⅛ teaspoon ground black pepper
½ teaspoon salt
1 tablespoon olive oil
1 small onion, finely chopped
2 cups Arborio rice (Italian short-grain
  rice) or medium-grain rice
½ cup dry white wine
1 cup frozen baby peas
¼ cup chopped fresh parsley

◆ Shell and devein shrimp (see page 90), reserving shells. In 3-quart saucepan, combine broth, *4 cups water*, and reserved shells. Heat to boiling over high heat. Reduce heat to low; simmer 20 minutes. Strain broth through sieve; if necessary, add *water* to equal 5½ cups. Return broth to clean saucepan and heat to boiling over high heat. Reduce heat to low to maintain simmer; cover.

◆ In 4-quart saucepan, melt margarine over medium-high heat. Add shrimp, pepper, and salt; cook, stirring, 2 minutes, or just until shrimp are opaque. Transfer to bowl.

◆ In same saucepan, heat oil over medium heat. Add onion; cook 5 minutes, until tender. Add rice and cook, stirring often, until grains are opaque. Add wine; cook until absorbed. Add ½ cup simmering broth; stir until absorbed. Continue cooking, adding broth, ½ cup at a time, and stirring after each addition, about 25 minutes, until all liquid is absorbed and rice is tender and creamy but still firm. Stir in peas and cooked shrimp and heat through. Stir in parsley.

Each serving: About 645 calories, 30g protein, 100g carbohydrate, 8g total fat (2g saturated), 183mg cholesterol, 565mg sodium

MUSHROOM RISOTTO

Prep: 20 minutes plus standing
Cook: 50 minutes
Makes 4 main-dish servings

½ ounce dried porcini mushrooms
1 can (13¾ to 14½ ounces) reduced-
  sodium chicken or vegetable broth
2 tablespoons margarine or butter
1 pound white mushrooms, sliced
¼ teaspoon ground black pepper
½ teaspoon salt
Pinch dried thyme
1 tablespoon olive oil
1 small onion, finely chopped
2 cups Arborio rice (Italian short-grain
  rice) or medium-grain rice
½ cup dry white wine
½ cup freshly grated Parmesan cheese
2 tablespoons chopped fresh parsley

◆ In small bowl, combine porcini with *½ cup boiling water*; let stand 30 minutes. With slotted spoon, remove porcini; rinse and chop. Strain soaking liquid through sieve lined with paper towel. In 2-quart saucepan, heat broth, *3¼ cups water*, and porcini liquid to boiling over high heat. Reduce heat to low to maintain simmer; cover.

◆ In 4-quart saucepan, melt margarine over medium heat. Add white mushrooms, pepper, salt, and thyme; cook, stirring occasionally, 10 minutes. Stir in porcini. Transfer mushroom mixture to bowl.

◆ In same saucepan, heat oil over medium heat. Add onion; cook 5 minutes. Add rice and cook, stirring often, until grains are opaque. Add wine; cook until absorbed. Add ½ cup simmering broth; stir until absorbed. Continue cooking, adding broth, ½ cup at a time, and stirring after each addition, about 25 minutes, until all liquid is absorbed and rice is tender and creamy but still firm. Stir in mushroom mixture and Parmesan; heat through. Stir in parsley.

Each serving: About 645 calories, 17g protein, 102g carbohydrate, 14g total fat (4g saturated), 18mg cholesterol, 600mg sodium

BUTTERNUT SQUASH RISOTTO WITH SAGE

Prep: 20 minutes   *Cook:* 50 minutes
Makes 4 main-dish servings

1 medium butternut squash (2 pounds)
1 can (13¾ to 14½ ounces) reduced-
  sodium chicken or vegetable broth
2 tablespoons margarine or butter
¼ teaspoon ground black pepper
3 tablespoons chopped fresh sage
¼ teaspoon salt
1 tablespoon olive oil
1 small onion, finely chopped
2 cups Arborio rice (Italian short-grain
  rice) or medium-grain rice
⅓ cup dry white wine
½ cup freshly grated Parmesan cheese

◆ Cut squash into chunks; cut off peel. Cut enough squash into ½-inch pieces to equal 2 cups. Shred enough remaining squash to equal 2 cups. In 2-quart saucepan, heat broth and *3½ cups water* to boiling over high heat. Reduce heat to low to maintain simmer; cover.

◆ In 4-quart saucepan, melt margarine over medium heat. Add squash pieces, pepper, 2 tablespoons sage, and salt. Cook, stirring often, 10 minutes, or until squash is tender (add *2 to 4 tablespoons water* if squash sticks to pan before it is tender). Transfer to small bowl.

◆ Add oil, onion, and shredded squash to same saucepan; cook, stirring frequently, until vegetables are tender. Add rice; cook, stirring often, until grains are opaque. Add wine; cook until absorbed. Add ½ cup simmering broth; stir until absorbed. Continue cooking, adding broth, ½ cup at a time, and stirring after each addition, about 25 minutes, until all liquid is absorbed and rice is tender and creamy but still firm. (Add *½ cup water* if necessary.) Stir in squash pieces, Parmesan, and remaining 1 tablespoon sage; heat through.

Each serving: About 690 calories, 17g protein, 119g carbohydrate, 14g total fat (4g saturated), 18mg cholesterol, 470mg sodium

COUSCOUS

The grain-like semolina pasta called couscous, originally from North Africa, is quickly transformed into a refreshing main-course salad or an exotic side dish for chicken, lamb, or beef. The boxed supermarket version is ready in about five minutes (traditional couscous is soaked, steamed, and dried several times).

NUTTY COUSCOUS SALAD

◆◆◆◆◆◆◆◆◆◆◆◆◆◆◆◆◆◆◆◆◆◆◆◆◆◆◆◆

Prep: 20 minutes   *Cook:* 5 minutes
Makes 8 accompaniment servings

1½ cups (10 ounces) couscous (Moroccan pasta)
½ cup pitted dates
1 bunch flat-leaf parsley
1 large orange
2 tablespoons olive or vegetable oil
2 tablespoons cider vinegar
½ teaspoon sugar
¼ teaspoon salt
1 cup dried currants or dark seedless raisins
2 tablespoons coarsely chopped crystallized ginger
1 can (6 ounces) salted cashews

1 Prepare couscous as label directs. Cut each date crosswise into 3 pieces. Reserve a few sprigs parsley to use for garnish.

2 With large chef's knife, finely chop enough remaining parsley to equal 3 tablespoons. Set aside.

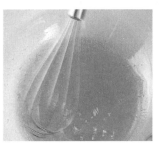

3 Prepare orange dressing: Grate peel and squeeze juice from orange. In large bowl, with wire whisk or fork, mix orange peel, orange juice, oil, cider vinegar, sugar, and salt until blended.

4 To dressing in bowl, add couscous, dates, chopped parsley, currants, ginger, and cashews; toss to mix well. Garnish with parsley sprigs. Cover and refrigerate if not serving right away.

DATES

With at least 50 percent sugar, dates are the sweetest of fruits. They are categorized as soft, semisoft, or dry according to how soft they are when ripe: The Deglet Noor, the most commonly available, is a medium-size semisoft date, while the Medjool, a very large premium date, is the best known of the soft dates.

Dates are available both fresh on the stem and dried; most supermarket dates have beeen dried and partially rehydrated. When buying, avoid very shriveled dates (though a wrinkled skin is normal) and any with mold or sugar crystals on the skin. Dates will last up to a year in an airtight container in the refrigerator and up to five years in the freezer.

Dates are frequently used in baking (you can substitute chopped dates for raisins), and are good in salads, pilafs, poultry stuffings, and lamb stews.

Medjool

Deglet Noor

EACH SERVING: ABOUT 410 CALORIES, 9g PROTEIN, 60g CARBOHYDRATE, 17g TOTAL FAT (4g SATURATED), 8mg CHOLESTEROL, 370mg SODIUM

FLAVORED COUSCOUS

Lime couscous Prepare 1 cup couscous (Moroccan pasta) as label directs, but add 1 tablespoon fresh lime juice and ½ teaspoon grated lime peel to water before boiling. Makes 4 accompaniment servings.

Each serving: About 210 calories, 6g protein, 36g carbohydrate, 5g total fat (1g saturated), 0mg cholesterol, 245mg sodium

Moroccan couscous Prepare 1 cup couscous (Moroccan pasta) as label directs, but add ¼ cup golden raisins, ¼ teaspoon ground cinnamon, ¼ teaspoon ground turmeric, and ¼ teaspoon ground cumin to water before boiling. Makes 4 accompaniment servings.

Each serving: About 245 calories, 6g protein, 44g carbohydrate, 5g total fat (1g saturated), 0mg cholesterol, 255mg sodium

Green onion and dried tomato couscous Prepare 1 cup couscous (Moroccan pasta) as label directs, but add 1 medium green onion, sliced, and 5 oil-packed dried tomato halves, chopped, to water before boiling. Makes 4 accompaniment servings.

Each serving: About 225 calories, 6g protein, 37g carbohydrate, 6g total fat (1g saturated), 0mg cholesterol, 270mg sodium

Lime couscous

Moroccan couscous

Green onion and dried tomato couscous

FRAGRANT VEGETABLE COUSCOUS

Prep: 10 minutes plus standing   *Cook:* 15 minutes
Makes 4 accompaniment servings

1 tablespoon olive or vegetable oil	⅛ teaspoon ground cinnamon
3 green onions, finely chopped	1 can (13¾ to 14½ ounces) chicken broth
2 medium carrots, diced	1 cup (7 ounces) couscous (Moroccan pasta)
¼ teaspoon salt	½ teaspoon grated orange peel (optional)
¼ teaspoon ground black pepper	

◆ In 3-quart saucepan, heat oil over medium-high heat; add green onions, carrots, salt, and pepper and cook, stirring occasionally, until carrots are tender-crisp. Stir in cinnamon.

◆ Add chicken broth to vegetable mixture; heat to boiling over high heat. Stir in couscous. Cover saucepan; remove from heat and let stand 5 minutes.

◆ With fork, fluff couscous mixture. Stir in grated orange peel, if you like.

Each serving: About 235 calories, 7g protein, 40g carbohydrate, 5g total fat (1g saturated), 8mg cholesterol, 585mg sodium

COUSCOUS SALAD WITH RADISHES

Prep: 15 minutes   *Cook:* 5 minutes
Makes 8 accompaniment servings

1½ cups (10 ounces) couscous (Moroccan pasta)	1 cup frozen peas, thawed
1 can (14½ ounces) vegetable broth	1 cup frozen whole-kernel corn, thawed
1 bunch radishes, coarsely chopped	3 tablespoons olive oil
	1 teaspoon grated lemon peel
	½ teaspoon salt

◆ Prepare couscous as label directs, but use vegetable broth plus *water* to equal amount of water called for on label, and do not use margarine or butter or salt.

◆ In large bowl, mix radishes, peas, corn, olive oil, grated lemon peel, and salt. Stir in couscous until mixed. Cover and refrigerate if not serving right away.

Each serving: About 220 calories, 6g protein, 36g carbohydrate, 5g total fat (1g saturated), 0mg cholesterol, 180mg sodium

CORNMEAL

Cornmeal – ground dried corn kernels – is the key ingredient of polenta, the silky cornmeal mush of Northern Italy. It's great served as a side dish, like mashed potatoes; layered with cheese; or cooled and sliced to be grilled, broiled, or fried. Spoonbread, a soufflé-like casserole, is the fancy Southern version of cornmeal mush. Always add cornmeal gradually to a liquid, and stir well to prevent lumps.

POLENTA WITH MUSHROOMS

◆◆◆◆◆◆◆◆◆◆◆◆◆

Prep: 15 minutes plus standing
Cook: 35 minutes
Makes 3 main-dish servings

1 package (0.35 ounce) dried porcini mushrooms
8 ounces shiitake mushrooms
8 ounces cremini or white mushrooms
2 tablespoons olive oil
1 medium onion, coarsely chopped
2 tablespoons margarine or butter
1 teaspoon minced fresh oregano or ¼ teaspoon dried oregano
¼ teaspoon coarsely ground black pepper
½ teaspoon salt
2 cups milk
1 cup yellow cornmeal
¼ cup freshly grated Parmesan cheese
Oregano sprigs for garnish

1 In bowl, combine porcini and *1 cup boiling water*; let stand 30 minutes. Meanwhile, cut stems from shiitakes; trim stem ends from cremini. Rinse and thickly slice shiitakes and cremini. In 12-inch skillet, heat 1 tablespoon olive oil over medium heat. Add onion and cook 5 minutes, or until tender; transfer to small bowl. In same skillet, heat margarine and remaining 1 tablespoon oil over medium-high heat.

2 Add shiitakes, cremini, minced oregano, and pepper to skillet; cook, stirring, 10 minutes. Meanwhile, drain porcini in sieve lined with paper towel; reserve ¾ cup liquid. Rinse porcini; chop.

3 Return onion to skillet. Stir in chopped porcini and reserved liquid; heat to boiling. Boil 1 minute. Remove from heat; keep warm.

PERFECT POLENTA

◆◆◆◆◆◆◆◆◆◆◆◆

This is our tried-and-tested method for lump-free polenta: In pan you intend to cook it in, place one-third of cold liquid called for in recipe, then gradually whisk in cornmeal. In another pan, heat remaining liquid to boiling. Add hot liquid to cornmeal mixture, whisking constantly.

4 Prepare polenta: In 3-quart saucepan, place salt and 1⅓ cups milk; gradually whisk in cornmeal until smooth. In 2-quart saucepan, heat remaining ⅔ cup milk and *2 cups water* to boiling over high heat; whisk into cornmeal mixture. Heat to boiling over medium-high heat, whisking. Reduce heat to low.

5 Cook polenta, stirring constantly, 5 minutes, or until thick. Stir in grated Parmesan until well combined. Serve polenta topped with mushroom mixture. Garnish with oregano sprigs.

EACH SERVING: ABOUT 545 CALORIES, 16g PROTEIN, 65g CARBOHYDRATE, 26g TOTAL FAT (8g SATURATED), 28mg CHOLESTEROL, 690mg SODIUM

ROSEMARY POLENTA WEDGES

Prep: 15 minutes plus standing
Broil: 5 to 10 minutes
Makes 8 accompaniment servings

1½ teaspoons salt	½ teaspoon minced fresh
1½ cups yellow cornmeal	rosemary or ¼ teaspoon
3 cups milk	dried rosemary, crushed
1 tablespoon margarine or	Rosemary sprigs for garnish
butter	

◆ Line two 8-inch round cake pans with foil; grease foil. In 3-quart saucepan, place salt and *1¼ cups water*. Gradually whisk in cornmeal.

◆ In 2-quart saucepan, heat milk to boiling over medium-high heat; whisk into cornmeal mixture. Heat to boiling over medium-high heat, whisking. Reduce heat to low and cook, stirring constantly, 3 to 5 minutes, until mixture is thick.

◆ Spoon mixture into prepared pans; let stand 10 minutes, or until firm. If not serving right away, cover and refrigerate.

◆ About 20 minutes before serving, preheat broiler. Grease rack in broiling pan. Remove polenta from pans; discard foil. Cut each polenta round into 8 wedges. Place polenta wedges on rack in broiling pan.

◆ In small saucepan, melt margarine with minced rosemary over medium heat. Brush polenta wedges with margarine mixture; garnish each with small rosemary sprig. Broil polenta about 5 to 7 inches from heat source 5 to 10 minutes, until lightly browned and heated through.

Each serving: About 165 calories, 5g protein, 24g carbohydrate, 5g total fat (2g saturated), 12mg cholesterol, 460mg sodium

SPOONBREAD

Prep: 15 minutes plus standing   *Bake:* 40 minutes
Makes 8 accompaniment servings

3 cups milk	1 cup yellow cornmeal
½ teaspoon salt	4 tablespoons margarine or
¼ teaspoon ground black	butter, cut up
pepper	3 large eggs, separated

◆ Preheat oven to 400°F. Grease shallow 1½-quart glass or ceramic baking dish. In 4-quart saucepan, heat milk, salt, and pepper to boiling over medium-high heat. Remove from heat; gradually whisk in cornmeal. Whisk in margarine until melted. Let stand 5 minutes.

◆ Whisk in egg yolks, one at a time. In medium bowl, with electric mixer at high speed, beat egg whites to soft peaks; fold half of whites into cornmeal mixture, then fold in remaining whites. Pour into baking dish. Bake 40 minutes, or until set. Serve immediately.

Each serving: About 200 calories, 7g protein, 18g carbohydrate, 11g total fat (4g saturated), 92mg cholesterol, 270mg sodium

THREE-CHEESE POLENTA

Prep: 45 minutes plus standing   *Bake:* 20 minutes
Makes 10 main-dish servings

Chunky Tomato Sauce (see	1 tablespoon margarine or
below)	butter
2 cups half-and-half or light	4 ounces mozzarella cheese,
cream	shredded (1 cup)
1 teaspoon salt	4 ounces Fontina cheese,
½ teaspoon ground black	shredded (1 cup)
pepper	1 cup freshly grated
3 cups yellow cornmeal	Parmesan cheese

◆ Prepare Chunky Tomato Sauce; keep warm. Meanwhile, in 5-quart Dutch oven, place half-and-half, salt, pepper, and *1 cup water*. Gradually whisk in cornmeal until smooth. Whisk in *7 cups boiling water*. Heat to boiling over medium-high heat. Reduce heat to low; cook, stirring constantly, about 5 minutes, until mixture is very thick. Stir in margarine until melted. Remove polenta from heat.

◆ Preheat oven to 425°F. Grease 13" by 9" glass baking dish. In medium bowl, mix all cheeses. Spread one-third of polenta in baking dish. Reserve ½ cup cheese mixture for topping; sprinkle polenta with half of remaining cheese. Top with one-third of polenta, remaining cheese, then remaining polenta. Sprinkle with reserved ½ cup cheese. Bake 20 minutes, or until top is browned. Remove from oven; let stand 10 minutes for easier serving.

◆ Cut polenta lengthwise into 2 strips. Cut each strip crosswise into 5 pieces. Serve with Chunky Tomato Sauce.

Each serving: About 500 calories, 17g protein, 50g carbohydrate, 26g total fat (11g saturated), 48mg cholesterol, 1355mg sodium

---

CHUNKY TOMATO SAUCE

In 4-quart saucepan, melt 2 tablespoons margarine or butter over medium heat; stir in 3 large celery stalks, diced, and 3 large carrots, diced, until coated. Cover and cook 20 minutes, stirring occasionally, until vegetables are very tender. Add 1 jar (48 ounces) marinara sauce; heat to boiling over high heat. Reduce heat to low; cover and simmer 15 minutes.

OTHER GRAINS

Whether you're looking for a flavor-packed side dish or a hearty, healthy lunch, delicious grains like quinoa, bulgur, barley, and wheat berries all offer unique texture and taste, and make a nice change of pace from ordinary rice. These wholesome grains are especially appealing when they're speckled with a variety of flavorful ingredients – from nuts and fresh herbs to crunchy vegetables and dried fruits.

QUINOA WITH CORN

Prep: 10 minutes   Cook: 20 minutes
Makes 6 accompaniment servings

1 cup quinoa	1 tablespoon margarine or
Salt	butter
3 medium ears corn, silk and	¼ teaspoon ground black
husks removed	pepper
4 green onions	½ teaspoon grated lemon peel

1 In fine-mesh sieve, thoroughly rinse quinoa with cold running water. In 2-quart saucepan, heat quinoa, ½ teaspoon salt, and *1¾ cups water* to boiling over high heat.

2 Reduce heat to low; cover saucepan and simmer 15 minutes, or until water is absorbed. Meanwhile, cut corn kernels from cobs. Thinly slice green onions.

3 In 10-inch skillet, melt margarine over medium-high heat. Add corn, green onions, pepper, and ¼ teaspoon salt. Cook, stirring often, 3 minutes, or until tender-crisp. Add quinoa and lemon peel; cook, stirring, until combined.

THE HIGH-PROTEIN GRAIN

Native to the Andes mountains in South America, quinoa was cultivated by the ancient Incas. Although it is considered a grain, quinoa is botanically an herb. Unlike any other grain or vegetable, however, quinoa is a complete protein (containing all eight essential amino acids). It is also high in iron.

Quinoa cooks quickly and has a light, springy texture. Rinse quinoa before using to remove the saponin, a bitter, soapy-tasting coating that acts as a natural insecticide.

Try lightly browning quinoa in a dry skillet for 5 minutes before cooking to give it a delicious toasted flavor. For a salad, toss cooked quinoa with finely chopped raw vegetables and a vinaigrette. Quinoa can also be served with fruit and a little sugar or honey as a breakfast cereal.

EACH SERVING: ABOUT 165 CALORIES, 5g PROTEIN, 29g CARBOHYDRATE, 4g TOTAL FAT (1g SATURATED), 0mg CHOLESTEROL, 300mg SODIUM

BULGUR PILAF

Prep: 10 minutes plus standing   *Cook:* 30 minutes
Makes 6 accompaniment servings

2 tablespoons margarine or
  butter
1 medium onion, finely
  chopped
1 cup bulgur wheat
1 can (13¾ to 14½ ounces)
  reduced-sodium chicken or
  vegetable broth
1 cinnamon stick (3 inches)

1 can (15 to 19 ounces)
  garbanzo beans, rinsed and
  drained
⅓ cup diced dried apricots
¼ teaspoon salt
⅛ teaspoon ground black
  pepper
¼ cup chopped fresh parsley

◆ In 3-quart saucepan, melt margarine over medium heat. Add onion and cook, stirring often, 5 minutes, or until tender. Add bulgur and cook, stirring, 2 minutes longer.

◆ Stir in broth, cinnamon stick, garbanzo beans, dried apricots, salt, and pepper; heat to boiling over high heat.

◆ Reduce heat to low; cover and simmer 15 minutes. Remove from heat and let stand 5 minutes. Stir in parsley; fluff bulgur mixture with fork.

Each serving: About 220 calories, 7g protein, 37g carbohydrate, 6g total fat (1g saturated), 5mg cholesterol, 350mg sodium

WHEAT BERRIES WITH BROWN BUTTER AND PECANS

Prep: 10 minutes plus soaking   *Cook:* 1 hour 15 minutes
Makes 6 accompaniment servings

1 cup wheat berries (whole-
  grain wheat)
2 tablespoons margarine or
  butter
1 medium onion, finely
  chopped
½ teaspoon salt

⅛ teaspoon ground black
  pepper
½ cup pecans, coarsely
  chopped (about 2 ounces)
2 tablespoons chopped fresh
  parsley

◆ In medium bowl, soak wheat berries overnight in enough *water* to cover by 2 inches.

◆ Drain wheat berries. In 3-quart saucepan, heat wheat berries and *3 cups water* to boiling over high heat.

◆ Reduce heat to low; cover and simmer 1 hour, or just until tender but still firm. Drain. Wipe saucepan clean.

◆ In same saucepan, melt margarine over medium heat. Add onion and cook, stirring frequently, 5 minutes, or until tender. Stir in salt, pepper, and pecans. Cook, stirring, about 3 minutes, until pecans are lightly toasted and margarine begins to brown.

◆ Add wheat berries and *1 tablespoon water* to pecan mixture; stir until well combined. Heat through, stirring. Remove from heat; stir in parsley.

Each serving: About 235 calories, 6g protein, 31g carbohydrate, 11g total fat (1g saturated), 0mg cholesterol, 225mg sodium

MUSHROOM-BARLEY PILAF

Prep: 15 minutes   *Cook:* 55 minutes
Makes 6 accompaniment servings

1 cup pearl barley
2 tablespoons margarine or
  butter
1 medium onion, finely
  chopped
2 medium celery stalks, cut
  into ¼-inch-thick slices
12 ounces mushrooms, sliced

1 can (13¾ to 14½ ounces)
  chicken or vegetable broth
½ teaspoon salt
⅛ teaspoon ground black
  pepper
⅛ teaspoon dried thyme
¼ cup chopped fresh parsley

◆ In 3-quart saucepan, toast barley over medium heat, shaking pan occasionally, 4 minutes, or until beginning to brown. Transfer to bowl.

◆ In same saucepan, melt margarine over medium heat. Add onion and celery and cook 5 minutes, or until tender. Stir in mushrooms; cook about 10 minutes, until tender and liquid has evaporated.

◆ Stir in barley, broth plus enough *water* to equal 2½ cups, salt, pepper, and thyme. Heat to boiling over high heat. Reduce heat to low; cover and simmer 30 minutes, or until barley is tender. Remove from heat; stir in parsley.

Each serving: About 190 calories, 6g protein, 32g carbohydrate, 5g total fat (1g saturated), 5mg cholesterol, 530mg sodium

DRY BEANS

Prized for their value and versatility, dry beans turn up in favorite dishes around the globe. Before cooking, soak dry beans overnight, or follow our quick (1-hour) method. For digestibility, it's best to drain soaked beans, then cook them in fresh water. Cooking time will vary with both age and variety; some beans, such as black-eyed peas, don't even require soaking.

CASSOULET

◆◆◆◆◆◆◆◆◆◆◆◆◆

Prep: 45 minutes plus standing
Bake: 1 hour 30 minutes
Makes 12 main-dish servings

1 package (16 ounces) dry Great Northern beans
¼ pound salt pork, diced
2 pounds boneless fresh pork butt, cut into 1½-inch chunks
1 pound lamb for stew, cut into 1½-inch chunks
4 parsley sprigs
2 bay leaves
6 whole cloves
1 kielbasa (smoked Polish sausage), cut into 1½-inch chunks (1 pound)
6 large carrots, cut into bite-size chunks
3 large celery stalks, thickly sliced
2 medium onions, each cut into quarters
1 can (6 ounces) tomato paste
1 cup dry white wine or chicken broth
1½ teaspoons salt
½ teaspoon dried thyme
Crusty bread (optional)

1 Rinse beans; discard any stones or shriveled beans. In large bowl, soak beans in *water* to cover by 2 inches overnight. (Or, to quick-soak: In 4-quart saucepan, heat beans and *7 cups water* to boiling over high heat; cook 3 minutes. Remove from heat. Cover; let stand 1 hour.) Drain beans. In 4-quart saucepan, heat beans and *5 cups water* to boiling over high heat. Reduce heat to low; cover and simmer 30 minutes.

4 In 5-inch square of cheesecloth, tie parsley, bay leaves, and cloves. Return meats to Dutch oven; add spice bag, beans with their liquid, kielbasa, and next 7 ingredients.

2 Meanwhile, in 8-quart Dutch oven, cook salt pork over medium heat until most of fat is rendered. Transfer to large bowl. Pour off all but 2 tablespoons fat from Dutch oven.

5 Heat mixture in Dutch oven to boiling over high heat, stirring occasionally. Cover Dutch oven and bake, stirring occasionally, 1½ hours, or until meat and beans are fork-tender. To serve, discard spice bag and skim fat from cassoulet. (Cassoulet will become very thick upon standing. Stir in enough *hot water* to reach desired consistency.) Serve in soup bowls with bread, if you like.

3 Preheat oven to 350°F. In fat in Dutch oven, cook pork butt and lamb, in small batches, over medium-high heat until browned, transferring pieces to bowl with salt pork.

BOUQUET GARNI

◆◆◆◆◆◆◆◆◆◆◆◆

The traditional bouquet garni is made of sprigs of thyme and parsley and 1 or 2 bay leaves, in a cheesecloth or muslin bag or tied together with string. The bouquet garni is always discarded at the end of cooking. To make it easy to remove, tie one end of the string to the pan handle.

EACH SERVING: ABOUT 415 CALORIES, 41g PROTEIN, 34g CARBOHYDRATE, 17g TOTAL FAT (6g SATURATED), 95mg CHOLESTEROL, 975mg SODIUM

TEXAS CAVIAR

Prep: 20 minutes plus standing and chilling
Cook: 45 minutes   *Makes* 10 accompaniment servings

1 package (16 ounces) dry black-eyed peas	1 small garlic clove, minced
½ cup cider vinegar	½ cup chopped fresh parsley
⅓ cup olive or vegetable oil	3 green onions, minced
1 tablespoon salt	2 medium celery stalks, thinly sliced
2 teaspoons sugar	1 large hard-cooked egg, chopped, for garnish
¼ teaspoon ground red pepper (cayenne)	

◆ Rinse black-eyed peas with cold running water and discard any stones or shriveled peas. In 5-quart Dutch oven, heat black-eyed peas and *6 cups water* to boiling over high heat. Reduce heat to low. Cover and simmer 40 minutes, or until black-eyed peas are tender; drain.

◆ Prepare dressing: In medium bowl, with wire whisk or fork, mix vinegar, oil, salt, sugar, ground red pepper, and garlic. Add black-eyed peas, parsley, green onions, and celery; toss gently to coat with dressing. Cover bowl and refrigerate for at least 2 hours to blend flavors, stirring occasionally. To serve, garnish with chopped egg.

Each serving: About 185 calories, 12g protein, 31g carbohydrate, 8g total fat (1g saturated), 21mg cholesterol, 675mg sodium

THREE-BEAN CASSEROLE

Prep: 20 minutes plus standing   *Cook:* 2 hours 45 to 50 minutes
Makes 8 main-dish servings

⅔ cup dry navy (pea) beans	⅓ cup dark molasses
⅔ cup dry red kidney or cranberry beans	¼ cup packed dark brown sugar
⅔ cup dry pinto beans	1 tablespoon Worcestershire sauce
2 tablespoons vegetable oil	
1 pound boneless fresh pork butt, cut into 1-inch chunks	2 teaspoons salt
½ cup catchup	1 teaspoon mustard seeds
	1 medium onion, thinly sliced

◆ Rinse all beans with cold running water and discard any stones or shriveled beans. In large bowl, soak beans in *water* to cover by 2 inches overnight. (Or, to quick soak: In 5-quart Dutch oven, heat beans and *6 cups water* to boiling over high heat; cook 3 minutes. Remove Dutch oven from heat; cover and let stand 1 hour.) Drain and rinse beans.

◆ Preheat oven to 350°F. In 5-quart Dutch oven, heat oil over medium-high heat; add pork and cook until well browned. Add beans to Dutch oven. Add *3¾ cups water*; heat to boiling over high heat. Cover; bake 1 hour. Stir in catchup and remaining ingredients; cover and bake 1 hour, stirring occasionally. Uncover; bake 45 to 50 minutes longer, until beans are tender, stirring occasionally.

Each serving: About 255 calories, 21g protein, 44g carbohydrate, 5g total fat (1g saturated), 28mg cholesterol, 790mg sodium

HOPPIN' JOHN

Prep: 15 minutes   *Cook:* 1 hour
Makes 8 main-dish servings

1 package (16 ounces) dry black-eyed peas	2 cans (13¾ to 14½ ounces each) reduced-sodium chicken broth
1 tablespoon vegetable oil	
2 medium celery stalks, coarsely chopped	¼ teaspoon crushed red pepper
1 large onion, coarsely chopped	1 bay leaf
	Salt
1 medium red pepper, coarsely chopped	2 cups regular long-grain rice
2 garlic cloves, minced	Hot-pepper sauce (optional)
1 large smoked ham hock (about 12 ounces)	

◆ Rinse peas with cold running water; discard any shriveled peas or stones. In 4-quart saucepan, heat oil over medium-high heat. Add next 3 ingredients; cook 10 minutes, or until golden. Add garlic; cook 30 seconds. Stir in peas, ham hock, next 3 ingredients, ½ teaspoon salt, and *4 cups water*; heat to boiling over high heat. Reduce heat to low; cover and simmer 40 minutes, or until peas are tender.

◆ Meanwhile, prepare rice as label directs, but use 1 teaspoon salt and do not add margarine or butter. Discard ham hock and bay leaf from black-eyed pea mixture. In large bowl, gently mix black-eyed pea mixture and rice. Serve with hot-pepper sauce, if you like.

Each serving: About 355 calories, 20g protein, 77g carbohydrate, 3g total fat (1g saturated), 11mg cholesterol, 525mg sodium

WHAT'S IN A NAME?

◆◆◆◆◆◆◆◆◆◆◆◆◆◆◆◆◆◆◆◆◆◆◆◆

Hoppin' John is an old Southern dish of black-eyed peas and rice, traditionally eaten on New Year's Day for luck. According to one story, it got its name after the custom of inviting guests to eat by saying "Hop in, John." Another story attributes it to a New Year's Day ritual in which children hopped once around the table before eating.

CANNED BEANS

Canned beans are the secret to many an easy meal, whether baked in a Greek-style pie or tucked into a hearty vegetarian burrito. Keep your pantry stocked with a variety. For best texture and appearance in the finished dish, rinse beans before using.

GREEK GREENS AND SPINACH PIE

Prep: 40 minutes   Bake: 30 minutes
Makes 8 main-dish servings

3 cans (15 to 19 ounces each) white kidney beans (cannellini)

2 tablespoons olive or vegetable oil

1 large bunch kale (about 1½ pounds), tough stems trimmed, leaves coarsely chopped

1 large bunch escarole (about 1¼ pounds), chopped

1 bunch (10 to 12 ounces) spinach, tough stems removed, leaves coarsely chopped

½ teaspoon salt

½ teaspoon coarsely ground black pepper

2 tablespoons minced fresh dill or 1 teaspoon dillweed

1 package (8 ounces) feta cheese, crumbled

5 sheets (about 16" by 12" each) fresh or frozen (thawed) phyllo (about 3½ ounces)

2 tablespoons margarine or butter, melted

Dill sprigs and chopped fresh dill for garnish

1 Rinse and drain 2 cans beans. In medium bowl, with potato masher, mash drained beans. Spread evenly in 13" by 9" glass baking dish. Rinse and drain remaining can of beans; set aside. In 8-quart Dutch oven or saucepot, heat oil over high heat; add greens, one-third at a time, and cook, stirring, just until wilted. While greens are cooking, stir in salt and pepper. Remove from heat.

2 To greens in Dutch oven, stir in the 1 can drained beans, minced dill, and feta. Spoon evenly over mashed beans in baking dish. Preheat oven to 375°F.

3 Place 1 sheet of phyllo on top of greens mixture in baking dish; brush phyllo sheet lightly with some of melted margarine.

4 Continue layering with 3 more sheets of phyllo, brushing each sheet lightly with some of melted margarine. Top with dill sprigs arranged in pretty design. Top with remaining sheet of phyllo; press down gently so dill is visible through phyllo. Brush lightly with remaining melted margarine.

5 Tuck ends of phyllo into baking dish. Bake pie about 30 minutes, until filling is heated through and phyllo is lightly golden. Garnish with chopped dill; cut into squares.

EACH SERVING: ABOUT 345 CALORIES, 18g PROTEIN, 39g CARBOHYDRATE, 14g TOTAL FAT (5g SATURATED), 25mg CHOLESTEROL, 1035mg SODIUM

SKILLET BEANS AND RICE

Prep: 15 minutes   Cook: 30 minutes
Makes 5 main-dish servings

¾ cup regular long-grain rice
1 tablespoon vegetable oil
1 medium green pepper, cut into ½-inch pieces
1 medium red pepper, cut into ½-inch pieces
1 medium onion, chopped
1 can (15 to 19 ounces) black beans

1 can (15 to 19 ounces) garbanzo beans
1 can (15 to 19 ounces) red kidney beans
1 can (15 to 19 ounces) pink beans
1 can (14½ ounces) stewed tomatoes
½ cup bottled barbecue sauce

◆ Prepare rice as label directs.

◆ Meanwhile, in 12-inch skillet, heat oil over medium heat; add green and red peppers and onion and cook until vegetables are tender.

◆ Rinse and drain all beans. Add beans, stewed tomatoes, barbecue sauce, and *1 cup water* to pepper mixture in skillet; heat to boiling over high heat. Reduce heat to low; cover and simmer 15 minutes.

◆ When rice is done, stir rice into bean mixture.

Each serving: About 465 calories, 21g protein, 88g carbohydrate, 6g total fat (1g saturated), 0mg cholesterol, 1215mg sodium

CORN, BLACK BEAN, AND RICE BURRITOS

Prep: 25 minutes   Bake: 15 minutes
Makes 4 main-dish servings

1 cup regular long-grain rice
1 can (15 to 19 ounces) black beans, rinsed and drained
1 can (15¼ to 16 ounces) whole-kernel corn, drained
1 can (4 to 4½ ounces) chopped mild green chiles, drained

4 ounces Monterey Jack or Cheddar cheese, shredded (1 cup)
¼ cup chopped fresh cilantro
1 package (10 ounces) flour tortillas (eight 6- to 7-inch tortillas)
1 jar (12½ ounces) mild salsa

◆ Preheat oven to 425°F. Prepare rice as label directs.

◆ Meanwhile, in large bowl, combine black beans, corn, chiles, cheese, and cilantro. When rice is done, stir into bean mixture. Spoon rounded ½ cup rice mixture across center of each tortilla.

◆ Spoon about 1 tablespoon salsa on top of rice mixture on each tortilla. Fold sides of tortilla over rice mixture, overlapping slightly.

◆ Grease 13" by 9" glass or ceramic baking dish. Place burritos, seam-side down, in dish. Spoon any remaining rice mixture down center of burritos; top with remaining salsa. Cover loosely with foil and bake 15 minutes, or until burritos are heated through.

Each serving: About 685 calories, 25g protein, 117g carbohydrate, 15g total fat (6g saturated), 25mg cholesterol, 1415mg sodium

BLACK BEAN AND VEGETABLE HASH

Prep: 15 minutes   Cook: 30 minutes
Makes 4 main-dish servings

1½ pounds all-purpose potatoes (about 4 medium), peeled and cut into ½-inch cubes
2 tablespoons vegetable oil
4 ounces Canadian bacon, cut into ½-inch pieces

1 large red pepper, cut into ½-inch pieces
1 can (15 to 19 ounces) black beans, rinsed and drained
4 large eggs
Salt and coarsely ground black pepper (optional)

◆ In 3-quart saucepan, heat potatoes and enough *water* to cover to boiling over high heat. Reduce heat to low; cover and simmer 4 minutes, or until potatoes are almost tender. Drain.

◆ In nonstick 12-inch skillet, heat oil over medium-high heat. Add Canadian bacon, red pepper, and potatoes; cook, stirring occasionally, about 15 minutes, until vegetables are tender and browned. Stir in black beans; heat through.

◆ Meanwhile, in 10-inch skillet, heat *1½ inches water* to boiling over high heat. Reduce heat to medium-low. One at a time, break eggs into custard cup, then, holding cup close to water's surface, slip each egg into simmering water. Cook eggs 3 to 5 minutes, until desired doneness. When done, with slotted spoon, carefully remove eggs from water. Drain each egg (still held in spoon) on paper towels. Serve poached eggs on vegetable hash. Sprinkle eggs with salt and pepper, if you like.

Each serving: About 420 calories, 22g protein, 53g carbohydrate, 15g total fat (4g saturated), 229mg cholesterol, 780mg sodium

LENTILS

The small, flat legumes called lentils are delicious, economical, and packed with nutrients. And, as a bonus, they do not require the lengthy soaking and cooking times of dry beans. In less than an hour, lentils are ready to serve as an aromatic Indian side dish, a warm salad, a hearty pasta stew, or an elegant French-style accompaniment.

INDIAN-STYLE LENTILS

◆◆◆◆◆◆◆◆◆◆◆◆◆◆◆◆◆◆◆◆◆◆◆◆◆◆◆◆◆◆

Prep: 20 minutes   Cook: 35 to 45 minutes
Makes 6 accompaniment servings

1 pound sweet potatoes	1 can (13¾ to 14½ ounces) chicken or vegetable broth
1 medium onion	¼ teaspoon salt
1 tablespoon vegetable oil	1 container (8 ounces) plain low-fat yogurt
1 tablespoon minced, peeled fresh ginger	¼ cup chopped fresh mint or cilantro
1 large garlic clove, minced	Mint or cilantro leaves for garnish
1½ teaspoons cumin seeds	
⅛ teaspoon ground red pepper (cayenne)	
1 cup lentils, rinsed and picked through	

1 Peel sweet potatoes and cut into ¾-inch pieces (you should have about 3 cups); set aside.

2 Finely chop onion. In 3-quart saucepan, heat oil over medium heat. Add onion and cook, stirring occasionally, 5 minutes, or until tender.

3 Stir in ginger, garlic, cumin seeds, and ground red pepper; cook, stirring, 30 seconds. Stir in sweet potatoes, lentils, chicken broth, salt, and *1 cup water*; heat to boiling over high heat.

4 Reduce heat to low; cover and simmer 20 to 30 minutes, stirring occasionally, until lentils are just tender. In small bowl, mix yogurt and chopped mint. Garnish and serve with lentils.

INDIAN LENTIL SOUP

Follow directions for Indian-Style Lentils, but cut sweet potatoes into ½-inch dice and use 2 cans (13¾ to 14½ ounces each) broth. Simmer 45 minutes or until lentils are very tender. Partly mash with potato masher, if you like. Or, blend in batches in the blender, or in food processor with knife blade attached. Reheat if necessary over low heat. Garnish with lemon slices.

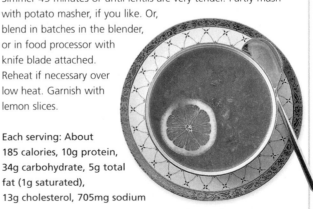

Each serving: About 185 calories, 10g protein, 34g carbohydrate, 5g total fat (1g saturated), 13g cholesterol, 705mg sodium

EACH SERVING: ABOUT 175 CALORIES, 9g PROTEIN, 33g CARBOHYDRATE, 4g TOTAL FAT (1g SATURATED), 8mg CHOLESTEROL, 415mg SODIUM

WARM LENTIL SALAD

Prep: 10 minutes   *Cook:* 30 to 40 minutes
Makes 4 accompaniment servings

1 cup lentils	2 tablespoons fresh lemon
1 bay leaf	juice
1 small carrot, shredded	2 tablespoons olive oil
1 tablespoon chopped fresh	¾ teaspoon salt
mint or 1 teaspoon dried	¼ teaspoon ground black
mint	pepper

◆ Rinse lentils with cold running water and discard any stones or shriveled lentils.

◆ In 2-quart saucepan, heat lentils, bay leaf, and enough *water* to cover lentils by 2 inches to boiling over high heat. Reduce heat to medium-low; cover and simmer 20 to 30 minutes, until lentils are just tender.

◆ When lentils are done, drain well; discard bay leaf. In medium bowl, mix lentils, shredded carrot, chopped mint, lemon juice, oil, salt, and pepper until blended.

Each serving: About 140 calories, 8g protein, 21g carbohydrate, 7g total fat (1g saturated), 0mg cholesterol, 410mg sodium

LENTILS AND PASTA

Prep: 15 minutes   *Cook:* 50 minutes
Makes 4 main-dish servings

1 cup lentils	¾ teaspoon salt
1 ounce pancetta or ham,	¼ teaspoon ground black
chopped (¼ cup)	pepper
1 small onion, chopped	1 cup ditalini or small shell
1 medium carrot, chopped	pasta
1 medium celery stalk,	¼ cup chopped fresh parsley
chopped	Flat-leaf parsley sprig for
1 garlic clove, chopped	garnish
1 tablespoon olive oil	

◆ Rinse lentils with cold running water and discard any stones or shriveled lentils. On cutting board, chop pancetta, onion, carrot, celery, and garlic together until very fine.

◆ In 3-quart saucepan, heat olive oil over medium heat. Add pancetta-vegetable mixture and cook, stirring often, 10 minutes, or until tender.

◆ Stir in lentils and *3 cups water*; heat to boiling over high heat. Reduce heat to low; cover and simmer 15 minutes. Stir in salt and pepper; cover and cook 15 minutes longer, or until lentils are just tender.

◆ Meanwhile, cook ditalini as label directs; drain. Stir ditalini and chopped parsley into lentils; garnish.

Each serving: About 235 calories, 14g protein, 44g carbohydrate, 5g total fat (1g saturated), 4mg cholesterol, 535mg sodium

FRENCH LENTILS WITH SHALLOTS AND BRANDY

Prep: 10 minutes   *Cook:* 30 to 35 minutes
Makes 6 accompaniment servings

1 cup small green French	⅓ cup finely chopped shallots
lentils	2 tablespoons brandy
Salt	¼ teaspoon ground black
2 tablespoons margarine or	pepper
butter	¼ cup chopped fresh parsley

◆ Rinse lentils with cold running water and discard any stones or shriveled lentils.

◆ In 2-quart saucepan, heat lentils and *2 cups water* to boiling over high heat. Reduce heat to low; cover and simmer 20 to 25 minutes, until lentils are just tender, adding ½ teaspoon salt halfway through cooking. Drain lentils. Wipe saucepan clean.

◆ In same saucepan, melt margarine over medium heat. Add shallots; cook 3 minutes, or until tender. Stir in brandy; cook 1 minute longer, until almost evaporated. Stir in lentils, pepper, and ¼ teaspoon salt and heat through. Stir in parsley.

Each serving: About 100 calories, 6g protein, 14g carbohydrate, 4g total fat (1g saturated), 0mg cholesterol, 315mg sodium

LENTILS FOR LUCK

◆◆◆◆◆◆◆◆◆◆◆◆◆◆◆◆◆◆◆◆◆

In Italy, lentils are an indispensable part of the festivities for New Year's Eve. Associated with money because they resemble tiny coins, they symbolize prosperity in the coming year. In Tuscany, stewed lentils are served with *cotechino*, a lightly spiced pork sausage that is boiled and served in slices. Further north, in Bologna and Modena, lentils accompany *zampone*, a boned pig's foot stuffed with the same cotechino-sausage mixture.

QUICK & YEAST BREADS

12

Quick breads are wonderfully simple to make: The batter (for muffins and tea loaves) or dough (for biscuits and scones) is mixed together in no time. Best of all, there's no rising time needed since they're leavened with baking soda or baking powder rather than yeast.

WHAT MAKES THEM RISE?

Baking soda Once it's combined with an acidic ingredient (e.g., buttermilk or yogurt), baking soda releases carbon dioxide gas that makes a dough or batter rise. Because it starts working as soon as it's moistened, bake the dough or batter immediately after mixing. Store baking soda in an airtight container in a cool, dry place up to 1 year.

Baking powder A mixture of baking soda and an acid (usually cream of tartar), baking powder releases some gas when it's moistened and the rest during baking. It should stay potent up to 6 months if stored in a cool, dry place. If you're not sure if your baking powder is still active, combine ½ teaspoon with ¼ cup hot water. If the mixture bubbles, the baking powder's fine.

SOURED MILK

If buttermilk is not on hand, don't worry. It's easy to make a "soured" milk that can stand in for buttermilk in any recipe. In a glass measuring cup, place 1 tablespoon fresh lemon juice or distilled white vinegar, then pour in enough regular milk to equal 1 cup. Stir; let stand about 5 minutes to thicken before using.

MIXING IT RIGHT

• Be sure the baking powder or soda is fresh (see above).
• Always start with room-temperature ingredients for easier blending and baking (unless margarine or butter is cut in).
• When mixing batters, always combine the wet and dry ingredients just until the flour is moistened. It's fine if there are lumps in the batter; they'll smooth out during baking.
• For the cut-in method, blend the solid shortening into the dry ingredients until coarse crumbs form. Stir in the liquid quickly, just until the dough clings together. Biscuit dough is sometimes kneaded briefly for a better texture.
• Don't overmix the batter or dough, or you'll have a dense, tough bread that's riddled with tunnels.

BETTER BAKING

• When making a quick bread, fill the baking pan about two-thirds full with batter. Smooth the top of the batter with a rubber spatula so it bakes uniformly.
• Fill muffin-pan cups two-thirds to three-quarters full with batter. If there are empty cups, half-fill them with water to prevent the pan from warping.
• Always bake quick breads in the center of the oven. If baking more than two loaves at once, be sure there's some space between the pans so the hot air can circulate.
• Don't worry if the finished loaf has a center crack – it's typical of quick breads and adds to their homey appeal.

TESTING FOR DONENESS

Insert a toothpick into the center of the loaf – it should come out clean and free of crumbs. If not, bake a few minutes longer, then test again.

COOLING, STORING, AND REHEATING

• Cool most quick breads in the pan 10 to 15 minutes so they can set. Then transfer to a wire rack to cool completely.
• Remove muffins, biscuits, and scones from the pan or cookie sheet right away to prevent sticking.
• In general, the richer the batter, the longer the bread will stay moist. Rich, dense quick loaves are even better if made a day ahead so their flavors can meld; they'll also be firmer for easier slicing. Most muffins, biscuits, scones, and corn breads are best eaten (or frozen) the day they're made.
• To store quick breads and muffins, cool completely on a wire rack, wrap in plastic wrap, overwrap in foil, and keep at room temperature. They should stay fresh up to 3 days.
• Quick breads and muffins freeze well. Wrap tightly, pressing out air. Freeze quick breads up to 3 months, muffins up to 1 month. Thaw, still wrapped, at room temperature.
• Reheat biscuits, scones, muffins, loaves, and coffee cakes, wrapped in foil, at 400°F. Muffins, scones, and biscuits will take about 10 minutes, loaves and coffee cakes 20 minutes.
• Muffins reheat well in the microwave. Loosely wrap in a paper towel and microwave for 20 seconds. Take care – sugary ingredients (e.g., jam, chocolate chips) get very hot and baked goods can become tough if reheated too long.
• Day-old muffins, biscuits, and quick breads are good split and toasted under the broiler or in a toaster oven.

QUICK BREADS AND TEA LOAVES

Luscious quick breads make a cheery breakfast or afternoon snack. For a tender texture, mix these breads (leavened with baking powder or soda, not yeast) just until combined. Let the baked bread rest briefly in the pan to set, then turn it out onto the rack to finish cooling. This prevents steam from collecting, which would make the bread soggy.

APRICOT-STREUSEL LOAF

◆◆◆◆◆◆◆◆◆◆◆◆◆

Prep: 25 minutes plus cooling
Bake: 60 to 70 minutes
Makes 1 loaf, 12 servings

1 package (6 ounces) dried apricots (1 cup)
½ cup pecans (about 2 ounces)
1½ teaspoons baking powder
1 teaspoon baking soda
2½ cups all-purpose flour
1¼ cups sugar
¾ cup margarine or butter
1 container (8 ounces) sour cream
3 large eggs, beaten
2 teaspoons vanilla extract

1 Preheat oven to 350°F. Grease 9" by 5" metal loaf pan. Chop dried apricots and pecans; set aside. In large bowl, mix baking powder, baking soda, 2 cups flour, and 1 cup sugar. With pastry blender or two knives used scissor-fashion, cut ½ cup margarine into flour mixture until mixture resembles coarse crumbs.

2 Stir in sour cream, eggs, and vanilla just until flour mixture is moistened. Stir in chopped apricots and pecans. Spoon batter evenly into loaf pan.

3 Prepare streusel: In bowl, with fingertips, mix remaining ½ cup flour, ¼ cup sugar, and ¼ cup margarine, softened, until mixture resembles coarse crumbs.

4 Sprinkle streusel topping over batter. Bake loaf 60 to 70 minutes, until toothpick inserted in center comes out clean. Cool in pan on wire rack 10 minutes; remove from pan. Cool completely on rack.

DRIED APRICOTS

Pitted unpeeled apricots are dried to produce a very sweet yet tangy fruit that is high in iron and niacin. They are usually treated with sulfur dioxide to preserve their rich orange color (below, left). Dried apricots from a health food store may be brown (below, far left) if they have not been treated. Dried apricot halves from California are firmer and more tart than the whole pitted dried apricots from Turkey, which are sweeter, softer, and milder in flavor. When chopping dried apricots, dip the knife frequently in hot water to prevent the fruit from sticking to the blade, or snip the fruit with kitchen shears.

EACH SERVING: ABOUT 375 CALORIES, 4g PROTEIN, 50g CARBOHYDRATE, 19g TOTAL FAT (5g SATURATED), 8mg CHOLESTEROL, 310mg SODIUM

BLUEBERRY-LEMON TEA BREAD

Prep: 20 minutes plus cooling   *Bake:* 1 hour 5 minutes
Makes 1 loaf, 12 servings

2 cups all-purpose flour	1⅓ cups sugar
2 teaspoons baking powder	2 large eggs
½ teaspoon salt	½ cup milk
½ cup margarine or butter, softened	1½ cups blueberries
	¼ cup fresh lemon juice

◆ Preheat oven to 350°F. Grease and flour 9" by 5" metal loaf pan. In medium bowl, combine flour, baking powder, and salt. In large bowl, with mixer at low speed, beat margarine and 1 cup sugar just until blended. Increase speed to medium; beat about 5 minutes, until light and creamy.

◆ Reduce mixer speed to low; add eggs, 1 at a time, beating after each addition until well blended, occasionally scraping bowl with rubber spatula.

◆ Alternately beat flour mixture and milk into egg mixture, mixing just until blended. Gently stir in blueberries. Spoon batter into loaf pan.

◆ Bake loaf 1 hour 5 minutes, or until toothpick inserted in center comes out clean. Place sheet of waxed paper under wire rack. Cool loaf in pan on wire rack 10 minutes. Remove from pan and place on rack.

◆ With cake tester or skewer, prick top and sides of warm loaf all over. Prepare lemon glaze: In small bowl, mix lemon juice and remaining ⅓ cup sugar. With pastry brush, brush top and sides of warm loaf with lemon glaze. Cool loaf completely on rack.

Each serving: About 255 calories, 4g protein, 41g carbohydrate, 9g total fat (2g saturated), 37mg cholesterol, 275mg sodium

◆◆◆◆◆◆◆◆◆◆◆◆◆◆◆◆◆◆◆◆◆◆◆◆◆◆

APPLYING A GLAZE

Besides adding flavor to a tea bread, cake, or tart, a glaze can give a smooth, lustrous finish and seal in its moisture. Glazes can be as simple as melted jam, or a mixture of sugar and liquid. Set the tea bread over waxed paper to catch drips. For a flavor that permeates, prick the bread all over, then brush glaze over the top and sides of the still-warm bread.

◆◆◆◆◆◆◆◆◆◆◆◆◆◆◆◆◆◆◆◆◆◆◆◆◆◆

GOLDEN DATE-NUT BREAD

Prep: 20 minutes plus cooling   *Bake:* 1 hour 30 minutes
Makes 1 loaf, 16 servings

2 cups all-purpose flour	1½ cups walnuts (about 6 ounces), coarsely chopped
¾ cup sugar	1½ cups pitted dates, chopped
1 teaspoon baking powder	1 cup milk
½ teaspoon salt	2 large eggs, lightly beaten
1 cup margarine or butter	

◆ Preheat oven to 325°F. Grease 9" by 5" metal loaf pan.

◆ In large bowl, mix flour, sugar, baking powder, and salt. With pastry blender or two knives used scissor-fashion, cut in margarine until mixture resembles coarse crumbs. Stir in walnuts, dates, milk, and eggs just until flour mixture is moistened. Spoon batter into loaf pan.

◆ Bake loaf 1½ hours, or until toothpick inserted in center comes out clean. Cool loaf in pan on wire rack 10 minutes; remove from pan and cool completely on rack.

Each serving: About 325 calories, 5g protein, 36g carbohydrate, 20g total fat (3g saturated), 29mg cholesterol, 245mg sodium

BANANA BREAD

Prep: 20 minutes plus cooling   *Bake:* 50 to 55 minutes
Makes 1 loaf, 12 servings

2 cups all-purpose flour	2 large eggs
¾ teaspoon baking soda	1 cup mashed bananas (about 2 large ripe bananas)
½ teaspoon salt	½ cup walnuts (about 2 ounces), coarsely chopped
¾ cup sugar	
6 tablespoons margarine or butter, softened	

◆ Preheat oven to 350°F. Grease and flour 9" by 5" metal loaf pan. In medium bowl, combine flour, baking soda, and salt. In large bowl, with mixer at low speed, beat sugar, margarine, and eggs just until blended. Increase speed to high; beat about 5 minutes, until light and creamy.

◆ Reduce speed to low. Add mashed bananas and ¼ *cup water*; beat until well mixed.

◆ Add flour mixture to banana mixture; beat just until blended, occasionally scraping bowl with rubber spatula. Stir in nuts. Spoon batter into loaf pan.

◆ Bake loaf 50 to 55 minutes, until toothpick inserted in center of bread comes out clean. Cool in pan on wire rack 10 minutes; remove from pan and cool completely on rack.

Each serving: About 235 calories, 4g protein, 34g carbohydrate, 10g total fat (2g saturated), 36mg cholesterol, 245mg sodium

QUICK COFFEE CAKES

These easy-to-make coffee-cake "quick breads" are just right for weekend brunches, mid-morning coffee breaks, or not-too-rich desserts. With their luscious fruit or chocolate toppings and fillings, there's a home-baked treat to tempt every taste. These coffee cakes are delicious served warm or at room temperature.

APPLE-NUT COFFEE CAKE

◆◆◆◆◆◆◆◆◆◆◆◆◆◆◆◆◆◆◆◆◆◆◆◆◆◆◆

Prep: 30 minutes plus cooling   Bake: 45 to 50 minutes
Makes 18 servings

1 cup walnuts (about 4 ounces), chopped

¼ cup packed brown sugar

1 teaspoon ground cinnamon

⅔ cup plus 2½ cups all-purpose flour

4 tablespoons plus 1 cup margarine or butter, softened

3 medium Golden Delicious apples

2 tablespoons plus 1½ cups granulated sugar

1 container (16 ounces) sour cream

1 tablespoon baking powder

2 teaspoons baking soda

2 teaspoons vanilla extract

4 large eggs

1 Prepare streusel topping: In bowl, knead walnuts, brown sugar, cinnamon, ⅔ cup flour, and 4 tablespoons margarine until mixture forms large pieces.

2 Peel, core, and thinly slice apples. In medium bowl, toss apples with 2 tablespoons granulated sugar. Preheat oven to 350°F. Grease 14" by 10" roasting pan.

3 In large bowl, with mixer at medium speed, beat remaining 1 cup margarine with remaining 1½ cups granulated sugar until light and fluffy. Add sour cream, baking powder, baking soda, vanilla, eggs, and remaining 2½ cups flour.

4 Beat mixture at low speed until blended, occasionally scraping bowl. Increase speed to medium; beat 1 minute. Spread batter in pan to corners. Arrange apple slices on top, to edge of pan (otherwise batter will bake up over apples).

5 Crumble streusel topping over apple layer. Bake 45 to 50 minutes, until cake pulls away from sides of pan. Cool in pan on wire rack 10 minutes to serve warm. Or, cool to serve later.

WHAT'S IN A NAME?

◆◆◆◆◆◆◆◆◆◆◆

The word "streusel" is German for "sprinkle" or "strew." In baking, it refers to a sweet, crumbly topping for breads, pies, muffins, or coffee cakes. Streusels are made from a mixture of flour, margarine or butter, sugar, and, often, nuts and spices, especially walnuts and cinnamon.

EACH SERVING: ABOUT 395 CALORIES, 5g PROTEIN, 43g CARBOHYDRATE, 23g TOTAL FAT (7g SATURATED), 59mg CHOLESTEROL, 400mg SODIUM

RHUBARB COFFEE CAKE

Prep: 20 minutes plus cooling   Bake: 45 minutes
Makes 15 servings

½ cup packed light brown
   sugar
2¾ cups all-purpose flour
1 teaspoon ground cinnamon
10 tablespoons margarine or
   butter
1 cup granulated sugar
1 tablespoon baking powder
1 teaspoon baking soda

½ teaspoon salt
2 large eggs
1 cup buttermilk or soured
   milk (see page 392)
2 teaspoons vanilla extract
1¼ pounds rhubarb, cut into
   1-inch chunks (4 cups)

◆ Prepare streusel topping: In medium bowl, with fingertips, mix brown sugar, ¾ cup flour, cinnamon, and 6 tablespoons margarine until mixture resembles coarse crumbs.

◆ Preheat oven to 375°F. Grease and flour 13" by 9" metal baking pan. In large bowl, combine remaining 2 cups flour, granulated sugar, and next 3 ingredients. With pastry blender or two knives used scissor-fashion, cut in remaining 4 tablespoons margarine until mixture resembles coarse crumbs.

◆ In small bowl, with fork or wire whisk, beat eggs with buttermilk and vanilla; stir into flour mixture just until flour is moistened. Spoon batter into baking pan.

◆ Place rhubarb chunks evenly over batter in baking pan. Sprinkle streusel topping over rhubarb. Bake cake 45 minutes, or until toothpick inserted in center comes out clean. Cool cake in pan on wire rack 10 minutes to serve warm. Or, cool completely to serve later.

Each serving: About 250 calories, 4g protein, 40g carbohydrate, 9g total fat (2g saturated), 29mg cholesterol, 370mg sodium

GINGER-PEACH COFFEE CAKE

Prep: 25 minutes plus cooling   Bake: 1 hour 15 minutes
Makes 15 servings

3 cups all-purpose flour
1½ teaspoons baking soda
1½ teaspoons baking powder
½ teaspoon salt
1½ cups sugar
¾ cup margarine or butter,
   softened
1 container (16 ounces) light
   sour cream

3 large eggs
2 teaspoons vanilla extract
½ cup crystallized ginger
   (about 3 ounces), finely
   chopped
4 medium peaches (about
   1½ pounds), peeled, pitted,
   and cut into ½-inch wedges

◆ Preheat oven to 350°F. Grease and flour 13" by 9" metal baking pan. In medium bowl, combine flour and next 3 ingredients. In large bowl, with mixer at low speed, beat sugar and margarine until blended.

◆ Increase speed to medium; beat 2 minutes, occasionally scraping bowl with rubber spatula. Add sour cream, eggs, and vanilla; beat 1 minute, or until blended.

◆ Reduce speed to low. Add flour mixture; beat until well mixed. Increase speed to medium; beat 2 minutes, occasionally scraping bowl. Stir in ginger.

◆ Spread batter in pan; arrange peach wedges in 3 lengthwise rows on top. Bake 1¼ hours, or until toothpick inserted in center comes out clean. Cool in pan on wire rack 10 minutes to serve warm. Or, cool completely to serve later.

Each serving: About 325 calories, 5g protein, 48g carbohydrate, 12g total fat (2g saturated), 53mg cholesterol, 390mg sodium

CHOCOLATE-CHERRY COFFEE CAKE

Prep: 30 minutes plus cooling   Bake: 1 hour 10 minutes
Makes 16 servings

½ cup semisweet-chocolate
   mini pieces
1 tablespoon unsweetened
   cocoa
2 teaspoons ground cinnamon
1⅓ cups sugar
¾ cup margarine or butter,
   softened
3 cups all-purpose flour
1½ teaspoons baking soda

1½ teaspoons baking powder
2 teaspoons vanilla extract
½ teaspoon salt
1 container (16 ounces) light
   sour cream
3 large eggs
⅔ cup dried tart cherries
Confectioners' sugar for
   garnish

◆ Preheat oven to 325°F. Grease and flour 10-inch Bundt pan. In small bowl, combine chocolate mini pieces, cocoa, cinnamon, and ⅓ cup sugar; set aside.

◆ In large bowl, with mixer at low speed, beat margarine and remaining 1⅓ cups sugar until blended. Increase speed to medium; beat 2 minutes, or until light and creamy, occasionally scraping bowl with rubber spatula. Reduce speed to low. Add flour and next 6 ingredients; beat until well mixed. Increase speed to medium; beat 2 minutes, occasionally scraping bowl. Stir in dried cherries.

◆ Spread one-third of batter in Bundt pan; sprinkle with half of chocolate mixture. Top with half of remaining batter; sprinkle with remaining chocolate mixture. Spread remaining batter on top.

◆ Bake cake 1 hour 10 minutes, or until toothpick inserted in center comes out clean. Cool cake in pan on wire rack 10 minutes. Invert cake onto rack to cool completely. To serve, sift confectioners' sugar over cake.

Each serving: About 345 calories, 5g protein, 50g carbohydrate, 14g total fat (3g saturated), 49mg cholesterol, 360mg sodium

MUFFINS

What better way to start the day than with warm, fragrant muffins packed with juicy berries, moist apples, or even luscious chocolate chips? What's more, muffins can be made in minutes. For a tender texture, use a light hand when mixing the wet and dry ingredients (stir the batter just until the flour is moistened), then gently fold in added extras, and bake. Don't forget to make the coffee.

APPLE-BUTTERMILK MUFFINS

◆◆◆◆◆◆◆◆◆◆◆

Prep: 20 minutes
Bake: 25 minutes
Makes 12

2 medium Golden Delicious or Winesap apples
2 cups all-purpose flour
½ cup packed light brown sugar
2 teaspoons baking powder
1 teaspoon baking soda
½ teaspoon salt
1 cup buttermilk or soured milk (see page 392)
¼ cup vegetable oil
2 teaspoons vanilla extract
1 large egg
½ cup walnuts (about 2 ounces), chopped (optional)
1 tablespoon granulated sugar
1 teaspoon ground cinnamon

1 Preheat oven to 400°F. Grease twelve 2½" by 1¼" muffin-pan cups. Peel, core, and dice apples (you should have about 2 cups). In large bowl, mix flour, brown sugar, baking powder, baking soda, and salt. In small bowl, with wire whisk or fork, mix buttermilk, oil, vanilla, and egg until blended.

2 Stir buttermilk mixture into flour mixture just until moistened (mixture will be lumpy). Fold in apples, and walnuts, if using. Spoon batter into muffin-pan cups.

3 In cup, mix granulated sugar and cinnamon; sprinkle over muffins. Bake 25 minutes, or until toothpick inserted in center comes out clean. Immediately remove muffins from pan; serve warm. Or, cool on wire rack; reheat if desired.

MUFFIN PANS

Muffin pans come in all shapes and sizes. Standard muffin pans are about 2½" wide by 1¼" deep, with 12 cups to the pan; you can also buy giant (4" by 2") and mini (1⅞" by ¾") versions. Muffin-top pans are extra shallow so you get lots of chewy crust and less interior.

Fill muffin pans two-thirds to three-quarters full with batter to allow for rising. (If you don't use all the cups, fill the empty ones halfway with water so the pan won't warp.) Always bake muffins as soon as the batter is mixed, before the leavening loses any of its rising power.

EACH MUFFIN: ABOUT 210 CALORIES, 4g PROTEIN, 30g CARBOHYDRATE, 8g TOTAL FAT (1g SATURATED), 19mg CHOLESTEROL, 305mg SODIUM

BASIC MUFFINS

Prep: 10 minutes   *Bake:* 20 to 25 minutes
Makes 12

2½ cups all-purpose flour
⅓ cup sugar
1 tablespoon baking powder
½ teaspoon salt
1 large egg
1 cup milk
⅓ cup margarine or butter, melted
1 teaspoon vanilla extract

◆ Preheat oven to 400°F. Grease twelve 2½" by 1¼" muffin-pan cups.

◆ In large bowl, mix flour, sugar, baking powder, and salt. In medium bowl, with wire whisk or fork, mix egg, milk, melted margarine, and vanilla; stir into flour mixture just until moistened (mixture will be lumpy).

◆ Spoon batter into muffin-pan cups. Bake 20 to 25 minutes, until toothpick inserted in center of a muffin comes out clean. Immediately remove muffins from pan; serve warm. Or, cool on wire rack to serve later; reheat if desired.

Each muffin: About 175 calories, 4g protein, 25g carbohydrate, 6g fat (2g saturated), 21mg cholesterol, 285mg sodium

MUFFINS PLUS

Try adding any of the following to the Basic Muffins batter just after mixing:

Blueberry or raspberry muffins Fold in 1 cup blueberries or raspberries.

Chocolate chip muffins Fold in ¾ cup semisweet-chocolate pieces.

Walnut or pecan muffins Fold in ½ cup chopped toasted walnuts or pecans (about 2 ounces). Sprinkle with a little sugar before baking.

Orange muffins Add 1 teaspoon grated orange peel with dry ingredients. Sprinkle with a little sugar before baking.

CARROT-BRAN MUFFINS

Prep: 15 minutes plus standing
Bake: 30 minutes
Makes 12

1 large egg
1 cup milk
¼ cup vegetable oil
1½ cups all-bran cereal
1 cup shredded carrots
1¼ cups all-purpose flour
⅓ cup sugar
1 tablespoon baking powder
½ teaspoon salt
¼ teaspoon ground cinnamon
1 cup dark seedless raisins

◆ Preheat oven to 400°F. Grease twelve 2½" by 1¼" muffin-pan cups.

◆ In medium bowl, with wire whisk or fork, combine egg, milk, oil, all-bran cereal, and carrots until blended; let stand 10 minutes.

◆ In large bowl, mix flour, sugar, baking powder, salt, and cinnamon. Stir bran mixture into flour mixture just until moistened (mixture will be lumpy). Fold in raisins.

◆ Spoon batter into muffin-pan cups. Bake 30 minutes, or until toothpick inserted in center of a muffin comes out clean. Immediately remove muffins from pan; serve warm. Or, cool on wire rack to serve later; reheat if desired.

Each muffin: About 190 calories, 4g protein, 34g carbohydrate, 6g total fat (1g saturated), 21mg cholesterol, 350mg sodium

BLUEBERRY CORN MUFFINS

Prep: 15 minutes   *Bake:* 20 to 25 minutes
Makes 12

1 cup all-purpose flour
1 cup yellow cornmeal
½ cup sugar
2 teaspoons baking powder
1 teaspoon baking soda
½ teaspoon salt
1 cup buttermilk or soured milk (see page 392)
¼ cup vegetable oil
2 teaspoons vanilla extract
1 large egg
1½ cups blueberries or 1¼ cups raspberries

◆ Preheat oven to 400°F. Grease twelve 2½" by 1¼" muffin-pan cups.

◆ In large bowl, mix first 6 ingredients. In small bowl, with wire whisk or fork, mix buttermilk, oil, vanilla, and egg until blended; stir into flour mixture just until moistened (mixture will be lumpy). Fold in berries.

◆ Spoon batter into muffin-pan cups. Bake 20 to 25 minutes, until toothpick inserted in center of a muffin comes out clean. Immediately remove muffins from pan; serve warm. Or, cool on wire rack to serve later; reheat if desired.

Each muffin: About 175 calories, 3g protein, 29g carbohydrate, 5g fat (1g saturated), 19mg cholesterol, 305mg sodium

Blueberry corn muffins

Carrot-bran muffins

Chocolate chip muffins

CORN BREAD

Quick to make and quick to bake, corn bread is at its best eaten warm and fresh. It's the classic accompaniment to a bowl of chili, but it goes well with practically any meal. While plain hot corn bread is delicious, flavorings such as cheese, chiles, and corn make an extra-special bread. For variety, bake a batch of crispy golden corn sticks.

CHEESE AND CHILE CORN BREAD

Prep: 20 minutes   *Bake: 25 to 30 minutes*
Makes 15 servings

8 ounces Monterey Jack cheese with jalapeño chiles
1½ cups all-purpose flour
1½ cups yellow cornmeal
¼ cup sugar
1 tablespoon baking powder
½ teaspoon salt
1 can (8½ ounces) cream-style corn

1 can (4 to 4½ ounces) chopped mild green chiles
1 small onion, grated
2 large eggs
¾ cup milk
4 tablespoons margarine or butter, melted

1 Preheat oven to 400°F. Grease 13" by 9" metal baking pan. Shred Monterey Jack cheese (you should have 2 cups). In large bowl, mix flour and next 4 ingredients.

2 In medium bowl, beat cheese, corn, chiles with their liquid, onion, eggs, milk, and melted margarine until blended; stir into flour mixture just until flour is moistened (batter will be lumpy).

3 Spread batter evenly in pan. Bake 25 to 30 minutes, until toothpick inserted in center comes out clean. Cut lengthwise into 3 strips, then cut each strip into 5 pieces. Serve warm, or cool in pan on wire rack to serve later.

THE ALL-AMERICAN BREAD

Corn bread is the classic American bread; native Americans made hundreds of different flat breads using ground corn, and later colonists developed their own myriad variations. Southerners prefer their corn bread unsweetened and use white rather than yellow cornmeal. For a browned, crisp crust, they bake it in a shallow pan or, better still, in a preheated, greased cast-iron skillet. In the North, corn bread is on the sweeter, fluffier side, and yellow cornmeal is the rule. Southwestern cooks often use blue cornmeal in the batter.

A higher proportion of flour makes a lighter corn bread, while more cornmeal makes a denser, drier bread with a more intense corn flavor. Buttermilk, which frequently appears in recipes of all regions, adds tenderness to the finished bread.

EACH SERVING: ABOUT 225 CALORIES, 8g PROTEIN, 28g CARBOHYDRATE, 9g TOTAL FAT (4g SATURATED), 46mg CHOLESTEROL, 455mg SODIUM

SWEET-POTATO CORN STICKS

Prep: 30 to 35 minutes plus cooling   *Bake:* 10 to 15 minutes
Makes 14

2 medium sweet potatoes (about 12 ounces), peeled and each cut into quarters	1 teaspoon salt
	4 tablespoons margarine or butter
1¼ cups all-purpose flour	1¼ cups milk
1 cup yellow cornmeal	⅓ cup packed brown sugar
2½ teaspoons baking powder	1 large egg

◆ In 3-quart saucepan, heat sweet potatoes and enough *water* to cover to boiling over high heat. Reduce heat to low; cover and simmer 15 to 20 minutes, until potatoes are fork-tender; drain well.

◆ Meanwhile, preheat oven to 400°F. Generously grease 14 corn-stick molds (2 pans, 7 molds each) or 11" by 7" metal baking pan.

◆ In large bowl, mix flour, cornmeal, baking powder, and salt. With pastry blender or two knives used scissor-fashion, cut in margarine until mixture resembles coarse crumbs.

◆ In small bowl, with potato masher, mash sweet potatoes with milk and brown sugar until smooth; stir in egg. Stir into flour mixture until batter is just blended. Spoon batter into corn-stick molds (or baking pan).

◆ Bake 10 to 15 minutes, until toothpick inserted in center of a corn stick comes out clean (if using baking pan, bake 15 minutes).

◆ Cool in molds on wire rack 5 minutes. Remove from molds (if using baking pan, cut into 14 pieces). Serve warm. Or, cool on wire rack; reheat just before serving, if desired.

Each piece: About 160 calories, 3g protein, 26g carbohydrate, 5g total fat (1g saturated), 18mg cholesterol, 295mg sodium

CORN-STICK MOLDS

The secret to making whimsically shaped corn sticks is a special cast-iron mold with depressions shaped like ears of corn. You can find these pans in specialty cookware shops. Grease the molds generously to prevent the batter from sticking, and to encourage a crunchy, nicely browned crust. Use a fork to ease the baked corn sticks from the pan.

SKILLET CORN BREAD

Prep: 10 minutes   *Bake:* 25 to 30 minutes
Makes 8 servings

1¼ cups all-purpose flour	2 large eggs
1¼ cups yellow cornmeal	1 can (8½ ounces) cream-style corn
1 tablespoon baking powder	
2 teaspoons sugar	4 tablespoons margarine or butter, melted
1 teaspoon salt	
1 cup milk	

◆ Preheat oven to 425°F. Generously grease 10-inch cast-iron skillet with oven-safe handle or 8" by 8" metal baking pan. In large bowl, mix flour, cornmeal, baking powder, sugar, and salt.

◆ In medium bowl, with fork or wire whisk, mix milk, eggs, corn, and melted margarine. Stir milk mixture into flour mixture just until combined; do not overmix.

◆ Pour batter into skillet. Bake 25 to 30 minutes, until toothpick inserted in center comes out clean. Serve warm. Or, loosen edge with knife, remove from pan, and cool on wire rack to serve later.

Each serving: About 260 calories, 7g protein, 39g carbohydrate, 9g total fat (2g saturated), 57mg cholesterol, 635mg sodium

SOUTHERN CORN BREAD

Prep: 10 minutes   *Bake:* 25 minutes
Makes 8 servings

4 tablespoons margarine or butter	¼ teaspoon baking soda
	1 teaspoon salt
1½ cups white or yellow cornmeal	2 large eggs
	1¾ cups buttermilk or soured milk (see page 392)
1 cup all-purpose flour	
2 teaspoons baking powder	

◆ Preheat oven to 450°F. Place margarine in 10-inch cast-iron skillet with oven-safe handle or 9" by 9" metal baking pan; place in oven 3 to 5 minutes, just until margarine is melted.

◆ Meanwhile, in large bowl, mix cornmeal, flour, baking powder, baking soda, and salt. In medium bowl, whisk together eggs and buttermilk. Add melted margarine to buttermilk mixture; stir into flour mixture just until moistened (batter will be lumpy; do not overmix).

◆ Pour batter into skillet. Bake 25 minutes, or until toothpick inserted in center comes out clean. Serve warm.

Each serving: 240 calories, 7g protein, 34g carbohydrate, 7g total fat (1g saturated), 55mg cholesterol, 565mg sodium

BISCUITS

Light, fluffy biscuits, served warm from the oven with golden honey or jam, promise to make any morning brighter. Our classic Buttermilk Biscuits are perfectly simple, but you'll also love our flavorful variations, flecked with fresh herbs, cheese, or smoky bacon. Or, try the whole-wheat, oatmeal, or sweet-potato biscuits.

BUTTERMILK BISCUITS

◆◆◆◆◆◆◆◆◆◆◆◆◆

Prep: 10 minutes
Bake: 12 to 14 minutes
Makes 13

2 cups cake flour or Southern soft wheat flour
1½ teaspoons baking powder
½ teaspoon baking soda
½ teaspoon salt
¼ cup shortening
¾ cup buttermilk or soured milk (see page 392)

1 Preheat oven to 450°F. In large bowl, mix flour, baking powder, baking soda, and salt. With pastry blender or two knives used scissor-fashion, cut in shortening until mixture resembles coarse crumbs.

2 Add buttermilk to flour mixture and stir just until moistened. Turn dough onto lightly floured surface and knead about 6 to 8 times, just until smooth. Roll or pat dough ¾ inch thick.

3 With floured 2-inch round biscuit cutter, cut out biscuits. Press trimmings together; roll and cut. Place biscuits, 1 inch apart, on ungreased cookie sheet. Bake 12 to 14 minutes, until lightly golden. Serve warm.

BISCUIT BASICS

◆◆◆◆◆◆◆◆◆◆◆◆◆◆◆◆◆◆◆◆◆◆◆◆

For the lightest biscuits, handle the dough as little as possible. When cutting them out, "punch" downward sharply with the cutter and don't twist, or you will seal the edges so the biscuits will not rise properly. If you don't have a biscuit cutter, just cut the dough into squares with a sharp knife.

Although you can make biscuits successfully with cake and all-purpose flour, the most tender of all are made with Southern soft wheat flour. Ground from winter wheat, it is lower in gluten than all-purpose and bread flours (both "hard" flours, preferable for baked goods that need a stronger structure) and makes lighter, fluffier biscuits.

BISCUITS PLUS

◆◆◆◆◆◆◆◆◆◆◆◆◆◆◆◆◆◆◆◆◆◆◆◆

Cheddar biscuits Reduce shortening to 2 tablespoons. Cut 4 ounces Cheddar cheese, shredded (1 cup), into flour mixture with shortening.

Black pepper and bacon biscuits Add ½ teaspoon coarsely ground black pepper to flour mixture. After cutting in shortening, stir 3 slices bacon, cooked and crumbled, into flour mixture.

Parsley-chive biscuits After cutting in shortening, stir 2 tablespoons chopped fresh parsley and 2 tablespoons chopped fresh chives into flour mixture.

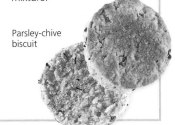

Parsley-chive biscuit

EACH BISCUIT: ABOUT 100 CALORIES, 2g PROTEIN, 14g CARBOHYDRATE, 4g TOTAL FAT (1g SATURATED), 1mg CHOLESTEROL, 200mg SODIUM

WHOLE-WHEAT SESAME BISCUITS

Prep: 15 minutes   *Bake: 12 to 15 minutes*
Makes 12

2 tablespoons sesame seeds
1 cup whole-wheat flour
1 cup all-purpose flour
1 tablespoon baking powder
¾ teaspoon salt
4 tablespoons margarine or butter
¾ cup plus 3 tablespoons milk

◆ In small skillet, toast sesame seeds over medium heat, stirring occasionally, about 5 minutes, until lightly browned.

◆ Preheat oven to 425°F. Reserve 1 teaspoon sesame seeds. In large bowl, mix both flours, baking powder, salt, and remaining sesame seeds. With pastry blender or two knives used scissor-fashion, cut in margarine until mixture resembles coarse crumbs.

◆ Stir in ¾ cup plus 2 tablespoons milk just until mixture forms soft dough that leaves side of bowl.

◆ Turn dough onto lightly floured surface; knead 6 to 8 times, just until smooth. With floured rolling pin, roll dough ½ inch thick.

◆ With floured 2½-inch round biscuit cutter, cut out biscuits. Gently press trimmings together; roll and cut. With pancake turner, place biscuits, about 1 inch apart, on ungreased large cookie sheet.

◆ Brush tops of biscuits with remaining 1 tablespoon milk; sprinkle with reserved sesame seeds. Bake 12 to 15 minutes, until golden. Serve warm, or cool on wire rack to reheat later.

Each biscuit: About 125 calories, 3g protein, 16g carbohydrate, 5g total fat (1g saturated), 3mg cholesterol, 310mg sodium

OATMEAL BISCUITS

Prep: 15 minutes   *Bake: 12 to 15 minutes*
Makes 20

1 cup old-fashioned or quick-cooking oats, uncooked
3½ cups all-purpose flour
⅓ cup packed brown sugar
4 teaspoons baking powder
1½ teaspoons salt
½ teaspoon baking soda
½ cup margarine or butter
1½ cups pecans (about 6 ounces), chopped
½ teaspoon imitation maple flavor (optional)
1½ cups plus 2 tablespoons buttermilk or soured milk (see page 392)

◆ Preheat oven to 450°F. Reserve 2 tablespoons oats. In large bowl, mix flour, next 4 ingredients, and remaining oats. With pastry blender or two knives used scissor-fashion, cut in margarine until mixture resembles coarse crumbs; stir in pecans.

◆ Stir maple flavor, if using, into 1½ cups buttermilk; stir buttermilk mixture into flour mixture just until soft dough that leaves side of bowl forms.

◆ Turn dough onto lightly floured surface; knead 6 to 8 times, just until smooth. With floured rolling pin, roll dough ½ inch thick.

◆ With floured 3-inch round biscuit cutter, cut out biscuits. Gently press trimmings together; roll and cut. With pancake turner, place biscuits, about 1 inch apart, on 2 ungreased large cookie sheets.

◆ Brush tops of biscuits with remaining 2 tablespoons buttermilk; sprinkle with reserved oats. Bake 12 to 15 minutes, until golden, rotating cookie sheets between upper and lower racks halfway through baking time. Serve warm, or cool on wire rack to reheat later.

Each biscuit: About 220 calories, 5g protein, 27g carbohydrate, 11g total fat (2g saturated), 1mg cholesterol, 365mg sodium

SWEET POTATO BISCUITS

Prep: 30 minutes plus cooling
Bake: 12 to 15 minutes   *Makes 20*

2 medium sweet potatoes (1 pound), peeled and cut into 2-inch chunks
4 cups all-purpose flour
½ cup packed light brown sugar
5 teaspoons baking powder
1 teaspoon salt
10 tablespoons margarine or butter
⅓ cup milk

◆ In 3-quart saucepan, heat sweet-potato chunks and enough *water* to cover to boiling over high heat. Reduce heat to low; cover and simmer 12 to 15 minutes, until potatoes are fork-tender. Drain well.

◆ In small bowl, with potato masher, mash sweet potatoes until smooth. Set aside to cool.

◆ Preheat oven to 425°F. In large bowl, combine flour, brown sugar, baking powder, and salt. With pastry blender or two knives used scissor-fashion, cut in margarine until mixture resembles coarse crumbs.

◆ Stir in milk and cooled mashed sweet potatoes; mix just until combined.

◆ Turn dough onto lightly floured surface; pat into an 8½-inch square. Cut dough in half. Cut each half into 10 equal pieces. With pancake turner, place biscuits, 1 inch apart, on 2 ungreased large cookie sheets.

◆ Place cookie sheets on 2 oven racks; bake biscuits 12 to 15 minutes, until golden, rotating cookie sheets between upper and lower racks halfway through baking time. Serve warm, or cool on wire rack to reheat later.

Each biscuit: About 175 calories, 3g protein, 28g carbohydrate, 6g total fat (1g saturated), 1mg cholesterol, 300mg sodium

SODA BREAD AND SCONES

Although rarely baked today in the traditional cast-iron pot over an open hearth, soda bread is still the staff of life in Ireland. A plain whole-wheat version appears at most meals, but the addition of raisins and caraway seeds makes it special. Scones, made from a similar, very lightly kneaded dough, are often richer – especially when served with strawberry jam and clotted cream at a "cream tea."

WHOLE-GRAIN SODA BREAD

◆◆◆◆◆◆◆◆◆◆◆◆◆◆◆◆◆◆◆◆◆◆◆◆◆◆◆

Prep: 15 minutes plus cooling   Bake: 1 hour
Makes 1 loaf, 12 servings

1½ cups all-purpose flour
1½ cups whole-wheat flour
1 cup quick-cooking oats, uncooked
¼ cup sugar
1 tablespoon baking powder
1½ teaspoons salt

1 teaspoon baking soda
6 tablespoons margarine or butter
1½ cups golden raisins
2 teaspoons caraway seeds
1½ cups buttermilk or soured milk (see page 392)

1 Preheat oven to 350°F. In large bowl, mix 1½ cups all-purpose flour and next 6 ingredients. With pastry blender or two knives used scissor-fashion, cut in margarine until mixture resembles coarse crumbs.

2 Stir in raisins and caraway seeds. Stir in buttermilk just until flour is moistened (dough will be sticky). Grease cookie sheet.

3 Turn dough onto well-floured surface; with floured hands, knead 8 to 10 times to mix thoroughly. (Do not overmix, or bread will be tough.) Shape into ball; place on cookie sheet.

4 Sprinkle ball lightly with all-purpose flour. In center, cut a 4-inch cross, about ¼ inch deep. Bake 1 hour, or until toothpick inserted in center comes out clean. Remove from cookie sheet; cool on wire rack.

BUTTERMILK

◆◆◆◆◆◆◆◆◆◆◆◆◆◆◆◆◆◆◆◆◆◆◆◆◆◆◆

In the past, buttermilk was the liquid left over when cream was churned into butter. Now commercially produced buttermilk is made by adding special bacterial cultures to low-fat milk. These turn the milk's natural sugar to acid, producing a thicker milk with a tangy taste. Dry or powdered buttermilk is also available. You can also substitute yogurt, or milk soured with lemon juice or vinegar (see page 392).

Buttermilk is a traditional ingredient in Irish soda bread, and is often used in other quick breads; its acidity causes the baking powder or soda to release carbon dioxide gas so the bread can rise. It makes extra-tender pancakes, biscuits, and cakes. Or, add buttermilk to cold soups and salad dressings for a creamy effect with less fat.

EACH SERVING: ABOUT 300 CALORIES, 8g PROTEIN, 54g CARBOHYDRATE, 7g TOTAL FAT (2g SATURATED), 1mg CHOLESTEROL, 595mg SODIUM

RICH SCONES

Prep: 15 minutes   ***Bake:*** *15 to 20 minutes*
Makes 8

3⅓ cups all-purpose flour
2 tablespoons baking powder
½ teaspoon salt
½ cup plus 1 tablespoon sugar
6 tablespoons margarine or
   butter

2 large eggs, beaten
1 cup plus 1 tablespoon half-
   and-half or light cream

◆ Preheat oven to 400°F. Grease large cookie sheet.

◆ In large bowl, mix flour, baking powder, salt, and ½ cup sugar. With pastry blender or two knives used scissor-fashion, cut in margarine until mixture resembles coarse crumbs.

◆ Stir eggs and 1 cup half-and-half into mixture in bowl just until ingredients are blended.

◆ Spoon dough onto floured surface (dough will be sticky). With lightly floured hands, pat dough into 9-inch round. Brush remaining 1 tablespoon half-and-half over dough; sprinkle with remaining 1 tablespoon sugar.

◆ With knife, cut dough into 8 wedges. With pancake turner, place scones, 2 inches apart, on cookie sheet.

◆ Bake scones 15 to 20 minutes, until golden. Serve scones warm, or remove from cookie sheet and cool on wire rack to reheat later.

Each scone: About 365 calories, 8g protein, 54g carbohydrate, 14g total fat (4g saturated), 65mg cholesterol, 630mg sodium

---

SCONES PLUS

Lemon-walnut scones
Prepare Rich Scones as above, but add 1 teaspoon grated lemon peel with flour mixture; add 1 cup chopped walnuts (about 4 ounces) with eggs and half-and-half.

Currant scones Prepare Rich Scones as above, but add ¾ cup dried currants with eggs and half-and-half.

Lemon-walnut
scone

Currant scone

OLIVE-ROSEMARY SCONES

Prep: 15 minutes plus cooling   ***Bake:*** *20 to 25 minutes*
Makes 12

3 cups all-purpose flour
4 tablespoons margarine or
   butter, cut into 4 pieces
1 tablespoon sugar
1 tablespoon baking powder
2 teaspoons chopped fresh
   rosemary or ¼ teaspoon
   dried rosemary, crushed

1 teaspoon baking soda
½ teaspoon salt
¼ cup plus 1 tablespoon
   olive oil
1 cup milk
1 large egg
½ cup Kalamata olives, pitted
   and coarsely chopped

◆ Preheat oven to 425°F. Lightly grease large cookie sheet. In food processor with knife blade attached, blend flour, margarine, sugar, baking powder, rosemary, baking soda, salt, and ¼ cup olive oil, pulsing processor on and off until mixture resembles coarse crumbs.

◆ In small bowl, mix milk and egg; pour mixture through feed tube into flour mixture, pulsing just until blended. Turn dough onto lightly floured surface; with floured hands, press olives into dough. Place dough on cookie sheet; pat into 10-inch round (dough will be sticky).

◆ With floured knife, cut round into 12 wedges, but do not separate wedges. Brush top with remaining 1 tablespoon olive oil. Bake scones 20 to 25 minutes, until golden. Remove from cookie sheet; cool slightly on wire rack to serve warm.

Each scone: About 230 calories, 4g protein, 25g carbohydrate, 12g total fat (2g saturated), 21mg cholesterol, 475mg sodium

BEER BREAD

Prep: 10 minutes plus cooling   ***Bake:*** *40 minutes*
Makes 1 loaf, 12 servings

3 cups all-purpose flour
¼ cup packed light brown
   sugar
1 tablespoon baking powder
¾ teaspoon salt

1 can or bottle (12 ounces)
   beer
4 tablespoons margarine or
   butter, melted

◆ Preheat oven to 375°F. Grease 9" by 5" loaf pan. In large bowl, mix flour, brown sugar, baking powder, and salt until evenly combined. Stir in beer and melted margarine just until moistened (batter will be lumpy).

◆ Spoon batter into loaf pan and bake 40 minutes, or until golden and toothpick inserted in center comes out clean. Cool in pan on wire rack 5 minutes; remove from pan and cool completely on rack.

Each serving: 170 calories, 3g protein, 28g carbohydrate, 4g total fat (1g saturated), 0mg cholesterol, 305mg sodium

YEAST BREADS <u>KNOW-HOW</u>

There's a world of scrumptious breads, rolls, coffee cakes, and flat breads that take their rising power from yeast. While they're not as fast to prepare as quick breads, most yeast breads can be mixed, kneaded, and shaped in less than half an hour – the rest is simply unattended rising time. What's more, quick-rise yeast speeds the traditional process considerably.

TYPES OF YEAST

Yeast is the tiny living organism that makes bread rise. It works by converting the natural sugars in flour into bubbles of carbon dioxide gas, which expand during baking to make dough rise and give it a yeasty flavor.

Dry yeast Active dry yeast – dehydrated granules of baker's yeast – is the type most commonly used in baking. It comes in ¼-ounce foil packages and in jars. Quick-rise yeast is a high-activity dry yeast that makes dough rise about 50 percent faster. It can replace active dry yeast in equal amounts; follow the package directions for water temperatures. Store either type in a cool, dry place until opened, then refrigerate.

Fresh yeast These moist, crumbly cakes are extremely perishable. Store in the refrigerator up to 2 weeks (or until the expiration date) or freeze up to 3 months. Use any thawed yeast cakes right away.

DEMYSTIFYING YEAST

• Yeast should be reliable until the expiration date.
• Since yeast works best in a moderately warm environment, have all ingredients at room temperature before you begin.
• To activate yeast, combine it with warm liquid. However, liquid that's too hot kills yeast, while cold liquid slows its growth. To avoid guesswork, use a thermometer to check.
• Yeast doughs require a warm place to rise – ideally 80° to 85°F – so the yeast can grow and the dough expand. Avoid drafty areas, or the dough will rise unevenly. Dough will rise successfully in an unheated oven: Place the dough in a covered bowl on the upper rack with a large bowl of hot water below it on the lower rack.
• Sugar speeds yeast growth, so some is usually added to the liquid. (Fat slows yeast growth, which is why rich doughs are slower to rise.) Salt inhibits rising, but a little salt helps control the rate of yeast fermentation.
• Extra yeast is sometimes added to speed leavening, but this produces a more porous loaf with a yeastier flavor. Batter bread recipes often call for more yeast than other types.

• Yeast doughs rise faster at high altitudes. At 5000 feet, use half the yeast specified. Check rising early, and bake dough as soon as it tests correctly (see Rising and Shaping, page 406), even if it doesn't look doubled.

KNOW YOUR FLOURS

A variety of flours can be used for breadmaking, but not all flours are alike. Flours vary in the amount of gluten – a protein that gives bread its strength and elasticity – they contain. Wheat flours milled from hard winter wheat are high in gluten and create the best breads. Soft-wheat flours, such as cake flour and pastry flour, are low in gluten and are better used for delicate cakes and cookies.

Breads typically call for either bread flour (made entirely from hard wheat) or all-purpose flour (a blend of hard and soft wheat). Whole-wheat and rye flours can also be used, usually combined with all-purpose flour for a lighter loaf (cornmeal, oats, and semolina flour may also be added to all-purpose flour to vary a basic dough). Stone-ground flours lend a nutty taste and coarse texture.

Store all-purpose flour in an airtight container in a cool, dry place up to 12 months; whole-grain varieties up to 3 months. For longer storage, keep flour in the freezer.

All-purpose · Rye · Stone-ground · Whole-wheat

KNEADING

Strong, steady kneading develops the gluten in dough to create an evenly textured loaf that's free of holes or dense spots. Knead for 5 to 10 minutes, working in just as much flour as the dough can handle (too much flour makes a dry, heavy loaf). Dough is ready when it's smooth and elastic and tiny blisters appear just below the surface. You can also use a food processor or heavy-duty mixer for kneading, but take care not to overload it, or you could damage the motor.

Place dough on lightly floured surface. With heel of hand, push dough down and away with rolling motion. Give it a quarter turn; fold, then push down again. Repeat until dough is smooth and tiny blisters appear.

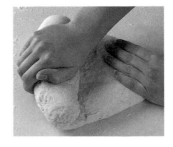

RISING AND SHAPING

1 Dough should rise until it doubles in size. To test, press a finger ½ inch into center. If the dent stays, dough has risen sufficiently. If the dent fills in, dough needs more rising time.

2 To punch dough down, push your fist into the center (this distributes carbon dioxide for a fine-textured bread), then work the edges of dough to the center. Batter breads are stirred down.

For easier shaping, place risen dough on a lightly floured surface and let rest 15 minutes. For a round loaf, gently pull sides under dough until rounded. Place on a cookie sheet and flatten slightly. The shaped dough usually rises a second time, until it's almost doubled in size.

For a rectangular loaf shape, with floured rolling pin, roll dough into rectangle. From a narrow end, roll dough tightly, jelly-roll style. Pinch seam and ends to seal; turn ends under. Place, seam-side down, in greased loaf pan.

WHICH CRUST?

• For a soft, tender crust, brush the unbaked loaf with milk, buttermilk, cream, or melted margarine or butter.
• For a crisp, chewy crust, brush (or spray, with a clean mister) loaf with water occasionally during baking.
• For shine and color, brush loaf with beaten egg (or yolk or white, sometimes mixed with water).

BETTER BAKING

• Some loaves are slashed just before baking. This allows carbon dioxide gas to escape and helps prevent cracks.
• Bake breads on the center rack of oven. If baking several pans at once, allow at least 2 inches between each pan.
• If top of loaf is overbrowning, cover it loosely with foil.
• Bread baked on a baking stone (from gourmet stores) will bake evenly and be extra crisp. Or try unglazed terracotta tiles from tile stores – make sure they're lead-free.

TESTING FOR DONENESS

Bread is done when it pulls away from the sides of the pan, is nicely browned, and sounds hollow when the bottom is lightly rapped with knuckles. Also check the sides of the loaf – they should feel crisp and firm when pressed.

COOLING AND STORING

• Bread that's cool cuts into neater slices. Most breads should be removed promptly from the pan and cooled right-side up on a wire rack; keep the bread away from drafts, which can cause shrinkage. Cooling can take as long as 3 hours.
• Be sure bread is completely cool before wrapping or freezing. If it's not cool, condensation can form on the inside of the wrapper and hasten spoilage.
• Store breads tightly wrapped. Soft breads stay freshest in plastic bags, while crusty breads stay crispest in paper bags.
• Always store breads at room temperature, not in the refrigerator, where they'll turn stale more quickly. Most breads are fine if used within 5 days.
• To freshen a stale loaf, heat in a 350°F oven for 5 to 7 minutes. Or, use stale bread as is to make bread pudding, toast, croutons, or bread crumbs.
• Most breads freeze well for up to 3 months. Cool completely, then place in a freezer bag, pressing out air, or tightly wrap in heavy-duty foil. To thaw, let stand at room temperature for about 1 hour, or wrap frozen bread in foil (with an opening at the top so steam can escape) and heat in a 300°F oven for about 20 minutes.

TROUBLESHOOTING

Dough overrises in bowl To fix (otherwise, loaf could collapse in oven or be heavy-textured), turn dough onto lightly floured surface and knead 2 to 3 minutes. Cover, let rest 15 minutes, and shape as directed.
Bread is too pale Place loaf directly on oven rack and bake 5 to 10 minutes longer.
Bread is dry and crumbly Dough had too much flour or dough overrose.
Bread collapses in oven The shaped dough overrose in the pan. Don't let dough rise above the pan's edges.
Cracks in bread Dough had too much flour or there was too much dough in the pan.
Holes in bread Dough wasn't kneaded enough – it's almost impossible to overknead by hand – or rising time was too long or in too warm a place.

Basic yeast breads

Nothing quite compares to a loaf of homemade bread. There's something satisfying in the mixing and kneading, and especially in the eating. The combination of yeast, liquid, and flour is found in all yeast breads; beyond that, the choice of flours alone makes for marvelous variety.

Big onion bread

◆◆◆◆◆◆◆◆◆◆◆◆◆

Prep: 1 hour plus rising and cooling
Bake: 1 hour 40 minutes
Makes 1 loaf, 20 servings

3 tablespoons plus ½ cup margarine or butter
5 large onions (about 2½ pounds), chopped
Salt
2 packages quick-rise yeast
About 8¾ cups all-purpose flour
2 cups milk
¼ cup light molasses
4 large eggs

1 In 12-inch skillet, melt 3 tablespoons margarine over medium-high heat. Add onions and 1 teaspoon salt; cook, stirring often, about 30 minutes, until very tender and browned. Remove from heat. In large bowl, combine yeast, 2 cups flour, and 4 teaspoons salt. In 1-quart saucepan, heat milk, molasses, and remaining ½ cup margarine over low heat until very warm (120° to 130°F); margarine need not melt.

2 With mixer at low speed, gradually beat liquid into flour mixture just until blended. Increase speed to medium; beat 2 minutes, occasionally scraping bowl with rubber spatula. Beat in 3 eggs and 3 cups flour to make a thick batter; beat 2 minutes longer, scraping bowl often. Reserve ⅓ cup onions. With wooden spoon, stir in remaining onions, then 3¼ cups flour to make a soft dough. Turn dough onto lightly floured surface.

3 Knead dough about 10 minutes, until smooth and elastic, working in about ½ cup flour while kneading. Shape into ball; place in greased large bowl, turning dough to grease top.

4 Cover dough; let rise in warm place (80° to 85°F) about 30 minutes, until doubled. To test, press two fingers about ½ inch into dough; remove. The indentation should remain.

5 Preheat oven to 350°F. Grease 10-inch tube pan with removable bottom. Punch down dough by pushing your fist into center. Turn onto lightly floured surface; divide in half.

6 With hands, roll each half of dough into a 15-inch-long rope. Twist ropes together. Place dough in tube pan; tuck ends under. Bake 40 minutes.

7 In cup, with fork, lightly beat remaining egg. When bread has baked 40 minutes, brush top with beaten egg; sprinkle with reserved onions. Bake bread 20 to 25 minutes longer, until loaf is browned and sounds hollow when lightly tapped with fingers. Cool bread in pan on wire rack 10 minutes; remove side of tube pan. Cool completely on rack.

EACH SERVING: ABOUT 300 CALORIES, 8g PROTEIN, 47g CARBOHYDRATE, 9g TOTAL FAT (2g SATURATED), 46mg CHOLESTEROL, 635mg SODIUM

WALNUT OATMEAL BREAD

Prep: 25 minutes plus rising and cooling   Bake: 35 to 40 minutes
Makes 1 loaf, 12 servings

1 package quick-rise yeast	1 large egg
⅓ cup packed light brown sugar	1 cup old-fashioned or quick-cooking oats, uncooked
1½ teaspoons salt	1 cup walnuts (about 4 ounces), coarsely chopped
About 4½ cups all-purpose flour	1 tablespoon milk
2 tablespoons margarine or butter	

◆ In large bowl, combine yeast, brown sugar, salt, and 1½ cups flour. In 1-quart saucepan, heat margarine and *1¼ cups water* over low heat until very warm (120° to 130°F); margarine need not melt.

◆ With mixer at low speed, gradually beat liquid into flour mixture just until blended. Increase speed to medium; beat 2 minutes, occasionally scraping bowl with rubber spatula.

◆ Beat in egg and 1 cup flour to make a thick batter; beat 2 minutes longer, scraping bowl often. Reserve 1 tablespoon oats for top of loaf. With wooden spoon, stir in walnuts, 1½ cups flour, and remaining oats to make a soft dough.

◆ Turn dough onto lightly floured surface; knead about 10 minutes, until smooth and elastic, working in about ½ cup more flour while kneading. Grease large cookie sheet.

◆ Shape dough into 5-inch ball; place on cookie sheet. Cover loosely with plastic wrap; let rise in warm place (80° to 85°F) about 30 minutes, until doubled.

◆ Preheat oven to 350°F. With sharp knife or single-edge razor blade, cut 3 slashes across top of loaf. Brush with milk; sprinkle with reserved oats.

YEAST AND TEMPERATURE
◆◆◆◆◆◆◆◆◆◆◆◆◆◆◆◆◆◆◆◆◆◆◆◆◆◆◆

Yeast is the living organism that makes dough rise. Warm liquid activates yeast, allowing it to begin fermentation. Liquid that is too hot will kill the yeast, but if it's not hot enough, the yeast will remain dormant. Yeast may be dissolved directly in liquid that is 105° to 115°F, or first combined with dry ingredients (as in most of these recipes) and dissolved with 120° to 130°F (hot to the touch) liquid. If using the dry-ingredient method with active dry yeast, which has larger particles than quick-rise yeast, beat for 1 minute with an electric mixer after adding liquid. For the most accurate results – and the best bread – test the temperature of the liquid with an instant-read thermometer.

◆ Bake 35 to 40 minutes, until loaf is golden and bottom sounds hollow when lightly tapped with fingers. Remove loaf from cookie sheet; cool loaf on wire rack 30 minutes to serve warm. Or, cool completely to serve later.

Each serving: About 320 calories, 9g protein, 50g carbohydrate, 10g total fat (1g saturated), 18mg cholesterol, 300mg sodium

PORTUGUESE PEASANT BREAD

Prep: 20 minutes plus rising and cooling   Bake: 35 minutes
Makes 2 loaves, 12 servings each

4 cups instant barley cereal, uncooked (available in the baby-food section of supermarkets)	About 4¾ cups all-purpose flour
	2 packages active dry yeast
	2 tablespoons sugar
2½ cups stone-ground white cornmeal	4 teaspoons salt

◆ In large bowl, combine barley cereal, cornmeal, and 4 cups flour. In another large bowl, combine yeast, sugar, salt, and 3 cups flour mixture.

◆ With mixer at low speed, gradually beat *3 cups very hot tap water* (120° to 130°F) into yeast mixture just until blended.

◆ Increase speed to medium; beat 2 minutes, scraping bowl frequently with rubber spatula. Beat in 2 cups flour mixture; beat 2 minutes longer, scraping bowl often. With wooden spoon, stir in remaining flour mixture to make a soft dough.

◆ Cover bowl loosely with plastic wrap and let rise in warm place (80° to 85°F) about 1 hour, until doubled.

◆ With floured hands, punch down dough and turn onto well-floured surface (dough will be sticky). Knead about 5 minutes, until smooth and elastic, working in about ¾ cup more flour. Grease large cookie sheet.

◆ Cut dough in half; shape each half into a 6-inch round. Dip each round in flour to coat well; place on cookie sheet. Cover loaves loosely with plastic wrap and let rise in warm place about 1 hour, until doubled.

◆ Preheat oven to 400°F. Bake loaves about 35 minutes, until golden brown, spraying loaves with water after first 5 minutes of baking, and again 10 minutes later to give crisp, chewy crust. Remove loaves from cookie sheet; cool on wire racks.

Each serving: About 155 calories, 5g protein, 32g carbohydrate, 1g total fat (0g saturated), 0mg cholesterol, 355mg sodium

WHOLE-GRAIN BREAD

Prep: 25 minutes plus rising and cooling   *Bake:* 50 to 60 minutes
Makes 1 loaf, 16 servings

2 cups rye flour	¾ cup milk
1 cup unprocessed bran	½ cup margarine or butter
½ cup wheat germ	⅓ cup dark molasses
About 4¼ cups whole-wheat flour	2 large eggs
2 packages active dry yeast	2 tablespoons yellow cornmeal
3 tablespoons sugar	1 teaspoon caraway seeds
1 tablespoon salt	

◆ In large bowl, combine rye flour, unprocessed bran, wheat germ, and 3 cups whole-wheat flour. In another large bowl, combine yeast, sugar, salt, and 3 cups flour mixture. In 2-quart saucepan, heat milk, margarine, molasses, and *1 cup water* over low heat until very warm (120° to 130°F); margarine need not melt.

◆ With mixer at low speed, gradually beat liquid into yeast mixture just until blended. Increase speed to medium; beat 2 minutes, occasionally scraping bowl with rubber spatula.

◆ Separate 1 egg and reserve white in refrigerator, covered. Beat remaining egg, egg yolk, and 2 cups flour mixture into yeast mixture; beat 2 minutes longer, scraping bowl often. With wooden spoon, stir in remaining flour mixture and ¾ cup whole-wheat flour to make a soft dough.

◆ Lightly sprinkle work surface with whole-wheat flour; turn dough onto surface and knead about 10 minutes, until smooth and elastic, working in about ½ cup more whole-wheat flour while kneading. Shape dough into ball; place in greased large bowl, turning dough to grease top. Cover loosely with plastic wrap; let rise in warm place (80° to 85°F) about 1 hour, until doubled.

◆ Punch down dough; turn onto surface lightly floured with whole-wheat flour. Cover loosely with plastic wrap and let rest 15 minutes for easier shaping. Sprinkle cookie sheet with cornmeal.

◆ Shape dough into 10" by 5" oval loaf, tapering ends; place on cookie sheet. Cover loosely with plastic wrap; let rise in warm place about 1 hour, until doubled.

◆ Preheat oven to 350°F. With sharp knife or single-edge razor blade, cut 3 diagonal slashes in top of loaf. In cup, with fork, beat reserved egg white with *1 tablespoon water*; brush over bread. Sprinkle with caraway seeds. Bake loaf 50 to 60 minutes, until bottom sounds hollow when lightly tapped with fingers. Remove from cookie sheet; cool on wire rack.

Each serving: About 270 calories, 9g protein, 45g carbohydrate, 8g total fat (2g saturated), 28mg cholesterol, 485mg sodium

HONEY-WHEAT BREAD

Prep: 20 minutes plus rising and cooling   *Bake:* 30 minutes
Makes 1 loaf, 12 servings

2 packages quick-rise yeast	¼ cup vegetable oil
3 cups whole-wheat flour	1 large egg
1½ teaspoons salt	About 4 cups all-purpose flour
½ cup honey	

◆ In large bowl, combine yeast, whole-wheat flour, and salt.

◆ With mixer at low speed, gradually beat *1⅔ cups very hot tap water* (120° to 130°F) into flour mixture just until blended. Increase speed to medium; beat 2 minutes, occasionally scraping bowl with rubber spatula.

◆ Beat in honey, oil, egg, and 1 cup all-purpose flour to make a thick batter; beat 2 minutes longer, scraping bowl often. With wooden spoon, stir in 2½ cups all-purpose flour to make a soft dough.

◆ Turn dough onto floured surface and knead about 10 minutes, until smooth and elastic, working in about ½ cup more all-purpose flour. Cover loosely with plastic wrap and let rest 10 minutes for easier shaping.

◆ On large cookie sheet, shape dough into 10" by 5" oval loaf. Cover loaf loosely with plastic wrap; let rise in warm place (80° to 85°F) about 30 minutes, until doubled. With sharp knife or single-edge razor blade, cut three 3-inch-long diagonal slashes across top of loaf.

◆ Preheat oven to 375°F. Sprinkle loaf lightly with all-purpose flour. Bake 30 minutes, or until bottom of loaf sounds hollow when lightly tapped with fingers. Remove loaf from cookie sheet; cool on wire rack.

Each serving: About 335 calories, 9g protein, 63g carbohydrate, 6g total fat (1g saturated), 18mg cholesterol, 275mg sodium

BUTTERMILK BREAD

Prep: 20 minutes plus rising and cooling **Bake:** *25 to 30 minutes*
Makes 2 loaves, 12 servings each

1 package active dry yeast	¼ cup sugar
2 teaspoons salt	1¾ cups buttermilk or soured
About 4¾ cups all-purpose	milk (see page 392)
flour	½ cup margarine or butter

◆ In large bowl, combine yeast, salt, and 2 cups flour. In 1-quart saucepan, heat sugar, buttermilk, and 6 tablespoons margarine over medium-low heat until very warm (120° to 130°F); margarine need not melt.

◆ With mixer at low speed, gradually beat buttermilk mixture into flour mixture just until blended. Increase speed to medium; beat 2 minutes longer, scraping bowl often with rubber spatula.

◆ Beat in 1 cup flour to make a thick batter; beat batter 2 minutes longer, scraping bowl often. With wooden spoon, stir in 1½ cups flour to make a stiff dough.

◆ Turn dough onto lightly floured surface and knead about 10 minutes, until smooth and elastic, working in about ¼ cup more flour while kneading.

◆ Shape dough into a ball; place in greased large bowl, turning dough to grease top. Cover dough loosely with plastic wrap; let rise in warm place (80° to 85°F) about 1 hour, until doubled.

◆ Punch down dough. Turn dough onto lightly floured surface and cut in half; cover loosely with plastic wrap and let rest 15 minutes for easier shaping.

◆ Grease two 8½" by 4½" loaf pans. Shape each piece of dough into a loaf (see page 406); place, seam-side down, in loaf pans. Cover loosely with plastic wrap; let rise in warm place about 1 hour, until doubled.

◆ Preheat oven to 375°F. Melt remaining 2 tablespoons margarine. With sharp knife or single-edge razor blade, slash top of each loaf lengthwise, cutting about ¼ inch deep. Brush slashes with melted margarine.

◆ Bake 25 to 30 minutes, until loaves are golden and bottoms sound hollow when lightly tapped with fingers. Remove loaves from pans; cool on wire racks.

Each serving: About 135 calories, 3g protein, 20g carbohydrate, 4g total fat (1g saturated), 1mg cholesterol, 240mg sodium

"SOURDOUGH" BREAD

Prep: 20 minutes plus rising and cooling **Bake:** *25 to 30 minutes*
Makes 2 loaves, 16 servings each

2 packages quick-rise yeast	About 7 cups all-purpose flour
2 tablespoons sugar	1 container (16 ounces) plain
2 teaspoons salt	low-fat yogurt

◆ In large bowl, mix yeast, sugar, salt, and 6 cups flour. In 2-quart saucepan, heat yogurt and ⅔ *cup water* over medium heat until very warm (120° to 130°F); stir into flour mixture, mixing until blended and dough forms a ball.

◆ Turn dough onto lightly floured surface; knead about 10 minutes, until smooth and elastic, working in about 1 cup flour while kneading. Cut dough in half; cover and let rest 10 minutes for easier shaping. Grease large cookie sheet.

◆ Shape each piece of dough into 5-inch round loaf. Place loaves on opposite ends of cookie sheet. Cover loosely with plastic wrap; let rise in warm place (80° to 85°F) about 45 minutes, until doubled.

◆ Preheat oven to 400°F. With sharp knife or single-edge razor blade, cut 3 parallel slashes in each loaf; brush loaves with *water*. Bake 25 to 30 minutes, until bottoms of loaves sound hollow when lightly tapped with fingers. Remove loaves from cookie sheet; cool on wire racks.

Each serving: About 105 calories, 4g protein, 21g carbohydrate, 1g total fat (0g saturated), 1mg cholesterol, 145mg sodium

THE PIONEER BREAD

◆◆◆◆◆◆◆◆◆◆◆◆◆◆◆◆◆◆◆◆◆◆◆◆◆◆◆◆◆

Before commercial yeast became available in 1868, homemade yeast starters were used to make bread rise. These were made from flour and water, and sometimes sugar; the mixture would attract wild yeasts present in the air and, after a few days, start to ferment. The pioneers on the trail west depended on sourdough starters – so called because they give bread a sour taste – for all their bread, and sourdough bread is still associated with California (although bakers in Europe and the eastern Mediterranean have used sourdough starters for thousands of years). For a tasty loaf made without the fuss of a starter, try our "sourdough," above.

SAVORY FILLED BREADS

Our trio of filled breads takes the basic yeast bread to new heights. And each recipe is quite easy to prepare: Mix the dough as usual, roll into a rectangle, and then sprinkle it with chopped Kalamata olives, walnuts, dried tomatoes, pepperoni, or mozzarella cheese. Roll up jelly-roll fashion and let rise before baking – the reward will be a truly impressive loaf.

1 Coarsely chop walnuts. In 10-inch skillet, cook walnuts over medium heat, stirring occasionally, until toasted. Remove skillet from heat. In large bowl, combine yeast, salt, sugar, pepper, and 2 cups flour.

2 In 1-quart saucepan, heat oil and *1½ cups water* over low heat until very warm (120° to 130°F). With wooden spoon, stir liquid into flour mixture until well blended. Stir in 2 cups flour to make a soft dough. Turn dough onto lightly floured surface; knead about 5 minutes, until smooth and elastic, working in about ½ cup more flour while kneading. Shape dough into a ball. Cover loosely with plastic wrap; let rest 10 minutes.

OLIVE AND WALNUT BREAD

Prep: 30 minutes plus rising and cooling   Bake: 35 to 40 minutes
Makes 1 loaf, 16 servings

1 cup walnuts (about 4 ounces)	About 4½ cups all-purpose flour plus additional for dusting
1 package quick-rise yeast	
1 teaspoon salt	3 tablespoons extra-virgin olive oil
1 teaspoon sugar	
½ teaspoon coarsely ground black pepper	¾ cup Kalamata olives, pitted and chopped

3 Grease large cookie sheet. On lightly floured surface, with floured rolling pin, roll dough to 15" by 12" rectangle; sprinkle with chopped olives and toasted walnuts. Starting from a short side, tightly roll dough jelly-roll fashion; pinch seam to seal.

4 Place loaf, seam-side down, on cookie sheet; tuck ends under. With sharp knife or single-edge razor blade, make parallel ⅛-inch-deep slashes in top of loaf. Cover loosely with plastic wrap; let rise in warm place (80° to 85°F) 15 minutes.

5 Meanwhile, preheat oven to 400°F. Bake 35 to 40 minutes, until bottom of bread sounds hollow when lightly tapped with fingers. Cool on wire rack slightly to serve warm. Or, cool completely to serve later.

EACH SERVING: ABOUT 210 CALORIES, 5g PROTEIN, 27g CARBOHYDRATE, 9g TOTAL FAT (1g SATURATED), 0mg CHOLESTEROL, 250mg SODIUM

TOMATO AND OLIVE BREAD

Prep: 35 minutes plus rising and cooling   Bake: 1 hour
Makes 1 loaf, 20 servings

2 packages quick-rise yeast
1 cup sugar
1 teaspoon salt
About 8 cups all-purpose flour
1½ cups milk
1 cup margarine or butter
3 large eggs
½ cup Kalamata olives, pitted
   and chopped

1 jar (8½ ounces) oil-packed
   dried tomatoes, drained and
   chopped
1 tablespoon chopped fresh
   rosemary or 1 teaspoon
   dried rosemary, crushed
Coarse salt (optional)

◆ In large bowl, combine yeast, sugar, salt, and 2 cups flour. In 1-quart saucepan, heat milk and margarine over low heat until very warm (120° to 130°F); margarine need not melt.

◆ With mixer at low speed, gradually beat liquid into flour mixture just until blended. Increase speed to medium; beat 2 minutes, occasionally scraping bowl with rubber spatula. Separate 1 egg and reserve white in refrigerator, covered. Beat in remaining eggs, egg yolk, and 1½ cups flour to make a thick batter; beat 2 minutes longer, scraping bowl often. With wooden spoon, stir in 4 cups flour to make a soft dough.

◆ Turn dough onto lightly floured surface and knead about 10 minutes, until smooth and elastic, working in about ½ cup more flour while kneading. Shape dough into ball; cover loosely with plastic wrap and let rest about 10 minutes for easier shaping.

◆ Meanwhile, prepare filling: In small bowl, mix olives, dried tomatoes, and rosemary.

◆ Grease 10-inch tube pan. On lightly floured surface, with floured rolling pin, roll dough into 20" by 15" rectangle. Spread filling evenly over dough, leaving 1-inch border. Starting from a long side, tightly roll dough jelly-roll fashion; pinch seam to seal. Place roll, seam-side down, in tube pan; press ends together to seal. Cover loosely with plastic wrap and let rise in warm place (80° to 85°F) about 1 hour, until doubled.

◆ Preheat oven to 350°F. In cup, with fork, beat reserved egg white with *2 teaspoons water*. Brush bread with egg-white mixture; sprinkle with coarse salt, if using. Bake 1 hour, or until bread sounds hollow when lightly tapped with fingers. When bread turns golden (after about 20 minutes), cover loosely with tent of foil to avoid overbrowning. Cool bread in pan on wire rack 10 minutes; remove from pan and cool completely on rack.

Each serving: About 350 calories, 7g protein, 50g carbohydrate, 13g total fat (3g saturated), 34mg cholestrol, 325mg sodium

CHEESE AND PEPPERONI BREAD

Prep: 30 minutes plus rising and cooling   Bake: 45 minutes
Makes 1 loaf, 16 servings

1 package quick-rise yeast
1 tablespoon sugar
1 teaspoon salt
About 4¼ cups all-purpose
   flour
1 cup milk
½ cup margarine or butter
2 large eggs

½ cup chopped pepperoni
8 ounces mozzarella cheese,
   shredded (2 cups)
½ teaspoon dried oregano
½ teaspoon coarsely ground
   black pepper

◆ In large bowl, combine yeast, sugar, salt, and 1 cup flour. In 1-quart saucepan, heat milk and margarine over low heat until very warm (120° to 130°F); margarine need not melt.

◆ With mixer at low speed, gradually beat liquid into flour mixture just until blended. In cup, with fork, beat eggs lightly; reserve 1 tablespoon beaten egg in refrigerator, covered. Beat remaining eggs into batter. Increase speed to medium; beat 2 minutes, occasionally scraping bowl with rubber spatula. Beat in 1 cup flour to make a thick batter; beat 2 minutes longer, occasionally scraping bowl. With wooden spoon, stir in 2 cups flour to make a soft dough.

◆ Turn dough onto lightly floured surface and knead about 10 minutes, until smooth and elastic, working in about ¼ cup more flour while kneading. Shape dough into ball; cover loosely with plastic wrap and let rest 10 minutes for easier shaping.

◆ Meanwhile prepare filling: In small bowl, with fork, mix pepperoni, shredded cheese, and oregano.

◆ Grease 9-inch round cake pan. On lightly floured surface, with floured rolling pin, roll dough into 23" by 6" rectangle. Evenly spoon filling lengthwise down center of dough. Starting from a long side, tightly roll dough jelly-roll fashion; pinch seam to seal. Place roll, seam-side down, in cake pan to make a ring, overlapping ends slightly; pinch ends together to seal and tuck under. Cover loosely with plastic wrap; let rise in warm place (80° to 85°F) about 30 minutes, until doubled.

◆ Preheat oven to 375°F. Brush loaf with reserved beaten egg; sprinkle with pepper. With sharp knife or single-edge razor blade, cut several slashes in top of bread. Bake 45 minutes, or until bread is golden and bottom sounds hollow when lightly tapped with fingers. Remove bread from pan immediately. Let cool on wire rack at least 15 minutes for easier slicing; serve warm. Or, cool completely on rack; refrigerate to reheat and serve later.

Each serving: About 260 calories, 9g protein, 26g carbohydrate, 13g total fat (5g saturated), 40mg cholestrol, 410mg sodium

Rolls and Breadsticks

Homemade rolls have an honored place on the dinner table or at a special breakfast or brunch. Making them is fun and easy: Just shape the basic yeast dough into small rounds, spirals, or knots, or twirl long ropes together for breadsticks. Brushing them with egg before baking will give an appetizing golden sheen.

SPIRAL ROLLS

◆◆◆◆◆◆◆◆◆◆◆◆◆◆

Prep: 30 minutes plus
rising and cooling
Bake: 15 to 20 minutes
Makes 12

1 package quick-rise yeast
2 tablespoons sugar
1½ teaspoons salt
3 cups plus 2 to 3 tablespoons all-purpose flour
1 cup milk
3 tablespoons margarine or butter
1 large egg beaten with 1 teaspoon water
Coarse salt

1 In large bowl, combine yeast, sugar, 1½ teaspoons salt, and 3 cups flour. In 1-quart saucepan, heat milk and margarine over low heat until very warm (120° to 130°F); margarine need not melt. With wooden spoon, gradually stir liquid into flour mixture, adding 2 to 3 tablespoons more flour if necessary to make a soft dough. Turn onto lightly floured surface; knead about 5 minutes, until smooth and elastic. Shape into ball.

2 Place dough in greased bowl, turning to grease top. Cover; let rise in warm place (80° to 85°F) about 30 minutes, until doubled. Preheat oven to 375°F. Grease large cookie sheet.

3 Punch down dough; cut into 12 equal pieces. On lightly floured surface, roll each piece into 12-inch rope. Coil each into spiral; tuck end under. Place 2 inches apart on cookie sheet.

BREAD BASKET BONUSES

Once you've made the basic dough, you can easily create other shapes. Try either of the following variations (pictured above with Spiral Rolls) – or make all three rolls from one batch of dough.

Knot rolls Prepare dough as in Steps 1 and 2 above; cut into 12 equal pieces. On lightly floured surface, roll each piece of dough into 9-inch-long rope; tie each rope into a knot. Place rolls, 2 inches apart, on greased large cookie sheet. Dust each roll with flour (omit egg mixture and coarse salt). Bake as directed.

Poppy-seed rolls Prepare dough as in Steps 1 and 2 above; cut into 12 equal pieces. Place 3 tablespoons poppy seeds on plate. On lightly floured surface, shape each piece of dough into a ball; brush top of each with some egg mixture (omit coarse salt). Dip rolls, egg-side down, into poppy seeds. Place rolls, poppy-seed-side up, 2 inches apart, on greased large cookie sheet. With kitchen shears or knife, cut an "X" in top of each roll. Bake as directed.

4 Brush each roll with some egg mixture and sprinkle lightly with coarse salt. Bake 15 to 20 minutes, until golden. Serve rolls warm. Or, cool completely to serve later.

EACH ROLL: ABOUT 165 CALORIES, 5g PROTEIN, 26g CARBOHYDRATE, 4g TOTAL FAT (1g SATURATED), 21mg CHOLESTEROL, 495mg SODIUM

MRS. BARBETTA'S BREADSTICKS

Prep: 30 minutes plus rising and cooling
Bake: 25 minutes   Makes 24

1 package active dry yeast
1 teaspoon fennel seeds,
   crushed
1 teaspoon salt
1 teaspoon cracked black
   pepper
2 cups all-purpose
   flour
½ cup shortening
1 large egg

◆ In large bowl, combine yeast, fennel seeds, salt, pepper, and 1 cup flour. In 1-quart saucepan, heat shortening and *½ cup water* over low heat until very warm (120° to 130°F); shortening need not melt.

◆ With mixer at low speed, gradually beat liquid into flour mixture just until blended. Increase speed to medium; beat 3 minutes, occasionally scraping bowl with rubber spatula. With wooden spoon, stir in remaining 1 cup flour to make a soft dough. With hands, knead dough in bowl 2 to 3 minutes, until smooth and elastic. Cover loosely with plastic wrap; let rise in warm place (80° to 85°F) about 2 hours, until doubled.

◆ Grease 2 cookie sheets. Turn dough onto lightly floured surface. Cut dough into quarters, then cut each quarter into 12 equal pieces. Roll each piece into a 12-inch-long rope. Twist 2 ropes loosely together; place on cookie sheet. Repeat to make 24 breadsticks in all, placing breadsticks 1 inch apart on cookie sheets.

◆ Preheat oven to 350°F. In small bowl, beat egg; brush over breadsticks. Bake breadsticks 25 minutes, or until browned and crisp, rotating cookie sheets between upper and lower racks halfway through baking time. Remove from cookie sheets; cool on wire racks. Store in tightly covered container.

Each breadstick: About 75 calories, 1g protein, 8g carbohydrate, 5g total fat (1g saturated), 9mg cholesterol, 90mg sodium

POTATO ROLLS

Prep: 1 hour 30 minutes plus rising and chilling
Bake: 25 to 30 minutes   Makes 24

3 medium all-purpose
   potatoes (about 1 pound),
   peeled and cut into 1-inch
   chunks
2 packages quick-rise yeast
2 tablespoons sugar
1 tablespoon salt
About 9¾ cups all-purpose
   flour
4 tablespoons margarine or
   butter
2 large eggs

◆ In 2-quart saucepan, heat potatoes and *4 cups water* to boiling over high heat. Reduce heat to low; cover and simmer 15 minutes, or until potatoes are fork-tender. Drain potatoes, reserving 1 cup potato cooking water. Return potatoes to saucepan. With potato masher, mash potatoes until smooth.

◆ In large bowl, combine yeast, sugar, salt, and 3 cups flour. In 1-quart saucepan, heat margarine, *1 cup water*, and reserved potato water over low heat until very warm (120° to 130°F); margarine need not melt.

◆ With mixer at low speed, gradually beat liquid into flour mixture just until blended. Increase speed to medium; beat 2 minutes, occasionally scraping bowl with rubber spatula. Separate 1 egg and reserve white in refrigerator, covered. Gradually beat remaining egg, egg yolk, and 1 cup flour into flour mixture to make a thick batter; beat 2 minutes longer, scraping bowl often. With wooden spoon, stir in mashed potatoes, then 5 cups flour, 1 cup at a time, to make a soft dough. (You may want to transfer mixture to a larger bowl for easier mixing.)

◆ Turn dough onto well-floured surface and knead about 10 minutes, until smooth and elastic, working in about ¾ cup more flour. Cut dough into 24 equal pieces; cover with plastic wrap and let rest 15 minutes for easier shaping. Grease 17" by 11½" roasting pan.

◆ Shape dough into balls and place in roasting pan. Cover pan loosely with plastic wrap and let rise in warm place (80° to 85°F) about 40 minutes, until doubled. (Or, if you like, cover and refrigerate overnight. When ready to bake, let rise in warm place, still covered loosely with plastic wrap, about 30 minutes, until doubled).

◆ Preheat oven to 400°F. With fork, beat reserved egg white. Brush rolls with egg white. Bake 25 to 30 minutes, until rolls are golden and sound hollow when lightly tapped with fingers. Cool 10 minutes; serve warm. Or, remove rolls from pan and cool on wire rack to serve later; reheat if desired. To serve, pull rolls apart.

Each roll: About 215 calories, 6g protein, 41g carbohydrate, 3g total fat (1g saturated), 18mg cholesterol, 295mg sodium

FLAT BREADS

Rustic, peasant-style flat breads are enjoyed the world over. Focaccia, a favorite from Italy, is a large, flattened yeast bread that is drizzled with olive oil and sometimes sprinkled with savory toppings before baking. From the Middle East comes the soft, mild-flavored pocket bread called pita. Split for sandwiches, or serve with appetizers, soups, or salads.

GOLDEN ONION FOCACCIA

Prep: 30 minutes plus rising   *Bake:* 20 to 25 minutes
Makes 8 servings

1 package quick-rise yeast
1 teaspoon salt
About 2 cups all-purpose flour
4 tablespoons olive oil
1 cup whole-wheat flour
1 tablespoon yellow cornmeal
1 medium red onion, thinly sliced

2 tablespoons freshly grated Parmesan cheese
1 tablespoon fresh rosemary or 1 teaspoon dried rosemary, crushed
¼ teaspoon cracked black pepper
Coarse salt (optional)

1 In large bowl, combine yeast, 1 teaspoon salt, and 1 cup all-purpose flour. In 1-quart saucepan, heat 2 tablespoons oil and *1 cup water* over medium heat until very warm (120° to 130°F). With mixer at low speed, gradually beat liquid into flour mixture just until blended. Increase speed to medium; beat 2 minutes. Add ½ cup all-purpose flour; beat 2 minutes. With wooden spoon, stir in whole-wheat flour to make a soft dough.

2 Knead dough in bowl 8 minutes, working in about ½ cup more all-purpose flour. Cover loosely with plastic wrap; let rest 15 minutes. Grease 13" by 9" metal baking pan; sprinkle with cornmeal.

3 Pat dough into pan, pushing into corners. Cover loosely with plastic wrap; let rise in warm place (80° to 85°F) 30 minutes, or until doubled. In 10-inch skillet, heat 1 tablespoon oil over medium heat. Add onion; cook until tender. Preheat oven to 400°F. With finger, make deep indentations 1 inch apart over entire surface of dough, almost to bottom of pan; drizzle with remaining 1 tablespoon oil.

4 Spoon onion evenly over dough in pan; sprinkle with remaining ingredients. Bake focaccia 20 to 25 minutes, until golden. Cool 10 minutes in pan on wire rack. Serve warm. Or, remove from pan and cool completely to serve later.

OTHER TOPPINGS

Sweet pepper In 10-inch skillet, heat 1 tablespoon olive oil over medium heat; add 2 red or yellow peppers, sliced, and ¼ teaspoon salt; cook, stirring often, 15 minutes, or until tender.

Dried tomato and olive Mix 6 oil-packed dried tomatoes, slivered, and ⅓ cup chopped, pitted Kalamata olives.

EACH SERVING: ABOUT 235 CALORIES, 6g PROTEIN, 36g CARBOHYDRATE, 8g TOTAL FAT (1g SATURATED), 1mg CHOLESTEROL, 300mg SODIUM

SEMOLINA FOCACCIA WITH FENNEL AND GOLDEN RAISINS

Prep: 20 minutes plus rising and cooling   Bake: 25 minutes
Makes 12 servings

1 package quick-rise yeast
2 tablespoons sugar
2 teaspoons salt
1½ cups plus 2 tablespoons semolina flour
¼ cup plus 2 tablespoons olive oil
¾ cup golden raisins
1 tablespoon fennel seeds, crushed
About 1½ cups all-purpose flour

◆ In large bowl, combine yeast, sugar, salt, and 1½ cups semolina flour. In 1-quart saucepan, heat ¼ cup oil and *1 cup water* over low heat until very warm (120° to 130°F).

◆ With mixer at low speed, gradually beat liquid into flour mixture just until blended, scraping bowl often with rubber spatula. Increase speed to medium; beat 2 minutes, scraping bowl often. With wooden spoon, stir in raisins, fennel, and 1 cup all-purpose flour to make a soft dough.

◆ Turn dough onto lightly floured surface and knead about 8 minutes, until smooth and elastic, working in about ½ cup more all-purpose flour. Shape dough into a ball; cover with plastic wrap and let rest 15 minutes.

◆ Grease 15½" by 10½" jelly-roll pan; sprinkle with remaining 2 tablespoons semolina flour. On lightly floured surface, with floured rolling pin, roll dough into 15" by 10" rectangle. Place in jelly-roll pan, pushing dough into corners. Cover loosely with plastic wrap and let rise in warm place (80° to 85°F) about 30 minutes, until doubled.

◆ Preheat oven to 400°F. With finger, make indentations 1 inch apart over surface of dough, almost to bottom of pan. Drizzle with remaining 2 tablespoons oil. Bake 25 minutes, or until golden. Remove from pan and cool on wire rack.

Each serving: About 220 calories, 4g protein, 35g carbohydrate, 7g total fat (1g saturated), 0mg cholesterol, 360mg sodium

---

SEMOLINA

Semolina flour is a high-protein, high-gluten flour milled from durum wheat. It has a nutty flavor and somewhat granular texture that resembles cornmeal. Commonly used for making commercial dried pastas, it is also suited for breads, gnocchi, and various confections. Semolina flour is available in Italian grocery stores or by mail-order (see page 30).

WHOLE-WHEAT PITAS

Prep: 1 hour 45 minutes plus cooling, standing, chilling, and rising
Bake: 5 minutes per batch   Makes 16

2 medium all-purpose potatoes (about 10 ounces), peeled and cut into 1-inch chunks
1 package active dry yeast
1 teaspoon salt
¾ cup whole-wheat flour
About 3¼ cups all-purpose flour
1 container (8 ounces) plain low-fat yogurt
1 tablespoon honey

◆ In 2-quart saucepan, heat potatoes and enough *water* to cover to boiling over high heat. Reduce heat to low; cover and simmer 15 minutes, or until potatoes are fork-tender. Drain potatoes; return to pan. With potato masher, mash potatoes until smooth; let potatoes cool to room temperature.

◆ In large bowl, mix yeast, salt, whole-wheat flour, and ¾ cup all-purpose flour. In 1-quart saucepan, heat yogurt, honey, and ¼ cup *water* over medium-low heat until very warm (120° to 130°F); stir into flour mixture until blended.

◆ Stir in potatoes and 1½ cups all-purpose flour to make a soft dough. Knead dough in bowl; shape into a ball. Cover bowl loosely with plastic wrap and refrigerate overnight.

◆ When ready to bake, turn dough onto well-floured surface and knead about 10 minutes, until smooth and elastic, working in about 1 cup more all-purpose flour while kneading. Cut dough into 16 equal pieces; shape each piece into a ball. Cover loosely with plastic wrap and let rise in warm place (80° to 85°F) about 40 minutes, until doubled.

◆ Preheat oven to 450°F. Place oven rack in center of oven. Working with 4 pieces of dough at a time, on lightly floured surface, with floured rolling pin, roll each piece of dough into a 6-inch round, being careful to keep thickness of dough even. (If dough is too thick or too thin, pitas will not rise uniformly when baked.) With pastry brush, brush excess flour from pitas.

◆ Heat large cookie sheet in oven 5 to 7 minutes. Place 4 pita rounds on preheated cookie sheet; bake 5 minutes, or until golden and puffed. Cool on wire rack. Repeat with remaining dough, heating cookie sheet for each batch.

Each pita: About 135 calories, 4g protein, 28g carbohydrate, 1g total fat (0g saturated), 1mg cholesterol, 145mg sodium

HOMEMADE PIZZAS

Pizza is a dish that inspires healthy appetites and plenty of creativity – we've topped ours with such ingredients as marinated artichokes, eggplant, and mild goat cheese. We've even grilled pizza for an extra-crisp crust and a slightly smoky flavor. Or, try adding flavorings to the crust itself for a simple but delicious change of pace.

ARTICHOKE AND CHEESE PIZZA

◆◆◆◆◆◆◆◆◆◆◆◆◆

Prep: 40 minutes plus resting
Bake: 25 to 30 minutes
Makes 4 main-dish servings

Basic Pizza Dough (see page 418)

Yellow cornmeal, for sprinkling

¼ cup loosely packed fresh basil leaves

1 jar (6 ounces) marinated artichoke hearts

1 small eggplant (12 ounces), cut lengthwise in half, then cut crosswise into ¼-inch-thick slices

3 small tomatoes or 1 medium tomato, cut into thin wedges

6 ounces goat cheese such as Montrachet, broken into chunks, or mozzarella cheese, thinly sliced

1 Prepare Basic Pizza Dough as in Step 1. Sprinkle large cookie sheet with cornmeal. Shape dough into 2 balls; place in opposite corners of cookie sheet, each about 3 inches from edges of sheet. Cover with plastic wrap and let rest 15 minutes. Meanwhile, preheat broiler. Reserve a few basil leaves for garnish; thinly slice remaining basil. Drain artichokes, reserving marinade. Cut each artichoke lengthwise in half.

2 In 15½" by 10½" jelly-roll pan, toss eggplant slices with 2 tablespoons reserved artichoke marinade. Arrange slices in jelly-roll pan. Place pan in broiler 5 to 7 inches from heat source; broil eggplant, turning once, 7 to 10 minutes, until tender and brown. Remove from broiler. Turn oven control to 425°F. In bowl, toss eggplant, artichokes, tomatoes, and half of sliced basil with remaining artichoke marinade.

3 On cookie sheet, pat 1 ball dough from center outward to make 10-inch round. (Dough will extend over edge of sheet until you form rim.) If dough shrinks back, let it rest a few minutes.

4 Arrange half of eggplant mixture and half of goat cheese on the patted-out pizza crust, leaving 1-inch border.

5 Pinch and press edge up to make a high rim. Repeat to make second pizza. Cover pizzas; let rest 15 minutes. Bake on bottom rack 25 to 30 minutes, until crust is browned. Sprinkle with remaining sliced basil; garnish with basil leaves.

FLAVORED CRUSTS

◆◆◆◆◆◆◆◆◆◆◆

To vary the Basic Pizza Dough on page 418, add any of the following:

• 1 teaspoon cracked black pepper or crushed fennel seeds

• 1 tablespoon finely chopped fresh rosemary or 1 teaspoon dried rosemary, crushed

• ⅓ cup chopped, pitted Kalamata olives

EACH SERVING: ABOUT 435 CALORIES, 18g PROTEIN, 56g CARBOHYDRATE, 16g TOTAL FAT (9g SATURATED), 33mg CHOLESTEROL, 695mg SODIUM

BASIC PIZZA DOUGH

◆◆◆◆◆◆◆◆◆◆◆◆◆

2 cups all-purpose flour
1 package quick-rise yeast
¾ teaspoon salt

2 teaspoons olive oil
Yellow cornmeal

1. In large bowl, combine flour, yeast, and salt. Stir in ¾ cup very hot tap water (120° to 130°F) and oil until blended and dough comes away from side of bowl. Turn onto lightly floured surface; knead 5 minutes.

2. Sprinkle cookie sheet with cornmeal. Shape dough into 1, 2, or 4 balls (for 1 large rectangular, two 10-inch, or four 6-inch pizzas); place on large cookie sheet (for 4 balls, use 2 cookie sheets). Cover with plastic wrap; let rest 15 minutes.

3. Shape dough: To make 1 large pizza, roll dough ball into 14" by 10" rectangle on cookie sheet; add topping. Bring edges of dough up; fold to make 1-inch rim. For two 10-inch pizzas, pat and stretch 1 ball into 10-inch round. Add topping; make 1-inch rim. Repeat to make second pizza. For four 6-inch pizzas, pat and stretch 1 ball into 6-inch round. Add topping; make ½-inch rim. Repeat to make 3 more pizzas.

BISTRO PIZZA

Prep: 55 minutes plus resting   *Bake:* 20 to 30 minutes
Makes 4 main-dish servings

2 medium red peppers, roasted and peeled (see page 310) or 1 jar (7 ounces) roasted red peppers, drained
Basic Pizza Dough (see above)
1 pound thin asparagus, trimmed

1 teaspoon olive oil
¼ teaspoon salt
6 ounces smoked mozzarella cheese, shredded (1½ cups)
¼ teaspoon coarsely ground black pepper

Prepare roasted red peppers; cut into strips. Set aside. Prepare pizza dough as in Steps 1 and 2, making 1, 2, or 4 balls as desired. While dough is resting, cut asparagus into 2-inch pieces. In small bowl, toss asparagus with olive oil and salt. Shape dough as in Step 3; top with mozzarella, red-pepper strips, and asparagus. Sprinkle with black pepper. Let rest 15 minutes. Meanwhile, preheat oven to 425°F. Bake on bottom rack in oven 20 to 30 minutes, until crust is browned.

Each serving: About 425 calories, 18g protein, 50g carbohydrate, 14g total fat (6g saturated), 33mg cholesterol, 740mg sodium

GARDEN PIZZA

Prep: 30 minutes plus resting   *Bake:* 20 to 30 minutes
Makes 4 main-dish servings

Basic Pizza Dough (see left)
1 tablespoon vegetable oil
1 small zucchini (6 ounces), diced
1 small yellow straightneck squash (6 ounces), diced
1 package (10 ounces) frozen chopped spinach, thawed and squeezed dry

1 large tomato, seeded and diced
½ teaspoon dried oregano
¼ teaspoon ground black pepper
8 ounces part-skim mozzarella cheese, shredded (2 cups)

Prepare pizza dough as in Steps 1 and 2, making 1, 2, or 4 balls as desired. While dough is resting, in 12-inch skillet, heat oil over medium-high heat; add zucchini and yellow squash; cook until tender. Stir in spinach, tomato, oregano, and pepper; remove from heat. Shape dough as in Step 3; top with vegetable mixture and mozzarella. Let rest 15 minutes. Preheat oven to 425°F. Bake on bottom rack in oven 20 to 30 minutes, until crust is browned.

Each serving: About 450 calories, 24g protein, 55g carbohydrate, 16g total fat (7g saturated), 32mg cholesterol, 730mg sodium

GRILLED PIZZA

Prep: 15 minutes plus resting   *Grill:* 5 to 10 minutes
Makes 4 main-dish servings

Basic Pizza Dough (see above left)
2 tablespoons olive oil
8 ounces fresh mozzarella cheese, thinly sliced

12 basil leaves
2 small tomatoes, thinly sliced
Salt and ground black pepper

◆ Prepare outdoor grill. Prepare pizza dough as in Step 1. Let rest 15 minutes, then shape into two 10-inch rounds or four 6-inch rounds on work surface as in Steps 2 and 3, but do not add toppings or form rims.

◆ Place crusts on grill rack; grill over medium heat 2 to 5 minutes, until underside turns golden and grill marks appear. With tongs, turn crusts. Brush lightly with some of olive oil. Top with mozzarella, then basil and tomato slices. Grill 3 to 5 minutes longer, until cheese begins to melt. Transfer pizzas to plates. Drizzle with remaining olive oil; sprinkle with salt and pepper.

Each serving: About 470 calories, 18g protein, 49g carbohydrate, 22g total fat (9g saturated), 44mg cholesterol, 750mg sodium

PREPARED-CRUST PIZZAS

When time is of the essence, who says you can't make a "homemade" pizza with a store-bought crust? With these tasty time-savers you can assemble creative pizzas that are just as quick as – and immensely more satisfying than – ordering out. Thanks to refrigerated pizza dough (which needs only rolling out) and ready-to-use Italian bread shells, all of your energy can go toward preparing tempting toppings: tangy feta cheese and crisp salad greens, sweet caramelized onions and nutty-tasting Gruyère, smoked salmon and cream cheese, and more. To avoid a soggy crust, it's best to serve these pizzas right away.

1 Preheat oven to 425°F. Grease large cookie sheet. Divide pizza dough in half. On lightly floured surface, with floured rolling pin, roll each half into an 11" by 6" rectangle.

2 Place both rectangles on cookie sheet. Sprinkle dough with all of basil and half of feta cheese. Bake on bottom rack of oven 12 to 15 minutes, until crust is golden brown.

SUMMER SALAD PIZZAS

◆◆◆◆◆◆◆◆◆◆◆◆◆◆◆◆◆◆◆◆◆◆◆◆◆◆◆◆◆

Prep: 20 minutes *Bake:* 12 to 15 minutes
Makes 2 main-dish servings

1 package (10 ounces) refrigerated pizza dough
½ cup loosely packed fresh basil leaves, chopped
1 ounce feta cheese, crumbled (¼ cup)
¼ cup low-fat mayonnaise dressing
2 tablespoons milk

¼ teaspoon coarsely ground black pepper
1 small head romaine lettuce (about 12 ounces)
1 small red onion
2 tablespoons freshly grated Parmesan cheese

3 Meanwhile, prepare dressing: In large bowl, with fork, mix mayonnaise dressing, milk, pepper, and remaining feta cheese.

4 Thinly slice lettuce and onion; toss with dressing in bowl. Pile salad on top of hot pizza crusts; sprinkle with Parmesan.

EXTRA-QUICK CRUSTS
◆◆◆◆◆◆◆◆◆◆◆◆◆◆

You can whip up a pizza in no time using supermarket pizza dough or Italian bread shells and any of our tempting toppings. But don't stop there – other kinds of breads can be used to make an instant pizza crust. Try plain or whole-wheat pitas, Armenian cracker bread, flour tortillas, matzoh, or toasted English muffins. Add the topping and bake at 425°F for about 10 minutes, until heated through.

EACH SERVING: ABOUT 570 CALORIES, 21g PROTEIN, 77g CARBOHYDRATE, 18g TOTAL FAT (5g SATURATED), 29mg CHOLESTEROL, 1005mg SODIUM

CARAMELIZED ONION AND GRUYÈRE PIZZA

Prep: 40 minutes   *Bake:* 10 to 12 minutes

Makes 4 main-dish servings

**2 jumbo onions (about
    12 ounces each)**
1 tablespoon olive oil
**½ cup packed fresh basil
    leaves, chopped**

**1 large Italian bread shell
    (16 ounces)**
**5 ounces Gruyère or Swiss
    cheese, shredded (1¼ cups)**

◆ Preheat oven to 450°F. Cut each jumbo onion into ¼-inch-thick slices. In nonstick 12-inch skillet, heat olive oil over medium heat. Stir in sliced onions until they are well coated with oil.

◆ Cook onions, stirring occasionally, 25 minutes, or until they are deep golden brown and very tender. Remove skillet from heat; stir in chopped basil.

◆ Place bread shell on large ungreased cookie sheet. Spoon onion mixture on bread shell; sprinkle with cheese. Bake pizza 10 to 12 minutes, until cheese is melted.

Each serving: About 540 calories, 25g protein, 65g carbohydrate, 22g total fat (7g saturated), 41mg cholesterol, 735mg sodium

HAVE-IT-YOUR-WAY INDIVIDUAL PIZZAS

MUSHROOM AND CHEESE Preheat oven to 450°F. Place 1 small Italian bread shell (4 ounces) on ungreased cookie sheet. Spread with 1 tablespoon bottled spaghetti sauce or pizza sauce; sprinkle with ¼ cup shredded Cheddar-and-mozzarella cheese blend (1 ounce). Top with ¼ cup thinly sliced mushrooms, another ¼ cup cheese, and 1 teaspoon chopped fresh parsley. Bake 10 minutes, or until cheese is melted and bubbly. Makes 1 serving.

Each serving: About 500 calories, 27g protein, 55g carbohydrate, 20g total fat (9g saturated), 42mg cholesterol, 990mg sodium

BASIL, OLIVE, AND TOMATO Preheat oven to 450°F. Place 1 small Italian bread shell (4 ounces) on ungreased cookie sheet. Arrange 1 plum tomato, very thinly sliced, on bread shell; sprinkle with ½ cup shredded mozzarella cheese (2 ounces). Top with 2 tablespoons chopped fresh basil, 2 tablespoons sliced pitted ripe olives, and ⅛ teaspoon cracked black pepper. Bake 10 minutes, or until cheese is melted and bubbly. Makes 1 serving.

Each serving: About 500 calories, 24g protein, 57g carbohydrate, 21g total fat (8g saturated), 46mg cholesterol, 980mg sodium

PEPPER AND PEPPERONI Preheat oven to 450°F. Place 1 small Italian bread shell (4 ounces) on ungreased cookie sheet. Spread bread shell with 1 tablespoon bottled spaghetti sauce or pizza sauce; sprinkle with ¼ cup shredded mozzarella cheese (1 ounce). Top with ¼ (3¼-ounce) package sliced pepperoni and ¼ small green pepper, cut into thin slices; sprinkle with another ¼ cup shredded mozzarella. Bake 10 minutes, or until cheese is melted and bubbly. Makes 1 serving.

Each serving: About 590 calories, 28g protein, 55g carbohydrate, 30g total fat (11g saturated), 46mg cholesterol, 1360mg sodium

SMOKED SALMON Preheat oven to 450°F. Place 1 small Italian bread shell (4 ounces) on ungreased cookie sheet; bake 8 minutes. Spread hot crust with 2 tablespoons whipped cream cheese. Top with ½ (3-ounce) package smoked salmon, cut into bite-size pieces, 1 tablespoon minced red onion, and 1 teaspoon capers, drained and chopped. Garnish with fresh parsley. Makes 1 serving.

Each serving: About 455 calories, 22g protein, 52g carbohydrate, 19g total fat (6g saturated), 42mg cholesterol, 1135mg sodium

Basil, olive, and tomato

Mushroom and cheese

Smoked salmon

Pepper and pepperoni

BATTER BREADS

Batter breads, which can be sweet or savory, are the easiest of all yeast breads to prepare. The dough is simply beaten – not kneaded – and turned into a casserole or baking pan, so no shaping is required. For best results, beat the batter (which will be stickier than standard yeast-bread doughs), until it's very stiff – you should be able to stand a spoon in it.

ONION-DILL BATTER BREAD

◆◆◆◆◆◆◆◆◆◆◆◆◆◆◆◆◆◆◆◆◆◆◆◆◆◆◆

Prep: 35 minutes plus rising and cooling   Bake: 30 to 35 minutes
Makes 2 loaves, 8 servings each

2 tablespoons margarine or butter	1 package active dry yeast
1 large bunch green onions, chopped	2 tablespoons sugar
	2 teaspoons salt
2 tablespoons chopped fresh parsley	½ cup yellow cornmeal plus additional for sprinkling
1 tablespoon chopped fresh dill or 1 teaspoon dillweed	4 cups all-purpose flour
	2 cups buttermilk or soured milk (see page 392)

1 In 10-inch skillet, melt margarine over medium heat; add chopped green onions and cook, stirring frequently, 5 minutes, or until tender. Remove skillet from heat; stir in chopped parsley and dill. In large bowl, combine yeast, sugar, salt, ½ cup cornmeal, and 2 cups flour. In 1-quart saucepan, heat buttermilk and ¼ *cup water* over low heat until very warm (120° to 130°F).

2 With mixer at low speed, gradually beat liquid into flour mixture just until blended. Increase speed to medium; beat 2 minutes.

3 Beat in ½ cup flour to make a thick batter. Beat 2 minutes longer, scraping bowl frequently with rubber spatula. With wooden spoon, stir in green-onion mixture and remaining 1½ cups flour to make a stiff batter. Cover bowl loosely with plastic wrap; let rise in warm place (80° to 85°F) about 1 hour, until doubled. Grease two 1½-quart round casseroles; sprinkle evenly with cornmeal.

4 With wooden spoon, stir down batter; divide in half and turn into casseroles. Cover loosely with plastic wrap; let rise in warm place about 45 minutes, until doubled.

5 Preheat oven to 375°F. Sprinkle tops of loaves lightly with cornmeal. Bake 30 to 35 minutes, until loaf sounds hollow when lightly tapped with fingers. Remove loaves from casseroles; cool on wire rack.

WHAT'S IN A NAME?

◆◆◆◆◆◆◆◆◆◆◆◆◆◆◆◆◆◆◆◆◆◆◆◆◆◆◆

Batter breads provide a quick way to enjoy yeast breads. Because they don't require kneading, the relatively soft, sticky batter usually calls for vigorous beating to develop the gluten, which gives the bread its structure and allows it to rise. Batter breads have a rustic appearance. Although the texture won't be as fine-crumbed as bread that has been kneaded, the taste will be just as delicious.

EACH SERVING: ABOUT 155 CALORIES, 5g PROTEIN, 29g CARBOHYDRATE, 2g TOTAL FAT (1g SATURATED), 1mg CHOLESTEROL, 315mg SODIUM

DOUBLE-CHEESE BATTER BREAD

Prep: 25 minutes plus rising and cooling
Bake: 35 minutes
Makes 1 loaf, 12 servings

1 package quick-rise yeast
6 ounces extra-sharp Cheddar cheese, shredded (1½ cups)
¼ cup freshly grated Parmesan cheese
1 tablespoon sugar
½ teaspoon salt
2½ cups all-purpose flour
2 large eggs
½ teaspoon poppy seeds

◆ In large bowl, combine yeast, Cheddar cheese, Parmesan cheese, sugar, salt, and 1½ cups flour.

◆ With mixer at low speed, gradually beat ¾ cup very hot tap water (120° to 130°F) into flour mixture just until blended. Separate 1 egg and reserve white in refrigerator, covered. Beat remaining egg and egg yolk into batter.

◆ Increase speed to medium; beat 3 minutes, scraping bowl often with rubber spatula. With wooden spoon, stir in remaining 1 cup flour to make a stiff batter that leaves side of bowl.

◆ Cover bowl loosely with plastic wrap; let dough rise in warm place (80° to 85°F) 20 minutes. Grease 1½-quart round casserole. With wooden spoon, stir down batter; turn into casserole. Cover loosely with plastic wrap; let rise in warm place 15 minutes.

◆ Preheat oven to 350°F. In cup, with fork, beat reserved egg white; brush over top of loaf. Sprinkle with poppy seeds. Bake 35 minutes, or until loaf sounds hollow when lightly tapped with fingers. Remove loaf from casserole; cool on wire rack.

Each serving: About 175 calories, 8g protein, 20g carbohydrate, 6g total fat (4g saturated), 52mg cholesterol, 225mg sodium

OATMEAL BATTER BREAD

Prep: 20 minutes plus rising and cooling
Bake: 40 minutes
Makes 2 loaves, 12 servings each

2 packages active dry yeast
2 teaspoons salt
5 cups all-purpose flour
1 cup quick-cooking oats, uncooked
½ cup light molasses
1 tablespoon margarine or butter plus 2 teaspoons (optional) for glazing

◆ In large bowl, combine yeast, salt, and 2 cups flour. In 2-quart saucepan, mix oats, molasses, 1 tablespoon margarine, and 2¼ cups water. Heat over low heat until very warm (120° to 130°F); margarine need not melt.

◆ With mixer at low speed, gradually beat liquid into flour mixture just until blended. Increase speed to medium; beat 2 minutes. Beat in ½ cup flour to make a thick batter; beat 2 minutes longer, scraping bowl frequently with rubber spatula. With wooden spoon, stir in remaining 2½ cups flour to make a stiff batter that leaves side of bowl.

◆ Cover bowl loosely with plastic wrap; let dough rise in warm place (80° to 85°F) about 1 hour, until doubled. Grease two 2-quart round, shallow casseroles. With wooden spoon, stir down batter. Divide in half and turn into casseroles; with greased fingers, turn to grease tops and shape each into a ball. Cover loosely with plastic wrap; let rise in warm place about 45 minutes, until doubled.

◆ Preheat oven to 350°F. Bake 40 minutes, or until loaves sound hollow when lightly tapped with fingers. Remove loaves from casseroles. If you like, for a soft crust, rub tops with remaining 2 teaspoons softened margarine; cool on wire racks.

Each serving: About 135 calories, 4g protein, 27g carbohydrate, 1g total fat (0g saturated), 0mg cholesterol, 185mg sodium

RAISIN BATTER BREAD

Prep: 20 minutes plus rising and cooling
Bake: 50 minutes
Makes 1 loaf, 20 servings

2 packages active dry yeast
¾ cup sugar
1 teaspoon salt
5 cups all-purpose flour
1½ cups milk
6 tablespoons margarine or butter, cut up
2 large eggs
1½ cups dark seedless raisins

◆ In large bowl, combine yeast, sugar, salt, and 2 cups flour. In 1-quart saucepan, heat milk and margarine over low heat until very warm (120° to 130°F); margarine need not melt.

◆ With mixer at low speed, gradually beat liquid into flour mixture just until blended. Increase speed to medium; beat 2 minutes. Beat in eggs and 1½ cups flour; beat 2 minutes longer, scraping bowl frequently with rubber spatula. With wooden spoon, stir in raisins and remaining 1½ cups flour to make a stiff batter that leaves side of bowl.

◆ Cover bowl loosely with plastic wrap; let dough rise in warm place (80° to 85° F) 1 to 1½ hours, until doubled.

◆ Grease 10-inch tube pan. With wooden spoon, stir down batter; turn into pan. Cover loosely with plastic wrap; let rise in warm place 45 to 60 minutes, until doubled.

◆ Preheat oven to 350°F. Bake 50 minutes, or until loaf is golden and sounds hollow when lightly tapped with fingers. Remove from pan; cool on wire rack.

Each serving: About 215 calories, 5g protein, 39g carbohydrate, 5g total fat (1g saturated), 24mg cholesterol, 165mg sodium

DANISH AND SWEET ROLLS

A fresh, warm sweet roll with coffee is one of life's simple pleasures. These old-world Danish pastries and rich, spice-scented buns also freeze well for treats another morning.

EASY DANISH PASTRIES

◆◆◆◆◆◆◆◆◆◆◆◆

Prep: 1 hour plus standing and chilling overnight
Bake: 30 minutes
Makes 18

2 packages active dry yeast
1 teaspoon plus ⅓ cup granulated sugar
4 cups all-purpose flour
½ teaspoon salt
¾ cup margarine or butter, cut up
4 large eggs
½ cup plus 2 tablespoons heavy or whipping cream
1 cup plus 2 tablespoons cherry or apricot jam or Danish Filling (see below)
½ cup confectioners' sugar

1 In medium bowl, stir yeast and 1 teaspoon granulated sugar into *½ cup warm water* (105° to 115°F); let stand 5 minutes, until foamy. In large bowl, mix flour, remaining ⅓ cup granulated sugar, and salt. With pastry blender or two knives used scissor-fashion, cut in margarine until mixture resembles coarse crumbs. Whisk 3 eggs and ½ cup cream into yeast mixture; stir into flour mixture until moistened. Cover; refrigerate overnight.

4 In cup, beat remaining egg with *1 tablespoon water*; brush over pastries. Bake pastries 30 minutes, or until golden, switching cookie sheets on oven racks halfway through baking. Transfer pastries to wire racks set over waxed paper; cool. In small bowl, mix confectioners' sugar with remaining 2 tablespoons cream to make thick glaze. Drizzle over pastries.

2 Preheat oven to 350°F. Grease 2 large cookie sheets. Divide dough in half. On floured surface, with floured rolling pin, roll half of dough into 12" square. Cut into nine 4-inch squares.

3 Place 1 tablespoon filling in center of each square. Make a 2-inch cut from each corner toward center; fold every other tip in to center. Arrange on cookie sheet. Repeat with remaining dough and jam.

◆◆◆◆◆◆◆◆◆◆◆◆◆◆◆◆◆◆◆◆◆◆◆◆◆

FOLDOVERS

Prepare pastries as in Steps 1 and 2 above. Place 1 tablespoon jam in center of each 4-inch square. Fold one corner in 2 inches to cover jam; fold opposite corner to edge. Arrange on cookie sheets and repeat with remaining dough and jam. Proceed as in Step 4.

◆◆◆◆◆◆◆◆◆◆◆◆◆◆◆◆◆◆◆◆◆◆◆◆◆

DANISH FILLINGS

Almond In bowl, with mixer at low speed, beat 1 tube or can (7 to 8 ounces) almond paste, 4 tablespoons margarine or butter, softened, 1 large egg, and ½ teaspoon grated lemon peel until smooth.

Cheese In bowl, with mixer at low speed, beat 1 package (8 ounces) cream cheese, softened, ⅓ cup confectioners' sugar, 1½ teaspoons vanilla extract, and 1 large egg yolk until smooth.

EACH PASTRY: ABOUT 285 CALORIES, 5g PROTEIN, 41g CARBOHYDRATE, 12g TOTAL FAT (4g SATURATED), 59mg CHOLESTEROL, 165mg SODIUM

HOT-CROSS BUNS

Prep: 45 minutes plus rising and cooling   Bake: 20 to 25 minutes
Makes 25

2 packages active dry yeast	½ cup margarine or butter
½ cup granulated sugar	2 large eggs
1½ teaspoons ground cardamom	½ cup golden raisins
About 4¾ cups all-purpose flour	½ cup diced mixed candied fruit
Salt	1 cup confectioners' sugar

◆ In large bowl, combine yeast, granulated sugar, cardamom, 1½ cups flour, and 1½ teaspoons salt. In 1-quart saucepan, heat margarine and *1 cup water* over low heat until very warm (120° to 130°F); margarine need not melt.

◆ With mixer at low speed, gradually beat liquid into flour mixture just until blended. Increase speed to medium; beat 2 minutes, occasionally scraping bowl with rubber spatula. Separate 1 egg and reserve white in refrigerator, covered.

◆ Beat remaining egg, egg yolk, and ½ cup flour into flour mixture to make a thick batter; beat 2 minutes longer, scraping bowl often. With wooden spoon, stir in 2½ cups flour to make a soft dough.

◆ Turn dough onto lightly floured surface and knead about 10 minutes, until smooth and elastic, working in about ¼ cup more flour if needed to keep dough from sticking to work surface. Shape dough into a ball; place in greased large bowl, turning dough to grease top. Cover bowl loosely with plastic wrap; let rise in warm place (80° to 85°F) about 1 hour, until doubled.

◆ Punch down dough. Knead in raisins and candied fruit. Cut dough into 25 equal pieces; let rest 15 minutes for easier shaping.

◆ Grease large cookie sheet. Shape dough into balls. Arrange buns in square, ½ inch apart, on cookie sheet. Cover loosely with plastic wrap; let rise about 40 minutes, until doubled.

◆ Preheat oven to 375°F. In cup, with fork, beat reserved egg white with ⅛ teaspoon salt. Brush buns with egg white. Bake 20 to 25 minutes, until buns are golden and sound hollow when lightly tapped with fingers. Slide onto to wire rack; cool.

◆ When buns are cool, prepare icing: In small bowl, mix confectioners' sugar and *4 teaspoons water* until smooth. Spoon icing into small zip-tight plastic bag; snip off one corner and pipe crosses on buns.

Each bun: About 170 calories, 3g protein, 30g carbohydrate, 4g total fat (1g saturated), 17mg cholesterol, 190mg sodium

OLD-FASHIONED STICKY BUNS

Prep: 1 hour 10 minutes plus rising and cooling   Bake: 25 to 30 minutes
Makes 20

2 packages quick-rise yeast	3 large eggs
⅔ cup granulated sugar	2 cups walnuts (about 8 ounces), chopped
2 teaspoons salt	1½ cups golden raisins
2 teaspoons ground cardamom (optional)	1½ cups packed dark brown sugar
About 7½ cups all-purpose flour	2 tablespoons corn syrup
1¾ cups milk	¾ cup confectioners' sugar
1 cup plus 2 tablespoons margarine or butter	

◆ In large bowl, combine first 4 ingredients and 3 cups flour. In 2-quart saucepan, heat milk and 6 tablespoons margarine over low heat until very warm (120° to 130°F); margarine need not melt.

◆ With mixer at low speed, gradually beat liquid into flour mixture just until blended, scraping bowl often. Beat in eggs. Increase speed to medium; beat 3 minutes. With wooden spoon, stir in 4 cups flour to make a soft dough.

◆ Turn dough onto lightly floured surface; knead about 10 minutes, until smooth and elastic, working in about ½ cup more flour. Shape into ball. Cover loosely with plastic wrap; let rest 15 minutes. Meanwhile, prepare filling: In 1-quart saucepan, melt 6 tablespoons margarine over low heat; set aside. In medium bowl, mix walnuts, raisins, and 1 cup brown sugar. Grease 17" by 11½" roasting pan.

◆ Cut dough in half. On lightly floured surface, with floured rolling pin, roll half of dough into 18" by 12" rectangle. Brush dough with half of melted margarine; sprinkle with half of filling. Starting from a long side, roll dough jelly-roll fashion; pinch seam to seal. With serrated knife, slice roll crosswise into 10 pieces. Repeat with remaining dough, margarine, and filling. Arrange buns, cut-side down, in roasting pan. Cover loosely with plastic wrap; let rise in warm place (80° to 85°F) about 30 minutes, until doubled.

◆ Preheat oven to 350°F. Bake 25 to 30 minutes, until buns are golden and sound hollow when lightly tapped with fingers.

◆ Prepare glaze: In 1-quart saucepan, heat corn syrup, remaining ½ cup brown sugar, and remaining 6 tablespoons margarine over medium heat until margarine is melted and sugar is completely dissolved; spoon over hot buns. Cool buns in pan on wire rack. When buns are cool, in small bowl, mix confectioners' sugar and *1 tablespoon water* until smooth; with spoon, drizzle icing over buns.

Each bun: About 495 calories, 9g protein, 74g carbohydrate, 19g total fat (3g saturated), 35mg cholesterol, 365mg sodium

COFFEE BRAIDS AND TWISTS

These special-occasion breads are enhanced with chocolate, sweet apples, and other luscious fillings before they're baked into pretty shapes. Perfect with coffee or tea, they also make a delicious and thoughtful gift.

DATE-NUT TWIST

◆◆◆◆◆◆◆◆◆◆◆◆◆

Prep: 1 hour plus rising and cooling
Bake: 40 minutes
Makes 1 twist, 16 servings

2 packages quick-rise yeast
⅓ cup granulated sugar
1 teaspoon salt
About 4½ cups all-purpose
  flour
1 cup milk
6 tablespoons margarine or
  butter
3 large eggs
1 cup walnuts (about
  4 ounces), chopped
1 cup pitted dates (5 ounces),
  chopped
⅓ cup packed brown sugar
2 teaspoons ground cinnamon
½ cup apricot jam, melted

1 In large bowl, mix first 3 ingredients and 1 cup flour. In 1-quart saucepan, heat milk and 4 tablespoons margarine over low heat until very warm (120° to 130°F); margarine need not melt. With mixer at low speed, beat liquid into flour mixture just until blended. Increase speed to medium; beat 2 minutes, occasionally scraping bowl. Separate 1 egg; reserve yolk in refrigerator, covered. Beat remaining 2 eggs, egg white, and 1 cup flour into flour mixture to make a thick batter.

2 Beat 2 minutes, scraping bowl often. With wooden spoon, stir in 2 cups flour to make a soft dough. Turn dough onto floured surface; knead about 10 minutes, until smooth and elastic, working in about ½ cup more flour. Shape into ball; place in greased large bowl, turning to grease top. Cover loosely with plastic wrap; let rise in warm place (80° to 85°F) 30 minutes, or until doubled. Grease 10-inch springform pan.

3 Preheat oven to 350°F. In 2-quart saucepan, melt remaining 2 tablespoons margarine over low heat. Remove from heat; stir in walnuts and next 3 ingredients.

4 Punch down dough. Turn onto lightly floured surface; cover; let rest 10 minutes. With floured rolling pin, roll into 18" by 10" rectangle; brush with all but 2 tablespoons jam.

5 Sprinkle walnut mixture evenly over dough; press into dough lightly with rolling pin. Starting from a long side, tightly roll dough jelly-roll fashion; cut roll lengthwise in half.

6 Keeping cut sides up, carefully twist halves of dough roll together; place in springform pan, shaping twist into a ring. Tuck ends under to seal. Bake twist 25 minutes.

7 In cup, with fork, beat reserved egg yolk and *1 teaspoon water*. When twist has baked 25 minutes, brush with egg-yolk mixture. Bake 15 minutes longer. Cool in pan on wire rack 5 minutes. Carefully remove side of pan; brush hot bread with remaining 2 tablespoons jam. Cool on rack slightly to serve warm. Or, cool completely on rack to serve later; reheat if desired.

EACH SERVING: ABOUT 320 CALORIES, 7g PROTEIN, 51g CARBOHYDRATE, 11g TOTAL FAT (2g SATURATED), 42mg CHOLESTEROL, 205mg SODIUM

APPLE-FILLED COFFEE BRAID

Prep: 50 minutes plus rising and cooling   *Bake: 30 minutes*
Makes 1 braid, 12 servings

5 tablespoons margarine or butter

2 Rome Beauty apples, peeled, cored, and diced

¼ cup dark seedless raisins

¼ teaspoon ground cinnamon

½ cup granulated sugar

1 package quick-rise yeast

¼ teaspoon salt

About 2¾ cups all-purpose flour

⅓ cup plus 4 teaspoons milk

1 large egg

¾ cup confectioners' sugar

◆ In 10-inch skillet, melt 2 tablespoons margarine over medium-high heat; add next 3 ingredients and ¼ cup granulated sugar. Cook 10 minutes, or until apples are tender; set aside. In large bowl, combine yeast, salt, ½ cup flour, and ¼ cup granulated sugar. In 1-quart saucepan, heat ⅓ cup milk, remaining 3 tablespoons margarine, and *2 tablespoons water* over low heat until very warm (120° to 130°F); margarine need not melt.

◆ With mixer at low speed, gradually beat liquid into flour mixture just until blended. Increase speed to medium; beat 2 minutes, scraping bowl. Beat in egg and ½ cup flour to make a thick batter; beat 2 minutes, scraping bowl often. Stir in 1½ cups flour to make a soft dough. On floured surface, with floured hands, knead dough about 10 minutes, until smooth and elastic, working in about ¼ cup more flour. Shape into ball. Cover; let rest 10 minutes.

◆ On greased 17" by 14" cookie sheet , with floured rolling pin, roll dough into 14" by 10" rectangle (damp towel under sheet will prevent slipping). Place apples in 3-inch-wide strip lengthwise down center. Shape braid (see below). Cover; let rise in warm place (80° to 85°F) 40 minutes, or until doubled. Preheat oven to 350°F. Bake braid 30 minutes, or until golden. Cool on wire rack. In cup, mix confectioners' sugar and remaining 4 teaspoons milk. Drizzle over braid.

Each serving: About 230 calories, 4g protein, 41g carbohydrate, 6g total fat (1g saturated), 19mg cholesterol, 110mg sodium

◆◆◆◆◆◆◆◆◆◆◆◆◆◆◆◆◆◆◆◆◆◆◆◆◆◆

SHAPING A BRAID

Cut dough on both sides of filling into 1-inch-wide strips just to filling. Place strips at an angle across filling, alternating sides; end of each strip should be covered by next strip. Pinch last strip to bottom of braid to seal.

◆◆◆◆◆◆◆◆◆◆◆◆◆◆◆◆◆◆◆◆◆◆◆◆◆◆

CHOCOLATE-ALMOND COFFEE BRAID

Prep: 55 minutes plus rising and cooling   *Bake: 50 minutes*
Makes 1 braid, 16 servings

1 package active dry yeast

½ teaspoon salt

About 5⅓ cups all-purpose flour

½ cup plus 2 tablespoons sugar

¾ cup milk

7 tablespoons margarine or butter

3 large eggs

1 package (8 ounces) cream cheese, softened

1 tube or can (7 to 8 ounces) almond paste

4 ounces sweet baking chocolate, chopped

◆ In large bowl, combine yeast, salt, 1 cup flour, and ½ cup sugar. In 1-quart saucepan, heat milk, 5 tablespoons margarine, and ¼ *cup water* over low heat until very warm (120° to 130°F); margarine need not melt. With mixer at low speed, gradually beat liquid into flour mixture just until blended. Increase speed to medium; beat 2 minutes, scraping bowl often. Beat in 2 eggs and 2 cups flour; beat 2 minutes longer. Stir in 1½ cups flour to make a soft dough.

◆ Turn dough onto floured surface. With floured hands, knead about 10 minutes, until smooth and elastic, working in about ½ cup more flour. Shape into ball; place in greased large bowl, turning to grease top. Cover; let rise in warm place (80° to 85°F) 1 hour, until doubled.

◆ Prepare filling: Separate remaining egg; reserve white in refrigerator, covered. In large bowl, with mixer at low speed, beat cream cheese, almond paste, and egg yolk until smooth. Stir in 3 ounces chopped chocolate. Refrigerate.

◆ Prepare streusel topping: In bowl, with fingertips, mix ⅓ cup all-purpose flour, remaining 2 tablespoons sugar, and remaining 2 tablespoons margarine until mixture resembles coarse crumbs. Refrigerate. Punch down dough. Turn onto lightly floured surface. Cover; let rest 15 minutes.

◆ On greased 17" by 14" cookie sheet, with floured rolling pin, roll dough into 16" by 12" rectangle (place damp towel under sheet to prevent slipping). Spread filling in 4-inch-wide strip lengthwise down center. Shape braid (see left). Cover; let rise in warm place (80° to 85°F) 30 minutes.

◆ Preheat oven to 325°F. Beat reserved egg white and *1 tablespoon water* lightly; use to brush over braid. Sprinkle streusel topping down center of braid. Bake braid 50 minutes, or until browned, covering with foil after 30 minutes to prevent overbrowning. Cool completely on wire rack. In small saucepan, melt remaining 1 ounce chocolate over low heat. Drizzle over cooled braid.

Each serving: About 380 calories, 8g protein, 49g carbohydrate, 17g total fat (6g saturated), 57mg cholesterol, 190mg sodium

COMPANY COFFEE CAKES

Make one of these heartwarming coffee cakes the centerpiece of your brunch. Each of our tempting recipes can be made ahead – wrap the cooled coffee cake well and freeze up to 1 month (if you like, cut in half or into serving portions before freezing). Thaw cake, still wrapped, at room temperature and reheat, if desired, before serving.

APRICOT-PECAN COFFEE CAKE

◆◆◆◆◆◆◆◆◆◆◆◆◆◆◆◆◆◆◆◆◆◆◆◆◆◆◆◆

Prep: 50 minutes plus rising and cooling   *Bake:* 30 minutes
Makes 12 servings

6 tablespoons margarine or butter	1 teaspoon salt
1½ cups pecans (about 6 ounces), finely chopped	About 4½ cups all-purpose flour
⅓ cup packed brown sugar	1 cup milk
1 teaspoon ground cinnamon	2 large eggs
2 packages quick-rise yeast	½ cup apricot jam, melted
⅓ cup granulated sugar	1 large egg yolk

1 Grease 10-inch springform pan. Prepare filling: In 2-quart saucepan, melt 2 tablespoons margarine over low heat. Remove saucepan from heat. Stir in pecans, brown sugar, and cinnamon until well blended; set aside. In large bowl, combine yeast, granulated sugar, salt, and 1 cup flour. In 1-quart saucepan, heat milk and remaining 4 tablespoons margarine over low heat until very warm (120° to 130°F); margarine need not melt.

2 With mixer at low speed, gradually beat liquid into flour mixture just until blended. Increase speed to medium; beat 2 minutes. Add whole eggs; beat until blended. With wooden spoon, stir in 3 cups flour to make a soft dough. Turn dough onto lightly floured surface; knead about 10 minutes, until smooth and elastic, working in about ½ cup more flour. Cover; let rest 10 minutes.

3 With floured rolling pin, roll dough into 18" by 10" rectangle; brush evenly with some of melted jam. Sprinkle filling evenly over dough; press lightly into dough with rolling pin.

4 Cut dough lengthwise into 2-inch-wide strips. Loosely roll up 1 strip and place in center of pan, cut-side down. One at a time, loosely wrap remaining strips around center strip to make a spiral, matching ends of strips as you work. Cover dough loosely with plastic wrap; let rise in warm place (80° to 85°F) about 30 minutes, until doubled.

5 Preheat oven to 350°F. In cup, with fork, beat egg yolk lightly. Brush coffee cake evenly with egg yolk. Bake 30 minutes, or until golden. Cool coffee cake in pan on wire rack 5 minutes; brush with remaining melted jam. Carefully remove side of pan. Serve warm. Or, cool on wire rack to serve later; reheat, if you like.

EACH SERVING: ABOUT 410 CALORIES, 8g PROTEIN, 58g CARBOHYDRATE, 17g TOTAL FAT (3g SATURATED), 56mg CHOLESTEROL, 270mg SODIUM

ORANGE-CARDAMOM SWEET BREAD

Prep: 35 minutes plus rising and cooling   Bake: 50 minutes
Makes 1 loaf, 20 servings

1 large orange	4 tablespoons margarine or
2 packages quick-rise yeast	butter
1 teaspoon salt	3 large eggs
About 7½ cups all-purpose	1½ teaspoons ground
flour	cardamom
1¼ cups buttermilk or soured	1 tablespoon milk
milk (see page 392)	½ cup sliced almonds (about
⅔ cup honey	2 ounces)

◆ Grease 10-inch springform pan. Grate 2 teaspoons peel and squeeze ¼ cup juice from orange. In large bowl, combine yeast, salt, and 2 cups flour. In 2-quart saucepan, heat buttermilk, honey, margarine, and orange juice over medium heat until very warm (120° to 130°F); margarine need not melt.

◆ With mixer at low speed, gradually beat liquid into flour mixture just until blended. Increase speed to medium; beat 2 minutes, occasionally scraping bowl with rubber spatula.

◆ In cup, with fork, beat eggs lightly; reserve 1 tablespoon beaten egg in refrigerator, covered. Add remaining beaten eggs with cardamom, orange peel, and 1½ cups flour to flour mixture; beat 2 minutes, scraping bowl often. With wooden spoon, stir in 3½ cups flour to make a soft dough.

◆ Turn dough onto lightly floured surface and knead about 10 minutes, until smooth and elastic, working in about ½ cup more flour while kneading. Shape dough into ball; place in center of springform pan, turning to grease top. Cover loosely with plastic wrap; let rise in warm place (80° to 85°F) about 1 hour, until doubled.

◆ Preheat oven to 350°F. In cup, with fork, mix milk and reserved beaten egg. Brush top of loaf with some of egg mixture. Sprinkle with sliced almonds; brush almonds lightly with more egg mixture. Bake 50 minutes, or until bread sounds hollow when lightly tapped with fingers, covering with foil after about 20 minutes to prevent overbrowning. Remove side of pan; cool bread on wire rack 30 minutes to serve warm. Or, cool completely to serve later.

Each serving: About 250 calories, 7g protein, 45g carbohydrate, 5g total fat (1g saturated), 33mg cholesterol, 160mg sodium

CREAM-CHEESE-SWIRL LOAVES

Prep: 50 minutes plus rising and cooling   Bake: 30 to 35 minutes
Makes 2 loaves, 12 servings each

2 packages active dry yeast	1 large egg
⅓ cup granulated sugar	2 packages (8 ounces each)
¾ teaspoon salt	cream cheese, softened
About 3½ cups all-purpose	⅔ cup confectioners' sugar
flour	1 tablespoon grated orange
½ cup margarine or butter	peel
¼ cup milk	2 large egg yolks

◆ In large bowl, combine yeast, granulated sugar, salt, and 1 cup flour. In 1-quart saucepan, heat margarine, milk, and *½ cup water* over low heat until very warm (120° to 130°F); margarine need not melt.

◆ With mixer at low speed, gradually beat liquid into flour mixture just until blended. Increase speed to medium; beat 2 minutes, occasionally scraping bowl with rubber spatula. Beat in whole egg and ¾ cup flour to make a thick batter; beat 2 minutes. With wooden spoon, stir in 1¼ cups flour to make a soft dough.

◆ Turn dough onto lightly floured surface and knead about 8 minutes, until smooth and elastic, working in about ½ cup more flour while kneading. Shape dough into ball; place in greased large bowl, turning dough to grease top. Cover loosely with plastic wrap; let rise in warm place (80°F to 85°F) about 1 hour, until doubled.

◆ Prepare filling: In small bowl, with mixer at low speed, beat cream cheese, confectioners' sugar, grated orange peel, and egg yolks until smooth. Refrigerate. Grease large cookie sheet.

◆ Punch down dough. Turn dough onto lightly floured surface. Cut dough in half; cover and let rest 15 minutes. With floured rolling pin, roll half of dough into 13" by 9" rectangle; spread half of filling to within 1 inch of edge.

◆ Starting from a long side, roll dough jelly-roll fashion; pinch seam to seal. Press ends to seal; tuck ends under. Repeat with remaining dough and filling. Place loaves, 3 inches apart, on cookie sheet; with sharp knife or single-edge razor, cut several slashes in tops. Cover loosely with plastic wrap; let rise in warm place about 45 minutes, until doubled.

◆ Preheat oven to 350°F. Bake 30 to 35 minutes, until loaves are golden and sound hollow when lightly tapped with fingers. Remove loaves from cookie sheet; cool slightly on wire racks to serve warm. Or, cool completely and refrigerate loaves to serve later; reheat, if you like.

Each serving: About 195 calories, 4g protein, 19g carbohydrate, 11g total fat (5g saturated), 48mg cholesterol, 170mg sodium

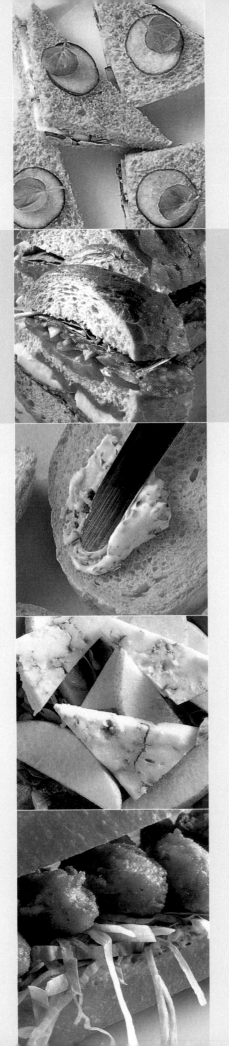

SANDWICHES 13

SANDWICHES <u>KNOW-HOW</u>

From peanut butter and jelly to hearty steak and mushroom, whether it's a light snack or informal supper, sandwiches make the perfect no-fuss meal. We've rounded up the latest on enticing fillings, crusty loaves, slender substitutes, and packaging tips for sandwiches to go.

YOU CAN TAKE IT WITH YOU

Brown-bagging a sandwich for a school lunch, work, or picnic is a time-honored tradition. But unless you pack with care, you could end up with soggy results, or even something dangerous to eat. Here, the best way to take it with you.

Save time with an assembly line If you're making several sandwiches at once, use a production-line technique: Line up bread slices in rows; apply spreads; top with fillings.

Wrap it up To keep sandwiches fresh and moist, wrap them in plastic wrap, waxed paper, zip-tight plastic bags, or aluminum foil immediately after you've prepared them.

Watch out for watery ingredients Lettuce, sliced tomatoes, or cucumbers can make bread soggy. For best results, omit these ingredients, or wrap separately and add just before serving.

Choose the right bread Certain sturdy, dense-textured loaves are made specifically to cradle fillings without turning mushy – and actually taste better after they absorb flavorful dressings. Best bets include focaccia, Italian ciabatta, hero rolls, sturdy baguettes, and semolina bread.

Keep sandwiches safe To prevent the growth of harmful bacteria such as salmonella, never allow fillings containing poultry, meat, fish, or eggs to sit at room temperature for longer than 2 hours.

MAKE A SLIMMER SANDWICH

Be choosy with condiments Avoid oil-laden spreads in favor of reduced-fat varieties (you can boost the flavor with chopped herbs or a touch of hot-pepper sauce), or stick with low-fat condiments like mustard or chutney. Or, create your own spread with pureed dried tomatoes or roasted garlic.

Be skimpy with cheese If you must add it, stick with reduced-fat varieties. Or, get a "creamy" texture from plain nonfat yogurt mixed with mustard.

Pick a lean protein Steer clear of fatty meats such as corned beef, pastrami, or sausage; opt instead for skinless chicken or turkey breast, shrimp, or water-packed tuna.

Pile on (fat-free) high-flavor foods Good bets include roasted peppers, chopped artichoke hearts (water-packed), pepperoncini (pickled Italian peppers), or capers. Skip bland lettuces like iceberg in favor of arugula or watercress.

IRRESISTIBLE COMBINATIONS

• Hummus, sliced tomatoes and cucumber, and hot-pepper sauce in warm whole-wheat pita bread.
• Sliced vine-ripened red and yellow tomatoes, mayonnaise, sea salt, and freshly ground pepper on crustless white bread.
• Olive paste, roasted peppers, sliced hard-cooked egg, arugula, and anchovies on a crisp-crusted baguette.
• A grilled sandwich made with mushrooms and spinach sautéed in olive oil with Fontina cheese on peasant bread.
• Smoked turkey, cream cheese with green onions, and cranberry relish or chutney on toasted raisin-walnut bread.
• Creamy avocado with sliced red onion, tomato, cucumber, alfalfa sprouts, and mayonnaise on multi-grain bread.
• Roasted eggplant, arugula, and goat cheese on focaccia.
• Sliced pork, caramelized onions, apple butter, and fiery mustard on multi-grain bread or a sturdy French roll.

A WELL-BREAD SANDWICH

These days there's an incredible range of breads available, providing delicious options for sandwich lovers. Most breads can be paired with virtually any ingredient from robust meats (e.g., pastrami, roast beef) to delicate fillings like egg salad or smoked salmon. But you'll find that grilled sausage or other oily add-ins call for sturdy-crusted loaves. For extra flavor, try breads filled with olives, nuts, or herbs. To improve day-old bread, toast the slices and slather on a moist condiment.

Peasant bread   Rye   Semolina   Ciabatta

Whole-grain   Sourdough   Focaccia   French roll   Pita

HOT SANDWICHES

When there's no time to cook, a simple sandwich is the obvious solution. Crowned with melted cheese or dripping with spicy barbecue sauce, these hot sandwiches provide new inspiration for a fast supper or a weekend brunch. Our Reuben has two kinds of meat, and our California grilled cheese has everything, including avocado.

SALTIMBOCCA CHICKEN SANDWICHES

Prep: 15 minutes   Broil: 3 to 5 minutes
Makes 4 main-dish servings

1 tablespoon all-purpose flour	4 thin slices prosciutto or cooked ham
Coarsely ground black pepper	
4 skinless, boneless chicken-breast halves (1¼ pounds)	1 medium tomato, thinly sliced
1 tablespoon vegetable oil	2 ounces Provolone or mozzarella cheese, shredded (½ cup)
¼ cup mayonnaise	
2 tablespoons chopped fresh basil	
4 slices Italian bread, each ¾ inch thick	

1 On waxed paper, mix flour and ¼ teaspoon pepper; use to coat chicken. In 12-inch skillet, heat oil over medium-high heat; add chicken and cook about 10 minutes, turning once, until tender and golden brown and juices run clear when chicken is pierced with tip of knife.

2 Meanwhile, preheat broiler. In small bowl, mix mayonnaise, basil, and ⅛ teaspoon pepper. Spread mayonnaise mixture over bread slices; place on cookie sheet.

3 Place cookie sheet in broiler at closest position to heat source. Broil bread 1 to 2 minutes, until mayonnaise mixture is lightly browned and bubbly. Remove cookie sheet; keep broiler on. Place 1 slice prosciutto on each slice of bread; top with chicken, then sliced tomato. Sprinkle evenly with shredded Provolone. Broil sandwiches 2 to 3 minutes, until cheese melts.

BEYOND MAYO

Mayonnaise is a favorite spread for all kinds of sandwiches, and can be endlessly varied – here we've added basil for a fresh Italian flavor. But there's a whole range of other spreads for you to experiment with:

• Try whole-grain mustard for texture, or flavored mustard with herbs or honey – great with meat or cheese.

• Tasty bean spreads or dips such as hummus are delicious with crisp greens.

• Olive spreads such as French tapenade or Italian olivada pack plenty of flavor and are especially good with tuna, fresh mozzarella, or roasted peppers.

• A little pesto is the perfect partner for a tomato and mozzarella sandwich on a crusty Italian roll – or try it with bacon, roasted turkey, or egg salad.

EACH SERVING: ABOUT 455 CALORIES, 42g PROTEIN, 19g CARBOHYDRATE, 23g TOTAL FAT (6g SATURATED), 124mg CHOLESTEROL, 585mg SODIUM

CALIFORNIA GRILLED SANDWICHES

Prep: 10 minutes   Cook: 8 minutes
Makes 2 main-dish servings

4 slices white or sourdough bread, each ¾ inch thick
4 ounces Monterey Jack cheese, thinly sliced
4 ounces thinly sliced roasted turkey
1 medium tomato, thinly sliced
½ medium avocado, thinly sliced
1 tablespoon Dijon mustard
1 tablespoon margarine or butter

◆ On 2 bread slices, layer cheese, turkey, tomato, and avocado. Spread remaining 2 slices of bread with mustard; place on top of filling, mustard-side down, to make 2 sandwiches.

◆ In 10-inch skillet, melt margarine over medium heat. Add sandwiches; cover and cook, carefully turning sandwiches once, until golden brown on both sides.

◆ To serve, with serrated knife, cut each sandwich in half.

Each serving: About 640 calories, 39g protein, 44g carbohydrate, 34g total fat (14g saturated), 98mg cholesterol, 1015mg sodium

BARBECUED BEEF SANDWICHES

Prep: 10 minutes   Cook: 30 minutes
Makes 4 main-dish servings

1 beef flank steak or top round steak (1 pound)
2 tablespoons olive or vegetable oil
2 medium red peppers, cut into ½-inch-wide strips
1 large onion, cut into ¼-inch-thick slices
1 tablespoon chili powder
1 can (8 ounces) tomato sauce
2 tablespoons Worcestershire sauce
2 tablespoons cider vinegar
1 tablespoon brown sugar
4 hamburger buns, split

◆ Holding knife almost parallel to cutting surface, cut steak crosswise into paper-thin slices.

◆ In 12-inch skillet, heat 1 tablespoon oil over high heat; add steak and cook, stirring frequently, about 2 to 3 minutes, until steak loses its pink color throughout. Transfer steak to bowl.

◆ In drippings in skillet, heat remaining 1 tablespoon oil over high heat; add peppers and onion and cook, stirring frequently, until tender-crisp and lightly browned.

◆ Stir chili powder into vegetables in skillet; cook, stirring, 1 minute. Add tomato sauce, Worcestershire, vinegar, brown sugar, and *¾ cup water*; heat to boiling. Reduce heat to low;

cover and simmer 15 minutes, until vegetables are very tender. Return steak to skillet; heat through. Serve barbecued beef in hamburger buns.

Each serving: About 455 calories, 36g protein, 39g carbohydrate, 18g total fat (5g saturated), 50mg cholesterol, 730mg sodium

SKILLET REUBEN DELUXE

Prep: 10 minutes   Cook: 8 minutes
Makes 4 main-dish servings

1 can (8 ounces) sauerkraut (1 cup)
¼ cup bottled Thousand Island salad dressing
4 slices rye bread
8 ounces sliced roasted turkey
8 ounces sliced corned beef
2 ounces Jarlsberg cheese, thinly sliced
2 tablespoons margarine or butter
Pickles and potato chips (optional)

◆ In strainer, place sauerkraut; rinse with cold running water. Drain, pressing down on sauerkraut to remove as much liquid as possible.

◆ Spread 1 tablespoon salad dressing on 1 slice rye bread. Top with half of turkey, half of corned beef, half of sauerkraut, half of Jarlsberg cheese, and 1 more tablespoon salad dressing. Top with another slice rye bread. Repeat to make second sandwich.

◆ In nonstick 12-inch skillet, melt 1 tablespoon margarine over medium heat. Add sandwiches; cover and cook until golden brown on both sides and cheese melts, carefully turning sandwiches once and adding 1 more tablespoon margarine to skillet.

◆ To serve, with serrated knife, cut each sandwich in half; place on 4 plates, with pickles and potato chips, if you like.

Each serving: About 390 calories, 36g protein, 23g carbohydrate, 17g total fat (3g saturated), 116mg cholesterol, 1375mg sodium

WHAT'S IN A NAME?

Corned beef, Swiss cheese, sauerkraut, and rye bread are the ingredients of the original Reuben sandwich, said to have been invented in 1914 by Arthur Reuben, the owner of Reuben's delicatessen in New York. The Reuben gained fame when a restaurant cook from Omaha entered his version in the National Sandwich Idea contest in 1956 and won. Reubens can be served cold, or grilled in a skillet like ours, which adds slices of roasted turkey for a sandwich so substantial that each one serves two.

OPEN-FACED SANDWICHES

These sandwiches may have originated on a Swedish smorgasbord table, but the possibilities go well beyond. Knife-and-fork specialties, our grown-up sandwiches include sliced steak with mushrooms, tender eggplant and mozzarella, and a classic pairing of smoked salmon and dill.

OPEN-FACED EGGPLANT AND MOZZARELLA SANDWICHES

◆◆◆◆◆◆◆◆◆◆◆◆◆

Prep: 15 minutes
Broil: 10 to 12 minutes
Makes 4 main-dish servings

1 medium eggplant (about 1½ pounds), cut crosswise into ¼-inch-thick slices

4 tablespoons olive or vegetable oil

1 loaf (8 ounces) semolina or Italian bread

1 package (9 ounces) fresh mozzarella cheese balls, drained, or 1 package (8 ounces) mozzarella cheese

1 teaspoon dried oregano

¼ teaspoon crushed red pepper

¼ teaspoon salt

8 oil-packed dried tomatoes, drained

1 small bunch basil

1 Preheat broiler. Place eggplant slices on rack in broiling pan; use 2 tablespoons oil to brush both sides. Broil 10 to 12 minutes, until tender and browned, turning slices once.

2 Diagonally slice both ends from loaf of bread; reserve ends for another day. Cut remaining bread diagonally into 8 slices. Thinly slice mozzarella cheese. In small bowl, with fork, mix oregano, crushed red pepper, salt, and remaining 2 tablespoons oil. Brush herb mixture over bread slices. Top bread with broiled eggplant, mozzarella slices, and dried tomatoes. Tuck basil leaves in between mozzarella slices.

QUICK SANDWICH TOPPINGS

A selection of open-faced sandwiches makes great party fare. Here are some easy ideas to try:

• Shrimp over dill mayonnaise

• Broiled cheese (Fontina, Monterey Jack, sharp Cheddar) over tomato or pickle slices

• Crispy cooked bacon strips over guacamole

• Sardines with minced red onion and parsley over mayonnaise mixed with whole-grain mustard

• Prosciutto and thinly sliced fresh figs over mascarpone cheese (shown above)

• Pear slices and Stilton cheese over a layer of watercress (shown above)

EACH SERVING: ABOUT 560 CALORIES, 20g PROTEIN, 53g CARBOHYDRATE, 31g TOTAL FAT (10g SATURATED), 44mg CHOLESTEROL, 825mg SODIUM

SMOKED SALMON SANDWICHES WITH DILL-CAPER CREAM CHEESE

Prep: 20 minutes   *Makes 4 main-dish servings*

1 package (3 ounces) cream
  cheese, softened
1 tablespoon finely chopped
  shallot
1 tablespoon capers,
  drained and chopped
1 tablespoon chopped
  fresh dill

1 teaspoon fresh lemon juice
4 slices pumpernickel bread
6 ounces thinly sliced
  smoked salmon
Ground black pepper
4 teaspoons salmon caviar
  (optional)
Dill sprigs for garnish

◆ Prepare dill-caper cream cheese: In small bowl, mix cream cheese and next 4 ingredients until blended.

◆ Spread dill-caper cream cheese evenly over bread. Arrange smoked salmon on top. Sprinkle with pepper. Place 1 teaspoon caviar on each sandwich, if you like. Garnish with dill sprigs.

Each serving: About 205 calories, 12g protein, 16g carbohydrate, 10g total fat (5g saturated), 33mg cholesterol, 690mg sodium

OPEN-FACED SPINACH AND GOAT-CHEESE SANDWICHES

Prep: 20 minutes   *Broil: 4 to 5 minutes*
Makes 4 main-dish servings

1 tablespoon olive oil
1 garlic clove, minced
3 large plum tomatoes
  (12 ounces), diced
½ teaspoon salt
¼ teaspoon ground black
  pepper

1 bunch (10 to 12 ounces)
  spinach, rinsed and well
  drained
4 large slices peasant bread
  (each 4" by 3" by ½")
2 ounces goat cheese,
  crumbled (½ cup)

◆ Preheat broiler. In 5-quart Dutch oven, heat olive oil over medium-high heat. Add minced garlic and cook, stirring frequently, about 15 seconds, until fragrant. Stir in diced tomatoes, salt, and pepper and cook about 2 minutes, until tomatoes are juicy and slightly softened. Add spinach and cook, stirring, just until spinach is wilted.

◆ Place peasant bread on cookie sheet; place in broiler at closest position to heat source. Broil about 1 minute per side, or until lightly toasted. Spoon spinach mixture evenly over toasted bread. Sprinkle goat cheese on top. Broil 4 to 5 minutes, just until cheese begins to turn golden.

Each serving: About 195 calories, 9g protein, 22g carbohydrate, 9g total fat (4g saturated), 11mg cholesterol, 560mg sodium

OPEN-FACED STEAK AND MUSHROOM SANDWICHES

Prep: 15 minutes   *Cook: 25 to 30 minutes*
Makes 4 main-dish servings

2 tablespoons margarine or
  butter, softened
1 tablespoon plus 1 teaspoon
  chopped fresh tarragon
Ground black pepper
1 loaf French bread
  (8 ounces), cut horizontally
  in half

1 beef flank steak (about
  1¼ pounds)
3 teaspoons vegetable oil
Salt
1 medium onion, thinly sliced
12 ounces mushrooms, sliced
Pinch dried thyme
⅓ cup dry red wine

◆ In small bowl, mix margarine, 1 tablespoon tarragon, and ⅛ teaspoon pepper until blended. Spread margarine mixture over cut sides of French bread. Cut each half into 4 pieces; place 2 pieces each on 4 plates.

◆ Pat flank steak dry with paper towels. In 10-inch skillet, heat 2 teaspoons oil over medium-high heat. Add steak, sprinkle with ¼ teaspoon salt and ⅛ teaspoon pepper, and cook 12 minutes, turning once, for medium-rare, or until desired doneness. Transfer steak to cutting board; keep warm.

◆ Reduce heat to medium. Add remaining 1 teaspoon oil to drippings in skillet; add sliced onion and cook, stirring often, 5 minutes, or until tender and browned.

◆ Stir in mushrooms, thyme, ½ teaspoon salt, and ⅛ teaspoon pepper. Increase heat to medium-high and cook 8 minutes, or until mushrooms are tender and liquid has evaporated. Stir in wine and heat to boiling; boil 2 minutes.

◆ Holding knife almost parallel to cutting board, slice steak thinly across grain; arrange steak on bread. Spoon mushroom mixture on top and sprinkle with remaining 1 teaspoon tarragon.

Each serving: About 540 calories, 45g protein, 38g carbohydrate, 22g total fat (6g saturated), 62mg cholesterol, 890mg sodium

HERO SANDWICHES

While a hero sandwich goes by many names, the basic concept's always the same: Take a crusty loaf of good French, Italian, or semolina bread, split it in half, and stuff it with assorted fillings – the delicious result is guaranteed to satisfy the hungriest diner. Hero fillings can be hot or cold; our assortment includes crispy fried oysters with herbed mayonnaise; sweet sausages sautéed with peppers and onions; and an extravagant Italian meat and cheese combination drizzled with a red wine vinaigrette. Cold heroes travel very well and are great to pack for picnics or tailgate parties.

1 In 3-quart saucepan, heat 2 inches oil to 375°F on deep-frying thermometer. In small bowl, mix mayonnaise, next 3 ingredients, and ¼ teaspoon hot-pepper sauce.

2 On sheet of waxed paper, combine cracker crumbs and ground red pepper. Drain oysters. Coat 6 oysters with cracker-crumb mixture.

OYSTER PO' BOY

Prep: 20 minutes   Cook: 30 seconds per batch
Makes 4 main-dish servings

Vegetable oil for deep frying
¼ cup mayonnaise
1 tablespoon minced shallot
1 tablespoon chopped fresh parsley
1 tablespoon capers, drained and chopped
¼ teaspoon hot-pepper sauce plus additional for serving
1 cup fine cracker crumbs

¼ teaspoon ground red pepper (cayenne)
2 dozen oysters, shucked (see page 89)
4 French bread rolls (each about 6 inches long), split horizontally and lightly toasted
1 cup very thinly sliced iceberg lettuce

3 With slotted spoon, add coated oysters to hot oil. Cook about 30 seconds, until golden; drain on paper towels. Coat and cook remaining oysters, 6 at a time.

4 Spread mayonnaise mixture on bottoms of toasted rolls. Top with lettuce and oysters; replace tops of rolls. Serve with hot-pepper sauce.

CLAM ROLL

The clam roll is to New England what the oyster po' boy is to Louisiana. Follow the recipe above, but use 4 frankfurter rolls instead of French bread rolls and 2 dozen clams, shucked, instead of oysters. Serve rolls with Tartar Sauce (see page 119) instead of spreading with mayonnaise mixture given above.

Each serving: About 435 calories, 13g protein, 48g carbohydrate, 21g total fat (3g saturated), 23mg cholesterol, 370mg sodium

EACH SERVING: ABOUT 675 CALORIES, 34g PROTEIN, 57g CARBOHYDRATE, 33g TOTAL FAT (6g SATURATED), 8mg CHOLESTEROL, 710mg SODIUM

DOUBLE-TOMATO-BRIE HEROES

Prep: 20 minutes   *Makes 8 main-dish servings*

1 jar (6½ ounces) oil-packed
  dried tomatoes (¾ cup),
  drained and finely chopped
2 tablespoons extra-virgin
  olive oil
2 tablespoons white wine
  vinegar

2 long loaves Italian bread
  (about 8 ounces each)
1 pound Brie cheese, sliced
  (with rind left on)
1 cup packed fresh basil
  leaves
2 medium tomatoes, sliced

◆ In small bowl, with wire whisk or fork, mix dried tomatoes, olive oil, and vinegar.

◆ Cut each loaf of bread horizontally in half. Spread dried-tomato mixture evenly on cut sides of bread. Arrange Brie on bottom halves of bread; top with basil leaves and tomato slices. Replace tops of loaves. If not serving right away, wrap each hero in plastic wrap and refrigerate. To serve, cut each hero crosswise into 4 pieces.

Each serving: About 430 calories, 18g protein, 36g carbohydrate, 25g total fat (11g saturated), 56mg cholesterol, 750mg sodium

SAUSAGE, PEPPER, AND ONION HEROES

Prep: 10 minutes   Cook: 30 minutes
Makes 4 main-dish servings

1 pound sweet Italian-sausage
  links, pricked all over with
  fork
2 medium onions, halved
  lengthwise and cut into
  ½-inch-thick slices

2 green peppers, cut into
  ½-inch-wide strips
4 hero rolls (each about
  6 inches long), split
  horizontally

◆ In 10-inch skillet, heat sausages and ¼ *cup water* to boiling over high heat. Reduce heat to low; cover and cook 5 minutes. Uncover skillet; increase heat to medium and cook, turning occasionally, until sausages are browned and cooked through. Drain on paper towels.

◆ Discard all but 1 tablespoon drippings from skillet. To drippings in skillet, add onions and peppers and cook, stirring frequently, 15 minutes, or until tender. Slice sausage diagonally into ½-inch pieces; add to pepper mixture with ⅓ *cup water*, stirring until brown bits in bottom of pan are loosened. To serve, spoon sausage mixture into hero rolls.

Each serving: About 585 calories, 21g protein, 41g carbohydrate, 37g total fat (11g saturated), 89mg cholesterol, 1360mg sodium

ANTIPASTO HEROES

Prep: 15 minutes   Makes 6 main-dish servings

¼ cup extra-virgin olive oil
2 tablespoons red wine
  vinegar
1 teaspoon sugar
¾ teaspoon dried oregano
¼ teaspoon crushed red
  pepper
2 loaves semolina bread (each
  16 inches long)
½ small head escarole,
  coarsely chopped

½ small head radicchio,
  coarsely chopped
6 ounces Provolone cheese,
  sliced
½ pound sliced salami
½ pound sliced cooked ham
2 medium tomatoes, sliced
6 peperoncini peppers

◆ Prepare dressing: In small bowl, with wire whisk or fork, mix olive oil, vinegar, sugar, oregano, and crushed red pepper until blended.

◆ Cut each loaf of bread horizontally in half. Spoon dressing onto cut sides of bread. Arrange escarole and radicchio on bottom halves of bread. Top with Provolone, salami, ham, tomatoes, and peperoncini. Replace tops of loaves. If not serving right away, wrap each hero in plastic wrap and refrigerate. To serve, cut each hero crosswise into 3 pieces.

Each serving: About 615 calories, 32g protein, 45g carbohydrate, 34g total fat (12g saturated), 61mg cholesterol, 2225mg sodium

WHAT'S IN A NAME?

A large French or Italian loaf, split and stuffed with slices of meat and cheese, peppers, pickles, lettuce, and just about anything else you like, is known to most Americans as a hero sandwich, but it goes by different names in different parts of the country: a submarine in New York, a hoagie in Philadelphia, or a po' boy in New Orleans. It may also be called a wedge or grinder. In Miami a version called a Cuban sandwich is filled with pork and pickles. Other popular hero fillings include meatballs and tomato sauce, eggplant with Parmesan, and breaded, fried veal cutlets with mozzarella cheese and tomato sauce.

TEA SANDWICHES

Tea sandwiches are pretty little morsels of crustless bread and a savory or sweet filling, meant to be enjoyed in a bite or two. Try our shrimp-filled hearts, cucumber and watercress sandwiches, or simple pinwheels. You can prepare them early in the day, and refrigerate them until teatime – or serve with cocktails, if you like.

SHRIMP TEA SANDWICHES

◆◆◆◆◆◆◆◆◆◆◆◆◆◆◆

Prep: 30 minutes
Cook: 2 minutes
Makes 24

8 ounces medium shrimp, shelled and deveined (see page 90)
1 small celery stalk, coarsely chopped
¼ cup mayonnaise
¼ teaspoon salt
3 drops hot-pepper sauce
12 very thin slices white bread

1 In 2-quart saucepan, heat *2 cups water* to boiling over high heat. Add shrimp; heat to boiling, stirring occasionally. Cook 1 minute, or until shrimp turn opaque throughout.

2 Drain shrimp. In food processor with knife blade attached, finely chop shrimp and celery. Add mayonnaise, salt, and hot-pepper sauce; process until blended, scraping sides with rubber spatula.

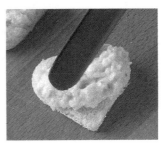

3 With 2" by 1½" heart-shaped cookie cutter, cut 4 hearts from each bread slice. Spread shrimp filling on half of hearts, using about 2 teaspoons per sandwich. Top with remaining hearts.

4 If not serving right away, line 15½" by 10½" jelly-roll pan with damp paper towels. Place tea sandwiches in jelly-roll pan; cover with damp paper towels to keep bread from drying out. Cover jelly-roll pan tightly with plastic wrap and refrigerate until ready to serve.

PINWHEEL SANDWICHES

1 Trim crusts from 1-pound loaf unsliced whole-wheat or white bread; cut lengthwise into ¼-inch-thick slices. With rolling pin, slightly flatten each slice; spread with 2 tablespoons favorite smooth filling (we used soft spreadable cheese with garlic and herbs). From a short side, roll up each slice jelly-roll fashion.

2 Cut each roll crosswise to make pinwheels.

EACH SANDWICH: ABOUT 50 CALORIES, 2g PROTEIN, 5g CARBOHYDRATE, 2g TOTAL FAT (0g SATURATED), 16mg CHOLESTEROL, 105mg SODIUM

CUCUMBER AND WATERCRESS TEA SANDWICHES

Prep: 30 minutes plus chilling
Makes 16

⅓ seedless European cucumber (4 ounces), unpeeled
¼ teaspoon salt
½ bunch watercress
1 tablespoon mayonnaise
8 very thin slices whole-wheat bread
2 tablespoons margarine or butter, softened

◆ From cucumber, cut 16 paper-thin slices for garnish; wrap with plastic wrap and refrigerate. Peel remaining cucumber; cut into paper-thin slices. In small bowl, toss peeled cucumber slices with salt; let stand 30 minutes, stirring occasionally.

◆ Meanwhile, remove stems from watercress. Reserve 16 small leaves for garnish; wrap with plastic wrap and refrigerate. Finely chop remaining watercress leaves. In another small bowl, mix chopped watercress with mayonnaise.

◆ Trim crusts from bread slices; lightly spread 1 side of each slice with margarine. Press salted cucumber slices with hand to drain liquid; pat dry.

◆ Spread watercress mixture on 4 bread slices; top with cucumber slices. Place remaining bread slices on top. Cut each sandwich diagonally into quarters.

◆ If not serving right away, line 15½" by 10½" jelly-roll pan with damp paper towels. Place tea sandwiches in jelly-roll pan; cover with damp paper towels to keep bread from drying out. Cover pan tightly with plastic wrap and refrigerate until ready to serve.

◆ To serve, garnish each sandwich with a cucumber slice and watercress leaf.

Each sandwich: About 45 calories, 1g protein, 5g carbohydrate, 3g total fat (0g saturated), 1mg cholesterol, 115mg sodium

DATE-NUT TEA SANDWICHES

Prep: 20 minutes   Makes 12

1 package (3 ounces) cream cheese, softened
¼ cup finely chopped dates
¼ cup finely chopped toasted walnuts (about 1 ounce)
¼ teaspoon grated orange peel
6 very thin slices whole-wheat bread, crusts trimmed

In small bowl, mix cream cheese and next 3 ingredients until evenly combined. Spread mixture evenly on 3 slices bread. Top with remaining bread. Cut each sandwich into 4 squares or triangles. If not serving right away, cover with damp paper towels, then plastic wrap; refrigerate.

Each sandwich: About 70 calories, 2g protein, 7g carbohydrate, 4g total fat (2g saturated), 8mg cholesterol, 75mg sodium

DILLED EGG TEA SANDWICHES

Prep: 20 minutes   Makes 18

3 large hard-cooked eggs
¼ cup mayonnaise
2 tablespoons chopped fresh dill
¼ teaspoon grated lemon peel
¼ teaspoon ground black pepper
12 very thin slices white or whole-wheat bread, crusts trimmed

In medium bowl, mash eggs with fork; stir in mayonnaise, dill, lemon peel, and pepper. Spread egg mixture evenly on 6 slices bread. Top with remaining bread. Cut each sandwich crosswise into 3 rectangles. If not serving right away, cover with damp paper towels, then plastic wrap; refrigerate.

Each sandwich: About 70 calories, 2g protein, 7g carbohydrate, 4g total fat (1g saturated), 37mg cholesterol, 105mg sodium

CHEDDAR AND CHUTNEY TEA SANDWICHES

Prep: 15 minutes   Makes 16

3 tablespoons margarine or butter, softened
3 tablespoons mango chutney, finely chopped
8 very thin slices white or whole-wheat bread
4 ounces Cheddar cheese, shredded (1 cup)

In small bowl, mix margarine and chutney until combined. Trim crusts from bread slices. Spread chutney mixture evenly on all bread slices. Sprinkle cheese evenly on 4 bread slices; top with remaining bread. Cut each sandwich into 4 squares or triangles. If not serving right away, cover with damp paper towels, then plastic wrap; refrigerate.

Each sandwich: About 80 calories, 3g protein, 7g carbohydrate, 5g total fat (2g saturated), 7mg cholesterol, 120mg sodium

CLUB SANDWICHES

A club sandwich traditionally begins as three slices of bread or toast, which allows you to layer it with the maximum amount of fillings, from Italian antipasto to a garden of vegetables to a spicy Southwestern take on the classic club. If these hearty sandwiches seem unwieldy, secure them with toothpicks.

ITALIAN LOAF SANDWICH

◆◆◆◆◆◆◆◆◆◆◆◆◆◆◆◆◆◆◆◆◆◆◆◆◆◆◆◆◆◆◆

Prep: 25 minutes plus chilling   Cook: 20 minutes
Makes 6 main-dish servings

4 tablespoons olive or vegetable oil
2 medium onions, cut into ½-inch-thick slices
One 12-inch-long loaf whole-grain bread (about 5" wide and 3" high)
3 tablespoons red wine vinegar
1 bunch arugula
6 ounces thinly sliced salami

8 ounces fresh mozzarella cheese, thinly sliced
2 medium red peppers, roasted and peeled (see page 310), or 1 jar (7 ounces) roasted red peppers, drained
2 medium tomatoes, sliced
½ (9½-ounce) jar Italian hot-pepper slices, drained

1 In 10-inch skillet, heat 2 tablespoons oil over medium heat. Add onions; cook, stirring occasionally, 20 minutes, or until tender and golden. Set aside. Cut bread horizontally into 3 slices.

2 In large bowl, with wire whisk or fork, mix vinegar and remaining 3 tablespoons oil. Brush some of oil mixture over cut sides of bread. To remaining oil mixture in bowl, add arugula; toss to coat.

3 To assemble: Arrange half of arugula on bottom of loaf; top with half of salami, all of cheese, and all of roasted peppers.

4 Place middle slice of bread over peppers and arrange tomato slices on bread; top with sautéed onions and hot-pepper slices, salami, and arugula. Replace top of loaf. For easier slicing, wrap sandwich tightly in plastic wrap; refrigerate 1 hour to allow juices from ingredients to moisten and flavor bread. To serve, cut sandwich into thick slices. Serve with knife and fork.

SAVORING SALAMI

A staple on antipasto platters and in robust deli sandwiches, salamis make some of the most tempting meats around. Salami is typically made from pork or beef that has been seasoned, cured, and air-dried. Some of the best known are Genoa (seasoned with black peppercorns and red wine), cotto (seasoned with white peppercorns), and varieties flavored with garlic, herbs, hot pepper, or fennel. Salamis are high in fat, but just a few slices add an incredible amount of taste. Once salami is cut, store it in airtight plastic wrap in the refrigerator for up to 3 weeks.

Salami with hot pepper

French herb salami

Roman-style flat salami

EACH SERVING: ABOUT 505 CALORIES, 21g PROTEIN, 38g CARBOHYDRATE, 29g TOTAL FAT (10g SATURATED), 52mg CHOLESTEROL, 1390mg SODIUM

HEALTH CLUB SANDWICH

Prep: 25 minutes   *Cook:* 2 minutes
Makes 4 main-dish servings

1 teaspoon honey
⅛ teaspoon ground black
 pepper
2 tablespoons olive oil
2 teaspoons plus 1 tablespoon
 fresh lemon juice
3 medium carrots, shredded
 (1 cup)
2 cups alfalfa sprouts
1 garlic clove, minced
½ teaspoon ground cumin

Pinch ground red pepper
 (cayenne)
1 can (15 to 19 ounces)
 garbanzo beans, rinsed and
 drained
12 slices multi-grain bread,
 lightly toasted if you like
1 large tomato, thinly sliced
1 bunch watercress, tough
 stems removed

◆ In medium bowl, mix honey, pepper, 1 tablespoon olive oil, and 2 teaspoons lemon juice. Add carrots and alfalfa sprouts; toss until evenly combined.

◆ In 2-quart saucepan, heat remaining 1 tablespoon olive oil with garlic, cumin, and ground red pepper over medium heat; cook 30 seconds, or until very fragrant. Stir in garbanzo beans and remove from heat. Add remaining 1 tablespoon lemon juice, and *1 tablespoon water*; with potato masher, mash until well blended.

◆ Spread garbanzo mixture evenly on 8 slices bread. Top 4 slices with tomato; top with watercress. Top the other 4 slices with carrot mixture. Place garbanzo-tomato layers on garbanzo-carrot layers. Top with remaining bread. To serve, cut each sandwich in half.

Each serving: About 405 calories, 15g protein, 64g carbohydrate, 12g total fat (2g saturated), 0mg cholesterol, 695mg sodium

---

SPROUTS

Low in calories and high in nutrients, sprouts add a bit of crunch to sandwiches, salads, and stir-fries. Most common are the fine, threadlike alfalfa sprouts, which taste slightly nutty, and mung bean sprouts (usually called "bean sprouts"), which are larger, crunchier, and milder in flavor. Alfalfa sprouts are best eaten raw; mung bean sprouts may be used raw or cooked briefly. You may also find radish sprouts, with leafy tops and a peppery taste, and lentil sprouts, which have a large seed and small sprout. All sprouts are very perishable, so use within a few days of purchase.

| Mung bean sprouts | Radish sprouts | Lentil sprouts | Alfalfa sprouts |

ROAST-BEEF WALDORF CLUB

Prep: 20 minutes plus standing   *Makes* 4 main-dish servings

4 very thin slices red onion
2 celery stalks
½ medium Golden Delicious
 apple
½ teaspoon fresh lemon juice
4 tablespoons reduced-fat
 mayonnaise
2 tablespoons sour cream

1 tablespoon prepared white
 horseradish
12 slices pumpernickel bread,
 lightly toasted if you like
8 ounces thinly sliced rare
 roast beef
1 bunch watercress, tough
 stems removed

◆ In small bowl, combine red onion with *ice water* to cover; let stand 15 minutes. Drain. Meanwhile, finely chop celery. Peel, core, and finely chop apple.

◆ In another small bowl, combine celery, apple, lemon juice, 2 tablespoons mayonnaise, and 1 tablespoon sour cream. In cup, mix horseradish, remaining 2 tablespoons mayonnaise, and remaining 1 tablespoon sour cream.

◆ Spread horseradish mixture evenly on 4 slices bread. Top with roast beef, red onion, and watercress.

◆ Spread celery mixture evenly on 4 slices bread and place on top of roast-beef layer. Top with remaining bread. To serve, cut each sandwich in half.

Each serving: About 445 calories, 27g protein, 52g carbohydrate, 14g total fat (4g saturated), 59mg cholesterol, 765mg sodium

SOUTHWEST TURKEY CLUB

Prep: 20 minutes   *Makes* 4 main-dish servings

4 tablespoons reduced-fat
 mayonnaise
1 chipotle chile in adobo (see
 page 30), finely chopped
12 slices sourdough bread,
 lightly toasted if you like
8 ounces thinly sliced roasted
 turkey

1 cup loosely packed cilantro
 sprigs
1 large tomato, thinly sliced
8 slices bacon, cooked and
 drained

◆ In small bowl, mix mayonnaise and chipotle. Spread chipotle mayonnaise evenly on 8 slices bread; top 4 slices evenly with turkey, then cilantro. Top the other 4 slices with tomato, then bacon.

◆ Place tomato-bacon layers on turkey-cilantro layers. Top with remaining 4 slices bread. To serve, cut each sandwich in half.

Each serving: About 410 calories, 28g protein, 42g carbohydrate, 13g total fat (3g saturated), 63mg cholesterol, 725mg sodium

DESSERTS 14

Anyone who has tasted a warm, fluffy soufflé, perfectly creamy custard, or a tender fruit shortcake knows that there's an art to great dessert making. The following time-honored tricks will help you master all the right methods. Because let's face it, every occasion is sweeter when a spectacular dessert is involved.

COOKING WITH FRUIT

Choosing the best fruit Choose ripe (but not mushy) fruit that's in season. When selecting fruit, the heavier it feels in your hand, the juicier and better tasting it will be. Smell it: If there's no aroma, there will be little flavor. Feel it: Fruit should yield slightly to gentle pressure. To ripen fruit, store it at room temperature in a dark place, or speed the process by placing it in a paper bag containing a whole lime.

Reasons to rinse Pesticides, waxy coatings, or even bacteria can linger on the skin of fruit, so rinse it well before using. (Don't forget to scrub citrus fruit if you're going to use the peel.) Never soak fruit in water, however; this leaches out flavor and encourages rotting. Instead, wash it quickly with gently running water, and dry immediately. Unless they are very sandy, avoid washing soft berries such as raspberries and blackberries, since they tend to become waterlogged.

A spoonful of sugar The sweetness of individual fruits can vary greatly, depending on ripeness, variety, and growing conditions, so you may need to adjust the amount of sugar called for in a recipe. Simply taste the fruit, or the fruit mixture, before cooking and adjust the sugar as necessary.

Prevent discoloration When exposed to air, tannins and enzymes in fruits such as apples, peaches, pears, and bananas cause them to turn brown. To prevent this, rub the fruit with a cut lemon, or briefly place it in a bowl of water with approximately 2 tablespoons of lemon juice added.

Cook it gently When you want to retain the shape and texture of a fruit, cook it gently just until it's tender. For poaching, keep the water at a low simmer. Sauté fruit only until it softens and begins to release its juices.

CREAMY CUSTARD EVERY TIME

Don't overbeat the eggs Overbeating can make the custard foamy and cause bubbles to appear on the surface as it bakes. Beat the eggs just till yolks and whites are blended.

Easy does it Custards, both baked and stove-top, require gentle heat so they don't separate. For silky stove-top custards, use low heat and stir constantly to prevent boiling (and subsequent curdling). Cook baked custards in a water bath – a larger pan of hot water. This method insulates them from the oven's direct heat so they cook evenly, without separating.

Is it ready? Overbaked custards may separate and turn watery. Remember that the custard is done even if the center is still jiggly; it will firm as it cools. To check, insert a knife ½ inch into the custard about 1 inch from the center; it should come out clean. A stove-top custard is ready when it's thick enough to coat a spoon well. Run your finger across the spoon; it should leave a track (see page 474).

Be careful with cooling Always remove the baked custard promptly from its water bath (otherwise, it will continue to cook), and then cool. Cool stove-top custards with a piece of plastic wrap pressed directly on top so a skin doesn't form.

SOUFFLÉ SUCCESS

• It's easier to separate eggs when they're cold, so separate them straight from the refrigerator, but let the whites stand 30 minutes before beating for maximum volume.

• Perfectly beaten egg whites are a must for a light, fluffy texture; beat the whites until they're stiff but not dry.

• The best way to blend: Mix in one third of the beaten egg whites to lighten batter. Add the remaining whites, half at a time, gently folding into the batter with a rubber spatula.

• Soufflés rely on a blast of quick, even heat to rise properly, so it's essential that the oven is heated to the correct temperature before baking. Only keep the oven door open for an instant when you put in the soufflé, and open it as little as possible during baking.

• Be sure to set the soufflé dish on a low rack in the oven so the mixture has plenty of room to rise.

• How to tell when the soufflé is done? It should be puffed and golden with a slightly soft, barely set texture.

• Come and get it! For the most dramatic presentation, call everyone to the table *before* you take the soufflé out of the oven; cool air will start to shrink it in 3 to 5 minutes.

Preparing soufflé dishes

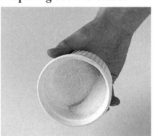

Use butter, margarine, or nonstick cooking spray to grease soufflé dishes, then sprinkle with just enough sugar to coat dishes lightly.

Folding in egg whites

Using a rubber spatula, gently fold one third of beaten egg whites into mixture. Then fold in the remaining egg whites, half at a time.

MAKING CHOUX PASTRY

This light, airy pastry is used for cream puffs and éclairs.
Beware of boiling Bring the water with the margarine or butter to a full boil, but don't let the water simmer away, or you'll have a dry dough.
Egg essentials For best results, use room-temperature eggs (they'll blend better and rise higher). Add the eggs to the batter one at a time, beating well after each addition to incorporate them thoroughly.
The heat is on Shape and bake choux pastry immediately, while it is still warm, for maximum expansion and lightness.
Go for the gold Pale, underbaked puffs will be raw inside and may collapse after they're removed from the oven. Aim for a rich, golden color.
Get a jump on entertaining Unfilled puffs freeze beautifully in zip-tight plastic bags; simply recrisp them in the oven.

High-rising choux puffs produce – and retain – a lot of steam as they bake. To help them dry into a golden-crisp shell, use a paring knife to cut a small slit into the side of each puff as soon as they come out of the oven.

PUFF PASTRY BASICS

• When buying frozen puff pastry, check the ingredients on the package. The best brands contain only flour, butter, salt, and water.
• Frozen puff pastry thaws very quickly, making it handy for last-minute treats. Figure on 10 to 20 minutes' thawing time.
• When cutting puff pastry dough, be sure your knife or pastry wheel is very sharp – clean cuts will ensure maximum puffing. Always cut straight down, never at an angle, or the dough will puff unevenly as it bakes.
• If you don't want puff pastry to rise too much, prick it in several places with a fork before baking.
• Save puff-pastry trimmings; they can be rerolled and used to make quick desserts (see page 466).
• Puff pastry demands a quick blast of heat at the beginning of baking; this melts the butter while it converts the water in the dough to steam, making it rise. To ensure that your oven is hot enough, preheat it at least 20 minutes ahead.

PHYLLO FACTS

• Fragile and tissue-thin, phyllo dries out quickly and becomes unusable, so keep it covered with plastic wrap until you are ready to use it. Any phyllo you don't use can be refrigerated, well wrapped, up to 2 weeks.

• Frozen phyllo will keep for 3 to 6 months; thaw overnight in the refrigerator. Never refreeze thawed phyllo dough, or it will become dry, brittle, and crumbly.
• Fresh phyllo dough, available at some specialty food stores and Greek and Middle Eastern markets, can be refrigerated, well wrapped, for 5 days, or frozen up to 3 months.
• Before baking, brush phyllo layers with a thin coating of melted margarine or butter for extra flavor and a crisp, golden crust – and to help guard against drying.
• Let phyllo bake until deep golden; this gives it a toasted flavor and a wonderfully crisp crust.
• Phyllo pie crusts and cups can be baked a day ahead. Store them in airtight containers, and recrisp (if necessary) in the oven before filling and serving.

GETTING TO KNOW GELATIN

• What exactly is gelatin? It's an odorless, tasteless, and colorless thickening agent derived from beef and veal bones; some gelatin is a by-product of pig skin.
• For best results, measure carefully. Too much gelatin makes a mixture rubbery; with too little, it will not set firmly.
• To soften gelatin, sprinkle it over a small quantity of cold liquid; leave it without stirring for 5 minutes, or until it softens and swells to a spongy consistency that will dissolve smoothly when heated. The mixture to which dissolved gelatin is added must be warm enough to prevent the gelatin from immediately setting and clumping.
• Dissolve gelatin completely during heating, but never let the mixture boil, or its setting ability will diminish. Stirring is essential to prevent the mixture from lumping or separating.
• When adding fruit to gelatin, keep the pieces small – gelatin will pull away from larger pieces. Raw pineapple, kiwifruit, and papaya contain enzymes that break down gelatin.
• To quick-chill gelatin, set the bowl in a larger bowl of ice water, stirring frequently with a rubber spatula, just until the mixture begins to mound but is not lumpy. (Don't try to speed this process in the freezer; the mixture may crystallize.)
• Once set, molded gelatin desserts have to be loosened from the mold. To do this, lower the base of the mold into a bowl of warm water and leave for 10 seconds (no longer, or the gelatin may melt). Place the serving plate on top of the mold, quickly invert it, and shake to release the dessert.
• Gelatin math: 1 envelope = about 2½ teaspoons (¼ ounce) powdered gelatin; 1 envelope will set up to 2 cups of liquid.

To check that all the gelatin crystals have fully dissolved, lift a little of the gelatin in a spoon – there should be no visible crystals.

MAKING THE MOST OF MERINGUE

A simple mixture of beaten egg whites and sugar, meringue is essential to any dessert repertoire. There are two basic types of meringue: soft and hard. The consistency depends on the proportion of sugar to egg whites. Soft meringue has less sugar and is most often used as a swirled topping for pie. Hard meringue has more sugar; it's piped into shapes such as disks or shells (to cradle fruit or cream fillings) and baked to a crisp, brittle finish.

Properly beaten egg whites form stiff (but not dry) peaks. When the beaters are lifted from the bowl, the peaks hold their shape.

If under- (or over-) beaten, egg whites will be too soft and syrupy and will not hold their shape during the baking process.

For better blending and a light, fluffy texture, it's important to add the sugar to the softly beaten whites gradually – two tablespoons at a time – and to make sure it is completely incorporated. Continue beating on high speed until the mixture forms stiff, glossy peaks. To ensure that the sugar has completely dissolved, follow the foolproof test at right.

Rub a little meringue mixture between your thumb and finger to make sure all the sugar has dissolved; it should feel smooth, not gritty.

Tricks of the trade
• Don't make meringues on a humid or rainy day; they will absorb too much moisture from the air and end up soggy or "weeping" (exuding little beads of moisture).
• If adding ingredients such as ground nuts, be sure to fold them in gently to avoid deflating the egg whites.
• To give meringue extra crispness and a pretty sparkle, sprinkle with granulated sugar before baking.
• Is it done yet? A soft topping is ready when the peaks are brown; hard, crisp meringue will sound hollow when tapped.
• Let hard meringues dry completely in the oven for crisp results. They'll have a gummy texture if removed too soon.
• Meringue pies are best served within a few hours of baking; hard meringues can be stored up to a week in an airtight container.

ALL ABOUT ICE CREAM

STORE-BOUGHT
• A sticky container most likely means the product has thawed, leaked, and been refrozen; choose another carton.
• For easier serving, soften ice cream in the refrigerator about 30 minutes. For speedier results, microwave rock-hard ice cream at medium-low for about 30 seconds.
• The container should be well sealed to prevent the ice cream from absorbing odors from other foods, or forming ice crystals on its surface. It's a good idea to place a sheet of plastic wrap directly against the surface of the ice cream to seal it from air. Reseal the container tightly after opening.
• Low-fat ice creams and frozen yogurt melt faster than full-fat varieties. So prechill serving bowls, or add the scoops at the very last minute – or you may end up with a milky puddle over warm pies or hot, bubbling cobblers.

HOMEMADE
• For the creamiest texture (and a maximum yield), make and chill the ice-cream mixture the day before you plan to freeze it (the chilled mixture will also freeze faster).
• Fill ice-cream machines only two-thirds full – the mixture expands as it freezes and needs room to incorporate air.
• A fresh-frozen mixture thaws quickly, so handle it as little as possible before getting it into the freezer.
• If using an old-fashioned-style churn, add more ice and salt as needed (the faster the freezing process, the smoother the texture of the ice cream).

ICE-CREAM CLINIC (HOW TO AVOID…)
Lumpy mixture Chances are the mixture was too warm when the freezing process began. This increases churning time, which creates a less-smooth texture, as well as the likelihood of flecks of butter forming. A better approach? Make sure the mixture is completely cooled (either slowly in the refrigerator or more quickly in an ice-water bath) before churning.
Grainy texture Pitfalls that prevent smooth results: Sloppy measuring (never add extra water or alcohol to the mixture); churning the mixture too slowly (to help avoid this, add ice and salt when necessary to an old-fashioned-style churn to keep the mixture cold); or simply storing the finished ice cream too long.
Bland taste The most common culprit is a lack of sweetener. (However, if you're making sorbet, it's also possible that you didn't add enough lemon juice, which brightens the flavor.) To avoid this, taste the mixture prior to freezing and sweeten as necessary. You can also enhance the taste by allowing ice cream to "ripen" in the freezer for at least four hours before serving; this helps it fully develop its flavor and texture.
Ice crystals These occur in ice cream that has been stored for too long (a practice that also creates a thick, heavy texture). To prevent ice crystals, add 1 envelope unflavored gelatin for each 6 cups liquid in the ice cream base. Let the gelatin soften in ¼ cup of the liquid, then heat until the gelatin dissolves and stir it into the rest of the liquid.

FRUIT SALADS

When fruit is in its peak season, there's no better way to show it off than with a fabulous fruit salad. Choose fully ripe fruit, then treat it simply: A little sugar brings out its flavor; a touch of an acidic ingredient (such as wine or citrus) brightens it. Serve your favorite after a rich meal or at a special brunch.

1 Prepare coconut: Preheat oven to 350°F. With hammer and screwdriver or large nail, puncture 2 eyes of coconut. Drain coconut liquid; discard. Bake coconut 15 minutes.

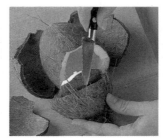

2 Remove coconut from oven and wrap in kitchen towel. With hammer, hit coconut to break into large pieces. With paring knife, pry coconut meat from shell.

3 With paring knife or vegetable peeler, peel outer skin from coconut meat. With large holes of grater or vegetable peeler, shred 1 cup coconut (reserve remainder for use another day).

AMBROSIA

◆◆◆◆◆◆◆◆◆◆◆◆◆

Prep: 40 minutes
Bake: 15 minutes
Makes 10 servings

1 fresh coconut
1 ripe pineapple
6 navel oranges

4 Prepare pineapple: Cut off crown and bottom from pineapple. Stand pineapple upright on cutting board; with large chef's knife, slice off rind and remove eyes. Cut pineapple lengthwise into quarters. Cut out core. Cut each quarter lengthwise in half; slice into chunks. Place in large bowl.

5 Prepare oranges: With paring knife, cut off ends from oranges; stand on cutting board and slice off rind, removing all white pith.

6 Holding oranges over pineapple in bowl, cut sections and add to bowl. Squeeze juice from membranes into bowl; discard membranes. Add coconut to fruit in bowl; toss gently to combine.

EACH SERVING: ABOUT 105 CALORIES, 1g PROTEIN, 19g CARBOHYDRATE, 4g TOTAL FAT (3g SATURATED), 0mg CHOLESTEROL, 25mg SODIUM

FRUIT AND WINE CUP

Prep: 10 to 15 minutes   *Makes* 4 servings

⅓ cup white wine (for strawberries) or red wine (for peaches)

2 tablespoons sugar

1 pint strawberries, hulled and each cut in half, or 2 cups peeled sliced peaches (3 to 4 peaches)

In small bowl, mix white or red wine and sugar until sugar dissolves. Place strawberries or peaches in 4 goblets. Pour wine mixture over fruit.

Each serving: About 60 calories, 0g protein, 12g carbohydrate, 0g total fat, 0mg cholesterol, 0mg sodium

FRUIT WITH MARSALA CREAM AND TORTILLA CRISPS

Prep: 25 minutes   *Cook:* 6 to 8 minutes
Makes 4 servings

⅓ cup sugar

½ teaspoon ground cinnamon

2 flour tortillas (7 inches each)

Vegetable oil

1 pint strawberries

2 medium kiwifruit

2 medium peaches

½ cup heavy or whipping cream

2 tablespoons confectioners' sugar

1 tablespoon sweet Marsala wine

◆ In small shallow bowl, mix sugar and cinnamon. Cut each tortilla into 6 triangles. In 10-inch skillet, heat ¼ inch oil over medium heat; add tortilla triangles, a few at a time, and cook, turning once, until golden. Drain on paper towels. Immediately toss in sugar mixture; set aside. If not using right away, store triangles in tightly covered container.

◆ Hull strawberries and cut each in half. Peel kiwifruit and cut into bite-size chunks. Peel and slice peaches. Place fruit in 4 dessert bowls.

◆ Prepare Marsala cream: In small bowl, with mixer at medium speed, beat heavy cream and confectioners' sugar until soft peaks form; gradually beat in Marsala. Spoon Marsala cream alongside fruit; serve with tortilla crisps.

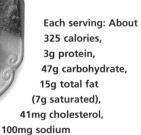

Each serving: About 325 calories, 3g protein, 47g carbohydrate, 15g total fat (7g saturated), 41mg cholesterol, 100mg sodium

BLUEBERRY-MANGO SALAD

Prep: 15 minutes   *Makes* 6 servings

1 tablespoon sugar

1 tablespoon dark rum

1 tablespoon fresh lime juice

2 large mangoes, peeled and diced

1 pint blueberries

In medium bowl, combine sugar, rum, and lime juice. Add mangoes and blueberries; toss to coat.

Each serving: About 95 calories, 1g protein, 24g carbohydrate, 0g total fat, 0mg cholesterol, 5mg sodium

SUMMER FRUIT BASKET

Prep: 1 hour 20 minutes   *Makes* 16 servings

1 oblong watermelon, about 20 pounds, chilled

2 large navel oranges

½ cup sugar

1 medium pineapple

1 pint strawberries

4 large kiwifruit

2 medium nectarines

½ pound red seedless grapes

Green florist wire, herb sprigs, clear thread or nylon fishing line, and tiny nontoxic flowers such as baby's breath and sweetheart roses for handle (optional)

◆ Prepare watermelon basket: With sharp knife, cut lengthwise slice about 2 inches from top of watermelon. Scoop out pulp from both sections; cut into bite-size chunks. Place 10 cups watermelon in large bowl (save remainder for another day). Cut a thin slice of rind from bottom of watermelon shell, if needed, so it will stand level. Cut scalloped edge around rim of watermelon shell.

◆ With vegetable peeler, remove peel from 1 orange. In blender, process peel with sugar until peel is finely chopped. Cut white pith from orange; cut peel and pith from remaining orange. Cut sections from oranges. Cut off crown and bottom from pineapple. Cut off rind; remove eyes. Cut pineapple lengthwise into quarters; cut out core. Cut pineapple into bite-size chunks. Hull strawberries; cut each in half if large. Peel kiwifruit; cut into bite-size chunks. Cut nectarines into wedges.

◆ Place fruit in bowl with watermelon. Add grapes and orange sugar and toss to mix. Fill watermelon shell with fruit; cover with plastic wrap and refrigerate until ready to serve.

◆ Meanwhile, if you like, make a handle for basket: Cut florist wire into three 18-inch lengths. Wrap herb sprigs completely around wire; secure with clear thread. Tuck in flowers. Wrap with damp paper towels and plastic wrap; refrigerate. To serve, loosely twist wires together and insert ends into watermelon basket.

Each serving: About 115 calories, 2g protein, 29g carbohydrate, 1g total fat, 0mg cholesterol, 5mg sodium

POACHED FRUIT AND COMPOTES

Poaching is an easy and classic way to transform firm fresh or dried fruits into a deliciously succulent dessert. The fruit first gently simmers in a sugar syrup; the flavorful poaching liquid is then reduced to create an even richer syrup that will accompany the fruit. In these recipes we've infused the syrup with spices, herbs, and citrus peel to complement different fruits. Try serving any leftover fruit for breakfast.

HONEY-POACHED PEARS AND ORANGES

Prep: 30 minutes plus chilling   *Cook:* 35 to 45 minutes
Makes 8 servings

½ cup honey	8 firm, ripe pears (about
¼ cup sugar	4¼ pounds)
2 tablespoons fresh lemon	4 small navel oranges
juice	1 small lemon, sliced
6 whole cloves	Mint leaves for garnish

1 In 5-quart Dutch oven or saucepot, stir together honey, sugar, lemon juice, cloves, and *4 cups water*. Peel pears. With melon baller, remove cores from bottom of pears; do not remove stems. Immediately place pears in honey mixture, turning to coat. Heat to boiling over high heat.

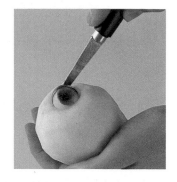

2 Reduce heat to low; cover and simmer 10 to 20 minutes, until pears are tender when pierced with knife. With slotted spoon, transfer pears to large bowl. Meanwhile, with paring knife, cut peel and white pith from oranges; discard.

3 To poaching liquid, add oranges; heat to boiling over high heat. Reduce heat to medium-low; simmer, uncovered, 5 minutes, turning occasionally.

4 With slotted spoon, add oranges to bowl with pears. Heat poaching liquid to boiling over medium-high heat; cook 10 minutes, uncovered, to reduce slightly. Pour hot syrup over fruit. Cool slightly. Cover and refrigerate, turning fruit occasionally, at least 3 hours, until well chilled. To serve, stir in lemon slices. Garnish with mint sprigs.

HONEY

One of the first sweeteners known to man, honey is made by bees from flower nectar. It is available in three forms: comb honey, complete with the wax honeycomb, which may also be eaten; cream or spun honey, which is finely crystallized; and liquid honey, which is free of crystals. The flavor of honey varies according to the flower it comes from; in general, the darker the color, the stronger the flavor. Kept covered in a cool, dark place, honey will last indefinitely. If it crystallizes, it can be liquefied by standing the opened jar in a bowl of hot water. When measuring honey for cooking, oil the cup or spoon first so the honey slips out easily.

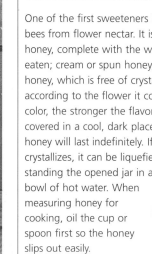

EACH SERVING: ABOUT 260 CALORIES, 2g PROTEIN, 67g CARBOHYDRATE, 1g TOTAL FAT (0g SATURATED), 0mg CHOLESTEROL, 0mg SODIUM

AUTUMN FRUIT COMPOTE

Prep: 20 minutes plus chilling
Cook: 35 to 40 minutes
Makes 8 servings

1 medium orange
1 medium lemon
4 medium Golden Delicious or Jonagold
  apples, peeled, cored, and each cut
  into 16 wedges
1 package (8 ounces) mixed dried fruit
  (with pitted prunes)
½ (8-ounce) package dried Calimyrna figs
¼ cup dried tart cherries or cranberries
½ cup sugar
1 cinnamon stick (3 inches)

◆ With vegetable peeler, remove peel from orange and lemon in 1-inch-wide strips. Squeeze 2 tablespoons juice from lemon.

◆ In 4-quart saucepan, heat orange and lemon peels, lemon juice, apples, mixed dried fruit, figs, dried cherries, sugar, cinnamon stick, and *3 cups water* to boiling over high heat, stirring to dissolve sugar. Reduce heat to low; cover and simmer 15 to 20 minutes, until apples are tender. Cool slightly.

◆ Pour fruit mixture into bowl; cover and refrigerate at least 4 hours to blend flavors. Serve chilled or at room temperature.

Each serving: About 225 calories,
1g protein, 55g carbohydrate, 0g total fat,
0mg cholesterol, 40mg sodium

HERB-POACHED PEACHES

Prep: 20 minutes plus chilling
Cook: 35 to 40 minutes
Makes 8 servings

4 large lemons
½ cup sugar
1 bay leaf
3 thyme sprigs
8 firm, ripe peaches (about 3 pounds)
2 tablespoons peach jam
1 small lemon, thinly sliced,
  for garnish

◆ Grate peel from 1 large lemon. Squeeze ½ cup juice from large lemons.

◆ In 5-quart Dutch oven or saucepot, stir together lemon peel, lemon juice, sugar, bay leaf, 2 thyme sprigs, and *4½ cups water*.

◆ Peel peaches. As each peach is peeled, immediately place in lemon-juice mixture, turning to coat completely to help prevent darkening.

◆ Heat peach mixture to boiling over high heat, stirring to dissolve sugar. Reduce heat to low; cover and simmer 5 to 10 minutes, until peaches are tender. With slotted spoon, transfer peaches to large bowl.

◆ Heat poaching liquid to boiling over high heat; cook, uncovered, about 15 minutes, until liquid is reduced to about 1½ cups. Stir in peach jam until dissolved. Pour hot syrup over peaches in bowl. Cool slightly.

◆ Cover and refrigerate, turning peaches occasionally, at least 4 hours, until well chilled.

◆ To serve, discard bay leaf. Serve peaches with syrup; garnish with lemon slices and remaining thyme sprig.

Each serving: About 140 calories,
1g protein, 38g carbohydrate, 0g total fat,
0mg cholesterol, 0mg sodium

LEMON-ANISE POACHED PEARS

Prep: 20 minutes plus chilling
Cook: 40 to 50 minutes
Makes 8 servings

2 medium lemons
8 firm, ripe pears (about 4¼ pounds)
1 cup sugar
2 tablespoons whole star anise or
  2 cinnamon sticks (3 inches each)
1 small navel orange, thinly sliced, for
  garnish

◆ Squeeze juice from 1 lemon into 8-quart Dutch oven. Thinly slice remaining lemon. Peel pears. With melon baller, remove cores from bottom of pears; do not remove stems.

◆ Add pears, lemon slices, sugar, star anise, and *6 cups water* to Dutch oven. Heat to boiling over high heat, stirring to dissolve sugar. Reduce heat to low; cover and simmer 10 to 20 minutes, until pears are tender. With slotted spoon, transfer pears to large bowl.

◆ Heat poaching liquid to boiling over high heat; cook, uncovered, 15 minutes, or until reduced to about 3 cups. Pour hot syrup over pears. Cool slightly. Cover; refrigerate, turning occasionally, at least 4 hours, until pears are well chilled. Serve pears with syrup; garnish with orange slices.

Each serving: About 250 calories,
1g protein, 65g carbohydrate, 1g total fat
(0g saturated), 0mg cholesterol,
0mg sodium

STAR ANISE

A star-shaped seed pod from a type of magnolia shrub, star anise has a mild licorice flavor and is a common ingredient in Chinese cooking. It is generally used whole for its attractive appearance. You will find star anise in the spice section of some supermarkets or in Asian food markets.

FRUIT SHORTCAKES

Shortcakes may look fancy, but they're simply biscuits or cakes dressed up with sweet, juicy fruit and thick whipped cream. We have a cake-based summer classic, a strawberry shortcake; a peach and blueberry version; and a giant shortcake showcasing mixed berries. Be sure to serve shortcakes right after they're assembled.

1 In 3-quart saucepan, mix lemon juice and corn-starch until smooth. Stir in blueberries and ⅔ cup sugar; heat to boiling over medium-high heat. Reduce heat to medium; cook 1 minute. Stir in peaches; set aside.

2 Preheat oven to 425°F. In bowl, mix flour, baking powder, salt, and ⅓ cup sugar. With pastry blender or two knives used scissor-fashion, cut in 9 tablespoons margarine until mixture resembles coarse crumbs.

3 Stir in milk just until mixture forms a soft dough that leaves side of bowl. On lightly floured surface, knead dough 6 to 8 times, just until smooth. With lightly floured hands, pat dough ¾ inch thick.

BLUEBERRY-PEACH SHORTCAKES

◆◆◆◆◆◆◆◆◆◆◆◆◆

Prep: 30 minutes
Bake: 16 to 22 minutes
Makes 8 servings

2 tablespoons fresh lemon juice
1 tablespoon cornstarch
1½ pints blueberries (about 3½ cups)
1 cup plus 3 tablespoons sugar
2 pounds peaches (about 6 medium), peeled (see right) and each cut into 8 wedges
3 cups all-purpose flour
4½ teaspoons baking powder
¾ teaspoon salt
10 tablespoons cold margarine or butter
1 cup plus 2 tablespoons milk
1 cup heavy or whipping cream

4 With floured 3-inch round biscuit cutter, cut out shortcakes. With pancake turner, place shortcakes 1 inch apart on ungreased large cookie sheet.

5 Press trimmings together; cut to make 8 shortcakes in all. Melt remaining 1 tablespoon margarine; brush over shortcakes. Sprinkle with 1 tablespoon sugar. Bake 16 to 22 minutes, until golden. In small bowl, with mixer at medium speed, beat cream with remaining 2 tablespoons sugar to soft peaks. With fork, split warm shortcakes in half. Spoon some fruit into each; top with cream, then more fruit.

PEELING PEACHES
◆◆◆◆◆◆◆◆◆◆◆◆◆

Plunge peaches into pan of boiling water for 30 seconds. With slotted spoon, transfer to large bowl filled with ice water to cover; cool. With fingers or small paring knife, slip off skin. If desired, rub peeled peaches with lemon juice to prevent discoloration.

EACH SERVING: ABOUT 610 CALORIES, 8g PROTEIN, 89g CARBOHYDRATE, 27g TOTAL FAT (10 g SATURATED), 45mg CHOLESTEROL, 670mg SODIUM

BERRIES AND CREAM SHORTCAKE

Prep: 25 minutes plus cooling   *Bake:* 25 to 30 minutes
Makes 10 servings

½ cup margarine or butter, softened
1 cup plus 1 tablespoon sugar
1½ cups cake flour (not self-rising)
½ cup milk
1½ teaspoons baking powder
1 teaspoon vanilla extract
¼ teaspoon salt

2 large eggs
1 pint blueberries
½ pint strawberries, hulled and each cut in half
½ pint raspberries
½ pint blackberries
¼ cup strawberry jam
1 cup heavy or whipping cream

◆ Preheat oven to 350°F. Grease and flour two 8-inch round cake pans.

◆ In large bowl, with mixer at low speed, beat margarine and 1 cup sugar just until blended. Increase speed to high; beat about 5 minutes, until light and creamy. Reduce speed to low; add flour, milk, baking powder, vanilla, salt, and eggs; beat until well mixed, frequently scraping bowl with rubber spatula. Increase speed to high; beat 2 minutes longer, occasionally scraping bowl.

◆ Spoon batter into pans. Bake 25 to 30 minutes, until toothpick inserted in centers of cakes comes out clean. Cool cake layers in pans on wire racks 10 minutes. Remove from pans; cool completely on racks. Meanwhile, in large bowl, gently toss all berries with strawberry jam.

◆ In small bowl, with mixer at medium speed, beat cream with remaining 1 tablespoon sugar until stiff peaks form.

◆ Place 1 cake layer on plate. Spread with half of whipped cream; top with half of fruit mixture. Place second cake layer on fruit mixture; top with remaining cream and fruit.

Each serving: About 385 calories, 4g protein, 50g carbohydrate, 20g total fat (8g saturated), 77mg cholesterol, 265mg sodium

CLASSIC STRAWBERRY SHORTCAKE

Prep: 30 minutes plus cooling   *Bake:* 30 to 35 minutes
Makes 12 servings

1 cup milk
4 tablespoons margarine or butter
4 large eggs
1½ cups plus ⅓ cup granulated sugar
1½ teaspoons vanilla extract
1¾ cups all-purpose flour

1 tablespoon baking powder
½ teaspoon salt
3 pints strawberries
2 cups heavy or whipping cream
¼ cup confectioners' sugar
Mint sprigs for garnish

◆ Preheat oven to 350°F. Grease 13" by 9" metal baking pan. In 1-quart saucepan, heat milk and margarine over medium heat until margarine melts. Set aside.

◆ In large bowl, with mixer at high speed, beat eggs, 1½ cups granulated sugar, and 1 teaspoon vanilla 2 to 3 minutes, until very thick and lemon-colored. Reduce speed to low. Add flour, baking powder, and salt; beat 1 minute, frequently scraping bowl with rubber spatula. Add hot milk mixture; beat 1 minute longer, or until batter is smooth.

◆ Pour batter into pan. Bake 30 to 35 minutes, until cake is golden and top springs back when lightly pressed. Cool cake completely in pan on wire rack.

◆ Hull and thinly slice strawberries. In large bowl, mix sliced strawberries with remaining ⅓ cup granulated sugar.

◆ Cut cake lengthwise into 3 strips, then cut each strip crosswise into 4 pieces. In small bowl, with mixer at medium speed, beat cream, confectioners' sugar, and remaining ½ teaspoon vanilla until soft peaks form. To serve, place each piece of cake on a dessert plate; top with some sliced strawberries with their syrup, then with some whipped cream. Garnish with mint.

Each serving: About 420 calories, 6g protein, 53g carbohydrate, 21g total fat (11g saturated), 128mg cholesterol, 300mg sodium

WHAT'S IN A NAME?

Probably originating in New England, strawberry shortcake has been an all-American favorite since the 1850s. The most traditional version is made with fluffy, warm baking-powder biscuits, split and buttered, then filled with fruit. The permutations are endless, however. The biscuit may be individual or large, sweeter or richer, buttered or not.… It might not be a biscuit at all, but sponge or pound cake, piecrust, or even sweet, rich bread. Peaches and other berries also make a luscious filling, with ice cream or whipped cream to top it off.

CRISPS AND COBBLERS

These old-fashioned desserts are pure comfort food. What's more, neither crisps nor cobblers require any special ingredients; just choose the best and ripest fruit you can find. It takes mere minutes to make the fruit filling and to mix up the biscuit or crumb topping – then just pop the pan in the oven and dessert is done. Ice cream is perfect on the side.

RHUBARB-STRAWBERRY COBBLER WITH SPICE BISCUITS

◆◆◆◆◆◆◆◆◆◆◆◆◆◆

Prep: 20 minutes plus cooling
Bake: 20 minutes
Makes 8 servings

1¼ **pounds rhubarb, cut into 1-inch chunks (4 cups)**
¾ **cup plus 1 teaspoon sugar**
1 **tablespoon cornstarch**
1 **pint strawberries, hulled and each cut into quarters**
1½ **cups all-purpose flour**
1½ **teaspoons baking powder**
½ **teaspoon baking soda**
¼ **teaspoon salt**
¼ **teaspoon ground cinnamon**
⅛ **teaspoon ground nutmeg**
4 **tablespoons margarine or butter**
¾ **cup plus 1 tablespoon heavy or whipping cream**

1 In 3-quart saucepan, heat rhubarb and ½ cup sugar to boiling over high heat, stirring constantly. Reduce heat to medium-low; cook about 8 minutes, until rhubarb is tender.

2 In cup, mix cornstarch and *¼ cup water.* Stir cornstarch mixture and strawberries into cooked rhubarb; cook 2 minutes longer, or until slightly thickened. Keep warm.

3 Preheat oven to 400°F. Prepare biscuits: In large bowl, mix flour, next 5 ingredients, and ¼ cup sugar. With pastry blender or two knives used scissor-fashion, cut in margarine until mixture resembles coarse crumbs. Add ¾ cup cream; stir just until mixture forms a soft dough that leaves side of bowl. Turn onto lightly floured surface.

4 Knead dough 6 to 8 times, just until smooth. With floured rolling pin, roll dough ½ inch thick. With 3-inch star-shaped cookie cutter, cut out biscuits.

5 Reroll trimmings; cut to make 8 biscuits in all. Pour hot rhubarb mixture into shallow 2-quart casserole or 11" by 7" glass baking dish. Place biscuits on top.

6 Brush biscuits with remaining 1 tablespoon cream; sprinkle with remaining 1 teaspoon sugar. Place sheet of foil under baking dish; crimp edges to form rim to catch any drips during baking. Bake 20 minutes, or until biscuits are golden brown and rhubarb mixture is bubbly. Cool slightly on wire rack, about 15 minutes, to serve warm.

EACH SERVING: ABOUT 315 CALORIES, 4g PROTEIN, 43g CARBOHYDRATE, 15g TOTAL FAT (7g SATURATED), 33mg CHOLESTEROL, 315mg SODIUM

COUNTRY APPLE CRISP

Prep: 30 minutes plus cooling   Bake: 30 to 35 minutes
Makes 8 servings

1 large orange
2½ pounds Golden Delicious
   or Cortland apples (about
   7 medium), peeled, cored,
   and cut into 1-inch slices
½ cup dried cherries or raisins
1 teaspoon ground cinnamon
½ teaspoon salt
¼ teaspoon ground nutmeg

⅓ cup plus ¼ cup packed light
   brown sugar
2 tablespoons plus ⅓ cup all-
   purpose flour
½ cup quick-cooking or old-
   fashioned oats, uncooked
3 tablespoons margarine or
   butter

◆ Preheat oven to 425°F. Grate ½ teaspoon peel and squeeze
⅓ cup juice from orange. In shallow 2-quart glass or ceramic
baking dish, toss orange peel, orange juice, apples, next
4 ingredients, ⅓ cup brown sugar, and 2 tablespoons flour.

◆ Prepare topping: In small bowl, mix oats and remaining
⅓ cup flour and ¼ cup brown sugar. With pastry blender or
two knives used scissor-fashion, cut in margarine until mixture
resembles coarse crumbs. Sprinkle over apple mixture.

◆ Bake 30 to 35 minutes, until apples are tender and
topping is lightly browned, covering with foil if necessary to
prevent overbrowning. Cool slightly on wire rack to serve
warm. Or, cool completely to serve later; reheat if desired.

**Each serving: About 260 calories, 2g protein, 53g carbohydrate,
5g total fat (1g saturated), 0mg cholesterol, 190mg sodium**

NECTARINE AND CHERRY CRISP
WITH OATMEAL TOPPING

Prep: 30 minutes plus cooling   Bake: 1 hour to 1 hour 15 minutes
Makes 12 servings

½ cup sugar
3 tablespoons cornstarch
3 pounds ripe nectarines
   (about 10 medium), each
   cut into 6 wedges
1½ pounds dark sweet
   cherries, pitted
2 tablespoons fresh lemon
   juice
8 tablespoons margarine or
   butter

⅔ cup packed light brown
   sugar
1 large egg
2 teaspoons vanilla extract
1½ cups old-fashioned oats,
   uncooked
¾ cup all-purpose flour
¼ teaspoon salt
¼ teaspoon baking soda

◆ Preheat oven to 375°F. In large bowl, with wire whisk or
fork, mix sugar and cornstarch. Add nectarines, cherries,
and lemon juice and toss until fruit is evenly coated. Spoon
fruit mixture into 13" by 9" glass baking dish; dot with
2 tablespoons margarine. Cover with foil; bake 40 to 50
minutes, until fruit mixture is gently bubbling.

◆ Meanwhile, prepare oatmeal topping: In large bowl, with
mixer at medium-high speed, beat brown sugar and
remaining 6 tablespoons margarine, softened, until smooth.
Add egg and vanilla; beat until light and creamy. With
wooden spoon, stir in oats and remaining ingredients until
mixed. Cover and refrigerate until ready to use.

◆ Drop topping by scant ¼ cups over baked fruit. Bake
nectarine crisp, uncovered, 20 to 25 minutes longer, until
topping is browned. Cool slightly on wire rack to serve
warm. Or, cool completely to serve later; reheat if desired.

**Each serving: About 325 calories, 5g protein, 58g carbohydrate,
10g total fat (2g saturated), 18mg cholesterol, 170mg sodium**

LIGHT PLUM COBBLER

Prep: 20 minutes plus cooling   Bake: 50 to 60 minutes
Makes 10 servings

2½ pounds ripe red or purple
   plums (about 10 medium),
   each cut into 4 wedges
2 tablespoons all-purpose
   flour

½ cup sugar
1¾ cups reduced-fat all-
   purpose baking mix
¼ cup yellow cornmeal

◆ Preheat oven to 400°F. In large bowl, toss plums with
flour and sugar. Spoon plum mixture into shallow 2-quart
ceramic or glass baking dish. Cover loosely with foil. Bake
30 to 35 minutes, until plums are very tender.

◆ In medium bowl, mix baking mix and cornmeal with
¾ cup water until just combined. Drop 10 heaping spoonfuls
of batter randomly over baked plums. Bake cobbler,
uncovered, 20 to 25 minutes longer, until biscuits are
browned and plum mixture is bubbling. Cool slightly on
wire rack to serve warm. Or, cool completely to serve later;
reheat if desired.

**Each serving: About 200 calories, 3g protein, 43g carbohydrate,
2g total fat (0g saturated), 0mg cholesterol, 240mg sodium**

WHAT'S IN A NAME?
◆◆◆◆◆◆◆◆◆◆◆◆◆◆◆◆◆◆◆◆◆◆◆◆◆◆

It's easy to be confused by the variety of names for
cooked fruit desserts. A *cobbler* is fruit baked with a
biscuit crust, while a *crisp* is baked with a rich crumb
topping. To make a *slump* or *grunt*, spoonfuls of dough
are steamed atop a hot fruit mixture in a saucepot. A
pandowdy is made with fruit topped with pastry; before
the crust is baked completely, it's cut up and pressed
back into the fruit to absorb the juices. *Brown Betty* is a
dessert of fruit (especially apples) layered with buttered
bread crumbs and spices and baked until tender.

BAKED FRUIT DESSERTS

Baking heightens the flavor of many fruits and gives them a pleasing mellow texture. Here we've wrapped apples in pastry to create tempting dumplings; given pears an Italian nuance with sweet Marsala and lemon; and enhanced ripe plums with a crumbly almond topping. These desserts are best served warm, with half-and-half or light cream, or ice cream, if you like.

OLD-FASHIONED APPLE DUMPLINGS

◆◆◆◆◆◆◆◆◆◆◆◆◆◆◆◆◆◆◆◆◆◆◆◆◆◆◆◆

Prep: 40 minutes Bake: 35 to 40 minutes
Makes 6 servings

2½ cups all-purpose flour	1½ teaspoons ground
1 teaspoon salt	cinnamon
8 tablespoons light brown	6 small Golden Delicious
sugar	apples (6 ounces each)
1 cup shortening	1 large egg, beaten
½ cup diced mixed dried fruit	6 whole cloves
2 tablespoons margarine or	
butter	

1 In large bowl, mix flour, salt, and 2 tablespoons brown sugar. With pastry blender or two knives used scissor-fashion, cut in shortening until mixture resembles coarse crumbs. Stir in *5 to 6 tablespoons cold water* until dough holds together; set aside. In small bowl, mix dried fruit, margarine, 4 tablespoons brown sugar, and 1 teaspoon cinnamon.

2 Peel apples. With melon baller, remove cores but do not go all the way through to bottom. Press dried-fruit mixture into cavities. Preheat oven to 400°F. Grease 15½" by 10½" jelly-roll pan.

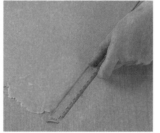

3 Reserve ⅓ cup dough. On floured surface, with floured rolling pin, roll out remaining dough, using a ruler to help push and shape dough into 21" by 14" rectangle. Cut dough into six 7-inch squares.

4 On waxed paper, mix remaining 2 tablespoons brown sugar and ½ teaspoon cinnamon. Roll an apple in sugar mixture. Center apple on a dough square; brush edges of dough with some beaten egg.

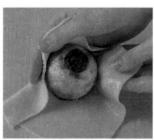

5 Bring dough up over top of apple. Press to shape; seal edges. Place dumpling in jelly-roll pan. Repeat with remaining apples, sugar mixture, and dough squares, and more beaten egg, to make 6 dumplings in all.

6 Roll reserved dough ¼ inch thick. Using knife, cut out as many leaves as possible (see page 489); reroll scraps and cut out more leaves. Score leaves with back of knife to make veins. Brush dumplings with egg. Attach leaves; brush with egg. Press in cloves for stems. Bake dumplings 35 to 40 minutes, until pastry is golden and apples are tender when pierced with knife.

EACH SERVING: ABOUT 730 CALORIES, 7g PROTEIN, 90g CARBOHYDRATE, 40g TOTAL FAT (10g SATURATED), 36mg CHOLESTEROL, 435mg SODIUM

ROASTED ALMOND-CRUST PLUMS

Prep: 15 minutes   *Bake:* 25 to 35 minutes
Makes 6 servings

1½ pounds ripe plums, each cut in half
⅓ cup sliced natural almonds
⅓ cup packed brown sugar
¼ cup all-purpose flour
3 tablespoons margarine or butter, softened
Vanilla ice cream (optional)

Preheat oven to 425°F. Arrange plums, cut-side up, in one layer in shallow baking dish. In medium bowl, with fingertips, mix almonds and next 3 ingredients until mixture comes together. Sprinkle over plums. Bake 25 to 35 minutes, until plums are tender. Serve hot, with ice cream, if you like.

Each serving: About 205 calories, 3g protein, 31g carbohydrate, 9g total fat (1g saturated), 0mg cholesterol, 70mg sodium

CLAFOUTI

Prep: 20 minutes   *Bake:* 40 to 45 minutes
Makes 12 servings

1 pound dark sweet cherries, pitted
⅔ cup all-purpose flour
⅓ cup granulated sugar
2 tablespoons amaretto (almond-flavor liqueur)
4 large eggs
2 cups half-and-half or light cream
Confectioners' sugar for garnish

◆ Preheat oven to 350°F. Grease 10" by 1½" round ceramic baking dish. Place cherries in dish. In blender at low speed, blend flour, granulated sugar, amaretto, eggs, and 1 cup half-and-half 30 seconds. With motor running, gradually add remaining 1 cup half-and-half; blend 30 seconds longer.

◆ Pour egg mixture over cherries in baking dish. Bake 40 to 45 minutes, until custard is set and knife inserted 1 inch from edge comes out clean (center will still jiggle). Serve hot, sprinkled with confectioners' sugar.

Each serving: About 160 calories, 4g protein, 20g carbohydrate, 7g total fat (3g saturated), 86mg cholesterol, 40mg sodium

---

CHERRY PITTER

This pliers-like tool made from aluminum or stainless steel makes short work of pitting cherries and gives a cleaner result than using a paring knife. It can also be used for pitting olives.

CARIBBEAN BAKED BANANAS

Prep: 10 minutes   *Bake:* 15 minutes
Makes 4 servings

2 tablespoons dark rum
½ teaspoon grated lime peel
4 large ripe bananas, cut into ½-inch slices
2 tablespoons brown sugar
2 tablespoons margarine or butter, melted
½ cup flaked coconut
Vanilla ice cream (optional)

◆ Preheat oven to 425°F. In 9-inch pie plate or shallow baking dish, combine rum and lime peel. Add bananas, tossing to coat.

◆ In small bowl, mix brown sugar and melted margarine until smooth. Stir in coconut. Spoon coconut mixture evenly over bananas. Bake 15 minutes, or until coconut is golden brown. Serve hot, with ice cream, if you like.

Each serving: About 280 calories, 2g protein, 46g carbohydrate, 10g total fat (5g saturated), 0mg cholesterol, 100mg sodium

BAKED PEARS WITH MARSALA

Prep: 25 minutes plus cooling   *Bake:* 40 to 50 minutes
Makes 8 servings

1 medium lemon
8 firm Bosc pears
2 teaspoons plus ⅓ cup sugar
½ cup sweet Marsala wine
2 tablespoons margarine or butter, melted

◆ Preheat oven to 450°F. With vegetable peeler or small knife, remove peel from lemon in 2½" by ½" strips; squeeze juice from lemon.

◆ With melon baller or small knife, remove cores from bottom of unpeeled pears but do not remove stems. With pastry brush, brush insides of pears with lemon juice, then sprinkle insides with a total of 2 teaspoons sugar.

◆ In shallow 1½- to 2-quart ceramic or glass baking dish, mix lemon-peel strips, Marsala, and ⅓ *cup water*. Place remaining ⅓ cup sugar on sheet of waxed paper.

◆ With pastry brush, brush pears with melted margarine, then roll in sugar to coat. Place pears, cored-ends down, in baking dish. Sprinkle any sugar remaining on waxed paper around pears in baking dish.

◆ Bake pears, basting occasionally with syrup in dish, 40 to 50 minutes, until fork-tender. Cool slightly to serve warm. Or, cool pears completely; cover and refrigerate up to 1 day and reheat to serve warm.

Each serving: About 170 calories, 1g protein, 34g carbohydrate, 3g total fat (2g saturated), 8mg cholesterol, 30mg sodium

RICE PUDDINGS

These creamy, mild-flavored puddings are made of the simplest ingredients – basically rice, milk, and sugar. Short-grain rice such as Italian Arborio gives an especially creamy texture, but regular long-grain rice also makes a delicious pudding. Avoid using parboiled rice, which will never become as soft. Each of these puddings is as comforting served warm as it is cold.

VANILLA RICE PUDDING WITH DRIED CHERRIES

◆◆◆◆◆◆◆◆◆◆◆◆

Prep: 15 minutes plus chilling
Cook: 1 hour 30 minutes
Makes 12 servings

½ **vanilla bean or 1 tablespoon vanilla extract**

6 **cups milk**

¾ **cup sugar**

¾ **cup Arborio rice (Italian short-grain rice) or regular long-grain rice**

½ **cup dried cherries or raisins**

2 **tablespoons dark rum**

¼ **teaspoon salt**

½ **cup heavy or whipping cream**

1 With knife, cut vanilla bean lengthwise in half. Scrape out and reserve seeds from inside of both halves. Place bean halves and seeds in 4-quart saucepan. (If using vanilla extract, stir in with rum in Step 3.)

2 Add milk and sugar to saucepan; heat to boiling over medium-high heat, stirring occasionally. Stir in rice; heat to boiling. Reduce heat to low.

3 Cover; simmer 1¼ hours, stirring occasionally, until very creamy and slightly thickened. Discard vanilla-bean halves. Spoon into large bowl; stir in cherries, rum, and salt.

VANILLA BEANS

◆◆◆◆◆◆◆◆◆◆◆◆◆◆◆◆◆

The dried pod of an orchid native to Central America, vanilla adds its familiar but intriguing aroma to a vast range of sweet dishes. The bean is usually split before use and the seeds scraped out; both bean and seeds are added to the dish. Pure vanilla extract provides flavor in a more convenient form. Vanillin (unless labeled "natural"), imitation vanilla, and "vanilla flavor" are based on synthetic vanillin, which is strong in flavor and may have a harsh aftertaste. You can make vanilla sugar by placing a split bean in a storage jar with 1 to 2 cups of sugar; leave 24 hours before using. Top up the sugar each time you use some; the bean will last up to 1 year.

4 Cool slightly; cover and refrigerate at least 6 hours. Up to 2 hours before serving, whip cream until stiff peaks form. Fold whipped cream, half at a time, into rice pudding.

EACH SERVING: ABOUT 230 CALORIES, 5g PROTEIN, 33g CARBOHYDRATE, 8g TOTAL FAT (5g SATURATED), 30mg CHOLESTEROL, 110mg SODIUM

LEFTOVER-RICE PUDDING

Prep: 5 minutes   *Cook:* 25 minutes

Makes 4 servings

2 cups milk
1 cup cooked rice
1 cinnamon stick (3 inches) or
  ⅛ teaspoon ground
  cinnamon

2 tablespoons sugar
¼ cup raisins or dried cherries
  (optional)

In 3-quart saucepan, heat milk, rice, cinnamon stick, and sugar to boiling over high heat. Reduce heat to medium-low; boil gently 20 minutes, stirring occasionally. Stir in raisins, if using, during last 5 minutes of cooking. Remove from heat. Discard cinnamon stick. Serve warm, or cover and refrigerate to serve cold later.

Each serving: About 150 calories, 5g protein, 23g carbohydrate, 4g total fat (3g saturated), 17mg cholesterol, 60mg sodium

COCONUT RICE PUDDING

Prep: 5 minutes plus standing   *Cook:* 35 minutes

Makes 6 servings

⅔ cup regular long-grain rice
½ teaspoon salt
1 can (15 ounces)
  unsweetened coconut milk

⅓ cup sugar
Toasted flaked coconut
  (optional)

In 3-quart saucepan, heat rice, salt, and *2 cups water* to boiling over medium-high heat. Reduce heat to low; cover and simmer 15 minutes. Stir in coconut milk and sugar. Cook, uncovered, 10 minutes longer, stirring occasionally. Remove from heat. Let stand 20 minutes. Serve warm, or cover and refrigerate to serve cold later. Just before serving, sprinkle with toasted coconut, if you like.

Each serving: About 280 calories, 3g protein, 32g carbohydrate, 17g total fat (15g saturated), 0mg cholesterol, 190mg sodium

---

COCONUT MILK

◆◆◆◆◆◆◆◆◆◆◆◆◆◆◆◆◆◆◆◆◆◆◆

Canned unsweetened coconut milk (not to be confused with the thin, milky liquid that drains from a fresh coconut when you crack the shell) is a blend of coconut meat and water processed to a paste and strained. A basic ingredient in Thai and other Asian cuisines, it adds a rich and exotic flavor to soups, sauces, meat and seafood curries, and desserts. Cream of coconut, a richer mixture containing sugar and stabilizers, is used in drinks and desserts. Once opened, canned coconut milk can be refrigerated in an airtight container for up to 1 week or frozen for 6 months.

CREAMY CARDAMOM RICE PUDDING

Prep: 5 minutes   *Cook:* 1 hour 15 minutes

Makes 6 servings

4 cups milk
⅓ cup regular long-grain rice
⅓ cup sugar
5 cardamom pods

½ teaspoon salt
2 large egg yolks
⅓ cup heavy or whipping
  cream

◆ In 5-quart Dutch oven, heat milk, rice, sugar, cardamom, and salt to boiling over medium-high heat, stirring occasionally. Reduce heat to low; cover and simmer 1 hour, stirring occasionally.

◆ In medium bowl, whisk egg yolks with cream. Gradually whisk in 1 cup hot rice pudding. Return mixture to Dutch oven; cook over low heat, stirring constantly, 3 minutes, or until mixture just begins to bubble. Pour into serving bowl. Serve warm, or cover and refrigerate to serve cold later.

Each serving: About 245 calories, 7g protein, 28g carbohydrate, 12g total fat (7g saturated), 111mg cholesterol, 265mg sodium

BAKED CUSTARD RICE PUDDING

Prep: 20 minutes plus cooling   *Bake:* 1 hour 15 minutes

Makes 8 servings

½ cup regular long-grain rice
4 strips (3" by 1" each)
  orange peel
½ teaspoon salt

3 large eggs
½ cup sugar
3 cups milk
1 teaspoon vanilla extract

◆ Preheat oven to 350°F. In 2-quart saucepan, heat rice, orange peel, salt, and *2 cups water* to boiling over medium-high heat. Reduce heat to low; cover and simmer 15 minutes. Remove and discard orange peel.

◆ In large bowl, whisk eggs and sugar until well blended. Whisk in milk and vanilla. Stir in hot rice. Pour mixture into shallow 1½-quart glass baking dish, stirring to distribute rice. Place baking dish in larger roasting pan; carefully pour *boiling water* into roasting pan to come halfway up sides of baking dish.

◆ Bake 1¼ hours, or until knife inserted halfway between center and edge of pudding comes out clean. Remove baking dish from roasting pan; cool on wire rack 30 minutes. Serve pudding warm, or cover and refrigerate to serve cold later.

Each serving: About 180 calories, 6g protein, 27g carbohydrate, 5g total fat (3g saturated), 92mg cholesterol, 205mg sodium

BAKED PUDDINGS

Baked puddings owe much of their charm to their simplicity. We've included a British toffee pudding with a sticky brown-sugar topping; a delicate orange pudding that forms its own sauce; and a rich, rich chocolate pudding. For maximum pleasure, serve warm.

STICKY TOFFEE PUDDING

◆◆◆◆◆◆◆◆◆◆◆◆◆

Prep: 20 minutes plus standing and cooling
Bake: 30 minutes
Makes 12 servings

1 cup chopped pitted dates
1 teaspoon baking soda
10 tablespoons margarine or
   butter, softened
1 cup granulated sugar
1 large egg
1 teaspoon vanilla extract
2 cups all-purpose flour
1 teaspoon baking powder
1 cup packed brown sugar
¼ cup heavy or whipping cream
Whipped cream (optional)

1 Preheat oven to 350°F. Grease a 13" by 9" broiler-safe baking pan. In medium bowl, combine dates, baking soda, and *1½ cups boiling water*; let stand 15 minutes.

2 In large bowl, with mixer at medium speed, beat 6 tablespoons margarine until creamy. Beat in granulated sugar. Add egg and vanilla; beat until blended.

3 At low speed, add flour and baking powder. Add date mixture and beat until evenly combined (batter will be thin). Pour batter into pan. Bake 30 minutes, or until golden and toothpick inserted in center comes out clean. Meanwhile, in 2-quart saucepan, heat brown sugar, cream, and remaining 4 tablespoons margarine to boiling over medium heat; boil 1 minute. Set aside. Turn oven control to broil.

WHAT'S IN A NAME?
◆◆◆◆◆◆◆◆◆◆◆◆◆◆◆◆◆◆◆◆◆

The word "pudding" often describes a creamy, soft stovetop dessert made with milk, sugar, and eggs, and thickened with a starch, such as flour, rice, or cornstarch. It also applies to a wide range of sweet dishes, including bread pudding and steamed or baked cakelike desserts such as plum pudding or the Sticky Toffee Pudding on this page. In England, desserts in general may be referred to as "pudding," although two of the country's best-known puddings are savory: steak and kidney pudding (a pastry crust filled with meat) and Yorkshire Pudding (recipe on page 184), the traditional accompaniment to roast beef.

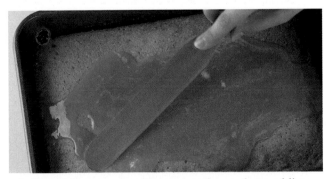

4 Spread brown-sugar mixture evenly over hot pudding. Broil at closest position to heat source about 30 seconds, or until bubbly. Cool in pan on wire rack 15 minutes. Serve warm, with whipped cream, if you like.

EACH SERVING: ABOUT 355 CALORIES, 3g PROTEIN, 61g CARBOHYDRATE, 12g TOTAL FAT (3g SATURATED), 25mg CHOLESTEROL, 270mg SODIUM

CHOCOLATE FUDGE PUDDING

Prep: 25 minutes   Bake: 40 minutes
Makes 8 servings

1 cup milk
4 large eggs, separated
½ cup plus 2 tablespoons
  granulated sugar
⅓ cup all-purpose flour
3 squares (3 ounces)
  unsweetened chocolate,
  melted

1 teaspoon vanilla
  extract
¼ teaspoon salt
Confectioners' sugar
Vanilla ice cream or whipped
  cream (optional)

◆ Preheat oven to 350°F. Grease 8" by 8" glass baking dish.

◆ In 3-quart saucepan, heat milk to boiling over medium-high heat. Meanwhile, in medium bowl, whisk egg yolks with ½ cup granulated sugar until smooth. Whisk in flour until combined. Gradually whisk hot milk into yolk mixture. Return mixture to saucepan; heat to boiling over medium-high heat, whisking constantly. Reduce heat to low; cook 1 minute, whisking. Remove from heat and whisk in melted chocolate, vanilla, and salt.

◆ In small bowl, with mixer at high speed, beat egg whites until soft peaks form; beat in remaining 2 tablespoons granulated sugar. Whisk one-third of whites into chocolate mixture until smooth; fold in remaining whites (batter will be stiff). Spoon evenly into baking dish.

◆ Place baking dish in roasting pan; carefully pour *boiling water* into roasting pan to come halfway up sides of dish. Bake 40 minutes, or until firm. Sift confectioners' sugar on top. Serve warm, with ice cream, if you like.

Each serving: About 190 calories, 6g protein, 25g carbohydrate, 9g total fat (4g saturated), 111mg cholesterol, 115mg sodium

◆◆◆◆◆◆◆◆◆◆◆◆◆◆◆◆◆◆◆◆◆◆◆◆◆◆◆◆

MELTING CHOCOLATE

You can melt chocolate in a heavy saucepan or double boiler on the stove top. The pan must be dry, as moisture will make the chocolate grainy. Melt over low heat, stirring constantly to prevent scorching. To microwave, place 1 to 4 ounces chocolate in a microwave-safe container; cook on Medium (50% power) for 1½ to 2 minutes.

Chocolate melted in the microwave retains its shape, so it won't look melted until it's stirred (above).

◆◆◆◆◆◆◆◆◆◆◆◆◆◆◆◆◆◆◆◆◆◆◆◆◆◆◆◆

INDIAN PUDDING

Prep: 30 minutes plus cooling   Bake: 2 hours
Makes 8 servings

⅔ cup yellow cornmeal
4 cups milk
½ cup light molasses
4 tablespoons margarine or
  butter, cut up
¼ cup sugar

1 teaspoon ground ginger
1 teaspoon ground cinnamon
½ teaspoon salt
¼ teaspoon ground nutmeg
Vanilla ice cream

◆ Preheat oven to 350°F. Grease shallow 1½-quart glass or ceramic baking dish. In small bowl, stir together cornmeal and 1 cup milk. In 4-quart saucepan, heat remaining 3 cups milk to boiling over high heat. Stir in cornmeal mixture; heat to boiling. Reduce heat to low and cook, stirring often, 20 minutes. Remove from heat. Stir in molasses and next 6 ingredients.

◆ Pour batter into baking dish. Cover with foil. Place dish in roasting pan; carefully pour *boiling water* into roasting pan to come halfway up sides of dish. Bake 1 hour. Remove foil; bake 1 hour longer. Remove from roasting pan; cool on wire rack 30 minutes. Serve warm with ice cream.

Each serving (without ice cream): 245 calories, 5g protein, 34g carbohydrate, 10g total fat (4g saturated), 17mg cholesterol, 265mg sodium

ORANGE PUDDING-CAKE

Prep: 20 minutes   Bake: 40 minutes
Makes 6 servings

¾ cup sugar
¼ cup all-purpose flour
⅛ teaspoon salt
1 cup milk
3 large eggs, separated

4 tablespoons margarine or
  butter, melted
¼ cup fresh lemon juice
¼ cup fresh orange juice
2 teaspoons grated orange peel

◆ Preheat oven to 350°F. Grease 8" by 8" glass baking dish. In large bowl, whisk sugar, flour, and salt until combined. Whisk in milk, egg yolks, and next 4 ingredients until smooth.

◆ In small bowl, with mixer at high speed, beat egg whites to soft peaks. Fold one-fourth of orange mixture into whites; fold whites back into orange mixture until evenly combined.

◆ Pour batter into baking dish. Place dish in roasting pan; carefully pour *boiling water* into roasting pan to come halfway up sides of dish. Bake 40 minutes, or until top is golden and set (dessert will separate into pudding and cake layers). Serve warm.

Each serving: About 250 calories, 5g protein, 33g carbohydrate, 11g total fat (3g saturated), 112mg cholesterol, 185mg sodium

BAKED CUSTARDS

Crème brûlée, crème caramel, and flan are nothing more than baked custards with elegant names. They can be varied with a wide range of flavors; here we've used butterscotch, chocolate, basic vanilla, and the surprise ingredient of pumpkin. For best results, take care not to overbake, or the mixture may become watery and start to separate. Baked custards are done even if the centers are still slightly jiggly – remember, they'll firm up as they cool.

BUTTERSCOTCH CRÈME BRÛLÉE

◆◆◆◆◆◆◆◆◆◆◆◆◆◆◆◆◆◆◆◆◆◆◆◆◆◆◆◆◆◆◆◆◆◆◆

Prep: 20 minutes plus cooling and chilling   Bake: 1 hour
Makes 12 servings

3 cups half-and-half or light cream

4 tablespoons margarine or butter

¾ cup plus 2 tablespoons packed light brown sugar

9 large egg yolks

1½ teaspoons vanilla extract

Strawberries for garnish

1 Preheat oven to 325°F. In 2-quart saucepan, heat half-and-half over medium heat until tiny bubbles form around edge of pan.

2 Meanwhile, in heavy 3-quart saucepan, heat margarine and ¾ cup packed brown sugar to boiling over medium heat; boil 2 minutes, stirring constantly. Gradually whisk in warm half-and-half until mixture is completely smooth. Remove from heat. In medium bowl, with wire whisk or fork, beat egg yolks and vanilla until blended.

3 Slowly beat half-and-half mixture into egg-yolk mixture until well mixed. Pour into twelve 4-ounce ramekins or custard cups. Place ramekins in small roasting pan; place in oven.

4 Carefully pour *boiling water* into roasting pan to come halfway up sides of ramekins. Bake 1 hour, or just until set (mixture will be slightly soft in center). Remove ramekins from roasting pan; cool on wire rack. Refrigerate at least 3 hours, until well chilled.

5 Up to 4 hours before serving, preheat broiler. Place remaining 2 tablespoons brown sugar in small sieve. With spoon, press brown sugar through sieve over top of chilled custards.

6 Place ramekins in jelly-roll pan for easier handling. With rack in broiler at closest position to heat source, broil crème brûlée 3 to 4 minutes, just until sugar melts. Refrigerate until ready to serve. The melted brown sugar will form a shiny, crisp crust over the custard. Serve within 4 hours, or the crust will lose its crispness. To serve, arrange ramekins on platter and garnish platter with strawberries.

EACH SERVING: ABOUT 220 CALORIES, 4g PROTEIN, 19g CARBOHYDRATE, 15g TOTAL FAT (6g SATURATED), 182mg CHOLESTEROL, 80mg SODIUM

LOW-FAT CRÈME CARAMEL

Prep: 15 minutes plus cooling and chilling   *Bake:* 30 minutes
Makes 8 servings

1½ cups sugar	4 cups low-fat milk (1%)
3 large eggs	1 teaspoon vanilla extract
3 large egg whites	

◆ Preheat oven to 350°F. Grease eight 8-ounce custard cups. In 2-quart saucepan, heat 1 cup sugar and *2 tablespoons water* over medium heat until sugar is melted and a light caramel color. Immediately pour into custard cups.

◆ In large bowl, with wire whisk or fork, beat eggs, egg whites, and remaining ½ cup sugar until well blended. Beat in milk and vanilla; pour into custard cups. Skim foam from tops. Place cups in large roasting pan; place in oven. Carefully pour *boiling water* into roasting pan to come halfway up sides of cups. Bake 30 minutes, or until centers are just set. Remove cups from roasting pan; cool on wire rack. Refrigerate 3 hours, or until well chilled.

◆ To serve, with small spatula, carefully loosen custard from cups and invert each custard onto a dessert plate, allowing caramel syrup to drip from cup onto custard.

Each serving: About 235 calories, 8g protein, 44g carbohydrate, 3g total fat (1g saturated), 85mg cholesterol, 110mg sodium

CHOCOLATE POTS DE CRÈME

Prep: 15 minutes plus cooling and chilling   *Bake:* 30 to 35 minutes
Makes 6 servings

3 squares (3 ounces)	2 large egg yolks
semisweet chocolate	¼ cup sugar
2½ cups milk	1 teaspoon vanilla extract
2 large eggs	

◆ Preheat oven to 350°F. In 3-quart saucepan, heat chocolate and ¼ cup milk over low heat, stirring frequently, until chocolate is melted; remove from heat. In 2-quart

saucepan, heat remaining 2¼ cups milk to boiling over medium-high heat; stir into chocolate mixture. In large bowl, whisk eggs, egg yolks, sugar, and vanilla until well blended. Gradually whisk in chocolate mixture. Pour evenly into six 6-ounce ramekins or custard cups. Place ramekins in roasting pan; place in oven.

◆ Carefully pour *boiling water* into roasting pan to come halfway up sides of ramekins. Cover roasting pan with foil, crimping edges loosely. Bake custards 30 to 35 minutes, until knife inserted halfway between edge and center of custard comes out clean.

◆ Remove foil; remove ramekins from roasting pan. Cool on wire rack. Refrigerate 3 hours, or until well chilled. Serve custards in ramekins.

Each serving: About 210 calories, 7g protein, 22g carbohydrate, 11g total fat (6g saturated), 156mg cholesterol, 75mg sodium

PUMPKIN FLAN

Prep: 15 minutes plus cooling and chilling   *Bake:* 50 minutes
Makes 12 servings

⅓ cup plus ¾ cup sugar	1 can (12 ounces) evaporated
8 large eggs	milk
2 cups milk	¾ teaspoon ground cinnamon
½ (16-ounce) can solid-pack	¼ teaspoon ground ginger
pumpkin (not pumpkin-pie	¼ teaspoon ground nutmeg
mix)	

◆ Preheat oven to 325°F. In 10-inch skillet, heat ⅓ cup sugar over medium heat, stirring constantly, until melted and a light caramel color. Immediately pour caramel syrup into 9" by 5" loaf pan, tilting pan to cover bottom completely.

◆ In large bowl, with wire whisk or fork, beat eggs and remaining ¾ cup sugar until well blended. Beat in milk, pumpkin, evaporated milk, cinnamon, ginger, and nutmeg until well mixed; pour mixture into loaf pan.

◆ Place loaf pan in 13" by 9" baking pan; place in oven. Caefully pour *boiling water* into baking pan to come halfway up sides of loaf pan. Bake about 50 minutes, until knife inserted in center of flan comes out clean.

◆ Remove loaf pan from baking pan. Cool on wire rack. Refrigerate flan 3 hours, or until well chilled.

◆ To serve, with small spatula, carefully loosen flan from loaf pan and invert onto a chilled large platter, allowing caramel syrup to drip from pan onto flan.

Each serving: About 190 calories, 8g protein, 25g carbohydrate, 7g total fat (3g saturated), 156mg cholesterol, 95mg sodium

SOUFFLÉS

Dessert soufflés are dazzling whether they're baked as puffy individual servings or as one giant soufflé. Despite their mystique, they are amazingly simple – follow our straightforward recipes for guaranteed light and airy results. Be sure to serve soufflés immediately from the oven, before they deflate.

APRICOT SOUFFLÉ

◆◆◆◆◆◆◆◆◆◆◆◆◆

Prep: 20 minutes plus cooling
Bake: 12 to 15 minutes
Makes 6 servings

1 package (6 ounces) dried apricots (about 1 cup)
¾ cup orange juice
About 2 tablespoons plus ¼ cup sugar
6 large egg whites
½ teaspoon cream of tartar
1 teaspoon vanilla extract

1 In small saucepan, heat apricots and orange juice to boiling over high heat. Reduce heat to low; cover and simmer 10 minutes, or until apricots are softened. In blender or food processor with knife blade attached, blend apricots with any liquid in pan until pureed. Place in large bowl; set aside to cool to room temperature. Preheat oven to 375°F. Grease six 6-ounce soufflé dishes or custard cups; sprinkle with about 2 tablespoons sugar.

2 In large bowl, with mixer at high speed, beat egg whites and cream of tartar until soft peaks form. Beat in vanilla. Beating at high speed, gradually sprinkle in remaining ¼ cup sugar until mixture holds stiff peaks when beaters are lifted.

3 With rubber spatula, gently fold one-third of beaten egg whites into apricot mixture to lighten mixture. Fold in remaining whites, half at a time. Spoon mixture into soufflé dishes.

FRESH PEAR SOUFFLÉ

Prepare Apricot Soufflé as recipe directs, but instead of the apricot-orange juice mixture in Step 1, make pear puree: In 2-quart saucepan, toss 4 cups peeled, coarsely chopped fully ripe pears (5 to 6 pears) with 1 tablespoon fresh lemon juice. Cook over high heat, covered, 15 minutes, or until pears are very tender. Uncover and cook 10 to 15 minutes longer, stirring occasionally, until mixture is almost dry. Transfer to blender or food processor with knife blade attached and blend until pureed. Place in large bowl; cool to room temperature. Proceed as recipe directs.

Each serving: About 165 calories, 4g protein, 39g carbohydrate, 1g total fat (0g saturated), 0mg cholesterol, 55mg sodium

4 With metal spatula held at a 45-degree angle to soufflé, make a domed peak on each soufflé. Place dishes on jelly-roll pan for easier handling. (If not serving right away, soufflés can be refrigerated for up to 3 hours before baking.) Bake soufflés 12 to 15 minutes, until puffed and golden. Serve immediately.

EACH SERVING: ABOUT 150 CALORIES, 5g PROTEIN, 34g CARBOHYDRATE, 0g TOTAL FAT, 0mg CHOLESTEROL, 60mg SODIUM

CHOCOLATE SOUFFLÉ

Prep: 20 minutes plus cooling   *Bake:* 30 minutes
Makes 6 servings

⅓ cup all-purpose flour
1 tablespoon instant espresso-coffee powder
About 1¼ cups granulated sugar
1 cup milk
3 tablespoons margarine or butter, softened

6 squares (6 ounces) unsweetened chocolate, coarsely chopped
6 large eggs, separated
2 teaspoons vanilla extract
¼ teaspoon salt
Confectioners' sugar for garnish

◆ In 3-quart saucepan, mix flour, espresso powder, and 1¼ cups granulated sugar; gradually stir in milk until blended. Cook over medium heat, stirring constantly, until mixture thickens and boils; boil 1 minute. Remove from heat.

◆ Stir in margarine and chocolate until melted and smooth. Beat in egg yolks all at once until well mixed. Stir in vanilla. Cool to lukewarm. Preheat oven to 350°F. Grease six 8-ounce soufflé dishes; sprinkle lightly with granulated sugar.

◆ In large bowl, with mixer at high speed, beat egg whites and salt to stiff peaks. With rubber spatula, gently fold one-third of beaten egg whites into chocolate mixture; gently fold back into remaining whites. Pour into soufflé dishes. Bake 30 minutes (centers will be fudgy). When soufflés are done, sprinkle with confectioners' sugar; serve immediately.

Each serving: About 485 calories, 11g protein, 60g carbohydrate, 27g total fat (9g saturated), 219mg cholesterol, 240mg sodium

RASPBERRY SOUFFLÉ

Prep: 25 minutes plus cooling   *Bake:* 20 minutes
Makes 4 servings

3 tablespoons margarine or butter
3 tablespoons all-purpose flour
⅛ teaspoon salt
¾ cup milk
About 5 tablespoons granulated sugar
3 large egg yolks

2 tablespoons orange-flavor liqueur
4 large egg whites
Three ½-pints raspberries
¼ cup red currant jelly
1 teaspoon cornstarch
Confectioners' sugar for garnish

◆ In 2-quart saucepan, melt margarine over low heat. Stir in flour and salt until blended. Gradually stir in milk and cook, stirring constantly, until mixture thickens slightly and boils; boil 1 minute. Remove from heat.

◆ With wire whisk, beat in 3 tablespoons sugar. Rapidly whisk in egg yolks. Cool to lukewarm. Stir in orange liqueur. Preheat oven to 375°F. Grease four 10-ounce soufflé dishes or custard cups; sprinkle lightly with granulated sugar.

◆ In large bowl, with mixer at high speed, beat egg whites to stiff peaks. With rubber spatula, fold one-third of beaten egg whites into egg-yolk mixture; gently fold back into remaining whites. Fold in ½ pint raspberries. Spoon into soufflé dishes; place on jelly-roll pan for easier handling. Bake 20 minutes, or until knife inserted in soufflés comes out clean.

◆ Meanwhile, prepare raspberry sauce: Reserve ½ cup raspberries for garnish. Press remaining raspberries through sieve to remove seeds. In 1-quart saucepan, heat raspberry puree, currant jelly, cornstarch, and remaining 2 tablespoons granulated sugar over medium heat until mixture thickens and boils; boil 1 minute. Keep sauce warm.

◆ When soufflés are done, sprinkle with confectioners' sugar; serve immediately with sauce and reserved berries.

Each serving: About 370 calories, 9g protein, 50g carbohydrate, 14g total fat (4g saturated), 166mg cholesterol, 250mg sodium

HAZELNUT SOUFFLÉ

Prep: 25 minutes plus cooling   *Bake:* 45 minutes
Makes 6 servings

½ cup hazelnuts, toasted and skinned (see page 522)
About ½ cup granulated sugar
1½ cups milk
4 tablespoons margarine or butter
¼ cup all-purpose flour

4 large egg yolks
2 tablespoons hazelnut-flavor liqueur
¼ teaspoon salt
6 large egg whites
Confectioners' sugar for garnish

◆ In food processor with knife blade attached, process hazelnuts with ¼ cup sugar until very finely ground.

◆ In 1-quart saucepan, heat milk to boiling over medium-high heat. Meanwhile, in 3-quart saucepan, melt margarine over low heat; add flour and cook, stirring frequently, 2 minutes. Whisk in milk; heat to boiling. Cook, whisking constantly, 1 minute. Remove from heat. Whisk in egg yolks, 1 at a time. Stir in ground hazelnut mixture, hazelnut liqueur, and salt. Cool to lukewarm. Preheat oven to 375°F. Grease 2½-quart soufflé dish; sprinkle lightly with granulated sugar.

◆ In large bowl, with mixer at high speed, beat egg whites until soft peaks form. Gradually sprinkle in remaining ¼ cup granulated sugar, beating until mixture holds stiff peaks when beaters are lifted. Fold one-fourth of whites into hazelnut mixture until blended; gently fold back into remaining whites. Pour into soufflé dish. Bake 45 minutes, or until just set. When soufflé is done, sprinkle with confectioners' sugar; serve immediately.

Each serving: 330 calories, 9g protein, 28g carbohydrate, 20g total fat (5g saturated), 150mg cholesterol, 265mg sodium

CHOUX PASTRIES

A stovetop batter, full of eggs, choux pastry puffs up dramatically when baked to give deliciously light, crisp pastries. To ensure crispness, bake until thoroughly golden.

CHOCOLATE CREAM-PUFF RING

◆◆◆◆◆◆◆◆◆◆◆◆◆

Prep: 40 minutes plus standing and cooling
Bake: 40 minutes
Makes 12 servings

Basic Choux Pastry (see page 464)
1 package (12 ounces) semisweet-chocolate pieces (2 cups)
¼ cup plus 1½ teaspoons milk
3 tablespoons margarine or butter
2 large eggs
2 cups heavy or whipping cream
1½ teaspoons light corn syrup
1 pint strawberries

1 Preheat oven to 400°F. Lightly grease and flour cookie sheet. Using 7-inch plate as guide, trace circle in flour on cookie sheet. Prepare Basic Choux Pastry.

2 Drop batter by heaping tablespoons into 12 mounds, inside circle, to form a ring. With moistened finger, smooth tops. Bake 40 minutes, or until golden. Turn off oven; let ring stand in oven 15 minutes. Remove ring from oven; cool on cookie sheet on wire rack.

3 Meanwhile, prepare chocolate mousse filling: In heavy 3-quart saucepan, heat 1½ cups semisweet-chocolate pieces (reserve remaining ½ cup for glaze), ¼ cup milk, and 2 tablespoons margarine over low heat, stirring occasionally, until smooth. Add eggs, one at a time, stirring constantly with wire whisk.

4 Continue whisking chocolate mixture about 5 minutes longer, until slightly thickened. Transfer to bowl, cover surface with plastic wrap, and refrigerate 30 minutes until cool.

5 In large bowl, with mixer at medium speed, beat cream until stiff peaks form. With rubber spatula, fold whipped cream into cooled chocolate mixture, half at a time, until blended.

6 With long serrated knife, cut cooled ring horizontally in half. Spoon chocolate mousse filling into bottom of ring. Replace top of ring. Refrigerate until ready to serve. Prepare glaze: In heavy 1-quart saucepan, heat reserved ½ cup semisweet-chocolate pieces, remaining 1 tablespoon margarine, remaining 1½ teaspoons milk, and light corn syrup over low heat, stirring occasionally, until smooth. Spoon over ring. Fill center of ring with strawberries.

EACH SERVING: ABOUT 445 CALORIES, 7g PROTEIN, 31g CARBOHYDRATE, 34g TOTAL FAT (12g SATURATED), 162mg CHOLESTEROL, 235mg SODIUM

CREAM PUFFS WITH HOT FUDGE SAUCE

Prep: 30 minutes plus standing and cooling   *Bake:* 40 to 45 minutes
Makes 8 servings

Basic Choux Pastry (see below right)

Hot Fudge Sauce (see page 482)

1 quart vanilla ice cream

◆ Preheat oven to 400°F. Grease and flour large cookie sheet. Prepare Basic Choux Pastry. Drop batter by slightly rounded ¼ cups, 3 inches apart, onto cookie sheet into 8 large mounds. With moistened finger, gently smooth tops to round slightly.

◆ Bake 40 to 45 minutes, until golden. Remove puffs from oven; with knife, poke a hole into side of each puff to let out steam. Turn off oven. Return puffs to oven and let stand 10 minutes. Transfer puffs to wire rack to cool.

◆ With serrated knife, cut each cooled puff horizontally in half; remove and discard any moist portion inside puffs.

◆ Prepare Hot Fudge Sauce. To serve, place ½-cup scoop vanilla ice cream in bottom half of each cream puff; replace tops. Spoon Hot Fudge Sauce over cream puffs.

Each serving: About 610 calories, 9g protein, 55g carbohydrate, 43g total fat (18g saturated), 176mg cholesterol, 330mg sodium

ÉCLAIRS

Prep: 1 hour plus chilling, cooling, and standing   *Bake:* 40 minutes
Makes about 24

3 cups milk
6 large egg yolks
1 cup sugar
⅓ cup cornstarch
4 teaspoons vanilla extract

Basic Choux Pastry (see right)
3 squares (3 ounces) semisweet chocolate
3 tablespoons heavy or whipping cream

◆ Prepare pastry cream: In 4-quart saucepan, heat milk to boiling over high heat. Meanwhile, in large bowl, whisk egg yolks with sugar until smooth; whisk in cornstarch until combined. Gradually whisk hot milk into yolk mixture.

◆ Return mixture to saucepan; cook over high heat, whisking constantly, until mixture thickens and boils. Reduce heat to low and cook, whisking, 2 minutes.

◆ Remove saucepan from heat and stir in vanilla. Pour pastry cream into shallow dish. Press plastic wrap onto surface of pastry cream to keep skin from forming as it cools. Refrigerate at least 2 hours, or overnight. Preheat oven to 400°F.

◆ Grease and flour large cookie sheet. Prepare Basic Choux Pastry. Spoon batter into large decorating bag fitted with ½-inch round tip. Pipe batter into strips about 3½ inches long and ¾ inch wide, 1 inch apart, onto cookie sheet to make 24 éclairs. With moistened finger, smooth any tails. Bake 40 minutes, or until golden. Transfer to wire rack to cool.

◆ With serrated knife, cut each cooled éclair horizontally in half, leaving one side intact, or, with small knife, make a hole in each end. Whisk pastry cream until smooth; spoon into large decorating bag fitted with ¼-inch round tip. Pipe into éclairs (reserve extra pastry cream for use another day).

◆ In 1-quart saucepan, melt chocolate with cream over very low heat, stirring often; remove from heat. Dip top of each éclair in chocolate mixture, smoothing with small metal spatula if necessary. Let stand until chocolate sets.

Each éclair: 160 calories, 4g protein, 18g carbohydrate, 9g total fat (3g saturated), 95mg cholesterol, 95mg sodium

BASIC CHOUX PASTRY

◆◆◆◆◆◆◆◆◆◆◆◆◆◆

½ cup margarine or butter
¼ teaspoon salt

1 cup all-purpose flour
4 large eggs

1 In 3-quart saucepan, heat margarine, salt, and *1 cup water* over medium heat until margarine melts and mixture boils. Remove from heat. With wooden spoon, vigorously stir in flour all at once until mixture forms ball and leaves side of pan.

2 Add eggs to flour mixture, one at a time, beating well after each addition, until mixture is smooth and satiny. Shape and bake warm batter as directed.

PUFF PASTRIES

Dozens of paper-thin layers of dough and butter make puff pastry light and flaky; we've used frozen puff pastry to create ultra-easy, elegant desserts. The rich, delicate pastry is lovely with a fragrant apple filling for a French-style treat or baked into little fruit-filled bundles for a less formal dessert.

APPLE-ALMOND PASTRY

Prep: 30 minutes plus cooling
Bake: 25 to 30 minutes
Makes 10 servings

1 large egg
½ (7- to 8-ounce) tube or can almond paste
2 teaspoons vanilla extract
3 medium Golden Delicious apples (about 1 pound), peeled, cored, and thinly sliced
2 teaspoons all-purpose flour
1 package (17¼ ounces) frozen puff-pastry sheets, thawed
2 teaspoons sugar

1 In medium bowl, with fork, beat egg. Transfer 1 tablespoon egg to cup; mix in *1 tablespoon water*. Set aside. To egg in bowl, add almond paste and vanilla; with fork, break up almond paste and blend mixture. In large bowl, toss apple slices with flour. Unfold 1 pastry sheet on lightly floured large cookie sheet. With floured rolling pin, roll pastry to about a 13-inch square. (Place damp towel under cookie sheet to help prevent it from moving.)

2 Invert an 11-inch round bowl onto pastry, lightly pressing to make circle. With pastry wheel or sharp knife, trim pastry, leaving 1-inch border around circle; discard trimmings.

3 With small spatula, spread almond mixture to cover 11-inch circle. Arrange apple slices on top. Unfold second pastry sheet on lightly floured surface; roll, mark, and trim as in Steps 1 and 2.

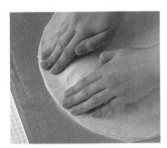

4 Preheat oven to 375°F. With pastry brush, brush some egg mixture in cup on pastry border around apples. Place second pastry circle on top of apples; press all around edge to seal.

5 With tip of sharp knife, cut ½-inch triangles from edge of pastry, about 2 inches apart; discard triangles.

6 Lightly score top crust with curved lines, starting at center and working toward edge (do not cut all the way through). Brush crust with remaining egg mixture in cup; sprinkle with sugar. (Dessert can be prepared to this point and refrigerated up to 4 hours before baking.) Bake pastry 25 to 30 minutes, until crust is golden brown. Cool pastry on wire rack at least 30 minutes before serving.

EACH SERVING: ABOUT 335 CALORIES, 6g PROTEIN, 41g CARBOHYDRATE, 17g TOTAL FAT (3g SATURATED), 21mg CHOLESTEROL, 170mg SODIUM

FRUIT BUNDLES

Prep: 35 minutes plus cooling   *Bake:* 20 to 25 minutes
Makes 8 servings

¾ cup pitted prunes (about
   4 ounces), coarsely chopped
¾ cup dried apricots (about
   4 ounces), coarsely chopped
¾ cup apple juice
1 tablespoon all-purpose flour
½ teaspoon ground cinnamon

1 medium Golden Delicious
   apple, peeled, cored, and
   cut into ½-inch pieces
¼ cup plus 1 tablespoon sugar
1 package (17¼ ounces)
   frozen puff-pastry sheets,
   thawed

◆ In 1-quart saucepan, heat prunes, apricots, and apple juice to boiling over high heat. Reduce heat to low; simmer 8 to 10 minutes, until fruit is soft and liquid is absorbed. Cool completely; transfer to large bowl. Stir in flour, cinnamon, apple pieces, and ¼ cup sugar.

◆ Preheat oven to 425°F. Unfold 1 pastry sheet on lightly floured surface. With floured rolling pin, roll pastry to a 12-inch square. With sharp pastry wheel or knife, trim edges of sheet; cut square into four 6-inch squares. Spoon one-eighth of fruit mixture onto center of each square.

◆ Brush edges of 1 pastry square with some *water*. Bring corners of pastry square over fruit; gently squeeze and twist pastry together to seal in filling and form a bundle. Fan out corners of pastry. Repeat to make 3 more bundles.

◆ Repeat with second pastry sheet, remaining fruit mixture, and more *water* to make 4 more bundles. Place bundles, 2 inches apart, on ungreased large cookie sheet. (If desired, refrigerate bundles on cookie sheet to bake later in day.)

◆ Brush tops of bundles with *water*, then sprinkle with remaining 1 tablespoon sugar. Bake 20 to 25 minutes, until bundles are puffed and golden. Serve warm or transfer bundles to wire rack to cool.

Each serving: About 415 calories, 5g protein, 65g carbohydrate, 17g total fat (4g saturated), 0mg cholesterol, 205mg sodium

QUICK PUFF-PASTRY DESSERTS

Frozen puff pastry is great to have on hand for impressive no-fuss desserts. When working with puff pastry, remember that clean edges are important for maximum puffing. Use a cookie cutter with very sharp edges or very sharp knife or pastry wheel and cut straight down. If necessary, trim edges of the pastry sheets after you've rolled them out. The following method is easy and adapts to many ideas:

On lightly floured surface, unfold puff-pastry sheet. With cookie cutter, cut out hearts, stars, or other shapes. Or, with sharp knife or pastry wheel, trim edges of pastry sheet and then cut out small squares, rectangles, or triangles. Place on an ungreased cookie sheet and prick several times with a fork.

If desired, sprinkle pastry with a little sugar or a few crushed sugar cubes. Or, brush pastry (tops only) with 1 large egg white beaten with 1 tablespoon water (if egg mixture drips on cut edges, pastry won't puff fully), then sprinkle with finely chopped pistachios or other nuts. Bake 10 to 15 minutes at 375°F, until pastry is puffed and golden. Cool on wire rack.

With serrated knife, carefully split each cooled pastry horizontally in half or thirds. Fill with sweetened whipped cream (flavored with a little liqueur or vanilla extract, if you like), ice cream, berries or other fruit, or Marsala Cream Cheese (see below). Try serving with any of the sauces on page 482.

Marsala cream cheese In large bowl, with mixer at low speed, beat 1 package (8 ounces) cream cheese, softened, with ½ cup confectioners' sugar until smooth. Gradually beat in ¼ cup sweet Marsala wine until blended; set aside. In small bowl, with mixer at medium speed, beat 1 cup heavy or whipping cream until stiff peaks form. Fold whipped cream into cream-cheese mixture. Makes about 1½ cups.

Each tablespoon: About 80 calories, 1g protein, 3g carbohydrate, 7g total fat (4g saturated), 24mg cholesterol, 30mg sodium

Puff-pastry hearts filled with whipped cream cheese, served with hot fudge sauce

Nut-topped puff-pastry rectangles filled with kiwifruit, banana slices, and whipped cream

PHYLLO PASTRIES

Phyllo pastry, purchased fresh or frozen, makes spectacular desserts like our delicate phyllo cups with a fruit-and-ricotta filling. Phyllo dries out quickly; keep it covered until you are ready to use it. Wrap unused phyllo and refrigerate it up to 2 weeks; do not refreeze thawed dough, or it will become dry and brittle.

PHYLLO CUPS WITH HONEY-RICOTTA AND MIXED BERRIES

◆◆◆◆◆◆◆◆◆◆◆◆◆◆◆◆◆◆◆◆◆◆◆◆◆◆◆◆

Prep: 45 minutes plus draining and cooling
Bake: 12 minutes   **Makes 6 servings**

2 containers (15 ounces each) part-skim ricotta cheese
6 sheets (about 16" by 12" each) fresh or frozen (thawed) phyllo (about 4 ounces)
2 tablespoons margarine or butter, melted
¼ cup honey
1 teaspoon grated orange peel
1 cup blueberries
1 cup raspberries
1 cup blackberries
Confectioners' sugar for garnish

1 In food processor with knife blade attached, blend ricotta cheese about 1 minute, or until smooth. Place double-thick layer of white paper towels in medium strainer set over small bowl. Spoon ricotta cheese onto paper towels; cover with plastic wrap, place in refrigerator, and let drain at least 2 hours or overnight (whey will drop into bowl and ricotta will thicken).

2 Meanwhile, preheat oven to 375°F. On work surface, stack phyllo sheets one on top of the other. With knife, cut stack lengthwise, then crosswise in half (you will have twenty-four 8" by 6" pieces).

3 Keep phyllo stack covered with plastic wrap to prevent it from drying out while assembling phyllo cups. Lightly brush six 10-ounce custard cups with melted margarine. On work surface, place 2 pieces of phyllo, one on top of the other; brush top piece with some melted margarine. Arrange phyllo in custard cup.

4 Repeat with 2 more pieces of phyllo, placing crosswise over phyllo in cup. Fold phyllo overhang to make pretty edge. Repeat with remaining phyllo and melted margarine to make 6 phyllo cups in all.

5 Place custard cups in jelly-roll pan for easier handling. Bake phyllo cups about 12 minutes, until phyllo is crisp and golden.

6 Cool phyllo cups in custard cups on wire racks about 15 minutes; carefully remove from custard cups. (Phyllo cups can be made 1 day ahead and kept in airtight container.) Just before serving, remove ricotta from refrigerator. Discard whey in bowl. Transfer drained ricotta to same bowl.

7 Add honey and orange peel to ricotta and mix well. In medium bowl, toss blueberries, raspberries, and blackberries. Spoon ricotta mixture into phyllo cups; top with berries. Sprinkle with confectioners' sugar. Serve immediately.

EACH SERVING: ABOUT 370 CALORIES, 18g PROTEIN, 38g CARBOHYDRATE, 16g TOTAL FAT (8g SATURATED), 44mg CHOLESTEROL, 315mg SODIUM

SPICED PEAR STRUDEL

Prep: 30 minutes plus cooling   Bake: 40 minutes
Makes 16 servings

3 large pears (1¾ pounds),
   peeled and thinly sliced
½ cup pitted dates, diced
⅓ cup granulated sugar
½ teaspoon ground cinnamon
¼ teaspoon ground ginger
⅛ teaspoon salt
¾ cup plain dried bread
   crumbs

12 sheets (about 16" by
   12"each) fresh or frozen
   (thawed) phyllo (about
   8 ounces)
½ cup margarine or butter,
   melted
Confectioners' sugar for
   garnish

◆ Grease large cookie sheet. In large bowl, toss pears with next 5 ingredients and ¼ cup bread crumbs.

◆ Cut two 24-inch lengths of waxed paper; overlap 2 long sides about 2 inches. On waxed paper, arrange 1 sheet of phyllo; brush with some melted margarine, then sprinkle with scant tablespoon bread crumbs. (Keep remaining phyllo covered with plastic wrap to prevent it from drying out.) Continue layering phyllo, brushing each sheet with some margarine and sprinkling every other sheet with crumbs.

◆ Preheat oven to 375°F. Starting along 1 long side of phyllo, spoon pears to about ½ inch from edges to cover half of rectangle. From pear-side, roll phyllo, jelly-roll fashion.

◆ Place roll on cookie sheet seam-side down; tuck ends under. Brush with remaining margarine. Cut 16 diagonal slashes in top. Bake 40 minutes, covering with foil during last 20 minutes if necessary to prevent overbrowning. Cool on cookie sheet on wire rack 30 minutes. Sprinkle cooled strudel lightly with confectioners' sugar; serve warm or cold.

Each serving: About 175 calories, 2g protein, 27g carbohydrate, 7g total fat (1g saturated), 0mg cholesterol, 195mg sodium

HONEY-LEMON BAKLAVA

Prep: 30 minutes plus cooling   Bake: 1 hour 15 minutes
Makes 24 servings

4 cups walnuts (about
   16 ounces)
1 teaspoon ground cinnamon
¼ teaspoon ground cloves
1 cup sugar
1 package (16 ounces) fresh or
   frozen (thawed) phyllo (each
   sheet about 16" by 12")

10 tablespoons margarine or
   butter, melted
1 cup honey
1 cinnamon stick (3 inches)
4 teaspoons fresh lemon juice

◆ Grease 13" by 9" glass baking dish. In food processor with knife blade attached, place first 3 ingredients and ½ cup sugar. Pulse until walnuts are finely chopped; set aside.

◆ Preheat oven to 300°F. Cut phyllo sheets into 13" by 9" rectangles. In baking dish, place 1 sheet phyllo; brush with some melted margarine. (Keep remaining phyllo covered with plastic wrap to prevent it from drying out.) Repeat with 5 more sheets; sprinkle with about 1 cup walnut mixture.

◆ Place 1 sheet of phyllo in baking dish over walnuts; brush with some margarine. Repeat with 5 more sheets of phyllo; sprinkle with about 1 cup walnut mixture. Repeat layering 2 more times, ending with walnuts. Place 1 sheet of phyllo on top of last walnut layer; brush with some margarine. Repeat until all phyllo sheets are used, brushing with remaining margarine.

◆ With sharp knife, cut almost but not all the way through layers to make 24 servings: Cut lengthwise into 3 strips; cut each strip crosswise into 4 rectangles. Then cut each rectangle diagonally into 2 triangles. Bake 1¼ hours, or until golden.

◆ Prepare syrup: About 15 minutes before baklava is done, in small saucepan, heat honey, cinnamon stick, *1 cup water*, and remaining ½ cup sugar to boiling over medium heat; boil 5 minutes, stirring often. Reduce heat to low. Add lemon juice; simmer 5 minutes longer. Discard cinnamon stick; spoon hot syrup over hot baklava. Cool baklava in pan on wire rack at least 1 hour. Let stand at room temperature until ready to serve. To serve, finish cutting through layers.

Each serving: About 305 calories, 4g protein, 34g carbohydrate, 18g total fat (2g saturated), 0mg cholesterol, 150mg sodium

PHYLLO NAPOLEONS

Stack 6 sheets (about 16" by 12" each) fresh or frozen (thawed) phyllo (about 4 ounces), lightly brushing every second sheet with melted margarine. With pizza wheel or knife, cut stack lengthwise in half; cut each half crosswise into 6. Bake on cookie sheet at 375°F 10 minutes; cool on sheet on wire rack.

Spread 4 rectangles with half of Marsala Cream Cheese (see page 466) or sweetened whipped cream; top with some berries mixed with jam. Layer with 4 more rectangles, remaining cream cheese, and more berry mixture. Sprinkle remaining rectangles with confectioners' sugar; place on top to make 4 Napoleons.

CREPES AND BLINTZES

These thin pancakes make a lovely dessert when wrapped around sweet fillings. Freeze crepes for up to 4 months, stacked with a sheet of waxed paper between each one. Thaw for about an hour before using. Crepes used for blintzes are made from the same batter but are browned on one side only.

APPLE-CALVADOS CREPES

◆◆◆◆◆◆◆◆◆◆◆◆◆

Prep: 50 minutes plus chilling batter
Bake: 5 minutes
Makes 6 servings

Basic Crepes (see page 82)
5 tablespoons margarine or butter
3 pounds Golden Delicious apples (6 large), peeled, cored, and diced
½ cup plus 1 tablespoon sugar
¼ cup Calvados or applejack brandy

1 Prepare Basic Crepes. Preheat oven to 400°F. In 12-inch skillet, melt 4 tablespoons margarine over medium-high heat. Stir in apples and ½ cup sugar; cover and cook 10 minutes, or until apples are tender.

2 Uncover and cook about 10 minutes longer, until apples begin to caramelize. Stir in Calvados. Remove skillet from heat.

3 Spread scant ¼ cup filling down center of each crepe. Roll up; arrange in shallow baking dish. Dot with remaining 1 tablespoon margarine; sprinkle with remaining 1 tablespoon sugar. Bake 5 minutes.

PEAR- AND PLUM-FILLED CREPES

Pear filling In 12-inch skillet, melt 4 tablespoons margarine or butter over medium-high heat. Add 3 pounds ripe Bosc pears (7 to 8 pears), peeled and diced; cook, uncovered, 10 to 15 minutes, stirring occasionally, until tender. Stir in ¼ cup packed brown sugar, ¼ teaspoon ground cinnamon, and 2 strips (3 inches each) lemon peel; cook 1 minute longer. Discard lemon peel. Fill and bake crepes as directed in Step 3. Makes 6 servings.

Each serving with crepes: About 390 calories, 7g protein, 56g carbohydrate, 17g total fat (6g saturated), 125mg cholesterol, 370mg sodium

Plum filling In 12-inch skillet, melt 3 tablespoons margarine or butter over medium-high heat. Add 2½ pounds ripe plums (10 large), each cut into quarters, ⅔ cup granulated sugar, and a pinch ground cloves. Cook, stirring occasionally, 15 to 20 minutes, until plums are tender. Fill and bake crepes as directed in Step 3. Makes 6 servings.

Each serving with crepes: About 395 calories, 8g protein, 60g carbohydrate, 15g total fat (6g saturated), 125mg cholesterol, 345mg sodium

EACH SERVING: ABOUT 465 CALORIES, 7g PROTEIN, 65g CARBOHYDRATE, 19g TOTAL FAT (6g SATURATED), 125mg CHOLESTEROL, 390mg SODIUM

CREPES SUZETTE

Prepare Basic Crepes (see page 82). In 10-inch skillet, melt 4 tablespoons margarine or butter with ⅓ cup orange juice, 2 tablespoons sugar, and ¼ teaspoon grated orange peel over low heat. Fold each crepe into quarters; arrange in sauce, turning to coat. Simmer 10 minutes. Pour ¼ cup orange-flavor liqueur evenly over crepes (do not stir).

Heat 1 to 2 minutes. With long wooden match, carefully ignite. When flames subside, transfer crepes to plates. Makes 6 servings.

Each serving: 275 calories, 7g protein, 22g carbohydrate, 16g total fat (6g saturated), 125mg cholesterol, 365mg sodium

CHEESE BLINTZES

Prep: 40 minutes plus chilling batter   *Cook:* 20 minutes
Makes 6 servings

Basic Crepes (see page 82)	¾ teaspoon vanilla extract
2 packages (8 ounces each) cream cheese, softened	1 large egg
1 container (8 ounces) cottage cheese	Blueberry Sauce (see page 482)
3 tablespoons confectioners' sugar	2 tablespoons margarine or butter
	Sour cream (optional)

◆ Prepare batter as directed in Steps 1 and 2 of Basic Crepes. While batter is chilling, prepare filling: In medium bowl, with mixer at medium speed, beat cheese, confectioners' sugar, vanilla, and egg until smooth. Cover and refrigerate filling until ready to use.

◆ Cook crepes as directed in Steps 3 and 4 of Basic Crepes, but cook crepe on bottom side only. Stack cooked crepes, browned-side up, between waxed paper. Prepare sauce. Place ¼ cup filling in center of browned side of each crepe. Fold left and right sides over filling and overlap ends to make a package. In 10-inch skillet, heat 1 tablespoon margarine over medium heat. Add 6 blintzes, seam-side down; cook until golden on both sides. Transfer to plates. Repeat with remaining margarine and blintzes. Serve hot with sauce, and sour cream, if you like.

Each serving: About 595 calories, 18g protein, 38g carbohydrate, 42g total fat (23g saturated), 250mg cholesterol, 715mg sodium

CREPES WITH STRAWBERRIES AND CREAM

Prep: 30 minutes plus chilling batter   *Cook:* 20 minutes
Makes 6 servings

Basic Crepes (see page 82)	1 cup heavy or whipping cream
4 tablespoons granulated sugar	1 tablespoon margarine or butter, melted
1 pint strawberries, hulled and thinly sliced	Confectioners' sugar for garnish
1 to 2 tablespoons orange-flavor liqueur	

◆ Prepare Basic Crepes, adding 1 tablespoon granulated sugar to batter in Step 1. While batter is chilling, in medium bowl, mix strawberries, liqueur, and 2 tablespoons granulated sugar. Let stand 20 minutes to allow sugar to dissolve and berries to marinate.

◆ In small bowl, with mixer at medium speed, beat heavy cream with remaining 1 tablespoon granulated sugar until soft peaks form. Spoon cream into serving bowl.

◆ Strain syrup from strawberries into small bowl. Stir in melted margarine; use to brush on crepes. Fold each crepe into quarters. Dust crepes lightly with confectioners' sugar. Place strawberries in small serving bowl. Serve crepes with strawberries and whipped cream.

Each serving: About 365 calories, 8g protein, 27g carbohydrate, 25g total fat (14g saturated), 179mg cholesterol, 315mg sodium

BROWN SUGAR CREPES

Prep: 25 minutes plus chilling batter   *Cook:* 3 to 6 minutes
Makes 6 servings

Basic Crepes (see page 82)	6 teaspoons margarine or butter
12 rounded teaspoons brown sugar	

◆ Prepare Basic Crepes. Press 1 rounded teaspoon brown sugar through sieve evenly over 1 crepe. Fold crepe into quarters. Repeat with remaining brown sugar and crepes.

◆ In nonstick 10-inch skillet, melt 2 teaspoons margarine over medium-high heat, swirling to coat bottom of pan. Add 4 crepes and cook 30 to 60 seconds per side, until heated through. Transfer to 2 dessert plates. Repeat with remaining margarine and crepes in 2 more batches.

Each serving: About 225 calories, 7g protein, 22g carbohydrate, 12g total fat (5g saturated), 125mg cholesterol, 325mg sodium

BREAD PUDDINGS

One of the most homey desserts, bread pudding is simply bread baked in a custard of eggs, milk, and sugar. Thrifty cooks make it as a way of using up day-old or stale bread – dry bread soaks up the egg mixture and all the flavors better than fresh bread would. Our Bread and Butter Pudding is an old-fashioned favorite, and we've created new versions with apples and cinnamon, with dried cherries, and with chocolate for a touch of luxury. For the white chocolate called for in our Black-and-White Bread Pudding and White-Chocolate Custard Sauce, you can substitute the equivalent weight in Swiss confectionery bars or white baking bars.

BLACK-AND-WHITE
BREAD PUDDING

Prep: 30 to 40 minutes plus standing and cooling
Bake: 1 hour 15 minutes   *Makes 16 servings*

1 loaf (16 ounces) sliced firm white bread	3 ounces bittersweet chocolate (not unsweetened), grated
4 cups milk	3 ounces white chocolate, grated
½ cup sugar	
1 tablespoon vanilla extract	White-Chocolate Custard Sauce (optional, see below)
½ teaspoon salt	
9 large eggs	

WHITE-CHOCOLATE CUSTARD SAUCE

Place 3 ounces white chocolate, finely chopped, in large bowl; set aside. In small bowl, with wire whisk, beat 4 large egg yolks and ¼ cup sugar until combined. In heavy 2-quart saucepan, heat 1 cup milk and ¾ cup heavy or whipping cream to boiling over high heat. Into egg mixture, beat small amount of hot milk mixture. Slowly pour egg mixture back into milk mixture, stirring rapidly to prevent lumping. Reduce heat to low; cook, stirring constantly, about 5 minutes, until mixture thickens slightly and coats back of spoon well. (Mixture should be about 160°F, but do not boil, or it will curdle.) Pour mixture over white chocolate, stirring to combine (white chocolate will not melt completely). Serve sauce warm, or refrigerate to serve cold. Makes about 2½ cups.

Each tablespoon: About 40 calories, 1g protein, 3g carbohydrate, 3g total fat (2g saturated), 28mg cholesterol, 5mg sodium

1 Preheat oven to 325°F. Place bread slices on large cookie sheet; lightly toast in oven 20 to 30 minutes, turning once. Grease 13" by 9" glass or ceramic baking dish.

2 Arrange bread in baking dish, overlapping slightly. In very large bowl, with wire whisk or fork, mix milk, sugar, vanilla, salt, and eggs until blended. Whisk in grated chocolates.

3 Pour milk mixture over bread; let stand 30 minutes, occasionally spooning liquid over bread. Bake, covered, 1 hour. Uncover; bake 15 minutes longer, or until golden. Cool on wire rack 30 minutes. Prepare sauce, if using. Serve pudding warm, or refrigerate to serve cold later.

EACH SERVING: ABOUT 240 CALORIES, 9g PROTEIN, 28g CARBOHYDRATE, 10g TOTAL FAT (5g SATURATED), 128mg CHOLESTEROL, 285mg SODIUM

BREAD-AND-BUTTER PUDDING

Prep: 15 minutes plus standing and cooling   Bake: 55 to 60 minutes
Makes 8 servings

4 tablespoons margarine or
   butter, softened
12 slices firm white bread
¾ teaspoon ground cinnamon
3 cups milk

⅓ cup sugar
1½ teaspoons vanilla extract
¼ teaspoon salt
4 large eggs

◆ Preheat oven to 325°F. Grease 8" by 8" glass baking dish. Spread margarine on bread slices. Arrange 4 slices of bread in dish in one layer, overlapping slightly; sprinkle with ¼ teaspoon cinnamon. Repeat, making 2 more layers.

◆ In medium bowl, with wire whisk or fork, mix remaining ingredients until well blended. Pour mixture over bread slices; let stand 10 minutes. Bake 55 to 60 minutes, until knife inserted in center of pudding comes out clean. Cool on wire rack 30 minutes. Serve warm, or refrigerate to serve cold later.

Each serving: About 270 calories, 9g protein, 30g carbohydrate, 13g total fat (4g saturated), 119mg cholesterol, 385mg sodium

LIGHT CHERRY BREAD PUDDING

Prep: 20 minutes plus standing and cooling   Bake: 1 hour 30 minutes
Makes 12 servings

4 ounces dried tart cherries
   (¾ cup)
1 loaf (12 ounces) Italian
   bread
6 cups low-fat milk (1%)
¾ cup packed light brown sugar

1 tablespoon vanilla extract
2 teaspoons ground cinnamon
4 large egg whites
3 large eggs
Confectioners' sugar for
   garnish

◆ In 2-quart saucepan, heat dried cherries and ¾ *cup water* to boiling over high heat. Reduce heat to low; cover and simmer 10 minutes, or until cherries are tender.

◆ Meanwhile, grease shallow 3-quart casserole. Cut bread into 1-inch-thick slices. In very large bowl, with wire whisk or fork, mix milk and next 5 ingredients until well blended. Drain cherries, adding any liquid to egg mixture. Set cherries aside. Add bread slices to egg mixture; let stand 10 minutes, carefully turning slices occasionally for even soaking.

◆ Preheat oven to 350°F. Arrange enough bread slices in casserole in one layer, pushing slices together, to cover bottom; sprinkle all but ¼ cup cherries over bread. Arrange remaining bread, overlapping slices to fit, on top. Pour any egg mixture remaining in bowl over bread.

◆ Bake bread pudding 1½ hours, or until knife inserted in center comes out clean, covering loosely with foil during last 10 to 15 minutes of baking if top browns too quickly.

◆ Sprinkle pudding with remaining cherries. Dust with confectioners' sugar. Cool on wire rack 30 minutes. Serve warm, or refrigerate to serve cold later.

Each serving: About 240 calories, 10g protein, 42g carbohydrate, 4g total fat (1g saturated), 58mg cholesterol, 270mg sodium

APPLE BREAD PUDDING

Prep: 40 minutes plus standing and cooling
Bake: 1 hour 15 to 30 minutes   Makes 12 servings

8 ounces unsliced rich egg
   bread, such as challah, cut
   into 1-inch cubes (6 cups)
3 tablespoons margarine or
   butter
6 large Golden Delicious
   apples (3 pounds), peeled,
   cored, and sliced

1 teaspoon ground cinnamon
½ cup plus ⅔ cup plus
   1 tablespoon sugar
2 tablespoons cornstarch
5 cups milk
5 large eggs
1½ teaspoons vanilla extract

◆ Preheat oven to 350°F. Spread bread cubes in jelly-roll pan; bake 15 to 20 minutes, until lightly toasted. Meanwhile, in 12-inch skillet, melt margarine over medium-high heat. Stir in apples and ½ teaspoon cinnamon; cover and cook 10 minutes. Uncover; stir in ½ cup sugar. Cook, stirring often, 5 to 10 minutes, until apples are lightly caramelized. In cup, mix cornstarch and ½ cup milk until smooth; stir into apples. Reduce heat to low and cook, stirring constantly, 1 minute.

◆ Place half of bread in 13" by 9" glass baking dish. Spoon apple mixture over bread; top with remaining bread. In large bowl, with wire whisk or fork, mix eggs, vanilla, ⅔ cup sugar, and remaining 4½ cups milk until well blended; pour over bread. Let stand 10 minutes, pressing bread into liquid. In cup, combine remaining 1 tablespoon sugar with remaining ½ teaspoon cinnamon; sprinkle over bread.

◆ Place baking dish in larger roasting pan. Carefully pour *boiling water* into roasting pan to come halfway up sides of dish. Bake 1¼ to 1½ hours, until knife inserted in center comes out clean. Cool on wire rack 30 minutes. Serve warm.

Each serving: 325 calories, 8g protein, 53g carbohydrate, 10g total fat (4g saturated), 112mg cholesterol, 205mg sodium

STOVETOP CUSTARDS

These easy stirred custards make simple puddings or form the basis for festive desserts like our trifle, laced with almond liqueur. There are also delicate brown-sugar custards, left alone to cook gently on the stovetop, plus a foolproof method for classic custard sauce.

RASPBERRY-PEAR TRIFLE

Prep: 1 hour plus chilling   Cook: 10 minutes
Makes 16 servings

2¼ cups milk
¾ cup plus 3 tablespoons sugar
¼ cup cornstarch
⅛ teaspoon salt
6 large egg yolks
¼ cup almond-flavor liqueur (amaretto)
3 cans (16 ounces each) pear halves in extra-light syrup
1 package (10 ounces) frozen raspberries in light syrup, thawed

1 cup heavy or whipping cream
1 store-bought pound cake (10¾ to 12 ounces), cut into 1-inch cubes
8 pairs amaretti cookies, coarsely crushed (about 1¼ cups)
Fresh raspberries for garnish

1 In 3-quart saucepan, heat 1¾ cups milk and ¾ cup sugar just to boiling over medium heat. Remove from heat. In medium bowl, with wire whisk, mix cornstarch, salt, and remaining ½ cup milk until smooth; beat in egg yolks.

2 Into yolk mixture, stir small amount of hot milk mixture; gradually stir yolk mixture back into milk mixture in saucepan. Cook over medium heat, stirring constantly, until mixture thickens and boils.

3 Remove custard from heat; stir in liqueur. Pour custard into clean bowl. Press plastic wrap onto surface of hot custard to keep skin from forming as custard cools. Refrigerate at least 3 hours, until chilled.

4 Drain pear halves, reserving ⅓ cup syrup. In blender at low speed, blend thawed frozen raspberries with their syrup and reserved syrup from pears. In small bowl, with mixer at medium speed, beat heavy cream, gradually adding remaining 3 tablespoons sugar, until stiff peaks form. Reserve 1 rounded cup whipped cream for garnish.

5 Gently fold remaining whipped cream into chilled custard. In 4-quart glass trifle or serving bowl, place half of cake cubes; top with half of raspberry mixture.

6 Arrange half of pear halves over raspberry mixture. Reserve ¼ cup cookie crumbs for garnish; sprinkle pear halves with half of remaining cookie crumbs.

7 Spread half of custard over crumb layer. Repeat layering. Garnish trifle with reserved whipped cream, fresh raspberries, and reserved cookie crumbs. Cover and refrigerate at least 2 hours or up to 24 hours to blend flavors.

EACH SERVING: ABOUT 375 CALORIES, 6g PROTEIN, 51g CARBOHYDRATE, 15g TOTAL FAT (6g SATURATED), 116mg CHOLESTEROL, 140mg SODIUM

CHOCOLATE PUDDING

Prep: 10 minutes plus chilling *Cook:* 20 minutes
Makes 8 servings

¾ cup sugar
⅓ cup cornstarch
½ teaspoon salt
3¾ cups milk
5 large egg yolks
2 teaspoons vanilla extract

3 squares (3 ounces) unsweetened chocolate, melted
2 tablespoons margarine or butter
Whipped cream (optional)

◆ In 3-quart saucepan, mix sugar, cornstarch, and salt until blended; gradually stir in milk. Cook over medium heat until mixture thickens and boils, stirring constantly; boil 1 minute, stirring. In small bowl, with wire whisk or fork, beat egg yolks lightly. Into yolks, beat small amount of hot milk mixture.

◆ Gradually pour yolk mixture back into milk mixture in saucepan, stirring rapidly to prevent lumping. Cook over low heat, stirring constantly, about 2 minutes, until very thick (mixture should be about 160°F).

◆ Remove from heat; stir in vanilla, melted chocolate, and margarine. Pour pudding into shallow bowl; press plastic wrap onto surface to prevent skin from forming as pudding cools. Refrigerate at least 4 hours, until chilled and set. Serve with whipped cream, if you like.

Each serving: About 280 calories, 6g protein, 32g carbohydrate, 15g total fat (6g saturated), 149mg cholesterol, 225mg sodium

---

THE PERFECT CUSTARD SAUCE

This classic sauce, also known as "crème anglaise," goes beautifully with pies, tarts, plain cakes, or fruit: In 2-quart saucepan, heat 1¼ cups milk to boiling. Meanwhile, in medium bowl, whisk 4 large egg yolks with ¼ cup sugar until smooth. Gradually whisk hot milk into egg-yolk mixture. Return mixture to saucepan; cook over medium heat, stirring constantly (do not boil), just until mixture thickens slightly and coats back of wooden spoon well. (A finger run across the custard-coated spoon should leave a track.)

Remove from heat; strain through sieve into clean bowl. Stir in 1 teaspoon vanilla extract, 1 tablespoon liqueur or brandy, or ½ teaspoon grated lemon peel. Refrigerate if not serving right away. Makes 1½ cups.

Each tablespoon: About 25 calories, 1g protein, 3g carbohydrate, 1g total fat (0g saturated), 37mg cholesterol, 5mg sodium

---

BROWN-SUGAR SKILLET CUSTARDS

Prep: 10 minutes plus chilling *Cook:* 1 hour
Makes 6 servings

4 large eggs
½ cup packed dark brown sugar

2 teaspoons vanilla extract
Pinch salt
3 cups milk

◆ In large bowl, with wire whisk, mix eggs with brown sugar, vanilla, and salt until sugar is dissolved. Whisk in milk.

◆ Fold a kitchen towel in half to line bottom of 12-inch skillet; set six 6-ounce custard cups or ramekins in skillet. Carefully pour milk mixture into custard cups; pour *cold water* into skillet to come halfway up sides of custard cups.

◆ Heat water to boiling over medium heat (it will take about 45 minutes). Cover skillet and remove from heat; let stand 15 minutes. Remove custard cups from skillet and refrigerate at least 2 hours, until chilled, or overnight.

Each serving: About 200 calories, 8g protein, 24g carbohydrate, 7g total fat (4g saturated), 159mg cholesterol, 145mg sodium

LEMON PUDDING

Prep: 10 minutes plus chilling *Cook:* 15 minutes
Makes 6 servings

⅔ cup sugar
¼ cup cornstarch
1 teaspoon grated lemon peel
Pinch salt

2½ cups milk
2 large egg yolks
⅓ cup fresh lemon juice
Assorted berries (optional)

◆ In 2-quart saucepan, with wire whisk, stir sugar, cornstarch, lemon peel, and salt until blended. Stir in a little milk until smooth; stir in remaining milk. Cook over medium-high heat, whisking constantly, until mixture thickens and boils. Boil 1 minute, whisking. Remove from heat.

◆ In small bowl, whisk egg yolks and lemon juice. Into yolks, gradually whisk half of hot milk mixture. Pour yolk mixture back into milk mixture in saucepan, stirring rapidly to prevent lumping. Cook over low heat, stirring constantly, about 2 minutes, until very thick (mixture should be about 160°F).

◆ Spoon pudding into shallow bowl. Press plastic wrap onto surface of pudding to prevent skin from forming as pudding cools. Refrigerate at least 2 hours, until chilled and set. Serve with assorted berries, if you like.

Each serving: About 190 calories, 4g protein, 33g carbohydrate, 5g total fat (3g saturated), 85mg cholesterol, 90mg sodium

GELATIN-BASED DESSERTS

Gelatin works magic, turning simple cream or fruit mixtures into smooth mousses or showpiece molded desserts. We've included a delicately flavored cooked-cream dessert from Italy, two very different mousses, and an elegant Raspberry Charlotte. The golden rules: Always dissolve the gelatin completely during heating, and never allow a gelatin mixture to boil.

PANNA COTTA WITH RASPBERRY SAUCE

◆◆◆◆◆◆◆◆◆◆◆◆◆◆

Prep: 20 minutes plus chilling
Cook: 15 minutes
Makes 8 servings

1 envelope unflavored gelatin
1 cup milk
½ vanilla bean or
   1½ teaspoons vanilla extract
1¾ cups heavy or whipping
   cream
¼ cup sugar
1 strip (3" by 1") lemon peel
1 cinnamon stick (3 inches)
1 container (10 ounces)
   frozen raspberries in syrup,
   thawed
2 tablespoons red currant jelly
2 teaspoons cornstarch
Fresh raspberries and mint
   sprigs for garnish

1 In 2-cup glass measuring cup, sprinkle gelatin over milk; let stand 5 minutes. Meanwhile, with knife, cut vanilla bean lengthwise in half. Scrape out and reserve seeds.

2 In 1-quart saucepan, heat bean halves and seeds, cream, and next 3 ingredients to boiling over high heat, stirring occasionally. (If using vanilla extract, stir in after removing lemon peel.) Reduce heat to low; simmer, stirring occasionally, 5 minutes.

3 Stir milk mixture into saucepan; heat 2 to 3 minutes, stirring constantly, until gelatin is completely dissolved (do not boil). Remove lemon peel, cinnamon stick, and vanilla bean. Pour mixture into medium bowl set in large bowl of *ice water*.

4 Stir mixture often, 10 to 12 minutes, just until beginning to mound when dropped from spatula. Immediately remove from ice bath.

5 Pour into eight 4-ounce ramekins or custard cups; place on jelly-roll pan for easier handling. Refrigerate at least 4 hours, until well chilled, or overnight.

6 Prepare sauce: Into 2-quart saucepan, press thawed raspberries through sieve. Stir in jelly and cornstarch. Heat to boiling over medium heat, stirring; boil 1 minute. Transfer to bowl; cover and refrigerate.

7 To unmold panna cotta, run warm knife around edge of each ramekin, then tap side of ramekin sharply to break seal; invert onto a dessert plate. Spoon some sauce around each panna cotta and garnish.

EACH SERVING: ABOUT 280 CALORIES, 3g PROTEIN, 23g CARBOHYDRATE, 20g TOTAL FAT (13g SATURATED), 75mg CHOLESTEROL, 35mg SODIUM

CAPPUCCINO MOUSSE

Prep: 30 minutes plus chilling   *Cook:* 2 to 3 minutes
Makes 8 servings

1 envelope plus 1 teaspoon unflavored gelatin
⅓ cup plus ½ cup milk
1 cup freshly brewed espresso coffee, or 2 tablespoons instant espresso-coffee powder dissolved in 1 cup boiling water
½ cup plus 1 teaspoon sugar
2 tablespoons coffee-flavor liqueur
1⅓ cups heavy or whipping cream
Pinch ground cinnamon
Chocolate-covered coffee beans for garnish

◆ In 1-quart saucepan, sprinkle gelatin over ⅓ cup milk; let stand 5 minutes. Stir in espresso. Heat over low heat, stirring constantly, 2 to 3 minutes, until gelatin is completely dissolved (do not boil). Remove from heat and stir in ½ cup sugar until dissolved. Stir in liqueur and remaining ½ cup milk. Transfer mixture to large bowl.

◆ Set bowl in larger bowl of *ice water*. With rubber spatula, stir often just until mixture mounds slightly when dropped from spatula. Immediately remove from ice bath.

◆ Meanwhile, in medium bowl, with mixer at medium speed, beat 1 cup cream to soft peaks. Fold one-third of cream into espresso mixture until incorporated. Fold in remaining whipped cream. Spoon into 8 coffee cups or 6-ounce custard cups. Cover and refrigerate at least 4 hours, until well chilled, or overnight.

◆ To serve, beat remaining ⅓ cup cream with cinnamon and remaining 1 teaspoon sugar to stiff peaks; spoon a dollop onto each mousse. Garnish with coffee beans.

Each serving: 220 calories, 3g protein, 17g carbohydrate, 16g total fat (10g saturated), 58mg cholesterol, 30mg sodium

MANGO MOUSSE

Prep: 20 minutes plus chilling   *Cook:* 3 minutes
Makes 8 servings

1 envelope unflavored gelatin
2 large ripe mangoes, peeled and cut into bite-size chunks (about 3 cups)
1 can (15 ounces) cream of coconut
½ cup fresh lime juice

◆ In 1-quart saucepan, sprinkle gelatin over ¼ *cup cold water*; let stand 5 minutes. Meanwhile, in blender at medium speed, blend remaining ingredients until smooth.

◆ Heat gelatin mixture over low heat, stirring constantly, 2 to 3 minutes, until completely dissolved (do not boil). Add to mango mixture in blender and blend until combined. Pour mixture into eight 4-ounce custard cups. Cover and refrigerate 4 hours, until well chilled, or overnight.

Each serving: 225 calories, 3g protein, 16g carbohydrate, 19g total fat (16g saturated), 0mg cholesterol, 5mg sodium

RASPBERRY CHARLOTTE

Prep: 25 minutes plus chilling   *Cook:* 4 minutes
Makes 8 servings

1 tablespoon plus ¼ cup sugar
2 tablespoons orange-flavor liqueur
1 package (3 to 4½ ounces) sponge-type ladyfingers
1 envelope unflavored gelatin
3 tablespoons fresh lemon juice
2 containers (10 ounces each) frozen raspberries in syrup, thawed
1 cup heavy or whipping cream
Fresh raspberries for garnish

◆ Line 9" by 5" loaf pan with plastic wrap. In 1-quart saucepan, heat 1 tablespoon sugar and *2 tablespoons water* to boiling, stirring to dissolve sugar. Remove from heat; stir in liqueur.

◆ Separate ladyfingers into halves. Lightly brush flat sides of ladyfinger halves with liqueur mixture. Line long sides and bottom of loaf pan with ladyfingers, flat sides in (they will not completely cover bottom).

◆ In clean 1-quart saucepan, sprinkle gelatin over ¼ *cup cold water*; let stand 5 minutes. Heat over low heat, stirring constantly, 2 to 3 minutes, until gelatin is completely dissolved (do not boil). Remove from heat; stir in lemon juice.

◆ In blender at medium speed, blend thawed frozen raspberries until smooth. Into large bowl, press raspberries through sieve; stir in gelatin mixture and remaining ¼ cup sugar. Set bowl in larger bowl of *ice water*. With rubber spatula, stir often, just until mixture mounds slightly when dropped from spatula; immediately remove from ice bath.

◆ In small bowl, with mixer at medium speed, beat cream to soft peaks. Fold one-third of cream into raspberry mixture until completely incorporated; gently fold in remaining cream. Spoon into ladyfinger-lined pan. Cover and refrigerate 4 hours, until well chilled, or overnight.

◆ To serve, trim ladyfingers level with raspberry filling. Unmold charlotte onto serving plate and remove plastic wrap. Garnish with fresh raspberries.

Each serving: About 255 calories, 2g protein, 36g carbohydrate, 11g total fat (7g saturated), 52mg cholesterol, 40mg sodium

Meringues

A mixture of stiffly beaten egg whites and sugar, meringue can be baked into many shapes. For best results, add the sugar very gradually while beating the egg whites, and beat until they stand straight in peaks when the beaters are lifted. Avoid making meringues on a humid day, because they'll absorb moisture from the air and turn soggy. They can be stored for up to a week in an airtight container at room temperature.

HAZELNUT DACQUOISE

◆◆◆◆◆◆◆◆◆◆◆◆◆◆◆◆◆◆◆◆◆◆◆◆◆◆◆◆◆◆

Prep: 1 hour 30 minutes plus cooling and chilling
Bake: 45 minutes plus drying in oven   *Makes 12 servings*

1 cup (about 4 ounces) hazelnuts (filberts), toasted and skinned (see page 522)	1 teaspoon vanilla extract
2 tablespoons cornstarch	3 squares (3 ounces) semisweet chocolate, melted and slightly warm
1½ cups plus 4 tablespoons confectioners' sugar	1 tablespoon instant espresso-coffee powder
6 large egg whites	Chocolate Curls for garnish (see page 551)
½ teaspoon cream of tartar	
3 cups heavy or whipping cream	

1 Preheat oven to 300°F. Line 2 large cookie sheets with foil. Using 8-inch round cake pan as a guide, with toothpick, outline 2 circles on foil on each sheet. In food processor with knife blade attached or in blender, blend hazelnuts, cornstarch, and ¾ cup confectioners' sugar until nuts are ground.

2 In large bowl, with mixer at high speed, beat egg whites and cream of tartar to soft peaks. Sprinkle ¾ cup confectioners' sugar, 2 tablespoons at a time, into egg whites, beating well after each addition, until sugar dissolves and whites stand in stiff, glossy peaks.

3 With rubber spatula, fold hazelnut mixture into egg whites. With metal spatula, spread one-fourth of meringue mixture inside each circle on cookie sheets. Bake meringues 45 minutes. Turn oven off; leave meringues in oven 1 hour to dry.

4 Transfer meringues with foil to wire racks; cool completely. With metal spatula, carefully loosen and remove meringues from foil.

5 Prepare chocolate cream: In small bowl, with mixer at medium speed, beat 1½ cups heavy cream, 1 tablespoon confectioners' sugar, and ½ teaspoon vanilla just to soft peaks. With rubber spatula, fold half of whipped cream into slightly warm melted chocolate just until combined. Fold in remaining whipped cream. Reserve ¼ cup chocolate cream.

6 Prepare coffee cream: In cup, dissolve espresso in 2 tablespoons heavy cream. In small bowl, beat remaining heavy cream and 3 tablespoons confectioners' sugar until soft peaks form. Add espresso mixture; beat until stiff peaks form.

7 On cake stand or plate, place 1 meringue layer; spread with half of chocolate cream. Top with another meringue layer and half of coffee cream. Repeat layering, ending with coffee cream. Spoon reserved ¼ cup chocolate cream on top. Refrigerate dacquoise at least 5 hours, or overnight, for easier cutting. Prepare Chocolate Curls. Just before serving, arrange curls on top of dacquoise.

EACH SERVING: ABOUT 365 CALORIES, 5g PROTEIN, 24g CARBOHYDRATE, 30g TOTAL FAT (16g SATURATED), 82mg CHOLESTEROL, 50mg SODIUM

STRAWBERRY-LEMON MERINGUE NESTS

Prep: 35 minutes plus chilling and cooling
Bake: 2 hours 30 minutes plus drying in oven
Makes 6 servings

3 large lemons	½ cup heavy or whipping
1 tablespoon cornstarch	cream
6 tablespoons butter	1 pint strawberries, hulled
1¼ cups sugar	and each cut into quarters
4 large eggs, separated	1 tablespoon strawberry jam
¼ teaspoon cream of tartar	

◆ Prepare lemon curd: Grate 1 tablespoon peel and squeeze ½ cup juice from lemons. In 2-quart saucepan, with wire whisk, mix cornstarch, lemon peel, and lemon juice until smooth. Add butter and ¾ cup sugar; heat to boiling over medium heat. Boil 1 minute, stirring constantly.

◆ In small bowl, beat egg yolks lightly. Into yolks, beat small amount of hot lemon mixture; pour egg mixture back into lemon mixture in saucepan, beating rapidly. Reduce heat to low; cook, stirring constantly, 5 minutes, or until thick (do not boil). Pour into medium bowl; cover surface with plastic wrap. Refrigerate 3 hours, until chilled, or up to 3 days.

◆ Meanwhile, prepare meringue nests: Preheat oven to 225°F. Line large cookie sheet with foil. In small bowl, with mixer at high speed, beat egg whites and cream of tartar until soft peaks form. Sprinkle in remaining ½ cup sugar, 2 tablespoons at a time, beating well after each addition until sugar dissolves and whites stand in stiff, glossy peaks.

◆◆◆◆◆◆◆◆◆◆◆◆◆◆◆◆◆◆◆◆◆◆◆◆◆◆◆◆◆◆◆◆

PIPING MERINGUE STARS

For a dessert sensation, pipe any meringue mixture into stars: Preheat oven to 225°F. Line large cookie sheet with foil. Using 3-inch star-shape cookie cutter as a guide, with toothpick, trace star outlines on foil. Spoon two-thirds of meringue into decorating bag fitted with coupler and large star tip. Pipe meringue around outline of traced stars on foil; fill centers of stars with meringue. Change tip on decorating bag to medium star tip; spoon remaining meringue into bag.

Pipe slightly smaller star on top of each existing star. With spoon, form small indentation in center of each meringue star. Bake 2½ hours. Transfer meringues with foil to wire rack; cool completely. Top with lemon curd or whipped cream and fruit.

◆◆◆◆◆◆◆◆◆◆◆◆◆◆◆◆◆◆◆◆◆◆◆◆◆◆◆◆◆◆◆◆

◆ Spoon meringue into 6 mounds on cookie sheet. With back of spoon, form a well in center of each mound to create a nest. Bake 2½ hours. Turn oven off; leave nests in oven 1 hour to dry completely.

◆ Transfer nests with foil to wire rack; cool completely. With metal spatula, carefully loosen nests and remove from foil. Store in airtight container at room temperature until ready to use (up to 1 week).

◆ Just before serving, in small bowl, with mixer at medium speed, beat cream to stiff peaks. Gently fold into lemon curd. In medium bowl, toss strawberries with jam. Spoon lemon-curd mixture into nests; top with strawberry mixture.

Each serving: About 415 calories, 5g protein, 52g carbohydrate, 22g total fat (13g saturated), 200mg cholesterol, 165mg sodium

BERRIES AND CREAM MERINGUES

Prep: 25 minutes plus cooling   Bake: 45 minutes plus drying in oven
Makes 8 servings

4 large egg whites	2 tablespoons sweet Marsala
¼ teaspoon cream of tartar	wine (optional)
¾ cup plus 1 tablespoon	1 pint blueberries
granulated sugar	½ pint raspberries
1½ cups heavy or whipping	½ pint blackberries
cream	Confectioners' sugar
¼ teaspoon vanilla extract	

◆ Preheat oven to 225°F. Line 2 large cookie sheets with foil. In small bowl, with mixer at high speed, beat egg whites and cream of tartar until soft peaks form. Sprinkle in ¾ cup granulated sugar, 2 tablespoons at a time, beating well after each addition until sugar completely dissolves and whites stand in stiff, glossy peaks.

◆ With small metal spatula, spread meringue on foil-lined cookie sheets into eight 6-inch rounds, about ½ inch apart. Bake 45 minutes. Turn oven off; leave meringues in oven 1 hour longer to dry completely.

◆ Transfer meringues with foil to wire racks; cool completely. With metal spatula, carefully loosen and remove meringues from foil. Store in airtight container at room temperature until ready to use (up to 1 week).

◆ Just before serving, in small bowl, with mixer at medium speed, beat heavy cream, vanilla, and remaining 1 tablespoon granulated sugar until soft peaks form. Beat in Marsala, if using. Spread whipped cream on meringues. Top with berries; sprinkle berries with confectioners' sugar.

Each serving: About 280 calories, 3g protein, 32g carbohydrate, 17g total fat (10g saturated), 61mg cholesterol, 45mg sodium

ICE-CREAM DESSERTS

Create impressive but easy desserts with store-bought ice cream and sorbets. Use to fill a cake roll or top a cookie-crumb crust, put it in the freezer – and relax.

CINNAMON ICE-CREAM ROLL

◆◆◆◆◆◆◆◆◆◆◆◆◆

Prep: 40 minutes plus cooling, freezing, and standing
Bake: 12 to 15 minutes
Makes 16 servings

⅔ cup cake flour (not self-rising)
1 teaspoon baking powder
½ teaspoon salt
About ⅓ cup unsweetened cocoa
½ teaspoon plus 2 tablespoons ground cinnamon
4 large eggs, separated
¾ cup plus 2 tablespoons sugar
¾ teaspoon vanilla extract
1 quart vanilla ice cream
1 cup heavy or whipping cream
Quick Chocolate Curls (see page 551) for garnish

1 Preheat oven to 375°F. Grease 15½" by 10½" jelly-roll pan; line pan with waxed paper. Set aside. Sift flour, baking powder, salt, ⅓ cup cocoa, and ½ teaspoon cinnamon through medium-mesh sieve into small bowl. In another small bowl, with mixer at high speed, beat egg whites until soft peaks form. Gradually sprinkle in ¼ cup sugar, beating until sugar completely dissolves and whites stand in stiff peaks.

2 In large bowl, with same beaters and with mixer at high speed, beat egg yolks, vanilla, and ½ cup sugar until very thick and lemon-colored.

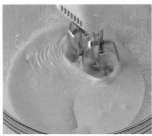

3 With rubber spatula or wire whisk, fold in flour mixture and egg whites (this will take patience). Spread evenly in pan. Bake 12 to 15 minutes, until top springs back when lightly touched.

4 Sprinkle clean cloth kitchen towel with cocoa. When cake is done, immediately invert onto towel. Remove waxed paper. If you like, cut off crisp edges. From a narrow end, roll cake with towel, jelly-roll fashion. Cool cake completely, seam-side down, on wire rack, about 1 hour.

5 Place ice cream in large bowl; let stand at room temperature to soften slightly. Stir in remaining 2 tablespoons cinnamon. Unroll cooled cake; spread with ice cream. From same end, roll cake without towel. Place cake, seam-side down, on freezer-safe long platter. Freeze at least 4 hours, until firm. In small bowl, with mixer at medium speed, beat heavy cream and remaining 2 tablespoons sugar until stiff peaks form.

6 Spoon whipped cream over top of cake. (If not serving right away, freeze cake uncovered until whipped cream hardens. Wrap; return to freezer. To serve, let cake stand at room temperature 15 minutes for easier slicing.) Garnish with Quick Chocolate Curls.

EACH SERVING: ABOUT 200 CALORIES, 4g PROTEIN, 25g CARBOHYDRATE, 11g TOTAL FAT (6g SATURATED), 88mg CHOLESTEROL, 145mg SODIUM

SORBET-AND-CREAM CAKE

Prep: 30 minutes plus cooling, freezing, and standing   *Bake:* 10 minutes
Makes 20 servings

30 vanilla wafers	1 pint mango sorbet
4 tablespoons margarine or butter	1 pint lemon sorbet
½ teaspoon grated lime peel	1 ripe mango, peeled and thinly sliced, for garnish
2 pints vanilla ice cream	Fresh raspberries or strawberries for garnish
1 pint raspberry or strawberry sorbet	

◆ Preheat oven to 375°F. In food processor with knife blade attached or in blender at medium speed, blend vanilla wafers until fine crumbs form. (You should have about 1 cup crumbs.)

◆ In small saucepan, melt margarine over low heat; stir in lime peel. In 9" by 3" springform pan, with fork, stir wafer crumbs and margarine mixture until crumbs are moistened. With hand, press mixture firmly onto bottom of pan. Bake crust 10 minutes. Cool completely in pan on wire rack.

◆ While crust is cooling, place 1 pint vanilla ice cream and all sorbets in refrigerator 30 minutes to soften slightly.

◆ Spoon alternating scoops of softened vanilla ice cream and sorbets over crust in 2 layers; press mixture down to eliminate air pockets. Place pan in freezer about 30 minutes to harden mixture slightly.

◆ Meanwhile, place remaining vanilla ice cream in refrigerator to soften slightly.

◆ With metal spatula, evenly spread remaining vanilla ice cream over frozen layer. Cover and freeze at least 4 hours, until firm.

◆ To unmold, place warm dampened towels around side of pan for about 20 seconds to soften ice cream slightly. Remove side of pan and place cake on platter. (If you like, remove pan bottom also.) Cover cake and keep frozen if not serving right away; let stand at room temperature about 15 minutes for easier slicing. Before serving, garnish top of cake with mango slices and raspberries.

Each serving: About 160 calories, 1g protein, 23g carbohydrate, 8g total fat (2g saturated), 15mg cholesterol, 85mg sodium

VANILLA-PECAN ICE-CREAM TORTE

Prep: 20 minutes plus cooling, freezing, and standing   *Bake:* 8 minutes
Makes 16 servings

1 cup pecan halves, toasted and cooled	3 pints vanilla ice cream
20 gingersnap cookies	2 tablespoons plus 1 teaspoon pumpkin-pie spice
2 tablespoons sugar	
3 tablespoons margarine or butter, melted	

◆ Preheat oven to 375°F. Reserve 16 pecan halves for garnish. In food processor with knife blade attached or in blender at medium speed, blend remaining pecan halves with gingersnaps and sugar until mixture is finely ground.

◆ In 9-inch springform pan, with fork, stir cookie mixture and melted margarine until crumbs are moistened. With hand, press mixture firmly onto bottom of pan. Bake crust 8 minutes. Cool completely in pan on wire rack.

◆ While crust is cooling, let ice cream stand at room temperature 20 minutes to soften slightly. In large bowl, mix ice cream and pumpkin-pie spice until blended; spread over crust. Place pecan halves around top edge of torte. Cover torte and freeze at least overnight, or up to 1 week.

◆ To serve, let frozen torte stand at room temperature about 15 minutes for easier slicing. Remove side of pan.

Each serving: About 210 calories, 3g protein, 22g carbohydrate, 13g total fat (4g saturated), 22mg cholesterol, 125mg sodium

ICE-CREAM SPECIALS

◆◆◆◆◆◆◆◆◆◆◆◆◆◆◆◆◆◆◆◆◆◆◆◆◆

For almost-instant desserts, layer ice cream, fruit, and sauce; top with crumbled cookies, chopped candy, or nuts

• Strawberry and vanilla ice cream layered with sliced strawberries, topped with crumbled macaroon cookies

• Peach ice cream with fresh raspberries, Blueberry Sauce (see page 482), and toasted slivered almonds

• Cinnamon ice cream (mix in 1 tablespoon ground cinnamon per pint of softened vanilla ice cream) with warmed maple syrup and pecans

HOMEMADE ICE CREAM

There's nothing difficult about making scrumptious ice cream yourself, whether it's with an old-fashioned hand-crank ice-cream maker or with an electric model. Our classic, custard-based Vanilla-Bean Ice Cream is irresistible; so are the easy variations on page 482. Alternatively, make our super-simple No-Cook Vanilla Ice Cream – just stir. To add crunch, stir in 1½ cups coarsely chopped Gold-Rush Nut Brittle (see page 524) or other chopped candy immediately *after* churning.

VANILLA-BEAN ICE CREAM

Prep: 5 minutes plus chilling and freezing   *Cook:* 15 to 20 minutes
Makes about 5 cups

1 vanilla bean or 1 tablespoon vanilla extract	4 large egg yolks
¾ cup sugar	⅛ teaspoon salt
3 cups half-and-half or light cream	1 cup heavy or whipping cream
	Butterscotch Sauce (optional, see page 482)

1 Chop vanilla bean into ¼-inch pieces. In blender, process vanilla bean and sugar until mixture is very finely ground; set aside. (If using vanilla extract, stir in with heavy cream in Step 4.) Prepare custard: In 3-quart saucepan, heat half-and-half to boiling. Meanwhile, in medium bowl, whisk egg yolks, salt, and vanilla-sugar until smooth.

 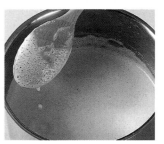

2 Gradually whisk hot half-and-half into egg-yolk mixture.

3 Return mixture to saucepan and cook over medium heat, stirring constantly, just until mixture coats back of wooden spoon (do not boil, or mixture will curdle). Remove from heat.

4 Strain custard mixture through sieve into clean large bowl. Stir heavy cream into custard; refrigerate at least 2 hours, until chilled, or overnight.

5 Churn and freeze in ice-cream maker as manufacturer directs. Prepare Butterscotch Sauce, if you like. Serve ice cream with warm sauce.

NO-COOK VANILLA ICE CREAM

In large bowl, stir 2 cups half-and-half or light cream, 2 cups heavy or whipping cream, ¾ cup sugar, 1 tablespoon vanilla extract, and ⅛ teaspoon salt until sugar is completely dissolved. Pour mixture into ice-cream maker; churn and freeze as manufacturer directs. Makes about 6¾ cups.

Each ½ cup: 225 calories, 2g protein, 14g carbohydrate, 18g total fat (11g saturated), 64mg cholesterol, 50mg sodium

EACH ½ CUP: ABOUT 260 CALORIES, 4g PROTEIN, 19g CARBOHYDRATE, 19g TOTAL FAT (11g SATURATED), 145mg CHOLESTEROL, 70mg SODIUM

PEACH OR STRAWBERRY ICE CREAM

Prep: 20 minutes plus chilling and freezing   *Cook:* 15 to 20 minutes
Makes about 6 cups

Vanilla-Bean Ice Cream or No-
Cook Vanilla Ice Cream (see
page 481)
8 medium peaches, peeled
and sliced (4 cups), or
2 pints strawberries, hulled

½ cup sugar
2 tablespoons fresh lemon
juice

Prepare Vanilla-Bean Ice Cream as directed in Steps
1 through 4 or prepare No-Cook Vanilla Ice Cream, but
omit vanilla and use only ½ cup sugar. In medium bowl,
mash peaches or strawberries with sugar and lemon juice;
cover and refrigerate 30 minutes. Before churning, stir fruit
mixture into ice-cream mixture; churn and freeze in ice-
cream maker as manufacturer directs.

**Each ½ cup: About 275 calories, 4g protein, 31g carbohydrate,
16g total fat (9g saturated), 120mg cholesterol, 55mg sodium**

CHOCOLATE ICE CREAM

Prep: 10 minutes plus chilling and freezing   *Cook:* 15 to 20 minutes
Makes about 6 cups

Vanilla-Bean Ice Cream or No-
Cook Vanilla Ice Cream (see
page 481)
3 squares (3 ounces)
unsweetened chocolate

2 squares (2 ounces)
semisweet chocolate
1 teaspoon vanilla extract

◆ Prepare Vanilla-Bean Ice Cream as directed in Steps
1 through 4 or prepare No-Cook Vanilla Ice Cream, but
omit vanilla and reserve ¼ cup heavy cream.

◆ In top of double boiler, melt unsweetened and semisweet
chocolate with reserved ¼ cup heavy cream; remove from
heat. Stir in vanilla.

◆ Stir 1 cup ice-cream
mixture into melted
chocolate; stir chocolate
mixture back into ice-
cream mixture. Churn
and freeze in ice-cream
maker as manufacturer
directs.

**Each ½ cup: About 280 calories,
4g protein, 21g carbohydrate,
21g total fat (12g saturated),
120mg cholesterol, 55mg sodium**

ICE-CREAM SAUCES

These no-fuss sauces are great over ice
cream and can be used for our Ice-
Cream Special ideas (see page 480).
Serve a selection with different ice-
cream flavors and let guests
assemble their own dessert.
These sauces are
equally delicious
with pound cake,
bread pudding,
dessert crepes, or
cream puffs.

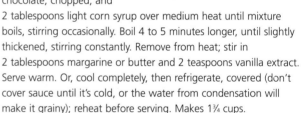

Hot fudge sauce

Blueberry sauce

Hot fudge sauce
In heavy 2-quart
saucepan, heat 1 cup
heavy or whipping
cream, ¾ cup sugar, 4 squares
(4 ounces) unsweetened
chocolate, chopped, and
2 tablespoons light corn syrup over medium heat until mixture
boils, stirring occasionally. Boil 4 to 5 minutes longer, until slightly
thickened, stirring constantly. Remove from heat; stir in
2 tablespoons margarine or butter and 2 teaspoons vanilla extract.
Serve warm. Or, cool completely, then refrigerate, covered (don't
cover sauce until it's cold, or the water from condensation will
make it grainy); reheat before serving. Makes 1¾ cups.

**Each ¼ cup: About 330 calories, 2g protein, 32g carbohydrate,
24g total fat (12g saturated), 47mg cholesterol, 55mg sodium**

Blueberry sauce
In 2-quart saucepan, stir ⅓ cup sugar,
2 teaspoons cornstarch, and ¼ cup cold water until smooth. Heat
to boiling over medium heat, stirring. Add 2 cups fresh or frozen
blueberries and heat to boiling, stirring. Reduce heat to low and
cook 1 minute longer. Remove from heat and stir in 1 teaspoon
fresh lemon juice. Serve warm. Makes 1¾ cups.

**Each ¼ cup: About 65 calories, 0g protein, 16g carbohydrate,
0g total fat, 0mg cholesterol, 5mg sodium**

Butterscotch sauce
In 3-quart saucepan, heat 1 cup packed
brown sugar, ½ cup heavy or whipping cream, ⅓ cup light corn
syrup, 2 tablespoons margarine or butter, 1 teaspoon distilled
white vinegar, and ⅛ teaspoon salt to boiling over high heat,
stirring occasionally. Reduce heat to low and cook 2 minutes.
Remove from heat and stir in 1 teaspon vanilla extract. Serve
warm. Makes 1⅓ cups.

**Each ¼ cup: About 355 calories, 1g protein, 60g carbohydrate,
13g total fat (6g saturated), 33mg cholesterol, 150mg sodium**

GRANITAS AND SORBETS

Fruity, refreshing, and fat-free, granitas and sorbets are made from similar mixtures of pureed fruit and sugar syrup, but granitas have a coarser texture (granita is derived from the verb "to granulate" in Italian). You don't even need an ice-cream maker: Just whirl up the sorbets in a food processor or, for the granitas, freeze in a metal pan (metal makes the mixture freeze faster). Any of the flavors here would make a light ending to a rich meal, perhaps with a crisp cookie on the side.

PEACH GRANITA

◆◆◆◆◆◆◆◆◆◆◆◆◆◆◆◆◆◆◆◆◆◆◆◆◆◆◆◆

Prep: 20 minutes plus freezing and standing
Makes about 8 cups

1 cup sugar
1¾ pounds peaches or
    nectarines (about
    5 medium), unpeeled, cut
    into wedges

2 tablespoons fresh lemon
    juice
Almond-Anise Biscotti
    (optional, see page 518)

1 Prepare sugar syrup: In 1-quart saucepan, heat sugar and *1¼ cups water* to boiling over high heat, stirring occasionally. Reduce heat to medium; cook, stirring, 1 minute, or until sugar dissolves completely. Transfer to small bowl to cool. In blender at medium speed, blend peach wedges until smooth; pour into medium-mesh sieve set over medium bowl.

2 With spoon, press peach puree through sieve; you should have 3 cups puree. Into puree, stir lemon juice and syrup. Pour into 9" by 9" metal baking pan. Cover with foil or plastic wrap. Freeze 2 hours; stir with fork.

3 Freeze at least 3 hours longer, until fully frozen, or overnight. To serve, let stand 20 minutes at room temperature; with fork or spoon, scrape surface to create pebbly texture. Serve with biscotti, if you like.

MORE FRUIT GRANITAS

Raspberry or blackberry granita Prepare granita as above but substitute 3 pints raspberries or blackberries and 2 tablespoons fresh lime juice for peaches and lemon juice. Makes about 8 cups.

Each ½ cup: About 55 calories, 0g protein, 14g carbohydrate, 0g total fat, 0mg cholesterol, 0mg sodium

Raspberry granita

Watermelon granita Prepare granita as above but substitute 5½-pound piece watermelon, seeded and cut into chunks (about 9 cups), and 2 tablespoons fresh lime juice for peaches and lemon juice; when making the sugar syrup, use only ¾ cup water instead of 1¼ cups. Makes about 9 cups.

Each ½ cup: About 70 calories, 1g protein, 17g carbohydrate, 0g total fat, 0mg cholesterol, 0mg sodium

Watermelon granita

EACH ½ CUP: ABOUT 70 CALORIES, 0g PROTEIN, 18g CARBOHYDRATE, 0g TOTAL FAT, 0mg CHOLESTEROL, 0mg SODIUM

LEMON-ROSEMARY SORBET

Prep: 25 minutes plus standing and freezing
Makes about 4 cups

1¼ cups sugar
¼ cup light corn syrup
2 tablespoons coarsely
  chopped fresh rosemary
1⅓ cups fresh lemon juice
  (about 7 large lemons)

2 teaspoons grated lemon
  peel
Rosemary sprigs and lemon
  slices for garnish

◆ In 2-quart saucepan, heat sugar, corn syrup, and *4 cups water* to boiling over high heat, stirring occasionally until sugar dissolves. Remove saucepan from heat; stir in chopped rosemary. Cover pan and let stand 20 minutes.

◆ Pour mixture through sieve set over medium bowl; stir in lemon juice and peel. Pour lemon mixture into 9" by 9" metal baking pan; cover with foil or plastic wrap. Freeze, stirring occasionally, about 3 hours, until partially frozen.

◆ In food processor with knife blade attached, blend lemon mixture until smooth but still frozen. Return mixture to baking pan; cover and freeze at least 3 hours, or until firm.

◆ To serve, let sorbet stand at room temperature 10 to 15 minutes to soften slightly for easier scooping; garnish.

Each ⅓ cup: About 110 calories, 0g protein, 28g carbohydrate, 0g total fat, 0mg cholesterol, 5mg sodium

BLUEBERRY SORBET

Prep: 10 minutes plus freezing and standing
Makes about 3⅓ cups

½ cup sugar
2 tablespoons fresh lemon
  juice

1 bag (20 ounces) frozen
  unsweetened blueberries

◆ Prepare sugar syrup: In 1-quart saucepan, heat sugar, lemon juice, and *1 tablespoon water* to boiling over high heat. Reduce heat to low and cook, stirring occasionally, until sugar dissolves. Remove from heat.

◆ In food processor with knife blade attached, blend frozen blueberries until fruit resembles finely shaved ice, stopping processor occasionally to scrape down side. (If fruit is not finely shaved, sorbet will not be smooth.)

◆ With processor running, slowly pour hot sugar syrup in a thin stream through feed tube and process until mixture is smooth but still frozen. Spoon into freezer-safe container and freeze until firm.

◆ To serve, let sorbet stand at room temperature 10 to 15 minutes to soften slightly for easier scooping.

Each ⅓ cup: About 70 calories, 0g protein, 17g carbohydrate, 0g total fat, 0mg cholesterol, 0mg sodium

MORE FRUIT SORBETS

Peach sorbet Prepare as for Blueberry Sorbet (below left) but use ¼ cup sugar, 1 tablespoon fresh lemon juice, and 1 tablespoon water for sugar syrup, adding ½ teaspoon almond extract to cooked syrup; instead of blueberries, use 1 bag (20 ounces) frozen unsweetened peach slices. Makes about 3 cups.

Each ⅓ cup: About 50 calories, 0g protein, 13g carbohydrate, 0g total fat, 0mg cholesterol, 0mg sodium

Cantaloupe sorbet Prepare as for Blueberry Sorbet (left) but use ½ cup sugar, 2 tablespoons fresh lemon juice, and 1 tablespoon water for sugar syrup; instead of blueberries, use 1 small ripe cantaloupe (2 pounds), seeded, cut into small chunks, spread on jelly-roll pan, and frozen overnight. Makes about 4 cups.

Each ⅓ cup: About 55 calories, 1g protein, 15g carbohydrate, 0g total fat, 0mg cholesterol, 15mg sodium

Strawberry sorbet Prepare as for Blueberry Sorbet (left) but use ⅓ cup sugar, 1 tablespoon fresh lemon juice, and 1 tablespoon water for sugar syrup; instead of blueberries, use 1 bag (20 ounces) frozen unsweetened strawberries. Makes about 2⅓ cups.

Each ⅓ cup: About 65 calories, 0g protein, 17g carbohydrate, 0g total fat, 0mg cholesterol, 0mg sodium

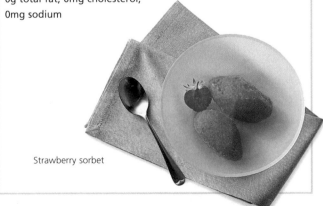

Strawberry sorbet

PIES & TARTS

15

Simple or elegant, fruit-filled or fudgy, pies and tarts are wonderfully welcome after practically any meal. A light, flaky crust is a pie's crowning glory and surprisingly easy to make, as long as you use the right ingredients and follow our foolproof mixing and rolling techniques.

PERFECT PASTRY

• Start with cold ingredients (e.g. chilled margarine or butter, ice-cold water). The kitchen should be cool too.
• Generally, handle the dough as little as possible, or you'll overdevelop the gluten in the flour and make a tough crust.
• For best results, use a mix of fat – margarine or butter for flavor and color and shortening for flakiness.
• When cutting fat into the flour, work quickly so the fat remains firm and cold.
• Sprinkle in ice water just until the dough is moistened. Toss quickly and lightly with a fork; do not stir. (Use the least amount of water to avoid a tough crust.)
• Chilling dough for at least 30 minutes will make it easier to roll and also help prevent shrinkage. Wrap tightly so the edges don't dry out and crack when rolled.
• To prevent sticking, roll dough on a lightly floured surface; sprinkle surface with additional flour as necessary. Roll dough from the center forward and back; rotate the dough a quarter-turn and repeat rolling and rotating to make an even circle.
• If dough tears, just moisten the edges and press together. Or, brush a small piece of dough with water; use as a patch.
• When fitting dough into a pie plate, gently ease it onto the bottom with your fingertips or a small ball of dough, taking care to press out air pockets. Never stretch or pull the dough to fit, or the crust may shrink during baking.

WHICH PIE PAN?

Crisp, flaky crusts aren't dependent only on a good dough – the pan also makes a difference. For a crisp, well-browned crust, choose a glass pie plate, or a metal one with a dull

finish (shiny pans are fine for crumb crusts). Use a regular pie plate (9 inches across by 1 inch deep) or a deep-dish one (9½ inches by 1½ to 2 inches) as directed so the filling won't overflow. For tarts, use a fluted pan with a removable bottom, which makes for easy removal of the tart.

BLIND BAKING

Crusts with moist fillings are often partially or completely baked before they're filled for crisp results. This is called "blind baking." Line the crust with foil and weight it with pie weights, dry beans, or uncooked rice to prevent puffing or slipping during baking. Cool completely before filling.

For tarts and pies, remove the foil and weights after the crust is set, then return to the oven to brown.

For tartlets, weight the crust with another tart pan before baking. Or, prevent puffing by piercing crust with a fork.

BETTER BAKING

• For non-soggy double-crust pies, cut slits in the top crust before baking so steam can escape during cooking.
• For easy handling – and to catch drips – bake the pie on a sheet of foil with crimped edges, or use a cookie sheet.
• Bake in the lower third of the oven so the bottom crust becomes crisp and the top doesn't overbrown (if pie still browns too quickly, just cover it loosely with foil).
• To check a custard pie for doneness, insert a knife about 1 inch from the center; it should come out clean. A starch-thickened fruit pie is ready when it bubbles in the center.
• Let pies cool before cutting so the filling can set.

NO-FUSS CRUMB CRUSTS

Cookie crumb crusts take no time to make – all you need is a blender or food processor. Or, crush cookies in a zip-tight bag with a rolling pin. Chocolate or vanilla wafers, gingersnaps, or graham crackers are a good base. For added richness, replace some of the cookies with ground nuts such as pecans, macadamias, or almonds, or with amaretti cookies. For spicy flavor, add a bit of ground ginger, cinnamon, or nutmeg.

Regular pie plate   Deep-dish pie plate

PIECRUSTS

Tender, flaky piecrust is a work of art – and surprisingly easy to master. For best results, chill the ingredients before mixing, and handle the pastry as little as possible (overworking develops the gluten in the flour, making the pastry tough). To create a glaze, brush the top crust (not the edge) with milk, cream, or slightly beaten egg white and sprinkle with sugar. Each piecrust takes about 10 minutes to prepare, plus chilling time.

PASTRY FOR 2-CRUST PIE

❖❖❖❖❖❖❖❖❖❖❖❖❖

2¼ cups all-purpose flour
½ teaspoon salt
¼ cup shortening

½ cup cold margarine or butter, cut up

1 In large bowl, mix flour and salt. With pastry blender or two knives used scissor-fashion, cut in shortening and margarine until mixture resembles coarse crumbs.

2 Sprinkle in *4 to 6 tablespoons ice water*, a tablespoon at a time. Mix lightly with fork after each addition, until dough is just moist enough to hold together.

3 Shape dough into 2 balls, one slightly larger. Wrap and refrigerate 30 minutes, or overnight (if chilled overnight, let stand at room temperature 30 minutes before rolling). On lightly floured surface, with floured rolling pin, roll larger ball 2 inches larger all around than inverted 9-inch pie plate.

4 Roll dough round gently onto rolling pin; gently ease into pie plate. Trim edge, leaving 1-inch overhang. Reserve trimmings for decorating pie, if you like. Fill piecrust.

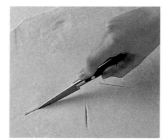

5 Roll small ball of dough into 10-inch round. Cut several slashes; center over filling. Trim edge, leaving 1-inch overhang; fold overhang under. Make decorative edge (see page 488).

PASTRY FOR 1-CRUST PIE

1¼ cups all-purpose flour
¼ teaspoon salt
2 tablespoons shortening

4 tablespoons cold margarine or butter, cut up

Prepare pastry as directed for 2-Crust Pie, but in Step 2 sprinkle in *3 to 5 tablespoons ice water*, and in Step 3 make only 1 ball of dough.

PASTRY FOR 11-INCH TART

1½ cups all-purpose flour
½ teaspoon salt
2 tablespoons shortening

½ cup cold margarine or butter, cut up

Prepare pastry as directed for 2-Crust Pie, but in Step 2 sprinkle in *3 to 4 tablespoons ice water*, and in Step 3 make only 1 ball of dough and, after chilling, roll dough to a 14-inch round. Ease dough into 11" by 1" round tart pan with removable bottom. Fold overhang in and press against side of tart pan to form rim ⅛ inch above pan edge.

PASTRY FOR 9-INCH TART

1 cup all-purpose flour
¼ teaspoon salt
1 tablespoon shortening

6 tablespoons cold margarine or butter, cut up

Prepare pastry as directed for 2-Crust Pie, but in Step 2 sprinkle in only *2 to 3 tablespoons ice water*, and in Step 3 make only 1 ball of dough and, after chilling, roll dough to an 11-inch round. Use to line 9" by 1" round tart pan with removable bottom as directed for 11-inch tart.

FOOD PROCESSOR METHOD

In food processor with knife blade attached, combine flour, salt, shortening, and margarine. Process for 1 to 2 seconds, until mixture forms fine crumbs. Add smaller amount of *ice water* all at once; process for 1 to 2 seconds, until dough leaves sides of bowl. Remove dough from bowl; with hands, shape into ball.

DECORATIVE PIE EDGES

From classic to creative, these borders are the perfect way to add a professional finish to homemade pies. The forked, fluted, sharp fluted, and rope edges are pretty on any pie, whether one- or two-crust. The appliqué leaf edge is best for one-crust pies (but you will need enough pastry for a two-crust). For neat results, chill the pastry so that it is firm (not hard) when you work with it.

◆ ◆ ◆ ◆ ◆ ◆ ◆ ◆ ◆ ◆ ◆ ◆

PREPARING PIE EDGES

1 Trim dough edge (or top crust for 2-crust pie) with kitchen shears to leave 1-inch overhang. (For forked or leaf edge, trim edge even with rim of pie plate; omit Step 2 below).

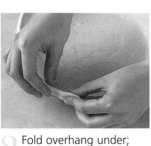

2 Fold overhang under; pinch to make stand-up edge. Shape decorative edge as desired (right).

◆ ◆ ◆ ◆ ◆ ◆ ◆ ◆ ◆ ◆ ◆ ◆

Forked edge Trim dough edge as in Step 1 (below left) even with rim of pie plate. With floured 4-tine fork, press dough to rim of plate; repeat around edge.

Fluted edge Push one index finger against outside edge of rim; with index finger and thumb of other hand, pinch to form ruffle. Repeat around edge, leaving ¼-inch space between each ruffle.

Sharp (or pinched) fluted edge Push one index finger against inside edge of rim; with index finger and thumb of other hand, pinch to make flute. Repeat around edge, leaving ¼-inch space between each flute.

Rope edge Press thumb into dough edge at an angle, then pinch dough between thumb and knuckle of index finger. Place thumb in groove left by index finger; pinch as before; repeat around edge.

Leaf edge Prepare Pastry for 2-Crust Pie (see page 487). Use larger ball of dough to line pie plate; trim even with rim. Roll smaller ball ⅛ inch thick. With knife or small cookie cutter, cut out leaves (see page 489). Lightly brush piecrust edge with water. Press shapes onto edge.

DOUBLE-CRUST PIES

A double-crust pie, which lends itself to decorative edges and adornments of cutouts made from dough trimmings, is a beautiful – and delicious – way to encase a fruit filling. Be sure to cut a few slits in the top to allow the steam to escape. Always cool the pie for a short time as the recipe directs (even when serving it warm) so the filling can firm up for easier cutting.

DEEP-DISH APPLE PIE

◆◆◆◆◆◆◆◆◆◆◆◆◆◆◆◆◆◆◆◆◆◆◆◆◆◆◆◆◆◆

Prep: 40 minutes plus chilling and cooling   *Bake:* 50 to 55 minutes
Makes 10 servings

Pastry for 2-Crust Pie (see page 487)
9 medium Golden Delicious or Newtown Pippin apples (about 3 pounds), peeled, cored, and cut into ⅛-inch-thick slices

½ cup sugar
3 tablespoons all-purpose flour
2 tablespoons coarsely chopped crystallized ginger
2 tablespoons margarine or butter, cut into small pieces

1 Prepare Pastry for 2-Crust Pie through chilling. Preheat oven to 425°F. In large bowl, toss apple slices with sugar, flour, and ginger.

2 Use larger ball of dough to line 9½-inch deep-dish pie plate. Spoon apple mixture into piecrust; dot with margarine.

3 Roll dough for top crust into 11-inch round. Place on filling as directed; make decorative edge (see page 488). Reroll trimmings. Make shapes (see below); brush with water. Place on pie. Place sheet of foil underneath pie plate; crimp foil edges to form a rim to catch drips during baking.

4 Bake pie 50 to 55 minutes, until apples are tender when pierced with a knife. Cover pie loosely with foil after 30 minutes to prevent overbrowning. Cool pie on wire rack 1 hour to serve warm. Or, cool completely to serve later.

◆◆◆◆◆◆◆◆◆◆◆◆◆◆◆◆◆◆◆◆◆◆◆◆◆◆◆◆

DECORATIVE PASTRY SHAPES

Apple Roll out the dough trimmings. Use a small knife dipped in flour to cut a free-form apple shape.

Leaves Reflour knife; cut out leaves from remaining dough. Use back of the knife to mark veins in the leaves.

◆◆◆◆◆◆◆◆◆◆◆◆◆◆◆◆◆◆◆◆◆◆◆◆◆◆◆◆

EACH SERVING: ABOUT 370 CALORIES, 3g PROTEIN, 53g CARBOHYDRATE, 17g TOTAL FAT (4g SATURATED), 0mg CHOLESTEROL, 240mg SODIUM

STRAWBERRY-RHUBARB PIE

Prep: 30 minutes plus chilling and cooling   Bake: 1 hour 35 to 45 minutes
Makes 10 servings

Pastry for 2-Crust Pie (see
  page 487)
¼ cup cornstarch
1 cup plus 1 tablespoon sugar
1 pint strawberries, hulled,
  each cut in half if large

1¼ pounds rhubarb, cut into
  ½-inch pieces (4 cups)
2 tablespoons margarine or
  butter, cut up

◆ Prepare Pastry for 2-Crust Pie through chilling. Preheat oven to 425°F. In large bowl, mix cornstarch and 1 cup sugar. Add strawberries and rhubarb; toss to combine.

◆ Use larger ball of dough to line 9-inch pie plate. Spoon fruit mixture into piecrust; dot with margarine. Roll top crust and place on filling as directed; make decorative edge (see page 488). Sprinkle with remaining 1 tablespoon sugar.

◆ Place sheet of foil underneath pie plate; crimp edges to form a rim to catch drips. Bake pie 15 minutes. Turn oven control to 375°F; bake 1 hour 20 to 30 minutes longer, until filling is bubbly in center. Cool pie on wire rack 1 hour to serve warm. Or, cool completely to serve later.

Each serving: About 355 calories, 4g protein, 49g carbohydrate, 17g total fat (4g saturated), 0mg cholesterol, 240mg sodium

PEAR-CRANBERRY PIE

Prep: 45 minutes plus chilling and cooling   Bake: 1 hour 20 to 30 minutes
Makes 10 servings

Pastry for 2-Crust Pie (see
  page 487)
3 tablespoons cornstarch
⅛ teaspoon ground cinnamon
¾ cup plus 1 tablespoon sugar
1½ cups cranberries, chopped

6 large fully ripe pears (about
  3 pounds), peeled, cored,
  and sliced
2 tablespoons margarine or
  butter, cut up

◆ Prepare Pastry for 2-Crust Pie through chilling. Preheat oven to 425°F. In large bowl, mix cornstarch, cinnamon, and ¾ cup sugar. Add cranberries and pears; toss to combine.

◆ Use larger ball of dough to line 9-inch pie plate. Spoon pear mixture into piecrust. Dot with margarine. Roll top crust and place on filling as directed; make decorative edge (see page 488). Sprinkle with remaining 1 tablespoon sugar.

◆ Place sheet of foil underneath pie plate; crimp foil edges to form a rim to catch drips. Bake pie 20 minutes. Turn oven control to 375°F; bake 60 to 70 minutes longer, until filling is bubbly in center. Cool pie on wire rack 1 hour to serve warm. Or, cool completely to serve later.

Each serving: About 400 calories, 3g protein, 61g carbohydrate, 17g total fat (4g saturated), 0mg cholesterol, 240mg sodium

HOME-STYLE PEACH AND CHERRY PIE

Prep: 50 minutes plus chilling and cooling   Bake: 1 hour 30 minutes
Makes 10 servings

Pastry for 2-Crust Pie (see
  page 487)
¾ cup packed light brown
  sugar
⅓ cup cornstarch
½ teaspoon salt
6 medium-size ripe peaches
  (about 2½ pounds), peeled,
  pitted, and thinly sliced

1 pound tart cherries,
  pitted (about 2 cups), or
  ½ (20-ounce) bag frozen
  pitted tart cherries, thawed
1 tablespoon milk
1 tablespoon granulated
  sugar

◆ Prepare Pastry for 2-Crust Pie through chilling. Preheat oven to 375°F. In large bowl, mix brown sugar, cornstarch, and salt. Add peaches and cherries; toss to combine.

◆ Use larger ball of dough to line 9½-inch deep-dish pie plate. Spoon fruit mixture into piecrust. Roll remaining dough into an 11-inch round; use to make lattice top (see page 500). Brush pastry with milk and sprinkle with granulated sugar.

◆ Place sheet of foil underneath pie plate; crimp foil edges to form a rim to catch drips during baking. Bake pie 1½ hours, or until filling is bubbly in center. Cover pie loosely with foil during last 40 minutes to prevent overbrowning. Cool pie on wire rack 1 hour to serve warm. Or, cool completely to serve later.

Each serving: About 375 calories, 4g protein, 59g carbohydrate, 15g total fat (3g saturated), 0mg cholesterol, 330mg sodium

SINGLE-CRUST PIES

A single crust can cradle luscious fruits, rich chocolate-nut creations, or silky custards. Be sure to mend any cracks that appear in the pastry during rolling: Moisten the torn edges, lay a patch of dough over the tear, and carefully press into position.

SWEET SUMMER PIE

◆◆◆◆◆◆◆◆◆◆◆◆◆◆◆◆◆

Prep: 55 minutes plus chilling and cooling
Bake: 1 hour
Makes 10 servings

Pastry for 1-Crust Pie (see page 487)
1 large orange
1 large lemon
4 large eggs, separated
⅛ teaspoon salt
⅔ cup plus ¼ cup sugar
⅓ cup all-purpose flour
8 medium nectarines (about 2½ pounds), peeled, pitted, and sliced
½ pint raspberries

◆◆◆◆◆◆◆◆◆◆◆◆◆◆◆◆◆◆◆◆◆◆◆◆◆

GRATING PEEL

When grating peel from oranges, lemons, or limes, avoid waste, messy scraping, and jammed grater holes by pressing a piece of plastic wrap over the fine side of the grater first. When you're finished, the peel will come off the wrap without any trouble – and the grater will be easier to clean.

1 Prepare Pastry for 1-Crust Pie through chilling. Grate 2 teaspoons peel and squeeze ⅓ cup juice from orange. Grate 1½ teaspoons peel from lemon, then squeeze enough juice to add to orange juice to equal ½ cup juice in total. In small bowl, with mixer at high speed, beat egg yolks, salt, and ⅓ cup sugar about 3 minutes, until thick and lemon-colored. Gradually beat in juice mixture and all of grated peel.

2 In 1-quart saucepan, cook yolk mixture over low heat, stirring constantly, 8 to 10 minutes, until thick (do not boil or mixture will curdle). Spoon into medium bowl; cool completely. Preheat oven to 425°F. In large bowl, mix flour and ⅓ cup sugar. Add nectarine slices; toss to combine. Gently stir in raspberries. Use pastry to line 9-inch pie plate; make decorative edge (see page 488).

3 Spoon fruit mixture into piecrust. Cover loosely with lightly greased foil; bake 45 minutes, or until bubbly in center and crust is lightly browned. Remove from oven. Turn oven control to 350°F.

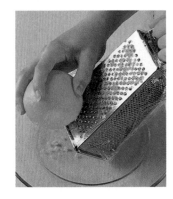

4 In clean small bowl, with mixer at high speed, beat egg whites to soft peaks. Sprinkle in remaining ¼ cup sugar, beating until whites stand in stiff peaks. Fold whites into cooled yolk mixture, one-third at a time.

5 Spread topping over filling right to edges. Return pie to oven; bake 15 minutes, or until topping is set and lightly browned. Cool pie completely on wire rack. Cover and refrigerate any leftovers.

◆◆

EACH SERVING: ABOUT 295 CALORIES, 6g PROTEIN, 49g CARBOHYDRATE, 10g TOTAL FAT (2g SATURATED), 85mg CHOLESTEROL, 160mg SODIUM

PEACH TARTE TATIN

Prep: 1 hour plus chilling and cooling
Bake: 25 minutes
Makes 12 servings

Pastry for 1-Crust Pie (see page 487)
1 cup sugar
6 tablespoons margarine or butter
1 tablespoon fresh lemon juice

11 medium-size firm, slightly ripe peaches (about 3¾ pounds), peeled, pitted, and each cut in half

◆ Prepare Pastry for 1-Crust Pie through chilling.

◆ In heavy 12-inch skillet with oven-safe handle, heat sugar, margarine, and lemon juice to boiling over medium-high heat. Place peaches in skillet, pitted side down. Cook 10 minutes. Carefully turn peaches; cook 8 to 12 minutes longer, until syrup is caramelized and thickened.

◆ Meanwhile, preheat oven to 425°F. Just before peaches are done, on lightly floured surface, with floured rolling pin, roll dough into a 14-inch round. Place dough on top of peaches in skillet; tuck edge under to form a rim. With knife, cut six ¼-inch slits in dough so steam can escape during baking. Bake 25 minutes, or until crust is golden.

◆ When tarte tatin is done, place large platter over top of skillet; carefully invert onto platter. Cool 1 hour to serve warm. Or, cool completely to serve later.

Each serving: 270 calories, 2g protein, 42g carbohydrate, 12g total fat (2g saturated), 0mg cholesterol, 155mg sodium

CHOCOLATE-PECAN PIE

Prep: 45 minutes plus chilling and cooling   *Bake: 1 hour 5 minutes*
Makes 12 servings

Pastry for 1-Crust Pie (see page 487)
4 tablespoons margarine or butter
2 squares (2 ounces) unsweetened chocolate

¾ cup packed dark brown sugar
¾ cup dark corn syrup
1 teaspoon vanilla extract
3 large eggs
1¾ cups pecan halves (about 7 ounces)

◆ Prepare Pastry for 1-Crust Pie through chilling.

◆ Preheat oven to 425°F. Use pastry to line 9-inch pie plate. Make decorative edge (see page 488). Line pie shell with foil and fill with pie weights, dry beans, or uncooked rice.

◆ Bake piecrust 10 minutes. Remove foil with weights; bake 10 minutes longer, or until lightly golden. Cool piecrust on wire rack at least 10 minutes. Turn oven control to 350°F. Meanwhile, in heavy 1-quart saucepan, melt margarine and chocolate over low heat, stirring frequently. Cool slightly.

◆ In large bowl, with wire whisk, mix chocolate mixture, brown sugar, and next 3 ingredients until blended. Coarsely chop 1 cup pecan halves; leave remaining pecans as halves. Stir all pecans into chocolate mixture; pour into cooled crust.

◆ Bake pie 45 minutes, or until edges are set (center should jiggle slightly). Cool completely on wire rack. Cover and refrigerate any leftovers.

Each serving: About 390 calories, 5g protein, 42g carbohydrate, 24g total fat (4g saturated), 53mg cholesterol, 170mg sodium

GRANDMA'S SWEET-POTATO PIE

Prep: 1 hour 10 minutes plus chilling and cooling   *Bake: 40 minutes*
Makes 10 servings

Pastry for 1-Crust Pie (see page 487)
4 medium sweet potatoes (about 2 pounds), unpeeled, or 2 cans (16 to 17 ounces each) sweet potatoes, drained
2 cups half-and-half or light cream

1 cup packed dark brown sugar
4 tablespoons margarine or butter, melted
1 teaspoon ground cinnamon
¾ teaspoon ground ginger
½ teaspoon ground nutmeg
½ teaspoon salt
3 large eggs

◆ Prepare Pastry for 1-Crust Pie through chilling.

◆ If using fresh sweet potatoes, in 3-quart saucepan, heat sweet potatoes and enough *water* to cover to boiling over high heat. Reduce heat to low. Cover and simmer 30 minutes, or until fork-tender; drain. Cool potatoes until easy to handle; peel and cut into chunks.

◆ Preheat oven to 400°F. In large bowl, with mixer at low speed, beat sweet potatoes until smooth. Add half-and-half and remaining ingredients; beat until well blended.

◆ Use pastry to line 9½-inch deep-dish pie plate. Make decorative edge (see page 488). Spoon sweet-potato mixture into piecrust.

◆ Bake pie 40 minutes, or until knife inserted 1 inch from edge comes out clean. Cool 1 hour to serve warm. Or, cool slightly, then refrigerate to serve later. Cover and refrigerate any leftovers.

Each serving: About 400 calories, 6g protein, 52g carbohydrate, 19g total fat (6g saturated), 82mg cholesterol, 320mg sodium

CRUMB-CRUST PIES

These foolproof crusts are simple to make. Cookie crumbs, melted margarine or butter, and sugar are simply mixed together and pressed into the pie plate – no rolling required. To set the mixture, the crust is briefly baked before filling. For firm, easy-to-cut slices, these pies should be chilled before serving.

STRAWBERRY-RHUBARB MOUSSE PIE

◆◆◆◆◆◆◆◆◆◆◆◆◆◆◆◆◆◆◆◆◆◆◆◆◆◆◆◆

Prep: 20 minutes plus chilling and cooling **Bake:** *15 minutes*
Makes 10 servings

1 pound rhubarb, cut into
  1-inch chunks (3½ cups)
1 cup sugar
2 envelopes unflavored gelatin
1 pint strawberries, hulled
1 tablespoon fresh lemon juice
6 tablespoons margarine or
  butter, melted

2 cups shortbread-style cookie
  crumbs (about thirty-six
  1½-inch square cookies) or
  vanilla wafer crumbs
1 cup heavy or whipping
  cream
Mint sprigs and strawberry
  halves for garnish

1 In 2-quart saucepan, heat rhubarb, sugar, and ¼ *cup water* to boiling over high heat, stirring constantly. Reduce heat to medium-low; cook 10 minutes, or until very tender. In food processor with knife blade attached, blend rhubarb mixture until smooth; return to saucepan. In small bowl, sprinkle gelatin over ½ *cup cold water*; let stand 2 minutes to soften.

2 In bowl, with potato masher or fork, mash strawberries. Stir into rhubarb with gelatin and lemon juice; cook 3 minutes over low heat, until gelatin dissolves completely.

3 Pour rhubarb mixture into bowl; refrigerate, stirring occasionally, about 2½ hours, until mixture mounds slightly when dropped from a spoon. (Or, for quicker setting, place bowl with rhubarb mixture in a larger bowl of *ice water* and stir every 10 minutes for about 1 hour.)

4 Meanwhile, preheat oven to 350°F. In deep-dish 9½-inch pie plate, mix margarine with crumbs. Press onto bottom and up side of pie plate. Bake 15 minutes; cool on wire rack.

5 In medium bowl, with mixer at medium speed, beat cream to soft peaks. With rubber spatula, fold whipped cream into rhubarb mixture until blended. Spoon into piecrust. Refrigerate at least 3 hours, or overnight. Garnish.

◆◆◆◆◆◆◆◆◆◆◆◆◆◆◆◆◆◆◆◆◆◆◆◆◆◆◆◆

WHIPPING CREAM

Heavy or whipping cream will double in volume when whipped, so use a bowl that is large enough. Soft peaks (right), when the cream forms gentle folds, are best for folding into other mixtures to add volume, as in our Strawberry-Rhubarb Mousse Pie. Stiff peaks (right), when the cream keeps its shape, can be used to top cream pies, frost cakes, or stack layers of pastry.

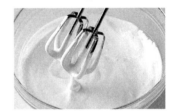

Soft peaks

Stiff peaks

◆◆◆◆◆◆◆◆◆◆◆◆◆◆◆◆◆◆◆◆◆◆◆◆◆◆◆◆

EACH SERVING: ABOUT 315 CALORIES, 3g PROTEIN, 34g CARBOHYDRATE, 19g TOTAL FAT (8g SATURATED), 36mg CHOLESTEROL, 155mg SODIUM

DOUBLE BLUEBERRY PIE

Prep: 30 minutes plus cooling and chilling   *Bake:* 8 minutes
Makes 10 servings

30 gingersnap cookies
2 tablespoons plus ½ cup sugar
5 tablespoons margarine or butter, melted

2 tablespoons cornstarch
3 pints blueberries
Whipped cream (optional)

◆ Preheat oven to 375°F. In food processor with knife blade attached or in blender at high speed, process gingersnap cookies and 2 tablespoons sugar until fine crumbs form.

◆ In 9-inch pie plate, with fork, mix cookie crumbs with melted margarine. With hand, press mixture onto bottom and up side of pie plate, making a small rim. Bake crust 8 minutes. Cool on wire rack.

◆ Meanwhile, in 2-quart saucepan, mix cornstarch with *2 tablespoons cold water* until blended. Stir in half of blueberries and remaining ½ cup sugar; heat to boiling over medium-high heat, pressing blueberries against side of saucepan with back of spoon. Boil 1 minute, stirring constantly. Remove saucepan from heat; stir in remaining blueberries.

◆ Pour blueberry mixture into piecrust. Cover with plastic wrap and refrigerate at least 5 hours, or overnight. Serve with whipped cream, if you like.

Each serving: About 240 calories, 2g protein, 43g carbohydrate, 8g total fat (2g saturated), 0mg cholesterol, 210mg sodium

CHOCOLATE CREAM PIE

Prep: 25 minutes plus cooling and chilling   *Bake:* 8 minutes
Makes 10 servings

1¼ cups chocolate wafer cookie crumbs (24 cookies)
5 tablespoons margarine or butter, melted
2 tablespoons sugar

Chocolate Pudding (see page 474)
1 cup heavy or whipping cream

◆ Preheat oven to 350°F. In 9-inch pie plate, with fork, mix cookie crumbs, melted margarine, and sugar. Press mixture onto bottom and up side of pie plate. Bake 8 minutes; cool on wire rack.

◆ Prepare Chocolate Pudding; pour warm pudding into piecrust. Place plastic wrap directly on surface to prevent skin from forming. Refrigerate at least 4 hours, or overnight. To serve, in medium bowl, with mixer at medium speed, beat cream until stiff peaks form. Spoon onto pie.

Each serving: About 430 calories, 7g protein, 40g carbohydrate, 29g total fat (12g saturated), 152mg cholesterol, 340mg sodium

BANANA CREAM PIE

Prep: 30 minutes plus cooling and chilling   *Bake:* 15 minutes
Makes 10 servings

8 tablespoons margarine or butter
2 cups shortbread-style cookie crumbs (about thirty-six 1½-inch square cookies) or vanilla wafer crumbs
¾ cup sugar

⅓ cup cornstarch
¼ teaspoon salt
3¾ cups milk
5 large egg yolks
1¾ teaspoons vanilla extract
3 medium-size ripe bananas
¾ cup heavy or whipping cream

◆ Preheat oven to 350°F. In small saucepan, melt 6 tablespoons margarine over low heat. In 9-inch pie plate, with fork, mix cookie crumbs with melted margarine. Press mixture onto bottom and up side of pie plate. Bake 15 minutes, or until golden; cool on wire rack.

◆ Prepare filling: In 3-quart saucepan, mix sugar, cornstarch, and salt; stir in milk until smooth. Cook over medium heat, stirring constantly, until mixture thickens and boils; boil 1 minute. In small bowl, beat egg yolks lightly; beat in small amount of hot milk mixture. Slowly pour yolk mixture back into milk, stirring rapidly. Cook over low heat, stirring constantly, 2 minutes, or until very thick.

◆ Remove from heat; stir in 1½ teaspoons vanilla and remaining 2 tablespoons margarine. Slice 2 bananas. Pour half of filling into piecrust. Arrange sliced bananas on top; spoon remaining filling over. Place plastic wrap directly on surface of filling; refrigerate at least 4 hours, or overnight.

◆ To serve, in small bowl, with mixer at medium speed, beat cream and remaining ¼ teaspoon vanilla to stiff peaks; spread over filling. Slice remaining banana; arrange around edge of pie. Cover and refrigerate any leftovers.

Each serving: About 410 calories, 6g protein, 42g carbohydrate, 25g total fat (10g saturated), 147mg cholesterol, 280mg sodium

FREE-FORM TARTS

These rustic-looking tarts suggest backroad bistros and homey farmhouse suppers. The dough is simply rolled into a circle and then folded up over the fruit mixture. To prevent leaking, pinch closed any cracks that form during assembly.

FARMSTAND CHERRY TART

◆◆◆◆◆◆◆◆◆◆◆

Prep: 45 minutes plus chilling and cooling
Bake: 45 to 50 minutes
Makes 6 servings

1½ cups all-purpose flour
⅓ cup plus 1 tablespoon yellow cornmeal
⅔ cup plus 1 teaspoon sugar
Salt
½ cup cold margarine or butter
2 tablespoons plus 1 teaspoon cornstarch
1½ pounds dark sweet cherries, pitted
1 large egg white

WHAT'S IN A NAME?

Galette is the French term for any round, flat, free-form tart that is baked on a cookie sheet. The pastry can be either a yeast dough or a simple unleavened pastry dough, as in the recipes here. A galette may be sweet or savory; possible toppings include jam, nuts, meat, or cheese, as well as fruit.

1 In medium bowl, mix flour, ⅓ cup cornmeal, ⅓ cup sugar, and ½ teaspoon salt. With pastry blender or two knives used scissor-fashion, cut in margarine until mixture resembles coarse crumbs.

2 Sprinkle in *4 to 5 tablespoons ice water*, 1 tablespoon at a time, mixing lightly with hand until dough comes together (dough will feel very dry at first). Shape into a ball.

3 Sprinkle large cookie sheet with remaining 1 table-spoon cornmeal. Place dampened towel under cookie sheet to prevent it from slipping while rolling dough. With floured rolling pin, roll dough on cookie sheet into a 13-inch round. With long metal spatula, gently loosen dough from cookie sheet. In large bowl, mix ⅓ cup sugar with cornstarch.

4 Sprinkle half of sugar mixture over center of dough, leaving a 2½-inch border all around. Add cherries to sugar mixture remaining in bowl; toss well.

5 Spoon cherry mixture over sugar on dough round. Fold dough up around cherries, leaving a 4-inch opening in center. Pinch to seal any cracks.

6 In cup, mix egg white and ⅛ teaspoon salt. Brush over dough; sprinkle with remaining 1 teaspoon sugar. Refrigerate 30 minutes, or until well chilled. Preheat oven to 425°F.

7 Place 2 sheets of foil under cookie sheet; crimp foil edges to form a rim to catch any drips during baking. Bake tart 45 to 50 minutes, until crust is golden and filling is gently bubbling, covering loosely with foil during last 10 minutes to prevent overbrowning. As soon as tart is done, with long metal spatula, loosen tart from cookie sheet. Cool tart 15 minutes on cookie sheet, then slide onto wire rack to cool completely.

EACH SERVING: ABOUT 460 CALORIES, 6g PROTEIN, 74g CARBOHYDRATE, 17g TOTAL FAT (3g SATURATED), 0mg CHOLESTEROL, 410mg SODIUM

LITTLE PEAR TARTS

Prep: 35 minutes plus chilling and cooling   Bake: 30 minutes
Makes 2 tarts (4 servings)

Pastry for 1-Crust Pie (see page 487)
3 small ripe pears (1¼ pounds), peeled, cored, and cut into ¼-inch-thick slices
2 tablespoons all-purpose flour
2 tablespoons dried currants or chopped raisins
4 teaspoons fresh lemon juice
½ teaspoon ground cinnamon
⅓ cup plus 6 teaspoons sugar
2 tablespoons milk
2 tablespoons chopped pecans

◆ Prepare Pastry for 1-Crust Pie through chilling, but shape dough into 2 equal balls. Preheat oven to 400°F. In large bowl, toss pear slices with flour, currants, lemon juice, cinnamon, and ⅓ cup sugar. Set aside.

◆ On lightly floured surface, with floured rolling pin, roll 1 dough ball into 10-inch round. Transfer to one half of large cookie sheet. Mound half of pear mixture in center of round; fold dough up around pears, leaving a 2½-inch opening in center.

◆ Repeat with remaining dough and pear mixture to make a second tart on same cookie sheet. Brush each crust with 1 tablespoon milk; sprinkle each with 2 teaspoons sugar.

◆ Place 2 sheets foil under cookie sheet; crimp foil edges to form a rim to catch any drips during baking. Bake tarts 20 minutes.

◆ In cup, mix pecans with remaining 2 teaspoons sugar; sprinkle over filling in centers of tarts. Bake 10 minutes longer, or until crust is browned. Cool tarts on cookie sheets on wire rack 10 minutes to serve warm. Or, slide tarts onto rack after 10 minutes and cool completely to serve later.

Each ½ tart: About 515 calories, 5g protein, 80g carbohydrate, 21g total fat (4g saturated), 1mg cholesterol, 270mg sodium

PEACH-BLUEBERRY TART

Prep: 30 minutes plus chilling and cooling   Bake: 40 minutes
Makes 8 servings

Pastry for 1-Crust Pie (see page 487)
2 tablespoons cornstarch
⅓ cup plus 2 tablespoons sugar
1 cup blueberries
6 large peaches (2 pounds), peeled, pitted, and each cut into 6 wedges
2 teaspoons fresh lemon juice
1 tablespoon margarine or butter, cut up

◆ Prepare Pastry for 1-Crust Pie through chilling. Preheat oven to 425°F. In large bowl, mix cornstarch and ⅓ cup sugar. Add blueberries, peaches, and lemon juice; toss to combine.

◆ On lightly floured surface, with floured rolling pin, roll dough to 14-inch round. Trim jagged edges; reserve scraps. Transfer round to large cookie sheet. Spoon fruit mixture with juices in center of round, leaving a 2-inch border. Dot fruit mixture with margarine. Fold dough up around fruit. Brush any cracks with *water*; patch with reserved scraps.

◆ Sprinkle dough and exposed fruit with remaining 2 tablespoons sugar. Place 2 sheets foil under cookie sheet; crimp foil edges to form rim to catch any drips during baking. Bake tart 40 minutes, or until bubbly in center. Cool on cookie sheet on wire rack 30 minutes to serve warm.

Each serving: About 270 calories, 3g protein, 42g carbohydrate, 11g total fat (2g saturated), 0mg cholesterol, 150mg sodium

APPLE GALETTE

Prep: 40 minutes plus chilling and cooling   Bake: 45 minutes
Makes 8 servings

Pastry for 1-Crust Pie (see page 487)
5 medium Golden Delicious apples (2 pounds)
¼ cup sugar
2 tablespoons margarine or butter, cut up
2 tablespoons apricot jam, melted

◆ Prepare Pastry for 1-Crust Pie through chilling. Preheat oven to 425°F. On lightly floured surface, with floured rolling pin, roll dough to 15-inch round. Transfer to large cookie sheet.

◆ Peel apples; cut each in half. With melon-baller, remove cores. Cut crosswise into ¼-inch-thick slices. Fan apple slices in concentric circles on dough round, leaving a 1½-inch border. Sprinkle apples evenly with sugar and dot with margarine. Fold dough up around apples.

◆ Place 2 sheets foil under cookie sheet; crimp edges to form a rim to catch any drips during baking. Bake galette 45 minutes, or until apples are tender. Place cookie sheet on wire rack. Brush apples with jam. Cool slightly to serve warm.

Each serving: About 270 calories, 2g protein, 40g carbohydrate, 12g total fat (3g saturated), 0mg cholesterol, 165mg sodium

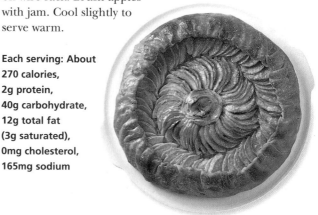

TARTS

Bursting with colorful fruit, creamy custards, nuts, or silky chocolate mixtures, tarts make a dazzling dessert. Unlike a piecrust, a tart shell must be sturdy enough to stand on its own when removed from the pan.

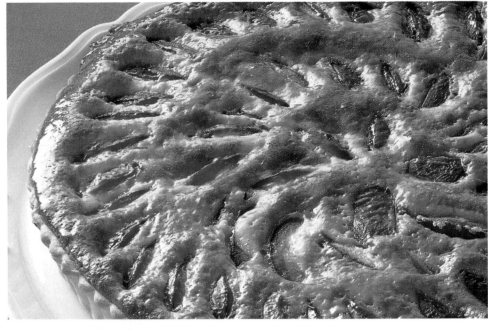

PLUM FRANGIPANE TART

◆◆◆◆◆◆◆◆◆◆◆◆

Prep: 30 minutes plus chilling and cooling
Bake: 1 hour 10 to 25 minutes
Makes 12 servings

Pastry for 11-inch Tart (see page 487)
1 tube or can (7 to 8 ounces) almond paste, cut up
½ cup sugar
4 tablespoons margarine or butter, softened
¼ teaspoon salt
2 large eggs
2 teaspoons vanilla extract
¼ cup all-purpose flour
1¼ pounds ripe plums (about 5 large), pitted and each cut into 6 wedges

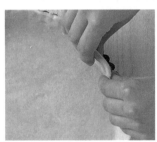

1 Prepare Pastry for 11-inch Tart and use to line tart pan as directed. Preheat oven to 425°F.

2 Line tart shell with foil and fill with pie weights, dry beans, or uncooked rice. Bake tart shell 15 minutes; remove foil with weights and bake 5 to 10 minutes longer, until golden. (If crust puffs up during baking, gently press it to tart pan with back of spoon.) Remove tart shell from oven; turn oven control to 375°F.

3 Meanwhile, prepare filling: In large bowl, with mixer at low speed, beat almond paste, sugar, margarine, and salt until crumbly. Increase speed to medium-high; beat 3 minutes, frequently scraping bowl with rubber spatula. (There may be some tiny lumps.) Add eggs and vanilla; beat until smooth. With wooden spoon, stir in flour until blended.

CRANBERRY-ALMOND TART

Prepare Plum Frangipane Tart as directed, but omit plums and bake almond filling only 20 minutes, until golden. Cool in pan on wire rack. In 2-quart saucepan over high heat, heat 1 cup cranberries, ¾ cup sugar, ⅓ cup water, and ½ teaspoon grated orange peel to boiling. Reduce heat to medium-low; simmer 5 minutes, until mixture thickens slightly and cranberries pop. Stir in additional 2 cups cranberries. Set aside until cool. When tart is cool, carefully remove side of pan; spoon cranberry topping over almond filling. Makes 12 servings.

Each serving: About 370 calories, 5g protein, 46g carbohydrate, 19g total fat (3g saturated), 36mg cholesterol, 280mg sodium

4 Pour filling into warm tart shell. Arrange plum wedges in concentric circles over filling. Bake tart 50 to 60 minutes, until golden. Cool tart completely in pan on wire rack. When tart is cool, carefully remove side from pan. Cover and refrigerate any leftovers.

EACH SERVING: ABOUT 335 CALORIES, 5g PROTEIN, 36g CARBOHYDRATE, 19g TOTAL FAT (3g SATURATED), 36mg CHOLESTEROL, 280mg SODIUM

RASPBERRY TART

Prep: 20 minutes plus chilling and cooling   *Bake:* 50 to 60 minutes
Makes 8 servings

Pastry for 9-inch Tart (see page 487)
⅔ cup sugar
¼ cup all-purpose flour

¼ teaspoon ground cinnamon
Four ½-pints raspberries
1 cup heavy or whipping cream (optional)

◆ Prepare Pastry for 9-inch Tart, but fit dough onto bottom and 1 inch up side of 9-inch springform pan. Preheat oven to 400°F.

◆ In small bowl, combine sugar, flour, and cinnamon; sprinkle half of sugar mixture over dough. Top with 4 cups raspberries; refrigerate remaining raspberries for topping. Sprinkle remaining sugar mixture evenly over raspberries in pastry. Bake tart on lowest oven rack 50 to 60 minutes, until raspberry mixture is bubbly.

◆ Cool tart completely in pan on wire rack. When tart is cool, carefully remove side of pan; top tart with reserved raspberries. To serve, pour 2 tablespoons cream on each plate, if you like; arrange a wedge of tart on cream.

Each serving: About 250 calories, 3g protein, 38g carbohydrate, 11g total fat (2g saturated), 0mg cholesterol, 165mg sodium

MIXED BERRY TART

Prep: 25 minutes plus chilling and cooling   *Bake:* 22 to 27 minutes
Makes 8 servings

Pastry for 9-inch Tart (see page 487)
1 cup milk
2 large egg yolks
⅓ cup granulated sugar
2 tablespoons cornstarch
2 teaspoons orange-flavor liqueur

1 teaspoon vanilla extract
3 cups assorted berries, such as blueberries, raspberries, and blackberries
Confectioners' sugar for garnish

◆ Prepare Pastry for 9-inch Tart; use to line tart pan as directed. Preheat oven to 425°F. Line tart shell with foil; fill with pie weights, dry beans, or uncooked rice. Bake 15 minutes. Remove foil with weights; bake 7 to 12 minutes longer, until golden. (If crust puffs up during baking, press it against tart pan with back of spoon.) Cool completely on rack.

◆ Meanwhile, prepare pastry cream: In 2-quart saucepan, heat milk to boiling over medium-high heat. In medium bowl, whisk egg yolks with granulated sugar until smooth; whisk in cornstarch. Gradually whisk hot milk into yolk mixture. Return to saucepan. Cook, whisking constantly, until mixture thickens and boils. Reduce heat to low and cook, whisking, 2 minutes. Remove from heat; stir in

liqueur and vanilla. Pour into clean bowl; press plastic wrap directly onto surface to prevent skin from forming. Refrigerate at least 2 hours, until cold.

◆ When tart shell is cool, carefully remove side of pan. Whisk pastry cream until smooth; spread in tart shell. Spoon berries on top. Sift confectioners' sugar over berries. Cover and refrigerate any leftovers.

Each serving: About 250 calories, 4g protein, 30g carbohydrate, 13g total fat (3g saturated), 57mg cholesterol, 185mg sodium

FIG AND CUSTARD TART

Prep: 25 minutes plus chilling and cooling   *Bake:* 34 to 42 minutes
Makes 8 servings

Pastry for 9-inch Tart (see page 487)
1½ cups sour cream
⅓ cup sugar
2 tablespoons all-purpose flour
1 teaspoon vanilla extract

⅛ teaspoon salt
1 large egg
6 large or 12 small figs or 3 cups assorted berries
¼ cup apricot jam

◆ Prepare Pastry for 9-inch Tart and use to line tart pan as directed. Preheat oven to 425°F. Line tart shell with foil; fill with pie weights, dry beans, or uncooked rice. Bake 15 minutes. Remove foil with weights; bake 7 to 12 minutes longer, until golden. (If crust puffs up during baking, gently press it against tart pan with back of spoon.) Cool slightly on wire rack. Turn oven control to 400°F.

◆ In medium bowl, with wire whisk or fork, beat sour cream, sugar, flour, vanilla, salt, and egg until smooth and well blended; pour into baked tart shell. Bake 12 to 15 minutes, just until set. Cool tart completely in pan on wire rack. Cover and refrigerate 2 hours, or until cold.

◆ Carefully remove side of pan. Cut each fig into quarters, or halves if small. Arrange figs on tart. In small saucepan, melt apricot jam over low heat. Brush jam over figs. Cover and refrigerate any leftovers.

Each serving: About 335 calories, 4g protein, 36g carbohydrate, 20g total fat (8g saturated), 46mg cholesterol, 230mg sodium

LEMON TART

Prep: 20 minutes plus chilling and cooling   Bake: 52 to 57 minutes
Makes 8 servings

Pastry for 9-inch Tart (see page 487)
4 large lemons
4 large eggs
1 cup granulated sugar

⅓ cup heavy or whipping cream
Confectioners' sugar for garnish

◆ Prepare Pastry for 9-inch Tart and use to line tart pan as directed. Preheat oven to 425°F. Line tart shell with foil and fill with pie weights, dry beans, or uncooked rice.

◆ Bake tart shell 15 minutes. Remove foil with weights and bake 7 to 12 minutes longer, until golden. (If crust puffs up during baking, gently press it against tart pan with back of spoon.) Cool tart shell completely on wire rack. Turn oven control to 350°F.

◆ Grate 1½ teaspoons peel and squeeze ⅔ cup juice from lemons. In medium bowl, whisk together eggs, sugar, lemon peel, and lemon juice until well combined. Whisk in cream. Carefully pour lemon mixture into cooled tart shell.

◆ Bake on cookie sheet 30 minutes, or until barely set. Cool completely on wire rack.

◆ Carefully remove side of pan; just before serving, sprinkle with confectioners' sugar. Cover and refrigerate any leftovers.

Each serving: About 320 calories, 5g protein, 39g carbohydrate, 16g total fat (5g saturated), 120mg cholesterol, 200mg sodium

CHOCOLATE TRUFFLE TART

Prep: 20 minutes plus chilling and cooling   Bake: 42 to 47 minutes
Makes 12 servings

Pastry for 9-inch Tart (see page 487)
½ cup margarine or butter
6 squares (6 ounces) semisweet chocolate
¼ cup sugar

1 teaspoon vanilla extract
½ cup heavy or whipping cream
3 large eggs
White-chocolate hearts (see page 552) for garnish

◆ Prepare Pastry for 9-inch Tart and use to line tart pan as directed, but trim edge even with rim of pan. Preheat oven to 425°F. Line tart shell with foil and fill with pie weights, dry beans, or uncooked rice.

◆ Bake tart shell 15 minutes. Remove foil with weights and bake 7 to 12 minutes longer, until golden. (If crust puffs up during baking, gently press it against tart pan with back of spoon.) Cool tart shell in pan on wire rack 15 minutes. Turn oven control to 350°F.

◆ While crust is cooling, prepare filling: In heavy 1-quart saucepan, melt margarine and chocolate over low heat, stirring frequently. Stir in sugar and vanilla; remove from heat. In small bowl, with fork or wire whisk, lightly beat cream and eggs. Blend some warm chocolate mixture into egg mixture; stir egg mixture back into chocolate mixture until blended.

◆ Pour warm mixture into tart shell. Bake 20 minutes, or until just set (center will appear jiggly). While tart is baking, prepare white-chocolate hearts. Cool tart in pan on wire rack; refrigerate to serve cold. Carefully remove side of pan; garnish with hearts. Cover and refrigerate any leftovers.

Each serving: About 300 calories, 4g protein, 21g carbohydrate, 24g total fat (8g saturated), 67mg cholesterol, 220mg sodium

HOLIDAY NUT TART

Prep: 20 minutes plus chilling and cooling   Bake: 48 to 55 minutes
Makes 12 servings

Pastry for 11-inch Tart (see page 487)
½ cup packed light brown sugar
½ cup light corn syrup
3 tablespoons margarine or butter, melted

2 teaspoons vanilla extract
2 large eggs
1 can (10 to 11 ounces) salted deluxe mixed nuts (about 2 cups)
Whipped cream (optional)

◆ Prepare Pastry for 11-inch Tart and use to line tart pan as directed. Preheat oven to 375°F. Line tart shell with foil and fill with pie weights, dry beans, or uncooked rice.

◆ Bake tart shell 15 minutes; remove foil with weights and bake 8 to 10 minutes longer, until golden. (If crust puffs up during baking, gently press it against pan with back of spoon.)

◆ Meanwhile, in medium bowl, whisk together brown sugar and next 4 ingredients until smooth. Stir in nuts. Pour mixture into tart shell. Bake tart 25 to 30 minutes, until set and deep golden brown. Cool tart in pan on wire rack.

◆ Carefully remove side of pan. Serve tart with whipped cream, if you like. Cover and refrigerate any leftovers.

Each serving: About 405 calories, 7g protein, 35g carbohydrate, 26g total fat (5g saturated), 36mg cholesterol, 340mg sodium

LATTICE-TOPPED PECAN TART

Prep: 30 minutes plus chilling and cooling
Bake: 50 to 55 minutes
Makes 16 servings

Pastry for 2-Crust Pie (see page 487)
3 tablespoons margarine or butter
1½ cups light corn syrup

1 cup sugar
1½ teaspoons vanilla extract
4 large eggs
2½ cups pecans (10 ounces), coarsely chopped

◆ Prepare Pastry for 2-Crust Pie through chilling. Preheat oven to 350°F. On lightly floured surface, with floured rolling pin, roll larger ball of dough to 14-inch round. Use to line 11" by 1½" tart pan with removable bottom. In 3-quart saucepan, melt margarine over low heat; remove from heat. Stir in corn syrup, sugar, and vanilla. Separate 1 egg; set yolk aside. With wire whisk or fork, beat remaining 3 eggs and egg white into margarine mixture just until blended. Stir in pecans; pour mixture into tart shell.

◆ In cup, mix remaining egg yolk with *2 teaspoons water*. Roll remaining dough into an 11-inch round. Make lattice top (see right); brush with yolk mixture. Bake tart 50 to 55 minutes, until knife inserted in filling 1 inch from edge comes out clean. Cool tart in pan on wire rack. To serve, carefully remove side of pan. Cover and refrigerate any leftovers.

Each serving: About 430 calories, 5g protein, 51g carbohydrate, 24g total fat (4g saturated), 53mg cholesterol, 195mg sodium

LATTICE-TOPPED FRUIT TART

Prep: 45 minutes plus chilling and cooling   Bake: 55 to 60 minutes
Makes 12 servings

Pastry for 2-Crust Pie (see page 487)
3 medium Golden Delicious apples (about 1¼ pounds), peeled, cored, and cut into ½-inch cubes
1 tablespoon margarine or butter

3 tablespoons plus ⅔ cup sugar
Salt
2 cups cranberries
½ cup golden raisins
1 teaspoon vanilla extract
2 tablespoons all-purpose flour
1 large egg, lightly beaten

◆ Prepare Pastry for 2-Crust Pie through chilling. On lightly floured surface, with floured rolling pin, roll larger ball of dough to 14-inch round. Use to line 11" by 1½" tart pan with removable bottom. Cover with plastic wrap and refrigerate.

◆ In 10-inch skillet, mix apples, margarine, 3 tablespoons sugar, and ¼ teaspoon salt; cover and cook over medium heat about 10 minutes, until very tender, mashing occasionally with fork. Uncover; increase heat to medium-high and cook, stirring frequently, until all liquid evaporates and apples form a thick puree. Remove skillet from heat; cool completely.

◆ Preheat oven to 375°F. In medium bowl, mix cranberries, raisins, vanilla, flour, remaining ⅔ cup sugar, and ¼ teaspoon salt. Spread apple puree evenly over bottom of tart shell. Top with cranberry mixture.

◆ Roll remaining dough into an 11-inch round. Make lattice top (see below); brush lightly with beaten egg.

◆ Bake tart 55 to 60 minutes, until filling begins to bubble and crust is golden. Cover with foil if necessary during last 30 minutes of baking to prevent overbrowning. Cool in pan on wire rack. To serve, carefully remove side of pan.

Each serving: About 315 calories, 3g protein, 47g carbohydrate, 14g total fat (3g saturated), 18mg cholesterol, 285mg sodium

◆◆◆◆◆◆◆◆◆◆◆◆◆◆◆◆◆◆◆◆◆◆◆◆◆◆◆◆

LATTICE TOP

1 With pastry wheel or knife, cut dough round into twenty ½-inch-wide strips. Place 10 strips, about ½ inch apart, over tart or pie filling; do not seal ends.

2 Fold every other strip back three-fourths of its length. Place center cross strip at right angle to first ones (place on a diagonal, if you like, for diamond lattice), and replace folded part of strips.

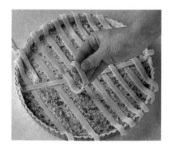

3 Now fold back alternate strips; place second cross strip in place, parallel to first and about ½ inch away. Replace folded part of strips.

4 Repeat to weave cross strips into lattice. Trim strips almost even with pan or dish; press to inside edge of crust to seal.

◆◆◆◆◆◆◆◆◆◆◆◆◆◆◆◆◆◆◆◆◆◆◆◆◆◆◆◆

TARTLETS

These dainty little desserts provide a festive end to dinner parties and holiday gatherings, not to mention tea parties. The delicate shells should be cooled in their pans. Do not fill them more than four hours in advance, or the pastry will get soggy. However, you can bake the pastry shells ahead and freeze them (just re-crisp before filling).

LEMON-RASPBERRY TARTLETS

◆ ◆ ◆ ◆ ◆ ◆ ◆ ◆ ◆ ◆ ◆

Prep: 40 minutes plus chilling and cooling
Bake: 15 minutes
Makes 6 tartlets (12 servings)

4 medium lemons
¾ cup sugar
¾ cup butter
1 tablespoon cornstarch
6 large egg yolks
Pastry for 2-Crust Pie (see page 487)
Three ½-pints raspberries

CORNSTARCH

Extracted from corn kernels, cornstarch thickens juicy pies, puddings, and sauces; it also may be mixed with flour in cookies, cakes, and pastry for extra-tender results. Dishes thickened with cornstarch are clear and glossy; those thickened with flour are opaque.

1 Prepare filling: Grate 1 tablespoon peel and squeeze ½ cup juice from lemons. In 2-quart saucepan, heat peel, juice, sugar, butter, and cornstarch over medium heat, stirring, until sugar dissolves and butter melts. In small bowl, beat egg yolks lightly. Beat small amount of lemon mixture into yolks; slowly pour egg mixture back into lemon mixture. Cook over low heat, stirring constantly, about 5 minutes, until thick enough to coat back of spoon.

2 Pour filling into a bowl; press plastic wrap directly onto surface to prevent skin from forming. Refrigerate 3 hours, or until well chilled. Meanwhile, prepare Pastry for 2-Crust Pie through chilling, but divide dough into 6 portions before refrigerating.

3 Press dough onto bottom and up sides of six 4-inch fluted tartlet pans.

4 Place tartlet pans in jelly-roll pan for easy handling. With fork, prick pastry all over. Refrigerate tartlet shells 20 minutes. Preheat oven to 400°F. Bake tartlet shells 15 minutes, or until golden.

5 Transfer tartlet pans to wire rack to cool. When tartlet shells are cool, carefully remove from pans. Spoon lemon filling into tartlet shells and top with raspberries. Cover and refrigerate any leftovers.

EACH ½ TARTLET: ABOUT 350 CALORIES, 3g PROTEIN, 34g CARBOHYDRATE, 24g TOTAL FAT (10g SATURATED), 31mg CHOLESTEROL, 295mg SODIUM

CHOCOLATE TARTLETS

Prep: 50 minutes plus chilling, cooling, and standing
Bake: 9 to 12 minutes
Makes 36

Pastry for 1-Crust Pie (see page 487)
3 tablespoons apricot jam
2 squares (2 ounces) semisweet chocolate
3 tablespoons plus ¼ cup heavy or whipping cream
1 tablespoon margarine or butter, cut up

1 teaspoon vanilla extract
1 teaspoon confectioners' sugar
Assorted berries, very thinly sliced kumquats, or shaved chocolate for garnish

◆ Prepare Pastry for 1-Crust Pie through chilling. Preheat oven to 425°F. On lightly floured surface, with floured rolling pin, roll dough less than 1/16 inch thick. With 2½-inch round cutter, cut out 36 pastry rounds (if necessary, reroll scraps). Fit into 3 dozen mini muffin-pan cups or 1¾-inch tartlet pans.

◆ Bake tartlets 9 to 12 minutes, until golden. Cool in pans on wire rack. Remove tartlet shells from pans; spoon ¼ teaspoon jam into each. In top of double boiler over simmering water, melt chocolate with 3 tablespoons cream. Remove from heat; stir in margarine until smooth. Stir in vanilla. Spoon mixture evenly into tartlets, covering jam. Let stand until set.

◆ In small bowl, with mixer at medium speed, beat remaining ¼ cup cream with confectioners' sugar to stiff peaks. Spoon small dollop of cream onto each tartlet; garnish.

Each tartlet: About 60 calories, 1g protein, 5g carbohydrate, 4g total fat (1g saturated), 4mg cholesterol, 35mg sodium

HAZELNUT TARTLETS

Prep: 1 hour plus chilling and cooling   Bake: 15 minutes
Makes 36

Pastry for 1-Crust Pie (see page 487)
1 cup (about 4 ounces) hazelnuts (filberts), toasted and skinned (see page 522)

1 cup confectioners' sugar plus extra for garnish
1 large egg
3 tablespoons margarine or butter, softened
1 teaspoon vanilla extract

◆ Prepare Pastry for 1-Crust Pie through chilling. Preheat oven to 400°F. In food processor with knife blade attached, process nuts with 1 cup confectioners' sugar until very finely ground. Add remaining ingredients; process until smooth.

◆ On lightly floured surface, with floured rolling pin, roll dough less than 1/16 inch thick. With 2½-inch round cutter, cut out 36 pastry rounds (if necessary, reroll scraps). Fit pastry into 3 dozen mini muffin-pan cups or 1¾-inch tartlet pans.

◆ Spoon hazelnut filling into tartlet shells. Bake tartlets 15 minutes, or until golden. Remove tartlets from pans and cool on wire rack. To serve, sift confectioners' sugar on top. Cover and refrigerate any leftovers.

Each tartlet: About 70 calories, 1g protein, 6g carbohydrate, 5g total fat (1g saturated), 6mg cholesterol, 40mg sodium

CREAM CHEESE AND FRUIT TARTLETS

Prep: 45 minutes plus chilling and cooling   Bake: 15 minutes
Makes 24

Pastry for 9-inch Tart (see page 487)
1 container (8 ounces) soft cream cheese
3 tablespoons sugar
1 tablespoon milk

¾ teaspoon vanilla extract
Kiwifruit, strawberries, canned mandarin-orange sections, and small seedless red and green grape halves
Mint leaves for garnish

◆ Prepare Pastry for 9-inch Tart through chilling. Preheat oven to 425°F.

◆ Divide dough in half. Roll one half into a 12-inch rope; cut rope into twelve 1-inch pieces. Repeat with other half of dough. Press each piece of dough evenly into bottom and up sides of twenty-four mini muffin-pan cups. Prick each tartlet shell several times with toothpick. Bake 15 minutes, or until golden. Cool tartlet shells 5 minutes in pans on wire rack. Remove shells from pans; cool completely on wire rack.

◆ Prepare filling: In small bowl, with fork, beat cream cheese, sugar, milk, and vanilla until blended. Spoon filling into tartlet shells. Top each tartlet with some fruit. Refrigerate until ready to serve; garnish.

Each tartlet: About 100 calories, 1g protein, 9g carbohydrate, 7g total fat (3g saturated), 11mg cholesterol, 85mg sodium

COOKIES & CAKES

16

COOKIES KNOW-HOW

A batch of fragrant, warm-from-the-oven cookies is a simple pleasure few can resist. Cookies come in six basic types: drop, shaped or molded, pressed, rolled, icebox, and bar (which includes brownies). Drop and bar cookies are made with a soft dough. All the others are made with a stiffer dough for ease of shaping. Although cookie making is not complicated, you'll achieve better results if you're ready with the best ingredients, equipment, and know-how. The following tips promise to help deliver delicious results.

MAKING AND SHAPING

• Avoid adding more flour than is necessary to a cookie dough or batter, or overmixing once the flour is added, or you'll have hard, tough cookies.
• For even baking, shape cookies to roughly the same thickness.
• For shaped or rolled cookies, chilled dough is easier to handle. Doughs made with butter chill to a firmer consistency and hold their shape better than doughs made with margarine or shortening.
• Roll out a small amount of cookie dough at a time; keep remainder covered with plastic wrap to keep it moist.

Icebox cookies can be shaped, chilled, and cut at your convenience. To bake, cut desired number of cookies in even slices from log, and arrange slightly apart on cookie sheets.

ABOUT COOKIE SHEETS

• Cookie sheets with only 1 or 2 turned-up edges allow for the best air circulation. If using a jelly-roll pan, invert it and place dough on the flip side.
• Cookie sheets should be at least 2 inches smaller in length and width than your oven, so air circulates.
• Grease cookie sheets only when a recipe calls for it. Some cookies have a high fat content, so greasing isn't always necessary. When greasing is required, use a light hand, and crumpled waxed paper for even spreading.

• Heavy-gauge metal cookie sheets with a dull finish result in the most evenly browned cookies. Aluminum is ideal. Dark-colored sheets can overbrown the bottoms of cookies.

BETTER BAKING

• If baking with margarine, make sure it contains 80 percent fat. Spreads (which may be labeled diet, whipped, liquid, or soft) have a high water content, which will result in cookies that are less tender and buttery.
• To make bar cookies easier to serve, and to aid cleanup, line the pan with foil before adding the batter; baked cookies can simply be lifted out of the pan, then cut.
• For best results, bake one sheet of cookies at a time on the center rack of the oven. If baking two at a time, switch sheets halfway through baking so the cookies bake evenly.
• When baking cookies in batches, cool the cookie sheet to room temperature before placing more cookies on it. A hot cookie sheet will melt the dough. If the recipe calls for greasing the sheet, regrease for each batch.
• To avoid overcooking, check cookies at the minimum baking time suggested in the recipe, and then watch them closely during their last few minutes in the oven.
• Straight from the oven, most drop cookies are too soft to handle. Let them cool slightly before transferring to a rack.
• To test bar cookies for doneness, insert a toothpick into the center of pan; it should come out clean (unless the recipe specifies otherwise). Other cookies are done when they're just firm at the edges.
• Bar cookies should be cooled in the pan before cutting, or they'll crumble.

STORING AND SHIPPING COOKIES

• To store cookie dough, place in an airtight container or plastic bag (wrap logs for icebox cookies first in plastic wrap); chill up to 1 week or freeze up to 6 months (if necessary, let stand at room temperature until easy to slice).
• To store cooled baked cookies, arrange a single layer in an airtight container; cover with waxed paper. Repeat layers; seal container. Store at room temperature up to 3 days.
• Freeze unbaked drop cookies directly on cookie sheets. Once cookies are frozen, transfer to heavy-duty zip-tight bags.
• To freeze baked cookies, place in zip-tight plastic bags, pressing out air. Or, place in airtight containers; for cushioning, layer with crumpled waxed paper. Freeze up to 3 months.
• Avoid mailing brittle cookies – chewy, soft drop cookies or bars will survive best. Line a sturdy cardboard box or tin with waxed paper or bubble wrap. Wrap cookies individually – or in pairs, back to back – with plastic wrap. Cushion each layer with crumpled newspaper. Fill empty spaces in the box with crumpled paper or bubble wrap; mark the package "fragile."

DROP COOKIES

These run the gamut from elegant, fragile Anise Wafers (see right) to cookie-jar favorites like oatmeal cookies. Drop cookies are formed by dropping spoonfuls of soft unchilled dough onto a cookie sheet. For even baking, distribute the dough in equal portions.

ANISE WAFERS

◆◆◆◆◆◆◆◆◆◆◆◆◆

Prep: 1 hour plus cooling
Bake: 5 to 7 minutes per batch
Makes about 2½ dozen

3 large egg whites
¾ cup confectioners' sugar
½ cup all-purpose flour
6 tablespoons butter, melted
¾ teaspoon anise extract
¼ teaspoon salt

ALMOND TUILES

Prepare batter as directed in Steps 1 through 3 above, but substitute ¼ teaspoon almond extract for anise extract and, before baking, sprinkle each cookie generously with a single layer of sliced almonds; you will need about ⅔ cup almonds (about 2½ ounces). Bake as directed in Step 4; but remove warm cookies from cookie sheet and drape over rolling pin to curve. When firm, transfer to wire racks. Makes about 2½ dozen.

Each cookie: About 50 calories, 1g protein, 4g carbohydrate, 3g total fat (2g saturated), 6mg cholesterol, 45mg sodium

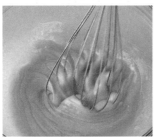

1 Preheat oven to 350°F. Grease large cookie sheet. In large bowl, with wire whisk, beat egg whites, confectioners' sugar, and flour until blended and smooth. Beat in remaining ingredients.

2 Drop 1 heaping teaspoon batter onto cookie sheet. Repeat to make 4 cookies in all, about 3 inches apart.

3 With small spatula, spread each cookie to a 3-inch round. (Do not place more than 4 on cookie sheet because, after baking, cookies must be shaped quickly before hardening.)

5 Repeat shaping with remaining cookies on cookie sheet. If cookies become too hard to shape, return cookie sheet to oven to soften cookies slightly. Repeat Steps 2 through 4 with remaining batter. (Batter will become slightly thicker upon standing.) Store cookies in tightly covered container.

4 Bake cookies 5 to 7 minutes, until edges are golden. With pancake turner, quickly transfer 1 cookie to wire rack. Gently shape warm cookie to flute edges; leave on rack to cool. (If you like, omit shaping the cookies and cool flat.)

EACH COOKIE: ABOUT 40 CALORIES, 1g PROTEIN, 4g CARBOHYDRATE, 2g TOTAL FAT (1g SATURATED), 6mg CHOLESTEROL, 45mg SODIUM

CHOPPING NUTS

Nuts can be tricky to keep in place while chopping. The best way: Using a chef's knife, hold down the tip of the knife with one hand while raising and lowering the handle with the other. Work the blade of the knife fanwise back and forth across the nuts.

JUMBO PECAN-DATE OATMEAL COOKIES

Prep: 30 minutes plus cooling
Bake: 20 to 25 minutes per batch
Makes about 2 dozen

1 cup margarine or butter, softened
¾ cup granulated sugar
¾ cup packed light brown sugar
1½ cups all-purpose flour
1 teaspoon baking soda
1 teaspoon vanilla extract
½ teaspoon salt
½ teaspoon ground cinnamon
2 large eggs
3 cups quick-cooking or old-fashioned oats, uncooked
2 cups pitted dates (10 ounces), chopped
1 cup pecans (about 4 ounces), chopped

◆ Preheat oven to 350°F. In large bowl, with mixer at medium speed, beat margarine and both sugars about 5 minutes, until light and creamy. Reduce speed to low; add flour and next 5 ingredients. Beat just until blended, occasionally scraping bowl with rubber spatula. With wooden spoon, stir in oats, dates, and pecans.

◆ Drop dough by level ¼ cups, about 3 inches apart, on ungreased large cookie sheet. Bake cookies 20 to 25 minutes, until golden. With pancake turner, transfer to wire rack to cool. Repeat with remaining dough. Store cookies in tightly covered container.

Each cookie: About 250 calories, 4g protein, 35g carbohydrate, 12g total fat (2g saturated), 18mg cholesterol, 195mg sodium

PEANUT-BRITTLE COOKIES

Prep: 25 minutes plus cooling
Bake: 15 to 20 minutes per batch
Makes about 1½ dozen

1 cup creamy peanut butter
½ cup margarine or butter, softened
½ cup packed light brown sugar
¼ cup granulated sugar
1 teaspoon baking soda
½ teaspoon vanilla extract
¼ teaspoon salt
1 large egg
1 cup all-purpose flour
8 ounces peanut brittle, coarsely chopped

◆ Preheat oven to 350°F. In large bowl, with mixer at medium speed, beat first 8 ingredients until blended, occasionally scraping bowl with rubber spatula. Reduce speed to low. Add flour; beat just until blended.

◆ Drop dough by heaping tablespoons, about 2 inches apart, on ungreased large cookie sheet. Top dough with chopped peanut-brittle pieces, gently pressing brittle halfway into dough.

◆ Bake cookies 15 to 20 minutes, until lightly browned. Cool 2 minutes on cookie sheet on wire rack; with pancake turner, transfer to wire rack to cool completely. Repeat with remaining dough and peanut brittle. Store cookies in tightly covered container.

Each cookie: About 245 calories, 6g protein, 26g carbohydrate, 14g total fat (3g saturated), 12mg cholesterol, 235mg sodium

DOUBLE-CHOCOLATE CHUNK COOKIES

Prep: 30 minutes plus cooling
Bake: 25 to 30 minutes per batch
Makes about 1½ dozen

1 package (12 ounces) semisweet chocolate chunks or 12 ounces coarsely chopped semisweet chocolate bars (2 cups)
1 cup margarine or butter, softened
⅔ cup packed light brown sugar
⅓ cup granulated sugar
1 teaspoon baking soda
2 teaspoons vanilla extract
½ teaspoon salt
1 large egg
2 cups all-purpose flour
2 cups walnuts (about 8 ounces), coarsely chopped

◆ In heavy small saucepan, heat 1 cup chocolate chunks over low heat, stirring frequently, until melted and smooth. Remove saucepan from heat; cool to room temperature.

◆ Preheat oven to 350°F. In large bowl, with mixer at low speed, beat margarine, both sugars, baking soda, vanilla, and salt until crumbly. Add melted chocolate and egg; beat until well blended, occasionally scraping bowl with rubber spatula. With wooden spoon, stir in flour, walnuts, and remaining chocolate chunks.

◆ Drop dough by level ¼ cups, about 3 inches apart, on ungreased large cookie sheet. Bake cookies 25 to 30 minutes, until edges are set but centers are still soft. With pancake turner, transfer cookies to wire rack to cool completely. Repeat with remaining dough. Store cookies in tightly covered container.

Each cookie: About 360 calories, 5g protein, 37g carbohydrate, 24g total fat (3g saturated), 12mg cholesterol, 255mg sodium

CHOCOLATE-ESPRESSO WALNUT CLUSTERS

Prep: 30 minutes plus cooling   Bake: 15 minutes per batch
Makes about 3 dozen

3 squares (3 ounces)
  unsweetened chocolate,
  melted
1 cup all-purpose flour
1 cup sugar
½ cup margarine or butter,
  softened
1 tablespoon instant espresso-
  coffee powder

2 teaspoons vanilla extract
1 teaspoon salt
½ teaspoon baking powder
2 large eggs
4 cups walnuts (about
  16 ounces), coarsely broken

◆ Preheat oven to 350°F. In large bowl, combine all ingredients except walnuts. With mixer at low speed, beat ingredients until well mixed, occasionally scraping bowl with rubber spatula. With wooden spoon, stir in walnuts.

◆ Drop dough by rounded tablespoons, about 1 inch apart, onto ungreased large cookie sheet. Bake 15 minutes, until set. Transfer to wire rack to cool. Repeat with remaining dough. Store cookies in tightly covered container.

Each cookie: About 160 calories, 3g protein, 11g carbohydrate, 12g total fat (2g saturated), 12mg cholesterol, 100mg sodium

FRUITCAKE COOKIES

Prep: 50 minutes plus cooling   Bake: 12 minutes per batch
Makes about 5½ dozen

1½ cups all-purpose flour
1 cup packed dark brown
  sugar
6 tablespoons margarine or
  butter, softened
½ teaspoon salt
½ teaspoon baking soda
½ teaspoon baking powder
½ teaspoon almond extract

2 large eggs
1 cup red candied cherries
  (8 ounces), coarsely
  chopped
½ cup green candied cherries
  (4 ounces), coarsely
  chopped
1 cup walnuts (about
  4 ounces), coarsely chopped

◆ Preheat oven to 400°F. In large bowl, with mixer at low speed, beat first 8 ingredients until well blended, occasionally scraping bowl with rubber spatula.

◆ Reserve ½ cup chopped red and green candied cherries. With spoon, stir walnuts and remaining candied cherries into cookie dough. Drop dough by heaping teaspoons, about 1 inch apart, onto ungreased large cookie sheet. Decorate tops of cookies with some of reserved cherries.

◆ Bake cookies 12 minutes, or until golden. With pancake turner, carefully transfer cookies to wire rack to cool. Repeat with remaining dough and candied cherries. Store cookies in tightly covered container.

Each cookie: About 60 calories, 1g protein, 10g carbohydrate, 2g total fat (0g saturated), 6mg cholesterol, 45mg sodium

MCINTOSH-OATMEAL COOKIES

Prep: 25 minutes plus cooling   Bake: 20 minutes per batch
Makes about 4 dozen

1½ cups sugar
1 cup margarine or butter,
  softened
1½ cups all-purpose flour
1 teaspoon baking soda
1 teaspoon ground cinnamon
1 teaspoon vanilla extract
½ teaspoon salt
2 large eggs

2 medium McIntosh apples,
  peeled, cored, and diced
  (about 2 cups)
3 cups quick-cooking or old-
  fashioned oats, uncooked
1 cup dark seedless raisins
¾ cup walnuts (about
  3 ounces), chopped

◆ Preheat oven to 350°F. In large bowl, with mixer at medium speed, beat sugar and margarine about 5 minutes, until light and creamy. Add flour, baking soda, cinnamon, vanilla, salt, and eggs; beat just until blended, occasionally scraping bowl with rubber spatula. With wooden spoon, stir in apples and remaining ingredients.

◆ Drop dough by heaping tablespoons, about 3 inches apart, onto ungreased large cookie sheet. Bake cookies 20 minutes, until golden. With pancake turner, transfer to wire rack to cool.

◆ Repeat with remaining dough. Store cookies in tightly covered container.

Each cookie: About 120 calories, 2g protein, 16g carbohydrate, 5g total fat (1g saturated), 9mg cholesterol, 95mg sodium

McIntosh-oatmeal cookies   Fruitcake cookies   Chocolate-espresso walnut clusters

LACY PECAN CRISPS

Prep: 40 minutes plus cooling   *Bake:* 6 to 8 minutes per batch
Makes about 5 dozen

1½ cups pecan halves (about 6 ounces)

6 tablespoons butter, softened

½ cup packed light brown sugar

⅓ cup light corn syrup

¾ cup all-purpose flour

½ teaspoon vanilla extract

◆ Preheat oven to 375°F. Grease large cookie sheet. Set aside 60 pecan halves; finely chop remaining pecans.

◆ In 2-quart saucepan, heat butter, brown sugar, and corn syrup to boiling over medium heat (do not use margarine, because it would separate from sugar during cooking); remove from heat. With wooden spoon, stir in chopped pecans, flour, and vanilla.

◆ Drop 1 level teaspoon mixture onto cookie sheet; top with a pecan half. Repeat to make 8 cookies, placing them about 3 inches apart. Bake cookies 6 to 8 minutes, until lightly browned.

◆ Remove cookie sheet from oven; let cool about 30 seconds to set slightly. With pancake turner, quickly loosen cookies and transfer to wire rack to cool completely. Repeat with remaining dough and pecan halves. Store cookies in tightly covered container.

Each cookie: About 45 calories, 0g protein, 5g carbohydrate, 3g total fat (1g saturated), 3mg cholesterol, 15mg sodium

COCONUT-ALMOND MACAROONS

Prep: 15 minutes plus cooling   *Bake:* 20 to 25 minutes per batch
Makes about 1½ dozen

1 bag (7 ounces) shredded coconut (2⅔ cups)

1 cup sliced natural almonds (about 4 ounces)

⅓ cup sugar

¼ teaspoon salt

4 large egg whites

1 teaspoon almond extract

◆ Preheat oven to 325°F. Grease large cookie sheet. In large bowl, with wooden spoon, mix coconut, almonds, sugar, and salt until combined. Stir in egg whites and almond extract until well blended.

◆ Drop mixture by heaping tablespoons, about 2 inches apart, on cookie sheet. Bake 20 to 25 minutes, until golden. With pancake turner, transfer cookies to wire rack to cool completely. Repeat with remaining dough. Store cookies in tightly covered container.

Each cookie: About 110 calories, 3g protein, 11g carbohydrate, 7g total fat (3g saturated), 0mg cholesterol, 45mg sodium

SESAME CRISPS

Prep: 20 minutes plus cooling   *Bake:* 8 minutes per batch
Makes about 3 dozen

6 tablespoons butter, softened

⅓ cup sugar

1 teaspoon vanilla extract

¼ teaspoon salt

¼ teaspoon baking powder

1 large egg

½ cup plus 2 tablespoons all-purpose flour

4 teaspoons white sesame seeds, toasted (see page 318)

4 teaspoons black sesame seeds (available in Asian markets; or, use all white sesame seeds)

◆ Preheat oven to 350°F. Grease large cookie sheet. In large bowl, with mixer at medium speed, beat first 5 ingredients until blended. Add egg; beat until well combined. With wooden spoon, stir in flour.

◆ Spoon half of dough into a small bowl; stir in toasted white sesame seeds. Stir black sesame seeds into dough remaining in large bowl. Drop doughs by rounded teaspoons, about 3 inches apart, onto cookie sheet. Bake cookies about 8 minutes, until set and edges are golden.

◆ Remove cookie sheet from oven; let cookies cool on sheet about 30 seconds to set slightly. With pancake turner, transfer to wire rack to cool completely. Repeat with remaining cookie doughs. Store cookies in tightly covered container.

Each cookie: About 45 calories, 1g protein, 5g carbohydrate, 2g total fat (1g saturated), 11mg cholesterol, 40mg sodium

Sesame crisps

Lacy pecan crisps

Coconut-almond macaroons

SHAPED AND PRESSED COOKIES

The dough for shaped cookies should be firm enough to be molded by hand. If it's too soft to handle, refrigerate it for 1 hour and try again. The dough for pressed cookies should be soft enough to be forced through a decorating bag or cookie press, but firm enough to hold its shape when baked.

WALNUT CRESCENTS

◆◆◆◆◆◆◆◆◆◆◆◆◆

Prep: 45 minutes plus chilling and cooling
Bake: 20 minutes per batch
Makes about 6 dozen

1 cup walnuts (about 4 ounces)
½ cup granulated sugar
1 cup butter, softened
2 cups all-purpose flour
½ cup sour cream
2 teaspoons vanilla extract
¼ teaspoon salt
½ cup confectioners' sugar

1 In 10-inch skillet, lightly toast walnuts over medium heat, shaking skillet frequently. Set skillet aside until walnuts are cool.

2 In food processor with knife blade attached, blend walnuts and ¼ cup granulated sugar until walnuts are very finely chopped. In large bowl, with mixer at low speed, beat butter and remaining ¼ cup granulated sugar until blended, occasionally scraping bowl with rubber spatula.

3 Increase speed to high; beat about 5 minutes, until light and fluffy. Reduce speed to low; gradually beat in flour, sour cream, vanilla, salt, and walnut mixture until blended. Divide dough in half; wrap each half in plastic wrap and refrigerate 1 hour, or until dough is firm enough to handle. (Or, place dough in freezer 30 minutes.) Meanwhile, preheat oven to 325°F.

TEACAKES

Instead of shaping these rich, short cookies into crescents, in Step 4 simply roll the dough into 1-inch balls; bake and roll in confectioners' sugar as directed. If you like, substitute pecans or almonds for the walnuts. Or, try toasted, skinned hazelnuts (see page 522) and omit skillet-toasting in Step 1.

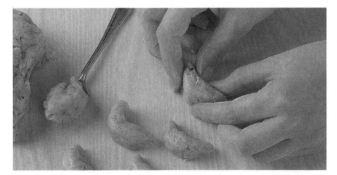

4 Working with half of dough at a time, with lightly floured hands, shape dough by rounded teaspoons into 1" by ½" crescents. Place crescents, about 1½ inches apart, on ungreased large cookie sheet. Bake cookies 20 minutes, or until lightly browned around edges. Cool cookies on sheet on wire rack 2 minutes. Place confectioners' sugar in small bowl.

5 While still warm, gently roll cookies, one at a time, in confectioners' sugar to coat. Cool completely on wire rack. Repeat with remaining dough and confectioners' sugar. Store cookies in tightly covered container.

EACH COOKIE: ABOUT 55 CALORIES, 1g PROTEIN, 5g CARBOHYDRATE, 4g TOTAL FAT (2g SATURATED), 8mg CHOLESTEROL, 35mg SODIUM

ALMOND LOGS

Prep: 25 minutes plus cooling   Bake: 20 to 25 minutes per batch
Makes 2 dozen

2 tubes or cans (7 to 8 ounces
    each) almond paste, cut into
    1-inch chunks
⅔ cup confectioners' sugar

2 large egg whites
2 cups sliced natural almonds
    (about 8 ounces)

◆ Preheat oven to 325°F. Grease and flour large cookie sheet. In small bowl, with mixer at low speed, beat almond paste until crumbly. Add confectioners' sugar and egg whites; beat until well blended (dough will be sticky and wet). Place sliced almonds on sheet of waxed paper. With lightly floured hands, roll 1 level tablespoon dough into a 3-inch-long log. Place dough log on almonds; gently press and stick almonds into dough to cover.

◆ Repeat with more dough and almonds to make 12 logs, placing logs on cookie sheet, about 1 inch apart, as they are formed. Bake cookies 20 to 25 minutes, until golden and set. Transfer to wire rack to cool. Repeat with remaining dough and almonds. Store cookies in tightly covered container.

Each cookie: About 140 calories, 4g protein, 13g carbohydrate, 8g total fat (1g saturated), 0mg cholesterol, 10mg sodium

GINGER MOLASSES COOKIES

Prep: 40 minutes plus cooling   Bake: 7 to 10 minutes per batch
Makes about 4 dozen

1 cup packed brown sugar
⅔ cup shortening
½ cup light molasses
¼ cup milk
2 teaspoons baking powder
1½ teaspoons ground ginger
1 teaspoon ground cinnamon
¾ teaspoon baking soda

½ teaspoon salt
¼ teaspoon ground cloves
1 large egg
3½ cups all-purpose flour
¼ cup granulated sugar
¼ cup crystallized ginger
    (about 1½ ounces), cut into
    ¼-inch pieces (optional)

◆ Preheat oven to 350°F. In large bowl, with mixer at low speed, mix first 11 ingredients and 2 cups flour until blended. With wooden spoon, stir in remaining 1½ cups flour. Place sugar in small bowl. Roll cookie dough into 1½-inch balls; roll each ball in sugar to coat. Place 12 balls, 2 inches apart, on ungreased large cookie sheet.

◆ Gently press 1 piece of crystallized ginger, if using, into center of each ball on cookie sheet, flattening slightly. Bake 7 to 10 minutes, or until bottoms are lightly browned. Transfer to rack to cool. Repeat with remaining dough and crystallized ginger. Store cookies in tightly covered container.

Each cookie: About 85 calories, 1g protein, 14g carbohydrate, 3g total fat (1g saturated), 4mg cholesterol, 65mg sodium

CHOCOLATE-RASPBERRY ALMOND SPRITZ

Prep: 50 minutes plus cooling and chilling
Bake: 12 to 14 minutes per batch
Makes about 2½ dozen

½ cup blanched whole almonds
    (about 2 ounces)
¾ cup sugar
2¼ cups all-purpose flour
1 cup butter, softened
1½ teaspoons almond extract
¼ teaspoon salt
1 large egg

¼ cup plus 2 tablespoons
    heavy or whipping cream
6 squares (6 ounces)
    semisweet chocolate, finely
    chopped
3 tablespoons seedless red
    raspberry jam

◆ Preheat oven to 350°F. In food processor with knife blade attached, blend almonds with sugar, pulsing processor on and off, until almonds are finely ground. (Or, in blender, grind almonds with sugar in batches.)

◆ In large bowl, with mixer at low speed, beat almond mixture, flour, and next 4 ingredients just until blended, scraping bowl occasionally with rubber spatula. Spoon dough into large decorating bag with large star tip (about ¾ inch in diameter) or cookie press fitted with desired template.

◆ Pipe teardrop shapes (about 2" by 1½") or press through cookie press, 1 inch apart, onto ungreased large cookie sheet. Bake cookies 12 to 14 minutes, until lightly browned around edges. Cool slightly on cookie sheet. With pancake turner, transfer cookies to wire rack to cool completely. Repeat with remaining dough.

◆ Prepare filling: In 1-quart saucepan, heat cream to boiling over low heat. Place chocolate in small bowl with jam. Pour hot cream over chocolate mixture; let stand 1 minute. Stir until smooth. Refrigerate 15 to 18 minutes, until firm enough to spread. (If mixture becomes too firm, let stand at room temperature until slightly softened.)

◆ With small spatula, spread about 1 rounded teaspoon filling onto flat side of half of cooled cookies. Top with remaining cookies, flat-side down. Store cookies in refrigerator.

Each cookie: About 160 calories, 2g protein, 17g carbohydrate, 10g total fat (6g saturated), 28mg cholesterol, 85mg sodium

ROLLED COOKIES

These cookies are rolled out and cut into myriad shapes with decorative cutters, a pastry wheel, or a sharp knife. They require a firm dough that is often refrigerated (this relaxes the gluten and yields a more tender cookie). Cookies made with butter (instead of margarine or a spread) hold their shape best. Cut out the cookies as close to one another as possible to reduce excessive rerolling of the scraps.

TWO-TONE COOKIES

◆◆◆◆◆◆◆◆◆◆◆◆◆◆◆◆◆◆◆◆◆◆◆◆◆◆

Prep: 1 hour plus cooling   Bake: 12 to 15 minutes per batch
Makes 3 dozen

¾ cup margarine or butter, softened	½ teaspoon salt
⅔ cup plus 3 teaspoons sugar	1 large egg
1 teaspoon baking powder	2 cups all-purpose flour
1½ teaspoons vanilla extract	¼ cup unsweetened cocoa

1 Grease and flour 2 large cookie sheets. In large bowl, with mixer at low speed, beat margarine and ⅔ cup sugar until blended. Increase speed to high; beat until light and creamy. Reduce speed to low. Add baking powder, vanilla, salt, egg, 1½ cups flour, and *2 tablespoons water*; beat until blended.

2 Place half of dough in medium bowl; with wooden spoon, stir in remaining ½ cup flour. Stir cocoa into dough remaining in large bowl. On lightly floured surface, with floured rolling pin, roll vanilla dough ⅛ inch thick.

3 Preheat oven to 350°F. With floured 3-inch round scallop-shaped cookie cutter, cut vanilla dough into as many cookies as possible. Reserve trimmings. Place cookies on 1 cookie sheet, about ¼ inch apart. Repeat with chocolate dough, placing chocolate cookies on second cookie sheet.

4 With 1½-inch round scallop-shaped cookie cutter, cut out small round in center of each vanilla and chocolate cookie.

5 Fit a small vanilla cookie cutout into center of each chocolate cookie and a small chocolate cookie cutout into center of each vanilla cookie to make two-tone cookies.

6 Sprinkle cookies lightly with 2 teaspoons sugar. Bake cookies on 2 oven racks 12 to 15 minutes, until golden, rotating cookie sheets between upper and lower racks halfway through baking time. With pancake turner, transfer cookies to wire racks to cool. Gather trimmings, reroll, and cut out more cookies. Sprinkle cookies with remaining 1 teaspoon sugar and bake as above. Store cookies in tightly covered container.

EACH COOKIE: ABOUT 75 CALORIES, 1g PROTEIN, 9g CARBOHYDRATE, 4g TOTAL FAT (1g SATURATED), 6mg CHOLESTEROL, 90mg SODIUM

CLASSIC SUGAR COOKIES

Prep: 45 minutes plus chilling, cooling, and decorating
Bake: 12 to 15 minutes per batch   *Makes about 4 dozen*

¾ cup sugar
10 tablespoons butter,
  softened
1 teaspoon baking powder
½ teaspoon salt
2 tablespoons milk

2 teaspoons vanilla extract
1 large egg
2 cups all-purpose flour
Ornamental Frosting
  (optional, see below)

◆ In large bowl, with mixer at low speed, beat first
4 ingredients until blended. Increase speed to high; beat
until mixture is light and creamy. Reduce speed to low. Add
milk, vanilla, and egg; beat until blended. (Mixture may
appear curdled.)

◆ With wooden spoon, stir in flour until blended. Shape
dough into 2 balls; flatten each slightly. Wrap each in plastic
wrap and refrigerate 1 hour, or until firm enough to roll.
(Or, place dough in freezer 30 minutes.)

◆ Preheat oven to 350°F. On lightly floured surface, with
floured rolling pin, roll 1 piece of dough ⅛ inch thick,
keeping remaining dough refrigerated.

◆ With floured assorted 3- to 4-inch cookie cutters, cut
dough into as many cookies as possible; refrigerate
trimmings. Place cookies, about 1 inch apart, on ungreased
large cookie sheet.

◆ Bake cookies 12 to 15 minutes, until golden around
edges. Transfer cookies to wire rack to cool. Repeat with
remaining dough. Reroll trimmings; cut out more cookies
and bake as above.

◆ When cookies are cool, prepare Ornamental Frosting, if
you like, and use to decorate. Set cookies aside at least
1 hour to allow frosting to dry completely. Store cookies in
tightly covered container.

**Each cookie: About 55 calories, 1g protein, 7g carbohydrate,
3g total fat (2g saturated), 11mg cholesterol, 60mg sodium**

DECORATING COOKIES

These frosted holiday cookies (made from Classic Sugar Cookies on
this page and Gingerbread Cutouts, page 513) are pretty enough to
be used as tree or wreath decorations. If you like, with skewer or
toothpick, make 1 or 2 holes in top of each cookie before baking.
Thread ribbon, string, or clear nylon fishing line through finished
cookies for hanging.

ORNAMENTAL FROSTING   In bowl, with mixer at medium
speed, beat 1 package (16 ounces) confectioners' sugar, 3 tablespoons
meringue powder (see page 30), and ⅓ cup warm water about
5 minutes, until mixture is stiff and knife drawn through it leaves a
clean-cut path.

  If you like, tint frosting with assorted food colorings as desired;
keep covered with plastic wrap to prevent drying out. With small
metal spatula, artists' paintbrushes, or decorating bags with small
writing tips, decorate cookies with frosting. (Thin frosting with a little
warm water if necessary to obtain the right consistency.) Makes
about 3 cups.

**Each tablespoon: About 40 calories, 0g protein, 9g carbohydrate,
0g total fat, 0mg cholesterol, 5mg sodium**

HAZELNUT SPICE CUTOUTS

Prep: 45 minutes plus chilling and cooling
Bake: 10 to 12 minutes per batch   Makes about 2 dozen

½ cup (about 2 ounces) hazelnuts (filberts), toasted and skinned (see page 522), or walnuts	6 tablespoons margarine or butter, softened
½ cup packed light brown sugar	½ teaspoon ground cinnamon
1¼ cups all-purpose flour	½ teaspoon vanilla extract
	¼ teaspoon ground allspice
	¼ teaspoon salt
	1 large egg

◆ In food processor with knife blade attached or in blender at high speed, blend nuts with sugar until finely ground.

◆ In large bowl, with mixer at low speed, beat nut mixture with remaining ingredients just until mixed, occasionally scraping bowl with rubber spatula. Divide dough in half; pat each half into a 1-inch-thick disk. Wrap each half in plastic wrap and refrigerate 1 hour, or until firm enough to roll. (Or, place dough in freezer 30 minutes.)

◆ Preheat oven to 350°F. Grease large cookie sheet. On well-floured surface, with floured rolling pin, roll half of dough ⅛ inch thick. With floured assorted 3- to 4-inch cookie cutters, cut dough into as many cookies as possible; reserve trimmings.

◆ Place cookies, about 1 inch apart, on cookie sheet. Bake cookies 10 to 12 minutes, until edges are golden. Transfer cookies to wire rack to cool. Repeat with remaining dough. Reroll trimmings and cut out more cookies. Store cookies in tightly covered container.

Each cookie: About 80 calories, 1g protein, 10g carbohydrate, 5g total fat (1g saturated), 9mg cholesterol, 60mg sodium

TOASTED-WALNUT CRISPS

Prep: 30 minutes plus cooling   Bake: 20 minutes
Makes about 16

2 cups walnuts (8 ounces)	¾ cup margarine or butter, cut into small pieces
1⅓ cups all-purpose flour	
1 cup confectioners' sugar	1 tablespoon vanilla extract
2 tablespoons cornstarch	1 tablespoon milk
¼ teaspoon salt	1 tablespoon granulated sugar

◆ Reserve ⅓ cup walnuts for topping. In 12-inch skillet, toast remaining walnuts over medium heat, shaking skillet frequently, until golden brown; cool and chop walnuts.

◆ Preheat oven to 325°F. In large bowl, stir chopped toasted walnuts, flour, confectioners' sugar, cornstarch, and salt until well mixed. With hand, knead margarine and vanilla into flour mixture until well blended and mixture

holds together. On floured surface, with floured hands, gently knead dough 5 or 6 times, until smooth, sprinkling with extra flour if needed.

◆ With floured rolling pin, roll dough ¼ inch thick. With floured 3-inch fluted round cookie cutter, cut dough into as many rounds as possible; reserve trimmings. Place cookies on ungreased large cookie sheet, about 1 inch apart.

◆ Reroll trimmings and cut out more cookies. Brush cookies with milk; sprinkle with granulated sugar. Press 1 walnut into each. Bake 20 minutes, or until golden. Transfer to wire rack to cool. Store in tightly covered container.

Each cookie: About 240 calories, 3g protein, 18g carbohydrate, 18g total fat (3g saturated), 0mg cholesterol, 135mg sodium

GINGERBREAD CUTOUTS

Prep: 45 minutes plus cooling and decorating
Bake: 12 minutes per batch   Makes about 3 dozen

½ cup sugar	½ cup margarine or butter, cut into chunks
½ cup light molasses	
1½ teaspoons ground ginger	1 large egg, beaten
1 teaspoon ground allspice	3½ cups all-purpose flour
1 teaspoon ground cinnamon	Ornamental Frosting (optional, see page 512)
1 teaspoon ground cloves	
2 teaspoons baking soda	

◆ Preheat oven to 325°F. In 3-quart saucepan, heat first 6 ingredients to boiling over medium heat, stirring occasionally. Remove saucepan from heat; stir in baking soda (mixture will foam up in the pan). Stir in margarine until melted. With fork, stir in egg, then flour.

◆ On floured surface, knead dough until thoroughly mixed. Divide in half. Wrap half in plastic wrap; set aside.

◆ With floured rolling pin, roll remaining half of dough slightly less than ¼ inch thick. With floured assorted 3- to 4-inch cookie cutters, cut dough into as many cookies as possible; reserve trimmings. Place cookies, about 1 inch apart, on ungreased large cookie sheet.

◆ Bake cookies 12 minutes, or until edges begin to brown. Transfer to wire rack to cool. Repeat with remaining dough. Reroll trimmings and cut out more cookies.

◆ When cookies are cool, prepare Ornamental Frosting, if you like, and use to decorate. Set cookies aside at least 1 hour to allow frosting to dry completely. Store in tightly covered container.

Each cookie: About 90 calories, 1g protein, 14g carbohydrate, 3g total fat (1g saturated), 6mg cholesterol, 100mg sodium

LINZER WREATHS

Prep: 45 minutes plus chilling and cooling
Bake: 10 to 12 minutes per batch   **Makes** about 20

1 cup blanched whole
    almonds (about 4 ounces)
⅔ cup granulated sugar
1 teaspoon vanilla extract
2¼ cups all-purpose flour
½ teaspoon baking soda

1 cup margarine or butter,
    softened
¼ cup confectioners' sugar
⅔ cup seedless red raspberry
    jam

◆ In food processor with knife blade attached or in blender at medium speed, blend almonds, ⅓ cup granulated sugar, and vanilla until almonds are finely ground.

◆ In large bowl, stir together almond mixture, flour, baking soda, and remaining ⅓ cup granulated sugar. With pastry blender or two knives used scissor-fashion, cut in margarine until mixture resembles coarse crumbs. With hand, knead until dough forms a ball. Divide ball into 2 pieces; wrap each in plastic wrap. Refrigerate 1 hour, or until firm enough to roll. (Or, place dough in freezer 30 minutes.)

◆ Preheat oven to 350°F. On lightly floured surface, with floured rolling pin, roll 1 piece of dough ⅛ inch thick; keep remaining dough refrigerated. With floured 3-inch round fluted cookie cutter, cut dough into as many rounds as possible; reserve trimmings. With 1½-inch round fluted cutter, cut out center of half of cookies. With pancake turner, place cookies, about 1 inch apart, on ungreased large cookie sheet.

◆ Bake cookies 10 to 12 minutes, until lightly browned. With pancake turner, transfer cookies to wire rack to cool completely. Repeat with remaining dough. Gather trimmings and cutout centers, reroll, and cut out more cookies.

◆ Sprinkle confectioners' sugar over cookies with cutout centers. In small saucepan, heat jam over low heat until melted. Brush whole cookies with jam and top with cutout cookies. Store, between sheets of waxed paper, in tightly covered container.

Each cookie: About 220 calories, 3g protein, 27g carbohydrate, 12g total fat (2g saturated), 0mg cholesterol, 140mg sodium

APRICOT-RASPBERRY RUGELACH

Prep: 1 hour plus chilling and cooling   **Bake:** 30 to 35 minutes
Makes 4 dozen

1 cup margarine or butter,
    softened
1 package (8 ounces) cream
    cheese, softened
1 teaspoon vanilla extract
¼ teaspoon salt
2 cups all-purpose flour
¾ cup granulated sugar
1 cup walnuts (about
    4 ounces), chopped

¾ cup dried apricots, chopped
¼ cup packed light brown
    sugar
1½ teaspoons ground
    cinnamon
½ cup seedless red raspberry
    jam
1 tablespoon milk

◆ In large bowl, with mixer at low speed, beat margarine with cream cheese until blended and smooth. Beat in vanilla, salt, 1 cup flour, and ¼ cup granulated sugar until blended. With wooden spoon, stir in remaining 1 cup flour.

◆ Divide dough into 4 equal pieces. Wrap each piece in plastic wrap; refrigerate at least 2 hours, until firm enough to roll, or overnight.

◆ Prepare filling: In medium bowl, stir walnuts, apricots, brown sugar, 6 tablespoons granulated sugar, and ½ teaspoon cinnamon until well mixed. Line 2 large cookie sheets with foil; grease foil.

◆ Preheat oven to 325°F. On lightly floured surface, with floured rolling pin, roll 1 piece of dough into a 9-inch round; keep remaining dough refrigerated. Spread dough with 2 tablespoons jam. Sprinkle with about ½ cup filling; gently press filling onto dough.

◆ With pastry wheel or sharp knife, cut dough into 12 equal wedges. Starting at curved edge, roll up each wedge, jelly-roll fashion. Place cookies on cookie sheet, point-side down, about ½ inch apart. Repeat with remaining dough, jam, and filling.

◆ In cup, mix remaining 2 tablespoons sugar with remaining 1 teaspoon cinnamon. Brush rugelach with milk; sprinkle with cinnamon-sugar.

◆ Bake rugelach on 2 oven racks 30 to 35 minutes, until golden, rotating cookie sheets between upper and lower racks halfway through baking time. Immediately remove to wire racks to cool. Store in tightly covered container.

Each cookie: About 115 calories, 1g protein, 12g carbohydrate, 7g total fat (2g saturated), 5mg cholesterol, 70mg sodium

Linzer wreaths

Apricot-raspberry
rugelach

ICEBOX COOKIES

The beauty of these cookies, also called refrigerator or slice-and-bake cookies, is that you can have warm-from-the-oven treats anytime: Just prepare the dough and store, wrapped, in the refrigerator for up to 1 week (or freeze for up to 2 months), then bake cookies as you want them.

COCONUT BUTTONS

◆◆◆◆◆◆◆◆◆◆◆◆◆◆

Prep: 45 minutes plus chilling and cooling
Bake: 20 to 25 minutes per batch
Makes about 6½ dozen

1 cup butter, softened
½ cup sugar
2 tablespoons milk
1 teaspoon coconut extract
¾ teaspoon baking powder
½ teaspoon salt
2⅔ cups all-purpose flour
1½ cups flaked coconut, chopped
4 squares (4 ounces) semisweet chocolate
1 tablespoon shortening

1 In large bowl, with mixer at medium-high speed, beat butter, sugar, milk, coconut extract, baking powder, and salt until light and creamy. With wooden spoon, stir in flour and chopped coconut (dough will be crumbly). With hands, squeeze dough together. Divide dough into 4 equal pieces. Shape each piece into a 10" by 1" log. Wrap each log in plastic wrap and slide onto small cookie sheet for easier handling. Refrigerate dough overnight, or freeze at least 2 hours, until firm enough to slice.

2 Preheat oven to 325°F. Cut 1 log into ½-inch-thick slices (keep remaining logs refrigerated). Place slices, 1 inch apart, on ungreased large cookie sheet. With toothpick, make 4 holes in each cookie to resemble a button.

3 Bake cookies 20 to 25 minutes, until lightly golden. Transfer to wire rack to cool. Repeat with remaining dough. When cookies are cool, in small heavy saucepan, melt chocolate with shortening over low heat, stirring frequently.

COOKIE TIP

◆◆◆◆◆◆◆◆◆◆◆◆

Although margarine and butter are equally suitable for most purposes, some cookie recipes, such as the one above, call for butter only. This is because the dough would spread too much during baking if made with margarine. Always use butter if the recipe specifically calls for it.

4 Dip bottom of each cooled cookie into melted chocolate so that chocolate comes slightly up side of cookie.

5 With small metal spatula, scrape excess chocolate from bottom of cookie, leaving a thin layer. Place cookies, chocolate-side down, on waxed paper; set aside to allow chocolate to set completely. Store finished cookies in tightly covered container.

EACH COOKIE: ABOUT 55 CALORIES, 1g PROTEIN, 6g CARBOHYDRATE, 3g TOTAL FAT (2g SATURATED), 6mg CHOLESTEROL, 45mg SODIUM

POPPY-SEED PINWHEELS

Prep: 40 minutes plus chilling and cooling
Bake: 8 to 10 minutes per batch   Makes about 7 dozen

2½ cups all-purpose flour	1 teaspoon salt
1 cup sugar	1 teaspoon vanilla extract
¾ cup margarine or butter, softened	2 large eggs
1 teaspoon baking powder	1 can (12 ounces) poppy-seed filling

◆ In large bowl, with mixer at low speed, beat all ingredients except poppy-seed filling until well blended, occasionally scraping bowl with rubber spatula. Divide dough in half; wrap each half in plastic wrap and refrigerate 1 hour, or freeze 30 minutes, until firm enough to handle.

◆ On sheet of waxed paper, with floured rolling pin, roll half of dough into a 12" by 8" rectangle; spread with half of filling. From a long side, roll dough jelly-roll fashion. Repeat with remaining dough and filling. Wrap in plastic wrap; refrigerate overnight or freeze at least 2 hours, until firm enough to slice.

◆ Preheat oven to 350°F. Grease large cookie sheet. Cut 1 log into ¼-inch-thick slices (keep remainder refrigerated). Place slices, about 1 inch apart, on cookie sheet. Bake 8 to 10 minutes, until edges are golden brown. Cool slightly on cookie sheet on wire rack. With pancake turner, transfer to wire rack to cool completely. Repeat with remaining dough. Store cookies in tightly covered container.

Each cookie: About 55 calories, 1g protein, 8g carbohydrate, 2g total fat (0g saturated), 5mg cholesterol, 55mg sodium

SPICY ALMOND SLICES

Prep: 25 minutes plus chilling and cooling
Bake: 10 to 12 minutes per batch   Makes about 6½ dozen

1 cup margarine or butter, softened	½ teaspoon ground cloves
1 cup granulated sugar	½ teaspoon ground nutmeg
¾ cup packed dark brown sugar	½ teaspoon salt
1 tablespoon ground cinnamon	2 large eggs
1 teaspoon baking soda	3½ cups all-purpose flour
1 teaspoon vanilla extract	2 cups sliced blanched almonds (about 8 ounces)

◆ In large bowl, with mixer at low speed, beat first 10 ingredients and 2 cups flour until well mixed. With wooden spoon, stir in almonds and remaining 1½ cups flour; mix thoroughly with hands, if necessary. (Dough will be stiff.)

◆ Divide dough in half. Shape each half into 10" by 3" by 1" brick; wrap each brick in plastic wrap. Refrigerate overnight or freeze at least 2 hours, until firm enough to slice. Preheat oven to 375°F. Cut 1 brick into ¼-inch-thick slices (keep remainder refrigerated).

◆ Place slices, 1 inch apart, on ungreased cookie sheet. Bake 10 to 12 minutes, until browned around edges. With pancake turner, transfer cookies to wire rack to cool. Repeat with remaining dough. Store in tightly covered container.

Each cookie: About 75 calories, 1g protein, 9g carbohydrate, 4g total fat (1g saturated), 5mg cholesterol, 60mg sodium

PECAN SQUARES

Prep: 30 minutes plus chilling and cooling
Bake: 12 to 15 minutes per batch   Makes about 5 dozen

¾ cup packed dark brown sugar	2 teaspoons vanilla extract
½ cup margarine or butter, softened	2½ cups all-purpose flour
1 large egg	½ teaspoon baking soda
2 tablespoons milk	½ teaspoon salt
	1¼ cups pecans (5 ounces), toasted and chopped

◆ In large bowl, with mixer at medium-high speed, beat brown sugar and margarine until light and fluffy. Add egg, milk, and vanilla; beat until smooth. With wooden spoon, stir in flour, baking soda, and salt. When flour is almost incorporated, stir in pecans. (Dough will be very stiff.)

◆ Divide dough in half. On lightly floured surface, shape each half of dough into an 8" by 1½" by 1½" bar, using pancake turner to help flatten sides. Wrap each bar in plastic wrap and slide onto small cookie sheet for easier handling. Refrigerate dough overnight or freeze at least 2 hours, until very firm.

◆ Preheat oven to 350°F. Grease large cookie sheet. Cut 1 bar into slightly less than ¼-inch-thick slices (keep remainder refrigerated). Place slices, about 1½ inches apart, on cookie sheet. Bake cookies 12 to 15 minutes, until browned around edges. Transfer cookies to wire rack to cool. Repeat with remaining dough. Store cookies in tightly covered container.

Each cookie: About 60 calories, 1g protein, 7g carbohydrate, 3g total fat (0g saturated), 4mg cholesterol, 50mg sodium

FROSTED PECAN SQUARES

Prepare Pecan Squares as above. In medium bowl, mix 2 cups confectioners' sugar and 2 tablespoons plus 2 teaspoons milk to make a thick icing, adding more milk if necessary. With small metal spatula or knife, spread some icing of top of each cooled cookie; top each with a toasted pecan half (you will need about 1¼ cups toasted pecan halves). Set aside to allow icing to dry.

Each cookie: About 90 calories, 1g protein, 11g carbohydrate, 5g total fat (1g saturated), 4mg cholesterol, 50mg sodium

BISCOTTI

Biscotti are irresistible Italian cookies that involve a unique cooking process. The dough is baked twice, first in a loaf shape, then again after the loaf is cut into slices. The result is a dry, crunchy cookie perfect for dipping into coffee or sweet wine. Flavors range from the traditional almond and anise to modern variations made with chocolate, ginger, or dried fruit.

CRANBERRY-HAZELNUT BISCOTTI

◆◆◆◆◆◆◆◆◆◆◆◆◆◆◆◆◆◆◆◆◆◆◆◆◆◆◆

Prep: 1 hour plus cooling Bake: 45 to 55 minutes
Makes about 4½ dozen

3¾ cups all-purpose flour
2 cups sugar
1 teaspoon baking powder
½ teaspoon salt
5 large eggs
2 teaspoons vanilla extract

1⅓ cups (about 5½ ounces) hazelnuts (filberts), toasted and skinned (see page 522), chopped
½ cup dried cranberries or currants

1 Preheat oven to 350°F. Grease and lightly flour 2 large cookie sheets. In large bowl, combine first 4 ingredients. Separate 1 egg; reserve white for glaze. In small bowl, with wire whisk or fork, beat 4 whole eggs, 1 egg yolk, vanilla, and *1 tablespoon water*. Pour egg mixture into flour mixture; with wooden spoon, stir until blended.

2 With hands, knead dough until it comes together (dough will be very stiff). Knead in hazelnuts and dried cranberries. Divide dough into 4 equal pieces.

3 On lightly floured surface, with floured hands, shape each piece of dough into an 11" by 2" log. Place 2 logs, about 4 inches apart, on each cookie sheet.

4 In cup, with fork, lightly beat reserved egg white. With pastry brush, brush logs with egg white. Bake logs on 2 oven racks 35 to 40 minutes, until toothpick inserted in center comes out clean, rotating cookie sheets between upper and lower racks halfway through baking time (logs will spread during baking and become loaf shaped). Cool loaves 10 minutes on cookie sheets on wire racks.

6 Place slices, cut-side down, on same cookie sheets in single layer. Bake slices on 2 oven racks 10 to 15 minutes, until golden, turning slices once and rotating cookie sheets between upper and lower racks halfway through baking time. Transfer biscotti to wire racks to cool completely. (Biscotti will harden as they cool.) Store in tightly covered container.

5 Transfer loaves to cutting board. With serrated knife, cut each loaf crosswise into ½-inch-thick diagonal slices.

EACH SERVING: ABOUT 85 CALORIES, 2g PROTEIN, 15g CARBOHYDRATE, 2g TOTAL FAT (0g SATURATED), 20mg CHOLESTEROL, 35mg SODIUM

CHOCOLATE BISCOTTI

Prep: 45 minutes plus cooling and chilling
Bake: 45 to 50 minutes   Makes about 4 dozen

1 cup sugar
1 cup margarine or butter, softened
2½ cups all-purpose flour
1 cup unsweetened cocoa
1 tablespoon baking powder
1 teaspoon instant-coffee granules
1 teaspoon vanilla extract
½ teaspoon salt
4 large eggs
8 squares (8 ounces) semisweet chocolate
¼ cup sliced almonds (1 ounce), toasted

◆ Preheat oven to 350°F. In large bowl, with mixer at medium speed, beat sugar and margarine until light and creamy. With mixer at low speed, beat in 1 cup flour and next 6 ingredients until blended. With wooden spoon, stir in remaining 1½ cups flour until blended. Divide dough in half. On ungreased large cookie sheet, with well-floured hands, shape dough into two 12" by 3" loaves, 3 inches apart. Bake loaves 25 to 30 minutes, until firm. Cool on cookie sheet on wire rack 20 minutes.

◆ Transfer loaves to cutting board. With serrated knife, cut each loaf crosswise into ½-inch-thick diagonal slices. Place slices, cut-side down, on 2 ungreased large cookie sheets in single layer. Bake on 2 oven racks 20 minutes, turning slices once and rotating cookie sheets between upper and lower racks halfway through cooking time. Transfer to wire racks to cool completely.

◆ In heavy small saucepan, melt chocolate over low heat until smooth, stirring frequently. With pastry brush, brush top of each biscotti with some melted chocolate; sprinkle some almonds on chocolate. Refrigerate biscotti 30 minutes, or until chocolate is set. Store in tightly covered container.

Each cookie: About 110 calories, 2g protein, 13g carbohydrate, 6g total fat (2g saturated), 18mg cholesterol, 105mg sodium

ALMOND-ANISE BISCOTTI

Prep: 25 minutes plus cooling
Bake: 55 minutes   Makes about 7 dozen

1 cup whole almonds (about 4 ounces)
1 tablespoon anise seeds, crushed
1 tablespoon anise-flavor aperitif or liqueur
2 cups all-purpose flour
1 cup sugar
1 teaspoon baking powder
⅛ teaspoon salt
3 large eggs

◆ Preheat oven to 325°F. Place almonds on jelly-roll pan. Bake 10 minutes, until lightly toasted. Cool; chop very coarsely. Meanwhile, in medium bowl, combine anise seeds and aperitif; let stand 10 minutes.

◆ Grease large cookie sheet. In large bowl, combine flour, sugar, baking powder, salt, and almonds. Whisk eggs into anise mixture. With wooden spoon, stir egg mixture into flour mixture. Divide dough in half.

◆ With floured hands, shape dough on cookie sheet into two 15-inch logs, 3 inches apart (dough will be sticky).

◆ Bake logs 40 minutes, or until golden and toothpick inserted in center of log comes out clean. Cool on cookie sheet on wire rack 10 minutes.

◆ Transfer logs to cutting board. With serrated knife, cut each crosswise into ¼-inch-thick diagonal slices.

◆ Place slices, cut-side down, on 2 ungreased cookie sheets in single layer. Bake on 2 oven racks 15 minutes, turning slices once and rotating cookie sheets between upper and lower racks halfway through baking time. Transfer to wire racks to cool completely. Store in tightly covered container.

Each cookie: About 30 calories, 1g protein, 5g carbohydrate, 1g total fat (0g saturated), 8mg cholesterol, 15mg sodium

GINGER BISCOTTI

Prep: 25 minutes plus cooling
Bake: 48 to 50 minutes
Makes about 3½ dozen

3 cups all-purpose flour
1 tablespoon ground ginger
2 teaspoons baking powder
¼ teaspoon salt
½ cup margarine or butter, softened
½ cup granulated sugar
½ cup packed brown sugar
3 large eggs
½ cup minced crystallized ginger (about 3 ounces)

◆ Preheat oven to 350°F. Grease large cookie sheet. In medium bowl, combine first 4 ingredients.

◆ In large bowl, with mixer at medium speed, beat margarine with both sugars until light and creamy. Beat in eggs, 1 at a time.

◆ With mixer at low speed, beat in flour mixture until blended. With wooden spoon, stir in crystallized ginger. Divide dough in half.

◆ With floured hands, shape dough on cookie sheet into two 12-inch logs, 3 inches apart.

◆ Bake 30 minutes, or until toothpick inserted in center of log comes out clean. Cool on cookie sheet on wire rack 10 minutes. Transfer logs to cutting board. With serrated knife, cut each crosswise into ½-inch-thick diagonal slices.

◆ Place slices, cut-side down, on 2 ungreased cookie sheets in single layer. Bake on 2 oven racks 18 to 20 minutes, until golden, turning slices once and rotating cookie sheets between upper and lower racks halfway through baking time. Transfer to wire racks to cool completely. Store in tightly covered container.

Each cookie: About 80 calories, 1g protein, 13g carbohydrate, 3g total fat (1g saturated), 15mg cholesterol, 70mg sodium

BROWNIES

Brownies are the most famous – and irresistible – breed of bar cookies. Whether they're dense and chewy or light and cakelike, studded with nuts or frosted, they continue to reign as one of America's best-loved desserts. If not using brownies within 3 days, cover tightly and freeze for future treats.

ALMOND CHEESECAKE BROWNIES

◆◆◆◆◆◆◆◆◆◆◆◆◆

Prep: 30 minutes plus cooling
Bake: 40 to 45 minutes
Makes 2 dozen

¾ **cup margarine or butter**
4 **squares (4 ounces) unsweetened chocolate**
4 **squares (4 ounces) semisweet chocolate**
2 **cups sugar**
6 **large eggs**
2½ **teaspoons vanilla extract**
1½ **cups all-purpose flour**
¾ **teaspoon baking powder**
½ **teaspoon salt**
1½ **packages (8 ounces each) cream cheese, slightly softened**
¾ **teaspoon almond extract**

1 Preheat oven to 350°F. Line 13" by 9" metal baking pan with foil; lightly grease foil. In heavy 3-quart saucepan, melt margarine and all chocolate over low heat, stirring frequently. Remove from heat. With wooden spoon, beat in 1½ cups sugar, then beat in 4 eggs and 2 teaspoons vanilla until well blended. Stir in flour, baking powder, and salt just until blended; set aside.

2 In small bowl, with mixer at medium speed, beat cream cheese until smooth; gradually beat in remaining ½ cup sugar. Beat in almond extract, remaining 2 eggs, and remaining ½ teaspoon vanilla just until blended.

3 Spread 1½ cups chocolate batter evenly in baking pan.

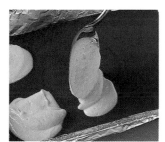

4 Spoon cream-cheese mixture in 6 large dollops on top of chocolate batter (cheese mixture will cover much of chocolate batter). Spoon remaining chocolate batter in 6 large dollops over and between cheese mixture.

5 With tip of knife, cut and twist through mixtures to create marble design. Bake 40 to 45 minutes, until toothpick inserted 2 inches from center comes out almost clean with a few moist crumbs attached. Cool brownies in pan on wire rack. When cool, cut brownies lengthwise into 4 strips, then cut each strip crosswise into 6 pieces.

EACH BROWNIE: ABOUT 260 CALORIES, 4g PROTEIN, 27g CARBOHYDRATE, 16g TOTAL FAT (7g SATURATED), 69mg CHOLESTEROL, 185mg SODIUM

CHOCOLATE AND PEANUT-BUTTER BROWNIES

Prep: 20 minutes plus cooling   Bake: 25 to 30 minutes
Makes 2 dozen

3 squares (3 ounces)
  semisweet chocolate
1 square (1 ounce)
  unsweetened chocolate
2½ cups all-purpose flour
1½ teaspoons baking powder
½ teaspoon salt
1¾ cups packed light brown
  sugar

1 cup creamy peanut butter
½ cup margarine or butter,
  slightly softened
3 large eggs
2 teaspoons vanilla extract
1 package (6 ounces)
  semisweet-chocolate pieces
  (about 1 cup)

◆ Preheat oven to 350°F. In heavy 1-quart saucepan, melt all chocolate squares over low heat, stirring frequently. Remove from heat. In medium bowl, mix flour, baking powder, and salt.

◆ In large bowl, with mixer at medium speed, beat brown sugar, peanut butter, and margarine about 2 minutes, until smooth. Reduce speed to low. Beat in eggs and vanilla until blended. Beat in flour mixture just until combined (dough will be stiff). Place one-third of dough (about 1¾ cups) in another large bowl. Stir in melted chocolate until blended; stir in ¾ cup semisweet-chocolate pieces.

◆ Pat half of remaining peanut-butter dough into ungreased 13" by 9" metal baking pan. Drop remaining peanut-butter dough and chocolate dough in random pattern on top; pat down with hand. Sprinkle with remaining chocolate pieces.

PRALINE-ICED BROWNIES

Prepare Classic Brownies (right). While brownies are cooling, prepare topping: In 2-quart saucepan, heat 5 tablespoons margarine or butter and ⅓ cup packed light brown sugar over medium-low heat about 4 minutes, until mixture melts and bubbles. Remove from heat. With wire whisk, beat in 3 tablespoons bourbon (or 1 tablespoon vanilla extract plus 2 tablespoons water), then beat in 2 cups confectioners' sugar until smooth. With metal spatula, spread topping over room-temperature brownies in pan. Sprinkle with ½ cup pecans (about 2 ounces), toasted and coarsely chopped. Cut brownies lengthwise into 8 strips; cut each strip crosswise into 8 pieces. Makes 64.

Each brownie: About 115 calories, 1g protein, 15g carbohydrate, 6g total fat (2g saturated), 20mg cholesterol, 65mg sodium

◆ Bake 25 to 30 minutes, until toothpick inserted in center comes out clean. Cool in pan on wire rack. When cool, cut lengthwise into 4 strips; cut each strip crosswise into 6 pieces.

Each brownie: About 265 calories, 5g protein, 34g carbohydrate, 14g total fat (3g saturated), 27mg cholesterol, 185mg sodium

COCOA BROWNIES

Prep: 10 minutes plus cooling   Bake: 25 minutes
Makes 16

½ cup margarine or butter
1 cup sugar
2 large eggs
1 teaspoon vanilla extract
½ cup all-purpose flour

½ cup unsweetened cocoa
¼ teaspoon baking powder
¼ teaspoon salt
1 cup coarsely chopped
  walnuts (4 ounces), optional

Preheat oven to 350°F. Grease 9" by 9" metal baking pan. In 3-quart saucepan, melt margarine over medium heat. Remove from heat; stir in sugar. With wooden spoon, stir in eggs, 1 at a time, and vanilla until well blended. In medium bowl, combine flour and next 3 ingredients; stir flour mixture into saucepan until blended. Stir in nuts, if using. Spread batter evenly in pan. Bake 25 minutes, or until toothpick inserted 2 inches from center comes out almost clean. Cool in pan on wire rack. When cool, cut brownies into 4 strips; cut each strip crosswise into 4 squares.

Each brownie: About 130 calories, 2g protein, 17g carbohydrate, 7g total fat (1g saturated), 27mg cholesterol, 115mg sodium

CLASSIC BROWNIES

Prep: 20 minutes plus cooling   Bake: 35 minutes
Makes 2 dozen

1 cup margarine or butter
4 squares (4 ounces)
  unsweetened chocolate
4 squares (4 ounces)
  semisweet chocolate

2¼ cups sugar
6 large eggs
2 teaspoons vanilla extract
½ teaspoon salt
1¼ cups all-purpose flour

Preheat oven to 350°F. Line 13" by 9" metal baking pan with foil; grease foil. In heavy 3-quart saucepan, melt margarine and all chocolate squares over low heat, stirring frequently. Remove from heat. With wire whisk, beat in sugar, then eggs, until well blended. Stir in vanilla, salt, then flour just until blended. Spread batter evenly in pan. Bake 35 minutes, or until toothpick inserted 2 inches from center comes out almost clean with a few moist crumbs attached. Cool brownies in pan on wire rack. When cool, cut lengthwise into 4 strips; cut each strip crosswise into 6 pieces.

Each brownie: About 230 calories, 3g protein, 28g carbohydrate, 13g total fat (4g saturated), 53mg cholesterol, 150mg sodium

Bar cookies

Homey bar cookies are the easiest of all to make. Just spread the dough in a pan and bake, then cut the cookies to size – as big or as dainty as you like. Our selection includes tart-sweet Citrus Bars, traditional Shortbread enriched with hazelnuts, moist, dense Date-and-Nut Squares, and walnut-studded Blondies.

1 Preheat oven to 400°F. In food processor with knife blade attached, blend flour, shortening, margarine, ¼ cup sugar, and ¼ teaspoon salt, pulsing processor on and off until crumbs form. With processor running, add *2 to 3 tablespoons cold water* through feed tube, 1 tablespoon at a time, pulsing processor on and off until dough comes together.

2 Press dough onto bottom and ¼ inch up sides of ungreased 13" by 9" metal baking pan. With fork, prick dough all over. Bake 20 to 25 minutes, until golden; remove from oven. Turn oven control to 375°F.

3 Squeeze ⅓ cup juice from limes. Grate 2 teaspoons peel and squeeze ¼ cup juice from lemons. In medium bowl, whisk sour cream with eggs, remaining 1 cup sugar, and ⅛ teaspoon salt. Mix in lime and lemon juice and lemon peel.

Citrus bars

◆◆◆◆◆◆◆◆◆◆◆◆

Prep: 35 to 40 minutes plus cooling and chilling
Bake: 30 minutes
Makes 32

1¾ **cups all-purpose flour**
¼ **cup shortening**
4 **tablespoons margarine or butter, cut up**
1¼ **cups sugar**
Salt
3 **limes**
2 **lemons**
½ **cup sour cream**
5 **large eggs**
Confectioners' sugar for garnish

ORANGE BARS

For an easy variation, make Citrus Bars as above, but in Step 1, add 1 teaspoon grated orange peel to dough. In Step 3, substitute 1 teaspoon grated orange peel for lemon peel, and substitute ⅓ cup orange juice for lime juice.

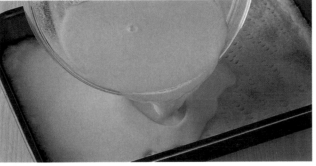

4 Pour citrus mixture over warm crust in baking pan; bake 15 minutes, or just until set (do not overbake, or surface of citrus filling may crack). Cool completely in pan on wire rack; refrigerate until well chilled.

5 When cool, sprinkle with confectioners' sugar. Cut lengthwise into 4 strips; cut each strip crosswise into 8 pieces. To store, cover pan and refrigerate.

EACH BAR: ABOUT 100 CALORIES, 2g PROTEIN, 13g CARBOHYDRATE, 5g TOTAL FAT (1g SATURATED), 35mg CHOLESTEROL, 55mg SODIUM

HAZELNUT SHORTBREAD

Prep: 45 minutes plus cooling   Bake: 50 to 60 minutes
Makes 3 dozen

1 cup (about 4 ounces) hazelnuts (filberts), toasted and skinned (see above)	**1 cup butter, softened**
2¼ cups all-purpose flour	**½ cup sugar**
	½ teaspoon vanilla extract
	¼ teaspoon salt

◆ Preheat oven to 300°F. In food processor with knife blade attached, finely chop hazelnuts with ¼ cup flour.

◆ In large bowl, with mixer at low speed, beat butter and sugar until light and creamy. Beat in vanilla, salt, hazelnut mixture, and remaining 2 cups flour just until blended. Pat dough evenly into ungreased 13" by 9" metal baking pan. With fork, prick dough all over.

◆ Bake shortbread 50 to 60 minutes, until lightly browned.

◆ While still warm, cut shortbread lengthwise into 3 strips; cut each strip crosswise into 12 pieces. Cool in pan on wire rack 10 minutes; remove pieces from pan. Cool shortbread completely on wire rack. Store in tightly covered container.

Each cookie: About 100 calories, 1g protein, 9g carbohydrate, 7g total fat (3g saturated), 14mg cholesterol, 65mg sodium

Blondies (below left), Hazelnut shortbread (below right), and Date and nut squares (bottom)

DATE AND NUT SQUARES

Prep: 15 minutes plus cooling   Bake: 30 to 35 minutes
Makes 16

1 cup packed light brown sugar	**1 cup pecans (about 4 ounces), chopped**
½ cup margarine or butter	**1 cup pitted dates (5 ounces), chopped**
1⅓ cups all-purpose flour	**2 large eggs**
1 teaspoon baking soda	

◆ Preheat oven to 350°F. Grease 9" by 9" metal baking pan. In 3-quart saucepan, heat brown sugar and margarine over medium-low heat, stirring occasionally, until melted and smooth. Remove saucepan from heat.

◆ With wooden spoon, beat in remaining ingredients until well blended. Spread batter evenly in pan.

◆ Bake 30 to 35 minutes, until toothpick inserted in center comes out clean. Cool in pan on wire rack. When cool, cut into 4 strips, then cut each strip crosswise into 4 squares. Store in tightly covered container.

Each cookie: About 220 calories, 3g protein, 30g carbohydrate, 11g total fat (2g saturated), 27mg cholesterol, 160mg sodium

BLONDIES

Prep: 15 minutes plus cooling   Bake: 35 minutes
Makes 1 dozen

1 cup walnuts, macadamia nuts, or pecans (about 4 ounces), coarsely chopped	**6 tablespoons margarine or butter, softened**
1¼ cups all-purpose flour	**1¼ teaspoons baking powder**
½ cup granulated sugar	**½ teaspoon salt**
½ cup packed light brown sugar	**1½ teaspoons vanilla extract**
	2 large eggs

◆ Preheat oven to 350°F. Grease 9" by 9" metal baking pan. Reserve ½ cup chopped nuts.

◆ In large bowl, with mixer at low speed, beat flour, remaining ingredients, and remaining ½ cup nuts until well blended, occasionally scraping bowl with rubber spatula.

◆ Spread batter evenly in pan; sprinkle reserved nuts on top. Bake 35 minutes, or until toothpick inserted in center comes out clean. Cool blondies in pan on wire rack.

◆ When cool, cut blondies into 3 strips; cut each strip crosswise into 4 pieces. Store in tightly covered container.

Each cookie: About 240 calories, 4g protein, 29g carbohydrate, 13g total fat (2g saturated), 36mg cholesterol, 220mg sodium

CANDY

Homemade candy is a holiday tradition. But you'll want to make these goodies year-round for birthdays, dinner parties, or even coffee-time treats.

TOFFEE ALMOND CRUNCH

◆◆◆◆◆◆◆◆◆◆◆◆◆

Prep: 1 hour plus cooling and standing
Cook: 30 minutes
Makes about 1¾ pounds

1¾ cups sugar
⅓ cup light corn syrup
1 cup margarine or butter
2 cups blanched slivered almonds (8 ounces), lightly toasted and finely chopped
2 squares (2 ounces) unsweetened chocolate
2 squares (2 ounces) semisweet chocolate
1 teaspoon shortening

1 Lightly grease 15½" by 10½" jelly-roll pan. In heavy 2-quart saucepan, heat sugar, corn syrup, and ¼ *cup water* to boiling over medium heat, stirring occasionally until sugar dissolves. Stir in margarine. Set candy thermometer in place and continue cooking, stirring frequently, about 20 minutes, or until temperature reaches 300°F, or hard-crack stage (see below right). (Temperature will rise quickly once it reaches 220°F, so watch carefully.) Remove from heat.

4 Transfer candy in one piece from pan to cutting board. Spread chocolate over candy; sprinkle with reserved almonds, pressing them gently into chocolate. Set candy aside about 1 hour to allow glaze to set.

2 Reserve ⅓ cup almonds for sprinkling on chocolate glaze. Stir remaining almonds into hot syrup. Immediately pour mixture into jelly-roll pan; working quickly, with metal spatula, spread evenly. (Pan will become very hot.)

5 With knife, cut into hardened candy to break it into pieces. Store in layers, separated by waxed paper, in tightly covered container up to 1 month. (Note: This almond crunch is also delicious without the chocolate layer.)

3 Cool candy in pan on wire rack. Meanwhile, prepare glaze: Coarsely chop all chocolate. In heavy 1-quart saucepan, melt chopped chocolate and shortening over low heat, stirring frequently. Remove from heat; cool slightly.

◆◆◆◆◆◆◆◆◆◆◆◆◆◆◆◆◆◆◆◆◆◆◆◆◆◆◆◆◆◆

TESTING CANDY

If you don't have a candy thermometer, use the cold-water test: Remove the syrup from the heat; drop a half spoonful into a cup or bowl of very cold water. Let stand 30 seconds.

Thread (230° to 234°F) Syrup forms a fine thread in the air as it falls from spoon

Soft ball (234° to 240°F) Syrup forms soft ball that flattens on removal from water

Firm ball (244° to 248°F) Syrup forms firm ball that does not flatten on removal from water

Hard ball (250° to 266°F) Syrup separates into hard, but not brittle, threads

Hard crack (300° to 310°F) Syrup separates into hard, brittle threads (above)

◆◆◆◆◆◆◆◆◆◆◆◆◆◆◆◆◆◆◆◆◆◆◆◆◆◆◆◆◆◆

EACH OUNCE: ABOUT 185 CALORIES, 2g PROTEIN, 19g CARBOHYDRATE, 13g TOTAL FAT (3g SATURATED), 0mg CHOLESTEROL, 80mg SODIUM

CHOCOLATE-WALNUT FUDGE

Prep: 25 minutes plus chilling
Makes 36 pieces, about 2¼ pounds

1 pound bittersweet chocolate or 2 packages (8 ounces each) semisweet chocolate, coarsely chopped
1 can (14 ounces) sweetened condensed milk
1 cup walnuts (about 4 ounces), coarsely chopped
1 teaspoon vanilla extract
⅛ teaspoon salt

◆ Line 8" by 8" metal baking pan with plastic wrap; smooth out as many wrinkles as possible. In heavy 2-quart saucepan, heat chocolate and condensed milk over medium-low heat, stirring constantly, until chocolate melts. Remove from heat; stir in remaining ingredients. Spoon chocolate mixture into pan; spread evenly. Refrigerate 3 hours, or until firm.

◆ Remove fudge from pan. Cut fudge into 6 strips; cut each strip crosswise into 6 pieces. Store in tightly covered container at room temperature up to 2 weeks.

Each piece: About 120 calories, 3g protein, 10g carbohydrate, 10g total fat (5g saturated), 4mg cholesterol, 20mg sodium

GOLD-RUSH NUT BRITTLE

Prep: 10 minutes plus cooling   Cook: 35 minutes
Makes about 1½ pounds

1½ cups sugar
1 cup light corn syrup
½ teaspoon salt
2 tablespoons margarine or butter
2 teaspoons vanilla extract
1 teaspoon baking soda
1 can (6 ounces) unsalted cocktail peanuts (1 cup)
1 cup sliced blanched almonds (about 4 ounces)
1 cup pecans (about 4 ounces)

◆ Grease large cookie sheet. In heavy 3-quart saucepan, heat sugar, corn syrup, salt, and *½ cup water* to boiling over medium heat, stirring occasionally until sugar dissolves.

◆ Set candy thermometer in place and continue cooking, stirring frequently, about 30 minutes, until temperature reaches 300°F, or hard-crack stage (see page 523).

◆ Remove saucepan from heat; stir in margarine, vanilla, baking soda, and all nuts. Immediately pour onto cookie sheet. With 2 forks, quickly lift and stretch nut mixture into about 14" by 12" rectangle.

◆ Cool brittle completely on cookie sheet on wire rack. With hands, break brittle into small pieces. Store in tightly covered container up to 1 month.

Each ounce: About 195 calories, 3g protein, 26g carbohydrate, 10g total fat (1g saturated), 0mg cholesterol, 120mg sodium

CHOCOLATE AND HAZELNUT TRUFFLES

Prep: 25 minutes plus chilling
Makes 32

8 ounces bittersweet chocolate or 6 squares (6 ounces) semisweet chocolate and 2 squares (2 ounces) unsweetened chocolate
½ cup heavy or whipping cream
3 tablespoons unsalted butter, softened and cut up
2 tablespoons coffee-, almond-, or orange-flavor liqueur (optional)
⅓ cup (about 1½ ounces) hazelnuts (filberts), toasted and skinned (see page 522), finely chopped
3 tablespoons unsweetened cocoa

◆ Line 8½" by 4½" metal loaf pan with plastic wrap. In food processor with knife blade attached, process chocolate until finely ground.

◆ In 1-quart saucepan, heat cream to boiling over medium-high heat. Add cream to chocolate in food processor and blend until smooth. Add butter, and liqueur, if using, and blend until incorporated. Spoon chocolate mixture into loaf pan; spread evenly. Refrigerate 3 hours, or until firm enough to handle.

◆ Spread hazelnuts and cocoa on separate sheets of waxed paper. Remove chocolate mixture from pan by lifting edges of plastic wrap and inverting mixture onto cutting board; discard plastic wrap. Cut chocolate mixture into 32 squares. Quickly roll each square into a ball.

◆ Roll half of truffles in chopped hazelnuts. Roll remaining truffles in cocoa. Refrigerate truffles up to 1 week. (Or, freeze in airtight container up to 1 month; remove from freezer 5 minutes before serving.)

Each truffle: About 65 calories, 1g protein, 3g carbohydrate, 7g total fat (4g saturated), 8mg cholesterol, 0mg sodium

CAKES

Few desserts match the feeling of festivity evoked by a homemade cake. Satisfying to prepare and a pleasure to serve, a cake made from scratch is a supremely rewarding way to put your creative energies to work. Always follow the recipe accurately for reliable – and delicious – results.

WHY USE CAKE FLOUR?

Made from soft wheat, cake flour has a high starch content and low gluten content, which produces tender cakes. If you don't have cake flour and the recipe calls for it, you can use all-purpose flour; substitute 2 tablespoons cornstarch for the same amount of flour for each 1 cup cake flour specified. Or, use 1 cup minus 2 tablespoons all-purpose flour per 1 cup of cake flour.

LINING A CAKE PAN

Greasing and flouring cake pans prevents most cakes from sticking, but some batters require a lining of waxed paper as well.

Place pan on waxed paper. Use a pencil to trace around bottom rim; cut out circle.

Fit paper in greased pan; grease paper. Lightly dust with flour; tap to remove excess.

BUTTER VERSUS FOAM CAKES

Cakes come in two basic groups: butter and foam cakes. Butter cakes rely on fat for moisture and richness; they're loved for their flavor and velvety crumb. Chocolate, layer, and pound cakes are the most common varieties. The "creaming" stage is crucial; butter and sugar should be beaten together until they take on a pale color and fluffy consistency. To ensure that all of the dry ingredients are evenly dispersed, they should be well combined before they're added to the creamed mixture.

Foam cakes – light, airy chiffon and angel-food cakes – depend on beaten eggs or egg whites for volume and a delicate texture. Chiffon and sponge cakes contain both egg yolks and whites, and may include vegetable oil, margarine, or butter; angel-food cakes use only whites and contain no added fat. Adding cream of tartar to the egg whites before beating gives them better stability; beat until stiff peaks form when beaters are lifted. When combining ingredients, blend the foam gently so it won't deflate. Never grease the pan for an angel or chiffon cake; the batter needs to cling to the sides to rise. Before baking, cut through the batter in the pan with a rubber spatula to remove any air bubbles.

BAKING BASICS

• Before you begin preparing a recipe, set out all the ingredients, measuring when necessary.
• Room temperature eggs yield the best volume, but for safety, don't leave them out more than 30 minutes. Or, warm chilled eggs in a bowl of warm tap water 5 minutes before using.
• Use softened (not melted) butter; it's easier to beat.
• Although butter cakes can be mixed by hand, electric mixers provide the most even blending. Scrape the bowl often while beating so ingredients are mixed well.
• To avoid air bubbles, gently tap pans on the work surface after filling with batter.
• Bake cakes in the center of the oven. If making more than two layers, switch the position of pans halfway through baking.
• To prevent a cake from falling, leave the oven door shut during the first 15 minutes of baking.

HIGH-ALTITUDE BAKING

Most cake recipes require adjustment when prepared at high altitudes. The guidelines given in the chart below will help you avoid disasters. High-altitude cakes tend to stick to the pan, so grease and flour pans well, or line with waxed paper. Fill pans only half-full of batter, as these cakes may overflow.

RECIPE ADJUSTMENTS

INGREDIENT	3000 FEET	5000 FEET	7000 FEET
For each cup of liquid, add	1–2 tbsp liquid	2–4 tbsp liquid	3–4 tbsp liquid
For each teaspoon of baking powder, remove	⅛ tsp baking powder	⅛–¼ tsp baking powder	¼ tsp baking powder
For each cup sugar, remove	½–1 tbsp sugar	½–2 tbsp sugar	1–3 tbsp sugar

TESTING TIPS

The best bakers gauge doneness by how a cake looks, smells, sounds, and feels, in addition to the suggested cooking time. Begin testing for doneness about 10 minutes before the end of the recommended baking time. A fully baked cake should have a toasty aroma and (except for chocolate cakes) a deeply golden crust; any cracks on the surface should look dry. Most cakes will start to pull away from the sides of the pan; a toothpick inserted into the center of the cake should come out clean and dry, unless the recipe specifies otherwise. Alternatively, use the test illustrated below.

The secret's in the spring: Most cakes can be tested for doneness by pressing the top lightly with a finger. When the cake is fully baked, the top should spring back.

UNMOLDING AND COOLING

• Before unmolding, butter cakes should be cooled in their pans on a rack for approximately 10 minutes. Don't skimp on this resting period; it allows the cake to stabilize and further shrink from the side of the pan – and steam to build around the cake – making it easier to unmold.
• After the butter cake has rested in its pan, unmold it without delay so air can circulate around it freely, allowing it to cool more quickly and not become soggy.
• To unmold a butter cake, carefully run a small knife around the cake to loosen it from the side of the pan. Top cake with a wire cooling rack. Holding both the pan and the rack (if necessary, protect hands with a kitchen cloth or oven mitts), invert cake onto rack. Carefully remove pan and sandwich cake with second rack; flip cake, right-side up, onto second rack.
• Foam cakes call for a slightly different approach. Angel-food and chiffon cakes are too delicate to be removed from the pan until they're completely cooled. In addition, they must be cooled upside-down in the pan, which should be

Before unmolding the cake, carefully run a small knife around the edge to loosen it from the side of the pan.

To unmold cake, place cooling rack over pan; carefully invert cake. Remove pan and flip cake back onto second rack.

inverted onto the neck of a bottle or a funnel. This position prevents the cake from falling in the pan, while the bottle or funnel allows air to circulate evenly round the cake, and prevents the cake from touching the counter if it has risen above the rim of the pan. Sponge cakes are sturdier and can simply be cooled in the pan on a wire rack.
• To unmold a foam cake, carefully loosen it from the side of the pan with a long metal spatula or knife, pressing it firmly against the side of the pan (to avoid tearing the cake), and turn out onto a plate.

STORING CAKES

• All cakes should be cooled completely before they're frosted or stored.
• Because of their fat content, butter cakes stay fresh-tasting for 2 to 3 days. Foam cakes are best eaten within a day or 2 of preparation; they contain little fat and will dry out quickly.
• Keep cakes left in the pan tightly covered. Layer cakes and frosted tube cakes are best kept under an inverted large bowl.
• Always refrigerate cakes with fillings and frostings made with whipped cream, cream cheese, sour cream, yogurt, or eggs.
• Freeze frosted cakes, unwrapped, until firm, then wrap in plastic and aluminum foil and freeze up to 2 months.
• Freeze unfrosted butter cakes on a baking sheet just until firm. Wrap layers in plastic wrap, then foil, and freeze up to 4 months.
• Freeze foam cakes in a freezer bag for up to 3 months.

WHAT WENT WRONG?

Curdled batter Each egg was not thoroughly incorporated into the batter before the next was added; batter was beaten at too high a speed. This usually corrects itself when the dry ingredients are added.
Cake overflowed in pan Pan too small; too much leavening.
Tough, flat, and heavy texture Too much liquid; too much shortening; too much flour; batter under- or overbeaten.
Sunken middle Batter was overbeaten, creating excess aeration that cake was unable to contain; too much sugar, liquid, or baking powder was added to batter; oven door was opened before cake was set – or closed with too much force.
Peaked or cracked center A hard (high-gluten) flour was used instead of a softer flour (e.g., cake flour); batter was overbeaten after flour was added (this overactivates the gluten in flour, creating a tough cake); the oven was too hot, causing the cake to rise too quickly.
Cake did not rise properly Too much liquid; too much fat; too large a pan; oven too cool.
Dry crumb Too much baking powder; too long a baking time.
Crumbly texture Underbeaten; too much shortening.
Pale color Too little sugar; too short a baking time.
Tunnels in dough Too much egg; too little sugar; poor mixing; oven too hot.

CLASSIC LAYER CAKES

For family gatherings, birthdays, and other special occasions, there's nothing like the sheer romance of a layer cake made from scratch. The tender crumb and homemade taste simply can't compare with commercial mixes or store-bought cakes. Try timeless cakes, such as buttery Yellow or Rich Chocolate, or fanciful finales like the playful Checkerboard Cake.

CHECKERBOARD CAKE

◆◆◆◆◆◆◆◆◆◆◆◆◆◆◆◆◆◆◆◆◆◆◆◆◆◆◆◆◆

Prep: 40 minutes plus cooling   *Bake: 25 to 30 minutes*
Make 16 servings

1 cup margarine or butter, softened

2 cups sugar

3½ cups cake flour (not self-rising)

1¼ cups milk

1 tablespoon baking powder

1 tablespoon vanilla extract

½ teaspoon salt

8 large egg whites

8 squares (8 ounces) semisweet chocolate, melted and cooled

Chocolate Butter Cream (see page 550)

Special equipment:
2 large decorating bags, each with ½-inch opening or ½-inch writing tip (or use a zip-tight plastic bag with corner cut to make ½-inch opening)

1 Preheat oven to 350°F. Grease three 8-inch round cake pans. Line bottoms of pans with waxed paper; grease paper. Dust pans with flour. In large bowl, with mixer at low speed, beat margarine and 1½ cups sugar until blended. Increase speed to high; beat about 5 minutes, until light and creamy. Reduce speed to low. Add flour and next 4 ingredients; beat just until combined. Increase speed to medium; beat 2 minutes, occasionally scraping bowl.

2 In another large bowl, with mixer at high speed, beat egg whites to soft peaks; gradually sprinkle in remaining ½ cup sugar, beating until stiff peaks form when beaters are lifted. Fold whites, one-third at a time, into flour mixture.

3 Spoon half of batter into medium bowl. Into batter in large bowl, fold melted chocolate. Spoon vanilla batter into a large decorating bag or zip-tight plastic bag with corner cut. Spoon chocolate batter into a second decorating bag.

4 Pipe 1½-inch-wide band of chocolate batter around inside edge of 2 cake pans. Pipe 1½-inch-wide band of vanilla batter next to each chocolate band; pipe enough chocolate batter to fill in center.

5 In third pan, repeat piping, alternating batters, but starting with vanilla around edge. Stagger pans on 2 oven racks, placing 2 on upper rack and 1 on lower rack, so that layers are not directly on top of one another.

6 Bake 25 to 30 minutes, until toothpick inserted in centers comes out clean. Cool in pans on wire racks 10 minutes. Run small knife around edges of pans to loosen cakes; invert onto racks. Remove waxed paper; cool completely. Prepare butter cream. Place one of the two identical layers on cake plate; spread with ½ cup butter cream. Top with the reverse-design layer. Spread with ½ cup butter cream; top with remaining layer. Frost side and top of cake with remaining butter cream. Store any leftover cake in refrigerator.

EACH SERVING: ABOUT 550 CALORIES, 6g PROTEIN, 72g CARBOHYDRATE, 29g TOTAL FAT (9g SATURATED), 3mg CHOLESTEROL, 430mg SODIUM

WHITE CHOCOLATE CAKE

Prep: 1 hour 15 minutes plus cooling   Bake: 25 minutes
Makes 16 servings

9 ounces white chocolate,
  Swiss confectionery bars, or
  white baking bars
1½ cups milk
1¼ cups sugar
¾ cup margarine or butter,
  softened
3¼ cups cake flour (not self-
  rising)
1½ teaspoons baking powder

1½ teaspoons vanilla extract
¾ teaspoon salt
3 large eggs
Quick Chocolate Curls made
  with white chocolate
  (optional, see page 551)
Lemon Butter Cream (see
  page 550)
⅔ cup seedless red raspberry
  jam

◆ In 2-quart saucepan, melt white chocolate with milk over low heat, stirring frequently, until mixture is smooth. Remove saucepan from heat; cool slightly.

◆ Preheat oven to 350°F. Grease and flour three 8-inch round cake pans.

◆ In large bowl, with mixer at low speed, beat sugar and margarine until blended. Increase speed to high; beat about 5 minutes, until light and creamy. Reduce speed to low; beat in flour, baking powder, vanilla, salt, eggs, and cooled white-chocolate mixture until blended, frequently scraping bowl with rubber spatula. Increase speed to medium; beat 2 minutes.

◆ Divide batter evenly among cake pans. Stagger pans on 2 oven racks, placing 2 on upper rack and 1 on lower rack, so that layers are not directly on top of one another. Bake 25 minutes, or until toothpick inserted in centers of layers comes out clean. Cool layers in pans on wire racks 10 minutes. Run small knife around edges of pans to loosen cakes; invert onto racks and cool completely.

◆ Meanwhile, prepare Quick Chocolate Curls, if you like, and refrigerate; prepare Lemon Butter Cream. With serrated knife, cut each layer horizontally in half to make 6 thin layers in all. Place 1 cake layer cut-side up on large cake plate. Spread with ⅓ cup butter cream. Top with second layer; spread with ⅓ cup jam. Repeat layering to make 3 layers of butter cream and 2 layers of jam in all, ending with sixth layer.

◆ Spread remaining butter cream over side and top of cake. With toothpick, carefully press chocolate curls, if using, into butter cream, completely covering cake. Store any leftover cake in refrigerator.

Each serving: About 550 calories, 6g protein, 70g carbohydrate, 28g total fat (9g saturated), 49mg cholesterol, 425mg sodium

RICH CHOCOLATE CAKE

Prep: 50 minutes plus cooling   Bake: 30 minutes
Makes 16 servings

2 cups all-purpose flour
1 cup unsweetened cocoa
2 teaspoons baking powder
1 teaspoon baking soda
½ teaspoon salt
1⅓ cups milk
2 teaspoons vanilla extract

2 cups sugar
1 cup margarine or butter,
  softened
4 large eggs
Fluffy White Frosting (see
  page 550) or other desired
  frosting

◆ Preheat oven to 350°F. Grease three 8-inch round cake pans. Line bottoms of pans with waxed paper; grease paper. Dust pans with flour. In medium bowl, combine flour, cocoa, baking powder, baking soda, and salt; set aside. In measuring cup, mix milk and vanilla.

◆ In large bowl, with mixer at low speed, beat sugar and margarine until blended. Increase speed to high; beat about 2 minutes, until creamy. Reduce speed to medium-low; add eggs, 1 at a time, beating well after each addition. Alternately add flour mixture and milk mixture, beginning and ending with flour mixture; beat until batter is smooth, occasionally scraping bowl with rubber spatula.

◆ Divide batter evenly among cake pans. Stagger pans on 2 oven racks, placing 2 on upper rack and 1 on lower rack, so that layers are not directly on top of one another. Bake 30 minutes, or until toothpick inserted in centers of layers comes out almost clean. Cool in pans on wire racks 10 minutes. Run small knife around edges of pans to loosen cakes; invert cakes onto racks. Carefully remove waxed paper; cool cakes completely.

◆ Prepare frosting. Place 1 cake layer on cake plate; spread with ½ cup frosting. Top with second layer and ½ cup frosting. Place remaining cake layer on top. Frost side and top of cake with remaining frosting.

Each serving: About 345 calories, 5g protein, 54g carbohydrate, 14g total fat (3mg saturated), 56mg cholesterol, 375mg sodium

AMBROSIA LAYER CAKE

Prep: 1 hour 30 minutes plus chilling and cooling
Bake: 35 to 40 minutes
Makes 20 servings

4 large oranges	**1 teaspoon baking soda**
1 tablespoon fresh lemon juice	**¼ teaspoon salt**
3 tablespoons cornstarch	**2 teaspoons vanilla extract**
2½ cups sugar	**3 large eggs**
1¼ cups margarine or butter, softened	**1 cup buttermilk or soured milk (see page 392)**
6 large egg yolks	**Fluffy White Frosting (see page 550)**
2½ cups cake flour (not self-rising)	**1 cup flaked coconut**
1½ teaspoons baking powder	**Orange-peel strips for garnish**

◆ Grate 1 tablespoon peel and squeeze 1⅓ cups juice from oranges. In heavy 3-quart saucepan, mix orange peel and juice, lemon juice, cornstarch, and 1 cup sugar. Add ½ cup margarine; heat to boiling over medium heat, stirring. Boil 1 minute. In small bowl, beat egg yolks lightly. Into yolks, beat small amount of orange mixture; beat yolk mixture into orange mixture in saucepan. Cook over low heat, stirring constantly, 3 minutes, or until very thick. Pour filling into medium bowl; cover surface with plastic wrap to prevent skin from forming. Refrigerate 2 hours, or until well chilled.

◆ Meanwhile, preheat oven to 350°F. Grease and flour 13" by 9" metal baking pan. In medium bowl, combine flour, baking powder, baking soda, and salt.

◆ In large bowl, with mixer at low speed, beat remaining 1½ cups sugar and remaining ¾ cup margarine just until blended. Increase speed to high; beat 5 minutes, until light and creamy, scraping bowl often with rubber spatula. Reduce speed to low; add vanilla and whole eggs, 1 at a time, until blended. Alternately add flour mixture and buttermilk, beginning and ending with flour mixture; beat until batter is well mixed, occasionally scraping bowl.

◆ Spread batter in pan. Bake 35 to 40 minutes, until toothpick inserted in center of cake comes out clean. Cool in pan on wire rack 10 minutes. Run small spatula around edges of pan to loosen cake; invert onto rack to cool completely.

◆ Prepare Fluffy White Frosting. With serrated knife, cut cake horizontally in half. To remove top cake layer, carefully place cookie sheet in between cut layers and lift off top layer. Slide bottom layer onto serving platter; with metal spatula, spread with chilled filling. Carefully transfer top layer of cake onto bottom layer by gently sliding cake onto filling. Frost sides and top of cake with frosting. Sprinkle with coconut; garnish. Refrigerate until ready to serve.

Each serving: About 360 calories, 4g protein, 52g carbohydrate, 16g total fat (4g saturated), 96mg cholesterol, 300mg sodium

YELLOW CAKE

Prep: 45 minutes plus cooling   Bake: 23 to 28 minutes
Makes 16 servings

3 cups cake flour (not self-rising)	**1 cup margarine or butter, softened**
1 tablespoon baking powder	**4 large eggs**
½ teaspoon salt	**Orange Butter Cream (see page 550) or other desired frosting**
1 cup milk	
2 teaspoons vanilla extract	
2 cups sugar	

◆ Preheat oven to 350°F. Grease three 8-inch round cake pans. Line bottoms of pans with waxed paper; grease paper. Dust pans with flour. In medium bowl, combine flour, baking powder, and salt; set aside. In measuring cup, mix milk and vanilla.

◆ In large bowl, with mixer at low speed, beat sugar and margarine until blended. Increase speed to high; beat 2 minutes, or until creamy. Reduce speed to medium-low; add eggs, 1 at a time, beating well after each addition. Alternately add flour mixture and milk mixture, beginning and ending with flour mixture; beat until batter is smooth, occasionally scraping bowl with rubber spatula.

◆ Divide batter evenly among pans. Stagger pans on 2 oven racks, placing 2 on upper rack and 1 on lower rack, so that layers are not directly on top of one another. Bake 23 to 28 minutes, until toothpick inserted in centers of layers comes out almost clean with a few moist crumbs attached. Cool in pans on wire racks 10 minutes. Run small knife around edges of pans to loosen cakes; invert onto racks. Remove waxed paper; cool completely.

◆ Prepare butter cream. Place 1 cake layer on cake plate; spread with ⅔ cup butter cream. Top with second cake layer and ⅔ cup butter cream. Place remaining cake layer on top. Frost side and top of cake with remaining butter cream. Store any leftover cake in refrigerator.

Each serving: About 475 calories, 5g protein, 59g carbohydrate, 25g total fat (6g saturated), 58mg cholesterol, 455mg sodium

CHOCOLATE BUTTERMILK CAKE

Prep: 30 minutes plus cooling   Bake: 30 minutes
Makes 16 servings

¾ cup unsweetened cocoa plus
    additional for dusting pans
2¼ cups all-purpose flour
1¾ cups sugar
1½ cups buttermilk or soured
    milk (see page 392)
1 cup vegetable oil

2 teaspoons baking soda
1½ teaspoons vanilla extract
1¼ teaspoons salt
3 large eggs
Chocolate Butter Cream (see
    page 550)

◆ Preheat oven to 350°F. Grease two 9-inch round cake pans. Dust pans with cocoa.

◆ In large bowl, mix flour, next 7 ingredients, and ¾ cup cocoa. With mixer at low speed, beat until mixed, frequently scraping bowl with rubber spatula. Increase speed to medium; beat 3 minutes, occasionally scraping bowl. Divide batter evenly between pans. Bake 30 minutes, or until toothpick inserted in centers of layers comes out clean. Cool layers in pans on wire racks 10 minutes. Run small knife around edges of pans to loosen cakes. Invert onto racks; cool completely. Prepare butter cream.

◆ Place 1 cake layer rounded-side down on cake plate; spread with ⅔ cup butter cream. Top with second layer, rounded-side up. Frost side and top of cake with remaining butter cream. Store any leftover cake in refrigerator.

Each serving: About 475 calories, 5g protein, 56g carbohydrate, 28g total fat (7g saturated), 41mg cholesterol, 465mg sodium

SPICE LAYER CAKE

Prep: 45 minutes plus cooling   Bake: 28 to 30 minutes
Makes 16 servings

1¾ cups all-purpose flour
1 teaspoon baking powder
¾ teaspoon ground cinnamon
½ teaspoon baking soda
½ teaspoon salt
½ teaspoon ground ginger
½ teaspoon ground nutmeg
Pinch ground cloves
1 cup sugar

½ cup margarine or butter,
    softened
2 large eggs
1 teaspoon vanilla extract
¾ cup buttermilk or soured
    milk (see page 392)
Vanilla Butter Cream (see
    page 550) or other desired
    frosting

◆ Preheat oven to 350°F. Grease three 8-inch round cake pans. Line bottoms with waxed paper; grease paper. Dust pans with flour. In bowl, mix flour and next 7 ingredients.

◆ In large bowl, with mixer at medium speed, beat sugar and margarine 5 minutes, or until light and creamy. Add eggs, 1 at a time, beating well after each addition. Beat in vanilla. With mixer at low speed, alternately add flour mixture and

buttermilk, beginning and ending with flour; beat just until batter is smooth. Divide batter among pans. Stagger pans on 2 oven racks, placing 2 on upper rack and 1 on lower rack, so that layers are not directly on top of one another.

◆ Bake 28 to 30 minutes, until toothpick inserted in centers comes out clean. Cool in pans on wire racks 10 minutes. Run knife around edges of pans to loosen cakes; invert onto racks. Remove waxed paper; cool completely. Prepare butter cream. Place 1 layer on cake plate; spread with ⅔ cup butter cream. Top with second layer, ⅔ cup butter cream, and remaining layer. Frost side and top of cake with remaining butter cream. Store any leftover cake in refrigerator.

Each serving: About 340 calories, 4g protein, 40g carbohydrate, 19g total fat (4g saturated), 30mg cholesterol, 365mg sodium

BANANA LAYER CAKE

Prep: 40 minutes plus cooling   Bake: 30 minutes
Makes 16 servings

1 cup mashed fully ripe
    bananas (2 to 3 bananas)
¼ cup buttermilk or soured
    milk (see page 392)
1 teaspoon vanilla extract
2 cups cake flour (not self-
    rising)
1 teaspoon baking powder
½ teaspoon baking soda

¼ teaspoon salt
⅛ teaspoon ground nutmeg
1¼ cups sugar
½ cup margarine or butter,
    softened
2 large eggs
Cream-Cheese Frosting (see
    page 550)

◆ Preheat oven to 350°F. Grease three 8-inch round cake pans. Line bottoms with waxed paper; grease paper. Dust pans with flour. In bowl, mix bananas, buttermilk, and vanilla. In medium bowl, mix flour and next 4 ingredients.

◆ In large bowl, with mixer at medium speed, beat sugar and margarine 5 minutes, or until light and creamy. Add eggs, 1 at time, beating well after each addition. At low speed, alternately add flour mixture and banana mixture, beginning and ending with flour mixture; beat just until smooth.

◆ Divide batter among pans. Stagger pans on 2 oven racks, placing 2 on upper rack and 1 on lower rack, so layers are not directly on top of one another. Bake 30 minutes, or until toothpick inserted in centers comes out clean. Cool in pans on wire racks 10 minutes. Run knife around edges of pans to loosen cakes; invert onto racks. Remove waxed paper; cool completely. Prepare frosting. Place 1 layer on cake plate; spread with ½ cup frosting. Top with second layer, ½ cup frosting, and remaining layer. Frost side and top of cake with remaining frosting. Store any leftover cake in refrigerator.

Each serving: About 335 calories, 3g protein, 49g carbohydrate, 14g total fat (5g saturated), 39mg cholesterol, 265mg sodium

RICH CHOCOLATE CAKES AND TORTES

These dazzling desserts look as if they came from an expensive bakery, but our straightforward recipes make them easy to prepare. Each one promises a deep chocolate flavor, as well as a distinctive taste all its own. The mocha torte offers tiers of espresso cream and crunchy toasted almonds, Chocolate Truffle Cake boasts a dense, decadent texture, and the prune-nut torte is moist and fruity. Remember that chocolate can easily scorch when heated, so melt it carefully, over low heat, and stir it often.

TRIPLE-LAYER MOCHA-ALMOND TORTE

◆◆◆◆◆◆◆◆◆◆◆◆◆◆◆◆◆◆◆◆◆◆◆◆◆◆◆◆◆◆

Prep: 45 minutes plus cooling   Bake: 45 to 50 minutes
Makes 16 servings

6 squares (6 ounces) semisweet chocolate	¼ cup all-purpose flour (yes, ¼ cup)
1 tablespoon plus 2 teaspoons instant espresso-coffee powder	1 teaspoon baking powder
	½ teaspoon salt
3 cups blanched whole almonds (about 12 ounces)	6 large eggs, separated
	½ teaspoon almond extract
¾ cup plus ⅓ cup sugar	2½ cups heavy or whipping cream

1 Preheat oven to 350°F. Grease 9" by 2½" springform pan. Line bottom of pan with waxed paper; grease paper. Dust with flour. In small saucepan, melt chocolate with 1 tablespoon espresso powder and ¼ *cup water* over low heat, stirring frequently, until smooth. Remove from heat.

2 In food processor with knife blade attached, or in blender in batches, grind 2 cups almonds with ¼ cup sugar. (Nuts should be finely ground but not pastelike.) Transfer nut mixture to medium bowl; stir in flour, baking powder, and salt.

3 In large bowl, with mixer at high speed, beat egg whites to soft peaks; sprinkle in ½ cup sugar, 2 tablespoons at a time, until whites stand in stiff peaks when beaters are lifted. In small bowl, with mixer at medium speed, beat yolks, chocolate mixture, and almond extract 3 minutes, frequently scraping bowl. Fold nut mixture and chocolate mixture into egg whites just until blended. Spread batter evenly in pan.

4 Bake 45 to 50 minutes, until toothpick inserted in center of cake comes out clean. Cool in pan on wire rack 10 minutes. Remove side and bottom of pan. Remove waxed paper; cool completely on rack.

5 Meanwhile, coarsely chop remaining 1 cup almonds. In small skillet, toast almonds over medium heat until golden. Cool. With serrated knife, cut cake horizontally into 3 layers. In cup, dissolve 2 teaspoons espresso powder in *1 tablespoon hot water.*

6 In large bowl, with mixer at medium speed, beat cream, remaining ⅓ cup sugar, and espresso mixture to stiff peaks. Place 1 cake layer on cake plate; spread with 1 cup cream. Top with second layer; spread with 1 more cup cream.

7 Top with third layer. Spread top and side of cake with remaining cream. Reserve 1 tablespoon almonds; press remaining almonds into side of cake. Garnish with reserved almonds. Refrigerate until ready to serve.

EACH SERVING: ABOUT 380 CALORIES, 9g PROTEIN, 27g CARBOHYDRATE, 29g TOTAL FAT (12g SATURATED), 131 mg CHOLESTEROL, 135mg SODIUM

CHOCOLATE TRUFFLE CAKE

Prep: 1 hour plus chilling overnight and standing   *Bake:* 35 minutes
Makes 24 servings

1 cup butter (do not use
   margarine)
14 squares (14 ounces)
   semisweet chocolate
2 squares (2 ounces)
   unsweetened chocolate

9 large eggs, separated
½ cup granulated sugar
¼ teaspoon cream of tartar
Confectioners' sugar for
   garnish

◆ Preheat oven to 300°F. Remove bottom from 9" by 3" springform pan and cover bottom with foil, wrapping foil around to the underside (this will make it easier to remove cake from pan). Replace bottom. Grease and flour foil bottom and side of pan.

◆ In heavy 2-quart saucepan, melt butter with all chocolate over low heat, stirring frequently. Pour chocolate mixture into large bowl.

◆ In small bowl, with mixer at high speed, beat egg yolks and granulated sugar about 5 minutes, until very thick and lemon-colored. With rubber spatula, stir egg-yolk mixture into chocolate mixture until blended.

◆ In another large bowl, with clean beaters, with mixer at high speed, beat egg whites and cream of tartar to soft peaks. With rubber spatula or wire whisk, gently fold beaten egg whites into chocolate mixture, one-third at a time.

◆ Spread batter evenly in pan. Bake 35 minutes. (Do not overbake; cake will firm on chilling.) Cool cake completely in pan on wire rack. Refrigerate overnight in pan.

◆ To remove cake from pan, run a hot knife around edge of cake; remove side of pan. Invert cake onto cake plate; unwrap foil on bottom and lift off bottom of pan. Carefully peel foil from cake.

◆ Let cake stand 1 hour at room temperature before serving. Just before serving, sprinkle confectioners' sugar through fine sieve over star stencil or doily for a pretty design (see page 552), or dust top of cake with confectioners' sugar. Store any leftover cake in refrigerator.

Each serving: About 200 calories, 4g protein, 15g carbohydrate, 16g total fat (9g saturated), 100mg cholesterol, 100mg sodium

CHOCOLATE, PRUNE, AND NUT TORTE

Prep: 1 hour plus chilling overnight   *Bake:* 35 minutes
Makes 12 servings

3 bittersweet chocolate bars
   (3 ounces each) or
   9 squares (9 ounces)
   semisweet chocolate
6 large egg whites
½ cup granulated sugar

½ teaspoon vanilla extract
2 cups pitted prunes, diced
1½ cups pecans (about
   6 ounces), coarsely chopped
1 tablespoon confectioners'
   sugar

◆ Grease 10" by 2½" springform pan; line bottom of pan with waxed paper.

◆ Finely grate chocolate. (Or, in food processor with knife blade attached, process chocolate until ground.)

◆ Preheat oven to 425°F. In large bowl, with mixer at high speed, beat egg whites until soft peaks form. Beating at high speed, sprinkle in granulated sugar, 2 tablespoons at a time, beating well after each addition, until whites stand in stiff peaks when beaters are lifted. Beat in vanilla.

◆ With rubber spatula, gently fold prunes and pecans into beaten egg whites; gently but thoroughly fold in grated chocolate. Pour batter into pan, smoothing top. Bake 35 minutes, or until top of torte is deep brown and edge pulls away from side of pan.

◆ Cool torte in pan on wire rack 15 minutes; remove side of pan. Invert torte and remove bottom of pan; peel off waxed paper. Cool torte completely on rack. Cover and refrigerate torte overnight.

◆ Just before serving, cut six 12" by ½" strips of waxed paper. Place strips 1 inch apart on top of torte. Sprinkle top of torte with confectioners' sugar, then carefully remove waxed-paper strips. Store any leftover torte in refrigerator.

Each serving: About 305 calories, 6g protein, 34g carbohydrate, 21g total fat (7g saturated), 0mg cholesterol, 30mg sodium

CAKE ROLLS

Alluring spirals of cake and filling make cake rolls among the prettiest desserts around. Best made in advance, they're perfect for company.

WHITE-CHOCOLATE YULE LOG

◆◆◆◆◆◆◆◆◆◆◆◆

Prep: 1 hour 10 minutes plus cooling and chilling
Bake: 10 to 15 minutes
Makes 20 servings

10 large eggs, separated
1 cup granulated sugar
3 teaspoons vanilla extract
1 cup all-purpose flour
¼ cup confectioners' sugar plus additional for sprinkling
White-Chocolate Butter Cream (see page 550)
1 pint heavy or whipping cream (2 cups)
¼ cup unsweetened cocoa
½ teaspoon ground cinnamon
Chocolate Leaves (see page 551) and cranberries for garnish

1 Preheat oven to 350°F. Grease two 15½" by 10½" jelly-roll pans. Line pans with waxed paper; grease paper. In large bowl, with mixer at high speed, beat egg whites until soft peaks form. Beating at high speed, gradually sprinkle in ½ cup granulated sugar, 2 tablespoons at a time, beating until whites stand in stiff peaks when beaters are lifted.

2 In small bowl, with mixer at high speed, beat egg yolks, remaining ½ cup granulated sugar, and 2 teaspoons vanilla until very thick and lemon-colored; at low speed, beat in flour just until combined. With rubber spatula, fold yolk mixture into beaten whites.

3 Spread batter evenly in pans. Bake on 2 oven racks 10 to 15 minutes, until cakes spring back when lightly touched, rotating pans between upper and lower racks halfway through baking time.

4 Sprinkle large cloth kitchen towel with confectioners' sugar. When cakes are done, immediately run spatula around edges of pans to loosen cakes; invert onto towel, slightly over-lapping a long side of each.

5 Carefully peel off waxed paper. Starting from a long side, roll cakes with towel jelly-roll fashion. Cool completely, seam-side down, on wire rack. Meanwhile, prepare White-Chocolate Butter Cream; set aside.

6 In large bowl, with mixer at medium speed, beat cream, cocoa, cinnamon, ¼ cup confectioners' sugar, and remaining 1 teaspoon vanilla to stiff peaks. Unroll cake; spread with cocoa cream, leaving ½-inch border.

7 From same long side, roll cake without towel. Cut a 2-inch-thick diagonal slice from each end of roll; trim each to 2½ inches in diameter. Place cake, seam-side down, on long platter.

8 With metal spatula, spread some butter cream over roll. Place end pieces on top of roll to resemble cut branches. Spread remaining frosting over roll and branches. With four-tined fork, score frosting to resemble bark of tree. Refrigerate cake at least 2 hours before serving. Garnish with Chocolate Leaves and cranberries. Store any leftover cake in refrigerator.

EACH SERVING: ABOUT 360 CALORIES, 5g PROTEIN, 33g CARBOHYDRATE, 23g TOTAL FAT (14g SATURATED), 166mg CHOLESTEROL, 145mg SODIUM

FALLEN CHOCOLATE SOUFFLÉ ROLL

Prep: 30 minutes plus cooling and chilling   *Bake: 15 minutes*
Makes 16 servings

5 squares (5 ounces) semisweet chocolate	¾ teaspoon ground cinnamon
1 square (1 ounce) unsweetened chocolate	¼ teaspoon salt
	⅛ teaspoon ground cloves
1 teaspoon instant espresso-coffee powder, dissolved in 3 tablespoons hot water	1½ cups heavy or whipping cream
	¼ cup coffee-flavor liqueur
6 large eggs, separated	5 tablespoons confectioners' sugar plus additional for sprinkling
¾ cup granulated sugar	
1 teaspoon vanilla extract	

◆ Preheat oven to 350°F. Grease 15½" by 10½" jelly-roll pan. Line with waxed paper; grease paper. Dust pan with flour. In top of double boiler set over simmering water, melt all chocolate with espresso mixture, stirring often; set aside.

◆ In large bowl, with mixer at high speed, beat egg whites until soft peaks form. Beating at high speed, gradually sprinkle in ¼ cup granulated sugar, 1 tablespoon at a time, beating well after each addition, until whites stand in stiff peaks when beaters are lifted.

◆ In small bowl, with mixer at high speed, beat egg yolks with remaining ½ cup granulated sugar until very thick and lemon-colored. Reduce speed to low; beat in vanilla, cinnamon, salt, and cloves. With rubber spatula, fold chocolate mixture into yolk mixture. Gently fold one-third of whites into chocolate mixture; fold chocolate mixture into remaining whites.

◆ Spread batter evenly in pan. Bake 15 minutes, or until firm to the touch. Cover cake with clean, dampened kitchen towel; cool in pan on wire rack 30 minutes.

◆ In large bowl, with mixer at medium speed, beat cream until soft peaks form. Beat in coffee liqueur and 3 tablespoons confectioners' sugar, then beat until stiff peaks form.

◆ Remove towel from cake; sift 2 tablespoons confectioners' sugar over cake. Run small spatula around edges of pan. Cover cake with sheet of foil and a large cookie sheet; invert cake onto cookie sheet. Carefully peel off waxed paper.

◆ Spread whipped cream evenly over cake, leaving ½-inch border. Starting from a long side and using foil to help lift cake, roll cake jelly-roll fashion (cake may crack). Place, seam-side down, on long platter. Refrigerate at least 1 hour, until ready to serve. Just before serving, sprinkle confectioners' sugar on top.

Each serving: About 215 calories, 4g protein, 21g carbohydrate, 14g total fat (8g saturated), 110mg cholesterol, 65mg sodium

BLUEBERRY GINGERBREAD ROLL

Prep: 30 minutes plus cooling   *Bake: 15 minutes*
Makes 8 servings

1 cup all-purpose flour	¼ cup light molasses
½ cup granulated sugar	1 large egg
2 teaspoons ground ginger	3 tablespoons confectioners' sugar plus additional for sprinkling
1 teaspoon baking soda	
½ teaspoon baking powder	
½ teaspoon ground cinnamon	1 cup heavy or whipping cream
¼ teaspoon salt	1 teaspoon vanilla extract
¼ teaspoon ground nutmeg	2 cups blueberries
6 tablespoons margarine or butter, melted	

◆ Preheat oven to 350°F. Grease 15½" by 10½" jelly-roll pan. Line with waxed paper; grease paper. Dust pan with flour.

◆ In large bowl, combine flour and next 7 ingredients. In medium bowl, whisk together melted margarine, molasses, egg, and ⅓ *cup hot water*. Whisk molasses mixture into flour mixture just until smooth. Spread batter evenly in pan. Bake 15 minutes, or until top springs back when lightly touched.

◆ Meanwhile, sprinkle confectioners' sugar onto large cloth kitchen towel. Run small spatula around edges of pan; invert hot cake onto towel. Peel off waxed paper. Trim ¼ inch from edges of cake. Starting from a long side, roll cake jelly-roll fashion. Cool completely on wire rack.

◆ In medium bowl, with mixer at medium speed, beat cream with vanilla and 3 tablespoons confectioners' sugar until stiff peaks form. With rubber spatula, fold in blueberries. Unroll cooled cake (cake may crack); spread whipped cream evenly on top, leaving ½-inch border. Starting from same long side, roll up cake and transfer, seam-side down, to long platter. Refrigerate until ready to serve.

Each serving: About 350 calories, 3g protein, 40g carbohydrate, 20g total fat (9g saturated), 67mg cholesterol, 375mg sodium

ANGEL FOOD AND SPONGE CAKES

Angel food, its cousin the chiffon cake, and sponge cake share a light, springy texture. With virtually no fat, angel food cake is the most ethereal. Its delicate crumb is the result of perfectly beaten egg whites. Sponge and chiffon cakes get a bit more richness from egg yolks; chiffon, made with oil as well, is the richest of these airy wonders. All are delicious on their own, lightly glazed, or simply dusted with confectioners' sugar and served with fresh fruit.

CHOCOLATE ANGEL FOOD CAKE

◆◆◆◆◆◆◆◆◆◆◆◆◆◆◆◆◆◆◆◆◆◆◆◆◆◆◆◆◆◆◆◆

Prep: 30 minutes plus cooling   Bake: 30 to 35 minutes
Makes 16 servings

1½ cups cake flour (not self-rising)

½ cup unsweetened cocoa

1⅔ cups egg whites
  (12 to 14 large egg whites)

1½ teaspoons cream of tartar

¾ teaspoon salt

1½ teaspoons vanilla extract

2 cups sugar

4 squares (4 ounces) semisweet chocolate

2 teaspoons shortening

1 Preheat oven to 375°F. Sift flour and cocoa through medium-mesh sieve into medium bowl. Set aside. In large bowl, with mixer at high speed, beat egg whites, cream of tartar, and salt until soft peaks form; beat in vanilla. Beating at high speed, gradually sprinkle in sugar, 2 tablespoons at a time, beating well after each addition, until whites stand in stiff peaks when beaters are lifted.

2 With rubber spatula or wire whisk, fold flour mixture into beaten whites just until flour mixture disappears. Do not overmix. Pour batter into ungreased 9- to 10-inch tube pan.

3 Bake 30 to 35 minutes, until cake springs back when lightly touched. Invert cake in pan on metal funnel or bottle; cool cake completely in pan.

4 Carefully run metal spatula around side of pan to loosen cake; remove from pan and place cake on cake plate.

5 Prepare chocolate glaze: In heavy small saucepan, melt semisweet chocolate with shortening over very low heat, stirring frequently, until smooth. Spread over top of cake, letting some run down side.

ANGEL FOOD CAKE TIPS

• Egg whites for beating are best at room temperature. The bowl in which you beat them should be perfectly dry and free from grease or any traces of yolk.

• Either over- or underbeating will cause loss of volume.

• For angel and chiffon cakes, never grease the pan; the batter must cling to the pan side as it bakes and cools. To cool, invert the pan over a funnel or bottle to let air circulate on all sides and prevent the cake from sinking.

• When loosening the cake from the pan, tightly press the spatula against the pan to avoid tearing the cake.

EACH SERVING: ABOUT 190 CALORIES, 4g PROTEIN, 39g CARBOHYDRATE, 3g TOTAL FAT (2g SATURATED), 0mg CHOLESTEROL, 145mg SODIUM

SUGAR 'N' SPICE ANGEL FOOD CAKE

Prep: 20 minutes plus cooling *Bake:* 30 to 35 minutes
Makes 16 servings

1 cup cake flour (not self-rising)
1 cup confectioners' sugar
1 teaspoon ground cinnamon
1 teaspoon ground ginger
¼ teaspoon ground allspice
Salt

1⅔ cups egg whites (12 to 14 large egg whites)
1 teaspoon cream of tartar
1 teaspoon vanilla extract
¾ cup granulated sugar
¼ cup packed dark brown sugar

◆ Preheat oven to 375°F. Sift flour, sugar, cinnamon, ginger, allspice, and ¼ teaspoon salt through medium-mesh sieve into medium bowl.

◆ In large bowl, with mixer at high speed, beat egg whites, cream of tartar, and ½ teaspoon salt until soft peaks form; beat in vanilla. Beating at high speed, sprinkle in granulated sugar and brown sugar, 2 tablespoons at a time, beating well after each addition, until whites stand in stiff peaks when beaters are lifted. With rubber spatula or wire whisk, fold in flour mixture just until flour mixture disappears. Do not overmix. Pour batter into ungreased 9- to 10-inch tube pan.

◆ Bake 30 to 35 minutes, until cake springs back when lightly touched. Invert cake in pan on funnel or bottle; cool completely in pan. Carefully run metal spatula around side of pan to loosen cake. Remove from pan; place on cake plate.

Each serving: About 115 calories, 3g protein, 25g carbohydrate, 0g total fat, 0mg cholesterol, 145mg sodium

VANILLA CHIFFON CAKE

Prep: 20 minutes plus cooling *Bake:* 1 hour 15 minutes
Makes 16 servings

2¼ cups cake flour (not self-rising)
1 tablespoon baking powder
1 teaspoon salt
1½ cups granulated sugar
½ cup vegetable oil

5 large egg yolks
1 tablespoon vanilla extract
7 large egg whites
½ teaspoon cream of tartar
Confectioners' sugar for garnish

◆ Preheat oven to 325°F. In large bowl, combine flour, baking powder, salt, and 1 cup granulated sugar. Make a well in center and add oil, egg yolks, vanilla, and ¾ *cup cold water*; whisk into flour mixture until smooth.

◆ In another large bowl, with mixer at high speed, beat egg whites and cream of tartar until soft peaks form. Beating at high speed, gradually sprinkle in remaining ½ cup granulated sugar, 2 tablespoons at a time, beating well after

each addition, until whites stand in stiff peaks when beaters are lifted. With rubber spatula, gently fold one-third of whites into yolk mixture; fold in remaining whites. Pour batter into ungreased 9- to 10-inch tube pan.

◆ Bake 1¼ hours, or until top springs back when lightly touched. Invert cake in pan on funnel or bottle; cool completely in pan. Carefully run metal spatula around side of pan to loosen cake; remove from pan and place on cake plate. Just before serving, sift confectioners' sugar on top.

Each serving: About 220 calories, 4g protein, 32g carbohydrate, 9g total fat (2g saturated), 67mg cholesterol, 250mg sodium

GOLDEN SPONGE CAKE

Prep: 20 minutes plus cooling *Bake:* 15 to 20 minutes
Makes 8 servings

¾ cup all-purpose flour
2 tablespoons cornstarch
3 large eggs
½ cup sugar

1 tablespoon margarine or butter, melted
Whipped cream and fresh fruit (optional)

◆ Preheat oven to 375°F. Grease and flour 9" by 9" metal baking pan. In small bowl, combine flour and cornstarch. In large bowl, with mixer at high speed, beat eggs and sugar about 10 minutes, until thick and lemon-colored, occasionally scraping bowl with rubber spatula. With rubber spatula, fold in flour mixture until well blended; fold in melted margarine. Pour batter into pan.

◆ Bake 15 to 20 minutes, until cake is golden and springs back when lightly touched.

◆ Cool cake in pan on wire rack 10 minutes. Run small knife around edges of pan to loosen cake; invert onto rack to cool completely. Serve cake with whipped cream and fruit, if you like.

Each serving: About 135 calories, 3g protein, 23g carbohydrate, 3g total fat (1g saturated), 80mg cholesterol, 40mg sodium

FANCY DECORATED CAKES

These spectacular cakes are for grand celebrations. They rely on special frosting techniques that require a steady hand and a bit of patience. But your guests will agree – the stunning results are well worth the effort.

DOTTED SWISS ALMOND CAKE

◆◆◆◆◆◆◆◆◆◆◆◆◆◆◆◆◆◆◆◆◆◆◆◆◆◆◆◆

Prep: 1 hour plus cooling Bake: 35 minutes
Makes 24 servings

2½ cups all-purpose flour
2½ teaspoons baking powder
½ teaspoon salt
½ cup margarine or butter, softened
1 tube or can (7 to 8 ounces) almond paste, cut up
1½ cups sugar
5 large egg whites
1 tablespoon vanilla extract
1¼ cups milk

Amaretto Butter Cream (see page 550)
6 tablespoons seedless red raspberry jam

Special equipment:
1 decorating bag with coupler
1 writing tip (⅛-inch opening)
1 writing tip (⅜-inch opening)

1 Preheat oven to 350°F. Grease two 8" by 8" metal baking pans. Line bottoms with waxed paper; grease paper. Dust pans with flour. In medium bowl, combine flour, baking powder, and salt; set aside. In large bowl, with mixer at low speed, beat margarine, almond paste, and sugar 2 to 3 minutes, until blended, scraping bowl often with rubber spatula.

2 Increase speed to medium; beat about 2 minutes, until well mixed, scraping bowl often (mixture may look crumbly). Gradually beat in egg whites and vanilla just until blended. Reduce speed to low; alternately add flour mixture and milk to almond-paste mixture, beginning and ending with flour mixture. Beat just until mixed.

3 Pour batter into pans. Bake 35 minutes, or until toothpick inserted in centers of cakes comes out clean. Cool layers in pans on wire racks 10 minutes. Run spatula around sides of pans to loosen cakes; invert onto racks. Remove waxed paper; cool completely. Prepare butter cream. Spoon 1 cup butter cream into decorating bag fitted with ⅛-inch writing tip; set aside.

4 With serrated knife, cut each cake layer horizontally in half. (Use ruler and toothpicks to mark halfway points.)

5 Place bottom half of 1 layer, cut side up, on cake plate; spread evenly with 2 tablespoons jam. Spread ⅓ cup butter cream on top of jam.

6 Repeat layering 2 times, then top with remaining cake layer. Spread remaining butter cream on top and sides of cake.

7 With butter cream in decorating bag, pipe clusters of small dots on top of cake.

8 With ⅜-inch writing tip, pipe rows of dots around bottom and top borders and down corners of cake. Store any leftover cake in refrigerator.

EACH SERVING: ABOUT 370 CALORIES, 4g PROTEIN, 40g CARBOHYDRATE, 22g TOTAL FAT (11g SATURATED), 43mg CHOLESTEROL, 180mg SODIUM

STRAWBERRY BASKET CAKE

Prep: 1 hour 15 minutes plus standing and cooling
Bake: 23 to 28 minutes   Makes 20 servings

Layers from Yellow Cake (see page 529)

2 pints heavy or whipping cream (4 cups)

1 tablespoon vanilla extract

1 envelope unflavored gelatin

⅔ cup confectioners' sugar

½ cup strawberry jam

2 pints strawberries

Special Equipment:
2 decorating bags
1 medium star tip (½-inch opening)
1 medium basket-weave tip (¾-inch opening)

◆ Prepare Yellow Cake. While cake layers are cooling, prepare frosting: In large bowl, combine cream and vanilla. In small saucepan, evenly sprinkle gelatin over *3 tablespoons cold water*; let stand 2 minutes to soften. Cook over medium-low heat, stirring frequently, about 3 minutes, until gelatin completely dissolves. (Do not boil.)

◆ Remove saucepan from heat; with mixer at medium-high speed, immediately begin beating cream mixture. Beat about 2 minutes, until thickened and soft peaks just begin to form. Beat in confectioners' sugar, then beat in dissolved gelatin in a thin, steady stream. Beat cream mixture until stiff peaks form but mixture is still soft and smooth; do not overbeat.

◆ Place 1 cake layer on cake plate; spread with half of jam, then spread with 1 cup frosting. Top with second cake layer, remaining jam, and 1 more cup frosting. Place remaining cake layer on top. Frost side and top of cake with a thin layer (about ⅛ inch thick) of frosting.

◆ Spoon about 1¼ cups frosting into decorating bag fitted with ½-inch medium star tip; set aside. Spoon about 2 cups of remaining frosting into decorating bag fitted with ¾-inch

medium basket-weave tip. Pipe basket-weave pattern around side of cake (see below). Add remaining frosting to decorating bag as necessary to complete basket weave.

◆ With frosting in bag with star tip, pipe decorative border around top edge of cake. Refrigerate cake until ready to serve. Just before serving, pile strawberries on top of cake. Remove berries before slicing cake; serve on the side.

Each serving: About 455 calories, 5g protein, 46g carbohydrate, 28g total fat (13g saturated), 110mg cholesterol, 270mg sodium

BASKET-WEAVE FROSTING

Creating the basket-weave effect for our celebration Strawberry Basket Cake is easier than it looks, and the results are stunning. If you're not sure of your piping skills, have a practice run on a sheet of waxed paper first, before you tackle the finished cake.

1 With basket-weave tip, serrated side of tip facing out, pipe vertical strip of frosting up side of cake.

2 Next, pipe 3 horizontal bars, evenly spaced, across vertical strip, extending ¾ inch to left and right sides of vertical strip.

3 Pipe another vertical strip of frosting to right of first one, just slightly overlapping ends of horizontal bars.

4 Starting at right edge of first vertical strip, pipe horizontal bars across second vertical strip in spaces between bars in first row, extending ¾ inch to right of second vertical strip. Repeat around cake to create a woven effect.

KIDS' CAKES

These whimsical creations are guaranteed crowd-pleasers at birthday parties and post-game celebrations. They're made from our simple layer cake recipes, then adorned with frostings and assorted candies. Your kids will love helping decorate – simply set out bowls of goodies and let their imaginations do the rest.

MONSTER SNAKE CAKE

◆ ◆ ◆ ◆ ◆ ◆ ◆ ◆ ◆ ◆ ◆ ◆

Prep: 1 hour 20 minutes plus cooling
Bake: 30 minutes
Makes 24 servings

2 layers from Rich Chocolate Cake (see page 528; freeze remaining layer for use another day) or 1 package cake mix for 2-layer cake, batter prepared as label directs

1 package (16 ounces) confectioners' sugar

1 cup margarine or butter, softened

5 tablespoons half-and-half or light cream

2 teaspoons vanilla extract

Green food-color paste (see page 30)

Candy garnishes: scallop-edged jelly candies, 1 small blue candy, ¼ cup multicolor nonmelting candy-coated chocolate pieces, and black, red, and white candy-coated licorice candies

1 Prepare Rich Chocolate Cake layers; cool as directed. (Or, if using cake mix, grease two 8-inch round cake pans. Line bottoms with waxed paper; grease paper. Dust pans with flour. Divide batter evenly between pans; bake and cool as label directs.)

2 While cakes are cooling, prepare frosting: In large bowl, with mixer at low speed, beat confectioners' sugar, margarine, half-and-half, and vanilla just until blended. Increase speed to medium and beat, frequently scraping bowl with rubber spatula, until frosting is smooth and an easy spreading consistency. Stir in enough green food-color paste to tint frosting bright green; set aside.

3 Cut 2½-inch round in center of each cake layer. Without removing round, cut each layer in half to make 4 C-shaped pieces and 4 small semicircles.

4 On cutting board or large piece of heavy cardboard covered with foil (finished cake is approximately 28" by 9"), place C-shaped pieces of cake end to end, alternating directions to create a curvy snake shape.

5 Place cut side of 1 cake semicircle against cut side of one end of snake to form tail. Repeat on other end for head. Place remaining 2 semicircles at head end of snake to form an open mouth. Frost side and top of cake.

6 Garnish cake: Cut all but 1 jelly candy in half. Place jelly-candy halves along top edge of cake for scales. Place whole jelly candy on head for eye, with blue candy in center for pupil. Use multicolor chocolate pieces to decorate body. Use black and red licorice candies for eyelashes and white licorice candies for teeth. Use brown candy-coated chocolate piece for nose. Store any leftover cake in refrigerator.

EACH SERVING: ABOUT 275 CALORIES, 2g PROTEIN, 37g CARBOHYDRATE, 14g TOTAL FAT (3g SATURATED), 26mg CHOLESTEROL, 255mg SODIUM

CIRCUS TRAIN

Prep: 2 hours plus cooling *Bake:* 35 to 45 minutes
Makes 15 servings

Batter for Banana Layer Cake
  (see page 530)
Cream-Cheese Frosting (see
  page 550)
Toothpicks

Candy garnishes: multicolor
  décors, assorted licorice
  candies, gummy animals,
  and licorice whips and twists
Drinking straws

◆ Preheat oven to 350°F. Grease and flour five 5¼" by 2¾"
mini-loaf pans (1½ cups capacity each) or 9" by 5" loaf pan.

◆ Prepare batter for Banana Layer Cake. Spread batter
evenly in mini-loaf pans. Bake 35 minutes, or until toothpick
inserted in centers of cakes comes out clean. Cool in pans on
wire rack 10 minutes. Run spatula around sides of pans to
loosen cakes; invert cakes onto rack and cool completely. (Or,
if using 9" by 5" loaf pan, bake 45 minutes; cool as above. Cut
cooled cake crosswise into five 1¾-inch-wide pieces.)

◆ While cake is cooling, prepare Cream-Cheese Frosting.

◆ To assemble: With serrated knife, cut rounded tops off
3 cakes; set aside. (Do not cut tops too thin.) For engine,
from 1 of the same 3 cakes, cut a ½-inch-thick horizontal
slice. Trim slice, rounding 2 corners of a short side; with
toothpicks, attach to one end of cake for back of engine.
Cut 1 rounded top crosswise in half. With toothpicks, attach
half to bottom front of engine to resemble a cowcatcher.
Cut 2-inch semicircle from second half of rounded top for
front of train; with toothpicks, attach to top front of engine.
Reserve remaining 2 rounded tops to make canopies.

◆ With small metal spatula, frost engine and cars and tops
and sides of canopies. Sprinkle canopies with décors.
Decorate engine and cars: Use round licorice candies for
wheels; black licorice pieces for coal car; red licorice pieces
for freight; assorted licorice candies for engine; and gummy
animals for animal cars. Outline train borders with licorice
whips. Attach canopies to animal cars with pieces of drinking
straws. Assemble train on long board or tray, using licorice
twists to attach cars. Store any leftover cake in refrigerator.

**Each serving: About 355 calories, 3g protein, 53g carbohydrate,
15g total fat (5g saturated), 41mg cholesterol, 280mg sodium**

GREAT-SPORT CUPCAKES

Prep: 1½ hours plus cooling *Bake:* 25 minutes per batch
Makes 36

Batter for Rich Chocolate
  Cake (see page 528)
Vanilla Butter Cream (see
  page 550)
Black, red, orange, and yellow
  food-color paste (see
  page 30)

Special Equipment:
3 small decorating bags
3 writing tips (1/16-inch opening
  each)

◆ Preheat oven to 350°F.
Line thirty-six 2½-inch muffin-
pan cups with fluted paper
liners. (If you do not have enough
muffin-pan cups, bake cupcakes in
batches.) Prepare batter; pour into
cups. (Bake only as many cupcakes as
1 rack in center of oven can hold.) Bake
25 minutes, or until toothpick inserted in centers comes out
almost clean. Cool in pans on wire racks 10 minutes.
Remove from pans; cool completely on racks. Repeat with
remaining batter.

◆ Prepare butter cream. Remove 1¼ cups butter cream;
divide it among 3 cups. With food-color paste, tint one-third
black and one-third red; leave one-third white. Cover with
plastic wrap; set aside. Divide remaining butter cream among
3 more cups. With food-color paste, tint one-third orange
and one-third yellow; leave one-third white. Frost 12 cupcakes
with orange butter cream, 12 cupcakes with yellow butter
cream, and 12 cupcakes with white butter cream.

◆ Spoon reserved black, red, and white butter creams into
decorating bags, each fitted with a 1/16-inch writing tip. Pipe
black butter cream onto each orange cupcake for basketballs.
Pipe red butter cream onto each white cupcake for baseballs.
Pipe white butter cream onto each yellow cupcake for tennis
balls. Store any leftover cupcakes in refrigerator.

**Each cupcake: About 210 calories, 3g protein, 25g carbohydrate,
12g total fat (3g saturated), 26mg cholesterol, 225mg sodium**

DRIED FRUIT AND NUT CAKES

Studded with dried and candied fruits and nuts, these dense, moist cakes have a rich, concentrated flavor that improves with time. A perennial favorite for the holidays, these cakes are also great for housewarming gifts and special brunches, or with afternoon coffee.

CHRISTMAS FRUITCAKE

◆◆◆◆◆◆◆◆◆◆◆◆◆◆◆◆◆◆◆◆◆◆◆◆◆◆◆◆◆

Prep: 30 minutes plus cooling and chilling   Bake: 1 hour 30 minutes
Makes 36 servings

1 cup pitted prunes, each cut in half	½ cup diced candied lemon peel (4 ounces)
1 package (10 ounces) dried figs (1 cup), chopped	1 cup sugar
1 package (6 ounces) dried apricots (1 cup), chopped	1 cup margarine or butter
½ (10-ounce) package pitted dates (1 cup)	2 cups all-purpose flour
2 cups pecans (about 8 ounces)	2 teaspoons baking powder
1 cup green candied cherries (8 ounces)	1 teaspoon salt
1 cup red candied cherries (8 ounces)	1 teaspoon vanilla extract
½ cup candied pineapple wedges (4 ounces)	5 large eggs
	¼ cup brandy (optional)
	¼ cup apricot jam, melted
	Dried fruit, green and red candied cherries, and pecans for garnish
	Wide ribbon for decoration

1 Preheat oven to 325°F. Grease 10-inch tube pan. Line bottom with foil; grease foil. In large bowl, combine first 9 ingredients. In another large bowl, with mixer at low speed, beat sugar and margarine just until blended. Increase speed to high; beat until light and creamy. Add flour, baking powder, salt, vanilla, and eggs. Reduce speed to low; beat until just blended, frequently scraping bowl.

2 Stir batter into fruit mixture until fruit is evenly distributed. Spoon batter into pan. Bake fruitcake 1½ hours, or until toothpick inserted near center of cake comes out clean.

3 Remove fruitcake from oven. With skewer, poke holes in warm cake and drizzle with brandy, if using. Cool cake completely in pan on wire rack.

4 Run small knife around edge of pan to loosen cake; remove from pan and carefully peel off foil. Wrap fruitcake tightly in plastic wrap or foil; refrigerate overnight so cake will be firm and easy to slice. Store in refrigerator up to 4 weeks.

5 To serve, brush fruitcake with half of melted jam; garnish with dried fruit, candied cherries, and pecans. Brush fruit and pecans with remaining jam. If you like, wrap ribbon around cake to decorate; secure with double-sided tape. To serve, slice cake very thin.

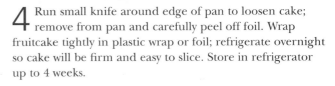

MINIATURE FRUITCAKE LOAVES

Prepare fruitcake as above, but spoon batter into six 5¾" by 3¼" mini-loaf pans and bake 50 to 60 minutes. Poke holes in warm cakes and drizzle with ½ cup brandy, if using; brush cakes with melted jam and garnish with fruit and pecans as directed.

EACH SERVING: ABOUT 255 CALORIES, 3g PROTEIN, 42g CARBOHYDRATE, 10g TOTAL FAT (2g SATURATED), 30mg CHOLESTEROL, 155mg SODIUM

COATING NUTS AND FRUIT WITH FLOUR

Tossing chopped nuts and dried or fresh fruit with a small amount of flour helps keep them separate – and suspended – in a cake batter. Otherwise, these ingredients tend to clump together and may sink to the bottom of the pan during baking.

APRICOT-PECAN FRUITCAKE

Prep: 20 minutes plus cooling   Bake: 1 hour 10 to 20 minutes
Makes 24 servings

2½ packages (6 ounces each) dried apricots (2½ cups), cut into ½-inch pieces	1 cup margarine or butter, softened
2 cups coarsely chopped pecans (about 8 ounces) plus ⅔ cup pecan halves (about 3 ounces)	5 large eggs
	½ cup brandy
	1 tablespoon vanilla extract
1 tablespoon plus 2 cups all-purpose flour	2 teaspoons baking powder
	1 teaspoon salt
1¼ cups sugar	⅓ cup apricot jam, melted and strained

◆ Preheat oven to 325°F. Grease 9- to 10-inch tube pan.

◆ In medium bowl, toss dried apricot pieces and chopped pecans with 1 tablespoon flour until coated; set aside.

◆ In large bowl, with mixer at low speed, beat sugar and margarine until blended. Increase speed to high; beat about 2 minutes, until light and creamy, frequently scraping bowl with rubber spatula.

◆ Reduce speed to low; add eggs, brandy, vanilla, baking powder, salt, and remaining 2 cups flour; beat mixture until well blended, occasionally scraping bowl. Stir in dried-apricot mixture.

◆ Spoon batter into pan. Arrange ⅔ cup pecan halves on top of batter in 2 concentric circles. Bake cake 1 hour 10 to 20 minutes, until toothpick inserted near center of cake comes out clean.

◆ Cool cake in pan on wire rack 10 minutes. Run small knife around edge of pan to loosen cake; remove cake from pan and cool completely on rack.

◆ To serve, brush top of cake with melted apricot jam. Or, wrap and refrigerate cake up to 1 week; brush with jam before serving.

Each serving: About 295 calories, 4g protein, 32g carbohydrate, 17g total fat (2g saturated), 44mg cholesterol, 235mg sodium

SPICE AND NUT CAKE

Prep: 20 minutes plus cooling   Bake: 50 to 60 minutes
Makes 12 servings

Unsweetened cocoa for dusting	1 tablespoon ground ginger
1 cup margarine or butter, softened	2 teaspoons baking soda
½ cup packed dark brown sugar	1½ teaspoons ground cinnamon
1 teaspoon vanilla extract	1 teaspoon salt
2 large eggs	¾ teaspoon ground allspice
3 cups all-purpose flour	1½ cups walnuts (about 6 ounces), coarsely chopped
1 cup buttermilk, soured milk (see page 392), or plain low-fat yogurt	1 cup pitted prunes, coarsely chopped
¾ cup dark molasses	Confectioners' sugar for garnish

◆ Preheat oven to 350°F. Grease 10-inch Bundt pan; dust with cocoa. In large bowl, with mixer at low speed, beat margarine and next 3 ingredients until blended. Increase speed to high; beat about 5 minutes, until light and fluffy.

◆ Reduce speed to low; add flour and next 7 ingredients. Beat until well blended, frequently scraping bowl with rubber spatula. Stir in walnuts and prunes.

◆ Spoon batter into pan, spreading evenly with back of spoon. Bake cake 50 to 60 minutes, until toothpick inserted near center of cake comes out clean.

◆ Cool cake in pan on wire rack 10 minutes. Remove cake from pan and cool completely on rack. Just before serving, sift confectioners' sugar through sieve over cake.

Each serving: About 480 calories, 7g protein, 57g carbohydrate, 26g total fat (4g saturated), 36mg cholesterol, 605mg sodium

APPLE, CARROT, AND SPICE CAKES

Chopped or shredded fruits and vegetables lend a subtle sweetness, moisture, and luscious texture to these varied cakes. Except for our apple upside-down cake, which is most delicious warm, all these cakes keep well.

CARROT CAKE

◆◆◆◆◆◆◆◆◆◆◆◆◆

Prep: 40 minutes plus cooling
Bake: 55 to 60 minutes
Makes 20 servings

2½ cups all-purpose flour
2 teaspoons baking soda
2 teaspoons ground cinnamon
1 teaspoon baking powder
1 teaspoon salt
½ teaspoon ground nutmeg
4 large eggs
1 cup granulated sugar
¾ cup packed light brown sugar
1 cup vegetable oil
1 tablespoon vanilla extract
3 cups lightly packed shredded carrots (about 6 medium)
1 cup walnuts (about 4 ounces), chopped
¾ cup dark seedless raisins
1 can (8 to 8¼ ounces) crushed pineapple in unsweetened juice
Cream-Cheese Frosting (see page 550)

1 Preheat oven to 350°F. Grease 13" by 9" metal baking pan. Line bottom with waxed paper; grease paper. Dust pan with flour. In medium bowl, combine flour, baking soda, cinnamon, baking powder, salt, and nutmeg.

2 In large bowl, with mixer at medium-high speed, beat eggs until blended. Gradually add granulated sugar, then brown sugar; beat 2 minutes, frequently scraping bowl with rubber spatula. Beat in oil and vanilla. Reduce speed to low; add flour mixture and beat about 1 minute, until smooth, frequently scraping bowl.

3 Fold in carrots, walnuts, raisins, and pineapple with its juice.

4 Pour batter into pan. Bake 55 to 60 minutes, until toothpick inserted in center of cake comes out clean, with a few moist crumbs attached. Cool cake in pan on wire rack 10 minutes. Invert cake onto rack and remove waxed paper. Cool cake completely on rack.

5 Prepare frosting. Transfer cake to large platter or tray. With metal spatula, spread frosting over sides and top of cake. Store any leftover cake in refrigerator.

ZUCCHINI CAKE

Prepare Carrot Cake as above, but substitute 3 cups shredded zucchini (about 2 medium) for carrots and add ⅛ teaspoon ground cloves to flour mixture. Omit pineapple. Garnish with chopped walnuts.

Each serving: About 415 calories, 5g protein, 51g carbohydrate, 22g total fat (5g saturated), 52mg cholesterol, 340g sodium

EACH SERVING: ABOUT 425 CALORIES, 5g PROTEIN, 54g CARBOHYDRATE, 22g TOTAL FAT (5g SATURATED), 52mg CHOLESTEROL, 345mg SODIUM

APPLE-WALNUT BUNDT CAKE

Prep: 25 minutes plus cooling   Bake: 1 hour 15 minutes
Makes 16 servings

3 cups all-purpose flour
1¾ cups granulated sugar
1 cup vegetable oil
½ cup apple juice
1 teaspoon baking soda
1 teaspoon ground cinnamon
2 teaspoons vanilla extract
¾ teaspoon salt
¼ teaspoon ground nutmeg
3 large eggs

3 medium Golden Delicious or Granny Smith apples (about 1¼ pounds), peeled, cored, and coarsely chopped
1 cup walnuts (about 4 ounces), coarsely chopped
1 cup golden raisins
Confectioners' sugar for garnish

◆ Preheat oven to 350°F. Grease and flour 10-inch Bundt pan. In large bowl, with mixer at low speed, beat flour and next 9 ingredients until well mixed, frequently scraping bowl with rubber spatula. Increase speed to medium; beat 2 minutes, occasionally scraping bowl. Stir in apples, walnuts, and raisins.

◆ Spoon batter into pan, spreading evenly. Bake 1¼ hours, or until cake pulls away from side of pan and toothpick inserted near center of cake comes out clean. Cool cake in pan on wire rack 10 minutes. Remove from pan and cool completely on rack. Just before serving, sprinkle with confectioners' sugar.

Each serving: About 405 calories, 5g protein, 55g carbohydrate, 20g total fat (3g saturated), 40mg cholesterol, 195mg sodium

APPLESAUCE-APPLE UPSIDE-DOWN CAKE

Prep: 25 minutes plus cooling   Bake: 35 to 40 minutes
Makes 8 servings

¾ cup margarine or butter, softened
3 medium Granny Smith apples (about 1¼ pounds), peeled, cored, and each cut into 8 wedges
½ cup packed brown sugar
2 cups all-purpose flour

1½ teaspoons baking soda
1 teaspoon ground cinnamon
½ teaspoon salt
¼ teaspoon ground nutmeg
Pinch ground cloves
⅔ cup granulated sugar
2 large eggs
1 cup applesauce

◆ Preheat oven to 350°F. In 10-inch skillet with oven-safe handle (or wrap handle in double thickness of foil), melt ¼ cup margarine over medium-high heat. Add apples and brown sugar and cook, stirring occasionally, 8 minutes, or until apples are tender. Remove from heat.

◆ In medium bowl, combine flour and next 5 ingredients. In large bowl, with mixer at medium speed, beat remaining ½ cup margarine with granulated sugar until light and creamy. Beat in eggs, 1 at a time. Reduce speed to low; alternately add flour mixture and applesauce, beginning and ending with flour mixture, beating just until smooth.

◆ Spoon batter evenly over apples in skillet. Bake 35 to 40 minutes, until cake springs back when lightly touched and toothpick inserted in center comes out clean. When cake is done, invert platter over cake. Quickly invert skillet to unmold cake; replace any apples left in skillet. Cool 30 minutes to serve warm.

Each serving: About 455 calories, 5g protein, 70g carbohydrate, 19g total fat (4g saturated), 53mg cholesterol, 590mg sodium

GINGERBREAD

Prep: 15 minutes plus cooling   Bake: 55 minutes
Makes 9 servings

½ cup sugar
½ cup margarine or butter, softened
2 cups all-purpose flour
1 cup light or dark molasses
1 tablespoon ground ginger

1 teaspoon ground cinnamon
½ teaspoon baking powder
½ teaspoon baking soda
½ teaspoon salt
¼ teaspoon ground cloves
1 large egg

◆ Preheat oven to 325°F. Grease 9" by 9" metal baking pan. Line bottom of pan with waxed paper; grease paper. Dust pan with flour. In large bowl, with mixer at low speed, beat sugar and margarine until blended. Increase speed to high; beat 1 minute, or until creamy. Reduce speed to low; beat in flour, remaining ingredients, and ¾ *cup hot water* until blended. Increase speed to high; beat 1 minute, occasionally scraping bowl with rubber spatula. Pour batter into pan.

◆ Bake 55 minutes, or until toothpick inserted in center of gingerbread comes out clean. Cool gingerbread in pan on wire rack 10 minutes. Invert onto rack. Remove waxed paper and serve warm, or cool completely to serve later.

Each serving: About 325 calories, 4g protein, 55g carbohydrate, 11g total fat (2g saturated), 24mg cholesterol, 345mg sodium

POUND CAKES

Dense and velvety, with a fine crumb, traditional pound cakes are leavened simply by beating air into the batter. The original pound cakes were made with a pound each of butter, sugar, flour, and eggs. Modern versions, with the addition of baking powder and liquid, are a bit lighter in texture. Try our lovely Southern pound cake, imbued with bourbon, go Italian-style with crunchy cornmeal, or just enjoy the classic, vanilla. Pound cakes keep well and, in fact, are better the next day.

BOURBON-BROWN SUGAR POUND CAKE

◆ ◆ ◆ ◆ ◆ ◆ ◆ ◆ ◆ ◆ ◆ ◆ ◆

Prep: 25 minutes plus cooling
Bake: 1 hour 20 to 25 minutes
Makes 24 servings

3 cups all-purpose flour
¾ teaspoon salt
½ teaspoon baking powder
½ teaspoon baking soda
¾ cup milk
2 teaspoons vanilla extract
¼ cup plus 2 tablespoons bourbon whiskey
1½ cups packed dark brown sugar
½ cup plus ⅓ cup granulated sugar
1 cup margarine or butter, softened
5 large eggs
2 tablespoons orange juice

1 Preheat oven to 325°F. Grease and flour 10-inch Bundt pan or fluted tube pan. In medium bowl, combine flour, salt, baking powder, and baking soda.

2 In measuring cup, mix milk, vanilla, and ¼ cup bourbon. In large bowl, with mixer at medium speed, beat brown sugar and ½ cup granulated sugar until free of lumps. Add margarine and beat 5 minutes, or until light and creamy. Add eggs, 1 at a time, beating well after each addition. Reduce speed to low; alternately add flour mixture and milk mixture, beginning and ending with flour mixture.

3 Pour batter into pan. Bake 1 hour 20 to 25 minutes, until cake springs back when lightly touched and toothpick inserted near center comes out clean. Cool cake in pan on wire rack 10 minutes. Remove cake from pan.

4 In small bowl, mix orange juice, remaining 2 tablespoons bourbon, and remaining ⅓ cup granulated sugar; brush mixture all over warm cake. Cool cake completely on rack. To serve, slice very thin.

LIGHT AND DARK BROWN SUGAR

At one time brown sugar was simply a less refined form of white sugar, containing molasses left over from the refining process. Today, it is usually made by combining white sugar with molasses, giving it added flavor, moisture, and color. Exposure to air causes brown sugar to dry out, but adding a slice of apple or bread to the box will soften it. Brown sugar is available in light or dark varieties; the latter is softer with a more intense molasses taste. Because brown sugar traps air between the coarse crystals, it should be firmly packed when measured.

EACH SERVING: ABOUT 230 CALORIES, 3g PROTEIN, 32g CARBOHYDRATE, 9g TOTAL FAT (2g SATURATED), 45mg CHOLESTEROL, 215mg SODIUM

VANILLA POUND CAKE

Prep: 20 minutes plus cooling   Bake: 1 hour to 1 hour 10 minutes
Makes 16 servings

2¼ cups granulated sugar
1½ cups margarine or butter, softened
1 tablespoon vanilla extract
¾ teaspoon salt

6 large eggs
3 cups cake flour (not self-rising)
Confectioners' sugar for garnish

◆ Preheat oven to 325°F. Grease and flour 10-inch Bundt pan. In large bowl, with mixer at low speed, beat granulated sugar and margarine just until blended. Increase speed to high; beat about 5 minutes, until light and creamy.

◆ Add vanilla, salt, and eggs. Reduce speed to low; beat until well blended, frequently scraping bowl with rubber spatula. Increase speed to high; beat 3 minutes, occasionally scraping bowl. With wire whisk, fold in flour just until smooth.

◆ Spoon batter into pan. Bake 60 to 70 minutes, until toothpick inserted near center of cake comes out clean. Cool in pan on wire rack 10 minutes. Remove from pan; cool completely on rack. Sprinkle with confectioners' sugar.

Each serving: About 365 calories, 4g protein, 45g carbohydrate, 19g total fat (4g saturated), 80mg cholesterol, 320mg sodium

CORNMEAL POUND CAKE

Prep: 20 minutes plus cooling   Bake: 1 hour 5 minutes
Makes 10 servings

1 cup all-purpose flour
½ cup yellow cornmeal
½ teaspoon baking powder
¼ teaspoon salt
1 cup margarine or butter, softened

1 cup sugar
4 large eggs
1 teaspoon grated orange peel
1 teaspoon vanilla extract

◆ Preheat oven to 325°F. Grease and flour 9" by 5" loaf pan or 6-cup fluted tube pan. In medium bowl, combine flour and next 3 ingredients. In large bowl, with mixer at medium speed, beat margarine with sugar 5 minutes, or until light and creamy. Add eggs, 1 at a time, beating well after each addition. Beat in orange peel and vanilla. Reduce speed to low; beat in flour mixture just until combined.

◆ Pour batter into pan. Bake 1 hour 5 minutes, or until cake pulls away from sides of pan and toothpick inserted in center comes out clean. Cool cake in pan on wire rack 10 minutes. Remove cake from pan and cool completely on rack. To serve, slice very thin.

Each serving: About 340 calories, 4g protein, 35g carbohydrate, 20g total fat (4g saturated), 85mg cholesterol, 315mg sodium

POPPY SEEDS

The tiny, bluish-gray seeds of a poppy plant lend a nutty taste and crunchy bite to a variety of cakes, breads, pastries, creamy dressings, salads, and noodle dishes. Because of their high oil content, poppy seeds can turn rancid quickly, so store them in an airtight container in the freezer.

LEMON-POPPY-SEED POUND CAKE

Prep: 25 minutes plus cooling   Bake: 1 hour 30 minutes
Makes 16 servings

2 cups all-purpose flour
2 tablespoons poppy seeds
½ teaspoon baking powder
¼ teaspoon baking soda
¼ teaspoon salt
3 large lemons

¾ cup margarine or butter, softened
1¾ cups sugar
4 large eggs
1 teaspoon vanilla extract
½ cup sour cream

◆ Preheat oven to 325°F. Grease and flour 9" by 5" loaf pan or 6-cup fluted tube pan. In medium bowl, combine flour and next 4 ingredients. Grate 1 tablespoon peel and squeeze 3 tablespoons juice from lemons.

◆ In large bowl, with mixer at medium speed, beat margarine with 1½ cups sugar about 5 minutes, until light and creamy. Add eggs, 1 at a time, beating well after each addition. Beat in lemon peel and vanilla. Reduce speed to low; alternately add flour mixture and sour cream, beginning and ending with flour mixture.

◆ Spoon batter into pan. Bake 1½ hours, or until toothpick inserted in center of cake comes out clean. Cool cake in pan on wire rack 10 minutes. Remove from pan. In small bowl, mix lemon juice and remaining ¼ cup sugar. Brush mixture over top and sides of warm cake. Cool completely on rack. To serve, slice very thin.

Each serving: About 255 calories, 4g protein, 34g carbohydrate, 12g total fat (3g saturated), 56mg cholesterol, 190mg sodium

CHEESECAKES

Few desserts are as popular as a rich, sumptuous cheesecake. So we've come up with recipes to suit every occasion. Purists will adore our Classic Cheesecake, a dense-textured delight that makes any get-together more festive. For variety, try the crunchy pecan and brown sugar topping as a delicious finishing touch. For dinner parties, Pumpkin-Swirl Cheesecake entices with mellow fall flavors and a dramatic design. Tart-sweet Lime Cheesecake is cool and creamy.

PUMPKIN-SWIRL CHEESECAKE

Prep: 30 minutes plus standing, cooling, and chilling
Bake: 1 hour 10 minutes
Makes 16 servings

8 cinnamon graham crackers (5" by 2½" each) or 1 cup graham-cracker crumbs
2 tablespoons margarine or butter, melted
3 packages (8 ounces each) cream cheese, softened
1 cup sugar
⅓ cup brandy
2 teaspoons vanilla extract

4 large eggs
1 can (16 ounces) solid-pack pumpkin (not pumpkin-pie mix)
2 tablespoons cornstarch
1 teaspoon ground cinnamon
½ teaspoon ground allspice
½ teaspoon salt
1 container (8 ounces) sour cream

1 Preheat oven to 325°F. In food processor with knife blade attached or in blender, process graham crackers until fine crumbs form. In 9" by 3" springform pan, with fork, stir graham-cracker crumbs and melted margarine until evenly moistened. With hand, press mixture onto bottom of pan. Bake crust 10 minutes. Cool crust completely in pan on wire rack.

2 Meanwhile, in large bowl, with mixer at medium speed, beat cream cheese until smooth; gradually beat in sugar. Reduce speed to low; beat in brandy, vanilla, and eggs just until blended, scraping bowl often with rubber spatula. In medium bowl, mix pumpkin, cornstarch, cinnamon, allspice, and salt. Stir half of cream-cheese mixture into pumpkin mixture until blended. Stir sour cream into remaining cream-cheese mixture.

3 Reserve ½ cup pumpkin mixture. Pour remaining pumpkin mixture onto crust. Carefully pour cream-cheese mixture on top of pumpkin layer.

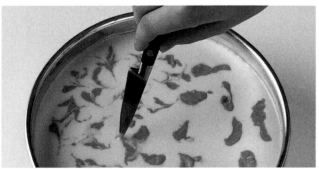

4 Spoon dollops of reserved pumpkin mixture onto cream-cheese layer. With knife, cut and twist through cream-cheese layer for swirl effect.

5 Bake cheesecake 1 hour, or until edges are set (center will jiggle). Turn off oven; let cheesecake remain in oven 1 hour. Remove cheesecake from oven. Run small knife around edge of pan to loosen cheesecake (this helps prevent cracking during cooling). Cool completely in pan on wire rack. Cover and refrigerate cheesecake at least 6 hours, or until well chilled. To serve, remove side of pan.

EACH SERVING: ABOUT 300 CALORIES, 6g PROTEIN, 21g CARBOHYDRATE, 21g TOTAL FAT (12g SATURATED), 107mg CHOLESTEROL, 255mg SODIUM

CLASSIC CHEESECAKE

Prep: 30 minutes plus chilling, standing, and cooling
Bake: 50 minutes   Makes 20 servings

¾ cup margarine or butter, softened
1¼ cups plus 2 tablespoons all-purpose flour
1¼ cups sugar
5 large eggs
2 teaspoons grated lemon peel
4 packages (8 ounces each) cream cheese, softened
3 tablespoons milk

◆ In small bowl, with mixer at medium speed, beat margarine, 1¼ cups flour, ¼ cup sugar, 1 egg yolk, and 1 teaspoon lemon peel until well mixed. Shape dough into ball; wrap with plastic wrap. Refrigerate 1 hour.

◆ Preheat oven to 400°F. Press one-third of dough onto bottom of 10" by 2½" springform pan. Bake 8 minutes, or until golden; cool on wire rack. Turn oven control to 475°F.

◆ In large bowl, with mixer at medium speed, beat cream cheese just until smooth; gradually beat in remaining 1 cup sugar. Reduce speed to low; beat in remaining 1 egg white and 4 eggs, milk, remaining 2 tablespoons flour, and remaining 1 teaspoon lemon peel. Beat 5 minutes. Press remaining dough around side of pan to within 1¼ inches of top; pour filling into dough.

◆ Bake 12 minutes. Turn oven control to 300°F; bake 30 minutes longer, until edges are set (center will jiggle). Turn off oven; let cheesecake remain in oven 30 minutes. Remove cheesecake from oven and cool in pan on wire rack. Refrigerate at least 6 hours, or until well chilled. To serve, carefully remove side of pan.

Each serving: About 320 calories, 6g protein, 20g carbohydrate, 24g total fat (12g saturated), 104mg cholesterol, 230mg sodium

LIME CHEESECAKE

Prep: 25 minutes plus cooling and chilling
Bake: 50 minutes   Makes 16 servings

8 honey graham crackers (5" by 2½" each) or 1 cup graham-cracker crumbs
½ cup walnuts (about 2 ounces), very finely chopped
⅓ cup margarine or butter, melted
¾ teaspoon ground cinnamon
3 medium limes
2 packages (8 ounces each) cream cheese, softened
4 large eggs
1 container (16 ounces) sour cream
1¼ cups sugar
1 teaspoon vanilla extract
½ teaspoon salt
Lime slices for garnish

◆ Preheat oven to 350°F. In food processor with knife blade attached or in blender, process graham crackers until fine crumbs form. In 9" by 2½" springform pan, with fork, mix graham-cracker crumbs, chopped walnuts, melted margarine, and cinnamon until well blended. Press mixture onto bottom and 1½ inches up side of pan; set aside.

◆ Grate 1 tablespoon peel and squeeze ⅓ cup juice from limes; set aside. In large bowl, with mixer at medium speed, beat cream cheese and eggs until smooth. Reduce speed to low; beat in sour cream, sugar, vanilla, salt, lime juice, and grated lime peel until well blended. Pour cream-cheese mixture into graham-cracker crust.

◆ Bake cheesecake 50 minutes. (Center may jiggle slightly.) Cool in pan on wire rack. Refrigerate cheesecake at least 6 hours, or until well chilled. To serve, carefully remove side of pan; garnish cheesecake with lime slices.

Each serving: About 315 calories, 5g protein, 22g carbohydrate, 24g total fat (11g saturated), 97mg cholesterol, 250mg sodium

NUT-AND-CRUMB-TOPPED CHEESECAKE

Prepare topping: In medium bowl, with fingertips, mix 1 cup pecans (about 4 ounces), chopped, ⅔ cup all-purpose flour, ½ cup packed brown sugar, 6 tablespoons margarine or butter, 2 tablespoons granulated sugar, and ½ teaspoon vanilla extract until mixture is crumbly. Prepare Classic Cheesecake as above, but before baking, sprinkle with topping. Bake as directed (if top browns too quickly, cover loosely with foil). Let stand in oven, cool, and refrigerate as directed. To serve, carefully remove side of pan. In small bowl, with mixer at medium speed, beat ½ cup heavy or whipping cream, 1 tablespoon brown sugar, and ½ teaspoon vanilla extract until stiff peaks form. Spoon whipped cream into decorating bag fitted with ½-inch star tip; pipe pretty design around top edge of cheesecake. Garnish with pecan halves, if you like.

Each serving: About 445 calories, 7g protein, 32g carbohydrate, 33g total fat (14g saturated), 112mg cholesterol, 275mg sodium

FROSTING AND DECORATING

Using a decorating bag and assorted tips, it's easy to pipe frosting or whipped cream into a vast range of whimsical shapes and playful designs. You may want to practice piping on a sheet of waxed paper before you decorate your cake.

◆◆◆◆◆◆◆◆◆◆◆◆

FILLING A DECORATING BAG

1 Place coupler base in decorating bag. Attach desired tip with ring.

2 Stand bag in measuring cup or sturdy glass. Fold bag over to make cuff; fill halfway with frosting.

3 Shake down frosting and twist bag shut. Hold bag closed with one hand; use writing hand to guide tip.

◆◆◆◆◆◆◆◆◆◆◆◆

WRITING TIP

Piping dots Hold bag fitted with small writing tip at a 90° angle, with tip just above cake. Gently squeeze bag, keeping tip in frosting, until the dot forms. Stop pressure and lift tip.

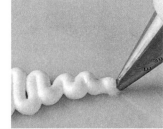

Smoothing dots If the tip leaves a small "tail" at the top of the dot, gently smooth it with finger dipped in confectioners' sugar or cornstarch.

Squiggles and lettering Use thinned frosting for a smooth flow. With tip at a 45° angle, touch surface to secure frosting then lift slightly to form squiggles. To finish, stop pressure and lift tip.

STAR TIP

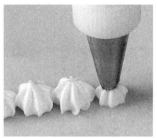

Stars With star tip at 90° angle and just above cake, squeeze to form star, then lift slightly, keeping tip in frosting. Stop pressure and lift tip.

Rosettes Position star tip as for stars, but as you squeeze, move tip up in a circular motion. Stop pressure and lift tip.

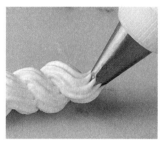

Ropes Holding bag at a 45° angle, pipe a C. Tuck tip under bottom portion of C; repeat, overlapping curves to form a rope.

A SELECTION OF OTHER TIPS

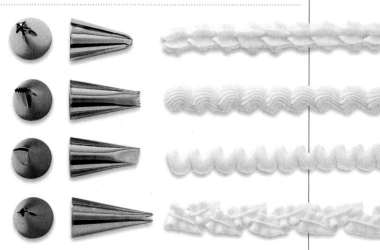

5-POINT STAR Use this smaller star to pipe small rosettes and fancy borders.

BASKET This tip forms the ridged lines that create the woven design for our basket cake.

PETAL With a wider opening at one end, petal tubes are used to make petals, ribbons, and bows.

LEAF The open "V" of this tube gives leaves, veins, and pointed tips.

EASY FROSTINGS

FLUFFY WHITE FROSTING In top of double boiler, over simmering water, with mixer at high speed, beat 2 large egg whites, 1 cup sugar, ¼ cup water, 2 teaspoons fresh lemon juice, 1 teaspoon light corn syrup, and ¼ teaspoon cream of tartar 7 to 10 minutes, until soft peaks form. Remove double-boiler top from bottom; beat 7 to 10 minutes longer, until stiff peaks form. Makes about 3 cups.

Each tablespoon: About 15 calories, 0g protein, 4g carbohydrate, 0g total fat, 0mg cholesterol, 5mg sodium

CREAM-CHEESE FROSTING In large bowl, with mixer at low speed, beat 3 cups confectioners' sugar, 2 packages (3 ounces each) cream cheese, softened, 6 tablespoons margarine or butter, softened, and 1½ teaspoons vanilla extract just until blended. Increase speed to medium. Beat 1 minute, or until smooth and fluffy, frequently scraping bowl. Makes about 2½ cups.

Each tablespoon: About 60 calories, 0g protein, 8g carbohydrate, 3g total fat (1g saturated), 5mg cholesterol, 35mg sodium

CHOCOLATE BUTTER CREAM In large bowl, with mixer at low speed, beat 2 cups confectioners' sugar, ¾ cup margarine or butter, softened, and 1 teaspoon vanilla extract until almost combined. Add 4 squares (4 ounces) semisweet chocolate, melted and cooled, and 2 squares (2 ounces) unsweetened chocolate, melted and cooled. Increase speed to high; beat about 1 minute, or until light and fluffy. Makes about 2½ cups.

Each tablespoon: About 70 calories, 0g protein, 7g carbohydrate, 5g total fat (2g saturated), 0mg cholesterol, 40mg sodium

WHITE-CHOCOLATE BUTTER CREAM In large bowl, with mixer at low speed, beat 1 cup butter, softened (do not use margarine), 3 tablespoons milk, 2 cups confectioners' sugar, and 6 ounces white chocolate, Swiss confectionery bars, or white baking bars, melted and cooled, just until mixed. Increase speed to high; beat 2 minutes, or until light and fluffy, scraping bowl often with rubber spatula. Makes about 2½ cups.

Each tablespoon: 85 calories, 0g protein, 8g carbohydrate, 6g total fat (4g saturated), 13mg cholesterol, 50mg sodium

VANILLA BUTTER CREAM In 2-quart saucepan, mix 1 cup sugar and ½ cup all-purpose flour until evenly combined. Gradually stir in 1⅓ cups milk until smooth. Cook over medium-high heat, stirring often, until mixture thickens and boils. Reduce heat to low; cook 2 minutes, stirring constantly. Remove from heat; cool completely. In large bowl, with mixer at medium speed, beat 1 cup margarine or butter, softened, until creamy. Gradually beat in milk mixture. Beat in 1 tablespoon vanilla extract. Makes about 3¼ cups.

Each tablespoon: About 55 calories, 0g protein, 5g carbohydrate, 4g total fat (1g saturated), 1mg cholesterol, 45mg sodium

LEMON BUTTER CREAM Prepare Vanilla Butter Cream as above, but replace vanilla extract with 1 tablespoon grated lemon peel.

ORANGE BUTTER CREAM Prepare Vanilla Butter Cream as above, but replace vanilla extract with 1 teaspoon grated orange peel.

AMARETTO BUTTER CREAM

Prep: 20 minutes   Cook: 10 minutes
Makes about 4 cups

1 cup sugar
4 large egg whites
2 cups unsalted butter,
  softened (no substitutions)

¼ cup amaretto liqueur or
  ½ teaspoon almond extract
Pinch salt

◆ In 1-quart saucepan, heat ¾ cup sugar and ⅓ *cup water* to boiling over high heat without stirring. Cover and cook 2 minutes longer. Uncover; set candy thermometer in place and continue cooking, without stirring, until temperature reaches 248° to 250°F, or hard-ball stage (see page 523). Remove from heat.

◆ Just before syrup is ready (temperature will be about 220°F), in large bowl, with mixer at high speed, beat egg whites until foamy. Gradually beat in remaining ¼ cup sugar and continue beating until soft peaks form.

◆ With mixer at low speed, slowly pour hot syrup in thin stream into beaten egg whites. Increase speed to high; beat 15 minutes longer, or until mixture forms stiff peaks and is cool to the touch.

◆ When mixture is cool, reduce speed to medium. Gradually add softened butter, 1 tablespoon at a time, beating after each addition. (If butter cream appears to curdle, increase speed to high and beat until mixture comes together, then reduce speed to medium and continue adding softened butter.) When butter cream is smooth, reduce speed to low; beat in amaretto and salt until incorporated.

Each tablepoon: About 65 calories, 0g protein, 4g carbohydrate, 6g total fat (4g saturated), 16mg cholesterol, 10mg sodium

CAKE GARNISHES

These elegant finishing touches transform home-style cakes into distinctive desserts. Arrange them to form a border or design, or simply scatter them on top. The chocolate decorations can be made ahead and stored in an airtight container, between layers of waxed paper, in the refrigerator. Stenciling with confectioners' sugar should be done shortly before serving, or the cake's moisture may dissolve the sugar.

CHOCOLATE CURLS

1 Melt 1 package (6 ounces) semisweet chocolate pieces and 2 tablespoons shortening (see page 552).

2 Scrape mixture onto cookie sheet with no sides; spread to cover evenly. Refrigerate 10 minutes, or until firm but not brittle.

3 Place cookie sheet on damp cloth (to keep it from slipping). Holding back of pancake turner at 45° angle, scrape chocolate into curls (if chocolate softens or sticks to pancake turner, chill several minutes). Transfer to jelly-roll pan; refrigerate until ready to use).

QUICK CHOCOLATE CURLS

Hold a 1-ounce square semisweet or white chocolate between palms of hands to warm, 5 minutes. Slowly and firmly draw vegetable peeler along smooth bottom of square for wide curls, or along sides for short curls. Refrigerate in jelly-roll pan until ready to use. With toothpick, place curls on cake.

CHOCOLATE LEAVES

1 Melt ½ cup semisweet chocolate pieces and 2 teaspoons shortening (see page 552). Meanwhile, rinse and dry 6 medium nontoxic leaves (see above).

2 With clean paintbrush, pastry brush, or small metal spatula, spread layer of melted chocolate on underside of each leaf.

3 Refrigerate chocolate-coated leaves 30 minutes, or until firm. With cool hands, carefully peel each leaf from chocolate.

GRATED CHOCOLATE

For an easy decoration to garnish the top or sides of cake, run a block of semisweet chocolate over the large holes of a grater.

MELTING CHOCOLATE

Melt semisweet chocolate (with shortening, if called for) in top of double boiler over simmering water, stirring occasionally. Or, melt in heavy 1-quart saucepan over very low heat, stirring constantly. White chocolate should always be melted in top of a double boiler over barely simmering water; stir constantly until smooth.

MAKING A PARCHMENT CONE

1 Cut 12" by 12" square of baking parchment; cut in half into 2 triangles. Lay one triangle on flat surface, wide side at top. Fold left-hand point down to bottom point.

2 Take right-hand point; wrap completely round folded left-hand point, forming cone. Both points should meet at bottom point of original triangle.

3 Grasp all thicknesses of paper where original three points meet and fold point in to secure cone. Fill cone not more than two-thirds full and fold top over to seal. Snip off tip to desired size opening.

FEATHERING

1 Frost cake. Before frosting sets, melt 2 ounces semi-sweet chocolate (see above). Spoon into parchment cone, small decorating bag with small writing tip, or zip-tight bag (cut one corner off); pipe spiral on top of cake, working outward from center.

2 Immediately run tip of paring knife through spiral, working from center to edge of cake. Repeat, working from center, to mark cake in 8 segments. Divide each segment again, this time working from edge to center for feathered effect.

CHOCOLATE SHAPES

1 With pencil, draw outline of 12 hearts or other shapes, each 1½ inches across, on piece of waxed paper. Place waxed paper, pencil-side down, on cookie sheet; tape to cookie sheet. Melt 1½ ounces chocolate or white chocolate.

2 Spoon warm chocolate into parchment cone, small decorating bag with small writing tip, or zip-tight plastic bag (cut one corner off); pipe in continuous line (not too thin, or shape will be fragile) over each tracing to form 12 shapes in all.

3 Refrigerate at least 15 minutes, or until set. Carefully peel off shapes and transfer to cake. (Create your own designs by making other shapes, such as leaves, scrolls, or flowers.)

QUICK PIPING BAG

If you don't have a decorating bag, just use a zip-tight plastic bag with corner cut off. With rubber spatula, scrape melted chocolate into bag. Seal bag, then snip off one corner with scissors to make a small opening.

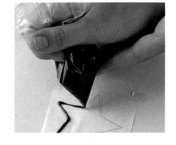

STENCILING

1 Cut lightweight cardboard or manila file folder at least 1 inch larger all around than cake. With mat knife or single-edge razor blade, cut out stars, triangles, or other shapes of different sizes.

2 Place stencil over unfrosted cake. Sift unsweetened cocoa, confectioners' sugar, or cinnamon-sugar over top. After decoration has been evenly dispersed in cutout holes, carefully lift off stencil to reveal design.

INDEX

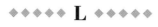

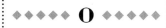

ADDITIONAL CREDITS

Food preparation Eric Treuillé,
Kathy Man, Maddalena Bastianelli
Additional art direction
Cherry Ramsayer
Photographers' assistant
Margaret-Ann Hugo
IT Manager John Clifford
Typesetting Sue Hill
Additional editorial assistance
Jennifer Rylaarsdam
Additional nutrition advice
Antonina Smith
Proofreading Pamela Ellis
Index Madeline Weston

EDITORS' ACKNOWLEDGMENTS

Many thanks to members of the food industry for their patient help and information: foremost to Marlys Bielunski of the National Cattleman's Beef Association for her knowledge and attention to detail, to Robin Kline of the National Pork Producers Council, Priscilla Root of the American Lamb Council, Howard Helmer of the American Egg Board, Linda Funk of the Wisconsin Milk Marketing Board, Nancy Tringali of the National Broiler Council, Mary Humann and Julie Hamilton of the National Honey Board, and Elizabeth Karmel and Betty Hughes of Weber-Stephen Products.

Thanks also to Delia Hammock, Sharon Franke, Mary Ann Svec, Marianne Marinelli, Lisa Troland, Lynda Gunn, Karen Kolnsberg, and Mary O'Connor of the Good Housekeeping Institute for their myriad contributions.

At Hearst Books, our thanks to Ann Bramson, Elizabeth Rice, Debbie Weiss-Geline, Jacqueline Deval, Richard Aquan, Jennifer Kaye, and Rachel Bailey.

Finally, to our indefatigable copy editor, Judith Sutton, our thanks and admiration.

ROASTING TIMES FOR POULTRY AND MEAT

POULTRY (OVEN TEMPERATURE 350°F)

POULTRY TYPE AND WEIGHT Start with bird at refrigerator temperature. Remove from oven when meat thermometer reads 175° to 180°F; temperature will continue to rise as bird stands.		COOKING TIME (UNSTUFFED)	COOKING TIME (STUFFED)
Chicken	2½–3 lbs	1¼–1½ hrs	1¼–1½ hrs
	3–4 lbs	1½–1¾ hrs	1½–1¾ hrs
	4–6 lbs	1¾–2 hrs	1¾–2 hrs
Capon (at 325°F)	5–6 lbs	2–2½ hrs	2½–3 hrs
	6–8 lbs	2½–3½ hrs	3–4 hrs
Cornish hen	1–2 lbs	1–1¼ hrs	1–1¼ hrs
Turkey (at 325°F)	8–12 lbs	2¾–3 hrs	3–3½ hrs
	12–14 lbs	3–3¾ hrs	3½–4 hrs
	14–18 lbs	3¾–4¼ hrs	4–4¼ hrs
	18–20 lbs	4¼–4½ hrs	4¼–4¾ hrs
	20–24 lbs	4½–5 hrs	4¾–5½ hrs
Duckling	4–5 lbs	2½–2¾ hrs	2½–2¾ hrs
Goose	10–12 lbs	2¾–3¼ hrs	3–3½ hrs

VEAL (OVEN TEMPERATURE 325°F)

CUT AND WEIGHT Start with meat at refrigerator temperature. Remove roast from oven when it reaches 5° to 10°F below desired doneness; temperature will continue to rise as roast stands.	MEAT THERMOMETER READING	APPROXIMATE COOKING TIME (MINUTES PER LB)
Boneless shoulder roast 3–5 lbs	160°F	35–40 mins
Leg rump or round roast (boneless) 3–5 lbs	160°F	35–40 mins
Boneless loin roast 3–5 lbs	160°F	25–30 mins
Rib roast 3–5 lbs	160°F	30–35 mins

BEEF

CUT Start with meat at refrigerator temperature. Remove roast from oven when it reaches 5° to 10°F below desired doneness; temperature will continue to rise as roast stands.	OVEN TEMPERATURE	WEIGHT	APPROXIMATE COOKING TIME	
			Medium-rare (145°F)	Medium (160°F)
Rib roast (chine bone removed)	350°F	4–6 lbs	1¾–2¼ hrs	2¼–2¾ hrs
		6–8 lbs	2¼–2½ hrs	2¾–3 hrs
Rib eye roast	350°F	4–6 lbs	1¾–2 hrs	2–2½ hrs
Whole tenderloin	425°F	4–5 lbs	50–60 mins	60–70 mins
Half tenderloin	425°F	2–3 lbs	35–40 mins	45–50 mins
Round tip roast	325°F	3–4 lbs	1¾–2 hrs	2¼–2½ hrs
		6–8 lbs	2½–3 hrs	3–3½ hrs
Eye round roast	325°F	2–3 lbs	1½–1¾ hrs	—